## INTERGENERATIONAL JUSTICE IN SUSTAINABLE DEVELOPMENT TREATY IMPLEMENTATION

Economic, technological, social and environmental transformations are affecting all humanity, and decisions taken today will impact the quality of life for all future generations. This volume surveys current commitments to sustainable development, analysing innovative policies, practices and procedures to promote respect for intergenerational justice. Expert contributors provide serious scholarly and practical discussions of the theoretical, institutional and legal considerations inherent in intergenerational justice on the local, national, regional and global scale. They investigate treaty commitments related to intergenerational equity, explore linkages between regimes, and offer insights from diverse experiences of national future generations' institutions. This volume should be read by lawyers, academics, policymakers, and business and civil society leaders interested in the economy, society, environment, sustainable development, climate change and other law, policy and practices impacting all generations.

MARIE-CLAIRE CORDONIER SEGGER is Leverhulme Visiting Professor at the University of Cambridge, Full Professor of Law at the University of Waterloo, Canada, Executive Secretary to the Climate Law & Governance Initiative, and laureate of the 2020 H.E. Judge C. G. Weeramantry International Justice Award. She serves as Senior Director of the Centre for International Sustainable Development Law (CISDL), as Chair of the Future Board for Bit Bio, on the Board of the International Law Association, as a Law Fellow and Director of Studies for Lucy Cavendish College, as a founding Fellow of the Centre for Environment, Energy and Natural Resources Governance (CEENRG) and as an affiliated Fellow of the Lauterpacht Centre for International Law (LCIL) in Cambridge. Author or editor of over twenty books and 120 papers, she edits the Treaty Implementation for Sustainable Development series for Cambridge University Press and serves on the editorial boards of several law journals, also advising countries and international organisation on treaty commitments on climate change, biodiversity, trade, investment and other Sustainable Development Goals.

MARCEL SZABÓ is Full Professor and Head of the Department of European Law at Pázmány Péter Catholic University. Besides his academic career, between 2011 and 2012 Professor Szabó represented the Hungarian Government in front of the International Court of Justice in the Hague, and between 2012 and 2016 he was the Deputy Commissioner for Fundamental Rights and Ombudsman for Future Generations in Hungary. Professor Szabó was elected as justice at the Constitutional Court of Hungary in 2016, for twelve years. He is Founder and Honorary Chair of the Network of Institutions of Future Generations. His main areas of research are international environmental law, rights of future generations, responsibility of states in public international law, and public international law and EU law in the case law of the Constitutional Court of Hungary. Professor Szabó is the founder and Editor-in-Chief of the *Hungarian Yearbook of International Law and European Law.*

ALEXANDRA R. HARRINGTON is Research Director and Lead Counsel (Peace, Justice and Governance) with the Centre for International Sustainable Development Law (CISDL) and Fulbright Canada Research Chair in Global Governance at the Balsillie School of International Affairs in Waterloo, Canada. She serves as Director of Studies for ILA Colombia, as a member of the IUCN World Commission on Environmental Law and as Visiting Professor at Albany Law School. Dr Harrington is the author of *International Organizations and the Law* and the forthcoming *International Law and Global Governance: Treaty Regimes and Sustainable Development Goals Interpretation*, as well as dozens of articles and book chapters.

## TREATY IMPLEMENTATION FOR SUSTAINABLE DEVELOPMENT

Over the past three decades, a series of international treaties have entered into force to address pressing global concerns of social and economic development and environmental protection. On climate change, biodiversity and biosafety, desertification, agriculture and seeds, and trade and investment liberalisation, new regimes have been established to implement global commitments related to sustainable development, many with nearly universal membership. Successful domestic implementation of these international treaty regimes is one of the most significant challenges facing international law today. Although much has been written on the content and form of treaty law, there is relatively little that examines the transition from international legal theory and treaty texts to domestic regulation and practice.

This series of books addresses this need and provides a serious contribution to ongoing global debates by conducting a detailed analysis of how myriad new treaty regimes that cover the future's most pressing concerns can be made to work in practice.

*Series Editors*

Marie-Claire Cordonier Segger
Markus Wilhelm Gehring

*Volumes in the Series*

Children's Rights and Sustainable Development edited by Claire Fenton-Glynn (2019)

*Sustainable Development, International Aviation, and Treaty Implementation* edited by Armand de Mestral, Paul Fitzgerald, and Tanveer Ahmad (2018)

*NAFTA and Sustainable Development* edited by Hoi L. Kong and L. Kinvin Wroth (2015)

*Legal Aspects of Implementing the Cartagena Protocol on Biosafety* edited by Marie-Claire Cordonier Segger, Frederic Perron-Welch, and Christine Frison (2013)

*Sustainable Development, International Criminal Justice, and Treaty Implementation* edited by Sébastien Jodoin and Marie-Claire Cordonier Segger (2013)

# Intergenerational Justice in Sustainable Development Treaty Implementation

## ADVANCING FUTURE GENERATIONS RIGHTS THROUGH NATIONAL INSTITUTIONS

Edited by

**MARIE-CLAIRE CORDONIER SEGGER**

University of Cambridge/University of Waterloo

**MARCEL SZABÓ**

Pázmány Péter Catholic University, Budapest

**ALEXANDRA R. HARRINGTON**

Albany Law School

CAMBRIDGE
UNIVERSITY PRESS

**CAMBRIDGE**
**UNIVERSITY PRESS**

University Printing House, Cambridge CB2 8BS, United Kingdom

One Liberty Plaza, 20th Floor, New York, NY 10006, USA

477 Williamstown Road, Port Melbourne, VIC 3207, Australia

314–321, 3rd Floor, Plot 3, Splendor Forum, Jasola District Centre, New Delhi – 110025, India

79 Anson Road, #06-04/06, Singapore 079906

Cambridge University Press is part of the University of Cambridge.

It furthers the University's mission by disseminating knowledge in the pursuit of education, learning, and research at the highest international levels of excellence.

www.cambridge.org
Information on this title: www.cambridge.org/9781108488020
DOI: 10.1017/9781108768511



First published 2021

*A catalogue record for this publication is available from the British Library.*

*Library of Congress Cataloging-in-Publication Data*
NAMES: Cordonier Segger, Marie-Claire, 1973– editor. | Szabó, Marcel, editor. | Harrington, Alexandra R., editor.
TITLE: Intergenerational justice in sustainable development treaty implementation / edited by Marie-Claire Cordonier Segger, University of Cambridge; Marcel Szabó, Pázmány Péter Catholic University, Hungary; Alexandra R. Harrington, Albany Law School.
DESCRIPTION: Cambridge, United Kingdom ; New York, NY : Cambridge University Press, 2019. | Series: Treaty implementation for sustainable development | Includes index.
IDENTIFIERS: LCCN 2020015977 (print) | LCCN 2020015978 (ebook) | ISBN 9781108488020 (hardback) | ISBN 9781108738354 (paperback) | ISBN 9781108768511 (epub)
SUBJECTS: LCSH: Sustainable development–Law and legislation. | Environmental law, International. | Intergenerational relations–Economic aspects.
CLASSIFICATION: LCC K3585 .I5823 2019 (print) | LCC K3585 (ebook) | DDC 344.04/6–dc23
LC record available at https://lccn.loc.gov/2020015977
LC ebook record available at https://lccn.loc.gov/2020015978

ISBN 978-1-108-48802-0 Hardback

# Contents

# Figures

# Tables

# Notes on Contributors

**Sumudu Atapattu** is Director of Research Centers and Senior Lecturer at University of Wisconsin Law School, where she teaches in the area of international environmental law and climate change and human rights. Selected books include *Human Rights Approaches to Climate Change: Challenges and Opportunities* (Routledge 2015), *International Environmental Law and the Global South* (Cambridge University Press 2015) (co-editor), and *Emerging Principles of International Environmental Law* (Transnational 2006). Affiliated with the University of Wisconsin-Madison's Nelson Institute for Environmental Studies, the Center for South Asia, and the 4W Initiative, she has also served as Visiting Professor at Doshisha University Law School, Japan, and Giessen University, Germany. Professor Atapattu is also the Executive Director of the Human Rights Program at the University of Wisconsin-Madison. In 2000, she was awarded a Senior Fulbright Scholarship for research on environmental rights and human rights at the New York University Law School and the George Washington University Law School, and from 2002 to 2006 she was a visiting scholar at the Institute for Legal Studies at University of Wisconsin Law School as part of the adjunct faculty. She serves as the Lead Counsel for Human Rights at the Centre for International Sustainable Development Law based in Montreal, Canada, and on the advisory board of the *McGill Journal of Sustainable Development Law*. She holds an LLM (Public International Law) and a PhD (International Environmental Law) from the University of Cambridge, and is an Attorney-at-Law of the Supreme Court of Sri Lanka.

**Tara Dawn Atleo** is a Doctoral Candidate on Sustainability Management, School of Environment, Enterprise and Development (SEED) at the University of Waterloo Faculty of the Environment. Ms Atleo is CEO of the Maaqutusiis Hahoulthee Stewardship Society and a member of the Ahousaht First Nation, whose territory in coastal British Columbia is part of the Emerald Edge, the world's largest intact coastal temperate rainforest. Ms Atleo holds a Governor General's Medal and won the Gold Award in the UNFCCC COP23 Climate Law & Governance International Essay Competition for her paper, 'The Importance of Locally Developed Indigenous Planning Tools and Policy for Climate Change Action in Ahousaht Traditional Territories'. Her Masters from the University of London focused on environmental economics, specifically how to use non-market valuation techniques for culturally significant areas in Ahousaht traditional territories, and she holds a BSc from Vancouver Island University.

**Günther Bachmann** is General Secretary of the German Council for Sustainable Development. Upon concluding his landscape planning studies at the Technical University Berlin, Dr Bachmann participated in a variety of research assignments. He joined the Federal Environment Agency in 1983 and was named head of the Soil Protection Department in 1992. In later years, Dr Bachmann was instrumental in the creation of the 1999 Federal Soil Protection Act. In February 2014, he was appointed honorary professor by Lüneburg University's foundation. Dr Bachmann regularly publishes looseleafs and writes commentaries on the Soil Protection Act as well as essays on a range of issues.

**Gyula Bándi** is Hungarian Ombudsman for Future Generations. He has been active in the field of environmental law research and education for more than three decades, and he assisted in the establishment of postgraduate environmental law education in Hungary. He is Jean Monnet Professor of EU Environmental Law, and founder and Director of a Jean Monnet Centre of Excellence. He received the Pázmány Péter High Education award for his activity.

**Gábor Bartus** is Secretary General of the National Council for Sustainable Development (Hungary) and a Lecturer at the Budapest University of Technology and Economics. He has served as a Senior Advisor to the Prime Minister of Hungary and has an extensive background in environmental policy issues.

**Christina Binder** is Chair for International Law and Human Rights Law at the Bundeswehr University Munich. Previously, she was Professor of International Law at the University of Vienna. Professor Binder is a member of the Executive Board and Vice President of the European Society of International Law and of the Executive Board of the EIUC (European Inter-University Centre for Human Rights and Democratisation). She is a member of the ILA Committees on the Implementation of the Rights of Indigenous Peoples, Human Rights in Times of Emergency, and Feminism and International Law. Professor Binder has offered classes on human rights law and international law at many universities throughout Europe, Latin America, Australia, and Asia. She was a visiting fellow at the Lauterpacht Center for International Law in Cambridge (2007–2008), the Max Planck Institute for Comparative Public Law and International Law in Heidelberg (2008–2010 and regularly since then), and McGill University (summer 2015). She acts as election expert for the Congress of Local and Regional Authorities of the

Council of Europe and has worked as legal and electoral expert for election observation missions with the EU and OSCE/ODIHR.

**Jonathan Boston** has published widely on a range of matters including public management, social policy, climate change policy, tertiary education policy, and comparative government. While at Victoria University of Wellington, he has served as Director of the Institute for Governance and Policy Studies and Director of the Institute of Policy Studies. Earlier in his career, Professor Boston worked for the New Zealand Treasury and taught at the University of Canterbury. From 2000 to 2001, he was a member of the Tertiary Education Advisory Commission, and he later helped to design, implement, and evaluate the Performance-Based Research Fund. More recently, Professor Boston served as Co-Chair of the Expert Advisory Group on Solutions to Child Poverty established by the Children's Commissioner. He was awarded a Fulbright Fellowship in 2014 to undertake research on 'Governing for the Future: Bringing Long-Term Policy Issues into Short-Term Political Focus'. Professor Boston serves on the boards of a number of organisations, including Oxfam New Zealand.

**Edith Brown Weiss** is Francis Cabell Brown Professor of International Law, Georgetown Law. In September 2002, she was appointed to a five-year term on the three-member Inspection Panel of the World Bank and from 2003 to 2007 served full-time as the Chairperson of the Inspection Panel, an appointment at the vice-presidential level. Since January 2012, Professor Brown Weiss has served as a Judge on the International Monetary Fund's Administrative Tribunal and is President of the Inter-American Development Bank's Administrative Tribunal. She is also a member of the nine-person United Nations Environment Programme's International Advisory Council on Environmental Justice. Her past professional experience includes positions as Associate General Counsel for International Activities at the US Environmental Protection Agency, 1990–1992, Assistant Professor of Civil Engineering and Politics at Princeton University, and Research Associate at Columbia University and the Brookings Institution. Her numerous professional activities have included positions as President of the American Society of International Law (April 1994–1996), US Special Legal Advisor to the North American Commission on the Environment (1996–2002), chair of the Committee for Research on Global Environmental Change of the Social Science Research Council (1989–1994), and elected member of the Council on Foreign Relations, the American Law Institute, and the Commission on Environmental Law of the IUCN. She has been a member of the National Academy of Science's Commission on Geosciences, Environment and Resources, the NAS Water Science and Technology Board, the NAS, Israel, Jordan, Palestinian Territories Panel on Sustainable Water Supplies in the Middle East, and the NAS Environmental Studies Board. In July 2017, Professor Brown Weiss presented the General Course on Public International Law at The Hague Academy of International Law. In 2010, she received the Manley O. Hudson Medal from the American Society of International Law, in 2008 the Award for International Environmental Law from the Center for International Environmental Law, in 2003 the American Bar Association (ABA) Award for Distinguished Achievement in Environmental Law and Policy, in 1996 the Prominent Women in International Law Award from the American Society of International Law, and in 1994 the Elizabeth Haub Prize for international environmental law given by the Free University of Brussels and the International Council of Environmental Law (ICEL).

**Gregorio Rafael P. Bueta** is Expert Legal and Policy Consultant with the Asian Development Bank's Law and Policy Reform Program. He has worked extensively with judiciaries and legal professionals across Asia on environment and climate change law and adjudication, particularly in Bangladesh, Bhutan, Cambodia, India, Myanmar, Malaysia, Nepal, Pakistan, the Philippines, and Sri Lanka. Mr Bueta has also been involved in legal and regulatory reforms in South Asia in areas such as energy trade and corporate governance. Prior to joining ADB, he headed the Strategic Initiatives Management Office in the Office of the President of the Philippines focusing on government policies and programmes related to environment and climate change. As a private legal practitioner and independent consultant from the Philippines, Mr Bueta is an advocate for environmental rights and justice, protection of biodiversity, promotion of human rights, development of good governance, and integrity in public service. He has written several published works on environment and natural resources law and human rights. Mr Bueta has also worked with the United Nations Development Programme, the Philippine Judicial Academy, the Ateneo School of Government, the Council for the Welfare of Children, Ayala Corporation, the EcoWaste Coalition, and various NGOs and private companies. He has a Bachelor of Arts degree in Political Science from the Ateneo de Manila University. He earned his Juris Doctor Degree from the same institution and was the recipient of the St Thomas More Most Distinguished Award for his graduating class.

**Marie-Claire Cordonier Segger** is Leverhulme Trust Visiting Professor at the University of Cambridge and Full Professor of Law at the University of Waterloo, Canada, and Executive Secretary to the Climate Law & Governance Initiative, a UNFCCC partnership of legal institutes, universities, intergovernmental organisations and others supporting implementation of the Paris Agreement. She serves as Senior Director of the Centre for International Sustainable Development Law (CISDL); and as a founding Fellow of the Centre for Environment, Energy and Natural Resources Governance (CEENRG) and Affiliated Fellow of the Lauterpacht Centre for International Law (LCIL) at the University of Cambridge. She has published over twenty law books in four languages with Oxford University Press, Cambridge University Press, Kluwer, Routledge and others; authored over 160 articles and reports; edits the Cambridge University Press Book Series on Implementing

Treaties for Sustainable Development; and serves on the editorial boards of seven law journals. Through the UN and for key countries, she negotiates and implements sustainable development treaties on biodiversity, climate change, natural resources, trade and investment, earning the international Justitia Regnorum Fundamentum and other awards, and serving as senior legal advisor to the UNFCCC, the Convention on Biological Diversity and the Ramsar Convention. She is laureate of the H.E. Judge C. G. Weeramantry International Justice Award, and serves on the International Law Association, the Voices of Future Generations Children's Initiative, and the World Bank's Law Justice and Development Environment and Natural Resources TWG, and has founded over a dozen organisations for justice, environment, human rights and sustainable development. She holds a DPhil of International Law from Oxford, a Masters of Environmental Management from Yale, the BCL and LLB law degrees from McGill, and a BA Hons, and she speaks six languages.

**Jona David** is an award-winning UN Child Author, and his fourth children's book, *The Cosmic Climate Invention*, has recently been released. His brightly illustrated volumes highlight children's rights to a clean environment and education. Jona David has been writing since he was 8. When he was told at 7 that he had dyslexia, he was determined to overcome it by memorising the 8,000 most common words in English, and then wrote his first story, *The Epic Eco-Inventions*. As Gold Award winner and Child Author for Europe and North America in a series of books to celebrate the UN Convention on the Rights of the Child, he published *The Epic Eco-Inventions* at the age of 9, *The Great Green Vine Invention* at the age of 10, and *The Mechanical Chess Invention* at 11. His books have been translated into four UN languages, with over 1,000 copies sold and downloads in forty countries. As part of this commitment, Jona speaks about the rights of future generations internationally. Jona addressed the UN Children's Summit in New York for the launch of the world's Sustainable Development Goals in 2015. He won Pupil of the Year 2016 in the Cambridge Education Awards, second place worldwide (twice) in the Trust for Sustainable Living international sustainability essay competitions and schools debates in Oxford and in Dubai, and the Justitia Fundamentum Junior prize in Europe, among other awards, for his writings and awareness-raising for children's rights, the environment, education, and empowerment.

**Kinga Debisso** is Political Advisor at the Hungarian Ministry of Justice. Previously, she was PhD student and lecturer at the Department of European Law at Pázmány Péter Catholic University, and was chief legal advisor at the Office of the Commissioner for Fundamental Rights of Hungary. She also served as international legal advisor at the Hungarian Ministry of Public Administration and Justice. Her main research areas are European foreign policy, development policy and environmental law.

**Ole Kristian Fauchald** is Professor at the Department for Public and International Law, University of Oslo. Previously, Dr Fauchald worked as an adviser to the

Ministry of Environment for two years, before returning to the Faculty as postdoctoral researcher and subsequently associate professor. From 2006 to 2007, Dr Fauchald spent a year as guest researcher at Peking University. Since 2009 he has been a part-time researcher at the Fridtjof Nansen Institute. Dr Fauchald focuses on national and international environmental law, international trade law (WTO), and international investment law. He has also published on human rights law, is a member of the Research Group on Internationalisation of Law and the Research Group on Natural Resources Law, and is on the steering group of the project 'The Legitimate Roles of the Judiciary in the Global Order' (awarded Centre of Excellence Status). He has teaching experience in public international law, international environmental law, international trade law, international investment law, constitutional law, environmental law, and administrative law. He graduated as cand. jur. at the Law Faculty, University of Oslo in 1991, and received his dr. juris from the Faculty for his thesis 'Environmental Taxes and Trade Discrimination', published by Kluwer International in 1998.

**Andrew Flynn** is Senior Lecturer in Environmental Policy and Planning. He has a background in policy analysis and environmental geography. His principal research interests have been in the making and delivery of policy on sustainable development, the implementation of policy, and its evaluation. In exploring the dynamics of policy and regulation, Professor Flynn pays particular attention to the food system. His work on food supply chains and technological innovations in the food system have provided insights into the relationships between the state and key economic interests and how these have led to new patterns of regulation. This, in turn, has helped to inform work on environmental regulation, particularly in relation to the role of supply chains.

**Sándor Fülöp** is President of the Hungarian Environmental Management and Law Association (EMLA) and was First Parliamentary Commissioner for Future Generations in Hungary from 2008 to 2012. Prior to this, he worked as a public prosecutor and executive director of Hungary's principal non-profit environmental law firm. Dr Fülöp has also been a member of the compliance committee of the Aarhus Convention, the first international convention on access to information, access to decision-making, and access to justice in environmental matters. He works on public interest environmental cases as a private attorney, teaches, and does international consultancy work in environmental law and policy matters. Dr Fülöp has authored numerous publications in the field of environmental protection legislation, including 'Environmental Protection Democracy in Practice: Handbook on Community Participation for Environmental Protection and Water Management Authorities' (2002), 'Some Internal Contradictions of the Environmental Protection Law: Is the Re-Codification Necessary?' (2002), and 'Preliminary Examination – Impact Study – IPPC' (2007).

**Markus W. Gehring** is Director of Studies in Law at Hughes Hall, Lecturer in Law and a Fellow of the Lauterpacht Centre for International Law at the University of Cambridge. Previously, he served for two years as Tutor in Sustainable Development Law, and he was also Fellow in Law at Robinson College from 2005 to 2012. He has been a Visiting Professor in several law faculties around the world and held a Jean Monnet Research Chair *ad personam* in Sustainable Development Law at the University of Ottawa Law Faculty in Canada. He is also affiliated Lecturer in European and International Law and Senior Research Associate in the Centre for Rising Powers in the Politics and International Studies Department, and an affiliated Lecturer in the Department of Land Economy, a Founding Fellow of the Centre for Environment, Energy and Natural Resources Governance (C-EENRG), and an Associate of the Centre for Climate Mitigation Research (4CMR). He serves as Lead Counsel for Sustainable Trade, Investment and Finance Law with the Centre of International Sustainable Development Law (CISDL), based at McGill University, and as Expert in the Centre for European Legal Studies (CELS) at the University of Cambridge. A member of the Frankfurt am Main and Ontario Bars, he practised European and international trade law with Cleary Gottlieb in their Brussels office. Prior to joining Robinson College, he was a tutor in Public International Law at University College, Oxford. He co-edits the Cambridge University Press book series on Implementation of Sustainable Development Treaties and is author of several publications on international law, the EU, and sustainable development. He holds a JSD and LLM from Yale, a Dr iur from Hamburg, and an MA from the University of Cambridge.

**Alexandra R. Harrington** is Research Director and Lead Counsel for Peace, Justice and Governance with the Centre for International Sustainable Development Law and Fulbright Canada Special Foundation Fellow at the Balsillie School of International Affairs in Waterloo, Canada. She held the 2018–2019 Fulbright Canada Research Chair in Global Governance, based at the Balsillie School of International Affairs, and holds a doctoral degree in law from McGill University Faculty of Law. Dr Harrington is the author of *International Organizations and the Law* and the forthcoming *International Law and Global Governance: Treaty Regimes and Sustainable Development Goals Interpretation*. She is the Director of Studies for the International Law Association Colombian branch, a member of the International Law Association Committee on the Role of International Law in Sustainable Natural Resource Management for Development, and a professor at Albany Law School. She also guest lectures globally on topics related to international law, environmental law, global governance, and sustainable development. Dr Harrington has served as a consultant for entities such as the Commission for Environmental Cooperation of the North American Agreement on Environmental Cooperation and the UNEP. Dr Harrington's publications address a variety of fields relating to international law, including environmental law, legal issues relating to climate change, natural resources regulation, international organisations, international human rights law, international child's rights, international trade law, corporate social responsibility, and criminal law.

**András Jakab** is Professor of Law at the University of Salzburg and former Director of the Institute for Legal Studies at the Hungarian Academy of Sciences in Budapest, where he also holds a tenured research chair. He served as Schumpeter Fellow at the MPIL, where he lead a five-year project on Constitutional Reasoning in a Comparative Perspective. Formerly, he held research and teaching positions at the Pázmány Péter Catholic University in Budapest (2010–2011), the Centro de Estudios Políticos y Constitucionales (CEPC) in Madrid (2008–2010), the University of Liverpool (2006–2008), Nottingham Trent University (2004–2006), the MPIL (2003–2004), and the Károli Gáspár University of the Reformed Church in Budapest (2001–2003).

**Sébastien Jodoin** is Assistant Professor at the Faculty of Law of McGill University, where he directs the Law, Governance & Society Lab. He is also a member of the McGill Centre for Human Rights and Legal Pluralism, an Associate Member of the McGill School of Environment, and a Faculty Associate of the Governance, Environment & Markets Initiative at Yale University. His research focuses on legal and policy solutions to complex environmental and social problems that cut across multiple fields and levels of governance. His areas of interest include sustainable development, transnational law, public policy, environmental law and governance, climate change, human rights, disability, social innovation, and socio-legal research. Professor Jodoin currently serves as a principal investigator for research grants awarded by the Social Sciences and Humanities Research Council of Canada and the Fonds québécois de recherche société et culture. He holds a PhD in environmental studies from Yale University, an MPhil in international relations from the University of Cambridge, an LLM in international law from the London School of Economics, and a BCL and LLB from McGill University. Professor Jodoin recently served as the president of Génération d'idées, a think tank focused on the interests and participation of Quebeckers aged 20–35. Prior to his appointment at McGill University, he worked for the Centre for International Sustainable Development Law, the Canadian Centre for International Justice, Amnesty International Canada, and the United Nations International Criminal Tribunals for Rwanda and the former Yugoslavia. Professor Jodoin has received numerous awards and honours, including the Transnational Environmental Law Fifth Anniversary Issue Prize, the 2012 Public Scholar Award from the Yale Graduate School of Arts & Sciences, a Doctoral Scholarship from the Pierre Elliott Trudeau Foundation, a Doctoral Fellowship from the Social Sciences and Humanities and Research Council of Canada, and a Public Interest Law Articling Fellowship from the Law Foundation of Ontario. He currently serves as the Principal Investigator for an SSHRC Insight Development Grant on the role of human rights in transnational climate change law and advocacy.

**Erick Kassongo** is Legal Research Fellow with the Centre for International Sustainable Development Law (CISDL), focusing on the issues of climate change governance, adaptation and mitigation, sustainable landscapes investments, and sustainable development. Mr Kassongo is also Director of Centre Congolais pour le Développement Durable (CODED) and national coordinator of Initiative Climat REDD (ICR) in the Democratic Republic of the Congo, as well as a member of the African Union expert working group on extractive industries and environmental and human rights violations. As a lawyer and climate activist from the Democratic Republic of Congo (DRC), he has fought environmental cases on behalf of indigenous communities and describes his legal battles to stop deforestation.

**Ludwig Krämer** is a leading expert on environmental law and policy in the European Union, Senior Counsel of Client Earth, and head of the EU's Aarhus Centre, where he is instrumental in promoting access to information and rights of participation. Dr Krämer was a judge at the Landgericht Kiel (1969–2004). He joined the European Commission in 1972, serving in a series of senior legal positions until his retirement in 2004 with the distinction of being the longest-serving official of the European Commission in the field of environmental protection.

**Friederike Kurre** is Research Assistant at the German Bundestag (Office to Dr Matthias Heider MP, Committee of Economic Affairs and Energy), and Legal Trainee at Oberlandesgericht (Higher Regional Court) Brandenburg an der Havel. Previously she worked as research assistant at the European Legal Studies Institute in Osnabrück, and was junior research fellow at the Office of the Hungarian Ombudsman for Future Generations.

**Antonio G. M. La Viña** is Executive Director of the Manila Observatory, a Jesuit scientific research institution with research work in the fields of atmospheric and earth science in the Philippines and the Southeast Asian region. For ten years, he was the Dean of the Ateneo School of Government, taking this position in 2006 when he returned to the Philippines after an eight-year stint in a Washington DC environmental think tank, the World Resources Institute (WRI). From 1996 to 1998, Dr La Viña was the Undersecretary for Environment and Natural Resources of the Philippines. He is co-founder of the Legal Rights and Natural Resources Center – Friends of the Earth Philippines. Dr La Viña is a lead negotiator for the Philippines in the climate change negotiations. He played prominent and leadership roles in Kyoto in 1997 as the chair of the land use change and forestry negotiations and in Copenhagen in 2009, where he chaired the negotiations on Reducing Emissions from Deforestation and Degradation (also known as REDD-plus). At the Durban Climate Change Conference last December 2011, Dr La Viña once again chaired REDD-plus negotiations and succeeded in getting 195 countries to an agreement on REDD-plus Finance, which has been characterised as the maximum, not least, common denominator. Aside from climate change, Dr La Viña is an authority on a range of subjects and has published dozens of books, papers, and articles on law and governance, including constitutional law, indigenous people's rights, biodiversity and biotechnology, sustainable agriculture, trade and environment, mining, public ethics, leadership, local governance, social accountability, and social entrepreneurship.

**Odeeth Lara Morales** is Post-Doctoral Fellow working for the project Implementing Sustainable Community Plans in the School of Environment, Enterprise and Development (SEED) at the University of Waterloo. She holds a PhD in the discipline of Marketing, Enterprise and Sustainable Tourism from Anglia Ruskin University (United Kingdom), and has taught Sustainable Tourism and Management courses at Lord Ashcroft International Business School (LAIBS) in Cambridge. Dr Morales is passionate about sustainability and about achieving the global Sustainable Development Goals on a local level through the implementation of sustainable community plans, and the development of environmental programmes, collaborative strategies, and market-based instruments and approaches. She has participated in international conferences such as the UNESCO Week for Peace and Sustainable Development, the Conference of the Parties to the Convention on Biological Diversity (COP13), and the United Nations Sustainable Development Summit.

**Peter Lawrence** is Senior Lecturer at the University of Tasmania (UTAS) Law School, where he teaches international law and supervises the *University of Tasmania Law Review*. He is interested in the interface between ethics, justice, climate change, and international law, and his interests include not just substantive justice but also procedural justice and the question of how institutions which purport to represent future generations can be justified in terms of legitimacy. Prior to joining UTAS, Professor Lawrence worked for the Australian Department of Foreign Affairs and Trade Canberra (1989–2004), which included working as the First Secretary for the Australian Permanent Mission to the United Nations in Geneva (1996–1999). This involved leading Australian delegations negotiating environment agreements and chairing a contact group which produced the first rolling text of the optional protocol to the UN Convention against torture. In 2011, Professor Lawrence was a visiting fellow at ANU Centre for Public and International Law. In 2013, he successfully defended his PhD at the University of Tilburg in the Netherlands, and in 2014 he published *Justice for Future Generations, Climate Change and International Law* (Edward Elgar Press 2014). Professor Lawrence has been an active member of the European Science Foundation network on Human Rights to a Green Future coordinated by the University of Utrecht Ethics Institute and was a visiting fellow at this Institute from October to December 2016. He has made presentations in recent years at the University of Oxford, the University of Kobe Japan, Australian National University, Monash University, University of

Sydney Law School, the University of Utrecht (Ethics Institute, Law Faculty, Middleburg Roosevelt College), and Tilburg University Law Faculty.

**Renato Machado** is Federal Prosecutor for Environmental Matters and Citizen's Rights in the state of Rio de Janeiro, Brazil, and specializes in environmental Brazilian law. He was appointed by the General Federal Prosecutor as member of the National Council of the General Prosecutor's environment commission and is the Ministério Público Federal's adjunct coordinator of environmental matters in the state of Rio de Janeiro. In 2009 he monitored Operation Oxossi, Brazil's largest ever nationwide operation against illegal hunting and trade in wildlife, led by the Brazilian Federal Police in cooperation with Interpol's Environmental Crime Programme.

**Jaykumar Menon** is Founder of the Open Source Pharma Foundation, which aims to generate affordable new cures in areas of great health need, and of the India Nutrition Initiative, which is developing DFS, a salt that is double-fortified with iron and iodine, to address malnutrition caused by iron deficiency. An international human rights lawyer working at the intersection of human rights and global health, Mr Menon is also a Visiting Scientist at the Harvard School of Public Health and a Research Fellow at the Centre for International Sustainable Development Law at McGill University. He holds a JD and a Master of International Affairs from Columbia University and a BA from Brown.

**James McKenzie** has been Associate Chair of the Ontario Municipal Board (OMB) since 2017. Mr McKenzie is a skilled mediator and adjudicator and is highly respected by peers and practitioners. He was appointed to the OMB as Vice Chair in 2007, bringing a wealth of knowledge and experience in the areas of conflict management and alternative dispute resolution to the Board. As a Vice Chair of the OMB, Mr McKenzie has played an important role in training Members, reviewing draft decisions and assisting with case management issues. He has also contributed to improving tribunal processes related to efficient adjudication and has enhanced tribunal processes related to the provision of mediation services. Mr McKenzie is a professional mediator and planner and has taught mediation, negotiation, and dispute resolution in the School of Urban and Regional Planning at Ryerson University, in the Faculty of Environmental Studies at York University, and in the Peace and Conflict Studies Program at Royal Roads University. He was formerly a member of the Canadian Institute of Planners and, until his appointment to the Board, was a Registered Professional Planner. Mr McKenzie holds a Master's degree in Environmental Studies from York University and a Bachelor of Arts degree in Urban and Regional Planning from Ryerson University.

**Salim Nakjavani** is Adjunct Professor at the University of University of the Witwatersrand. From 2011 to 2015, Professor Nakjavani served as a United Nations prosecutor in the criminal proceedings against the senior Khmer Rouge leaders in Cambodia, where he participated in investigations, a multi-year trial, and complex appeals. Between 2002 and 2003, as part of the team that established the Office of the Prosecutor of the International Criminal Court, he was responsible for the drafting of the first Code of Conduct for international prosecutors and helped to develop the suite of legal tools known today as the Case Matrix and Legal Tools Database. In the intervening periods, he has held academic posts in the two leading public universities in South Africa, where he taught and published in the areas of legal ethics, legal writing, constitutional law, public international law, and international criminal law. Professor Nakjavani holds qualifications in three legal systems and has advised on justice and rule of law efforts in Indonesia, East Timor, Cambodia, Bangladesh, and Uganda. He graduated magna cum laude in law at McGill University (Canada) and went on to the University of Cambridge, where he won the Whewell Scholarship in International Law in 2002. He serves on the editorial boards of the *Constitutional Court Review* and the *Forum for International Criminal and Humanitarian Law*. He is fluent in French, with working experience in the francophone civil law systems.

**Alan Netherwood** is Director of Cynnal Cymru: Sustain Wales and Honorary Research Fellow of the School of Geography and Planning, Cardiff University. He has worked in Wales since 1993 for local government (Cardiff Council), academia (BRASS Research Centre, Cardiff University), Environment Agency Wales, and voluntary bodies in the fields of sustainable development and climate change. Professor Netherwood chaired the Welsh local government sustainable development officers network SDCC for three years and served on the Environment Agency's UK Climate Change Science Board. He was a visiting research fellow at the BRASS Centre in Cardiff University in 2004 while developing the Ecological Footprint of Cardiff, and holds a PhD in Environmental Management from the University of Central Lancashire and an MSc in Natural Resources Management from Leicester University. Professor Netherwood has a range of publications in practitioner journals, books, and conference papers in this field. He is currently working as a consultant with Welsh Local Government Association on their Sustainable Development Framework and on Climate Change, providing policy support to the Public and Third Sector, and has co-authored the Review of the Effectiveness of the Welsh Assembly Government Sustainable Development Scheme, with Cardiff University.

**Damilola Olawuyi** is Associate Professor of Law at Hamad Bin Khalifa University Law School and Chancellor's Fellow and Director at the Institute for Oil, Gas, Energy, Environment and Sustainable Development (OGEES Institute), Afe Babalola University, Nigeria. A prolific and highly regarded scholar, Professor Olawuyi has practiced and taught law in Europe, North America, Asia, Africa, and the Middle East. His publications include three books and more than thirty articles, book chapters, and reports on petroleum law, energy, and international environmental law. His most recent publication is *The Human Rights-Based Approach to Carbon*

*Finance* (Cambridge University Press 2016). Professor Olawuyi was formerly an international energy lawyer at Norton Rose Fulbright Canada LLP, where he served on the firm's global committee on energy investments in Africa. He has delivered lectures on energy law in over twenty countries. Professor Olawuyi serves on the executive committees and boards of the American Society of International Law, the International Law Association, and the Environmental Law Centre, Alberta. He has been a visiting professor at Columbia Law School, New York, and China University of Political Science and Law. He is Editor-in-Chief of the *Journal of Sustainable Development Law and Policy*. Professor Olawuyi has been admitted as Barrister and Solicitor in Alberta, Canada; Ontario, Canada; and Nigeria.

**Julia Pitts** is Mediator and environmental law and governance consultant at Nature Resources. She has served as a Senior Manager on the Australian Office of the Commissioner for Sustainability and the Environment, as Senior Legislation Officer within both the Commonwealth and the ACT Government, and has worked with three independent ACT Commissioners for Sustainability and the Environment. Ms Pitts is a specialist trained in water governance, negotiation, and diplomacy with UNITAR, and environmental and public policy disputes with both CDR Associates in Boulder, Colorado and Duke University. She received an LLM from King's College London, University of London and an LLB from the University of Hull.

**Judit Pump** is Senior Advisor to the Ombudsman for Future Generations in Hungary since 2013, and Honorary Assistant Professor of the Faculty of Law and Political Sciences of Pázmány Péter Catholic University, has been working in the field of environmental law for thirty years. Dr Pump's research interests includes the regulatory system of environmental law, particularly civil law, the protection of natural resources, the public utility sector, and their relationships to human rights. She has teaching experience in graduate and postgraduate programmes of lawyers, economists, and engineers. Her main course is an introduction to the relationship between environmental law and civil law. She holds a PhD in environmental law and an LLM from ELTE Law School.

**Marisa Quaresma dos Reis** is Doctoral Candidate and Researcher at the Lisbon Research Centre of Public Law (Faculty of Law of the University of Lisbon). She is part of the International and European Law (IEL) research group and is a Research Fellow for the Portuguese Foundation for Science and Technology in the area of Political and Legal Sciences. Her interests are broad, covering international and European law, human and fundamental rights, constitutional and environmental law, and animal rights. She has a deep interest in applied ethics, political science, and philosophy, and has worked in the areas of family law, youth and children's rights, and criminal procedure law as a former deputy district attorney. While a Research Fellow at the Foundation for the Rights of Future Generations (FRFG) in

Frankfurt, she was also the Project Leader of the international conference 'Ways to Legally Implement Intergenerational Justice', participating as a speaker and editor of the peer-reviewed journal *Intergenerational Justice Review*. She was awarded the European Commission prize for Outstanding Project for her FRFG research. She speaks at conferences and publishes internationally, and serves as material leader of a research project on intergenerational justice and law at the Lisbon Research Centre of Public Law.

**Franz Reimer** is Liaison Lecturer at Katholischer Akademischer Ausländer-Dienst (KAAD) since 2015 and member of the board of the Erwin Stein Foundation. Dr Reimer served in the Justus-Liebig-Universität Gießen as Dean of Studies of the Department of Law from 2010 to 2013. From 2012 to 2018/2019, he was also executive director of the Rudolf von Jhering Institute for Fundamental Law Research at JLU Gießen. Dr Reimer studied law in Bonn, Oxford, and Freiburg, where his doctoral thesis, supervised by Dietrich Murswiek, was published in 2001 under the title *Constitutional Principles: A Standard Type in the Basic Law*. As an assistant at the Institute of Political Science and Philosophy of Law, he wrote the habilitation thesis 'Quality Assurance: Fundamentals of a Service Administration Law', which in 2007 led to the acquisition of venia for Public Law and Legal Theory.

**Dinah Shelton** has been Professor of Law, George Washington University Law School since 2004. Before her appointment, she was professor of international law and director of the doctoral programme in international human rights law at the University of Notre Dame Law School from 1996 to 2004. Professor Shelton previously taught at Santa Clara University and was a visiting lecturer at the University of California, Davis, Stanford University, University of California, Berkeley, the University of Paris, and the University of Strasbourg, France. From 1987 to 1989, she was the director of the Office of Staff Attorneys at the US Court of Appeals for the Ninth Circuit. Professor Shelton is the author or editor of three prize-winning books: *Protecting Human Rights in the Americas* (winner of the 1982 Inter-American Bar Association Book Prize and co-authored with Thomas Buergenthal), *Remedies in International Human Rights Law* (awarded the 2000 Certificate of Merit, American Society of International Law), and the three-volume *Encyclopedia of Genocide and Crimes against Humanity* (awarded a Best Research book award by the New York Public Library). She has also authored many articles and books on international law, human rights law, and international environmental law. Professor Shelton is a member of the board of editors of the *American Journal of International Law* and is a vice-president of the American Society of International Law. Professor Shelton serves on the boards of many human rights and environmental organisations. In 2006, she was awarded the prestigious Elizabeth Haub Prize in Environmental Law, and she has served as a legal consultant to the United Nations Environment Programme, UNITAR, the World Health Organization, the European Union, the Council of Europe, and the Organization of American States. In 2009, Professor Shelton became the first woman nominated by the United States to become a member of the Inter-American Commission on Human Rights, established by the Organization of American States to promote and protect human rights in the Western Hemisphere. She served a four-year term, during which she went on to become President of the Commission.

**Shlomo Shoham** is Chairman of the Sustainable Global Leadership Academy. Judge (ret.) Shoham served as the first Commissioner for Future Generations and as a legal advisor to the Constitution Law and Justice Committee in the Israeli Parliament. Judge (ret.) Shoham was also a lecturer in the Law Faculties of the Universities of Tel Aviv, Jerusalem, and Bar Ilan on a range of subjects in human rights and criminal law. He taught emotional intelligence at the executive MPA programme at the Hebrew University in Jerusalem and has taught meditation, bio-energy, future-oriented leadership, and holistic leadership to thousands of people worldwide. He also served as the head of the Israel delegation to the Commission on Sustainable Development of the UN. Judge (ret.) Shoham was an honorary fellow of the Bertelsmann Foundation; within this framework he wrote his book, *Future Intelligence*. He was the first leader to bring AUM meditation to Israel. Since then, Shlomo has guided many AUM meditations, some of them with 700–1,000 participants.

**Tyra Sioni** is UNESCO Voices of Future Generations Child Author for the Pacific Islands, lives in Papua New Guinea with her father, Ray, and Chilli, their cat. She is from Papua New Guinea and Australia, and attends Alotau International School, in Milne Bay province. She has a great passion for Politics, English, Science, and Environmental Studies, and also excels in and is talented in music and art, which runs in her family. Tyra's hobbies are playing guitar, songwriting, singing, reading, writing, drawing, and painting. She is fierce, selfless, and straight with people, but she cares deeply for those who suffer. Tyra continues to help develop her community and country by spreading awareness to multinational organisations such as the United Nations.

**Otto Spijkers** is Professor of International Law at the China Institute of Boundary and Ocean Studies (CIBOS) and Founding Staff Member of the International Water Law Academy (IWLA) of Wuhan University, China. Previously, he was Lecturer of Public International Law at Utrecht University, Senior Research Associate with the Netherlands Institute for the Law of the Sea (NILOS), and researcher with the Utrecht Centre for Water, Oceans and Sustainability Law (UCWOSL). He is a member of the Committee on the Role of International Law in Sustainable Natural Resource Management for Development of the International Law Association. Professor Spijkers has been a visiting lecturer at the University of Malta, the Grotius Centre for International Legal Studies of Leiden University,

Xiamen University's China International Water Law Programme (China), the Law School of the East China University of Political Science and Law (ECUPL) in Shanghai (China), the Università degli Studi di Salerno (Italy), and the Association pour la promotion des droits de l'homme en Afrique centrale (APDHAC) of the Université Catholique d'Afrique Centrale (Yaoundé, Cameroon). Previously, Professor Spijkers was a PhD candidate and lecturer at the Grotius Centre for International Legal Studies at the University of Leiden. His doctoral dissertation, *The United Nations, the Evolution of Global Values and International Law*, was published with Intersentia in 2011. Professor Spijkers worked as public services coordinator at the Peace Palace Library, as international consultant and coordinator for the United Nations International Law Fellowship Programme, as intern for the Appeals Chamber of the International Criminal Tribunal for Rwanda, and as intern for the Office of Legal Affairs of United Nations Headquarters. Professor Spijkers is editor and author of the Invisible College Blog, the blog of the School of Human Rights Research.

**Elisabeth Gording Stang** is Professor at Oslo University College and Akershus, or OsloMet, the city university. As a student, Dr Stang was a scientific assistant (1993–1994) at the Department of Public Law at the University of Oslo, where she wrote a thesis on forced adoption in the child welfare service. Stang became a cand. jur. in 1994 and became secretariat leader for the committee that evaluated the children's ombudsman scheme in the Ministry of Children and Family Affairs. Since then, Dr Stang has been a researcher (1996–1997) at the Department of Public Law (UiO) with a five-month pre-project on assistance measures in the child welfare fund funded by the Norwegian Research Council (NFR). Dr Stang became Dr Juris in 2007, and her thesis was published the same year. She became Associate Professor of Law at Oslo University College, at the Child Welfare Education in 2008. In the period 2011–2014, Dr Stang was on leave from the college and worked as a researcher at the research institute NOVA. Here she was also the initiator, and leader of, an interdisciplinary research group with a focus on children, the rule of law, and social work. Dr Stang was nominated by the Legal Association for the Academy Award 2016 and (by a student) for *Morgenbladet*'s prize for best lecturer that same year. Dr Stang was nominated by the *Journal of Family Law, Inheritance Law and Child Welfare Law* (FAB) for the best journal article for the year 2017 with 'The Proposal for a New Child Welfare Act: Rights Acquisition, Structural Change and Language Revision'. Through her career, Dr Stang has held several positions, including secretary for the Confidentiality Council and research, appointed by the Ministry of Justice (2004–2005), and she was an editorial member of the Nordic journal *Retferd* from 2008 to 2016. She was elected as a board member of the Scheibler Foundation in 2017. Dr Stang is also an active communicator to the field of practice and participates in the social debate related to cases involving vulnerable children.

**Katalin Sulyok** is Assistant Professor of Law at ELTE Law School and Head of Department at the Hungarian Office of the Ombudsman for Future Generations. She has served as a Visiting Researcher at the Cambridge University Centre for Environment, Energy, and Natural Resource Governance and as a Visiting Researcher at the Lauterpacht Centre for International Law. Dr Sulyok received a PhD in public international law from Eötvös Loránd University, and LLM degrees from ELTE Law School and Harvard Law School.

**Marcel Szabó** is Justice of the Constitutional Court from 2016, graduated from ELTE Law School in 1994 and pursued studies at Stanford University, Panthéon-Assas University of Paris, and the University of Cambridge and Stanford University. From 1998 to 2002, he served as the Head of the Legal Working Group in charge of the negotiation on the implementation of the judgment of the International Court of Justice in the *Gabcikovo-Nagymaros* case. Professor Szabó was Agent of Hungary before the International Court of Justice between 2011 and 2012. From 2012 to 2016, he served as the Ombudsman for Future Generations of Hungary. From 2015 to 2016, he acted as board member of the European Ombudsman Institute. In 2014, inspired by the report of UN Secretary-General on future generations, Professor Szabó initiated the establishment of the Network of National Institutions for Future Generations. He was elected Chairman of the Network in 2014 and Honorary Chairman in 2016. In 2016, Professor Szabó became a member of the International Court of Arbitration. Since 1997, he has lectured at the Pázmány Péter Catholic University. He earned his PhD in 2003 and obtained his habilitation in 2012. From 2003 to 2010, he was Deputy Dean for International Relations at the Faculty of Law and Political Sciences of Pázmány Péter Catholic University. He is currently full professor and head of the Department of European Law of Pázmány Péter Catholic University. Professor Szabó has been Editor-in-Chief of the *Hungarian Yearbook of European Law and International Law* since 2013. He was visiting professor at the Sacro Cuore University, Milan in 2001, at the University of San Francisco in 2008, and at Marymount College, Los Angeles, teaching public international law and European law. He is Chairman of the UNESCO Voices of Future Generations initiative and recipient of the 2018 Global Inspiration Award and the 2020 H.E. Judge C. G. Weeramantry International Justice Award.

**Paula Tiihonen** is Counselor for the Economic Affairs Committee, the Committee for Labor Affairs, and the Committee for the Future, Finnish Parliament. She received her doctorate in 1986 in administrative sciences, while working as a Counselor of Legislation in the Ministry of Justice. Dr Tiihonen has written several books on public administration, including *Democracy and Future* (The Finnish Parliament 2006, co-edited with M. Mannermaa and J. Dator), and *Russia 2017: Three Scenarios* (The Finnish Parliament 2007, co-edited with O. Kuusi and H. Smith).

**Joerg Chet Tremmel** is Associate Professor at the University of Tübingen, Germany, and a Research Fellow at the Grantham Institute on Climate Change and the Environment at the London School of Economics and Political Science (LSE). He holds a PhD from the University of Tübingen, a MA in Political Science from Johann-Wolfgang-Goethe-University of Frankfurt (2003), and an MBA in economics from the European Business School, Oestrich-Winkel (1998). His research interests include applied ethics (especially intergenerational justice and climate ethics), the 'short-termism' of political and business systems, and epistemology.

**Maria del Pilar Vanegas Guzman** is President of the International Law Association of Colombia. Ms Vanegas Guzman has had extensive international law experience, including as a delegate for the International Committee of the Red Cross, where she worked for the protection of victims of armed conflict and the respect of international humanitarian law. Among her postings with the ICRC were Peru, Rwanda, Central Asia, the Balkans, Guinea, and Israel and the Occupied Territories. Ms Vanegas Guzman has also worked as a legal advisor to corporations and individuals in Colombia and South Africa, and in conjunction with the University of Johannesburg has a research background in the interplay between international and local laws. She is also accredited by the Federation of Law Societies of Canada. She holds a LLM (McGill University), a DSU in Public International Law (Université Panthéon-Assas [Paris II]), a LLM in International Business Law (London School of Economics and Political Science), and a LLB (Universidad del Rosario).

**Halina Ward** has been Director of the Foundation for Democracy and Sustainable Development since 2009, having previously served as a trustee from 2006 to 2009. She has a strong leaning to policy-relevant, action-oriented research. Her interest in links between democracy and sustainable development was framed by periods spent working on projects in Azerbaijan, Kazakhstan, and Kosovo; by work on the relationship between public policy and responsible private enterprise; by experience as a mediator and facilitator; by extensive work on environmental and social implications of international trade liberalisation and its institutions; and through interactions with public authorities in the UK as an ordinary citizen. Before joining the Foundation for Democracy and Sustainable Development, Ms Ward was Director of the Business and Sustainable Development Programme at the International Institute for Environment and Development (IIED) in London. She has also worked as a Senior Fellow at the Royal Institute of International Affairs (Chatham House), as a Senior Consultant for the consultancy Environmental Resources Management, and as a solicitor practising commercial environment law. Ms Ward holds a LLB and a LLM (Law and Development) from the University of London. She is a member of the Scientific Committee of Vigeo, a Paris-based social ratings agency.

**H.E. C. G. Weeramantry** was Vice-President of the International Court of Justice. In the course of his professional career of over five decades as lawyer, legal educator, domestic judge, international judge, author, and lecturer, Judge Weeramantry touched on a wide variety of topics essential to peace, cross-cultural understanding and education. He wrote over twenty books and lectured extensively in over forty countries. He was the President of the International Association of Lawyers against Nuclear Arms (IALANA). The Weeramantry International Centre for Peace Education and Research (WICPER) is based on his philosophy and has his vast corpus of research and writing as an informational base from which to develop its programmes. Judge Weeramantry received the UNESCO Peace Education Prize 2006 in recognition of his commitment and concrete undertakings in support of the concept and culture of peace through his career, and was Chair Emeritus of the Centre for International Sustainable Development Law (CISDL) until he passed away in 2017.

**David Wright** is Full Professor at the University of Ottawa's Telfer School of Management. Professor Wright seeks to provide a business perspective on information and communications technology (ICT), currently focusing on its use in climate change mitigation and adaptation. His present work includes how ICT can enable greenhouse gas emissions reductions in power generation, data centres, transport, and buildings, and how the ICT sector can control emissions generated by its own products. Professor Wright has experience in government and in industry. In government, he developed systems dynamics models to evaluate the impact of industrial society on natural resource depletion and the ability of the environment to absorb pollution. In industry, he has worked with telecommunications equipment vendors and network operators on market analysis, network evolution, service requirements, distance education, and the strategic impact of new technology on business. Professor Wright is cited in *Who's Who in the World*, *Who's Who in Canadian Business*, and *Who's Who in Science and Engineering*, and holds an Engineering PhD.

# Foreword

*Jona David and Tyra Sioni*

UNESCO Voices of Future Generations Child Authors and Trust for Sustainable Living Medallist

We are grateful for the honour to recommend this volume on intergenerational justice to all readers, young and old, all over the world.

As Child Authors from the United Nations Education, Science and Culture Organization (UNESCO) Voices of Future Generations Children's Initiative, we believe it is crucial for all generations to respect each other's interests and needs.

One of us (Tyra) comes from Papua New Guinea, Singapore, and Australia, while the other (Jona) is a citizen of the UK, Canada, Germany, and Switzerland. Our own stories focus on children's rights to a voice in decision-making that concerns us, a right that is guaranteed globally in the UN Convention on the Rights of the Child. Ending poverty and hunger, protecting and restoring life on land and below water, securing gender equality, promoting eco-education, taking action to stop climate change, using science and technology innovations wisely – all of the UN Sustainable Development Goals are decisions of great importance for children today, and for all future generations. Actually, if we cannot achieve sustainable development on the ground and globally, it is unclear whether all of us children today will even have a future at all. Through our books, educational work, awareness-raising events, and local projects, all of us Child Authors are trying to speak out for our rights, for intergenerational equity, for the future we want. We are trying to say that it is important to have the courage to be ourselves, and to stand up for each other. Not just for children today, but for future generations of children, and for all species of our Earth. Our books are one way to raise awareness, to get our voices heard, but we can't make the scale of change required alone.

For a real chance of global sustainability and justice, we need present generations of leaders, experts, and practitioners to make a deep commitment to help transform all the inefficient, wasteful, destructive systems by which we currently live. In the light of the challenges faced by humanity today, this volume is very important. In its words and chapters, written by world-class experts and leaders, are found efforts to imagine new ways to deliver justice for future generations around the world. In particular, this volume helps everyone to understand the scale and scope of the changes that must come, why the transformations are so important, how countries and institutions for intergenerational justice all over the world are trying to help, and what more is needed. We think this is crucial for the survival of all life on our small, shared planetary home. We recommend this volume, as we can see it is part of the solutions we need now, worldwide. We believe that everyone can make a difference, and this book offers a very important and hopeful step forward towards a more sustainable future for our generation, and for all generations to come.

# Acknowledgements

The editors wish to acknowledge and offer their sincerest thanks to the contributors to this volume for their insights, brilliance, and patience in the long process of developing the initial papers and book concept into the current published academic volume.

Additionally, our sincere thanks and recognition must be extended to leaders, experts, and colleagues from the Hungarian Office of the Ombudsman for Future Generations, the Centre for International Sustainable Development Law, the Balsillie School of International Affairs, the Lauterpacht Centre for International Law at the University of Cambridge, the School of Environment, Enterprise and Development in the University of Waterloo, the International Law Association, the Voices of Future Generations Initiative, and the Weeramantry Centre for International Peace Education and Research. We also deeply appreciate the guidance and support of John Berger, Jackie Grant, Finola O'Sullivan, Jane Bowbrick, Vinithan Sethumadhavan and their team at Cambridge University Press. Finally, we must recognise and dedicate this volume to an extraordinary mentor, friend and elder, H.E. Judge C. G. Weeramantry. He is deeply missed, even as his wisdom, intellectual courage and invitation to the law continue.

The editors also extend their thanks and warmest appreciation to their kind, supportive, and talented families, particularly spouses, parents, and children, for their continuing support and inspiration. We are very grateful to the generations who came before us and helped shape this project and hope this book can serve as a catalyst for the promotion of sustainable development for future generations.

# Abbreviations and Acronyms

| | |
|---|---|
| ADB | Asian Development Bank |
| AfCHPR | African Court of Human and Peoples' Rights |
| ASEAN | Association of South East Asian Nations |
| AU | African Union |
| BIT | Bilateral Investment Treaty |
| CBD | Convention on Biological Diversity |
| CEDAW | Convention on the Elimination of All Forms of Discrimination Against Women |
| CIL | customary international law |
| CISDL | Centre for International Sustainable Development Law |
| CITES | Convention on the International Trade in Endangered Species |
| CJEU | Court of Justice of the European Union |
| CoE | Council of Europe |
| COP | Conference of the Parties |
| CRC | Convention on the Rights of the Child |
| CSD | Commission for Sustainable Development |
| CSR | corporate social responsibility |
| DSU | Understanding on Rules and Procedures Governing the Settlement of Disputes, or Dispute Settlement Understanding |
| ECtHR | European Court of Human Rights |
| ECOSOC | Economic and Social Council |
| EEC | European Economic Community |
| EIA | environmental impact assessment |
| EU | European Union |
| FAO | Food and Agriculture Organization |
| GATS | General Agreement on Trade in Services |
| GATT | General Agreement on Tariffs and Trade |
| GEF | Global Environment Facility |

| | |
|---|---|
| GHG | greenhouse gases |
| HDI | Human Development Index |
| IACHR | Inter-American Court of Human Rights |
| IAEA | International Atomic Energy Agency |
| ICESCR | International Covenant on Economic, Social and Cultural Rights |
| ICJ | International Court of Justice |
| IDLO | International Development Law Organization |
| IEL | international environmental law |
| IGO | intergovernmental organisation |
| ILA | International Law Association |
| ILC | International Law Commission |
| ILO | International Labour Organization |
| IPCC | Intergovernmental Panel on Climate Change |
| IR | international relations |
| IUCN | International Union for the Conservation of Nature |
| MDGs | Millennium Development Goals |
| MEAs | multilateral environmental agreements |
| MOP | Meeting of the Parties |
| MRV | measurement, reporting and verification |
| MTR | multilateral treaty regimes |
| NGOs | nongovernmental organisations |
| OAS | Organization of American States |
| OAU | Organization of African Unity |
| OECD | Organization for Economic Cooperation and Development |
| PCA | Permanent Court of Arbitration |
| PCIJ | Permanent Court of International Justice |
| PIL | public international law |
| RTAs | regional trade agreements |
| SDGs | Sustainable Development Goals |
| SIA | sustainability impact assessment |
| SIDS | Small Island Developing States |
| TEU | Treaty of European Unity |
| TFEU | Treaty on the Functioning of the European Union |
| TNC | transnational corporation |
| UK | United Kingdom |
| UN | United Nations |
| UNCCD | UN Convention to Combat Desertification |
| UNCED | United Nations Conference on the Environment and Development |
| UNCHR | UN Commission on Human Rights |
| UNCSD | UN Commission on Sustainable Development |
| UNDRIP | UN Declaration on the Rights of Indigenous Peoples |
| UNECE | UN Economic Commission for Europe |

| | |
|---|---|
| UNEP | UN Environment Programme/UN Environment |
| UNESCO | UN Educational, Scientific and Cultural Organization |
| UNFCCC | UN Framework Convention on Climate Change |
| UNGA | UN General Assembly |
| UNSC | UN Security Council |
| UNTS | UN Treaty System |
| US | United States |
| USD | US dollars |
| VCLT | Vienna Convention on the Law of Treaties |
| WCED | World Commission on Environment and Development |
| WHC | Convention Concerning the Protection of the World Cultural and Natural Heritage |
| WHO | World Health Organization |
| WSSD | World Summit on Sustainable Development |
| WTO | World Trade Organization |

# 1

# Introduction

*Marie-Claire Cordonier Segger, Marcel Szabó, and Alexandra R. Harrington*

It is the age of the Anthropocene. With far-reaching changes to economy and technology, society and the environment, humanity has gained the capacity to either foster or foreclose the quality of life for future generations. Through degradation of the Earth's marine and terrestrial ecosystems and its climate, including the natural resources upon which all people depend, human civilization holds the potential to deprive billions of their rights to life, taking millions of other species as well. Particularly as social, economic and environmental transformations and impacts of the recent global COVID-19 pandemic become more apparent, a growing recognition of the risks and threats is slowly changing perceptions of humankind's responsibility for its descendants.[1] Since the 1972 UN Conference in Stockholm, numerous international policy declarations have reflected increasing concern for the need to promote a more sustainable development that can take into account the needs and interests of future generations, including the global adoption of the 17 Sustainable Development Goals (SDGs) and their 169 targets in 2015 by Heads of State in New York.

The contours of global commitments to respect intergenerational equity remain unclear in international law. Sustainable development entails the integration of economic, social and environmental objects to improve the quality of life for the present generation without compromising the needs of future generations. It is possible that a customary legal principle of intergenerational equity is gradually gaining recognition, as part of States' attempts to promote more sustainable development.[2] It is certain, however, that concern for intergenerational equity is found in international treaty law on sustainable development. A legal commitment to protection of the interests of future generations is reflected in international law

[1] J. Locke, *Essays on Human Understanding* (Penguin Classics 1998); C. Darwin, *Descent of Man* (CreateSpace 2014).

[2] T. Cottier, S. Lalani, and C. Siziba, *Intergenerational Equity: Environmental and Cultural Concerns* (Brill 2019).

through three fundamental (and near-universal) conventions: the venerable UNESCO 1972 World Heritage Convention,[3] the 1992 Convention on Biological Diversity (CBD),[4] and the 1992 United Nations Framework Convention on Climate Change (UNFCCC).[5] These widely ratified treaties are an essential part of the legal framework and models for achieving greater intergenerational justice by setting forth obligations and measures to protect natural heritage for the benefit of present and future generations, and by making international cooperation and assistance a duty of the States to enable the full and effective implementation of their treaty obligations. A commitment to intergenerational equity is also found in the 1994 United Nations Convention to Combat Desertification and Drought (UNCCD)[6] and the 1998 UNECE Aarhus Convention on Access to Information, Public Participation in Decision-making and Access to Justice in Environmental Matters,[7] among other accords. Indeed, perhaps one of the most comprehensive definitions of sustainable development is found in treaty law, in the 2003 Tanganyika Convention, where intergenerational justice is highlighted in Article 5 paragraph 2: "[t]he natural resources of Lake Tanganyika shall be protected, conserved, managed, and used for sustainable development to meet the needs of present and future generations in an equitable manner."[8]

For the signatory States to such treaties, a legal duty arises to undertake domestic action for the protection and conservation of the elements of nature and the transmission of natural heritage to future generations. The motivation, means and metrics for implementing such treaty commitments, however, are worthy of a great deal more attention. With current gaps in effective global treaty enforcement mechanisms, national sustainability institutions and their efforts to implement international norms at domestic levels acquire crucial significance. As one small example, the Aichi Biodiversity Targets in the CBD's Strategic Plan for Biodiversity 2011–2020 may have been the most ambitious treaty norms for the protection of biological diversity,[9] but they did not offer more than a mere hope that the loss of biological diversity could be reduced by 50 percent by 2020.[10] Since 1965, the territory of national parks and other natural reserves increased by 700 percent, while simultaneously a 40 percent loss of biological diversity worldwide was recorded in non-maritime areas, and in the

[3] UNESCO 1972 World Heritage Convention, 1975 UNTS 1037 art. 4.
[4] 1992 Convention on Biological Diversity preamble.
[5] 1992 United Nations Framework Convention on Climate Change preamble, art. 3.
[6] 1994 United Nations Convention to Combat Desertification and Drought preamble.
[7] 1998 UNECE Aarhus Convention on Access to Information, Public Participation in Decision-making and Access to Justice in Environmental Matters preamble, art. 1.
[8] Convention on the Sustainable Management of Lake Tanganyika concluded on 12 June 2003, arts. 2, 5.
[9] CBD, Strategic Plan for Biodiversity 2011–2020, Aichi Biodiversity Targets, UNEP/CBD/COP/DEC/X/2 (29 October 2010).
[10] Aichi Biodiversity Targets, ibid. at Target 5.

seas, the loss of biological diversity has been estimated at 20 percent.[11] While global protection is failing to deliver the desired results, the development of national institutions entrusted with the protection of the interests of future generations may offer a suitable complementary means of implementing commitments. As such, the law and governance characteristics, competences and procedures of such implementing institutions merit careful consideration.

As noted in UN Secretary-General Ban Ki-moon's 2013 Report ('Intergenerational Solidarity and the Needs of Future Generations'),[12] it is possible to identify several key national institutions worldwide that play a pioneering role in the national implementation of sustainable development and intergenerational solidarity. Further, as the Secretary-General explains, there is a need to learn from the experiences of these institutions in order to create more effective instruments to assure our common future.[13] Given the commitments found in several key treaties that may require increased effort for effective implementation, a deeper cooperation between national human rights institutions committed to protecting the interests of future generations, and with economic and environmental institutions, could potentially contribute to the development of international legal principles and shape relevant state practice.

Starting from this concern – its premise and its promise – this volume provides a discussion of the theoretical, institutional and legal considerations inherent in the implementation of international treaties promoting intergenerational equity and justice. Implementing international conventions on sustainable development for future generations raises both conceptual and practical challenges. Conundrums are posed, for instance, by the status of beneficiaries (future generations) and their representation, the institutional implications of a duty of cooperation between States in promoting intergenerational justice, and the interpretation and enforcement of common but differentiated responsibilities.

Such questions are challenging and require an interdisciplinary response. The implementation of intergenerational equity and justice commitments is complex, not least owing to the abstract nature of the State obligations laid down in treaty law, but also because of the multiplicity of areas which intergenerational justice touches upon, ranging from environmental, social and economic sustainability to questions of demographical trends, public participation, fiduciary duties and the contours of a common heritage for humanity. To address these questions and more, this volume represents a multidisciplinary overview of the legal framework, the diverse mechanisms and possible challenges relating to the national implementation of intergenerational justice for the achievement of sustainable development. Against a background

[11] Protected Plant Report 2016: How Protected Areas Contribute to Achieving Global Targets for Biodiversity (UNEP 2016) 30–31.

[12] UN Secretary-General, 'Intergenerational Solidarity and the Needs of Future Generations: Report of the Secretary-General', UN Doc. A/68/322 (15 August 2013), items 39–48.

[13] Ibid. at 27–32.

of scant general consensus on the appropriate enforcement of intergenerational justice, the volume examines several national institutions that have been established worldwide with different focuses and spheres of competence for the protection of the interests of future generations. Within its pages, expert authors also comment on the rights of future generations in constitutions and courts, as this pertains to implementation of the treaties that commit to respect for intergenerational equity. The comprehensive study of such institutions, their competences and their specific areas of expertise yields valuable insights for a more grounded theory and more effective implementation of intergenerational justice commitments, with due attention to current regional and global trends and developments in the ambit of promoting sustainable development.

## OUTLINE OF THE VOLUME

The volume is structured in six parts, each discussing different aspects of implementing intergenerational law and policy departing from the relevant international treaties, through the challenges of sustainability and policy integration and the variety of national solutions to implement intergenerational justice commitments in the national framework.

Following this introductory note, in Chapter 2 the eminent Edith Brown Weiss asserts that the concept of intergenerational equity provides a valuable framework to address the most challenging issues featuring the new Anthropocene epoch, i.e. human activities that are shaping the planet's environment on an unprecedented scale. Since the temporal aspect of human activities has been understood, she argues, humankind's responsibility for its descendants became a major concern for many. The notion of intergenerational equity represents a tool for the reconciliation of solidarity between past, present and future generations. Basic principles of intergenerational equity are threefold, she explains: humanity must conserve the comparable quality, options and access to all basic resources of the Earth's environment for future generations to enjoy and to decide for themselves. Her chapter explores the substantial and institutional criteria of individual national institutions to take up their role in realizing these universal principles guaranteed by international law on a national level.

Part I then lays the foundations for the rest of the volume by exploring several relevant international conventions enshrining the basic exigencies of intergenerational justice and sustainable development, notably the 1992 CBD, the 1992 UNFCCC, the 1972 Convention Concerning the Protection of the World Cultural and Natural Heritage, and the 1998 UNECE Aarhus Convention on Access to Information, Public Participation in Decision-making and Access to Justice in Environmental Matters. This part defines and provides the theoretical background underpinning the principle of intergenerational equity in international law on sustainable development, and its implications.

Chapter 3 provides a further introduction to emerging trends in international law on sustainable development, with a focus on the principle of intergenerational equity as reflected in the New Delhi Declaration of the International Law Association (ILA), examining how its meaning and importance has become clearer over time, through global policy debates, through agreement of various international economic, human rights and environmental instruments which complement recent developments in the CBD and its protocols, the UNFCCC and its Paris Agreement, the Convention Concerning the Protection of the World Cultural and Natural Heritage (WHC) and the Aarhus Convention, and through the decisions of international courts and tribunals as interpreted by leading scholarly literature. It considers, from a perspective of international law on sustainable development, the meaning of current commitments to intergenerational equity, and the principal architecture for implementing these treaties in global, regional and local contexts.

Chapter 4 then provides a framework for the implementation of the norms of intergenerational justice envisioned by international treaty law. Introducing the most important references to intergenerational justice laid down in the CBD, the UNFCCC and the WHC, among others, the author concludes that there are three fundamental obligations of the state to comply with intergenerational provisions: (1) the obligation to protect natural heritage for future generations, (2) the legal duty to undertake domestic action aiming at the protection of the natural heritage and (3) a duty to cooperate internationally regarding the state's domestic actions. It also comments on the use of national constitutions, courts and institutions to defend the rights of future generations, including public trust doctrine.

Finally in Part I, Chapter 5 briefly surveys the jurisprudence that has developed in international human rights tribunals and how it has and may continue to improve environmental decisions and remediate environmental degradation, safeguarding our planet for future generations. It then turns to identify challenges for the future such as the capacity to use human rights law to prevent threats to the environment, especially long-term threats and harm to nature; the limits in tackling big questions like climate change and transboundary harm; and the limited jurisdiction of human rights tribunals that makes it impossible to address directly harm caused by non-state actors.

Shifting focus slightly, Part II of the volume focuses on the contours of intergenerational justice, equity and the rights of future generations, providing perspectives on the concept and its implications in law and policy. It scopes the international acceptance and dissemination of these norms, and focuses on the key issues of intergenerational justice awaiting national implementation with contributions concentrating on the main problems, relevant models, similarities and discrepancies.

With this in mind, in Chapter 6, the author argues that the principal challenge to be addressed by any institution for future generations is that of "embedded decision-making short-termism that is at odds with sustainable development." From this starting point, it is posited, responses to the conundrum of identifying 'how many generations,' 'where' and 'in relation to what issues' can be flexibly addressed and must, inherently, address social as well as environmental considerations. Institutions for future generations can provide a stimulus to, and decision-making tools and information for, deliberation over choices and trade-offs about the future in policy processes, and a judicial and administrative review function to guarantee ongoing accountability of decision-makers. However, the author recommends, their functions and ways of working need to be linked clearly to the notion of demos in the present.

Chapter 7 argues that national institutions for future generations are responsible for representing coming generations at the negotiating table. There are several international conventions that outline the duty of the state to 'take future generations into consideration' when implementing their principles. National institutions can channel the interests of future generations into the process of decision-making. Institutional design and relationship with the powers of decision can be varied; however, certain common features make these bodies capable of executing this international duty. In general, institutions (1) convey citizens' concerns on long-term issues, (2) serve as an interface for creating policy coherence among different strategies, (3) recommend solutions of sustainability and (4) trace blocks of implementation of the conventions. The article focuses on the example of the Hungarian Ombudsman to further explore the executive powers of national bodies in the implementation of international intergenerational commitments.

Part III then highlights the key challenges for national implementation of intergenerational equity and justice in principle, exploring recent trends and innovations in the development of constitutional legal norms and arrangements, economic instruments, mechanisms for transparent public participation and access to justice, and measures to address science, precaution and uncertainty.

Throughout Chapter 8, it is asserted that the concept of sustainability reflects long-term social challenges which cannot be efficiently dealt with in the framework of the traditional democratic mechanism, as democracy is based on elections held every four or five years, and is therefore necessarily short-sighted. Constitutions have the task of providing the rules of the political game, listing the taboos that politicians otherwise might break. Structurally, democratically elected politicians are focused on short-term consequences that impact on immediate election cycles, and are likely to go for the easy solution. In order to prevent them from being seduced, the author argues, constitutions must bind them, as Ulysses was bound to the mast so that he could resist the sirens, in order to protect current and future generations and provide for intergenerational equity and justice.

Chapter 9 observes that intergenerational solidarity appears in different constitutions of the world and can provide an important marker for cases in domestic courts, among other forums. Using the example of Portugal's constitutional experiences as a prism, the author outlines the potential impact of the implementation of the generally recognized international concepts of intergenerational solidarity and equity in the transformation of the constitutional system of human rights.

Chapter 10 explores the role of the individual person in the discussion of intergenerational justice, national institutions and sustainable development. It considers the legal concept of sustainable development and examines whether it does indeed allow valuable assessments of present actions and future developments. A perspective of future generations is necessarily a perspective that goes beyond the European continent and beyond the legal traditions of Western industrialized countries. The modern organization of societies and economies clearly favours institutions, collective rights, transboundary governance and general interference with the sphere of individuals, in the name of efficiency. The author draws conclusions for the present political and economic situation throughout the globe, focusing in particular on the individual as a consumer and as a user of the natural environment.

Chapter 11 then conveys the Brazilian legal experience with concepts of intergenerational equity and justice using the example of class actions and *actio popularis*, especially the solutions adopted to protect the collective interests in case of petitioner's neglect of the case. Furthermore, the importance of independent and specialized public institutions to defend the rights of future generations will also be highlighted and discussed in the context of developing robust systems which allow for the promotion and elevation of the voices of the public in matters that affect the present and the future.

Chapter 12 explains that several constitutional principles, rights and values support the idea of public participation, such as democracy, rule of law, human dignity, the collective or 'community' dimension, common concern of humanity, common heritage, common good, subsidiarity and environmental justice. It further notes that there are numerous practical reasons underlying public participation, such as building trust in connection with administration, enhancing legitimacy of decisions, promoting mutual learning through incorporation of public values into decisions, and facilitating conflict resolution. Public participation may be implemented in various forms, such as local and national elections, public hearings, referendums, ombudspersons, public prosecutors and NGOs. The author focuses on the constitutional and empirical underpinnings of environmental public participation as well as the very different forms it may take in the pursuit and advancement of intergenerational equity and justice.

Chapter 13 considers public participation for the interests of future generations and the role of young people in policy development and decision-making for the long term. It examines practical steps taken by the office of the Commissioner for Sustainability and the Environment in the Australian Capital Territory to involve young people in its work, and finishes by identifying the current trend of youth-initiated climate change litigation, for and on behalf of future generations.

In Chapter 14, the author argues that, despite a great number of international political agreements, the sustainability performance of societies is often very weak. Significant negative correlation between words and facts are fundamental economic challenges that have the potential to undermine sustainability and the rights of future generations, including concepts of intergenerational equity. First, he highlights certain economic problems regarding sustainability transitions such as discounting and selecting the appropriate social discount rates in decision-making processes, or the problem of transition costs. Then, he outlines possible institutional solutions to the problem of the long-term effects of decisions.

In Chapter 15, the author argues that Sustainability Impact Assessments (SIAs) can be valuable tools applied to foreign investment: they allow negotiators to identify aspects of agreements that require mitigation or enhancement measures in order to achieve the fullest benefits of investment. It is noted, however, that there are important differences between trade and investment liberalization commitments in their impacts on social and environmental concerns. The most notable difference is that investment liberalization can have both an impact on regulation and a localized effect.[14] While trade liberalization might impact an entire sector or sectors, investment liberalization can have very little impact overall but drive significant detrimental changes for one part of the country where sensitive sectors such as mining or forestry are considerably expanded because of investment liberalization. Drawing on this, the author analyses how impact assessment can, as an instrument of sustainable development, play a role in strengthening and improving world investment law.

Chapter 16 recognizes that both environmental law and policy-making face significant challenges due to scientific uncertainty. Scientific uncertainty, by inherently burdening and rendering less reliable scientific evidence, causes considerable problems in environmental cases. This is especially true for fact finding and establishing causality. The International Court of Justice, regional human rights courts and other international and domestic tribunals, as well as scholars, are still striving to develop effective legal tools for addressing uncertainty in the face of law. Such attempts range from the well-known precautionary principle to a selection of innovative methods applied in a variety of decisions. The author discusses leading public trust cases that deal with these problems directly, setting forth the precautionary principle as a fiduciary duty associated with a sovereign trustee. The effort is to look beyond the discussion of existing legal tools by providing insights into the ecological subject matter of environmental cases, then briefly present the main sources and types of scientific uncertainty manifest in ecological decision-making. In so doing, the author argues that the deeper understanding of the characteristics of natural sciences is pivotal for enhancing the efficiency of environmental law.

Chapter 17 advances from this to assert that sustainability policies focus on new transformation and trajectories, responsibility and governance. Providing scientific evidence and transformative knowledge is one of the main sources and tools for achieving sustainability through policy reform. The author argues, by way of an

[14] See K. von Moltke, *An International Investment Regime? Issues of Sustainability* (IISD 2000) 21.

example from the German Council for Sustainable Development, that such policies can trigger choice editing and raise awareness. Through this lens, the author provides experiences and new approaches that demonstrate the place of intergenerational equity in these transformations and trajectories, and how that place may become further refined in the future.

Part IV provides original case studies of prominent national sustainable development institutions of model character, analysing different solutions to the complex problems of policy integration and the representation of the interests of future generations in policy-making, implementation and reform. This part of the volume offers comparative insights from different domestic experiences and traditions, identifying areas of commonality and difference in efforts to activate domestic institutions in the interest of intergenerational equity.

Chapter 18 provides a case study of institutional reform in Israel, although the Israel Commission for Future Generations no longer exists as such. As the author explains, the competences of the Israeli Commission included advising the Parliament on issues of particular relevance for the interests of future generations and submitting opinions on the implication of laws for the needs of future generations. The Commission gave itself a broad scope of responsibilities and considered all policies and laws that may have significant long-term effects on the living conditions of future generations, including environmental issues, education of children, health care, medical research, national economy and pension funds. Although lacking decision-making power, the author suggests, the Commission had the ability to exert pressure on the government by raising awareness of the long-term consequences of harmful policies, laws and actions.

Chapter 19 examines the Norwegian Ombudsman for Children as an independent human rights institution with strong powers to investigate petitions and complaints, ensuring that the voices and opinions of children and young people are heard, and that their rights are adequately protected. As the author explains, the Ombudsman can monitor legislation and policies affecting the incorporation of the Convention on the Rights of the Child into all areas of society, including health, human rights education and cultural rights. Embedding responsibility towards children both in the legal and social systems forms the underlying premise of the work of this institution, which the author asserts is at the heart of intergenerational equity and justice.

Chapter 20 discusses the German Parliamentary Council on Sustainable Development as a case study of national implementation mechanisms for intergenerational equity. The Parliamentary Advisory Council on Sustainable Development works within the parliamentary system as a multi-stakeholder body. Its competences include supporting the Federal Government with recommendations on medium- and long-term planning, and developing goals, measures and instruments for longer-term strategies. It carries out SIAs that are mandated for all pieces of legislation. In general, the Council seeks to integrate and streamline the principles of sustainable development and long-term thinking in politics and policy-making, and engages in dialogue with other parliaments, the European Union and society as a whole to promote greater fairness between generations and the maintenance of the Earth's ecosystem.

Chapter 21 considers the functions of the Finnish Committee for the Future. The Committee for the Future is one of the sixteen parliamentary committees providing a basis for decisions taken by the Finnish Parliament. It prepares reports and statements to the Parliament upon request and undertakes analyses concerning future-related research and technological development. Its studies and statements are based on long-term issues, such as climate change, energy policy and population demographics, as well as the perspectives of the welfare state. By identifying future development trends and possible scenarios, the author posits, the Committee seeks to influence the government's decisions on actions that have long-term consequences for the living conditions of future generations.

Chapter 22 discusses the Welsh Commissioner for Sustainable Futures. The powers of the Commissioner include advisory functions and setting out principles to the Welsh Government on leadership for sustainable development aligned with the SDGs, as well as ensuring that the views and opinions of the wider public are channelled into its suggestions to the government. The Commission seeks to embed sustainable practices in the policies governing various sectors and communities, and convenes stakeholders to address difficult issues by creating a platform for cooperation. In this way, the author explains, the Commissioner plays an important bridging role between civil society and the government.

Chapter 23 provides an analysis of the experiences of the New Zealand Parliamentary Commissioner for Environment, including the functions and powers that have bearing on intergenerational equity. The functions of the Parliamentary Commissioner for the Environment include reviewing the system of agencies established to manage the country's natural resources and examining the effectiveness of management and planning. It also investigates situations in which the environment has been adversely affected on the basis of petitions or requests submitted by the House of Representatives. While conducting in-depth investigations, the Commissioner can obtain and disseminate information, summon individuals and question them under oath, report on findings to the wider community and make recommendations on remedial actions, as the author explains.

Chapter 24 considers the Canadian Commissioner of Environment and Sustainable Development. Situated in the Office of the Auditor General of Canada, the Commissioner of the Environment and Sustainable Development provides additional environmental aspects to the work of the Auditor General when reporting to the House of Commons, while assisting in its environmental auditing responsibilities. The Commissioner regularly monitors the federal departments' progress on the implementation of their respective sustainable development strategies, reporting on these to the Auditor General. It also receives and handles petitions on environmental and sustainable development matters and seeks responses to these from the relevant ministries. The author provides an overview of this work, taking into account both its value and its limits.

Chapter 25 provides a discussion of the ways in which intergenerational equity is included in the Colombian Peace Agreement with the FARC-EP. The authors note that explicit connections are made between the creation of conditions that are designed to foster peace and those which are meant to maintain peace in the long run and for those in the future, such as those fostering intergenerational equity through land distribution, infrastructural development and the enshrinement of essential rights – such as food and education – for all in society, including previously marginalized groups. In addition, the authors discuss how the formalized process of ensuring political participation and recognizing the many forms of victimization which took place during more than five decades of civil war that dominated the country can be viewed as enshrining intergenerational equity as a matter of law and reintegration for the community. Drawing on the case study of Colombia, the chapter asserts that there are important lessons that can be translated for intergenerational justice in other conflict and post-conflict settings.

Chapter 26 provides a case study from Mexico on the ways in which communities can rebuild themselves and their sense of identity for current and future generations by combining unique, lived experiences with tourism and economic development. It emphasizes the role that the interests of children and future generations can play in stemming the flow of dangerous conduct, and how this approach can lead to a renewed understanding of the indigenous community culture and heritage.

Chapter 27 examines intergenerational equity and justice in Cameroon and the Democratic Republic of Congo through the prism of policies governing mining and forestry initiatives in these two countries. It discusses key governance challenges in this context and how various commitments found within the SDGs might serve as points of analysis and motivation to overcome them and assist in achieving greater degrees of intergenerational equity. From the perspective of highly vulnerable least-developed countries which face important governance challenges, the chapter provides options to support more sustainable development that respects the needs and interests of future generations.

Chapter 28 explores the planning and policy tools developed by local indigenous communities to approach cultural significance valuation, and to consider their potential contributions to the promotion of intergenerational equity. The author argues that improving and understanding new and culturally appropriate approaches to non-marker valuation and issues of resource use in indigenous traditional territories is essential in achieving the SDGs, including SDG 13 on climate change, SDG 1 towards the eradication of poverty, SDG 3 for good health and well-being, and SDGs 14 and 15 for life below water and life on land.

In Chapter 29, the importance of diversity in reaching common goals among model institutions is thoroughly examined. Each institution has its own unique set of characteristics as a result of constitutional backgrounds, functions, organizational structures, etc. Also, each institution has found its own set of theoretical bases, principles upon which it pursues its activities and reaches its goals. The comparative study of the model institutions identifies the most important features (including not just references to legal frameworks and organizational structures, but also missions, aims and goals), theories and principles by which they can be characterized. By placing each institution within this set of criteria assessed and drawn from existing practice, links between the various aspects are highlighted, and it is shown how theories can be operational in practice. The chapter argues for and reflects on the innovative characteristics of model institutions for sustainable development when the theoretical basis (especially legal theory) is lagging behind.

In Chapter 30, drawing on the findings of a report prepared by legal experts from the Centre for International Sustainable Development Law (CISDL), the authors document and compare various intergenerational governance commitments in the constitutions of key countries, and the domestic practices and mechanisms for their implementation. In conjunction with this analysis, the authors discuss and evaluate international institutions for future generations and democratic legitimacy, noting key obstacles to progress and also opportunities to advance.

In Chapter 31, the author addresses the ways in which international organizations and institutions function to advance the interests of future generations. The author asserts that there are ways in which these organizations and institutions can and do further intergenerational equity at a structural level and in terms of policy generation.

Part V sheds light on current regional trends and innovations in this field, focusing on recent developments at regional levels and proposals for institutionalizing the representation of future generations in Europe, Africa, Asia, Latin America and the Caribbean.

Chapter 32 examines national sustainable development institutions through the lens of the jurisprudence of the European Court of Human Rights (ECtHR). It demonstrates that the ECtHR increasingly recognizes the "right to a healthy environment" in its dynamic interpretation of Articles 8 and 2 of the European Convention on Human Rights (ECHR). Drawing on the Court's case law, the chapter thus illustrates how a domestic legal concept such as the right to a healthy environment can be transferred into international law and how this can in turn fertilize domestic legal developments. It asks essential questions not only for those interested in European practices but for the broader topic of intergenerational equity *per se*.

Chapter 33 examines institutions for the rights of future generations in relation to the constitutions and case law of Africa, and the jurisprudence of the African Court of Human and Peoples' Rights (AfCHPR). It traces progress and setbacks in recognition and implementation of the rights of future generations. Drawing on national constitutions and the Court's case law, the chapter thus illustrates how the concept of intergenerational justice is being recognized and implemented in domestic and regional law, and asks what the emerging trends and legal developments are, and what can be learned from experiences, critiques and evaluative considerations.

Chapter 34 delves into the question of whether and how respect for future generations – along with intergenerational equity – is manifested in the terms and potentials of North American treaty law. Throughout time and across the various tribal compacts, relationships between countries and indigenous communities have changed dramatically. With the recognition of new negotiating relationships and parameters in, for example, the context of Canada, this chapter sheds vital light on the ways in which such changes have been and can be used to open spaces for intergenerational equity and the protection of future generations.

Finally, Chapter 35 examines national sustainable development institutions by considering recent developments in the constitutions of Asia and the jurisprudence of the Philippines and other Asian countries. It traces progress and setbacks in recognition and implementation of the rights of future generations. Drawing on national constitutions and recent public trust doctrine case law, the chapter thus illustrates how the concept of intergenerational justice is being recognized and implemented in domestic law in Asia, commenting on emerging trends and legal developments and asking what the most important lessons are.

Part VI scopes future directions and options, distilling lessons learned from current practices, for reform of political and legal institutions at the national, regional and global levels. It notes that education and the development of values-based legal institutions with effective authority on behalf of future generations could play key roles in delivering and disseminating intergenerational justice, and summarizes the findings of the volume.

Chapter 36 starts from the view that the fundamental principle of international water law is that of equitable and reasonable utilization of international watercourses. This principle is codified in Article 5 of the Convention on the Law of the Non-Navigational Uses of International Watercourses. It obliges States to use and develop an international watercourse equitably and reasonably, and "with a view to attaining optimal and sustainable utilization thereof and benefits therefrom." The link between 'sustainable utilization' and 'equitable and reasonable utilization' is unclear. Scholars have suggested that you cannot use an international watercourse equitably and reasonably without doing so sustainably. This chapter explores the link between sustainable utilization and equitable and reasonable utilization, in an attempt to promote a more 'future just' utilization of the world's international watercourses. Besides analysing the Watercourses Convention, the chapter analyses signs of evolution in regional and bilateral agreements of water law and in domestic water law and policy.

Chapter 37 discusses progress on intergenerational equity in implementing international law on climate change, including the 2015 Paris Agreement. The climate debate, and the climate negotiations, have made important strides in defining and understanding concerns for intergenerational and intragenerational equity, it argues.

The chapter focuses on the way that States have reflected an intergenerational equity principle in the shape and substance of the global climate change regime. From the recognition of intergenerational equity in the 1992 UNFCCC text, to its adoption and operationalization in the 2015 Paris Agreement and the 2018 Katowice outcomes the chapter considers how treaty law has advanced. It also mentions current developments in climate litigation, where the principle of intergenerational equity has contributed to the duty of countries to implement international commitments. The author concludes that the principle of intergenerational equity may be acquiring a legal binding status through treaty law on sustainable development in relation to climate change.

Chapter 38 surmises that even the best attempts to institutionalize the representation of future generations are falling short of what is necessary in the Anthropocene. The long-term success of the institutionalization of the interests/needs of future generations remains fragile as long as the classical separation of powers model dividing political power into legislative, executive and judicial branches is not called into question. The theoretical starting point for any attempts to institutionalize sustainability, the author suggests, should be an extension of the classical three-branches model of government into a new four-powers model including an institutional level that brings the interests of posterity into the decision-making processes of today. The author advises giving the new institution (the fourth branch of government) a proactive rather than a reactive role and connecting it to the legislature in order to formulate sustainable laws. Another decisive feature would be path-dependency, the author notes. The institutions needed to represent future generations will be different for different democracies, depending on the differences among existing political systems and the interplay of the institutions that exist to date. The chapter concludes that many of the counterarguments in the literature against the representation of future generations, such as the ignorance argument, the non-identity argument and the thesis of the rich future argument, are either unconvincing or they apply to veto-oriented new institutions but not to constructive and path-dependent ones. The chapter addresses the question of what institutions have the power to protect future generations if the present legislative and executive power structures lean towards present generations.

Chapter 39 looks forward, drawing on the leading works of World Future Council members and others, and considers ways and means to develop public international law with a view on future generations. Taking into account the extraordinary conditions and opportunities facing the world as it seeks the necessary policies and approaches to recovery from a global pandemic, the chapter provides a summary of the findings is provided, focusing on lessons learned in implementing international treaty obligations in relation to intergenerational equity. It compares the institutional arrangements across countries and regions, underlining key challenges and innovations, and then explores future directions for the development of international law on sustainable development in relation to intergenerational justice. It asks whether and how intergenerational equity and moral constructs can work together to function and thrive within a legal setting at the international level. It also considers, from a perspective of international law on sustainable development, priorities for future legal research in this field, and options for more effective interventions.

This book concludes with an Afterword in honour of the late Justice H.E. C.G. Weeramantry, a tireless advocate for the rights of future generations and the importance of intergenerational equity and justice. Justice Weeramantry's legacy, the Afterword demonstrates, is one which will indeed guide the lives and identities of future generations and will doubtless be manifested in the place granted to intergenerational equity as a matter of law and policy. The Afterword also notes the launch of a senior-level international justice award in memory of His Excellency Justice C.G. Weeramantry, and a global fellowship for international law and sustainable development that honours the legacy of the Judge and his wife, Mrs Rosemary Weeramantry.

2

# The Theoretical Framework for International Legal Principles of Intergenerational Equity and Implementation through National Institutions

*Edith Brown Weiss*

More than thirty years ago the article entitled 'A Planetary Trust: Conservation and Intergenerational Equity' appeared,[1] and the book *In Fairness to Future Generations* was published more than twenty-five years ago.[2] Since then much has happened. As society has gained greater scientific understanding of the environment and of climate change, it has become ever more aware that what is done today affects the future of the planet and that actions in one place have far-reaching effects elsewhere. Society has also turned its attention towards the local level and has begun to focus on what actions must be taken domestically, within and across countries, to ensure equity for both present and future generations. New institutions are now devoted to sustainable development and future generations, and the principle of intergenerational equity is included in many national and sub-national judicial decisions.

This chapter sets out a framework for considering intergenerational equity. It identifies three important contextual features shaping society's actions today, sets forth the elements of a principle of intergenerational equity and strategies for implementing the principle, develops criteria for evaluating institutions focused on sustainable development and future generations, and identifies and discusses the significance of judicial decisions within countries that have incorporated the principle of intergenerational equity explicitly. It adopts a 'bottom-up' approach in the sense that individuals, communities, non-governmental organizations,

1 E. Brown Weiss, 'A Planetary Trust: Conservation and Intergenerational Equity' (1984) 11 *Ecology Law Quarterly* 495–582.

2 E. Brown Weiss, *In Fairness to Future Generations: International Law, Common Patrimony and Intergenerational Equity* (Transnational Publishers and United Nations University Press 1989). The work benefited from a small, distinguished international advisory group under the auspices of the United Nations University. The group was responsible for drafting the Goa Guidelines on Intergenerational Equity. See ibid. at 293–295.

religious organizations, and businesses as well as governments have important roles in promoting values that foster intergenerational equity and sustainable development.[3]

## THE CONTEXT

At least three global contexts shape the environment today: (1) the transition from the Holocene Epoch to the Anthropocene; (2) the exploding effects of measures taken or not taken in one place on other places; and (3) the rapid development of information and communications technology, which empowers a bottom-up world while facilitating potentially mammoth controls over individual and collective behaviour.

### *The Anthropocene*

For the last twelve thousand years or so, the planet has been in the geological Holocene Epoch. This has been a relatively stable period. Scientists now believe that it has entered a new epoch, the Anthropocene Epoch, in which human beings have a central role in shaping the planet on a geological scale and in which change is taking place at a rate far faster than traditional geological speed.[4] Scientists have begun to warn that the carbon cycle, the nitrogen cycle, and now the hydrological cycle, which are fundamental cycles of the Earth, are speeding up.[5] The impacts of this acceleration could be devastating. The transition to the Anthropocene Epoch sharply conveys the fundamental message that everyone shares the global environment and responsibility for it for the foreseeable future. This inherently raises issues of intergenerational equity and makes them urgent as never before.

3 For other books on law and intergenerational equity, see e.g. E. Agius and S. Busuttil (eds.), *Future Generations and International Law* (Earthscan 1998); C. Redgwell, *Intergenerational Trusts and Environmental Protection* (Manchester University Press 1999); J.C. Tremmel (ed.), *Handbook of Intergenerational Justice* (Edward Elgar 2006); R. Bifulco, *Diritto e generazioni future* (Franco Angeli 2008); D. Ramos, Jr., *Meio ambiente e conceito jurídico de futuras gerações* (Juruá Editora Juvevê 2012); L.G. Ferrer Ortega, *Los derechos de las futuras generaciones desde la perspectiva del derecho internacional: el principio de equidad intergeneracional* (Universidad Nacional Autónoma de México 2014).

4 'Dawn of a New Epoch?', *The Economist*, 3 September 2016; P.J. Crutzen and E.F. Stoermer, 'The "Anthropocene"' (2000) 41 *Global Change Newsletter: International Geosphere-Biosphere Programme* 17–18.

5 'A Man-Made World', *The Economist*, 26 May 2011 www.economist.com/node/18741749 accessed 30 November 2017; P.J. Durack, S.E. Wijffels, and R.J. Matear, 'Ocean Salinities Reveal Strong Global Water Cycle Intensification during 1950–2000' (2012) 336 (6080) *Science* 455–458 (predicting that the hydrologic cycle may intensify by as much as 2.4 percent with a global temperature rise of 2–3 °C).

### *The Global Commons*

In the Anthropocene Epoch, we have to confront the evidence that what we do in one place individually or collectively may have effects locally, regionally, or globally. Interactions of different measures may produce unforeseen effects, and collectively they may produce even greater unforeseen effects. For example, the clear cutting of tropical forests or elimination of peat bogs to grow palm oil for energy purposes destroys invaluable sinks for carbon dioxide emissions.[6] While this has been known for some time, only now is society acknowledging on a collective scale that these effects are becoming pervasive and must be addressed on all human and physical scales. The advent of the Anthropocene Epoch makes us aware that we share a global commons to which everyone has access in some way and in which our actions, whether individually or collectively, may affect its robustness and resilience, and its long-term health and stability. Fairness to future generations is inherently part of the global commons.[7]

### *Bottom-Up Empowerment to Address Issues*

Information and communications technology is transforming the ways in which we interact. The world is more integrated, with about 68,000 intergovernmental, international, and non-governmental organizations, according to the *Yearbook of International Organizations* for 2016.[8] It is also more fragmented. It is more chaotic and less hierarchical than ever before. Certainly, States remain central, but the context in which they operate is in flux. Change occurs rapidly. Communications, locally or globally, are rapid, which lets informal groups or ad hoc coalitions arise quickly and also disappear quickly.

Recent data reveals the extent to which people are now participating in communication with people no longer linked physically to their own communities. Facebook has 1.59 billion monthly active users and 1.04 billion daily active users.[9] Facebook is blocked in China, but QQ, the most popular Chinese social media platform, has a

6 Y. Pan et al., 'A Large and Persistent Carbon Sink in the World's Forests' (2011) 333 (6045) *Science* 988–993; D. Biello, 'Peat and Repeat: Can Major Carbon Sinks Be Restored by Rewetting the World's Drained Bogs?', *Scientific American*, 8 December 2009 www.scientificamerican.com/article/peat-and-repeat-rewetting-carbon-sinks/ accessed 30 November 2017.

7 See Pope Francis, *Laudato Si': On Care for Our Common Home*, Encyclical Letter, 24 May 2015, 118–120 http://w2.vatican.va/content/francesco/en/encyclicals/documents/papa-francesco_20150524_enciclica-laudato-si.html accessed 30 November 2017.

8 Union of International Associations (2016–2017) *Yearbook of International Organizations* (Brill 2016).

9 As of December 2015. Facebook Annual Report 2015, 32 http://investor.fb.com/annuals.cfm accessed 30 November 2017.

similar reach with 899 million monthly active users.[10] Twitter has 288 million monthly active users, about 80 percent of whom accessed Twitter from a mobile device.[11] Blogs continue to be an immensely popular means for people to communicate with the world – for example, the hosting service WordPress reported 65.4 million new blog posts in August 2016.[12] The hosting service Tumblr had a total of 140 *billion* blog posts on 315.8 million blogs as of September 2016.[13] Mobile phone technology, which is spreading in Asia, Latin America, and Africa, is the most rapidly diffusing technology in history. The technology enables people to communicate with each other across boundaries and to develop innovative means to deal with long-standing social, bureaucratic, and economic obstacles.[14]

Bottom-up empowerment is taking place in many fields. For example, in the financial sector, mobile banking and bitcoin and other digital currencies provide radical alternatives to traditional commerce.[15] In the small business sector, the Internet empowers individuals and groups across the world to set up small businesses. This is a world in which it is becoming much easier for people to connect locally, regionally, and globally. Young people today are growing up with different expectations about their ability to communicate across national borders and they assume that they will be able to do so. Technology has helped break past physical boundaries. This has important implications for access to the commons and for managing it. It also has temporal implications, for it makes it easier to be aware of the problems of equity between and among present and future generations and potentially easier to confront them.

The world today may be characterized as kaleidoscopic. Change takes place rapidly and often unexpectedly. New constellations and patterns form and change shape. People, institutions, and governments are connected across physical boundaries. Bottom-up empowerment is part of this kaleidoscopic world. There are also multiple handles on the kaleidoscope that can exercise top-down control and cause patterns to shift. For future generations, it means that there is increased risk of dangers to the sustainability and integrity of the planet as well as more opportunities

[10] Tencent Holdings 2016 Interim Report, 6 www.tencent.com/en-us/ir/reports.shtml accessed 30 November 2017. QQ is owned by Tencent Holdings, which also owns the second and third most popular social media platforms in China, Qzone and WeChat/Weixin.

[11] As of fourth quarter 2014. Twitter Annual Report 2014, 43, 46 https://investor.twitterinc.com/annuals-proxies.cfm accessed 30 November 2017.

[12] 'A Live Look at Activity across WordPress.com', WordPress.com https://wordpress.com/activity/ accessed 30 November 2017.

[13] 'About Tumblr' www.tumblr.com/about accessed 30 November 2017.

[14] See, e.g., 'The Innovating Continent', *The Economist*, 25 April 2015 www.economist.com/news/middle-east-and-africa/21649516-innovation-increasingly-local-pioneering-continent accessed 30 November 2017.

[15] See, e.g., 'The End of a Monopoly', *The Economist*, 10 May 2014 www.economist.com/news/special-report/21601624-and-no-end-new-ways-pay-your-bills-end-monopoly accessed 30 November 2017.

to address them at many levels by many actors – civil society, the private sector, and governments.[16]

## THE NORMATIVE FRAMEWORK OF INTERGENERATIONAL EQUITY

Intergenerational equity provides a normative framework for considering our use of planet Earth, whether globally or locally, and its conservation for future generations. The framework has deep roots in diverse cultural and religious traditions: Judeo-Christian tradition, Islamic law, other religious traditions, common law, civil law, and African customary law. In international law, the principle of intergenerational equity builds upon a principle of equity, initially formulated by Aristotle and elaborated by Grotius as addressing concerns not covered by law. In the twentieth century, equity served as a basis for allocating and sharing resources or for distributing burdens.

The basic concept of the principle of intergenerational equity is that all generations – past, present, and future – are partners in caring for and using the Earth.[17] The present generation, which means everyone living today, must pass the Earth and its natural and cultural resources to future generations in at least as good condition as it received them so that future generations can meet their own needs. This concept is found in diverse theoretical writings and legal instruments. It applies both to the diversity of resources and to the quality of the environment. The principle fosters the robustness and resilience of the human environment and is key to sustainable development.

We can identify three elements of the principle: (1) comparable options, (2) comparable quality, and (3) comparable or non-discriminatory access.[18] These elements are consistent with the following criteria: (a) that they encourage equality among generations; (b) that they not require one generation to predict the values of future generations, which is not possible, but instead they give future generations flexibility to achieve their own goals; (c) that they be reasonably clear in their application to foreseeable situations; and (d) that they be generally shared by different cultural traditions and generally acceptable to different economic and political systems.

The Report of the UN Secretary-General released in September 2013 discusses the "fundamental principle of intergenerational equity," and notes three parts to it: conservation of options, conservation of quality, and conservation of access.[19] It is useful to consider each of these three elements briefly in order to understand how they might be applied by institutions, courts, or other groups.

16 E. Brown Weiss, 'International Law in a Kaleidoscopic World' (2011) 1 *Asian Journal of International Law* 21–32.

17 See Brown Weiss, *supra* note 2 at 17, for this and material that follows.

18 Ibid. at 38.

19 UN Secretary-General, 'Intergenerational Solidarity and the Needs of Future Generations: Report of the Secretary-General', UN Doc. A/68/322 (15 August 2013).

### *Comparable Options*

Comparable options call for conserving the diversity of the natural resources base (and cultural resources), so that future generations have a more robust and flexible heritage with which to achieve their own well-being. This means, for example, conserving biological diversity, respecting recharge rates in ground water aquifers, using renewable resources in preference to non-renewable, conserving germplasm and the local information about a plant's environment, conserving the productivity of soils, constraining the use of fossil aquifers according to certain criteria, and, in the case of helium – for which there are no known substitutes for certain uses – not releasing all of it to the atmosphere as a by-product of other resource exploitation. Conserving options is especially relevant as a guide for adapting to climate change.[20]

### *Comparable Quality*

Comparable quality calls for ensuring the quality of the environment is on balance in no worse condition than received. At any given time, it is possible to both degrade a particular environment and protect or improve the environment elsewhere. Hence the reference is to ensuring, on balance, comparable quality. However, there are limits to the concept of 'on balance'. Some of our actions generate long-term, irreversible harm, or harm that takes too long to reverse or that cannot be reversed at acceptable costs. For example, pollution of ground water is very difficult to reverse and often too costly. In Lake Superior, between Canada and the US, the flushing time to remove persistent toxic pollution is a century or more.[21] There are other examples. The disposal of nuclear wastes may lead to long-term degradation of the environment and harm to human health. The unsustainable use of soils, as from clearcutting of tropical forests or unsuitable agriculture, renders them unproductive for the future. Climate change may greatly exacerbate problems of environmental quality, as in the acidification of the oceans, prolonged droughts, or severe storms and floods.

### *Comparable Access*

Comparable access gives members of our generation a reasonable, non-discriminatory right of access to the environment and its resources to use for their own benefit, and provides for equitable non-discriminatory access to future generations. This element looks, for example, to assessing whether the real prices of

20 See Brown Weiss, *supra* note 2 at Appendix D, 345–351.

21 Ibid. at 233; see National Research Council of the United States, *The Great Lakes Water Quality Agreement: An Evolving Instrument for Ecosystem Management* (National Academy Press 1985) 52, 73–74.

resources for future generations will be comparable to the present. The need to ensure comparable, non-discriminatory access to the benefits of the environment to future generations calls for strong and effective adaptation measures to address climate change.[22]

### *Obligations or Also Rights?*

We can ask whether, under the principle of intergenerational equity, the present generation only has obligations to future generations, or whether future generations have rights which the present generation has an obligation to fulfill. Rights cannot exist without corresponding obligations, but obligations can exist without corresponding rights.[23] The 1997 UNESCO Declaration on the Responsibilities of Present Generations to Future Generations addressed only our obligations towards future generations,[24] and States intentionally did not reference rights of future generations.

One can argue, though, that future generations have rights, which are in the nature of collectively held rights and reflect their common interests in the robustness, integrity, and resilience of the Earth and the human environment. They do not depend upon knowing the number of individuals who will exist in the future, which cannot be known. Rather, they are group rights, which can be defined at a collective level.[25] When future generations emerge as members of the present generation, these members assume certain responsibilities towards still future generations. They may also hold individual rights, the protection of which ensures that future generations will also be able to have such rights fulfilled. For example, the right to safe drinking water, as adopted by the UNGA and the UN Human Rights Council, carries both the individual right and the obligation to ensure that future generations also have access to safe drinking water when a future generation becomes a present one.[26]

### *Intergenerational Equity and Intragenerational Equity*

An important theoretical and practical question is the relationship between intergenerational equity and intragenerational equity. One can argue that intergenerational

[22] See E. Brown Weiss, 'Climate Change, Intergenerational Equity, and International Law' (2008) 9 *Vermont Journal of Environmental Law* 615.

[23] Brown Weiss, *supra* note 2 at 99–103 (discussing philosophical and legal perspectives on the issue of rights and obligations). See also e.g. H. Kelsen, *Pure Theory of Law*, transl. M. Knight (University of California Press 1969) 62.

[24] Declaration on the Responsibilities of the Present Generations towards Future Generations, UNESCO Res. 44, 29th Sess., 12 November 1997.

[25] Brown Weiss, *supra* note 2 at 96; see also UN Secretary-General, *supra* note 19 (recognizing the rights of future generations).

[26] The Human Right to Water and Sanitation, GA Res. 64/292, UN Doc. A/RES/64/292 (28 July 2010); Human Rights and Access to Safe Drinking Water and Sanitation, UN Human Rights Council Res. 15/9, UN Doc. A/HRC/RES/15/9 (30 September, 2010).

equity encompasses intragenerational equity as an integral element. As we go further and further into time, the most that we can give future generations is the condition in which they will inherit the Earth. Certainly poor people, who have trouble meeting even basic needs, can be expected to respect their obligations to future generations only if they have the resources to do so. The quest for intergenerational equity requires addressing today's poverty issues.[27] Mitigating poverty is central and essential to sustainable development.

One can also contend that as future generations become members of the present generation they are entitled to realize the rights of future generations. Intergenerational equity and intragenerational equity are linked. To be sure, there will at times be trade-offs when resources needed to promote intragenerational equity take away from the resources needed to address long-term concerns. It is important to develop criteria to ensure that both intragenerational equity and intergenerational equity are addressed. Too often, long-term costs are accrued for short-term benefits, which often go only to the few.

## GENERAL STRATEGIES FOR IMPLEMENTING INTERGENERATIONAL EQUITY

To implement the normative framework of intergenerational equity, it is necessary to look through an intergenerational lens and identify needed strategies. There are many strategies referenced in the UN Secretary-General's report and elsewhere.[28] This essay identifies some strategies that can lead to immediate actions. In addressing general strategies, it is important to ask what one could do differently tomorrow to implement intergenerational equity.

### *Sustainable Use of Resources*

The intergenerational lens highlights the importance of sustainable use of resources, so that society conserves the diversity and the quality of the Earth's resources. There are many examples of such strategies. For ground water, these include ensuring that ground water is not exploited in excess of recharge rates resulting in depletion of the supply and that the recharge area of aquifers is protected. When nuclear wastes are disposed of, it is necessary to record the scientific assumptions made in

[27] The link between intergenerational and intragenerational equity stems from many moral frameworks. For example, the link is connected with a long-term utilitarian framework because of its indiscriminate treatment of human interests across space and time. Indeed, some utilitarians articulate a biological root to the altruistic tendencies of individuals to protect strangers as the safety of our families becomes certain. See P. Singer, *The Expanding Circle* (Princeton University Press 2011). These same arguments lead to the expansion of biological altruism to future generations once the safety of our generation becomes certain.

[28] UN Secretary-General, *supra* note 19; Brown Weiss, *supra* note 2 at 119–165.

accessing the safety of such disposals, so that future generations know what those assumptions were, and can reassess them if necessary. When society allows forests to be cut or engages in agriculture, it is necessary to maintain the productivity of soils. When biologically diverse areas are used, it is necessary to be very cautious so that biological diversity is conserved for future generations.[29] These strategies implement the 2030 SDGs, which States adopted at the UN in September 2015.[30]

### *Long-Term Strategic Impact Assessments*

The intergenerational lens suggests the need for strategic EIAs that consider the long-term effects of a given proposal and the complex interactions that the actions might trigger. Too often, EIAs address only more local and immediate effects and do not look holistically at identifying the global and long-term effects. It is important to avoid tunnel vision. As in the example given earlier in which tropical forests are destroyed to plant palm trees for biofuel, an assessment should not only address how the implementation of the project will limit GHG emissions, but should also address the consequences of destroying tropical forests. Tropical forests are very effective in absorbing carbon dioxide and cannot be recreated, a long-term effect which would be lost.

Strategic environmental assessments are designed to take a holistic view.[31] This makes it more likely that an EIA can identify long-term effects, especially systemic ones. From the intergenerational perspective, identifying long-term effects of proposed projects, whether the effects are direct or indirect, is essential and makes it at least theoretically possible to monitor them.

### *Monitoring and Warning Systems*

The intergenerational lens highlights the importance of adequately monitoring the human environment and putting warning systems in place to provide alerts when dangerous thresholds are about to be crossed. This is essential for the climate system, where the crossing of certain thresholds will trigger extremely damaging and likely

29 E.O. Wilson, *Half-Earth: Our Planet's Fight for Life* (Liveright 2016); N. Meyers, *The Sinking Ark* (Pergamon Press 1979); E.O. Wilson (ed.), *Biodiversity* (National Academy of Sciences 1988) (providing a comprehensive review of the global loss of species diversity); E.O. Wilson, *The Diversity of Life* (Harvard University Press 1992).

30 UN, Transforming Our World: The 2030 Agenda for Sustainable Development, GA Res 70/1, UN Doc. A/RES/70/1 (25 September 2015). The seventeen goals include achieving sustainable water use, sustainable consumption levels, sustainable use of land resources, and taking action to combat climate change. Ibid. at 14.

31 See, e.g., Council Directive 2001/42/EC (requiring European Community member states to prepare a strategic environmental assessment in certain circumstances).

irreversible effects.[32] Monitoring and warning systems are essential for assessing risks and for taking informed decisions in dealing with them. The more difficult questions relate to what phenomenon must be monitored, by whom, how and at what cost. While we may not be able to avoid crossing certain thresholds, a good warning system could buy time to try to figure out how to deal with the problems.

### *Scientific and Technical Research*

The intergenerational lens also highlights the importance of strong programs of scientific research and technological development, particularly for issues that would otherwise be neglected in the private sector, such as research on the transportation of pollutants in ground water. Scientific research and development will help present and future generations assess risks to the long-term health of our environment, increase efficiency in the extraction and development of resources, develop alternatives to scarce resources, forestall damaging resource practices, and develop technologies for using resources more efficiently. While the private sector will conduct some of this research, there is still a role for government-funded research that addresses the long-term issues.

The intergenerational lens also suggests a need for generating new ideas and practices to protect the welfare of future generations and for removing barriers to putting these into practice. Innovation centers could serve as incubators for such ideas and practices and as places for identifying and attacking the impediments to innovation.[33]

### *Maintenance of Plants, Equipment, Databases*

An intergenerational lens also asks that society change how it views maintenance. Glamour attaches to capital investments, not the maintenance of these investments. Intergenerational equity implies a commitment that goes beyond the immediate capital investment. It implies a commitment to the investments that may be required to maintain facilities, infrastructure, institutions, and databases. Otherwise renewable resources may be depleted or money spent on projects and equipment whose benefits

[32] See J. Rockström, et al., 'A Safe Operating Space for Humanity' (2009) 461 *Nature* 472–475 (proposing environmental thresholds beyond which the Earth may be less safe for human development); T.M. Lenton, et al., 'Tipping Elements in the Earth's Climate System' (2008) 105 *Proceedings of the National Academy of Sciences of the United States of America* 1786–1793. Some discuss the use of geoengineering, including both carbon sequestration and solar radiation management, to forestall the crossing of certain thresholds. See National Research Council, *Climate Intervention: Reflecting Sunlight to Cool Earth* (National Academies Press 2015); National Research Council, *Climate Intervention: Carbon Dioxide Removal and Reliable Sequestration* (National Academies Press 2015).

[33] For impediments to innovation, see e.g., W. Bonvillian and C. Weiss, *Technological Innovation in Legacy Sectors* (Oxford University Press 2015).

may accrue only to the present generation and sometimes only for a few years. Indeed, the benefits may accrue only to a handful of people with special interests in immediate capitalization and not long-term operations. One of the criteria in evaluating proposed projects should be the ease and the cost of maintenance.

### *Education about Future Generations*

The intergenerational lens focuses on the critical importance of educating all people about the effects of society's actions on future generations, their rights, and the measures needed to conserve our natural and also our cultural resources. This is especially important for youth. If it is believed that change can take place on the scale of a generation, then one generation identifies the problems, another takes measures to address them, and a third considers the measures adopted as routine. Indeed, youth have been at the international forefront of pressing for actions to protect themselves and future generations.[34]

## STRATEGIES FOR CONSIDERING FUTURE GENERATIONS IN DECISION-MAKING

### *Representation of the Interests of Future Generations*

One of the most fundamental problems is that the interests of future generations are not represented in current decision-making processes, whether internationally, nationally, or locally. Thus, it is easy to overlook their interests. If we want to consider their interests, we have to define them, and this poses problems. How do we know what the interests of future generations might be when there is a proposal to build a large hydroelectric power plant or to fertilize the oceans with iron filings to absorb more carbon dioxide? In these instances, one can identify criteria based in the concept of sustainable development and ensuring the robustness and integrity of our environment that could be used to clarify their interests. But in other cases, it may be more difficult, even if essential. We also need to guard against special interests cloaking their ambitions in a subterfuge of enriching future generations.

In 1989, the book *In Fairness to Future Generations* proposed an international commission on the future of the planet and representation of the interests of future generations at all levels of government decision-making. The preparations

[34] See K. Offerdahl, Speech, Expert Panel on Intergenerational Solidarity: 'Representing Youth and Future Generations in the United Nations', 9 May 2013 https://sustainabledevelopment.un.org/content/documents/3576offerdahl.pdf accessed 30 November 2017; see also 'Our Children's Trust' www.ourchildrenstrust.org accessed 30 November 2017 (advancing the interests of children in global litigation efforts to combat climate change); Order and Findings & Recommendation, *Kelsey Cascade Rose Juliana* v. *United States*, No. 6:15-cv-01517-TC (D. Ore. 8 April 2016) (recognizing the standing of children to sue on issue of climate change).

for the Rio+20 Conference in 2012 included a recommendation for a UN High Commissioner for Future Generations, which was deleted from the final outcome of the Conference.[35] The UN Secretary-General's report in 2013 identified several options for institutionalizing representation of future generations at the international level. These included a High Commissioner for Future Generations, a Special Envoy of the UN Secretary-General for future generations, the placement of future generations as a recurring agenda item at a high level political forum, and a directive from the UN Secretary-General to UN agencies to promote intergenerational solidarity.[36] These options are designed to address the issue of how to represent the interests of future generations in decision-making. As of the time of writing, none has been implemented.

### *Shared Values and Norms Regarding Future Generations*

Most importantly, to consider the interests of future generations in making decisions, it is critical to have shared values and shared norms regarding obligations to future generations. These norms and values provide the basis for all the actions that need to be taken to implement intergenerational equity and respect the rights of future generations. Governments as well as civil society have a crucial role. In a kaleidoscopic world it may be easier to foster such values, especially in younger generations, for whom communications across borders will be routine, if they are not already. On the other hand, it could also be challenging to do so because of the increasing ease of spreading false information and messages that would not foster responsibility towards future generations.

### *Institutions for Protecting the Interests of Future Generations*

The Oxford Martin Commission on the Future recognized the failure to manage the world for future generations and set forth recommendations intended to translate short-term choices into sustainable long-term decision-making.[37] The report recognized the importance of institutions in managing the world for future well-being. The preparatory material for the Rio+20 Conference included proposals for an Ombudsman for Future Generations, a UN High Commissioner for Future Generations, and a Commission on Future Generations.[38] The final Conference

[35] C. Pearce, 'Ombudsperson for Future Generations: A Proposal for Rio+20' (2012) 6 *Perspectives* 1–8.

[36] UN Secretary-General, *supra* note 19.

[37] *Now for the Long Term: The Report of the Oxford Martin Commission for Future Generations* (University of Oxford 2013) www.oxfordmartin.ox.ac.uk/downloads/commission/Oxford_Martin_Now_for_the_Long_Term.pdf accessed 30 November 2017. Members of the Commission were former high international and national government officials. Pascal Lamy, the former Director-General of the WTO, served as the Commission's chairman.

[38] UN Secretary-General, *supra* note 19.

document, adopted by the Conference body, did not reference a specific international institutional proposal. As noted, intergenerational equity is an issue for all people living today, especially for youth. The intergenerational lens suggests the need for a watchdog, for a place where civil society, the private sector, and others can raise concerns about problems that otherwise might be unseen at the local, national, regional, or even international level, and for a place to ensure accountability to future generations.

Intergenerational equity must be implemented at the national, sub-national, and local levels. One can consider two categories of institutions: (1) those associated with parliaments, ministries, or local authorities and (2) those represented by national and sub-national judicial bodies. Before highlighting recent important developments in both areas, it is useful to set forth some criteria for assessing the effectiveness of such institutions and their experience in considering the interests of future generations, whether through legislative or administrative measures or judicial decisions. There is a growing awareness of the need for institutions that specifically focus on the interests of future generations and society's obligations to them and for laws and regulations that provide for considering their interests. This awareness is integral to the effort to promote sustainable development.

### *Criteria for Assessing Institutions for Future Generations*

With the advent of institutions to implement sustainable development and intergenerational equity, criteria are needed to judge their utility and performance. This chapter proposes using the ACEEA criteria: Access, Competence and Credibility, Efficiency, Effectiveness, and Accountability. 'A' stands for accessibility of the institution at the intended level, whether international, national, or local. To whom is access intended? For what purposes? At what cost? More specifically, how is it accessible to those whose interests it is supposed to serve? If the purpose is to represent the interests of those who are not yet born, how do future generations gain 'virtual' access to the institution?

'C' stands for competence and credibility. Does the institution have the expertise or is it able to marshal the expertise to perform its functions? Is the quality of work high? Does the institution learn from experience or the experience of others? Is it open to innovation or does it provide an environment for innovation so as to maintain its competence? In dealing with the interests of future generations, is it able to integrate knowledge from the natural sciences with that from the social sciences in order to understand the impacts of actions on future generations and the measures required to address them? Can it consider the whole picture or does it rather have tunnel vision on only one aspect of a problem?

Credibility and competence are linked. Is the institution credible? This is a broad criterion which calls into play a suite of factors. In the context of future generations, is the institution independent of forces that would skew its deliberations in favour of special interests rather than the interests of future generations? Do the people in the institution have integrity and does the institution itself act with integrity? Is it objective and impartial in its assessments and actions? Is it transparent in its activities and assessments? Most importantly, both public and private actors have to trust the institution to take actions that have been carefully considered as in the interests of future generations.

The first 'E' stands for efficiency. There are only limited resources available to allocate to almost every activity that is undertaken. Similarly, institutions have limited resources, so that it is essential to use these resources efficiently in achieving the institution's purposes. Often the impediments to efficiency are administrative burdens or requirements. Sometimes the impediments relate to the use of obsolete technologies, to the lack of maintenance of equipment, or to the timing for receiving financial support. Other times they may relate to the way that the human resource system in the institution functions. Generally, an institution for protecting future generations will be more respected and accepted if it operates efficiently.

The second 'E' stands for effectiveness. Is the institution effective in identifying and protecting the interests of future generations? Does it influence decision-making? If it represents future generations in court cases, what happens as a result of that? What is the follow through? In sum, is the institution making a difference? And how does one know? Part of the problem of assessing effectiveness is creating the counter-factual narrative: what would happen if the institution had not been there? Sometimes effectiveness can be assessed on the basis of particular actions. At other times, it involves a much broader inquiry into the effect of having such an institution on public and private sector decision-making.

A final 'A' stands for accountability. This criterion is linked to the institution's credibility. The traditional approach to accountability is to ask whether the institution or individual staff members have fulfilled their obligations and, if they have not, for the institution or staff members to suffer consequences, in other words, to be held accountable. The relevant questions are: who is accountable, to whom, for what, when, and how. In the case of an institution devoted to future generations, the traditional calculus is somewhat more complicated. In theory, such an institution is accountable to future generations, but future generations do not exist to hold the institution accountable for meeting its obligations, which are directed to them as beneficiaries. Thus, the question arises as to whom the institution is accountable. One can argue that the problem is no different from that of accountability in other institutions, and that the 'to whom' question may be answered with reference to funders, to parliaments or executive departments setting up the institution, or to whomever established the institution and set forth its purposes and functions. Accountability to the beneficiaries, namely future generations, takes place through the criterion of effectiveness.

Institutions for the protection of future generations can be either public or private. In our new kaleidoscopic world, the protection of future generations also needs to take place at another level – namely, through bottom-up empowerment. This relates to the Internet and social media networks, to online educational courses that spread knowledge across the world, and to the millions of people who can be reached through this new media and who can serve as watchdogs and implementers in their own local communities. After all, for thousands of years local communities have been figuring out how to manage resources in a sustainable way, making voluntary commitments pursuant to shared values and even norms, even though they are not required by particular laws or legislation. One needs also to pay attention to what can be called 'bottom-up initiatives and empowerment' to ensure that individuals and ad hoc and informal coalitions in the new kaleidoscopic world can be mobilized to protect the interests of future generations. Bottom-up empowerment can also be effective in holding institutions accountable for their actions affecting future generations.

The criteria outlined above can be applied both to institutions that are parliamentary and/or executive in character and to judicial institutions. They apply more broadly beyond the institutional role in implementing intergenerational equity.

### *Parliamentary and Executive Implementation*

Institutions expressly focused on considering the interests of future generations date back less than twenty-five years. The public sector institutions with such a mandate are still few in number, but have increased in number since the turn of the century. Most, but not all, have been parliamentary initiatives. The analysis highlights particularly significant initiatives, some of which are explored in detail in other chapters of this book. They are presented chronologically in order to trace the historical development of institutions addressing intergenerational equity.

One of the earliest initiatives was in France in response to efforts by the renowned Jacques-Yves Cousteau. Cousteau was the author of a petition for the rights of future generations, which garnered thousands and thousands of signatures worldwide. In 1993, then President Mitterrand of France, sensitive to concerns about future generations, established the French Council on Future Generations. Initially, the Council focused primarily on nuclear issues. When Cousteau resigned as President of the Council in 1995 over the deliberation on nuclear issues, the Council lapsed.[39] More recently, the French Government established the Inter-Ministerial Committee for Sustainable Development, which submits reports on policies that affect future generations.

In 1993, about the same time as the launch of the French Council on Future Generations, Finland established the Committee for the Future as a parliamentary committee. The Committee, which is composed of seventeen members of Parliament

[39] J. Szarka, *The Shaping of Environmental Policy in France* (Berghahn Books 2002) 203.

representing different political parties,[40] selects its topics, submits reports on the future, and analyzes policies of other parliamentary committees that affect the future.

In 2001, the Knesset, Israel's parliamentary body, passed a law creating a Commission on Future Generations with a Knesset Commissioner for Future Generations to assess bills with "particular relevance for future generations," to advise Members of the Knesset, and to present recommendations on issues particularly relevant for future generations.[41] The original bill defined "particular relevance for future generations" as referring to an issue

> which may have significant consequences for future generations, in the realms of the environment, natural resources, science, development, education, health, the economy, demography, planning and construction, quality of life, technology, justice and any matter which has been determined by the Knesset Constitution, Law and Justice Committee to have significant consequences for future generations.[42]

The Knesset abolished the Commission in December 2007.[43]

In January 2004, the German Bundestag established the Parliamentary Advisory Council on Sustainable Development to serve as the advocate of long-term responsibility in the political process, structure policy for future generations, and support the work of the bodies created by the Federal Government.[44] In 2009, the Bundestag expanded the duties of the Advisory Council to include preparing sustainability impact reports for all pending legislation, to help achieve the goal of having all "motions, regulations, and draft legislation comply with the principles of sustainable development."[45]

In 2007, the Hungarian Parliament established an Ombudsman for Future Generations with the power to evaluate legislation and intervene in certain litigation, among other responsibilities. In 2011, the Parliament created the Office of the Commissioner for Fundamental Rights and turned the Ombudsman position into a Deputy Commissioner position under this broader rubric.[46] The Deputy Commissioner's duties include monitoring the enforcement of laws related to the interests of future generations, participating in the inquiries of the Commissioner for Fundamental Rights, and advising the Commissioner as to whether to institute

40 See 'Committee for the Future', Eduskunta Riksdagen www.eduskunta.fi/EN/lakiensaataminen/valiokunnat/tulevaisuusvaliokunta/Pages/default.aspx accessed 30 November 2017.

41 The Knesset Law 1994 (Amendment No. 14), 5761-2001.

42 Ibid. at § 8. For further discussion of the Commission for Future Generations and reproduction of the relevant legislation, see S. Shoham and N. Lamay, 'Commission for Future Generations in the Knesset: Lessons Learnt', in J.C. Tremmel (ed.), *Handbook of Intergenerational Justice* (Edward Elgar 2006) 244–281.

43 Knesset Legislation No. P/17/1629 (4 December 2007).

44 See Joint Motion, 15/2441, (9 January 2004). The Council presents a report of its efforts once every two years.

45 Motion, 18/559 (19 February 2014) (English translation).

46 Fundamental Law of Hungary, art. 30 (1 April 2013).

proceedings *ex officio* and to go to the Constitutional Court on any matter that may affect future generations.[47]

In March 2015, the National Assembly of Wales passed a widely heralded bill, entitled Well-Being of Future Generations. The legislation established the position of 'The Future Generations Commissioner for Wales,'[48] and provided for measures to implement sustainable development. The Commissioner's functions include the following: providing advice and assistance on the issues, encouraging best practices, undertaking needed research, reviewing the extent to which a public body is "safeguarding the ability of future generations to meet their needs," and preparing and publishing regular reports on the extent to which the legislation's objectives are being met.[49]

### *Regional and International Initiatives*

Since 2000, there has been movement within the EU to develop institutional programs to implement intergenerational equity. In 2003, twenty-six members of the EU from different political parties signed a motion for a resolution in the CoE Parliamentary Assembly to establish a Committee for Future Generations within the Assembly, which would issue opinions and guidelines on any matters affecting future generations.[50] The initiative did not succeed. In 2015, more than a decade later, the European Parliament began to explore such an initiative again. As noted previously, the UN Secretary-General's 2013 Report on Intergenerational Solidarity put forth options for institutional initiatives at the international level for considering the interests of future generations.[51]

This section of the chapter began with setting forth the ACEEA criteria for assessing institutions that are concerned with future generations. For most of the institutions, it is difficult to apply the criteria in full because they are new, have been limited in time, or have only limited functions. The criteria offer, however, a baseline for assessing these institutional initiatives and for strengthening them in their purpose to ensure consideration and protection of the interests of future generations.

47 The Deputy Commissioner's duties are defined in Act CXI of 2011, § 3. The new Fundamental Law of Hungary, entered into force in 2012, recognizes the need to protect natural resources at the constitutional level. The Amendment provides that "[n]atural resources, in particular arable land, forests and the reserves of water, biodiversity, in particular native plant and animal species, as well as cultural assets form the common heritage of the nation; it shall be the obligation of the State and everyone to protect and maintain them, and to preserve them for future generations." Fundamental Law of Hungary, art. P (1 April 2013). For the functions and powers of the Hungarian Ombudsman for Future Generations, see *infra* ch. 4 in this volume.

48 Well Being of Future Generations (Wales) Act 2015, pt. 3.

49 Ibid. at § 20.

50 See Parliamentary Assembly, EU Council, Doc. 9668 (22 January 2003).

51 See UN Secretary-General, *supra* note 19.

## THE PRINCIPLE OF INTERGENERATIONAL EQUITY IN INTERNATIONAL AND NATIONAL COURTS

Judicial bodies can consider the interests of future generations and hold those who would violate obligations to future generations to account. There is as yet little precedent in international tribunals for doing so. Research on national and sub-national courts, however, indicates that they are sometimes turning to a principle of intergenerational equity. The number of cases citing the principle since 1990 has increased rather dramatically. This chapter first looks at the record at the ICJ and then at national and sub-national tribunals. The IACHR and the ECtHR have also considered cases involving the interests of future generations.

### *International Court of Justice*

The ICJ first referenced the principle of intergenerational equity in 1993 in a concurring opinion by Judge Weeramantry. Although the ICJ later explicitly referenced the interests of future generations ("those yet unborn") in an advisory opinion, it has not yet based a decision on a principle of intergenerational equity. A brief review of the early cases before the ICJ follows to provide context for the recognition of the principle at the international judicial level.

In the ICJ's maritime boundary delimitation case of *Denmark* v. *Norway*, Judge Weeramantry discussed the principle of intergenerational equity in his concurring opinion. He wrote that principles of intergenerational equity "can build upon the increasing use by the ICJ of equitable principles to achieve a result that the Court views as fair and just."[52]

In the 1995 Nuclear Test Case, the ICJ declined to accept New Zealand's request for jurisdiction over France's proposed underground nuclear tests as constituting a violation of international law.[53] Two of the dissenting opinions, however, discussed the importance of intergenerational equity to the dispute. Judge Weeramantry wrote:

> The case before the Court raises, as no case ever before the Court has done, the principle of intergenerational equity – an important and rapidly developing principle of contemporary environmental law ... New Zealand's complaint that its rights are affected does not relate only to the rights of people presently in existence. The rights of the people of New Zealand include the rights of unborn posterity ... [T]his is therefore an important aspect not to be ignored.
>
> In the words of an important recent work on this question: "The starting proposition is that each generation is both a custodian and a user of our common natural

[52] *Denmark* v. *Norway* (1993) ICJ 38, 277 (J. Weeramantry, writing separately) (quoting Brown Weiss, *supra* note 2 at 37).

[53] *New Zealand* v. *France* (1995) ICJ 288.

and cultural patrimony. As custodians of this planet, we have certain moral obligations to future generations which we can transform into legally enforceable norms."[54]

On 8 July 1996, the ICJ handed down its Advisory Opinion on *Legality of the Threat or Use of Nuclear Weapons*, which responded to the UNGA request in December 1994.[55] In its opinion, the ICJ explicitly referred to the interests of future generations, stating "it is imperative for the Court to take account of the unique characteristics of nuclear weapons, and in particular ... their ability to cause damage to generations to come."[56] In his dissenting opinion, Judge Weeramantry discussed the damage to future generations and wrote:

> It is to be noted in this context that the rights of future generations have passed the stage when they were merely an embryonic right struggling for recognition. They have woven themselves into international law through major treaties, through juristic opinion and through general principles of law recognized by civilized nations.[57]

More recently, in *Pulp Mills on the River Uruguay*, Judge Cançado Trindade discussed the principle of intergenerational equity and observed that "[n]owadays, in 2010, it can hardly be doubted that the acknowledgment of intergenerational equity forms part of conventional wisdom in international environmental law."[58] In his Separate Opinion in *Whaling in the Antarctic* four years later, Judge Cançado Trindade concluded that "intergenerational equity marks presence nowadays in a wide range of instruments of international environmental law, and indeed of contemporary public international law."[59]

These opinions have set the stage for the application of a principle of intergenerational equity in future cases that may affect the well-being of future generations and the robustness and diversity of our environment.

### *National Courts*

Increasingly, national courts have referred to intergenerational equity in general or explicitly to the principle of intergenerational equity. These courts have invoked intergenerational equity in two ways. The first is as a procedural matter, for example by granting standing to children as representatives of future generations or by tolling a statute of limitations for a violation that involves significant harm to future

54 Ibid. at 341 (J. Weeramantry, dissenting) (quoting Brown Weiss, *supra* note 2 at 21).
55 *Legality of the Threat or Use of Nuclear Weapons, Advisory Opinion* (1996) ICJ 226.
56 Ibid. at 244.
57 Ibid. at 455 (J. Weeramantry, dissenting).
58 *Pulp Mills on the River Uruguay (Argentina* v. *Uruguay)* (2010) ICJ 14 (J. Cançado Trindade, writing separately, para. 122).
59 *Whaling in the Antarctic (Australia* v. *Japan; New Zealand intervening)* (2014) ICJ 226 (J. Cançado Trindade, writing separately, para. 47).

generations. The second is substantive, for example by finding that given actions threaten the well-being of future generations and therefore require that certain measures be taken.

National and lower level courts in at least twenty States have looked to a principle of intergenerational equity or discussed the interests of future generations in the case. Sometimes the decisions are based upon constitutional provisions or explicit legislative provisions referencing intergenerational equity. In other decisions, the court incorporates a principle of intergenerational equity without such reference. The number of judicial decisions concerned with intergenerational equity started to rise significantly in 2004 and thereafter.[60]

The judicial decisions fall within three major categories: (1) natural resources (including forests, biodiversity, and fauna conservation), (2) pollution, and (3) administrative challenges regarding construction of projects or granting of permits to exploit natural resources. Many cases in the latter two categories involve the exploitation of mineral resources. The judicial cases considered below represent only some of the relevant case law. They are intended to highlight the various ways in which courts have used the principle of intergenerational equity.

### *Procedural Applications*

A preliminary issue in national courts is who has standing to represent future generations, since future generations by definition cannot appear in person. One possibility would be a guardian *ad litem* for future generations. The analogy is to a guardian *ad litem* for children and for those unable to represent themselves. One problem with this approach is that the guardian is being asked to represent an inanimate object, in future generations, for members do not yet exist until they become part of the present generation. Some respond that this already happens for the inanimate bodies of corporations, which are routinely represented in courts. If a guardian *ad litem* could be appointed for future generations, the guardian would still need to define the interests of future generations in any given case. This requires consensus on the norms that can be applied to the facts of the case. Such guardians would need to have funding for their work, whether from the public or private sectors.

#### *Organizations as Having Standing to Represent Future Generations*

In a pathbreaking case from the Netherlands, the Urgenda Foundation, a NGO, brought a case on behalf of current and future generations of people living in the State, and the court accepted jurisdiction of the case.[61] However, the Court avoided

[60] Based on data compiled by and on file with the author.

[61] *Urgenda Foundation* v. *The State of the Netherlands Ministry of Infrastructure and the Environment*, C/09/456689/HA ZA 13-1396, Judgment of 24 June 2015.

taking on jurisdiction on behalf of future generations of people living in other States.[62] To date, it has been more common, as explained below, to see children as the appropriate class to represent future generations.

### *Children as Having Standing to Represent Future Generations*

The seminal case for granting standing to future generations is the *Minors Oposa* decision.[63] On 9 August 1993, the Supreme Court of the Republic of the Philippines granted standing to a group of children, as representatives of themselves and of future generations, to bring a case against the Environment and Natural Resources Department to seek cancellation of existing timber license agreements and to ban the approval of new ones. The Supreme Court said:

> [w]e find no difficulty in ruling that they can, for themselves, for others of their generation and for the succeeding generations, file a class suit. Their personality to sue in behalf of the succeeding generations can only be based on the concept of intergenerational responsibility insofar as the right to a balanced and healthful ecology is concerned. Such a right, as hereinafter expounded, considers the "rhythm and harmony of nature." Nature means the created world in its entirety ... Needless to say, every generation has a responsibility to the next to preserve that rhythm and harmony for the full enjoyment of a balanced and healthful ecology. Put a little differently, the minors' assertion of their right to a sound environment constitutes, at the same time, the performance of their obligation to ensure the protection of that right for generations to come.[64]

The Supreme Court found the right to a balanced and healthful ecology in the Constitution of the Philippines.[65]

In another groundbreaking case, this one from the US, the Children's Trust filed a lawsuit against the US in the federal district court in Oregon on the grounds that the atmosphere constitutes a public trust and the US must do more to combat climate change and ensure a stable climate system. After oral argument, the federal Magistrate judge issued findings and recommended denying motions to dismiss the complaint. He referred the matter to the US District for review and oral argument.[66]

[62] Ibid. at 4.92.

[63] *Minors Oposa* v. *Secretary of the Department of the Environment and Natural Resources*, 33 I.L.M. 173 (1994).

[64] Ibid. at 185.

[65] For analysis of the case, see T. Allen, 'The Philippine Children's Case Recognizing Legal Standing for Future Generations' (1994) 6 *Georgetown International Environmental Law Review* 713–741; D.B. Gatmaytan, 'The Illusion of Intergenerational Equity: *Oposa* v. *Factoran* as Pyrrhic Victory' (2003) 15 *Georgetown International Environmental Law Review* 457–485; M.S.Z. Manguiat and V.P.B. Yu III, 'Maximizing the Value of *Oposa* v. *Factoran*' (2003) 15 *Georgetown International Environmental Law Review* 487–496.

[66] Order and Findings & Recommendation, *Kelsey Cascade Rose Juliana* v. *United States*, No. 6:15-cv-01517-TC (D. Ore. 8 April 2016) http://ourchildrenstrust.org accessed

On 10 November 2016, US District Judge Aiken denied the defendant's motion to dismiss the case, which thus recognized standing for the children to raise the claim and allowed the case proceed to trial.[67] The District Court opinion is remarkable for its recognition of the importance of climate stability for present and future generations, specifically Judge Aiken's explanation that:

> Exercising my "reasoned judgment," . . . I have no doubt that the right to a climate system capable of sustaining human life is fundamental to a free and ordered society . . . a stable climate system is quite literally the foundation "of society, without which there would be neither civilization nor progress."

The opinion cites the *Minors Oposa* case from the Philippine Supreme Court to the effect that "without 'a balanced and healthful ecology,' future generations 'stand to inherit nothing but parched earth incapable of sustaining life.'"[68]

In the process of holding that there were no political question concerns to impede the decision, Judge Aiken found it important that the "plaintiffs are minors who cannot vote and must depend on others to protect their political interests."[69] The fact that they could not vote only created a greater need for the plaintiffs to have the case brought to a court, where their interests could be asserted in some form. Extending Judge Aiken's procedural posture towards the youth to future generations is a logically consistent next step, as members of future generations also have no capacity to vote in the present.

There are other relevant cases. In Pakistan, a case rests on a seven year old's claim that the government's failure to address climate change by planning to use Thar's coal reserves is a failure to uphold its responsibility to future generations.[70] On the other hand, in Bangladesh, judicial standing was denied to children as representatives of future generations.[71] The Appellate Division of the Supreme Court of Bangladesh explicitly declined to follow the precedent from the *Minors Oposa* case in the Philippines.

There is growing recognition that it is essential to include children in the dialogue about the future. Thus, it is likely that courts will increasingly be sympathetic to their

30 November 2017. The Magistrate's report denied the request to grant standing to an individual person as representing future generations.

67 Opinion and Order, *Kelsey Cascade Rose Juliana* v. *United States*, No. 6:15-cv-01517-TC (US District Court, District of Oregon, Eugene Division, 10 November 2016).

68 Ibid. at 32.

69 Ibid. at 16.

70 *Rabab Ali* v. *Federation of Pakistan & Another*, Supreme Court of Pakistan (Petition filed 6 April 2016).

71 *Faroque* v. *Secretary, Ministry of Communication, Government of the People's Republic of Bangladesh*, WP No. 300 of 1995 (flood action plan case) (stating "we do not accept Dr. Faroque's submission that the association represents not only the present generation but also the generation yet unborn. This claim is based on a case of the Philippines Supreme Court . . . Our Constitution does not contain an analogous provision").

concerns and to recognizing standing for them in courts, especially if the standing can be based in constitutional provisions relating to the environment.

### *Other Procedural Issues Relating to Future Generations*

There are potentially other procedural issues in hearing cases involving harm to future generations. One issue is whether the statute of limitations for hearing cases involving potentially serious and irreversible harm to present and future generations can be tolled or deemed not to apply.

In Brazil, in a case involving illegal logging in the Amazonian State of Acre, indigenous peoples raised the issue of whether the statute of limitations could bar environmental claims.[72] The Panel of the High Court unanimously held that the right to compensation for environmental damage does not lapse and that hence there is no statute of limitations. As Bryner described the case:

> the Court was particularly concerned with how, under a statute of limitations, past or present inaction would bind future owners of a common asset . . . [T]he Court asked: "How could the current generation assure its right to pollute, to the detriment of generations yet unborn?" As the High Court reasoned, eliminating a time limit on collective claims is in keeping with the principle of intergenerational equity in environmental law.[73]

The High Court has handed down several decisions that emphasized the constitutional duty to protect the environment for future generations.[74]

### *Substantive Application of Intergenerational Equity*

The material that follows highlights only some of the applications of a principle of intergenerational equity in national and, in some cases, sub-national courts. The cases do not include any decisions of separate environmental tribunals, which many countries have now established. The cases are intended to illustrate the broad range of environmental problems in which intergenerational equity has had a role in resolving the dispute: from controlling pollution to natural resource conservation and administrative decisions for permits to extract resources. They are divided below into four categories: (1) conservation of natural resources including limitations on mining, (2) control of pollution, (3) ensuring sustainable development, and (4) mitigating climate change.

72 STJ, REsp No. 1.120.117/AC (2d Panel), Relator: Min. Eliana Calmon, 10.11.2009 (19 October 2009) (Braz.).

73 N.S. Bryner, 'Brazil's Green Court' (2012) 29 *Pace Environmental Law Review* 470–537, 525.

74 See, e.g., *CCK Construtora e Incorporadora LTDA*, STJ, REsp 302.906/SP (2d Panel) Relator: Min. Antonio Herman Benjamin (26 August 2010) (Braz.); *H Carlos Schneider S/A Comércio e Indústria e Outro* v. *Ministério Público Federal*, STJ, REsp 650.728/SC (2d Panel) Relator: Min. Antonio Herman Benjamin (23 October 2007) (Braz.).

### *Conservation of Natural Resources*

Cases in India and Brazil illustrate the application of intergenerational equity to disputes about the use of natural resources, especially forests and minerals. Some of these cases are highlighted below.

The Supreme Court of India has referenced a principle of intergenerational equity in a number of cases. For example, in *Intellectual Forum, Tirupathi* v. *State of Andhra Pradesh and Others*, the dispute concerned the preservation of historical water reservoirs in the Tirupathi region and the use of the reservoir beds for construction and commerce despite the frequent droughts in the region.[75] The Court cited the development of the principle of intergenerational equity in international law and noted that

> [i]t is now an accepted social principle that all human beings have a fundamental right to a healthy environment, commensurate with their well-being, coupled with a corresponding duty of ensuring that resources are conserved and preserved in such a way that present as well as the future generations are aware of them equally.

In *State of Himachal Pradesh and Others* v. *Ganesh Wood Products and Others*, the Supreme Court upheld a petition to prohibit new manufacturing units using cut trees, on the grounds that excessive felling of trees had adversely affected the region's environment.[76] Drawing upon a principle of intergenerational equity, the Supreme Court observed that "[a]fter all, the present generation has no right to deplete all the existing forests and leave nothing for the next and future generations."[77]

The coal mining cases in the Indian state of Goa are of special note because the Supreme Court said that the interest of future generations had to be taken into account in such operations. Citing intergenerational equity, the Court limited the amount of minerals that could be mined and required, as a condition of the permit to mine, that a trust fund for the benefit of future generations be created.[78] Further, the Court established the Supreme Court Committee on Intergenerational Equity to conduct expert analysis to find an appropriate cap on coal mining in Goa. It specifically directed the Committee to keep in mind the principles of sustainable

[75] *Intellectuals Forum, Tirupathi* v. *State of Andhra Pradesh and Others*, (2006) 3 SCC 549.

[76] *State of Himachal Pradesh and Others* v. *Ganesh Wood Products and Others*, 6 SCC 363 (1995). Cited in J. Vinuales, *The Rio Declaration on Environment and Development: A Commentary* (Oxford University Press 2015) 146.

[77] *State of Himachal Pradesh and Others*, *supra* note 76 at 363 (noting that "it is contrary to the public interest involved in preserving forest wealth, maintenance of environment and ecology and considerations of sustainable growth and intergenerational equity").

[78] *Goa Foundation* v. *Union of India & Ors.*, Writ Petition (Civil) No. 435 of 2012, Judgment (21 April 2014). For background and recent developments of the case, see 'The State of Mining in Goa', Goa Foundation www.goafoundation.org/mining/ accessed 30 November 2017. The regulation that allows the current generation to use natural resources while using some of the proceeds to generate a trust fund has some precedent. The State of Montana has adopted a similar provision in 1976. See Montana Constitution art. IX § 5 (1976).

development and intergenerational equity in decisions and debates.[79] The question for the Court was not whether intergenerational equity should impact the decision, but how intergenerational equity would be applied. The Goa Foundation, which brought the case, has pushed for an expansive understanding of intergenerational equity and for measures to ensure that the trust fund is effective.[80] On 2 August 2017, the Supreme Court of India issued an historic judgment in a large-scale mining case in the State of Odisha, formerly Orissa. The Court addressed the principle of intergenerational equity and, while declining to impose specific limits on the amount of ore that could be mined annually, required the mining company to develop a policy to address intergenerational equity before the end of 2017.[81]

Like India, Brazil has been at the forefront of recognizing the interests of future generations in its laws and court decisions. Brazil's Constitution of 1988 includes a right to environment, with article 225 providing that "[a]ll have the right to an ecologically balanced environment, which is an asset of common use and essential to a healthy quality of life, and both the Government and the community shall have the duty to defend and preserve it for present and future generations."[82] Under the Constitution, Prosecutors' functions include bringing civil actions to protect "the environment and other diffuse and collective interests."[83] Between 2007 and 2011, the High Court handed down a number of decisions that emphasized the constitutional duty to protect the environment for future generations. In a case involving the protection of mangrove swamps in Brazil, the High Court noted that there is a legal duty to preserve the threatened ecosystem and equated the deprivation of its public use and use by future generations to the theft of chattel under criminal law.[84] Other judicial decisions in Brazil and other Latin American countries, and in North America, that discussed intergenerational equity involved a range of issues, from mining operations that threaten rivers to urban pollution problems.[85]

[79] *Goa Foundation, supra* note 78 at 81.

[80] Rahul Basu, a key figure in the Goa Foundation, urged the Expert Committee to embrace Hartwick's rule that "as mineral resources are extracted from the ground, investments in productive assets need to be made to leave future generations with as much assets as the present generation." R. Basu, 'Implementing Intergenerational Equity in Goa' (December 2014) XLIX *Economic & Political Weekly* 51.

[81] *Common Cause* v. *Union of India & Ors*, SC Writ Petition (Civil) No. 114 of 2014, Judgment (2 August 2017).

[82] Constituição Federal [Constitution] art. 225.

[83] Ibid. at art. 129.

[84] STJ REsp No. 650.728 (2d Panel), Relator: Min. Herman Benjamin, 23.10.2007 (2 December 2009) (Braz.).

[85] For analysis of intergenerational equity in Canadian judicial cases and legislation, see J.V. DeMarco, 'Law of Future Generations: The Theory of Intergenerational Equity in Canadian Environmental Law' (2004) 15 *Journal of Environmental Law and Practice* 1–46. For Brazil, see D. Ramos, Jr. *Meio ambiente e conceito juridico de futuras geracões* (Juruá Editora Juvevê 2012).

### *Pollution*

Court decisions in Latin America, South Asia, and Africa have applied intergenerational equity to pollution problems, including urban pollution problems. A case from Kenya illustrates this application. The High Court of Kenya – the country's second highest court – in *Waweru* v. *Republic of Kenya* (2006), applied the principle of intergenerational equity to water pollution.[86] The High Court ordered local authorities to construct sewerage treatment works so that overflow waste from septic tanks did not flow into open channels leading to the Kiserian River. It furthermore required property owners to comply with the health requirements concerning the disposal of wastewater and sewage, despite petitioners' claims that the cost would be prohibitive. The High Court ended its decision with a lengthy consideration of the role of intragenerational and intergenerational equity and concluded:

> [T]he need to formulate and maintain ecologically sustainable development that does not interfere with the sustenance, viability and the quality of the water table and the quality of the river waters ... [also gives] rise to the equally important principle of intergenerational equity because the water table and the rivers courses affected are held in trust by the present generation for future generations. Yes, the intergenerational equity obligates the present generation to ensure that health, diversity and productivity of natural resources are maintained or enhanced for the benefit of future generations. We observe that water tables and clean rivers are for this and future generations.[87]

The opinion ended with an exhortation to fight for environmental justice.

### *Sustainable Development*

National courts in several countries have invoked intergenerational equity in the context of sustainable development. The Indian Supreme Court is well known for its decision in the *Vellore* case, which invoked sustainable development and intergenerational equity, stating "[w]e have no hesitation in holding that Sustainable Development as a balancing concept between ecology and development has been accepted as a part of the Customary International Law."[88] The case concerned discharges by tanneries and other industries of untreated effluents into agricultural land, waterways, and other open areas.

Australian courts and, to a lesser extent, New Zealand courts have been at the forefront in applying intergenerational equity in the context of ecological sustainability. Australia has recognized the principle of intergenerational equity as a principle of 'ecological sustainability' in any development project through various

86 *Waweru* v. *Republic of Kenya* (2006) 1 KLR (E&L) 677–696 (High Court).

87 Ibid. at 694–695 (quoting at length from Brown Weiss, *supra* note 2).

88 *Vellore Citizens Welfare Forum* v. *Union of India* [1996] 5 SCC 647, 658.

statutes at the federal and state levels. The courts in New South Wales have frequently referenced a principle of intergenerational equity.[89] In New Zealand, the Resource Management Act, 1991 (RMA) brings intergenerational equity into these discussions through its statement of purpose, 'sustainable management,' which it defines as "sustaining the potential of natural and physical resources (excluding minerals) to meet the reasonably foreseeable needs of future generations."[90] A limited number of judicial decisions directly discuss intergenerational equity on this basis.

### *Climate Change*

As noted previously in the discussion of standing for children to bring cases involving effects on future generations, two important cases in national courts address a State's obligation to mitigate climate change.

Going back to the Netherlands Urgenda Foundation suit is useful. As stated earlier, the NGO brought suit on behalf of present and future generations against the Dutch Government for failing to take adequate measures to reduce GHG emissions. The District Court of The Hague ordered the Dutch Government to take greater precautionary measures to reduce the risk of dangerous climate change.[91] The Court addressed a question of first impression of whether the government had "breached its duty of care for taking insufficient measures to prevent dangerous climate change."[92] It concluded that the principle of fairness required the State to ensure that the costs of climate change are "distributed reasonably between present and future generations."[93] The case was decided at the trial level. In November 2016, the Government appealed the decision. In December 2019, the Dutch Supreme Court upheld the lower courts' findings that the government's climate change laws and rules were insufficient to meet the State's legal obligations under the Paris Agreement. Even in the middle of the pandemic, the Dutch government has used this decision as a spur to create new draft policies for implementing climate change reform.

In the US, the *Children's Trust* suit against the federal government for failing to take adequate measures to address climate change was discussed earlier. Both the opinion by the Federal District Court judge and the earlier report by the magistrate recognized the potential harm to children, now and in the future, from climate change. The case is highly significant because it recognizes that climate change is

89 See, e.g., *BGP Properties Pty Ltd* v. *Lake Macquarie City Council* [2004] NSWLEC 399, 2004 WL 2077431, 94 (12 August 2004).

90 Resource Management Act 1991, § 5(2)(a).

91 *Urgenda Foundation* v. *The State of the Netherlands*, The Hague, 24 June 2014, Case No. C/09/ 456689 / HA ZA 13-1396.

92 Ibid. at 4.53.

93 Ibid. at 4.76.

an intergenerational problem, and granted standing to plaintiffs to bring a claim to address it. In addition to the case in the US Federal District Court in Oregon, Our Children's Trust has brought cases in five other states in the US and at least ten other countries.[94]

## CONCLUSION

Within the last fifteen years, there has been increased awareness that we need to consider the future and the interests of future generations in our decision-making. The adoption and implementation of a principle of intergenerational equity by States and a growing number of judicial decisions reflect this. The Report of the UN Secretary-General in 2013, which confirms the principle, has set the stage for greater attention to the future and for the adoption of institutional measures to care for future generations. In the context of a bottom-up kaleidoscopic world, it is important that the public and private sectors, and civil society, implement our responsibilities to future generations and respect their entitlement to a diverse, robust, and healthy environment, at least no worse than today's.

[94] See 'Legal Action', Our Children's Trust www.ourchildrenstrust.org/Legal accessed 30 November 2017. Citizens suing their governments to force action on climate change is an environmental tactic seeing greater use around the world. See J. Schwartz, 'In Novel Tactic on Climate Change, Citizens Sue Their Governments', *New York Times*, 10 May 2016 www.nytimes.com/2016/05/11/science/climate-change-citizen-lawsuits.html accessed 30 November 2017.

# PART I

# Introduction to Treaty Law on Intergenerational Justice and Codifying Sustainability

# 3

# International Treaty Law and Policy for Future Generations

*Marie-Claire Cordonier Segger*

We assume a collective responsibility to advance and strengthen the interdependent and mutually reinforcing pillars of sustainable development – economic development, social development and environmental protection – at the local, national, regional and global levels.

2015 Johannesburg Declaration, WSSD

Intergenerational equity is, in principle, inherent in the concept of sustainable development, which seeks to ensure that social, environmental and economic progress does not foreclose on the needs of future generations, while still meeting the needs of present generations.

What exactly constitutes sustainable development, however, whether for present or future generations, remains unclear in fact and in law. Many economic development decisions have significant environmental and social implications, as has been recognized since *Our Common Future*, the report by the WCED, was released in 1987.[1] Through decades of global policy debates and in many treaties, State commitments to sustainable development play an important role in efforts to cooperatively advance economically while respecting human rights and environmental protection imperatives. However, when States commit 'to promote sustainable development' in a multilateral environmental accord, agree to conduct their economic relations 'in accordance with a principle of sustainable development' in a trade treaty, or promise to ensure 'sustainable development that respects the interests of future generations' in a natural resources contract, the implications of these commitments are not always clear in international law. The commitments themselves, however, become even more relevant as the world emerges from a wave of lockdowns driven by the global COVID-19 pandemic, and as countries and institutions consider the opportunities available for post-pandemic recovery strategies, economic stimulus and investments.

1 G.H. Brundtland et al., *Our Common Future: Report of the World Commission on Environment and Development* (Oxford University Press 1987).

In this chapter, the origins and meaning of State commitments to sustainable development in international law are briefly discussed, with a focus on the principle of intergenerational equity as it is found in many treaties, and on global policy commitments to reduce inequality as an important global SDG. It is argued that sustainable development, as a concept, can bridge the need for increased attention to ending poverty, on one hand, and the need to identify and respect environmental limits and social safeguards, on the other. First, building on other works,[2] an international concept of sustainable development which includes intergenerational equity is briefly summarized, noting that commitments to sustainable development in international law may best be characterized as part of the 'object and purpose' of many different and binding treaties. As the chapter highlights, a series of global SDGs have been adopted as common policy objectives by Member States of the UN,[3] and among these seventeen SDGs, the tenth focuses especially on the need to reduce inequality within and among countries, guiding governments and intergovernmental organizations that have committed to achieving them, as 'soft law'. Finally, the chapter argues, key principles of international law can assist in achieving intergenerational equity through binding treaties related to the SDGs. Indeed, among key principles recognized in the ILA's 2002 New Delhi Principles of International Law Relating to Sustainable Development [New Delhi Principles], and firmly reflected in international accords on sustainable development, the principle of respect for inter- and intra-generational equity is gaining recognition.

## MAKING DEVELOPMENT MORE SUSTAINABLE

Sustainable development refers to State efforts to achieve progress ('development'), qualified by the condition that these efforts should be possible to maintain over the long term ('sustainable'), rather than prejudicing the ability of future generations to meet their own needs. International understanding of both 'development' and 'sustainability' has evolved a great deal in recent decades, and like other important terms (i.e. peace, democracy, human rights), can mean different things in diverse contents. Finding one accepted definition of sustainable development is like trying to achieve a series of moving targets in all regions of the world, simultaneously and for all time – challenging.

To unpack the concept, it is first useful to consider what is meant by 'development'. Development scholarship and practice has evolved in recent years. Originally,

[2] This chapter shares thoughts with the author's work in M.-C. Cordonier Segger and A. Khalfan, *Sustainable Development Law: Principles, Practices and Prospects* (Oxford University Press 2004) and M.-C. Cordonier Segger, 'Commitments to Sustainable Development through International Law and Policy', in M.-C. Cordonier Segger and H.E. Judge C.G. Weeramantry (eds.), *Sustainable Development Principles in the Decisions of International Courts and Tribunals* (Routledge 2017), among other pieces.

[3] UN, Transforming Our World: The 2030 Agenda for Sustainable Development, GA Res 70/1, UN Doc. A/RES/70/1 (25 September 2015) [Sustainable Development Goals].

development efforts were intensely focused on increasing economic growth, and development policies aimed principally at increasing a State's gross domestic product (GDP). In the era of post–World War II reconstruction, it was believed that modernization and economic progress could help 'backward, traditional societies' to end poverty. Unsurprisingly, however, attempts to impose one model of development on many diverse countries and cultures were not entirely successful. Fierce debates raged between those who espoused modernization and industrialization as the path to development, and those who critiqued these theories as colonial impositions leading to under-development in the global south.[4] In the late 1980s and 1990s, inspired by *Our Common Future* (the Brundtland Report) and other international processes, a new model emerged which focuses on a human-centered approach – development is seen as an iterative process that seeks to improve human conditions and capabilities, creating viable livelihoods for people in poverty. This view is found in the Preamble to the 1986 Declaration on the Right to Development, which defines development as "a comprehensive, economic, social and cultural process which aims at the constant improvement and well-being of the entire population and of all individuals on the basis of their active, free and meaningful participation in development and in the fair distribution of the benefits resulting therefrom."[5] While debates still persist, most international institutions active in development theory and practice, as well as many developing finance agencies, have now adopted a variation of this approach. As such, development can be defined as the processes of expanding people's choices, enabling improvements in collective and individual quality of life, and in the exercise of full freedoms and rights.[6] This global concept of 'sustainable development' gained currency in the 1980s as a way to bridge between deadlocked views in developed and developing countries to address concerns about the long-term sustainability of international, national and local development policy objectives that focused overmuch on economic development and human aspirations. In its simplest form, the concept of sustainable development permits States to cooperatively improve the quality of life for their people in ways that could last over the long term by respecting environmental limits and social safeguards. As States have set new international policy directions and slowly come to a consensus on new, global SDGs up to 2030, they have also been conducting negotiations that have resulted in binding international law on sustainable development.

Just as for other important international declarations or guidelines related to peace, human rights, the environment, trade or investment, to reach international

4 See, e.g., UNDP, *Human Development Reports* http://hdr.undp.org/; see also G. Esteva, 'Development', in W. Sachs (ed.), *The Development Dictionary: A Guide to Knowledge as Power* (Zed Press 1992).

5 United Nations Millennium Development Goals www.un.org/millenniumgoals/; see also United Nations Millennium Declaration, GA Res. 55/2, UN GAOR, 55th Sess., Supp. No. 49, at 4, UN Doc. A/55/49 (2000).

6 A. Sen, *Development as Freedom* (Oxford University Press 1999) at 35.

consensus around public policy goals on sustainable development took many years. In order to understand what sustainable development means today, and how a commitment to intergenerational justice forms part of its foundations and its principles, it is useful to trace the origins and progress of these debates. Emphasis, especially, can be placed on the current commitments of the UN Member States, together with stakeholders and partners on all levels, to work collaboratively towards achieving the seventeen global SDGs. In light of these debates and the fragile consensus that has evolved, the status of sustainable development in international law can be clarified, including a consideration of how intergenerational equity, as an emerging legal principle, helps to achieve these SDGs and related binding legal instruments.

### *Prior to the 1987 Report of the UNCED*

The need for societies to develop while living within certain environmental limits has been recognized since ancient times and across diverse civilizations.[7] However, global concern about the direction of economic development practices increased dramatically in the twentieth century.[8] These early debates on the sustainability of development patterns gained currency and began to influence public opinion in many countries. As noted in the writings of political economists Thomas Malthus and David Ricardo, in the early 1900s concerns were raised about the prospect for economic growth continuing over the long term. A seminal report, *Limits to Growth*, was released by the Club of Rome in 1972, forecasting widespread economic, social and environmental collapse if countries did not recognize and respect absolute limits to growth, especially population control.[9] In the same year, the UN hosted the UNCHE, which resulted in the Stockholm Declaration on the Human Environment, the creation of the UNEP, and increased impetus to agree on certain MEAs such as the 1973 CITES. The Stockholm Declaration implicitly recognizes, in Principle 14, the need to reconcile conflicts "between the needs of development and the need to protect and improve the environment."

By the release of the 1980 World Conservation Strategy of the IUCN, which defines "the modification of the biosphere and the application of human, financial,

[7] D.W. Pearce and R.K. Turner, *Economics of Natural Resources and the Environment* (Johns Hopkins University Press 1990) at 6–7.

[8] Stockholm Declaration of the United Nations Conference on the Human Environment, UN Doc. A/C. 48/14 (1972), 11 ILM 1461 (1972) [hereinafter Stockholm Declaration]. For discussion, see, e.g. G.D. Meyers and S.C. Muller, 'The Ethical Implications, Political Ramifications and Practical Limitations of Adopting Sustainable Development as National and International Policy' (1996) 4 Buff. Envtl. L. J. 1 and A. Geisinger, 'Sustainable Development and the Domination of Nature: Spreading the Seed of the Western Ideology of Nature' (1999) 27 B.C. Envtl Aff. L. Rev. 43.

[9] Ibid. at 43.

living and non-living resources to satisfy human needs and improve the quality of human life," the term sustainable development was more generally recognized in global debates.[10] The World Charter for Nature, adopted by the UNGA two years later, calls for "optimum sustainable productivity," affirming that in "formulating long-term plans for economic development, population growth and the improvement of standards of living, due account shall be taken of the long-term capacity of natural systems to ensure the subsistence and settlement of the populations concerned, recognizing that this capacity may be enhanced through science and technology."[11]

In 1983, responding to increasingly heated debates between developed and developing countries, the UNGA established the WCED.[12] While focusing on the environment, the Resolution required equal representation of developing and developed countries on the special commission and referred specifically to the need for sustainable development in its terms of reference. This WCED undertook a global series of consultations and, through an Experts Group on Environmental Law, also designed a series of legal principles and recommendations on environmental protection and sustainable development. In 1987, the Commission delivered its Report to the UNGA, *Our Common Future*.[13] The most generally accepted definition of sustainable development is found in this 'Brundtland Report' where it is defined as "development that meets the needs of the present without compromising the ability of future generations to meet their own needs," which was drafted by a legal working group of the WCED in scant hours.[14] The Brundtland definition of sustainable development and the contents of the Report were accepted by the UNGA in Resolution 42/187 'Report of the World Commission on Environment and Development'. In this Resolution, the UNGA agreed that "an equitable sharing of the environmental costs and benefits of economic development between and within countries and between present and future generations is a key to achieving sustainable development." It also called upon all Governments to "ask their central and sectoral economic agencies to ensure that their policies, programmes and budgets encourage sustainable development and to strengthen the role of their environmental and natural resource agencies in advising and assisting central and sectoral agencies in that task," and for the "governing bodies of the organs, organizations and programmes of the United Nations system to review their policies, programmes,

[10] United Nations Framework Convention on Climate Change, opened for signature 4 June 1992 (entered into force 21 March, 1994), 1771 UNTS 107, 31 ILM 849.

[11] United Nations Convention on Biological Diversity, opened for signature 5 June 1992, 1760 UNTS 79, 143; 31 ILM 1004.

[12] UNGA Resolution A/38/161 on the Process of Preparation of the Environmental Perspective to the Year 2000 and Beyond.

[13] WCED, *supra* note 1.

[14] Ibid.

budgets and activities aimed at contributing to sustainable development."[15] Of key relevance, the WCED definition grounds the need for sustainable development with a claim for equitable opportunities for development between and among generations rather than, for instance, a claim about the need to prevent environmental damage as such. It focuses on 'needs', especially the essential needs of the world's poor, to which overriding priority should be given. Also, it emphasizes the 'carrying capacity' limits to development which must be understood and respected, while recognizing that these limits are imposed by the current state of technology and social organization on the environment's ability to meet human needs.

Overall, the Resolution makes it clear that in 1987, the UNGA did not see the concept of sustainable development as merely a 'compromise term' for more environmentally sound exploitation of natural resources, or a softer, more 'development-friendly' way to refer to new environmental policies in developing countries. It underscored how sustainable development is an objective for governments and the international system, one which implies design and implementation of a 'new kind of development' in certain specific economic sectors (such as agriculture, forestry, fisheries), one that can last over the long term by respecting the needs of future generations.

### *The 1992 UNCED and the UNCSD*

In 1992, in response to the Brundtland Report, the UN convened a global conference in Rio de Janeiro (the UNCED, or the Rio Earth Summit)[16] – on development needs and how to integrate environmental considerations into development planning and economic decision-making. In 1992, public awareness about environmental issues had reached an extremely high level, and it was also becoming clear that traditional strategies for development were not yielding adequate results in developing countries.

A scene of high tensions, vigorous debates and extremely active participation from civil society, scientists, business leaders and many others, the UNCED was broadly viewed as a global success. Specific outcomes included the 1992 Rio Declaration, a short consensus declaration agreed by the Heads of State assembled in Rio; the 1992 Agenda 21, which is annexed to the Declaration and contains an extensive global action plan on specific environment and development issues; and three international treaties signed by a record number of countries: the 1992,[17] the 1992 UN CBD,[18] and (two years later) the 1994 UNCCD.[19]

[15] WCED, *supra* note 1 at para. 90.

[16] See Sustainable Development Goals Knowledge Platform, UNCED, Earth Summit https://sustainabledevelopment.un.org/milestones/unced accessed 12 September 2019.

[17] United Nations Framework Convention on Climate Change (1992).

[18] United Nations Convention on Biological Diversity (1992).

[19] United Nations Convention to Combat Desertification (1994).

The Rio Declaration, a short document of twenty-seven principles, has a composite character.[20] These principles reflect the work of the WCED's Experts Group on Environmental Law, which is mentioned later in this chapter. There are several elements of the Rio Declaration which can elucidate key elements of the 'new kind of development' that was being contemplated by the world community. In particular, the Declaration focuses on procedural changes, such as building scientific knowledge, undertaking impact assessment and promoting public participation in decision-making, which permit governments to take environmental concerns into account in development planning.

Agenda 21 complements the Rio Declaration by providing an 800-page 'blueprint' for sustainable development. It contains hundreds of recommendations specific to various different sectors of economic and other activities that States can undertake in order to turn the principles agreed in the Declaration into strategies and programs.[21] The purpose of this 'blueprint' was to halt and reverse the effects of environmental degradation and to promote sustainable development in all countries.[22] However, most of the details on SDGs and standards, as well as commitments meant to achieve this objective, remained to be worked out through the specific conventions signed at the UNCED, and the new institutions recommended by the Conference.[23] In particular, the global treaties signed at the UNCED became one of the principal areas where new standards, rules and regimes helped to clarify the content of a commitment to sustainable development.

One follow-up mechanism which was recommended by the Brundtland Report and Agenda 21 was the creation of a specialized UN institution to carry the international sustainable development policy agenda forward. Its purpose would be to ensure the effective follow-up of decisions made at the Earth Summit, enhance international cooperation towards integration on environment and development, and examine progress in the implementation of Agenda 21.[24] It was meant to address questions of sustainable development which went beyond cooperation on environmental issues, as these were being undertaken by the UNEP. A second, equally important mechanism involved the UNCED's recommendation to create a global environmental fund which would support the incremental costs of ensuring that development initiatives were also environmentally sound, in four main areas agreed at the Rio Earth Summit. The UN responded by creating the GEF, hosted by the World Bank, the UNEP and the UN Development Programme

[20] United Nations, Rio Declaration on Environment and Development (1992).
[21] United Nations Sustainable Development, Agenda 21 (1992).
[22] Ibid.
[23] Ibid.
[24] Ibid.

(as implementing agencies), which was funded by voluntary contributions from States. The UNGA also created the UN CSD in 1992.[25]

Between 1992 and 2002, many countries began to implement specific commitments on sustainable development from the Rio outcomes. For instance, many governments have developed national or subnational Agenda 21s, authorized special bodies to implement Agenda 21,[26] or even negotiated regional blueprints for sustainable development, such as the 1996 Santa Cruz de la Sierra Summit of the Americas on Sustainable Development for the OAS, or indeed the complex treaty processes of the EU. Further, international organizations adopted sustainable development policies or objectives through their own internal decision-making procedures. These included international economic development institutions such as the World Bank, the OECD, the UN regional economic commissions and the regional development banks, in addition to environmental organizations such as the World Conservation Union (IUCN) and the UNEP.

### *The 2002 WSSD*

The WSSD, held from 26 August to 4 September 2002, brought together an estimated 45,000 participants in Johannesburg, South Africa. The UN objectives for the Summit were to review the 1992 UNCED and reinvigorate global commitment to sustainable development.[27] States hoped to focus on how best to *implement* sustainable development in a context of globalization and renewed commitments to international development assistance. The nature of the WSSD outcomes reflects this new focus. The Summit did produce a 2002 Johannesburg Declaration, and the Johannesburg Plan of Implementation (JPOI).[28] Further, however, the Johannesburg outcomes built on the 1992 and 1997 changes in the procedural aspects of development decision-making. Johannesburg witnessed the launch of more than 200 'Type II Outcomes'.[29] As specific sustainable development partnerships between governments, civil society and industry, agreed under the auspices of the WSSD process and supported by the CSD, these outcomes aimed to achieve a set of measurable objectives and results focused on the implementation of sustainable development in specific areas, and continue operating to this day.[30] Further, the WSSD process set in place a broadened institutional architecture for sustainable development, to further implement Agenda 21 and the WSSD outcomes, and to meet emerging

25 Sustainable Development Goals Knowledge Platform, CSD https://sustainabledevelopment.un.org/csd.html accessed 12 September 2019.

26 Agenda 21, *supra* note 21.

27 See Sustainable Development Goals Knowledge Platform, WSSD https://sustainabledevelopment.un.org/milesstones/wssd accessed 12 September 2019.

28 Johannesburg Declaration on Sustainable Development (2002); Johannesburg Plan of Implementation (2002).

29 Ibid.

30 Ibid.

sustainable development challenges.[31] JPOI Chapter XI lays out a multi-tiered international architecture for sustainable development governance, through which States seek to provide a strengthened and linked system of international bodies and organizations working towards sustainable development.

### *The 2012 UN Conference on Sustainable Development*

The UN Conference on Sustainable Development – or Rio+20 – took place in Rio de Janeiro, Brazil on 20–22 June 2012, and resulted in a focused political outcome document laying out clear and practical measures for implementing sustainable development.[32] In Rio, Member States launched a process to develop a set of SDGs, which build upon the MDGs and converge with the post-2015 development agenda. The Conference further adopted guidelines on green economy policies. Governments also decided to establish an intergovernmental process under the UNGA to prepare options on a strategy for sustainable development financing and agreed to strengthen the UNEP on several fronts.[33] The focus on technical implementation in specific sectors of development, rather than general principles or new international instruments, has become evident in the international outcomes of the 2002 WSSD and the 2012 Rio+20 Conference. Unlike the 1992 Rio Earth Summit, the Johannesburg WSSD and the Rio+20 UN Conference processes did not produce new international treaties. However, States specifically named over sixty international agreements in economic, environmental and social fields, at bilateral, regional and international levels, which play a role in achieving sustainable development and mentioned more than 200 others.[34] Further, specific commitments in the JPOI resulted in the development of a dedicated area of funding within the GEF for the implementation of the UNCCD.[35] In *The Future We Want*, the negotiated declaration that was the outcome of the 2012 UNCSD, similarly, over forty treaties and international instruments are specifically recognized, and the contributions of the judiciary are also highlighted.[36]

In Johannesburg, Rio and New York, the social and human rights aspects of the sustainable development agenda were recognized and strongly affirmed. For instance, the 2015 SDGs integrate international 'social development' institutions such as the WHO, the ILO and the UNDP to play a strong role in sustainable development. They focus on how to implement sustainable development, concluding that this

[31] Ibid.
[32] Ibid.
[33] WSSD, *supra* note 27.
[34] Ibid.
[35] UNCCD, *supra* note 19.
[36] *The Future We Want: Outcome Document on the United Nations Conference on Sustainable Development* (2012).

requires the integration and reconciliation of social, economic and environmental policies related to development.

## *The 2015 SDGs*

The Millennium Declaration of the UN was the forerunner of the 2015 SDGs, which identify several crucial targets for achieving greater equity – or at least reducing inequality – by 2030. Indeed, in SDG 10 to reduce inequality within and among countries, governments and a wide array of stakeholders prioritized several crucial targets, committing to adjust economic endeavors in order to increase equity among current generations; to reduce discrimination and promote greater inclusion; and to address the needs and voices of vulnerable developing countries and peoples, especially migrants. Addressing economic activities, for instance, in SDG 10 countries set a target at 10.1 to "progressively achieve and sustain income growth of the bottom 40 per cent of the population at a rate higher than the national average" by 2030; a target at 10.4 to "adopt policies, especially fiscal, wage and social protection policies, and progressively achieve greater equality"; and at 10.5 to "improve the regulation and monitoring of global financial markets and institutions and strengthen the implementation of such regulations."[37] To reduce discrimination through inclusion, for instance, in SDG 10 countries also set a target at 10.2 to "empower and promote the social, economic and political inclusion of all, irrespective of age, sex, disability, race, ethnicity, origin, religion or economic or other status" by 2030 and at 10.3 to "ensure equal opportunity and reduce inequalities of outcome, including by eliminating discriminatory laws, policies and practices and promoting appropriate legislation, policies and action in this regard."[38] They also prioritized, with regard to the most vulnerable countries at 10.6, to "ensure enhanced representation and voice for developing countries in decision-making in global international economic and financial institutions in order to deliver more effective, credible, accountable and legitimate institutions" and at 10.7 to "facilitate orderly, safe, regular and responsible migration and mobility of people, including through the implementation of planned and well-managed migration policies."[39] Among other means, as noted at 10.b, these targets are to be implemented by encouraging "official development assistance and financial flows, including foreign direct investment, to States where the need is greatest, in particular least developed countries, African countries, SIDS and landlocked developing countries, in accordance with their national plans and programmes."[40]

[37] Sustainable Development Goals Knowledge Platform, Sustainable Development Goal 10: Reduced Inequalities https://sustainabledevelopment.un.org/sdg10 accessed 12 September 2019.

[38] Ibid. at Target 10.2.

[39] Ibid. at Targets 10.6, 10.7.

[40] Ibid. at Target 10.b.

## INTERNATIONAL LAW ON SUSTAINABLE DEVELOPMENT

Where does this review of global policy-making processes leave international law? The WCED sought to bridge between developed and developing countries in order to resolve serious problems of environmental degradation and lack of social and economic development. The concept of sustainable development provided that bridge. However, not the 1992 Rio Declaration and Agenda 21, nor the 2002 Johannesburg Declaration and Plan of Implementation, nor 2012's *The Future We Want*, nor even the 2015 SDGs provide one universal definition of sustainable development that is agreed among States and covers all resources, all regions and all situations. The most accepted short description continues to be the one recommended in the 1987 Brundtland Report, which was adopted by the UNGA, when it stated that sustainable development "implies meeting the needs of the present without compromising the ability of future generations to meet their own needs," which does not precisely lay out the parameters of an international treaty commitment to 'sustainable development', or the precise normative content of sustainable development in international law.[41] As noted by Vaughan Lowe, how can one determine the needs of present generations? Are these needs also rights or entitlements? And how can one predict what will be the needs of generations to come?[42] Actually, the world's thousands of societies have diverse traditions and cultures, livelihoods, climates and living conditions. International development objectives continue to evolve, as does our understanding of sustainability for different sectors, societies and conditions. This may mean that one globally recognized definition for what constitutes 'sustainable development' is quite unlikely. And indeed, in global policy-making processes, especially through the Summits in Rio and Johannesburg, States have focused on developing greater global consensus on how to achieve it, signing and ratifying international treaties where necessary. Indeed, from the recommendations and targets found in the Brundtland Report, the outcomes of the Stockholm, Johannesburg, Rio and New York Summits, and the new global SDGs, a general concept of sustainable development can be distilled which emphasizes certain key elements. In essence, it focuses on a new type of development that does not irreversibly deplete essential natural capital, one that reconciles social, economic and environmental policies to enable improvements in present generations' quality of life, in a way that takes the interests of future generations into account.

This definition emphasizes certain aspects of the concept that have been recognized by States in the global policy-making process. First, it focuses on sustainable development as human-centered, in that it involves finding new ways to improve quality of life for people. Second, it focuses on the need to reconcile and integrate

[41] WCED, *supra* note 1.

[42] See V. Lowe, 'Sustainable Development and Unsustainable Arguments', in A. Boyle and D. Freestone (eds.), *International Law and Sustainable Development: Past Achievements and Future Developments* (Oxford University Press 1999).

environmental protection and social development with economic development. As such, sustainable development decision-making needs to take all three sets of priorities and rules into account in a balanced way. This can be done through procedures such as consultation among environment, social and economic development authorities; impact assessment; scientific collaboration and education; technical assistance and capacity building; and transparency and public participation. Third, development that is sustainable should be able to last over the long term. In order to do this, States need to determine and respect the environmental limits of ecosystems and resources. However, these limits are not static but rather are dynamic, and the relevant time horizon depends on the resource and ecosystem in question. That the concept is dynamic does not require that the status of sustainable development in international law must also remain unclear. As noted in the *Western Sahara* case, "in the development of the international legal system it may be more important to stress the imperative need to develop international law to comprehend within itself the rich diversity of cultures, civilizations and legal traditions."[43] Sustainable development has been the topic of a World Summit and the subject matter of at least a dozen international treaties. Sustainable development has also been part of the arguments before nearly all prominent international tribunals to date. In certain treaties and decisions, sustainable development has been characterized as an emerging principle of international law, while in others it serves as a goal or policy objective, the object and purpose of international treaties rather than a norm in itself.

International environmental advocates have argued that sustainable development is a new customary principle of international law, one that is in the process of being established as binding upon States.[44] Scholars have suggested that it is a "general principle that states should ensure the development and use of their natural resources in a manner which is sustainable,"[45] stating that "there can be little doubt that the concept of sustainable development has entered the corpus of international customary law."[46] H.E. Judge C.G. Weeramantry, while Vice-President of the ICJ, also argued that sustainable development was a principle of international law in his Separate Opinion in the *Gabčíkovo-Nagymaros* case, stating that he considers sustainable development to be "more than a mere concept, but as a principle with normative value which is crucial to the determination of this case."[47] In the 2005 *Iron Rhine* (*Belgium* v. *Netherlands*) award, the Arbitral Tribunal struck under the auspices of the PCA considered sustainable development an emerging principle in

43 *Western Sahara*, Advisory Opinion [1975] ICJ Reports 12.

44 See Cordonier Segger and Khalfan, *supra* note 2.

45 P. Sands, *Principles of International Economic Law*, 2nd edn. (Cambridge University Press 2003) 252–266.

46 Ibid.

47 *Case Concerning the Gabčíkovo-Nagymaros Project (Hungary/Slovakia)*, Separate Opinion of Vice President Weeramantry [1997] ICJ Reports 7.

international law, without prejudice to its status.[48] As argued by the Parties to several recent cases in international human rights tribunals, there may even be an international customary rule which grants a "right to sustainable economic development" to States or indigenous peoples under international law.[49] As has been argued elsewhere,[50] State practice demonstrating that sustainable development is now a principle of international law could be discerned from many sources, including broad ratification of treaties on sustainable development; the records or *travaux préparatoires* of international negotiations and conferences which document formal notes or statements by State representatives; votes and other acts in the UNGA and other international organizations; the pleadings of States before national and international tribunals and legal opinions by government lawyers; and national legislation and the decisions of national courts.[51] There is ample, significant and voluminous evidence of State practice making commitments to sustainable development. The answer to a question of *opinio juris* is, however, not quite so straightforward. To prove a norm of customary law, there is a need to show that State practice and *opinio juris* has been extensive and virtually uniform *in the sense of the provision invoked*. This element relates to the need for a "fundamentally norm-creating character such as could be regarded as forming the basis of a general rule."[52] For a State obligation on sustainable development to have been accepted as legally binding by a preponderance of States, it is necessary to define the specific legal norm that States must respect, even if this were simply to be defined in the context of one type of economic activity, or in the exploitation of a particular natural resource. What would be the content of such a norm? Would it be that States should ensure that certain development activities will not affect sustainability? That States must balance the needs of present and future generations when taking development decisions? Or that States shall identify and abandon unsustainable development policies, programs or projects? Much legal conceptual work remains. At present, if a sustainable development principle exists in international law, its clearest expression is likely as a 'shorthand' label for a principle requiring the integration of environment and socio-economic development: that States shall take environmental protection into account in the development process and vice versa. Europe, in particular, appears to have accepted an integration principle as its 'principle of sustainable development'. However, there is a lingering lack of clarity as to whether *most* States undertake such a commitment out of a sense of legal obligation, or simply because of a common commitment to a noble goal. It is not clear, essentially, that a principle of 'sustainable development' has yet emerged in international customary law.

48 Permanent Court of Arbitration (Belgium and the Netherlands, 24 May 2005).

49 Ibid.

50 Ibid.

51 See Cordonier Segger and Weeramantry, *supra* note 2.

52 See Lowe, *supra* note 42.

However, that is not the end of debates on the legal status of sustainable development. International law on sustainable development has mainly emerged in international treaties and accords. A search for one agreed customary norm of sustainable development might actually be a search in the wrong direction. Another possibility is that sustainable development could be characterized as an objective of States, and even an internationally recognized objective of the world community as a whole. As a global objective (or a set of goals and targets), similar to 'world peace', 'respect for human rights' and 'conservation of nature', sustainable development could be recognized as object and purpose of international treaty law. A commitment to sustainable development can be seen as a second, sometimes marginalized objective of multilateral environmental accords, phrased in different ways depending on the specific problem being addressed or resource being managed.[53] It can also be seen as one objective of international economic treaties, where States often note, in the Preamble, their joint commitment to promote sustainable development.[54] It can be found in new treaties on human rights and corruption.[55] And in some cases, such as recent treaties related to energy, desertification or food and agriculture, it might even be seen as a primary object of the international agreements themselves.[56] In international law, particular relevance is given to policy objectives when agreed in a treaty by States. Article 31 of the VCLT is the general rule of interpretation.[57] In essence, the terms of the treaty, in context and in accordance with its object and purpose, are taken together to guide a lawyer in understanding the intentions of the Parties, and are the prevailing elements for interpretation. These elements are not just legally relevant, but actually essential – *inter pares* to an international agreement, in any case. If sustainable development is object and purpose of more than thirty treaties which explicitly commit to achieve it since the Rio UNCED, it is also relevant in the regimes to implement further treaties that are related to sustainable development. As an object and purpose of these treaties alone, the concept becomes extremely important and influential in international law. It is important to the interpretation of treaty obligations in a dispute related to the environment or development issues, and guides the implementation of the agreements and even the further evolution of the treaty regimes themselves. This is important because few international treaties today, particularly in the field of sustainable development, are simply contracts among States. Rather, principles, norms, rules and decision-making procedures are all necessary parts of an international treaty regime which exists to achieve the common object and purpose of States, other international and non-State actors. As such, the emergence, evolution and effects of normative systems can coalesce around a particular object and purpose

53 Ibid.
54 Ibid.
55 Ibid.
56 Ibid.
57 Vienna Convention on the Law of Treaties (1980) at sec. III.

in international law, reinforced by 'epistemic communities' which share scientific information and data. In many treaties on sustainable development, both the CBD and the UNFCCC for instance, States essentially establish framework agreements which commit to certain common objectives and a process by which furthermore detailed and specific protocols are negotiated.

In conclusion on this point, the 'soft law' from the Stockholm Declaration, the UNGA Resolution on the Brundtland Report, the Rio Declaration and Agenda 21, and the Johannesburg Declaration and JPOI provide convincing evidence to justify finding sustainable development to be the object and purpose of international treaty law. This view is found, for instance, in Chapter 39 of Agenda 21 ('International Legal Mechanisms and Instruments'). By referring to international law in this context as 'international law on sustainable development', as 'international law concerning sustainable development' 'in the field of international law sustainable development', and as 'treaties relating to sustainable development', States have set sustainable development as a goal or subject matter of international law, rather than as a principle of international law in itself. Further evidence can be found in the decisions taken in the 1997 UNGASS Programme of Further Implementation of Agenda 21. In the 2002 WSSD,[58] and in the 2015 SDGs, this characterization of 'international law in the field of sustainable development' was not overturned, nor significantly modified. Rather, as noted above, the focus was on implementation.

A survey of the way that sustainable development is characterized in the grand majority of treaties which make specific reference to the concept further supports a characterization of sustainable development as 'purpose' of treaty law, whether or not it is also a 'principle'.[59] As one example, the UNFCCC sets the overall framework for intergovernmental efforts to tackle the challenge posed by climate change. The UNFCCC Preamble also affirms that "responses to climate change should be coordinated with social and economic development in an integrated manner with a view to avoiding adverse impacts on the latter, taking into full account the legitimate priority needs of developing countries *for the achievement of sustained economic growth* and the eradication of poverty" (emphasis added), recognizes that "all countries, especially developing countries, need access to resources required *to achieve sustainable social and economic development*" (emphasis added) and states that Parties are "determined to protect the climate system for present and future generations." The 1997 Kyoto Protocol and the 2015 Paris Agreement share UNFCCC objectives, principles and institutions, and recognize sustainable development as an objective in clear and straightforward

[58] States agreed, in the JPOI at paragraph 148 (e), to mandate the CSD to "[t]ake into account *significant legal developments in the field of sustainable development*, with due regard to the role of relevant intergovernmental bodies in promoting the implementation of Agenda 21 relating to international legal instruments and mechanisms" (emphasis added).

[59] Cordonier Segger and Khalfan, *supra* note 2.

way.[60] Indeed, both accords offer clear guidance for measures that States can take 'in order to promote sustainable development' in the area of climate change. The treaties aim to promote a different, more sustainable type of development of the world's natural resources and infrastructure, in a manner that attempts to take environmental, social and economic factors into account. In the context of the UNFCCC, taking account of regime theory, it can be argued that while an uneasy agreement existed to permit recognition of the right to promote sustainable development as a Principle in the UNFCCC negotiations of 1991–1992, from 1997 to 2015 consensus had sufficiently evolved among the Parties to recognize sustainable development as part of the 'object and purpose' of the regime, and to establish actual mechanisms to operationalize this commitment. As a second example, the UNCCD addresses desertification as a major economic, social and environmental problem of concern to many countries in all regions of the world.[61] In the UNCCD, States make over forty references to 'sustainable' development, use, management, exploitation, production and practices and/or unsustainable development and exploitation practices. While the Parties refer to sustainable use of land and water resources in the section on Principles at Article 3, States also clearly incorporated sustainable development as an 'Objective' of the UNCCD.

The commitment 'to promote sustainable development' is also found in international trade treaties, and indeed, has been interpreted by decisions of the Appellate Body of the WTO and other trade tribunals, as has been discussed elsewhere.[62] While certain tribunal decisions appear to support the contention that sustainable development is a customary principle of international law, others are clear that they view sustainable development as part of the object and purpose of their treaty, an interpretation which also fits more clearly with the approach taken by the UN in 2015 when adopting global SDGs for the world community. Of importance for this volume, while sustainable development may best be characterized as an object or purpose of treaty law rather than a principle in itself, States may agree on certain principles in order to achieve their SDGs.

## EQUITY AS A PRINCIPLE OF INTERNATIONAL LAW ON SUSTAINABLE DEVELOPMENT

Should sustainable development be recognized as a treaty objective, this does not preclude the existence of international legal norms (including treaty rules or customary principles) which serve to realize the treaty purpose. For instance, a requirement that development decision-making integrate environmental protection

60 Kyoto Protocol to the United Nations Framework Convention on Climate Change (1998); Paris Agreement on Climate Change (2015).

61 UNCCD, *supra* note 19.

62 M. Gehring and A. Genest, 'Disputes on Sustainable Development in the WTO Regime', in Cordonier Segger and Weeramantry, *supra* note 2 at 357–383.

objectives might have a specific normative character and serve the overall sustainable development use objective of the UN CBD. Such operational principles may gain recognition as customary international law, binding on all States that have not persistently objected, in order to achieve sustainable development. Their universal adoption in the context of particular resources or conditions, moreover, might support a contention that in the specific context, they have already reached such a status. The practical implications of such a contention, in some treaties which have near-universal membership and commit to these principles in their context, might be minimal, but it does not discount the value of examining the principles themselves, particularly, in the context of this volume, the principle of intergenerational equity.

In global governance structures, particularly with regard to the environment, consensus is still forming on which legal principles (and in the end, which values) will provide orientation for the integration of environmental, social and economic law. The process of uncovering principles of international law related to sustainable development has been reasonable, complex and comprehensive. The most important undertakings ran parallel to the global policy-making events outlined above, and included the process of elaborating the 1972 Stockholm Declaration, which sets out a series of (mainly environmental) principles,[63] and the 1987 Brundtland Commission's Legal Experts Group on Principles of International Law for the Protection of the Environment and Sustainable Development, which built on the Stockholm Declaration but included a detailed commentary and a clear 'norm-generating' facet to each of the proposed Principles.[64]

In 2002, the ILA's Committee on the Legal Aspects of Sustainable Development, after ten years of study, released the New Delhi ILA Declaration on Principles of International Law relating to Sustainable Development as a Resolution of its 70th Conference.[65] The New Delhi Declaration notes that "sustainable development is

[63] Stockholm Declaration on the Human Environment (1972).

[64] WCED, *supra* note 1.

[65] It is argued that States have a duty to respect the following principles: (1) sustainable use of natural resources whereby States have sovereign rights over their natural resources, and a corresponding duty not to cause, or allow, undue damage to the environment of other States in the use of these resources; (2) inter- and intra-generational equity and the eradication of poverty; (3) common but differentiated responsibilities and respective capabilities; (4) the precautionary approach to human health, natural resources and ecosystems, transferring the burden of proving lack of significant harm from an undertaking to the proponent, in cases of scientific uncertainty; (5) public participation, backed by access to information and justice; (6) good governance, with measures to support rule of law, coherence and anti-corruption; and (7) integration and interrelationship of human rights and social, economic and environmental objectives. See ILA, 'New Delhi Declaration on the Principles of International Law Related to Sustainable Development', Resolution 3/2002 available at www.cambridge.org/core/journals/netherlands-international-law-review/article/ila-new-delhi-declaration-of-principles-of-international-law-relating-to-sustainable-development/2B62D56A4AEF4667CFDEEBD5626BF6B5; N. Schrijver and F. Weiss (eds.), *International Law and Sustainable Development: Principles and Practice* (Martinus Nijhoff 2004) 1–152, 699–706; Cordonier Segger and Khalfan, *supra* note 2 at 95–191; D. French, *International Law and Policy of Sustainable*

now widely accepted as a global objective and that the concept has been amply recognized in various international and national legal instruments, including treaty law and jurisprudence at international and national levels."[66] Seven principles of international law are then highlighted which characterize treaties related to sustainable development,[67] and are reflected in decisions of international courts and tribunals.[68] In addition to six other principles which have been discussed elsewhere, it is argued that States have a duty to respect a principle of inter- and intragenerational equity and the eradication of poverty.[69]

According to the ILA New Delhi Principles, a commitment to equity includes both intragenerational equity and intergenerational equity. As the New Delhi Principles suggest at 2.1, a "principle of equity is central to the attainment of sustainable development. It refers to both intergenerational equity (the right of future generations to enjoy a fair level of the common patrimony) and intragenerational equity (the right of all peoples within the current generation of fair access to the current generation's entitlement to the Earth's natural resources)" and at 2.2 that the "present generation has a right to use and enjoy the resources of the Earth but is under an obligation to take into account the long-term impact of its activities and to sustain the resource base and the global environment for the benefit of future generations of humankind," and also that the "right to development must be implemented so as to meet developmental and environmental needs of present and future generations in a sustainable and equitable manner," which includes at 2.3 "the duty to co-operate for the eradication of poverty in accordance with Chapter IX on International Economic and Social Co-operation of the Charter of the UN and the Rio Declaration on Environment and Development as well as the duty to co-operate for global sustainable development and the attainment of equity in the development opportunities of developed and developing countries" (2.3). Indeed, the New Delhi Principles agree at 2.4 that "it is the primary responsibility of the State to aim for conditions of equity within its own population and to ensure, as a minimum, the eradication of poverty, all States which are in a position to do so have a further responsibility, as recognized by the Charter of the United Nations and the Millennium Declaration of the United Nations, to assist States in achieving this objective."[70]

*Development* (Manchester University Press 2005); see also seven CISDL Legal Working Papers detailing the meaning, scope and existing status in international law of each proposed ILA New Delhi Declaration Principle http://cisdl.org/public/docs/new_delhi_declaration.pdf accessed 12 June 2016.

66 ILA, 'New Delhi Declaration on the Principles of International Law Related to Sustainable Development' (2009).

67 M.-C. Cordonier Segger and C. J. Weeramantry (eds.), *Sustainable Justice* (Martinus Nijhoff 2004) 561–592.

68 Cordonier Segger and Weeramantry, *supra* note 2.

69 M.-C. Cordonier Segger, 'Sustainable Development in International Law', in D. Armstrong (ed.), *Routledge Handbook on International Law* (Routledge 2009) 355.

70 ILA, 'New Delhi Declaration on the Principles of International Law Related to Sustainable Development' (2009).

This principle is reflected in many examples of international treaty law on sustainable development. States shall promote a just distribution of resources among members of the present generation, as well as between this generation and the generations to come. It is the second *volet* of the equity principle which is most directly relevant to this current volume. In essence, as the ILA New Delhi Principles and many other systems have argued, the present generation has the obligation to refrain from depriving future generations of the means to meet their own environmental, social and economic needs,[71] and States shall take into account the needs of future generations in making decisions about sustainable development, especially those that might otherwise compromise their interests.[72]

While these seven rather functional principles, including the principle of intergenerational equity, may appear in most treaties related to sustainable development, it is not yet clear whether all seven have already been recognized as binding customary norms, both due to a lack of practice/*opinio juris* and, in some cases, a lack of specificity and 'normativity' in their formulation. However, the principles are present in nearly all international treaties which recognize sustainable development as an objective. As such, the principles can be welcomed as accepted tenets in the corpus of international law on sustainable development.

## CONCLUSION

In conclusion, the principle of intergenerational equity, as one of the tenets of international law on sustainable development, may still be emerging as a customary norm, though it is already well-recognized and accepted in university and other treaties on sustainable development. As part of a growing body of 'international law in the field of sustainable development' that is slowly and progressively being defined and implemented by States and other relevant actors, the principle that the interests, rights, and needs of future generations must be taken into account in decision-making on sustainable development, and measures set in place to ensure that its distributional and other requirements can be represented, is particularly well-recognized in treaty law. As discussed above, the importance of further codification and implementation of international law on sustainable development is supported by many references made by governments in agreed consensus statements, from the 1992 Rio Declaration and Chapters 38 and 39 of the 1992 Agenda 21, from the 1997 Programme of Further Implementation of Agenda 21, from the 2002 Johannesburg Declarations and Plan of Action from the WSSD from the 2012 Rio Declaration, *The Future We Want*, and from the 2015 SDGs. For the purposes of this volume, it is key to recognize that the

[71] Ibid.
[72] Ibid.

principle of intergenerational equity is central to the body of legal principles, treaties and instruments in the field of sustainable development which govern the area of intersection between social, economic and environmental law. Though the role of international law in promoting and securing sustainable development may still be in the process of definition, much progress has been made in recent decades. State commitments to equity, including intergenerational equity, must be respected early and often, both domestically and internationally.

In the past, sustainable development has been seen as a legal concept of some vagueness. It needed to be relevant in different local and global contexts, from many cultures and regions. This approach has outlived its usefulness, particularly in international law, and in many treaties one now finds commitments to a new type of development that does not irreversibly deplete essential natural capital, one that reconciles social, economic and environmental policies to enable improvements in present generations' quality of life, in a way that takes the interests of the future into account. Similarly, the normative consequences of a commitment to strengthen and respect intergenerational equity may not be the same as a straightforward prohibition or prescription, but States have begun to focus on implementation in different contexts, committing to the sustainable use or management of a particular resource, or to promote sustainable development by re-directing a specific type of economic activity.

As interactional treaty regimes are increasingly recognized and studied as part of international law, a legal commitment to sustainable development has meaning and normative force both in the implementation of international treaties, and in 'soft law' cooperation arrangements which support them, and may be taken up by international courts, tribunals and other dispute settlement mechanisms that implement those treaties and that cooperate on compliance. Further, principles of international law on sustainable development are emerging and gaining recognition to assist with implementation of the SDGs, and to help resolve disputes. In order to realize sustainable development, States have agreed inter alia to cooperate on common global concerns, including by jointly managing certain transboundary natural resources in a way that is equitable and sustainable; to ensure that social and economic development decision-making and environmental protection are integrated; to respect the common but differentiated responsibilities of developed and developing countries; to use precaution in the face of scientific uncertainty; to undertake development decision-making in a way that is transparent and participatory; to ensure accountability and good governance; and – of highest relevance here – to eradicate poverty while promoting greater intra- and inter-generational equity. In essence, a great deal of progress has been made since the 1987 Brundtland Report, though much more is needed. As international courts and tribunals are increasingly finding, when States commit to sustainable development in a treaty or international legal process, this is not legally meaningless. It involves an obligation to seek a balance between sometimes conflicting priorities in the development process, and in the interests of future generations. The balance can be achieved through procedures and substantive obligations which differ depending on the treaty instrument, the area of law and policy that it regulates, and the nature of the dispute in question. The challenge for future legal scholarship – and action – is to develop the understanding, wisdom and courage that are necessary to implement this global commitment in the interest of a common future.

# 4

# Intergenerational Justice under International Treaty Law: The Obligations of the State to Future Generations and the Example of the Hungarian Ombudsman for Future Generations

*Marcel Szabó*

Like the concept of sustainable development, the principle of intergenerational equity has long been part of modern international legal literature and has found its way into State practice. This element of international law, however, might not have gained as much attention as it rightfully deserves. This chapter – and indeed the entirety of the present volume – seeks to redress this deficit.

Public International Law (PIL) is a value-based legal order, which from the mid-twentieth century was intended to ensure the maintenance of peace between nations. Since the beginning of the twenty-first century, however, it has been faced with an even greater challenge: to ensure the survival of humanity on the planet. When UN Member States realized that the future of the natural environment and the living conditions of future generations were seriously threatened, they decided to balance economic development with environmental protection by implementing the principle of sustainable development. In so doing, the Member States hoped to see the principle used to limit destructive industrial development and create a long-term balance between environmental use and renewal. The notion of sustainable development as an independent legal category has already fulfilled its historical mission. It looks as if it is unable to further strengthen its protective function, as environmental considerations are often diluted by an ever-increasing need for economic growth. In light of growing dangers regarding the health of the natural and human environment, the international community is now in great need of expanded systems of effective legal protection.

The principle of intergenerational equity is often considered to be part of the concept of sustainable development. Nonetheless, the principle has a significant potential to become an independent tool for the protection of the natural heritage of the world and the interests of future generations. Intergenerational equity is closely linked with some of the basic building blocks of international law, including the premise of fairness and equity, and this strong moral foundation can contribute to its strength and binding quality.

It can be argued that Member States of the UN, by virtue of the principle of *jus cogens*, have a legal obligation not to destroy the physical foundations of the life of future generations by virtue of the guarantees of the right to life and associated rights that are enshrined in the UN Charter and subsequently enacted in UN-sponsored treaties such as the ICCPR. The principle of intergenerational equity is based on such legal standards. The exact content of the principle is illuminated by the hypothetical heritage concept of the domestic legislation of States, which aims to preserve the natural heritage of the nation for the benefit of future generations. Thus, the protection of the interests of future generations is based on three pillars in PIL.

The first pillar is a moral and legal requirement to preserve natural resources for the survival of our descendants, a claim that must be recognized within the scope of *jus cogens*. The second pillar is the principle of intergenerational equity, which is based on the first and can integrate it into the body of international law. The third pillar is the concept of natural heritage, which has already been incorporated into the domestic legal system of many States, and which has also become an important element of international law. The heritage concept implies that countries must properly manage the natural resources within their own territory keeping in mind the long-term needs of their citizens and succeeding generations. The universalization of this concept can strengthen the whole body of international law through an *opinio juris* that requires individual states to take responsibility for their own resources, while also providing a legal principle to preserve the natural heritage globally. It is through the patchwork of individual, national efforts that a strong international system of protections can be created. The integration of the concept of natural heritage into international law can also lay the foundations for the further development of the principle of intergenerational equity. In the following sections, this chapter will spell out the principle of intergenerational equity in greater detail and will elaborate on its significance in the protection of future generations for the twenty-first century.

## THE VALUES OF INTERNATIONAL LAW: CONTRIBUTIONS TO THE PROTECTION OF THE EARTH AND THE SURVIVAL OF FUTURE GENERATIONS

The focus of international law on human values started unequivocally with the legal processes following World War II. Participants in the San Francisco Conference in 1945 set out to protect humanity from another devastating war and to establish the UN. "Determined to save succeeding generations from the scourge of war," the UN Charter became the first instrument in international law that argued for taking a long-term responsibility for the well-being of future generations. Later the document became the basis of the new international legal order.

The ICJ acknowledged the need to protect future generations in its 1996 *Nuclear Weapons* Advisory Opinion, referring to "the unique characteristics of nuclear weapons, and in particular ... their capacity to cause untold human suffering, and their ability to cause damage to generations to come." The ICJ added that "[t]he destructive power of nuclear weapons cannot be contained in either space or time. They have the potential to destroy all civilization and the entire ecosystem of the planet ... Further, the use of nuclear weapons could be a serious danger to future generations."[1] Interpreting the words of the ICJ, Judge Weeramantry, in his Dissenting Opinion, argued: "[a]t any level of discourse, it would be safe to pronounce that no one generation is entitled, for whatever purpose, to inflict such damage on succeeding generations." At the same time, Judge Weeramantry emphasized the responsibility of the ICJ to exert its influence and put the principle of intergenerational equity into practice: "[t]his Court, as the principal judicial organ of the United Nations, empowered to state and apply international law with an authority matched by no other tribunal must, in its jurisprudence, pay due recognition to the rights of future generations."[2]

When the ICJ referred to future generations for the first time, it did so with regard to the disastrous harm that could be inflicted upon succeeding generations by the use of nuclear weapons. In the next twenty years, however, it became increasingly evident that many economic activities in their current form and at their present rate are also capable of fully undermining the living conditions of future generations. A 'business as usual' scenario in how environmental resources are used, in itself and without the use of any weapon of mass destruction, is likely to cause immeasurable suffering to the future of humanity.

Since Grotius, there is a principle in international law that States cannot, in treaties or customary law, derogate from certain, universally binding obligations.[3] Laws related to some of the most brutal violations of fundamental rights, including regulations against genocide and the basic norms of humanitarian law, belong to the category of such *jus cogens* obligations. It can be argued that environmental destruction that entirely diminishes the living conditions of future generations would also violate the universally binding rules of international law. One of the definitions of the crime of genocide is the deliberate attempt to inflict "conditions of life" on a group of people that would "bring about their physical destruction in whole or in part."[4] Destroying the living conditions of future generations differs from a crime of genocide in terms of intention but, unfortunately, not in terms of its consequences.

[1] Advisory Opinion on the Legality of the Threat or Use of Nuclear Weapons [1996] ICJ Reports 244.

[2] Ibid. at 233 (Dissenting Opinion of Judge Weeramantry).

[3] The initial name of the principle was *jus naturale necessarium*, whose origins can be traced back to natural law. R. Nieto-Navia, 'International Peremptory Norms (Jus Cogens) and International Humanitarian Law', in A. Cassese and L.C. Vohrah, *Man's Inhumanity to Man: Essays on International Law in Honour of Antonio Cassese* (Kluwer 2003) 598.

[4] UN Office of the High Commissioner for Human Rights, Convention on the Prevention and Punishment of the Crime of Genocide, 9 December 1948, pt. c, art. II.

In its resolution regarding the protection of biological diversity, the Hungarian Constitutional Court, for example, referred to the obligation to safeguard the living conditions of future generations as a peremptory norm of international law. Some authors argue that the maintenance of ecological sustainability should constitute a legally binding component of international law,[5] given that upsetting this ecological balance would cause unprecedented challenges to the whole of humanity. It is likely, however, that such a strong approach would not yet be supported by the majority of international legal scholars and national governments.

To sum up briefly, it can be presumed that there are foundational but nonexplicit norms in international law that would forbid present generations to undermine the living conditions of future generations, seriously threatening their survival. The balance between the economic activities of existing generations and the interests of the unborn in preserving environmental values can be achieved by the dual implementation of the concepts of sustainable development and intergenerational equity. The following section of this chapter addresses these concepts in greater detail.

## THE CONCEPT OF SUSTAINABLE DEVELOPMENT AND ITS CONSEQUENCES FOR THE PROTECTION OF FUTURE GENERATIONS

In the decades following World War II, many parts of the world have undergone considerable economic progress. GATT was established, and economically fruitful regional agreements were made, including European integration. While this was common among States in the West, many developing States remained under colonial rule for many more decades. Even when decolonization occurred, the years which followed were typically characterized by the marketization and cheap sale of valuable mineral resources and other raw materials. While it was assumed that this would lead to some form of economic upturn, the presumed or anticipated economic growth went unrealized, and many developing countries fell into widespread bankruptcy.

While in most industrialized economies the exhaustibility of the Earth's resources became increasingly apparent, in developing States a different kind of perception was growing. Many of these States felt that the Western European States were (and perhaps still are) to blame for their delayed economic development, and became concerned that endorsing the idea of a self-restraining economy in the name of environmental protection would only bring a new form of "green" imperialism.[6] The divide between States' economic development and the degradation of their natural

[5] R.E. Kim and K. Bosselmann, 'Operationalizing Sustainable Development: Ecological Integrity as a *Grundnorm* of International Law' (2015) 24:2 RECIEL 194–208.

[6] G. F. Maggio, 'Inter/Intragenerational Equity: Current Applications under International Law for Promoting the Sustainable Development of Natural Resources' (1996–1997) 4 *Buffalo Environmental Law Journal* 177.

environment has become an ever-increasing challenge. The political significance of this antagonism and the long-term threat it posed for the health of the natural environment has been recognized by many States and international organizations. Efforts have been made to further develop the international legal system to better respond to these tensions and mitigate their impact on the human and non-human environment.[7]

## *The Road to Rio*

One of the principles of the Stockholm Declaration, adopted at the 1972 UN Conference on the Human Environment, already mentions the responsibility of present generations to protect the natural environment for the future.[8] The Preamble, however, also makes it clear that environmental problems were viewed differently by developed and developing States. While the former considered environmental issues as a question of industrialization, the latter faced environmental concerns of a different nature, primarily originating from a lack of economic development. For developing countries, environmental problems entailed adequate access to clean drinking water, stable food supplies, the lack of waste-water treatment, and the growing problem of environmental health. The Preamble of the Declaration unmasks these opposing approaches even more clearly than the principles following it.

According to the developed States, problems originating from environmental degradation and diminishing resources needed to be solved in an urgent manner; however, developing States viewed these questions as problems of the affluent North and maintained that it was precisely their economic development that would better enable them to protect their natural environment. For example, once sewerage systems were built, it was argued that the pollution of the rivers could be prevented, and once adequate road networks were constructed, the rural population would be able to work in less environmentally destructive spheres. Instead, the reality was that developing States tended to industrialize their economies in the quickest and least capital-intensive way possible, using technologies that contributed considerably to the development or intensification of existing environmental problems. At the same time, their position that wealthier States should support their efforts to preserve their natural environment remained relevant.

The ultimate outcome of the Stockholm Conference was an attempt to harmonize the positions of developed and developing States in regard to environmental protection. Of the adopted principles, the first provides for humanity's responsibility

[7] S. Alam et al., *International Environmental Law and the Global South* (Cambridge University Press 2015).

[8] See Principle I of the Stockholm Declaration www.un-documents.net/aconf48-14r1.pdf accessed 9 June 2019.

to preserve the world's natural capital for future generations,[9] while the eighth lays down the prerequisite that economic development is necessary for environmental protection.[10]

### *Confronting the Disappointing Legal Trends and the Tragic Deterioration of Environmental Quality: Twenty Years after the Momentary Idyll of Rio*

During the 1992 Rio Earth Summit there was increasing hope that long-term progress on the key issues concerning the protection of present and future generations could be achieved through international legal instruments. Besides the concept of sustainable development, the principle of intergenerational equity also appears in the Rio Declaration on Environment and Development. Principle 3 of the Declaration states that "[t]he right to development must be fulfilled so as to equitably meet developmental and environmental needs of present and future generations."[11] It is worth noting that the first draft of the Declaration was unequivocally committed to the absolute preservation of the natural heritage of mankind, although this provision was not included in the final document. The original text referred to the natural and cultural heritage as 'public trust' which should be preserved for the benefit of present and future generations.[12] At the same time, the Declaration called attention to the inadequate structures of production and consumption, which could lead to the global collapse of the natural environment and thus the economy.[13]

According to public opinion at the time, through the adoption of the CBD and the UNFCCC, at least two of the three major planetary challenges (climate change, decreasing biodiversity, and the accumulation of waste and pollution) had been sufficiently addressed. It soon became clear, however, that the hopes associated with these developments were unsubstantiated. The decline of biological diversity could not be halted, and the 1997 Kyoto Protocol (which is the additional protocol to the UNFCCC) only entered into force in 2005. This Protocol was not renewed by

9 Ibid.: "Man has the fundamental right to freedom, equality and adequate conditions of life, in an environment of a quality that permits a life of dignity and well-being, and he bears a solemn responsibility to protect and improve the environment for present and future generations. In this respect, policies promoting or perpetuating apartheid, racial segregation, discrimination, colonial and other forms of oppression and foreign domination stand condemned and must be eliminated."

10 Ibid at Principle VIII: "Economic and social development is essential for ensuring a favorable living and working environment for man and for creating conditions on earth that are necessary for the improvement of the quality of life."

11 Ibid. at Principle 3.

12 B.H. Weston, 'The Theoretical Foundations of Intergenerational Ecological Justice: An Overview' (2012) 34 *Human Rights Quarterly* 256.

13 *Rio Declaration on Environment and Development*, Report of the United Nations Conference for Environment and Development, Principle 8 (2012).

the State Parties in 2012, and the subsequent Paris Agreement,[14] adopted in 2015, is markedly less ambitious. Further, the effectiveness and durability of the Paris Agreement has been called into question by the decision of key actors, notably the US, to publicly declare that they will withdraw following a prescribed period of time.[15]

Despite such international attempts at regulating key environmental issues, the perpetual deterioration of the state of the natural environment can be observed both regionally and globally. GHG emissions have increased at a faster pace between 2000 and 2010 than at any time over the previous three decades, propelling other harmful environmental processes.[16] The main emitters of GHGs are the US, China, the EU, Russia, India, Japan, and Brazil. Since these States account for two-thirds of the total emissions, they bear special responsibility for the adverse effects of climate change.[17] From 1965 onward, although the territory of national parks and other terrestrial protected areas increased by about 600 percent, biological diversity plummeted by 40 percent in non-maritime areas, and by 20 percent in the world's oceans.[18] The number of vertebrate species has halved in the last forty years because of unsustainable pressure on various natural habitats.[19]

Projections concerning the future state of the environment are also bleak. According to the 2017 UN Population and Vital Statistics Report, the world's population has more than doubled since the 1960s, and now exceeds 7.5 billion, with a future projection of further growth.[20] Some estimates show that world population will be between 8.3 billion and 10.9 billion by 2050.[21] According to the European Environmental Agency, annual global per capita consumption of meat has almost doubled over the past four decades,[22] and the projections of the UN FAO indicate a 60 percent increase in agricultural production by 2050.[23] This could lead to a large-scale expansion of cropland, mostly at the expense of forest and grassland

[14] Paris Agreement [4 November 2016] https://treaties.un.org/Pages/ViewDetails.aspx?src=TREATY&mtdsg_no=XXVII-7-d&chapter=27&lang=_en&clang=_en accessed 9 June 2019.

[15] See www.whitehouse.gov/blog/2017/06/01/president-donald-j-trump-announces-us-withdrawal-paris-climate-accord accessed 9 June 2019.

[16] O. Edenhofer et al. (eds.), *Mitigation of Climate Change – Summary for Policymakers, Contribution of Working Group III to the Fifth Assessment Report of the Intergovernmental Panel on Climate Change* (Cambridge University Press 2014) 6.

[17] J.H. Knox, 'Linking Human Rights and Climate Change at the United Nations' (2009) 23 *Harvard Environmental Law Review* 489.

[18] C. Mora and P. Sale, 'Ongoing Global Biodiversity Loss and the Need to Move Beyond Protected Areas: A Review of the Technical and Practical Shortcomings of Protected Areas on Land and Sea' (2011) *Marine Ecology Progress Series* 251–255.

[19] R. McLellan (ed.), *Living Planet Report 2014: Species and Spaces, People and Places* (WWF 2014) 16.

[20] *United Nations Population and Vital Statistics Report* 2017 https://unstats.un.org/unsd/demographic/products/vitstats/Sets/Series_A_2017.pdf accessed 9 June 2019.

[21] *Global Megatrends Assessment* 2015, European Environmental Agency (2015) 15.

[22] Increasing from around 23 kg per person to some 42 kg.

[23] *World Agriculture towards 2030/2050: The 2012 Revision*, ESA Working Paper (FAO 2012).

ecosystems. According to the projections of the OECD, human interference in the natural environment will continue to deplete biodiversity in the coming decades.[24] Drylands and wetlands have been identified as the two ecosystems most vulnerable to biodiversity loss. Environmental degradation and the loss of natural habitats not only diminish the structural and functional diversity of ecosystems but also erode nature's ability to support human societies.[25]

The WSSD, held in Johannesburg in 2002, aimed to facilitate the creation of a new global partnership between Member States in order to tackle environment-related global issues and promote international development under the aegis of the UN. However, scholars have often described the Johannesburg conference as a resounding failure. Given the above-discussed environmental changes and recent environmental harms suffered, it can be reasonably said that the preservation of natural resources and the protection of the interests of future generations is more topical than ever.

### *The Concept and Critique of Sustainable Development*

In 1984, more than a decade after the 1972 Stockholm conference, the UNGA established the WCED. The Commission's oversight and management was entrusted to the then Norwegian prime minister Gro Harlem Brundtland. In 1987, the Commission published the highly acclaimed 'Brundtland Report', entitled *Our Common Future*, which defined sustainable development for the first time. The report argued that sustainable development is a form of "development that meets the needs of the present without compromising the ability of future generations to meet their own needs."[26] This framing of sustainable development has shaped international environmental thinking ever since. In the last two decades, the notion of sustainable development has consolidated in international law, with its content becoming more unambiguous and concrete.[27] The concept has become part of several international agreements as an underlying principle of the State's action pertaining to the agreement. It has also inspired the SDGs, the successor entities to the MDGs, as a reflection of the most pressing needs and issues facing the international community.

Sustainable development is used in international conventions and agreements in three functionally different ways. In a considerable number of these documents,

[24] *OECD Environmental Outlook to 2050* (OECD 2012).

[25] *Global Megatrends Assessment 2015*, European Environmental Agency (2015) 123.

[26] WCED, *Our Common Future: Report of the World Commission on Environment and Development* www.un-documents.net/our-common-future.pdf accessed 9 June 2019, chapter 2.

[27] Opposing views can also be found in the literature. See V. Lowe, 'Sustainable Development and Unsustainable Arguments', in A. Boyle and D. Freestone (eds.), *International Law and Sustainable Development* (Oxford University Press 1999) 30–31.

the concept appears to function as a mere fig leaf, referring to sustainable development with no real tangible content or intention behind it. Agreements that do take the principle seriously can be divided into two categories. In the first group are the documents whose primary goal is the protection of the natural environment, but which also attempt to ensure that certain forms of economic activities are permitted. A good example is the 2007 Agreement on the Conservation of Gorillas and Their Habitats.[28] This Agreement aims to protect gorillas and their natural environment while also acknowledging and taking into account the interests of local populations who inhabit the same territory. The second group of agreements aims to regulate economic activity and ensure that investments are not made at the expense of environmental quality. This is especially relevant when different parties benefit from the same natural resource and therefore a more cautious management method is desirable. Recognizing that long-term economic activity is only possible by using resources in a sustainable manner and by allowing future generations to also have access to the resource forms the base of these agreements. Fisheries pacts typically fall within this category. Unfortunately, in the case of these agreements (and in general in the case of agreements within this group), it is often clear that the provisions concerning sustainable development and the sanctions (or lack thereof) implied by them are not sufficient to adequately consider key environmental aspects in the implementation of economic pursuits.

The legal role of the principle of sustainable development is usually strongest when one party is interested in the economic part of the agreement, while the other's main concern is the preservation of the natural environment. An apt example is the 1995 agreement regarding the use of the Mekong river basin,[29] in which downstream countries were interested in restraining the economic activity of upstream States and urged their adoption of stricter environmental measures. Keeping the river clean was important for downstream users to ensure their own economic and environmental well-being. In the case of international rivers it is common for downstream users to put pressure on their upstream neighbors to restrict and regulate their economic activity and to secure the sustainable development of the entire river basin.

Although the definition of sustainable development has become increasingly sophisticated in international agreements, due to the lack of an associated guarantee system the practical application of the principle did not yield satisfactory results. For example, although forward-looking provisions were made regarding the sustainable

[28] See www.cms.int/sites/default/files/instrument/Scanned_Agreement_text_E.pdf accessed 9 June 2019.

[29] Agreement on the Cooperation for the Sustainable Development of the Mekong River Basin, Ratified by Cambodia, The Lao People's Democratic Republic, Thailand and Viet Nam [5 April 1995] www.mrcmekong.org/assets/Publications/agreements/95-agreement.pdf accessed 9 June 2019.

use of Lake Tanganyika,[30] and the Mekong river basin,[31] the legal protection of these natural resources was not successful. Lake Tanganyika, for instance, has shrunk considerably because of excessive human use and is now threatened with a humanitarian crisis despite the fact that all Contracting Parties are equally interested in the use and preservation of the lake's natural resources.

Based on the experiences of the last three decades since the Brundtland Report in 1987, it can be questioned whether the concept of sustainable development is, in itself, a sufficient force for countries to undertake concrete measures for the protection of the natural environment. At the same time, the principle made one thing clear: sustainable development is a universally accepted goal of all Member States of the UN, and thus can serve as an important foundation for the further development of international law. The principle of intergenerational equity is closely tied to the definition of sustainable development. Yet, it can provide renewed hope that there may be legal instruments that are capable of carving out more concrete and more enforceable responsibilities for Member States.[32]

## INTERGENERATIONAL EQUITY: HOPE FOR CONCRETE REGULATIONS FOR THE LEGAL PROTECTION OF THE UNBORN

When it became increasingly evident that sustainable development as a legal principle would not be able to achieve many of the expected outcomes regarding environmental protection, several legal scholars and international environmental organizations turned to the principle of intergenerational equity as a potentially more forceful and demanding legal instrument.[33]

In jurisprudence, the notion of sustainable development is comprised of two principles: intergenerational and intragenerational equity.[34] Intergenerational equity refers to the first dimension of sustainable development and pertains to the term

[30] Convention on the Sustainable Management of Lake Tanganyika, Ratified by Burundi and the United Republic of Tanzania [23 August 2005] https://treaties.un.org/Pages/showDetails.aspx?objid=080000028006c247 accessed 9 June 2019.

[31] Agreement on the Cooperation for the Sustainable Development of the Mekong River Basin, *supra* note 29.

[32] Although, according to some authors, the system of international protection of human rights contains the notion of intergenerational equity, in the current article I do not discuss the implications of this approach. See M.-C. Cordonier Segger, 'Sustainability, Global Justice, and the Law: Contributions of the Hon. Justice Charles Doherty Gonthier' (2010) 55 *McGill Law Journal* 347.

[33] Intergenerational equity is referred to as a principle that "requires that we avoid actions with harmful and irreversible consequences for our natural and cultural heritage." See Goa Guidelines on Intergenerational Equity adopted by the Advisory Committee to the United Nations University Project on 'International Law, Common Patrimony and Intergenerational Equity', 15 February 1988.

[34] See E. Brown Weiss, *In Fairness to Future Generations: International Law, Common Patrimony and Intergenerational Equity* (United Nations University 1989).

'sustainable'.[35] This principle posits that in their development choices States must preserve the environmental capital they hold in trust for future generations and ensure that it is transmitted in conditions equivalent to those in which it was received. In other words, environmental preservation is necessary to ensure equity between generations because, without it, the 'sustainability' of development cannot be ensured.[36] Professor Edith Brown Weiss argues that each generation "would want to inherit the Earth in at least as good condition as it has been in for any previous generation and to have as good access to it as previous generations."[37] If a generation receives the planet in a degraded condition compared to how it was passed on to previous generations, this "would be contrary to the principles of intergenerational equity."[38] Thus, the idea of intergenerational equity incorporates both the obligation to safeguard natural resources, which can guarantee the preservation of the freedom of choice for future generations,[39] and the obligation to ensure access to these resources by present and future generations respectively.

The notion of intergenerational equity cannot be distinctly separated from the concept of intragenerational equity. Intragenerational equity is closely linked to the 'developmental' dimension of sustainable development.[40] It requires equity in the distribution of developmental outcomes within one generation at the national and international (between developed and developing States) levels. According to this principle, the obligation to ensure access to natural resources concerns not only future but also currently existing generations. This means that there should be no substantial difference among presently living human communities as to their access to natural resources and assets. The principle of intragenerational equity rests on the general understanding that societies are founded on a partnership among generations, which partnership assumes consideration for each other's interests.[41]

### *Does the Principle of Intergenerational Equity Demand More than the Concept of Sustainable Development?*

This question becomes relevant when the abundance and fairness of distribution of natural resources are examined, in other words, when determining how much of the

[35] See, e.g. E. Brown Weiss, 'Implementing Intergenerational Equity', in M. Fitzmaurice et al. (eds.), *Research Handbook on International Environmental Law* (Edward Elgar 2010) 100.

[36] V. Barral, 'Sustainable Development in International Law: Nature and Operation of an Evolutive Legal Norm' (2012) 23(2) *European Journal of International Law* 377–400.

[37] E. Brown Weiss, 'Our Rights and Obligations to Future Generations for the Environment' (1990) *American Journal of International Law* 201.

[38] Ibid.

[39] L.M. Collins, 'Revisiting the Doctrine of Intergenerational Equity in Global Environmental Governance' (2007) 30 *The Dalhousie Law Journal* 120.

[40] D.A. French, 'International Environmental Law and the Achievement of Intragenerational Equity' (2001) 31 *Environmental Law Reporter* 469.

[41] E. Burke, *Reflections on the Revolution in France* (Hackett 1987) 84–85.

available resources should be preserved for future generations. According to Serageldin, it would be foolish to require present generations to leave "to the next generation exactly the same amount and composition of natural capital as we found ourselves."[42] Indeed, what exactly does the concept of sustainable development demand in regard to the preservation of natural heritage? The standard legal approach is to satisfy the needs of the presently living first, "with due regard to the needs and benefits of future generations."[43] To use a metaphor, the concept of sustainable development does not require us to reject the cake or not to eat from it; it only tries to convince us that avoiding excessive eating is good both for us and for future generations. But the basis of this concept is the promise that there is a scenario where both present and future generations get full and the living conditions of human and non-human communities are still sufficiently maintained. Unfortunately, this understanding is most likely out of touch with present economic and environmental reality.

The notion of intergenerational equity requires that parts of the cake be left for future generations even if our present needs are not fully satisfied. Moreover, the amount of resources left for future generations should be comparable to the amount consumed by society. This means that the principle of intergenerational equity demands more regarding the safeguarding of the natural and cultural heritage than the concept of sustainable development. Intergenerational equity requires that the natural capital of the world be consumed at a rate that always leaves enough resources to maintain the living conditions of future generations. This applies even if the joint consumption of two separate generations would not allow for the full satisfaction of the needs of both present and future generations. Intergenerational equity calls for the proportionate use of non-renewable resources, and the sustainable use of renewable resources, so that they can replenish in sufficient quantity and time for the use of our descendants.

The realization of the demands of intergenerational equity poses considerable questions about society's moral duties towards the unborn. It is especially hard to evaluate society's moral responsibilities once the available resources have started to diminish permanently, creating gradually intensifying environmental problems for each succeeding generation. Whose duty is it to start tightening the belt? And if the degradation of natural resources causes exponentially growing challenges, which succeeding generation should we compare ourselves to in order to evaluate needs and opportunities? Furthermore, talking about our own consumption in the present will only be possible from a historical perspective, putting all members of the present generation into the same category. But there are tremendous inequalities

[42] I. Serageldin, 'Sustainability and the Wealth of Nations: First Steps in an Ongoing Journey' (1995) *The World Bank Conference on Environmentally Sustainable Development* 9–10.

[43] ILA New Delhi Conference (2002), *Fifth and Final Report of the Committee on Legal Aspects of Sustainable Development* (ILA 2002) 388.

within individual societies as well as among nations. Can society abandon its responsibility to mitigate these inequalities just because it still has more to consume than its descendants will? Intragenerational equity between nations and within states is indispensable for better environmental quality at the global scale.[44] For a viable future, many opposing interests will need to be harmonized. Humanity, however, has no other choice but to set out on this difficult journey. And the first step on this road is to do away with the false illusion of infinitude regarding environmental resources and societal consumption.

What gives authority to the idea of intergenerational equity? Why can it be said that it is a hope and an opportunity that society can protect the natural foundations of human life on Earth through this instrument of international law?

### *Moral Foundations*

The moral grounds of legal questions should not be underestimated in the practice of law. There are several examples of societies that collapsed because of the irresponsible management of their resources. The history of the ecological catastrophe of the Eastern Islands or the collapse of the Maya civilization of the Yucatán are apt reminders of our vulnerability, and of the nature of the risks we are facing.[45] It is becoming increasingly clear that humanity has reached a global tipping point that could result in the potential collapse of civilizations as they are currently known. It is no surprise, then, that participants at the Rio Conference in 1992 called for the immediate alteration of current patterns of production and consumption.

It is common knowledge that, in accordance with the genetic expression of the laws of nature, most vertebrate species aim to take care of their offspring. Humans are no exception.[46] Immanuel Kant argued that humanity has a sensitivity towards dangers threatening even its most remote descendants if there is full certainty about the occurrence of the threat.[47] By contrast, it seems that present societies are unable to change their practices that undermine the future of their children and grandchildren.

The behaviour that would urge society to better tend to its progeny, however, also has moral and spiritual underpinnings. Pope Francis' Encyclical *Laudato Si'* calls attention to the fact that the meaning of present existence can be questioned if the

44 R.M. Green, 'Intergenerational Distributive Justice and Environmental Responsibility' (1977) 27(4) *BioScience* 263.

45 G.F. Maggio, 'Inter/Intragenerational Equity: Current Applications under International Law for Promoting the Sustainable Development of Natural Resources' (1996–1997) 4 *Buffalo Environmental Law Journal* 174–175.

46 P.A. Barresi, 'Beyond Fairness to Future Generations: An Intragenerational Alternative to Intergenerational Equity in the International Environmental Arena' (1997) *Tulane Environmental Law Journal* 72–73.

47 I. Kant, 'Idea for a Universal History with a Cosmopolitan Purpose', in H. Reiss (ed.), *Kant's Political Writings* (Cambridge University Press 1970) 41, 50.

world left behind is not livable for our children and grandchildren.[48] Similarly, both Judaism and Christianity include notions of collective human ownership of the natural world, demanding stewardship over the natural heritage for future generations.[49] Islamic law is also consistent with contemporary notions of intergenerational equity, conceptualizing Muslims as stewards and trustees of the natural world with duties towards both current and future generations.[50]

Thus, it is evident that the principle of intergenerational equity that requires the preservation of environmental resources for future generations provides a clear moral command and an associated normative guideline. One of its greatest strengths is therefore its distinct ethical dimension.

### *Justice as a Conceptual Element of Intergenerational Equity*

As Morse remarked, if the UN Charter, with its Statute of the ICJ, is implemented by Member States, in keeping with the objectives of its preamble and the statement of purposes and principles, it can become a bridge to international justice leading mankind from the barbarism of recurrent wars to a just and permanent world order of enforceable peace.[51] Pursuant to the preamble of the UN Charter, Member States are to create the necessary conditions under which justice can be achieved and international conflicts can be settled.[52] As discussed earlier, international law became more values-oriented following the World War II, and justice, at least in theory, became one of the guiding principles of States' international relations.

According to Professor Edith Brown Weiss, international law has always been concerned with justice, and the doctrine of intergenerational equity merely extends this notion further into the intertemporal dimension.[53] Intergenerational equity is sometimes also called intergenerational justice. Legal philosophy differentiates between distributive justice and reciprocal justice.[54] The axiom of distributive justice is that the goods are distributed in a way that assumes the contractual agreement of

48 Pope Francis, *Laudato Si': On Care for Our Common Home*, Encyclical Letter, 24 May 2015, para. 160.

49 See D. Rosen, 'Judaism and Ecology', in E. Agius and L. Chircop (eds.), *Caring for Future Generations: Jewish, Christian, and Islamic Perspectives* (Westport 1998) 62; E. Agius, 'The Earth Belongs to All Generations: Moral Challenges of Sustainable Development', in E. Agius and L. Chircop (eds.), *Caring for Future Generations: Jewish, Christian, and Islamic Perspectives* (Westport 1998) 103.

50 See A. Nanji, 'The Right to Development: Social and Cultural Rights and Duties to the Community', *Proceedings of the Seminar on Islamic Perspectives on the Universal Declaration of Human Rights*, UN Doc. HR/IP/SEM/1999/1 (PART II Sec. 2), 1999, 346.

51 W.L. Morse, 'International Law: The Bridge to International Justice' (1972) 4(1) *Akron Law Review* 3.

52 Charter of the United Nations [1945] para. 1, art. I.

53 Brown Weiss, *supra* note 34, at 28, 34.

54 See Aristotle, *Nicomachean Ethics, Book V* (Cambridge University Press 2000).

unrestrained parties free of influence. The notion of reciprocal justice can have special significance in the interpretation of the principle of intergenerational equity. Naturally, future generations cannot give back, and only present generations can provide for them. The idea, however, that everything the present generation has received from its forebears will be inherited to posterity in equally good or better condition is in accordance with the general understanding of morality, and thus can serve as a sufficient foundation of intergenerational equity.

### *Equity and Intergenerational Equity*

According to its legal meaning, equity is a special form of expression of justice. As Vaughan Lowe stated, "[r]ecourse to general principles of justice in order to assist the 'just' application of law is a feature common to the major legal systems of the world."[55] Equity refers more to proportionality between stakeholders than to justice, but the two concepts cannot be fully separated. In substantive law a decision that does not take into account the equal interest of all stakeholders can still be lawful, while a decision based on the principle of equity has to pass the test of morality.

Equity has long been accepted as a general principle of international law. Equity is the "general principle of justice as distinguished from any particular system of jurisprudence or the municipal law of any State,"[56] as defined in a decision of the Arbitration Court in the claims between the US and Norway in 1922. This definition illustrates the centuries-old embeddedness of the concept of equity in international law. The weight given to equity in the international system also strengthens the advancement of the principle of intergenerational equity. The notion of equity represents concepts of proportionality and commensurability not only between subsequent generations, but also among communities and stakeholders of the presently living.

The full significance of the ruling of the ICJ in the Gabčíkovo-Nagymaros case is still waiting to be revealed in the international legal literature. The case related to the diversion of the Danube River as a natural resource on the border of Slovakia and Hungary. Slovakia unilaterally diverted a segment of the river into an artificial channel in order allow for the functioning of the Gabčíkovo dam constructed on Slovakian territory. Hungary argued that the entire body of water should remain in the original riverbed in order to provide, from an environmental point of view, sufficient amounts of water for the Danube's system of tributaries. The ruling of the ICJ in this case built on the concept of equity from two perspectives. On the one hand, it argued that, based on the principle of intragenerational equity, the waters of

[55] V. Lowe, 'The Role of Equity in International Law' (1989) *Australian Yearbook of International Law* 55.

[56] *Norwegian Shipowners' Claims (Norway v. United States), Permanent Court of Arbitration* (1922) Reports of International Arbitral Awards, Vol 1, 331.

the Danube must be shared between the two countries in a way that is in accordance with the principle of using an "equitable and reasonable share."[57] At the same time, the ICJ also considered the question from an intergenerational perspective. It stated that "[t]hroughout the ages, mankind has, for economic and other reasons, constantly interfered with nature. In the past, this was often done without the consideration of the effects upon the environment. Owing to new scientific insights and to a growing awareness of the risks for mankind – for present and future generations – of pursuit of such interventions at an unconsidered and unabated pace, new norms and standards have been developed."[58] Following this line of argument, the ICJ called for constant monitoring of the environmental impacts of the dam, enabling the protection of natural resources for future generations.

The principle of equity, as the ILA has articulated, is a "principle of international law of a rather more general nature, enabling the international community to take into account considerations of justice and fairness in the formation, application and interpretation of international law."[59] This means that when the joint consumption of present and future generations cannot fully satisfy the needs of both generations, it follows from the principle of equity that present generations have the legal obligation to use natural resources in a way that guarantees future generations access to the same level of environmental quality.

## *The Contractual Practice of Intergenerational Equity: The Obligation of States with Regard to Domestic Law*

It is worth recalling how the concept of intergenerational equity appears in international agreements. Given the remarkably high number of participating States, the most important documents from this perspective are certainly the 1992 CBD and the UNFCCC. Both conventions contain frameworks and fundamental terms that are very similar to that of the 1992 Rio Declaration. The rationale of these instruments as being "[f]or the benefit of present and future generations" appears in the Preamble in the CBD, and in Article 3 in the UNFCCC.[60] Both agreements aim to halt environmental destruction in the fastest way possible. The negative impacts originating from the degradation of natural habitats and the growing climate problem were already felt during the adoption of these documents, and it was understood that they would continue to threaten the living conditions of future generations. This means that with regard to the concrete agreements, the positions of present and future generations are the same and that differentiating between them is not necessary. Curbing environmental destruction serves the survival of humanity both in the

57 Ibid. at para. 140.
58 *Gabcikovo-Nagymaros Project (Hungary v. Slovakia)* [1997] ICJ Reports 178.
59 ILA New Delhi Conference (2002), *Fifth and Final Report of the Committee on Legal Aspects of Sustainable Development* (ILA 2002) 392.
60 UNFCCC [2012] art. 3; CBD [2012] preamble.

short and the long term. In this regard, both conventions satisfy the criteria of intragenerational and intergenerational equity, since, according to their terms, developed countries are required to facilitate the actions of developing countries to mitigate the consequences of climate change and fight biodiversity loss.

In theory, the concept of sustainable development should operate by means of exerting mutual pressure on other States to keep their economic activities in check and comply with the principles of sustainability. Otherwise, excessive use of natural resources and overexploitation by one State in the name of economic development can result in the depletion of resources held in common. States interested in economic development and the use of natural assets can, under an optimal scenario, ensure the long-term, sustainable use of resources by regulating one another's behaviour and economic pursuits. Intergenerational equity is based on the cooperation of States: individual States realize particular projects and goals, which together emerge as a patchwork of solutions achieving a desired end. This means that the protection of both the climate system and biodiversity takes place individually, on the national level, while the success of these efforts can only be evaluated in light of the results achieved globally. In order for the respective States to be able to take the necessary national measures, however, it is vital that the developed States provide financial and technical assistance for their less developed counterparts. It is through this assistance that the principles of intragenerational equity are put into practice. Without such help, however, achieving intergenerational justice would be considerably more difficult. Therefore, increasing intragenerational equity can result in the better protection of future generations, and can help achieve intergenerational equity.

### *Intergenerational Equity: The Concepts of Trust and Heritage*

As discussed earlier, the original draft of the Rio Declaration referred to natural and cultural heritage as 'public trust' in need of protection for the benefit of future generations. According to this approach, the currently living can be distinctly separated from coming generations. It follows from the definition of trust that the task of the present is to preserve the natural heritage for posterity, even if their interests and needs are conflicting.[61]

As a legal concept, intergenerational equity can be linked to the idea that each generation receives natural and cultural legacy from its predecessors and holds it in trust for the benefit of the next generation. According to Professor Edith Brown Weiss, this imposes certain planetary obligations upon each generation to conserve the quality and diversity of the natural and cultural resource base, while also giving certain planetary rights to each generation to use the legacy. These planetary obligations and rights form the basis of a proposed doctrine of intergenerational

[61] B.H. Weston, 'The Theoretical Foundations of Intergenerational Ecological Justice: An Overview' (2012) 34 *Human Rights Quarterly* 256.

equity. For these obligations and rights to be enforceable, they must be incorporated into international law or into national and subnational legal systems.[62]

The legal concept of intergenerational equity is further strengthened by its connection to the notion of trust. Trust, or more broadly the concept of heritage, is widely used in international law and in a number of domestic legal systems. Linking the heritage concept with the concept of intergenerational equity, therefore, can provide a more clearly defined legal avenue for determining how to use resources in the present in a way that does not foreclose future generations from the planetary legacy.

## THE CONCEPT OF NATURAL AND CULTURAL HERITAGE AS A GUIDING PRINCIPLE OF INTERGENERATIONAL EQUITY

As noted above, during the formulation of the principles of the Rio Declaration, natural and cultural heritage was still referred to as 'public trust'. The idea that the most valuable natural and cultural resources on the planet should be regarded as the common, hypothetical heritage of the world whose preservation is everyone's responsibility is not far from the conventional thinking of PIL.

### *The Concept of Heritage in International Law*

That there are values and treasured resources that unite countries over boundaries, and whose protection is in the interest of the whole of humanity and thus of all States, has long been part of international legal tenets.

### *Heritage of Every People*

The 1954 Convention for the Protection of Cultural Property in the Event of Armed Conflict was the first to protect the common heritage of mankind under international law.[63] The Convention considered the "immovable property of great importance to [be] the cultural heritage of every people." The heritage concept of the Convention only extends to the protection of cultural heritage and does not include the safeguarding of natural assets; however, it is worth mentioning the agreement as one of the first steps in the development of the concept of heritage in international law. It is interesting to note that, under the Convention, protection was ensured for all elements of cultural property that could be considered valuable for the whole of humanity, without the prior need to enlist, record, or catalogue the

[62] E. Brown Weiss, 'Intergenerational Equity in International Law' (1987) *American Society of International Law Proceedings* 127.

[63] Convention for the Protection of Cultural Property in the Event of Armed Conflict [1954] 249 UNTS 240, art. 1.

properties in question. The concept's strength could easily become its drawback, however, as it can often be debated whether a particular historical monument or cultural property is significant for the whole of humanity.

### *Common Heritage of Mankind*

The concept of the common heritage of mankind was first proposed by Arvid Pardo, the permanent representative of Malta to the UN. The proposal argued that the resources of the seabed should be considered the common heritage of mankind and that the exploitation of its subsoil should benefit all nations equally. While the distribution of benefits is important for the elimination of inequality between developed and developing States, the need to take into account the long-term interests of future generations was also emphasized in the proposal.[64] In 1970, the UNGA recognized the seabed of the high seas and its subsoil as the common heritage of mankind[65], and in 1982 the concept was incorporated into the UN Convention on the Law of the Sea.[66] The doctrine of the common heritage of mankind establishes that these resources and territories cannot become the sovereign part of any one country, and that free access has to be provided for everyone to take advantage of the available resources of the heritage. Any profit originating from them, however, must be equally and fairly shared among all countries of the world, taking into account the interests of future generations.

Typically, the concept of heritage is, both in a legal and a common sense, used under two circumstances. In the first case, one aims to ensure that rights as heirs are upheld *vis-à-vis* other heirs, while in the second case one seeks to safeguard the future of one's children by carefully handing over one's legacy. According to the Convention on the Law of the Sea, economic cooperation exploiting the common heritage must pay part of their revenue to the International Seabed Authority. Most of the payments are used to compensate developing States for the exploitation of resources by economic actors based in more developed and wealthier States, while a smaller part of the amounts received is used to finance research by the International Seabed Authority in order to designate areas of particularly high value where extraction is prohibited in view of the interests of future generations. Despite the latter regulation, the governance structure established by the Convention often depicts siblings quarreling over the parental legacy rather than the strong motives of States to safeguard the needs of future generations in their territory. A significant portion of the exploited resources should be spent on ensuring the maintenance of

64 See e.g. www.un.org/depts/los/convention_agreements/texts/pardo_ga1967.pdf accessed 9 June 2019.

65 Declaration of Principles Governing the Sea-Bed and the Ocean Floor, and the Subsoil Thereof, beyond the Limits of National Jurisdiction [1970] UNGA 2749 (XXV).

66 United Nations Convention on the Law of the Sea (UNCLOS) [1981] pt. XI.

adequate living conditions for future generations rather than simply on the satisfaction of the needs of the present generation.

The 1967 Outer Space Treaty recognizes the moon and other celestial bodies as part of the common heritage of mankind.[67] Similar to the Convention on the Law of the Sea, the Treaty declares that these natural objects do not fall under the sovereignty of any country, but rather that all States are entitled to exploit their resources in accordance with the regulations of international law.[68] In the history of international law, many other natural and cultural objects have been proposed for recognition as the common heritage of mankind. More recently, satellite orbits, the world's cultural heritage,[69] endangered species, genetic resources, tropical forests, the atmosphere, all food sources, and the living resources of the seas have been nominated to form part of the common heritage of mankind.[70]

States can only accept the concept of the common heritage of mankind if it relates to areas and resources that do not belong to any country's sovereign territory. This is an understandable prerequisite. There was an attempt in the international legal literature to include aquifers and groundwater resources under the category of the common heritage of mankind.[71] Unfortunately, many developed countries have already depleted their available water resources to enable irrigation and secure agricultural production. Those States that preserved their groundwater base can rightly argue that, under a common heritage regime, the aquifers belonging to their sovereignty would become freely available to exploit by the economic actors of other States. The concept of the common heritage of mankind is nevertheless a valuable doctrine of international law, because it asserts that natural resources that do not belong to any particular state must serve the benefit of the whole of humanity, including those living after us.

### *Cultural and Natural Heritage of the World*

There is another forward-looking example of the concept of heritage in international law, which was created under the aegis of UNESCO. The World Heritage Convention aims to preserve the world's most invaluable cultural and natural assets for future generations.[72] The State Parties to the Convention may nominate natural and cultural treasures of outstanding universal value to be added to the World Heritage List, declaring thereby that they wish to elevate the protection of the

67 Ibid. at art. 1.

68 Ibid. at arts. 2–3.

69 Ibid.

70 K. Baslar, *The Concept of Common Heritage of Mankind in International Law* (Brill 1998) 279.

71 R. Martin-Nagle, 'Fossil Aquifers: A Common Heritage of Mankind' (2011) *Journal of Energy & Environmental Law* 39–60.

72 UNESCO Convention Concerning the Protection of the World Cultural and Natural Heritage [16 November 1972] 1037 UNTS 151, 11 ILM 1358.

resource to the international level. It is clear that the purpose of the Convention is not the mitigation of intragenerational injustice through the adequate distribution of resources among present generations, but rather the preservation of cultural and natural value for the benefit of posterity. The weaknesses of the Convention are that it only regards listed and catalogued values and resources, and that the legal consequences of violating its provisions are relatively mild.

### *Common Concern of Humanity*

Another concept often referred to in the international legal literature is the common concern of humanity.[73] This concept makes it possible to implement the principle of intergenerational equity in relation to the State's sovereign natural heritage. The term 'common concern' was used by the chairman of the Brundtland Commission in the foreword of its 1987 report. Gro Harlem Brundtland highlighted that commissioners from diverse nations united under "a common concern for the planet and the interlocked ecological and economic threats with which its people, institutions, and governments now grapple."[74] This realization corresponds to the 1992 CBD, which recognizes biodiversity as the common concern of humanity, and to the UNFCCC and the 2015 Paris Agreement, which both considered climate change within this conceptual framework.

The UNFCCC and the CBD emphasize the common responsibility of States in matters pertinent to the outlined common concerns. Pursuant to the Rio Conventions, the common concerns of biodiversity loss and threats imposed by climate change impose concrete duties on each individual country and on the international community as a whole. For the realization of the concept of the common concern of humanity, several implementation mechanisms and financial schemes have been developed under international law. The GEF, the UN collaborative initiative on Reducing Emissions from Deforestation and Forest Degradation (UN-REDD Programme), and the Kyoto Protocol form part of these efforts. The advantage of the concept as a legal category is that it urges States' individual actions, while establishing a moral base for universal responsibility and creating the necessary financial incentives for action. The drawback is that it lacks what the heritage concept implicitly entails: a reference to future generations and a moral obligation to preserve resources for the benefit of our descendants.

[73] C. Bowling, E. Pierson, and S. Ratté, *The Common Concern of Humankind: A Potential Framework for a New International Legally Binding Instrument on the Conservation and Sustainable Use of Marine Biological Diversity in the High Seas* www.un.org/depts/los/biodiversity/prepcom_files/BowlingPiersonandRatte_Common_Concern.pdf accessed 9 June 2019.

[74] WCED, *supra* note 26, Chairman's Foreword.

### *Regional Natural Heritage*

In European law, which is a special subsystem of PIL, the Birds Directive and the Habitats Directive define the species of wild birds naturally occurring in the European territory as well as the threatened natural habitats and species as the natural heritage of the EU.[75] In its communication regarding these Directives, the European Commission noted that "[t]he environment is our life-support system and a common heritage. Preserving, protecting and improving is a shared European value, with EU environmental law establishing a common framework of obligations for public authorities and rights for the public."[76] On this basis, the EU can institute legal obligations to preserve the protected elements of the natural heritage in the region. It can also establish financial schemes and incentive mechanisms necessary for protections, without allowing Members of the EU to take advantage of the natural heritage found in the territory of another Member State.

### *Heritage of Individual States Held in Cooperation with Others*

Members of the Amazon Cooperation Treaty Organization[77] met in Quito in 1989 to adopt the Declaration of San Francisco de Quito.[78] The Declaration emphasizes the ecological significance of the Amazon rainforest and considers it to be one of the most important elements of the national heritage. It highlights the common goal of respecting the rights and preserving the living conditions of indigenous peoples who live in this high-biodiversity area.[79] The Declaration did not receive significant recognition in the legal literature, although an edited volume on *International Law and the Conservation of Biological Diversity* makes mention of it.[80] The realization of the rights of indigenous peoples is undoubtedly a highly important endeavor. Understanding the Amazon ecosystem, however, as the heritage of individual nations might seem contradictory to the view that natural heritage is part of the common heritage of mankind. Yet, from a legal perspective, declaring the Amazon to be part of the national heritage of States cannot be considered an exclusionary approach. Rather, it can be argued that through this Declaration, States seek to protect a biologically intertwined and organic entity by establishing a link

75 Directive 2009/147/EC; Directive 92/43/EEC.

76 Communication from the Commission of 28 April 2017: Commission Notice on Access to Justice in Environmental Matters, C(2017)2616 final, para. 1.

77 Amazon Cooperation Treaty [3 July 1978]. See D. Ware, 'The Amazon Treaty: A Turning Point in Latin America Co-operation?' (1980) 15 *Texas International Law Journal* 118–137.

78 1989 San Francisco de Quito Declaration, adopted at the Third Meeting of Ministers of Foreign Affairs, held in Quito, Ecuador.

79 B. Garcia, *The Amazon from an International Law Perspective* (Cambridge University Press 2011) 109.

80 M. Bowman and C. Redgwell, *International Law and the Conservation of Biological Diversity* (Kluwer Law International 1996) 264.

between the concept of heritage and the idea of the nation. This effort might seem to assume a sovereign claim over parts of the Amazon by individual States; in reality it aims to guarantee the protection of this highly valuable natural heritage through international cooperation and through the use of more effective international legal tools.

The concept of national heritage can also be found in other States' legal practice. In 2012, for example, Article P of the new Fundamental Law of Hungary declared that biodiversity, the soil, water reserves, and forests form the national heritage of the nation.[81] A 2014 declaration of the European Forum of Judges for the Environment provides an even more explicit interpretation of this concept, one that highlights its coherence with the provisions of international law. It states:

> [s]ignatories to the Declaration assign special significance to the general protection of biological diversity, recognizing that natural values are unique and irrecoverable parts of the national heritage; their management and the improvement of their condition, as well as their preservation is the common concern of humanity and as such has outstanding importance for the benefit of present and future generations.[82]

In sum, it can be argued that the idea of preserving and protecting the natural heritage for the benefit of future generations is more and more delineated in PIL. Part of this concept is the explicit responsibility of States to safeguard their natural heritage, as an important component part of the universal heritage under their own jurisdiction. States are also bound to cooperate with each other for the protection of the heritage, in part through the use financial instruments. Implementing the international legal heritage concept also implies the concretization of legal obligations following from the principle of intergenerational equity.

### *Legal Instruments for the Protection of the Natural Heritage and Future Generations in National Law*

In national law, the principles of intergenerational equity and the protection of natural heritage are implemented through the customary instruments of public law, relying on traditional legal principles and enforcement practices that characterize common democratic procedures. Some States, however, have experimented to protect the interests of future generations through the establishment of new institutions.

[81] Article P of the Fundamental Law of Hungary states that "Natural resources, in particular arable land, forests and the reserves of water, biodiversity, in particular native plant and animal species, and cultural artefacts shall form the common heritage of the nation; it shall be the obligation of the State and everyone to protect and maintain them, and to preserve them for future generations."

[82] See 'Principal Considerations' of the Declaration on Environmental Responsibility prepared by the European Forum of Judges for the Environment.

### *The Protection of Future Generations and the National Heritage through Traditional Legal Instruments*

Today, an increasing number of States incorporate the protection of future generations into their national legislation, often at the constitutional level. Protection can mean, for example, a kind of heritage concept that requires present generations to preserve natural resources in an unaltered States for the benefit of future generations. This can be seen as a growing practice,[83] which can be classified as a forming *opinio iuris*, according to which individual States are required to safeguard the heritage under their own jurisdiction.

Reviewing the constitutional provisions of individual States, the following observations can be made. At least twenty States have explicit provisions for the protection of future generations.[84] The interests of future generations can also be protected through the preservation of particular elements of the natural heritage. In several States, for example, maintaining the ecological balance is a constitutional legal requirement.[85] Other States include the rational use of natural resources,[86] or the preservation of biological diversity,[87] among their constitutional principles. Numerous States call for the constitutional protection of some of their specific environmental resources including water,[88] the soil,[89] or agricultural land.[90]

As the above list of provisions only considers constitutional protections, it can be assumed that the legal system of protections as well as the list of countries having such protections will be extended if the entire body and depth of domestic law in each State is taken into account. Additionally, it cannot be excluded that the domestic legal systems of most States in the world already acknowledge the interests and needs of future generations, and therefore aim to provide some form of safeguard mechanism for the preservation of natural resources. Constitutional and other national courts, as well as *sui generis* institutions, can all play a significant part

83 Some scholars argue that such regulations are rather the exception than the rule. See for example L.M. Collins, 'Revisiting the Doctrine of Intergenerational Equity in Global Environmental Governance' (2007) 30 *The Dalhousie Law Journal* 137.

84 Albania, Andorra, Brazil, Cuba, East Timor, Eritrea, Georgia, Germany, Guyana, Iran, Japan, Malawi, Namibia, Norway, Papua New Guinea, Poland, South Africa, Uganda, Vanuatu, and Zambia.

85 In sum, twenty-eight countries belong to this category. For example Brazil, Cape Verde, Costa Rica, Haiti, Mexico, Mongolia, Mozambique, and Paraguay.

86 Albania, Argentina, Andorra, Bulgaria, East Timor, Georgia, Guyana, Lithuania, Nicaragua, Panama, Portugal, Spain, Uganda, Uzbekistan, and Vietnam.

87 Argentina, Brazil, Bulgaria, Columbia, Ecuador, Finland, Hungary, Malawi, Namibia, Norway, Peru, and Thailand.

88 Albania, Algeria, Andorra, Austria, Cambodia, Cuba, Eritrea, Guatemala, Guyana, Hungary, Lao PDR, Lithuania, Mongolia, Panama, Switzerland, Tajikistan, Uganda, Uruguay, and Venezuela.

89 Andorra, Cambodia, Cape Verde, Eritrea, Finland, Guatemala, and Hungary.

90 Andorra, Cuba, and Mongolia.

in this endeavor, and indeed eight such *sui generis* institutions were highlighted by the Secretary-General of the UN in his 2013 report.[91]

### *Protecting the Interests of Future Generations through Dedicated Institutions*

The primary task of institutions for future generations is to embed long-term thinking in governance. This task is often not evident, given the structure of the parliamentary cycles (four- or five-year periods), evoking short-term political interests and a strong focus on immediate results. The task of promoting long-term thinking is fulfilled by a Parliamentary Committee in Finland,[92] an independent Ombudsman Office in Wales,[93] and a Deputy Auditor in Canada. In the Finnish system, it is members of Parliament who debate decisions meant to serve both present and future generations. In Wales, the Commissioner has a consultative and bridging role between the different actors of the State, the public and the economic sphere, while in Canada the Deputy Auditor investigates whether and how State spending serves the long-term interests of the Canadian people, including future generations.

In Israel, the Israeli Commission for Future Generations was in place between 2001 and 2006. Its role was to assess whether the laws and policies adopted by the Knesset satisfy the long-term interests and needs of present and future generations in matters related to the environment, education, and public health. The Parliamentary Advisory Council on Sustainable Development, which functions as part of the German Parliament, oversees the implementation of strategies concerning the future development of the country. It not only serves as a watchdog institution but can also provide recommendations on bills and legislation. The decisions made by the Council are arrived at by consensus, which provides additional significance to their proposals and statements. According to its mandate, the Norwegian Ombudsman for Children not only is concerned with support, education, and healthcare provision for children but also pays close attention to the rights of young and unborn children as a collective group of people who can easily find themselves in a more marginalized position. In New Zealand, the Parliamentary Commissioner for the Environment handles public complaints as an Ombudsman but also acts as a Guardian monitoring legislation and overseeing the work of public authorities regarding environmental matters. In terms of its legislative functions, the Commissioner tries to ensure that parliamentary decisions that concern the well-being of future generations are based on robust scientific information. In case scientific results show (or cannot eliminate the possibility) that a particular decision may adversely affect the living conditions of

[91] UN Secretary-General, 'Intergenerational Solidarity and the Needs of Future Generations: Report of the Secretary-General', UN Doc. A/68/322 (15 August 2013).

[92] The Committee for the Future was established in 1993.

[93] Future Generations Commissioner for Wales.

future generations, the Parliament is more likely to reject or revise the proposal in question. Objective, scientific information on the long-term consequences of present actions can go a long way in the institutional protection of future generations. It is important to mention the Hungarian Ombudsman for Future Generations, which is formally part of the office of the Commissioner for Fundamental Rights. It acts as a Deputy of the Commissioner but has a separate mandate. The goal of the Hungarian institution is to advocate for the preservation of natural resources and the protection of the interests of future generations. Further, its functions are strengthened by provisions of the Fundamental Law of Hungary that require the State to look after the unborn.

In the following part of this chapter the functions and powers of the Hungarian Ombudsman for Future Generations are outlined in some detail. The aim of this part is to serve as an illustration of how the establishment of a national institution for future generations could serve the implementation of obligations related to intergenerational equity based on public international law.

## THE EXAMPLE OF THE HUNGARIAN INSTITUTION FOR FUTURE GENERATIONS

Established by the Hungarian Parliament in 2007, the institution of Parliamentary Commissioner responsible for the protection of future generations started operations in December 2008. At its inception, the institution was entirely independent, with ample powers to police the enforcement of the constitutional right to a healthy environment. However, the institution was not enshrined in the former constitution of Hungary. The new Fundamental Law of Hungary adopted on 18 April 2011 (entering into force on 1 January 2012) constitutionally embedded the legal status of future generations within the framework of the Hungarian legal system. Transforming the system of future generations' protection, the independent ombudsman institutions were replaced by a single, unified institution, i.e. the Commissioner for Fundamental Rights. Within this institution, it is one of the Commissioner's deputies, referred to explicitly in the Fundamental Law, who is responsible for representing the rights and interests of future generations. In addition, the Fundamental Law introduced a number of provisions which expressly set forth the substantive legal basis for the protection of future generations.[94]

The conceptual basis of the Fundamental Law is laid down in the preamble, the so-called National Avowal. This states that the Fundamental Law "shall be an alliance among Hungarians of the past, present and future", thereby expressly referring to the future generations of Hungarians. Article 38 of the Fundamental Law prescribes the preservation of natural resources, "taking into account the needs

[94] See in detail Kinga Debisso's and Marcel Szabó's article in Vol. 9 (2021) of the Hungarian Yearbook of International Law and European Law (forthcoming).

of future generations." Article P of the Fundamental Law declares that natural resources shall form the common heritage of the nation, it shall be the obligation of the State and everyone to protect and maintain them, and to preserve them for future generations.

Thus, the Fundamental Law may be considered a 'living instrument' from the perspective of the protection of the interests of future generations. Article 30(3) of the Fundamental Law refers to the Ombudsman for Future Generations (*'jövő nemzedékek szószólója'*) as an institution dedicated to the protection of the interests of future generations. However, the Fundamental Law is silent on the factual and legal situations that may trigger the action of the Ombudsman in defence of future generations. Of course, all state measures may have an impact on the living conditions of future generations: education, health, economic and financial policies, public debt and the prevention of environmental degradation all affect the interests of future generations. So what are the concrete situations where it is incumbent upon the Ombudsman for Future Generations to take action? There are various temporal and legal aspects at play that make it difficult to determine the Ombudsman's scope of competence. Besides considering conflicts of interest between present and future generations, there is the further dilemma of tensions between successive future generations as well. How can the Ombudsman tailor his or her action to address these conflicts? Another important aspect is that while the Fundamental Law merely refers to the interests of future generations, the Ombudsman Act expressly mentions the rights of future generations, which are to be promoted by the Ombudsman for Future Generations. Meanwhile, the Ombudsman Act is silent on the specific substance of these rights. Finally, it is clear, that the Ombudsman for Future Generations is not a fourth branch of power, and cannot aspire towards counterbalancing other institutions of the Hungarian legal system. Owing to the uncertainties surrounding the scope of its constitutional mandate, the Ombudsman proceeded in the protection of future generations' interest by imposing some degree of self-limitation.

The legal framework detailing the activities of the Deputy Commissioner responsible for future generations is set out in Act CXI of 2011 (Ombudsman Act). This Act integrated the Ombudsman for Future Generations into the newly established Office of the Commissioner for Fundamental Rights. Although the Ombudsman was assigned the status of Deputy Commissioner, it boasts an autonomous organizational structure and a largely independent operational competence. It is because of this institutional structure that the Ombudsman for Future Generations is also referred to as Deputy Commissioner. The Ombudsman for Future Generations currently has a staff of 15, most of them lawyers, but he also has experts on staff with a degree in biology and media studies.

The institutional cohabitation of the Parliamentary Commissioner and the Ombudsman for Future Generations serves an important constitutional purpose. The Commissioner has long dealt with environmental issues, with the relevance of some cases being limited to present generations, such as for example noise complaints and other nuisances. While it is clear that these are also environmental issues, they do not fall within the framework of protecting the interests of future generations. The Ombudsman also deals with the types of citizens' complaints described above, but proceeds in such cases as the Deputy of the Commissioner for Fundamental Rights and not as the Ombudsman for Future Generations. A good example for this double hatted role was the case concerning the measure enacted by the mayor of the city of Ózd in 2013. During the terrible summer heat of 2013 the mayor shut down public wells, depriving the poorest families of their basic human right to drinking water. The Commissioner for Fundamental Rights and the Ombudsman for Future Generations underlined[95] that the measure constituted a grave instance intragenerational inequality, at the same time, the preservation of these wells and their water base was essential for future generations, drawing attention also to the intergenerational aspects of the case.

The Commissioner for Fundamental Rights acts on the basis of actual violations that have taken place, proceeding typically upon a petition submitted by a citizen, and proposing that authorities take specific measures to remedy the situation. By comparison, the Ombudsman for Future Generations has a broader range of powers: he or she acts *ex officio*, since members of future generations have not yet been born and cannot submit petitions. The Ombudsman for Future Generations must act at a time when only the remote chance of an infringement affecting future generations emerges, or more generally, the risk of a harm to their interests. As such, it is this institution that may somewhat counterbalance the serious shortcomings of today's economic system. The method of discounting, widely used in current economics, maximizes economic benefits that may be reaped in the present and significantly reduces long-term losses by discounting them. The approach of the Ombudsman for Future Generations is not based on discounted damage in line with contemporary economic thinking, but proceeds on the basis of effects that will actually affect future generations, and can direct the attention of state bodies and the public to actions threatening the interests future generations.

The most important instrument of the Ombudsman for Future Generations is his or her power to draw the attention of the public and state bodies to risks and threats via statements and reports. Ongoing dialogue with the relevant NGOs plays a crucial role in identifying threats to future generations. The Ombudsman may even come to a head with the entire institutional system in order to provide protection to future generations, therefore, it is of great importance that his or her position is also supported by science. The Ombudsman for Future Generations has repeatedly sought the position of the Hungarian Academy of Sciences on environmental issues, to present sound results and proposals to the public and decision-makers in an attempt to prevent harmful measures.

[95] Joint report No. AJB-5527/2013.

The Ombudsman for Future Generations has the right to issue statements independently on any topic and to put forward legislative proposals to remedy situations that are unfavourable to future generations. In particularly serious cases, the Ombudsman issues a joint report together with the Commissioner for Fundamental Rights. It is the responsibility of the Ombudsman for Future Generations to monitor the implementation of strategies developed by the Hungarian Parliament in respect of future generations and to present his or her findings to the public.

The most important instrument in the Ombudsman's toolkit is its access to the public. The Ombudsman for Future Generations' press releases, media appearances and statements made to parliamentary committees can significantly influence legislation and law enforcement. For example, the Ombudsman for Future Generations' statement detailing constitutional concerns and professional doubts regarding a 2015 bill which was to significantly and adversely affect the legal position of Hungarian national parks,[96] may have informed the preliminary norm control procedure initiated by the President of the Republic before the Hungarian Constitutional Court.

The Ombudsman for Future Generations may also turn to the Constitutional Court with the consent of, and via the Commissioner for Fundamental Rights, to request the posterior review of conformity with the Fundamental Law. The constitutional basis for this is the obligation to preserve the nation's natural resources and cultural artefacts for the benefit of future generations. In 2019, in connection with a law adversely affecting the condition and quantity of forests, the Ombudsman for Future Generations initiated the procedure of the Constitutional Court via the Commissioner for Fundamental Rights, requesting the annulment of provisions of the Forestry Act that threatened the preservation of forests as natural resources. In 2020 the Constitutional Court found in favour of the petition and annulled the relevant provisions of the Forestry Act.[97]

In other cases, it was the Constitutional Court that sought the input of the Ombudsman for Future Generations. One such high-profile case concerned the Constitutional Court's proceedings related to the expansion of the Paks Nuclear Power Plant (the only Hungarian nuclear power plant), or the proceedings regarding the sale of Natura 2000 areas without legal guarantees to secure the preservation of such areas. In both cases, the Constitutional Court relied heavily on the position elaborated by the Ombudsman for Future Generations. In the case of Natura 2000 sites, the Constitutional Court went so far as to state that the preservation of biological diversity for the benefit of future generations is not merely a legal obligation arising from the Hungarian Fundamental Law, but also a peremptory (*jus cogens*) norm of public international law.[98]

[96] For details see: Decision No. 16/2015. (VI. 5.) AB.

[97] Decision No. 14/2020. (VII. 6.) AB.

[98] Decision No. 28/2017. (X. 25.) AB, Reasoning [38].

It is safe to say that the institution of Ombudsman for Future Generations is a crucial pillar of the Hungarian legal system. Nevertheless, based on the Ombudsman's practice of the past decade we may conclude that while in principle there are no constitutional constraints on his or her action, an institution such as that of the Ombudsman for Future Generations cannot act as a fourth branch of power with the ambition to counterbalance all other state bodies. To ensure that his or her action remains effective and efficient, the Ombudsman for Future Generations must exercise certain self-restraint. The institution's activity is primarily geared towards protecting the essential interest of future generations, namely preserving the environmental foundations for life. This is what Edit Brown Weiss referred to as 'conservation of options'. Philosophical debates can be carried on whether we can even know how future generations will want to live and whether successive generations will come into conflict with one and other. However, there can be no doubt that preserving the foundations of life constitute the fundamental interest of future generations, and serve to guarantee their fundamental rights. Thus, the Ombudsman has a 'hypothetical heritage protection' function, serving as an institutional guarantee for the protection of our natural heritage for future generations.

Public international law, while recognizing the sovereignty of states over their natural resources, at the same time considers these values to be a common concern of humanity. Should national institutions providing a constitutional guarantee for the preservation of the environment for future generations spread throughout the world, a global network guaranteeing the protection of the natural heritage of mankind could be established through the national mosaics of natural heritage protection. It is in this endeavour that the Hungarian Ombudsman for Future Generations may play a key role, whose example could inspire other constitutional systems as well. Given the global acceptance of the institution of ombudsman, I am convinced that transplanting the Hungarian model of future generations' ombudsman in other jurisdictions would be easy to achieve.

## CONCLUSION

In 2003, Dirzo and Raven made memorable predictions about the state of the environment and biological diversity at the end of the twenty-first century.[99] According to their assessment, 7.9 million square meters of the planet are currently under legal environmental protection. This is approximately 5.3 percent of the Earth's surface. Only 10 percent of the tropical rainforests are protected and, as the authors argue, the level of protection is so unsatisfactory that only about 5 percent

99 R. Dirzo and P.H. Raven, 'Global State of Biodiversity and Loss' (2003) 28 *Annual Review of Environment and Resources* 137–167.

of them may remain intact by the end of the century. Two-thirds of the biological diversity currently existing on the planet will be lost by 2100.

It is society's common responsibility to prevent this unprecedented and irreversible process with the tools that are presently within its collective reach. This chapter has discussed ways that the concept of intergenerational equity in international law, in concert with the domestic regulation of individual states, can be a powerful instrument in the preservation of the natural heritage of the world and the long-term survival of humanity.

Legal instruments necessary for the protection of natural resources can be identified even if they are often scattered or abstract. Without strong political will and joint action on the part of States, however, the patchwork of individual national legislations and legal-philosophical concepts cannot form a coherent international legal framework. While the central questions of the twentieth century were how to create the necessary conditions for peace and avoid another war, one of the main challenges for international law in the twenty-first century is how to preserve the remaining natural resources for the future of humanity. The international legal regime was capable of setting up a more or less sufficient system for the prevention of armed conflict and the safeguarding of peace. The same is needed now for the protection of the interests of future generations. According to the Charter of the UN, one of the goals of the UN is "to save succeeding generations from the scourge of war."[100] In the twenty-first century the stakes are even higher: the goal is now to ensure that the vital resources of the planet are preserved so that human life can flourish long into the future.

[100] Charter of the United Nations [1945] preamble.

# 5

# The Use of International Human Rights Norms to Implement International Solidarity

*Dinah Shelton*

In the twentieth century, the international community increasingly recognized that constitutional guarantees of basic rights sometimes prove inadequate or even illusory when military coups, armed conflicts, or repressive governments disrupt or deliberately ignore the rule of law and constitutional limits on the exercise of power. International and regional organizations created or reformed after World War II thus concluded that human rights must be considered a matter of international concern if individuals and groups are to be ensured their fundamental rights and freedoms.

The UN Charter contains human rights obligations binding on each Member State, elaborated further when the UN almost immediately began drafting an international bill of rights. The first step was the adoption on 10 December 1948 of the Universal Declaration of Human Rights, a text cited in almost every subsequent human rights instrument and incorporated into the constitutions of many new States.[1] The Declaration was transformed into treaty law through the 1966 adoption of the ICCPR and the ICESCR.[2] Subsequent UN standard-setting has sought to protect particularly vulnerable groups (such as racial minorities, women, children, indigenous peoples, and persons with disabilities)[3] and prevent and punish particularly egregious human rights violations (such as slavery, torture, and forced disappearances).[4]

1 The Declaration is today considered to define the term human rights as used in the UN Charter and is the standard by which each UN member state is judged.

2 International Covenant on Civil and Political Rights [1966]; International Covenant on Economic, Social and Cultural Rights [1966].

3 See Convention on the Elimination of All Forms of Discrimination Against Women [1979]; Convention on the Rights of the Child [1989]; United Nations Declaration on the Rights of Indigenous Persons [2007]; Convention on the Elimination of All Forms of Racial Discrimination [1969]; Convention on the Rights of Persons with Disabilities [2006].

4 See Convention on the Prevention and Punishment of the Crime of Genocide [1951]; United Nations Conventions against Torture [1987].

The UN monitors the human rights performance of all its Member States through Universal Periodic Review conducted by the UN Human Rights Council (the Council).[5] The Council also appoints thematic working groups or rapporteurs to conduct studies or investigate particular human rights issues or situations in various countries, and it maintains a complaints procedure that allows anyone to denounce a situation of gross and systematic violations of human rights.[6] The studies authorized by the Council include the topic of human rights and the environment, undertaken by an Independent Expert appointed for a three-year term in 2012.[7]

Regional organizations reinforce the UN human rights program and offer courts jurisdiction to render binding judgments and award redress to victims of violations. In 1950, ten 'like-minded' governments adopted the European Convention for the Protection of Human Rights and Fundamental Freedoms (ECHR) and through it established the ECtHR.[8] Today, the ECtHR has mandatory jurisdiction over the forty-seven Member States of the CoE, allowing more than 800 million people the possibility of 'going to Strasbourg' after exhausting available local remedies.

The OAS, the body of regional cooperation in the Americas, adopted the American Declaration of the Rights and Duties of Man on May 2, 1948, simultaneously with concluding the constitutional Charter of the OAS.[9] In 1959, the OAS General Assembly created the independent expert body, the IACHR.[10] A decade later the OAS Member States adopted the American Convention on Human Rights, which expanded the jurisdiction of the IACHR and created the Inter-American Court of Human Rights.[11] Protection of socio-economic rights was added in 1988, with the adoption of the Protocol to the American Convention on Human Rights in the Area of Economic, Social and Cultural Rights (Protocol of San Salvador), a treaty that expressly recognizes environmental rights.[12]

In 1981, the OAU (now the AU) adopted the African Charter on Human and Peoples' Rights, now accepted by all fifty-three Member States, and therein created the African Commission of Human and Peoples' Rights.[13] The Charter explicitly

5 UN Human Rights Office of the High Commissioner (UN OHCHR), *Universal Periodic Review* www.ohchr.org/EN/HRBodies/UPR/Pages/UPRMain.aspx accessed 30 November 2017.

6 See UN OHCHR, *Special Procedures of the Human Rights Council* www.ohchr.org/EN/HRBodies/SP/Pages/Welcomepage.aspx accessed 30 November 2017.

7 See UN OHCHR, Current Mandates – Special Rapporteur on the Issue of Human Rights Obligations Relating to the Enjoyment of a Safe, Clean, Healthy and Sustainable Environment www.ohchr.org/EN/HRBodies/SP/Pages/Currentmandateholders.aspx accessed 30 November 2017.

8 See European Convention for the Protection of Human Rights and Fundamental Freedoms [1950].

9 American Declaration of the Rights and Duties of Man [1948].

10 Inter-American Commission on Human Rights [1959].

11 American Convention on Human Rights [1969].

12 Protocol to the American Convention on Human Rights in the Area of Economic, Social and Cultural Rights (Protocol of San Salvador) [1988].

13 African Charter on Human and Peoples' Rights [1982] 21 ILM 58.

mandates the African Commission to "draw inspiration from international law on human and peoples' rights."[14] In 2004, a protocol establishing the AfCHPR, designed to 'supplement' the work of the Commission, entered into force and its first judges were elected in 2006.[15]

Other regional and sub-regional intergovernmental organizations around the world have begun to address human rights in recent years. These include initiatives in Southeast Asia and the Arab-speaking world, as well as sub-regional bodies in Europe, the Americas, and Africa. The opportunities for civil society participation that the regional systems offer provides a bridge between the universality of human rights norms, on the one hand, and the cultural and political particularities of each region and State, on the other.

## THE ENVIRONMENT AS A HUMAN RIGHTS ISSUE

Environmental degradation became a matter of national and international concern beginning in the 1960s, some two decades after human rights emerged on the international agenda. The term sustainable development emerged even later to emphasize the interrelationship between the social, economic, and environmental aspects of development, as well as the need to consider intergenerational equity.[16] Given the timing of these developments, it is unsurprising there are few explicit references to the environment or sustainable development in the earlier-drafted international human rights instruments, which is cause for one of the limitations of to a human rights approach to such matters.

### *International Mechanisms*

The ICESCR contains a right to health in Article 12 that expressly calls on States Parties to take steps for "the improvement of all aspects of environmental and industrial hygiene."[17] The 1989 CRC refers to aspects of environmental protection in Article 24, which provides that States Parties shall take appropriate measures to combat disease and malnutrition "through the provision of adequate nutritious foods and clean drinking water, taking into consideration the dangers and risks of environmental pollution."[18] These two provisions are the only references to the environment in global human rights treaties.

[14] Ibid. at art. 60.

[15] Protocol to the African Charter on Human and Peoples' Rights on the Establishment of an African Court on Human and Peoples' Rights [1988].

[16] G.H. Brundtland et al., *Our Common Future: Report of the World Commission on Environment and Development* (Oxford University Press 1987).

[17] ICESCR, *supra* note 3 at art. 12.

[18] CRC, *supra* note 4 at art. 24.

Despite this lacuna, international recognition of the linkages between human rights and sustainable development has expanded considerably since the emergence of environmental protection as a legal issue. The links between human rights and environmental protection were acknowledged in the widely cited Principle 1 of the 1972 Stockholm Declaration.[19] Subsequently, in resolution 45/94 the UNGA recalled the language of Stockholm, stating that all individuals are entitled to live in an environment adequate for their health and well-being.[20] The resolution called for enhanced efforts to ensure a better and healthier environment.

As the UNGA's language suggests, many human rights tribunals and experts view environmental protection as a pre-condition to the short- and long-term enjoyment of several internationally guaranteed human rights, especially the rights to life and health. In this sense, the UNGA has called the preservation of nature "a prerequisite for the normal life of man."[21] The former UN Human Rights Commission, in appointing a Special Rapporteur on the adverse effects of the illicit movement and dumping of toxic and dangerous products and wastes on the enjoyment of human rights,[22] consistently recognized that environmental law violations "constitute a serious threat to the human rights to life, good health and a sound environment for everyone."[23] Other resolutions of the Commission referred explicitly to the right to a safe and healthy environment.[24] In recent years, the Human Rights Council has adopted resolutions on climate change as a human rights issue, and the UNGA has recognized the human right to safe drinking water and sanitation.[25]

If a healthy environment is essential to the enjoyment of human rights, the reverse is also true: enjoyment of certain human rights is an important tool to use in achieving sustainable development. This approach is well-illustrated by the Rio Declaration on Environment and Development, adopted at the conclusion of the 1992 Conference of Rio de Janeiro on Environment and Development.[26] Principle

[19] At the Stockholm concluding session, the preamble of the final declaration proclaimed that "Man is both creature and moulder of his environment, which gives him physical sustenance and affords him the opportunity for intellectual, moral, social and spiritual growth ... Both aspects of man's environment, the natural and the man-made, are essential to his well-being and to the enjoyment of basic human rights – even the right to life itself." Principle 1 of the Stockholm Declaration established a further connection between human rights and environmental protection, declaring that "Man has the fundamental right to freedom, equality and adequate conditions of life, in an environment of a quality that permits a life of dignity and well-being."

[20] GA Res. 45/94 (1990).

[21] GA Res. 35/48 of 30 October 1980.

[22] Resolution 2001/35, Adverse Effects of the Illicit Movement and Dumping of Toxic and Dangerous Products and Wastes on the Enjoyment of Human Rights, E/CN.4/RES/2001/35.

[23] Commission on Human Rights, Resolutions 199/23 and 2000/72.

[24] Resolution 2001/65, Promotion of the Right to a Democratic and Equitable International Order, the Commission affirmed that "a democratic and equitable international order requires, inter alia, the realization of ... [t]he right to a healthy environment for everyone".

[25] GA Res. 64/292 (2010).

[26] Rio Declaration on Environment and Development [1992].

10 formulates a link between human rights and environmental protection largely in procedural terms, declaring in Principle 10 that access to information, and public participation in and access to effective judicial and administrative proceedings, including redress and remedy, should be guaranteed because "environmental issues are best handled with the participation of all concerned citizens, at the relevant level."[27] These procedural rights, contained in all human rights instruments, are thus adopted in environmental texts in order to have better decision-making and enforcement.

Still other legal texts proclaim the existence of a right to a safe and healthy environment as a human right. The African Charter on Human and Peoples' Rights, Article 16, guarantees to every individual the right to enjoy the best attainable state of physical and mental health, while Article 24 was the first international treaty to proclaim that "[a]ll peoples shall have the right to a general satisfactory environment favorable to their development."[28] Article 24 thus merges human rights, environmental protection, and development, which together form the core concept of sustainable development.[29]

The 1988 Additional Protocol to the American Convention on Human Rights in the area of Economic, Social and Cultural Rights,[30] in Article 11, proclaims that "[e]veryone shall have the right to live in a healthy environment and to have access to basic public services" and that the States Parties shall promote the protection, preservation, and improvement of the environment.[31] Also at the regional level, the preambles of EU legal texts often state their aim as being "to protect human health and the environment."[32]

### *National and European Mechanisms*

On the national level, more than 100 constitutions throughout the world guarantee a right to a clean and healthy environment,[33] impose a duty on the State to prevent

[27] Ibid. at Principle 10.

[28] African Charter on Human and Peoples' Rights, *supra* note 14 at art. 16.

[29] Ibid. at art. 24.

[30] Additional Protocol to the American Convention on Human Rights in the Area of Economic, Social and Cultural Rights [17 November 1988] OAS T.S. 69.

[31] Ibid. at art. 11.

[32] EC Council Directive No. 85/201 on Air Quality Standards for Nitrogen Dioxide, 7 March 1985, L 87 O.J.E.C. (1985); EC Council Directive No. 80/779 on Air Quality Limit Values, 15 July 1980, L 229, O.J.E.C. 30 (1980).

[33] Examples include: Constitution of the Republic of Angola [2010] art. 24-1 ("all citizens shall have the right to live in a healthy and unpolluted environment"); Constitution of Argentina [1994] art. 41 ("all residents enjoy the right to a healthy, balanced environment which is fit for human development"); Constitution of Azerbaijan [1995] art. 225 ("everyone has the right to live in a healthy environment"); Constitution of Brazil [1988] ("everyone has the right to an ecologically balanced environment, which is a public good for the people's use and is essential for a healthy life").

environmental harm, or mention the protection of the environment or natural resources. Such provisions vary in the chosen description of the environmental quality that is protected. While many of the older provisions refer to a "healthy" or "healthful" environment, more recent formulations add references to ecology and/or biodiversity to the guarantee.

The scope and the contents of environmental rights have been the subject of litigation in many States, with the aim of protecting natural resources over the long term. The Supreme Court of Montana has provided the most detail about the substantive implications of a right to a specified environmental quality, indicating the value of constitutional rights in preventing harm to the environment. In *Montana Environmental Information Center et al* v. *Department of Environmental Quality*,[34] the plaintiffs contended that the constitutional guarantees of environmental protections were violated when the legislature amended state law to allow discharges from water wells without regard to the degrading effect that the discharges would have on the surrounding environment. The monitoring of well tests was also alleged to be inadequate because it was done without regard to the harm caused by those tests. The Montana Supreme Court concluded that because the right to a clean and healthful environment is a fundamental right in the State Constitution,

> any statute or rule which implicates that right must be strictly scrutinized and can only survive scrutiny if the State establishes a compelling state interest and that its action is closely tailored to effectuate that interest and is the least onerous path that can be taken to achieve the State's objective.[35]

Human health does not need to suffer before the guarantee can be invoked:

> The delegates [to the Constitutional Convention] did not intend to merely prohibit that degree of environmental degradation which can be conclusively linked to ill health or physical endangerment. Our constitution does not require that dead fish float on the surface of our state's rivers and streams before its farsighted environmental protections can be invoked ...[36]

[34] [1999] 296 Mont. 207.

[35] Ibid.

[36] The Montana Supreme Court further applied its constitutional provision in the case *Cape-France Enterprises* v. *The Estate of Peed* [2001] 305 Mont. 513, in which it held that "the protections and mandates of this provision apply to private action – and thus to private parties – as well" as to state action. Thus, "it would be unlawful for Cape-France, a private business entity, to drill a well on its property in the face of substantial evidence that doing so may cause significant degradation of uncontaminated aquifers and pose serious public health risks." The Court held that it would be a violation of the state's obligation under the constitution for it to grant specific performance of a contract for the sale of the land in question. See C. Naber, 'Murky Waters: Private Action and the Right to a Clean and Healthful Environment – An examination of Cape-France Enterprises v. Estate of Peed' (2003) 64 Mont. L. Rev. 357; B. Thompson, 'Constitutionalizing the Environment: The History and Future of Montana's Environmental Provisions' (2003) 64 Mont. L. Rev. 157.

Many lawyers concerned with either the environment or with human rights have concluded that this "rights-based approach" to environmental protection offers stronger guarantees than do the legal approaches of environmental regulation, private litigation, or market-based incentives, because human rights are generally seen as maximum claims on society, elevating concern for the environment above a mere policy choice that may be modified or discarded at will. All legal systems establish a hierarchy of norms. Constitutional guarantees usually are at the apex and "trump" any conflicting norm of lower value. Thus, to include respect for the environment as a constitutional right ensures that it will be given precedence over other legal norms that are not constitutionally based.

In addition, the moral weight afforded by the concept of rights as inherent attributes that must be respected in any well-ordered society exercises an important compliance pull. Finally, at the international level, enforcement of human rights law is more developed than are the procedures of international environmental law. For example, the availability of individual complaints procedures has given rise to extensive jurisprudence from which the specific obligations of States to protect and preserve the environment are detailed.

The danger of placing confidence in the regulatory process alone is illustrated by *Zander* v. *Sweden*,[37] where the applicants complained about contamination of their well water by cyanide from a neighboring dump-site. The municipality initially furnished temporary water supplies, but later, adhering to the normal regulatory procedures, the town raised the permissible level of cyanide in the city water supply. The permit for the dump was renewed and expanded, while the applicant's request for safe drinking water was denied.[38] The ECtHR found in favour of the individual, who had no redress before domestic courts for the deterioration of his water supply.[39]

Human rights, enshrined in international and constitutional law, thus set the limits of majority rule and provide protection against dictatorial repression. The scope and contours of substantive as well as procedural rights are sometimes detailed in legislation, but they are also given content through litigation. National courts and international human rights tribunals elaborate on the often generally stated rights whose implementation they monitor. The ECtHR, for example, has given indications of the quality of environment required to comply with the Convention's substantive

[37] *Zander* v. *Sweden*, App. No. 14282/88 (ECHR 1993). Concededly, it was the denial of judicial review of this decision that formed the basis of Lander's successful claim before the European Court. The Court, finding that the applicants had a right to clean water under Swedish law, held that the lack of judicial review violated the European Convention, Article 6(1) because the applicants were entitled as of right to seek precautionary measures against water pollution.

[38] The European Court did not actually have to reach a conclusion on the substance of this decision, because it found that the applicant's procedural right of access to justice under Article 6 was violated. The applicants had been unable to obtain judicial review by Swedish courts of the board's permitting decision; Ibid.

[39] Ibid.

guarantees,[40] especially as contained in Article 8 of the European Convention. Pollution need not reach the point of affecting health, if the enjoyment of home, private, and family life are reduced and there is no fair balance struck between the community's economic well-being and the individual's effective enjoyment of guaranteed rights.[41]

The European Court often imports environmental norms in its human rights judgments to ensure protection for the applicants and those whose rights could be violated in the future. *Taşkin and Others v. Turkey* involved challenges to the development and operation of a gold mine,[42] which the applicants alleged caused environmental damage to the detriment of people in the region. In reviewing the applicable legal framework, the European Court referred to the procedural rights set forth in Rio Principle 10 and the Aarhus Convention. In addition, however, the European Court also quoted from a CoE Parliamentary Assembly resolution on environment and human rights that recommended that Member States ensure appropriate protection of life, health, family and private life, physical integrity and private property,[43] taking particular account of the need for environmental protection, and that Member States recognize a human right to a healthy, viable, and decent environment. Given this recommendation and the domestic constitutional guarantees in Turkey, the European Court found a violation despite the absence of any accidents or incidents at the mine, because the mine was deemed to present an unacceptable risk of harm. The case indicates that in some circumstances human rights litigation can prevent future harm and not just redress victims once the harm has occurred.

In the case of *Tatar v. Romania*,[44] brought after a major gold mining accident contaminated the surrounding water, the European Court again considered the procedural rights to information, public participation, and redress, but it also assessed the government's substantive obligations pursuant to international environmental standards. The European Court relied on UN findings about the causes and consequences of the accident, as well as determinations of the WHO about the health consequences of exposure to sodium cyanide, placing heavy reliance on them in the absence of adequate domestic fact-finding. The European Court referred to international standards on best practices for the mining industry and, significantly, quoted extensively from the Stockholm Declaration on the Human Environment, the Rio Declaration on Environment and Development, and the Aarhus Convention.

40 See *Lopez Ostra* v. *Spain* (ECHR 1994) Ser. A, No. 303C.

41 In *Powell & Raynor* v. *United Kingdom* (ECHR 1990) Ser. A, No. 172, the European Court found that aircraft noise from Heathrow Airport constituted a violation of Article 8, but was justified as "necessary in a democratic society" for the economic well-being of the country and was acceptable under the principle of proportionality because it did not "create an unreasonable burden for the person concerned." The latter text could be met by the State if the individual had "the possibility of moving elsewhere without substantial difficulties and losses."

42 *Taşkin and Others* v. *Turkey*, App. No. 46117/99 (ECHR 1999).

43 Parliamentary Assembly Recommendation 1614 (2003) of 27 June 2003.

44 *Tatar* v. *Romania*, App. No. 6702/01 (ECHR 2009).

Two of the European Court's conclusions in the *Tatar* case were particularly important to the development of the law. First, the European Court declared that the 'precautionary principle' has become a European legal norm with applicable content, requiring the government to adopt reasonable and adequate measures capable of respecting the rights of individuals in the face of serious risks to their health and well-being, even where scientific certainty is lacking.[45] Second, the European Court reminded Romania of its obligations under Stockholm Principle 21 and Rio Principle 14 to prevent significant transboundary harm, in noting that both Hungary and Serbia were affected by the mining accident.[46] These international environmental norms, the European Court found, should have been applied by the Romanian government.[47]

Enforcement of environmental rights involves courts not only in determining the mandated environmental quality but also in assessing whether or not the government has taken the requisite actions to achieve that quality. Human rights tribunals have made clear that the State may be responsible regardless whether pollution or other environmental harm is directly caused by the State or whether the State's responsibility arises from its failure to regulate adequately private-sector activities.[48] Human rights instruments require States not only to respect the observance of rights and freedoms but also to guarantee their existence and the free exercise of all of them against private actors as well as the State. Any act *or omission* by a public authority which impairs guaranteed rights may violate a State's obligations.[49] This is particularly important in respect of the environment, where most activities causing harm are undertaken by the private sector.

The European Court's jurisprudence requires at a minimum that the State should have complied with its domestic environmental standards.[50] The issue of compliance with domestic law is particularly important when there is a domestic constitutional right to environmental protection. The European Court will review governmental actions in the light of the domestic law.[51] Beyond ensuring that any

45 See ibid.

46 See ibid.

47 Ibid.

48 See *Moreno Gómez* v. *Spain*, no. 4143/02 (ECHR 2004) para. 55; *Giacomelli* v. *Italy*, application no. 59909/00 (ECHR 2006) paras. 78–79; *Surugiu* v. *Romania*, no. 48995/99 (20 April 2004).

49 *Velasquez Rodriguez Case*, 4 Inter-Am. Ct. H.R. (ser. C) 155 (Judgment of 29 July 1988) (concerning disappearance of civilians perpetrated by the Honduran army); *Godinez Cruz Case*, 5 Inter-Am. Ct. H.R. (ser. C) 152-53 (Judgment of January 20, 1989).

50 See e.g. *Ashworth and Others* v. *United Kingdom*, App. No. 39561/98 (ECHR 2004); *Moreno Gómez* v. *Spain*, application no. 2004-X (ECHR 2005).

51 See e.g., *Okyay and Others* v. *Turkey*, App. 36220/97 (ECHR 2005) 57, wherein applicants alleged the failure of Turkish authorities to enforce constitutional environmental rights and environmental laws. They explicitly argued that Article 56 of the Turkish Constitution guaranteed them the right to life in a healthy and balanced environment.

domestic environmental rights are enforced, the European Court scrutinizes the domestic law to assess if the State has ensured a fair balance between the interests of the community and the rights of those affected. The European Court accords each State considerable deference in this respect through its 'margin of appreciation' doctrine because it has concluded that national authorities "are in principle better placed than an international court to assess the requirements" in a particular local context to determine the most appropriate environmental policies and individual measures while taking into account the needs of the local community,[52] especially in a technical sphere like environmental protection.[53]

The Committee hearing complaints under the European Social Charter also insists on compliance with domestic and international environmental norms. A complaint lodged on 4 April 2005 claimed violations of the Charter's right to health provisions because the State had not adequately prevented negative environmental impacts nor had it developed an appropriate strategy to prevent and respond to the health hazards stemming from lignite mining.[54] The complaint also alleged that there was no legal framework guaranteeing security and safety of persons working in lignite mines. The European Committee of Social Rights concluded that the government had violated the right to health,[55] after examining the Greek National Action Plan for GHG emissions, which it found was inadequate in the light of the State's obligations under the Kyoto Protocol and the principle requiring use of the "best available techniques."[56] While the Committee found that Greek regulations on information and public participation were satisfactory, the evidence showed "that in practice the Greek authorities do not apply the relevant legislation satisfactorily" and very little had been done to organize systematic epidemiological monitoring of those concerned and no morbidity studies have been carried out.[57]

52 *Giacomelli, supra* note 49 at para. 80.

53 *Fadeyeva* v. *Russia*, application no. 55723/00 (ECHR 2005) para. 104.

54 Complaint No. 30/2005 *Marangopoulos Foundation for Human Rights (MFHR)* v. *Greece*.

55 The Committee transmitted its decision on the merits to the Committee of Ministers and to the Parties on 6 December 2006. The Committee of Ministers adopted its resolution on the matter on 15 January 2008.

56 According to the Committee, "[t]he Greek National Action Plan for 2005–2007 (NAP1) provides for greenhouse gas emissions for the whole country and all sectors combined to rise by no more than 39.2% until 2010, whereas Greece was committed, in the framework of the Kyoto Protocol, to an increase in these gases of no more than 25% in 2010. When air quality measurements reveal that emission limit values have been exceeded, the penalties imposed are limited and have little dissuasive effect. Moreover, the initiatives taken by DEH (the public power corporation operating the Greek lignite mines) to adapt plant and mining equipment to the 'best available techniques' have been slow."

57 See ibid.

## LITIGATION HURDLES: CAUSALITY, EVIDENCE, AND PRECAUTION

Assessing risk is an important issue in litigating substantive environmental rights. Some human rights procedures limit standing to 'victims' of violations and there must be a sufficient threat for the applicants or petitioners to qualify as victims.[58] The precautionary principle has begun to play a role in bringing more risks within the ambit of human rights litigation.[59] It seems clear, as well, that if the environmental conditions at present are improved or protected from deterioration, the benefits will accrue to future generations as well, maximizing their options and reflecting the principle of intergenerational equity.

The *Taşkin* case described above was one based on risk, stemming from the use of cyanide in gold extraction.[60] The European Court referred to the various reports that had been done on site and which highlighted the risks. Domestic judicial findings also demonstrated the threat to the environment and lives of the neighboring population. The European Court found Article 8 to be applicable "where the dangerous effects of an activity to which the individuals *are likely to be exposed* have been determined as part of an environmental impact assessment procedure in such a way as to establish a sufficiently close link with private and family life for purposes of Article 8 of the Convention."[61] The European Court held that this broad reading was necessary to ensure the effectiveness of Article 8.

The problem of fact-finding and lack of expertise is frequently said to be a hurdle to giving substantive content to environmental rights. This has not proved to be a high hurdle thus far in human rights litigation, because in most cases domestic fact-finding has already revealed the risks or the consequent harm. This was the case in *Oneryildiz v. Turkey*,[62] *Taşkin* and *Fadeyeva*.[63] In the last-mentioned case, concerning pollution from a steel factory, a government decree had recited statistics on the increases in respiratory and blood diseases linked to air pollution, as well as the increased number of deaths from cancer.[64] The government had also determined by

58 See *Bordes and Temeharo* v. *France*, Comm. No. 645/1995, CCPR/C/57/D/645/1995 (30 July 1996). The risk of harm from nuclear radiation due to nuclear testing by France in the South Pacific was deemed too remote for the victims to qualify as victims.

59 Ibid.

60 *Taşkin and Others* v. *Turkey*, App. No. 46117/99 (ECHR 2004).

61 Ibid. at para. 113 (emphasis added).

62 41 EHRR 325. The case concerned a methane explosion at a waste disposal site. The government had been warned for two years before the explosion about the risk posed by the site and the threat this posed to the lives of those living nearby. The government was held responsible for the loss of life and property damage that resulted from the explosion.

63 *Fadeyeva* v. *Russia*, *supra* note 54. See also *Ledyayeva, Dobrokhotova, Zolotareva and Romashina* v. *Russia*, nos. 53157/99, 53247/99, 53695/00, and 56850/00 (ECHR 2006).

64 Constitution of the Russian Federation [1993] art. 42 guarantees as follows: "Everyone has the right to a favourable environment, to reliable information about its state, and to compensation for damage caused to his health or property by ecological disease." The provision was not invoked in the case.

legislation the safe levels of various polluting substances, many of which were exceeded in the security zone where the applicant lived. The mayor of the city said the steel plant was responsible for more than 95 percent of industrial emissions into the town's air,[65] while a State Report on the Environment indicated that the plant in question was the largest contributor to air pollution of all metallurgical plants in Russia. The two statements came close to eliminating questions about causality.[66]

In the end, both parties agreed that the applicant's place of residence was affected by industrial pollution caused by the steel plant, but they disagreed over the degree and effects of the pollution.[67] The government claimed that the disturbance caused by the pollution was not so severe as to raise an issue under Article 8. The applicant and the European Court disagreed, and the Court elaborated on its test for finding that environmental conditions are sufficiently severe to be encompassed within the guarantees of Article 8:[68]

> The assessment of that minimum is relative and depends on all the circumstances of the case, such as the intensity and duration of the nuisance, and its physical or mental effects. The general context of the environment should also be taken into account. There would be no arguable claim under Article 8 if the detriment complained of was negligible in comparison to the environmental hazards inherent to life in every modern city.

Causality was an issue on the applicant's health claims. Her medical records indicated problems, but did not attribute them to any specific causes. The doctors stated, however, that her problems would be exacerbated by working in conditions of vibration, toxic pollution, and an unfavourable climate.[69] The applicant also submitted an expert report which linked the plant specifically to increased adverse health conditions of persons residing nearby.[70] The European Court found that the medical evidence did not establish a causal link between the pollution at her residence and her illnesses, but accepted that the evidence, including submissions by the government, was clear about the unsafe and excessive pollution around her home. The European Court also made reference to the expert report and the findings of the domestic courts and noted that Russian legislation defined the maximum permissible concentrations as "safe concentrations of toxic elements."[71] Therefore,

65 The Court noted that this made the case different from and more easily definable than other air pollution cases where multiple minor sources cumulate to produce the problem.

66 The Court noted that the parties produced official documents containing generalized information on industrial pollution, because basic data on air pollution are not publicly available. *Fadeyeva v. Russia*, *supra* note 54 at para. 30.

67 Ibid.

68 Ibid. at para. 69.

69 Ibid. at para. 45.

70 The Court made it a point to recite the qualifications of the expert when discussing the report. See ibid. at para. 46 n. 1.

71 Ibid. at para. 87.

exceeding these limits produced a presumption of unsafe conditions potentially harmful to the health and well-being of those exposed to it. This presumption, together with the evidence submitted, led the European Court to conclude that the applicant's health deteriorated as a result of her prolonged exposure to the industrial emissions from the steel plant.[72] Alternatively, even if that harm could not be quantified, the pollution "inevitably made the applicant more vulnerable to various illnesses" and affected her quality of life at home.[73]

The analysis emphasises the question of what evidence is sufficient to raise the presumption the European Court creates in the *Fadeyeva* case. It should not be limited to legislative findings because, as *Zander v. Sweden* indicates, safe levels may be changed to accommodate economic interests without necessarily being based on sound science. The WHO and other scientific bodies have determined through epidemiological studies what constitutes safe levels of concentration of toxic, carcinogenic, mutagenic, and other hazardous substances.[74] Reliable evidence from such studies can and should be introduced to demonstrate presumed harm when such levels are exceeded, even if local legislation permits higher concentrations.

In the Greek case on lignite mining,[75] the European Social Charter Committee relied on what it called "ample and unambiguous scientific evidence" that lignite-caused air pollution has a harmful effect on human health and life, without specifying the health risks. Despite the beneficial impacts of lignite use in providing energy independence, access to electricity at a reasonable cost, and economic growth, the Committee found that the government's actions violated the State's national and international obligations to combat pollution that caused health problems.[76] It pointed to the right to environment in the Greek Constitution, as well as national environmental protection legislation and regulations, noting that these were not applied and enforced in an effective manner. In sum, Greece had not struck a reasonable balance between the interests of persons living in the lignite mining areas and the general interest and there was thus a violation of the right to protection of health under the Charter.[77]

72 See generally ibid.

73 Ibid. at para. 88.

74 The WHO has developed guidelines for safe and acceptable water quality and quantity. WHO, *Guidelines for Drinking Water Quality*, 3rd edn. (WHO 2004). Independent surveillance of water quality, quantity, accessibility, affordability, and long-term availability are part of the WHO framework.

75 *Marangopoulos Foundation for Human Rights* v. *Greece*, Complaint No. 30/2005, European Committee on Social Rights (2006).

76 Ibid.

77 Ibid.

## LIMITS OF THE RIGHTS-BASED APPROACH

Although the cases discussed herein reveal that human rights jurisprudence now encompasses risk as an element of harm sufficient to bring the danger of future harm within the jurisdiction of human rights tribunals, most cases are still brought after environmental damage has already occurred. The requirement in the European Court that applications be brought by 'victims' of a violation serves to exclude many cases where prevention of future harm is sought. Some human rights tribunals like the IACHR do have the power of initiative to promote as well as protect human rights, but the courts must respond to the cases brought before them. Moreover, the European Court's jurisprudence on 'just satisfaction' is extremely limited. If the European Court finds a violation, it often simply issues a declaratory judgment. Although the European Court may in its discretion choose to go beyond a declaratory judgment and afford some compensation, costs, and fees to a litigant, it does not always do so and never issues an order to a government to halt the violation. Thus, Ms. Fadeyeva is given the money to move away from the polluting steel factory, but the factory continues to pollute.

A second limitation in most States and human rights tribunals is that the environmental injury must harm humans. To make a claim under ECHR Article 8, an individual's home life must be directly affected, and harm to the surrounding environment, even protected areas, is not sufficient.[78] According to the European Court, Article 8(1) extends only to protection against "a harmful effect on a person's private or family sphere and not simply the general deterioration of the environment."[79] Thus, Article 8 has been useful primarily when the environmental harm consists of pollution. Issues of resource management and nature conservation or biological diversity are more difficult to bring before the European Court. A 1974 opinion of the European Commission of Human Rights indicates the present limits of the human rights approach. In rejecting an application alleging a violation of the applicant's right of privacy and family life insofar as it concerned a dog, the Commission stated:

> The Commission cannot however accept that the protection afforded by Art. 8 of the Convention extends to relationships of the individual with his entire immediate surroundings, in so far as they do not involve human relationships and notwithstanding the desire of the individual to keep such relationships within the private sphere. No doubt the dog has had close ties with man since time immemorial. However, given the above considerations this alone is not sufficient to bring the keeping of a dog into the sphere of the private life of the owner.[80]

[78] ECHR at Art. 8.

[79] *Kyrtatos* v. *Greece*, app. No. 41666/98, 40 EHRR 390 (2005) (finding no violation of Article 8 due to the destruction of a protected wetland adjacent to the applicant's property).

[80] *Eur. Comm'n H.R.*, Case 68/25/74, 5 D. & R. 86.

In the application of human rights law, the issue of a right to an environment of a certain quality is complicated by both temporal and geographic elements absent from other human rights protections. While most human rights violations affect only specific and identifiable victims in the present, environmental degradation may cause harm to many currently living, and to future generations of humanity as well. A right to environment thus implies significant, constant duties towards persons not yet born, a concept that human rights tribunals have difficulty applying.

The right to a healthy environment also implies a potentially vast territorial scope of State obligations. Presently, human rights instruments typically require each State to respect and ensure guaranteed rights "to all individuals within its territory and subject to its jurisdiction."[81] This geographic limitation reflects the reality that a State will normally have the power to protect or the possibility to violate human rights only of those within its territory and jurisdiction. Nature recognizes no political boundaries, however. A State polluting its coastal waters or the atmosphere may cause significant harm to individuals thousands of miles away. States that permit or encourage depletion of the tropical rain forest can contribute to global warming that threatens the entire biosphere.

Finally, as noted earlier, most environmental harm is caused by the private sector being inadequately regulated by the government, either because of gaps in the law or, more often, because the law is not enforced. Often, private economic interests have considerable political power or links to the government. Governments may encourage foreign investment or engage in major development projects that cause serious environmental degradation and human rights violations. The reaction of such governments to decisions of human rights bodies that call for halting, modifying, or delaying destructive investment and development projects can be strongly negative and can result in decreased funding, changes to the rules and composition of the tribunals, or at the least may have a chilling effect on decisions and judgments in environmental rights cases.

## CONCLUSION

Despite the limitations indicated, national and international tribunals are increasingly being asked to give effect to the link between sustainable environmental protection and internationally guaranteed human rights. In some instances, the complaints brought have not been based upon a specific right to a safe and environmentally sound environment, but rather upon rights to life, property, health, information, and family and home life. Underlying the complaints, however, are instances of pollution, deforestation, water pollution, and other types of environmental harm.

[81] See e.g. ICCPR, *supra* note 2; ICESCR, *supra* note 3; CRC, *supra* note 4; CEDAW, *supra* note 4.

International petition procedures thus allow those potentially harmed to bring international pressure to bear when governments lack the will to prevent or halt pollution that threatens the environment and human well-being. Petitioners have been afforded redress and governments have taken measures to remedy the violation. Petition procedures at the least can help to identify problems and encourage a dialogue to resolve them. In addition, the emphasis given rights of information, participation, and access to justice can encourage an integration of democratic values and promotion of the rule of law in broad-based structures of governance. Even where there is a guaranteed right to environment, it still must be balanced against other rights should there be a conflict. Human rights exist to promote and protect human well-being, to allow the full development of each person and the maximization of the person's goals and interests, individually and in community with others. This cannot occur without basic healthy surroundings, which the State must promote and protect. The benefits that accrue from such human rights and the litigation to enforce them are not limited to the specific litigants or to the present generation. A river preserved from pollution or soil from depletion will remain for the enjoyment of future generations and thus help to provide intergenerational justice.

Adjudicating cases under broadly worded standards is not new for judges nor is it uncommon for them to be faced with deciding highly technical matters. Courts must regularly, and on a case-by-case basis, define what constitutes 'reasonable', 'fair', or 'equitable' conduct. With the adoption of constitutional environmental rights provisions and increasing acceptance of the links between environmental degradation and the violation of other human rights, national and international tribunals struggle to give substance to environmental rights without overstepping the judicial function. In general, courts have taken the view that such enactments serve to place environmental protection in a position superior to ordinary legislation. Over time, courts tend to create a balancing test to avoid too readily undoing the deliberative decisions reached by the political branches of government.

Environmental law is not about stopping all human activities but about recognizing that they utilize scarce resources and produce emissions and waste that inevitably have individualized and cumulative environmental impacts. These impacts have to be considered, measured, and monitored, with the result that some activities will be limited or prohibited. Environmental science helps determine the causal links between the activities and the impacts, giving courts a set of data on which to base decisions about whether or not a proper balance of interests has been obtained, one which ensures an equitable outcome and minimizes the risk of harm to the environment and human rights. The substance of environmental rights involves evaluating ecological systems, determining the impacts that can be tolerated and what is needed to maintain and protect the natural base on which life depends. Environmental quality standards, precaution, and principles of sustainability can establish the limits of environmental decision-making and continue to give specific content to environmental rights in law.

Both national and international courts have used environmental law and science to give content to the level of environmental protection required by human rights law. This approach can involve reference to WHO standards on acceptable emissions levels, incorporation of the precautionary principle to judge the adequacy of measures taken by a government, or reference to environmental treaties and declarations. The breadth of the search for standards depends in part on whether or not there is a textual guarantee of environmental quality and, if there is, on the descriptions of that quality.

There remain many questions to be addressed, including issues about the scope of the guaranteed rights, the scope of State responsibility, accountability of non-State actors, and procedural mechanisms to give effect to or monitor compliance with environmental rights. These issues will undoubtedly be raised in future litigation and debated in academic journals. In both contexts, contributions from scientists, especially the medical profession, and other relevant disciplines will be necessary to ensure that the law and policy reflects knowledge about the environment and the consequences of pollution.

# PART II

# Key Challenges in Domestic Implementation of Intergenerational Justice

# 6

# What Should We Protect? Future Generations Institutions as Counterweights

*Halina Ward*

This chapter asks, 'what should we protect?' when designing institutions for future generations. First, it outlines an approach to defining a central 'problem' that such institutions might address, inspired by the ideas of democracy and of sustainable development. It then briefly considers the case for an institutional response to the problem and delves into three domains (political, intergovernmental, and legal) where reasoning about future generations reveals a variety of approaches to considering them. Finally, the piece sets out some thoughts on possible functions and ways of working for institutions for future generations so that they serve both democracy and sustainable development.

## WHAT IS THE PROBLEM?

The question 'what should we protect?' through institutions for future generations is closely linked to a foundational issue – what is the *problem* (or *problems*) that institutions for future generations might or ought to be designed to address?

A response to the question of problem definition needs to be inspired and underpinned by two key sets of principles and ideas: those of sustainable development on the one hand and those of democracy on the other. These two sets of principles and ideas should both set guideposts and provide the motivating force for the design of institutions for future generations. The attainment of each is hampered by obstacles that institutions for future generations are potentially uniquely placed to address. Each provides a distinct set of justifications for institutions for future generations, and the interplay between democracy and sustainable development offers a number of key design principles for institutions for future generations.

## *On Sustainable Development*

Sustainable development presents an essential guidepost for institutions for future generations. It is closely linked to 'future generations thinking' through the concept of intergenerational equity, and through the foundational idea that sustainable development is associated with the needs of future generations.

The concept of sustainable development was first and perhaps most clearly articulated in the 1989 report of the WCED, the so-called Brundtland Report, which defined it as "development which meets the needs of the present without compromising the ability of future generations to meet their own needs."[1]

The associated principle of intergenerational equity (that is, the idea of equity between present and future generations) has since come to be understood as among the core principles of sustainable development. Five years after the Brundtland Report, Principle 3 of the Rio Declaration on Environment and Development (one of the outcomes of the 1992 UNCED)[2] incorporated a version of the principle of intergenerational equity when it asserted that "[t]he right to development must be fulfilled so as to equitably meet developmental and environmental needs of present and future generations."[3]

Both the outcomes of the 2012 UN Conference on Sustainable Development and the 2015 adoption of the SDGs affirm the relevance of sustainable development, or 'sustainability', as an outcome with which endeavors at every level of human activity and governance ought at a minimum to be aligned and at best to be directed.[4]

For all that an essential core of sustainable development documents refer to future generations, these and other international instruments and core texts that reference sustainable development leave many major questions unaddressed, including those of timescale, future generations *of whom*, and how to deal with balancing acts between the needs of present and future generations. In none of these are the content of intergenerational equity adequately described, nor are principles to guide its application established by the idea of sustainable development. The most appropriate decision-making process through which to arrive at responses to

1 G.H. Brundtland et al., *Our Common Future: Report of the World Commission on Environment and Development* (Oxford University Press 1987) 8.

2 See UNGA, Rio Declaration on Environment and Development, Report of the United Nations Conference for Environment and Development, Annex I (1992) 31 ILM 874 www.un.org/documents/ga/conf151/aconf15126-1annex1.htm accessed 30 November 2017.

3 Ibid. at Principle 3.

4 UN, *The Future We Want*, UNGA A/RES/66/288, 11 September 2012, Annex www.un.org/ga/search/view_doc.asp?symbol=A/RES/66/288&Lang=E accessed 30 November 2017. UN, Transforming Our World: The 2030 Agenda for Sustainable Development, UNGA A/RES/70/1, 21 October 2015 www.un.org/ga/search/view_doc.asp?symbol=A/RES/70/1&Lang=E accessed 30 November 2017. Paragraph 18 declares that "We will implement the Agenda for the full benefit of all, for today's generation and for future generations."

these challenges presents the second guidepost for future generations institutions, namely democracy.

## *On Democracy*

The idea of 'democracy' must also set guideposts for institutions for future generations. This least flawed of all political systems yet devised breeds possibility (cf. Winston Churchill's much-quoted insight that "democracy is the worst form of government except all the others that have been tried").[5] It enables people to make decisions in ways that are both well-informed and accountable, and at its best it provides an inclusive pathway to accommodating competing values and ideas. It is a system that enables the realization of the imperative, recognized in the SDGs, to 'leave no-one behind'.[6]

Democracy's systems of feedbacks offer accountability that is not flawed by the self-deception of authoritarianism. Its freedoms allow people to express their concerns, to influence political processes, and to hold their representatives to account. Democracy has a powerful potential to serve the weakest people in any given society. It is also more closely aligned with the idea of sustainable development than any other political system currently in play.[7]

But democracy has not significantly advanced over the past decade, save for in Australasia and parts of Asia.[8] It is at best weakened and at worst threatened by apathy, disappointment, complacency, inequality, conflict, corruption, and manipulation.[9] If democracy matters for sustainable development, institutions for future generations need to be aligned with it to the greatest extent possible.[10]

A democracy entry point for future generations institutions can help to guard institutions from the risk of becoming 'undemocratic', 'technocratic', or 'elitist'. In

5 See Hansard, HC (5th Series), vol. 444, cols. 206–07, 11 November 1987 http://hansard.millbanksystems.com/commons/1947/nov/11/parliament-bill#column_206 accessed 30 November 2017.

6 UN, Transforming Our World: The 2030 Agenda for Sustainable Development, *supra* note 5 at preamble, and paras. 4, 26, 48, 72, and 74 (e) www.un.org/ga/search/view_doc.asp?symbol=A/RES/70/1&Lang=E accessed 30 November 2017.

7 For an overview of the links and tensions between sustainable development and democracy-as-currently-practiced, see A. Westall, *The Relationship between Democracy and Sustainable Development* (FDSD Briefing) (FDSD 2015) www.fdsd.org/site/wp-content/uploads/2015/06/The-relationship-between-democracy-and-sustainable-development.pdf accessed 30 November 2017.

8 Economist Intelligence Unit, *Democracy Index 2014: Democracy and Its Discontents* (The Economist 2015) www.eiu.com/democracy2014 accessed 30 November 2017.

9 See also *Manifesto for Democracy and Sustainability* (FDSD 2013) www.fdsd.org/site/wp-content/uploads/2015/11/Manifesto-for-Democracy-and-Sustainability.pdf accessed 30 November 2017.

10 For a fuller account of the 'democracy case' for future generations institutions, see G. Smith, *The Democratic Case for an Office for Future Generations* (FDSD, April 2015) www.fdsd.org/site/wp-content/uploads/2015/04/Office-for-Future-Generations-FDSD-format.81.pdf accessed 30 November 2017.

turn, ensuring that future generations institutions are part of the lived experience of democracy can itself help to strengthen democratic practice – for such institutions could help to model, cajole, inspire, and secure different, more inclusive, and more deliberative approaches to the practice of democracy.

Ensuring that future generations institutions serve both democracy and sustainability is likely to advance the conditions for each to be fully realized, for democracy is weakened by unsustainability[11] as surely as the prospects for sustainable development are weakened when democracy, or the motive force that it provides, are absent.

### *Future Generations as Counterweights*

Future generations institutions might, from the perspective offered by the twin entry points of democracy and of sustainable development, offer a partial counterweight to some of the principal obstacles associated with efforts to fully achieve the process and goals of sustainable development, highlighted further below. And they *ought*, if democracy is valued as the 'best flawed political system' through which to pursue sustainable development, to be designed in ways that are aligned to the greatest extent with the ideal and practices of democracy.

At first blush, that might appear challenging. For if democracy is decision-making 'of the people, by the people, for the people' how can it comfortably be aligned with institutions whose purpose is to consider people who have not yet been born and cannot therefore make decisions? Institutions for future generations can provide a stimulus to, and decision-making tools and information for, deliberation over choices and trade-offs about the future in policy processes. They can potentially provide a judicial and administrative review function to guarantee ongoing accountability of decision-makers. However, their functions and ways of working need to be clearly linked to the notion of *demos* in the present so that they support and serve, rather than undermine, democracy. That is among the key inspirations for this short chapter's suggestions for operating principles for institutions for future generations.

### *Future Generations as Counterweights and Sustainable Development*

Future generations institutions are potentially counterweights to the political and cultural challenges of short-termism, or of the failure to have due regard to intergenerational equity or to future generations. All of these are deeply embedded within the concept of sustainable development. Al Gore wrote in his book, *Earth in the Balance: Forging a New Common Purpose*, that "the future whispers while the

[11] For a version of this argument, which is derived from an assessment of the implications of climate change for democracy, see H. Ward, *Democracy in the Face of Climate Change: Exploring the Present, 2050, and Beyond* (FDSD, January 2016) www.fdsd.org/site/wp-content/uploads/2016/01/democracy-in-the-face-of-climate-change-Halina-Ward.pdf accessed 30 November 2017.

present shouts."[12] For whilst as a species humans have a great capacity for foresight, they also have a great capacity for expressing and acting on individual self-interest. Dominant contemporary economic and cultural models sustain those behaviours.

And so it often is, too, in the worlds of politics and of democracy. There is a thin notion of representation in representative democracy in which the 'public interest' to be served by our elected representatives can be formed simply by means of an aggregation of all self-interests held by present people – including those that are short-term. Challenges like climate change or natural resource scarcity shine a bright light on the negative consequences of short-termism in decision-making. In his book *The Clock of the Long Now*, Stuart Brand explores what it might take to stretch the idea of 'now' and to make it a 'long now'.[13] Brand reminds readers of the difference between *kairos* and *chronos*: the former the time of opportunity and the propitious moment, and the latter eternal or ongoing time.

As Professor Jonathan Boston puts it in a 2014 essay and lecture, a key question is "how can we increase the political salience today of long-term risks and looming policy crises given the human tendency to discount or ignore problems that seem distant, remote or abstract?"[14] In the words of the *Manifesto for Democracy and Sustainability*, "from the local to the global, the practice of democracy at every level urgently needs to overcome short-termism."[15] Here, then, is a central challenge both for democracy and for sustainable development. It is a challenge, also, that defines the symbiotic relationship between the two – for democracy and sustainable development are two sides of the same coin. Each is weakened in the absence of the other.

This is not to suggest that short-term thinking is unimportant, invaluable, or even non-essential. But the *systematization*, both politically and culturally, of short-termism presents a clear and present danger to the idea of intergenerational fairness that is embedded within sustainable development. If the role and functions of future generations institutions are placed in the context of sustainable development, they are charged with contributing to resolving the problem of short-termism and in ways that allow them to help to revitalize democracy.

One major choice, however, concerns whether the functions of future generations institutions should principally be environmental. This entry point offers another framing or problematization of the relationship between sustainable development and future generations that carries less immediate 'democracy' resonance.

12 A. Gore, *Earth in the Balance: Ecology and the Human Spirit* (Houghton Mifflin 1992) 170.

13 S. Brand, *The Clock of the Long Now* (Basic Books 1999).

14 J. Boston, 'Governing for the Future: How to Bring the Long-Term into Short-Term Political Focus', paper prepared for a seminar at the Centre for Environmental Policy, School of Public Affairs, American University, Washington DC (5 November 2014) www.american.edu/spa/cep/upload/jonathan-boston-lecture-american-university.pdf accessed 30 November 2017.

15 *Manifesto for Democracy and Sustainability* (FDSD 2013) www.fdsd.org/site/wp-content/uploads/2015/11/Manifesto-for-Democracy-and-Sustainability.pdf accessed 30 November 2017, at Principle 17.

In this alternative framing, future generations institutions might be understood as offering a counterweight to driving forces, such as population growth, consumption, and the associated values of consumerism that if unaddressed can lead to the breaching of environmental limits.

To expand a little on this idea, today, it is clear that the earth's natural systems are under enormous pressure. UNEP's 2012 GEO 5 assessment concluded that "scientific evidence shows that Earth systems are being pushed towards their biophysical limits, with evidence that these limits are close and have in some cases been exceeded."[16] Earlier, in 2005, the Millennium Ecosystem Assessment warned that: "Over the past 50 years, humans have changed ecosystems more rapidly and extensively than in any comparable period of time in human history, largely to meet rapidly growing demands for food, fresh water, timber, fiber and fuel."[17] In 2011, a cover piece in *The Economist* magazine wrote that "[h]umans have become a force of nature reshaping the planet on a geological scale – but at a far-faster-than-geological speed."[18]

In addition to the notion of 'environmental limits', the concept of 'planetary boundaries' that must not be transgressed, which was first proposed in 2009 in an article in the journal *Nature*, could also help to frame action to prevent human activities from causing unacceptable environmental change.[19] The article's authors described 'planetary boundaries' across nine Earth system processes, argued that the 'safe operating space for humanity' and therefore the precondition for sustainable development lay within those boundaries, and suggested that for three Earth systems – climate change, biodiversity, and nitrogen – thresholds had already been breached. This concept of 'planetary boundaries' is not uncontroversial. Yet whether the focus of discussion is 'planetary boundaries' or 'environmental limits', it is clear that a range of Earth systems are associated with thresholds beyond which potentially irreversible and abrupt disruptions could occur.

At the same time, the case for asking future generations institutions to work *only* to bring our decision-making outcomes back within natural limits or planetary boundaries is a weak one. In the first place, the task of disaggregation of limits to the local or national levels would very quickly become highly technical. Were that to be a principal quality of the institution's ways of working, it would struggle to demonstrate its integration with the decision-making 'by the people' and 'of the people' that is essential to democracy. Of the two framing options derived from the idea of sustainable development, the first (that of future generations institutions

[16] GEO 5 press release, *World Remains on Unsustainable Track despite Hundreds of Internationally Agreed Goals and Objectives*, UNEP (6 June 2012) www.unep.org/geo/pdfs/geo5/GEO5-Global_PR_EN.pdf accessed 30 November 2017.

[17] Millennium Ecosystem Assessment, *Ecosystems and Human Wellbeing: Synthesis* (Island Press 2005) 1 www.maweb.org/documents/document.356.aspx.pdf accessed 30 November 2017.

[18] The Economist, 'Welcome to the Anthropocene' (26 May 2011) www.economist.com/node/18744401 accessed 30 November 2017.

[19] J. Rockström et al., 'A Safe Operating Space for Humanity' (2009) 461(7263) *Nature* https://doi.org/10.1038/461472a accessed 30 November 2017.

as counterweights to short-termism) offers a preferable problem statement for future generations institutions. It offers greater potential for future generations institutions to align with both the proposed imperatives of democracy and sustainable development; and to do so in ways that are socially as much as environmentally progressive.

Perhaps it might be countered that a 'political short-termism' entry point for a future generations institution is too technical, or too broad, to help revitalize democracy 'of' and 'by' the people. Yet, on the other hand, if the 'systems' problem of democracy from a sustainable development perspective is that of short-termism, a future generations institution that addresses just one corner (namely environmental limits), leaving the remainder only indirectly touched, could have only limited catalytic value. A future generations institution designed around the challenge of environmental limits would have an insufficiently broad remit, for example, to deal with social issues such as those associated with health, education, or pension reform. These are all areas where short-termism threatens to undermine the ability of future generations to meet their needs.

If the narrow remit offered by the challenge of environmental limits is 'insufficient', a 'short-termism' framing of the problem that future generations institutions seek to address offers a potential basis for institutions that have 'enough' remit. From this perspective, the principal challenge to be addressed by institutions for future generations might be framed as 'embedded decision-making short-termism that is at odds with sustainable development'.

## TOWARDS AN INTEGRATED APPROACH

Once democracy and sustainable development guideposts are put in position, their contribution to defining the *problem* becomes clearer. This article has proposed that the problems around which future generations institutions should be designed are both 'the problem' of short-termism, which dogs decision-making in both the political and the private spheres in much of the contemporary world, and 'the problem' of lack of engagement and participation in decision-making that threatens to turn lack of active support for democracy into a condition for its gradual – or for that matter sudden – erosion.

### *Why Institutions?*

In order to rebalance the political system so that it does not so consistently 'discount the future' (to apply an economic framing),[20] counterweights are needed. Future generations institutions potentially provide those counterweights. At the same time,

[20] For an explanation of the term and its associated problems see e.g. T.J. Brennan, 'Discounting the Future: Economics and Ethics' (1995) 120 *Resources* 3–6 www.ce.cmu.edu/~hsm/bca2006/readings/rff-discounting-1995.pdf accessed 30 November 2017.

however, this chapter has not yet made the case for *institutions* as a counterweight rather than some other measure or policy instrument.

In the first place, policy, legal, and formal institutional innovations are among the key shapers of *democracies*' responses to unsustainable development. They can show the way, with institutions for future generations an important part of the mix. They can help to guard against the risk that political crises triggered by demographic shifts, or climate change, or resource scarcity – in all their varied manifestations – do not lead to even more 'short-termism', be it cultural, political, or institutional. At the same time, it is important not to over-emphasize the role of future generations institutions, for remedies to the current ailments of political systems must stem as much from cultural and social innovation as from institutional or legal 'fixes'.

Institutions and laws shape human behaviour. In general, one might suggest that they work well when they are grounded in strong social consensus, and if the current observed practices of people living in the consumerist cultures of much of the world are anything to go by, future generations institutions may not be grounded in strong social consensus. Superficial appearances, however, might be deceptive. Recent evidence from the UK-based Common Cause Foundation, for example, suggests that for Britons the sense that other people lack the compassionate values that they hold to be more important than selfish values may make them less positive about getting involved in civic and political activities such as joining meetings, voting, or volunteering.[21] And what could be less selfish than having regard to the needs of people who have not yet been born, regardless of their possible relationship to us?

Earlier polling commissioned in 2011 by the Foundation for Democracy and Sustainable Development and Intergenerational Foundation from Ipsos MORI also suggests that Britons do care about future generations – including those distant in both space and time.[22] Yet the Common Cause Foundation report hints that they may be prevented from getting involved in securing their needs through the political system because they think that *other people* do not care about them. Institutions for future generations can help to redress that imbalance. These insights, which are connected to the methods of social psychology, suggest that, by only knowing where to look, a far stronger social consensus for future generations institutions than at first blush might appear to be the case might be found. And even if that were not so, there are also plenty of examples of laws (or institutions) that are applied or designed to quash competing values or social beliefs. The removal of capital

[21] Common Cause Foundation, *Perceptions Matter: The Common Cause UK Values Survey* (Common Cause Foundation 2016).

[22] Foundation for Democracy and Sustainable Development (FDSD) and Intergenerational Foundation (IF), *British Public Opinion on the Needs of 'Future Generations'* (FDSD and IF 2011) www.fdsd.org/site/wp-content/uploads/2014/11/british-public-opinion-on-future-generations .pdf accessed 30 November 2017.

punishment from the statute books of many democracies – despite widespread public support for the death penalty – is one example.[23]

In his book *Why People Obey the Law*,[24] Tom Tyler argues that people obey the law not through fear of punishment, but if (and when) they believe that the law is legitimate. This finding helps to explain why people often obey laws that do not directly match their own (personally held) values. Similar reasoning might be applied to institutions too. Institutions for future generations must be, and be seen to be, legitimate. They need to be 'of' democracy, not separate from it. Far from simply being among the outputs of democratic process, laws and public institutions are part of the fabric of democracy. They have the potential to alter the character of democracy and the values that enfranchised people bring to their own engagement with one other. Future generations institutions need to be understood this way too.[25]

### *What Future Generations Institutions Should Protect*

What is it that these institutions for future generations should protect? Whilst it is both difficult and unwise to seek to aggregate across nations and legal and constitutional cultures, it is suggested that the task generally should be to 'promote and protect the interests of future generations understood in the context of the imperative to meet the needs of the present without compromising the ability of future generations to meet their own needs'. Promotion of the interests of future generations, then, is the mission – but its boundaries are set by sustainable development, and that, in turn, connects future generations institutions to 'needs'.

There are a number of remaining challenges. After all, as mentioned earlier, the definition of sustainable development proposed in the Brundtland Report and foundational international documents addressing sustainable development leave major questions unaddressed, including 'which future generations?' 'over what timescale?' and 'how to deal with balancing acts between the needs of present and future generations?'

This said, if one makes the context for the mission of future generations institutions sustainable development, it is clear that 'longer-term thinking' alone, unguided by other norms, cannot be the sole response to short-termism. It must be longer-term thinking and evidence *that can secure intergenerational equity* and its counterpart, intragenerational equity. In short, the response lies with institutions

[23] See e.g. Lexington's Notebook, 'Democracy and the Death Penalty: An Evolving Debate', *The Economist* (8 February 2013) www.economist.com/blogs/lexington/2013/02/democracy-and-death-penalty accessed 30 November 2017.

[24] T. Tyler, *Why People Obey the Law* (Princeton University Press 2006).

[25] For two different approaches to grappling with this problem, see R. Read, *Guardians of the Future: A Constitutional Case for Representing and Protecting Future People* (Green House 2012); G. Smith, *The Democratic Case for an Office for Future Generations* (FDSD Report) (FDSD, April 2015) www.fdsd.org/site/wp-content/uploads/2015/04/Office-for-Future-Generations-FDSD-format.81.pdf accessed 30 November 2017.

for *future generations*, not institutions for *long-term thinking* alone. This formulation does not make use of 'rights' language (such as 'guaranteeing or securing the rights of future generations'). Nor does it speak of 'representing' future generations. Both 'rights' and 'representation' lead to significant practical difficulties. There is a persistent and commonly held perception, for example, that rights must necessarily operate as 'trumps' over other considerations that cannot be associated with 'rights'.[26] Furthermore, charging institutions for future generations with protection of the 'rights' of future generations would be uncomfortable in the absence of some founding constitution articulating such rights – and currently the precedents are limited.

There are also both practical and potentially constitutional difficulties that stem from the idea of formally 'representing' future generations (in the sense of 'being' them, or 'speaking accurately for them'). And there is quite simply no need to do so. It is possible to sharpen our ability to think about, and care for, future generations without seeking to have them 'represented'. 'Representation' of future generations is a conceit that risks paternalism if it is used in any more than its theatrical sense. Democracy is inherently tied to a *demos* of people who are already alive. Yes, these 'already-living' people are people with futures, connected to other people in time and space, people with moral obligations to those who have not yet been born. But they are people in the present nonetheless. In this sense the vision of future generations institutions that is proposed in this chapter is 'presentist'.[27] But it is not 'short-termist'.

### *How Politicians, International Instruments and Legal Reasoning Invoke 'Future Generations'*

Further inspiration for the 'what' of future generations institutions might also be taken from the ways in which future generations are currently addressed in the worlds of politics and law. A simple review of three types of sources strengthens the value of linking future generations institutions to sustainable development. A first set of sources is a review of the language and associated values invoked by UK politicians referring to future generations in the period from 2008 to 2011 carried out by members of a 'narratives and frames' working group of the UK Alliance for Future Generations.[28] Second, a review of some forty-five references to future generations in international instruments. And third, a partial review of the range

[26] The idea of rights as 'trumps' was described in R. Dworkin's influential work, *Taking Rights Seriously* (Harvard University Press 1977).

[27] See e.g. D. Thompson, 'Representing Future Generations: Political Presentism and Democratic Trusteeship' (2010) 13(1) *Critical Review of International and Political Philosophy* 17–37.

[28] See www.allianceforfuturegenerations.org. The review was not published.

of ways in which legal reasoning and courts in the UK have invoked future generations. Each is discussed briefly in turn.

To begin with the politicians, there was a huge resurgence in the political currency of 'future generations' in the UK over the period from 2008–2011. For example, during a debate on the sale of woodlands, the then Secretary of State for the Environment spoke of strengthening national and social capital *for future generations*.[29] At the same time, the opposition spoke of retaining forests in public ownership *in order to protect them* for future generations.[30] In political debate on relaxation of planning rules, motivated in part by rapid population growth and the nation's housing crisis, the reduction in restrictions was justified in terms of its benefits for future generations.[31] When speaking of the budget deficit, government ministers referred, variously, to "the previous Government max[ing] out the nation's credit card, landing future generations with a record budget deficit";[32] or of ensuring that "future generations can thrive without being burdened with the dead weight of our debt, our failings."[33] Future generations here were invoked to support budget cuts. At the same time, former Prime Minister Gordon Brown feared for 'the *future*' "*if it means we are to return to the short-sighted austerity politics of the* 1930s."[34] Elsewhere, a speech by the then NATO Secretary-General in 2004 had referred to NATO as an 'Alliance for Future Generations' and "an indispensable instrument to protect and promote our most fundamental values and to pass them on to future generations."[35]

The 'needs' of future generations in the UK in the period from 2008–2011 tended to have been considered favourably by politicians in those cases where they militated towards reduced state expenditure, or to intensifying or promoting economic activity in the present. In this respect, they were used as a 'sword', and only less frequently as

[29] C. Spelman, quoted in *New Direction for England's Public Forest Estate* (27 January 2011) www.gov.uk/government/news/new-direction-for-england-s-public-forest-estate accessed 30 November 2017.

[30] Labour motion on forests debate, Hansard, HC, vol. 522, part 110, cols. 925–970, 2 February 2011 www.publications.parliament.uk/pa/cm201011/cmhansrd/cm110202/debtext/110202-0003.htm accessed 30 November 2017.

[31] G. Clark, 'Reforming Planning for Future Generations', *Huffington Post* (5 August 2011) www.huffingtonpost.co.uk/greg-clark/reforming-planning-for-fu_b_918391.html accessed 30 November 2017.

[32] G. Osborne, February 2011, reported in 'George Osborne Orders Squeeze on Labour's Controversial Funding Scheme for Schools and Hospitals', *Daily Mail* (16 February 2011) www.dailymail.co.uk/news/article-1357403/George-Osborne-orders-squeeze-Labours-controversial-funding-scheme-schools-hospitals.html accessed 30 November 2017.

[33] N. Clegg (then Deputy Prime Minister), *Governing for the Long-Term*, speech, 9 September 2010 www.gov.uk/government/speeches/governing-for-the-long-term-deputy-pm-speech accessed 30 November 2017.

[34] G. Brown, speech, University of St Andrews (10 February 2011) www.st-andrews.ac.uk/news/archive/2011/title,64629,en.php accessed 30 November 2017.

[35] J. de Hoof Scheffer, *An Alliance for Future Generations* (27 June 2004) www.nato.int/docu/speech/2004/s040627e.htm accessed 30 November 2017.

a 'shield' to guard against harmful interventions. The UK referendum on membership of the EU, however, led to a partial shift, with significant 'shielding' invocations and public and political discussion of future generations as losers in a 'Brexit' referendum outcome, both before and after the vote itself,[36] and also retorts that argued the case for Brexit in terms of benefits to future generations.[37]

In conclusion, there is nothing inherently 'pro sustainable development' in the ways in which future generations are invoked in political discourse, nor anything inherently 'environmental'. One might even go so far as to suggest that the invocation of future generations is potentially a frontier battleground for sustainable development.

Second, the realm of law. Four years ago, pooling sources with Peter Roderick and Sebastien Duyck, research found some forty-five references to future generations in international legal instruments. In an article subsequently published in the 2011 *Yearbook of International Environmental Law*, it was suggested that international references to future generations reveal a systemic attempt to provide a counterweight to the tendency towards short-termism in global and national governance. But

> they do so with a lack of specificity that diminishes the attempt. What is revealed are the broad contours of a systematic challenge to operationalize 'long-termism', which includes a set of commitments, some soft and some hard, that are in search of a dedicated institutional setting to provide a counterweight to the bias to short-termism of both domestic politics and the reality of statehood in inter-governmental negotiations.[38]

There are a number of ways to typologize these references, but the article made use of two. First, the normative force for *states* that is reflected in the future generations language used subdivided into texts that refer to present and future generations alongside one another, and those that contain stand-alone reference to future generations. None of these references contain any explicit commitment to fairness or equity for future generations. In that sense, whilst they can be understood as helping to form the normative content of the idea of international equity, none of them are themselves direct or explicit commitments to intergenerational *equity*, even if they reflect the international community's understanding, in different settings, of what that concept might entail. What is clear, however, is that references to future generations

[36] See e.g. B. Chu, 'Brexit Is One More Example of the Older Generation Financially Bankrupting the Young', *The Independent* (28 June 2016) www.independent.co.uk/voices/brexit-eu-referendum-financial-economic-impact-older-generation-bankrupting-young-a7107666.html accessed 30 November 2017.

[37] See e.g. 'Britain's Bright Future after Brexit', *Get Britain Out* campaign website (17 October 2016) http://getbritainout.org/britains-bright-future-after-brexit/ accessed 30 November 2017.

[38] H. Ward, 'Beyond the Short Term: Legal and Institutional Space for Future Generations in Global Governance' (2012) 22(1) *Yearbook of International Environmental Law* 1–34, 14.

in international instruments contain little echo of the day-to-day tendency systematically to bias towards the present. When States choose to refer to future generations in international instruments, they do so in terms that express a high regard for future generations and for the long term.

The second means of typologizing the references was to assess the nature of the claims that future generations might have upon the present, divided into 'interests', 'needs', and 'rights'. Here, only a few of the international instruments referring to future generations touch upon the nature of the claims that future generations might have upon the present through references to the 'interests', 'needs', or 'rights' of future generations. As between the three terms, it is perhaps unsurprising (given the incorporation of this word within the Brundtland definition of sustainable development) that more references exist to the needs of future generations than to their interests or rights. Interestingly, none of the existing formulations in international instruments establishes a time horizon over which future generations are to be considered: implicitly it is determined by the subject matter under consideration. There is only one reference to rights. And it is also significant that whilst some of the provisions appear in the operational parts of the relevant instruments, most references to future generations are preambular, or incorporated within overall statements of principles or objectives.[39]

Third, and briefly, one might look to how legal reasoning – through court cases and academic analysis – has already developed multiple ways of engaging with future generations. This analysis focuses on common law cases and the European context. In relation to the controversial EU biopatenting Directive, one commentator highlights at least three moral approaches inherent in the text, reflecting its difficult legal passage.[40] When it comes to legal reasoning, it seems that decisions of the European Patent Office give more force to utilitarian than human rights or dignitarian arguments. As a result, the outcome in a number of cases has been described as 'crude' and 'absolutist' or open to ethical criticism.[41] Shawn Harmon argues that 'solidarity' should be adopted as one of the Patent Office's touchstones, so as to "heed the manifold claims that ... genes are the 'heritage of humanity,'"[42] thereby ensuring that the European Patent Office would consider the moral responsibility to preserve genetic information for the benefit of humanity and to embed this into its morality assessments.

In the common law concerning the disposition of property, case law expresses a distaste for thinking too far ahead in the minefield that is the 'rule against perpetuities', which regulates the time frame within which property rights arising in the future must vest. Its aim originally was to balance the interest in retaining land, at

39 Ibid. at 9.

40 See S. Harmon, 'From Engagement to Re-Engagement: The Expression of Moral Values in European Patent Proceedings, Past and Future' (2006) 31(5) *European Law Review* 642–666.

41 Ibid.

42 Ibid.

the time of Europe's great estates, within lines of descent versus the wider public interest in keeping it marketable so as not to tie up huge portions of the nation's wealth. The principle works to restrict the freedom of current landowners to contract in ways that bind future generations, thereby locking in a current judgment of the future.[43] A similar line of reasoning, broadly, can be seen at work in rules that prevent 'positive covenants' passing/running with ownership of land.[44]

In the field of spatial planning, planners make decisions based on an attempt to estimate "the consequences that will flow or follow from a change of use or operations" – potentially with major implications for both present and future generations of residents or users of the area concerned.[45] Difficult choices ensue when implicitly they are asked to choose a 'sustainable' level of housing provision or to consider the wider effects of a decision for biodiversity, particularly in relation to environmental limits. Courts considering immigration cases concerned with citizenship – as well as legislatures considering the allocation of citizenship rights – must in effect engage in debate about who constitute 'future generations' of citizens. For it is citizenship laws that decide who will belong to future generations of any given nation.[46]

Discussion of euthanasia can proceed on the basis that relaxation of existing prohibitions may lead to persons in the future – including future generations – behaving in ways that are ethically repugnant.[47] Here is a representation of an idea that future generations must be protected from the risk that they could develop a less refined sense of ethical discrimination than currently used.

Law related to the preservation of cultural and architectural heritage is presented with a dilemma when it is asked – for example in cases about the preservation of graffiti as street art – to consider the 'prospective' heritage of the present rather than the preservation of the historic.[48] Is cultural heritage about preserving the past for the future, or also recognizing the value of what one has in the present?

The field of intellectual property balances the economic interests of those whose interests are protected, and the possible economic and societal benefits of protected exploitation of those interests, against the wider value of the protected subject matter to future generations. Here, too, one finds a tension between short-term economic

43 See generally L.-A. Buckley, 'Perpetuities Reform in Ireland? The Law Reform Commission's Proposals' (2002) 37 *Irish Jurist* 143–166.

44 See P. O'Connor, 'Careful What You Wish For: Positive Freehold Covenants' (2011) 3 *The Conveyancer and Property Lawyer* 191–207.

45 See for example Case Comment, 'Webbs Country Foods Ltd v Secretary of State for the Environment (Unreported) (QBD)' (1995) *Journal of Planning and Environment Law* 33–38.

46 See S. Mullally, 'Defining the Limits of Citizenship: Family Life, Immigration and 'Non-Nationals' in Irish Law' (2004) 39 *Irish Jurist* 334–351.

47 See for example C. Gavaghan's book review of 'Euthanasia and Law in Europe', (2009) 13(2) *Edinburgh Law Review* 360–361.

48 See for example J. Webster, 'Should the Work of Banksy Be Listed?' (2011) 4 *Journal of Planning and Environment Law* 374–385.

interests and a broader array of interests over the long-term, extending into future generations of interest-holders. And since this is principal among the core tensions of sustainability, it ought also to benefit from the existence of institutions for future generations.

In conclusion, it is clear that there are many ways to 'do things with future generations', or to 'do things with time', that are already written into legal frameworks or that have evolved through the common law. Their treatment is context-specific, and consideration of those contexts makes it clear that it must remain so: no consistent vision of time and its passage can be superimposed on the law as it relates to future generations. And so too for the mandate of future generations institutions.

### *The Qualities and Ways of Working of Future Generations Institutions*

This chapter has considered the 'why' of future generations institutions, and the 'what' of different forms of reasoning. But what of the 'how' in the sense of 'how' they might work? What of the *qualities* of future generations institutions?

The detailed mandates and procedures of future generations institutions ought quite properly to be shaped by their particular national settings, as in the case of the establishment in 2015 of the office of Commissioner for Future Generations pursuant to the Well-being of Future Generations (Wales) Act 2015.[49] Standing back, however, the working methods and mandates of future generations institutions could usefully be designed through reflection on ten principles. These might help them not only to be counterweights to short-termism but also to the affliction of democracy sclerosis that is a constant irritant, and potentially a major disruptor, of established democracies. The ten principles are derived from the foundational ideas set out in this chapter:

First, the quality of all that future generations institutions do should be guided by sustainable development. In particular, they should seek ways of working that both emphasize the equity dimension of intergenerational fairness and are guided by the pledge in the 2030 Agenda for Sustainable Development to 'leave no-one behind'.[50]

Second, future generations institutions should be embedded within the political institutions and practices of democracy – 'of democracy', not apart from it. This is the way both to legitimize them and to ensure that they strengthen, rather than weaken, democracy 'by, of and for' the people. This might mean, for example, that they are accountable to parliaments, or that their leaders are appointed by parliaments – taking account of the recommendations of mixed panels of ordinary citizens and experts – rather than governments. Future generations institutions must find ways to work as an accelerator for *democratic* decision-making for sustainable

[49] Well-being of Future Generations (Wales) Act 2015.

[50] UN, Transforming Our World: The 2030 Agenda for Sustainable Development, *supra* note 5 at preamble, paragraphs 4, 26, 48, 72.

development so that 'we the people' and our elected representatives have sources of inspiration for a system of democracy that is 'other-regarding' and 'future generations-respecting'. They must be 'of the people', even when their staff are appointed on the basis of professionally recognized competence.

Third, future generations institutions should be mandated to contribute to legislative and policy processes, in particular to bring insights about the choices and pathways associated with 'future-impacting' decision-making. This function could be carried out through a standing mandate, potentially to support specialist parliamentary committees or a separate 'future generations committee', or a duty to respond to requests from parliamentarians to assist decision-making on future generations, or even a right to intervene when the shout of the short-term threatens to drown out the whisper of the long-term. They could also be integrated within the emerging toolkit of 'e-government', both as sources of insight and as advocates for (though not 'representatives of') future generations.

Fourth, future generations institutions should be empowered to stall or suspend legislative proceedings until materials or insights needed for legislators to take account of long-term perspectives, and the potential implications of decisions for future generations, can be prepared. Future generations institutions must certainly be charged with acting as policy advocates – offering advice, and insights, and reasoning, to accompany legislative proposals with implications for future generations and intergenerational equity.

Fifth, on request from local communities or their elected representatives, future generations institutions should be enabled to contribute analysis or problem-solving facilitation to local decision-making on matters with an impact on future generations, including for example spatial planning or infrastructure development.

Sixth, future generations institutions should have administrative and, potentially, judicial review functions, to scrutinize public decision-makers in relation to decisions that may significantly impair the ability of future generations to meet their needs. But this is difficult territory. Give too much power to these institutions and you disrupt a balance of power that would ordinarily lie with the legislature, helping to trigger a pushback that in times of crisis could be worse than the ill which the institution chose to repair.

Seventh, future generations institutions will need monitoring capacities to seek out the implications of legal and policy developments for, and their impact on, future generations. Such capacities might be realized for example through periodic 'review reports' that address through a variety of future generations lenses thematic issues such as biodiversity, or education, or food, or climate change.[51]

[51] The Finnish Parliament's Committee for the Future already reflects broadly similar functions. See www.eduskunta.fi/EN/lakiensaataminen/valiokunnat/tulevaisuusvaliokunta/Pages/default.aspx accessed 30 November 2017.

Eighth, future generations institutions should carry the hallmarks of living, learning institutions – seeking continually to refresh democratic practice and internal learning as they refine and develop their working methods. They should be both adaptive and reflexive. If, for example, it ceases to be the job of elected representatives to take account of future generations – for instance, because more is returned to the people in the form of referendums or direct democracy, including modern forms of e-democracy – then one must be capable of inserting the institutions within those evolving practices. It follows from this that institutions for future generations should be multidisciplinary in both constitution and staffing. They should apply a mix of qualitative and quantitative analysis and methods, particularly since the challenges that block decision-making that is 'future generations-regarding' are often behavioural, and the challenges cultural. They should have multiple forms and ways of reasoning and engaging, but a strong and unyielding mission.

Ninth, future generations institutions could be open to receiving complaints from citizens or interested individuals about public decisions or policies that threaten future generations in significant ways with a power to investigate those that raise the most pressing or significant issues. How this idea is implemented will, however, necessarily differ from legal and constitutional context to context.

Tenth, and finally, future generations institutions should actively seek to transmit their knowledge beyond the confines of the institution, so that they make it more likely that the conditions and problems that led to their creation (particularly those associated with short-termism) are progressively addressed not simply at the political level, but also at deeper societal and cultural levels.

## CONCLUSION

The argument for future generations institutions that is proposed in this chapter is grounded in the suggestion that future generations institutions can act as a counterweight to short-term decision-making that undermines sustainable development. For practical purposes, what are needed are institutions to 'do things with future generations' in the context of sustainable development. From this starting point, responses to the challenges of identifying challenges that vex theorists, such as 'how many generations', 'where', and 'in relation to what issues', can be flexibly addressed.

Taking inspiration from an undergraduate law text, *How to Do Things with Rules*,[52] it is striking that a similar text on 'how to do things with future generations', or 'how to do things with the future', might offer a useful guide to the different interpretive and decision-making techniques and principles that can be, and are, applied by institutions, lawyers, and decision-makers when considering future

[52] W. Twining's book *How to Do Things with Rules* sets out principles of legal interpretation and legal reasoning – sufficient to get a law student started. W. Twining and D. Miers, *How to Do Things with Rules*, 4th edn. (Butterworths 1999).

generations. Such a volume might clearly set out the points of departure and convergence between different 'theories of future generations' and their implications for decision-making from reproductive rights to competition policy, biopatenting, cultural heritage, and climate change. One could expect that future generations institutions would, in part and after a while, offer many of the examples of 'how to do things with future generations.' All that is needed is simply to get started, as existing future generations institutions addressed elsewhere in this volume have done.

The anchor for future generations institutions are the principles and idea of sustainable development, not any particular theory of future generations. That is potentially an expansionist perspective (in the sense that it potentially gives future generations institutions a broad remit), but one in which the *quality* of what is brought by the institution must be guided by sustainable development. At the same time, the sustainable development framing of future generations institutions also points to the essential need for them to address social as well as environmental considerations.

There are other arguments in favour of this practical 'just get started, and work from there' approach. Certainly, there are plenty of theoretical approaches to future generations, including approaches grounded in contractarian, utilitarian, dignitarian, and communitarian thinking. But Tim Mulgan's book *Ethics for a Broken World* underscores the wisdom of hesitation before choosing one over another.[53] The book imagines 'philosophy after catastrophe'. Its most striking insight is just how many existing theoretical starting points, in their assumption that the world is generally likely to get better, are ill-equipped to provide guidance from what he calls a 'broken world' that is hit by catastrophic events that test democracy to its limits. Any theory that is unlikely to stand the test of time is inherently unlikely to work well for institutions for future generations.

At the same time, with the adoption of the SDGs in 2015, it might be feasible to attain the broad goal of developing a set of general guiding principles that embody the absolute essentials of 'how to do things with future generations.' An initial set of principles might be derived directly from the SDGs themselves, and potentially supplemented thereafter through processes of consultation and engagement at national or as appropriate sub-national or city levels.

One cannot expect any institution to make consistently wise decisions. No matter what precepts it is given, it will be of 'this time'. There are people and peoples among our ancestors who certainly had perceptions of time that were different from ours, just as perceptions of time are partly culturally determined even by people alive today. Our perceptions of time will likely be different to those of future generations. Society must do its best to avoid paternalism towards future generations, but do our best we certainly must.

[53] T. Mulgan, *Ethics for a Broken World: Imagining Philosophy after Catastrophe* (Routledge 2014) (first published as an e-book in 2011 by Acumen).

# 7

# Future Generations Institutions to Implement International Obligations towards Future Generations

*Sándor Fülöp*

As a starting point, this chapter examines how frequently future generations language is used in international legal documents. It finds that in the last few decades surprisingly many binding and less-than-binding international legal documents – and not only environmental ones – refer to future generations. However, since these references are seldom made in the main body of the binding international treaties, the force of 'future generations language' is questionable. Even so, these declarations of the will of the international legal community impact laws on all levels, most importantly the use of future generations language in the national constitutions that were created or amended recently. Unfortunately, the impulse for development of international law on intergenerational justice has broken after the splendid years of the 1990s. The international community has experienced a significant decline in mentioning and dealing with future generations in the sources of international law since then. The negative socio-economic developments since the 1990s served as the major hindrance to continuation of intergenerational features in our laws, as policy focused elsewhere.

However, there is a certain level of positive inertia in the trajectory of the related scientific research and social thinking in which policies relating to future generations has developed amidst less receptive social and political circumstances, especially because the quickly changing natural environment serves as a constant warning about the fragility of the future. Honest assessments from scientific, civil, religious and other communities, and the sobering facts of ecological degradation, will together make society more receptive to its moral responsibility towards future generations and towards survival of its culture, in order to ensure societies with acceptable living standards that are based in freedom and dignity.

A mere expression of the desire of the legislature to protect the rights (needs or interests) of future generations, however, in itself will not result in the necessary changes in social and economic life and will not make consumption and other decisions more responsible. Proper institutions with acceptable budgets can implement effective procedures based on effective laws. There is no such thing as good law with poor implementation – a failure to reach the will of the legislation happens because of poorly designed legal regimes. In this respect, scholars question whether it is possible or necessary to use the term 'rights of the future generations' or whether to use the phrase 'the responsibility of the government' instead. In the discourse about this basic issue that determines the quality of laws about intergenerational justice there are several concepts such as the non-existence argument, how to foresee the needs, interests and preferences of future generations, and whether rights and obligations can exist separately.

Specific institutional arrangements for implementing future generations laws seem to be indispensable because the compartmentalized, short-term thinking administrative bodies of the 'modern' State are not able to handle the complex, multidisciplinary tasks of sustainable development. This practice is sometimes seen in countries that allocate new tasks to old institutions in order to implement future generations laws, while other States form brand new institutions for these tasks. Internationally, certain European institutions are considered to have the most potential to become at least partly intergenerational ones. This chapter will discuss the general features of future generations institutions as well.

Once there is a proper future generations institution in place, the next question is the methodology for its work. The most obvious solution is to use existing legal tools from plans, programs and policies at all levels of legislation, administrative decision-making procedures and domestic law. While the relevant literature seems to be quite colourful in this respect, it appears that the idea of this systematic work seems to be a core element of the majority of them. Naturally, if the social and political climate allows, the future generations institutions will campaign for further, more effective legislation in the field of intergenerational justice. This new future generations law most probably would need to be globalized and focused on local communities, while giving less role to the State level – similar to the developments visible in the field of economics.

## INTERNATIONAL LAW TAKING NOTE OF FUTURE GENERATIONS

### *Future Generations Language in International Legal Documents*

There are numerous surveys in the environmental and sustainable development literature about the appearance and use of the term 'future generations'. Several binding and non-binding, though highly influential, documents contain not only environmental but many other topics in connection with the due consideration of the needs and interests of future generations. Biodiversity, climate, peace and security, nuclear safety, industrial safety and catastrophe prevention, health, education, cultural heritage, scientific and technological progress, values and traditions are some of issues on the substantive side, while on the procedural side future generations language can be found in topics such as the establishment and operation of proper institutions.[1] The international treaties, declarations and other instruments that mention future generations are the forerunners of a much larger mass of legal documents which refer to sustainable development as a term in which intergenerational justice is a defining element. For example, Dire Tladi establishes that the vast majority of environmental agreements contain the term 'sustainable development' either directly or in a circumscribed manner using other words but having the same meaning and sustainable development "has been included in virtually every recent treaty and policy document on the environment."[2]

### *The Binding Force of the Future Generations Related Provisions*

The problem with this international legal commitment is that the references to future generations are made mostly in the preambles, or in the text body but in aspirational language. International legal scholars and tribunals agree that preambles are usually not binding: "they are not intended to contain provisions or dispositions of substance (in short they are not operative clauses)." Nevertheless. it is generally accepted that they may be relevant and important as guides to the manner in which the treaty should be interpreted,[3] or, going a little further, the preamble may justify a wider interpretation of the text body and/or at least the rejection of a narrower interpretation.[4] These are very strong arguments, especially if it is considered that the most important principle of the international public law is good faith interpretation of the law.[5] What could be more important for the parties to a treaty than its goals? Unfortunately, in the field of environmental protection, many States follow the free rider strategy even during the drafting of international laws and other documents and

1 H. Ward, *Committing to the Future We Want: A High Commissioner for Future Generations at Rio+20* (Foundation for Democracy and Sustainable Development/World Future Council 2012) 1, annex C; K. Cook and R. Taylor, 'The Rights of Future Generations in International Law', in B. Jávor and J. Rácz (eds.), *Do We Owe Them a Future?* (Védegylet 2006) 145–151; J. Anstee-Wedderburn, 'Giving a Voice to Future Generations: Intergenerational Equity, Representation of Generations to Come, and the Challenge of Planetary Rights' (2014) 1(1) AUJlEnvLaw 3, 42–50. M-C. Cordonier Segger and A. Khalfan, *Sustainable Development Law: Principles, Practices and Prospects* (Oxford University Press 2004), at 3; C. Raffensperger, *Models for Protecting the Environment for Future Generations* (Harvard Law School 2008) 3 and Annex C; M. Orellana et al., *The High Commissioner for Future Generations: The Future We Want* (Center for International Environmental Law & World Future Council 2012) 7.

2 Similarly to the precautionary principle that shares widespread inclusion in international legal documents. D. Tladi, *Sustainable Development in International Law: An Analysis of Key Environmental Instruments* (Pretoria University Law Press 2007) 42–43.

3 *Beagle Channel Arbitration* (cited by Cook and Taylor, *supra* note 1).

4 Anstee-Wedderburn, *supra* note 1 at 46.

5 Vienna Convention on the Law of Treaties [1969] art. 31.

also in the process of their implementation.[6] Several authors acknowledge that this is a hypocritical situation in which intergenerational justice is placed on one side; such short-termism on the part of the State calls out for clarification and, if possible, should be accompanied by substantial professional and public media attention. Based on the pending, probably developing, status of interpretation of intergenerational justice provisions, Kate Cook and Rachel Taylor suggest that preambular obligations in the intergenerational context should be tested in international legal disputes, although they acknowledge that this has not happened so far.[7]

### *National Constitutions: A Good Start*

Researchers have found that national constitutions, especially those enacted in the last two and a half decades, also contain, as a rule, a certain level of reference to the needs and/or interests of future generations or sustainable development or both. On the level of national constitutions, Joerg Tremmel differentiates between general, ecological and financial considerations in connection with intergenerational justice.[8] Naturally, the more detailed topics are very similar to the above-mentioned topics; however, Tremmel has found several additional ones, for instance references to spiritual values (using the Czech Constitution as an example), to natural beauty (using the Italian Constitution as an example) and in many instances to public health.[9] Others have found that the constitutional definitions of sustainable development, where they exist, in themselves describe the content of intergenerational justice, such as environmental, social, political, developmental elements or even anything that influences the coming generations.[10]

While the connections between international laws, future generations, sustainable development provisions and similar content in national constitutions are most obviously circular, analysis should not exclude international legal regimes and good examples from the motivating forces of the national constitutional legislatures as a kind of cascading down of the ideas and moral considerations. It is another thing, however, to determine how far the national constitutions permeate lower-level

[6] S. Fülöp, 'The Institutional Representation of Future Generations', in G. Bos and M. Düwell (eds.), *Human Rights and Sustainability: Moral Responsibilities for the Future* (Routledge 2016).

[7] Ibid. at 146.

[8] J. Tremmel, 'How Can Future Generations Be Protected by Changing Constitutions?', in Jávor and Rácz, *supra* note 1 at 36.

[9] The strong interrelationship between environmental rights and rights in connection with public health in the history of the development of the constitution in many countries shows clearly the anthropocentric origin of the 'right to a healthy environment'. This statement can be generalized in concert with E. Pirjatanniemi, who notes that "human rights with their inevitable anthropocentric bias have sometimes been regarded as a significant cause of environmental problems." Ibid. at 21.

[10] M. Sheridan, 'The Possible Approaches and Possibilities of Institutional Representation of Future Generations in Europe', in Jávor and Rácz, *supra* note 1 at 160.

laws and regulations and the actual legal practice that follows these constitutional undertakings.

## *The Rise and Fall of Future Generations*

As a small experiment, the research for this chapter mapped out the intensity in time of future generations and common heritage language in international law. The results demonstrate that in the decades after World War II the international community was occupied with other issues, such as human rights, and that knowledge about environmental degradation and resource depletion was relatively scarce. Thereafter, in the 1970s and 1980s, a definite increase occurred, and in the 1990s there are peak numbers. Unfortunately, the following decades show a clear-cut decline in references to future generations.[11]

Examining the data behind the numbers up to the mid-2000s, Halina Ward established that all treaties contained equal handling or preferences regarding the needs of the future generations while none of them preferred present generations to future ones.[12] With such references peaking and ebbing since then, in the present decade she could not be so optimistic. The same time pattern can be detected in the use of future generations languages in national constitutions.[13]

Two years after Joerg Tremmel's article appeared in Benedek Jávor's famous book, *Do We Owe Them a Future?*, the fragility of international financial systems and the astounding recklessness of financial networks in blowing up empty financial balloons showed itself in its full strength. Even if the enthusiasm of international legislative entities for intergenerational justice decreased in that decade, it appears that without this economic and social cataclysm a mutual connection between the international and national levels acknowledging and ensuring the rights of future generations would have exerted growing pressure from both sides in a virtuous circle and soon would have made intergenerational justice a mandatory principle of international law.

## *The Short History of the Idea of Sustainable Development*

Compared to the case of future generations, the broader, more complex (arguably contradictory) term 'sustainable development' has followed a similar development line with a very similar time pattern. With the help of Tladi's thorough survey, the development of the idea and support for sustainable development in the international community can be described as a steeply rising curve in the 1970s and 1980s that reached its plateau in the 1990s and started to decline over the last two decades. The first stage was the twenty years between Stockholm and Rio, where

[11] Ward, *supra* note 1 at Annex C.

[12] Ibid. at 1.

[13] Tremmel, *supra* note 8 at 32–37.

the Stockholm Conference represented a very well-prepared strong start.[14] In the Stockholm Declaration, one can already find clear language for intergenerational justice together with intragenerational justice as the building blocks of the concept of sustainable development. It was followed by the creation of the UNEP and a series of important international conventions, such as CITES on the international trade of endangered species (1973)[15] and the Basel Convention on hazardous wastes (1989).[16] Between Stockholm and Rio further major milestones included the UN Charter of Economic Rights and Duties (1975),[17] the Lomé Conventions (concerning the intragenerational justice pillar),[18] the Montevideo Programme on the development and periodic review of environmental law (1981),[19] the World Charter for Nature (1982)[20] and the Brundtland Commission Report (1997).[21] The latter Report, apart from the frequently quoted definition of sustainable development that integrates the needs of the present generations and the ability of future generations to meet their own needs, contains suggestions in six important areas: (1) strengthening the integration principle; (2) further institutionalization; (3) networking between politics, science and the public; (4) public participation in environmental decision-making; (5) a sustainable development convention; and (6) finances with the involvement of multilateral financial institutions.[22]

The plateau in this time sequence is the UNCED, during which the Rio Declaration was used to craft the basic principles of sustainable development that have served as a universal reference in environmental legislations and legal disputes. Additionally, Agenda 21 and the Forest Principles were the non-binding but very influential instruments of the UNCED, while the UNFCCC and the CBD were the basis of further developments in international (thereafter regional and national) environmental law.[23] In close connection with the UNCED, in 1991 the GEF was created by the World Bank, UNEP and the UN Development Programme to ensure financial support for the implementation of the most important environmental

[14] United Nations Declaration on Human Environment [1972].

[15] Convention on International Trade in Endangered Species of Wild Fauna and Flora [1973].

[16] Basel Convention on the Control of Transboundary Movements of Hazardous Wastes and Their Disposal [1989].

[17] United Nations Charter of Economic Rights and Duties of States [1975].

[18] The series of Lomé Conventions is the world's largest financial and political framework for North–South cooperation between the EU Member States and the African, Caribbean and Pacific (ACP). First agreed in 1975, and renewed in 1979, 1984 and 1990, since 2000 it has been called the Cotonou Agreement.

[19] UNEP programme for the development and periodic review of environmental law, started in 1981.

[20] Decision 37/7 of the 48th plenary meeting of the UNGA on 28 October 1982.

[21] G.H. Brundtland et al., *Our Common Future: Report of the World Commission on Environment and Development* (Oxford University Press 1987).

[22] Tladi, *supra* note 2 at 17–25.

[23] United Nations Framework Convention on Climate Change [1992]; Convention on Biological Diversity [1992].

conventions. Tladi points out, however, that the signs of decline were already noticeable in the Rio documents. First, while the Stockholm Declarations clearly recognized the link between human rights and the environment, the Rio documents avoided this issue.[24]

Second, as noted by Tladi, "Stockholm emphasizes the responsibility to protect the environment, while Rio emphasizes the right to utilise the environmental resources."[25] Compared to Stockholm and Rio, the following decades produced meager results in the field of sustainable development and intergenerational justice apart from the two cornerstones, the 2002 Johannesburg WSSD and the 2012 Rio UN Conference on Sustainable Development.[26] Notably, the 2000 MDGs and the newest developments in 2015 could not produce a boost in international law concerning institutionalization and finances similar to that brought about by the previous events. Neither the Paris Agreement nor the Agenda for 2030 could have these ambitions; they aimed rather at reinforcing the commitments of the world's States towards sustainable development, and they probably represent a new start for the so-far-declining trends.[27]

### *The Relatively Independent Trajectory of Sustainable Development*

As has been seen, there was a similar history in the development of intergenerational justice and sustainable development in international law. The 2008 economic crises dramatically refocused already dwindling social attention and a tapering down of resources from environmental protection, future generations and sustainable development as such.[28] Yet, this could not prevent the network of environmental sciences, international NGOs, and national academic, civil and political forces from attempting to develop the knowledge basis and social understanding of the most important facts of sustainable development. In addition, the imminent system of ecological threats has become perceptible; for example, with extreme weather conditions, it has become apparent that some basic social problems are closely

[24] Tladi notes revealing titles in the relevant literature: 'What Happened in Rio to Human Rights' by D. Shelton and 'International Environmental Law from Stockholm to Rio: Back to the Future' by M. Pallemaerts; Tladi, *supra* note 2 at 27.

[25] Ibid. at 28.

[26] See Johannesburg World Summit of Sustainable Development [2001]; United Nations Conference on Sustainable Development [2012].

[27] The Paris Climate Accord, an agreement within the UNFCCC, adopted on 12 December 2015 and the SDG document 'Transforming Our World: The 2030 Agenda for Sustainable Development' adopted on 25 September 2015.

[28] Bándi writes, "the economic crisis that started in 2008 unambiguously pushed into the background several viewpoints that were not in connection with economic growth, especially the viewpoints of the environment." Gy. Bándi, A *fenntarthatóság értelmezésének egyes szempontjai* (Certain Viewpoints of Interpretation of Sustainability) 2 (dissertation, Hungarian Academy of Sciences 2013) http://real-d.mtak.hu/651/7/dc_618_12_doktori_mu.pdf accessed 30 November 2017.

connected to environmental degradation, including migration and related phenomena such as water shortages and desertification. Similarly, connections can be made between loss of biodiversity and the growing susceptibility of human communities to new types of pandemics.

The time has come to restructure our social perceptions, political readiness and legal-institutional-financial tools in connection with a new understanding of sustainable development and intergenerational justice. However, further bolstering from scientific side, and not only physics, biology and other hard sciences but also sociology and law, is also necessary. Cook and Taylor underline that, even if we accept these rights and/or are ready to safeguard the needs or interests of future generations, it remains unclear what the precise content and the extent of these concepts should be.[29]

It should be agreed that in light of the lessons of the past four-plus decades, the concept of sustainable development should be rephrased because it has become too broad and vague. This is in accordance with the emergence of two dichotomies that have come to accompany the concept of sustainable development – the nature of North–South relationships and the alleged contradiction between anthropocentric and ecocentric approaches. The signs of the former dichotomy began to appear during the preparation for the Stockholm Conference, namely at the 1968 UNESCO Conference on the Scientific Basis for Rational Use and Conservation of the Resources of the Biosphere.[30] According to Tladi, developing countries did not support the idea of a global conference on the world's resources, and another preparatory conference in Founex, Switzerland was needed to forge a consensus and secure their participation and the success of the Stockholm Conference. This latter dichotomy appears on the surface as tension between the social-economic and the environmental sides of sustainable development. The Stockholm Declaration on the Human Environment, as the title itself shows, quite clearly put almost all the emphasis on the anthropogenic, social-economic side.[31] For instance, Principle 9 states that environmental problems "can best be remedied by accelerated development." Since then, a line of governments and economic leaders have echoed this principle as an argument for postponing environmental measures until the level of economic development allows them, in practice meaning never.

### *Reinforcing Our Moral Responsibilities towards Future Generations*

There must be a way – or several ways – out of this situation of conceptual stalemate. One of the most pressing of these issues is, undoubtedly, our moral responsibility

[29] Ibid. at 28.

[30] The 'Biosphere Conference' was organized by UNESCO, with the active participation of FAO and WHO, from 4 to 13 September 1968 in Paris on "the scientific basis for the rational use and conservation of the resources of the biosphere."

[31] UN Declaration on Human Environment, *supra* note 14.

towards our offspring. Professor Agius eloquently states that "[t]hroughout human history a sense of responsibility for the immediate future, namely the future of our own children and grandchildren has always been an inherent part of human nature. The next generation has always represented hope, continuity and progress. Each generation has taken pride in leaving a heritage which the next generation could use to advance the society."[32] From this perspective, national constitutions can be understood as an interface of law and the moral theses commonly agreed in societies. Several constitutions underline the unity of the past, present and future generations of a nation, in which natural resources are inherited and also bequeathed by each generation.[33] Others establish responsibility for future generations simply based on the fact that the current generation determines their fate.[34] Starting out from the religious morality perspective, some national constitutions encompass a responsibility based in religious tenets.[35] Many constitutions invoke the definition of sustainable development in a moral context, therefore implicitly accepting the concept of intergenerational justice,[36] although they mostly put the stress on the balance between social and economic development and environmental protection. Given these variations, one might wonder if such deep moral issues can tolerate too many compromises.

### *Human Rights and Intergenerational Justice*

On the international level, human rights law weaves basic moral considerations into the tissue of law.[37] After the first decades of silence, the concept of intergenerational justice has found expression in the most important human rights documents starting with the Charter of the UN, the ICCPR and the ICESCR. Later documents make this connection more explicit. The 2013 Report of the Secretary-General of the UN establishes in the simplest and strongest way that the extent of someone's human rights cannot depend on when they are born.[38] Human rights, however, have a balancing nature, and other rights, such as the rights of future generations and the basic economic rights of the present generations, could limit the scope of a human right. Karen Moir argues that extending human rights to future generations would not undermine the rights of the most vulnerable in the world today, and, similarly, that the extension of human rights to women did not violate those of men, nor did

[32] E. Agius, 'A European Ombudsman for the Rights of Future Generations', in Jávor and Rácz, *supra* note 1 at 16.

[33] E.g. Ukraine.

[34] E.g. Czech Republic.

[35] E.g. Switzerland.

[36] E.g. Argentina and France.

[37] E. Pirjatanniemi, 'Greening Human Rights Law – A Focus on the European Convention on Human Rights', in Bos and Düwell, *supra* note 6 at 20.

[38] UN Secretary-General, 'Intergenerational Solidarity and the Needs of Future Generations: Report of the Secretary-General', UN Doc. A/68/322 (15 August 2013).

the extension of human rights to ethnic and religious minorities violate those of majority groups. Moir's central argument is the balancing nature of human rights and the fact that these rights can only be considered legitimate once all human beings are accounted for.[39]

### *Survival as a Moral Command*

The recent significant decline of global and national undertakings towards future generations raises a practical question for lawyers who are committed to justice, including intergenerational justice. Should they preach high moral values in connection with their undeniable responsibilities towards the coming generations or simply to point out that humankind is on a path of self-eradication with an accelerating speed? Probably a good mixture of the two sets of argument would be the most effective solution. For instance, Gaillard argues plausibly that oil extraction in the Niger River delta in Nigeria ruining vital natural lands has hurt the rights of present and future generations at the same time.[40] Furthermore, nuclear waste creates serious disadvantages for present and future generations, as well as climate change that generates hurricanes, inundations, refugees and new conflicts.[41] Yet, very few legal texts identify the protection of future generations and the survival of society as clearly as the 1992 Czech Constitution in its use of the words "responsibility for the future generations as well as for the fate of life on this Earth."[42] It is apparent that the interconnection of these two concepts has basic importance for spreading them into legal systems and practices. Without this, society could end up having strong future generations legal texts and institutions that are neglected, under-budgeted and bypassed in everyday administrative practice while the major function of the concept of the protection of future generations is to postpone the problems of the immediate future to the remotely further future.

As Professor Agius writes, the accumulating environmental threats "will soon lead to breakdowns in vital support systems for life on Earth."[43] The environmental threats themselves form a part of a larger system of survival issues, such as nuclear weapons and other weapons of mass destruction that can easily fall into the hands of unpredictable and unreliable regimes, as can biotechnology and other life sciences, terrorism, organized crime and uncontrolled migration, in the frames of globalization and the dangerous divisions between rich and poor countries.[44]

39 Ibid. at 2.
40 Ibid. at 40.
41 Tremmel, *supra* note 8 at 32, 34.
42 Constitution of the Czech Republic, preamble [1992].
43 Agius, *supra* note 32 at 1.
44 Ibid. at 2.

## THE CONTENT AND QUALITY OF LAWS TARGETING INTERGENERATIONAL JUSTICE

### *There Is No Such Thing as Good Laws/Poor Implementation*

When examining the possibilities of effective implementation of international norms of intergenerational justice, the first thing to look at is the quality of those norms. As Tremmel has pointed out, even where the legislature ensures institutional guarantees of intergenerational justice, without solid legal background an institution itself is not worth much.[45] Implementation of weak legal language cannot reflect strong, vague phrases about the needs and interests of future generations without specifying their actual content. As Jane Anstee-Wedderburn points out following a survey of several Australian laws, while the State's sustainable development laws seem impressive on the surface, there is little noticeable impact on social-economic practices.[46]

### *The Rights of Future Generations or the Responsibility of Present Governments*

The basic legal structure that determines the strength of future generation laws seems to be built around the existence or non-existence of rights of future generations. Therefore, at the first step of 'legal quality auditing' a basic structural weakness of future generations' laws must be assessed. Indeed, rights language is very seldom used either at the national or at the international level. At the international level, examples include the Aarhus Convention,[47] while at the national level examples include the Constitution of Finland,[48] Latvia,[49] Portugal,[50] and Slovenia.[51] It must be noted, however, that at the national level the scope of the 'right' phrase is dubious. Once it is used with a general subject, such as 'everyone', one must interpret whether it refers to the present and future generations equally depending on the context. However, this logic was challenged by the development of the Hungarian Constitution, in which the right to a healthy environment has existed since 1976 and was ensured to everyone, while the new 2011 Constitution (Fundamental Law) made it clear that this should be understood only for present

45 Ibid. at 35.
46 Ibid. at 42.
47 UNECE (Pan-European) Convention on Access to Information, Participation and Justice in Environmental Decision-Making Procedures [1998] art. 1.
48 Ibid. at art. 20.
49 Ibid. at art. 115.
50 Ibid.
51 Ibid. at art. 72; see also Tremmel, *supra* note 8 at 36–38.

generations, because it contains separate provisions regarding future generations that do not address rights in this manner.

In many cases, the national constitutions establish a duty of the States to protect the material bases of future generations in a way that is not the equivalent of rights language but theoretically is very close to it based on the generally accepted rule that rights and obligations exist together. However, this presupposed right, if it exists at all, is weaker: without further detailed stipulations, no one will be in a good position to claim the implementation of these rights in concrete cases, with concrete content, since the extent and measures of protection are to be determined solely by the State. Even so, it can be argued that the discretionary power of the State is limited by the aim of the legislature in determining the obligation to protect the rights of the future generations.

### *The Non-Existence Argument*

Tremmel seems to be right when saying that, if future generations cannot have rights simply based on widely shared arguments that non-existent, even more the "not-sure-that-will-exist" persons cannot have any rights, then future generations might not have needs and interests either, and that would be nonsensical.[52] This closely relates to his other argument that moral convictions will sooner or later determine the content of laws related to a given field of social life. If one generally thinks that one's offspring will enjoy at least the basic conditions of life on Earth – that is, the basic conditions to live with dignity and joy – this moral conviction will need to appear in law at the international and national levels.[53]

### *Needs and Interests of Future Generations*

It can be argued that the present language of needs and interests of future generations does not ensure enough concrete protection because of a lack of meaningful claims and definite procedures to fulfill them should they be infringed or threatened with infringement. However, some legal scholars see the possibility of developing proper legal practice relating to the interests of future generations once careful analysis of the alternatives takes place and the precautionary principle prevails in cases when there is a need to balance the interests of the present and future generations.[54] In fact, a continuous line might be drawn to describe the rising level of commitment of societies to future generations, starting with (1) identifying needs and interests, continuing with (2) establishing State obligations that are subject to certain conditions which the States can consider, and reaching the top level of

[52] Tremmel, *supra* note 8 at 49–50.
[53] Ibid.
[54] Raffensperger, *supra* note 1 at 3.

commitment with (3) the legislature declaring *expressis verbis* the rights of future generations. Naturally, the machinery of the institutes that are partly or wholly responsible for fulfilling longer-term goals should not start moving only at stage (3). Time is short, the irreversible changes in the major ecological systems have begun already,[55] and the future generations will not have any enjoyment of their rights if society does not immediately begin to allocate and implement the tasks of arranging time-dimensional social-environmental conflicts.

### *Rights and Obligations Somehow Separate*

Some assert that it is no use arguing whether future generations have rights: we definitely have responsibilities beyond the short-term. The merits of separating rights and obligations are questionable, however.[56] As in the case of property rights, where the right-holder is faced with an indefinite number of obligations to let him/her enjoy her/his property, the obligation towards future generations might have the same structure. Additionally, the strong and natural relationship between rights and obligations will not be broken simply by the fact that the fulfillment of obligations and the enjoyment of rights shift in time considerably.[57] These conservative, legalistic arguments are in harmony with the philosophical justice theories Professor Agius refers to: apart from the individual level, so-called commutative justice that is based on mutual connections of persons here and now, there are other, higher level forms of justice.[58] In the frames of these social justice theories regarding what the individual owes society in general and vice versa, society has responsibilities to individuals in general and in particular when they are not in a position to see beyond their own lives – future generations belong to this category.[59] Others turn the close relationship of rights and responsibilities upside down in order to argue for the existence of and need to protect the rights of future generations.[60]

[55] J. Rockström, 'A Safe Operating Space for Humanity' (2009) 461(7263) *Nature* 461.

[56] As Emilie Gaillard states, "[a] silent and dominant juridical paradigm is present: juridical reciprocity. By virtue of this paradigm every right entails a corresponding obligation." E. Gaillard, 'Avoiding the Tragedy of Human Rights: How Complex Thought May Open the Way to Recognising Human Rights for Future Generations', in Bos and Düwell, *supra* note 6 at 43. However, Elina Pirjatanniemi concludes from the fact that for example the Finnish Constitution unilaterally declares that protection of nature and environment is the responsibility for all, without saying a word about the rights of nature or the environment that it is possible to form legal obligations without having identifiable right-holders. Pirjatanniemi, *supra* note 37 at 22.

[57] Let me propose here the profane civil law example of the future contract (forward transaction).

[58] Agius, *supra* note 32 at 20.

[59] Ibid.

[60] Raffensperger, *supra* note 1 at 4.

### The Unforeseeable Preferences of the Future Generations

Another problem in connection with conceptualizing the rights of the future generations is that right-holders can usually express choices and preferences.[61] This problem differs from the problem of lack of representation, which is a substantive law problem about the extent of rights rather than solely a procedural one. Here, the question should be carefully phrased in order to find meaningful answers. If, for instance, one asks "how could one know the needs of generations sometime in the remote future?" one might have difficulty answering. But the narrower question "what are the minimum requirements of the future generations?" leads to more easily achieved and reasonable answers, because from the basic physical, psychological and social features of the human race one can conclude what future generations will need for sustenance and a dignified life.[62] Cook and Taylor also suggest taking into account not only the most necessary physical conditions of life such as water, clean air and biodiversity, but also their security and conditions of fair and equitable economic development.[63]

Finally, Tremmel asserts that the minimum set of rights of future generations will be at once detailed and concrete enough in order to achieve meaningful implementation.[64] However, this should not simply occur in a national constitution, but rather, in the spirit of the integration principle, should be integrated into the entire body of national law in a systematic way.

## FUTURE GENERATION INSTITUTIONS FOR THE FACILITATION OF INTERNATIONAL LEGAL OBLIGATIONS TOWARDS FUTURE GENERATIONS

### Inappropriate Governance

The administrative system of the State that is otherwise primarily aimed at implementing international and national legislation seems to be inefficient in designing and running programs for intergenerational justice or deciding individual cases by striking the right balance between the interests of present and future generations. On the surface there is the inherent short-termism of political systems and the silo thinking of administrative offices. On deeper analysis, it can be established that the government is a central part of those social-psychological processes that hide, deny

[61] Cook and Taylor, *supra* note 1 at 152.

[62] Understood here as also a life that is not deprived of the possibility of continuing to cultivate certain customs, habits, joys, and challenges that their antecedents had.

[63] Cook and Taylor, *supra* note 1 at 152.

[64] Tremmel, *supra* note 8 at 55.

and soften the threatening messages about the international science[65] of the system of ecological degradation.[66]

## *New Tasks for Old Institutions in Order to Implement Future Generations' Laws*

For better implementation of the existing legal constructions of intergenerational justice, new kinds of institutions, preferably separate and independent from governments, are needed. There are basically two institutional solutions in connection with intergenerational justice: (1) to establish clear rights and responsibilities for future generations through an existing state body as part of its portfolio or (2) to create a new organization focusing solely or mostly on intergenerational justice. For the first solution, the most obvious candidates are the constitutional court and the state auditor's office, because they are, at least in theory, independent from the government and have considerable power to control governmental operations. In addition, in the first solution there is a strong moral-constitutional background to intergenerational justice topics, while in the second situation the budgetary and financial aspects of the topic of intergenerational justice are reflected. As an in-between solution, in several States a parliamentary council has been created for future generations, involving prestigious and committed members of parliament, although with their portfolios they tend not to have the ability to focus fully on the intergenerational justice portfolio, thereby diminishing the value of this institutional solution.

Additionally, parliamentary committees are sites of political compromises in which, according to practical experience, intergenerational justice has a tendency to be on the losing side. When existing institutions undertake tasks related to intergenerational justice, it is important to solidify this part of their mandate, for example by writing a strong future generations chapter into their by-laws or guiding establishing documents. These documents should contain the substantial responsibilities of the given body, for instance the systematic evaluation of the time dimensions of relevant decision-making procedures, reporting and networking. On the institutional-procedural side, measures that seem to be necessary include appointing a future generations deputy, co-chair or other officials and departments within the organization to perform the tasks that need more flexibility and new approaches. Examples include watchdog activities, networking, think-tank functions, advocacy, public campaigns and capacity-building programs.

65 Intergovernmental efforts, such as the 2005 Millennium Ecosystem Assessment (MA), the serial Global Environmental Outlook from UNEP/UNEA (GEOs), the reports of the IPCC, or the reports, comments and messages of private, but highly prestigious, groups such as the Club of Rome, the Balaton Group, the World Future Council and the Oxford Martin Commission.

66 S. Fülöp, 'Clarification and Networking: Methodology for an Institution Representing Future Generations', in Gy. Bándi (ed.), *Environmental Democracy and Law* (European Law Publishing 2014) 159–161.

### European Institutions with the Potential to Become Intergenerational Institutions

Sheridan made a wide survey of international organizations in which a future generations institution (FGI) could possibly be located.[67] The EU seems to be the most likely candidate with its strong constituent principles, deep and detailed environmental and other relevant branches of legislation and, not least, a relatively easy procedure for creating the new institutions necessary for the operation of the Union.[68] The scientific policy network of the European Environmental Agency (EEA) would also be an asset for an FGI within the EU. European institutions including the UNECE, the CoE (both of which are pan-European rather than clearly and geographically European only), and the OECD (where the bulk of members are from Europe are committed, and expect, to act for intergenerational justice).[69]

Additionally, several previously mentioned organizations already have strong commitments to future generations in their respective by-laws and other constituting and/or ruling documents, as well as the professional and institutional capacity and, in some cases, even the legal authority to stand up for the rights or interests of the future generations. It is another question whether any of these organizations has the political will to form a FGI – but times change. Until then, Sheridan would not exclude an environmental NGO network either.[70] Specifically, he mentions the European Environmental Bureau,[71] which has a large network of national environmental NGOs (in which 'environmental' means many things, ranging from general democracy issues to gender issues), a well-staffed office in Brussels, and several decades of history of professional work and prestige. Further, in speaking about NGO networks, several others could be imagined as playing an FGI role, especially if they are able and willing to form and operate a functioning network for the purpose of institutional representation of the future generations.

### Forming Brand New Institutions for Intergenerational Justice

For a new future generations organization, an independent committee seems to be a good solution, because sustainability is inherently multidisciplinary, even transdisciplinary, and there must be strong links with other stakeholders and with the rest of the

[67] Sheridan, *supra* note 10 at 161–166.
[68] Ibid.
[69] Ibid.
[70] In harmony with Pirjatanniemi, who says that in intergenerational equity cases "the scope of those having standing should be widened." See Pirjatanniemi, *supra* note 37 at 21.
[71] Ibid. at 166.

society.[72] A smaller, say three-person, committee could enhance the personal prestige of the participants, but hides the danger of personal rivalries. Finally, appointing an individual would be risky because of his/her personal biases, however benign, and unavoidable professional limitations. Naturally, a good staff can counterbalance such disadvantages.

Individual officials include guardians and ombudspersons, but naturally they should also be understood together with their offices.[73] Guardians seem to have a narrower scope of activity, mostly focused on the representation of the interests of future generations with an advocacy type of work only. An ombudsman can use a much wider set of tools, starting from his/her basic tasks of handling community complaints concerning environmental (or intergenerational) conflicts, the advocacy function and several other functions mostly in connection with collecting information about the best relevant scientific results and informing society about them. This might be called a 'bridging function'. According to Anstee-Wedderburn, the ombudsman has a more investigative and advisory role at an international level, monitoring compliance with international agreements, investigating alleged violations and publicizing findings.[74] Naturally, this latter task makes sense at a national level too; however, a more assertive, possibly confrontational positioning of the new institutions seem to be unnecessary, even counterproductive for the time being.

### *General Features of Future Generations Institutions*

Based on a wide survey of existing solutions and suggestions, Anstee-Wedderburn reaches the conclusion that the representative of the future generations should act as an international advocate and moral persuader, raise public awareness, generate public debate, signal the importance of considering the long-term effects of actions, and in general work to enhance intergenerational solidarity.[75] Sheridan ranked the features of FGIs in terms of the power they can exercise, such as advisory, consultative, cooperative, decision-making, determinative and even authoritative functions.[76] Some authors would wish to see as much administrative or constitutional power in the hands of the future generations organization.[77] Veto power seems to be a very plausible solution for protecting the rights of the future generations against obviously selfish and short-sighted investments and other steps taken by our

[72] K. Töpfler et al., *Transgovernance: The Quest for Governance of Sustainable Government* (Institute for Advanced Sustainability Studies 2011).

[73] The first Hungarian Ombudsman for Future Generations has not issued any statements in his own name, but always in the name of the FGO Office – not out of some special modesty, but with the aim of lending more prestige to the outputs of a compound, multidisciplinary staff of the highest available professional level and also to underline the network nature of the office.

[74] Anstee-Wedderburn, *supra* note 1 at 52.

[75] Ibid. at 69.

[76] Sheridan, *supra* note 10 at 168.

[77] Tremmel, *supra* note 8 at 45.

decision-makers that endanger the natural resources. However, this could turn out to be a double-edged sword.

If the majority of society is not convinced of the rightfulness of the veto, the machinery of public democracy could easily turn against the FGI, especially because it is new and has not yet achieved a fixed place in the State's system. It is easier to give the power of veto to older, powerful and highly prestigious institutions such as the constitutional court or state auditor. Anstee-Wedderburn also considers it desirable to have a strong, "more inquisitorial" representative for future generations, but realizes after careful analysis that this power of enforcement is unlikely to be given.[78] Therefore, she continues, "any international representative of future generations will be limited to performing an educative, consultative and advocacy role."[79] It is arguable that an authoritative power is not only impossible but also undesirable. By using administrative (or quasi-administrative) power, an FGI would become 'part of the system' and would be forced to use the logic of the system, with all its procedural constraints, professional limitations and even biases.

In legal systems different from the European system, ombudspersons might be appointed by the government and enjoy only a relative independence.[80] An exception is the Austrian provinces in Europe, where independence from the government counts as one of the most important features of ombudspersons, since their major role is control of the government's administrative work and influence over its legislative or legislative drafting work in the case of parliamentary acts. Other traits are common between the European and the American approaches, such as evaluation and advice concerning governmental policies and decisions typically made in order to ensure that certain disadvantaged social groups do not suffer harm. In these systems, ombudspersons are often tasked with writing reports – to the parliament, the government, the general public or to all of these – and serving as liaisons or mediators between the government and the group they represent. On occasion, they are also given standing to sue. Human rights ombudsmen usually have quasi-judicial roles too, serving as investigators of citizens' complaints. In connection with this function, they have investigative powers and access to relevant information, usually with no constraints, in contrast to other legal subjects.[81]

The legitimacy of FGIs derives from direct election or appointment by the parliament or the president/head of state. Even a wide NGO network,[82] especially at the international level, can achieve significant prestige, enough in principle to perform meaningful tasks in connection with future generations. Whatever form it takes, the legitimacy of an FGI at the international or national level is strongly enhanced by several very prestigious new international legal documents. The 2013 Report of the UN

78 Anstee-Wedderburn, *supra* note 1 at 37.

79 Ibid.

80 Raffensperger, *supra* note 1 at 15.

81 Ibid.

82 See Tremmel, *supra* note 8 at 45.

Secretary-General on 'Intergenerational Solidarity and the Needs of Future Generations', the 2014 John Knox report on the interrelationship of human rights and sustainable development, and the 2015 'Road to Dignity by 2030' – the SDGs – have all reached the level of making concrete suggestions about ways of achieving sustainable development, and intragenerational and intergenerational justice.[83]

As a summary of many sources in the literature, the common features of the FGIs are as follows. First, with regard to the values they represent, there are several key features, including: (1) long-termism rather than short-termism, intergenerational solidarity – interconnecting the past, present and future generations as builders of our human civilization who continue to inherit and bequeath the resources of the Earth in what is hoped to be an endless process; (2) system thinking, integration, multilevel (global, regional, national and local) and multidisciplinary networking; and (3) independence and legitimacy ensuing from, *inter alia*, transparency, accountability, accessibility and effectiveness.

Second, in terms of the tasks and functions the FGIs perform, there are further key features, including (1) watchdog functions – being alert for the negative, dangerous tendencies in social and economic developments, supporting whistle-blowers, seeking remedies and sanctions against those who recklessly endanger natural resources; (2) investigation functions – upon complaints of local communities or NGOs, with wide access to any kind of administrative files and other data (e.g. expert opinions), interrogation, fact-finding with the help of special experts, making suggestions, and calling the attention of decision-makers and the wider public; (3) advocacy functions – arguing for better laws and legal practices that consider the interests of both the present and future generations and strike the right balance, but under all circumstances avoiding any plans and decisions that significantly harm the interests of any of the stakeholders without their consent; (4) remedy functions – typically through mediation, but sometimes with the right to sue for the interests of the future generations in administrative, civil, criminal or petty offense cases; (5) bridging functions – learning the most relevant messages from the science and conveying them to society, performing awareness-raising and capacity-building activities; (6) think-tank functions – in the field of scarcely researched issues that are important for sustainable development, examining and recommending solutions for sustainability;[84] (7) networking functions with the general public – using civil input, such as workshops, conferences and NGO meetings, as key elements in selecting and implementing FGI policies, applying the legal tools of public participation, and enhancing the level of public participation with various capacity-building tools; (8) further international and national networking functions with all other relevant stakeholders – such as churches, trade unions, pressure groups and expert groups;

[83] Fülöp, *supra* note 6.

[84] The two major think-tank programs of the HFGO were sustainable local communities and alternative indicators.

and (9) media outreach functions – in hard copy and in electronic formats, as well as through community media.

In addition, Sheridan calls attention to a point that is seldom raised, although it is of great practical importance: a FGI seeks to make a difference, meaning that "it shall add something that is not happening at present."[85] Indeed, a FGI should not be a mere third instance environmental administrative body and should not copy the methodology of any existing silos of the present administrative system. The methodological independence of an FGI ensues from its system thinking and systematic clarification of environmental and other intergenerational conflicts, as well as its networking with all the stakeholders.[86]

## A SYSTEMATIC APPROACH TO LAW ENFORCEMENT WORK OF INSTITUTIONS FOR INTERGENERATIONAL JUSTICE

### *Several Approaches, Similar Results in the Literature*

After having detailed many high-quality future generations laws and specialized institutions or parts of institutions that are committed to implementing them, it is necessary to concentrate on the operation of those institutions that might ensure that the new institutions will perform their new tasks effectively. Suggestions from the literature tend in one direction: system thinking, systematic work. Tladi determined the essence or normative content of sustainable development in the following way: it is about the "questions relating to the right thing to do in the face of global problems."[87]

One could probably add that these problems are not only global – in the sense of wherever they are handled – but also systemic in nature. Environmental problems themselves represent a system;[88] moreover, when societies try to tackle them they should put the system of ecological threats into the context of other systems. Sustainable development is mainly about reconciling the contradictions between social and economic interests and environmental interests. As Tladi himself says later, international efforts to protect the environment, starting from the 1880 Behring Sea Fur Seals dispute between the US and the UK, have always been concerned with constraining certain economic activities.[89]

Jávor sees at least a minimal opportunity in the existing institutional systems to fairly represent the rights (needs and interests) of future generations:

[85] Fülöp, *supra* note 66 at 61.
[86] Ibid.
[87] Ibid. at 11.
[88] Rockström, *supra* note 58.
[89] Tladi, *supra* note 2 at 13.

> [e]nvironmental regulations, sustainable development strategies, development plans, institutions to control financial equilibrium (such as national banks and audit offices) of states or the opportunities available for civil society to represent basic social values outside traditional political decision-making processes are on the whole suitable to set the delicate balance between the interests of future and present generations.[90]

Attention should be called to the phrase 'on the whole', since it means that there is a need to seek holistic, systematic solutions. At the same time, this necessitates a harmonized, concerted operation of the elements Jávor listed as part of the system that might ensure intergenerational justice.

### *Systematic Work at the EU level*

In the same spirit, but even more concretely, Agius highlights that the EU can achieve sustainable development only if it (a) sets out a vision of what is sustainable – this has to be thoroughly discussed with all stakeholders and agreed at a nearly unanimous level, (b) improves its methods of policy-making, first of all with tools of informed decision-making and ensuring a better coherence between policies, and (c) addresses several non-sustainable social and economic trends, such as climate change, energy, social exclusion and poverty, natural resource management, land use and transport.[91] Later he adds more concretely that the EU and its Member States should use governance tools in order to achieve sustainable development, such as mechanisms, processes and institutions through which citizens and organizations articulate their interests, exercise their rights, meet their obligations and mediate their differences.[92] Unfortunately, he asserts, in the world at present, inhuman governance prevails that fails to meet basic human needs, discriminates against and denies rights to women, fails to protect the environment and to safeguard the interests of future generations, makes no progress in abolishing war, and cannot get close to creating "transnational democracy."[93]

### *An Empty Niche at the National Level*

As already noted, the core reason for the present inability of administrative systems to handle issues with broader timespans lies in silo thinking in designing and operating the various administrative bodies responsible for several aspects of environmental protection and of other branches of administration relevant for future generations.[94]

90 B. Jávor, 'Introduction', in Jávor and Rácz, *supra* note 1 at 7.
91 Agius, *supra* note 32 at 20.
92 Ibid. at 26.
93 Ibid.
94 Such as cultural heritage, city planning, construction, energy systems, water management or land protection.

While in fact the management and protection of major natural resources is a very complex professional task, these compartmentalized authorities seldom seek close cooperation with each other – indeed, they tend to compete for resources and for the attention of the media and the politics – let alone performing the long-term interdisciplinary planning and implementation thereof.[95]

Unlike present governmental work, the system nature of the work of FGIs should be mirrored in their scope of activity, in the material sense (all kinds of plans, policies, strategies, programs, legislative acts, individual administrative decisions and other kinds of act should be monitored and influenced), in the territorial sense (global and regional, if possible, but in all cases national and local matters) and in the personal sense (state, economic and civil stakeholders should be partners of the FGI).[96]

### *Inherent System Nature of the Concept of Sustainable Development*

If it appears that the system approach is the most important trait, rather a *differentia specifica* of FGIs, the concept of sustainable development should be revisited. Marie-Claire Cordonier Segger offers a definition of sustainable development that also mirrors the system nature of the tasks facing us,[97] and at the same time includes the joint task of ensuring the proper living standards of future generations and the survival of the present generations and our civilization as such:

> Development can be defined as a collective process of change toward improvements in quality of life for human beings and their communities, and sustainability can be seen to refer to the need for development to be integrated, socially, economically and environmentally sound, oriented to the long-term, and hence, *able to last*.[98]

This argument overcomes the black and white approach used by many who have discussed whether the principle of sustainable development and the principle of intergenerational justice has already reached the status of obligatory international legal norms. Cordonier Segger establishes that, although it is not clear that sustainable development has as yet the character of a customary norm of international

[95] S. Fülöp, 'The System Nature of Environmental Law', in A. Boiko (ed.), *Human Rights and Environment in a New Ukraine: In Honour of Prof. Svitlana Kravchenko* (Lviv 2015); S. Fülöp, 'Wilderness Protection in Hungary', in K. Bastmeijer (ed.), *Wilderness Protection in Europe: The Role of International and National Law* (Cambridge University Press 2016).

[96] Sheridan, *supra* note 10 at 160.

[97] As a contrast to the system nature of sustainable development, several authors underline that human rights lack this system approach; rather, they "concentrate on the interests of particular, identifiable human beings." Pirjatanniemi, *supra* note 37 at 11, 17; J. Knox, *Report of the Independent Expert on the Issue of Human Rights Obligations Relating to the Enjoyment of Safe, Clean, Healthy and Sustainable Environment* (United Nations 2013).

[98] M.-C. Cordonier Segger, 'What Is Sustainable Development Law? A CISDL Concept Paper', in Cordonier Segger and Khalfan, *supra* note 1 at 1 (emphasis added).

law, this does not mean that it is void of all meaning or normative value.[99] Continuing this line of thought, it can be said that even if very few countries and other international stakeholders hold themselves to this principle, even if no one is able or willing to obey it, sustainable development could be the most obvious method for legal actors as a result of common-sense striving based on the survival instinct of any individual or community.

### *The System of International Legal Principles*

In 2006, when the coming economic, social and, beneath the surface, environmental decline was not foreseen, scientists doubted that the principle of intergenerational justice could be accepted as binding and brought into harmony with basic principles of international law such as the intragenerational justice principle and the principle of the sovereignty of States to use their natural wealth.[100] Again, it could be added that even within those frameworks of international law there are no rights without responsibility and there is no such thing as clear right without accompanying responsibilities of the right-holder. Similarly, the rights of poor nations to international support, for instance, should be handled together with the responsibility to spend their resources and donations in a sustainable way. Also, the right of a State to freely manage its natural resources cannot be separated from the responsibility to honor intergenerational justice.

### *Global Networking*

Taking into consideration that the majority of ecological and resource-management problems are inherently global in nature, no organization with the task of representing future generations can be successful without a global network in which it can exchange experiences, synchronize policies and cooperate on programs. Agenda 21, when calling on States to prepare their national strategy for sustainable development and referring to intergenerational justice in close connection, also warns them of the importance of cooperation with each other and with international organizations.[101] This trend is reinforced in Agenda for 2030, where a whole chapter is spent on this issue.[102] Cordonier Segger also highlights the inherent networking elements of sustainable development: "it inspires cooperation, coherence and innovative governance systems."[103] Social innovation in the present age means first of all of abandoning linear or pyramid structures in favour of networks.[104]

99 Ibid. at 2.
100 Cook and Taylor, *supra* note 1 at 156.
101 Paragraph 8.7, cited in ibid.
102 Goal 16.
103 Cordonier Segger, *supra* note 98.
104 M. Castells, *The Rise of the Network Society* (Wiley-Blackwell 2010).

## CONCLUSION

Forty-four years ago, the Stockholm Declaration, Principle 1 declared that humans bear a solemn responsibility to protect and improve the environment for present and future generations.[105] The international community has committed itself to the cause of intergenerational justice, not only in words but also by creating a very strong global institution, the UNEP, with strong legal commitments as well. Twenty years later, in Rio, the heads of States reinforced and further developed the principles of sustainable development, accepted basic obligatory international laws and (a year prior) ensured a strong financial basis for better implementation through the GEF. Yet, the status of the environment has drifted to the edge of a system of catastrophes, and the efforts of the global community have turned out to be relatively ineffective. Humankind must find new paths: it should rephrase the principles of environmental protection and renew its global, national and lower-level institutions.[106] Attention should be paid to the most successful segment of the world: the multinational, globalized economy. This sector has developed effective communication networks, recognizes no borders (similarly to environmental pollution) and successfully interconnects localities across the world. Environmental protection is a must at this time and carries the highest urgency for the sake of future generations and for the survival of the present civilization. The example of climate change raises the specter of social and environmental calamities, such as city air not fit to breathe, pandemics in connection with loss of biodiversity, famine caused by poisoning of fertile soils, and desertification. A well-designed, effectively facilitated environmental monitoring, protection and adaptation network should be put in place with the strongest possible global institutions, adaptive and interconnected local communities,[107] and States that are willing to prevent these developments. This network could be called a network of intergenerational justice, but it would be better to call it simply the network of survival of our culture.

As far as connections between the laws of intergenerational justice and their implementation are concerned, prima facie it should be agreed that weak laws lead to weak implementation. However, time is scarce, and institutions that are willing

[105] The United Nations Declaration on Human Environment, adopted in Stockholm (1972).

[106] Decleris claimed for a new system of public values based on sustainability, justice and economical life, with the support of quick development of the sustainability sciences. However, he counts very much on the State to control the markets and reform itself as a strong, moral, intelligent and effective State ruled by an open, just and effective legal system. M. Decleris, *The Law of Sustainable Development, Report to the Commission* (2000). Bándi notes, however, that the present States are currently very far from the ideas of Decleris. As a way of bolstering this aim, he proposes the ILA New Delhi Declaration of Principles of International Law Relating to Sustainable Development, 2 April 2002, which were reinforced in 2012 by the same body. Ibid.

[107] In the same spirit, Bándi claims that sustainable development and the principle of subsidiarity are closely related and mutually reinforcing concepts. Bándi, *supra* note 28 at 202.

and able to consider the rights (interests and needs) of future generations should not wait until these laws are perfected. It has been seen that State responsibilities are less than rights, and also that the needs and interests of future generations are vague concepts. But there are legal scholars who suggest a brave, benign interpretation of these concepts that would let our moral convictions prevail. This chapter agrees with these sentiments as a method for preserving and protecting the rights of future generations.

# PART III

# Law and Policy Innovations for Intergenerational Justice

*Constitutional Challenges and Innovations for Future Generations*

# 8

# Sustainability in European Constitutional Law

*András Jakab*

Now civilisations, I believe, come to birth and proceed to grow by successfully responding to successive challenges. They break down and go to pieces if and when a challenge confronts them which they fail to meet.[1]

Sustainability, as compared to the rule of law, human rights, sovereignty or democracy, is a relatively new constitutional key concept.[2] It is mentioned explicitly more and more in constitutional discourses, and – even more importantly – it helps to reconstruct a number of current constitutional debates under one conceptual umbrella.[3] Sustainability comprises different responses to long-term social challenges which cannot efficiently be responded to via democratic mechanisms. Democratic mechanisms are based on election terms and are, consequently, structurally short-sighted. By

[1] A.J. Toynbee, *Civilization on Trial* (Oxford University Press 1948) 56.

[2] For critical remarks and advice on literature, I am grateful to the participants of the 'Sustainability as a Legal Principle' workshop at the IVR XXVIth World Congress of Philosophy of Law and Social Philosophy in Belo Horizonte (Brazil) on 22 July 2013, of the conference 'Model Institutions for a Sustainable Future' in Budapest on 25 April 2014 and of the workshops at the Centre for Social Sciences of the Hungarian Academy of Sciences on 11 September 2014 and 26 March 2015, and of the *Dienstagsrunde* on 27 July 2015 at the Max Planck Institute for Comparative Public Law and International Law, further to Carlino Antpöhler, Armin von Bogdandy, Lídia Balogh, Attila Bartha, Eszter Bodnár, Péter Cserne, Giacomo Delledonne, Róbert Iván Gál, Matthias Goldmann, Rainer Grote, Michael Ioannidis, Béla Janky, Klára Katona, Alexandra Kemmerer, Lando Kirchmair, Zsolt Körtvélyesi, Károly Mike, Pier Pigozzi, Ekkehart Reimer, András Simonovits, Pál Sonnevend, Ákos Szalai, Joerg Chet Tremmel, Leonie Vierck and David Wineroither. This chapter is based on a research project funded by the Hungarian Scientific Research Fund OTKA (K112900).

[3] On doctrinal reconstruction as one of the main tasks of legal scholarship see A. von Bogdandy, 'The Past and Promise of Doctrinal Constructivism' (2009) 7 *International Journal of Constitutional Law* 364–400; A. Jakab, 'Seven Role Models of Legal Scholars' (2011) 2 *German Law Journal* 757–784, esp. 758–765.

'European constitutional law', this chapter refers to both the primary law of the EU and domestic constitutional documents.[4]

This first part of this chapter sketches the nature and types of sustainability challenges that contemporary societies face, with a special focus on Europe. The second part demonstrates possible constitutional responses to these challenges. Finally, the third part summarizes the main argument of the chapter.

A short preliminary terminological remark – this chapter uses the expression 'sustainability' instead of the more popular 'sustainable development'.[5] The concepts are almost identical, the former being slightly less ambitious in that sustainability does not require an improvement, it merely requires that a situation does not deteriorate.

## SUSTAINABILITY CHALLENGES

The moral instinct and common sense of most people would likely suggest that sustainability should be aimed for in every society. One approach that could be used to justify sustainability would be to refer to the idea of distributive justice (more precisely, intergenerational justice);[6] another approach would be to refer to the long-term interests of the political community. Instead of the first, moral philosophical approach, this chapter employs the second, rather pragmatic one in the hope of minimizing overheated emotional debates. Sustainability requires nothing more than following the *long-term* interest of the political community. 'Long' basically means anything that is beyond the usual four- or five-year election period that is the primary time span of democratic politicians.

There are several factors that might endanger sustainability. For example, the EU Sustainable Development Indicator (prepared by Eurostat on the basis of the 2006 EU Sustainable Development Strategy) consists of 106 individual indicators (some of them being composite themselves) including education, public health, fertility rate, different aspects of environmental protection and public debt, to name

[4] For more details on the concept of democracy see A. Jakab, *European Constitutional Language* (Cambridge University Press 2016) ch. 9.

[5] See e.g. "Sustainable development means that the needs of the present generation should be met without compromising the ability of future generations to meet their own needs . . . It aims at the continuous improvement of the quality of life and well-being on Earth for present and future generations." Sustainable Development Strategy (2006) European Council DOC 10917/06 para. 1.

[6] For excellent overviews of the intergenerational justice approach see A. Gosseries, 'What Do We Owe to Next Generations?' (2001) 35 *Loyola of Los Angeles Law Review* 293–355; L.B. Solum, 'To Our Children's Children: The Problems of Intergenerational Ethics' (2001) 35 *Loyola of Los Angeles Law Review* 163–234; A. Gosseries and L.H. Meyer (eds.), *Intergenerational Justice* (Oxford University Press 2009); L. Meyer, 'Intergenerational Justice', in E.N. Zalta (ed.), *Stanford Encyclopedia of Philosophy* (Stanford 2008) http://plato.stanford.edu/entries/justice-intergenerational/ accessed 30 November 2017.

just a few.[7] Composite indicators imply 'weak sustainability', meaning the (at least partially) mutual substitutability of the different types of capitals (environmental, demographic, etc.).[8] This chapter refers only to the aspects considered the most pressing and that have constitutional relevance.[9]

## *Environmental Challenge*

The concept of sustainability stems from *environmental protection* or, more precisely, from eighteenth-century German forest economics literature.[10] The originally ethical,[11] later economical, concept was later widely dispersed in legal thinking by UN documents in the twentieth century.[12] It is usually defined in environmental protection as the prohibition of the use of natural resources in ways which would impede the satisfaction of comparable future needs (typically through exhaustion or through pollution).[13] For the present chapter, this is not primarily relevant and is mentioned only because it shows the origin and the multifaceted nature of the concept. As there are numerous analyses of this aspect of sustainability (and the fundamental scholarly opinion is probably the least divided on these issues, thus the debates are more of a technical nature), the rest of the chapter will concentrate rather on other types of challenges.

[7] For further aggregated sustainability indicators see A. Grunwald and J. Kopfmüller, *Nachhaltigkeit*, 2nd edn. (Campus Verlag 2012) 81–86.

[8] On the concept in general see E. Neumayer, *Weak versus Strong Sustainability: Exploring the Limits of Two Opposing Paradigms*, 4th edn. (Edward Elgar 2013).

[9] For another usual classification (ecological, economic and social components) see e.g. G. Beaucamp, *Das Konzept der zukunftsfähigen Entwicklung im Recht* (Mohr Siebeck 2002) 19–31 with further references.

[10] A. Glaser, *Nachhaltige Entwicklung und Demokratie: Ein Verfassungsrechtsvergleich der politischen Systeme Deutschlands und der Schweiz* (Mohr Siebeck 2006) 42; D. Klippel and M. Otto, 'Nachhaltigkeit und Begriffsgeschichte', in W. Kahl (ed.), *Nachhaltigkeit als Verbundbegriff* (JCB Mohr 2008) 39–59 (esp. 44–45 referring to Hans-Carl von Carlowitz, *Sylvicultura Oeconomica* [Leipzig 1713]).

[11] For an analysis of the ethical issues of environmental sustainability see H. Jonas, *Das Prinzip Verantwortung* (Frankfurt am Main 1979). On Jonas from a legal perspective see J. Schubert, *Das 'Prinzip Verantwortung' als verfassungsstaatliches Rechtsprinzip: rechtsphilosophische und verfassungsrechtliche Betrachtungen zur Verantwortungsethik von Hans Jonas* (Nomos 1998); O. Fuchs, 'Le principe responsabilité de Hans Jonas, Contribution à l'étude de la médiation juridique des rapports de l'homme à la nature' (2006) 2 *Revue de la recherche juridique – droit prospectif* 1027–1045.

[12] On the history of the concept of 'sustainable development' in UN documents since the 1970s see U. Beyerlin, 'Sustainable Development', in R. Wolfrum (ed.), *Max Planck Encyclopedia of Public International Law* (Oxford University Press 2017) marginal numbers 2–6 www.mpepil.com/ accessed 21 June 2019; K. Gehne, *Nachhaltige Entwicklung als Rechtsprinzip* (Mohr Siebeck 2011) 11–71.

[13] See e.g. the Brundtland Commission's definition: sustainable development is 'development that meets the needs of the present without compromising the ability of future generations to meet their own needs'. G.H. Brundtland et al., *Our Common Future: Report of the World Commission on Environment and Development* (Oxford University Press 1987) 43.

### *Fiscal Challenge*

Accumulating public debt redistributes the resources of future generations amongst members of the present generation,[14] and democracies actually do tend to accumulate debts.[15] It is normally more popular to spend than to save money, and people like to enjoy public services but they do not like to pay taxes to finance them.[16] And democracies, by their nature, tend to engage in popular things. As a matter of fact, the more competitive a democracy, the more likely its public deficit will grow, as in a hard competition parties feel forced to (promise to) buy votes in order to win.[17] Another explanation for public debt in democracies is that they tend to be less centralized, meaning that their politics are fragmented.[18] If politics are fragmented then every political group will try to spend the common money on its own electorate and/or supporters.[19] The more fragmented politics are (for example, coalition governments instead of one-party governments, second chambers with budgetary powers, etc.), the more likely it is that public debt will grow.[20]

Public debt, however, is not necessarily a bad thing, and Lorenz von Stein even famously stated that "a state without public debt is either doing too little for the future or it requires too much from the present."[21] Public debt on its own does not contradict the principle of sustainability, unless it reaches an excessive level. Unsustainable public debt leads to sovereign default (for example, Mexico 1982, Russia 1998 and Argentina 2001), which normally coincides with a banking crisis (no more loans for the private economy, thus no more private investments), an economic crisis (flight of foreign capital, combined with decreasing internal demands) and a currency crisis (either in an attempt to repay debts the state is printing its own money at an excessive

[14] G. Haverkate, *Verfassungslehre* (Beck 2007) 324–328; J.M. Buchanan, 'The Constitution of Economic Policy' (1987) 77(3) *American Economic Review* 243–250. On the economic nature of public debt and on its future effects see G. Brennan, 'The Political Economy of Public Debt' (2012) 23(3) *Constitutional Political Economy* 182–198.

[15] J.M. Buchanan and R.E. Wagner, *Democracy in Deficit: The Political Legacy of Lord Keynes* (Academic Press 1977) 98–105.

[16] P. Kirchhof, *Deutschland im Schuldensog. Der Weg vom Bürgen zurück zum Bürger* (C.H. Beck 2012) 5.

[17] J. Cullis and P. Jones, *Public Finance & Public Choice*, 3rd edn. (Oxford University Press 2009) 327–328.

[18] A. Alesina and R. Perotti, 'The Political Economy of Budget Deficit', *IMF Staff Papers* 42/1995, 1–31.

[19] A. Velasco, 'Debts and Deficits with Fragmented Fiscal Policymaking' (2000) 76(1) *Journal of Public Economics* 105–125; R. Ricciuti, 'Political Fragmentation and Fiscal Outcome' (2004) 118(3–4) *Public Choice* 365–388.

[20] L.P. Feld, 'Nachhaltige Finanzverfassung aus ökonomischer Perspektive', in W. Kahl (ed.), *Nachhaltige Finanzstrukturen im Bundesstaat* (Mohr Siebeck 2011) 56.

[21] L. von Stein, *Lehrbuch der Finanzwissenschaft*, 2nd edn. (FA Brockhaus 1871) 666.

rate, which leads to inflation,[22] and/or the economic crisis or the cancellation of the repayment of debts in foreign currency lead to the devaluation of the domestic currency in relation to foreign currencies).

What is excessive, meaning what is likely to lead to sovereign default, is, however, not entirely clear. Some say sovereign debt is excessive if it endangers credibility on the credit market, referring to whether the creditors believe it to be too high.[23] There is definitely a psychological element in financial sustainability (think of situations giving rise to bank runs), but this should not beg the actual question of when creditors should *rightly* believe a public debt to be too high.

Even if the somewhat better question 'when should creditors rightly believe that a public debt is too high?' is asked, the question might still be the wrong one. The mere number (usually the GDP ratio of the public debt) is not conclusive on whether public debt is sustainable. Looking at the latest global financial crisis, it can be seen that those European countries which suffered the most from it (such as Ireland or Spain) had considerably lower public debt (in GDP ratio) than Japan or the US. But in these countries, just as in the whole of the Eurozone, the internal mechanisms were missing which would have been necessary to tackle public debt issues and which are present in the US or in Japan (for example, fiscal union or efficient European intervention mechanisms into Member State budgetary matters).[24] On the one hand, there were no effective methods to enforce the purely numerical Maastricht criteria (public debt, deficit and inflation) after a country joined the Eurozone, but on the other hand, these numbers on their own did not predict whether an economy was sustainable.

Further factors which should also be considered are the origin of public debt (whether it was spent on investment or whether it was spent for non-productive purposes; pensions belong to the second category but in some other cases separating the two is not easy at all), the demographic perspectives of a country (for example, whether the workforce is shrinking or expanding),[25] the interest rate at which new loans are given to the State (for example, the debt interest is actually decisive, and the actual debt is only relevant as far as it can predict the payable interests),[26] the growth of the

22 This is a real threat only if central banks are under the influence of the government. On the benefits of independent central banks, see A. Alesina and R. Perotti, 'The Political Economy of Budget' Deficits, *IMF Staff Papers* 42/1 (1995) 26.

23 E. Reimer, 'Nachhaltigkeit durch Begrenzung der Staatsverschuldung – Bilanz und Perspektiven', in Kahl, *supra* note 20 at 147–166, esp. 147.

24 C. Cottarelli, 'Sovereign Debt Crisis: Why in Europe and Not Elsewhere?' (2012) 47(2) *Intereconomics* 74–75.

25 C. Wyplosz, 'Fiscal Policy: Institution versus Rules' (2005) 191(1) *National Institute Economic Review* 64–78.

26 D. Velculescu, 'Some Uncomfortable Arithmetic Regarding Europe's Public Finances', *IMF Working Paper* 10/177, 2010 http://core.ac.uk/download/pdf/6671906.pdf accessed 30 November 2017. If the payable interest rate is more than the total income then we are dealing with terminal debt; see N.K. Frederiksen, 'Long-Term Fiscal Indicators: Sustainability versus Terminal Debt Constraints', Danish Ministry of Finance Working Paper 14/2005.

economy (a growing economy supports higher public debt ratio than a shrinking one)[27] and who controls debt bonds (whether it is national or foreign creditors).

Public debt is thus an important, but incomplete, indicator of fiscal sustainability. One cannot give a simple number that shows the threshold of unsustainability, and there are other factors which should be considered to make the judgment lack transparency. There is no *simple* final fiscal sustainability formula.

### *Demographic Challenge*

Two hundred years ago, overpopulation was feared.[28] In the twentieth century, the population of the world grew from 1.6 billion to 6.1 billion.[29] Today, the situation is rather the opposite: low fertility rates and longer life expectancies have led to a shrinking and ageing population in Europe,[30] and it is predicted that in several decades most of the world will suffer from this social problem.[31] Despite slight recent improvements in the countries with the lowest fertility rates,[32] the problem seems to persist.

Long life expectations are due to better and free health services;[33] low fertility rates are due to secularization (and, consequently, a growing emphasis on individual responsibility), education which allows for new life options (and for family planning), the medical advancement of contraception methods, the fact that children have become a financial burden instead of a financial investment, government-run

[27] Sustainable debt is when the growth rate of the economy is greater than the interest rate of the debt; see H.H. Zee, 'On the Sustainability and Optimality of Government Debt', *IMF Working Paper* 87/83, 1–25, 2 http://papers.ssrn.com/sol3/papers.cfm?abstract_id=885013 accessed 30 November 2017; C. Cottarelli and L. Forni et al., 'Defaults in Today's Advanced Economies', *IMF Staff Position Note* SPN 10/12, 5 September 2010.

[28] T.R. Malthus [under the pseudonym Joseph Johnson], *An Essay on the Principle of Population* (1798).

[29] N. Eberstadt, 'The Demographic Future. What Population Growth – and Decline – Means for the Global Economy' (2010) *Foreign Affairs* 54–64, 54.

[30] Half of the world's population lives in countries (all European countries, but not the US) in which the fertility rate is below 2.1 births per woman (replacement level), see ibid. at 55, 62; F.-X. Kaufmann, *Schrumpfende Gesellschaft: Vom Bevölkerungsrückgang und seinen Folgen* (Suhrkamp 2005).

[31] D. Dorling, *Population 10 Billion: The Coming Demographic Crisis and How to Survive It* (Constable 2013).

[32] J.R. Goldstein et al., 'The End of "Lowest-Low" Fertility?' (2009) 35 *Population and Development Review* 663–699. Explanations for the improvement of the situation range from the realization of formerly postponed children (J. Bongaarts and T. Sobotka, 'A Demographic Explanation for the Recent Rise in European Fertility' [2012] 38 *Population and Development Review* 83–120) through the increasing level of socioeconomic development (M. Myrskylä et al., 'Advances in Development Reverse Fertility Declines' [2009] 460 *Nature* 741–743) until more comprehensive gender equity (J. Feyrer et al., 'Will the Stork Return to Europe? Understanding Fertility within Developed Nations' [2008] 22[3] *Journal of Economic Perspectives* 3–22).

[33] Global life expectancy rose from 30 to 65 in the twentieth century; see Eberstadt, *supra* note 29 at 55.

general pension systems (no need for children when we grow old),[34] and the imbalance between the partial emancipation of women in work life and the lack of their emancipation in private life.[35]

The human working force is expected to shrink even more than the actual population, as longer life expectancies do not necessarily mean longer working years.[36] In order to avoid this, European countries can try to drive fertility rates higher, extend the active working years of the elderly, encourage immigration,[37] and invest in education, as fewer people can only produce the same if they are more productive and better educated.[38] Demographic challenges lead to probably the most difficult questions of constitutional theory, as these concern the nature of the political community (as seen in later parts of this chapter).

## POSSIBLE CONSTITUTIONAL RESPONSES TO THE SUSTAINABILITY CHALLENGE

This section will first show why the response to the sustainability challenges has to be a constitutional one, and then examine one by one possible constitutional solutions (general principles, fundamental rights, institutional rules on elections and referendums, and rules on public finance) which might contribute to tackling these challenges better.

### *Why Does the Response Have to Be Constitutional?*

Constitutions have the task of providing the rules of the political game, to establish taboos that politicians might otherwise perpetrate.[39] Structurally, democratically

[34] "A PAYGO system may serve as insurance against not having children and as an enforcement device for ungrateful children who are unwilling to pay their parents a pension." H.-W. Sinn, 'The Pay-as-You-Go Pension System as Fertility Insurance and an Enforcement Device' (2004) 88 *Journal of Public Economics* 1335.

[35] Grunwald and Kopfmüller, *supra* note 7 at 46; K. Leisinger, 'Bevölkerungspolitik', in *Online Handbook Demografie*, 2007 www.berlin-institut.org/online-handbuchdemografie/bevoelkerungspolitik/bevoelkerungspolitik-als-entwicklungspolitik.html accessed 30 November 2017. B. Hobson and L. Sz. Oláh, 'Birthstrikes? Agency and Capabilities in the Reconciliation of Employment and Family' (2006) 39(3–4) *Marriage and Family Review* 197–227; B. Hobson, S. Fahlén, and J. Takács, 'Agency and Capabilities to Achieve a Work–Life Balance: A Comparison of Sweden and Hungary' (2011) 18(2) *Social Politics* 168–198.

[36] Eberstadt, *supra* note 29 at 62.

[37] J. Henseler, 'Mobilität und Migration in der Einwanderungsgesellschaft und der dazu gehörigen sozialpädagogischen Fragestellung' (Habilitation Thesis, University of Erfurt 2006) www.db-thueringen.de/servlets/DerivateServlet/Derivate-11077/henseler.pdf accessed 30 November 2017. On the integration of immigrants see W. Kahl, 'Nachhaltigkeit, Migration und Integration', in Kahl, *supra* note 10 at 242–264.

[38] Eberstadt, *supra* note 29 at 62, 64.

[39] For more details on the function of constitutions, see A. Jakab, 'On the Legitimacy of a New Constitution: Remarks on the Occasion of the New Hungarian Basic Law of 2011', in

elected politicians are focused on short-term (election-period) consequences, and they are likely to go for the easy solution which buys votes for them.[40] In order to prevent them from being seduced, constitutions ought to bind them, like Ulysses was bound to the mast so he could resist the sirens.[41] This is an admittedly paternalistic solution (constitutions in general can be considered as paternalistic tools) since it indirectly also prohibits voters from voting in favour of the wrong solutions, because their judgment is not trusted on certain issues.[42]

Traditionally, constitutions have only contained sustainability provisions concerning the protection of the environment,[43] but during the last decade (mainly due to the financial crisis) financial or economic sustainability clauses have also become more common,[44] and with the aggravation of the European demographic situation, it is very likely that demographic sustainability provisions will also increasingly appear in constitutions. The constitutional requirements following from different types of sustainability provisions can possibly contradict each other, as stronger environmental protection requires *ceteris paribus* lower production, whereas financial sustainability requires higher production levels. There are currently no constitutional tests on how to balance or weigh these different aspects, which can partly be explained by the novelty of the issue, partly by general factual uncertainties about what actually leads to sustainability and partly by moral disagreement about the relative weight of these aspects. The latter two factors also inhibit the development of such a test in this chapter; however, below is a sketch of substantive constitutional arguments on the topic with some institutional recommendations.

The most natural guardians of financial sustainability, such as financial markets, cannot, unfortunately, do the job the population would like to be done: financial markets 'penalize fiscal profligacy in a discontinuous fashion and only with

M.A. Jovanović and Đ. Pavićević (eds.), *Crisis and Quality of Democracy in Eastern Europe* (Eleven 2012) 61–76 http://ssrn.com/abstract=2033624 accessed 30 November 2017.

40 W.A. Niskanen, 'The Case for a New Fiscal Constitution' (1992) 6(2) *Journal of Economic Perspectives* 13–24.

41 J. Elster, *Ulysses and the Syrens: Studies in Rationality and Irrationality* (Cambridge University Press, Maison des Sciences de l'Homme 1984) 36–37, 87–96.

42 For constitutions as tools to protect future generations, see A.P. Gosseries, 'The Intergenerational Case for Constitutional Rigidity' (2014) 27(4) *Ratio Juris* 527–539, esp. 536–538; A.P. Gosseries, 'Constitutions and Future Generations' (2008) 2 *The Good Society* 32–37.

43 See e.g. A. Touzet, 'Droit et développement durable' (2008) 2 *Revue de droit public et de la science politique* 453–488.

44 For a large number of such clauses see J.C. Tremmel, 'Establishing Intergenerational Justice in National Constitutions', in J.C. Tremmel (ed.), *Handbook of Intergenerational Justice* (Edward Elgar 2006) 187–214; P. Häberle, 'Nachhaltigkeit als Gemeineuropäisches Verfassungsrecht: eine Textstufenanalyse', in Kahl, *supra* note 10 at 180–203; J. Schubert, *Das 'Prinzip Verantwortung' als verfassungsstaatliches Rechtsprinzip: rechtsphilosophische und verfassungsrechtliche Betrachtungen zur Verantwortungsethik von Hans Jonas* (Nomos 1998) 231–247.

significant lags', and very often first when society is already in an extreme stage.[45] The fact that a constitutional response to the sustainability challenges is needed does not mean, however, that traditional (lawyerly) constitutional courts should have a major role in sustainability issues. The chapter will return to this seemingly paradoxical institutional problem later.

### General Principles

Probably the most obvious, but technically least sophisticated, way to deal with such an issue is to insert a general principle into a constitution. The principle can be conceptualized as a 'general principle of intergenerational justice' (which might be viewed as a subcategory of the constitutional principle of social justice or *Sozialstaatlichkeit* – if this is adopted by the respective constitution) or as a 'general principle of sustainability'. As to the former, in the Preamble of the 1946 Bavarian Constitution there is a general precursor of this idea, without explicitly mentioning the word 'sustainability': "firmly intending moreover to secure permanently for future German generations the Blessing of Peace, Humanity and Law." As to the latter, the Preamble of the EU Charter of Fundamental Rights can be used as an example: "[the EU] seeks to promote balanced and sustainable development" and "[e]njoyment of these rights entails responsibilities and duties with regard to other persons, to the human community and to future generations," or in the context of the protection of environment, Article 11 of TFEU with an explicit reference to a general principle of 'sustainable development'.[46] A similarly general principle is to be found in Art. 2(2) of the Swiss Constitution: "(2) [The Swiss Confederation] shall promote the common welfare, sustainable development, internal cohesion and cultural diversity of the country."[47]

With enough doctrinal effort, one can deduce from the vaguest constitutional provisions the solutions for the most concrete problems.[48] In this case, however,

[45] X. Debrun, D. Hauner, and M.S. Kumar, 'Independent Fiscal Agencies' (2009) 23(1) *Journal of Economic Surveys* 44–81, esp. 45, 51.

[46] "Environmental protection requirements must be integrated into the definition and implementation of the Union policies and activities, in particular with a view to promoting sustainable development." See B. Sjåfjell, 'The Legal Significance of Article 11 TFEU for EU Institutions and Member States', *University of Oslo Faculty of Law Research Paper* No. 2014-38 http://ssrn.com/abstract=2530006 accessed 30 November 2017.

[47] There are further provisions on environmental sustainability in Art. 2(4), 73 and 104 Swiss Constitution; see A. Petitpierre-Sauvain, 'Que fait le développement durable dans la Constitution fédérale?', in A. Auer et al. (eds.), *Aux confins du droit* (Helbing & Lichtenhahn 2001) 553–567.

[48] Between 1992 and 1997, in lack of a fundamental rights catalogue, the Polish Constitutional Court decided most cases based on a simple 'rule of law clause' of the constitution; see B. Banaszak and T. Milej, *Polnisches Staatsrecht* (Beck 2009) 11–12. Activist examples deducing content from extremely vague concepts such as 'human dignity' or 'general personality rights' can be collected from the case law of most European constitutional courts.

such a deduction is not possible. On the one hand, this area of law is too doctrinally and judicially undeveloped to build a coherent conceptual system and, even more importantly, it is unlikely to be substantially developed either. This is the case because constitutional lawyers and constitutional courts (with some exceptions)[49] tend to be deferential if a case is about complicated financial issues, the implications of which they normally do not entirely grasp.[50]

### *Fundamental Rights*

It is possible to generate the impression that the language of rights encourages the overuse of resources, that it necessarily has a short time span, and that it does not consider the wider concepts of the common good. This is, however, not true – the language of rights is a *language* which can be used for very different purposes. There are impressive doctrinal attempts to express sustainability issues in the emotionally (and legally) strong language of rights.[51] These attempts use lawyerly finesse and sophistication to conceptualize sustainability issues as rights instead of environment protection, such as discussing the right to a healthy environment,[52] or – in an even more radical turn – the rights of (wild) animals.[53]

For the purpose of financial and demographic sustainability, new right-bearers can be introduced and will be considered under the headings of suffrage for children and the rights of future generations. Or, as shown in the last point in this part of the chapter, it is possible to introduce new rights, and new limitation tests for existing rights, specifically concerning the issues of financial intergenerational sustainability.

[49] Cf. A. Sajó, 'How the Rule of Law Revolution Killed Hungarian Welfare Reform' (1996) 1 *East European Constitutional Review* 31–41; C.M. Akrivopoulou, 'Striking Down Austerity Measures: Crisis Jurisprudence in Europe' (June 2013) Int'l J. Const. L. Blog 25 www.iconnectblog.com/2013/06/striking-down-austerity-measures-crisis-jurisprudence-in-europe/ accessed 30 November 2017. In all these cases, constitutional courts protected the social rights of those who had already been born, and it is questionable whether they would have been ready to do so for generations who would be born in the future.

[50] The judicial deference resulting from factual (financial) uncertainty is a part of what the ECHR calls 'margin of appreciation'; see A. Legg, *The Margin of Appreciation in International Human Rights Law* (Oxford University Press 2012) 17–66. Other courts behave similarly without conceptualizing this issue so openly.

[51] D. Birnbacher, 'What Does It Mean to Have a Right?' (2009) 9(4) *Intergenerational Justice Review* 128–132, 128. We translate interests into rights in order to make them stronger; see M. Tushnet, *The Constitution of the United States: A Contextual Analysis* (Hart 2009) 188.

[52] See e.g. A. Postiglione, 'Human Rights and the Environment' (2010) 14(4) *International Journal of Human Rights* 524–541; A. Boyle, 'Human Rights and the Environment: Where Next?' (2012) 23(3) *European Journal of International Law* 613–642, esp. 641–642.

[53] C.R. Sunstein and M.C. Nussbaum (eds.), *Animal Rights: Current Debates and New Directions* (Oxford University Press 2004).

### New Right-Bearers I: Suffrage for Children

The electoral system in modern democracies only allows those citizens who have reached a certain age to vote, and children are excluded from this right. It also means that their interests are less represented than those of retired people,[54] which makes the emergence of structurally biased social security systems more likely (and in fact they are biased).[55] By giving suffrage to children – so the argument goes – this structural bias could be corrected,[56] as the population is growing older and it is consequently more interested in shorter-term goals.[57] By granting a stronger say to children, it is also likely that the social security system (including social benefits) for families will be more favorable, which could encourage them to have more children,[58] an issue especially pressing in countries with extremely low fertility rates like Germany, Japan and Hungary.[59]

Besides the justification with reference to demographic sustainability (or intergenerational justice) there are also arguments for the suffrage of children based on democracy. As democracy is considerably more established as a constitutional

54 Suffrage of children in order to avoid gerontocracy: P. van Parijs, 'The Disenfranchisement of the Elderly, and Other Attempts to Secure Intergenerational Justice' (1998) 27(4) *Philosophy and Public Affairs* 292–333. More and more of these pensioners will have no children: this also makes the probability of the consideration of children's interests lower; see ibid. at 315.

55 P.E. Peterson, 'An Immodest Proposal: Let's Give Children the Vote' (1992) 121(4) *Daedalus* 151–174; R.I. Gál, E. Szabó, and L. Vargha, *Children Cost to Parents, the Old Cost to Taxpayers: An Application of National Transfer Accounts and National Time Transfer Accounts* (Budapest Demographic Research Institute 2013).

56 R.H. Pantell and M.T. Shannon, 'Improving Public Policy for Children: A Vote for Each Child' (2009) 9(4) *Intergenerational Justice Review* 139–144.

57 See van Parijs, *supra* note 55 at 293 and 298 on the unavoidably short-term self-interest of the elderly and on the empirical evidence that age-related self-interest affects voting behaviour (with further references).

58 Cf. A.H. Gauthier and J. Hatzius, 'Family Benefits and Fertility: An Econometric Analysis' (1997) 51(3) *Population Studies* 295–307, 302 (explaining that a 25 percent increase in the benefits given to the first two children raises fertility by 0.01 percent per woman in the short run and 0.07 percent in the long run) and K. Hinrichs, 'Do the Old Exploit the Young? Is Enfranchising the Young a Good Idea?' (2002) 43(1) *European Journal of Sociology* 35–58, 48 stating that pronatalist policies are hardly effective with regards to their original aims, but they normally do reduce the risk of child poverty (with further references). For an optimistic view on the question, stating that it *is* possible to improve low fertility rates through public policies, J.M. Hoem, 'The Impact of Public Policies on European Fertility' (2008) 19(10) *Demographic Research* 249–260, with further references. For the sake of testing the argument we suppose in this paper that pronatalist policies *do* positively influence fertility rates.

59 R. Aoki and R. Vaithianatham, 'Is Demeny Voting the Answer to Low Fertility in Japan?' (2009) *Center for Intergenerational Studies, Institute of Economic Research, Hitotsubashi University*; B. Schanda, 'Családi választójog – alkotmányjogi képtelenség vagy a fenntartható demokrácia biztosítéka?' (2010) 57(10) *Magyar Jog* 608–611; J. Fröhlich, 'Alapkérdések a családi választójog vitájában' *Pázmány Law Working Papers* 2011/20; P. Kirchhof, *Das Gesetz der Hydra* (Droemer 2006) 184–185. For a wider overview including the French, Austrian, Belgian and Swiss debates see I. Rupprecht, *Das Wahlrecht für Kinder. Verfassungsrechtliche Zulässigkeit und praktische Durchführbarkeit* (Nomos 2012) 26–44.

principle in the constitutional discourse than sustainability or intergenerational justice (indeed, many doubt that that latter two are constitutional principles at all),[60] justifications based on democracy seem to be stronger legal arguments. The history of democracy can basically be reconstructed as an ever-broadening suffrage. Originally only the white, the male and the rich had suffrage, and step by step this was broadened to include the poor, the colored and female citizens.[61] Children are also citizens; they are also part of the 'people' from which all state power is supposed to stem.[62] Today, children have remained the only major group of citizens that does not have representation in the legislature.[63]

A further possible argument for the suffrage of children would be to state that children also pay taxes, and consequently they should also have suffrage.[64] This is, however, a weak argument. Many foreigners (including tourists) pay taxes in every country, and they do not have suffrage either; connecting suffrage to taxes is an outdated view which would (if turned around) lead to disenfranchising poor people.

There are basically three ways to achieve some form of child suffrage: (1) children themselves exercise the right to vote (for example, by lowering the age limit to 16, 14 or even to 0); (2) their parents can receive proxy votes for them; or (3) children collect their unexercised votes until they reach the minimum age and then they use all their 'stored' votes at once. The second and third solutions can be combined with the first one.

There is, in theory, also a fourth way – granting the right to vote to the parents who would not simply substitute their children but have the extra suffrage on their own rights *because* they have children.[65] This fourth option is, however, in open

[60] See W. Kluth, 'Demographischer Wandel und Generationengerechtigkeit' (2009) 68 *Veröffentlichungen der Vereinigung der Deutschen Staatsrechtslehrer* 247–289, 282 (denying the constitutional nature of the requirement of intergenerational justice).

[61] A. Jakab, 'Full Parliamentarisation of the EU without Changing the Treaties. Why We Should Aim for It and How Easily It Can Be Achieved', *Jean Monnet Working Papers* 2012/3, 4–13 http://papers.ssrn.com/sol3/papers.cfm?abstract_id=1958111 accessed 30 November 2017.

[62] Hinrichs, *supra* note 59; L.M. Peschel-Gutzeit, 'Unvollständige Legitimation der Staatsgewalt oder: Geht alle Staatsgewalt nur vom volljährigen Volk aus?' (1997) *Neue Juristische Wochenschrift* 2861–2862.

[63] Hinrichs, *supra* note 59 at 40; K. Löw, 'Kinder und Wahlrecht' (2002) *Zeitschrift für Rechtspolitik* 448–450.

[64] R.H. Pantell and M.T. Shannon, 'Improving Public Policy for Children: A Vote for Each Child' (2009) 94 *Intergenerational Justice Review* 139–143, 141.

[65] Between the two World Wars, each father of four children or more received an extra vote in the French colonies Tunisia and Morocco; see A. Toulemon, *Le suffrage familial ou suffrage universel intégral* (Sirey 1933) 121–122; A.M. Simon-Holtorf, *Geschichte des Familienwahlrechts in Frankreich (1871 bis 1945)* (Peter Lang 2004) 168–169. For the similar Belgian system (combining it with financial and educational aspects for extra votes) from 1893 until 1919, see L. Dupriez, *L'organisation du suffrage universel en Belgique* (Larose 1901); M. Mauranges, *Le vote plural, son application dans les élections belges* (Larose 1899); J. Barthélémy, *L'organisation du suffrage et l'expérience belge* (Giard & Brière 1912); L. de Briey, A. Héraut, and E. Ottaviani, 'On Behalf of Children? Plural Voting System in Belgium from 1893 to 1919' (2009) 9 *Intergenerational Justice Review* 144–145.

conflict with the equality of suffrage, a basic tenet of modern democracies, so it will not be considered further. Besides this, it would also open up the debate for further weighing systems (more suffrage for those who pay more taxes, who have higher education etc.) which have all been tried and rejected in legal history. For both of these reasons, proposals suggesting fractional votes for children are not considered in this chapter.[66]

There is an obvious paradox about establishing any of these measures, nicely explained by Claus Offe: if there is a majority to vote for the children's suffrage then there is no need for it, and if there is no majority then it is unclear how to introduce it.[67] For the sake of the argument, this problem will be ignored until later in this chapter.

### Option 1: Lowering the Minimum Age for Suffrage

In most European countries, the minimum age required for suffrage is 18, but in Austria this has recently been lowered to 16, just like in certain German *Länder*.[68] There are proposals to lower this to 14 in some countries (or even lower if the child can express his/her will to vote in front of an authority),[69] but this has not yet been implemented. Besides the general democracy arguments mentioned above, the arguments for such a change range from synchronizing the age of criminal liability with the minimal age of suffrage,[70] to the full realization of children's rights,[71] to the

66 A. Rehfeld, 'The Child as Democratic Citizen' (2011) 633 *The Annals of the American Academy of Political and Social Science* 141–166, 158 ("Imagine that upon turning 12, a child received 1/7 of a vote, with an additional 1/7 added for every year after [at 18 they have a full vote]").

67 C. Offe, 'Zusatzstimmen für Eltern. Ein Beitrag zur Reform von Demokratie und Wahlrecht?', in Evangelische Akademie (ed.), *Zukunft wählen – Zusatzstimmen für Eltern?* (Evangelische Akademie 1993) 1–26. This kind of objection can be brought against most legislative reform proposals, though.

68 For further examples outside of Europe with age limits of 16 (Brazil, Cuba, Somalia, Nicaragua) or 17 (East Timor, Indonesia, Sudan, North Korea), see R.I. Gál, A. Gulyás, and M. Medgyesi, 'Intergenerációs alkotmány' (2011) 5 *Nemzeti Fenntartható Fejlődési Tanács Műhelytanulmányok* 25. For proposals lowering the voting age to 16 in the UK and the US, see A. Folkes, 'The Case for Votes at 16' (2004) 1 *Representation* 52–56; D. Hart and R. Atkins, 'American Sixteen- and Seventeen-Year-Olds Are Ready to Vote' (2011) 633 *The Annals of the American Academy of Political and Social Science* 201–222.

69 W. Gründinger, 'Wer wählt, der zählt', in Stiftung für die Rechte zukünftiger Generationen (ed.), *Wahlrecht ohne Altersgrenze? Verfassungsrechtliche, demokratietheoretische und entwicklungspsychologische Aspekte* (Oekom 2008) 21–52. Before that time, the parent can exercise the suffrage for the child. For 14 as the lowest acceptable age of suffrage see H. Meyer, 'Wahlrechtsgrundsätze', in J. Isensee and P. Kirchhof (eds.), *Handbuch des Staatsrechts der Bundesrepublik Deutschland. Band III*, 3rd edn. (C.F. Müller 2005) 543–604. For a proposal to abolish age limits in general (without any formal procedure for expressing the will to vote), M. Weimann, *Wahlrecht für Kinder: Eine Streitschrift* (Beltz 2002) 1–23.

70 Rupprecht, *supra* note 60 at 209.

71 Weimann, *supra* note 70 at 1–23.

denial of maturity or intellectual capacity as a precondition of suffrage.[72] A general reference to children's rights is unconvincing since fundamental rights can be limited if they conform to the tests of rights limitation (in this case the proportionality test), the first step of which is to establish the rationale for the limitation. Synchronizing age limits does not really seem a convincing argument *on its own* either, since for different legal possibilities (such as being elected president or senator, or being able to sell properties) most legal orders require very different ages, because there are different rationales behind the different age limits.

The question, rather, is whether there is a rationale behind having a minimum of age for suffrage and what age this rationale would require to be set as a minimum age of suffrage. Throughout history, there seems to have been a tendency to have lower and lower age limits. The question about the 'right' minimum age is not a strictly constitutional one, as introducing a minimum age of 40 would probably violate most international human rights instruments, but the question as to whether 14, 16 or 18 is the right one seems to be left to political decision. The real issue is, however, whether there is a rationale at all behind any age limit. The most obvious answer would be to say that the rationale is that voters should have a minimum level of maturity (implying intellectual capacity). This would, however, be an unsatisfying answer because the right to vote is in fact not based on intellectual capacities in any democracy. If it was, then a good proportion of the mature population should be excluded from suffrage (and possibly substituted with intelligent teenagers). Introducing a minimum level of intellectual capacity as a precondition of suffrage leads to the situation in which there is no reason why this level should not be higher and higher, leading to the exclusive suffrage of a handful of professors in each country. Such a system would, however, result in governments which would protect the interests of professors in the name of the public interest.[73]

The fact that the majority of children would not want to vote or that they are easily influenced (other possible counter-arguments against the suffrage of children) can also be applied to many mature voters, yet no one proposes their exclusion. Another possible counter-argument is that lowering the age limit increases the number of voters who are actually not paying taxes, so it would lead to higher public debt again. As we noted above, however, sustainability arguments have a weaker legal force than democracy or fundamental rights arguments, so this would not outweigh the argument for the suffrage of children.

The equality of suffrage is based on the moral equality of citizens and not on their equal intellectual capacity. The only argument which seems strong enough is self-protection: adults protect children from their own bad choices. Just as in many

[72] S. Leece, 'Should Democracy Grow Up? Children and Voting Rights' (2009) 9(4) *Intergenerational Justice Review* 133–139, 133 ("excluding children from the franchise normally rests explicitly on the premise that political authority should be knowledge-based").

[73] See the masterful critique of Plato by R.A. Dahl, *Democracy and Its Critics* (Yale University Press 1989) 52–79.

Continental European contract laws children are not allowed to sell their properties (under market price) *as long as they are children*, adults can also protect them constitutionally from possibly making bad political choices *as long as they are children*. This paternalistic argument seems to be sufficient for a temporary limitation of the right to vote. But it is very difficult to explain why *nobody* can exercise this right for them. In the current electoral systems, it is possible to use two conceptualizations to describe the legal situation:[74] (1) children do not have suffrage at all as long as they are children (this would contradict the principle of the moral equality of citizens) or (2) children have suffrage but they are not allowed to exercise it as this is in their own best interest as long as they are children. The key question thus becomes whether it should be possible for someone (in practice for the parents) to exercise the right to vote for the children.

**Option 2: Proxy Votes by Parents (Demeny Voting)**

Parents voting vicariously for their children is often referred to as Demeny Voting, as it was (also) proposed by demographer Paul Demeny in 1986.[75] This means that children do have suffrage but they cannot exercise it themselves and their parents exercise it for them vicariously. The situation is similar to contract law in that parents make contracts in the name of and for their children. With this solution, the 'one man one vote' principle is not violated. Similar solutions are known in the UK and in France, where relatives can vote on one's behalf if one is unable to attend the elections, but this substitution can only happen if one already has the right to exercise suffrage.[76] Sometimes proxy voting is referred to in the literature as 'family suffrage', but I am going to use the expression 'suffrage for children' as this more precisely expresses the actual doctrinal suggestion. In most European countries, this proposal has a political color, namely a conservative one, except for Germany, where you find supporters of this idea from all over the political spectrum.[77]

Possible counter-arguments are manifold. First, some objections concern the directness of votes, such as whether someone can exercise the right to vote for someone else at all. Certain legal acts (marriage, executing a will) can only be done personally, and votes – so the objection goes – are similar. Second, others concern the equality of votes, as parents in many cases would cast two votes. Third, some

[74] On the undertheorized nature of the question in political (and constitutional) theory, see F. Schrag, 'The Child's Status in the Democratic State' (1975) 3(4) *Political Theory* 441–457, 443: "Children are a nuisance to most adults; they are a particular nuisance to the democratic theorist who wishes to exclude them from having a voice in the direction of the policy with as much vehemence as he wishes to include every adult (except, of course, felons, the insane, the mentally retarded, and aliens)."

[75] P. Demeny, 'Pronatalist Policies in Low-Fertility Countries: Patterns, Performance and Prospects' (1986) 12 *Population and Development Review* (supplement) 335–358.

[76] Called *proxy voting* in the UK; see Representation of the People Act 2000, section 12(1). In French law, it is called *vote par procuration*; see Code électoral, article 147 bis.

[77] Van Parijs, *supra* note 55 at 311.

object to the implied presupposition that parents would act in the interest of their children. Finally, some doubt whether there can be any solutions for the technical details (conflict between parents, etc.).

**Argument 1: Directness.** A usual answer to the first objection is to refer to a blind person for whom someone else is marking the ballot paper. This answer can, however, be countered with reference to the fact that the blind person can give a direct order about the vote, whereas children cannot do so. Another answer could be to refer to postal votes. This, again, is not really a convincing answer, as postal votes express the will of the voters, whereas in the case of children they normally would not express any such wish. A third answer would be to refer to doubts concerning the requirement of directness of votes in a democracy. We can do this either by using comparative law arguments (such as in the UK and France) or by referring to the fact that this requirement was historically introduced only to avoid the sale of votes (purposive interpretation of the concept)[78] or by referring to the general system of democracy, with the words of Jane Rutherford: "Proxies are a common system for delegating the right to vote. In fact, the entire system of democracy can be seen as giving elected representatives proxies for their constituents."[79] As a matter of fact, any of the three arguments seems a strong counter-objection.

**Argument 2: Equality.** The objection concerning equality is probably the strongest of all the concerns.[80] There are two strategies to counter it. The first one is to admit that Demeny Voting would indeed encroach upon the principle of equality but to state that the universality of elections is more important.[81] In this case a conflict between two principles is shown, that of equality of suffrage and that of universality of suffrage, and the principle of universality is judged to be more

[78] D. Krebs, 'Wider die amputierte Wahl. Physiker und Philosophen als Hebammen einer echten Demokratie', in Stiftung für die Rechte zukünftiger Generationen (ed.), *Wahlrecht ohne Altersgrenze? Verfassungsrechtliche, demokratietheoretische und entwicklungspsychologische Aspekte* (Oekom 2008) 267–300, 283.

[79] J. Rutherford, 'One Child, One Vote: Proxies for Parents' (1998) 82 *Minnesota Law Review* 1463–1525, 1502.

[80] Even though doctrinally different, *in practice* it means that certain citizens have more than one vote, which downgrades all other citizens in comparison to them; see R. Wernsmann, 'Das demokratische Prinzip und der demographische Wandel. Brauchen wir ein Familienwahlrecht?' (2005) 44 *Der Staat* 43–66, 55–56, 66. Some go even further and suggest that it would be such a grave breach of the constitutional principle of democracy that not even a constitutional amendment could introduce it; see M. Pechstein, 'Wahlrecht für Kinder?' (1991) 3 *Familie und Recht* 142–146, 146; W. Schreiber, 'Wahlrecht von Geburt an – Ende der Diskussion?' (2004) *Deutsches Verwaltungsblatt* 1341–1348; W. Schroeder, 'Familienwahlrecht und Grundgesetz' (2003) *JuristenZeitung* 917–922. The latter argument is a very local (German) objection, though, probably inapplicable to other European countries. For an argument *contra* this objection see H. Quintern, *Das Familienwahlrecht* (Lit 2009) 167–235. Under US law, a constitutional amendment would be necessary to introduce it; see the detailed analysis by R.W. Bennett, 'Should Parents Be Given Extra Votes on Account of Their Children?' (2000) 94 *Northwestern University Law Review* 503–565.

[81] Krebs, *supra* note 79 at 267–300.

important as it is more directly connected to the principle of democracy. The universality – so the argument goes – is logically prior, as it concerns the 'whether', whereas the equality only concerns the 'how'.[82]

The second strategy is to deny the encroachment upon the principle of equality and to stick strictly to the doctrinal reasoning: everyone only has one vote, and parents merely exercise votes vicariously for their children. This second reasoning is probably what is behind the existing French and UK (adult) proxy voting systems, and from a strictly legal point of view it also sounds more convincing than the first answer.

**Argument 3: Interests.** The objection concerning doubts about whether parents would actually cast their votes in the interests of their children is a weak one: "Arguing that parents cannot act as their children's representative because they might abuse their position becomes absurd in comparison to all the other powers parents already have over their children."[83] Parents represent their children in court and they receive and spend the subsidies for their children.[84] It can also be legitimately asked: if not the parents, then who else could represent them?[85]

**Argument 4: Technical details.** The objection concerning technical details (especially which parent should exercise the right to vote) is also unconvincing. As a matter of fact, there are a number of proposals with different technical solutions.[86] Referring to the technical details as an objection just begs the real question of whether it should be introduced. All technical details (such as separated or divorced parents, step-parents, disappeared parents and children in state custody) are logically secondary and by no means insurmountably difficult questions.

### Option 3: Storable Votes

A further possibility to give suffrage to children without facing the objections applicable to proxy votes is to apply so-called storable votes[87] This would mean that

82 Ibid. at 281.

83 S. Olsson, 'Children's Suffrage: A Critique of the Importance of Voters' Knowledge for the Well-Being of Democracy' (2008) 16 *The International Journal of Children's Rights* 55–76.

84 U. Hermann, *Ökonomische Analyse eines Kinderwahlrechts* (Dissertation, Freie Universität Berlin 2010) 204.

85 Krebs, *supra* note 79 at 274.

86 Van Parijs, *supra* note 55 at 312–313 (listing different technical proposals concerning who can exercise the vote [with references]: only the father, only the mother, until 10 years the mother and then the father, fathers for their sons and mothers for their daughters, half vote to each parent, father for first child and mother for second [or the other way around]). According to F. Reimer, 'Nachhaltigkeit durch Wahlrecht? Verfassungsrechtliche Möglichkeiten und Grenzen eines Wahlrechts von Geburt an' (2004) *Zeitschrift für Parlamentsfragen* 322–339, every parent should only be able to exercise one additional vote, and the parents should agree who exercises the vote for the first child (in case of a lack of agreement, neither of them can exercise it).

87 For the concept see A. Casella, 'Storable Votes' (2005) 51 *Games and Economic Behavior* 391–419.

children collect their uncast votes until they reach 18 and then they can cast four or five votes at once. In this way, nobody would exercise their votes for them but they could still keep all of their votes. This ensures that the moral equality of all citizens (including children) is abided and avoids the problems associated with parents vicariously exercising their children's votes, thus no vote would be lost.

Such a suggestion is, however, conceptually flawed. A vote at a parliamentary election is not capital that you can collect and store like money, but it is an *act of deciding about somebody (or a group of people) at a certain time*. The concept of storable votes was developed as a decision-making technique for expressing the intensity of preferences by minority groups about *certain issues* and not about setting up a decision-making organ.

It would probably also mean – as a conceptual side effect – that everybody should have the possibility of not going to ballots in order to collect his/her vote for future elections. Or one could even take a 'vote loan' and exercise one's future votes immediately. Why not?

### Conceptual Side-Effects

The actual social purpose of suffrage for children only necessitates active suffrage (the right to vote), but for the sake of conceptual coherence, some also suggest passive suffrage for children (the right to be elected).[88] A further conceptual side effect is that if suffrage for children is accepted then – with the same arguments – suffrage for (mentally) disabled people must also be accepted. As a matter of fact, such arguments have already been used by the ECtHR for mentally disabled people but not for children,[89] so this could be turned around. A conceptual side effect of the suffrage of mentally disabled people is the suffrage of children – at least in the form of children voting for themselves without any age limit, since proxy voting is not suggested in the discourse of mentally disabled people.

### Practical Consequences for the Sustainability Challenge

All the above could lead to the conclusion that suffrage for children should be introduced. As a matter of fact, from the perspective of the conceptual coherence of democracy, suffrage for children (more precisely proxy votes, possibly combined with lowering the minimum age for suffrage) seems more favorable than the current situation. But for the actual issue of this chapter, namely sustainability, the situation is much less clear.[90] To put it shortly, it seems to be a *useful but actually not decisive* change.

88 Gründinger, *supra* note 70 at 31. Cf. Rupprecht, *supra* note 60 at 15 (calling such proposals 'not serious').

89 *Alajos Kiss* v. *Hungary*, judgment of 20 May 2010, no. 38832/06.

90 On the inconclusiveness of statistical models on the practical effects see also A. Goerres and G. Tiemann, 'Kinder an die Macht? Die politischen Konsequenzen des stellvertretenden Elternwahlrechts' (2009) *Politische Vierteljahresschrift* 50–74.

On the one hand, even children can be outvoted with or without suffrage for children if the ageing population is large enough, and on the other hand, if we accept the premise of self-interest then children (or their parents) will only be interested in sustainability as long as they are alive.[91] This means that the time span will be longer, but structurally it just delays the problems for a few decades.[92] According to model counting in Germany, as an example, the amount of child subsidies would be only 10 percent higher than it is currently.[93] Depending on the voting model (probabilistic vs. median voter model), pensioner voters will take over the electoral system either in 2016 or in 2030.[94] Both of these data are very disappointing from a sustainability perspective.

Besides these problems, there is also a questionable implied presupposition about voting behavior behind every suggestion on suffrage for children, according to which 'citizens are following their own interest' (instrumental voting). This presupposition has been criticized both from an epistemological point of view ('citizens do not know and cannot actually know what their own best interest is') and an anthropological point of view ('citizens very often vote against their personal interest, if they think that it is the interest of the political community').[95] A further possible, rarely discussed, argument against children's suffrage is that they often behave deliberately against the parents' will.[96] If this is true, a question that will be left open here, then it raises further doubt about the actual impact of children's suffrage on demographic sustainability.

Suffrage for children might thus be useful (and doctrinally probably more coherent than the current exclusion), but for the purposes of this chapter is definitely not a decisive suggestion, so the search for further constitutional solutions must continue. Given the practical difficulty of introducing such a change, the fierce ideological debates and the paradox by Claus Offe as shown above, it is probably not worth fighting – from the perspective of sustainability – for this change at all. Instead, intellectual time and effort should be concentrated on constitutional solutions which serve the purpose of sustainability more efficiently.

[91] For example, they might want child subsidies to be very high *now*, even if this causes long-term debt for future generations; see Goerres and Tiemann, *supra* note 91 at 58.

[92] T. Krieger, 'Generationenergerechtigkeit und das "Wahlrecht von Geburt an" – kritische Anmerkungen aus Sicht der Public-Choice-Theorie', in Stiftung, *supra* note 70 at 301–330.

[93] Hermann, *supra* note 85 at 138. The usual distortion of electoral systems favouring educated and rich people because they are more likely to vote also applies to parents voting for their children; see ibid. at 125.

[94] Ibid. at 202; H.-W. Sinn and S. Übelmesser, 'Pensions and the Path to Gerontocracy in Germany' (2002) 19 *European Journal of Political Economy* 153–158.

[95] A.A. Schuessler, *A Logic of Expressive Choice* (Princeton University Press 2000); J.M. Guttman, N. Hilger, and Y. Shachmurove, 'Voting as Investment vs. Voting as Consumption: New Evidence' (1994) 47(2) *Kyklos* 197–207; K. Kan and C.C. Yang, 'On Expressive Voting: Evidence from the 1998 US Presidential Election' (2001) 108(3–4) *Public Choice* 295–312.

[96] Cf. S. Müller-Franken, *Familienwahlrecht und Verfassung* (Mohr 2013) 45, with further references to psychological literature.

### *New Right-Bearers II: Rights of Future Generations*

To ensure long-term sustainability, social or environmental rights should *also* be given to those generations which have not yet been born.[97] As noted above, the language of rights is supposed to provide a stronger emotional and legal force to the argument.[98] The conceptualization of certain interests as rights is done in order to give them more weight.

It would be difficult to argue an inability to establish *grosso modo* at least certain interests of future generations. Certain interests of future generations can be established and can be given heavier weight by conceptualizing them as rights. Before discussing possible objections, a short terminological note. Tremmel recently suggested talking about 'succeeding' generations, as both unborn generations and present children should be considered.[99] While he is right in substance, the terminology of future generations seems to be very much established, so this chapter keeps using it while noting that 'future generations' should be understood as including also present children.

Possible objections against the conceptualization of sustainability as 'rights of future generations' are the following: (1) every new right is by definition a reason to limit another (old) one, meaning that it can lead to the limitation of traditional fundamental rights; (2) it is unclear who is empowered to represent future generations (ombudsman, special committees, children, anybody), and how it can be ensured that these organs or people really do represent the rights of future generations; (3) it is conceptually flawed to talk about the rights of *future* generations, as (depending on whether we include currently living children) either all of them or a very large proportion of them actually do not exist, so the subjects or bearers of rights are actually non-existent;[100] and (4) it is conceptually flawed because only individuals, not *generations*, can have rights, so one can only talk about the rights of 'future humans'.[101]

**Argument 1.** This is a legitimate objection, even if doctrinally it is possible to differentiate between the importance of different rights by having different rights limitation tests for them. In any case, introducing a new right or introducing the same rights for new bearers necessarily does provide for reasons to limit the rights of others. Rights are trumps, and if we have more and more trumps then we inflate the

[97] P. Saladin and C.A. Zenger, *Rechte künftiger Generationen* (Helbing & Lichetnhahn 1988).

[98] M. Könczöl, 'Future Generations: An Almost Rawlsian Perspective', in M. Jovanović and B. Spaić (eds.), *Jurisprudence and Political Philosophy in the 21st Century: Reassessing Legacies* (Peter Lang 2012) 130–136, 131 ("In moral and legal thinking, references to rights have to be countered by references to other rights, references to interests with references to interests").

[99] Tremmel, *supra* note 45 at 206.

[100] M. Könczöl, 'Future Generations and Deliberative Democracy: What and How to Represent?' (2014) http://ssrn.com/abstract=2487082 accessed 30 November 2017.

[101] H. Unnerstall, *Rechte zukünftiger Generationen* (Königshausen & Neumann 1999) 63–67, 117–126.

old (traditional) ones. The question is thus not whether new rights lead to the inflation of old ones (and they do), but whether there are good reasons to do so, such as whether we gain enough by conceptualizing the interests of future generations as rights when we give up certain rights of the present generations. Stripped of the language of rights, the question is thus transformed into a question of weighing the interests of future generations and the interests of the present generations,[102] a question to which there is no easy legal answer (there are no generally accepted doctrines or case law on the issue) but which requires careful balancing. The objection is, to conclude, legitimate and strong but inconclusive.

**Argument 2.** The objection concerning representation is a relevant but not particularly strong one. It can either be done in a decentralized way in which everybody can step up in the interest of future generations,[103] or a central authority, ombudsman or council can be established to do so. The latter issue will be revisited below.

**Arguments 3 and 4.** References to the non-existence or the collective nature of the right-bearers are interesting conceptual objections.[104] According to traditional legal doctrine, for a 'right' one needs (at least as a fetal form) existing and individual bearers. With the conceptualization as 'right' comes not a heavier weight but certain conceptual constraints. One of the virtues of law as a method of social control is precisely its conceptual coherence and thus its systematic nature, which is necessary for legal certainty. Law can be changed in many ways, and its conceptual system can even be rewritten, but it always has a price – the legal machinery (courts, authorities, solicitors, enforcement agencies, legal academics) has to accommodate and to learn the novelties. If the novelties do not fit the old system, if the old conceptual system is questioned, then the solution of new and not explicitly regulated cases will be difficult when applying the law. The concept of 'rights' is a fundamental one in modern constitutional democracies, and they are perceived as *individual* rights of *existing* people. It is possible to change this, but it is a highly risky undertaking which should only be done if no other options are available to achieve sustainability and if the gains (in sustainability) are more important than the potential losses in rights

[102] M.D. Adler, 'Future Generations: A Prioritarian View' (2009) 77 *George Washington Law Review* 1478–1520.

[103] A Filipino lawyer represented forty-three children who were considered as representatives of future generations at the Federal Constitutional Court of the Philippines. He was granted *locus standi* on 30 July 1993 with the following explanation: "We find no difficulty in ruling that they [the children] can, for themselves, for others, in their generation and for succeeding generations, file a class suit. Their personality to sue on behalf of succeeding generations can only be based on the concept of inter-generational responsibility ... [to make the natural resources] equitably accessible to the present as well as to future generations." Antonio Oposa, 'In Defence of Future Generations' (2002) 2(3) *Intergenerational Justice Review* 7.

[104] For an overview on the arguments of the debate see S. Tattay, 'Making Sense of a Nonsense: Representation of the 'Rights' of Future Generations', in M. Belov (ed.), *Global Governance and Its Effects on State and Law*, Central and Eastern European Forum for Legal, Political, and Social Theory Yearbook Vol. 6 (Peter Lang 2016).

protection. Fundamentally redefining the conceptual structure of basic and established terms such as rights is reminiscent of Lewis Carroll's tale of Alice, and it seems similarly absurd:[105]

> "And only one for birthday presents, you know. There's glory for you!"
> "I don't know what you mean by 'glory,'" Alice said.
> Humpty Dumpty smiled contemptuously. "Of course you don't – till I tell you. I meant 'there's a nice knock-down argument for you!'"
> "But 'glory' doesn't mean a 'nice knock-down argument.'" Alice objected.
> "When I use a word," Humpty Dumpty said in a rather scornful tone, "it means just what I choose it to mean – neither more nor less."
> "The question is," said Alice, "whether you can make words mean different things."
> "The question is," said Humpty Dumpty, "which is to be master – that's all."

Thus, while not doubting that a new conceptual system would be possible,[106] it is suggested that the question of the 'rights of future generations' is left open and that other possible constitutional solutions which could achieve the same result without destroying traditional doctrinal frameworks should be concentrated on.[107]

### *New Fundamental Rights and New Interpretations of Traditional Fundamental Rights*

The most well-known sustainability right is the 'right to a healthy environment',[108] which, according to a recent study by David R. Boyd, is mentioned in ninety-two constitutions all around the world.[109] As a disappointing result of Boyd's study, it has

[105] L. Carroll, *The Annotated Alice (Alice's Adventures in Wonderland & Through the Looking Glass)* (Bramhall House 1960) 269.

[106] For a general attempt to conceptualize collective rights, see M. Jovanović, *Collective Rights. A Legal Theory* (Cambridge University Press 2011). For advocating rights of future persons, see A. Gosseries, 'On Future Generations' Future Rights' (2008) 16(4) *Journal of Political Philosophy* 446–474. For a conceptualization as 'rights of future individuals' (but not those of generations), see O.J. Herstein, 'The Identity and (Legal) Rights of Future Generations' (2009) 77 *George Washington Law Review* 1173–1215. The concrete doctrinal operationalization (esp. in cases of conflicts of fundamental rights) remains, however, in all these cases unclear.

[107] Some constitutions do contain references to the rights of future generations, but their doctrinal operationalization still remains unclear. See e.g. Japanese Constitution (1946) art. 11; Norwegian Constitution (as amended in 1992) art. 110b; Bolivian Constitution (2009) arts. 33, 108(15).

[108] For recent works on environmental fundamental rights see e.g. R.P. Hiskes, *The Human Right to a Green Future: Environmental Rights and Intergenerational Justice* (Cambridge University Press 2009); D.L. Shelton (ed.), *Human Rights and the Environment* (Edward Elgar 2011); T. Hayward, *Constitutional Environmental Rights* (Oxford University Pree 2005); L. Hajjar Leib, *Human Rights and the Environment* (Martinus Nijhoff 2011); S.J. Turner, *A Global Environmental Right* (Routledge 2014).

[109] D.R. Boyd, *The Environmental Rights Revolution: A Global Study of Constitutions, Human Rights, and the Environment* (University of British Columbia Press 2012) 251.

been established that there is actually no causal relationship between mentioning this right in a constitution and the level of environmental protection that actually exists. The right's value is limited to giving impetus to the legislator by emphasizing the topic in public discourse, and in some cases it can help against backsliding.[110] The level of environmental protection that exists in a given State correlates much more strongly with whether there are detailed statutory rules on environmental protection and whether individuals have the right to enforce these rules in independent courts.[111]

More specifically, although constitutions do not mention fundamental rights to financial sustainability, in international law recently – as a more general and partly financial right – the 'right to development' has emerged.[112] This, however, is convincingly criticized because it conceptually lacks an actual obliged party,[113] so, like the above-mentioned rights of future generations, it would be difficult to apply.

What seems to be more promising on a conceptual level is constitutionally guaranteeing family subsidies or tax deductions. These make family planning easier by reducing financial risks, thus increasing the likelihood of a growth in the fertility rate. Almost all authors agree that such measures are legitimate, with many even regarding them as a constitutional imperative deducible from the provisions concerning family protection or the protection of minors to be found in many constitutions.[114] The constitutional imperative can either be conceptualized as a duty of the State to act, or in an even stronger form as the fundamental right of those concerned (implying a better *locus standi* and a proportionality test in case of limitations).[115] The difference between direct subsidies and tax deductions is, unfortunately, normally not considered to be constitutionally relevant, even though from a demographic point of view cash benefits are clearly more effective than tax allowances.[116] Only very few think that these are not legitimate on the grounds that the state should remain neutral in questions of family planning,[117] an argument

[110] Ibid. at 233–252.
[111] Ibid. at 117–123.
[112] See the Resolution of UN Assembly General 41/128.
[113] A. Ausprich, 'Entschuldung, Menschenrechte und das Recht auf Entwicklung', in M. Dabrowski et al. (eds.), *Die Diskussion um ein Insolvenzrecht für Staaten. Bewertungen eines Lösungsvorschlages zur Überwindung der Internationalen Schuldenkrise* (Duncker & Humblot 2003) 81–88.
[114] C. Seiler, 'Entwicklung der Bevölkerung und Familienpolitik', in J. Isensee and P. Kirchhof (eds.), *Handbuch des Staatsrechts der Bundesrepublik Deutschland. Band IV*, 3rd edn. (C.F. Müller 2008) 507–529.
[115] Cf. the statement that the living costs of those who have no children are considerably lower, see BVerfGE 103, 242, 263f.
[116] Van Parijs, *supra* note 55 at 318 with further references.
[117] G. Roellecke, 'Geburtenrückgang, Volk, Recht, Moral' (1990) 45(19) *JuristenZeitung* 877–883. *Contra* F. Ekart, 'Familienförderung durch Steuerrecht?' (2004) *Kritische Justiz* 116–131 (referring to the state's [supposed] obligation to remain neutral in questions of family planning).

which seems to be blind to the demographic challenges that European societies face, and which consequently has to be discarded.

A different problem is how pensions and related demographic changes can be conceptualized in constitutional law. In most legal orders, pensions are generally not protected by the right to property,[118] but rather by general principles of predictability and legal certainty. A protection by the right to property is only applicable as far as the pension is based on the pensioner's own former financial contribution.[119] This conceptualization seems to be a harmful legal fiction, or to put it more bluntly, a systemic lie, as in most European countries pension systems run *in fact* on a pay-as-you-go basis. Consequently, even though public pension contributions are paid and the pensions received after retirement depend on the amount paid under this title, in fact the money paid in is a type of tax that will basically be spent immediately at the moment of payment on the pensions of other people. If the goal is to be more pragmatic about sustainability challenges, then pension systems should also recognize that bringing up children is at least as important for establishing the just amount of pensions as the amount of contributions paid – a principle which has also been considered by the German Federal Constitutional Court.[120] In this way the external cost of not having children can partially be internalized.

Both child subsidies (tax allowances) and pension issues are relevant, and their above-mentioned constitutional reconceptualizations help in the sustainability issues that are presented in this chapter. But they suffer from the same problem as suffrage for children, since they only concern those generations which are already alive. And if attempts are made to include future generations, there will be serious doctrinal problems concerning the concept of rights.

### Institutional Rules on Elections and Referendums

Proportional electoral systems tend to lead to coalition governments, which normally result in higher deficits. This is because the compromises that the parties in government have to make normally include extra payments for their specially favored social groups.[121] So first-past-the-post voting systems (as in the UK) are more

[118] For an exception see the case law of the ECtHR, e.g. *Stec* v. *UK*, judgment of 12 April 2006, nos. 65731/01 and 65900/01.

[119] BVerfGE, 58, 81, 109ff, see Kluth, *supra* note 61, esp. 256, 260–261 with further references.

[120] Based on arts. 3(1) and 6(1) GG, see BVerfGE 87, 1 (41f); 103, 242 (263). G. Haverkate, *Die Zukunft der sozialen Sicherungssysteme* (DVBl 2004), 1061–1070.

[121] L.P. Feld, 'Nachhaltige Finanzverfassung aus ökonomischer Perspektive', in Kahl, *supra* note 10 at 52–53, with further references.

likely to generate lower public debts.[122] We also know that veto referendums on major public investments are effective in curbing public deficits.[123]

There are also empirically unsubstantiated (so far), but plausible, theses about institutional electoral rules concerning sustainability. For example, it is quite possible that prohibiting the re-election of politicians would result in politicians who are somewhat less likely to buy votes,[124] but the organizations (parties) behind them will still have the same motivations that would work against such changes. And it is also possible that politicians would pay more attention to the common good if voters could change their ranking on the party lists,[125] but no empirical research has confirmed this suggestion yet. All these are interesting, and in some cases definitely useful, suggestions for financial sustainability in general.[126]

### *Rules on Public Finance*

There is a very strong tendency in the Member States of the EU to establish more and more legal (mostly constitutional) rules in order to achieve financial sustainability.[127] The existence and the strength of such rules normally correlates with the

[122] T. Persson, G. Roland, and G. Tabellini, 'How Do Electoral Rules Shape Party Structures, Government Coalitions, and Economic Policies?', *CESifo Working Papers* No. 1115 (2004).

[123] L.P. Feld and J.G. Matsusaka, 'Budget and Government Spending: Evidence from Swiss Cantons' (2003) 87(12) *Journal of Public Economics* 2703–2724; J.G. Matsusaka, 'Fiscal Effects of the Voter Initiative' (1995) 103(3) *Journal of Political Economy* 587–623.

[124] W.S. Glaeser, 'Abhängigkeit der Politiker als Funktionsmangel der Demokratie' (2006) 39(1) *Zeitschrift für Rechtspolitik* 10–15.

[125] V. von Prittwitz, 'Wahl ohne Auswahl? Probleme des deutschen Wahlrechts im europäischen Vergleich', in H.H. von Arnim (ed.), *Die deutsche Krankheit: Organisierte Unverantwortlichkeit?* (Duncker & Humblot 2005) 73–80.

[126] For general financial sustainability purposes, a similarly useful suggestion (which is not electoral in its nature) might be to let subnational entities go bankrupt in order to reward responsible (and to punish irresponsible) financial decision-making on a local level; see C. B. Blankart and A. Klaiber, 'Subnational Government Organisation and Public Debt Crisis' (2006) 26(3) *Economic Affairs* 48–54. For further institutional solutions helping to lower public deficit, see M. Shi and J. Svensson, 'Conditional Political Budget Cycles' (April 2002) *CEPR Discussion Paper* No. 3352 http://ssrn.com/abstract=315248 accessed 30 November 2017 (the higher the rent for the politicians (e.g. via corruption), the higher the probability of buying votes); J. Rodden, 'The Dilemma of Fiscal Federalism: Grants and Fiscal Performance around the World' (2002) 46(3) *American Journal of Political Science* 670–687 (long-term balanced budgets in subnational governments are most likely if (1) either the center imposes borrowing restrictions or (2) subnational governments have wide-ranging taxing and borrowing autonomy. If you have no restrictions, but also no autonomy, then large and persistent deficits are likely to occur); J. Wehner, 'Cabinet Structure and Fiscal Policy Outcomes' (2010) 49 *European Journal of Political Research* 631–653 (the fewer members the cabinet has, the lower the deficit is likely to be).

[127] For a quantification of the strength of such rules, showing growing numbers, see the regularly updated Fiscal Rule Index of the European Commission: http://ec.europa.eu/economy_finance/db_indicators/fiscal_governance/documents/nfr_2012_graph_3.pdf accessed 30 November 2017.

financial sustainability of a country, but it is unclear whether financial sustainability is caused by such rules or the other way around, whether the existence of a rule is just a symptom of a political climate which would care anyway about financial sustainability. Those rules which either seem to be very innovative or *prima facie* directly relevant to sustainability are analyzed in this Part.[128]

### *Transparency Rules*

There are thoughtful suggestions about how to increase transparency on both the side of the taxpayers and the side of the government in order achieve financial sustainability. Making public the amount of tax paid by everybody (natural and legal persons) would definitely make tax evasion more difficult and therefore help in achieving a balanced budget.[129] There are, however, legitimate privacy concerns, which would also have to be balanced in a proposal for such a change, and the suggestions do not address this possible objection.

On the other side, transparency of budgetary numbers, especially public debt figures, might shock the public and politicians into paying more attention to financial sustainability. A usual way of hiding government spending is to use separate special accounts and funds, which is proven to lead to higher public debt.[130] The ageing of government infrastructure could be discounted in order to have a more realistic description of the situation,[131] and the obligation to pay pensions should also be discounted in public debt figures.[132] Leaving the future pension obligations of the government out of the public debt figure amounts to systemic lying and self-deception;[133] on average, the public debt figures of Western states are around 130 percent higher than the official figures.[134] Such rules could also be enshrined into constitutions so that governments can resist the temptation to meddle with the numbers.

[128] We are not going to analyze medium term budgetary frameworks, 'rainy day' funds and different budgetary procedures which might indirectly be relevant to our topic. For these issues, see *Report on the Public Finances in EMU* (European Commission 2010).

[129] Kirchhof, *supra* note 60 at 278–280; K. Tripke, *Die Steuerrechtsordnung*, Vol. I, 2nd edn. (Schmidt 2000) 213–214. For Norway, see http://skattelister.no/ accessed 30 November 2017.

[130] J.E. Alt and D.D. Lassen, 'Transparency, Political Polarization, and Political Budget Cycles in OECD Countries' (2006) 50(3) *American Journal of Political Science* 530–550. The authors claim that the other main factor explaining stronger political budget cycles in advanced democracies is the level of political polarization.

[131] Reimer, *supra* note 23 at 165.

[132] For a suggestion to take discounted future income and expenditure flows into account, see A.J. Auerbach et al., 'Generational Accounting: A Meaningful Way to Evaluate Fiscal Policy' (1994) 8(1) *Journal of Economic Perspectives* 73–94.

[133] G. Eusepi and R.E. Wagner, 'Indebted State versus Intermediary State: Who Owes What to Whom?' (2012) 23(3) *Constitutional Political Economy* 199–212, esp. 209–210.

[134] Data from P. van den Noord and R. Herd, *Pension Liabilities in the Seven Major Economies* (OECD 1993) 31 (which, because of demographic changes, has probably become worse in the meantime).

More transparency about the amount of pension obligations is definitely necessary for any constitutional response to sustainability challenges. But information on its own, without institutional enforcement mechanisms, is insufficient. The electorate cannot function in elections as an enforcement agency, as it is often just as short-sighted as politicians, as the last few years in Europe have shown.[135]

### *Fiscal Rules*

A fiscal rule is often defined as a *permanent (mostly constitutional) constraint* on fiscal policy, expressed in terms of a summary indicator of fiscal performance such as the government budget deficit, borrowing, debt or a major component thereof.[136] There are three types of such rules which are relevant here: (a) balanced budget rules (deficit brakes), (b) debt brakes, and (c) expenditure brakes.[137]

In practice, there is very often a combination of these rules, and even the Maastricht criteria (EMU member states public deficit below 3 percent and total public debt under 60 percent of GDP) contain a combination of deficit brake and debt brake for the Member States,[138] which – to illustrate one of the main problems of these rules – many of the EMU Member States have never actually achieved. The purpose of establishing such rules is normally twofold. On the one hand, these rules can express a genuine intention to achieve financial sustainability, and on the other hand, they can help to signal to financial markets that a country is trying hard,

[135] But on the other hand, once politicians are successful in fiscal adjustments, then these do not decrease the chances of re-election (suggesting that politicians actually underestimate the ability of voters to understand the need for adjustments), see A. Alesina et al., 'The Political Economy of Fiscal Adjustments' (1998) 1 *Brookings Papers on Economic Activity* 1 (1998) 197.

[136] G. Kopits and S.A. Symanski, 'Fiscal Policy Rules', *IMF Occasional Paper* (1998) No. 162. The definition is widely used; see e.g. X. Debrun et al., 'Tied to the Mast? National Fiscal Rules in the European Union' (2008) *Economic Policy* 297–362.

[137] *Report on the Public Finances in EMU* (European Commission 2010) 103, 149. A fourth type, revenue rules, will not be considered here. Revenue rules are about higher-than-expected revenues *ex ante* in the budget law; e.g. they prescribe to allocate such unexpected revenues to the purpose of debt reduction. Examples are to be found in France, Lithuania and the Netherlands. See ibid. 103.

[138] For the excessive deficit procedure, see art. 126(1) TFEU deficit brake, and the special Deficit Protocol (Protocol No. 12 on the Excessive Debt Procedure, 9 May 2008 OJ C115 279), which according to art. 51 TEU is part of primary EU law. For the debt brake see art. 3 Fiscal Compact (Treaty on Stability, Coordination and Governance in the Economic and Monetary Union, 2 March 2012) which prescribes for twenty-five Member States (all but the UK and the Czech Republic) that they must have a debt brake on a constitutional level by 1 January 2014. For more details see A. Levade, 'Les normes de l'Union européenne et l'équilibre budgetaire des Etats', *Revue française de finances publiques* n. 112 2012/February 66–84; L. Azoulai et al., 'Another Legal Monster? An EUI Debate on the Fiscal Compact Treaty' *EUI Working Paper. Department of Law* 2012/9. 4–5; S. Peers, 'The Stability Treaty: Permanent Austerity or Gesture Politics?' (2012) 8(3) *European Constitutional Law Review* 404–441; P. Craig, 'The Stability, Coordination and Governance Treaty' (2012) 37 *European Law Review* 231–248.

consequently taking into account its hopefully bright future, and its interest rates should sink lower.

There are inherent limits to such rules which must be borne in mind. First, without applying similar rules to subnational units,[139] and without the prohibition of the bailout of subnational units,[140] debts and deficits will climb their way up to the central government.[141] Second, these rules are normally good for prevention, but once the public debt is high, they do not seem to be particularly effective.[142] And third, introducing these rules also means limiting parliamentarism and democracy,[143] just as all fundamental rights and other constitutional provisions do.

### *Balanced Budget Rules (Deficit Brakes)*

A well-known European constitutional example of the balanced budget rule is to be found in articles 109 and 115 of the German *Grundgesetz*.[144] These articles explicitly state that revenues and expenditures shall in principle be balanced without revenue from credits, and that this principle shall be satisfied when revenue obtained by the borrowing of funds does not exceed 0.35 percent in relation to the nominal [GDP].[145] This seems to be even stricter than the 0.5 percent allowed by article 3(1)(b) of the Fiscal Compact,[146] but in fact, the German constitutional provisions also contain an escape clause which is very easy to apply: a simple majority of the lower house (Bundestag) can exempt from the application.

139 L.P. Feld and G. Kirchgässner, 'On the Effectiveness of Debt Brakes: The Swiss Experience' *Crema Working Paper* 2006/21, 18/19 www.crema-research.ch/papers/2006-21.pdf accessed 30 November 2017.

140 H. Pünder, 'Gerechte Lastenverteilung zwischen den Generationen' (2008) *Deutsches Verwaltungsblatt* 946–956.

141 In theory, there is a no-bailout clause in EU law (art. 125 TFEU), but in practice it is ineffective; see M. Adams et al., 'Introduction', in M. Adams et al. (eds.), *The Constitutionalization of European Budgetary Contraints* (Hart 2014), 1–15, 2.

142 Reimer, *supra* note 23 at 153.

143 L.J. Quesada, 'La reforma del artículo 135 de la Carta Magna Española' (2012) 30 *Teoría y Realidad Constitucional* 335–356; O.S. Benítez, 'La constitcíón domesticada: Algunas reflexiones críticas sobre la reforma del artículo 135 CE' (2012) 29 *Teoría y Realidad Constitucional* 409–432.

144 Rules on borrowing existed even in the 1919 Weimar Constitution (art. 87), although without any enforcement mechanism. Later attempts to curb public debt (before 2009) also failed, see Reimer, *supra* note 23 at 148–150.

145 M. Koemm, *Eine Bremse für die Staatsverschuldung? Verfassungsmäßigkeit und Justiziabilität des neuen Staatsschuldenrechts* (Mohr Siebeck 2012); C. Seiler, 'Konsolidierung der Staatsfinanzen mithilfe der neuen Schuldenregel' (2009) 14 *JuristenZeitung* 721–728; C. Lenz and E. Burgbacher, 'Die neue Schuldenbremse im Grundgesetz' (2009) 35 *Neue Juristische Wochenschrift* 2561–2567; L.P. Feld and T. Baskaran, 'Federalism, Budget Deficits and Public Debt: On the Reform of Germany's Fiscal Constitution' (2010) 3 *Review of Law & Economics* 365–393.

146 F. Fabbrini, 'The Fiscal Compact, the "Golden Rule," and the Paradox of European Federalism' (2013) 36(1) *Boston College International & Comparative Law Review* 1–38, 11.

A similar logic is behind the Italian regulation (articles 81, 117 and 119 of the Italian Constitution; Statute No. 243/2012 of 24 December 2012) enshrining the balanced budget principle from which it is possible to deviate only after a cumbersome procedure in which both chambers agree on the change.[147]

The rules contained in articles 135 of the Spanish Constitution are more complicated.[148] Even though they were also inspired by the German rules,[149] they explicitly refer to EU requirements ('the limits established by the EU for their member states') containing both the 3 percent deficit brake and the 60 percent debt brake (and have been doing so since 2011, so well before the Fiscal Compact). And, of course, the article contains the usual escape clause concerning natural disasters, economic recession or extraordinary emergency.[150]

### *Debt Brakes*

Debt brakes are to be found in European national constitutions, for example in article 216(5) of the Polish Constitution and in article 36(4)–(5) of the Hungarian Fundamental Law. Additionally, in Slovakia a special constitutional statute, No. 493 of 2011, regulates the issue. These rules concentrate on public debt expressed in the ratio of the GDP and they basically prohibit the adoption of budgets which would result in overstepping the threshold of 60 percent (Poland) or 50 percent of GDP (Hungary and Slovakia).

### *Expenditure Brakes*

Expenditure brakes consider spending that is within the control of the government, which is notable since public debt and deficit also depend on economic growth or interest rates which are outside government control. In this sense, it is fairer in terms of the responsibility of the government concerning financial sustainability because the revenue forecast in the budgets will cover the appropriations included in them. The most well-known example is article 126 of the Swiss Constitution,[151] but Estonia

[147] T. Groppi, I. Spigno, and N. Vizioli, 'The Constitutional Consequences of the Financial Crisis in Italy', in X. Contiades (ed.), *Constitutions in the Global Financial Crisis* (Ashgate 2013) 89–113; A. Arroyo Gil and I.M. Giménez Sánchez, 'La incorporación constitucional de la cláusula de estabilidad presupuestaria en perspectiva comparada: Alemania, Italia y Francia' (2013) 98 *Revista Española de Derecho Constitucional* 149–188, 167–171.

[148] For further details see *Organic Law 2/2012 on Budgetary Stability and Financial Sustainability* (27 April 2012).

[149] V.R. Almendral, 'The Spanish Legal Framework for Curbing the Public Debt and the Deficit' (2013) 9 *European Constitutional Law Review* 189–204, 195.

[150] A. Ruiz Robledo, 'The Spanish Constitution in the Turmoil of the Global Financial Crisis', in Contiades, *supra* note 148 at 141–165.

[151] For more details see S. Danninger, 'A New Rule: The Swiss Debt Brake' *IMF Working Papers* WP/02/18 (January 2002) www.imf.org/external/pubs/ft/wp/2002/wp0218.pdf accessed 30 November 2017; L.P. Feld and G. Kirchgässner, 'On the Effectiveness of Debt Brakes:

(article 116 of the Constitution) and Finland (article 84 of the Constitution) apply similar rules. Since a mere expenditure brake would over-encourage tax deductions, as they fall outside of the scope of the brake,[152] expenditure brakes normally appear in combination with other rules, such as with balanced budget rules.

## CRITICISMS OF STRICT NUMERICAL APPROACHES

There are several problems with strict numerical brakes.[153] First, they fail to encourage procyclical expansion, but they encourage procyclical contractions, making a crisis even graver.[154] In order to avoid a crisis being aggravated by cuts, the numerical brakes often contain escape clauses. The problem on a substantive level, however, is that the mathematical counting in these cases is far from obvious, and this combined with the political weight of the counting makes it vulnerable to populist criticism. On the procedural level, one often finds a seemingly strict fiscal rule with a very soft escape clause making the whole institution questionable. Second, these rules are mostly silent on the composition of the required fiscal adjustment, and thus cuts are normally made in areas which are detrimental in the long term but which are politically less risky, such as education, research and infrastructural investment.[155] Allowing the growth of deficit/debt in the case of investment, it is a simple question of accountancy to label any investment as the cause of the deficit/debt, while registering welfare payments in the normal budget.[156] Third, with a lack of genuine commitment these brakes just encourage creative accounting, which makes finances non-transparent, in turn making democratic accountability more difficult regarding these issues.[157] Fourth, it is largely unclear how the exact number is chosen, and once the number is chosen, it encourages the debt/deficit to grow

The Swiss Experience', in R. Neck and J.-E. Sturm, *Sustainability of Public Debt* (MIT Press 2008) 223–255; J.-F. Aubert and P. Mahon, *Petit commentaire de la Constitution fédérale de la Confédération suisse du 18 avril 1999* (Schulthess 2003) 1002–1007; T.P. Stauffer, 'Art. 126', in B. Ehrenzeller et al. (eds.), *Die schweizerische Bundesverfassung* (Dike–Schulthess 2002) 1284–1294.

[152] Report on the Public Finances in EMU (European Commission 2010) 102.

[153] Debrun et al., *supra* note 46 at 53.

[154] International Monetary Fund, 'Has Fiscal Behavior Changed under the European Economic and Monetary Union?' *World Economic Outlook* 2004/September, 103–118; L. Summers and J.B. DeLong, 'Fiscal Policy in a Depressed Economy' (2012/Spring) *Brookings Papers on Economic Activity* 233–274.

[155] Criticising the Stability and Growth Pact of the EU: O.J. Blanchard and F. Giavazzi, 'Improving the SGP through a Proper Accounting of Public Investment', *International Macroeconomics* 4220 www.cepr.org/pubs/dps/DP4220.asp accessed 30 November 2017.

[156] M. Heintzen, *Das neue deutsche Staatsschuldenrecht in der Bewährungsprobe* (De Gruyter 2012) 22.

[157] J. von Hagen and G. Wolff, 'What Do Deficits Tell Us about Debts? Empirical Evidence on Creative Accounting with Fiscal Rules' (2006) 30 *Journal of Banking and Finance* 771–779.

until that number, even if the debt/deficit was previously below that number. Fifth, they are overly simplistic, since actual financial sustainability depends on too many factors (for example, perception of sustainability; demographic, educational and growth factors; tax/expenditure policy; capital market; and the possibility of bailout) which cannot be included in a simple rule.[158] Finally, it is difficult to ensure a politically independent but at the same time effective control.[159]

In order to respond to all these questions, it is probably better not to have simple numbers. Instead, either an aggregate index or just a list of factors to be considered should be measured. As regards the latter, the enforcing body needs to have some discretion to weigh the different factors,[160] which makes conclusions politically vulnerable. As regards the former, for example using the aggregate index, has the advantage that statements about it are somewhat easier to falsify. There are different possible aggregate indices, one of which is the so-called Economic Sustainability Indicator. This indicator takes into account real capital, human capital considering both the number and the education of the workforce, natural capital considering natural resources, structural capital considering formal and informal rules in society, and intergenerational debt considering all future promises of payments. It considers the starting year of measurement as 100 percent (current capital level), and on the basis of this, every year one can calculate whether it is increasing or decreasing.[161] This indicator can handle changes where one type of capital is transformed into another one: "If the state finances goods that will benefit future generations as well (for example expensive bridges), it then makes perfect sense that they should pay their share of burden, too."[162] Measures that would lead to a lower (or to a substantively lower) indicator could be deemed unconstitutional. A public methodology as detailed as possible is, of course, necessary to falsify any statement about counting on the Economic Sustainability Indicator.

The exact formulae that should be used to count such an indicator is beyond the capabilities of lawyers (such as the present author), but there are some typically lawyerly considerations that should be taken into account when setting up such a body. In the following, we are going to do exactly this.

[158] K. Mause and F. Groeteke, 'New Constitutional "Debt Brakes" for Euroland? A Question of Institutional Complementarity' (2012) 23(4) *Constitutional Political Economy* 279–301.

[159] G. Kopits, 'Fiscal Rules: Useful Policy Framework or Unnecessary Ornament?' *IMF Working Paper* 2001/145, 16; X. Debrun and M.S. Kumar, 'The Discipline-Enhancing Role of Fiscal Institutions: Theory and Empirical Evidence', *IMF Working Paper* 2007/171.

[160] Debrun et al., *supra* note 46 at 44–81.

[161] A further advantage is that, by using one single aggregate number, it also attempts to connect expert knowledge to political communication; see P. Ederer et al., 'The Economic Sustainability Indicator', in Tremmel, *supra* note 45 at 129–147, esp. 131.

[162] Tremmel, *supra* note 45 at 207.

## ENFORCING BODY: A CONSTITUTIONAL COURT CONSISTING OF ECONOMISTS

One option would be to place the competence of reviewing the effect of government measures – including statutes – on the sustainability indicator with a judicial body, such as with a constitutional court.[163] This would have different advantages. First, in many States such a body already exists, so it would institutionally be easier. As such a control over government powers is obviously anti-democratic, an already established anti-democratic institution like a constitutional court is more likely to be successful. In questions of constitutional design, it is mostly constitutional lawyers who are asked. As a specialized lobby group of the constitutional courts, they are interested in strong constitutional courts,[164] and so are more likely to support the use of these courts for this purpose than the setting up of new institutions which are beyond their influence. Second, there are functioning mechanisms to ensure that such bodies are politically independent and that they do not abuse their power, such as (a) a culture of detailed reasoning in order to explain the reasons behind decisions, (b) dissenting opinions which help the judges to control each other, and (c) traditions of selecting senior academics for such positions whose motivational background is different from that of politicians.[165]

The problem is, however, that lawyers are not up to this task, since the opinions here would need to consist of mathematical counting, debates about statistical methodology and other technical mechanisms. Lawyers are well-trained in conflict solving when there are debates about fundamental rights but, as seen above, financial and demographic sustainability problems cannot plausibly be conceptualized in terms of fundamental rights.[166] Experience also shows that, perhaps because of the inaptness mentioned above, courts are shy in enforcing fiscal rules regardless of whether they include external economic experts.[167] Essentially, a new institution

[163] For a similar proposal concentrating on natural resources, see K. Skagen Ekeli, 'Green Constitutionalism: The Constitutional Protection of Future Generations' (2007) *Ratio Juris* 378–401.

[164] M. Shapiro and A. Stone, 'The New Constitutional Politics of Europe' (1994) 4 *Comparative Political Studies* 397–420.

[165] It would also strengthen constitutional courts, whether we take that as an advantage or not, just like constitutional debt brakes in some countries do; see G. Delledonne, 'Financial Constitutions in the EU: From the Political to the Legal Constitution?' *Sant' Anna Legal Studies (STALS) Research Paper* 5/2012.

[166] "Or if they are conceptualised in terms of fundamental rights, then they should not: changes in the social security institutions are typically framed in terms of 'liberty and individual responsibility' on the one hand and 'solidarity and justice' on the other hand. This sort of debate typically overrides pragmatic concerns about efficiency and sustainability." P. Ederer et al., 'The Economic Sustainability Indicator', in Tremmel, *supra* note 45 at 129–147, esp. 130.

[167] See P.-A. Van Malleghem, '(Un)Balanced Budget Rules in Europe and America', in Adams, *supra* note 142 at 151–180 on US state fiscal constitutional limits, with further references.

would be needed that functions like a constitutional court, with clear, constitutionally defined competences and goals, limited terms for members (to avoid the accusation of a Platonic philosophers' kingdom), with a special emphasis on transparency,[168] and consisting of non-lawyer experts (mostly economists).[169] In some States there are already similar expert bodies, such as fiscal councils, budget councils and stability councils,[170] but their competences are more limited than what is being suggested here.[171] The existing bodies normally monitor, advise and can exceptionally veto budgets, but they cannot invalidate government measures – including statutes *a posteriori* – and they cannot stop payments either.[172] Instead of conceptualizing this as a new chamber of the legislature,[173] it is preferable to conceive of it as a new type of constitutional court, where every citizen should have a *locus standi* to initiate procedures (*actio popularis*).[174] As disagreement cannot be excluded, just like in traditional constitutional courts but contrary to decision-making bodies in most national banks or courts of auditors, dissenting opinions should be possible so that judges can control each other.

An obvious problem with the idea of such an economic constitutional court is that politicians are generally not so keen on limiting their own power. It is a valid practical objection, but it also applies to constitutional courts, and in most European States there is some kind of constitutional court or judicial review by ordinary courts. They have either been set up (on rare occasions) as a result of the rational self-limitation of politicians, or as a result of external economic pressure, which can

[168] On the role of transparency in such matters see M. Goldmann, The 'Financial Crisis as a Crisis of Democracy: Towards Prudential Regulation through Public Reasoning' (15 July 2011) http://ssrn.com/abstract=1886518 accessed 30 November 2017.

[169] J. Tremmel, 'Institutionelle Verankerung der Rechte nachdrückender Generationen' (2004) 37(2) *Zeitschrift für Rechtspolitik* 44–46.

[170] R. Hagemann, 'Improving Fiscal Performance through Fiscal Councils, OECD 2010' www.oecd.org/eco/surveys/46673013.pdf accessed 30 November 2017; D. Fromage, 'Le Haut Conseil des finances publiques: quelles conséquences deux ans après sa création?' (2015) 131 *Revue du droit public* 1107–1126; G. Kopits and B. Romhányi, 'A Költségvetési Tanács indulásának tanulságai' (2010) 57 *Közgazdasági Szemle* 573–590.

[171] Also other (ombudsperson-type) expert institutions possess only soft competences and tasks, like investigation and initiation of procedures by other organs, public awareness measures, reports and recommendations, but no tough sanctions. On the examples of Israel, New Zealand and Hungary, see M. Göpel, 'Guarding Our Future: How to Protect Future Generations?' (2011) 1(6) *Solutions* www.thesolutionsjournal.com/node/821 accessed 30 November 2017.

[172] On the importance of constitutionally guaranteed veto rights concerning the implementation of budget (i.e., stopping payments), based on examples from US states, see H. Bohn and R.P. Inman, 'Balanced-Budget Rules and Public Deficits: Evidence from the US States' (1996) 45(1) *Carnegie-Rochester Conference Series on Public Policy* 13–76.

[173] Explicitly suggesting this, Beaucamp, *supra* note 9 at 205–209.

[174] M. Leschke, 'Nachhaltigkeit und Institutionen – eine wirtschaftwissenschaftliche Sicht', in Kahl (ed.), *supra* note 10 at 297–325, 320. On the importance of *locus standi* rules in sustainability issues (as opposed to substantive fundamental rights issues), see K. Skagen Ekeli, 'Green Constitutionalism: The Constitutional Protection of Future Generations' (2007) 20(3) *Ratio Juris* 378–401.

originate from an international organization (IMF), the EU or financial markets. In the long run, the principles of financial self-limitation can even be internalized in the political cultures of the countries affected with the help of these institutions.[175]

### *European Integration and Financial Sustainability: 'Never Waste a Good Crisis'*

The problem of financial sustainability emerged with the recent economic crisis in Europe but it is also an opportunity. The existence of the US in its current constitutional structure is to be explained by a huge debt crisis after the War of Independence – the need for an efficient central government brought the federal government into existence instead of a loose confederation of states (cf. 1777 Articles of Confederation vs. 1787 Constitution).[176] The budget question even helped eighteenth- and nineteenth-century European countries to advance the idea of representative democracy.[177]

To some extent, the EU is financially already more centralized than the US, since in the US there are no federal provisions about what a state constitution should contain on the issue, whereas in the EU the novelty of the Fiscal Compact (besides restating the existing duties of Member States) was precisely this.[178] Moreover, the Fiscal Compact showed that new quasi-primary law can be created without unanimity since, although two states (the UK and the Czech Republic) opted out, for the rest of the members the Fiscal Compact applies in the form of a traditional international treaty.[179]

## CONCLUSION

Recent developments in both European domestic and supranational constitutional laws mirror the idea of sustainability, which seems to be the most important upcoming principle in European constitutional thought. The reason for the emergence of these constitutional ideas is that sustainability challenges are textbook situations for establishing constitutional rules which bind present and future

[175] In the long run, however, institutions also form mentality; see D. Acemoglu and J. Robinson, *Why Nations Fail: The Origins of Power, Prosperity and Poverty* (Random House 2012) 302–334, 404–427.

[176] A. Loubert, 'Sovereign Debt Threatens the Union: The Genesis of a Federation' (2012) 8(3) *European Constitutional Law Review* 442–455.

[177] C. Gröpl, 'Schritte zur Europäisierung des Haushaltsrechts' (2013) 52(1) *Der Staat* 1–25.

[178] Fabbrini, *supra* note 147. The other difference (partly explaining the first one) is that there is no bailout of Member States in the US.

[179] C. Closa Montero, 'Moving Away from Unanimity: Ratification of the Treaty on Stability, Coordination and Governance in the Economic and Monetary Union' *Reconstituting Democracy in Europe Working Paper* 2011/38 http://papers.ssrn.com/sol3/papers.cfm?abstract_id=2005894 accessed 30 November 2017.

political decision makers. Some of these ideas seem to fit the constitutional language that we speak in Europe better.

The general attempt of talking about the 'rights of future generations' is conceptually not reconcilable with the current language of rights. Fundamental rights seem to work only for the environmental aspects, but even here, any rights of present generations suffer from a short-sightedness, albeit to a lesser extent. Certain institutional rules on elections and referendums have been considered as useful instruments to help financial sustainability.

It seems that specific fiscal constitutional rules are also needed, but not the usual simplistic numerical debt, deficit or expenditure brakes. Instead, some kind of aggregate number has to be developed – and not by lawyers – in order to take into account the many factors of sustainability. Furthermore, appropriate constitutional transparency rules are needed, and an independent institution similar to constitutional courts in structure, functioning and transparency, but consisting of economists, should be established with the ability to invalidate government measures (including statutes) and stop government payments. And as with constitutional courts, these institutions could be established either as a result of the rational self-limitation of politicians or as a result of external (economic) pressure.

# 9

# The Principle of Intergenerational Solidarity in Reshaping Constitutional Rights and Obligations: An Example from Portugal

*Marisa Quaresma dos Reis*

We may consider each generation as a distinct nation, with a right, by the will of its majority, to bind themselves, but none to bind the succeeding generation, more than the inhabitants of another country.

Letter of Thomas Jefferson to John Wayles Eppes Monticello, 1813

In Southern Europe, the advent of new democracies had severe constitutional implications concerning the catalogue of social, economic and cultural rights in States such as Greece, Spain or Portugal.[1] In fact, Portuguese constitutional rights should be interpreted as a consequence of the Carnation Revolution.

The recently implemented Portuguese socio-political State model suggests the emergence of a new range of needs. Individuals began to demand positive actions from public authorities instead of simply protection of their freedoms. Jorge Miranda, father of the Portuguese Constitution of 1976, argued that 'social equality' is a viable element of effectiveness of 'legal equality', since the formal existence of rights is not enough to guarantee them.[2]

It seems true that the basic principle of a social – or even venturing further, of a socialist – constitution, should be the prohibition of so-called social retrogression,[3] meaning that the degree of normative concretization of social rights may not be reduced.

In 1997, the fourth constitutional revision also included the concept of 'solidarity' and linked it to social security. Another constitutional reference to 'solidarity' in article 66 linked to the concept of generations, in view of the fact that individuals

[1] J.C. Loureiro, 'Constitucionalismo, bem-estar e crises' (2014) 1(3) *e-Pública: Revista Eléctronica de Direito Público* 41–58.

[2] J. Miranda, 'Direitos fundamentais e ordem social' (2006) *Escritos vários sobre direitos fundamentais* 45–84.

[3] On this principle, T.F. de Freitas, 'O princípio da proibição de retrocesso social' (2006) 2 *Estudos em homenagem ao Professor Doutor Marcello Caetano* 783.

in both present and future generations are endowed with the same dignity, a principle that goes along with the fundamental rights system and a criterion that can be used when claiming new rights or revisiting existing ones.

These ideas lead to another discussion, because life expectancy is currently much higher than in previous times owing to technological evolution and biomedical advances. For example, in 2011, the global population reached seven billion people.[4] On the other hand, we have an equal concern of population decline in more developed countries, mainly because of lower birth rates.[5] How can national constitutions deal with these rapid demographic alterations?

## CRISIS AND SOCIAL RIGHTS

As a starting point, it is important to reflect on the extent of the application of article 63 of the Portuguese Constitution, paragraph 1 of which reads: '1. Everyone shall have the right to social security'.[6] Before the 2016 presidential elections in Portugal, austerity measures imposed by the EU troika provoked public debate on the reduction of pensions. This caused social turmoil, as pensions had been perceived to be untouchable, acquired rights.[7]

A thesis known as 'dogmatic unity' *claims* that both liberty and social rights are of the same value at the constitutional level.[8] This thesis is far from doctrinal consensus. Blanco de Morais rejected the traditional doctrine, understanding that rights, freedoms and guarantees would be purely negative rights (i.e. defensive) while social rights would be positive rights (i.e. entitlement to benefits, for they would require legal conditions, and above all, financial and material provisions for the realization of those benefits).[9] Of this difference in nature, the dominant doctrine would argue

4 2011, World Population Data Sheet, Population Reference Bureau www.prb.org/pdf11/2011population-data-sheet_eng.pdf accessed 30 November 2017.

5 Ibid.

6 Constitution of Portugal art. 63(1) (1911).

7 L. Pereira Coutinho, 'A "convergência de pensões" como questão política' (2014) 1(1) *e-Pública: Revista Eléctronica de Direito Público* 50–68; J. Reis Novais, 'O direito fundamental à pensão de reforma em situação de emergência financeira' (2014) 1(1) *e-Pública: Revista Eléctronica de Direito Público* 69–96.

8 A. Salgado Matos, 'O Direito ao Ensino – Contributo para uma dogmática unitária dos direitos fundamentais' (1998) FDUL 7; J. Reis Novais, *Direitos Sociais* (Coimbra 2010); J. Reis Novais, *As Restrições a Direitos Fundamentais não Expressamente Autorizadas pela Constituição* (Coimbra 2003) 125; J. Reis Novais, 'Direito, Liberdade e Garantia: uma noção imprestável na justiça administrativa?' (2009) 73 *Cadernos de Justiça Administrativa* 229. See also V. Pereira da Silva, *A Cultura a Que Tenho Direito – Direitos fundamentais e cultura* (Almedina 2007); I. Moreira, *A Solução dos Direitos, Liberdades e Garantias e dos Direitos Económicos, Sociais e Culturais na Constituição Portuguesa* (Almedina 2007).

9 C. Blanco de Morais, 'De novo a querela da "unidade dogmática" entre direitos de liberdade e direitos sociais em tempos de "exceção financeira"' (2014) 1(3) *e-Pública: Revista Eléctronica de Direito Público* 59–85.

that while rights, freedoms and guarantees would be directly and immediately invoked without depending on financial conditions, social rights would depend not only on legal conditions but also on financial benefits. Their effectiveness would be conditioned by the financial availability of the State, that is, by the 'reserve for contingencies'.

On the other hand, for the unitarians, there is no difference between the two types of rights, since both depend on the 'reserve for contingences'. This is to say that the amount of the pensions could not be drastically affected, even if presuppositions behind these provisions undergo drastic changes.

However, it is true that some rights have high costs. And who would pay those costs? Hans Zacher, using the contractualist metaphor, argues that the social contract in a pension scheme, for instance, should not be understood as a bilateral agreement between those retired and those who are still actively contributing to the scheme; the social contract should instead be viewed as a generational contract including a third generation composed of children and youngsters.

Edmund Burke[10] also considered the contract theory as being cross-generational.[11] His concept of social contract comes out of his belief that good government is a gift from God. Thus, morality and government should not be separate. As a member of a governing body, no one should act according to their own selfish purposes. On the contrary, legislators should take into account the potential impact on future generations of legislating for the moment.

Constitutional case law has been essential to the construction of implicit fundamental rights, grounded on the principle that fundamental rights do not have to have a proper legal basis (*princípio da não-tipicidade*), as expressed in article 16, paragraph 1 of the Portuguese Constitution.[12]

Some authors argue that social rights are not covered by this principle. However, three great Portuguese constitutionalists, Gomes Canotilho, Vital Moreira and Jorge Miranda,[13] believed the contrary. The rationale is also related to the continuity of the welfare state, despite the financial and economic crisis which occurred in Portugal. Alexy's conception of the division of fundamental rights results from the functions of the legal-constitutional order and the normative structures which

[10] "Society is indeed a contract. It is a partnership ... not only between those who are living, but between those who are living, those who are dead, and those who are to be born." E. Burke, *Reflections on the Revolution in France* (1790).

[11] H. Zacher, 'Das Wichtigste: Kinder und ihre Fähigkeit zu leben – Anmerkungen zur intergenerationellen Solidarität', in H. Zacher (ed.), *Abhandlungen zum Sozialrecht II* (Heidelberg 2008) 281.

[12] Constitution of Portugal, art. 16 (1911) (Scope and Interpretation of Fundamental Rights): "1. The fundamental rights enshrined in the Constitution shall not exclude any others set out in applicable international laws and legal rules. 2. The constitutional precepts concerning fundamental rights must be interpreted and completed in harmony with the Universal Declaration of Human Rights."

[13] J. Joaquim Gomes Canotilho and V. Moreira, *Fundamentos da Constituição* (Coimbra 1991) 116–117; J. Miranda, *Manual de direito constitucional* , 5th edn., Vol. IV (Coimbra 2012) 199.

consecrated them. This leads to a triadic fragmentation: rights to something, freedoms and competences. Canotilho adapted these concepts into the Portuguese context.[14] As noted by Márcia Cruz, Canotilho made a new distinction between an original entitlement to benefits (already determined at the constitutional level, which has a normative structure) and a derived entitlement (dependent on an infra-constitutional mediation).[15]

One cannot go further on this path without first approaching Carl Schmitt's theory of 'exceptions'.[16] To Schmitt, an exception is not formally codified in law – instead, the sovereign is the one who decides if there is an exception, and it is admissible for the sovereign to stand outside the legal system to deal with an exception. In case of emergency, a constitution may decide who can act in response to the emergency, but nothing more. This means that the sovereign – normally, the government – consistently decides on situations that may constitute exceptions and could potentially suspend the constitution.

This said, could a financial crisis be understood as an exception, leading the government to decide against 'expensive' rights (such as social rights), based on the argument of sustainability and linked to the principle of intergenerational solidarity? That was exactly what happened in Portugal.[17]

## PORTUGUESE CONSTITUTIONAL CASE LAW

From 2010 on, the principles of 'intergenerational solidarity' and 'intergenerational justice' – both expressions were used interchangeably – arose in Portuguese Constitutional case law, mainly within the socio-economic context and linked to other broader principles such as solidarity and sustainability, while reviewing the constitutionality of reforms adopted by the government.[18]

In Ruling 187/13, the Constitutional Court stated that, in order to pursue intergenerational justice and assure the sustainability of the social security system, the 90 percent cut in the vacation subsidy and the payment of an extraordinary solidarity contribution by pensioners (Contribuição Extraordinária de Solidariedade, CES)[19]

[14] R. Alexy, *Teoria de los derechos fundamentales* (Centro de Estudios Constitucionales 1993) 89.

[15] See M. Raquel Madruga Cruz, *Concretização progressiva dos direitos sociais-Na perspectiva da justiça intergeracional: uma ótica orientada pela sustentabilidade* (Faculdade de Direito, Universidade de Coimbra 2014) 83.

[16] C. Schmitt, *Political Theology: Four Chapters on the Concept of Sovereignty* (University of Chicago Press 2005) 7.

[17] See C. Blanco de Morais, *Teoria da Constituição em Tempo de Crise do Estado Social*, Curso de Direito Constitucional Vol. II Coimbra 2015).

[18] Rulings 353/2012 www.tribunalconstitucional.pt/tc/acordaos/20120353.html accessed 30 November 2017, 187/13 www.tribunalconstitucional.pt/tc/acordaos/20130187.html accessed 30 November 2017, 474/13 www.tribunalconstitucional.pt/tc/acordaos/20130474.html accessed 30 November 2017, 862/13 www.tribunalconstitucional.pt/tc/acordaos/20130862.html accessed 30 November 2017.

[19] In Portuguese, 'Contribuição Extraordinária de Solidariedade'.

did not violate any fundamental right consecrated in the Constitution. This decision went against a strong opposing trend,[20] and it was severely criticized. The dissenting opinions asserted that CES was extraordinary and not structural revenue, and therefore not an adequate measure to protect future generations from an unfair burden.[21]

In Ruling 474/2013,[22] Justice Maria Lúcia Amaral's concurring opinion reads:

> Let's be clear: no constitutional order lasts beyond the sustainability of the State, as there is no constitution that rationally elects irresponsibility as a guiding principle of public policy of the present generation towards the autonomy of future generations.

This case was related to measures that would collide with the protection of the right to work. The Court decided that these measures were unconstitutional based on the principles of legitimate expectations and of legal certainty.

In 2013, the Constitutional Court used the same arguments to declare that a measure which imposed a 10 percent cut in pensions of the beneficiaries of the public social security system (Caixa Geral de Aposentações, CGA)[23] was unconstitutional. According to a study presented by the government, pensioners of the CGA (Public System) had revenues at least 10 percent superior to other pensioners. The Court argued that the government failed to demonstrate that CGA pensioners had a patrimonial advantage when compared to others. This means that it would be a mere budgetary cut with no structural character and not able to foster the sustainability of the social security system. Consequently, it would not promote intergenerational justice or equity.

The government came back in 2014 with a proposal that included a permanent pension cut, called a 'sustainability contribution' (*contribuição de sustentabilidade*), as well as other measures that could lead to more efficient budgetary options. Again, the Constitutional Court concluded that the pension cut would lead to internal inequality and inequity and to intragenerational injustice while violating legitimate expectations again.[24] For all these decisions, the Portuguese Constitutional Court has been accused by numerous scholars of judicial activism and of interfering with political decisions.

[20] In this case, the Court declared that the Constitution protects the right to a pension but does not protect the 'right to a certain amount'.

[21] Justice Catarina Sarmento's concurring opinion stated: "I do not accept the argument that the ECS [Extraordinary Contribution of Solidarity] is also justified by a duty of intergenerational solidarity: such a goal can never be pursued by a merely ad hoc, isolated measure. ECS was designed as extraordinary income; it is not a structural measure, designed for the solvency of the system and cannot therefore be regarded as a measure for the purpose of reducing burdens on future generations."

[22] Acordão N.° 474/2013 (N° 27) www.tribunalconstitucional.pt/tc/acordaos/20130474.html accessed 30 November 2017.

[23] In Portuguese, 'Caixa Geral de Aposentações'.

[24] Ruling 575/2014 www.tribunalconstitucional.pt/tc/acordaos/20140575.html accessed 30 November 2017.

## SAVING THE WELFARE STATE: AN *INTERGENERATIONAL* WELFARE STATE?

Inter- and intra-generational justice may become increasingly prominent issues in the constitutional debate around the world in the coming decades. The great changes in the demographic pyramid of many developed states and the rapid increase of the population in developing countries raise several issues concerning justice between the older, the younger and the unborn. This new discussion will be as important as other questions of social justice, notably justice between the rich and the poor. In fact, the issues cannot be separated, since each influences the other, and the concept of fundamental rights may determine the future of a welfare or social state.

A new legal paradigm considering the rights of future generations is under development by several legal scholars in the international academic arena. This paradigm seeks to address the far-reaching consequences of the present governmental decisions and legislative acts.

In politics, intergenerational justice has become a pressing topic, included in several political programs but generally used in a demagogic and populist approach. From another perspective, democracy itself may, in its conventional form, conflict with the interests of future generations. In order to attract votes, political parties focus their programs on the needs and desires of the present generation because the present generation constitutes the electorate. Young and unborn people are disenfranchised and are not able to choose their political representatives.

Currently, modern science stands at a point that can apprehend the consequences of our present actions and decisions into the far future. These present actions and decisions may impact and even exert a strong negative influence on the well-being of future individuals and whole generations.

Law should not be myopic and ought to adapt to new ethical and moral premises. A new theory is needed to reconcile law and ethics for the future. Emilie Gaillard has already gone further in this mission,[25] developing an innovative thesis proposing a new legal perspective: the recognition of a principle of temporal non-discrimination in the application of fundamental rights. She stated:[26]

> Recognition of a non-discrimination principle that transcends time, based on which the absence of temporal existence no longer results in an absence of rights or legal safeguards, may truly be considered an intellectual conversion. Thus, the implementation of crimes against future generations becomes possible by rendering

[25] E. Gaillard, *Générations futures et droit privé. Vers un droit des générations futures* (Librairie Générale de Droit et de Jurisprudence 2008).

[26] E. Gaillard, 'Des crimes contre l'humanité aux crimes contre les générations futures: Vers une transposition du concept éthique de responsabilité transgénérationnelle en droit pénal international?' (2011) 7(2) *McGill Journal of Sustainable Development Law* 1.

> more complex traditional legal concepts. Formulating crimes against future generations is also an impressive feat in that it upholds a principle of dignity of the future generations. Such a principle has the further potential of propelling forward the domain of human rights law by opening it to discussions of a trans-generational perspective.

In the future, a trans-generational approach to fundamental rights will be essential in order to keep constitutional rights, mainly environmental and social rights, vivid. With a new demographic scenario, and taking into account the possibility of new financial crisis, it is clear that it will not be possible to keep the welfare state as we knew it.

Law must be understood on a space-time axis. Accepting this conception will bring new perspectives to welfare rights. In order to save social rights, one must accept the unitarian doctrine and understand that all fundamental rights have a trans-temporal dimension, being applicable to several generations in a row (in line with Emilie Gaillard's principle of temporal non-discrimination). The legislator ought to safeguard future individuals' social rights at the same time she creates laws that promote them in the present. This is a proportionality exercise and it demands a self-transcendence vision.[27]

The so-called *non-identity problem*,[28] and the question of the non-recognition of legal personhood to people not yet born (or conceived) and for that reason not entitled with legal rights, can be approached from this new and creative point of view. It is the principle of human dignity as well as the principle of equality that is behind a *post mortem* protection of certain fundamental rights. Specifically, it is important to recall cases for the protection of the memory of a deceased person and the right to a deceased's name, image or copyright. In terms of statutes, the Portuguese Criminal Code foresees a crime of offenses to the remembrance of a deceased person setting a limit of fifty years.[29] It appears that, treating equal situations equally, if society should protect the memory of a deceased person, it should also protect an expectation – and thus recognize a so-called *ante natalem* protection – of fundamental rights to future people.

In the abstract, these comparisons may solve the issue concerning the legal status of future individuals, but it is necessary to have another approach towards entire generations. If the re-creation of the 'welfare state', thereby turning it into an

[27] E. Partridge, 'Why Care about the Future?', in E. Partridge (ed.), *Responsibilities to Future Generations* (Prometheus Books 1981).

[28] On the non-identity problem see D. Parfit, *Reasons and Persons* (Clarendon Press 1987).

[29] Art. 185 (offences to the memory of a deceased person): "1 – Who, in any way, seriously offend the memory of a deceased person shall be punished with imprisonment up to six months or a fine up to 240 days . . . 3 – The offence is not punishable when it has been more than 50 years on the person's death." See www.pgdlisboa.pt/leis/lei_mostra_articulado.php?nid=109&tabela=leis accessed 30 November 2017.

'Intergenerational Welfare State', prevails, it would be advisable to create a new Parliamentary Committee or similar entity to evaluate the potential future impact of laws, because future generations are better represented by a committee than by a sole individual.[30] Of the existing models, the Finnish model seems to be the most effective in protecting the interests of future generations,[31] a group of uncertain and unidentified individuals whose interests are vast, because it takes into account such varied issues as economy and social policies, environment, public debt and biomedicine.

## CONCLUSION

In the view of this author, the legal concepts should be understood and recreated from a space-time axis perspective, for the concept of humanity includes past, present and future generations, and all the possible realities that can be fulfilled by human societies. The protection of future generations is a universal value, visible across countries and cultures. More and more, it finds expression in domestic laws, constitutions and international agreements.

Most crises of the present time are the symptoms of slow-burning, long-term lack of vision. However, institutions and political parties remain under the tyranny of the present. The discussions on the protection of future generations' interests are related to the question of public debts. The urgency of this legal debate is evident. Juridical concepts such as 'duties', 'rights' or 'damage' are still unclear in the intergenerational context. Nevertheless, there is a consensus that future generations have moral meaning. One of the main threats to future generations' interests is political short-termism. There is an urgent need to promote legal debate in an innovative way of thinking to find solutions that can overcome today's legal architecture, surpassing at the same time our restricted way of thinking.

As Axel Gosseries would say, constitutions may be a doubled-edged sword.[32] On the one hand, constitutions may consecrate the recognition of an intergenerational perspective (and protection) concerning fundamental rights. On the other hand, the rigidity of a constitution may become an obstacle preventing the ability of future people to respond properly to problems that do not exist today. It is desirable that constitutions promote guarantees of fundamental rights to future generations. At the same time, those same guarantees should not become legal burdens on future

[30] For a detailed analysis of the different existing institutions see M. Szabó, 'National Institutions for the Protection of the Interests of Future Generations' (2015) 2(2) *e-Pública: Revista Eléctronica de Direito Público* 7–24.

[31] P. Tiihonen, 'A Committee for the Future', Future Justice Blog www.futurejustice.org/blog/guest-contribution/guest-article-a-committee-for-the-future/ accessed 30 November 2017.

[32] A. Gosseries, 'Constitutions and Future Generations' (2008) 17(2) *The Good Society* 32.

generations or disrespect their sovereignty.[33] It is also true that some rigidity may be favorable to the protection of certain rights of future generations, and this could be the case with social rights.

This is to say that an activist court, such as the Portuguese Constitutional Court, in times of financial crisis, may also act as a double-edged sword – it can make political and legislative progress unfeasible or it may protect future generations from arbitrariness. Increasingly, a number of institutions and bodies all over the world (mainly in developed countries, where the demographic pyramid is changing drastically) have been created to promote the rights of future generations. At the same time, national constitutions and international legal texts more and more frequently include provisions which address the interests of future generations.

Nevertheless, methodological caution is required. Scholars should find a balance between intra- and inter-generational justice, preventing a certain political and ideological promiscuity in times of financial and social crisis. After the terrible earthquake of 1755, which destroyed the entire downtown of Lisbon, the Marqués de Pombal, then State Secretary of the Portuguese Crown, stated that the priorities of the Kingdom were to "Bury the dead and care for the living." Within a financial crisis, with major destructive social impacts, it becomes necessary to all of us – not only scholars – to find new ways to help the living to continue living with dignity, but at the same time not forgetting to respect the future's sovereignty.

[33] "As we are not to live for ever ourselves, and other generations are to follow us, we have neither the power nor the right to govern them, nor to say how they shall govern themselves . . . [It is] the summit of human vanity . . . to be dictating to the world to come." Thomas Jefferson's 1789 letter to James Madison. Jefferson stated that no constitution should last more than nineteen years in order to allow each generation to organize itself with a freedom comparable to the preceding one.

*Promoting the Voice of the Public*

# 10

# Time to Think: Sustainable Development, Future Generations and the Individual

*Ludwig Krämer*

For approximately three decades, the magic term of 'sustainable development' has played a key role in discussions on environmental policy and law. Though the UN WCED, chaired by Gro Harlem Brundtland (the Brundtland Commission), was not the first to introduce the notion of sustainability into the political discussions,[1] its findings created a large echo and were widely quoted in legal agreements and policy statements. The Brundtland Commission stated:

> Sustainable development is development that meets the needs of the present without compromising the ability of future generations to meet their own needs. It contains within it two key concepts: the concept of 'needs', in particular, the essential needs of the world's poor, to which overriding priority should be given; and the idea of limitation, imposed by the state of technology and social organisation on the environment's ability to meet present and future needs.

Quickly, the term 'sustainable development' was spread worldwide and became fashionable. The original objective of the Brundtland Report – to show that developing States could strive for economic development, but were not obliged to sacrifice their environmental assets to that development – was soon set aside. 'Sustainable development' was declared to be a political orientation based on three pillars, economic development, social progress and environmental protection. This led first to the suggestion that progress should be achieved in all three sectors, economy, social issues and environmental protection. Economic operators then tried to interpret the concept in the sense that measures in one sector should only be allowed when they satisfied the needs of the other two sectors. In practice, this was aimed at the environmental sector, where protection measures were only possible where they contributed to economic growth and the creation of jobs; in

[1] P.H. Sands, 'Sustainable Development of Forests, Ships and Law: Some Historical Annotations' (2007) *Environmental Policy and Law* 203; P. Sands, *Principles of International Environmental Law* (Cambridge University Press 2003) 25.

contrast, it was not considered necessary that measures to stimulate economic development – trade agreements, tax reliefs, investment programs and many others – were also beneficial for the environment.

The concept of sustainable development is not applied in fairness, in particular not with regard to the North–South divide (for example, in agriculture, fisheries, trade and other sectors).[2] Discussions, in particular in Western industrialized States,[3] clearly show that the concept is far from being respected. And alternative suggestions which argue, for example, that the environment – the biosphere – is the foundation on which economic and social activities are based,[4] or that the environment – the ecosphere – can well survive without humans but humans cannot survive without the environment, stand little or no chance of becoming a mainstream political or societal orientation for sustainable development.

The inflationary use of the term 'sustainable', a true case of linguistic pollution, contributed to largely emptying the Brundtland term of meaningful content in practice.[5] Every activity can be declared to be sustainable, whether it is sustainable dentistry, sustainable publicity, sustainable education, sustainable criminal law or sustainable nuclear energy. As 'sustainable' is not sharply defined, there is no risk in using the term, as no responsibility is linked to its use. In policy, the term is mostly used as meaning 'long-term'. Thus, a sustainable development policy means a policy whose positive effects are felt over a longer period of time – though nobody dares specify for how long.

As 'sustainable development' is more a slogan than anything else, in practice, measures are taken without any serious consideration for such development. For example, US and German authorities both require that a site which stores nuclear waste must be safe against water breaking, landslides, earthquakes, etc. for one

[2] For a legal overview of the concept from an environmental law perspective, see D.B. Magraw and L.D. Hawke, 'Sustainable Development', in D. Bodansky, J. Brunnée, and E. Hey (eds.), *The Oxford Handbook of International Environmental Law* (Oxford University Press 2007) 614. They see four core elements enshrined in 'sustainable development': intergenerational equity; intragenerational equity; the need to protect the environment; and the need to integrate economic, social and environmental policies. Ibid. at 637. See also, R. Wolfrum, 'International Environmental Law: Purposes, Principles and Means of Ensuring Compliance', in F. Morrison and R. Wolfrum (eds.), *International, Regional and National Environmental Law* (Hague 2000) 3. Wolfrum declares four similar elements to be comprised in the principle: the need to preserve natural resources for the benefit of future generations; the aim to exploit natural resources in a manner which is rational; the equitable use of natural resources; and the integration of environmental requirements into development plans and programs.

[3] The EU should not be forgotten in this context. The Juncker Commission, in office since the end of 2014, has as its official priority 'growth and jobs' and considers this approach as perfectly compatible with the EU's strategy on sustainable development.

[4] G. Winter, 'A Fundament and Two Pillars: The Concept of Sustainable Development 20 Years after the Brundtland Report', in H.C. Bugge and C. Voigt (eds.), *Sustainable Development in International and National Law* (Groningen 2008) 25.

[5] Magraw and Hawke, *supra* note 2 at 637.

million years. Other States may be less demanding,[6] but even where there is a safety requirement of only some 10,000 years, this period is long enough to oblige future generations to live with the deposited nuclear waste in their neighborhood. Arguing that future generations have a free choice to live next to such nuclear waste sites or not is just cynical.

Scientists declare that the warming of the planet Earth by more than 2 °C compared to pre-industrial levels will bring very considerable climate changes all over the world. Yet, since 1990, when the objective of keeping the warming within two degrees was first formulated and measures were initiated to stop the warming of the planet, the emission of GHG, responsible for the warming, increased from 38 to 53 gigawatt $CO^2$-equivalents, thus by some 30 percent.

The Via Appia, a road leading from Rome to Brindisi in the south of Italy, was built about 2,300 years ago. Yet, we still see today its outlines and the villages and cities which were built next to it. Transferring this experience to the future, we have to realize that motorways that are built today might influence the lives of future generations in the next 2,000 years. It is unrealistic to assume that these future generations may decide on alternative lines for their motorways or develop the landscape according to their own preferences.

Perhaps the most disappointing aspect of the 'sustainable development' discussion is the fact that the qualification of a policy, a strategy or of measures as 'unsustainable' has no consequences at all. No nuclear installation was ever stopped because its nuclear waste disposal was considered unsustainable. The EU's transport policy has been, according to Commission declarations, unsustainable since 1995,[7] but nothing has changed. The global loss of biodiversity continues, despite numerous warnings from the UN and other persons, bodies and institutions that this loss is unsustainable. The loss of tropical forests, the pollution of oceans, the overfishing of fish stocks, progressive desertification and soil erosion – wherever one looks, one sees clear signs of a degrading environment without serious steps being undertaken to stop the degradation. This is not due to the fact that the term 'sustainable development' has gained such importance at the level of public international law (PIL), which suffers from notorious enforcement difficulties. Omissions of the need to abide by sustainable development commitments are also numerous in national law and policies and normally remain without consequences.

For politicians, the term 'sustainable' is attractive, as it gives a green color to the policy as a whole or to individual measures ('greenwashing'). For a legal discussion, the time has perhaps come to conclude that the term is almost empty of content and allows the pursuance of whatever objectives the political power-circles have in mind.

6 See E. Rehbinder, 'Disposal of High-Level Nuclear Waste: A Never-Ending Story?' (2014) *Environmental Policy and Law* 256.

7 Commission, COM(96) 624 p. 32; COM(2009) 279 p. 3.

In order to orient policy towards greater sustainability, a number of countries have set up commissions, advisory boards, foundations, an ombudsman or a similar body for sustainable development, a sustainable future or for future generations. The common task of all these offices or bodies is to advise governments on the long-term effects of their political measures, to draw attention to negative implications that their policies might have and to suggest less impairing measures. Naturally, the influence of such offices or bodies on national policy or on individual measures varies from country to country. The bodies are set up by the political group in power and may therefore not be too critical of policy decisions. Staff policy, the embedding of the body in the administrative structure, or their greater or lesser autonomy all leave sufficient possibilities to ensure behavior that is not too critical.

Hereafter, it will be examined to what extent such bodies are capable of ensuring that future generations live in a decent environment, benefit from sustainable development or have the ability to satisfy their own needs.

## A *RIGHT* OF FUTURE GENERATIONS

This 'ability of future generations', solemnly invoked in the Brundtland formula, has provoked a considerable amount of legal, political, philosophical and other literature, which is not to be retraced here as this contribution concentrates on legal aspects. Often enough, the term 'ability' in the Brundtland formula was transposed as meaning 'rights' of future generations. In law, though, it creates considerable difficulties to consider that natural or legal persons that do not yet exist have rights. This does not concern the rights of an embryo or, in succession law, of a *nasciturus*.[8] To perceive the problem, one has rather to think of a person who will live in 100 or 200 years from today. This makes it obvious that the attribution of legal rights or of a general right to sustainable development is not only a legal problem but raises at the same time considerable problems of legal philosophy.

Lawyers have deployed a lot of intellectual creativity to address the question of rights of those who live in future times. Only some of the ideas which were launched can be retraced here, in a rather arbitrary selection. The most renowned pioneer with regard to rights of future generations is Edith Brown Weiss, whose book *In Fairness to Future Generations*, which was followed by several concurrent publications,[9] broke new ground.[10] Brown Weiss argued that each generation

[8] On the private law aspects see E. Gaillard, *Générations futures et droit privé. Vers un droit des générations futures* (Librairie générale de droit et de jurisprudence 2011).

[9] E. Brown Weiss, 'Our Rights and Obligations to Future Generations for the Environment' (1990) AJIL 198; A. D'Amato, 'Do We Owe a Duty to Future Generations to Preserve the Global Environment?' (1990) AJIL 190; L. Gündling, 'Our Responsibility to Future Generations' (1990) AJIL 207.

[10] E. Brown Weiss, *In Fairness to Future Generations: International Law, Common Patrimony and Intergenerational Equity* (Oxford University Press 1989).

"would want to inherit the earth in at least as good condition as it has been in for any previous generation and to have as good access to it as previous generations."[11] She concluded that "intergenerational equity calls for equality among generations in the sense that each generation is entitled to inherit a robust planet that on balance is at least as good as that of previous generations." Where a generation receives a degraded planet and would thus be treated worse than previous generations, this "would be contrary to the principles of intergenerational equity."

Brown Weiss has no remedy against such a breach of the principle of intergenerational equity. And, of course, this makes sense, as one cannot well imagine somebody taking action against previous generations for the degradation of the environment caused by the invention of cars, for example. Brown Weiss is, though, of the opinion that in the principle of intergenerational equity future generations is enshrined a real 'right' of future generations. She conceives these rights as

> group rights, as distinct from individual rights, in the sense that generations hold these rights as groups in relation to other generations past, present and future ... it does not matter who the individuals are or how many they may be. Only at the point where the individuals are born and by definition become members of the present generations do the generational rights attach to individuals.[12]

Consequently, she opined that "enforcement of these intergenerational rights is appropriately done by a guardian or representative of future generations as a group, not of future individuals, who are necessarily indeterminate."[13]

Brown Weiss's concept is referred to by Dinah Shelton[14] without further comment. However, Shelton quotes by way of example a judgment of the Philippines Supreme Court of 1993, where the Court gave a right of standing to plaintiffs which had brought the action also in the name of future Filipino generations.[15] This case will further be discussed below. Other lawyers are more reserved as regards rights of future generations. D.B. Magraw and L.D. Hawke,[16] as well as Marie-Claire Cordonier Segger,[17] are of the opinion that intergenerational equity is enshrined in the notion of 'sustainable development', but abstain from commenting on a *right* of future generations or individuals. Peter Sands also refers to Brown Weiss's concept that "we hold

[11] Brown Weiss, *supra* note 9 at 201.

[12] Ibid. at 204 *et seq*.

[13] Ibid. at 205.

[14] D. Shelton, 'Equity', in Bodansky, Brunnée, and Hey, *supra* note 2 at 644.

[15] *Minors Oposa v. Secretary of the Department of Environment and Natural Resources* www.elaw.org/node/1343 accessed 30 November 2017. For a history and the follow-up of that case see O.A. Houck, 'Light from the Trees: The Story of *Minors Oposa* and the Russian Forest Cases' (2006) law.bepress.com/cgi/viewcontent.cgi?article=7656&context=expresso accessed 30 November 2017.

[16] Magraw and Hawke, *supra* note 2.

[17] M.-C. Cordonier Segger, 'Sustainable Development in International Law', in Bugge and Voigt, *supra* note 4 at 87.

the earth in trust for future generations," but is silent on any mentioning of a *right* which is given to the future generations.[18]

In 2002, the ILA published principles on sustainable development.[19] In section 2.2 it stated:

> The present generation has a right to use and enjoy the resources of the Earth, but is under an obligation to take into account the long-term impact of its activities and to sustain the resource base and the global environment for the benefit of future generations.

In 2008, the International Human Rights Clinic at Harvard University published provisions on rights of future generations.[20] These provisions state:

> Article 1 §1(1): Present and future generations of citizens of the State have the right to an ecologically healthy environment. This right includes but is not limited to: the enjoyment of clean air, pure water, and scenic lands; freedom from unwanted exposure to toxic chemicals and other contaminants; and a secure climate … Article §1 (3): Individuals and groups who believe their environmental right has been violated may seek redress in state courts against alleged violators, both public and private. The State Attorney General is also charged with the enforcement of this provision, with or without additional legislative guidance, in behalf of all citizens, including future generations.

As can be seen from these different quotations, not all lawyers talk of 'rights', and some are more selective in their choice of words. However, before these different opinions are discussed further, two court judgments will be introduced into the discussion which might have some impact on this discussion, the above-mentioned *Minors Oposa* case and the Dutch climate change case.

## THE *MINORS OPOSA* CASE

In the *Minors Oposa* case,[21] the plaintiffs, Filipino minors, brought a class action against the Philippine Secretary of State, arguing that the Philippine Government had concluded timber license agreements which would allow the license holders to fell all the remaining rainforests in the Philippines; these rainforests had been reduced, owing to licensed as well as illegal felling, from some 16 million hectares in 1965 to some 850,000 hectares in the early 1990s. The plaintiffs brought the action

[18] Sands, *supra* note 1 at 258.

[19] ILA, New Delhi Declaration of Principles of International Law Relating to Sustainable Development (2 April 2002) cisdl.org/tribunal/pdf/NewDelhiDeclaration.pdf accessed 30 November 2017.

[20] The International Human Rights Clinic at Harvard Law School: An Environmental Right for Future Generations. Model State Constitutional Provisions & Model Statute (Harvard Law School 2008) www.law.harvard.edu/programs/hrp accessed 30 November 2017.

[21] See *Minors Oposa, supra* note 15.

in the name of the present living population of the Philippines, in particular the children, but also in the name of future generations. They argued that the devastating consequences of the deforestation would be felt by present and future generations and that the Secretary of State had grossly exceeded his discretionary power by granting the licenses.

The Supreme Court granted standing, without limiting the right of standing to the presently living Filipinos. It held that the right of standing was derived from the right to a clean environment, as laid down in Section 16, Article II of the Philippine Constitution,[22] and referred to the principle of intergenerational equity,[23] though without elaborating on it.[24] The Supreme Court did not decide whether a case brought in the name of future generations alone, would have to be considered admissible. This might have been less important for the Court, as the Court was only confronted with questions of the admissibility of a class suit, and such class suits sometimes follow specific rules. However, generally it appears strong to argue that a right to a clean environment, where it exists in constitutional law, is also a presently existing right of generations to come.

In order to discuss the rights of future persons further, we might consider that the case had continued in the Philippines,[25] and that the plaintiffs not only asked deforestation via timber license agreements to be stopped, but had also claimed compensation for the loss of rainforests from the companies which had practiced the licensed or illegal tree felling.[26] What would the rights of the future generations then be?

Brown Weiss submitted that there is a right of each generation to inherit an environment in as good a state as the one the previous generation inherited.[27] It is not clear, though, where this 'right' is derived from. The cases of the Via Appia or the megacity mentioned above demonstrate that our natural environment changes constantly, sometimes for the better and sometimes for the worse. The diversion

[22] Section 16 Article II of the Philippines Constitution of 1987: "The State shall protect and advance the right of the people to a balanced and healthful ecology in accord with the rhythm and harmony of nature."

[23] Houck, *supra* note 15 at fn. 111, mentions that the Court had received one of Brown Weiss's articles on intergenerational equity, as proof that "such an animal existed."

[24] Supreme Court ruling, *supra* note 15: "The adverse effects ... of ... deforestation to the plaintiff minors' generation and to generations yet unborn are evident and incontrovertible. Petitioners minors assert that they represent their generation as well as generations yet unborn. We find no difficulty in ruling that they can, for themselves, for others of their generation and for the succeeding generation, file a lawsuit. Their personality to sue in behalf of the succeeding generations can only be based on the concept of intergenerational responsibility insofar as the right to a balanced and healthful ecology is concerned ... The minors' assertion of their right to a sound environment constitutes, at the same time, the performance of their obligation to ensure the protection of the right for the generations to come."

[25] According to Houck after the Supreme Court Judgment, the case did not continue.

[26] Again, the case is constructed so as to allow the identification of all those companies.

[27] In the same sense, see A. Gosseries, 'On Future Generations' Future Rights' (2008) 446 *Journal of Political Philosophy* 461.

of rivers, the construction of infrastructure projects, the building of dikes on the shoreline or the development of urban agglomerations all change the environment. Why should there be a right to inherit an environment in as good a state as the one inherited by the previous generation?

And who decides what is 'as good a State'? Parts of a generation might see a dense network of motorways, airports and ports in a specific region or country as an improvement (for example in Siberia or Africa); others might see it as a deterioration of the environment. The construction of dikes in the Netherlands to protect against the North Sea was and is seen as a 'good' measure, whereas the construction of dikes along some rivers in Europe turned out to increase the present risk of floods and may thus not be seen as 'good' by everybody.

The model provisions of the Harvard Clinic suggest that the General Attorney of the US States should have the right to enforce the right of future generations.[28] But how does the attorney know what is in the interest of future generations, and whether there is not a discrepancy of opinion between people living in 2100 and people living in 2300? He has no way of finding out. He can only project into the future his present opinion on what those interests would be – and this means that we are back to speculation.

The children of Oposa who brought the case to the courts might have a right to see the deforestation stopped, derived from their right to a sound environment. But it is already more complicated to construct a right of compensation for past deforestation measures. Should this right refer to 1965, or to the pristine state of the Philippines in the seventeenth, eighteenth or nineteenth century? And how could any compensation be distributed among the plaintiffs? The number of questions increases when we talk of future generations: of which generation are we talking, the one that is following the present one, or also generations that live in the next hundred years? Furthermore, suppose that some compensation is granted; who will decide on its distribution among future generations?

Gosseries tries to solve a number of these problems by limiting the right of future generations to the next, overlapping generation.[29] Moreover, he suggests not talking of a right of future generations, but using formulations such as "[e]ach generation has against the previous one a right to" or "[e]ach generation has to the next one the obligation to." This approach might help to overcome some of the difficulties mentioned above. It is submitted, though, that it does not yet help future Filipino generations in a claim against the companies that practiced deforestation.[30]

[28] See The International Human Rights Clinic at Harvard Law School, *supra* note 20.

[29] Gosseries, *supra* note 27 at 463.

[30] Also, Gosseries' suggestion of setting up a fund for future victims constitutes a solution from the present point of view. Future individuals might prefer reforestation or other restoration measures or might disagree on the distribution of the compensation. Ibid. at 468.

## THE *URGENDA* CLIMATE CHANGE CASE

In a judgment of 24 June 2015, a Dutch court decided that the Dutch Government had to reduce its GHG emissions until 2020 by at least 25 percent compared to 1990, and that its present measures, aimed at a reduction of 17 percent, were not in compliance with the law.[31] The action had been brought by Urgenda, a Dutch organization which, according to its statutes, works towards a sustainable society for the benefit of present and future generations.

The Court found that Urgenda had standing, as Dutch law allowed organizations to take court action when their statutory objectives were impaired. And it found in substance that there was a duty of care which the Dutch Government had towards Urgenda which obliged it to distribute the charges and costs of climate policy measures reasonably between present and future generations: "if it turns out to be cheaper to act now, the State has a serious obligation, arising from due care, towards future generations, to act accordingly."

For the purposes of this chapter, however, the question again is whether Urgenda would have been given standing by the Court if it was only defending the interests of future generations. Of course, the Dutch Court did not answer, or even discuss, whether it was sufficient for the court that the standing was derived from Urgenda's statutory rights to aim for a sustainable society. However, it arrives at its judgment in substance by examining a large number of legal provisions and policy statements of public international, EU and national law. Thus, when the Court states that "[t]he principle of fairness means that the policy should not only start from what is most beneficial to the current generation at this moment, but also what this means for future generations, so that future generations are not exclusively and disproportionately burdened with the consequences of climate change," it interprets the 'principle of fairness', the 'duty of care', and/or the 'precautionary principle'. These, and other legal rules and principles interpreted by the court, are *present* legal rules. They apply *at present*, in a quite specific and present case involving Urgenda and the Dutch Government. Rights which are derived from these provisions cannot be the future generations' own rights, because nobody knows whether the provisions in question will still exist when the future generations come into existence; they might be abolished in the meantime.

The Court did not specify that future generations had rights of their own. Rather, it held that the present international, EU and national law contained an obligation of duty of care, of fairness and of taking preventive measures, and that these present rules also extended to fairness and duty of care towards future generations.

It is apparent that the Court came rather close to the title of Brown Weiss's book *In Fairness to Future Generations*, mentioned above: it held that the present legal

[31] Rechtbank Den Haag, case C/09/456689/HAZA13–1396, judgment of 24 June 2015, ECLI:NL: RBDHA:2015:7145.

rules contain an obligation of fairness towards future generations. In other words, by judging the present rights of Urgenda to defend a sustainable society – a term which, as the Court stated, also has an intergenerational dimension – the Court, by way of a reflex, also provided for protection of future generations. Urgenda's own right to protect and promote a sustainable society also had the long-term effect of protecting future generations. Like the Philippines Court, the Dutch Court did not talk of future generations' own rights but discussed present (legal or natural) persons' own rights.

Gosseries' suggestion of limiting rights to the next following generation will not help in the Dutch case either: it is the present scientists who argued that a reduction of GHG emissions by 25 percent by 2020 is necessary, based on the present state of knowledge. It may turn out that the melting of the polar ice caps accelerates so much that the 'correct' reduction would have been 50 percent – or, conversely, that climate change is progressing much more slowly than anticipated, so that only a 10 percent reduction by 2020 would have been necessary. These examples show that the requirement of a 25 percent reduction is based on the *present* state of knowledge, which influences the *present* state of law, of what 'fairness', 'duty of care', 'sustainable development' and other legal terms mean.

In 2019, the Dutch Supreme Court issued the final ruling in the *Urgenda* case. The opinion recognized the duties of the Dutch State to its citizens for climate change in the territories under the jurisdiction of the Netherlands and the larger global community.

## A *PRESENT* RIGHT FOR *FUTURE* GENERATIONS?

Is it thus possible to talk of a right of future generations? The answer largely depends on what is understood as a 'right'. Gosseries indicated that the existence of a right does not depend on the possibility of defending it in court;[32] governments, ombudsmen, guardians, parliamentary committees, commissioners and other persons or bodies may be called to defend or promote a right. The difference in the climate change case is, and remains, that Urgenda and the Oposa children were defending *present* rights. In the case of future generations, it is difficult to reason in the same way, as future generations do not yet exist and therefore cannot have *present* rights.

Nobody disputes that the Philippines Constitution and the Dutch law on climate change are intended to have long-term effects, which might reach far into the future and affect the people who will be living then. And when Philippine or Dutch law allows an ombudsman, a group of citizens or an environmental organization to defend future generations in court already today, this depends on the *present* state of law. It seems, however, impossible that the Oposa children would have received standing in a case where they claimed that the constitutional right to a healthy

[32] Gosseries, *supra* note 27 at 464.

environment of a person living, let us say in 2080 (but not yet living in 1993), was impaired by the timber licenses issued by the competent Secretary of State. This fundamental right to a sound environment of that person of 2080 did not yet exist in 1993.

To this has to be added the uncertainty on the content of such a 'right' of future generations "[n]o one can know what life will be like in future centuries or how future generations will view our present concerns."[33]. Perhaps the Philippines Constitution is amended in future, so that it does not contain a right to a sound environment any more. Perhaps future Philippines generations or persons are quite happy to see the Philippines islands without rainforests, because they can use the soil for other purposes opened up by synthetic biology. Perhaps they all decide to emigrate and settle elsewhere. Perhaps climate change brings about a new form of vegetation that creates high income for the population. Admittedly, these examples are far-fetched. However, they serve as illustrations that when present persons or bodies try to claim rights of future persons or generations, they project their own present preferences, wishes and rights onto those in the future. One might look back for a moment and consider whether, in classical Greece or Rome, people imagined humans flying, going to the moon, providing chemical birth control or inventing robots. Considering what the interests – and, derived from that, the 'rights' – of future persons or generations will be is speculation.

A right in a legal sense is something quite different from a moral right. A legal right is a right which has been attributed to a person or a group of persons by a norm or a complex of norms.[34] A right is a legal rule, in the sense that, when the facts which are stipulated by the rule are given, the rule applies – and the right may be exercised.[35] Persons who live in the future or future generations have not been attributed rights in the present. It is therefore not appropriate to talk of 'rights'. The formula suggested by Gosseries, that one should rather talk of obligations which the presently living persons have towards future persons or generations, appears more correct. These obligations, though, stem from the present legal provisions.

Therefore, the choice of words of the ILA that present actions should consider the 'long-term impact' is preferable to the choice of the word 'rights'. The terms used by the Harvard Law Clinic are, to say the least, misleading and erroneous and raise expectations – among the presently living persons! – which cannot be satisfied by governments, courts or other bodies.

33 J.G. Merrills, 'Environmental Rights', in Bodansky, Brunnée, and Hey, *supra* note 2 at 672.

34 Presumably, the adepts of a theory of 'natural rights' will object to this statement. However, even they would have to admit that the concept of natural rights in a society depends on the consensus in this society that such natural rights shall apply – which is a sort of normative concept.

35 This follows the concept developed on legal rules by R. Dworkin, *Taking Rights Seriously* (Duckworth 1977).

## A REPRESENTATIVE OF THE INTERESTS OF FUTURE GENERATIONS

This brings the discussion back to the question of the effects of measures which are taken today on persons or generations of the future. It is completely undisputed that the long-term effect of measures on humans and on the environment must be taken into consideration when a specific measure is taken.[36] Of course, this also requires consideration of what effects a measure will have on persons or generations which live at a later time. This is precisely what is stated by the *Minors Oposa* case and by the *Urgenda* case. In both cases, though, it is the law as it lies at present which was examined by the courts and which was the parameter for assessing whether the effects of the measure – the timber licenses and the 17 percent reduction in GHG emissions – had sufficiently taken into account the long-term effects.

Is the discussion on 'sustainable development' changing the situation with regard to persons or generations who live in future? It was submitted earlier that the term has degenerated into a slogan. The formula used by the Rechtbank Den Haag, that the term has an intergenerational dimension, demonstrates that the notion of sustainable development can be used as guidance to interpret and orient legal requirements. However, the Rechtbank Den Haag did not base its judgment on the fact that the 17 percent reduction in GHG emissions that the Dutch government had fixed as a policy orientation was a breach of the 'right to a sustainable development'. The Court did not even mention the existence of such a right, and quite rightly so, as such a right does not exist. Rather, the Court found legal obligations for the Netherlands, derived from public international, EU and national legal provisions, which were not respected and which did not sufficiently take into consideration the long-term effects of the Dutch policy decisions on humans and the environment.

The lesson to draw from this judgment is thus that where a will exists at political level or in a courtroom to apply concretely and practically the numerous provisions which aim at protecting preserving and improving the quality of the environment, there is a broad field of applying the presently existing legal norms and principles in a way that gives them a long-term effect on the protection of the environment. Examples of such provisions are the 'high level of environmental protection', the 'sustainable development', the need to integrate environmental requirements into other policies, the common but differentiated policy, the taking into consideration the precautionary principle, to substitute dangerous by less dangerous substances, stop biodiversity loss, minimize negative impacts on the environment, make the

[36] A good drafting requirement of EU Directive 2011/92 on the EIA of certain public and private projects, OJ 2012, L 26 p.1, which provides in annex IV fn. 1 that the impact assessment shall take into consideration "the direct effects and any indirect, secondary, cumulative, short, medium and long-term, permanent and temporary, positive and negative effects of the project."

polluter pay, rectify environmental impairment at source or eradicate poverty. If this will existed and were materialized, present actions would very largely also benefit future persons and generations. In this sense, the terms 'long-term effect' and 'benefit for future generations' are equivalent in meaning.

In terms of legal policy, this means that actions should be taken *now* against measures, plans and programs which grossly neglect the application of presently existing environmental legal provisions. The most flagrant examples aside from the climate change issue are the evolution of Lake Aral and Lake Baikal, the distribution of water from the River Jordan, the oil sands extraction in Canada, the fracking methods used throughout the world, the construction of new nuclear installations, the handling of nuclear waste, and then, in a broader non-environmental context, the migration of people in Africa, Asia and the Americas – all of which call for a radically different environment-oriented development policy and the realization of the commonly agreed objective that poverty should be eradicated. Turning these policy issues in legal battlefields is, it is submitted, the primary task of environmental lawyers.

The preceding lines may be understood as questioning the usefulness of institutions such as the 'Ombudsman for future generations' or similar bodies. However, this is not the case, on the contrary. It is a commonplace that the environment has no voice. At a time when increased communication, intensified trade, new technologies and other tendencies make globalization trends obvious and at the same time increase competition, the efforts to ensure economic growth become more and more the first priority of societies. Long-term environmental effects of planning, economic or structural measures are all too easily and frequently neglected. The value of a butterfly, measured in economic terms, is considered negligible, all the more as the greed for economic growth does not even lead to researching and finding parameters for assessing the value of environmental assets for society. And the saying that the biosphere can survive without humans but humans cannot survive without the biosphere is perceived as of little *economic* value.

An Ombudsman for future generations can be of use in this context. It has the potential to give a voice to the environment, to draw attention to long-term *environmental* effects of measures and their societal consequences, which may go beyond mere economic concerns. It may defend an environmental status quo against destruction which comes from short-term changes.

It is not the purpose of this chapter to describe or defend the function of an Ombudsman for future generations (for long-term environmental effects of measures). Other contributions are better placed to fulfill this function. It is visible, though, that the need for a body which thinks today of the environmental impacts that present policies, plans, programs and measures might have on societies of tomorrow, is obvious to any attentive observer. This author comes from Europe and will therefore take examples from European policy. In this context, a body reflecting on the role of cars in our society, the future of nuclear energy, the development policy which creates more and more migrants daily, the demographic development in the world, not to mention the five big environmental challenges,[37] would be desirable and necessary.

The encyclical *Laudato Si'* of Pope Francis of June 2015 voiced the concern that humankind is on a path towards destroying the home in which we live and in which generations who come after us will have to live. Independently of religious beliefs, it is time to think where we are going and where we want to go. And somebody who thinks about the long-term environmental effects of political or economic measures, beyond the election cycle, is not only welcome but needed.

## CONCLUSION

From the above discussion, several key points and conclusions merit particular attention. First, there is no present right for people who live in the future, or for future generations as such, although there are many fields in which this has been advocated and there have been many attempts to define it. Second, the meaning of 'rights of future generations' includes the need to take into consideration the long-term (environmental) effects of measures, as they can be assessed today. However, the construct of the rights of future generations necessarily extends beyond purely environmental concerns. Third, and finally, bodies or ombudsmen for future generations are essentially think tanks for bringing into the discussion the long-term effects of present policies, plans, programs and measures. They serve many functions and purposes, but their roles are by no means limited to the immediate legislative session.

[37] The fight against climate change, the loss of biodiversity, the omnipresence of chemicals, the management of resources and the eradication of poverty.

# 11

# Claims and Petitions Regarding Environment Preservation for Future Generations

*Renato Machado*

This chapter seeks to demonstrate how the Brazilian legal system regulates the role of individuals and institutions in preserving and defending the environment and other important assets for future generations. In the first part, the chapter begins by addressing how the interests of future generations and the preservation of the environment are viewed under the Brazilian Constitution, and how the mechanisms that protect collective rights and interests work in general.

Following this, the chapter presents the instruments that individuals have at their disposal to protect the interests of future generations, be it by themselves, through a non-governmental organization, or through Brazil's Ministério Público, a public institution that is independent from the Government. As it is essential to achieving justice, the chapter will discuss how the checks and balances involved in the Brazilian legal system operate and coexist in ways that can impact intergenerational equity.

## ENVIRONMENT PRESERVATION AND FUTURE GENERATIONS

Brazil's current Constitution, written in 1988, was the first Brazilian legal document to mention the interests of future generations, stating:

> All have the right to an ecologically balanced environment, which is an asset of common use and essential to a healthy quality of life, and both the Government and the community shall have the duty to defend and preserve it for present and future generations.[1]

In order to ensure the effectiveness of this right, it also states that it is incumbent upon the Government to preserve and restore the essential ecological processes and

[1] Constituição da República Federative do Brasil 1988 Art. 225 *caput*.

provide for the ecological treatment of species and ecosystems; preserve the diversity and integrity of the genetic patrimony of the country and to control entities engaged in research and manipulation of genetic material; and control the production, sale and use of techniques, methods or substances which represent a risk to life, the quality of life or to the environment.[2] One of its main obligations is to demand, in the manner prescribed by law, that works and activities which may potentially cause significant degradation of the environment conduct an environmental impact study (EIS) prior to the commencement of any activity or project, and that the EIS must be made public.[3] The government is also to promote environmental education in all school levels and provide public awareness of the need to preserve the environment.[4]

Besides that, the State is required to define, in all units of the Federation, territorial spaces and their components which are to receive special protection.[5] This designation entails that any alteration and suppression of these spaces would be allowed only by means of law, and any use of which that may harm the integrity of its natural attributes would be forbidden.[6] Last but not least, the fauna and the flora are to be protected through prohibition of all practices which represent a risk to their ecological function, cause the extinction of species or subject animals to cruelty.[7]

As is evident, the Brazilian Constitution views the environmental balance as a right that belongs to all, and also highlights the role of the community in defending it alongside the responsibilities upon the State in relationship to it. At the same time, it considers the environment a collective right, of common use, and it establishes a duty which, if interpreted a bit further, exists not only for the community, but also for the individuals who are part of it.

It is important to note that the term 'collective rights' is used in a broader sense, including all kinds of *trans-individual* rights and interests as well as standard collective rights. As an example, from another aspect of Brazilian law, the Consumers Defense Code (Federal Law 8078), in Article 81, categorizes collective rights in three forms: (1) Diffuse interests or rights: *trans-individual*, with an *indivisible* nature, whose owners are an *indeterminate* group of people, linked by factual circumstances; (2) Collective interests or rights: *trans-individual*, with *indivisible* nature, whose owners are a group, category or class of people linked to themselves or to an adverse party by a legal relationship base – in this case, the group may be

[2] Ibid. at 225 § 1 I, II, V.
[3] Ibid. at 225 § 1° IV.
[4] Ibid. at 225 § 1° VI.
[5] Ibid. at 225 § 1° III.
[6] Ibid.
[7] Ibid. at 225 § 1° VII.

*determined*; and (3) Homogeneous individual interests or rights: individual, which arise from a common source.

This classification, though, can be applied to any collective rights, not only consumer rights, because the Public Class Action Act (Federal Law 7347), in Article 21, states that the provisions from Title III of the Consumers Defense Code will be applied, as far as possible, to the defense of any diffuse, collective and individual rights which can be protected in court through the public class action.

It is perhaps axiomatic that future generations will always benefit from environmental preservation. Even though many laws about environmental protection were written before the 1988 Brazilian Constitution, this was the first time the future generations were ever mentioned. The main consequence is that, in all cases involving the environment, the law must be interpreted with this final goal in mind – there must be protections for present *and future* generations. Bearing that in mind, at least regarding environmental protection, it can be argued that there is no need of any additional legal mandate or special representative for future generations' interests.

Given the interactions between environmental protections and future generations under the Brazilian Constitution, this chapter does not make further mention of details such as how individuals and institutions can defend future generations' interests particularly because, in many ways, these interests are already included in the interpretative sector in the Brazilian legal system in areas such as the preservation of natural resources, as well as any asset that requires a principle of preservation, such as cultural and historical heritage, public patrimony and social security systems.

One of the main reasons for global society's current crisis is excessive individualism, which has been driving people and States to desire more than the world can give, therefore compromising the interests of future generations. This reflects not only the need for rigid social security systems but also for the preservation of natural resources, which are scarce. As a consequence, many legal systems have already developed theories about a *principle of intergenerational equity*, or *solidarity*, that should be borne in mind for any public policy.

Therein lies the necessity of thinking about the role of present individuals and institutions in defending the interests of future generations, and of considering the existence, in every country, of a public institution with the responsibility to defend, although not necessarily exclusively, the interests of future generations.

Have governments shown themselves capable of providing for the needs of our future generations? What have private companies accomplished so far in this regard? How should an institution created for such a purpose be designed? There cannot be uniform answers to these questions, as each country will have its own institutional design to match its historical, cultural, social and political aspects. In the sections that follow, this chapter demonstrates how the Brazilian legal system has evolved so that individuals and institutions have many means of defending the interests of future generations.

## MINISTÉRIO PÚBLICO: A PUBLIC INSTITUTION INDEPENDENT FROM THE GOVERNMENT, ESSENTIAL FOR ACHIEVING JUSTICE

Ministério Público is a Brazilian institution which already existed before the 1988 Constitution, but was given a new design, which considers it an essential institution to the achievement of justice:

> Article 127. Ministério Público is a permanent institution, essential to the jurisdictional function of the State, and it is its duty to defend the juridical order, the democratic regime and the inalienable social and individual interests.
>
> Paragraph 1. Unity, indivisibility and functional independence are institutional principles of the Public Prosecution.[8]

The Constitution further ensures the existence of *functional and administrative autonomy* for the institution, as the Ministério Público may propose remuneration policies and offices, the creation and extinction of its offices and auxiliary services, and "prepare its budget proposal within the limits established in the law of budgetary directives," all to be approved by the Congress. Only career officers, admitted through a civil service entrance examination, which demand at least three years of legal practice, can execute its functions, thereby ensuring participation by the Brazilian Bar Association in the examination.

Regarding the Ministério Público's functions, according to Article 129 of the Brazilian Constitution and Article 6 of Complimentary Law 75/1993, it is responsible not only for criminal charges, as part of the accusatory system, but also for protecting and defending collective rights (*lato sensu*), such as environment, cultural heritage, education, social security, sanitation and public health, consumer rights, and for representing the interests of individuals who cannot express their will completely, such as children, people with mental disorders and, in some cases, indigenous populations. It also exercises external control over police activities, and, further, other functions may be conferred upon it, provided that they are compatible with this purpose.[9] It is forbidden for the Ministério Público to enter into

[8] All the cited legal documents in Portuguese were transcribed from the official translation, and can be found at www.mpf.mp.br/atuacao-tematica/sci/normas-e-legislacao/legislacao/legisla cao-em-ingles-1 accessed 12 October 2016.

[9] Article 129. The following are institutional functions of the Public Prosecution: "I – to initiate, exclusively, public criminal prosecution, under the terms of the law; II – to ensure effective respect by the Public Authorities and by the services of public relevance for the rights guaranteed in this Constitution, taking the action required to guarantee such rights; III – to institute civil investigation and public civil suit to protect public and social property, the environment and other diffuse and collective interests; IV – to institute action of unconstitutionality or representation for purposes of intervention by the Union or by the states, in the cases established in this Constitution; V – to defend judicially the rights and interests of the Indian populations; VI – to issue notifications in administrative procedures within its competence, requesting information and documents to support them, under the terms of the

judicial representation and juridical consultation for governmental entities.[10] This prohibition highlights the independence of the institution, regarding the Government, and Public Administration in general, since it is not rare for the Ministério Público to file lawsuits against the Government for disrespecting collective rights, and on these occasions, the Government will rely on its own staff of public lawyers.

Therefore, is a public institution, inside the structure of the State, but independent from the Government, and from Public Administration in general, with an independent budget, proposed by itself and approved by the Congress. It functions then, as a fourth power, apart from Executive, Legislative and Judiciary, and it is responsible for bringing to justice through the protection of the main public and collective interests and inalienable rights, which cannot depend on individual decisions about wanting to defend them or not.

respective supplementary law; VII – to exercise external control over police activities, under the terms of the supplementary law mentioned in the previous article; VIII – to request investigatory procedures to the institution of police investigation, indicating the legal grounds of its procedural acts; IX – to exercise other functions which may be conferred upon it, provided that they are compatible with its purpose, with judicial representation and judicial consultation for public entities being forbidden."

[10] Article 6. The Federal Public Prosecutor's Office is responsible for: "I – fostering the direct action of unconstitutionality and the respective request of writ of prevention; II – fostering the direct action of unconstitutionality due to inaction; III – fostering the Allegation of disobedience of key precept resulting from the Federal Constitution; IV – fostering the representation for federal intervention in the States and the Federal District; V – fostering, exclusively, the public criminal action, pursuant to the law; ... VII – fostering the civil investigation and the public class action for: a) the protection of the constitutional rights; b) the protection of the social and public heritage, the environment, the assets and rights of artistic, aesthetic, historical, tourist and landscape value; c) the protection of the individual, diffuse and collective non-disposable interests, related to the native communities, the family, the children, the youth, the elderly, the ethnic minorities and the consumer; d) other non-disposable individual, homogeneous, social, diffuse and collective interests; VIII – fostering other actions, including the writ of injunction amongst them whenever there is lack regulating rule that makes the exercise of the rights and constitutional freedoms, as well as the prerogatives inherent to the nationality, sovereignty and citizenship infeasible when the interests to be protected are diffuse; ... XI – judicially defending the rights and interests of the native populations, including those related to the lands traditionally inhabited by them, filing the adequate actions; XII – bringing class actions for the defense of homogeneous individual interests; XIII - filing liability actions against the suppliers of products and services; XIV – promoting other actions necessary to the exercise of its institutional functions, in defense of the legal order, of the democratic system and the non-disposable social and individual interests, especially as for: a) the rule of law and the democratic institutions; b) the economic and financial order; c) the social order; d) the Brazilian cultural heritage; e) the manifestation of thought, of creation, of expression or information; f) administrative probity; g) the environment; ... XIX - the promotion of the responsibility: a) of the competent authority, for lack of the exercise of the incumbencies, constitutionally and legally imposed to the Federal Government, in the defense of the environment, its preservation and its recovery; b) of individuals or legal entities, for the practice of harmful activity related to the environment, considering the application of criminal penalties and the compensation of the damages that have been caused."

The Ministério Público's main reason to exist has, then, two foundations. The first is the principle of inertia, also linked to the accusatory criminal system: the judicial branch, ultimate guardian of the Constitution and of everyone's rights, cannot commence a lawsuit to protect any right, in order to guarantee its own independence and impartiality. The second is a fact. At the time the Constitution was written, Brazil was still recovering from a dictatorial regime; civil society was not well organized and needed an institution to guarantee that the protection of these rights could be brought to justice and that society's freedom and social rights were guaranteed in face of government omission or abuse.

The Ministério Público's role in defending collective rights is analogous to that of the Defensorias del Pueblo in Spain and in Latin American countries or the Ombudsman figure that exists in other countries, but also includes the power to bring cases to the courts. It was the Constituent Assembly's choice in 1988 to confer these functions on an already established institution, instead of creating a new structure.

The institution is organized similarly to the judicial branch, meaning that there is a Ministério Público unit or branch which functions in respect of each unit or branch of the judiciary. In other words, there is a federal branch that acts in federal justice, a labor branch that acts in labor justice, a state branch in each of Brazil's states, and also military and federal district branches. As a guarantee of the institution's independence and impartiality, the Ministério Público's members have the same guarantees as the judges, under Article 128, paragraph 5 of the Brazilian Constitution, namely: (a) *life tenure*, after two years in office, with loss of office only by a final and unappealable judicial decision; (b) *irremovability*, save for reason of public interest, through the decision of the competent collegiate body, by the vote of the absolute majority of its members, with full defense being ensured; and (c) *irreducibility of compensation*.

On the other hand, to guarantee their independence and impartiality, the members are also prohibited from the following: (a) receiving, on any account or for any reason, fees, percentages or court costs; (b) practicing the legal profession; (c) participating in a commercial company, under the terms of the law; (d) exercising, even when on paid availability, any other public function, except for a teaching position; (e) engaging in political or party activities; and (f) receiving, on any account or for any reason, financial aid or contribution from individuals, and from public or private institutions, save for the exceptions set forth in law. Even though the members are not elected, they are selected through a very difficult series of public exams and, within the scope of the checks and balances system, the Ministério Público´s actions are controlled through many means. Its actions and decisions cannot be automatically executed, as they depend on Court's decisions, and therefore are always submitted to control by the judicial branch.

According to Article 128 of the Constitution, its Chief, the Federal General-Prosecutor, is chosen by the Brazilian President, usually from the candidates receiving the three highest votes in an election in which only members vote.[11] Another form of control is exercised by the Ministério Público's National Council, which is composed of representatives from many public and also private sectors, with the responsibility to investigate any abuse of power by the Ministério Público's members, as provided in Article 130-A of the Constitution.[12]

## CLAIMS AND PETITIONS REGARDING ENVIRONMENTAL PRESERVATION

In Brazil, people have many means of presenting claims and petitions to defend collective interests, including those of future generations. One of the oldest and most important is the popular action, which can be presented directly to a judge.

Since 1965, years before the Ministério Público's current design was elaborated, through Article 1 of the Popular Action Act (Federal Law 4717) any Brazilian citizen has had a legitimate role in presenting a petition of nullity declaration or annulment of public acts that may cause damage to public patrimony to the Court, including any asset of economic, touristic, artistic, aesthetic or historical value. Since then, the

[11] Article 128. The Public Prosecution comprises: "I – the Public Prosecution of the Union, which includes: a) the Federal Public Prosecution; b) the Labor Public Prosecution; c) the Military Public Prosecution; d) the Public Prosecution of the Federal District and the Territories; II – the Public Prosecutions of the states. Paragraph 1. The head of the Public Prosecution of the Union is the Attorney-General of the Republic, appointed by the President of the Republic from among career members over thirty-five years of age, after his name has been approved by the absolute majority of the members of the Federal Senate, for a term of office of two years, reappointment being allowed. Paragraph 2. The removal of the Attorney-General of the Republic, on the initiative of the President of the Republic, shall be subject to prior authorization by the absolute majority of the Federal Senate. Paragraph 3. The Public Prosecutions of the states, of the Federal District and the Territories shall prepare a list of three names from among career members, under the terms of the respective law, for the selection of their Attorney-General, who shall be appointed by the Head of the Executive Power for a term of office of two years, one reappointment being allowed."

[12] Article 130-A. The National Council of the Public Prosecution is composed of fourteen members appointed by the President of the Republic, after their nomination has been approved by an absolute majority of the Federal Senate, for a two-year term of office, one reappointment being permitted, as follows: "I – the Attorney-General of the Republic, who chairs the Council; II – four members of the Public Prosecution of the Union, representing each one of its careers; III – three members of the Public Prosecution of the States; IV – two judges, one of whom nominated by the Supreme Federal Court and the other one by the Superior Court of Justice; . . . V – two lawyers, nominated by the Federal Board of the Brazilian Bar Association; VI – two citizens of notable juridical learning and spotless reputation, one of whom nominated by the Chamber of Deputies and the other one by the Federal Senate. Paragraph 1. The members of the Council who are members of the Public Prosecution shall be nominated by their respective bodies, under the terms of the law. Paragraph 2. It is incumbent upon the National Council of the Public Prosecution to control the administrative and financial operation of the Public Prosecution and the proper discharge of official duties by its members . . ."

popular action has frequently been used by citizens to defend the environment and to claim annulment of environmental licenses when they were issued against the law, especially after the 1988 Constitution also guaranteed, in Article 5, LXXIII, any citizen the right to propose a popular action to protect the environment.

The popular action has its origins in the Roman Empire's *actiones populares*, through which citizens defended public causes.[13] The kind of relationship that was developed between citizen and State at that time made it a common phenomenon.[14] The citizen, acting in his personal interest, would safeguard the interests of all, defend the community's rights and the rights of the State.[15]

In Brazil, it is understood that the popular action is a civic and political guarantee, as well as an instrument against improbity and administrative abuse as part of the citizen's power of public participation, assuring them the right to promote the responsibility of public administrators. It is a form of direct exercise of political rights and popular sovereignty, as a kind of derogation of the principle that indicates that this participation should be exercised only by the elected representatives.[16] According to Articles 11 and 12 of the Popular Action Act, if the sentence is determined to be in favor of the claimant, it will decree the invalidity of the impugned act, and condemn those responsible for the act – as well as any beneficiary – to recover or indemnify the damage, and also to determine the reimbursement of expenses including judicial costs and lawyers. To inform the petition, the citizen can require from any public entity the necessary information and public certificates, as long as their goal is specified, and they have to be provided within fifteen days.

The interpretation of the popular action by the Superior Courts has evolved, accepting that it may be proposed not only against illegal acts but also against omissions, in which case the judge may determine other appropriate injunctions, as well as preventive measures when the damage is yet to occur.[17] This is especially important in popular actions proposed to defend the environment, in which the judge may determine any measure able to guarantee the effectiveness of the protection claimed.[18]

Brazilian citizens have, then, three different possibilities regarding claims and petitions to defend and protect the environment for future generations. The first and oldest, as stated, would be as an individual, by their own means, through the Popular Action Act. The second possibility, as part of an association or non-governmental organization, would be for a public class action. As stated in the

[13] José Afonso da Silva, *Ação Popular Constitucional: Doutrina e Processo*, 2nd edn. (Malheiros 2007) 17–19.
[14] Ibid.
[15] Ibid.
[16] Ibid. at 83–85.
[17] STJ Resp 889766-SP 2ªT DJ 18/10/2007 333.
[18] STJ Resp 1098028/SP 1ª T 09/02/2010.

Public Class Action Act, Article 5, any association that exists for at least one year and includes in its institutional goals the protection of environment, consumer rights, artistic, historical, aesthetic and touristic patrimony may file a lawsuit to defend these rights and interests in Court.

The other possibility is that a public class action can also be brought by the Ministério Público, the Public Defense, the Union, the states, the federal district and the municipalities, any governmental agency or public company, or public foundations. In this case, instead of presenting the claim directly to court, the citizen would first exercise their right of petition, presenting it to any of these public institutions. The right of petition is also a means of exercising political rights, guaranteed by the 1988 Constitution in Article 5, XXXIV, and assuring all citizens the right of petition to the public authorities in the defense of rights or against abuse of power. This instrument will naturally be used prior to the institution of a popular action, through which the citizen will require information and demand measures. If the authority does not comply with the demands, the citizen will be able either to file a popular action lawsuit directly to a court, or to present a petition to the Ministério Público, requesting it to open a civil investigation or to file a public class action.

Environmental protection, though, is a very difficult task, as environmental law is difficult to understand and interpret, and the causes demand a good deal of technical support. In Brazil, for instance, there may be Federal, state and/or municipal legislation regarding the environment and cultural heritage, but also legal regulations from a great variety of agencies for each sector. Rather than filing class actions lawsuits by themselves, civil society organizations in Brazil often count on the Ministério Público to do this job, especially because of the lack of transparency in the government at all its levels and the concomitant difficulty in obtaining public information, which often requires going through long bureaucratic procedures.

All these issues created the need to promulgate a specific law regulating the right of access to information in 2011, Federal Law 12527, which also applies to the Ministério Público, as well as to all public institutions. In its tenth article, this law states that an interested party can present a petition to access information from public institutions for any legitimate means. The petition should contain the identification of the applicant and the specification of the required information. If not complied with, the same law provides for sanctions to the agent responsible.

In addition, Federal Law 7347, which regulates public class actions regarding responsibility for damage caused to the environment, consumer rights, any asset of artistic, cultural, historic, or touristic value, urban order, public patrimony, the honor and dignity of ethnic, racial or religious groups, and infractions of the economic order, as well as any other collective or diffuse interests, states in Article 6 that any person can, and any public functionary shall, initiate a Ministério Público initiative by providing information and elements of facts that may be the object of a public class action.

Another issue that should be highlighted is that the Brazilian Constitution, in the chapter that regulates the Ministério Público's functions, expressly says that:

> Art. 129. Paragraph 1. Legitimation by Ministério Público for the civil actions set forth in this article shall not preclude those of third parties in the same cases, according to the provisions of this Constitution and of the law.

In Brazil, because of its independence and its main constitutional attributions, the Ministério Público is a fundamental institution to guarantee the protection of environmental balance and natural resource preservation for future generations and is also a third alternative through which citizens can access juridical measures to protect these interests without having the weight and responsibility of doing so on their own. On the other hand, granting the individual the power to petition in favor of future generations' interests can also be considered a form of democracy, which is not only attained through voting or by occupying public office. The role of public institutions in this matter must not be one of substituting the action of citizenship, but rather of promoting it. Furthermore, if the individual feels the need to defend a collective interest, they should not feel obliged or compelled to join an association or any form of NGO – the power to foster the popular action, in this aspect, serves to strengthen the right to freedom of association.

The problem does not lie, then, in the legitimacy the system assigns to individuals, but on how it is exercised and controlled.[19] The Brazilian procedures for environmental protection, therefore, have already positively solved the fundamental question of whether one individual member of society can act in favor of an entire community of unborn people. The system also provides solutions in case of the petitioner's neglect of the cause. Indeed, the Public Class Action Act (Law 7347) states in Article 5, Paragraph 1 that, when the Ministério Público is not the petitioner, it can adhere to the petition, or it will act, mandatorily, as the law supervisor or *custos juris*, meaning that it can demand evidential instruction in the same way as any petitioner but also that, before the final sentence, it has to give its legal opinion on the case. Also, in Paragraph 3, there is a fail-safe mechanism through which, in case of non-justified abandonment of the cause by the petitioner association, the Ministério Público, or other legitimate actor, will assume the claim. Further, in Article 16, it is stated that the civil sentence will provide *erga omnes res judicata* effect except if the petition is rejected after the instruction phase for lack of evidence, in which case any other legitimate actor will be able to file another class action lawsuit with the same purpose but based on new evidence. Such a possibility does not exist within lawsuits that concern individual rights.

The Popular Action Act (Law 4717) provides in Article 18 exactly the same mechanisms as found in Article 16 of the Public Class Action Act in terms of

[19] E. Ferraresi, *Ação Popular, Ação Civil Pública e Mandado de Segurança Coletivo: Instrumentos Processuais Coletivos* (Forense 2009) 263.

avoiding damage to the collective interests in case of eventual abandonment of the cause or weak evidential instruction by the petitioner. In Article 6 § 4, the Act also states that the Ministério Público must follow the case and collaborate with the production of evidence, and, in Article 9, that if the petitioner abandons the case or manifests the intent to reject the petition for lack of evidence, the judge will publish notifications, after which any citizen or the Ministério Público will be able to assume the case, substituting as the petitioner from that point on. The role of the Ministério Público in the popular action, as defender of the juridical order, is that of an autonomous public party, responsible for ensuring the regularity of the process, hastening the production of evidence, and promoting civil and criminal responsibility of the guilty.[20] Furthermore, according to the Popular Action Act in Article 13, and in Article 5, LXXIII of the Brazilian Constitution, if the judge verifies that the petitioner presented the demand in bad faith or recklessly, after the popular action legal procedure, it can be condemned to pay a fee equivalent to ten times the judicial costs.

These are some of the instruments that the Brazilian legal system has developed to control individual action in the defense of collective interests. But there are also forms of control regarding Ministério Público, especially in case of inaction. Indeed, if the Ministério Público is asked to open a civil investigation to propose a public class action and the prosecutor has already exhausted the preparatory inquiries and is convinced that there is no plausible cause to file the lawsuit, the case may be dismissed through a decision with reasonable grounds. The petitioner can appeal to the Ministério Público's High Council or Coordination and Revision Chambers, depending on the structure of the relevant branch of the Ministério Público. After the dismissing decision, the records of the civil inquiry will be mandatorily sent to the High Council or Coordination and Revision Chambers for homologation, even if the petitioner does not appeal, which is an important form of control to prevent the collective right being left unprotected arbitrarily, as stated in Article 9 of Federal Law 7347. In spite of this, since the Ministério Público does not hold exclusive jurisdiction to propose the public class action, the petitioner will still be able to resort to any other legitimate parties.[21]

Regarding the effects of the final sentence, in both the popular action and public class action, to remove any doubt, if the decision is in favor of the petitioner or if the case is dismissed because the judge concludes that the claim is unfounded, the sentence will have *res judicata erga omnes* and *ultra partes* effect, meaning the object of the claim cannot be raised again in any lawsuit, and the effects of the sentence can be imposed on citizens who did not participate in the lawsuit. Only if the case is

[20] H.L. Meirelles, *Mandado de segurança, ação popular, ação civil pública, mandado de injunção, habeas data e ação direta de inconstitucionalidade*, 23rd edn. (Malheiros 2001) 133–134.

[21] H.N. Mazzilli, *A Defesa dos Interesses Difusos em Juízo*, 16th edn. (Saraiva 2003).

dismissed because of lack of evidence will the sentence not have this effect, meaning any other legitimate citizen or institution may be able to file another lawsuit with identical foundation, but based on new evidence: what the doctrine usually refers as *res judicata secundum eventum litis vel probationem*.[22] Obviously, all these different lawsuits and possibilities of initiation that coexist in the Brazilian legal system presuppose that the problem cannot be solved by the entity responsible for the law violation, or for the environmental damage, be it a person, a company or the government, and that the measures taken by the environmental agencies were not sufficient to avoid or contain the damage.

## LEGAL INSTRUMENTS OF ENVIRONMENTAL PROTECTION

As previously stated, environmental cases can be brought through a popular action by an individual citizen or through a public class action, either by an association or by a public institution such as the Ministério Público. However, besides the public class action, Brazilian prosecutors have many other instruments at their disposal to defend collective rights. According to Articles 7 and 8 of Complimentary Law 75/1993, prosecutors can initiate formal civil investigations, through which they can request information, technical reports and inspections, take formal testimonies and summon public hearings.[23]

Refusing, postponing or omitting information requested by the Ministério Público to instruct a public class action constitutes a crime, under Federal Law 7347, Article 10, and in that lies the advantage for Brazilian society in being defended by the Ministério Público: unlike society and individuals, it has adequate tools to handle private companies and government cases of abuse and neglect. In many cases, the problem is solved only by starting the investigation and notifying the public or private agent responsible.

[22] R. de Camargo Mancuso, *Ação Popular*, 8th edn. (Revista dos Tribunais 2015) 366–372.

[23] Article 7: "It is responsibility of the Federal Public Prosecution Service, whenever it is necessary to the exercise of its institutional functions: I – to institute civil investigation and other administrative correlated procedures; II – to request investigations and the institution of police investigation and military police investigation, and it may follow them up and to present evidences; III – to request to the competent authority the institution of administrative procedures, except for the disciplinary procedures, and it may follow them up and adduce evidence." Article 8: "For the exercise of its duties, the Federal Public Prosecution Service may, in the procedures under its competency: I – notify witnesses and request their bench warrant, in the case of groundless absence; II – request information, examinations, expert investigations and documents from authorities of the direct or indirect Public Administration; III – request, from the Public Administration, transient services from its servants and necessary material means for the accomplishment of specific activities; IV – request information and documents from private entities; V – carry out inspections and investigations; VI – have free access to any public or private place, respecting the constitutional rules related to dwelling defense; VII – issue notifications and summons necessary for the procedures and investigations it institutes; VIII – have unconditional access to any data bank of public character or related to service of public relevance; IX – request the aid of police force . . ."

When the investigation is concluded, another interesting instrument at the disposal of the Ministério Público is to issue Recommendations to Public Administration to improve the quality of public services, as well as to respect interests, rights and assets, establishing a reasonable time frame for the adoption of the necessary actions, and notifying it of any violation of the Constitution or the Law. This also helps to solve problems before bringing them to court, which is very positive, as judicial lawsuits demand time and entail significant costs. Even though compliance with the Ministério Público's Recommendations is not mandatory, after the agent responsible for any legal violation is notified, if this violation constitutes an act of impropriety or a crime, the agent cannot claim lack of knowledge about the facts or the law applied in the case, which is very important for the effectiveness of collective rights protection.

In the same manner, Complimentary Law 75, Articles 11–16, which organizes the Ministério Público at the federal level and concerns the defense of constitutional rights – including environmental preservation for future generations – establishes that the defense of citizens' constitutional rights aims to guarantee the effective respect of those rights by all public institutions. In cases where these issues arise, the Citizen's Rights Prosecutor may act by request or *motu proprio*, notifying the authority responsible to provide information in timely fashion. Regardless of whether the information is received, if the Citizen's Rights Prosecutor concludes that constitutional rights were, or are still, disrespected, it shall notify the responsible entity to cease the violation or take measures to guarantee that it will not happen again.

Another important form of extrajudicial settlement of conflicts is the Adjustment of Conduct Commitment Term which, if not complied with, can be executed directly in the courts without a prior lawsuit. It is a formal settlement term through which any private or public agent that caused damage to the environment or any other collective interest assumes a commitment to execute an environmental remediation project or to indemnify the violation. In this way, it is an alternative method to protect collective rights, complementing the judicial system in a faster, more efficient and economical fashion.

To avoid possible collusion or fraud, the individuals or associations who may be about to file a popular action or public class action lawsuit are not allowed to participate in Adjustment of Conduct Compromise Terms, as Federal Law 7347 Article 5 § 6 states:

> The legitimate public entities can take from those interested a commitment of conduct adjustment to the legal requirements, with penalty provision, which will have effectiveness of extrajudicial executive title.

Even the Ministério Público can only argue about forms of compliance and deadlines, not about the environmental recovery itself, otherwise the Term would be illegal, since environmental balance is an inalienable right.[24] Society, the academy

[24] E. Ferraresi, *supra* note 19 at 228.

and other interested parties can be called to public hearings to collaborate on the instruction of civil investigations as well as on the elaboration of these commitment terms, give them more popular legitimacy, and also give opinions on any polemical case investigated by the institution.

Last but not least, the Ministério Público also has exclusive jurisdiction to file criminal lawsuits for crimes against the environment, in light of criminal charges being classically its primary function. These criminal aspects will not be explored further, since they are not related to this chapter's direct object of study, even though the role of criminal law in preventing new violations of future generations interests cannot be denied.

## CONCLUSION

Having a public institution that is independent from the government receive and analyze claims and petitions regarding environmental protection for future generations, as well as other collective rights and interests, is desirable, since no citizen, in case of conflict of interests, should have to feel the weight of facing the government and/or private companies by himself. That does not mean it should exclude the possibility of any citizen presenting claims and petitions directly to the Court.

The role of individuals in the protection of future generations' interests cannot be underestimated, as it will always rely on the individual's decisions, whether through a public institution or an NGO. The best way to ensure that the needs of future generations are well provided for is, in democratic countries, to create a hybrid checks and balances system, through which individuals, NGOs and public institutions can work together to achieve these goals.

Therefore, legal systems should predict mechanisms through which deliberate abandonment of the cause, neglect, collusion or fraud are prevented. There should also be adequate instruments of extrajudicial conflict settlements at their disposal to prevent long and protracted lawsuits over an efficient answer to the violation. Finally, it is desirable that the means to present claims and petitions, as well as the means to obtain the public information that enables the exercise of these rights, be accessible and simple enough to be understood by all citizens, with as little bureaucracy as possible.

# 12

# Rationale and Means of Public Participation

*Gyula Bándi*

Sustainable development might have several constituents, among which the different aspects of public participation have a paramount relevance. If one examines the given topic – sustainable development and its constituents – there are always some vital new elements worth talking about, among which public participation is at the core. A vital fresh and illuminating element in the field of environmental sustainability is the Encyclical Letter of Pope Francis of May 2015,[1] which discusses sustainable development and environmental issues in detail. A kind of motto for the whole Encyclical is provided in point 13: "The urgent challenge to protect our common home includes a concern *to bring the whole human family together* to seek a sustainable and integral development, for we know that things can change." It is not our task to introduce this remarkable document in detail, but we must point to the special role of public participation in the whole enigma.

First, the theoretical foundation for the discussion of any further details – among others of public participation – is provided for in the document, highlighting the role of people at all possible levels:

> 142. If everything is related, then the health of a society's institutions has consequences for the environment and the quality of human life … In this sense, social ecology is necessarily institutional, and gradually extends to the whole of society, from the primary social group, the family, to the wider local, national and international communities.

After that the special role of the public is strongly underlined again:

> 179. … *public pressure* has to be exerted in order to bring about decisive political action. Society, through non-governmental organizations and intermediate groups,

[1] Pope Francis, *Laudato Si': On Care for Our Common Home*, Encyclical Letter, 24 May 2015 w2.vatican.va/content/francesco/en/encyclicals/documents/papa-francesco_20150524_enciclica-laudato-si.html accessed 30 November 2017.

must put pressure on governments to develop more rigorous regulations, procedures and controls. Unless citizens control political power – national, regional and municipal – it will not be possible to control damage to the environment.

And later we learn:

181. … in the absence of pressure from the public and from civic institutions, political authorities will always be reluctant to intervene, all the more when urgent needs must be met.

There is no better way of explaining why public participation is always a matter of great concern and shall be taken as an indispensable element of sustainable development. It is undoubtedly also connected with our introductory statement: public participation is a core component of sustainable development, and shall also be taken as a legally comprehensible component.

## THE TRIANGLE OF SUSTAINABLE DEVELOPMENT, LAW AND PUBLIC PARTICIPATION

Accordingly, first it is necessary to examine the legally comprehensible elements of sustainable development. The examples below do not provide a full picture, but rather focus on the most characteristic examples, as several attempts made by different organizations and academics to put legal flesh on the bones of sustainable development will only be mentioned here for illustration.

From among the several attempts following UNCED in 1992, sustainable development was studied in many forms and forums, one of them in 1995 focusing on the identification of the Principles of International Law for Sustainable Development.[2] This Report applies the following groups of 'principles and concepts' (the relevant numbering of the document is in brackets):

- Principles of interrelationship and integration (15–18)
- Principles and concepts relating to environment and development (19–74)
- Principles and concepts of international cooperation (75–122)
- Principles and concepts of participation, decision-making and transparency (123–139)
- Principles and concepts of dispute avoidance and resolution (140–160)

The Report may not be regarded as a homogeneous conceptual document; rather it is a mix of principles and instruments, of different special sustainable development

[2] Expert Group, 1995, *Report of the Expert Group Meeting on Identification of Principles of International Law for Sustainable Development*, Geneva, Switzerland, 26–28 September 1995, prepared by the Division for Sustainable Development for the Commission on Sustainable Development Fourth Session 18 April–3 May 1996, New York www.un.org/documents/ecosoc/cn17/1996/background/ecn171996-bp3.htm accessed 30 November 2017.

aspects versus general concepts of international cooperation. Still, the Report is a vital source of further legal development, a solid and widely accepted foundation for establishing and improving sustainable development law.

Using a different classification than that of the above-mentioned structure of the paper, the several constituent principles of the Report may be divided into three major classes, on the basis of their direct or less direct relationship with sustainable development as such:

- First, some constituents of the Report have a clear, direct link to sustainable development; consequently they may be taken as specific legal principles and concepts of sustainable development law, and within this, primarily also of environmental interests;
- Second, there is a group of principles and concepts that may have a less direct impact on sustainable development, covering mostly the reasonable use of resources, but this is closer to the material interests;
- Third, there is a group of principles and concepts with a less direct, looser connection to sustainable development, representing rather the principles and concepts of international law.

Within the first – and, from the point of view of sustainable development, most important – group of principles and concepts, *public participation* has also been listed with its three well-known pillars (access to information, informed decision-making and access to justice),[3] together with prevention and precaution, integration or equity. One may also point to many other components of the Report that have an impact on public participation, such as the following:

- There is a problem concerning common but differentiated responsibilities, which may mostly be taken as an international concept, while reference to the common tasks also requires public participation.
- Similarly, the requirement of notification to and consultations with neighboring and potentially affected States may not be managed without equal rights provided for the public of the affected countries or neighbors.
- Under the heading of 'Duty to cooperate in the spirit of global partnership' of the Report: "80. The principle of cooperation in the spirit of global partnership not only refers to cooperation among States, but should also be extended to non-State entities, ranging from business associations through non-governmental organizations to the academic world."

These are just some examples that refer to the web of many similar interrelated problems.

[3] See UNECE Convention on Access to Information, Public Participation in Decision-Making and Access to Justice in Environmental Matters (Aarhus Convention).

One important further aspect of the Report of the Expert Group that is also essential from the point of view of public participation is the reference to the right to (a healthy) environment: "The right to a healthy environment provides a focus to guide the integration of environment and development. Development is sustainable where it advances or realizes the right to a healthy environment."[4] As with the issue of the right to a healthy environment, the interests of future generations necessitate public participation. This is clearly articulated by the fact that future generations need representation:

> ... our conversation is one-sided. However, we are the speakers and future generations are the listeners. Just as the past speaks to us with many voices and through many idioms, so too do we now speak to the future.[5]

Therefore, the wording of the Report should be very rational, as it is in point 44: "It also entitles each generation to diversity comparable to that enjoyed by previous generations." Thus, there is a chance to compare interests and needs, even if they are different from those of the present generations.

The ILA also played a substantial role in the discussion over the legal substance of sustainable development, releasing a declaration at its conference held in New Delhi in April 2002 on the international legal principles applicable to sustainable development.[6] This Declaration was reinforced ten years later in Sofia.[7] The Sofia document did not modify the content of the original Declaration, but adopted an implementation guide in addition.[8] The Declaration considers sustainable development as a common concern of humanity, and takes human rights as a central part of sustainable development. The New Delhi Declaration of the ILA distinguished seven principles that constitute different elements of the concept of sustainable development.[9] Principle No. 5 of the Declaration is the principle of public participation together with access to information and justice. As in the Report of the Expert Group, these principles also construct sustainable development law around the

[4] Expert Group, *supra* note 2 at point 31.

[5] J.L. Olmsted, 'Representing Nonconcurrent Generations: The Problem of Now' (2008) 23 *Journal of Environmental Law & Litigation* 463.

[6] ILA, New Delhi Declaration of Principles of International Law in the Field of Sustainable Development (2 April 2002).

[7] Resolution No. 7/2012, Committee on International Law on Sustainable Development, 75th Conference of the ILA held in Sofia, Bulgaria, 26–30 August 2012.

[8] 2012 Sofia Guiding Statements on the Judicial Elaboration of the 2002 New Delhi Declaration of Principles of International Law Relating to Sustainable Development, annex to the Resolution No. 7/2012.

[9] The principles of ILA 2012 Sofia are: (1) the duty of states to ensure the sustainable use of natural resources; (2) the principle of equity and the eradication of poverty; (3) the principle of cooperation, the principle of common but differentiated responsibilities and the principle of precaution; (4) the principle of the precautionary approach; (5) the principle of public participation and access to information and justice; (6) the principle of good governance; (7) the principle of integration.

elements of equity (inter- and intra-generational equity), precaution, public participation (as procedural guarantees of the right to environment) and integration.

The European Community also wanted to create meaningful content for sustainable development or sustainable development law. They commissioned a study on the law of sustainability in 2000, formulated by a Greek author, Michael Decleris.[10] There are twelve 'principles' discussed in the study, the first of which may also be taken as a broader concept of public participation: the public environmental order, indicating the methods of finding the voice of the environment. The last principle is also different from the others, and moreover might be taken as a rather direct vision of public participation: environmental awareness, which means here the need to involve the society as a whole, and as a consequence one may also mention environmental democracy as a method of improving awareness.

Amongst the several conceptual papers one should also mention the attempts of the IUCN in designing a draft covenant, for the first time in 1995, while a fourth version has been issued in 2010.[11] This is not the place to reiterate all the elements, from equity to precaution, proportionality to eradication of poverty, etc. There is one additional element in the new Art. 9: resilience, meaning here the adaptive capacity of natural systems and human communities to survive and restore their systems. Resilience, being a flexible method, should also encompass the support and participation of the public.

While this chapter will not enter here into the discussion of sustainable development law in detail, one may not forget that there have been many attempts in legal theory to formulate the content of sustainable development law. In summing up the development of international law of sustainable development one should apply the words of Bosselmann:[12]

> The continued existence of the principle of sustainability has two important consequences. The first is that sustainable development is given meaning and direction ... The second consequence is that existing treaties, laws and legal principles need to be interpreted in the light of the principle of sustainability.

Public participation is an indisputable component of sustainable development in most of the legal writings:

> Public participation, supported by transparency and access to justice, is one of the most recognised principles of sustainable development ... This is based on social laws, such as respect for the human rights to assembly, freedom of speech and

[10] M. Decleris, *The Law of Sustainable Development*, Report to the Commission (2000) 42–43 www.woodlandleague.org/documents/sustainability/sustlaw.pdf accessed 30 November 2017.

[11] Draft International Covenant on Environment and Development, Fourth Edition: Updated Text, Environmental Policy and Law Paper No. 31 Rev. 3, 2010.

[12] K. Bosselmann, *The Principle of Sustainability: Transforming Law and Governance* (Ashgate 2008) 41.

> expression ... A corollary to this requirement is the need for access to justice for individuals and groups, comprising effective judicial or administrative procedures to redress allegations of violations of entitlements or rights.[13]

## JUSTIFICATION OF PUBLIC PARTICIPATION

Based on the above-mentioned examples of documents, reports and papers of different authors, one does not have to be very bold to state that public participation is an essential component/principle of sustainable development. Still, in order to create an even stronger vision in this regard, this chapter collects below those major underlying principles or grounds for public participation, mostly connected with other components of sustainable development, which support our statement. The main constituents to be discussed in detail below are: (1) democracy; (2) rule of law; (3) collective or community dimension (covering also equity and the concept of human rights); (4) common heritage of mankind; (5) common concern of humanity; (6) common good; (7) subsidiarity; and (8) environmental justice.

The first general and most obvious foundation is democracy, either direct or representative democracy. Both have their role to play in society, but direct democracy, meaning the real theater of public participation, must always have an obvious share. This is a solid basis for public participation. If one mostly focuses on environmental aspects, Principle 10 of the Rio Declaration shall be taken into consideration, which begins with the following verdict:[14] "Environmental issues are best handled with participation of all concerned citizens, at the relevant level." This is the real essence of democracy. Environmental democracy is taken in practice as how public participation is managed: "Environmental democracy is rooted in the idea that meaningful public participation is critical to ensure that land and natural resource decisions adequately and equitably address citizens' interests."[15] Many people agree that environmental democracy is made for balancing the failures of economic development.

As an example of basic democratic requirements, we turn to the TEU of the Treaty of Lisbon,[16] which contains references to and conditions of democracy in several instances:

> Art. 1: This Treaty marks a new stage in the process of creating an ever closer union among the peoples of Europe, in which decisions are taken as openly as possible and as closely as possible to the citizen.

[13] M.-C. Cordonier Segger and A. Khalfan, *Sustainable Development Law: Principles, Practices and Prospects* (Oxford University Press 2006) 156.

[14] UN, Rio Declaration (2012) www.unep.org/Documents.Multilingual/Default.asp?documentID=78&articleID=1163 accessed 30 November 2017.

[15] Environmental Democracy Index, Background and Methodology www.environmentaldemocracyindex.org/about/background_and_methodology accessed 30 November 2017.

[16] OJ 2007, C306, consolidated version OJ 2010 C83.

Art. 10 (1): The functioning of the Union shall be founded on representative democracy.

Art. 10 (3): Every citizen shall have the right to participate in the democratic life of the Union. Decisions shall be taken as openly and as closely as possible to the citizen.

Art. 11 (1): The institutions shall, by appropriate means, give citizens and representative associations the opportunity to make known and publicly exchange their views in all areas of Union action.

Democratic society is one of the fundamental clauses within the Earth Charter, too, at least according to principle I.3:[17]

> Build democratic societies that are just, participatory, sustainable, and peaceful.
> a. Ensure that communities at all levels guarantee human rights and fundamental freedoms and provide everyone an opportunity to realize his or her full potential.
> b. Promote social and economic justice, enabling all to achieve a secure and meaningful livelihood that is ecologically responsible.

A second, also obvious and general, concept similarly providing the groundwork for public participation is the rule of law. Assuming that this legal concept is self-evident,[18] let us point to a UN report in this respect:

> For the United Nations, the rule of law refers to a principle of governance in which all persons, institutions and entities, public and private, including the State itself, are accountable to laws that are publicly promulgated, equally enforced and independently adjudicated, and which are consistent with international human rights norms and standards. It requires, as well, measures to ensure adherence to the principles of supremacy of law, equality before the law, accountability to the law, fairness in the application of the law, separation of powers, participation in decision-making, legal certainty, avoidance of arbitrariness and procedural and legal transparency.[19]

Accountability, transparency of decisions and equality of human rights all form essential components of public participation.

Sustainable development, and, within this, environmental protection as its heart, belongs to the collective or 'community' dimension entailing a holistic vision. The rights of future generations or intergenerational equity simultaneously with

[17] Adopted in March 2000; see www.earthcharterinaction.org/content/pages/Read-the-Charter.html accessed 30 November 2017.

[18] A popular and easily manageable summary of the rule of law concept on the internet is provided for by the World Justice Project at http://worldjusticeproject.org/what-rule-law accessed 30 November 2017.

[19] UN Security Council, (S/2004/616) Report of the Secretary-General on the Rule of Law and Transitional Justice in Conflict and Post-Conflict Societies, 23 August 2004 www.ipu.org/splz-e/unga07/law.pdf accessed 30 November 2017.

intragenerational equity indicate the best way of transforming this collective dimension into practice, not allowing the interests of the poor or the coming generations to be marginalized. This may also be coupled with the right to environment. A good example of this highly complex vision is a commission opinion within the CoE:[20]

> 9. Bearing in mind that society as a whole and each individual in particular must pass on a healthy and viable environment to future generations, in accordance with the principle of solidarity between generations, the Assembly invites the governments of member states to: 9.1 provide adequate protection for the life, health, bodily integrity and property of the individual as guaranteed by Articles 2, 3 and 8 of the European Convention on Human Rights; 9.2 establish information systems concerning the environment and, wherever possible, foster public participation in decision-making processes; 9.3 co-operate and share responsibility in the event of damage to the environment.

As Edith Brown Weiss wrote:

> The basic concept is that all generations are partners caring for and using the Earth. Every generation needs to pass the Earth and our natural and cultural resources on in at least as good condition as we received them. This leads to three principles of intergenerational equity: options, quality and access.[21]

The above-mentioned CoE document, while focusing on the right to environment, makes a clear reference to such procedural guarantees as public participation: "19. … It is now generally accepted that the right to a healthy environment includes two complementary dimensions: a procedural and a material or substantive dimension." So, the community dimension, the two types of generational equity and the practical implementation of a human right to the environment – without labeling or naming this right (clean, healthy, safe, worthy for humans, etc.) – all entail public participation as a primary condition or procedural guarantee of sustainable development.

In recent decades, international environmental law has generated two special constituents of community dimension, one of which is common heritage of mankind. Common heritage was first codified in the Cultural Heritage Convention (1972) in Article 6:

> 1. Whilst fully respecting the sovereignty of the States on whose territory the cultural and natural heritage mentioned in Articles 1 and 2 is situated, and without prejudice

[20] Doc. 12003 Parliamentary Assembly, 11 September 2009, Drafting an Additional Protocol to the European Convention on Human Rights concerning the Right to a Healthy Environment, Report https://assembly.coe.int/nw/xml/XRef/Xref-XML2HTML-en.asp?fileid=17777&lang=en, Reference 3497 of 28 November 2008, Draft recommendation adopted unanimously by the committee on 4 September 2009.

[21] E. Brown Weiss, 'Climate Change, Intergenerational Equity, and International Law' (2008) 9 *Vermont Journal of Environmental Law* 616.

> to property right provided by national legislation, the States Parties to this Convention recognize that such heritage constitutes a world heritage for whose protection it is the duty of the international community as a whole to co-operate.[22]

The Max Planck Encyclopedia of Public International Law provides an easy and clear summary as follows:

> 26. The common heritage principle comprises the following elements: the common heritage can neither be occupied nor appropriated, it is open for use by all; it entails the obligation to cooperate, this obligation goes beyond the obligation to cooperate under general international law. Under the common heritage principle, there exists the obligation to actively share benefits. Further, the principle embraces the obligation to preserve the area and resources in question for future generations, which includes the concept of sustainable development. There is also the obligation to use the area in question for peaceful purposes only.[23]

A parallel constituent of community dimension in international environmental law is the concept of common concern of humanity. According to the principles of the UN Expert Group:[24]

> 82. . . .The foundation of the concept is the recognition of a legitimate interest of the international community to concern itself with certain issues and values which, by their nature, affect the community as a whole. The scientifically-based reality of ecological interdependence, and the concomitant recognition of the global nature of environmental problems, made it only a logical step to apply the concept of common concern to the environment of the planet, or elements thereof.

A clear abstract of the concept is provided by Dinah Shelton:

> Common concern is related to, but different from the concepts of commons areas and the common heritage of mankind . . . Common concerns are different because they are not spatial, belonging to a specific area, but can occur within or outside sovereign territory.[25]

The most important characteristic of both of these grounds is the term 'common'. Common interests require environmental democracy, otherwise the rigid concept of sovereignty prevails and the need for the careful balancing of interest is lost. The 'common' dimension within both of the above-mentioned concepts of international law clearly necessitates public involvement, providing the indispensable framework and conditions for direct democratic decision-making.

[22] Convention Concerning the Protection of the World Cultural and Natural Heritage (1972).

[23] R. Wolfrum, *Common Heritage of Mankind*, Max Planck Encyclopedia of Public International Law (Max Planck Institute for Comparative Public Law and International Law and Oxford University Press 2000).

[24] Expert Group, *supra* note 2.

[25] D. Shelton, 'Common Concern of Humanity' (2009) 1:V *Iustum, aequum, salutare* 34–35.

It is also widely accepted that our activities, legislation and societal action shall serve the common good, which has a deep moral content. Let us use the fifty-five-year-old wording of Pope Paul VI:

> 26. . . . the common good, that is, the sum of those conditions of social life which allow social groups and their individual members relatively thorough and ready access to their own fulfilment, today takes on an increasingly universal complexion and consequently involves rights and duties with respect to the whole human race. Every social group must take account of the needs and legitimate aspirations of other groups, and even of the general welfare of the entire human family.[26]

As one might observe, most of the above listed elements are covered under the concept of common good (see, for example, other groups, intragenerational equity, rights and duties of the human race, intergenerational equity), but it would not be difficult to identify the common heritage or common concern of humanity doctrines here and also in other manifestations of the concept. No wonder that common good may also be taken as ammunition for public participation.

Subsidiarity is the next yardstick, not being necessarily only a guiding principle of European integration.[27] While we do not analyze the concept of subsidiarity here, it is without doubt that this principle, as it is commonly referred to nowadays, was first mentioned in 1931 as a managerial principle of the Catholic Church:[28]

> 79. . . . Just as it is gravely wrong to take from individuals what they can accomplish by their own initiative and industry and give it to the community, so also it is an injustice and at the same time a grave evil and disturbance of right order to assign to a greater and higher association what lesser and subordinate organizations can do.

Of course, subsidiarity is not a clear or simple requirement. According to Carozza:[29]

> Subsidiarity is therefore a somewhat paradoxical principle. It limits the state, yet empowers and justifies it. It limits intervention, yet requires it. It expresses both a positive and a negative vision of the role of the state with respect to society and the individual.

26 Pastoral Constitution on the Church in the Modern World, *Gaudium et Spes*, Promulgated by His Holiness, Pope Paul VI on December 7, 1965 www.vatican.va/archive/hist_councils/ii_vatican_council/documents/vat-ii_cons_19651207_gaudium-et-spes_en.html accessed 30 November 2017.

27 TEU Art. 5 ("3. Under the principle of subsidiarity, in areas which do not fall within its exclusive competence, the Union shall act only if and in so far as the objectives of the proposed action cannot be sufficiently achieved by the Member States, either at central level or at regional and local level, but can rather, by reason of the scale or effects of the proposed action, be better achieved at Union level.").

28 Quadragesimo Anno, Encyclical of Pope Pius XI on Reconstruction of the Social Order, 15 May, 1931.

29 P.G. Carozza, 'Subsidiarity as a Structural Principle of International Human Rights Law' (2003) 97 *American Journal of International Law* 44.

In terms of public participation, subsidiarity definitely means the involvement of regional and local communities, different groups of society, NGOs and other associations in the decision-making processes, giving them the chance to express their opinion or even challenge the decisions of governmental institutions.

Finally, the concept of environmental justice as a special component of environmental protection somehow summarizes democracy, the above-mentioned different 'commons', generational equity and non-discrimination. The US EPA's views are commonly quoted in this respect: "Environmental Justice is the fair treatment and meaningful involvement of all people regardless of race, colour, national origin, or income with respect to the development, implementation, and enforcement of environmental laws, regulations, and policies." The involvement of people definitely requires public participation with all its constituents.[30]

A clear message for us from all the fundamentals listed above is that public participation is by all means a vital part of sustainable development as a whole and of all its constituents. The different common dimensions, the two major generational equity concepts, right to environment or broader issues as democracy, rule of law and subsidiarity all have public participation as a prerequisite.

## PRACTICAL RATIONALES AND MANIFESTATIONS OF PUBLIC PARTICIPATION

Beside the fundamentals and guiding principles, several practical rationales of public participation, which usually end up in the advancement of the quality of decision-making, should not be forgotten.[31] Accordingly, there are several explanations as to why public participation is not only an abstract requirement but also contributes to the betterment of environmental administration:

> Justifications for public participation may be both instrumental and non-instrumental. None-instrumental emphasise that public participation is inherently beneficial, whereas instrumental rationales by contrast emphasize the link between public participation and improved substantive outcomes.[32]

[30] There are several studies in this respect. See e.g. J. Ebbesson and P.N. Okowa (eds.), *Environmental Law and Justice in Context* (Cambridge University Press 2009); B. Vanheusden, 'The Relevance of Environmental Justice for the Legal Framework in the European Union' (2019) 7.2 *Journal for European Environmental and Planning Law* 163–175.

[31] From among the many articles, see e.g. P.J. Balint et al., *Wicked Environmental Problems: Managing Uncertainty and Conflict* (Island Press 2011) 108; M.B. Mihaly, 'Citizen Participation in the Making of Environmental Decisions: Evolving Obstacles and Potential Solutions Through Partnership with Experts and Agents' (2009–2010) 27 *Pace Environmental Law Review* 164–165; F. Coenen, 'Conclusions', in F. Coenen (ed.), *Public Participation and Better Environmental Decisions* (Springer 2009) 184.

[32] R. Moules, *Environmental Judicial Review* (Hart Publishing 2011) 18.

From among these various multipurpose benefits of public participation, the most important ones can be highlighted. First, public participation may create trust towards public administration, as transparency and consistent decision-making are vital prerequisites of society. Public participation will enhance the legitimacy of decisions, as a next stage of trust, as a consequence of transparent procedures. Public participation may improve the quality of decisions and may generate better substantive decisions by providing relevant and accurate information, mostly in connection with local issues and also by adding the dimension of mutual learning when incorporating public values into decisions. As with the encouraging effects of mediation, public participation may also assist in conflict resolution among divergent interests, or at least may reduce the level of conflicts by avoiding misunderstandings and clarifying the views of the different actors. A clear outcome of the above-mentioned components is the increasing acceptance of decisions by the public, better commitments for implementing these decisions, a widening of the control function of the public, and, accordingly, generally speaking a broadening of public support. Further, public participation may promote democratic and civic values within public administration and society as a whole; the list continues.

The individual areas of public participation according to Principle 10 of the Rio Declaration are taken as the common ground for understanding:

> Environmental issues are best handled with participation of all concerned citizens, at the relevant level. At the national level, each individual shall have appropriate access to information concerning the environment that is held by public authorities, including information on hazardous materials and activities in their communities, and the opportunity to participate in decision-making processes. States shall facilitate and encourage public awareness and participation by making information widely available. Effective access to judicial and administrative proceedings, including redress and remedy, shall be provided.

The well-known distinction related to the three cornerstones of public participation:

- access to information (first of all, environmental information);
- participation in decision-making;
- access to judicial and administrative proceedings; in other words, access to justice.

At the end of this short survey, it is necessary to focus again on simple practicalities.[33] Consequently, here is a simple list of examples of how public participation may be exercised at the three main levels of government.

[33] A concise summary of the Aarhus results may be found in the paper presented at the Joint UNEP-OHCHR Expert Seminar on Human Rights and the Environment, 14–16 January 2002, Geneva, Background Paper No. 5. by J. Ebbesson. See also J. Jendrośka, 'Information, Participation and Access to Justice: The Model of the Aarhus Convention Citizen's Rights in

At the local government level, there are several well-known elements of public participation, mostly as constituents of local democracy. First, and easiest, is the division of competences between the different levels of public administration, based on subsidiarity. Second, the election of representatives and the participation of NGOs or local professionals in committees and councils. In addition, local governments may conclude direct agreements with interested representations (e.g. about their participation in legal regulation). There may, furthermore, be public hearings (general and specific) or referendums as a decision-making forums.

The special responsibility of local governments for the establishment of environmental sustainability, and in particular for promoting public participation, is clearly demonstrated by the International Council for Local Environmental Initiative (ICLEI):[34]

> All local and regional governments in Europe to:
>
> 1. Continue their leading role in the transition to an economically smart, socially inclusive and environmentally sustainable Europe by contributing to the green economy, resource efficient urban and regional development and sound ecosystem management, more specifically by taking an integrated approach regarding: . . . h. Involving citizens in the implementation of the above goals through structured participatory processes.

The same applies at the regional level of governance, thus same or similar instruments may be used, adding the involvement of local governments, including division of competences between the different levels of public administration, based on subsidiarity, representation of local governments in the regional level institutions, participation of local governments, NGOs or local professionals in committees, councils, direct agreements with interest representations (e.g. about their participation in legal regulation) and possibly referendums, in case the regional level has a regulatory competence.

Finally, at the central level of government, there are even more options open for public participation, either direct or indirect. These include the basics of democratic governance, but also some other opportunities. The most common method is the election itself. Regulatory participation usually means commenting the drafts by the public (today, this is typically undertaken via the Internet). There are several possible direct agreements with interest representations (e.g. about their participation in legal regulation or authorizing NGOs or other private/public bodies with

European Environmental Law: Stock-Taking of Key Challenges and Current Developments in Relation to Public Access to Information, Participation and Access to Justice' (2012) 9.1 *Journal for European Environmental Policy and Law*, 71–90.

[34] International Council for Local Environmental Initiative, ICLEI European Convention Declaration, Brussels (13 September 2011) http://convention2011.iclei-europe.org/fileadmin/templates/files/Press_corner/Press_releases/Microsoft_Word_-_ICLEI_European_Convention_2011_Draft_Declaration_final.pdf accessed 30 November 2017.

special functions – control functions or registry functions, for example in connection with eco-labeling or the Eco-Management and Audit Scheme [EMAS], etc.). There are also several types of public forums, convened occasionally or regularly, and the referendum is always available. Indeed, in many countries there is access to a Constitutional Court or similar judicial body/organ (Supreme Court, Conseil d'État, etc.). A further example may be the use of institutions, the functions of which are connected with the representation of public interests, including through ombudsman-type (general or specialized) organs, the public prosecutor (e.g., as in Hungary, with a special competence in protecting the public interest and access to courts; or the Brazilian example of the specific role of the prosecutor), or similar 'official' representatives of public interest. There is also participation in consultative bodies or councils (such as the National Environmental Council in Hungary),[35] or public auditing (see the example of Canada in this volume). Of course, this list of options does not necessarily include all available means and methods, but it does indicate the most frequently applied instruments.

## CONCLUSION

In conclusion, it must be asserted that public participation is an indispensable element of sustainable development, and what is even more important, public participation shall also be taken as a legally comprehensible component of sustainable development. Public participation is not a gift from the state or government; on the contrary, it represents an essential pressure towards sustainable decision-making. There are several underlying conceptual constituents of public participation, besides

35 The Hungarian National Environmental Council was established by the environmental act in 1995 (Act. LIII of 1995). The Council is the advisory, proposing, opinion-making body of the Government, set up according to Art. 45 of the Act to provide a wide public, scientific and professional foundation of environmental protection. This is a maximum twenty-two-member body, of which twenty-one shall be independent from the Government. The twenty-second is the minister responsible for environmental issues (today the Minister of Agriculture) and is also the co-chair of the Council. The other members represent the following stakeholder groups on an equal footing: the environmental associations, foundations and alliances, elected by the rules established by themselves; the professional and business interest-representation organizations, also selected by the rules established by themselves; and the scientific community, the representatives of which are nominated by the president of the Hungarian Academy of Sciences. The most important functions of the Council according to Art. 45 of the environmental act are as follows: (a) to express its opinion and consult it with the decision-makers in connection with the regulatory impact assessment (the Hungarian variation of strategic environmental assessment), (b) to express its opinion in connection with the strategic environmental assessments and the draft of the original plans and programs, (c) to formulate an opinion to the Government how to make environmental protection more effective, such as in terms of the environmental information system, scientific research, education, development of necessary industrial background and financial instruments related to environmental and nature protection interests, (d) to formulate an opinion related to the strategic issues of environmental legislation of the European integration.

the general roots in democracy or rule of law, of which the right to environment takes precedence, in line with both sides of generational equity. Certainly, there are other vital grounds in the field of ecological sustainability which should also be mentioned, such as the common concern of humanity, common heritage of mankind or environmental justice, or good governance as a wider concept. Besides the fundamentals and guiding principles, we should not fail to remember the numerous practical rationales of public participation, which usually result in improvements in the quality of decision-making and in environmental administration.

# 13

# Are We Giving the Voice of the Future a Word in the Present?

*Julia Pitts*

Just like adults, children and young people live in, interact with and think about their environment on a daily basis. Despite this children and young people traditionally have had little say in the decisions being made by adults about the environment, at a local, national and international level.[1]

This chapter seeks to demonstrate that institutions and NGOs need to interact with children and young people in a way that recognizes them as 'citizen stakeholders' now and on behalf of the future. A central tenet of the principle of sustainability includes responsibility for future generations. The principle provides that current generations hold the environment in trust for the benefit of future generations. According to the principle, there exists a moral and ethical obligation to hand over to subsequent generations a stock of environmental wealth, comparable to that which was handed on to us by our forebears.

Then UN Secretary-General Ban Ki-moon stated in his 2013 Report *Intergenerational Solidarity and the Needs of Future Generations* that "few would question the responsibilities the world owes to its children and grandchildren, at least in the moral sense, if not strictly in the law, there is a realisation that future generations are vulnerable to our acts and policies."[2] Yet we often see the 'real politics' of business as usual taking precedence. In her 1987 WCED report, *Our Common Future*, Gro Harlem Brundtland recognized this, saying "we act as we do,

[1] Talking with Children and Young People about the Environment. A Report by the ACT Commissioner for Children and Young People with the ACT Commissioner for Sustainability and the Environment (September 2015).

[2] Ban Ki-moon, *Intergenerational Solidarity and the Needs of Future Generations – Report of the Secretary-General* 5 August 2013 A/68/322 http://sustainabledevelopment.un.org/content/documents/2006future.pdf accessed 30 November 2017.

because we can get away with it: future generations do not vote, they have no political or financial power, they cannot challenge our decisions."[3]

At the same time, 46 percent of today's global population is under 25 years old,[4] and 51 percent is under 30 years old. In these age groups there is a sense of supporting changes to current business as usual practices, and young people are increasingly understanding their ability to function as change-makers. As highlighted in the 2016 words of Ban Ki-moon, "You have unlimited power, unlimited authority, legitimate prerogative to raise your voice. Make your governors, your mayors, national assembly members, even professors and business communities; make them accountable."[5]

Current climate litigation, run through the ENGO Our Children's Trust based in the US State of Oregon, is a clear demonstration of children and young people taking action on behalf of themselves and for future generations. They recognize that despite Ban Ki-moon's encouraging words, adults have been slow to take effective steps or make clear decisions to protect the planet in the long term. These legal challenges have generated much interest across the wider population, and cases are in the courts in Norway,[6] Holland,[7] Pakistan,[8] the Philippines and Sweden. Additionally, discussions are currently underway in other parts of the globe.

## CHILDREN AND YOUNG PEOPLE'S PARTICIPATION AT INTERNATIONAL ENVIRONMENTAL CONFERENCES

Whilst the 1992 UNCED in Rio de Janeiro, colloquially known as the Earth Summit, is widely regarded as the point when children and young people's voices were first clearly heard clearly in the environmental context, it is worth noting that some twenty years earlier an International Youth Conference on the Human Environment was held in Hamilton, Canada in the lead up to the Stockholm meeting, sponsored in part by UNESCO.[9] This 1971 conference studied ways in

[3] G.H. Brundtland et al., *Our Common Future: Report of the World Commission on Environment and Development* (Oxford University Press 1987).

[4] According to Mr. Ahmad Alhendawi, the UN Secretary-General Ban Ki-moon's Special Envoy on Youth.

[5] UN News, DPI/NGO: "You Have Unlimited Power," Ban Tells Youth, Rallying Support for UN 2030 Agenda (30 May 2016) https://news.un.org/en/story/2016/05/530752-dpingo-you-have-unlimited-power-ban-tells-youth-rallying-support-un-2030-agenda accessed 30 November 2017.

[6] The Norwegian lawsuit over arctic oil exploration plans was initiated by an alliance of Greenpeace, Indigenous activists, youth groups and ex-NASA scientist James Hansen. See 'Norway Oil: Environmentalists Lose Arctic Exploration Case', BBC (8 January 2018) www.bbc.com/news/world-europe-42569104 accessed 19 June 2019.

[7] *Urgenda Foundation* v. *State of the Netherlands*, [2015] HAZA C/09/00456689.

[8] In June 2016 the Supreme Court of Pakistan ruled in favor of seven-year-old plaintiff Rabab Ali and allowed her constitutional climate change case to proceed. See *Ali* v. *Federation of Pakistan*, Constitutional Petition [undated] of 2016.

[9] See International Youth Conference on the Human Environment, Hamilton, Canada, August 1971.

which young people and youth organizations could participate in the campaign in 'favor of the environment'. Attended by 166 delegates and 102 observers, this was the first conference of its kind to include a large number of young people from developing countries. The Hamilton Declaration was then submitted by an appointed youth delegate to the Stockholm Conference. The Hamilton Declaration gave 'particular regard' to young people and the importance of ecological education.

The Stockholm Declaration of the UN Conference on the Human Environment in 1972 identified, in Principle 1, that humans bear a solemn responsibility to protect and improve the environment for present and future generations, whilst Principle 19 noted that education in environmental matters for the younger generation as well as adults is essential.

Twenty years later, at the 1992 Earth Summit, the "intensely passionate, personal and provocative plea" to delegates by twelve-year-old Severn Cullis-Suzuki was, according to Al Gore, the "best speech" at the Summit. Cullis-Suzuki strongly reminded delegates that this was her world too: "We figured it was going to be mostly old men sitting around, making decisions that are going to affect our future, and future generations. So we wanted to go as the conscience, as the reminder to those decision makers, who their decisions would truly affect."

Eleven years later, in 2003, the Governing Council of the UNEP adopted a long-term strategy for engaging young people in environmental activities and the work of UNEP. More recently, Paragraph 50 of *The Future We Want*, the final document of the Rio+20 conference,[10] reads:

> We stress the importance of the active participation of young people in decision making processes, as the issues we are addressing have a deep impact on current and future generations and as such the contribution of children and youth is vital to sustainable development. We also recognise the need to promote intergenerational dialogue and solidarity by recognising their views.[11]

Sixteen-year-old Advocate Gertrude Clement,[12] while addressing the UNGA at the Paris Agreement on climate change signing ceremony in 2016,[13] made it clear to the delegates that more paperwork is not the answer, stating "that we as youth are leading our communities in taking action, we expect action on a big scale, we expect action today, not tomorrow."[14]

Recent participatory initiatives include youth as 'Observers' to the UNFCCC COP, Youth 20 alongside the G20 and UN Youth. These initiatives were part of

[10] Resolution 66/288, *The Future We Want* adopted by the UNGA at its Sixty Sixth session on 27 July 2012.

[11] Ibid.

[12] Gertrude Clement, radio reporter from Tanzania and climate advocate with UNICEF. Gertrude represented the youth of Tanzania at the Conference of the Youth (COY11) held prior to COP 21.

[13] Signed at the UNGA in New York on 22 April 2016.

[14] Ibid.

efforts at capacity-building, in which many young people learned to be advocates and leaders, creating their own visions for the future in many countries around the globe. The momentum is building toward the recognition of children and youth as citizen stakeholders.

In September 2016,[15] before he stepped down from his UN Secretary-General role, Ban Ki-moon said:

> For me and you the old era where existing elders have been making prominent roles in every way of our life has gone. You are the leaders of today . . . The old era has gone now; the new era has come. Youth played a pivotal role in pushing government to adopt the 2030 Agenda for Sustainable development. You raised your voice for the Paris agreement on climate change. You have been speaking out. And I have really been asking you,[16] raise your voice. You have unlimited power, unlimited authority, legitimate prerogative to raise your voice. Make your governors, your mayors, national assembly members, even professors and business communities; make them accountable.

## A RIGHT TO BE HEARD, A RIGHT TO PARTICIPATE

Under article 12 of the CRC, children and young people have both a substantive and a procedural right to be heard in all matters affecting them.[17] The right of all children to be heard and taken seriously constitutes one of the fundamental values of the CRC.[18] It is the right of every child, without exception. The Committee on the Rights of the Child has identified the right to be heard as one of the four general principles of the Convention. As such, the right to be heard is not only a right in itself, but also should be considered in the interpretation and implementation of all other rights.

At the international level, the involvement of children in the work of the Committee has particular relevance, including in the reporting process of State Parties for implementation of the CRC and its Optional Protocols, the development of general comments,[19] the days of general discussion, in-country visits and other events.[20] With regard to the reporting process, State Parties have an obligation to ensure that children are encouraged and enabled to participate in the preparation of State reports to the Committee. The Committee adopted its working methods paper

15 DPI/NGO Conference Youth Caucus in Korea.

16 UN Secretary-General Ban Ki-moon appointed for the first time in history to the UN a Special Envoy on Youth of the UN Secretary-General in 2012.

17 Convention on the Rights of the Child (1990) art. 12.

18 Ibid. at arts. 12, 13, 14, 15, and 17.

19 The Committee publishes its interpretation of the content of human rights provisions in the form of general comments on thematic issues.

20 CRC Working methods for the participation of children in the reporting process of the Committee on the Rights of the Child, CRC/C/66/2, 16 October 2014.

in June 2014.[21] A paper covering the protocol for participation in the days of general discussion has yet to be prepared.

These requirements for child participation in the preparation of State reports to the Committee has to be effective and meaningful at the international level, and must be understood as an overall process rather than as a single event. To the extent possible, children should be given support and encouragement to form their own organizations and initiatives, which will create an environment for them to discuss their rights and express their own views on their State's progress in implementing the CRC and its Optional Protocols as part of the ongoing monitoring process.

At the time of the country review, NGOs were strongly encouraged to facilitate children's participation in the reporting process. Including State Parties, NGOs and UNICEF should ensure that the interests and priorities represented in the reporting process are those of the children themselves and not of the adults or organization they work with. In accordance with the Committee's General Comment No. 12, the following nine requirements must be respected for all processes in which children are heard and participate, including the reporting process. It is fair to say that these requirements should be applicable across all levels of governance:

(a) **Transparent and informative:** Children must receive full, accessible, diversity-sensitive and age-appropriate information about their right to express their views freely and about how their participation will take place, as well as its scope, purpose and potential impact. Their views have to be given due weight;
(b) **Voluntary:** Children should not be coerced into expressing views against their wishes and must be informed that they can cease involvement at any stage;
(c) **Respectful:** Children's views have to be treated with respect, and children should be provided with opportunities to initiate ideas and activities. Persons and organizations working for and with children should respect children's views with regard to participating in events and meetings;
(d) **Relevant:** Children should draw on their knowledge, skills and abilities to express their views on relevant issues. Space needs to be created to enable children to highlight and address issues they have identified as relevant and important;
(e) **Child-friendly environment:** Environments and working methods should be adapted to children's capacities. Adequate time and resources should be available to ensure that children are well prepared and have the confidence and opportunity to contribute their views to the process;

[21] Ibid.

(f) **Inclusive:** Children are not a homogeneous group and participation needs to provide for equality of opportunity for all, including marginalized children, without discrimination on any grounds, including age, and be culturally sensitive to children from all communities. Special measures should be taken to include very young children and children from marginalized communities;

(g) **Supported by training:** Adults need preparation, skills and support to facilitate children's participation effectively. Children also require capacity-building to strengthen their skills relevant to the reporting process, for example, in effective participation, awareness of their rights, public speaking and advocacy;

(h) **Safe and sensitive to risk:** Adults have a responsibility towards the children with whom they work and must take every precaution to minimize the risk of violence, exploitation or any other negative consequences of their participation. Organizations facilitating child participation in the reporting process must have a clear child-protection policy in place for all the children who take part in activities related to this process.

(i) **Accountable:** Child-led organizations, children's groups, NGOs and UNICEF should ensure that children have a clear understanding of their role in the reporting process and, more specifically, in meeting with the Committee. A commitment to follow-up and evaluation is essential. Children who have taken part in the reporting process – be it in research, consultations, drafting the report or meeting the Committee – should be informed about how their views will be interpreted and used.

## CRC DAY OF GENERAL DISCUSSION ON CHILDREN'S RIGHTS AND THE ENVIRONMENT

In September 2016,[22] the 73rd Session of the Committee of the CRC held its Day of General Discussion on Children's Rights and the Environment (DGD). This is the first time the environment and children's rights have been discussed in this forum.[23] The DGD is held once every two years to foster a deeper understanding of the content and implications of the CRC as they relate to specific articles or topics. Two working groups were formed, one focusing on children's exposure to environmental toxicants and the other on children and the effects of environmental degradation, in particular the impacts of climate change on children. The agenda included children

[22] Held at the UN Office in the Palais de Nations, Geneva, Switzerland, on 23 September 2016.

[23] The overall objective of the discussion day was "to promote the understanding of the relationship between children's rights and the environment, identify what needs to be done for child rights related laws, policies and practices to take adequate account of environmental issues and for the environment related laws and policies and practices to be child sensitive."

and young people speaking on behalf of themselves (and on behalf of future generations), an important, poignant,[24] and timely milestone. Discussion included the rights that directly and indirectly correlate with the right to a clean and healthy environment,[25] including the recognition of procedural rights (such as standing and access to justice). The report by the Child Rights International Network (CRIN),[26] one of the co-sponsors of the event, noted that each of the panelists stressed that children needed to be included in discussions on the environment, as they agreed that threats to natural resources affected health, life, survival and development, and play and leisure for children. Clarence Nelson,[27] a member of the Committee, noted that there were few mechanisms to support children's meaningful participation and decision making in climate change dialogue or policy. The recommendation that followed suggested that States place children's rights at the center of national and international programs to ensure that children are fully involved in the policy dialogue on climate change. As yet there have been no specific or further outcomes from the DGD. However, it will be an interesting space to watch to see what evolves from this milestone event.

### *Participation, Children and Young People*

> Young people are very action based so we want to see stuff happen but I think for lots of young people it's hard to know where to start, hard to know how to get involved with this kind of stuff or how they can directly make a difference. So I think things like this where we can contribute and young peoples' questions are taken into account are really good, because it is going to be our world. This is where we are growing up and we are going to take the reins at some point.[28]

Children and young people often raise a host of transformative and practical ideas. However, to deliver success, care must be taken in the overall design and evaluation of engagement, as so easily participation activities can become more concerned with process rather than product, seen as tokenistic, or as a mechanism for purely listening rather than providing effective ways for acting on the information.

Governments around the globe have sought the advice and involvement of children and young people through a wide array of participatory models at local, national and international levels. This has included highly structured and centralized

[24] Caleb Mulenga from Zambia shared his experience. He grew up near a mine and was constantly exposed to lead in the water supplies and the soil. He said: "I cannot shower away the lead."

[25] See CRC, *supra* note 20 at art. 24.

[26] See Day of General Discussion special edition – weekly newsletter, 6 October 2016 www.crin.org/ accessed 30 November 2017.

[27] Clarence Taylor is an independent expert from Samoa and CROC Committee Member until 2019.

[28] In the words of a student representative at the ACT Parliament of Youth on Sustainability, Canberra, Australia, 2013; see www.see-change.org.au/ accessed 30 November 2017.

youth advisory panels and groups, and regional youth parliaments, for example the European Youth Parliament, National Youth Parliaments,[29] State Government Youth Advisory Groups, and the Children and Young Peoples' Advisory Panels to various Commissioners.[30] A commitment to children's participation recognizes children as a source of strength and invaluable insight from their own perspective. Meaningful participation has the capacity to make a difference and to produce long-term or institutional change. However, it takes time and dedicated resources.[31] But are children, in the words of Kay Tisdall,[32] "treated as citizens in waiting rather than citizens in their own right," so that their participation is seen as training for future engagement as full citizens rather than providing a valuable contribution at the present moment? Feedback suggests that once participation activities conclude,

[29] Children's Parliaments in Slovenia, Zimbabwe, Spain, and example of a Millennium Young People's Congress, Hawaii, 1999 – to decide a program of action for a sustainable future over the next 1,000 years.

[30] At a different, more local level, two initiatives closer to home in the Australian Capital Territory, worth mentioning are the Youth Ambassadors program run between 2008 and 2013 and the annual SEE-Change Parliament of Youth on Sustainability (commenced 2013, ongoing). (1) Youth Ambassador Program – Office of the Commissioner for Sustainability and the Environment (OCSE). The catalyst was an exploratory workshop hosted jointly with the ACT Commissioner for Children and Young People and the Commissioner for Sustainability and the Environment and a wide range of young people. Water, public transport, cycle ways and friendly infrastructure were seen as most pressing environmental issues for youth in Canberra. This led to the then Commissioner for Sustainability and the Environment introducing a Youth Ambassadors program. The aim was to engage young people and make the work of the (environment) commissioner's office more accessible to them. It also acted as a conduit between the OCSE and the youth sector in the ACT. This advisory group of Youth Ambassadors comprised a mix of school students, university students and young professionals aged between 12 and 25. One youth representative from the initial reference group, who later became an ambassador, recounted how it was a pleasure to work with a group of people who cared so passionately about putting sustainability into practice and empowering young people to become community leaders and 'champions' for the environment. (2) Australian Capital Territory – Parliament of Youth on Sustainability. Another successful and ongoing initiative in the ACT has been the Parliament of Youth on Sustainability. Students of all ages from colleges, high schools and primary schools have come together to develop proposals for action and debate and deliver their recommendations to politicians. In 2013, the challenge of how Canberra should change by 2020 to meet its ambitious carbon emission targets and become more sustainable resulted in twenty-four recommendations that included the restructuring of ministerial portfolios to specific deliverables and a proposal for an ongoing youth advisory panel. In 2015 the Youth Parliament addressed 'Action for our Future,' where 162 students delivered forty-three proposals of which eleven were selected on what is the one key action for our future that needs to be taken to address climate change. The 2017 Youth Parliament will focus on 'How to Reduce Canberra's (Rather Large) Environmental Footprint'.

[31] The "Wales We Want" was an extensive two-year national conversation that included children and young people, to inform the development of the Wellbeing of Future Generations Act; see www.cynnalcymru.com/ accessed 30 November 2017.

[32] K. Tisdall, Centre for Research on Families and Relationship (CRFR), Professor of Childhood Policy in the School of Social and Political Science University of Edinburg cited in the Australian Research Alliance for Children and Youth (ARACY) review *Weathering the Future: Climate Change, Children and Decision Making.*

nothing more is heard by the young people about the outcomes and, sadly, any evaluation of the process is rare. Has participation led to quantifiable and measurable change in policy direction, decisions and outcomes?

In the words of the Australian Youth Affairs Coalition's report,[33] *Maximising Young Peoples' Impact on Organisational and Public Policy*, "where are you going with that?" Expressing an opinion is not the same as taking a decision, but it implies the ability to influence decisions. A process of dialogue and exchange is encouraged in which children assume increasing responsibilities and become active, tolerant and democratic. Not surprisingly, feedback reveals that young people really want to know the likelihood that their views will have an impact on the process, to have feedback provided to them on a regular basis and that the final outcome(s) of the process is communicated to them.[34] Research also reveals that they often felt limited when confined to opportunities for input on youth issues only,[35] and this diminished their experience and thoughts on other areas critical to their community, such as taxation and legislative reform.

### *Where Are You Going with That? Translating Listening into Action*

A 2011 review conducted by the Australian National University in Canberra for the Australian Research Alliance for Children and Youth (ARACY) titled *Weathering the Future: Climate Change, Children and Decision Making* recognized that policy responses to climate change in Australia have not been built with a child focus or voice in mind.[36] *Weathering the Future* asked how the voices and needs of children and young persons, both in their current status and as future adults, are to be heard. Participants were asked to identify any examples where the interests and views of young people are already reflected in Australian decision and policy making, both

[33] The Australian Youth Affairs Coalition (AYAC) is Australia's national peak body on representing young people aged 12–25 and the sector that supports them.

[34] AYAC, *Where Are You Going with That? Maximising Young People's Impact on Organisational and Public Policy* (2010). See *Australia's Youth Matters Report 2013: Young People Talk about What Is Important to Them* www.ayac.org.au/ accessed 30 November 2017. Interestingly, the environment and climate change did not appear in the top five issues, although they were raised in the survey question.

[35] This issue is addressed in R. Heath, *Please Just F. . .k Off: It's Our Turn Now – Holding Baby Boomers to Account* (Pluto Press 2016) (arguing that in Australia the views, ideas and energy of young people have been systematically ignored owing to adults perceiving young people's views as less worthy of consideration in policy debates and the wider community).

[36] Dr. L. Strazdins and H. Skeat, National Centre for Epidemiology and Population Health, Australian National University, Canberra, Australia. For ARACY, see *Weathering the Future: Climate Change, Children and Decision Making*, where climate change, child and youth, as well as health and well-being experts and young people were interviewed. They identified that little is known about the particular social, emotional and health impacts of climate change on children and young people, and that the views and interests of children and young people are not being adequately considered in crucial policy decisions that will ultimately shape their future.

generally and with regard to climate change. Most interviewees supported the idea that Australia has well-developed mechanisms for hearing the voices of young people – at least for teenagers and older children. Mechanisms such as summits, forums, surveys, conferences and access to relevant ministers all exist; however, what appeared to be lacking in Australia were mechanisms for translating the listening into action –"we've heard the message, we've changed the policy or our action, this is what we are thinking now, what do you think?" This appeared to be a constant theme from the interviews.

Views varied as to whether a 'top-down' approach, such as a Minister for Youths' "Australian Youth Forum" or a bottom-up self-advocacy approach is more effective in translating outcomes into action. Whilst the report revealed a sense of pessimism about how to do this, it went on to identify some core ideas, relevant for those of us working on intergenerational and future generations matters. These ideas specifically included a Children's Commissioner for Future Generations and the need for a greater emphasis to be placed on ensuring that the voices of young people are included in mainstream consultation and advocacy.

Interestingly, this included challenging the environment movement about why they are not seeking the views of children and young people. In Australia particularly, the environment movement has an 'educate and activate' strategy: that is, ensuring environmental education is included in schools and presentations by key environmental players to children, rather than seeing children and young people as key citizen stakeholders in climate change. Only relatively recently have child-focused NGOs such as Save the Children and Oxfam, which both work extensively with climate issues in the Australasian Oceania region, established Children and Youth Ambassador roles. One might have expected that the mechanisms to listen to the voices of children and young people, consider their interests, and promote their participation in decision making with regard to climate-change-related policy should, in theory, raise their status as legitimate stakeholders. However, academic and childhood expert Kay Tisdall noted in the ARACY paper that whilst some success had been celebrated, there is a view that children are often treated as citizens in waiting rather than citizens in their own right, so their participation is seen as training for future engagement as full citizens, rather than providing a valuable contribution now.[37]

For participation to be successful it has to be meaningful to young people, effective in bringing about change and sustained – that is embedded in the process rather than a one-off. Tisdall suggests that, in designing effective participation, the potential has to be retained for children and young people's participation to be political, to challenge and to insist on change. This may in part explain the explosion of grassroots youth-led participation models, such as the Australian Youth Climate Coalition

[37] E.K.M. Tisdall, *Governance and Participation*, in B. Percy-Smith, N. Thomas, A *Handbook of Children and Young People's Participation: Perspectives from Theory and Practice* (Routledge 2010).

(AYCC), which have attracted a large number of young people around the world, and why these grassroots youth groups are seeking other avenues for change-driven participation via the courts, for example the climate change litigation I briefly mentioned earlier run by Our Children's Trust in the USA.[38]

### *Other Avenues for Participation: Legal Challenges on Behalf of Future Generations*

Principle 10 of the Rio Declaration on Environment and Development remains a founding principle today and declares that

> environmental issues are best handled with the participation of all concerned citizens, at the relevant level. At a national level, each individual shall have appropriate access to information concerning the environment that is held by public authorities, including information on hazardous materials and activities in their communities, and the opportunity to participate in decision making processes. States shall facilitate and encourage public awareness and participation by making information widely available. Effective access to judicial and administrative proceedings, including redress and remedy, shall be provided.[39]

Obligations towards generations unborn, and taking the longer-term view, have been and are currently being explored and litigated in various contexts internationally. In terms of participatory and procedural rights for and on behalf of future generations, there appears to be a clear role and moral duty for commissioners and ombudspersons to act on their behalf in these or similar cases. If scientist James Hansen, legal academic Edith Brown Weiss, and other esteemed experts and academics can provide amicus briefs in current climate public trust cases, then national commissioners for future generations, commissioners for the environment and ombudspersons can also act as amicus curiae for children and young people and those not yet born, in similar court proceedings. In the words of Our Children's Trust the current climate cases are a "game changing youth driven global climate recovery campaign to secure the legal right to a stable and healthy climate."[40]

With this in mind, there are three cases of particular interest. First, the early 1993 Philippines case of *Minors Oposa* v. *Secretary of the Department of Environment and Natural Resources*, in which the Philippine Supreme Court found that present generations have standing (*locus standi*) to represent future generations, followed by the recent atmospheric trust action where the right of present and future generations to enjoy a livable planet with the atmosphere is held in trust as a vital

[38] Our Children's Trust is currently in the courts and has been brought by five teenagers and two not-for-profits. See *Juliana* v. *United States*, arguing the public trust doctrine www.ourchildrenstrust.org/ accessed 30 November 2017.

[39] Rio Declaration on the Environment (1992) Principle 10.

[40] Ibid.

life support system.[41] Second, the Dutch *Urgenda* case, in which the national Supreme Court ultimately affirmed that the Dutch government's efforts to reduce the country's GHG emissions were inadequate and ordered the government to reduce the GHG by at least 25 percent compared to 1990 levels.

The third case is from the US, where senior academics, scientists and experts are acting as amicus in the current intergenerational climate justice cases (brought by Our Children's Trust).[42] The supporting amicus briefs detailed the significant threats that climate change presents to the availability of water and food, national security, economic stability and important cultural values. In the words of friend to the court James Hansen, the former head of NASA Goddard Institute for Space Studies:

> the science is crystal clear. If emissions continue unabated, resulting warming of the ocean will lock in a continuing acceleration of climate extremes. We would subject young people and future generations to irreparable harm, with irreversible effects including the loss of many species and continually rising sea level out of control.[43]

Hansen then went on to say that "Governments are shirking their responsibility, pretending they do not understand the urgency of actions – so we must count on the wisdom of the judicial system to protect the rights of young people."[44]

One promising sign in the case of *Juliana* v. *United States* is the recent 'green light' to proceed to trial. In the words of Federal Court Judge Ann Aikens, "exercising my reasoned judgment I have no doubt that the right to a climate system capable of sustaining human life is fundamental to a free and ordered society."[45]

## CONCLUSION

This chapter has sought to demonstrate that over the past twenty-five years, institutions and NGOs have started to recognize the need to participate with children and young people and are slowly moving towards recognizing them as 'citizen stakeholders'. The CRC and DGD on children's rights and the environment, coupled with the passionate words of the previous UN Secretary-General Ban Ki-moon, are, hopefully, positive indicators of the emergence of a more mature conversation with children and young people. In the words of Tisdall, "in designing effective participation, the potential has to be retained for children and young people's participation to be political, to challenge and to insist on change."

41 *Minors Oposa* v. *Secretary of the Department of Environment and Natural Resources*, 224 SCRA 792 (1993).

42 See *Juliana* v. *United States*, *supra* note 38.

43 Ibid.

44 Ibid.

45 *Juliana* v. *United States* (with twenty-one youth plaintiffs), Judge Ann Aiken US Federal Court, November 2016.

*Economic Aspects of Intergenerational Justice*

# 14

# Unsustainability as an Economic Problem

*Gábor Bartus*

While intelligent people around the world naturally embrace the notion of sustainable development, strongly emphasize the need to safeguard the interests of future generations, and strive to fulfill the normative obligation of intergenerational equity, it is apparent that most personal, business and community decisions continue to be made based purely on the desire to achieve maximum short-term benefits. This generates contradiction between the normative ideas defined at the political level and the reality of actions in daily life. This chapter explains the potential causes of such a contradiction. The theory of this chapter is that people using the norm set of 'sustainable development,' 'rights of future generations,' and 'intergenerational equity' have failed to fully explore these norms and define the limitations and implications of their practical application. The problems will be explained through concepts and interrelations of economics.

## SUSTAINABILITY AND THE POSSIBILITIES OF FUTURE GENERATIONS REPRESENTED IN ECONOMICS

Initially, it should be noted that the following three terms are not interchangeable but are closely related to the subject matter of this chapter and to one another, and should be defined in terms of economics: sustainable development, the rights of future generations and intergenerational equity.

### *Sustainability*

The easiest term to define for economists is most likely *sustainable development.* The UN WCED, also known as the Brundtland Commission, defined sustainable development in its report published in 1987 as "development that meets the needs of the present generation without compromising the ability of future generations to meet their own needs."[1] This means that people living at any moment in the future will have a combination of assets at their disposal that help produce the goods (products and services) then required or demanded as economic resources and factors of production. For the present generation, this implies that people living now invest not only in their own well-being and actual consumption but also in the future, by accumulating capital and managing exhaustible natural assets in ways that protect both their quality and quantities.

This chapter prefers the capital approach to sustainability because the term *needs* used in the Brundtland definition makes operationalization very difficult or impossible. Needs do not remain constant over time, including the most trivial instances that are the biological necessities of human existence (such as air, fresh water, food, shelter, and movement), and needs are addressed by varying specific solutions (such as products and services and their varying technological solutions). What does not change over time is that goods to meet these needs may only be created with assets available to produce such goods. As a result, future generations will also need resources (capital) available to combine in certain ways to meet needs that the present generation is currently unfamiliar with. The present generation knows that future generations will need capital but is unable to predict the required quantity and quality.

Modern economics distinguishes four groups of factors of production capital:[2]

- economic or man-made capital, $K_m$: the classical definition of capital, including produced goods and production assets that contribute to production;
- human resources, $K_h$: workforce quantity (size of productive population, number of work hours), knowledge, skills and health of workforce – the more developed a society, the higher the importance of the latter over the former;
- social capital, $K_s$: human values, certain features of human relations (e.g. trust), the quality of institutions established by people; and
- natural resources, $K_n$: mineral resources, energy resources, renewable species and their systems, ecosystems and their diversity, i.e. biodiversity.

As a result, the available total stock of capital is:

$$K = K_m + K_h + K_s + K_n \tag{1}$$

[1] G.H. Brundtland et al., *Our Common Future: Report of the World Commission on Environment and Development* (Oxford University Press 1987) 43.

[2] N. Hanley and G. Atkinson, 'Economics and Sustainable Development: What Have We Learnt and What Do We Still Have to Learn?', in F. Berkhout, M. Leach, and I. Scoones (eds.), *Negotiating Environmental Change: New Perspectives from the Social Sciences* (Edward Elgar 2003).

*Sustainability* – in economic terms – simply means that production possibilities (allowing for short-term fluctuations) do not decrease in the long term. This is often referred to as the weak sustainability condition.[3]

The weak sustainability condition is as follows:

$$\delta K(t)/\delta t \geq 0, \tag{2}$$

in every case of t > t(0) where t is time and t(0) is the present moment. This large volume of factors includes increasing or degrading ones. Increasing factors of production contribute to expanding production possibilities while degrading ones reduce them. What is important for production possibilities is their root: if the overall expansion effect of the increasing factors is bigger than the reduction factor of degrading ones, the expansion of production possibilities takes place despite certain degrading factors. For example, many developed States have been able to achieve economic growth despite a decline in their population. This is exactly why Acemoglu and Robinson,[4] alongside Fukuyama,[5] stressed the importance of successful societies and the institutional foundation of their prosperity (the significance of inclusive institutions, the state, the rule of law and accountable governments).[6]

This is true for natural resources as well. In recent decades, we have increased our production possibilities in the world in general while gradually depleting natural resources. Based on OECD data, 25 percent of biodiversity had disappeared by 2000 and biodiversity loss is estimated to affect one-third of our original ecological capital by 2030.[7] The reason for this is that the expansion effect of the other three factors of production offset the reduction effect of degrading natural resources on production possibilities. Consequently, there is a tradeoff between the factors of production: a decline in one may be compensated by the increase of another factor.

According to World Bank figures, natural capital use contributed only approximately 6 percent to the income generated in 2005 on global average, with 18 percent generated by the use of physical capital and land and 77 percent by the mobilization of human and social capital. However, dependence on natural capital is distributed unevenly across countries. In the wealthiest countries, only 2 percent of income was generated by the use of natural resources while this indicator stood at 36 percent in the poorest economies.[8] Low percentage rates disclose high absolute values. The global estimated value of pollination services provided by insects (especially bees)

3 J.M. Hartwick, 'Intergenerational Equity and the Investing of Rents of Exhaustible Resources' (1977) 67 *American Economic Review* 972.

4 D. Acemoglu and J.A. Robinson, *Why Nations Fail* (Profile Books 2012).

5 F. Fukuyama, *The Origins of Political Order: From Prehuman Times to the French Revolution* (Profile Books 2011).

6 See ibid.

7 OECD, *Towards Green Growth* (OECD 2011).

8 K. Hamilton and E. Naikal, 'Comprehensive Wealth Accounting and Sustainable Development', in G. Atkinson et al. (eds.), *Handbook of Sustainable Development*, 2nd edn. (Edward Elgar 2014).

vital to food production is between USD 235 billion and USD 577 billion.[9] Sustainable use of natural resources would be especially critical in developing countries as people's livelihood – at least in the short term – depends heavily on the quality of the environment and steady revenues from ecosystem services.

*Strong sustainability* responds to this problem by advocating management systems where natural resources are substituted and maintained to ensure that production possibilities do not decrease in the long term even if the other factors of production remain unchanged. In other words, strong sustainability prohibits substitution: natural resources must remain intact, and their potential decline cannot be offset by increasing the other three factors of production.[10]

The strong sustainability condition is as follows:

$$\delta K(t)/\delta t \geq 0 \text{ and } \delta K_n(t)/\delta t \geq 0, \text{ in every case of } t > t(0) \quad (3)$$

It means that the sustainability condition must be met separately for natural capital as well and substitution is only allowed between other types of capital.

This may seem simple and easy to do, but this is not at all the case, as the relationship between various generations is inevitably asymmetric. Knowledge capital, for example, is constantly growing as each generation expands the pool of knowledge in basic science or applied technology. As a result, future generations can rely on more knowledge to help establish their own well-being. Similarly, the stock of man-made capital, buildings, passenger and freight transport infrastructure or financial capital may also be increased. Today's people live under incomparably better conditions – in most aspects of life – than any previous generation. For example, life expectancy at birth is higher, well-being as expressed by GDP per capita is higher, and poverty has never been so low (although inequalities have been growing in the past decade). The yield of capital available to people has been constantly rising since the beginning of the history of mankind.

However, capital accumulation has also led to severe problems, including in particular the depletion of natural resources, population decline in developed countries, and government debts growing at a very rapid pace. Looking back into the past, we can see cases where the exhaustion or lack of increase of certain types of capital resulted in local or regional disasters. There were civilizations, for example, whose demise was caused by the ultimate depletion of their natural resources,[11] while others, lacking the capabilities to protect themselves, were destroyed by hostile

[9] Intergovernmental Science-Policy Platform for Biodiversity and Ecosystem Services, *Pollinators Vital to Our Food Supply under Threat*, Press Release (26 February 2016) www.ipbes.net/article/press-release-pollinators-vital-our-food-supply-under-threat accessed 30 November 2017.

[10] R.U. Ayres, J.C.J.M. van den Bergh, and J.M. Gowdy, 'Strong versus Weak Sustainability: Economics, Natural Sciences and "Consilience"' (2001) 23 *Environmental Ethics* 155.

[11] The author studies many such examples: J. Diamond, *Collapse: How Societies Choose to Fail or Succeed* (Viking Penguin 2005).

armies or disappeared after their state structure collapsed.[12] The sustainability of civilizations does not depend exclusively upon natural resources.[13] According to Acemoglu and Robinson,[14] "[t]he growth generated by extractive institutions is very different in nature from growth created under inclusive institutions, however. Most important, it is not sustainable."[15]

While it seems evident that we should avoid exhausting capital that is essentially important for future generations, there are several trends which illustrate a history of practice to the contrary. First, experience from the past suggests that generations living at a later time are generally in a more privileged situation than their predecessors, meaning, for example, that the value of yield generated by capitals is growing as time moves forward in history. Second, these advancements have been achieved despite the fact that natural capital is decreasing and its degradation is accelerating. Third, while it is not guaranteed that these trends will continue until the end of time and natural capital does not have a critical level at which or below which the first trend goes into reverse and future generations will face less favorable conditions, we do not know exactly what the future will be like, and what the critical level of natural capital is at that point. For example, it is indeterminate how far the tradeoff among the different types of capital may be allowed and in general how much and what type of capital will any future generation need to establish its own well-being.

### *Rights of the Future Generations and Intergenerational Equity*

The concept of *intergenerational equity* or the *protection of the rights of future generations* broadens the scope of sustainable development by establishing moral – in practice primarily egalitarian – requirements with regard to the preservation of resources for the future. Which requirements are not crucially needed to ensure sustainability as resources supplying the needs of future generations should not necessarily match today's resources and should also not naturally be equally shared among the members of future societies. Intergenerational equity includes three principles: (1) conservation of options, (2) conservation of quality and (3) conservation of access.[16] Norton and Thompson stress that the relationship between

[12] Acemoglu and Robinson, *supra* note 4; Fukuyama, *supra* note 5.

[13] The majority of literature on sustainable development is expressly centered around natural capital. "Consequently, sustainable development can be viewed as a holistic approach to the relationship between man and the environment," A.E. Egelston, *Sustainable Development* (Springer 2013). "This concept of sustainability ... is based on the notion that depletion of natural resources and environmental degradation conspire to depress economic growth and development," K.E. Portney, *Sustainability* (MIT Press 2015).

[14] Acemoglu and Robinson, *supra* note 4 at 150.

[15] Ibid.

[16] E. Brown Weiss, 'Intergenerational Equity: A Legal Framework for Global Environmental Change', in E. Brown Weiss (ed.), *Environmental Change and International Law: New Challenges and Dimensions* (United Nations University Press 1992).

generations "has an important normative dimension that cannot be captured by economic valuations alone, but one that involves important questions of intergenerational equity."[17]

In specific cases, the principle of intergenerational equity has been naturally incorporated into the concept of sustainable development, and that process is genuinely reflected by the changes in the extension of the dictionary entry on sustainable development over time in the *Hungarian Dictionary of Environmental Protection and Nature Conservation*. While the definition of sustainable development in the first edition of 1993 exclusively focused on the preservation of natural resources for future generations, it was extended in the second edition in 2002 to include economic and social criteria, particularly fair distribution of access to resources on a global scale, reduction of poverty, and 'bridging the social gap' between certain groups within the society.

The present generations cannot be adequately informed about the future to ensure that their current resource allocation is organized in a way capable of removing asymmetry between various generations. If we are not completely informed, some type of inequality is very likely to be generated. Either the present or the future generations will be more privileged. Consequently, the conservation of options imposes much more rigorous requirements than simply ensuring the availability of some kind of stock of natural resources and other types of capital for future generations. This leads us to the issue of discounting.

## EQUITY BETWEEN GENERATIONS OR THE ISSUE OF DISCOUNTING

Another significant obstacle in the field of economics restricting the assessment or planning of equity between generations is the extreme difficulty of the comparison of present and distant future values. If there was an appropriate discount rate at our disposal, we could effectively compare costs and benefits relevant at various points in time. However, for the time being economics lacks any unanimously accepted theory or methodology to determine a correct (i.e. fair) discount rate while it could critically contribute to making just, sustainable decisions ensuring intergenerational equity.

In principle, two fundamental mistakes can be made. On the one hand, the present generation may use a larger share of the income at their disposal to create their own present wealth or increase it (current consumption) while reducing their investments, for example spending less on sustaining capital allowing future generations to supply their own well-being. On the other hand, it is also possible that investment into the future is so important for the present generation that it changes the rate of consumption and investment to benefit the latter. This way creates

[17] B.G. Norton and A. Thompson, 'Ethics and Sustainable Development: The Virtues of an Adaptive Approach to Environmental Choice', in Atkinson, *supra* note 8 at 119.

enormous stocks of capital for future generations, resulting in significantly better quality of life and higher income than today's to be enjoyed by their descendants. Nowadays, seeing the extremely fast degradation of natural capital and threatened by the impacts of climate change, it is obvious that future generations will live under less favorable conditions, which means they need to be protected, but it could also happen that they turn out to be the beneficiaries and will have a better quality of life than present generations. How to make smart decisions, how to decide the amount of available income that should be spent on our own consumption, and how much should be invested to support the consumption of future generations?

In order to assess the outcomes of these decisions, the relevant costs and benefits should be assigned to the various alternatives in each case considering the occurrence of those costs and benefits in time. As people inherently tend to weigh their losses and benefits against their occurrence in time, the selected time preference is crucial. The difference between the value of a present benefit and its worth when realized at a later point in time is measured by the discount rate. Two alternatives whose costs and benefits occur in various time periods may only be compared due to the time preference if the cash stream is measured for a specific point in time which is usually the present. In other words, compare the present value of the costs and benefits of the alternatives.

Yields of natural capital are created over an extremely long period of time and they remain valuable for people for an equally long period of time. If the stream of yields approaches infinity, it is called annuity and its present value will equal the nominal value of the yield due each year divided by the discount rate. As a result, the sum of the discount rate will significantly affect the present value of the maintenance and preservation of natural capital: the lower the discount rate, the higher the present value of the yields of natural capital (ecosystem services); the closer the discount rate is to zero, the more the present value of the yield (annuity) approaches infinity; and the higher the present value of the yield of natural capital, the less favorable compared with this alternative is a utilization option that decreases the amount of capital.

In relation to intergenerational equity, a low discount rate means that a decision to benefit the increase of future consumption possibilities is more reasonable, while a higher discount rate supports larger consumption by present generations. Remember that income can only be spent on consumption or investment where investment corresponds with the consumption of future generations and consumption of present generations realized at a later point in time. In other words, the use of income always includes weighing between present and future consumption. And the measurement of this weighing is discount rate.

Until now, this chapter has noted that the social discount rate may be 'lower' or 'higher,' but what is its precise value? This is the question that economics has not yet been able to find a definitive answer to. Advocates of different methodologies and various normative approaches continue to argue. The most eloquent example of this unresolved issue and the nature of this discussion it has generated is the debate triggered by the economics of climate change and the Stern review.[18] The research team headed by Nicholas Stern concluded in its report, commissioned by the British government, that climate change will cause enormous social damage identical to damage prompted by the two World Wars combined.[19] The loss Stern's team estimated significantly exceeded any previous estimates, and the large difference was mostly explained by the use of a lower discount rate that was close to zero.[20]

The value of the discount rate is the sum of its components, known as the Ramsey equation:

$$r = \delta + \eta * g \tag{4}$$

where r is the discount rate, $\delta$ is the rate of pure time preference, $\eta$ is the coefficient of relative risk aversion (or the elasticity of the marginal utility of consumption),[21] and g is the per capita growth rate of consumption.

The Ramsey equation suggests that the calculation of present value should consider not only the rate of pure time preference but also the degree of risk assumption and the growth rate of wealth in societies. For example, the wealthier future societies are, the more effectively they will be able to address certain problems, so we can use a higher discount rate.

Returning to the Stern example, while most other studies on climate change estimated the value of $\delta$, $\eta$ and g at around 2 percent, causing a discount rate of approximately 6 percent, the Stern review set $\delta$ at almost zero (0.1 percent), $\eta$ at 1 (which reflects absolute risk aversion) and future growth (g) at 1.3 percent, generating a discount rate of 1.4 percent. The difference is substantial, and the discount rates of 1.4 percent and 6 percent cause a nearly 100 times discrepancy with present values.[22]

Before hastily committing to a discount rate close to zero and arguing that in order to ensure intergenerational equity it is necessary to avoid treating generations differently by discounting benefits realized in the future by calculating them at a lower present value, one must carefully consider the following. On the one hand, looking back at the history of mankind, people living at a later point in time were in a more favorable position than their predecessors almost without exception, ignoring local and regional declines: they lived longer, they were richer, had more

18 N. Stern, *Stern Review on the Economics of Climate Change* (Her Majesty's Treasury 2006).

19 Ibid.

20 Ibid.

21 The value of relative risk sensitivity ($\eta$) usually settles between 1 and 4, where 1 represents absolute risk aversion.

22 See also W.D. Nordhaus, *The 'Stern Review' on the Economics of Climate Change*, Working Paper 12741 (National Bureau of Economic Research, 2006); T. Sterner and U.M. Persson, *An Even Sterner Review*, Discussion Paper 07-37 (Resources for the Future, 2007); M. Weitzman, 'A Review of the Stern Review of the Economics of Climate Change' (2007) 45(3) *Journal of Economic Literature* 703.

information about the world and had more production possibilities even if the natural capital might have been decreasing in the meantime. On the other hand, production possibilities are basically determined by human and social capital that induces technology changes, potentially promoting more efficient and economical use of natural capital in turn. While the finiteness of natural capital restricts the sustainability of economic growth, human and social capital and the resulting technology innovation may be endlessly increased, meaning that it may be a lasting source of economic development in time. Even if economic growth is affected by cyclical fluctuations, the tendency of growth may be continuous; for example, g is most probably a positive number, significantly different from zero. The coefficient of relative risk sensitivity is also definitely above 1, as the idea of people totally averting risks defies our overall experience: people experiment, start businesses, explore unchartered territories and choose from savings options with different risks.

The value of the discount rate is above zero, and a rate close to zero does not help prevent injustice against future generations but forces present generations to make unnecessary sacrifices. This is because a discount rate of zero makes all problems emerging in the future today's problem, with its present value equaling its future value. Current generations would be obliged to solve the problems of not only one but any future generation at the present moment if the cost–benefit analysis based on the nominal value of the future problem shows a better result than the cost–benefit value of the present problem of today's generation. A discount rate close to zero envisions a world without technology and social innovation, where people try to avert any potential threat using today's solutions even 100 years later. The world of zero discount rate is not a fair world; it is a dead world.

Another pitfall is a mistake that would apply short-term business discount rates significantly above zero (e.g. two-digit rates) in cases where, for example, natural capital is also affected. Then, the pitfall would continue by assuming that the yield (the ecosystem service) of the natural capital used will not have any beneficiaries in the distant future, e.g. as early as in two to three decades. The world of high discount rates is based on the false idea that any amount of innovation is possible at any time without any significant endeavor, costs or time.

While it is possible to argue that the correct discount rate is to be found in a relatively narrow range between maybe 1 percent and 7 percent, in reality this range is still too broad, causing significant discrepancies in the present value. An example of this can be seen in reactions to climate change connected with the Stern review, which prompted a huge upheaval by reducing the discount rate from 'only' 6 percent to 1.5 percent.

The situation becomes even more complex when considering cases where a future outcome is highly uncertain, but this potential event whose occurrence is highly uncertain will have severe impacts and consequences. In relation with such cases, Weitzman concludes that

> [t]he point of all of this is that economic analysis is not completely helpless in the presence of deep structural uncertainty and potentially unlimited exposure. The analysis is more frustrating and more subjective – and it looks a lot less conclusive – because it requires some form of speculation (masquerading as an 'assessment') about the extreme bad-fat-tail probabilities and utilities.[23]

Together, this leads to the following four conclusions. First, intergenerational equity is not a straightforward issue, as no automatically applicable, unquestionable, and fully verified formula exists to determine an optimal balance between current consumption and investments serving future interests. Second, the factors potentially determining the optimal balance should nevertheless be considered based on common sense and proper moral values, the examination of alternatives should also focus on the interests of future generations, and their presumed interests should also be represented. Third, it is not necessarily true that choices are always made to the detriment of future generations, as the application of a discount rate lower than the optimal level will harm current generations. Fourth, it is falsely believed that intergenerational equity is ensured by a discount rate close to zero. If the present value of costs or benefits occurring in the distant future is set to almost equal, their nominal future value, ignoring the potential impacts of technological development, the growth of knowledge, the improvement of institutions or economic growth (that obviously benefit future and not present generations), this may easily have clearly negative impacts on the current generation.

## THE PROBLEM OF SUSTAINABILITY TRANSITION

Assuming the problem of choosing the correct discount rate has been successfully tackled, the ratio of consumption and investment can be optimal in principle. Certainly, it is possible to describe a theoretical future state that is optimal from the aspect of sustainability. The necessary technologies are in a large part available, but they are currently not used to the extent required in theory. What is more, it is easily possible to imagine and describe more than one such sustainable social states.

There are multiple scientific works and political documents designed to do just that, describe optimal, sustainable state and structures. The problem, of course, is that no, or only marginal, adjustments have been made in the actual way societies work to approach that potentially optimal state. And that leads to the problem of sustainability transition.

[23] M. Weitzman, *Structural Uncertainty and the Value of Statistical Life in the Economics of Catastrophic Climate Change*, Working Paper 13490 (National Bureau of Economic Research, 2007) 31.

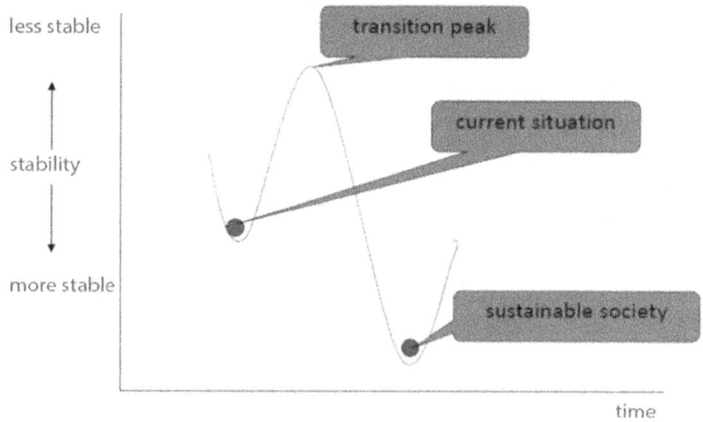


FIGURE 14.1 The problem of sustainability transition

### *Barriers of the Transition to Sustainability*

Consider the model in Figure 14.1.

In this model, time is the independent variable in relation to which a society's stability or resilience (the ability to efficiently respond to or withstand external shocks) is measured. Assume that the society examined is in a relatively less stable or resilient, non-sustainable state and that the more familiar state is considered to be much more stable, resilient and sustainable. It is clear that the transition from one state into the other involves time and costs and that a transition peak must be passed. This transition may imply temporary losses, as former status quos dissolve and the creation of a new status quo is time-consuming. A certain part of the capital must find new fields of utilization, and people must adjust some of their consumption habits.

Frequently, transition is challenging because the former system has not yet reached the end of its lifetime and the capital invested has not yet been recovered. For example, the lifetime of energy infrastructure assets ranges between forty years (power plants) and eighty years (grids).[24] Transition to renewable energy sources is essentially required to create a sustainable energy system, but adaptation to an energy system based dominantly on renewable energy sources does not only involve the replacement of coal power plants by solar panels and wind turbines, it requires major changes in the system itself and the system management as well. In other words, at times an operational system (which is not sustainable in the long term) must be transformed before the invested capital is recovered resulting in transition costs.

Transition time and costs increase if new technologies need to be developed. Remaining in the field of energy, a significant rise in the share of renewable – mostly

[24] J. Cortekar and M. Groth, 'Adapting Energy Infrastructure to Climate Change: Is There a Need for Government Interventions and Legal Obligations within the German "Energiewende?"' (2015) 73 *Energy Procedia* 12.

weather-dependent – energy sources is impossible without the development of energy storage technologies. In recent years, a number of parallel studies have been financed from public or private funds to improve the efficiency of energy storage. According to *Nature*, these efforts will soon pay off, as the price of batteries may be reduced by 50 percent and the density of energy stored may be up to ten times higher,[25] potentially facilitating higher penetration of electric vehicles and the transition of households to renewable energy systems.

The adjustment of patterns of production and consumption will potentially require education, training and promotional campaigns. Regulations should also be adapted to reflect the unique features of new technologies generating institutional costs. While a transition to a sustainable society generates welfare benefits for the whole of the society, it will harm certain members. These players may potentially block the transition process and the removal of these blocks may also be costly and time-consuming. The idea that sustainability transition is a win–win situation is a myth that limits the ability to face the real challenges and prevents the precise preliminary assessment of the actual costs of transition.[26]

Understanding the time and cost implications of sustainability transition helps realize why politicians frequently discuss the issue, but there is little government action to implement the transition to a sustainable society. As the time required for the transition is typically longer than normal democratic government cycles, it is almost certain that a government launching such a transition will have nothing to give voters, only the costs and efforts involved, and the benefits will not materialize in the same government cycle or before the next general election. If politicians are primarily interested in collecting as many votes as possible, they will be reluctant to make commitments generating only costs until the next general election, while the benefits are only available in calculations and forecasts and the fruits may potentially be reaped by the next government possibly formed by opposition parties.

Naturally, this does not fully prevent sustainability transition but strongly limits the range of possible interventions. Transition to sustainability is possible if the impacts of the non-action alternative are obvious and alarming and the sustainable solution along with a substitution technology is available and affordable. In this case, transition may be completed even if the results only appear at a later point in time. A good example for that is the ban of chlorofluorocarbons that deplete the stratospheric ozone layer and their substitution by other substances regulated by the Montreal Protocol. Agreement on transition was also possible to reach when it was supported by broad political consensus typically meaning that the parties in opposition at the time did not build their election campaign on the costs of starting the transition

[25] K. Bourzac, 'Batteries: 4 Big Questions' (2015) 526 *Nature* S105.

[26] U. Pisano, K. Lepuschitz, and G. Berger, *Vienna +10: National Sustainable Development Strategies in Europe: Taking Stock, New Developments and Future Challenges* (European Sustainable Development Network 2013) box 1.3 at 9.

process but chose to endorse the ruling party's efforts. Such interventions have been made to create a sustainable pension system in many Nordic countries. Another exception is the German energy policy reform, 'Energiewende,' based on the awareness and willingness to pay of Germany's large high-income middle-class population. In Germany, the installation of photovoltaic panels on residential buildings was financed from private household savings and public funds through the energy price system.

## CONCLUSION

In democratic political systems based on free elections every four or five years, the strategy of political forces focusing on the collection of the largest possible number of votes as dictated by the system causes a systemic error. This implies that that the sustainability transition is typically excessively costly and time-consuming to implement, even if it the process results in a more resilient society. This creates a collective action problem – although the sustainability transition would benefit the entire society in the long term, it may induce partial losses for players the implementation of the transition depends upon.

In order to remove the barriers of transition, a suitable catalyst to reduce transition costs (or at least to minimize the potential losses of key players) is necessary to shorten the time needed for transition and to accelerate the materialization of benefits. To make that shortcut, sustainability institutions need to be established.

Hungary's National Framework Strategy on Sustainable Development offers the following definition of sustainability institutions:

> The interests of our successors may be represented by the following three types of possible institutional solutions:
>
> - personalisation of future generations;
> - implementation of constitutional and other institutional constraints;
> - incorporation of automatic control mechanisms.

In the first case, since children and the unborn do not participate in decision-making that also affects them, the mentioned institutional solutions introduce such actor(s) into the political processes, who are mandated to represent them specifically.

The other form of the representation of future generations is the implementation of constitutional or other legal constraints. Constraints incorporated into the fundamental law are present in numerous countries or at least have surfaced as recommendations. In some countries, the constitution declares the right of future generations to a healthy, livable environment. In other cases, the fundamental law contains provisions about the financial stability, such as maximum public debt, some kind of spending constraint, annual budget deficit limit or the requirement of a balanced budget.

The third type of solution is the algorithmic regulation, or in other words automatic governance. It means that in certain issues the government or the legislation is not making decisions based on certain cases, but defines a formula, which then determines what actions should be taken. If the algorithm contains feedback elements based on long-term balance, automatic governance may be applied as a protection for future generations.[27]

The introduction of sustainability institutions seemingly contradicts a world where politicians exclusively concentrate on winning the highest possible number of votes as governments basically choose to restrict their own leeway by such interventions. Nevertheless, many exceptional instances may stimulate such self-restriction. The adoption of a constitutional limit on budgetary indebtedness in Hungary's legal system in 2011 was the consequence of the radical increase in government debt in preceding years and the high risk of sovereign default. In other words, conditions on the brink of disaster may help promote the establishment of sustainability institutions. A disaster is not necessarily a prerequisite, as broad public consensus and pressure on the political elite may be equally effective.

Sustainability institutions (or institutions in charge of safeguarding the interests of future generations) are not mandated – as parties having genuine knowledge about the future – to address the sensitive and as currently available information suggests presumably impossible challenge of making decisions in favor of the present or future generations but are established to importantly ensure that concerns about future generations are never disregarded and their interests are represented in the current consumption versus investment into the future debate. Societies will not necessarily be able to choose the correct discount rate in the discussion about selection alternatives, but they may certainly use experience from former wrong or right choices to make more successful decisions in the future. However, former optimal choices cannot ensure, even if the right selection pattern is applied, that an efficient balance between the present and the future is maintained. A number of factors (including scientific discoveries and technological innovations) affecting the decision may change whose future development is difficult to predict. While a fair intergenerational distribution of the burden to resolve the relevant issues cannot be promised, we can ensure that this challenge is addressed in every significant decision substantially affecting the future.

[27] National Framework Strategy on Sustainable Development of Hungary, Resolution 18/2013 of the Parliament of Hungary (28 March 2013).

# 15

# Intergenerational Equity and the European Constitution

*Markus W. Gehring and Alexandra R. Harrington*

How are concepts related to intergenerational equity reflected in the European constitutional order? This chapter will offer answers to this challenging and constantly emerging question and shed light on the interrelationship between intergenerational solidarity and sustainable development within the European constitutional system.

At a fundamental level, the objectives of intergenerational equity and sustainable development can and should be entwined in order for them to be achieved. In fact, global cooperation on sustainable development is a significant way to deliver intergenerational equity in order to address inequalities between developed and developing States. Intergenerational equity also provides one of the basic foundations for sustainable development, functioning as a key aspect of the 'social pillar' of sustainable development. Within the European constitutional order, the European Commission considers the concept of intergenerational equity and sustainable development to be important values, goals and principles for the European system, stating that they "are part of how European society works and how Europe engages with the rest of the world."[1]

In order to provide structure and governance background, the first section of this chapter provides an overview of the European Constitution, notably what is meant by the 'European Constitution' in itself, and why it is considered to exist even though the Constitutional Treaty has been rejected. Next, the chapter explains the history and key provisions on intergenerational equity in the European treaties, the reasons why intergenerational equity is so important within the European system, and which aspects/facets of intergenerational equity are relevant for sustainable

[1] See European Commission, *Renewed Social Agenda: Opportunities, Access and Solidarity in 21st Century Europe*, COM 412 (2008) 6. See also Y. Borgmann-Prebil and M. Ross, 'Promoting European Solidarity: Between Rhetoric and Reality?', in M. Ross and Y. Borgmann-Prebil (eds.), *Promoting Solidarity in the European Union* (Oxford University Press 2010) 1.

development. The chapter then provides an explanation of the history and definition of sustainable development in the European context, describing the key provisions in sustainable development in the European treaties, and also examining the relevant jurisprudence on the subject. The final section of the chapter offers tentative conclusions on some of the important implications for Europe, notably how the concepts of intergenerational equity and sustainable development relate to each other at European level and how important they have become over time.[2]

## THE EUROPEAN CONSTITUTION

The EU, currently comprised of twenty-seven Member States throughout the European region, was born in the early 1950s in the form of the European Community, created when six European States (France, Germany, Italy, Belgium, Luxembourg, and the Netherlands) signed the first founding treaties: the European Coal and Steel Community (ECSC) in 1952, followed by the EEC in 1957, and the European Atomic Energy Community (EURATOM) in 1957. In 1963, the various institutions created under the auspices of these treaties were harmonized into one central entity.[3] Accordingly, this European Community originated as an international organization of States linked together for economic purposes through several international treaties. Unlike other States or forms of federations, from the outset the European Community did not have a Constitution, or at least a constitution intended in conventional terms, through which to provide guidance or a source of rights and obligations to the same extent that is typically associated with a constitutional system.

After the Euro-impasse of the 1970s, when issues of the value and effectiveness of a potential European constitutional system, among other aspects of European integration, were solved only in part by the Single European Act of 1986,[4] a renewed constitution was generated during the adoption of the Treaty of Maastricht (or Treaty of the European Union) in 1992. The Treaty of Maastricht created the EU as "an ever closer union among the peoples of Europe, in which decisions are taken as closely as possible to the citizen."[5]

Following Maastricht, the EU began to transform into an entity far beyond an international organization of States linked by economic interests, although it continued to be ruled by a series of treaties and not by a 'real' constitution per se. After subsequent reforms through the treaties of Amsterdam (1999) and Nice (2003), which brought vital integration elements, such as the inclusion of the Schengen

[2] D. French, *Global Justice and Sustainable Development* (Legal Aspects of Sustainable Development) (Martinus Nijhoff 2010).

[3] P. Craig and G. de Búrca, *European Union Law*, 4th edn. (Oxford University Press 2011).

[4] The Single European Act brought major changes to the 1957 Treaty of Rome and established the common internal market in 1992.

[5] See Article A of the Treaty of Maastricht (original version) (1992).

Agreement in the EU framework, into existence, this "closer union among the peoples of Europe" concluded that a new 'constitutional foundation' was necessary to be functional for the future.

In December 2000, the Nice Charter of Fundamental Rights was adopted. This Charter represented a new era of protection for the designated fundamental rights, as prior to this there had been no formalized and concerted protection as such, with the rights granted being instead "fragmented and piecemeal"[6] and partially based on laws and treaties external to the EU or general principles of law. As a result of the Nice Charter, human rights at the European level were finally promoted by an organic text created by and for the EU and those living in it. The Nice Charter was also novel in that it provided for the protection of economic and social rights,[7] as well as 'new' rights such as the environment, and not only of 'traditional' political and civil rights.

In terms of political and legal power structures, the Treaty of Nice was meant to give a new balance to the European institutions. However, the reforms were not seen as sufficient, so it was decided to proceed with the approval of a true European Constitutional text.[8] In 2003, the Constitutional Convention, created by the Declaration of Laeken of December 2001, resulted in the Treaty Establishing a Constitution for Europe, subsequently modified and signed during the 2004 Intergovernmental Conference of Rome. However, not all Member States were ready to accept this new European Constitution, with States such as France and the Netherlands rejecting the Treaty in national referendums. This led to significant reflection on the necessity of a European Constitution, resulting in the Reform Treaty adopted as the Treaty of Lisbon in 2007, which subsequently entered into force on 1 December 2009. The Treaty of Lisbon rejected all references to the word "Constitution" and to all its symbols, yet confirmed many of the substantive provisions already included in the failed Constitutional Treaty.[9] With the Lisbon Treaty, the EU order is now founded on the new Treaty on the European Union ("TEU") and Treaty on the Functioning of the European Union ("TFEU").[10]

In light of the above, is it possible to say that a European constitution exists? One of the first endorsements of this constitutional discourse occurred in the 1980s through the CJEU, created by the ECSC and the EEC, which quickly became

[6] P. Craig, *The Lisbon Treaty: Laws, Politics, and Treaty Reform* (Oxford University Press 2010) 196.

[7] Ibid. at 196–197.

[8] Craig and de Búrca, *supra* note 3 at 654 and ff.

[9] For more details on this process, see for example F. Laursen, 'Introduction: Overview of the Constitutional Treaty and Main Elements of the Treaty', in F. Laursen, ed., *The Rise and Fall of the EU's Constitutional Treaty* (Martinus Nijhoff 2008) 1 ff.; Craig, *supra* note 6 at 1 ff and Craig and DeBurca, *supra* note 3 at 653 and ff (affirming that "the Convention deliberations, and the drafting of a Constitutional Treaty, warrant the appellation 'constitutional moment,'" even if the outcome of the ratification process is negative).

[10] Treaty on the Functioning of the European Union, OJ 2010/C 83/01 (2010).

an essential institution in the development of European law.[11] Significantly, with regard to the EU constitutional order, the CJEU declared the founding treaties to be akin to a constitutional charter:

> It must first be emphasized in this regard that the European Economic Community is a Community based on the rule of law, inasmuch as neither its Member States nor its institutions can avoid a review of the question whether the measures adopted by them are in conformity with *the basic constitutional charter, the Treaty*.

Additionally, while some Member States rejected a European Constitution, in 2008 the European Parliament endorsed the concept that the EU does indeed have a constitution:

> [T]he new Treaty substantially clarifies the definition of the values, principles and objectives which guide the actions of the European Union (EU); it describes the Union's competences; it lays down what institutions the EU will have, outlines its decision-making procedures, and stipulates what form its acts will take; it defines citizens' rights vis-à-vis the EU; it lays down the rules governing its own revision, etc. In that respect, it could be said that the Treaties on which the Union is founded in some way establish its *constitution*, taking the word 'constitution' in its material sense. After all, the role of a constitution is precisely that of laying down the conditions governing, and the limits to, the exercise of power in the context of a political entity and safeguarding citizens' rights, something which the new Treaty does.[12]

Thus, while it does not have a written constitution *strictu sensu*, it is possible to conclude that the EU does have a form of constitution.[13] It is this understanding of constitutional terms that allows for a fuller discussion of principles and the constitutional dimension of the EU and the principle of intergenerational equity and objective of sustainable development among them.

## INTERGENERATIONAL EQUITY IN THE EU CONSTITUTIONAL ORDER

As a principle, intergenerational equity has been linked to intergenerational justice and solidarity and has played a dual role over the past few decades: (a) a negative intergenerational equity construct, meaning a response to dangers or events, such as

[11] Through some landmark decisions, the ECJ considerably contributed to shaping and forging the law of the European Communities. This includes two essential decisions from the 1960s: case 26/62*Van Gend en Loos* and *Costa*. *N.V. Algemene Transport en Expeditie Onderneming Van Gend en Loos* v. *Nederlandse Administratie der Belastingen* [1963] ECR 1; case 6/64 *Flaminio Costa* v. *ENEL* [1964] ECR 585.

[12] European Parliament, *Report on the Treaty of Lisbon 2007/2286 (INI) of 29 January 2008*, EP-Doc A6–0013/2008, 17 (emphasis added). On this point, see also P. Kirchhof, 'The European Union of States', in A. von Bogdandy and J. Bast (eds.), *Principles of European Constitutional Law*, 2nd edn. (Hart Publishing 2010) 737.

[13] Craig and de Búrca, *supra* note 3.

climate change and (b) a positive intergenerational equity construct, through the creation of rights and obligations, for example in some State constitutions and in the 2015 Paris Agreement.[14] Within this dichotomy, the stages of development reached by intergenerational equity vary in the various branches of international law.[15]

At its heart, one of the core aspects of EU policy under the Pillar of Social Rights is the promotion of intergenerational solidarity.[16] Beyond this, however, recent actions of the EU have demonstrated a commitment to intergenerational equity, thereby preserving the interests of current and future generations to a more robust extent. The many decisions of the EU's organizational bodies to include sustainable development in legal and policy definition and implementation are some evidence of this, as they demonstrate a commitment to the ideals of sustainable development as a whole, necessarily including intergenerational equity.[17]

The EU's constitutional system has been used to establish express links between generations that are meant to promote understanding, exchange and a fostering of equity at all stages of the aging spectrum.[18] The European Parliament and Council have not only noted the systemic obligations of the EU to ensure and promote this balance but also noted the goals of the EU's mandate as including the creation of organic and societal exchanges between generations.[19] This is particularly focused on the relationships between the elderly population and the youth of the EU.[20]

In 2013, the European Council issued a guidance to assist in the implementation of the Horizon 2020 research funding scheme through which innovative and potentially groundbreaking research and collaborations were to be supported with the EU and between institutions in the EU and outside the region.[21] As a part of this, it was specified that supported activities are to prioritize "making use of the innovative, creative and productive potential of all generations," including the use of undertakings which

[14] See K. Wellens, 'Revisiting Solidarity as a (Re-)Emerging Constitutional Principle: Some Further Reflections', in R. Wolfrum and C. Kojima (eds.), *Solidarity: A Structural Principle of International Law* (Springer-Verlag, 2010) 4; Paris Agreement to the United Nations Framework Convention on Climate Change (2015).

[15] Wellens, *supra* note 15.

[16] European Parliament, Council and Commission, Interinstitutional Proclamation on the European Pillar of Social Rights, OL J 428, 13.12.2017, 1 (2017).

[17] Ibid. at 9.

[18] Decision No 940/2011/EU of the European Parliament and of the Council of 14 September 2011 on the European Year for Active Aging and Solidarity between Generations (2012), OJ L 246, 23.9.2011, 5.

[19] Ibid.

[20] Ibid.

[21] Council Decision of 3 December 2013 establishing the specific programme implementing Horizon 2020 – the Framework Programme for Research and Innovation (2014–2020) (2013/743/EU), OJ L 347, 20.12.2013, 965; Regulation (EU) No 1291/2013 of the European Parliament and of the Council of 11 December 2013 establishing Horizon 2020 – the Framework Programme for Research and Innovation (2014–2020) and repealing Decision No 1982/2006/EC, OL J 304, 20.12.2013, 104.

> enhance taking advantage of the potential of all generations by fostering the development of smart policies to make active aging a reality in an evolving intergenerational context and by supporting the integration of the generations of young Europeans in all domains of social, political, cultural and economic life, taking into account, amongst others, perception of opportunities for innovation in the context of high unemployment in many Union regions.[22]

Also, the Charter of Fundamental Rights and Freedoms of the EU contains an entire chapter on solidarity, which is directly linked to intergenerational equity. Specifically, Article 37 on environmental protection provides that "[a] high level of environmental protection and the improvement of the quality of the environment must be integrated into the policies of the Union and ensured in accordance with the principle of sustainable development."

Not only does the concept of intergenerational equity appear in the Treaty provisions, it extends to European case law.[23] For example, in *Herrmann* v. *Germany*, the ECtHR addressed issues of laws relating to the protection of animals and particular species through the lens of, among other concepts, intergenerational equity. Here, the Court stated that

> animals are viewed by the Convention as a constitutive part of an ecologically balanced and sustainable environment, their protection being incorporated in a larger framework of intra-species equity (ensuring healthy enjoyment of nature among existing humans), inter-generational equity (guaranteeing the sustainable enjoyment of nature by future human generations) and inter-species equity (enhancing the inherent dignity of all species as "fellow creatures").[24]

## SUSTAINABLE DEVELOPMENT IN THE EU CONSTITUTIONAL ORDER

A well-known and universally accepted definition of sustainable development is the one coined by the Brundtland Commission in 1987, whereby sustainable development is construed as "development that meets the needs of the present without compromising the ability of future generations to meet their own needs."[25] Yet, as

[22] Council Decision of 3 December 2013 establishing the specific programme implementing Horizon 2020 – the Framework Programme for Research and Innovation (2014–2020) (2013/743/EU), OJ L 347, 20.12.2013, p. 965 at 6.2.3.

[23] For a thorough analysis of the ECJ jurisprudence on solidarity, see C. Barnard, 'Solidarity and the Commission's "Renewed Social Agenda"', in Ross and Borgmann-Prebil, *supra* note 1, 75 ff.

[24] *Herrmann* v. *Germany*, Application No. 9300/97, 26 June 2012.

[25] G.H. Brundtland et al., *Our Common Future: Report of the World Commission on Environment and Development* (Oxford University Press 1987), Chapter 2: Towards Sustainable Development. In an interesting article on intergenerational equity, Professor Dinah Shelton asks whether the concept of "future generations" is limited to generations of humans only, or

with the definition of intergenerational equity, it is difficult to comprehensively define sustainable development.[26]

As has been posited, sustainable development is "founded upon the argument that economic development and environmental protection are not mutually exclusive goals, but that both must be concurrently attained if improvements are to be seen in global human welfare."[27] Thus, one of the key ideas of sustainable development is to maintain choice for future generations, reinforcing essential tenets of intergenerational equity.[28] As such, the concepts of intergenerational equity between generations and sustainable development are directly linked – one is an essential part of the other.

As a concept, sustainable development emerges from a general aspiration to a global responsibility towards "the interdependent societies and economies, the environment and natural resources, and the conditions of humanity."[29] In other words, sustainable development "provides a 'conceptual bridge' between the right to social and economic development, and the need to protect the environment."[30]

The importance of sustainable development in Europe has been emphasized several times by European institutions. For example, borrowing the Brundtland definition of sustainable development mentioned above, in 2001 the European Commission affirmed that "sustainable development is a global objective" and that "the European Union has a key role in bringing about sustainable development."[31] Also, in 2005 the European Commission affirmed that "[t]he essence of the European Union is to work for *sustainable development* as an overarching objective that aims at meeting the needs of the present without compromising the ability of future generations to meet their own needs."[32] Similarly, sustainable development is at the basis of the EU's promotion of international growth.[33]

whether it encompasses future life as well as the well-being of other species. See D. Shelton, 'Intergenerational Equity', in Wolfrum and Kojima, *supra* note 15 at 128.

26 See the difficulties identified in V. Lowe, 'Sustainable Development and Unsustainable Arguments', in A. Boyle and D. Freestone (eds.), *International Law and Sustainable Development* (Oxford University Press 2001) 25.

27 D. French, *International Law and Policy of Sustainable Development* (Manchester University Press, 2005) 2.

28 Shelton, *supra* note 65 at 134, citing B. Norton, 'Ecology and Opportunity: Intergenerational Equity and Sustainable Options', in A. Dobson (ed.), *Fairness and Futurity: Essays on Environmental Sustainability and Social Justice* (Oxford University Press 1999) 122 ff.

29 M.-C. Cordonier Segger and C.G. Weeramantry, 'Introduction to Sustainable Justice: Implementing International Sustainable Development Law', in M.-C. Cordonier Segger and Judge C.G. Weeramantry (eds.), *Sustainable Justice* (Martinus Nijhoff 2005) 2.

30 Ibid. at 2–3.

31 Communication from the European Commission, *A Sustainable Europe for a Better World: A European Union Strategy for Sustainable Development*, 15 May 2001, COM 264 (2001) 2.

32 European Commission, *Strategic Objectives 2005–2009, Europe 2010: A Partnership for European Renewal Prosperity, Solidarity and Security*, 26.1.2005 COM 12 (2005) 8 (emphasis added).

33 Ibid. at 12.

In a 2006 joint statement, sustainable development was discussed in the context of poverty eradication.[34] The document affirms that "[t]he primary and overarching objective of EU development cooperation is the eradication of poverty in the context of *sustainable development*,"[35] where sustainable development includes "good governance, human rights and political, economic, social and environmental aspects."[36] Sustainable development was also at the basis of the recent reform of the Common Agricultural Policy of the EU.[37]

Similar to the case of intergenerational equity, sustainable development is an idea that also appears prominently in the European treaties. For example, Article 2 of the Treaty establishing the European Community (as amended by the Treaty of Amsterdam) introduced sustainable development as an objective of the Union:

> The Community shall have as its task, by establishing a common market and an economic and monetary union and by implementing common policies or activities ... to promote throughout the Community a harmonious, balanced and *sustainable development* of economic activities, a high level of employment and of social protection, equality between men and women, sustainable and non-inflationary growth, a high degree of competitiveness and convergence of economic performance, a high level of protection and improvement of the quality of the environment, the raising of the standard of living and quality of life, and economic and social cohesion and solidarity among Member States. (emphasis added)

The Preamble of the TEU refers to sustainable development as one of the principles that should inspire the promotion of economic and social progress of the EU peoples.[38] Article 3 TEU mentions sustainable development twice. In paragraph 3 it is affirmed that:

> The Union shall ... work for the *sustainable development* of Europe based on balanced economic growth and price stability, a highly competitive social market economy, aiming at full employment and social progress, and a high level of protection and improvement of the quality of the environment. (emphasis added)

Article 3(5) TEU affirms that:

> [The Union] shall contribute to peace, security, the *sustainable development* of the Earth, solidarity and mutual respect among peoples, free and fair trade, eradication of poverty and the protection of human rights, in particular the rights of the child, as

[34] Joint statement by the Council and the representatives of the governments of the Member States meeting within the Council, *European Parliament and the Commission on European Union Development Policy: 'The European Consensus'* (2006/C 46/01), The European Consensus on Development, para. 1.

[35] Ibid. at para. 5 (emphasis added).

[36] Ibid. at para. 7.

[37] See European Commission, *Green Paper: Adapting to Climate Change in Europe – Options for EU Action*, COM 354 (29 June 2007) 14.

[38] Treaty on the European Union (Lisbon Version), OJ 2010/C 83/01, preamble (2010).

> well as to the strict observance and the development of international law, including respect for the principles of the United Nations Charter. (emphasis added)

Additional references to sustainable development in the TEU are contained in Article 21(2) pertaining to the Union's external action:

> The Union shall define and pursue common policies and actions, and shall work for a high degree of cooperation in all fields of international relations, in order to:
>
> (d) foster the *sustainable economic, social and environmental development* of developing countries, with the primary aim of eradicating poverty; . . .
> (f) help develop international measures to preserve and improve the quality of the environment and the sustainable management of global natural resources, in order *to ensure sustainable development.* (emphasis added)

Several references to sustainable development are also contained in the TFEU.[39] For example, Article 11 provides that:

> Environmental protection requirements must be integrated into the definition and implementation of the Union policies and activities, in particular with a view to promoting *sustainable development.* (emphasis added)

Title XX of TFEU is entirely dedicated to the environment. Specifically, Article 191(1) provides that:

> Union policy on the environment shall contribute to pursuit of the following objectives: preserving, protecting and improving the quality of the environment, protecting human health, prudent and rational utilisation of natural resources, promoting measures at international level to deal with regional or worldwide environmental problems, and in particular combating climate change.

Finally, the Charter of Fundamental Rights of the EU also refers to sustainable development. The Preamble mandates that the Union "seeks to promote balanced and sustainable development,"[40] while Article 37 of the Charter on environmental protection refers to the principle of sustainable development in these words:

> A high level of environmental protection and the improvement of the quality of the environment must be integrated into the policies of the Union and ensured in accordance with the principle of *sustainable development.* (emphasis added)

The CJEU also had limited occasion to interpret the objective of sustainable development. While at least 224 cases contain some reference to "sustainable development," the great majority mention sustainable development only in relation

[39] Treaty on the Functioning of the European Union, OJ 2010/C 83/01 (2010).
[40] Charter of Fundamental Rights and Freedoms, OJ 2010/C 83/02 (2010) preamble.

to a certain treaty article or directive/regulation. In other words, there are arguments based on the sustainable development objective, or that explain more thoroughly the idea of sustainable development, in only a few cases.

Specifically, it is worth mentioning the opinion of Advocate General Ruiz-Jarabo Colomer, who explains that the concept of sustainable development as used in the EC Treaty is often linked to that of environment, thus:

> alluding to a human dimension which cannot be overlooked when mention is made of protecting and improving the environment. In the geophysical medium which our natural surroundings represent, quality of life asserts itself as a citizenship right emanating from various factors, some of them physical (the rational use of resources and *sustainable development*) and some more intellectual (progress and cultural development).[41]

In another case, Advocate General Léger refers to the concept of sustainable development as defined by the Brundtland Commission to affirm that sustainable development

> does not mean that the interests of the environment must necessarily and systematically prevail over the interests defended in the context of the other policies pursued by the Community ... On the contrary, it emphasises the necessary balance between various interests which sometimes clash, but which must be reconciled.[42]

Further elaborating on the Brundtland Commission's report, Léger continues by stating that

> the concept [of sustainable development] means that the conduct of the various policies must, at the very least, not endanger the natural systems which give us life, the atmosphere, water, earth and living creatures. The report stresses that it is necessary not to set development against the environment but on the contrary to let them evolve in coordinated fashion.[43]

Additionally, Advocate General Léger explains that

> to reconcile these diverse interests in the context of sustainable development, the TEU introduced the *principle of "integration"* in Article 130r(2) *in fine*. That principle requires the Community legislature to conform with environmental protection requirements in the definition and implementation of other policies and actions. Integration of the environmental dimension is thus the basis of the strategy

[41] Opinion of Advocate General Ruiz-Jarabo Colomer, Case C-176/03, *Commission of the European Communities* v. *Council of the European Union*, delivered on 26 May 2005, para. 66 (emphasis added).

[42] Opinion of Advocate General Léger, Case C-371/98, *The Queen* v. *Secretary of State for the Environment, Transport and the Regions ex parte First Corporate Shipping Ltd*, delivered on 7 March 2000, para. 54.

[43] Ibid. at para. 55.

of sustainable development enshrined in both the Treaty on European Union and the Fifth Environment Programme, entitled "Towards Sustainability."[44] (emphasis in the original)

In another opinion, Advocate General Léger discussed the objectives of sustainable development inherent in the common policy on the environment as needing to be "understood in the light of the rule that natural resources must be used in a rational manner. The emphasis here is on the necessity of implementing measures to preserve the quantity of natural resources."[45]

In *Calì & Figli* v. *SEPG*, Advocate General Cosmas offers a definition of sustainable development as "development that meets current needs without prejudicing the ability of future generations to meet their needs," thus using a wording that is reminiscent of those employed by the Brundtland Commission.[46] Finally, in *Commission* v. *Council*, the Commission asked the CJEU to annul the 2004 Council decision implementing the Joint Action 2002/589/ (the "contested decision") in the area of Common Foreign and Security Policy mandating an EU contribution to the Economic Community of West African States (ECOWAS)'s Moratorium on Small Arms and Light Weapons, and to declare it illegal and inapplicable.[47] The problem was that the preamble of the contested decision made a reference to sustainable development,[48] and it was thus successfully argued by the Commission that this measure is not just a security measure but rather a development cooperation measure.[49] In other word the concept has been used to determine the competences of the Union. While the case law does not yet correspond to the importance of sustainable development in the Treaties, it can safely be concluded that it is one of the principles that should inspire the activities of the various European institutions in several sectors, such as environment, economic growth, and social policy.

European institutions and legislation seem to have an all-encompassing idea of sustainable development in mind. In fact, both in the treaties and in the CJEU jurisprudence, sustainable development as an informing principle or objective is recurrent not only in relation to the environment, but also with reference to economic growth and social policies and issues. In this regard, the Commission has explained that there are three interrelated components in sustainable

44 Ibid. at para. 57.

45 See case C-36/98, *Kingdom of Spain* v. *Council of the European Union*, Opinion of Advocate General Léger delivered on 16 May 2000, para. 77.

46 See case C-343/95, *Diego Calì & Figli Srl* v. *Servizi ecologici porto di Genova SpA (SEPG)*, Opinion of Advocate General Cosmas delivered on 10 December 1996, ff 58.

47 See case C-91/05 *Commission of the European Communities* v. *Council of the European Union*, Judgment of the Court of 20 May 2008, para. 1.

48 Ibid. ("the excessive and uncontrolled accumulation and spread of small arms and light weapons poses a threat to peace and security and reduces the prospects for sustainable development particularly in West Africa").

49 See ibid. at para. 19.

development: economic, social, and environmental.[50] Moreover, EU institutions seem to be concerned about sustainable development both within European borders and in the wider world (in particular, in less developed countries). This is particularly evident in the EU's embracing and incorporation of the SDGs into legal and political actions and decisions.

## CONCLUSION

This chapter began by asking an intriguing question: How can the concepts of intergenerational equity and sustainable development be linked together and how they are reflected in the constitutional order of the EU? In the previous sections, we have tried to outline in detail how each of these concepts is reflected as constitutional principles in European treaties and jurisprudence.

The strong linkage between intergenerational equity and sustainable development in international law has been argued by Karen Wellens: "the two core elements of . . . sustainable development – common but differentiated responsibilities and intergenerational equity – have been powerful tools towards further development and clarification of the principle of solidarity [in international law]."[51]

This chapter demonstrated the close connection between intergenerational solidarity and sustainable development in the European constitutional order. Solidarity between generations is part of sustainable development and sustainable development is part of solidarity between Member States. But there are also more practical connections. With regard to European law on natural resources, various official documents and provisions on sustainable development, energy, climate change, and disaster assistance refer to intergenerational solidarity.[52]

In the European constitutional order, equity is not limited to equity between the EU and Member States, or between Member States or between EU citizens, but rather it extends to intergenerational equity with other parts of the world. Moreover, the EU has explained that

> intergenerational solidarity must not end with Union citizens. A common approach concerning the rights and obligations of immigrants should be developed, and migrants from inside and outside the Union require support with integration into their new societies in full respect of human dignity.[53]

[50] Communication from the Commission to the European Parliament, Council, Economic and Social Committee and Committee of the Regions. *Towards a Global Partnership for Sustainable Development*, COM 82 (2002) 6.

[51] K. Wellens, 'Revisiting Solidarity as a (Re-)Emerging Constitutional Principle: Some Further Reflections', in R. Wolfrum and C. Kojima, *supra* note 15, 4.

[52] C. Hilson, 'EU Environmental Solidarity and the Ecological Consumer: Towards a Republican Citizenship', in Ross and Borgmann-Prebil, *supra* note 1, 137.

[53] European Commission, Strategic Objectives 2005–2009, *Europe 2010: A Partnership for European Renewal: Prosperity, Solidarity and Security*, COM 12 (26 January 2005), 9.

Similarly, from the analysis of European provisions and policies on this subject, it is clear that a proper understanding of sustainable development requires intergenerational equity between generations and within generations. At the same time, both sustainable development and intergenerational equity require environmental protection, social cohesion, and economic fairness.

The European constitutional order is based on the concepts of intergenerational equity and sustainable development and has developed principles, operational treaty provisions, policy and governance strategies, and jurisprudence to realize them. These concepts have become very important over time but, even more than that, they have evolved from political slogans into justiciable legal concepts. Indeed, the choice to include sustainable development (and, by extension, intergenerational equity) into treaty provisions, whether in the Preamble or elsewhere, implies some "legal significance" and a "potential normative impact."[54]

Specifically, Parties to the treaty at issue can rely upon the concept in interpreting the treaty, but they can also try to rely upon it to "justify their actions or question the actions of other before other parties or in formal adjudication."[55] The two concepts are intertwined and interlinked. It is thus not surprising that their development followed similar paths. The full realization of the potential legal impact of intergenerational equity or more concretely sustainable development on the jurisprudence in the CJEU is still outstanding, but we easily imagine that the Court of Justice will find them to be justiciable in the future.

[54] D. French, *supra* note 28, 44.
[55] Ibid.

*Addressing Science, Scientific Uncertainty, and Precaution*

# 16

# Scientific Uncertainty as a Key Obstacle to Efficient Legal Protection of the Environmental Interests of Future Generations

*Katalin Sulyok*

Making environmental policy is essentially an act of balancing the short-term economic interests of present generations and the long-term environmental benefits of posterity. Such balancing ultimately rests on a value judgment, which is formed on the basis of economic, ethical, and scientific considerations of stakeholders. This chapter focuses on the latter aspect of environmental policy-making, namely, the problems that arise in taking into due account the scientific facts in such balancing. It will explore the reasons why scientific warnings on environmental degradation or the risk thereof are often incapable of driving policy decisions, and it will discuss how invoking trust obligations of States may promote a balance that is more sensitive to scientists' inputs.

A key obstacle to science-based policy-making lies in the fact that scientists cannot predict with absolute certainty to what extent environmental benefits would actually accrue should a given policy measure be implemented and, vice versa, what changes would be entailed by omitting those protective measures. To comply with rigorous scientific methods, scientists can only make probabilistic statements on the possible outcomes of a given measure. Scientists term this phenomenon 'scientific uncertainty'. The fundamental problem with channelling uncertain scientific facts into policy-making is that lay decision-makers often seek yes-or-no answers, which scientists simply cannot provide.

Moreover, this chapter shows that scientific uncertainty is a more complex problem than scientists' inability to provide clear-cut answers *at a given point in time*. In fact, uncertainty to some degree will *always* remain inherent in scientific results, irrespective of scientific progress.[1] This persistent uncertainty requires innovative solutions from lawyers in order to provide a legitimate basis for taking actions to safeguard the interests of future generations. These tools may involve

[1] R.A. Carpenter, 'Uncertainty in Managing Ecosystems Sustainably', in J. Lemons (ed.), *Scientific Uncertainty and Environmental Problem Solving* (Blackwell Science 1996), 126.

changing entrenched doctrines and settled institutional processes for the sake of providing effective legal protection to the environmental needs of future generations. One such approach is invoking States' public trust obligations to justify precautionary fiduciary measures that are taken to preserve natural resources held by the State in trust for future generations. This so-called public trust doctrine is increasingly used, both at the domestic[2] and international levels,[3] to call for a more just balance between the interests of present and future generations.

The present chapter provides an overview of how the public trust doctrine can be used as an innovative legal tool for legitimizing protective measures despite extensive uncertainties inherent in the underlying scientific advice. First, it describes the various forms of scientific uncertainty in order to demonstrate its pervasive nature and outline its consequences for environmental policy-making. Then it discusses the public trust doctrine that appears to provide an appropriate framework for balancing intergenerational interests. Finally, it focuses on public trust cases where courts have discerned precautionary fiduciary duties of States for preserving natural resources. In conclusion, the chapter will discuss the potential of such judicial tools in promoting intergenerational equity by strengthening environmental protection for the benefit of generations to come.

## FORMS OF SCIENTIFIC UNCERTAINTY AS OBSTACLES TO SAFEGUARDING ENVIRONMENTAL INTERESTS OF FUTURE GENERATIONS

Promoting the interests of future generations necessitates, as a prerequisite, defining these interests. This task is pervaded by uncertainties on numerous levels. On the one hand, it is virtually impossible to predict what resources future generations will need. In this respect, the chapter presumes that, at a minimum, they will need a planet which is capable of providing them with a satisfactory level of 'ecosystem services'.[4] On the other hand, there are certain forms of uncertainty that will be faced on account of some specific characteristics of the scientific inquiry. This section will address and analyse these latter types of uncertainty.

2 Domestic applications of the doctrine will be discussed in detail below.

3 K. Baslar, *The Concept of the Common Heritage of Mankind in International Law* (Martinus Nijhoff Publishers 1998) 65–68.

4 J. Nickel and D. Magraw, 'Philosophical Issues in International Environmental Law', in S. Besson and J. Tasioulas (eds.), *The Philosophy of International Law* (Oxford University Press 2010) 457. Ecosystem services are defined as the benefits that nature provides human society with (such as food, fibres, raw materials, clean water, fertile soil, climate regulation, carbon capture, and many more). TEEB, *An Interim Report, European Communities* (TEEB 2008) 9.

*Uncertainty and the Environmental Interests of Future Generations*

Describing some hypothetical situations may be useful at this point to illustrate the typical dilemmas governmental agencies face while crafting environmental policies based on scarce scientific information.[5] Would abolishing quotas on private agricultural water withdrawals threaten the long-term existence of thermal aquifers, when the recharge rate of the affected aquifer is very uncertain on account of our limited understanding of hydrological dynamics? And, accordingly, does maintaining this quota system serve a compelling interest of future generations? Would a governmental development project extirpate a genetically isolated endemic rodent species if its only known population lives on the project's designated site, but only limited research has been carried out on the overall size of the species population? This factual situation would mean that there may be other populations scattered on the species' former range.

In the overwhelming majority of such cases, scientists cannot deliver conclusive answers to these types of questions, as some key uncertainties shadow their findings, which disrupts the process of science-based policy-making. The problems arising on the science–policy interface can to a certain extent be traced back to some structural differences between science and law. First, while statistical evidence is treated as normal in science, it is conceived only as 'a second best' option in law.[6] Moreover, politicians and lawyers tend to subscribe to a 'myth of certainty' with respect to science,[7] a false hope that scientists are able to tell the 'right' answer for policy dilemmas, and if they cannot provide credible, confident, and timely warning, there is no need for action. Furthermore, courts tend to assume a constant expansion of scientific knowledge,[8] and to hold associated belief to a view that uncertainty can be fully eliminated. As a consequence, many of them seem to be reluctant to accept the concept of irreducible uncertainty.[9]

However, scientists call on us not to treat the intuitive urge to reduce uncertainty as a justification for delaying policies.[10] Quite the contrary, they emphasize that taking protective action to preserve future options even in the absence of full scientific certainty renders policies easier to modify later, if subsequent scientific information so warrants. As a group of climate scientists, including the Nobel Laureate Paul

[5] These hypotheticals were formed on the basis of the practice of the Office of the Ombudsman for Future Generations of Hungary, which is tasked with advocating for an ambitious environmental protection by appearing as a spokesperson of future generations.

[6] T.A. Brennan, 'Causal Chains and Statistical Links: The Role of Scientific Uncertainty in Hazardous-Substance Litigation' (1987) 73 Cornell L Rev 490.

[7] D. Kriebel, 'How Much Evidence Is Enough? Conventions of Causal Inference' (2009) 72:1 *Law and Contemporary Problems* 132.

[8] Brennan, *supra* note 6 at 478–479.

[9] Ibid. at 490–491.

[10] B.C. O'Neill et al., 'Learning and Climate Change' (2006) 6 *Climate Policy* 585–589, 586.

Crutzen,[11] notes, 'the fewer irreversible commitments we have made, the more fully we can take advantage of whatever new information we obtain'.[12]

Such an approach squares well with one of the main requirements of the theory of intergenerational equity, namely to conserve as many options as possible for upcoming generations. Edith Brown Weiss, in the seminal book where she laid down the theoretical foundations of intergenerational equity, proposes three main requirements of safeguarding the interests of posterity: the conservation of options, the conservation of quality, and the conversation of access.[13] Without aspiring to achieve the impossible task of predicting the exact preferences of posterity, the principle of the conservation of options aims to ensure 'a reasonably secure and flexible resource base for future generations'.[14] In terms of policy-making, this principle resonates well with the proposed approach to make policy choices that try to maximize the policy options of future stakeholders.

### *Taxonomy of Sources of Scientific Uncertainty*

Environmental law scholars repeatedly take note of the challenges that scientific uncertainty poses in their field,[15] yet legal literature rarely engages in more in-depth discussion on the specific sources of uncertainty. In the following, the chapter presents a brief taxonomy of these sources in order to show the factors that make science essentially and irreducibly uncertain. Better understanding the root causes of uncertainty helps society fully face the extent and nature of the problems it entails. Moreover, in order to make an optimal decision, stakeholders should be able to evaluate the emerging forms of uncertainty and to attach different weights to different kinds of ambiguities.

Scientific uncertainty can be traced back to certain attributes of scientific facts and the scientific inquiry that produces them, which are usually termed 'types' or 'sources' of uncertainty. These sources vary across different fields of natural sciences. The following discussion focuses on those that are typical in environmental sciences, since these are the crucial driving force of environmental policy-making.

[11] The Nobel Prize in Chemistry 1995 was awarded jointly to P.J. Crutzen, M.J. Molina, and F. Sherwood Rowland for their work in atmospheric chemistry, particularly concerning the formation and decomposition of ozone.

[12] O'Neill et al., *supra* note 10 at 587.

[13] E. Brown Weiss, *In Fairness to Future Generations: International Law, Common Patrimony, and Intergenerational Equity* (United Nations University 1989) 40–45.

[14] Ibid. at 39.

[15] D.A. Farber, 'Uncertainty' (2011) 99 Geo LJ 901; C. Smith, 'Policy Implications of Uncertainty' (2011) *Philosophical Transactions of the Royal Society* 69; J. Peel, *Science and Risk Regulation in International Law* (Cambridge University Press 2010) 378–379.

### Natural Variation across Time and Space

This type of uncertainty arises in systems that change in ways that are difficult to predict[16] and, thus, are exceptionally hard to account for in models. An apposite example of the difficulties entailed by natural variation is making predictions of a species' population size. This prediction is inevitably uncertain, as populations vary depending on many factors, such as availability of food, abundance of predators, or disease spread.[17] For all these reasons, any predictions as to future population sizes will always be burdened with uncertainty flowing from background natural variation. Moreover, this type of uncertainty makes the detection of environmental trends difficult even in light of data collected for decades.[18]

### Extremely High Complexity of Environmental Systems

Simply put, a great deal of uncertainty is a result of the extremely high complexity of environmental systems, which are not fully understood. It is virtually impossible to describe all relevant connections and feedback in ecosystems. Food web research well illustrates this challenge. In marine ecosystems that comprise dozens of species, there can be up to 28 million pathways between two particular species throughout the ecosystem's food web.[19] Such an extreme level of complexity can be represented in models only if the natural system is grossly simplified,[20] which entails a great deal of uncertainty as to the convergence between model results and the real behaviour of the system.

Prior lessons of food web research for the purposes of fisheries management also warn us that indirect connections are often overlooked by scientists.[21] This may result in fundamentally mistaken policies. If one considers only direct connections, it seems to be an intuitively appealing management option to cull top predators (such as seals or whales) of an industrially important fish species (target species) in order to increase attainable fishery yields. However, in complex food webs, where fish predators also prey on the target species at a lower level of the food chain, the population of the target species will in fact be decreased if top predators are removed from the ecosystem, since these predators also prey on the fish predator itself. Consequently, decreasing the number of top predators via culling will decrease the population of the target species, which is exactly the opposite of the desired outcome.

16 H.M. Regan, M. Colyvan, and M.A. Burgman, 'A Taxonomy and Treatment of Uncertainty for Ecology and Conservation Biology' (2002) 12:2 *Ecological Applications* 618.

17 Ibid.

18 C.N. Cook et al., 'Achieving Conservation Science that Bridges the Knowledge–Action Boundary: Achieving Effective Conservation Science' (2013) 27:4 *Conservation Biology* 671.

19 P. Yodzis, 'Must Top Predators Be Culled for the Sake of Fisheries?' (2001) 16:2 *Trends in Ecology & Evolution* 80.

20 Ibid.

21 Ibid.

With regard to the extreme complexity of living networks, this cause of uncertainty remains pervasive and dominant. Therefore it is vital for decision-makers to become familiar with and recognize this type of uncertainty.

### Model Uncertainty

On the one hand, model uncertainty results from the necessary simplification inherent in every model.[22] Such simplification may lead to omitting from the model a variable that will later prove to be a relevant factor in the system's behaviour. On the other hand, uncertainty may also arise from constructing imprecise models of relatively known processes.[23] This takes place when scientists describe essentially stochastic natural systems with deterministic models.[24]

Moreover, uncertainty may also flow from the fact that we do not always know all the relevant processes of the real world, which may give rise to multiple working hypotheses for the same phenomenon, and thus different models for representing the same process.[25] This type of uncertainty is well illustrated by the historic example of modelling ozone depletion in the 1980s. Initially, there were three competing scientific theories for explaining the decay of atmospheric ozone: a dynamic, a solar, and a chemical theory.[26] However, all these models dismissed the role of heterogeneous reactions, which later turned out to be precisely the driving mechanism behind ozone hole formation.[27]

Another subset of model uncertainty is called parametric uncertainty, and it arises from using uncertain parameters in a model,[28] for example when a model relies on uncertain thresholds of an otherwise known relationship.[29] Parametric uncertainty may also be a result of abstractions in a model, which generate parameters that cannot be translated for direct biological interpretation.[30] As alluded to above, many forms of model uncertainty cannot be fully eliminated and, thus, it emerges as one of the most pervasive types of uncertainty.

22 Regan, Colyvan, and Burgman, *supra* note 16 at 620.

23 D. Ludwig, M. Mangel, and B. Haddad, 'Ecology, Conservation, and Public Policy' (2001) 32:1 *Annual Review of Ecology and Systematics* 489.

24 Ibid.

25 M.R. Payne et al., 'Uncertainties in Projecting Climate-Change Impacts in Marine Ecosystems' (May 2016) 73:5 *ICES Journal of Marine Science: Journal du Conseil* 1274.

26 J. O'Reilly et al., 'Characterizing Uncertainty in Expert Assessments: Ozone Depletion and the West Antarctic Ice Sheet: Characterizing Uncertainty in Expert Assessments' (2011) 2:5 *Wiley Interdisciplinary Reviews: Climate Change* 731.

27 Ibid.

28 Payne et al., *supra* note 25 at 1277.

29 A. Grubler, Y. Ermoliev, and A. Kryazhimskiy, 'Coping with Uncertainties: Examples of Modeling Approaches at IIASA' (2015) 98 *Technological Forecasting and Social Change* 214.

30 Payne et al., *supra* note 25 at 1277.

### Measurement Error

Measurement error manifests as one of three main types: operator error, instrument error, or systematic error.[31] Operator error can be traced back to imperfections in handling the measurement device, and instrument error covers random problems with the device itself.[32] Systematic errors arise from biased sampling procedures,[33] which may be a result of unintentional erroneous calibration of the device or consistent, incorrect recordings of the results.[34] This observational bias may also be a result of entrenched theories, which can influence the observation itself.[35] The observer's error can largely be eliminated with appropriate training,[36] and systematic errors occurring on theoretical grounds can also be reduced if properly recognized by the observer.[37]

### Ambiguity of Resulting Data

Uncertainty also arises from the fact that observations and modelling often can only provide scarce or ambiguous data. Estimation error may also occur: inaccuracies in data due to erroneous choice of statistical methods.[38] The absence of long-term consistent datasets is indeed one of the regular challenges that regulatory scientists face.

### Judgment Uncertainty: Subjective Elements in Drawing Inferences

In circumstances lacking proper data, scientists need to make extrapolations and interpolations, which inevitably include making subjective judgments.[39] Subjective inferences may bring significantly biased results. A classic example of such bias can be witnessed in the history of recording the ozone hole. Notably, scientists consistently dismissed data evidencing a growing ozone hole initially,[40] when the data contradicted all accepted scientific theories on ozone dynamics. Scientists also warn that, because of psychological factors, one may have a preference for making less ambiguous statements,[41] or for processing information selectively to confirm the observer's expected outcome.[42]

31 Regan, Colyvan, and Burgman, *supra* note 16 at 619.
32 Ibid.
33 Ibid.
34 Ibid.
35 Ibid. at 618–619.
36 Ibid. at 619.
37 Ibid.
38 J. Harwood and K. Stokes, 'Coping with Uncertainty in Ecological Advice: Lessons from Fisheries' (2003) 18:12 *Trends in Ecology & Evolution* 618.
39 O'Reilly et al., *supra* note 26 at 737; Regan, Colyvan, and Burgman, *supra* note 16 at 618, 621.
40 Grubler, Ermoliev, and Kryazhimskiy, *supra* note 29 at 215.
41 J.D. Brown, 'Prospects for the Open Treatment of Uncertainty in Environmental Research' (2010) 34:1 *Progress in Physical Geography* 79.
42 Ibid.

**Linguistic Uncertainty**

This type of uncertainty arises from the often ambiguous, vague, or underspecific scientific vocabulary.[43] Besides this, certain terms carry different meanings in natural and social science, which gives rise to additional linguistic uncertainty.[44] Interestingly, the terms 'cause' and 'causal inference' have divergent meanings in legal and natural sciences. Causes in natural sciences are naturally occurring factors that lead to the same outcome, whereas causes for the purposes of law are of narrower scope, hence, not all causes in science will be legally appreciable causes.[45] For instance, through the lens of science, weather conditions leading to a slippery road are a 'cause' of a resulting car accident; however, in terms of establishing legal responsibility for the accident, the weather is a causal factor that is not necessarily regarded as a legally relevant cause.

Legal and natural sciences also use different concepts of causation.[46] Legal tests that identify the relevant causes favour a 'mechanistic understanding of causation' which is predicated upon the metaphor of a causal chain consisting of discrete events, where each event is dependent upon the previous one.[47] However, in the scientific world causal relations are better conceived as a 'complex set of conditions' and not as a linear chain of events.[48]

**Unknown Unknowns**

Last but not least there are parameters, relevant relationships, and feedback that society is not even aware of.[49] In surprisingly many fields of science, society simply 'does not know enough about' the underlying processes to be able to meaningfully describe the system's behaviour.[50] This is the terrain of scientific surprises.

### *Implications for Policy-Making*

It should be clear from the discussion thus far that certain sources of uncertainty can be reduced or even minimized, but that others are more pervasive and, therefore, scientific information will to some extent always be burdened with scientific uncertainty.[51] As a result, scientific research can only provide probabilistic results, as some uncertainty will always remain as to the precise value of a given parameter.[52]

43 Regan, Colyvan, and Burgman, *supra* note 16 at 618.
44 Grubler, Ermoliev, and Kryazhimskiy, *supra* note 29 at 215.
45 H.L.A. Hart and T. Honoré, *Causation in the Law* (Oxford University Press 1985) 112–113.
46 Brennan, *supra* note 6 at 471.
47 Ibid. at 485–486.
48 Hart and Honoré, *supra* note 45 at 72.
49 Grubler, Ermoliev, and Kryazhimskiy, *supra* note 29 at 214.
50 K. Beven, 'Facets of Uncertainty: Epistemic Uncertainty, Non-Stationarity, Likelihood, Hypothesis Testing, and Communication' (2016) 61:9 *Hydrological Sciences Journal* 1652.
51 Carpenter, *supra* note 1 at 118–159, 126.
52 Ludwig, Mangel, and Haddad, *supra* note 23 at 487.

Revealing uncertainties inherent in scientific advice reminds us that scientists cannot aspire to be the final arbiter of policy dilemmas. Scientists should answer to legitimacy concerns with respect to their decisions as to how to treat uncertainties in assessing risks associated with the alternative actions.[53]

Against this background, the question arises as to what policy-makers could and should do to better tackle scientific uncertainty. Without providing a silver bullet, this chapter will offer some suggestions as to the conduct of the actors involved. Intergenerational balancing is an interdisciplinary venture across boundaries of social and natural sciences, which calls for an open and adaptive approach from all players involved. Scientists should be honest about uncertainties and reveal them in discussions with policy-makers.[54] In turn, lawyers and policy-makers should be able to grasp key uncertainties and understand their sources so as to be able to evaluate their magnitude and pervasive nature. They should come to terms with making decisions based on uncertain information and not expect scientists to deliver yes-or-no answers to their questions.

Emphatically, pervasive uncertainty does not in any way legitimize practices that would use ambiguity in science as a reason for challenging its epistemic authority and would entail a wholesale rejection of scientific warnings. Bearing in mind that achieving scientific certainty remains impossible,[55] we should aim to design processes for decision-making and corresponding legal frameworks that, notwithstanding their ever-uncertain nature, allow stakeholders to take them into due account and to take protective actions when necessary.

## BALANCING INTERGENERATIONAL INTERESTS: INVOKING TRUST OBLIGATIONS OF STATES TO PRESERVE THEIR NATURAL RESOURCES

Scientific inputs are translated into environmental policy decisions in accordance with applicable domestic legal rules. Hence, in order to make environmental policy that takes scientific uncertainty into due account, we need a legal framework that can adapt appropriately to irreducible uncertainty. Besides this scientific aspect of policy-makers' dilemmas, the framework should also be suitable for considering how decision-makers value and take into account future benefits today (such as the question of discounting,[56] which represents the economic aspect of intergenerational dilemmas) and the extent to which they owe moral obligations towards the future (creating the moral aspect of intergenerational dilemmas). These non-scientific

[53] S. Jasanoff, *The Fifth Branch* (Harvard University Press n.d.), 45–46; J. Peel, *Science and Risk Regulation in International Law* (Cambridge University Press 2010) 384.

[54] Brown, *supra* note 41 at 87.

[55] Jasanoff, *supra* note 53 at 250.

[56] The question of choosing the exact discount rate is addressed in more detail by Gábor Bartus in this volume.

aspects of these questions also warn us that environmental policy decisions ultimately constitute value judgments,[57] which are informed, but not determined solely, by science.[58]

## *Balancing Economic and Environmental Interests for Intergenerational Equity*

For the balancing exercise, we need a normative framework that is flexible enough to take into due account all these considerations, the interests of all players involved, and the specificities of each case. First of all, the environmental needs of future generations are not uniform across time and place, as they may change over time and with geographic locations. Ecosystems are exposed to different threats caused by natural and anthropogenic factors. For instance, in regions that experience growing water scarcity, increased protection of water reserves may be seen as a more pressing concern than in humid regions.[59]

Second, the gravity and imminence of a given environmental risk or concern also needs to be taken into account in the balancing exercise. Certain environmental problems are so pressing that they justify taking aggressive measures for the sake of future generations.[60] However, highly uncertain threats or those on a smaller scale may not justify taking costly measures at the material time, since in that case the costs borne by present generations would exceed the possible benefits gained in the distant future. Economists grasp this problem through the concept of discount rates. Discount rates are used to account for the time value of future benefits today.[61] Through the lens of economics, the discount rate chosen determines the stringency of the environmental measures taken. Higher discount rates mean that present gains are valued more than possible benefits in the future. As opposed to this, by choosing lower discount rates, decision-makers attach a higher value to possible benefits in the future. Cass Sunstein and Arden Rowell argue that imminent environmental threats justify choosing a lower discount rate, which would ensure that no excessive costs would be conferred on posterity.[62] The specific discount rate is not a matter of objective choice, but a subjective judgment influenced by numerous considerations and assumptions of the decision-maker.[63] The chosen discount rate could then be accounted for in the balancing framework of the public trust approach.

57 Peel, *supra* note 53 at 379.
58 R.J. Lazarus, *The Making of Environmental Law* (University of Chicago Press 2004) 22.
59 R. Kundis Craig, 'A Comparative Guide to the Western States' Public Trust Doctrines: Public Values, Private Rights, and the Evolution Toward an Ecological Public Trust' (2010) 37 Ecology LQ 58.
60 C.R. Sunstein and A. Rowell, 'On Discounting Regulatory Benefits: Risk, Money, and Intergenerational Equity' (2007) *University of Chicago Law Review* 206.
61 Arden Rowell, 'Time in Cost–Benefit Analysis' (2014) 4 *UC Irvine Law Review* 1215.
62 Sunstein and Rowell, *supra* note 60 at 206–207.
63 Ibid. at 171.

Third, as shown above, the balancing framework needs to be responsive to different types of uncertainty in the underlying scientific information. This chapter proposes that, given that uncertainty is not a homogeneous category, the legal framework should allow decision-makers to distinguish between its sources. As a consequence, striking a fair balance would ensure that certain measures may be instituted despite irreducible uncertainty, while also remaining sensible in terms of allowing economic activity to proceed to an extent that does not exert excessive environmental risks.

Fourth, efficient environmental protection requires a holistic approach, where the target of protection is broadly defined in light of growing scientific understanding of the interconnected nature of environmental systems. The sectoral approach of environmental statutory laws often falls short of achieving such protection,[64] as it tends to protect a specific species or habitat. Such schemes cannot tackle multi-rooted problems, which are dominant in managing ecosystems and natural resources.

### *The Public Trust Doctrine and Its Benefits for Intergenerational Balancing*

In the following section, it will be argued that the so-called public trust doctrine appears to be a suitable tool for such balancing. The doctrine imposes fiduciary duties on States to preserve their natural resources as trust assets for the benefit of present and future generations. Having its roots in ancient Roman law,[65] and in English common law[66], the doctrine is increasingly used in various jurisdictions around the world. In the US, it is derived from state common law,[67] but some federal statutes are also based on the public trust doctrine.[68] In India, the doctrine is regarded as part of common law,[69] while in the Philippines it was discerned from the

64 M.C. Wood and D. Galpern, 'Atmospheric Recovery Litigation: Making the Fossil Fuel Industry Pay to Restore a Viable Climate System' (2015) 45 *Environmental Law* 282.

65 The Institutes of Justinian declared that 'the following things are by natural law common to all – the air, running water, the sea, and consequently the seashore'. Institutes of Justinian, *Book II On the Law of Things, Title I Of the Different Kinds of Things*, translated into English by J.B. Moyle, 5th edn. (Oxford 1913) 1.

66 A.B. Klass, 'Modern Public Trust Principles: Recognizing Rights and Integrating Standards' (2006) 82 *Notre Dame Law Review* 702.

67 Craig, *supra* note 59 at 58.

68 For instance the Endangered Species Act, the National Environmental Policy Act, and the Clean Water Act are US federal legislative acts that ultimately reflect some public trust obligations of the government.

69 M.C. Blumm and R.D. Guthrie, 'Internationalizing the Public Trust Doctrine: Natural Law and Constitutional and Statutory Approaches to Fulfilling the Saxion Vision' (2011) 45 *U. C. Davis Law Review* 760. A leading case is the Supreme Court of India's decision in *MC Mehta v. Kamal Nat* [1997] 1 SCC 388 [1996].

constitutionally enshrined right to a healthy environment.[70] South Africa enacted several statues that codify public trust obligations.[71]

There is also an emerging international trend of enshrining public trust provisions in national constitutions.[72] The concept of public trust already appears in the constitutions of several States in Africa, Asia, and South America, specifically Tanzania, Uganda, Ethiopia, Papua New Guinea, Ghana, Swaziland, Bhutan,[73] Kenya,[74] Brazil,[75] and Ecuador.[76] In Europe, only Hungary has adopted a public trust provision in its Constitution.[77] In Sri Lanka, courts have read the doctrine into the Constitution since the beginning of the 1990s.[78] In North America, several states of the US incorporated such provisions in their constitutions,[79] while Canada discerned trust obligations from common law.[80] The doctrine's wide recognition in the international arena has even led some scholars to suggest that the doctrine has become a general principle of international law,[81] although others regard the widespread invocation of intergenerational equity as a mere signal of a convergence between domestic laws.[82] In any event, the interests of future generations are recognized in a good number of international environmental soft law documents and in preambular paragraphs of international conventions.[83]

Originally, the public trust doctrine was used in US common law for balancing intragenerational interests, that is to safeguard certain public uses of particularly

70 Blumm and Guthrie, *supra* note 69 at 771.

71 E. van der Schyff, 'Unpacking the Public Trust Doctrine: A Journey into Foreign Territory' (2010) 13:5 *PER: Potchefstroomse Elektroniese Regsblad* 122.

72 J.R. May and D. Daly, *Global Environmental Constitutionalism* (Cambridge University Press 2015) 267.

73 Ibid. at 340–342.

74 Blumm and Guthrie, *supra* note 69 at 783.

75 Ibid. at 794.

76 Ibid., at 797.

77 Article P of the Fundamental Law of Hungary, as adopted in 2011, enshrines the following: '(1) Natural resources, in particular arable land, forests and the reserves of water, biodiversity, in particular native plant and animal species, as well as cultural assets shall form the common heritage of the nation; it shall be the obligation of the State and everyone to protect and maintain them, and to preserve them for future generations.' In Decision No. 14/2020 (VII. 6.) AB, the Constitutional Court of Hungary explicitly underlined that Article P(1) can be considered as a constitutional recognition of the public trust doctrine. For the functions and powers of the Hungarian Ombudsman for Future Generations, see *infra* ch. 4 in this volume.

78 D. Samararatne, *Public Trust Doctrine the Sri Lankan Version* (International Centre for Ethnic Studies 2010) 26.

79 E.g. state constitutions of Hawaii, Pennsylvania, North Dakota, Montana, Alaska, and Texas have trust-like provisions.

80 Blumm and Guthrie, *supra* note 69 at 801–802.

81 Ibid. at 750.

82 For a detailed list of such international instruments see C. Redgwell, 'Principles and Emerging Norms in International Law Intra- and Inter-Generational Equity', in C. Carlarne, K. Gray, and R. Tarasofsky (eds.), *The Oxford Handbook on International Climate Change Law* (Oxford University Press 2016) 192.

83 Ibid. at 195–196.

important resources against private ownership, such as by granting public access to seashores, where beachside real estate was privately owned,[84] or by reserving fishing rights of sportsmen.[85] In this chapter's proposal, the public trust doctrine, on a lengthier time scale, may also serve intergenerational balancing; it provides an appropriate framework for this task, as it is flexible enough to allow sovereign trustees to factor in all relevant considerations and to strike a fair balance with regard to all interests involved in a particular case.

First of all, the doctrine is responsive to local needs, as reflected by a survey of US case practice showing that the scope of the doctrine, for example the assets encompassed, varies from state to state in line with the most pressing ecological issues and the public's needs of each state.[86] The California Supreme Court explicitly found the doctrine to be evolving 'in tandem with the changing perception of the values and uses' of respective trust assets.[87] This feature makes the trust approach feasible for crafting tailor-made solutions for local problems, which is particularly important given the apparent lack of one-size-fits-all solutions for such dilemmas.

Second, the doctrine allows taking precautionary measures in the face of irreducible scientific uncertainty. Courts increasingly use the public trust doctrine as a vehicle to establish precautionary fiduciary obligations of sovereign trustees.[88] Moreover, the public trust doctrine has been frequently referred to as a basis for allowing climate change claims to proceed that were brought on behalf of groups of minors as spokesperson of future generations. This aspect of the trust framework will be discussed in more detail below.

Third, the doctrine may provide an additional ethical ground for the government to take protective measures by redefining the role and mindset of stakeholders and civil servants, who make day-to-day decisions about permits, measures, and management of ecosystems. Mary Christina Wood envisages a transformative role of the trust approach, which will turn 'bureaucrats into trustees' who are willing to implement fiduciary duties to protect natural resources.[89] The trust framework, thus, may also appeal to the ethical sense of obligation of governmental stakeholders, which could then guide agency discretion to realize a more efficient protection.[90] This feature may sound like a mere rhetorical benefit of the doctrine. However, as the Supreme Court of the Philippines put it so clearly in *Manila Bay*, the lack of commitment on part of bureaucrats constitutes a major deficiency in the legal protection of the environment, hence there is a significant room for improvement in this respect:

84 *Oregon ex rel. Thornton*, 462 P.2d (2011) 73–75.
85 *Radich* v. *Fredrickson*, 10 P.2d 352, 355 (Or. 1932).
86 Craig, *supra* note 59 at 71–73.
87 *National Audubon Society* v. *Superior Court*, 658 P.2d 709, 719 (Cal. 1983).
88 For a more detailed discussion, see below.
89 M.C. Wood, 'Advancing the Sovereign Trust of Government to Safeguard the Environment for Present and Future Generations (Part II): Instilling a Fiduciary Obligation in Governance' (2009) 39:1 *Environmental Law* 91 at 130–131.
90 Ibid. at 103.

> This case turns on government agencies and their officers who, by the nature of their respective offices or by direct statutory command, are tasked to protect and preserve, at the first instance, our internal waters, rivers, shores, and seas polluted by human activities. To most of these agencies and their official complement, the pollution menace does not seem to carry the high national priority it deserves, if their track records are to be the norm. Their cavalier attitude towards solving, if not mitigating, the environmental pollution problem, is a sad commentary on bureaucratic efficiency and commitment.[91]

Therefore, by redefining the attitude and mindset of decision-makers, the public trust doctrine can bring significant added value in terms of promoting better environmental decision-making.

Fourth, some suggest that the public trust approach renders government decision-making more legitimate by democratizing its process in jurisdictions where decisions affecting natural resources are brought by administrative bodies that are not directly responsive to the wider public. As Professor Joseph L. Sax, father of the modern public trust doctrine in the US, emphasized, this approach can 'counteract the influence which private interest groups may have with administrative agencies and encourage policy decisions to be made openly at the legislative level'.[92] Hence, the public trust doctrine can be used to make natural resource decisions more accountable to the public.[93]

Lastly, a significant benefit of the public trust framework lies in the fact that it is a suitable vehicle for adopting a holistic approach towards natural resource protection. Trust obligations have a 'macro focus',[94] meaning that they focus on the overall integrity of the ecological assets as a whole and may trigger or justify protective actions to be taken irrespective of what the specific cause is that threatens the healthy state of the asset.

The above attributes prove the flexible nature of the trust approach, which renders it a particularly suitable normative framework for making sensible and, at the same time, effective measures for balancing intergenerational interests.

### *Various Obligations Conferred upon Sovereign Trustees*

The doctrine poses limitations on State policies regarding the use, exploitation, and transfer of ownership over natural resources constituting trust assets. Traditionally, the public trust doctrine has only included tidelands and submerged lands underneath

[91] *Metropolitan Manila Development Authority* v. *Concerned Residents of Manila Bay*, G.R. No. 171947-48, 574 S.C.R.A. 661 (S.C., 18 December 2008) (Phil).

[92] J.L. Sax, 'The Public Trust Doctrine in Natural Resource Law: Effective Judicial Intervention' (1970) *Michigan Law Review* 492.

[93] M.C. Blumm, 'Public Property and the Democratization of Western Water Law: A Modern View of the Public Trust Doctrine' (1989) 19 *Environmental Law* 573 at 580.

[94] Wood and Galpern, *supra* note 64 at 282.

navigable waters in its scope;[95] however, after its revival in the 1970s,[96] courts gradually started to expand its reach and now it protects all types of water,[97] including groundwater,[98] endangered species,[99] national parks, and ecological integrity of ecosystems.[100] The scope of constitutional public trust provisions varies among different States, yet they tend to be widely defined.[101]

At its core, the public trust doctrine imposes duties of a trustee on the government, which should then act under fiduciary obligations with respect to assets of the trust. Traditional trust law concerns the management of financial assets and defines certain obligations for the trustee owed to present and future beneficiaries of the trust.[102] By way of analogy, rules applicable to financial trusts are invoked in relation to public trusts as well.[103] Such obligations traditionally include a duty to protect the assets from damage, and to prevent waste of the trust assets.[104] As a consequence, in a public trust context, fiduciary obligations entail that a public trustee cannot allow the trust assets to 'fall into ruin on his watch',[105] and the trustee should 'exercise continuing supervision' of the assets concerned.[106]

In addition to these traditional fiduciary obligations, courts discerned specific obligations for sovereign trustees in relation to public trusts. They also defined certain rights for the trustee to interfere with private rights in relation to the assets.

As a consequence, the public trust doctrine is used both for imposing limits on State's policies affecting trust assets and also for defending governmental actions to preserve those assets.[107] Some examples are reiterated here to illustrate the doctrine's diverse contents when applied in the context of protecting ecosystems and managing natural resources. First, the public trust doctrine served as a restraint on a state's ability to alienate trust assets;[108] the Pennsylvania Supreme Court used the public

[95] Klass, *supra* note 66 at 703.

[96] Professor Sax is held to be the father of the modern, more expansive doctrine. He wrote a seminal article in which he laid down the foundations of a public trust doctrine that can be used as a meaningful tool in US law to advance environmental protection.

[97] *Mono Lake*, 658 P.2d 709 (Cal. 1983).

[98] *Waiahole Ditch Decision, Water Use Permit Applications*, 94 Hawaii 97, 9 P.3d 409 (2000).

[99] *Morimoto* v. *Board of Land&Natural Resources*, 113 P.3d 172 (Haw. 2005).

[100] *Nat'l Parks & Conservation Ass'n* v. *Bd. of State Lands*, 869 P.2d 909, 919 (Utah 1993).

[101] Blumm and Guthrie, *supra* note 69 at 748.

[102] *Kelsey Cascadia Rose Juliana et al.* v. *United States of America, et al.*, No. 6:15-cv-1517, No. 6:15-cv-01517-TC (D. Or. 10 November 2016).

[103] Wood, *supra* note 89 at 94–96.

[104] Ibid. at 94–95.

[105] *United States* v. *White Mountain Apache Tribe*, 537 U.S. 465, 475 (2002). See Wood and Galpern, *supra* note 64 at 282–283.

[106] Ibid.

[107] Klass, *supra* note 66 at 730–734.

[108] Craig, *supra* note 59 at 69; *Illinois Central*, 146 U.S. 387, 460 (1892); *Scott* v. *Chicago Park District*, 360 N.E.2d 773 (Ill. 1977) in which a state senate bill that aimed to convey land underneath Lake Michigan to a steel plant was declared void under the public trust doctrine. The court found that although the senate would have created jobs and other economic benefits, still it was barred from meeting its trust obligations through these benefits.

trust provision enshrined in the state constitution to ban hydraulic fracking;[109] and Sri Lankan courts employed the doctrine to put a limit on the government's discretionary power, when it suspected that the divestiture of public land did not serve the 'public good'.[110] Later, it was confirmed that discretionary powers could only be exercised for public benefit.[111] These courts also emphasized that conservation measures should be guided by 'a long term view of such [assets] being conserved for intergenerational use'.[112] Further, the doctrine was used to prevent a private owner of a tideland, which was regarded as a trust asset, from filling, as it would have threatened the ecological integrity of this important habitat.[113] The doctrine may also require agencies to adopt particular management measures to protect the trust asset.[114] The Louisiana Court of Appeals ordered a state agency to reduce the level of organic matter in a lake in order to improve its ecological health.[115] The doctrine may even require agencies to revoke permits that violate public trust assets. In the landmark *Mono Lake* case, the California Supreme Court compelled an agency to reconsider the allocation of the water of Mono Lake, in order to protect the health and stability of a fragile ecosystem dependent upon the lake, even to the detriment of the city of Los Angeles, which had a permit to withdraw much of the water from the tributaries of Mono Lake to satisfy its increasing demand for water.[116] Further, the public trust approach may also serve as an action-forcing tool, compelling governmental measures to restore the asset. In the much-cited *Manila Bay* decision, the Supreme Court of the Philippines relied on the doctrine to order the government agency to take various actions, such as constructing a sewage treatment facility, restocking indigenous fish species, and fostering environmental education of local people.[117] Finally, scholars suggest that the doctrine may also be used to prevent overexploitation of resources,[118] and to promote a duty of the trustee against wasteful use.[119]

[109] *Robinson Township et al.* v. *Commonwealth of Pennsylvania* case.
[110] Samararatne, *Public Trust Doctrine the Sri Lankan Version* at 27.
[111] *Bandara* v. *Premachandra* (1994) 1. Sri. L.R. 301.
[112] *Watte Gedara Wijebanda* v. *Conservator General of Forests and Others case*, cited by Samararatne, *Public Trust Doctrine the Sri Lankan Version* at 33.
[113] *California Supreme Court's decision in Marks* v. *Whitney*, 491 P.2d 374, 378 (Cal. 1971)
[114] Wood, *supra* note 89 at 115.
[115] *Lake Bistineau Pre. Soc'y, Inc.* v.*Wildlife & Fisheries Comm'n*, 895 So 2d 821, 191 (2004).
[116] *Mono Lake*, 658 P.2d 709, 711 (Cal. 1983).
[117] *Metropolitan Manila Development Authority Concerned Residents of Manila Bay*, G. R. No. 171947-48, 574 S.C.R.A. 661 (S.C., 18 December 2008).
[118] Lucas Bento, 'Searching for Intergenerational Green Solutions: The Relevance of the Public Trust Doctrine to Environmental Preservation' (2010) 11 *Common Law Review* 9.
[119] Wood, *supra* note 89 at 127. Interestingly, the explicit denial of the right of present generations to the wasteful use of natural resources was explicitly recognized as early as in 1910, by Theodore Roosevelt, in his New Nationalism Speech (31 August 1910): 'I recognize the right and duty of this generation to develop and use the natural resources of our land; but I do not recognize the right to waste them, or to rob, by wasteful use, the generations that come after us. I ask nothing of the nation except that it so behave as each farmer here behaves with

As is clear from the aforementioned examples, the public trust framework can be used to pursue environmental interests in many different forms. Importantly though, the public trust doctrine does not constitute an absolute ban on pursuing economic interests, for it allows 'rational and balanced' development.[120] As a necessary corollary of its balancing function, the public trust doctrine only prohibits the impairment of the trust assets above a certain threshold.[121]

## OPERATIONALIZING THE PUBLIC TRUST DOCTRINE IN THE FACE OF SCIENTIFIC UNCERTAINTY

The public trust doctrine's responsiveness to irreducible uncertainty manifests in two distinctive applications of the doctrine. On the one hand, courts in various jurisdictions increasingly use the public trust doctrine as a vehicle to establish precautionary fiduciary obligations of sovereign trustees. On the other hand, there has been a strategic use of the doctrine in climate change litigation, where it serves to force governments' more stringent climate actions.

### *Invoking Precautionary Fiduciary Obligations of Sovereign Trustees*

According to the most accepted formulation from Principle 15 of the 1992 UN Rio Declaration, the precautionary principle allows cost-effective measures to proceed in order to prevent environmental degradation, despite the lack of full scientific certainty, where there are threats of serious or irreversible damage to the environment. Following the Rio Declaration, the principle gained international and domestic acceptance and became known as an ambitious, yet in certain jurisdictions contested,[122] approach for dealing with uncertainty in environmental law.

The precautionary principle does not compel a certain type of policy answer; therefore, it is better conceived as a framework that enables decision-makers to institute preventive policies even when faced with incomplete science.[123] The

reference to his own children. That farmer is a poor creature who skins the land and leaves it worthless to his children. The farmer is a good farmer who, having enabled the land to support himself and to provide for the education of his children, leaves it to them a little better than he found it himself. I believe the same thing of a nation. Moreover, I believe that the natural resources must be used for the benefit of all our people, and not monopolized for the benefit of the few, and here again is another case in which I am accused of taking a revolutionary attitude.' http://teachingamericanhistory.org/library/document/new-nationalism-speech/ accessed 23 September 2017.

[120] V.P. Nanda and W.R. Ris Jr., 'The Public Trust Doctrine: A Viable Approach to International Environmental Protection' (1975) 5 *Ecology Law Quarterly* 304.

[121] *State* v. *Public Service Commissioners*, 275 Wis. 112, 81 N.W.2d 71 (1957).

[122] C.R. Sunstein, 'The Paralyzing Principle' (2002) 25 *Regulation* 32.

[123] D. Hunter, J. Salzman, and D. Zaelke, *International Environmental Law and Policy*, 5th edn. (Foundation Press, 2015) 479.

precautionary principle thus justifies actions that are taken in situations including scientific uncertainty.

In order to provide meaningful answers to scientific warnings on irreversible damage to ecosystems and natural resources, courts have started to discern precautionary fiduciary duties of States by using the public trust doctrine. As one of the most widely cited public trust decisions, adopted by the Hawaiian Supreme Court, stated: '[t]he absence of firm scientific proof should not tie the [trustee's] hand in adopting reasonable measures designed to further the public interest'.[124] The underlying lawsuit was filed to challenge the diversion of water from the Waiahole Ditch to sugar plantations. The Court used remarkably strong language when it found that '[t]he duty to protect public water resources is a categorical imperative and the precondition to all subsequent considerations'.[125] This shows the public trust potential to rebalance ecological needs when the existing balance fails to pay adequate considerations to environmental interests vis-à-vis private interests.

Other courts have used the public trust doctrine to require a more cautious planning procedure from government agencies when making decisions about allocating natural resources. Here the doctrine served as a vehicle for demanding appraisal of the 'potential effects' of affirming a new water appropriation on present and future needs in relation to the trust asset, for example the water, before making a decision.[126]

In the same vein, precautionary duties embraced under the public trust concept have led courts to require EIA by stressing that environmental law duties 'must be construed … against the recognition that, in addressing environmental issues, we often have imperfect knowledge as to the potential impact of activities on the environment'.[127]

## USING THE PUBLIC TRUST DOCTRINE IN CLIMATE CHANGE LITIGATION

The present decade, which is increasingly affected by the adverse effects of climate change, has seen a rise in the number of novel lawsuits termed 'climate change litigation'. Such claims are diverse, ranging from petitions urging more aggressive governmental policies to reduce GHG emissions,[128] through those opposing more

[124] *Waiahole Ditch Decision, Water Use Permit Applications*, 94 Hawaii 97, 9 P.3d 409, 2000).

[125] Ibid.

[126] *United Plainsmen Association* v. *North Dakota Conservation Commission*, 247 N.W.2d 457, 458 (N.D. 1976).

[127] *Labrador Inuit Association* v. *Newfoundland (Minister of Environment and Labour)* 1997 155 Nfld. & P.E:I.R. 93 (Can.), para. 11.

[128] J. Peel and H.M. Osofsky, *Climate Change Litigation* (Cambridge University Press 2015) 4.

lenient regulatory measures,[129] to litigation seeking to establish liability of a State or industrial player for the injurious consequences of climate change impacts.[130]

A noteworthy application of the public trust doctrine appears in the climate change litigation context. More precisely, the doctrine is used to allow claims forcing stricter measures to combat climate change filed in the name of groups of children as representatives of future generations that are most harmed by the lack of stringent climate policies of certain States.

Such strategic reliance on the public trust doctrine first appeared in the highly innovative claim brought by Anthony Oposa, an environmental and civil rights activist in the Philippines, who filed a class action with a group of minors, including his own children and his friends' children,[131] against the Department of Environmental and Natural Resources to challenge their timber licence agreements, which seriously impaired the Philippines rainforests. This lawsuit led the Philippine Supreme Court to hand down its landmark *Oposa* v. *Factoran* decision.[132]

The *Oposa* case soon became a point of reference and source of inspiration for other courts around the world, which found it persuasive enough to grant similarly broad standing to representatives of future generations. A reference to this decision was made in November 2016 by a US District Court Judge in Oregon,[133] who allowed public trust claims to proceed that were brought by a group of children and James Hansen, a renowned climate scientist acting as a guardian for future generations. The lawsuit alleges that the US federal government, by permitting, authorizing, and subsidizing the exploitation, production, transport, and burning of fossil fuels played a significant role in creating the current climate crisis that would 'significantly endanger plaintiffs, with the damage persisting for millennia'. Claimants submitted that the federal actions violated their rights to life, liberty, property, the equal protection of the law, and as a substantive due process claim, and infringed the federal government's public trust obligations. Plaintiffs sought to enjoin the defendant from violating these rights and to direct the government to develop a plan to reduce $CO_2$ emissions.

The District Court judge denied the motions of the federal government and the fossil fuel industry, as intervenors, that sought dismissal of the claims on account of its constituting a non-justiciable political question. Even though this District Court decision is far from constituting a binding precedent, it signals a novel way in which the public trust doctrine may be actively used by litigants in the future to challenge the unambitious climate policies of governments.

[129] Ibid.

[130] R. Lefeber, 'Climate Change and State Responsibility', in R. Rayfuse and S.V. Scott (eds.) *International Law in the Era of Climate Change* (Edward Elgar 2012) 321.

[131] May and Daly, *supra* note 72 at 116.

[132] *Oposa* v. *Factoran*, G.R: NO. 101083, 224 S.C.R.A. 792, 797-98 (9 August 1993) (Phil.).

[133] *Kelsey Cascadia Rose Juliana et al.* v. *United States of America, et al.*, No. 6:15-cv-1517, No. 6:15-cv-01517-TC (D. Or., 10 November 2016) 50.

## CONCLUSION

The in-depth discussion above concerning different sources of uncertainty aimed to illustrate that uncertainty is inextricably linked to scientific results and, to a certain extent, will always remain inherent in scientific facts. As a consequence, decision-makers and lawyers should be ready to find ways to take action that is legitimate but also ambitious enough to handle effectively the ubiquitous threats facing natural resources and ecosystems.

It was argued above that the public trust doctrine provides a flexible enough normative framework for sovereign decision-makers to balance competing intergenerational (and intragenerational) interests. This doctrine may also help to rebalance these needs by imposing broader duties on governments by its rhetorical force,[134] emphasizing the moral duties of current generations owed to posterity. Consequently, the public trust doctrine has the potential to turn sovereigns' 'discretion to destroy' its natural capital and ecosystems into an 'obligation to defend' them.[135]

This chapter has aimed to show that the public trust doctrine appears to be a useful tool for an increasingly pressing concern for societies, namely, finding a fair balance between the health, stability, and resilience of ecosystems and the need for economic development. Scientific uncertainty will always be part of the task of policy-making, and therefore it has to be addressed, handled, and factored into our policy decisions in a transparent manner. As noted above, the decisions made on the basis of uncertain scientific facts are ultimately guided by the decision-makers' value judgments. Where scientific evidence is not clear enough to legitimately compel a specific course of action, lawyers and stakeholders are, often tacitly, making a choice in favour of one of the competing interests.

Given that our decisions fundamentally affect the lives of future generations, and all the other forms of life on Earth, if science remains irreducibly uncertain concerning possible adverse but significant consequences of societal actions in the present, it is proposed that we aim to strike a fair balance that takes into due account ethical obligations owed to posterity. To paraphrase the late Judge Herczegh, a former member of the ICJ,[136] such an approach would call for decisions to be made 'in dubio pro futuro'.

[134] Craig, *supra* note 59 at 83.
[135] Wood, *supra* note 89 at 139.
[136] *Dissenting Opinion of Judge Herczegh, Case Concerning the Gabcikovo-Nagymaros Project (Hungary/Slovakia)*, ICJ Reports 1997, p. 7, 187. See also J. Crawford, 'In Dubio Pro Natura: The Dissent of Judge Herczegh', in P. Kovács (ed.) *International Law: A Quiet Strength* (Pázmány Press 2011) 251–270.

# 17

# Transformative Knowledge and Solutions in Sustainability Governance

*Günther Bachmann*

Sustainability policies are about new transformation and trajectories, responsibility and governance. Providing scientific evidence and transformative knowledge is one of its main sources and tools. Germany is well placed to share experiences with building institutions for sustainable development, although it must be noted that institutionalization is never completed or finalized. Choice editing and raising awareness form crucial parts of transformative knowledge that can be offered through the process of building institutions for sustainable development.

Governance is key for successfully delivering on the goals and commitments of the 2030 Agenda for Sustainable Development. The sustainability institutions established in Germany since 2001 are 'light' ones and set the scene for further steps and institutionalizing. Hybridizing, networking, and a better use of anchoring are key elements for future institutions, and reflect first-hand insights into practice and modalities. The process of shaping institutional answers to an increasing challenge has only just started, and coordinating the public–private interface and democratically resolving conflicts of interest are crucial tasks. Although this is an early stage, those institutions are frequently considered as a reference, if not a role model, in the international arena. This chapter presents a practitioner's view on institution building, keeping in mind that other societal arrangements or corporate responsibility might be of similar or even sometimes greater importance.

## FRAMING INSTITUTION BUILDING

There is reason to believe that visions and aspirational goals can catalyse change. For transformative processes to be operative (and successful), the role of institutions, however, is important. More often than not, institutions get in the way of change and foreclose practical steps. Judging from examples, transformation is not necessarily a one-way current of events. Change may also get stuck, sometimes even against its promising nature. But, under certain preconditions, institutional dynamics may also have a share in disrupting development otherwise thought unchangeable or locked in. In that case, institutions may accelerate transformative processes, for example the German unification,[1] the jumpstarting of the German Energy Transition (*Energiewende*),[2] or the European creation of the euro.[3]

Despite what administrators often assume, no institutional setup lasts forever. In fact, more often than not institutions are subject to fundamental change. Institutional change may be adaptive or disruptive, gradual or fragmented. It may be as slow as the turnover of staff and human resources or it may be turbulent and ready to impact. It may be doctored from within or imposed by the outside world. Redundancies, mutuality, and complementarity often accompany change, although institutions change even when no action is being taken. They may suffer from procrastination and lock-ins, and thus degenerate. From a practitioner's view, in the long run any institution will surely change over time, as is its earthly fate.

For catalysing change in modern societies, however, visions and goals need new performance frameworks. A different set of institutions and a different type of activity are necessary. To that extent, reasonable sustainability policies need underpinning by quantified subtargets and metrics.[4] For the usual political attitude, quantifying political commitment is a long shot and finding political engagement that can be publicly measured and exposed adds a new layer to political practice. The conventional design of policies works with programmes and projects, and legitimate measures (such as the ProMeas approach) have been used, however the TarTim approach involving targets and timetables is an additional and new feature,[5] and part of the overall trend in meta-governance.[6] Quantifying political goals – and subjecting them to monitoring, review, and supervision – shifts the paradigm of governance. It adds a different angle to the antagonism of regulation versus

[1] The German reunification was started by the fall of the Berlin Wall in 1989. Under the diplomatic umbrella of negotiations with Russia, the US, France, and the UK, this was followed by legal, social, and economic unification arrangements in Germany.

[2] Ethics Commission for a Safe Energy Supply (ed.), *Germany's Energy Transition – A Collective Project for the Future* (2011) www.bundesregierung.de/ContentArchiv/DE/Archiv17/_Anlagen/2011/05/2011-05-30-abschlussbericht-ethikkommission_en.pdf;jsessionid=4ABD206413F0971009BE256A2C3051E9.s7t1?__blob=publicationFile&v=2 accessed 30 November 2017.

[3] As of 1 January 2002.

[4] In the German context, a Parliamentary commission first developed this concept; see Abschlußbericht der Enquete-Kommission 'Schutz des Menschen und der Umwelt' Bt-Drucksache 1311200 (26.06.1998) dipbt.bundestag.de/doc/btd/13/112/1311200.pdf accessed 30 November 2017.

[5] 'Management by objectives' means establishing normative goals and numeric targets and tracking their completion. The goals may be broken down to inform downstream facilities and organizations. Introduced for steering business, the concept was later adopted in the public sector.

[6] R.J. In't Veld et al., *Transgovernance. The Quest for Governance of Sustainable Development*. IASS Institute for Advanced Sustainability Studies, Potsdam, November 2011 www.iass-potsdam.de/sites/default/files/transgovernance_-_the_quest_-_nov_2011_0.pdf accessed 30 November 2017.

deregulation and to what is often regarded as smart regulation, effective or lean management, and multi-level governance. Additionally, it adds to the concept of management by objectives.

Combined with independently checked metrics and reviews, the TarTim approach is a relatively new feature of the system of policy making. This paradigm, in line with the rule of law and democracy, calls for fundamentally checking conventional approaches and policy portfolios.[7] In particular, it refers to the interface of the private and the public sectors, where it provides new options. The recently emerging voluntary sustainability standards for commodities like cacao, coffee, timber, fish, palm oil, soy, and banana generate new action models that can be linked to developments such as the TarTim approach. These sustainability standards do not result from academic policy designs but rather take into account stakeholder dialogues and are driven by a sense of urgency and of a collectively shared responsibility to make a difference.[8]

## GERMANY

In a recent survey, the European Sustainable Development Network collected best practices for achieving horizontal (across sectors), vertical (across levels), temporal (across time), and open (across societal sectors, e.g. public, private, academia, civil society) policy coordination and integration from public servants.[9] As might be expected, approaches to these issues and practices varied from country to country, and so far there is no simplified, uniform blueprint for best practices. Once again, a study provided by the European Network of Advisory Councils shows that institutional arrangements may structure leadership in society.[10] Compared to conventional economic development plans or other sector programmes, sustainability strategies feature new elements. For example, any sustainable development strategy

7 In 2015, the German Council for Sustainable Development analysed the national implementation of (then upcoming) SDGs and informed the Government by a first gap analysis: Deutsche Nachhaltigkeits-Architektur und SDGs Stellungnahme des Rates für Nachhaltige Entwicklung an Herrn BM Peter Altmaier nach § 1 (2)b RNE-Geschäftsordnung, 26. Mai 2015, vgl. www.nachhaltigkeitsrat.de/fileadmin/_migrated/media/RNE_Stellungnahme_Deutsche_Nachhaltigkeits-Architektur_und_SDG_26-05-2015.pdf accessed 30 November 2017.

8 G. Bachmann, 'The Political Challenge of Voluntary Standard Systems', in C. Schmitz-Hoffmann et al. (eds.), *Voluntary Standard Systems: A Contribution to Sustainable Development* (Springer 2014) 431–440.

9 ESDN, National Sustainable Development Strategies in Europe: Status Quo and Recent Developments; Quarterly Report authored by N. Gjoksi, M. Sedlacko, and G. Berger www.sd network.eu/quarterly%20reports/report%20files/pdf/2010-September National_Sustainable_Development_Strategies_in_Europe.pdf accessed 30 November 2017.

10 M. de Vries, The Role of National Sustainable Development Councils in Europe in Implementing the UN's Sustainable Development Goals. Overview and Conclusions (2015) www.eesc.europa.eu/resources/docs/the-role-of-national-sustainable-development-councils-in-europe-in-imple.pdf accessed 30 November 2017.

can deliver essential tools to set priorities, bundle and coordinate activities, and incentivize additional action.[11]

In this respect, Germany can build on prior lessons and practices. Long before launching the German Sustainability Strategy in 2002, the German Federal Government and other administrative entities attempted to use several different tools that failed in their application.[12] Additionally, Parliamentary Enquête Commissions ensured up-to-date scientific evidence and produced well-accepted reports but triggered no immediate policies. At the local level, citizens' action campaigns and efforts to bring forward the agenda of sustainable development produced well-accepted results in many cases but did not achieve a cross-cutting effect.[13]

As regards sustainable development itself, the German history of political thought and institutionalization is poorly documented. The general trends in modern society are well covered and broadly discussed;[14] however, specifics regarding sustainability are almost tacit forms of knowledge. With roots going back as far as the Enlightenment, the modern history of sustainability begins in the 1970s.[15] In the 1980s and 1990s, it meandered through mixed experiences, failures, and successes, finally becoming embedded in institutional intelligence. In Germany, a national strategy on sustainability has been in place since 2002, prompted by independent monitoring, reports on progress, and aligning measures, and two Peer Reviews by international experts in 2009 and 2013.[16] The Sustainable Development Strategy unites key sector strategies in a parallel, complementary, or additive manner including, for example, the biodiversity strategy, the strategy on demography, and the strategy concerning resources and commodities.[17] Also important are programmes on improving the quality of life

[11] Deutsche Nachhaltigkeitsstrategie 2016 www.bundesregierung.de/Content/Infomaterial/BPA/Bestellservice/Deutsche_Nachhaltigkeitsstrategie_Neuauflage_2016.html?nn=437032 accessed 30 November 2017.

[12] For instance, the implementation (ownership) of comprehensive strategies by single departments never reached federal cabinet level.

[13] E. Göll, N. Kampfhenkel, E. Mohrbach, and K. Nolting, 'Lokale Agenda 21-Projekte und ihre Wirkungen. Evaluation und Einschätzungen' (2007) IZT WerkstattBericht Nr 81 www.stadtentwicklung.berlin.de/agenda21/de/service/download/izt_wb81_agenda.pdf accessed 30 November 2017.

[14] U. Beck et al., *Reflexive Modernization: Politics, Tradition and Aesthetics in the Modern Social Order* (Stanford University Press 1994) 228; In't Veld et al., *supra* note 6; W. Lepenies, *The Seduction of Culture in German History* (Princeton University Press 2014) 272; P. Watson, *The German Genius. Europe's Third Renaissance, the Second Scientific Revolution and the Twentieth Century* (Simon & Schuster 2010) 964; H. Welzer and B. Sommer, *Transformationsdesign. Wege in eine zukunftsfähige Moderne* (Oekom 2014) 240.

[15] G.H. Brundtland et al., *Our Common Future: Report of the World Commission on Environment and Development* (Oxford University Press 1987).

[16] Rat fur Nachhaltige Entwicklung, Peer Review www.nachhaltigkeitsrat.de/en/projects/projects-of-the-council/peer-review/ accessed 30 November 2017.

[17] German Resource Efficiency Programme II, *Programme for the Sustainable Use and Conservation of Natural Resources* (2012) www.bmub.bund.de/en/service/publications/downloads/details/artikel/german-resource-efficiency-programme-ii/ accessed 30 November 2017.

in Germany, as well as the emerging National Action Plan on Business and Human Rights.

The approval of the UN SDGs in 2015 strengthens this paradigm shift and puts even more weight on it. While poverty eradication and inequality forms the central focus of the Agenda 2030, it also deals with critical issues such as unsustainable consumption and production, common goods, and resources such as the oceans, forests, and biodiversity. It introduces new key benchmarks, such as the aspiration to strive for land degradation neutrality. As a bottom line, the implementation of the UN SDGs is challenging institutional patterns, in particular as far as open-mindedness, coherence, and coordination are concerned. The UN's tagline, 'delivering as one', calls for exactly those institutional 'virtues', plus visibility and significance, and the rule of law (as expressed by another of the goals).[18] Institution-wise this is a huge and demanding undertaking, requiring bold new tools and ready-to-use instruments.

The UN calls for a universal, comprehensive, and integrated concept of development in which the idea of universality replaces the notion of a divided world. Until now, development has often been seen as something for the developing countries (the political South) in which the developed world (the political North) would set the default, cementing the North–South divide. The UN SDGs now set a new standard, one of universality. They connect well with the experience gathered in running national strategies for sustainable development all over the world.

The question at hand is how the existing setup of institutions fits into this picture. How can new tasks be taken on without being sidelined by self-contained bureaucracies? How would they benefit from coordination and coherence?

There is a debate on how to implement SDGs into domestic policies. Partly, non-governmental organizations advocate an authoritative and generally binding implementation based on legal responsibility and liability. The argument is valid, but has its limitations. For the implementation of specific SDG targets, stipulating legally binding obligations may not be ruled out; however, supersizing administrative enforcement will not deliver an entry into overall SDG implementation.

## NEOPHYTES IN THE INSTITUTIONAL LANDSCAPE

There are three institutions in Germany dedicated solely to the issue of sustainability. Beyond that, systems of rules, such as the quantification of goals and indicators, management rules, and monitoring, as well as sustainable development research, should also be considered as institutional frameworks. In this respect, the definition of the term 'institution' is very broad. Following a series of unsuccessful efforts in the 1990s, Germany settled on introducing three new and innovative institutions,

[18] UNGA 2015, *Transforming Our World* www.un.org/ga/search/view_doc.asp?symbol=A/RES/70/1&Lang=E accessed 30 November 2017.

dedicated solely to serving the purpose of sustainable development, which have run the national sustainability strategy since 2002:[19]

- The State Secretary Committee on sustainable development. Chaired by the Chancellery and supported by the sustainable development working group of the Heads of the Directorates, the cross-cutting Committee for 'Sustainability Indicators', and the cross-cutting Steering Group 'Sustainable Cities', this Committee is responsible for the federal sustainability strategy (as of 2002) and respective measures.
- The German Council for Sustainable Development. Since 2001, the Council advises the Federal Government on all issues of sustainability. The Chancellor appoints members in their personal capacity, and they do not carry an imperative mandate from their home organization. The Council in turn reports back to the Federal Chancellery. Its fifteen members and staff are tasked with setting the agenda for sustainability, addressing change agents in society and the public, and creating projects and dialogues.
- The Parliamentary Advisory Council for Sustainable Development. Established in 2014, this is the continuous instrument of legislative impact assessment and routinely informs the Parliament regarding sustainability policies.

These institutions are new, and they are 'light' institutions as opposed to enforcement administrations. The latter create an understanding of what an institution should look like and, rightly so, as they dominate the landscape of institutions. Unlike those, the light sustainable development institutions are relative neophytes within governmental parameters. The current practice is that the neophyte institutions are to be re-established regularly.[20]

High-level decisions have to be taken, and for this to happen sound political reasoning on pros and cons, and the modality of work, is a precondition. Those institutions have lots of room to manoeuvre and experiment. In the case of the Parliament, this is provided by the consensus principle and the introduction of the legal sustainability impact assessment.[21] The State Secretary Committee combines regular decision making and discovery meetings with invited experts and representatives of the Council and of Parliament. The Council, with senior leadership and established practice, advises the Government, and is mandated to pursue its

[19] *(First) National Strategy for Sustainable Development 2002* www.nachhaltigkeitsrat.de/nachhaltigkeit/strategie/strategie-2002/ accessed 30 November 2017.

[20] Three-year terms for the Council for Sustainable Development. The Parliamentary Commission is being re-established according to general Parliamentary terms of four years.

[21] Deutscher Bundestag, Parlamentarischer Beirat für nachhaltige Entwicklung/Unterrichtung – 20.06.2017 (hib 381/2017) www.bundestag.de/presse/hib/2017_06/-/511204 accessed 30 November 2017.

own agenda. It grew into a change making body with an (in this context) unprecedented work profile. With Members from all different civil society arenas including the private and academic sectors, its statements and interventions are based on established evidence. The Council also gets involved in other strategic decision-making bodies, such as in the arenas of high tech, education, research, and innovation.[22] For the purpose of restructuring civil society's engagement in the sustainability agenda, the Council established four regional network hubs in the provinces, and strengthened its international outreach.[23]

The portfolio of the three institutions is a new canvas, and they have developed their working modality mainly through experimentation and policy loops centring on the issue of the sustainable development strategy. This is a transformative agenda from which new institutional features will have to emerge, and civil society will play an important role. This is true for the public as well as for the private sector. Quite a few examples are already in place and thriving, such as the Sustainability Code, the German Sustainability Award, and the Peer Review.

The Sustainability Code forms an essential part of the newly emerging institutional setup. It is robust and easy to access but still uses a very ambitious reporting standard addressing primarily the private sector.[24] It is also applicable to public institutions, as demonstrated by declarations of compliance issued by publicly owned enterprises, the Council itself, and a few advanced universities.[25] Neither the administration nor the corporate and financial rating communities have institutionalized the Code, but the Council for Sustainable Development has succeeded in bringing together a meaningful civil society-based, multi-stakeholder approach. Through its continuing activities, the Council is building up coaching capacities and stakeholder contributions.[26] In a series of non-legally binding agreements, the Council and industrial sector associations agreed on implementation features and, thus, increased support and exchange of experience – all of which lead to a new kind of institution 'in the making'.

Not-for-profit organizations are another field of practice. Established in 2008, the Foundation German Sustainability Award (2008) assigns the German Sustainability Award, Europe's most prestigious award in the field of sustainable development, in different categories to corporations, cities, and best practice, but also to eminent personalities for outstanding contributions to sustainability in

[22] The Federal Government, 'The New High-Tech Strategy Innovations for Germany' www.bmbf.de/pub/HTS_Broschuere_eng.pdf accessed 30 November 2017.

[23] Rat für Nachhaltige Entwicklung, *Regionale Netzstellen Nachhaltigkeitsstrategien (RENN)* www.nachhaltigkeitsrat.de/en/renn-netzwerk/ accessed 30 November 2017.

[24] Deutscher Nachhaltigkeits, *Kodex* www.deutscher-nachhaltigkeitskodex.de/de/startseite.html accessed 30 November 2017.

[25] HOCH, *Sustainability at HEI* www.hochn.uni-hamburg.de/en.html 30 November 2017.

[26] A comprehensive overview is provided by the *Sustainability Almanac*, see www.nachhaltigkeitsrat.de/fileadmin/user_upload/dokumente/publikationen/broschueren/German_Almanac_of_Sustainability_text_No_52_March_2017.pdf 30 November 2017.

Germany or worldwide. The idea of the Award is to encourage social and ecological responsibility and to identify role models in this area.[27]

Peer Reviews and blended learning are adding value to the emerging institutional governance. Germany has invited international Peers to assess domestic performance in the field of sustainable development three times. Those reviews built on experiences with reviews held earlier in the Netherlands and France in particular. In terms of the mandate and selection of Peers, the preparation process and stakeholder involvement, the drafting of assessments, and the high-level presentation of the result, the German procedure featured some new elements. Established review schemes for economic or environmental politics, such as those created by the OECD, were amended and adjusted in order to account for the comprehensive character of sustainability politics and the multi-level aspects. The newly institutionalized UN High Political Forum for Sustainable Development,[28] provides the arena for the presentation of Voluntary National Reports and invites the sharing of experiences. In the future this arena will perhaps serve as a light form of benchmarking of institutional progress. As of today, the VNRs take the form of governments reporting about their own performance. While this already provides serious insights and sometimes provokes deep thinking, the real conversation will only start if the HLPF institution reaches the next level by putting independently conducted Peer Reviews on display.

## A TRIPLE APPROACH

For determining which of the total set of SDGs applies to national circumstances and needs to be implemented, probably every country in the world will have to think about institutional adjustments, be they referred to as alignment or by any other term expressing the need for rendering governance fit for purpose. There is as yet no blueprint, and individual solutions and approaches may well differ significantly. It is hardly a prophecy to assume that coordination and coherence will be at the centre.

The German Council for Sustainable Development has subjected the SDGs to an initial screening and assessment of whether and how the German institutional system would have to address gaps and could approach opportunities and chances. The SDGs are most relevant to the further advancement of Germany's sustainable

[27] The German Sustainability Awards, see www.nachhaltigkeitspreis.de/sonstige/english-summary/ accessed 30 November 2017.

[28] UN, *High-Level Political Forum on Sustainable Development* https://sustainabledevelopment.un.org/hlpf accessed 30 November 2017. The HLPF is part of the institutional reforms to the UN system. It replaces the UN Commission on Sustainable Development. There are, of course, more institutional reforms and deeper cuts in the UN Development System needed, as a Team of International Advisors, chaired by Klaus Töpfer and Juan Somavia recommended in 2016; see *The Future We Want – The United Nations We Need* www.un.org/ecosoc/sites/www.un.org.ecosoc/files/files/en/qcpr/ita-findings-and-conclusions-16-jun-2016.pdf accessed 30 November 2017.

development strategy, and they stand alongside other important policies, such as those emanating from the EU and those relating to the unfinished business of domestic sustainable management, to which an updating of Germany's sustainable development strategy will respond.

In this context, Germany is in demand in three respects. First, because there are gaps and unsolved problems and there is a need for action domestically in Germany. Thanks to its skills in finding solutions and transferring them elsewhere, German constructs of sustainability are well placed to deliver on the SDGs. As with all States formerly known (in the pre-SDG world) as 'donors', there is reason for a portfolio alignment of approaches to official development 'aid' that would facilitate adequate SDG governance in other States. The differentiation between 'in', 'by', and 'with' is introduced as a triple approach to implementation, and henceforth, to institutionalizing sustainability. The 'triple' concept is quite broadly accepted throughout the SDG debate in Germany including organized civil society.

The National Sustainable Development Strategy, continuously updated since 2002, is the essential framework for the national implementation of Agenda 2030, and the SDGs are to henceforth be included in the further development of national targets and indicators. Content-wise, the National Sustainable Development Strategy goes beyond some requirements of the SDGs. Examples include the limitation of national debt, the energy transition policy, climate protection, and aspects of education. Sustainable mobility is not at all addressed in the SDGs, whereas Germany's sustainable development policy has, in recent years, focused significantly on this issue. Time-wise, the relaunch of the National Sustainable Development Strategy, informed by the SDGs, will enlarge its existing horizons and set targets for 2030. Those national 2020 targets that are still unfinished, and will probably not be reached until 2020 or beyond, need to be dealt with very seriously.

On the other hand, the SDGs address requirements that are, in terms of international comparison, regarded as having largely been met in Germany. Examples include peacekeeping, water and sanitation, means of implementation, the fight against extreme poverty, mortality, and primary education. Other SDGs mean that, in the German context, the national agenda must be processed further, since Agenda 2030 rightly addresses key issues such as prosperity beyond GDP, the perspective of decoupling growth and resources, limits to planetary boundaries, and the social divide via income disparities and constricted access to commons.

## TOOLING UP

With the 'triple' approach, Germany faces manifold challenges, both institutionally and practically. Hybridising, networking in hubs, and anchoring form key elements for shaping next steps. Work is under way for each of these, and studies and practice are advancing, as shown in the following.

## *Anchoring*

The fundamental requirements toward which SDG 16 (peace and inclusion) in particular is geared are generally regarded as givens for Germany in the national context, especially when it comes, for example, to the rule of law, election law, social security, freedom of association, anti-corruption, and freedom of information. This is not the case to the same extent with regard to the recognition of ecological services, resource constraints, or carbon restrictions in the equal ranking of the three dimensions of sustainability. There are deficits here which have a negative impact on the implementation of national sustainable development objectives and may possibly interfere with the implementation of the SDGs. Furthermore, the rules and procedures of the National Sustainable Development Strategy are still relatively new and often still unknown among broad sections of the public.

Top-level commitment towards sustainability goals and targets is an important part of any governance system, be it in the public sector or in the corporate community. However, there is no explicit and legally binding anchoring in Germany, although this was never perceived as a deficit. Only recently has the Council started a debate about the pros and cons of amending the constitutional law, thus legally strengthening the case for cross-cutting sustainability efforts.

One obvious possibility is constitutional anchorage. Even now, the German Basic Law dictates that the State should protect natural resources and wildlife in the context of constitutional order and on behalf of future generations. However, this is insufficient and does not meet the requirements of sustainable development. Rather, the *principle of sustainability* must be made mandatory for national policy and Germany's role in the world. Constitutional anchoring of the sustainability principle allows the State, the people and their elected leaders, and the business world to work towards sustainable development more reliably than ever before. Rule of law principles would be strengthened, and other options could target the use of the 'soft' instruments of information dissemination and presentation. For the State, what could also come into question are informal standards in the form of voluntary obligations which could also be used by third parties. The German Sustainability Code would be a possible instrument.

In light of the demographic change and the migration of people, Germany requires long-term, sustainability based action, an integrated perspective, and the genuine involvement of citizens in political decisions. Today, this is an issue of actual politics, but it has already been mentioned by the most recent Peer Review. Providing housing, access to education, and language skills are amongst the first principles of any integration, in line with human rights and the rule of law. In a longer-term perspective, sustainable urban development, degradation-neutral land use, and facilitation of green growth for all present challenges. Germany has ample experience with Peer Reviews. Focusing mainly on the federal level of sustainability policies in Germany, Peers from countries such as South Africa, Korea, Canada, the

US, and several European states were invited and given full and free access to scrutinize the German political and institutional landscape. The Council acted as facilitator. In terms of anchoring sustainable development and bringing in institutional competence and transparency, both Reviews made valuable observations. The findings of the Peers were discussed by Parliament and the Government, and by stakeholders, resulting in detailed feedback and conclusions. Generally, if designed and managed properly, Peer Reviews can generate important momentum and facilitate institution building processes.

### *Hybrids*

For future institutional setups, hybridizing is essential. Making the utmost use of the overlap between 'pure' institutions and the quasi-institutional systems of rules and rule-based decision making is the most promising way forward. Liability and due diligence are, in that sense, not restricted to the corporate community, but rather can be very actively pursued by the next generation of leaders in both the public and private sectors.

Aims may always be conflicting. Old and vested interests are regularly in conflict with new goals – otherwise the goal setting exercise would not make sense in the first place – but now those conflicts are entering the next stage. With sustainability governance leaving the political niche and hitting the mainstream, the resolution of conflicts becomes tricky and increases in frequency and significance. Interestingly, sustainability objectives may now also have a run-in with objectives equally rooted in sustainability concepts. The conventional 'resolution' via alpha structures, turfing, old-style power brokerage, or self-display communication, by contrast, is not immediately promising for the delivery of good solutions, the more so as they often appear as part of the problem. That is exactly why there is a need to combine programming, goal setting, and new approaches for institutional modalities. Against this backdrop, the anchoring of sustainability strategies in politics and society is crucial.

### *Networks*

The idea of an extra importance of coordination and of a specific need for new forms of societal dialogue is rooted in the 1987 report *Our Common Future* issued by the UNCED led by Gro Harlem Brundtland, which stands out from the long line of sustainability reports and statements. For any real societal dialogue, it is mandatory to reach out to ordinary people and local communities; however, by its design, the German federal structure does not envisage any direct participation procedures in matters relating to the German Sustainability Strategy.

However, sustainable strategies affect municipalities significantly, and, at the level of local government, there are also many procedures to help people exchange views and compare experiences that are of considerable importance. The Council has already developed a routine in bringing together Lord Majors with an ambitious sustainability agenda and fostering sustainable urbanism. Within the German sustainability strategy, in a *pars pro toto* way, this issue is represented by the fact that the strategy aims at reducing the sealing and consumption of land for the purpose of urban settlement. At the same time, the exchange of experience and the coordination of sustainability activities at all federal levels must be fundamentally improved through German governance systems. On behalf of the Federal Chancellery and with extra funds provided by the Parliament, the Council is establishing four regional sustainability network hubs tasked with encouraging and strengthening civil society engagement and action.

Science could help make goals and targets measurable, but this principle still remains to be implemented. As regards the SDGs, the potential (and necessary) role of science is much greater than the one currently taken, as there is a need for global monitoring and reporting on the progress being achieved through national SDG implementation. Recalibrating national means of implementation and global partnerships needs benchmarks and evidence on where things stand. For the area of climate change, the IPCC fulfils this task of watching and advising. The establishment of an IP-SDG in parallel would face serious difficulties and does not appear as natural option. Thus, the role of science is yet to be made clear.

Science may discover unexpected choices or scenarios, and research may increase the understanding of lock-ins or dynamic developments, which are essential ingredients for a sustainable development. That science and politics are interrelated seems to be basic knowledge, and research on the science–policy interface has recently proliferated. However, what a successful science–policy interface actually entails is not yet clearly understood, let alone shared and communicated. The system of science and research is still steered and managed mainly via input of funds, which is promising but needs a correlation with the output and scaling of results. The incentivization of a debate on science and sustainability between the German Federal Government and the scientific community has made valuable progress in recent years and provides an institutional framework for science and sustainability that is still, nevertheless, unmarked territory.

## *Coordination*

In principle, the notion of coordination is alien to institutional functionality. The issue is that everyone supports and demands coordination, but no one wants to be coordinated. This is what might be called the coordination mismatch; it is embedded into the functionality of institutions, and it produces all kinds of administrative performance features.

'Opting out' of the coordination radar seems to be one of the favourite concepts. A 'yes, but' attitude would pro forma accept the overall reason for coordinated action but emphasize particularities and special circumstances in a way that coordination would not suit. The classic 'Napoleonic' strategy creates a top-down chain of command and control. Classically, coordination is enforced by fiscal plans or central policy programming, as, for example, in five-year plans or development plans. Mainstreaming and aligning are made possible but also restricted to mostly fiscal contents. Voluntary 'opting in' based on knowledge and insight into the urgency of problems and the need for coordination is often seen as last resort. The political narrative of climate change is a good example. So far, it is mostly illusionary. Interministerial units and working parties tasked with cross-cutting missions sometimes work and sometimes fail, depending on circumstantial effects. A clear and transparent division of work promises efficiency and increased ownership. More institutions are responsible for less and less, and none is responsible for the grand total. As collateral side effect, unproductive turf battles and hidden agendas may occur and limit the discharge of duties.

Not surprisingly, those instruments are all part of the reality of governance, and they do not measure up to what they are designed to deliver. The interesting point in terms of governance for sustainability, however, is that they must not be ignored or ruled out. They may rather be given a place in sustainability toolboxes, and be completed by new out-of-the-ordinary (out-of-institution) approaches. Political leadership works out best and can often functions as some kind of attractor to coordinated action. Coordination by convening is a promising feature. It builds on the dedication of leaders, or on the calling power of people, on voluntary benchmarking, or competitive advantages. The coordination momentum will not appear from the outset, but will evolve as a matter of course. Clustered and intermediary approaches work, for example, by transparent sharing of information, access, and opportunities to be on public display. Councils for Sustainable Development are most likely to use this approach, opening up discourse arenas, establishing room for experiments, and encouraging science and advanced studies. This approach assumes competences in processes and with the actors.

## *New Features of Collaboration*

The challenges of decarbonization, fair trade and innovation, the circular economy, urban development, and social sustainability are crucial. Sustainability goals and measures must directly relate to one another, and nations must cater to the context of the UN's 2030 Agenda for Sustainable Development. The German SDGs will evolve from purely domestic targets into a larger framework taking account of Germany's responsibility on the international stage. The institutional framework should be enhanced with a view to integrating sustainability into every policy area, to networking actors, and to encouraging new actions. Governance capacities must be raised and better anchored, and research efforts as well as the education scheme must be aligned to the German Sustainability Strategy. Co-design approaches involving civil society should be applied to tie research activities more closely to real change processes.

The universal nature of the 2030 Agenda targets the common sharing of responsibility by all States that needs to be organized through more intensified partnerships. The worldwide sharing of knowledge and expertise needs to be bolstered. There is a need to forge new responsibility partnerships and to design corresponding funding models. Shared responsibility transcends national borders and will have to be fashioned, for example, along the lines of supply chains, material flows, or cultural norms.

Uncertainty prevails in long-term decisions. Emergencies are often the consequence of unforeseen development; however, addressing emergencies is not part of the Agenda 2030 and, at any rate, is not being addressed by the UN SDGs. The consciousness of threats or emergencies creates the sense of urgency that is often necessary to take decisions at all. The whole domain of sustainable development is filled with dangers, threats, risks, emergencies, and related phenomena, but also with options, opportunities, chances, beginnings, and stories of success and progress. Often, environmental emergencies may serve in a lens-like way to clarify options and problems. In order to make governance systems fit for transformation, they have to onboard the possibility of a 'sudden chance' as an unforeseen impact.

## CONCLUSION

Form follows function, institutionalizing follows purpose. Empowering people, promoting sustainable growth, respecting ecosystem limits, and protecting human rights are the core purposes of sustainable development that demand a great deal from institutional arrangements. Currently, developments such as the 2030 Agenda and SDGs signal the start of major institutional and governance changes, which will require engagement with all existing institutions but will also typecast new features. Any replica of what today is the institutional mainstream is not an option. Within the area of climate, Germany's role model institutions have developed over fifteen years not by design but mainly by practice, and further steps may be expected.

German practice highlights new institutions establishing a set of sustainable management tools, such as agenda setting, instigating steering and coordination, convening capacities, and inciting societal arrangements. While there is no one-size-fits-all institutional practice, experience such as hybridizing, working modality, networking, and scaling can be used to put together toolboxes. The open questions addressed in this chapter, such as the role of science or societal arrangements, demonstrate the importance of further institution design thinking.

# PART IV

# Implementing Sustainability through National Institutions: Case Studies

*National Case Studies*

# 18

# Institutions for a Sustainable Future: The Former Israeli Commission for Future Generations

*Shlomo Shoham and Friederike Kurre*

In this chapter, the former Commission for Future Generations in Israel, working from 2001 through 2006, is reviewed. The chapter explores the Commission's five years of operation and gives a broad overview of the historical background, how the Commission was created and then dissolved, and general information regarding powers, authority, fields of action, and mandate. In the end, the achievements and niche created by the Commission are also discussed in order to provide a better insight into its work. Furthermore, the chapter describes the role of the Commissioner during its five years of operation.

The Commission was intended to help the Israeli Parliament – the Knesset – to seriously take into account the goals of intergenerational justice. With specific focus on the creation of 'a dimension of the future that would be included in the primary and secondary legislation of the State of Israel', the Commission operated to defend the needs and the rights of future generations. The Commission proved how highly important and valuable the involvement of the future is, especially in times when people are stuck into day-to-day events and are hard-pressed to anticipate or plan even tomorrow's activities. Therefore, a sincere concern for fashioning the future of the generations to come has an altruistic dimension of a sort not found here. And it deserves every sort of praise.[1]

Similar to an experiment, the success of this venture was mixed; however, after some time the Commissioner and his group of experts developed real influence across a wide policy spectrum. Likewise, they brought an unusual and often controversial perspective – the claims of intergenerational justice – to debates ordinarily shaped by rival ideologies, conflicting datasets, or competing political interest groups. The idea of the Commission was grounded in the sustainable development movement, which has achieved substantial influence in environmental policy circles.[2]

1 R. Reuven, 'Endorsements', in S. Shoham, *Future Intelligence* (Bertelsmann Stiftung 2010) 7.

2 E. Andreas, 'Preface', in Shoham, *supra* note 1, 14.

Therefore, the Commission of Future Generations in Israel linked Israeli society's past and present with its future. This opportunity enabled the Commission to create legislation that would give significance to the existence of the people in this region and their future generations.

The looming environmental crises give a new urgency to the discussion of what we owe our future generations.[3] Fortunately, in recent decades, different institutions with the aim of protecting future generations have been established, and these were endorsed in the UN Secretary-General's 2013 Report, *Intergenerational Solidarity and the Needs of Future Generations*.[4] The Commission for Future Generations in Israel was, even if only for a limited period, among these institutions, and for this reason it deserves to be mentioned in the content of the still existing ones.

## HISTORICAL BACKGROUND

Israel has a relatively young and dynamic society which is constantly redefining its priorities. In its mere seventy years of existence as a State it already has achieved much. Israel is considered to be a developed Western state, is an OECD member, has a prosperous economy, ranked thirty-seventh largest in the world,[5] and an impressive development momentum. The State benefits from a highly skilled workforce and is among the most educated countries in the world. Furthermore, Israel has the highest standard of living in the Middle East and one of the highest life expectancies in the world.[6]

However, these considerable achievements in one of the most crowded States in the world have taken a heavy toll in terms of a problematic view of the future and considerable environmental costs. Although Israel's founders had a well-formulated ideological vision, its fulfilment was not achieved in a very sustainable way. The founders 'postponed' the needs of future generations because of an existential need to found a state under difficult circumstances. Policymakers saw the territory as a desolate expanse that needed to be made to prosper. Therefore, pioneering was expressed in concepts such as building a whole settlement in only one night. The same pioneers saw construction as the essence of their founding vision with an outlook of 'conquering the land'. Hundreds of thousands of new immigrants lived by this ideology without taking into consideration the future consequences of such quick development. The result of this was an increasing consumption of natural

[3] M. Tim, *Future People: A Moderate Consequentialist Account of our Obligations to Future Generations* (Clarendon Press 2006).

[4] Ban Ki-moon, *Intergenerational Solidarity and the Needs of Future Generations*, Report of the Secretary-General, 5 August 2013 A/68/322. https://sustainabledevelopment.un.org/content/documents/2006future.pdf accessed 30 November 2017.

[5] By nominal gross domestic product as of 2014.

[6] A. Schleicher, *Israel – Education at a Glance* (OECD Country Note 2013); 'WHO: Life Expectancy in Israel among Highest in the World', *The Associated Press* (24 May 2009).

resources, discharge of pollutants, and pressure on the land. Furthermore, urbanization, rapid economic development, growth of physical infrastructure, accelerated industrialization, and intensive agriculture destabilized and harmed the reciprocal correlation between human and nature.[7]

Thus, the first decades of the State of Israel were marked by unsustainable development. Besides this, the danger of recent conflicts and the related threats to the State's security and economy have delayed future-oriented policies as well. These threats made, and continue to make, it difficult for Israeli society to believe in positive thoughts that might envision the land as quiet and free of struggle.

Throughout all of this it is clear to see that Israel was (and still is) steeped in a constant fight for its existence, which made the Israeli public accustomed to heated debates over short-term issues. As a result of this, recently elected decision-makers often feel that the public is demanding solutions to current problems immediately even if swift action means disregarding future ramifications, conflict with other government policies, or postponing attention to essential long-term subjects. For these reasons, there was a profound need for the creation of a body like the Commission for Future Generations in Israel.[8]

### *The Knesset Law Amendment: Creating the Commission for Future Generations*

The establishment of the Israeli Commission was not preceded by a public campaign or even a public discussion arising outside parliament. It was not a result of a bottom-up process but rather was a totally top-down driven process imposed directly by parliament.

The Commission for Future Generations was born out of a great vision of the future in March 2001. The law concerning the Commission, however, started as a private bill which was the result of a personal revelation, initiated by Mr Joseph Lapid in October 2000, when he presented it to the parliament. At that point, Lapid was the leader of the middle-class liberal party, 'Shinui' (literally: change), a politician in the centre of the political arena and a Member of the Knesset. The bill stated:[9]

> A Commissioner for Future Generations ... will be given the opportunity to examine each legislative act and to appear before the relevant Knesset committee, wherever there is suspicion of possible prejudice against future generations. This may take the form of soil or air pollution, harm caused to pension funds, the implications of genetic biology or results of a technological development.[10]

[7] Shoham, *supra* note 1, 166–167.

[8] Ibid. at 98–100.

[9] B. Jávor and J. Rácz (eds.), *Do We Owe Them a Future? The Opportunities of a Representation for Future Generations in Europe* (Védegylet 2006) 90.

[10] K. Fodor, 'Institutional Representation of Future Generations: Successes and Barriers' (Master of Science Thesis, Central European University 2013) 48–49.

Lapid's intention was to establish an honourable position for the Israeli Parliament among the nations of the developed world. After presenting the bill to the parliament, it was subsequently adopted by the members of the Knesset. Nevertheless, there were several amendments to the original bill which showed that even a strongly positioned politician like Lapid could not create an institution that would have authority over both parliament and government. The maximum that the coalition government at that time, and probably a coalition of any time, would agree to was to permit the Knesset to have its own internal body that would advise it regarding the legislation process and carry out an audit of ramifications that could affect future generations, and which would be funded from the Knesset's own budget.[11] Ultimately, the Commission was established in 2001 as a result of the conviction that those who formulate the legislation shaping the Israeli society ought to consider the consequences of that legislation, and that the various interests shaping legislation should remain beholden to an overriding principle – protecting the interests of the children and grandchildren of future generations and preserving a broad scope of choices for them.[12]

Subsequently, the Commission was established according to the Knesset Law, the statute regulating the internal proceedings of the parliament. The Commission therefore was an organ of Parliament acting under the same articles defining the operation of the Legal Chamber, the Parliamentary Committees, the Opposition, the Speaker, and the Speaker's deputies. The idea at the base of the law was that the creation of an entity within the Parliament that had a comprehensive view of the Knesset legislative picture with regard to any potential negative effect on the needs and rights of future generations together with the means to prevent such legislation from taking place.[13] Such an institution was needed to an even greater extent in a State that has to cope with serious issues concerning its very survival, which also influences legislation and proposed legislation. At the head of the Commission was a Commissioner, chosen by an ad hoc public committee constituted of the three heads of the main Knesset committees and three well-known experts from the universities, appointed by the Speaker of the Parliament. The Commissioner, Justice (ret.) Shlomo Shoham, had specialized in the legislative process within the parliament, as the legal advisor of the Constitution, Law and Justice Committee.[14] Ultimately, the amendment to the Knesset Law provided the Commission for Future Generations with the authority to become involved in any bill that it reasoned would have significant impact on future generations and provide

[11] Jávor and Rácz, *supra* note 9 at 91.

[12] The Knesset Commission for Future Generations www.worldfuturecouncil.org/fileadmin/user_upload/Maja/Future_Justice_Library/Knesset_Paper.pdf accessed 30 November 2017.

[13] Ibid. at 3.

[14] Ibid.

its opinion on the bill. From a legal perspective, the Commission for Future Generations was defined in the 8th Chapter of the Knesset Law.[15]

### *Beginning and End: Reasons for Dissolving the Commission*

The Commission began operating in late 2001. In 2006, with the conclusion of the Commissioner's term, no new commissioner was appointed in his stead and the Commission's work ceased.[16] In December 2010, a bill was approved in the Knesset Plenum to dissolve the Commission. Members of the Knesset raised two primary reasons for dissolution of the Commission during deliberations on the topic: (1) the costs of its operations and (2) their feelings that the Commission received too much authority to interfere in their work. For example, in the explanation to the Knesset Bill,[17] it was argued that the

> activity of the Knesset Commission for Future Generations in addition to the above-listed departments [the Knesset Research and Information Center and the Knesset Legal Department] create redundancy in costs which can be saved without detracting from information provided to MKs (Member of Knesset).

While presenting the bill for a second and third reading, MK Yariv Levin noted that

> it was a real failure when this bill (Knesset Law Amendment No. 14) was passed and no proper differentiation was made between providing facts and a spectrum of positions, and determining morally what is good and what is bad. This is exactly the difference between what we have at our service from the Research and Information Center, which we must have, and depriving us of our role and interference in it by an external party.[18]

In the end, the Commission for Future Generations was abolished by the Knesset in 2011 on the ground that the role of the Commissioner had too much impact on their free choice as the representatives of the people to decide what is good or bad for future generations.[19]

The Israeli Commission for Future Generations was a significant initiative, the first explicit representation of future generations within governmental bodies. The Commissioner took a systematic and integrated approach in opinions and challenged

[15] T. Naama, 'Official Bodies that Deal with the Needs of Future Generations and Sustainable Development' (2013) *Comparative Review* www.knesset.gov.il/mmm/data/pdf/me03194.pdf accessed 30 November 2017.

[16] Ibid.

[17] Knesset Law (Amendment) – Dissolution of the Knesset Commission for Future Generations, 5770-2010.

[18] Naama, *supra* note 15.

[19] G. Dror, 'Cancellation of Commission for Future Generations – between Politics and Ethics. Ecology and Environment' (2012) 3:2 *Journal of Environmental Science and Policy* 161–165; K. Fodor, *supra* note 10 at 48–49.

the business-as-usual approach.[20] After the Commissioner's term ended, a smaller unit was empowered to issue reports, but without a mandate to represent future generations in the same manner.[21]

## ABOUT THE COMMISSION FOR FUTURE GENERATIONS

According to the Knesset Law, the Commission focused on raising the legislative branch's awareness of the future consequences of legislation and secondary legislation in Israel in a variety of fields: (1) the environment; (2) natural resources; (3) science; (4) development; (5) education; (6) health; (7) the economy; (8) demography; (9) planning and construction; (10) quality of life; (11) technology; and (12) law. In addition, it could address any issue that the Knesset Constitution, Law and Justice Committee determined as having a significant impact on future generations.[22]

The law determined that the Commission was to: (1) provide data and opinions on topics of particular interest to future generations; (2) provide its assessment of bills in the bill's explanations or as an appendix; (3) provide consultation to Members of Knesset; (4) be invited to deliberations in Knesset Committees; and (5) receive information from all supervisory bodies and submit an annual report on its activities each year.[23] The Commission would, for example, initiate conferences and workshops to increase public awareness on the connection between air pollution and morbidity with the participation of academic experts and deliberations in the Knesset Internal Affairs and Environment Committee. The Commission also initiated legislation, including an attempt to promote legislation of the Basic Law Sustainable Development,[24] which could have been a perfect fit for action in protecting future generations' interests.[25]

However, one of the first steps in establishing the Commission for Future Generations was the significant need to explain and define what constitutes *of particular interest to future generations*, as stipulated in the wording of the law. In the beginning it was defined in terms of the understanding of the term *sustainability*, which expressed the values on which responsibility to future generations is based. Surprisingly, although the concept of sustainability was not a concept the initiators of the law were aware of, the twelve areas which legally fell within the Commission's

20 G. Maja and P. Catherine, *Guarding Our Future – How to Include Future Generations in Policy Making* (World Future Council 2013) 7; Dror, *supra* note 19 at 161–165.

21 Dror, *supra* note 19 at 161–165.

22 Knesset Law (Amendment No. 14), 5761-2001, section 8; The Knesset Commission for Future Generations, *Report Obtained via the Freedom of Information Law* (2002 Annual) 5758-1998 (in Hebrew).

23 Knesset Law (Amendment No. 14), 5761-2001, section 8.

24 Naama, *supra* note 15; The Knesset Commission for Future Generations, *The World as a Deposit for Our Children: Parliamentary Activity for Sustainable Development* (in Hebrew).

25 Jávor and Rácz, *supra* note 9 at 103.

authority matched the principle components that make up the concept, as it is described in scholarly literature.[26]

### *Powers and Authority*

From 2001 to 2006, the Commission for Future Generations operated pursuant to enabling legislation passed by the Knesset.[27] According to the section 32 of the Knesset Law, the Commission had the authority to: (1) voice opinions on bills, secondary legislation, and regulations of interest to future generations; (2) provide the Knesset with recommendations on any issue the Commissioner considered relevant to the rights of future generations; (3) demand any information from ministries, state corporations, and local authorities; and (4) operate under the right to be given enough time to prepare an opinion on a bill.[28]

The Commission might best be described as an advisory or consultative body restricted to the legislative work of the Israeli Parliament, with little legal authority to propose bills, carry out enquiries, or pass judgment in the event of dispute. In practice, however, the Commissioner claimed the right to issue an informed opinion even when the Knesset was bound by law to make a decision within a given time frame. This effectively led to the Commission having informal veto power over lawmaking, which could be seen similar to the impact of the American filibuster in the US Congress.[29] The enabling legislation furthermore gave the Commission the authority to demand information – any document, piece of information, or report – from all governmental entities, such as ministries, public companies, state institutions, or government corporations, to carry out its duties. This authority, which gave the Commissioner an advantage over members of Parliament and government ministers, was similar to the authority of the State Comptroller.[30]

One of the key powers of the Commission was to request a 'reasonable time' from a parliamentary committee to collect data and prepare evaluation regarding certain bills or secondary legislation with particular relevance for future generations. The enabling statute even required committee chairs, if necessary, to delay their discussion in order to allow this. This implied authority could have been crucial, particularly when it came to budgetary bills.[31] For example, the law states that if Israel's annual budget is not voted on by March of the preceding year, the Parliament must dissolve itself and new elections have to be held. In this context, the Commissioner could have introduced uncomfortable delays into the process on issues he deemed

[26] Maja and Pearce, *supra* note 20 at 7.
[27] Knesset Law (Amendment No. 14), 5761-2001, section 8.
[28] The Knesset, Commission for Future Generations, *supra* note 22 at 4–5.
[29] Göpel and Pearce, *supra* note 20 at 7.
[30] State Comptroller Act 5718-1958 (State Comptroller Law); Jávor and Rácz, *supra* note 9 at 94.
[31] Ibid. at 95.

critical – which would have risked drawing antagonism from all sides, hence this authority had rarely been invoked.[32]

Furthermore, the Commission had been authorized to act in policy areas falling within three broader areas that often involve interrelated issues: society, economics, and the environment. And indeed, one of the Commission's successes was to raise public awareness of sustainability in a way that encompassed all three in a period when the idea of sustainability was associated almost exclusively with environmental issues. These main functions show that the Commission's power had a great deal to do with how it was perceived in the Parliament and among the public. Not being a democratically elected body, its opinions and recommendations were non-binding and thus it could only raise awareness in a way that put pressure on the committee discussing the legislation and on the voting Parliament.

### *Role of the Commissioner*

Appointing a Commissioner for Future Generations brought sustainable development straight to the heart of government's policy-making and intra-governmental expertise.[33] He was able to directly engage in the policy-making process and assess the long-term effects of policies from an integrated perspective.[34] As regards the Commission for Future Generations in Israel, the Commissioner was appointed by a respected public committee, in a process similar to the selection of Parliament's legal advisor and served a full five-year term. Through all of these conditions, the Commission and its employees were provided with the security and immunity they needed to express their positions without fear.[35] The Commissioner was provided with the power to examine bills and review draft legislation that addressed the potential for future harm and to bring concrete data and recommendations in the form of a report to the Parliament.[36] He could express his opinion during the deliberation of legislative committees or submit it as an attachment to bills being discussed in committee or voted on by the Parliament in plenum. No legislation in connection with future generations could have been adopted until the Commissioner submitted his report.[37] Moreover, the Commissioner had the authority to express his opinion and make recommendations on various topics unrelated to specific bills as well as on secondary legislation brought to vote in the Knesset. Furthermore, he had the authority to advise members of the Knesset on any topic

32 Shoham, *supra* note 1 at 103.

33 UK Sustainable Development Commission, About Us www.sd-commission.org.uk/pages/aboutus.html accessed 30 November 2017.

34 *Models for Protecting the Environment for Future Generations* (Harvard Law School 2008) 16.

35 Shoham, *supra* note 1 at 92.

36 R. Laster and D. Livney, *Environmental Law in Israel* (Kluwer Law International 2011) 37–38.

37 The Knesset Commission for Future Generations www.worldfuturecouncil.org/fileadmin/user_upload/Maja/Future_Justice_Library/Knesset_Paper.pdf accessed 30 November 2017.

that had special relevance to future generations. The given authority also allowed him to participate in all top-level debates on the legislation. Crucial to the effective functioning of the Commission was the Commissioner's right to access relevant information:[38]

> The Knesset Commissioner for Future Generations may request from any organization or body being investigated … any information, document or report … in the possession of that body and which is required by the Commissioner for the implementation of his tasks; the aforesaid body will give the Commissioner the requested information.[39]

These powers gave the Commissioner broad authority to act effectively as an Ombudsman for Future Generations.[40]

Judge (ret.) Shoham was appointed Commissioner during the Commission's five-year term after working as a legal advisor to the Constitution, Law and Justice Committee, which was to approve the bill.[41] During his term, he reported that every bill tabled in Parliament was presented to the Commission. As the Commissioner, he had the statutory authority to announce the involvement of the Commission in a particular bill. When this happened, he was invited to the meetings of the relevant committee to offer a written and oral opinion. He stated that over the five years of his tenure as Commissioner, the Commission submitted hundreds of reports, wrote opinions on bills, and initiated comprehensive thinking in critical areas for the future of the State, working with Israel's best researchers, academics, organizations, and other government bodies. Furthermore, civil servants skilled at synthesizing information sources, together with specialists at the top of their field, were hired. From the Commissioner's view, it was more important that employees have a professional rather than a political character.[42] Additionally, while active, the Commissioner considered children as a part of future generations and acted as their spokesman in the Israeli Parliament.[43]

### *Creating a Mandate and First Principles for the Commission*

Through the Knesset law amendment, the Commission was granted a broad and comprehensive scope of activity in a variety of fields. This gave the Commission

[38] *Models for Protecting the Environment for Future Generations*, *supra* note 34 at 18.

[39] Knesset Law, art. 35(a), unofficial translation reprinted in The Knesset Commission for Future Generations, *supra* note 17 at 16.

[40] *Models for Protecting the Environment for Future Generations*, *supra* note 34 at 18.

[41] The Knesset, Commission for Future Generations www.worldfuturecouncil.org/fileadmin/user_upload/Maja/Future_Justice_Library/Knesset_Paper.pdf accessed 30 November 2017.

[42] Shoham, *supra* note 1 at 92.

[43] S. Shoham and N. Lamay, 'Commission for Future Generations in the Knesset: Lessons Learnt', in J.C. Tremmel (ed.), *The Handbook of Intergenerational Justice* (Edward Elgar 2006) 244–281.

authority to work, but no guiding principle, which is crucial for such a body to affect change. In this context, the Commission started with an assessment of the political environment to establish one.

Since the politics in Israel are dominated by the survival mentality of *we are obligated to find solutions for today's problems without the luxury of considering tomorrow*, this left the State with a perceived mandate to *put out today's fire while creating those of tomorrow*.[44] One part of the problem, therefore, was rooted in information flows. There was and continues to be a broad amount of knowledge available on topics with which the Knesset is involved, but it does not always find its way to policymakers. Because of this issue, the Commission saw its role in part as bringing this information to policymakers' doors and enabling those individuals in the lawmaking process to become more forward-looking. The Commission saw more broadly a need to adopt future long-term thinking, which might have allowed it to ascertain the impact of legislative processes in the future. The adoption of future thinking would advance long-term planning, and the Commission felt its role should be to establish the practice of creating futures both within the Knesset and the Israeli public at large. For this reason, it was quickly agreed upon that the guiding principles and declared the mandate of the Commission for Future Generations would be:[45]

> Enhancing long-term and sustainable thinking among policymakers and in the State of Israel at large and ensuring that these considerations are included in primary and secondary legislation.

During this process of defining the Commission's mandate and how it should operate, the members settled on three central guiding principles:[46]

- **Scope of effect**: Since theoretically every subject on the Parliament's agenda could impact future generations, the Commission decided to test the scope of effect. Only when the subject discussed promised substantial impacts on the future would the Commission intervene. Because of this, the Commission decided to intervene in topics that had the power to impact lives of a large group of people in a positive or negative way and irrevocably.
- **Effectiveness**: Because of the obligation to use their limited resources optimally, the Commission decided to intervene only in areas in which its involvement would be effective and efficient, although the second condition could not be achieved in all cases. The Commission examined, throughout the entire period of its activity, the probable effectiveness of intervention with respect to every subject under discussion in the Knesset.

[44] Shoham, *supra* note 1 at 103–104.
[45] Ibid.
[46] Ibid. at 104–106.

- **Spectrum of choice**: There have been a lot of questions as to whether the Commission would have the authority to make any kind of decision for future generations and, if yes, where this would come from. Did the Commission have the right to decide what core values they would live by, what their priorities would be, what their urban and rural areas would look like, what kind of water they would drink? They did not have the right or the authority to make these decisions. But as a result, the Commission sought to ensure that future generations would have the broadest spectrum of choices possible. Therefore they defined the Commission's role as 'protecting the scope of this spectrum in the face of political decisions threatening to narrow it'.[47] By working out these principles, the Commission made clear that it is necessary for societies today to leave a wide and differentiated enough spectrum of choices for future generations to create their desired future.

## AN ATTEMPT TO CREATE 'VALUES OF SUSTAINABILITY'

The Commission for Future Generations was authorized to act in policy areas which fell in the three broad areas of society, economics, and the environment. A key element within this was to solve the conflict between short-term development forces and sustainability. Therefore, a policy striving for sustainability required multidimensional planning that took social, economic, and environmental issues and long-term considerations into account, while short-term development was forced to act within the immediate time frame in order to solve 'burning' problems. Furthermore, the act of legislation almost always brought up this conflict, obliging the Commission to consider steps so that the legislation would be sustainable. For the Commission, this concept of sustainability offered a platform of ideas for its work. But before it could adopt this concept in practice, it had to examine its significance for the various policy areas within the Commission's purview, specifically, within the context of what was meant by 'sustainable economics, health, education, scientific development and environment'. Inside the Commission, it began to see legislation focusing on sustainability as a critical tool which was able to help implanting future and long-term thinking into Israel's decision-making process and governmental policy design.[48]

After the Johannesburg Summit in 2002, the Commission worked out a proposed government bill to create a strategic plan for reaching sustainable development,[49] and presented it on 30 January 2003. Likewise, in the Knesset, the Commission pressed for the advancement of a basic law which would raise the issue to the status of constitutional law. Through this, the Commission saw the possibility of creating a

47 Ibid.
48 Ibid. at 107–108.
49 Jávor and Rácz, *supra* note 9 at 106–107.

counterweight to those who opposed sustainable development.[50] Moreover, this bill was intended to establish that all economic, social, and environmental development would be conducted in a sustainable manner, since the UN Joint Plan of Implementation signed in Johannesburg specifically spoke of an institutional framework as a proper way to embed and advance sustainable development at all levels of government. It called for governments to use all available means to embed the principles, specifically mentioning the use of legislation and the rule of law alongside the activity of governmental institutions.[51]

However, certain prominent Israeli politicians were concerned that a basic law on sustainable development could stop the wheels of development. This resulted in a narrower version of the bill than originally intended, but there was still hope that even a merely declarative clear law would be recognized as a principle to be taken into account in setting action priorities. Eventually, the bill was discussed in the Constitution, Law and Justice Committee, but despite wide agreement as to the importance of legislation of this sort, the bill was never passed.

Despite this, the Commission's initiative of a right to sustainability found its way into the map of rights contained in the proposed bill for the Israeli constitution. And even with this early legislative setback, the post-Johannesburg campaign bore fruit. Public conversation started after the idea of embedding the concept of sustainability in government action and the examination of the conflict between development and sustainability, and this brought a new dimension to decision-makers' discussion. Moreover, the new terms 'sustainability, sustainable development, future thinking and concern for future generations' entered public and political conversations and were found in almost every public debate over decisions with long-term significance. This strengthening of the conversation about sustainability in Israel can be seen as a result of the effort and work of the Commission for Future Generations.[52]

## FIELDS OF ACTION: EDUCATION, HEALTH, AND THE ENVIRONMENT

The following section of this chapter focuses on three fields of actions of the Commission for Future Generations – education, health, and environment. Certainly, there were more than nine other topics on which the Commission worked during its five years. Yet, the Commissioner was convinced that having a deeper view in these topics would give the best possible insight in the practical aspect of this kind of body and that it could emphasize the need to establish and maintain such a body in every parliament.

[50] Shoham, *supra* note 1 at 107–110.

[51] UN, *Plan of Implementation of the World Summit on Sustainable Development* (2010) www.un.org/esa/sustdev/documents/WSSD_POI_PD/ENGLISH/ accessed 30 November 2017.

[52] Shoham, *supra* note 1 at 108–109.

### *Education*

As regards education, one of the most popular calls during debates in 2005 over education in Israel was the call to support education reform by giving education a budgetary priority on par with that for infrastructure development. Very soon it was evident that there was a need to make education itself sustainable and to educate our children for sustainability. Therefore, the Commission defined four principles that organized this field.[53]

The Commission for Future Generations defined sustainable education as much more than education for sustainability. Rather, it sought for a new raison d'être of education itself, stating:

> *if sustainable education is education aimed at realization of a world vision, it must nurture creativity in thought and action while, at the same time, facilitate the individual and collective capacity to be proactive.*

The Commission's definition of sustainable education was embedded in the fundamental affirmation of the power of life, whereas mainstream references to sustainable development were grounded in a survivalist mentality. Sustainable education was therefore future-oriented education. Likewise, the Commission saw the cornerstones of sustainable education as the task to render up an intellectual and emotional flexibility to the students and children, and to give them a multidisciplinary, multicultural, and empowering education, as well as an education for creativity. Moreover, the work of the Commission focused on providing for the special needs of youth in primary and secondary education systems in Israel and on the rights of those with special needs to receive support to be integrated within the education system – in the best possible way. For this reason, in 2005 the Commission initiated the project Education 2025, where more than 150 researchers, academics, students, and teachers were engaged to define the kind of education Israel should have by the year 2025.

#### Israel's Future Education System

The Commissioner was a member of the legislation committee for the Dovrat National Task Force in Education, whose mission was to update the education legislation. He helped in drafting the Public Education Law, which would contain the majority of educational legislation and allow Israel's general public to take a more active role in the education system. He sought to integrate equal rights into public education, with the idea that the education system would sow the seeds of the country's future. The Commission established a joint forum with the Israeli Center for Management, in which they reached agreements on goals and developed the wording of a document. In testimony in front of the Knesset's Education Committee, the Commission pressed for more resources to be invested into pre-school education

[53] Ibid. at 112–114.

and therefore in the children's long-term future. Moreover, the Commission recommended creating a legislative framework to cover the rights of talented children, as an important part of the country's future human capital. Eventually the Commission also worked on a document calling for the creation of an authority concerned with strategic thought in education, which would be made up of teachers, students, philosophers, pupils, and experts from the Ministry and academia. But while the Commission was gathering support for this legislation, its tenure came to an end before it could complete its work in this field.

**Child Welfare**

As part of its activities in the area of education, the Commission worked on various levels to advance legislation for the preservation of child welfare and children's rights. It dealt with various subjects in that connection, including the status of minors in criminal proceedings, children, and families and the rights of children in civil procedures. Additionally, the Commission initiated a discussion in partnership with the Committee for the Rights of the Child on the absence of educational frameworks for young children in Arab society, recommending that the Israeli State be part of breaking the cycle of poverty and address the lack of educational opportunities in Arab settlements. In this context, the Commission meant not only certain actions required to improve the situation but also the establishment of a broad day-care infrastructure in Arab settlements.

**Promotion of Youth Involvement in the Democratic Process**

In addition, the Commission was involved in initiatives to familiarize children and young people with governance and the decision-making process that affects their lives, thus strengthening their commitment to the democratic process in Israel. Therefore, the Commission supported the establishment of a youth parliament, with the idea of serving as an advisory council alongside the Knesset. Moreover, it tried to promote public involvement by students in the Tel Aviv school district, developing a model in which young leaders would work with the Knesset and local government figures. Four regional conferences were organized, in cooperation with the educational administration of the city, and children visited the Knesset several times and participated in the activities of the Knesset and its committees. Through this, the young people were given the chance to influence the public agenda from their points of view as young leaders.[54]

### *Health*

With the aim of developing a conception of sustainable health, the Commission focused on advancing preventive medicine. Not only in Israel, but in most of the

54 Ibid.

Western world, national resources are invested in treating morbidity and not in prevention. For example, during the tenure of the Commission, more than 96 per cent of Israel's resources for health and medicine were dedicated to the needs of medicine as a profession, including expenditures on medical services, research, development, and investments in medical technology and infrastructure. The remaining 4 per cent, and in reality even less, of the overall health expenditures were actually allocated to programmes targeting healthy lifestyles or individual health. For this reason, the Commission tried to advance a better balance between health and medicine and chose to advance the issue of health in two areas: the relationship between public health and the environment and strengthening preventive services.[55]

**Public Health and the Environment**

To raise awareness in this area, the Commission worked together with different civil society organizations, public leaders, policymakers, and the medical community in shaping a policy on pollution. The first initiative was targeting air pollution. The Commission called on the Ministry of Environment to replace the 'Industrialists' Treaty', an agreement between the Ministry of Environment and the Industrialists Association in existence since 1986, which constituted nothing more than a voluntary commitment on the part of industrialists to implement standards for discharging pollutants to the air, without the binding power of a law and phrased in vague terms. Obviously, this agreement had little effect in terms of reducing pollution. That is why the Commission, although criticized by the Industrialists and the Ministry, was advocating a clean air act for Israel and initiated a workshop on the topic of clean air legislation in the Interior and Environment Committee of the Knesset. Professor Joel Schwartz from Harvard University, who worked on the US Clean Air Act and who helped on the Israel's Clean Air Act as well, gave a presentation in this session. Eventually, on 16 May 2005, a Clean Air Act for Israel was introduced in the Knesset and signed by forty-seven members. In a second initiative, the Commission convoked a conference on health and the environment at Tel Aviv University, cooperating with the Porter School for Environmental Studies and intended for medical doctors and opinion leaders among them, as well as Israel's decision-makers who were entangled in the topic. After three years of heated debates, the Knesset finally passed Israel's Clean Air Act in 2008.

**Strengthening Preventive Services**

With the aim of advancing preventive medicine, the Commission issued an opinion on a pilot programme to transfer preventive services in ten communities from the Ministry of Health to Health Maintenance Organizations (HMOs). However, the Commission recommended that the programme should be rejected in order

[55] Ibid. at 115–117.

to avert mortal injury to preventive services. On the other hand, the Commission recommended generating long-term thinking on the character of future infant health services. Further topics regarding the strengthening of preventive services were to confront and combat the issue of obesity, which was a serious problem for Israeli society.[56]

## *Environment*

Israel is faced with many difficult and serious environmental problems, which demand appropriate treatments and rapid responses. To give only a few examples: a serious lack of open spaces; pollution of the sea, coastline, water resources, and rivers; pollution from infrastructure, industry, and energy production; noise pollution; an increase in the amount of waste; and radiation. The awareness of environmental problems in Israel is still low, and there is barely any supervision or enforcement of environmental laws. Therefore, the environment became one of the main working areas for the Commission, as it was seen as the core of sustainable thinking.[57]

The Commission for Future Generations created the mindset that a sustainable environment should be an environment which maintains the life within it and leaves a range of resources to sustain the existence of future generations. In this context, the Commission set the creation and promotion of an infrastructure of preliminary legislation for a sustainable environment in Israel as its goal, as well as being intensively involved in the legislative processes addressing the preservation of the environment and natural resources. They tried to focus on different core issues, including health and environment, open spaces, land policy, parks, and coastal policy, as well as the relationship between land, capital, and governance. Two of the Commission's key conditions for intervention – only being involved in areas where there was a clear influence on future generations and in which it saw a way its work could be effective – were commonly satisfied when those issues emerged in parliament. Moreover, the Commission's environmental principles were almost identical to the principles defined at the UN Rio summit in 1992 (and improved in Johannesburg at the 2002 summit). Additionally, the Commission's work ranged inside and outside of Parliament, and involved private sectors. It participated regularly in Knesset committee meetings and conferences on environmental topics, which it also organized, and worked together with environmental organizations and academic authorities to advance the environmental agenda in the press and other media. As a result of all this, the Commission became identified with the theme of environmental defence.

Regarding their environmental projects, the most representative is its work to protect Israel's coastline, which also stands as an example for the deep conflict of

[56] Ibid.

[57] Ibid. at 167–168.

interests between environmental concerns and the driving forces of capitalist society.[58] The Commission was established three years after the first discussion about coastal protection arose. Israel's Mediterranean coast is 197 kilometres long, of which 49 kilometres are closed to the public and designated for security and infrastructure use only. If the approved areas for construction are added to this, only 58 kilometres of open seashore are left for public use. Even this limited coastal land is threatened by the wasteful use of coastal resources, real estate, sewage runoff, pollution of the water and coastline, and the destruction of coastal cliffs. For the Commission, it was clear that Israel needed an unambiguous and immediate plan to stop the destruction of open coastal areas. Legislation on this issue was required, and the need for a comprehensive and responsible law which would oblige the authorities to protect and preserve the coastal environment for future generations was unmistakable. A first private bill was presented to the Knesset in November 1999, formulated by a leading non-profit environmental organization, which emphasized the urgent need for the preservation of the coastal land. The Commission's involvement first began with participation in a committee meeting on 27 May 2002. The bill expressed many of the central principles which were also supported by the Commission. Overall, it found substantial support for these principles. The only pressing issue was the property ownership. The Commission recommended that the coastline should be defined as public property. As a result, the government created its own bill. In the following session, many further conflicts were generated, and the topic of coastal protection went public. Then the private bill that was supported by the Commission was dropped, and the conversations moved on with the governmental bill. In the final version of the bill, after further disputes, the way was paved for the creation of a Committee to Preserve the Coastal Environment (CPCE), but, to the chagrin of the Commission, without any declarative guiding principles like the ones contained in the original bill. On 11 November, the law came into force. Although the Commissioner referred to it as a 'farce' because it contained almost nothing of the original Commission bill, the Commission did not give up and tried to discuss possibilities of passing series of amendments to the law to make it conform to the original one.[59]

From all this, it is clear that the path to instilling future thinking among decision-makers remains a long one and that short-term thinking is still stronger than independent thinking. But there were also indirect successes with the new law, which should not be ignored. Of primary importance is that concern for the needs of future generations and the principles of sustainable development became part of common parlance.

[58] Jávor and Rácz, *supra* note 9 at 106–107.
[59] Shoham, *supra* note 1 at 168–175.

## CREATING A PUBLIC STATUS

Establishing a public status for an institution which was created to act for the interests of a public that did not exist yet was one of the first issues that had to be addressed. For this reason, one of the main responsibilities of the Commission was to raise public awareness in a way that would make an impact on committees discussing legislation and on individual parliamentarians. By exposing the Commission to the media, four main effects were brought about.

First, the Commission started to be appreciated by parliamentarians as an institution which had the power to cultivate public interest in issues. Therefore, the Commission gained recognition as a body within legislative activities. Second, by raising public awareness, people started to show interest in the concept of sustainable thinking and suggested input. Israelis were apparently concerned about the future and saw the Commission for Future Generations as a potential vehicle through which they could express their anxieties, which encouraged the Commission to introduce its parliamentary powers to the public. As a third effect, information – primarily from academia – was directed at the Commission, which lead to a wealth of exploratory research on issues relating to future generations. Eventually, as a fourth effect, the mere expression of the concepts of future generations and future thinking, which had not been introduced to public before, helped these ideas to find a broader footing in public life. To sum up, the media became an important tool for the Commission, allowing it to gather public support, although there were always the voices of both biting criticism and reassuring support.[60]

## ACHIEVEMENTS AND THE IMPACT ON KNESSET'S LEGISLATIVE PROCEEDINGS AND DECISION MAKING

Looking back at a report published by the Commission, it was clear that the activities bore fruit. After five years of operation, the Commission began to implant future thinking within the Parliament, the government, and the public. There was very substantial activity in each of the areas of action for which the Commission was responsible. Furthermore, the impact on Knesset legislative proceedings and on decision-makers in general was significant.

Looking at the achievements of the Commission, successes and fruitful activities worth mentioning might include the *Sustainable Development Bill* (2003); the Israel Clean Air Act; the Clean Air workshop for the Knesset's Committee on the Interior and Environment; the Workshop on the links between health and the environment for the Committee on the Interior and the Environment; the Conference on health and the environment in cooperation with the Porter School of Environmental Studies (University of Tel Aviv); co-launching the national programme for preventing

[60] Ibid. at 106–107; Jávor and Rácz, *supra* note 9 at 96–98.

obesity; establishing a steering committee to deal with the obesity epidemic, including representatives from government offices, the IDF, the HMOs, pediatricians, the Israel Medical Organization, and the Central Parents' Committee; promoting legislation on the topic of excess weight within the framework of the task force of the Ministry of Health (e.g. Amendment of the Ordinance on Public Health, trans fatty acids, the Consumer Protection Act addressing food advertising directed at children); structuring the vision of future education in Israel (Education 2025); promoting legislation on education and children's rights (e.g. Law for Mainstreaming Children with Special Needs; Special Education Law [Amendment No. 7]; hosting the Free Education for Sick Children Law; Public Library Law, Amendment of the Long School Day and Enrichment Studies; Evidence Amendment Law – Protection of the Children); promoting the Fund for Children at Risk, a social insurance bill; examining the national economy and government policies in terms of sustainable development; promoting a balanced development that considers all externalities (direct and indirect) from a macroeconomic perspective and seeks to improve intra- and intergenerational equality; promoting the design of a long-term, future-oriented budget, analyzing how to achieve it and allocating the appropriate resources for this purpose; promoting the State's economy basic law bill (i.e. amendments, budget deliberations, appropriation acts, and reconciliation legislation); promoting the Coastal Preservation Law; advocating in the Knesset the Mediterranean Coast Act (proposed Members' bill) and presenting a paper on the protection, management, and preservation of the coast; and proposing the Preservation of the Coastal Environment Law and initiating a rewording of the amendment to include the coast of the Bay of Eliat.[61]

After the Commission was dissolved in 2010, no other Commission was appointed. But, fortunately, there are other forecasts and assessment models for the physical state of the environment in the future which are further used in the decision-making process. The forecast of these models is based on assumptions regarding the rate of economic growth, globalization, and environmental standards. This scenario-building methodology is meant to assess future possibilities, locate opportunities, and identify risks. A very prominent and leading example is the Israel 2020 Project,[62] a national long-term project prepared by the Technion for the government, which was meant to sketch a combined economic, social, and environmental outlook on Israel's physical development in the twenty-first century and point to policy tools for implementation.[63]

[61] Shoham, *supra* note 1 at 191–198.

[62] Israel Ministry of Foreign Affairs, 'Israel 2020: A New Vision' (1995) 18:2 *Israel Environmental Bulletin* www.mfa.gov.il/MFA/Archive/Communiques/1995/ISRAEL%202020-%20A%20NEW%20VISION%20-%20-May95 accessed 30 November 2017.

[63] A. Mazor, *Israel 2020: Master Plan for Israel in the 21st Century* (in Hebrew) (Samuel Neaman Institute and the Technion 1997); Naama, *supra* note 15.

Furthermore, the Sustainability 2030 Project was the product of cooperation between the Ministry of Environmental Protection and the Jerusalem Institute for Israel Studies. Development of the measures, scenarios, and operative strategies was meant to enable decision-makers in Israel to understand sustainability trends, locate the factors hindering the implementation of a sustainable vision, and identify the paths that should be taken in order to implement it. The scenarios were developed based on expert opinions on a number of central topics, such as commerce and economy, land and space, the water market, the energy market, ecological systems, and sustainable management of raw materials for industry.[64]

## CONCLUSION

With the creation of the Commission for Future Generations in Israel, the Knesset showed courage. Although it did not bring all of the hoped-for change in consciousness within the Knesset, nevertheless the Commission represented a spirited human attempt in the right direction. Several important attempts in bringing bills to the Knesset showed how serious sustainable development was as a goal for the Commission. Furthermore, the success in influencing legislation and bringing a new concept into the legislative realm constituted a unique milestone. Moreover, the creation of a public status not only helped the Commission to gain a voice in the Parliament, but finally the public also gained a voice through which it could express itself and its concerns regarding the future. Although it is very unfortunate that the Commission's first term ended in dissolution, the idea of protecting future generations has been planted and the way for a sustainable development paved.

[64] Sustainability 2030, the project's website www.kayamut2030.org/ (in Hebrew); Naama, *supra* note 15.

# 19

# Norway: Norwegian Ombudsman for Children

*Ole Kristian Fauchald and Elisabeth Gording Stang*

The interests of future generations and the associated concept of sustainable development are closely linked to Gro Harlem Brundtland. Through her leadership of the Brundtland Commission and the report *Our Common Future*,[1] she is widely seen as the main person promoting 'sustainable development' as the key to resolving the world's environmental, social, and economic development challenges. Her government was subsequently instrumental in adopting a provision to protect the interests of future generations in the Norwegian Constitution.[2] Prior to these events, her government became the first in the world to appoint an Ombudsman for Children.[3] The combination of these events illustrates the links between the issues of this chapter – in what ways and to what extent should and has the Norwegian Ombudsman for Children contributed to protection and promotion of the interests of future generations?

While the 'interests of future generations' is frequently associated with environmental sustainability, we will use the concept in a broader sense in this chapter, extending to the three main dimensions of sustainable development: environmental, social' and economic sustainability.[4] Hence, the topic of this chapter is closely related not only to how the Ombudsman has addressed environmental issues as related to

[1] G.H. Brundtland et al., *Our Common Future: Report of the World Commission on Environment and Development* (Oxford University Press 1987).

[2] Brundtland was Norway's Prime Minister during three periods (1981, 1986–1989 and 1990–1996). She had also been a Minister of the Environment (1974–1979). The provision was adopted in 1992, just before the Rio Conference on Environment and Development. The provision was originally adopted as Article 110b and was amended and moved to Article 112 during a major revision of the Constitution in 2014. An English translation of the Norwegian Constitution is available at www.stortinget.no/globalassets/pdf/english/constitutionenglish.pdf accessed 30 November 2017.

[3] The first Ombudsman, Målfrid Grude Flekkøy, was appointed by the Government on 21 August 1981.

[4] See UNGA resolution 66/288, *The Future We Want* (1992).

future generations, but also whether the Ombudsman addresses intergenerational economic and social conditions.

Protecting and promoting the rights of the children that exist today may be viewed as safeguarding the now-living future generation of adults. Investing in children and childhood today – materially, economically, psychologically, legally, culturally' and emotionally – is in fact investing in one future generation's ability to run future societies in a sustainable way. Thus, investing in the children of today is the first step in safeguarding the interests of coming generations. This chapter seeks to look beyond the current generation of children by exploring how and to what extent the Ombudsman for Children seeks to promote longer-term interests of future generations of children.

The Ombudsman for Children Act[5] was prepared in parallel with the first general Norwegian legislation to protect the interests of children,[6] both of which were prepared and adopted concurrently with the negotiation of the UN Convention of the Rights of the Child (CRC).[7] The CRC contains several provisions relating to economic, social, and environmental rights, and Norway's implementation of the CRC has become a key task of the Ombudsman. In the second section of this chapter, we explore how Norway has followed up on these and other obligations and commitments, such as the Rio Declaration on Environment and Development,[8] by contributing to the implementation of the CRC and the interests of future generations in Norway.

Against this background, the chapter examines the mandate of the Ombudsman and associated practices in the third section. The aim is to establish the extent to which it is within the Ombudsman's mandate to promote the interests of future generations and how this element of the mandate has been followed up. On the basis of these findings, the fourth section asks whether there are specific challenges associated with the way in which the Ombudsman is organized that would need to be addressed in order to facilitate a more extensive focus on the interests of future generations in the practices of the Ombudsman. In the concluding section, the chapter sets out some ideas on how the Ombudsman can proceed to strengthen the

5 The Act relating to the Ombudsman for Children, adopted 6 March 1981. An English translation of the original Act as well as the associated Instructions is available at http://app.uio.no/ub/ujur/oversatte-lover/data/lov-19810306-005-eng.pdf accessed 30 November 2017. The current versions of the Act and Instructions are available at http://barneombudet.no/wp-content/uploads/2014/03/ACT-and-instructions.doc accessed 30 November 2017.

6 Act relating to Children and Parents, adopted 8 April 1981, an English translation is available at www.regjeringen.no/en/dokumenter/the-children-act/id448389/ accessed 30 November 2017.

7 Convention on the Rights of the Child, 20 November 1989, 1577 UNTS 3. The UN General Assembly endorsed the initiative of the UN Commission on Human Rights to consider a draft convention on the rights of the child in 1978, see UN General Assembly resolution 33/166. While the objective was to adopt a convention during the International Year of the Child in 1979, negotiators needed another decade to finalize the CRC.

8 UN Doc. A/CONF.151/26 (vol. I), 31 ILM 874 (1992).

work of the Office in terms of promoting the interests of future generations of children.

## LEGISLATIVE REFORM, CHILDREN, AND FUTURE GENERATIONS

Three significant events mark major legislative reform relevant to the interests of future generations in Norway since the appointment of the Ombudsman for Children in 1981: (1) Norway's ratification of the CRC in 1991 and incorporation of the CRC into Norwegian law by the amendment to the Human Rights Act in 2003; (2) the inclusion of protection of the environmental interests of future generations in the Norwegian Constitution in 1992; and (3) the constitutional reforms of 2014–2016, during which inclusion and revision of environmental, social, and economic rights were major issues.

### *Implementation of the CRC*

When Norway ratified the CRC in 1991, not much attention was paid to the need for legislative reform.[9] Such considerations have mainly come up in the context of subsequent more general discussions of how to implement human rights treaties. When the Norwegian Parliament adopted the Human Rights Act in 1999, along with a constitutional amendment, the CRC was not among the treaties that were incorporated through the Act.[10] However, the Parliament asked the Government to return to the issue within a reasonable time.[11] The Ombudsman for Children did not at the time comment on whether the CRC should be incorporated.[12]

It took another four years before the issue was ready for decision by the Parliament. The main discussion concerned whether the CRC should be implemented through incorporation, transformation, or both.[13] Despite the hearing document suggesting that the CRC be implemented through transformation, the conclusion of the Government on the basis of the hearing was to use incorporation. The Government also used the occasion to propose amendments to five acts,[14]

[9] The assessment of need for legislative reform was limited to articles 37c and 40 of the CRC, and concerned in essence the need for entering reservations upon ratification, see St.prp.no.104 (1989–1990) 4–6.

[10] Act relating to the Strengthening of the Status of Human Rights in Norwegian Law (1999). An English translation of the original version is available at www.jus.uio.no/ior/personer/vit/olefa/dokumenter/lov-19990521-030-eng.pdf accessed 30 November 2017.

[11] Ot.prp. no. 45 (2002–2003) 20–21.

[12] Ot.prp. no. 3 (1998–1999) 27–31.

[13] Ot.prp. no. 45 (2002–2003) 21–26.

[14] The amended acts were the following: The General Civil Penal Code (1902), Act relating to Mediation and Procedure in Civil Disputes (1915), Act relating to Procedure in Cases concerning the Public Administration (1967), Act relating to Adoption (1986), and Act relating to Child Welfare Services (1992). Ot.prp. no. 45 (2002–2003) 64–65 contains the Government's

amendments that arguably should have been adopted when Norway ratified the CRC in 1991.

The CRC is based on four main principles: the prohibition of all forms of discrimination (Article 2); the principle of the best interest of the child (Article 3); the right to life and survival for the child (Article 6); and the right to participation of the child (Article 12). While these four principles emphasize individual rights, they may relate to the interests of future generations as defined here. For example, the best interest principle and the right to participation must be an integrated part of the process of local political decisions in planning for new buildings, roads, playgrounds, schools, or other changes in children's physical environment. During such processes, which result in decisions that have significant implications for future generations, children are entitled to be given the right to express their views. The right to participation makes it possible for children to have a voice in political processes that affect the conditions of future generations.

Although most of the rights included in the CRC are individual rights that should be implemented in the direct interest of the existing generation of children, there are several provisions of the CRC that concern longer-term efforts to ensure the interests of future generations. Such provisions, which essentially encompass economic, social, and environmental rights, include Articles 3.2 (ensuring protection and care necessary for the child's well-being), 24 (the child's enjoyment of the highest attainable standard of health), 26 (the child's ability to benefit from social security), 27 (a standard of living adequate for the child's physical, mental, spiritual, moral, and social development), and 28 and 29 (education).

The Optional Protocol to the CRC on a communications procedure was adopted in December 2011 and entered into force in April 2014.[15] The Protocol allows children, or others acting on their behalf, to submit complaints to the CRC Committee after having exhausted national remedies. Despite significant initiatives of the Ombudsman to encourage Norway to ratify,[16] Norway has not yet done so. The reluctance of Norway to ratify the Protocol may be indicative of a general concern regarding human rights complaints procedures, as well as reflecting more specific concerns regarding compliance with all aspects of the CRC.[17] One issue

discussion of the amendments. See also the critical comment of the Ombudsman for Children regarding lack of implementation of the CRC as one of the reasons why the treaty had been invoked in few cases, ibid. at 22.

[15] Adopted by the Human Rights Council, 14 July 2011, A/HRC/RES/17/18.

[16] See Barneombudet, Årsrapport 2012, 10.

[17] Resolution adopted by the UNGA on 19 December 2011 [on the report of the Third Committee (A/66/457)], 66/138. Optional Protocol to the Convention on the Rights of the Child on a Communications Procedure, 27 of January 2012. The Parliament requested that the Government present a proposal for ratification during 2015, see Innst. 24 S (2014–2015). The Government proposed not to ratify the Protocol. The Parliament agreed and stated as its main reason uncertainty regarding the interpretation of the CRC by the Committee. A proposal to request that the Government reassess ratification on the basis of an assessment of future

that remains unresolved is whether the mandate of the Ombudsman will be revised so that it can pronounce on individual complaints or in some way be given a role to support children when they use domestic remedies.

## *The Interests of Future Generations in the Constitution*

The new provision on environmental rights that was added to the Norwegian Constitution in 1992 states that:

> Every person has the right to an environment that is conducive to health and to a natural environment whose productivity and diversity are maintained. Natural resources shall be managed on the basis of comprehensive long-term considerations which will safeguard this right for future generations as well.

While the first sentence is formulated as a right, the second sentence is phrased in terms of a duty, without clarifying who are the duty-bearers. The general formulation indicates that the duty is directed to both public authorities and private parties. The duty reflects the general principle that the current generation is to be regarded as the guardian or trustee of natural resources and the environment to the extent that these are important for the environment-related health, productivity, and biological diversity of future generations.

One way in which this provision has been followed is by including references to 'sustainable development' and the interests of future generations in almost all recent legislation related to natural resources.[18] However, questions can be raised regarding the effectiveness of initiatives to follow up such provisions. Except for some previous efforts at engaging the responsibility of other authorities, the Ministry of Climate and Environment has not followed up such legislative provisions in any significant manner beyond the field of climate change policy.[19] In general, the Ministry has

practice of the Committee was rejected. See Meld. St. 39 (2015–2016) and Innst. 161 S (2016–2017).

[18] See, of particular interest: the Local Government Act (1992), the Gene Technology Act (1993), the Act relating to Land (1995), the Act relating to the Protection of the Environment in Svalbard (2001), the Aquaculture Act (2005), the Forestry Act (2005), the Planning and Building Act (2008), the Marine Resources Act (2008), the Nature Diversity Act (2009), and the Minerals Act (2009). Two noteworthy exceptions are the Act relating to Petroleum Activities (1996) and the Water Resources Act (2000). English translations of Norwegian these acts are available at http://app.uio.no/ub/ujur/oversatte-lover/english.shtml accessed 30 November 2017.

[19] The early efforts include a series of seven reports from the Government to the Parliament between 1997 and 2007: St.meld. no. 58 (1996–1997); St.meld. no. 8 (1999–2000); St.meld. no. 24 (2000–2001); St.meld. no. 42 (2000–2001); St.meld. no. 25 (2002–2003); St.meld. no. 21 (2004–2005); St.meld. no. 26 (2006–2007). However, these reports vary significantly as to the extent to which they address the responsibility of authorities other than the Ministry of Climate and Environment. Only one report examines the responsibilities of other authorities in a systematic manner: St.meld. no. 42 (2000–2001) on biodiversity. Numerous reports have been produced on the Government's climate policy, some of which include significant sections

ignored the constitutional provision on environment.[20] Moreover, the main institution set up to oversee the Government's duty to follow up decisions of the Parliament, the Office of the Auditor General, which has produced a large number of reports on environmental and sustainability issues, frequently cites general legislative clauses setting out the objective of the relevant legislation but hardly ever refers to the constitutional clause.[21] The failure of relevant institutions to follow up the clause was a main reason why the Parliament amended the provision in 2014 as part of the general constitutional reform.[22]

## *Constitutional Reforms*

One major function of a constitution is to ensure long-term respect for and achievement of fundamental rights. Hence, it is an essential instrument for securing and promoting the interests of future generations. Some of the above-mentioned social and economic rights were included in the Norwegian Constitution during a general constitutional reform that started with the adoption of a series of amendments in May 2014. One of the major discussions during the reform was in what ways and to what extent constitutional protection should extend to economic, social, and cultural rights.[23] Extending rights to future generations, which is closely related to the concept of 'collective rights',[24] was not discussed during the reform process beyond the link made between children's rights and the interests of future generations,[25] and the discussion of environment-related rights.[26]

The reform has resulted in the adoption of two provisions of particular interest concerning the rights of children: the duty to create conditions that provide adequate economic, social, and health conditions for children (Article 104[3]) and the right to education (Article 109). The reform also included an amendment of

on the responsibilities of other authorities, most recently Meld. St. 21 (2011–2012) on Norwegian Climate Policy.

20 See O.K. Fauchald, 'Forfatning og miljøvern – en analyse av Grunnloven § 110 b', 120(1–2) *Tidsskrift for rettsvitenskap* (2007) 1–84; see also Innst. 187 S (2013–2014) 25–26.

21 Examples of reports that follow up legislative provisions include Document 3:9 (2011–2012) 32 on aquaculture and Document 3:17 (2011–2012) 37 on forestry. As regards the constitutional clause, see O.K. Fauchald, 'Hva er konsekvensene av Grunnlovens miljøparagraf?' (2015) 200 *PrivIus Journal of Private Law* 30–31.

22 Innst. 187 S (2013–2014) 25.

23 Ibid. at 2–4 and 12–17.

24 See St. Document 16 (2011–2012) 47.

25 Ibid. at 186.

26 Ibid. at 237 and 242–246 and Innst. 187 S (2013–2014) 25. Other issues regarding the interests of future generations were that inclusion of rights in the Constitution would be to the benefit of future generations (St. Document 16 [2011–2012] 61), and the concern that detailed rights in the Constitution could inappropriately limit available choices of future generations (St. Document 16 [2011–2012] 62 and 90, St. Document 12: 31 [2011–2012] 198, and Innst. 187 S [2013–2014] 4).

interest to Article 110 concerning labour rights by adding the following: 'Those who cannot themselves provide for their own subsistence have the right to support from the state.' Among the proposals that did not receive sufficient support to be adopted was the right to a decent standard of living (proposal for Article 111).[27]

The Parliament also adopted amendments to the environmental clause (Article 112). The amendment made clearer the duty of public authorities to implement the rights by changing the wording of the final paragraph from '[t]he State authorities shall issue further provisions for the implementation of these principles' to '[t]he authorities of the state shall take measures for the implementation of these principles'. Despite the amendment, recent developments indicate that the Ministry of Climate and Environment, the Government, and even the Parliament remain reluctant to follow up on the amendment.[28]

## THE NORWEGIAN OMBUDSMAN FOR CHILDREN AND FUTURE GENERATIONS

> We may give children a good reason to feel that they are part of the solution to problems regarding environmental degradation and climate change, and give them the opportunity to come forward with their opinions.[29]

The constitutional and legislative reforms since the establishment of the Ombudsman in 1981 indicate increased emphasis on protection and promotion of the interests of future generations at a general level. However, the way public authorities have followed up the reforms seem inadequate in many respects, and there exists no well-established framework to ensure effective implementation of policies to protect the interests of future generations. Against this background, there has been significant room for the Ombudsman for Children to act in support of the interests of future generations based in particular on the CRC and the new and amended constitutional provisions.

[27] St. Document 12: 31 (2011–2012) 199 and 203–205 and Innst. 187 S (2013–2014) 23–25.

[28] The Government adopted revised Instructions for Official Studies and Reports on 19 February 2016, in which the reference to the constitutional clause and to environmental issues were left out, see www.regjeringen.no/en/dokumenter/Instructions-for-Official-Studies-and-Re/id107582/ (the former Instructions, in English) accessed 30 November 2017; www.regjeringen.no/no/dokumenter/instruks-om-utredning-av-statlige-tiltak-utredningsinstruksen/id2476518/ (the new Instructions, no translation available) accessed 30 November 2017. See also O.K. Fauchald, 'Plikt til å utrede miljøkonsekvenser av lovgivning', in H.C. Bugge, H. Indreberg, A. Syse, and A. Tverberg (eds.), *Lov, Liv og Lære. Inge Lorange Backer 70 år*, (Universitetsforlaget 2016) 187–200.

[29] Norwegian Ombudsman for Children, Anne Lindboe and the Secretary General of World Wild Fund of Nature Norway, Nina Jensen, 'Det er dine unger, det er vår planet' ('It's Your Kids, It's Our Planet'), *Dagbladet* 24 March 2015 (authors' translation).

### *The Background and Mandate of the Ombudsman*

The idea of an Ombudsman for Children was launched in 1969 by late professor of criminal law Anders Bratholm.[30] Professor Bratholm's suggestion was later followed up by the commission preparing the Act relating to Children and Parents in its 1977 report.[31] Interestingly, one main task that the commission pointed out as central for the new Ombudsman was to secure children's interests in land planning processes and decisions regarding the localization of industry.[32]

The Ombudsman was originally appointed by the Government for a term of four years with the possibility of reappointment, but is currently appointed for six years and cannot be reappointed (Section 2 of the Act).[33] Despite the Government's power to appoint the Ombudsman, his/her office is an independent institution (Section 6 of the Act). Her Office employs twenty people of different backgrounds, including lawyers, psychologists, and sociologists.[34]

The Ombudsman Act and the Instructions for the Ombudsman for Children of 1981 (adopted in the form of a Government regulation) define the mandate of the Ombudsman.[35] Section 3 of the Ombudsman Act states (unofficial translation):

> The duties of the Ombudsman are to promote the interests of children *vis-à-vis* public and private authorities and to follow up the development of conditions under which children grow up.
>
> In particular the Ombudsman shall:
>
> (a) On own initiative or as a hearing instance protect the interests of children in connection with planning and study-reports in all fields,
> (b) Ensure that legislation relating to the protection of children's interests is observed, including if Norwegian law and administrative routines are in accordance with Norway's obligations according to the UN convention on the Rights of the Child,
> (c) Propose measures that can strengthen children's safety under the law,

30 A. Bratholm, *Umyndige personer* (Universitetsforlaget 1969) 103–104. The background of the establishment of the Ombudsman is further elaborated in Bratholm's speech at the twenty-fifth anniversary of the Ombudsman, as reproduced in the Ombudsman's annual report for 2006: Barneombudets årsrapport (2006) 18.

31 NOU 1977:35 Lov om barn og foreldre (barneloven) (The Act Relating to Children and Parents).

32 NOU 1977:35, 99. See also NOU 1995:26 Barneombud og barndom i Norge (The Ombudsman for Children and Childhood in Norway) 17.

33 All the four Ombudsmen appointed prior to 2009 were reappointed. These include Målfrid Grude Flekkøy (1981–1989), Trond Viggo Torgersen (1989–1996), Trond Waage (1996–2004), and Reidar Hjermann (2004–2012).

34 See http://barneombudet.no/ accessed 30 November 2017.

35 See *supra* note 6.

> (d) Put forward proposals for measures that can solve or prevent conflicts between children and society,
> (e) Ensure that sufficient information is given to the public and private sectors concerning children's rights and measures required for children.
>
> The Ombudsman may act on own initiative or at the request of other people.
>
> The Ombudsman for Children himself decides whether an application offers sufficient grounds for action.

The Instructions do not contain further rules of interest regarding the Ombudsman's mandate beyond a statement in Section 1 that '[t]he Ombudsman does not have the authority to decide cases or set aside decisions in the administration'.

Section 3 of the Act does not define the term 'conditions under which children grow up'. The specific tasks listed in the second paragraph indicate that a broad range of 'conditions' may be relevant, including social, economic, and environmental.[36] Moreover, the focus in the second paragraph of Section 3 on general policy measures indicates that satisfactory conditions shall be safeguarded in the long term. The reference to the CRC, which was added in 1998, and the reference to legislation imply that social, economic, and environmental rights shall be safeguarded. It can therefore be concluded that it is within the Ombudsman's mandate to criticize policies that are contrary to and recommend measures to promote the interest of future generations in all three dimensions of sustainable development.

To what extent the Ombudsman not only has a mandate but also a duty in these regards is less clear. The translation of Section 3 of the Act is misleading in this regard, as the Norwegian text refers to the 'tasks' (in Norwegian '*oppgaver*') of the Ombudsman rather than the 'duties' (in Norwegian '*plikter*'). The extent of the duties of the Ombudsman must therefore be determined by interpreting the provision in light of other provisions in the Act and Instructions. The starting points are that the Ombudsman 'takes up cases on his own initiative or at the request of other people' (Section 2 of the Instructions) and that he or she 'decides whether an application offers sufficient grounds for action' (Section 3 *in fine* of the Act). Hence, the Ombudsman enjoys significant discretion when deciding how to follow up the mandate. Nevertheless, it can be argued that where environmental, social, or economic conditions are deteriorating or are likely to deteriorate to an extent that future generations of children will suffer significantly or disproportionately, the Ombudsman fails to fulfil the tasks if choosing not to act. Under such circumstances it can be argued that the Ombudsman has a duty and not merely a mandate to act. The following are examples where there are strong arguments that the Ombudsman has such a duty.

Among the Ombudsman's most important tasks is to monitor the implementation of the CRC. The Committee on the Rights of the Child carries out reviews of

[36] See also the reference to 'all areas of society' in section 1 of the Instructions. Moreover, the reference to municipal planning and location of industrial activities in the preparatory works of the Act indicate the relevance and importance of environmental issues. See *supra* note 33.

national reports on the status of children's rights in the member states,[37] and it falls within the mandate and duty of the Ombudsman to play an important role in contributing to and reviewing the reports.

The focus on health in Articles 104 and 112 and the Constitution and the Article 24 of the CRC is particularly important in terms of long-term sustainability issues. The scope of Article 24 of the CRC is broad. The provision is closely related to Article 12(2)(a) of the UN Covenant on Economic, Social and Cultural Rights, which provides for the duty to take 'steps … necessary for … the healthy development of the child'. The General Comment adopted by the Committee on Economic, Social and Cultural Rights in 2000 stresses that the highest attainable standard of health 'is not confined to the right to health care'. The right embraces

> a wide range of socio-economic factors that promote conditions in which people can lead a healthy life, and extends to the underlying determinants of health, such as food and nutrition, housing, access to safe and potable water and adequate sanitation, safe and healthy working conditions, and a healthy environment.[38]

The provisions contained in the Constitution and the treaties are relevant to the impact of environmental and social conditions on children's health. An increasing number of Norwegian children suffer from asthma, allergies, poor air quality, and noise. Many children grow up in areas without appropriate access to nature and associated health benefits. High concentrations of chemicals in products and the environment trigger allergic reactions in children, and high levels of noise affect children's development. As is demonstrated by the 2007 adoption of a ten-year national strategy to improve children's environment and health, such issues need to be addressed through systematic and long-term policies.[39] However, as is shown in a recent report covering the status and risks associated with air pollution, noise, and chemicals in products in a Norwegian context, the strategy has not been successful in resolving these concerns.[40] Such issues are within the core of the Ombudsman's mandate and there is arguably a duty for the Ombudsman to address them.

More broadly, Article 104 of the Constitution and Article 6 of the CRC cover children's right to development. It ensures children's survival and ability to realize

37 Norway has submitted five reports to the UN Committee on the Rights of the Child; 2016, 2008 (CRC/C/NOR/4), 2003 (CRC/C/129/Add.1), 1998 (CRC/C/70/Add.2) and 1993 (CRC/C/8/Add.7).

38 General Comment No 14, *The Right to the Highest Attainable Standard of Health (Art. 12)* (2000), E/C.12/2000/4, para. 4.

39 Ministry of Health and Care Services, Barnas framtid – Nasjonal Strategi for barn og unges miljø og helse 2007–2016.

40 See Folkehelseinstituttet, *Barn, miljø og helse. Risiko- og helsefremmende faktorer* (2016) 69-83. An English summary of the report is available at www.fhi.no/en/mp/children-and-adolescents/childhood-family-and-well-being/childrens-health-and-the-environment—risk-and-health-promoting-factors—/ accessed 30 November 2017.

the full development of their personality, materially and spiritually.[41] The right to life, survival, and development for the individual child is necessarily strongly linked to future generations of children's survival and development, as well as to how the national and global political responsibility for effective measures securing sustainable development is exercised. Moreover, the right to education as set out in Article 109 of the Constitution and Article 29 of the CRC shall, *inter alia*, be directed to the development of respect of human rights and the principles enshrined in the Charter of the UN, the development of respect for national values and for civilizations different from their own, and the preparation of the child for responsible life in a free society, as well as the development of respect for the natural environment. Such broader issues associated with children's long-term prospects for development and education also fall within the core of the Ombudsman's mandate and are arguably covered by a duty to act.

The above elements of the Ombudsman's mandate are directly and indirectly relevant to the interests of future generations in all three dimensions of sustainable development. It is clear that the short-term fulfilment of such rights are within the Ombudsman's core mandate and that the Ombudsman has not only a right but also duty to act where such rights are seriously threatened. The recent constitutional reforms and the role of the Ombudsman in the implementation of the CRC are important reasons why the Ombudsman's duties in this regard arguably extend to future generations.

### *The Practice of the Ombudsman*

Since it was created in 1981, the activities of the Ombudsman for Children have been primarily documented through annual reports. This assessment of the extent to which the Ombudsman has contributed to the promotion of sustainable development and the interests of future generations is essentially based on studies of these reports. For the purposes of this inquiry, the activities of the Ombudsman have been divided into five main categories: (1) specific cases dealt with by the Ombudsman subsequent to communications from the public; (2) statements of the Ombudsman in the context of public hearings; (3) policy initiatives initiated by the Ombudsman; (4) general projects initiated by the Ombudsman; and (5) the Ombudsman's activities in relation to the CRC.

### *Specific Cases*

The main means for the Ombudsman to determine topics deserving particular attention has been to solicit the opinion of children. The challenge of establishing

[41] S. Detrick, A *Commentary on the United Nations Convention on the Rights of the Child* (Martinus Nijhoff 1999) 131.

good links of communication with children has varied over time. A significant proportion of the communications, in particular in the early years, came from parents and other adults. In order to increase communications from children, the Ombudsman established various platforms of communication, including free phone message services, radio and TV shows, and websites and various social media. The first major change in the ratio between communications from children and adults took place in 1990. The ratio had been approximately 1:10 during the first decade but changed to approximately 1:3 in subsequent years. The change, which has persisted with some variation over time, seems to be the combined result of the establishment of an arrangement for free telephone messages as part of the initiative 'Klar melding', and the appointment of a new Ombudsman (Trond Viggo Torgersen), who was well known to children as an artist and TV celebrity.

In order to identify general concerns and issues in need of the Ombudsman's attention, the approach has essentially been to encourage all kinds of submissions and to systematize them into categories. The reports of the Ombudsman have varied significantly in whether and how they categorize individual communications. Moreover, when categories are used, it is generally hard to determine the extent to which the Office receives communications relating to sustainable development, environmental issues, and the interests of future generations. Hardly any of the categories that have been used by the Ombudsman mention the environment or directly mention social or economic inequality.[42] The reports of the Ombudsman indicate that environment-related issues were more important among the communications in the early years than more recently.[43] A major change seems to have taken place in the early 1990s. At the beginning of the 1990s, when communications from children and youth increased significantly, one of the four main topics children focused on was the environment.[44] However, such issues more or less disappeared in 1992 and have not reappeared.[45] In more recent years, there seems to be an increase in communications of relevance to social inequity, such as health, drugs, alcohol, and violence.[46] Hence, while the political engagement of children and youth in political parties and environmental NGOs demonstrate that they have significant concerns regarding the future of the planet and the interests of future generations,[47]

[42] Two reports mention environmental issues as a major concern, see Barneombudet, Årsmelding 1990, 11, and Barneombudet, Årsmelding 1991, 6.

[43] Among the six subject areas used in the first years of the Ombudsman's reports (1982–1992) were 'culture and consumption' and 'planning and administration'. See also concerning children as consumers in Barneombudet, Årsrapport 2000, 17. The subject areas introduced and used since 2009 include only one category of some interest: 'health', but a closer reading of the reports indicate that focus has not been on environment-related health issues.

[44] See Barneombudet, Årsmelding 1990, 11 and Barneombudet, Årsmelding 1991, 6.

[45] See Barneombudet, Årsmelding 1992, 6.

[46] See Barneombudet, Årsrapport 2011, 4–5 and the reports in subsequent years.

[47] Relevant NGOs organized by children and youth in Norway are Nature and Youth https://nu.no/english accessed 30 November 2017, and Spire http://spireorg.no/english accessed 30 November 2017. Norwegian political parties have their respective 'youth parties', many of

this is not reflected in the Ombudsman's list of concerns expressed in the communications. It seems that children do not perceive the Ombudsman as a relevant institution for such concerns.

While the Ombudsman thus can claim to be soliciting children and youth and focusing on the concerns they raise, it can also be argued that the content of communications depends significantly on how the Ombudsman is perceived among children and others. The way that the Ombudsman systematizes and responds to communications is most likely a major driver in terms of shaping the perception of the Office among potential communicators. Hence, low numbers of communications concerning the environment and structural social and economic inequity is not necessarily a sign that such concerns are less important among children and youth, but may also be the result of choices and priorities of the Ombudsman.

## *Participation in Hearings*

The Ombudsman has generally listed all or the most important statements it has submitted in hearing processes in its annual reports. During the first two decades, the Ombudsman focused significantly on land planning issues, and such issues have remained on the agenda of the Ombudsman until quite recently.[48] Among the achievements of particular interest are the establishment of 'children's representatives' in planning cases at the municipal level during the early 1990s,[49] and the adoption of national guidelines to safeguard the interests of children in planning.[50] However, despite initiatives to strengthen children's interests in planning processes in the revised Planning and Building Act prepared during the 2000s, the rules and guidelines remained unchanged in the new Act.[51]

Beyond engagement in cases concerning land planning, the Ombudsman has only on very rare occasions engaged in hearings concerning environmental

which are generally regarded as having more 'progressive' views on environmental and social issues. Norwegian schools have organized voting in the context of general elections. Reports since 2001 show that significantly more school students than adults voted in favour of political parties with a particularly strong environmental profile (SV, V, and MDG) in every election. On average, 13.4 per cent of adults voted for these parties in the eight general elections during the period, compared to 19.9 per cent among school students.

[48] See, in particular, Barneombudet, Årsmelding for 1982, 36–41; Barneombudet, Årsmelding for 1983, 44–45 and 52–53; Barneombudet, Årsmelding 1989, 8 (summing up the achievements of the first Ombudsman); Barneombudet, Årsmelding 1994–1995, 63–64; Barneombudet, Årsrapport 2001, 8, Barneombudet, Årsrapport 2003, 7–8, Barneombudet, Årsrapport 2009, 16–17.

[49] See sections 3-3 and 5-1 of the Planning and Building Act (2008 no. 71) and St.meld. no. 39 (2001–2002) 44–47.

[50] See Rikspolitiske retningslinjer for å styrke barn og unges interesser i planleggingen (20 September 1995). The first such guidelines were adopted in 1988, see Barneombudet, Årsmelding 1987, 24, and Barneombudet, Årsmelding 1988, 13.

[51] See notes 50 and 51.

protection.[52] Examples where the Ombudsman has participated in hearings concerning legislation and policy initiatives regarding exploitation and management of natural resources have not been found. The Ombudsman has been more active in providing input to legislation and policies concerning health, economic, and social issues which could be of importance in a long-term sustainability perspective.[53] However, in recent years the Ombudsman's initiatives to strengthen children's interests seem to have moved in the direction of individual rights rather than broader systemic issues regarding social inequities.[54]

One issue of particular interest has been the Ombudsman's engagement in Norway's implementation of the CRC. The Ombudsman started work on the CRC before its adoption.[55] When Norway presented its first report to the Committee on the Rights of the Child, the Ombudsman sent a letter to the Committee commenting on Norway's treatment of refugee children and presented the views orally to the Committee.[56] The same year, the Ombudsman was central in establishing the Forum for the CRC among relevant Norwegian NGOs and interested individuals for which the Ombudsman acted as the secretariat.[57] Section 3 of the Ombudsman Act was amended in 1998 to ensure that the Ombudsman examines whether Norwegian law and administrative routines are in accordance with Norway's obligations, and the Ombudsman followed the procedures for Norwegian reporting to the Committee the same year.[58] Subsequently, the Ombudsman has produced separate reports to the Committee on the Rights of the Child in parallel with Norwegian reports.[59] The first such report in 2005 was brief and the only issue addressed by the Ombudsman of interest here related to inequalities and poverty due to differences in social security in municipalities. The second report from the Ombudsman in 2009 was much more elaborate and focused on most main aspects of the CRC, including Articles 3, 24, and 27–29. The main issues of relevance here concerned differences in health due to social conditions (Article 24), poverty among children (Article 27), and access to and

[52] The Ombudsman has on occasions participated in hearings concerning local pollution and outdoor recreation. See Barneombudet, Årsrapport 2004, 6 and Barneombudet, Årsrapport 2009, 16–17.

[53] Examples include child poverty (Barneombudet, Årsrapport 2009) 10 and commercials directed at children (Barneombudet, Årsrapport 2008) 10.

[54] See the Ombudsman's references of the most important statements in public hearings set out in its annual reports since 2010.

[55] Barneombudet, Årsmelding 1986, 113.

[56] Barneombudet, Årsmelding 1994–1995, 43–44.

[57] Ibid. at 44–45. See also http://forumforbarnekonvensjonen.no/ accessed 30 November 2017.

[58] Barneombudet, Årsrapport 1998, 13. On this occasion, the Forum for the CRC produced a supplementary report to the Committee for the Rights of the Child.

[59] The 2009 report is available at http://barneombudet.no/english/publications/ accessed 30 November 2017. A Norwegian version of the first report is available at http://barneombudet.no/for-voksne/barnekonvensjonen/rapportering-til-fns-barnekomite-i-geneve/ accessed 30 November 2017. The Forum for the CRC (note 58) submitted separate reports.

the psychological and physical environment of education (Article 28).[60] The Ombudsman has spent significant resources on following up the recommendations from the Committee on the Rights of the Child vis-à-vis Norwegian authorities.[61] Norway submitted its combined fifth and sixth reports to the Committee in October 2016, and the Ombudsman is at this juncture participating in preparing a joint 'shadow report' together with NGOs.

### *Policy Initiatives*

One of the most important policy initiatives of the Ombudsman has been the promotion of an act to safeguard and promote the physical and social environment of children.[62] However, the initiative proved unsuccessful and was shelved during the 2000s.[63] As a follow-up, the Ombudsman worked actively to promote legislation to improve children's physical environment, with a focus on schools and kindergartens.[64]

Another significant initiative has been to promote the participation of children in decision-making processes, which is reflected by the attention paid by the Ombudsman to Article 12 of the CRC in its annual reports.[65] The early initiatives focused on participation in land planning.[66] Subsequent initiatives include the creation of a fund to support projects to be determined by children,[67] the Ombudsman's focus on the 'competent child',[68] the creation of an 'Internet

60 The Ombudsman for Children in Norway, Supplementary Report to the UN Committee on the Rights of the Child (2009) 21–23.

61 See e.g. Barneombudet, Årsrapport 2009, 12 and Barneombudet, Årsrapport 2011, 8.

62 See Barneombudet, Årsmelding 1982, 20; Barneombudet, Årsmelding 1983, 6, 19, 29–30 and 46–47; Barneombudet, Årsmelding 1985, 48–49 (labelled a 'Constitution for Children'); Barneombudet, Årsmelding 1986, 12, 19–20, 21 and 27–28; and Barneombudet, Årsrapport 2000, 4–5 and 19–20.

63 See St.meld. no. 39 (2001–2002) which represented the Government's thorough and broad discussion of and plans for addressing children's interests. Despite the initiatives of the Ombudsman, the document does not discuss the idea of adopting a separate act to safeguard and promote children's physical and social environment. Only one political party supported the idea of such an act, see Innst. S. no. 282 (2002–2003) 23.

64 Barneombudet, Årsrapport 2003, 10; Barneombudet, Årsrapport 2004, 9–10; Barneombudet, Årsrapport 2005, 9; and Barneombudet, Årsrapport 2007, 16.

65 See e.g. Barneombudet, Årsrapport 1999, 11, and Barneombudet, Årsrapport 2006, 7.

66 See Barneombudet, Årsmelding 1991, 16, and Barneombudet, Årsmelding 1993, 12–13. The duty to appoint a representative for children in planning at the municipal level was added to Section 9-1 of the Planning and Building Act (1985) in 1993. Prior to this arrangement, children were allowed to have a representative in the council responsible for land planning issues. On challenges associated with the functioning of the representative, see Barneombudet, Årsrapport 2004, 8; Barneombudet, Årsrapport 2006, 8–9; and Barneombudet, Årsrapport 2008, 13.

67 'Barneombudets fremtidsfond', Barneombudet, Årsmelding 1989.

68 Barneombudet, Årsrapport 1998, 2–3.

Parliament',[69] initiation of a 'Youth Council',[70] voting rights of 16 year olds in municipal elections,[71] and the establishment of a national parliament for youth.[72] Such initiatives have made it possible for children to raise general issues of interest to future generations. It has not been possible to systematically examine the extent to which such issues have been raised through the initiatives promoted by the Ombudsman, but the annual reports of the Ombudsman indicate that such issues have not been important.

Finally, since 2012 the Ombudsman has sent letters to public authorities regarding issues of particular concern. Such letters address urgent situations that require attention in the short to medium term or issues of general interest. Few such letters have directly concerned long-term issues of interest to future generations.[73]

### *Projects*

From an early stage, the Ombudsman regarded the generation of reliable information and data about children as an important task, and the Office regularly produced factual reports,[74] and contributed to facilitate research activities.[75] Moreover, many of the initiatives to promote children's participation in decision-making processes have been project-based and essentially conducted by the Ombudsman.[76]

In recent years, the working procedures of the Ombudsman have become increasingly project-oriented.[77] The current Ombudsman initiated a process to elaborate visions for the Office once she was appointed in 2012.[78] The vision statement of the Ombudsman for 2012–2018 contains twenty-one long-term goals, none of which is directly related to the interests of future generations. Nevertheless, a number explicitly concern the implementation of the CRC,[79] and some concern long-term

69 Barneombudet, Årsrapport 1999, 8 and Barneombudet, Årsrapport 2000, 11–13.

70 Barneombudet, Årsrapport 2006, 8.

71 Barneombudet, Årsrapport 2010, 7.

72 Ibid. and Barneombudet, Årsrapport 2011, 10.

73 Examples include health issues among youth (Barneombudet, Årsrapport 2013), access of children to public hearings of the Ministry of Climate and Energy, and amendments to the Constitution (Barneombudet, Årsrapport 2014).

74 Barneombudet, Årsmelding 1992, 15–16; Barneombudet, Årsmelding 1994–1995, 25–26; Barneombudet, Årsrapport 1998, 13; Barneombudet, Årsrapport 1999, 2 and 12; Barneombudet, Årsrapport 2000, 3; Barneombudet, Årsrapport 2001, 2; Barneombudet, Årsrapport 2004, 10; and Barneombudet, Årsrapport 2011, 6.

75 Barneombudet, Årsmelding 1986, 66–67; Barneombudet, Årsmelding 1994–1995, 25–28 and 60–61; Barneombudet, Årsmelding 1996, 6; Barneombudet, Årsmelding 1997, 8; Barneombudet, Årsrapport 2006, 8; and Barneombudet 2007, 7–8.

76 See notes 68, 70, 71, and 73.

77 See Barneombudet, Årsrapport 2011, 7 and subsequent reports.

78 See Barneombudet, Årsrapport 2012, 9–10.

79 Ibid. at Goals 1, 2, 4, 15, 17, 18, and 21.

health-related problems,[80] the welfare of vulnerable groups,[81] and education.[82] The goal that is most clearly relevant to the environment and management of natural resources states that the municipalities shall use the CRC in planning and decision-making processes and indicators shall be applied to measure achievements.[83]

The vision statement has been followed up through the annual selection of focus areas from the list of goals, and by reporting on relevant activities in the annual reports. One such project carried out in 2013–2014 concerned children and health. While this project did address some long-term social and economic issues, environment-related issues were absent.[84] The focus on project-based work and longer-term achievements could strengthen the Ombudsman's work in the interest of future generations.

## *Conclusions*

The mandate of the Ombudsman covers the interests of future generations. This has been reinforced in recent years through constitutional amendments. The practice of the Ombudsman is mixed in terms of fulfilling this part of the mandate. On the one hand, the Ombudsman is expected to take care of the short-term concerns voiced by children and others on their behalf. On the other hand, it was clear from the outset that the Ombudsman also needed to address broader and longer-term context and work towards systemic changes. Our examination of the practice indicates that the focus has been significantly affected by the priorities of at least four of the five Ombudsmen that have served so far.[85] Generally, the practice reflects the need to strike an appropriate balance between short-term and longer-term functions of the Ombudsman.

This discussion of the Ombudsman's practice has identified how and to what extent there has been a focus on and contribution to the interests of future generations. The findings presented indicate that contributions have mostly been in the fields of social and economic sustainability and much less, and decreasingly so, in the field of environmental sustainability. In particular, the limited and decreasing contribution of the Ombudsman to environmental sustainability is puzzling given the state of the environment and the associated engagement of children and youth. Further, the Ombudsman has not explicitly addressed the interests of future

80 Ibid. at Goals 5 and 6.
81 Ibid. at Goals 7, 8, 11, and 14.
82 Ibid. at Goal 10.
83 Ibid. at Goal 15. See also CRC art. 3 and GC/C/CRC/14, paras. 30 and 32.
84 Barneombudet, Årsrapport 2013, 8. See also *supra* note 43.
85 This is the case for the first four Ombudsmen, see Barneombudet, Årsmelding 1989 (the appointment of Trond Viggo Torgersen), Barneombudet, Årsmelding 1996 (the appointment of Trond Waage), and Barneombudet, Årsrapport 2004 (the appointment of Reidar Hjermann). The appointment of Anne Lindboe seems to have had less immediate impact on the priorities of the Ombudsman, see Barneombudet, Årsrapport 2012.

generations – such interests have only been addressed implicitly. Against this background, there is significant room for the Ombudsman to strengthen and make more explicit contributions to the interests of future generations. This would be in accordance with the Ombudsman's task to contribute to the implementation of the CRC.

## ADDRESSING THE CHALLENGES OF PROMOTING INTERESTS OF FUTURE GENERATIONS

Taking care of the interests of future generations requires the Ombudsman to focus on political and legal reform. It also requires the Ombudsman to be able and willing to enter into a dialogue with political decision-makers with the objective of affecting their long-term policy choices. This represents two major challenges for the Ombudsman which will be further discussed here – availability of resources and being perceived as a political actor.

### *Resources and Priorities*

The Ombudsman was originally promoted by political parties to the left of the political spectrum. Just as the Ombudsman Act had been adopted, there was a change in government to the Conservative Party, which had voted against the Act and promised during the election campaign to abolish the Ombudsman.[86] The funding of the Ombudsman was not increased during the first decade, and the Office only had four employees including the Ombudsman.[87] A significant increase in resources had to wait until the early 1990s, when the Office expanded to nine permanent employees. A second major expansion came in the late 2000s when the Office expanded from twelve to a maximum of twenty employees, not including project-based staff. In recent years, the permanent staff has been scaled back to seventeen. Both periods of expansion occurred under left-leaning governments.[88]

Another aspect of the availability of resources has been the formal working and reporting requirements that the Ombudsman is subject to.[89] The first major change in this respect started with the adoption and elaboration of 'result goals' in the budget decisions regarding the Ombudsman in the mid-1990s.[90] In 1999, the Ombudsman voiced significant dissatisfaction with the situation and stated that new

[86] Barneombudet, Årsmelding 1989, 3.

[87] The first complaints regarding resources can be found in Barneombudet, Årsmelding 1986, 6–7 and Barneombudet, Årsmelding 1987, 26–27.

[88] The governments headed by Gro Harlem Brundtland (3) and Jens Stoltenberg (2).

[89] The issue was on the table already in 1987, when the Ombudsman issued a simplified report due to lack of resources, see Barneombudet, Årsmelding 1987, 6–7.

[90] This started with St.prp. no. 1 (1992–1993) Barne- og familiedepartementet 48 and was significantly expanded in St.prp. no. 1 for 1997–1998 Barne- og familiedepartementet 87.

administrative tasks have been assigned to the Ombudsman without being accompanied by expanded resources.[91] A second major change started in 2007, when the Ministry of Children and Family Affairs announced that it had established a new Department to strengthen the Ministry's governance of three institutions including the Ombudsman.[92] Subsequent reports of the Ombudsman, starting in particular in 2010, show that the Ombudsman has been asked to report on a number of internal governance related issues, including based on user surveys.[93] As can be seen, increases in the resources of the Ombudsman have been followed by stricter formal working and reporting requirements. Hence, increased resources seem at least to some extent to be offset by more resource intensive working and reporting requirements. Overall, this examination of the practice of the Ombudsman has found no important correlation between the availability of resources and the Ombudsman's priority of issues associated with the interests of future generations.

### *Independence: The Ombudsman as a Political Actor*

Neither the Government nor the Parliament can instruct the Ombudsman in specific cases, and the Ombudsman has emphasized that the Office shall be 'politically neutral' in the sense of maintaining its neutrality in relation to political parties.[94] The administrative affiliation of the Ombudsman with the Ministry of Children and Equality is of a formal character. Nevertheless, the affiliation means that the Ministry can influence the Ombudsman's implementation of the mandate. There is clear evidence that this occurred in the period between 1993 and 2006 when the Ministry's budget proposals contained detailed statements regarding the prior and future implementation of the Ombudsman's mandate.[95] During the following decade, however, the budget proposals were much less detailed, and the opinion of the Ombudsman seems to have been essential in defining tasks to be undertaken.[96] Nevertheless, in recent years the Ministry seems to influence the Ombudsman through other less

91 Barneombudet, Årsrapport 1999, 5 and 15. See also Barneombudet, Årsrapport 2001, 11.

92 St.prp. no. 1 (2007–2008) Barne- og likestillingsdepartementet 23–24, currently the Department of Child Welfare Services.

93 See Barneombudet, Årsrapport 2010, 10–13. See also Barneombudet, Årsrapport 2015, 24, where resource issues reappear as a major concern of the Ombudsman.

94 See NOU 1995:26, 67 and Prop. 1 S 2015–2016 Barne-, likestillings- og inkluderingsdepartementet 113. See also Barneombudet, Årsrapport 2014, 15.

95 See St.prp. no. 1 (1992–1993) Barne- og familiedepartementet, 48 and St.prp. no. 1 (2005–2006) Barne- og familiedepartementet, 90–91. Statements in the Ombudsman's annual report for 1999 are particularly critical of the Ministry's tendency of governing the office, Barneombudet, Årsrapport 1999, 5 and 15.

96 The current budget practice was introduced by St.prp. no. 1 (2006–2007) Barne- og likestillingsdepartementet 72. For a recent example underlining this approach, see St.prp. no. 1 (2014–2015) Barne-, likestillings- og inkluderingsdepartementet 127. See, however, Prop. 1 S 2015–2016 Barne-, likestillings- og inkluderingsdepartementet 113 where the Ministry has 'rephrased' the Ombudsman's mandate.

visible channels such as budgetary letters[97] and regular meetings between officials of the Ministry and the Ombudsman.[98] Criticism has been raised concerning the affiliation of the Ombudsman with the Ministry, and some have argued that the Ombudsman should be administratively placed directly under the Parliament, as is the case for the Parliamentary Ombudsman.

One major crisis in the history of the Ombudsman occurred in 2008 when the Government was faced with the choice between reappointment of the current Ombudsman or nominating a new person. Despite a consistent practice of reappointments, the Government chose to appoint a new Ombudsman. However, when it appeared that there were close links between the Minister of Children and Family Affairs and the new candidate, the new candidate withdrew her candidacy, the newly appointed Minister left her office, and the current Ombudsman was reappointed.[99] At the time, many speculated about whether the Government had been dissatisfied with the Ombudsman because of criticisms of the Government's policy. Nevertheless, a proposal to reorganize the Ombudsman so that it would be placed directly under the Parliament was rejected by the majority of the Parliament in 2008.[100]

When considering the Ombudsman's interest and ability to act in the interest of future generations, the above organizational aspects are important. The Ombudsman faces a general challenge when determining how to allocate resources and attention. One such challenge is to strike a balance between the focus on individual cases ('users') and on general long-term systemic change needed to safeguard the interests of future generations. Engagement in individual cases is likely to be perceived as the Ombudsman performing 'services' to 'users', while issuing opinions on general policy measures needed for long-term sustainability can easily be perceived as interfering with political processes and being problematic from the perspective of the political neutrality of the Ombudsman. In the latter situations, the Government may perceive statements of the Ombudsman as critical to its policy or proposals. If the Government only has the support of a parliamentary minority, it may be particularly sensitive to critical statements owing to its need for support from other parties in the Parliament. Against this background, it is

[97] Budgetary letters are made available from 2011 at www.regjeringen.no/no/dokument/dep/bld/tildelingsbrev-2/tildelingsbrev_og_aarsrapporter/id2355719/ accessed 30 November 2017.

[98] Ibid. at 8. The subheading used for these meetings ('styringskalender') indicates that they are intended as a means for the Ministry to influence the activities of the Ombudsman. See also note 99.

[99] See press releases from the nominated Ombudsman www.regjeringen.no/no/aktuelt/ida-hjort-kraby-trekker-seg-fra-stilling/id500666/ accessed 30 November 2017 and from the Minister www.regjeringen.no/no/aktuelt/manuela-ramin-osmundsen-gar-av/id500664/ accessed 30 November 2017.

[100] This decision was at least partly based on a letter from the Ministry where it concluded that the current arrangement was unproblematic, see Innst. S. no. 35 (2008–2009) 4–8.

problematic that the Ministry has the possibility of influencing the Ombudsman's ability and interest in focusing on long-term policy-oriented issues.[101]

## CONCLUSION

The background of the Ombudsman, being appointed by a government headed by a prime minister who subsequently became the world's main promoter of sustainable development, should raise expectations that the Ombudsman will promote the interests of future generations. Such expectations are reinforced by the failure of Norwegian authorities to give high priority to implementing international and domestic obligations and commitments to promote the interests of future generations. However, this chapter shows that the Ombudsman has promoted the interests of future generations of children only to a limited extent and only implicitly, and that this essentially has occurred as a side effect of efforts to safeguarding the interests of the current generation.

While the chapter shows that the Ombudsman's contribution to the interests of future generations does not seem to have depended entirely or essentially on the availability of human and economic resources, it can still be found that access to such resources would be important for the Ombudsman's ability and willingness to address such issues in the future. More importantly, we find that the links between the Ombudsman and the Ministry of Children and Equality is likely to constitute a significant factor affecting the Ombudsman's ability and willingness to promote the interests of future generations. Even if the Ombudsman has proved to be relatively resilient to the influence of the Ministry, the broad range of means by which the Ministry may influence the Ombudsman and the costs to the Ombudsman in resisting constitute a major argument in favour of reconsidering the Ombudsman's affiliation with the Ministry.

The most important factor affecting the Ombudsman's approach to the interest of future generations is the priorities of the Ombudsman and the staff of the Office. The visions and goals identified by the current Ombudsman combined with broader awareness of the more systemic consequences of effective implementation of the CRC may provide the Ombudsman with a more solid basis for addressing the interests of future generations. It appears that the Ombudsman should pay more attention to Norway's implementation of Articles 3.2, 24, and 26–29 of the CRC, and do so from a longer-term perspective. In Article 4, the CRC includes a relative obligation for the states parties to implement the CRC at the level of their available resources with regard to 'economic, social and cultural rights'. States parties shall

[101] See, for example, Tildelingsbrev til Barneombudet 2016, 3 and 5 where the Ministry 'rephrases' the mandate of the Ombudsman and instructs the Ombudsman to carry out an evaluation of how 'users' experience the Ombudsman, assess measures that should be taken to improve its 'services', and to report to the Ministry through its annual report for 2016 on the measures taken or to be taken.

undertake all appropriate legislative, administrative, and other measures 'to the maximum extent of their available resources and, where needed, within the framework of international co-operation'. By implication, a developed country like Norway should base its legislation and policies on a high standard for implementing economic and social rights.

Further, the new and amended constitutional provisions – Articles 104, 109, 110, and 112 – require active follow-up by the Government and Parliament. So far, public authorities, courts, parliamentary control mechanisms, and the Parliament itself have paid very limited attention to such provisions when proposing and adopting legislation, budgets, and policies. There is significant need for independent review of how these provisions are implemented in the interest of future generations. The Ombudsman for Children should see the constitutional reforms as an opportunity to strengthen its contribution to the living conditions of future generations of children.

# 20

# Institutions for a Sustainable Future: The German Parliamentary Advisory Council on Sustainable Development

*Franz Reimer*

This chapter gives an outline of the Parlamentarische Beirat für nachhaltige Entwicklung (Parliamentary Advisory Council on Sustainable Development, PACSD) of the German '*Bundestag*' (Federal Parliament). Before exploring the creation, functions, and effectiveness of this institution, fairly unknown even in Germany itself, it sketches the development of ecological consciousness and environmental law in Germany as well as the constitutional context. This leads to an analysis of the strengths and the weaknesses of the Parliamentary Advisory Council. The chapter ends with a short legislative outlook and forecast. For the sake of clarity, it should be mentioned at the outset that since Germany is a highly industrial country with a long history of environmental problems the German perspective on sustainability stresses the ecological, rather than the economic or social, dimensions which in turn is mirrored in the work of the PACSD.

## ENVIRONMENTAL PROBLEMS AND ENVIRONMENTAL LAW IN GERMANY

By and large, environmental problems as objects of public attention and state legislation can in Germany be phased in four periods.[1] The first one concerns local environmental problems such as deforestation, water pollution, or air pollution causing obvious sicknesses to neighbours. This is the time of single pieces of environmental law *avant la lettre*. For instance, when growing industrialisation led to intense air pollution in certain hot spots in the nineteenth century, an early piece of environmental legislation was enacted following the French prototype under which the duty to obtain a permit to build and run certain harmful industrial facilities was imposed. This was the nucleus of modern German emission control law (and is still the heart of

[1] For a more detailed account, M. Kloepfer, *Zur Geschichte des deutschen Umweltrechts* (Duncker & Humblot 1994).

the Federal Emmission Control Act codified in 1974). At the same time, in the mid nineteenth century, the public perception of nature started to change from threat to treasure. Consequently, the first legal steps were taken to protect natural monuments or particular areas. It took, however, more time before legislation to protect landscape and nature was enacted. Although, in 1919, article 150 of the Constitution of the German Reich (Weimar Constitution) addressed the topic (Artistic, historical and natural monuments and the landscape enjoy state protection and care), it was only in 1935 that the Nature Conservation Act came into effect (replaced in 1976 and in 2009).[2] This epoch of nature conservation can be seen as the second phase of environmental law in Germany. When regional environmental problems – such as a greyish sky above agglomerations such as the Ruhr area – became visible or tangible in the 1960 and 1970s, the 'environment' became part of the political agenda, and legislation accelerated. In 1971 the Leaded Petrol Act was enacted, followed quickly in 1972 by the Federal Waste Removal Act,[3] in 1974 by the above-mentioned Federal Emission Control Act,[4] as well as the Federal Environment Agency Act,[5] and in 1976 by the Federal Nature Conservation Act[6] and the Waste Water Charges Act.[7]

In the 1980s, acid rain and *Waldsterben* (forest decline) boosted both public awareness and political activism in the field of environmental protection.[8] It is this third period which is often seen as the founding era of German environmental law. It should be noted, however, that at this very moment the process of Europeanisation of German environmental law starts.[9] It has transformed German environmental law by way of its integrative and procedural approach.[10] By now, the bulk of environmental legislation in Germany is European, either induced by European directives or consisting in European regulations.

[2] Act on Nature Conservation and Landscape Management (Federal Nature Conservation Act – BNatSchG) of 29 July 2009. www.bmub.bund.de/fileadmin/Daten_BMU/Download_PDF/Naturschutz/bnatschg_en_bf.pdf accessed 28 October 2016.

[3] Circular Economy Act 2012 www.bmub.bund.de/fileadmin/Daten_BMU/Download_PDF/Abfallwirtschaft/kreislaufwirtschaftsgesetz_en_bf.pdf accessed 28 October 2016.

[4] Federal Immission Control Act (2013) www.bmub.bund.de/N1912-1/ accessed 28 October 2016.

[5] For the German version, cf. www.gesetze-im-internet.de/ubag/BJNR015050974.html accessed 28 October 2016.

[6] Act on Nature Conservation and Landscape Management (Federal Nature Conservation Act – BNatSchG) of 29 July 2009 www.bmub.bund.de/fileadmin/Daten_BMU/Download_PDF/Naturschutz/bnatschg_en_bf.pdf accessed 28 October 2016.

[7] Promulgation of the Amendment to the Waste Water Charges Act of 18 January 2005 www.bmub.bund.de/fileadmin/Daten_BMU/Download_PDF/Binnengewaesser/abwag_engl.pdf accessed 28 October 2016. Note that the Federal Water Act dates back to 1957.

[8] Kloepfer, *supra* note 1 at 81–137.

[9] As one of the early European norms see the Council Directive 79/409/EEC of 2 April 1979 on the conservation of wild birds [1979] OJ L 103/1.

[10] See the Environmental Impact Assessment as imposed by the Council Directive 85/337/EEC of 27 June 1985 on the assessment of the effects of certain public and private projects on the environment [1985] OJ L 175/40; now Directive 2011/92/EU [2011] L 26/1.

The fourth phase – the phase of internationalisation – has its rationale in global environmental problems such as the depletion of the ozone layer or global warming. Accordingly, German environmental law transfers and concretises many international agreements or, indeed, EU law concretising international agreements. Amongst the most dynamic fields of German law is what has been dubbed Climate Protection Law (*Klimaschutzrecht*), including the law of renewable energies and energy efficiency law. In other words, there is a close-knit network of environmental legislation both of substantive and of procedural nature, though without almost any reference to 'sustainability',[11] and the state of the environment in Germany has, generally speaking, improved over the years. Amongst the remaining challenges are land consumption, release of nitrogen compounds, carbon dioxide emissions, and traffic noise.

## THE CONSTITUTIONAL CONTEXT

In substantive constitutional law (i.e. in the Basic Law),[12] while 'sustainable development' is neither mentioned by name nor implicitly incorporated as such, important aspects are touched upon. In the jurisdiction of the Constitutional Court, from article 2 section 2 of the Basic Law ('Every person shall have the right to life and physical integrity') flows a duty of all branches of public power to protect everyone's life and physical integrity. However, since Parliament has a wide margin of appreciation over how to discharge this duty, the duty and the corresponding individual right has had no far-reaching consequences, particularly in the field of environmental protection. The same is true for the constitutional objective (*Staatsziel*) of 'social state' in article 20, which has had little impact in the field of protection of the environment. Instead, its application has in the past focused on present social needs rather than future needs, such as intergenerational justice.[13] Therefore, in 1994 a pertinent clause was inserted in the Constitution at a prominent position. Article 20a of the Constitution reads:

> Mindful also of its responsibility toward future generations, the state shall protect the natural foundations of life and animals by legislation and, in accordance with law and justice, by executive and judicial action, all within the framework of the constitutional order.

[11] For example, only brief mention was made of the sustainability principle in Circular Economy Act 2012, s 6(2); sustainability as a requirement for biofuels in Federal Immission Control Act, ss 37a et seqq.

[12] Since the European Treaties form part of the constitutional order ('Verfassungsverbund') in Germany, arts. 6 and 191 TFEU as well as art. 37 ECHR should briefly be mentioned, as well as the pertinent clauses in the Länder constitutions (e.g. art. 26 of the Hessian Constitution).

[13] Wolfgang Kahl, 'Staatsziel Nachhaltigkeit und Generationengerechtigkeit' (2009) 62:2 *Die Öffentliche Verwaltung* 3.

This clause enshrines the sustainability principle[14] in its ecological dimensions.[15] It is an integral part of constitutional law and therefore takes part in the supremacy of the Constitution. As another 'constitutional objective', it addresses the legislative, the executive, and the judiciary functions. Taking into account the explicit gradation in the wording of the article as well as the legislature's wide margin of appreciation, Parliament certainly has the first and foremost responsibility to implement the objective and decide on matters of protection of the environment. Maybe owing to the ecological activism of the German legislature, the effect of Article 20a has mainly been symbolic. Nevertheless, laws falling short of minimum ecological requirements could be annihilated by the Federal Constitutional Court for not being compatible with Article 20a, and the evident failure of Parliament to legislate could equally be declared unconstitutional. What is more, all branches of federal, state, and local government have to take into consideration the requirements of Article 20a in their everyday work, particularly when using their discretionary powers. This is subject to far-reaching judicial review by the administrative courts, although of course neither plants nor animals have a standing, and collective action remains the exception in the German system.[16] Nevertheless, the constitutional objective of environmental protection appears to have its main relevance as a sword of Damocles.

This brief and necessarily incomplete sketch would be all too fragmentary if it did not at least make reference to two fields in which questions of sustainability have been intensely discussed during the last years in Germany: suffrage and debts. Whereas article 38(2) of the Basic Law states that '[a]ny person who has attained the age of eighteen shall be entitled to vote; any person who has attained the age of majority may be elected', it has been repeatedly pointed out that this excludes approximate 20 per cent of the German population from voting. Consequently, diverse models of children's, youths', and family suffrage have been, and still are, discussed,[17] in part explicitly as a means of ensuring intergenerational justice or sustainability.[18] It is highly controversial whether or not an amendment of the constitution introducing family suffrage (for example a parental proxy voting allowance) would violate the Constitutional cornerstone of article 79(3) of the Basic

[14] *Federal Constitutional Court, ruling of 13 March 2007*, 1 BvF 1/05, BVerfGE 118, 79 [110].

[15] D. Murswiek in M. Sachs (ed.), *Grundgesetz Kommentar*, 7th edn. (C.H. Beck 2014) art. 20a marg. no. 37; G. Deter, '"Nationale Nachhaltigkeitsstrategie" und Grundgesetz' (2012) 23 *Zeitschrift für Umweltrecht* 157, 160. The explicit incorporation of the principle of sustainability – as proposed in the 16th electoral period (see the motion Bundestag printed papers 16/3399 of 9 November 2006) and recently demanded by experts in a PACSD hearing on 20 May 2015 – would probably not make a big difference, vide infra.

[16] For example, the Federal Nature Conservation Act 2009 (2009) art. 64.

[17] As a recent contribution, see C. Schickhardt, 'Kinder im Wahlrecht und in Demokratien. Für eine elterliche Stellvertreterwahlpflicht' (2015) 2:1 *Zeitschrift für Praktische Philosophie* 191–248 www.praktische-philosophie.org/schickhardt-2015.html accessed 28 October 2016.

[18] See e.g. F. Reimer, 'Nachhaltigkeit durch Wahlrecht?' (2004) 35 *Zeitschrift für Parlamentsfragen* 322.

Law,[19] and equally, there is no political consensus as to the reasonableness of the different models.

Given the social and economic dimensions of sustainability, the Constitutional provision concerning budget management (both in the Federation and in the Länder) should at least be mentioned.[20] Article 109(3) of the Basic Law in its present wording states '[t]he budgets of the Federation and the Länder shall in principle be balanced without revenue from credits' and further elaborates the conditions of public borrowing. According to article 115(2) '[r]evenues and expenditures shall in principle be balanced without revenue from credits'; again the following detailed provisions concretise this maxim. Since 'sustainability needs institutions',[21] article 109a states that '[t]o avoid a budgetary emergency, a federal law requiring the consent of the Bundesrat shall provide for: 1. the continuing supervision of budgetary management of the Federation and the Länder by a joint body (Stability Council)'. The introduction of these rules has been justified, *inter alia*, by the notion of intergenerational justice.[22] They are, however (as will be seen instantly), almost irrelevant for the work of the PACSD.

Given that Parliament is the first addressee of the Constitutional objective of environment protection but the Constitutional Court is reluctant to interfere with Parliament's margin of appreciation, the *process* of legislation and its institutional framework is of paramount importance. The legislative procedure is mainly governed by two codes: the rules of procedure of Parliament (*Geschäftsordnung des Deutschen Bundestages*) and the Joint Rules of Procedure of the Federal Ministries, which prepare the majority of bills. While the Rules of Procedure of Parliament at present only require bills to have 'a short explanatory memorandum',[23] but do not contain specific provisions as to their sustainability (let alone codify the PACSD), there are at least hints in the Joint Rules of Procedure of the Federal Ministries. Its provisions refer, *inter alia*, to the preparation of norms on the Federal level in rules 40–76.

As far as bills drafted by the Federal Government are concerned, rule 43 contains a detailed list of topics to be covered in the statement of grounds attached to the bill and it includes a presentation of the results of the impact assessment (*Gesetzesfolgen*). This impact assessment is regulated in rule 44. The requirements include a presentation as to whether the effects are compatible with sustainable

[19] Arguing for compatibility with the constitution see ibid. For arguments against see H. Meyer, 'Wahlgrundsätze', in J. Isensee and P. Kirchhof (eds.), *Handbuch des Staatsrechts*, Vol. 3, 3rd edn. (C.F. Müller 2005) para. 46 marg. no. 11.

[20] For the constitutional *status quo ante* see T. Hebeler, 'Nachhaltigkeit im Haushaltsrecht', in K. Lange (ed.), *Nachhaltigkeit im Recht. Eine Annäherung* (Nomos 2003) 265, 266.

[21] T. Schomerus, 'Nachhaltigkeit braucht Institutionen – zur Institutionalisierung von Nachhaltigkeitsräten' (2011) 33 *Natur und Recht* 1, 7.

[22] Bundestag printed paper 16/12410, 6; the printed papers are accessible at http://dipbt.bundestag.de/doc/btd/16/124/1612410.pdf accessed 28 October 2016.

[23] See rule 76 (2): 'Bills must, motions may, be accompanied by a short explanatory memorandum.'

development, and which long-term effects the bill will have[24] under rule 44 (1)(4) – a provision inserted in 2009[25] following a proposal of the PACSD. The sections are applicable not only to bills but also to government ordinances (*Rechtsverordnungen*) and in part even for regulations (*Verwaltungsvorschriften*) so that the requirement of a sustainability impact assessment has quite a broad scope of application. It should in this connection be noted that amendments to the German Constitution are made by way of legislation (*verfassungsändernde Gesetze*) so that bills amending the Basic Law are equally subject to the sustainability assessment.[26] As will be seen in more detail, a meta-assessment of this regulatory impact assessment is the most important competence of the PACSD. Since the Parliamentary rules of procedure contain provisions about the committees (where the bulk of the parliamentary work is done)[27] and about the treatment of bills but no requirements whatsoever concerning impact assessments, or indeed the PACSD, there is gap between the two rules of procedures.

## THE INSTITUTIONAL CONTEXT

To give a rough picture of the institutional setting, mention should be made of some of the actors with competencies in the field of sustainability at federal level.[28] Within Parliament, there are – to name but three – the Committees on Economic Cooperation and Development, on Education, Research and Technology Assessment, and on Environment, Nature Conservation, Building and Nuclear Safety. Committees can be defined as specialised parliamentary bodies formally preparing decisions of the Parliament and the PACSD does *not* pretend to be a committee in this narrow sense. Although a subdivision of Parliament with a certain role in legislation, its tasks mainly concern the relationship towards the Federal Government.

On the government level, there are, *inter alia*, the Federal Ministry for the Environment, Nature Conservation, Building and Nuclear Safety and, as subordinated authorities – though with considerable factual independence – the Federal Environment Agency (*Umweltbundesamt*), as a major official think tank, and the Federal Agency for Nature Conservation. Again and again, the Federal Environment Agency, on the basis of internal or external research, suggests amendments of environmental law rules but does not itself draft bills. The German

24 'Es ist darzustellen, ob die Wirkungen des Vorhabens einer nachhaltigen Entwicklung entsprechen, insbesondere welche langfristigen Wirkungen das Vorhaben hat', rule 44 (1).

25 Joint Ministries' Official Journal (GMBl) 2009, 690.

26 See e.g. Bill amending the Basic Law (art. 91b), Bundestag printed paper 18/2710.

27 This includes the option of public ad hoc hearings, cf. rule 70 of the Bundestag Rules of Procedure.

28 For information about sustainability councils on Länder and local government levels see Schomerus, *supra* note 22 at 4–5.

Advisory Council on the Environment (*Sachverständigenrat für Umweltfragen*), consisting of seven external experts – currently all of them university professors in different subjects ranging from zoology to law – submits an Environmental Report to the Federal Government every four years and from time to time issues special reports on particularly relevant topics. The German Advisory Council on Global Climate Change (*Wissenschaftlicher Beirat Globale Umweltveränderungen*) was set up in 1992 by the Federal Government.[29] Its main task is 'to periodically assess global environmental change and its consequences and to help all institutions responsible for environmental policy as well as the public to form an opinion on these issues'.[30] To make the confusion complete, there is a Council for Sustainable Development (*Rat für nachhaltige Entwicklung*) established in 2001 by the Federal Government. Consisting of fifteen personalities from all strands of life (such as economics, churches, universities), it is meant to advise the government and stimulate a dialogue within society. Neither the German Advisory Council on the Environment nor the Council on Global Climate Change nor the Council on Sustainable Development, however, have a mandate in the official process of legislation; this is a unique feature of the PACSD.[31] The last entity to be mentioned here is the State Secretaries' Committee [or board] for sustainable development (*Staatssekretärsausschuss für nachhaltige Entwicklung*), which coordinates the work of the Federal Ministries concerning sustainability. In particular, it implements and further develops the 'Sustainable Development Strategy' of the Federal Government. This strategy is based on four guidelines: intergenerational equity, quality of life, social cohesion, and international responsibility.[32] This strategy, however, is also part of the PACSD's agenda (see below).

## CREATION AND FUNCTIONS OF THE PARLIAMENTARY ADVISORY COUNCIL

The PACSD was established for the first time in 2004 during the 15th electoral period (2002–2005).[33] In the absence of a statute governing the PACSD, its legal basis are recurrent parliamentary decisions, to be taken anew in every electoral

[29] German Advisory Council on Global Change, Joint Decree on the Establishment of the Council of April 8, 1992 www.wbgu.de/en/about-us/decree-of-establishment/ accessed 28 October 2016.

[30] See ibid. at art. 1.

[31] Bodies with far reaching constitutional powers have been discussed but not introduced. As a model, J. Rux, 'Der ökologische Rat – Ein Vorschlag zur Änderung des Grundgesetzes mit Begründung', in Stiftung für die Rechte zukünftiger Generationen (ed.), *Handbuch Generationengerechtigkeit*, 2nd edn. (ökom 2003) 471–490.

[32] For details see Federal Government, *Sustainability* www.bundesregierung.de/Webs/Breg/EN/Issues/Sustainability/_node.html accessed 28 October 2016.

[33] For basic information in English see Deutscher Bundestag, *Parliamentary Advisory Council on Sustainable Development* www.bundestag.de/en/committees/bodies/sustainability accessed 28 October 2016.

period.[34] These decisions define the goal, composition, and functions of the PACSD for the respective electoral period. The most recent establishment decision (taken unanimously by parliament on 20 February 2014)[35] defines as the PACSD's goal 'to monitor and assist[36] the sustainability policy of the Federal Government at parliamentary level in a suitable and multidisciplinary way'.[37] It is then stated that the PACSD has seventeen members coming from all factions.[38] For its procedure, the provisions for Parliamentary committees are taken as applicable, and the PACSD itself later adopted a special code of procedure. The decision explicitly assumes that the Parliamentary committees' constitutional right to require the presence of any member of the Federal Government (Article 43(1) of the Basic Law) is equally applicable.

More elaborately, the objectives of the PACSD in the actual electoral period are (quoted in full):

> parliamentary monitoring and support of the Federal Government's National Sustainability Strategy, in particular in relation to continuing to develop the indicators and objectives, setting and specification of measures and instruments to implement the sustainability strategy and dovetailing important policy approaches of relevance to sustainability; parliamentary monitoring and support of the Federal Government's sustainability policy at European level, in particular of the European Strategy for Sustainability; parliamentary monitoring and support of the Federal Government's sustainability policy at the level of the United Nations, in particular the activities and measures as part of the Rio follow-up process.

In connection with this, there are several functions, including monitoring and supporting consultations and discussions in other bodies of the German Bundestag related to sustainable development by being able to present opinions and recommendations to the lead committee in question for consideration in the discussions; examining other priority issues which affect sustainable development and are suited to promoting the process of sustainable development and if necessary submitting recommendations to the Bundestag or the Federal Government accordingly; and evaluating the Federal Government's sustainability impact assessment. The PACSD shall present the lead committee in each case with the result of its evaluation as an opinion, which must be discussed by the lead committee and appraised in writing; parliamentary monitoring and support of the activities of the State Secretaries Committee on Sustainable Development at the Federal Chancellery and other institutions created at the level of the Federal Government on sustainable

[34] Bundestag printed papers 15/2441 of 9 January 2004; 16/1131 of 6 April 2006; 17/245 of 16 December 2009; 18/559 of 19 February 2014.

[35] Bundestag plenary session protocol 18/17, 1319.

[36] The German term *begleiten* can mean monitor, supervise, and/or assist.

[37] Bundestag plenary session protocol 18/17, 1319.

[38] The composition is eight CDU/CSU, five SPD, two DIE LINKE, and two BÜNDNIS 90/DIE GRÜNEN.

development, in particular the Council for Sustainable Development; and staying in contact with and consulting other institutions to promote sustainable development, in particular with other national parliaments, the Länder and the institutions of the EU.[39]

The implicit mission is to spread the concept of sustainable development amongst the members of Federal Ministries, Parliament, and the public.[40] It is therefore somewhat of an understatement that the PACSD calls itself a parliamentary 'watch-dog' in issues concerning future generations,[41] since its overall tasks are not only negative, but also positive, and it has, within its objectives, a far-reaching right to take up an issue on its own initiative.

## THE PACSD'S APPRAISAL OF THE SUSTAINABILITY ASSESSMENT IN PARTICULAR

Probably the most important, though clearly limited, of these objectives is an evaluation of the Federal Government's sustainability impact assessment. As sketched above, the bills drafted by the government (comprising roughly two-thirds of all bills) and the draft government ordinances have to be checked and reasoned, *inter alia*, as to their sustainability. This impact assessment is in turn to be appraised by the PACSD. The substantive basis for this appraisal is the catalogue of Management Rules, Indicators, and Goals of the Federal Government's National Sustainable Development Strategy.[42] In their short form, they read as follows:

### Management Rules

(1) Golden rule – Each generation must solve its own problems itself.
(2) Exploitation of renewable natural resources only within the scope of their ability to regenerate. Exploitation of non-renewable natural resources only if their function cannot be replaced.
(3) Release of substances only within the scope of the capacity for adaptation of natural systems.
(4) Avoidance of hazards and unjustifiable risks to human health.

[39] Bundestag printed paper 18/559, 1, 2 www.bundestag.de/blob/286956/0c46e2e6e4ce2cac7d7422acd1675494/18_559-pdf-data.pdf accessed 28 October 2016.

[40] Nationwide and on the international level; therefore websites in French language will be added to the German and English websites of the PACSD.

[41] Deutscher Bundestag, *Parliamentary Advisory Council on Sustainable Development* www.bundestag.de/en/committees/bodies/sustainability accessed 28 October 2016.

[42] Enclosure 1 of the Rules of Procedure for the parliamentary appraisal of the sustainability impact assessment in the framework of regulatory impact assessment www.bundestag.de/blob/382874/80726832b28c50dd4acc5fdca976ce6b/18_procedure-data.pdf accessed 28 October 2016.

(5) Ecologically and socially compatible structuring of technical developments.
(6) Energy and resource consumption, transport: decoupling and improved efficiency – with the help of research and development.
(7) Preparation of intergenerationally equitable budgets.
(8) Productive, sustainable and environmentally compatible farming – and welfare-oriented animal husbandry.
(9) Social cohesion: prevention of poverty and exclusion, creation of opportunities, structuring of demographic change, participation in social life for all.
(10) Gearing of global action to Millennium Development Goals: human rights, economic development, environmental protection, responsible government action.[43]

**Indicators**

(1) Resource conservation – Using resources economically and efficiently
(2) Climate protection – Reducing greenhouse gases
(3) Renewable energy sources – Strengthening a sustainable energy supply
(4) Land use – Sustainable land use
(5) Species diversity – Conserving species and protecting habitats
(6) Government debt – Consolidating the budget and creating intergenerational equity
(7) Provision for future economic stability – Creating favourable investment conditions and securing long-term prosperity
(8) Innovation – Shaping the future with new solutions
(9) Education and training – Continuously improving education and vocational training
(10) Economic output – Combining greater economic output with environmental and social responsibility
(11) Mobility – Guaranteeing mobility and protecting the environment
(12) Farming – Environmentally sound production in our cultivated landscapes
(13) Air pollution – Keeping the environment healthy
(14) Health and nutrition – Living healthily longer
(15) Crime – Further increasing personal security
(16) Employment – Boosting employment levels
(17) Prospects for families – Improving the compatibility of work and family life
(18) Equal opportunities – Promoting equal opportunities in society

[43] Ibid.

(19) Integration – Integration instead of exclusion
(20) Development cooperation – Supporting sustainable development
(21) Opening markets – Improving trade opportunities for developing countries.[44]

On the basis of these indicators and mirroring the Government's sustainability policy, two rapporteurs – one from the coalition and one from the opposition – fill in a short form with the results of their respective appraisal. This Review Note (*Prüfvermerk*) has to be written within two weeks and is then, in preparation for the session, conveyed to the other members of the PACSD. If a project turns out to be controversial between the two rapporteurs, the matter should be settled between the rapporteurs and, if necessary, together with the spokespersons. The work of the PACSD is characterised by the principle of consensus,[45] and indeed this principle is held sacred by the members and produces substantial benefits rather than semantic compromises.[46] The PACSD then submits the result of its appraisal as soon as possible – in the case of bills ahead of the first reading – to the respective lead committee in the form of an Expert Opinion (*gutachtliche Stellungnahme*). It contains an opinion with or without a request for examination. In case of request the lead committee is asked

> to submit an enquiry to the Federal Ministry regarding the missing information on the sustainability impact, to include its deliberations on the subject in the committee's report, and to report back to the PBnE [i.e. PACSD] regarding the result of the deliberations. The lead Federal Ministry is notified of the actions of the PBnE. In the case of an Expert Opinion without a request for examination, the Expert Opinion is submitted to the lead committee, but without the lead Federal Ministry being notified.[47]

The information in the printed paper attached to the bill can read as follows (the example is taken from a recent legislation procedure concerning a social security bill):[48]

> The PACSD has asserted the sustainability relevance of the bill of the Federal Government and therefore, according to the establishment decision (printed paper 18/559), drawn up an Expert Opinion in its session of 28 January 2015. The PACSD refrains from a request for examination towards the Committee on Health

[44] Enclosure 2 of the PACSD Rules of Procedure, *supra* note 45, where the full version can be found as well.
[45] See Bundestag printed paper 17/6680, 6: 'consensual working practice'.
[46] Telephonic information by Chief of Secretary Dr J. Wettengel (5 October 2015).
[47] PACSD Rules of Procedure, *supra* note 45 at 2.
[48] *Entwurf eines Gesetzes zur Stärkung der Versorgung in der gesetzlichen Krankenversicherung (GKV-Versorgungsstärkungsgesetz* – *GKV-VSG*, Bundestag printed paper 18/4095.

for it regards the account of the sustainability assessment as elaborate and plausible (Committee printed paper 18(23)30-8).[49]

The result can also be that the account of the sustainability assessment is too short but that in substance the bill is compatible with the sustainability requirements.[50] In the case of the 2016 federal budget bill, the PACSD asserted that all management rules and all indicators were applicable but refrained from a request for lack of an appropriate procedure of appraisal.[51] At times, the PACSD reminds the Federal Government of its duty to present the results of the sustainability assessment even if the bill is presumed to have a positive sustainability impact.[52] In case of a request for examination, the answer of the Federal Ministry (or Ministries) will be incorporated in the printed paper so that the sustainability relevance is made clear.[53]

The PACSD cannot itself conduct a sustainability impact assessment – for want of both time and resources. Rather, it is an actor enforcing the Federal Government's duty to assess the sustainability of bills and draft ordinances, and it is in this respect that the label 'watchdog' seems apt. The accuracy of the sustainability assessment, however, cannot be checked either. Therefore, a typical result of the PACSD's appraisal is '[t]he presentation of the sustainability assessment is plausible'. The first available statistics show that the percentage of objected to impact assessments has decreased (cf. Table 20.1). This might indicate an improvement in the impact assessment practice of the Federal Ministries but could also point to a relaxation of the appraisal intensity on the side of the PACSD.

## STRENGTHS AND DEFICIENCIES OF THE PARLIAMENTARY ADVISORY COUNCIL

The greatest strength of the PACSD is its clear-cut role in the legislative procedure, and the PACSD thus contributes effectively to the institutionalisation of sustainability. The increase in competences, in particular the newly introduced impact assessment appraisal according to rule 44(1)–(4) of the Joint Rules of Procedure, is a success which might show the immanent dynamics of this young but promising body. The time restrictions caused by the legislation procedure entail a very efficient

49 Bundestag printed paper 18/5123, 107 (author translation, F.R.).

50 'Im Gesetzentwurf sei die Aussage zur nachhaltigen Entwicklung zwar nicht ausreichend detailliert, um diese nachvollziehen zu können, aber es werde ersichtlich, dass Auswirkungen auf eine nachhaltige Entwicklung untersucht worden seien. Eine Prüfbitte sei daher nicht erforderlich (Ausschussdrucksache 18(23)3-16)', Bundestag printed paper 18/1657, 52; Bundestag printed paper 18/3935, 7.

51 See Bundestag printed paper 18/2825, 35: 'Grundsätzlich sind alle Managementregeln und Indikatoren betroffen und sollten einzelplanweise geprüft werden. Hierfür muss im Parlamentarischen Beirat für nachhaltige Entwicklung erst noch ein Verfahren entwickelt werden. Eine Prüfbitte ist daher nicht erforderlich.'

52 See e.g. Bundestag printed paper 18/4453, 4.

53 See Bundestag printed paper 18/3141, 7, 8.

TABLE 20.1 *Government proposals (bills and ordinances) in the 17th electoral period (statistical overview)*

| Period | Number of proposals | Sustainability relevant[a] | Not sustainability relevant | Statements about sustainable development | Thereof | | No statements about sustainable development | Sustainability assessment OK | Sustainability assessment insufficient |
|---|---|---|---|---|---|---|---|---|---|
| | | | | | Plausible | Non-plausible | | | |
| 1.3.2010–10.6.2011 | 306 | 192 | 114 | 212 | 136 | 76 | 94 | 136 | 170 |
| | 100% | 62.75% | 37.25% | 69.28% | 64.15% | 35.85% | 30.72% | 44.44% | 55.56% |
| 1.3.2010–31.1.2013 | 602 | 358 | 244 | 474 | 329 | 145 | 128 | 329 | 273 |
| | 100% | 59.47% | 40.53% | 78.74% | 69.41% | 30.59% | 21.26% | 54.65% | 45.35% |

[a] I.e. related to the objectives and thematic priorities of the National Sustainability Strategy; see Bundestag printed paper 17/6680, 3. As a third category, *bedingt nachhaltigkeitsrelevant* (of limited sustainability relevance) has recently been introduced.

*Sources:* Bundestag Printed Papers 17/6680 p. 2 and 17/13064 p. 9

working mode; however, the PACSD seems to be able to cope with this situation. The ambitious timetable safeguards that the Expert Opinion on sustainability is available from the beginning of the committee consultations.

As a possible institutional weakness, the legal basis of the PACSD's existence should be recapitulated, since it is based on a simple parliamentary decision rather than on a statutory provision and thus valid only for the respective electoral period. This can endanger the continuity of the PACSD's work if only by way of lapse of time at the beginning of an electoral period. It can, however, also be seen as an opportunity, since the necessity of deciding anew makes it easier to develop the PACSD in the light of the experiences of the previous electoral periods and adapt it to the current challenges. This is true at least as long as the hitherto existing political consensus about the work of the PACSD lasts.

Since the PACSD is not governed by the parliamentary Rules of Procedure, the Expert Opinion of the PACSD could simply be ignored by the committees. The PACSD has neither procedural nor substantive rights or competences towards Parliament or its committees. The interesting question of what the Constitutional Court would make of a situation in which the committees bluntly ignore a critical Opinion of the PACSD must be answered in that this omission could at best be an indicator of non-consideration of sustainability aspects and therefore of a violation of article 20a of the Basic Law, for example – it would not in itself render the law or ordinance unconstitutional.

Also, the restriction to a rather formal check (for example, as to the existence and plausibility of a sustainability impact assessment) can be seen as a weakness of the PACSD. The current Chairman, Andreas Jung MP, has accordingly pleaded for an extension of the ambit, such as for a substantive appraisal.[54] This appears to be not only desirable but even necessary if, as a matter of political psychology, an approving vote of the PACSD on the basis of the Government's sustainability assessment would lead to an implicit discharge of responsibility on the side of the respective committee(s). The plausibility check of the 'experts' could turn out to be dysfunctional – given the fact that it is 'only' a speedy and formal appraisal of the proponent's own (!) assessment. There is no empirical evidence for this effect, and it seems difficult to obtain any, but the danger of pulverisation of responsibility certainly exists.

If the appraisal's ambit is therefore widened towards a substantial assessment, the challenge will be twofold. First of all, it seems almost impossible to implement a full examination of the sustainability effects of a bill or ordinance in the given (very short) time slot. Secondly, the concept of sustainability is highly multidimensional (as illustrated by the twenty-one indicators serving as appraisal criteria for the PACSD). In many cases, the question will not be whether or not a proposal is sustainable, as if this could easily be determined on a one-dimensional scale, but how to weigh and balance the different aspects of sustainability. This balancing can

[54] Bundestag plenary session of 20 February 2014, Pl.-Pr. 18/17, 1314 C.

hardly be seen as a simple scientific operation. It is, as the concept of integrative protection of the environment teaches us,[55] a genuinely political decision that raises serious questions, for instance, whether a decrease in public borrowing or a credit-based investment in public infrastructures would be the more sustainable option. Thus, a true 'assessment of the assessment' could only mark evident and/or gross violations of the principle of sustainability. And again, its effect could be counterproductive, since it is the task of the proposal's author to ensure the sustainability of the project, as adding a full sustainability assessment conducted by the PACSD would discharge the political actor of this responsibility. In other words, the speedy but restricted appraisal cannot be regarded as a deficiency because it ensures that the sustainability assessment is done fully and thoroughly 'at the origin'. However, if in the course of the legislative procedure the bill is modified, which happens very often, those changes are not subject to a sustainability assessment and the PACSD's appraisal. It is in such situations that most legislative accidents happen.

As far as the PACSD's other objectives are concerned, the effectiveness of its work seems to be impeded by the multitude of bodies dealing with sustainability. In public, the PACSD is – to put it mildly – not a high-profile actor. The Federal Government has access to a lot of advisory boards and it might therefore underrate the expertise of MPs. Nevertheless, a fusion with the Council for Sustainable Development would create constitutional problems owing to the mixture of internal and external members.[56] The judiciary, finally, has to watch the sustainability of legislation, and the executive acts *ex officio* as far as sustainability is part of the law (which, in Germany, as has been shown, is the case for important aspects of sustainability, such as ecology), but the courts are, generally speaking, quite sensitive in questions of sustainability and intergenerational justice.[57]

## LEGISLATIVE OUTLOOK

At the constitutional level, little can, and should, be done. The incorporation of an objective of sustainability into the constitution – demanded again and again[58] – would add little, if any, intergenerational justice safeguards to constitutional law, given the existing provisions in the Basic Law and, in particular, the constitutional objectives of social state and environmental protection as well as the rules about fiscal sustainability.[59] On the contrary, the resulting imponderability,[60] and the shift

55 U. Di Fabio, 'Integratives Umweltrecht. Bestand, Ziele, Möglichkeiten' (1998) 17 *Neue Zeitschrift für Verwaltungsrecht* 329, 337.

56 Schomerus, *supra* note 22 at 6.

57 Interestingly, the PACSD invited the President of the Constitutional Court in the 17th electoral period; the conversation is planned for the actual electoral period (see Bundestag printed paper 17/13064, 10).

58 See *supra* note 15.

59 Which could and should be interpreted in the sense of intergenerational solidarity.

60 See Deter, *supra* note 15 at 163.

in power from Parliament towards the Constitutional Court (being obliged to take the political decisions about how to balance the different aspects of sustainability), could turn out to be detrimental to the aim of securing long-term justice. It would mean underestimating democracy as a structure and the electorate as actors. The elaborate list of sustainability indicators laid down in the Sustainability Strategy and used by the PACSD as criteria for its work can be read as a self-commitment, since it makes sustainability operable but at the same time shows its multidimensionality, including its flexibility (not to say indulgence).

Equally, the PACSD should not be codified in the Constitution. Given the strict requirements for amendments, this would impede improvements in the institutional and procedural setting in a field where further experience and flexibility are welcome. The incorporation of a provision governing the PACSD in the Rules of Procedure of Parliament, however, seems to be highly desirable. The PACSD's recently proposed the following rule 56b Rules of Procedure:

> The objectives of the Parliamentary Advisory Council on Sustainable Development are, in particular, the parliamentary monitoring and assistance of the Federal Government's sustainability policy at national, European and international level and the appraisal of the Federal Government's sustainability assessment as part of the regulatory impact assessment.[61]

This would give the PACSD a firmer institutional basis even though the Rules of Procedure have to be adopted anew by Parliament in every electoral period but would still leave the sustainability impact assessment and its appraisal by Parliament restricted to bills proposed by the government. An alternative could be to widen the proposed rule 56b by deleting the reference to the Federal Government's assessment:

> The objectives of the Parliamentary Advisory Council on Sustainable Development are, in particular, the parliamentary monitoring and assistance of the Federal Government's sustainability policy at national, European and international level and the appraisal of the sustainability assessment as part of the regulatory impact assessment.

and add in rule 76(2) Rules of Procedure of Bundestag a short reference to the sustainability assessment of bills proposed by members of Parliament:

> Bills must, motions may, be accompanied by a short explanatory memorandum. The memorandum should comprise the result of a sustainability assessment.

The Federal Government's obligation to implement a sustainability assessment under rule 44 of the Joint Rules of Procedure would not be affected, but bills

[61] PACSD, 'Vorschlag für eine Verankerung des PBnE in der Geschäftsordnung des Deutschen Bundestages' www.bundestag.de/blob/388870/3781fe6945f143a2f88b1623e91ef445/vorschlag-fuer-eine-verankerung-des-pbne-data.pdf accessed 28 October 2016.

proposed by MPs would equally have to undergo a sustainability assessment, at least in ordinary cases – the wording (should comprise) would leave flexibility for cases in which the sustainability relevance is evidently low. To ensure the sustainability of modifications proposed later in the legislation procedure, rules 82(1) and 85(1) of the Rules of Procedures of Bundestag could be amended so as to include an obligation to add a short explanatory memorandum concerning sustainability. This needs, however, further discussion to make sure that such a provision is more than a dead letter. In comparison to those intraparliamentary rules, the added value of a Law on Sustainability Assessment (*Nachhaltigkeitsprüfungsgesetz*), which has been proposed in the past,[62] is unclear.

## CONCLUSION

The Parliamentary Advisory Council on Sustainable Development is a body which the German Federal Parliament has created anew in every electoral period since 2004 by way of an establishment decision – in other words, there is no reliable long-term basis for the Council's work. Consisting of Members of Parliament only, its present objective is to monitor and support the Federal Government's sustainability policy at national, European, and international level from a parliamentary angle. The most specific and most important means is the PACSD's appraisal of the sustainability assessment of bills by the Federal Government (cf. rule 44 of the Joint Rules of Procedure of the Federal Ministries). The PACSD shall, according to the actual establishment decision, 'present the lead committee in each case with the result of its evaluation as an opinion, which must be discussed by the lead committee and appraised in writing'. As criteria, the PACSD uses the indicators and goals set out in the 'National Sustainable Development Strategy' (cf. the Annex below). The results of this evaluation are normally reached unanimously, which contributes considerably to the authority of the Council's work so that the consensus principle is regarded as sacred by its members. Beyond this specific parliamentary function, the PACSD competes against a number of different entities such as the German Advisory Council on the Environment, the Federal Environment Agency, the German Advisory Council on Global Climate Change, and the Council for Sustainable Development. Compared to these bodies, the PACSD is almost invisible to the public, such that it seems tempting to heighten the Council's public profile. Considering its limited resources and its irreplaceable role in the process of legislation, the PACSD should instead strive to further increase its intraparliamentary influence.

[62] As proposed by K. Jacob, S. Veit, and J. Hertin, 'Gestaltung einer Nachhaltigkeitsprüfung im Rahmen der Gesetzesfolgenabschätzung. Studie im Auftrag der Bertelsmann-Stiftung' (2009) 83 www.bertelsmann-stiftung.de/fileadmin/files/BSt/Presse/imported/downloads/xcms_bst_dms_27523_27524_2.pdf accessed 28 October 2016.

## Annex

TABLE 20.2 *Indicators and goals of the National Sustainable Development Strategy as used by the PACSD*

| No. | Indicator areas<br>Sustainability axiom | Indicators | Goals |
|---|---|---|---|
| **I. Intergenerational equity** | | | |
| 1a | **Resource conservation** | Energy productivity | To be doubled between 1990 and 2020 |
| 1b | Using resources economically and efficiently | Primary energy consumption | To be reduced by 20% by 2020 and 50% by 2050 compared to 2008 |
| 1c | | Raw material productivity | To be doubled between 1994 and 2020 |
| 2 | **Climate protection**<br>Reducing greenhouse gases | Greenhouse gas emissions | To be reduced by 21% by 2008/12, 40% by 2020 and 80% to 95% by 2050, in each case compared to 1990 |
| 3a amended | **Renewable energy sources**<br>Strengthening a sustainable energy supply | Share of renewable energy sources in final energy consumption | To be increased to 18% by 2020 and 60% by 2050 |
| 3b | | Share of renewable energy sources in electricity consumption | To be increased to 12.5% by 2010, to at least 35% by 2020, and to at least 80% by 2050 |
| 4 | **Land use**<br>Sustainable land use | Built-up area and transport infrastructure expansion | Increase to be reduced to 30 hectares a day by 2020 |
| 5 | **Species diversity**<br>Conserving species - protecting habitats | Species diversity and landscape quality | To be increased to the index value of 100 by 2015 |
| 6a | **Government debt**<br>Consolidating budgets - creating intergenerational equity | General government deficit | Ratio of government deficit to GDP less than 3% |
| 6b new | | Structural deficit | Structurally balanced public spending, total national structural deficit of no more than 0.5% of the GDP |

(*continued*)

TABLE 20.2 (*continued*)

| No. | Indicator areas<br>Sustainability axiom | Indicators | Goals |
|---|---|---|---|
| 6c new | | Debt position | Ratio of government debt to GDP no more than 60% |
| 7 | **Provisions for future economic stability**<br>Creating favourable investment conditions - securing long-term prosperity | Gross fixed capital formation in relation to GDP | Increase in GFCF share in GDP |
| 8 | **Innovation**<br>Shaping the future with new solutions | Private and public R&D spending | To be increased to 3% of GDP by 2020 |
| 9a | **Education and training**<br>Continuously improving education and vocational training | 18- to 24-year-olds without a school leaving certificate | To be reduced to less than 10% by 2020 |
| 9b amended | | 30- to 34-year-olds with a tertiary or post-secondary level of education | To be increased to 42% by 2020 |
| 9c | | Proportion of students starting a degree course | To be increased to 40% by 2010, followed by further increase and stabilisation at a high level |
| **II. Quality of life** | | | |
| 10 | **Economic capacity**<br>Raising economic output in an environmentally and socially compatible way | GDP per capita | Economic growth |
| 11a | **Mobility**<br>Guaranteeing mobility – protecting the environment | Intensity of goods transport | To be reduced to 98% by 2010 and to 95% by 2020, compared to 1999 levels |
| 11b | | Intensity of passenger transport | To be reduced to 90% by 2010 and to 80% by 2020, compared to 1999 levels |
| 11c | | Modal share of rail transport | To be increased to 25% by 2015 |
| 11d | | Modal share of inland freight water transport | To be increased to 14% by 2015 |

| No. | Indicator areas<br>Sustainability axiom | Indicators | Goals |
|---|---|---|---|
| 12a | **Farming**<br>Environmentally sound production in our cultivated landscape | Nitrogen surplus | To be reduced to 80 kg/hectare of agricultural area by 2012, further reduction by 2020 |
| 12b | | Organic farming | Share of organic farming on land used for agriculture to be increased to 20% in coming years |
| 13 | **Air quality**<br>Keeping the environment healthy | Air pollution | To be reduced to 30% by 2010, compared to 1990 levels |
| 14a | **Health and nutrition**<br>Living more healthily for longer | Men: premature mortality (cases of death per 100,000 residents under 65) | To be reduced to 190 cases per 100,000 by 2015 |
| 14b | | Women: premature mortality (cases of death per 100,000 residents under 65) | To be reduced to 115 cases per 100,000 by 2015 |
| 14c | | Smoking rate amongst young people (12- to 17-year-olds) | To be decreased to under 12% by 2015 |
| 14d | | Smoking rate amongst adults (15 years and older) | To be decreased to under 22% by 2015 |
| 14e | | Proportion of adults suffering from obesity (18 years and older) | To be reduced by 2020 |
| 15 Definition amended | **Crime**<br>Further increasing personal security | Criminal offences | To be reduced in number of recorded cases per 100,000 inhabitants to under 7,000 by the year 2020 |
| **III. Social cohesion** | | | |
| 16a | **Employment**<br>Boosting employment levels | Employment rate (15- to 64-year-olds) | To be increased to 73% by 2010 and 75% by 2020 |
| 16b | | Employment rate (older people, 55- to 64-year-olds) | To be increased to 55% by 2010 and 57% by 2020 |

(*continued*)

TABLE 20.2 (*continued*)

| No. | Indicator areas<br>Sustainability axiom | Indicators | Goals |
|---|---|---|---|
| 17a | **Prospects for families**<br>Improving the work–life balance | All-day care provision for children (0- to 2-year-olds) | To be increased to 30% by 2010 and 35% by 2020 |
| 17b | | All-day care provision for children (3- to 5-year-olds) | To be increased to 30% by 2010 and 60% by 2020 |
| 18 | **Equal opportunities**<br>Promoting equal opportunities in society | Gender pay gap | To be reduced to 15% by 2010 and to 10% by 2020 |
| 19 | **Integration of foreigners**<br>Integration instead of exclusion | Foreign school leavers with a school leaving certificate | Proportion of foreign school leavers with at least a *Hauptschule* certificate (lower secondary schooling) is to be increased and brought into line with that of German school leavers by 2020 |
| **IV. International responsibility** | | | |
| 20 | **Development cooperation**<br>Supporting sustainable development | Official development assistance as a share of gross national income | To be increased to 0.51% by 2010 and 0.7% by 2015 |
| 21 | **Opening markets**<br>Improving trade opportunities for developing countries | German imports from developing countries | Further increase |

*Source*: The Federal Government, 'National Sustainable Development Strategy 2012 Progress Report' (2002) 28–30 www.bundesregierung.de/Content/DE/_Anlagen/Nachhaltigkeit-wiederhergestellt/2012-06-07-fortschrittsbericht-2012-englisch-barrierefrei.pdf?__blob=publicationFile&v=5 accessed 28 October 2016.

# 21

# Power over Coming Generations: Committee for the Future in the *Eduskunta*, the Parliament of Finland

*Paula Tiihonen*

Who has the power to decide on behalf of coming generations? Who has the right to speak in the name of coming generations?

Power – in politics and in the economy – is in the hands of human beings. We, the people, can use it in many ways, on many levels, with many objectives and for many purposes. It is humans who shape the values on which power is based. And humans also have the power to change power systems and even power structures. Rules for using power, encapsulated in rules of governance, are clearly entrenched in the political systems of the Western democracies. However, this only applies to discussions of power predicated on today – using power for coming generations is more complicated.

Democracy is important when considering the rights of coming generations. In a democratic society, discourse on the people's relationship to decision-making concerning themselves is eternal in the sense that every generation must create its own interpretation of democracy, in its various sectors and on its various levels, and do this in a democratic way. A series of stage settings depicting democracy is not enough. Not even a good democracy functions without errors in times of transition and upheaval. The long-term and fundamental character of democracy means that maintaining and renewing it can be compared to tending a garden – results can be seen only slowly and after hard work. One must take care of big old trees, but give opportunities for many new fragile small flowers to have the courage to encounter and support all kinds of new and wild things – even unknown unknowns – but at the same time be prepared all the time for risks.

For the sake of the democratic system's credibility and future prospects, it would be wise to start evaluating power structures and power centres to get a background for analysis of the different kinds of institutions working for the future. It is important to evaluate economic power from the perspective of democracy. Democracy and the economy should be spoken of using the same criteria of importance, with the same force, at the same time, and in the same forums.

## POWER CENTRES AND BALANCE

On the level of institutions there are two key power centres: politics and the economy, perhaps better referred to as democracy and business. These two main power centres constitute the majority of decisions that are needed to ensure that the future is positive for coming generations.

To properly make this evaluation, this chapter will first look at the development of these two powers and assess whether there is a rational, fair, and wise balance between them. Then it examines the kinds of new methods that exist to work for future generations and ensure a better life for them, keeping in mind the delicate and problematic balance between the interests of present and future generations. In the context of politics and democracy, what must be determined in order to have a good understanding of the issues involved is which models of organising work for coming generations are possible and realistic and which are not, which are worth trying even if it is a long hard process, and which may not be suitable or even wanted.

The aim of this analysis is, first of all, to bring out some basic problems experienced in the Finnish Committee for the Future using a 'visionary power' and, at the same time, to generate a background against which to analyse proposals made by the 'Roundtable of National Institutions for a Sustainable Future' network. The most demanding of these proposals relates to creating the post of UN High Commissioner for Future Generations or widening the mandate of the EU Ombudsman to represent the next generation. Are these proposals wise, rational, reasonable, realistic, acceptable, and sustainable? While society's responsibilities towards coming generations have already been endorsed in many international treaties, resolutions, and declarations, this recognition is only a moral principle. Legacy, and especially legitimisation of power over coming generations, is a difficult thing.

Stein Ringen, an expert in democracy, has assisted in the identification of five trends in the changing power relations between politics and the economy that are key to the analyses used in this chapter.[1] Very briefly, these trends are:

(1) With growth in the economy, individual economic power has increased compared with political power, in which each voter still has only one vote;
(2) Economic power has become concentrated in the hands of a small elite;
(3) With liberalisation of markets and the economy, the private has entered public arenas;

[1] See S. Ringen (ed.), *The Possibility of Politics: A Study in the Political Economy of the Welfare State* (Routledge 2006).

(4) Political power has been thrust out of economic arenas. Funding of political activities has shifted to those who have the ability and desire to pay for political activities and whose interests lie in doing so; and
(5) With globalisation, deregulation, and information technology, capital markets have slipped out of the control of nation states.

Additionally, this chapter notes that the linkage between credibility of political democracy and economic power is a long-term question. The following two development trends reduce national legislative power in all democracies. First, big actors in the economy have, as a part of globalisation, acquired a new and powerful means of exercising power, the possibility to transfer capital, production, jobs, head offices, taxes, innovations, research and development, and new thinking to other countries. This possibility existed earlier as well, but now the right of veto or power to exit is real and credible. Second, supranational and international legislation and the issuance of various norms (for example by the EU, UN, WTO, CoE, World Bank, IMF, G8, and so on) have increased. Overall, the chapter maintains that a vote is a key to a better future.

Global economic power and democracy are connected in a very interesting and paradoxical way. Globalisation has added to democracy and equality more than any individual political decision. It has given work and brought prosperity to hundreds of millions and, through the rapid economic growth that it has brought, given several states opportunities to develop education, health care, infrastructure, and other prerequisites for future economic growth, and at the same time the fundamentals for human well-being, at a vigorous pace. Nevertheless, particularly when examined in the light of the starting points of citizens in the developed countries and from the perspective of the increasingly higher goals set for democracy, globalisation has distanced people from decision-making affecting them. The weakness of legitimisation and the erosion of the foundation of trust, real or perceived, has also been reflected in the attitudes of citizens toward the leaders of their own country. All over the world, people are voting more and more against the elites.

Climate change is a future problem that everyone knows and is affected by. The basic question is again who has the right or/and the responsibility to decide on behalf of future generations. Currently, even some constitutions refer to generations to come. These constitutional clauses can be grouped into three categories: (1) general clauses for intergenerational justice,[2] (2) ecological generational justice,[3] and (3) financial generational clauses.[4] These clauses simply formulate a state objective; they do not lay down a public right or a right for each individual citizen. Values on

[2] See J.C. Tremmel, 'Establishing Intergenerational Justice in National Constitutions', in J.C. Tremmel (ed.), *Handbook of Intergenerational Justice* (Elgar 2006).

[3] Ibid.

[4] Ibid.

which power is based are not enough – the institutions, forums, and tools to use power are relevant. But first, some examples of problems relating to balance of powers.

On the European level there is a clear lack of balance between economic and political powers. The tasks of the EU, its organisations, and its methods of operation were certainly not built specifically from the starting point of democracy. An effort has been made, especially in the twenty-first century, to bring citizens' rights and obligations to the fore, but democracy as a matter on the system level is still one of the fundamental problems of the EU. The euro/EMU is based on interests of finance.[5] The only freedom of movement which is in real action is free movement of capital. The EU has a lot of power in the hands of the central bureaucracy, to the extent that some businesspeople think it is not worth investing in Europe, even for coming generations.[6] But from the point of the people and their rights it is a question of the legitimacy of the power structure. It is not an accident that populist parties and movements that want to get rid of the EU are gaining in strength.

In general, from the perspective of the powers of national parliaments, the focus of criticism in the 1990s was the division of legislative powers between the EU and national parliaments, while in the present decade it is budgetary power that has come in for criticism. Funding and financial crises have increased especially the EU's advance financial supervision and the EU Commission's bureaucratic power to exercise guidance over national budgets before governments have even been able to present the budgets to their national parliaments.[7]

Some of the biggest problems with the increased economic power and the development of supranational-level democracy are sociological and cultural: the frailty of European civil society as well as the weak identity and fragile solidarity of EU citizens. Still, the European economic crisis has had some effects that are positive from the point of view of democracy: an increased awareness both in the media and among the public in general of the community of destiny that the countries of Europe, or at least the Eurozone, share. An awareness of European intertwinement is an essential prerequisite for supranational, EU-level democracy. In elections, representatives of peoples and political parties are being given their mandates by ever-smaller proportions of both citizens and inhabitants. In many countries the franchise is de facto limited in a variety of ways, and even among those who can do so only one-third or so exercise their right to vote. Legitimacy is on unsteady legs also because party memberships have declined.

Democracy along with its parliamentary institutions is in a paradoxical situation at the global level as well. Political democracy has spread more widely and faster in the

5 See EU, EU Monetary Cooperation https://europa.eu/european-union/about-eu/money/euro_en accessed 30 November 2017.

6 European Central Bank, ESCB and the Eurosystem, European Central Bank www.ecb.int/ecb/orga/escb/html/index.en.html accessed 30 November 2017.

7 See ibid.

world than even the most optimistic of future visionaries had been able to foresee. Nearly the whole of Asia and Africa has embraced democracy, at least formally, in the space of a few decades. With the advent of new institutions, hundreds of millions of people have gained new freedoms and rights and above all prosperity. Within Europe, the disintegration of the Soviet Union and a desire for EU membership have transformed one Eastern European country after another very quickly into democracies. The change has been so intense that democracy has meant primarily the building of democratic organisations. After the building stage, however, enthusiasm is bound to ebb, and voting turnouts have started to decline. The empty rooms of democracy are not enough. Democracy is a garden which has to be tended all the time.

One of the most difficult changes that must be acknowledged is that national governments no longer have the means of safeguarding employment for their citizens. If masses of people do not have jobs or enough of a salary to have a home and a family, educate themselves, or consume anything, a lot follows from this. The responsibility to share – especially to share opportunities for some kind of positive future – is more important than ever. That is the basic task of politics.

Democracy researchers have warned us of the danger of 'broken promises'. In the Nordic model of democracy, the disproportion between the promises – as people have inferred them – of political democracy and the reality that has been accomplished will be especially great. The reason is simple: in the welfare model that has been embraced, the State has been strong and extensive. Ever since the 1960s, the political system has not been content with merely promising citizens opportunities to achieve prosperity and well-being. Instead, the State itself has in nearly every sphere of life distributed well-being to all, either directly or indirectly. Within the space of a few generations, citizens have become accustomed to knowing that the State will take care of them in good times and bad, from birth to death.

## LONG-TERM POLITICS IN PARLIAMENTS

To put it briefly, long-term politics in parliaments is gardening, taking care of all the opportunities and options of coming generations. A parliament's permanent task is to enact laws. For hundreds of years all over the world, it has become established practice for parliaments to legislate and approve international treaties, set taxes, and confirm the State budget as well as to express confidence or non-confidence in the government. Parliaments in several countries have also acquired more general functions, involving examination of the legal, financial, and administrative actions of ministries, relating to oversight of the government. In their fundamentals, however, parliaments have remained unchanged – within the separation of powers between three branches, they have generally stuck to legislation and left judicial and executive functions to the other organs. In the way they operate, parliaments represent institutions that are bound strictly by tradition. Power of initiative or vision, strategies, innovation, and rethinking are in the government's hands: the government governs.

However, parliaments have traditionally had their role to play when major questions facing the nation, such as deciding on war and peace, were being resolved. Taxation and the State budget have been important instruments of democracy in this respect as well. That is why they have not been allowed to remain only a strategic matter for the government. There is a tremendous need inside the system of democracy to handle all kinds of big future problems – and not only problems of one future, but of several of them. No one knows the future. In real democracy, it should be believed and seen that the future we want can be made, and made in a democratic way. Parliaments could use more of their visionary power.

In a situation where the legitimacy of parliaments and democracy is crumbling, more needs to be rethought than the apparatus and performance techniques. The great future choice that politics and parliaments will have to make is whether to let development roll on under its own momentum as though it were a law of nature, or rather to resist its bad sides and support its good ones.

It is people who make an economy. It is time to rethink conceptions of whose interests the State is pursuing. What are the general, common, and shared interests? What is democracy and equality? What should be assessed with respect to every decision and action of the State is whether it increases or reduces income differences. Both nation States and their collective organisations, such as the EU, the World Bank, or the UN, know the tough laws that rule the economy and competition in a global world. They all share the weak status of politics. If parliaments embark on a struggle for a fairer world and a more genuine democracy than currently exists, they will really need strong support. Only the direct support of people will be sufficiently strong.

## COMMITTEE FOR THE FUTURE

In Finland, more than twenty years ago, some Representatives had the insight that establishing a committee to deal with the future would be one means of revitalising the *Eduskunta* from within.[8] What is especially noteworthy is that the Committee for the Future is an original political innovation conceived by parliamentary democracy itself.[9] It came into being on Representatives' own initiative and in the face of opposition from many quarters.[10] It was not easy to establish a forum specialising in matters of the future and consolidate its position. It took legislative initiatives by a majority of Representative on two occasions (133 of the 200 Representatives in 1986

[8] See Eduskunta Riksdagen, Committee for the Future www.eduskunta.fi/EN/lakiensaataminen/valiokunnat/tulevaisuusvaliokunta/Pages/default.aspx accessed 30 November 2017.

[9] Ibid.

[10] Ibid.

and 167 in 1992) to come into being.[11] The idea of giving the Committee permanent status appeared when the Constitution was revised; however, this attempt encountered staunch opposition.[12] Overcoming it took a historic decision, through which a plenary session voted down the opposition that the Constitutional Law Committee and its experts had mounted.[13] Speaking in the plenary chamber after their victory, the Representatives who had pushed through the proposal to put the Committee on a permanent footing said simply 'the future is permanent'.[14]

The Committee for the Future is one of the *Eduskunta*'s sixteen standing committees.[15] As with any other standing committee in Finland, it has seventeen members, who are all Representatives, and is cross-party in composition.[16] Its functions are: (1) to prepare parliamentary documents entrusted to it, such as the *Eduskunta*'s response to the Government's Report on the Future (normally one report per parliamentary term); (2) to issue statements to other committees on matters related to the future; (3) to discuss issues pertaining to future development factors and development models; (4) to analyse research regarding the future, including methodology; and (5) to serve as the parliamentary body responsible for assessing technological development and its consequences for society.[17]

The Committee for the Future was for a long time unique in the world as an institution, and the seventeen parliamentarians themselves established policy priorities for the future. The time perspective is long and the scale of issues broad. In many countries, intergenerational problems are limited to some environmental norms and options, sustainable development strategies, sometimes to development plans, demographic crisis, or control of finance. The Finnish Committee's only task is to think about futures, a range of alternative futures, discuss them, and work for the best possible future for the people. It deliberates factors that influence the development of the future, futures research, and the impacts of technological development.[18] Situated at the core of political life, it has a lot of power – not legislative, not budgetary, but initiative and visionary.[19] While the time frame to be addressed is twenty to fifty years, it is working for the best of coming generations.[20] And it works – the Committee has meetings twice a week, two hours on Wednesdays and one hour on Fridays.

11 Ibid.
12 Ibid.
13 Ibid.
14 Ibid.
15 Ibid.
16 Ibid., Members.
17 Ibid.
18 Ibid. Recent issues tackled by the Committee include green growth, ensuring that future generations are included in the Finnish relations with other states, infrastructural planning, and technology changes.
19 Ibid.
20 Ibid.

The most significant efforts have been devoted to its own issues and projects. First of all, the *power to decide its own agenda* is one of the pillars of the strength of the Committee.[21] It has had the power of initiative from the very beginning. The Committee itself shapes its agenda and chooses the methods to be used in its work.[22] The only limit to thinking about and discussing issues of the future is resources. As with any other Committee of the *Eduskunta*, it only has one counsellor and a small secretariat. It also has a small research budget of its own. But the whole idea is based on the belief that experts consider it an honour to be able to work for democracy. Instead of a salary or fee, they have their report published by and deliberated in their national parliament.

Committees of the *Eduskunta* have very broad and strong rights to receive information. In order to gain more knowledge and wisdom, the Committee for the Future organises different kinds of hearings, analyses all kinds of information, travels abroad to get signals of new and important developments, and prepares studies on futures, different options, possible dangers, and scenarios mainly using methods of futures research. After a general election, every committee must itself create its success and earn esteem for its work in each four-year parliamentary term.[23] By virtue of its exceptional role and task, the Committee serves as the *Eduskunta*'s think tank. For all committees, the corresponding minister/corresponding ministry is important. The Prime Minister is the only appropriate choice as the corresponding minister for the Committee for the Future.

Given that parliaments everywhere in the world are quite similar, it is natural that the Committee for the Future receives visits from many politicians, researchers, officials, journalists and others with 'a thirst for the new', as it would be fitting to call them in the light of the interest they demonstrate. What surprises them most of all? One thing above everything else is that in Finland so many members of the legislative assembly spend many hours each week together in the same room giving some or other matter their joint deliberation. And when the visitors are told that they also jointly plan, on the basis of a theme index that they have themselves determined, the projects to be tackled during the coming four-year parliamentary term, decide on the level and mode of implementation of these projects, arrive at their conclusions, and publish the results of their thinking together, they shake their heads.

The Inter-Parliamentary Union (IPU), established in 1889, is one of the oldest, most broadly based international organisations still extant.[24] In 2006, it assessed the new tasks of parliaments and the ways in which they needed to renew themselves in this millennium and published the results in a practical guidebook, *Parliament and*

21 Ibid.
22 Ibid.
23 Ibid., Committees.
24 IPU, About Us www.ipu.org/about-us accessed 30 November 2017.

*Democracy in the Twenty-First Century: A Guide to Good Practice*.[25] The book concludes with the chapter 'Facing the Future' and notes that parliaments must be ready for many things: to represent and speak on behalf of the entire people in all its diversity, make public the choices and dilemmas facing policy-makers and help educate the public about them, provide national forums for canvassing and debating alternative views and policy proposals, promote conflict resolution and help smooth out differences in their role as experts on high-level dialogue, and ensure that human rights as well as economic, social, educational, and political rights are protected and promoted.[26]

The final paragraph of the 'Facing the Future' chapter is devoted to a discussion of planning and making the future.[27] It outlines models in which parliaments have moved from reacting to proactive engagement, from approving government bills to themselves presenting initiatives, from solving individual problems of the past or present to pondering long-term structural problems.[28] The examples outlined include the Subcommittee on the Future Development of Latvia established by the Latvian parliament in 2003, the Commission for Future Generations set up by the Israeli parliament in 2001, and the Committee for the Future in the *Eduskunta*.[29] The Committee for the Future is seen as positive proof of the fact that parliamentarians really can be a source of initiative not only in outlining the future, but also in managing it and thereby shaping their country's future.[30]

There are certainly many explanations as to why of these three prominent models only the Finnish case is still at work as of the time of writing. One explanation is that success in planning and shaping the future can only happen if parliamentarians themselves have the self-confidence to exercise the power they already possess. The power of vision is one of many forms of democratic power. Certainly, in work for next generations there are drawbacks. A few examples can be found in the latest reports of the CoE, which touch on the question of basic issues of democracy: freedom of expression and trust in the fairness of the political system, especially during an economic recession.[31]

According to the CoE, among others, increasingly restrictive measures are being focused in the old democratic European countries on the political liberties that are of key importance from the perspective of democracy.[32] The freedom of speech of

[25] D. Beetham (ed.), *Parliament and Democracy in the Twenty-First Century: A Guide to Good Practice* (IPU Geneva 2006).

[26] Ibid. at chapter 8.

[27] Ibid. at 195.

[28] See generally ibid.

[29] See generally ibid.

[30] See generally ibid.

[31] See CoE, Freedom of Expression – Reports www.coe.int/en/web/freedom-expression/reports accessed 30 November 2017.

[32] See e.g. Secretary General of the CoE, *State of Democracy, Human Rights and the Rule of Law* (CoE 2017).

journalists working in the traditional media has been narrowed, the right to demonstrate is being intervened in earlier than used to be the case, and above all communications of every kind in the internet environment have been made the subject of more extensive monitoring than hitherto.[33] The spending cuts associated with austerity policies have led to a running down of democratic structures and a weakening of the situation regarding human rights in some European countries.[34] This has in turn caused a crumbling of the general trust that state structures enjoy.[35] As a result, the pan-European legitimacy problem of representative institutional democracy is worsening. The CoE's Commissioner for Human Rights has expressed his concern that austerity policy has increased the number of people who are thrust outside society and accelerated the rate at which inequality between people's ability to function in society is developing.[36]

## WHERE SHOULD A FORUM FOR FUTURES POLICY BE SITUATED?

Politics is still in the position to affect and shape the future, and it should bear responsibility. Further, politics has an ethical responsibility towards future generations and in addressing intergenerational justice. There are two main approaches to institutionalising this responsibility. One approach focuses on constitutional rights written into the constitution; the other approach calls for organisational solutions. But, in the end, both approaches can be located in many possible homes. Examples include parliament, the prime minister's office or other governmental agency, a university or some other research institution, an independent think tank, an NGO, or outsourcing to the private sector.

On the national level, in Finland and Chile parliaments have been most active in organising new thinking, forecasting, and scenario working inside parliaments as a part of normal political and legal process in committees.[37] In April 2015, the Parliament of Ukraine decided to establish the Commission for the Future. In Uruguay, there are similar plans. In Scotland, the parliamentary future work model is organised in a more flexible way. In each of these different parliamentary models, the tasks of the future units cover actual sectors of politics and life.

On the international level, the EU has several bodies focusing mainly on future work connected to technology and science. The European Parliamentary Technology Assessment network (Epta) was founded to handle the challenge of

[33] See ibid.

[34] See generally ibid.

[35] See generally ibid.

[36] See CoE Commissioner for Human Rights, *Issue Paper: Austerity Measures across Europe Have Undermined Human Rights* (2013) www.coe.int/en/web/commissioner/-/austerity-measures-across-europe-have-undermined-human-rights accessed 30 November 2017.

[37] See Eduskunta Riksdagen, *supra* note 8, Members.

new technologies.[38] The OECD, UN, World Bank, and other large global political actors have their own solutions. In this context, the UN/World Future Council is already actively working, and in the near future the UN Secretary-General's proposed High Commissioner for Future Generations will perhaps also be in action.[39] The World Future Society (WFS), founded in 1966, has the largest membership in the futures field.[40] The World Futures Studies Federation (WFSF), founded in Paris in 1973, is a global network of leading futurists, scholars, teachers, researchers, foresight practitioners, policy analysts, activists, students, and others from sixty countries with a long-range view.[41] The Millennium Project is an old Washington-based network of future activists. In Europe, the most traditional, advanced, and appreciated actors are technology (science) assessment bodies. The basic difference between all these bodies relates to the right to use State power and make legally binding decisions – and, ultimately, also to wield the power of sanctions, and coercive power in the name of the State. There is also a strong movement towards the private in every sector of society, including all kinds of future-oriented work. Public–private choice means that the bodies that future generations rely on can act as a public or private or public–private entity. Their object can also be private, public, or public–private.

The Welsh Assembly has taken a much more important role than in any other case by writing the main principles and rules of work for coming generations directly into law. The Well-being of Future Generations (Wales) Act 2015 addresses improving the social, economic, environmental, and cultural well-being of Wales.[42] The aim of the Act is to make the public bodies listed in it (Welsh Ministers, local authorities, local health boards, Public Health Wales NHS Trust, Velindre NHS Trust, national park authorities, fire and rescue authorities, Natural Resources Wales, the Higher Education Funding Council for Wales, the Arts and Sports Councils of Wales, and the National Library and Museum of Wales) think more about the long-term, work with people, communities, and each other, look to prevent problems, and take a more joined-up approach. To make sure all are working towards the same vision, the Act puts in place seven well-being goals. Public bodies have to report on their work. The Auditor General and the Future Generations Commissioner have the power of scrutiny.[43]

In Finland, there are strong future bodies in every sector, but not in the sense of law and using exercising legal power as in Wales. The most important bodies in Finland are: (1) standing permanent Committee for the Future; (2) the University/

[38] See Epta, About www.eptanetwork.org/ accessed 30 November 2017.

[39] See World Future Council, Future Justice www.worldfuturecouncil.org/future-justice/ accessed 30 November 2017.

[40] See WFS https://wfs.org/ accessed 30 November 2017.

[41] See WFSF, About WFSF www.wfsf.org/about-us/wfsf accessed 30 November 2017.

[42] See Well-being of Future Generations (Wales) Act 2015.

[43] See ibid.

Future Research Institute at the University of Turku, which offers a doctorate in Future Studies; (3) the Foresight Network in the Prime Minister's Office, a body of civil servants and experts who report to the Prime Minister; (4) the Association of Future Research NGO, part of a citizens' movement in the 1970s; and (5) several think tanks such as Sitra, the Finnish Innovation Fund under the Parliament, a public fund aimed at building a successful Finland for tomorrow.

It is a great thing that all of these bodies are working for a better future. Keeping in mind the starting point – power – and the two main questions for this article – who has the power to decide for coming generations and who has the right to decide for coming generations – the best place is the parliament. In democracies, only parliaments can have the right to use, in addition to legislative and budgetary power, visionary power so that it can generate a binding goal, task, or action that the authorities have a duty to perform rather than merely a wish or a proposal. Certainly, it is not so clear where future work in the parliament should be assigned. Should it be to a committee or an ombudsman or something totally new? The debate on the status of our Committee for the Future that arose in the context of revision of the Constitution and the Rules of Procedure at the beginning of the twenty-first century clearly illustrated a number of fundamental problems associated with the Committee's work that still are the focus of discussion from time to time. The arguments in favour of giving the Committee permanent status that were presented in the plenary session debate were mainly pragmatic and can be placed in the following categories.

First, with respect to the work that it does, the Committee for the Future can be compared to the Grand Committee (in Finland, the EU Committee which handles the most important EU issues meets on a weekly basis before and after every important meeting in Brussels, with the Prime Minister/Ministers in attendance) as well as in part to the Foreign Affairs and Defence committees, which likewise deal with questions other than those associated with legislative and budgetary matters in their own sectors. Second, the long-term planning and deliberation of matters that the Committee for the Future carries out specifically for the legislature are important. Third, the continuity that giving the Committee permanent status would ensure would also bring greater esteem for its work. Fourth, the international interest that the Committee has prompted and the positive reputation that is has generated are important. Fifth, putting the Committee on a permanent footing is specifically a political solution and a staking-out of policy. Sixth, practical problems relating to resources and quorums would arise as long as the Committee's status remained different from that of the permanent committees. And seventh, despite opposition that the idea has encountered, giving the Committee permanent status was not, in the view of either experts or the Constitutional Law Committee, contrary to the Constitution.

Correspondingly, the arguments put forward by those who viewed the idea of permanent status in a negative light can be grouped into the following categories.

First, the role played by the Committee for the Future differs essentially from that of the other committees insofar as it does not have any legislation- or budget-related tasks. Second, matters relating to the future are indeed important to the *Eduskunta*, but a committee is not the right kind of body for dealing with them. Third, how future-related tasks could best be dealt with in some other way should be studied and the role of the Committee for the Future assessed on this basis. And fourth, the esteem that a committee and its members enjoy does not depend on its formal status, but rather on its work and the results achieved.

One of the most central arguments against the activities of the Committee for the Future has been repeated year after year, namely that all committees must examine the issue of future interests and impacts to a certain degree. This is a clear objective, but in fact growth in the workload of committees entrusted with legislative tasks, such as EU matters, means that very little time has been left for work on alternative futures. Discussions in plenary sessions sometimes really handle future policy, but this is usually when the Committee prepares a report for the session that is obliged to deliberate it.

However, what matters most when assessing the location of futures policy is the general division of labour within parliamentary democracy. As is the case everywhere in democracies, the division of labour within the political system means that the Government is a proactive political actor. What this means is that, taking the demands of the future into consideration, it makes proposals to the parliament, which in turn has the task of approving laws and the budget. The Government governs. The parliament can be active and a source of initiatives specifically in long-term futures policy, and for this it needs an empowered and capable body that concentrates, with the aid of the methods of futures research, on these often difficult and complex matters.

At a plenary session in 1999, when the status of the Committee was being decided, a clear argument in favour of giving it permanent status was presented. The starting point was that what was involved in futures policy was the *Eduskunta*'s prestige and Representatives' influence:[44]

> The Committee for the Future performs a service role in the legislature. It is a body that can comprehensively concentrate on examining the future, on articulating, from the perspectives of both parliamentary work and the general development of society, the present-day societal pressures to which also the law-making committees must find better answers than heretofore.
>
> In my view, putting futures work on a permanent footing is a matter of how active a relationship the Eduskunta adopts to not only appraising future courses of development, but also to the Government and the public service. After all, what is very largely involved at the moment is that we, as a parliament, are content with what the Government enacts within its Programme for Government as well as that,

[44] See Eduskunta Riksdagen, *supra* note 8.

> very largely, also citizens express criticism, asking whether public servants direct the Eduskunta. In my view, our attaching sufficient importance to futures work and giving it enough room in the legislature as a whole will also help us towards assuming the role that belongs to the Eduskunta. Namely, the legislature must remain, true to its traditions, the most important forum for the social discourse.

A point that has been emphasised on numerous occasions since then is that, in addition to legislative and budgetary power, the *Eduskunta* also has power of vision. In a world of turbulence, this form of power is more and more important.

## ANSWERS TO EARLIER QUESTIONS

Who has the power to decide for coming generations? Who has the right to speak in their name? The short answer is no one. Both economics and politics wield strong power over coming generations. Balancing between these powers and legacy, and especially the legitimacy of the power they wield, is a complicated but very important issue when keeping in mind the common and mutual good of people in the future.

Given that the Committee for the Future is a part of the parliament, it is in a certain sense easy to answer these questions, because in principle it derives all of its rights from the Finnish people, in practice living in today's representative democracy through voting. However, in a democracy – old or new – no one has the right to wield power over coming generations so strongly and in such a way that unborn generations lose the rights, means, tools, voice, or courage to decide on matters affecting their lives and well-being or the ability to plan and innovate for their children's future options.

The influence that the Committee for the Future wields is wider than the Committee itself, even within the parliament. In the Finnish system, Representatives are also members of one or two other parliamentary committees.[45] Some of them have discovered that it is innovative and effective to combine visionary power from a long-term perspective with practical legislative or budgetary power. In practice, all ministers are members of the parliament, and many of them have been part of the Committee for the Future.[46] All in all, long-term future work in the *Eduskunta* has acquired its flexible forms in the course of these last twenty-plus years.[47] A considerable proportion of ministers have been members of the Committee. In the period 2003–2007, its Chair, Jyrkki Katainen, was, as a young politician, elected as the leader of the biggest opposition party, the National Coalition, and became Minister of Finance after the election.[48] The Committee's

45 See Eduskunta Riksdagen, *supra* note 8, Members.

46 See Eduskunta Riksdagen, *supra* note 8.

47 Ibid.

48 Ibid.

report 'A Caring, Encouraging and Creative Finland', which appraised the information society, was incorporated, complete with name, into the Programme for Government. Mr Katainen later became Prime Minister and subsequently an EU Commissioner. Another Prime Minister also came from among the ranks of the Committee. Juha Sipilä, who also was a new politician, won election to the *Eduskunta* in 2011, chose to work on the Committee for the Future, and was selected some years later to lead another big party, the Centre Party. By the end of the parliamentary term he was number one in all polls, and then the winner in the general election in 2015 and Prime Minister.

The Committee for the Future is not one of the committees that parliamentarians most eagerly aspire to membership on after a general election, but it has proved itself to be a good vantage point from which to follow changes in the world and the challenges that coming generations will have to contend with. Visionary power is not easy to use, but when wielded wisely it offers a very strong position from which to practise politics. When it has worked well, the Committee's operational model has been an almost ideal way of creatively and critically combining scientific and technological information with a search for innovative new political solutions. The Committee has enjoyed fairly good success because sufficiently different politicians with broad minds and an interest in the new have sought membership of it. What is very important is that the Committee contains, on the one hand, very experienced, inquisitive, and bold politicians and, on the other, ambitious 'rising stars' with a thirst for knowledge. It is likewise important that they represent the Finns in all their diversity of education, from farmer to professor.

The second foundation stone for lasting success is that the aim in the Committee's reports is to be thorough and scientifically critical rather than trying to please the public or voters with showily produced pamphlet-style publications. Lighter versions of reports have been needed for information purposes, but the serious and thorough way that science deals with phenomena has not been overlooked.

## THE MOST CRITICAL POINT IS INDEPENDENCE: INDEPENDENCE FOR OR AGAINST

The most difficult thing in power that will affect coming generations is independence. Independence as freedom is important and clear, but with power it is another thing. Independence from what and with what justification and with what kind of tools? By its very nature, independence leads to knock-on problems in the instruments of the exercise of independent power, and naturally the most intractable problems concern such instruments as the right of veto, the power to prosecute, coercive power, and in general the right to impose sanctions.

When the status of institutions that will concern themselves with future generations is being determined, there is usually a specific desire for strong rights to intervene in the activities of the public authorities, to prevent authorities or other actors from doing something that is seen to conflict with the rights of future generations. The other approach to independence is the opposite: positive. It is to seek means of presenting – independent of the legislature and government, or perhaps more accurately in tandem with them – alternative choices for consideration in decision-making and to get decision-makers to act, in whatever position or sector they work, with the long-term implications in mind. Authorities can also be required (by law) to explain better than is ordinarily the case the long-term effects that their decisions will have and how they will impact on coming generations. This practice has long been followed in Europe when government bills with a bearing on environmental matters have been introduced in parliament.

The Nordic welfare model is based on an equal society – no differences of class.[49] Nordic countries are so-called low-hierarchy countries. This applies to politics, administration, business life, and social life. There are few hierarchies and those are very low and flexibly surmountable. The political-administrative system is founded on trust – the default assumption is always that the entire official apparatus will operate in accordance with the law and for the common good.[50] Additionally, it must be emphasised that the public service ethos is linked to the question of independence and governance, but in the Nordic countries from a slightly different starting point than is perhaps generally the case.[51] The administration has always been modest, the civil servants highly educated and democratic, and a mentality of equality has been dominant.[52] For this reason, most civil servants deal with their matters from the beginning until the decision, personally and without the interference of superiors. Civil servants are responsible for their actions in vertical and horizontal dimensions.

## CONCLUSION

To conclude, after dealing with institutional and organisational issues which actually led to some very critical points, work for coming generations is very important. It certainly is a fundamental task of democracy. Forerunning and foresight are extremely valuable in governance and in business, but also nowadays in the family and in the life of every citizen.

[49] See e.g. N. Brandal, O. Bratberg, and D. Thorsen (eds.), *The Nordic Model of Social Democracy* (Palgrave Macmillan 2013).

[50] See ibid.

[51] See ibid.

[52] See ibid.

# 22

# Welsh Commissioner for Sustainable Futures

*Alan Netherwood and Andrew Flynn*

This chapter explores Wales' sustainable development journey from the Earth Summit in Rio in 1992 to the groundbreaking legislation given Royal Assent in 2015 – The Well-being of Future Generations Act (Wales) 2015 (FGA).[1] This legislation places a legal duty on the Welsh public sector to maximise its contribution to sustainable development. It also establishes a Commissioner for Future Generations and a Commissioner's Office, innovations which will hold the public sector to account on its approach to sustainable development.[2] On its launch, Nikhil Seth, Director of Division for Sustainable Development, Department of Economic and Social Affairs at the UN said:

> The Act captures the spirit and essence of two decades of United Nations work in the area of sustainable development and serves as a model for other regions and countries. We hope that what Wales is doing today the world will do tomorrow. Action, more than words, is the hope for our current and future generations.[3]

The chapter describes and evaluates different phases of policy and implementation, as government at all levels in Wales has developed its ideas about how to respond to the sustainable development agenda. It also tracks the evolving nature of the various Commissioner roles in the past two decades, culminating in the current Office, and suggests how this role might influence Wales' journey toward sustainable development.

## STAGES OF WALES' SUSTAINABLE DEVELOPMENT JOURNEY

It is clear that Wales has gone through a series of distinct phases in developing its sustainable development policy, which has been strongly influenced by the

1 Well-being of Future Generations Act (Wales) 2015.
2 Ibid.; see also https://futuregenerations.wales/.
3 The Wales We Want, International Sustainable Development Event (Cardiff, 29 April 2015).

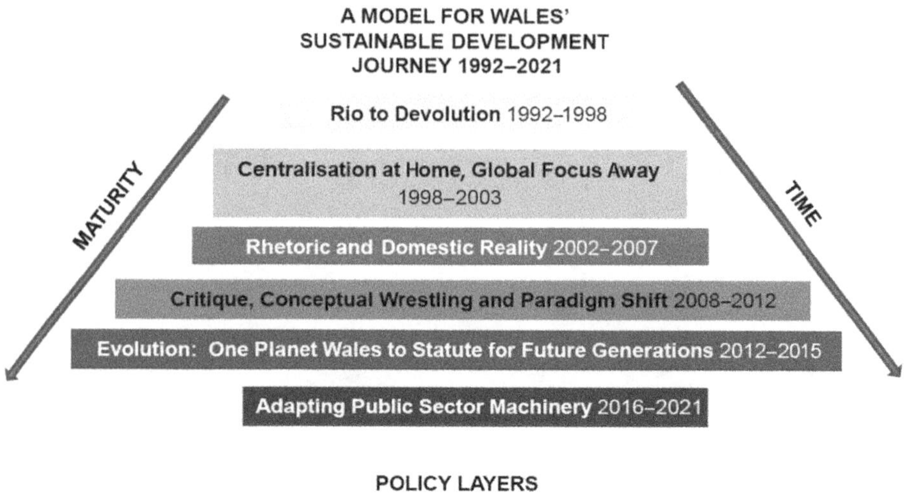


FIGURE 22.1 A model for stable development

establishment of devolved Welsh Government, local government reorganisations, an increasing centralisation of policy making, and a climate of increasing austerity within Government and the public sector. This journey has involved a wide range of actors, institutionally based, but also a number of policy entrepreneurs, acting as catalysts for change. This is a complex and multi-faceted chronology, covering over a quarter of a century. It should be noted that the FGA considers twenty-five years to equal a generation, so Wales has been involved in sustainable development policy making for a generation already.[4]

To provide some order to this complexity, the chapter suggests a model (below) to split the twenty-four years into six distinct phases, each with a descriptive title. Each phase has a set of specific characteristics which is explored in different sections in this chapter. Alongside this, a number of policy and implementation milestones are suggested in each of these phases in order to describe as succinctly as possible the change being seen on the ground. This is by no means a comprehensive analysis of activity, but is illustrative of the maturity of activity in each phase.

This approach could be used by any government or administration to provide some context to its own sustainable development journey, even though there may be different ways of describing activity in given time periods.

The making of policies to promote and deliver sustainable development has raised many challenges for established governmental bureaucracies. In Wales, those

[4] This covers the period from the commencement of devolution in 1998 to the initial publication of this chapter in 2018. During the drafting of the devolution legislation, debate was already taking place on how sustainable development should be promoted in Wales.

challenges have been multiplied because of the introduction of a new form of government.[5] The Government of Wales Act (1998)[6] created a devolved legislative body, the National Assembly for Wales, and under Section 121 of the Act required the new organisation to promote sustainable development in all of its work.[7] Devolution and the duty to promote sustainable development have had significant impacts upon the governance of Wales. A new institutional framework has had to grapple with a novel policy responsibility. It should be remembered, however, that even novel policy duties draw upon pre-existing agendas and perspectives, perhaps more so when the institutional capacity to deliver policy is limited.

Similarly, at an institutional level, the National Assembly for Wales, and its successor the Welsh Government, drew upon a predecessor body, the Welsh Office.[8] The drawing upon of former bureaucratic capacity, practices, and processes, alongside the unfolding of new policy approaches upon former ones matters in understanding how policy changes and the structure that it takes. For instance, a duty to promote sustainable development that proved challenging to mainstream has now become a commitment to the well-being of current and future generations that may well have more policy traction than anything before.[9] To develop an understanding of how sustainable development policy has developed in Wales since devolution, this chapter draws upon two concepts, *institutional layering* and *policy stretching*.

## INSTITUTIONAL LAYERING

In seeking to analyse how sustainable development has gained increasing traction in Welsh policy circles it is necessary to look for explanations that take into account structural elements of the situation. This means that the success of ideas such as sustainable development depends on political opportunity structures and the constellations of actors that are in a position to exert influence when a choice situation comes about.[10] These constellations are structured by institutional settings that shape the roles actors play, define the power they can command and the

[5] K. Bishop and A. Flynn, 'A Sustainable Development in Wales: Schemes, Structures, Debates and Delivery' (2015) 17 *Contemporary Wales* 92–112.

[6] UK Government of Wales Act (1998).

[7] Ibid.

[8] P. Chaney, T. Adrian, and A.J. Pithouse (eds.), *New Governance – New Democracy? Post Devolution Wales* (University of Wales Press 2001).

[9] Future Generations Commissioner for Wales, *Well-being in Wales: Planning Today for a Better Tomorrow* (Future Generations Commissioner for Wales 2017).

[10] P. Feindt and A. Flynn, 'Policy Stretching and Institutional Layering: British Food Policy between Security, Safety, Quality, Health and Climate Change' (2009) 4(3) *British Politics* 386–414.

processes they have to follow, and, in doing so, privilege certain interests over others and shield certain ideas from entering the arena. To understand the changing fortunes of sustainability in Welsh government, therefore, it is necessary to know something of the institutional context.

Quite often new policies and institutions are established without directly challenging the old ones. This creates what has been called institutional layering, a type of policy shift where new policies are created without the elimination of old ones.[11] Eric Schickler explains layering as the result of the accumulation of reforms, each of which is brought about by a different coalition of interests, a constellation he terms 'disjointed pluralism'.[12] This is certainly true in the case of devolution in Wales and what it meant for the early thinking on sustainable development and its delivery where there were attempts to follow on from longer standing ways in which UK government thinking and Welsh Office practiced had shaped policy.[13] Quickly, however, these efforts began to fall apart as devolution and a novel policy commitment to sustainable development began to challenge existing practices and agendas.[14]

Ideational and institutional tensions are not the only source of policy change. Often policies and institutions change in response to new (perceived) challenges for which existing institutions do not properly 'fit'.[15] Established institutions result from responses to past challenges and crises.[16] To become politically virulent, however, new problems must be translated into a language that resonates with some established norms, for example, equality or health and safety protection. As discussed below, there have been a series of changing circumstances, some responding to external events, which will trigger policy change because they can be presented as a deviation from an already embodied norm. In this process, however, norms and values, policies and paradigms are interpreted, allowing for their application or transposition to new areas.

The ways in which new meanings have been given to sustainable development has not only triggered new ideational and institutional layers, but has also helped to

[11] E Schickler, *Disjointed Pluralism: Institutional Innovation and the Development of the US Congress* (Princeton University Press 2001); J.S. Hacker, 'Privatizing Risk without Privatizing the Welfare State: The Hidden Politics of Social Policy Retrenchment in the United States' (2004) 98(2) *American Political Science Review* 243–260.

[12] Schickler, *supra* note 11 at 243–260.

[13] K. Bishop and A. Flynn, 'The National Assembly for Wales and the Promotion of Sustainable Development: Implications for Collaborative Government and Governance' (1999) 14(2) *Public Policy and Administration* 62–76.

[14] Bishop and Flynn, *supra* note 5.

[15] T. Skocpol, *Protecting Soldiers and Mothers: The Political Origins of Social Policy in the United States* (Harvard University Press 1992).

[16] D.C. North, *Institutions, Institutional Change and Economic Performance* (Cambridge University Press 1990).

expand thinking on sustainable development into new areas, such as that of future generations, and brought into play new institutions such as Cynnal Cymru: Sustain Wales, a Commissioner for Sustainable Futures, and in 2016 a Commissioner for Future Generations. The 'layering' metaphor therefore captures only a part of the processes, albeit a key one.

## POLICY STRETCHING

'Policy stretching' appears as a more accurate conceptual metaphor.[17] Policy stretching occurs where, over an extended period, elements of policy and governance are stretched to cover activities they were not intended to cover when they were designed.[18] This can cause problems, as incremental changes over time can incorporate contradictory goals or instruments, eroding key players' capacity to implement policy. When these tensions are found they often result in further 'tinkering' that may make the situation even worse. In the British context, policy stretching refers not only to new ideas, institutions, and players, but is inextricably linked to the emergence of a multilevel system of governance.[19]

The UK and Welsh Governments have shared individual responsibilities for sustainable development, and the EU has been active in policy making and legislation on the environment, whilst international commitments, such as those relating to climate change, are interpreted through a sustainability lens in Wales.[20] These commitments have, in turn, been interpreted by the Welsh Government for key agencies such as local authorities and non-government organisations.[21] These new arenas have opened up novel opportunities for a wider range of actors to engage with sustainable development policy, and in doing so have contributed to the process of policy stretching, confusion, and barriers to implementation. As the following sections reveal, changing governance structures, institutional layering, and policy stretching are interrelated processes with regard to Welsh policy on sustainable development. The extent to which a Commissioner for Future Generations role can address policy stretching and bring clarity to policy and delivery over coming years will be a litmus test of its success.

17 P. Feindt and A. Flynn, *supra* note 10.

18 Ibid.

19 B. Asare, P. Cairney, and D.T. Studlar, 'Federalism and Multilevel Governance in Tobacco Policy: the European Union, the United Kingdom, and Devolved UK Institutions' (2009) 29(1) *Journal of Public Policy* 79–102.

20 E. Royles, 'A Leader in a Changing World? Welsh Climate Change Policy' (2013) 63rd Political Studies Association Annual International Conference; A. Flynn, A. Kythreotis, and A. Netherwood, 'Climate Change Adaptation in Wales: Much Ado about Nothing?' (2016) 25(3) *Environmental Scientist* 32–39.

21 E. Royles and N. McEwen, 'Empowered for Action? Capacities and Constraints in Sub-State Government Climate Action in Scotland and Wales' (2015) 25(6) *Environmental Politics* 1034–1054.

## Rio to Devolution 1992–1998

Until devolution in 1998 there was little that was distinctive about a Welsh 'national' vision of sustainable development. The Welsh Office, the key governing institution, was part of the UK government, and Wales followed a UK policy lead.[22] Key international events such as the Rio Earth Summit of 1992 were led by the UK government.[23] Within Wales, economic interests were largely able to triumph over environmental ones in shaping policy problems and solutions.[24]

Indeed, it was in large part a reaction to the dominance of economic voices in the devolution debate of the 1990s that those concerned for environmental and sustainability issues began to organise themselves in the Sustainable Development Charter Group/Glamorgan Group.

The Group was a collection of over twenty-five environmental NGOs, key government agencies in Wales (Countryside Council for Wales, Environment Agency, and Welsh Development Agency),[25] and the Environmental Planning Research Unit at Cardiff University. It was established to debate the environmental policy implications of the devolution process and to co-ordinate attempts to lobby Parliament during the passage of the Government of Wales Bill.

The Government of Wales Bill received its First Reading in Parliament in November 1997.[26] Despite the commitment in the White Paper that the Assembly would promote sustainable development and subsequent ministerial statements reinforcing this point, the Bill did not contain any clause on sustainable development.[27] Concerns about the lack of a clause on sustainable development prompted the Sustainable Development Charter Group to publish a document outlining its proposals for a 'Greener National Assembly for Wales'.[28] Following further commitments given to Parliament during the passage of the Bill, a new clause 115 was tabled on 25 February 1998 which placed the Assembly under a duty to publish 'a scheme setting out its proposals for securing that its functions are exercised with due regard to the principle that sustainable development should be promoted'.[29] Whilst this amendment was welcomed in principle, there were considerable concerns about the wording of the clause. Following intense lobbying,

[22] A. Cole, J.B. Jones, and A. Storer, 'Inside the National Assembly for Wales: The Welsh Civil Service under Devolution' (2003) 74(2) *The Political Quarterly* 223–232.

[23] Bishop and Flynn, *supra* note 5.

[24] A. Flynn, T.K. Marsden, A. Netherwood, and R. Pitts, *Sustainable Development Effectiveness Report for the Welsh Assembly Government* (Welsh Assembly Government 2008).

[25] The Environment Agency Wales and Countryside Council were subsequently merged to become Natural Resources Wales, and the Welsh Development Agency was later incorporated into the Welsh Government.

[26] Bishop and Flynn, *supra* note 5.

[27] Bishop and Flynn, *supra* note 13.

[28] Ibid.

[29] Ibid.

notably by the RSPB, amendments to the 'sustainable development clause' were introduced by the Government during the Lords Committee stage that considerably strengthened it, and Section 121 was adopted.[30]

The commitment to promote sustainable development in Wales came at an opportune time, with environmental and sustainability issues high on policy agendas. Post-Rio, in some Welsh local authorities, there seems to have been a flurry of activity: 'visioning' for the future, practical community-based projects, and 'corporate' greening around resource efficiency. Research commissioned by WWF Cymru in 2012 suggests that that, prior to local government reorganisation in 1996, Rio had a 'galvanising' effect in Wales.[31] Authorities in Gwent, Cardiff, and Wrexham were described as early movers on Local Agenda 21 amongst others. Environmental co-ordinator posts were established in many local councils and, influenced by UK guidance from the Local Government Management Board, sustainable development through LA21 became established as a 'brand' to work though for local authorities, internally and externally.[32] This brand did not work for everybody, with some Councils seeing LA21 as woolly, unworkable, and never quite fitting into the aims of local authorities. This contrasted and mixed picture has been picked up in previous studies by the Joseph Rowntree Foundation[33] and by the BRASS Research Centre.[34]

Local Agenda 21 activity continued, despite local government reorganisation through 1995 and 1996, with a small group of Environmental Co-ordinators lobbying the Welsh Office to include LA21 as part of the 'makeup' of new Councils. In Caerphilly CBC's case, this ensured clear responsibility, resources, and staffing to pick up on the agenda developed in Gwent.[35] In Cardiff's case, innovative work such as the European SD Indicators project was dropped, as the City Council morphed into a new unitary authority.[36] Far from stalling activity, in many Councils the mandate of Agenda 21 was continued through reorganisation and became an established way of working.[37] This suggested a resilience around LA21 and the themes picked up on in Rio up until 2002. The role of organisations such as the Local Government Management Board, the Local Government International Bureau, and ICLEI had a clear role in this, providing guidance, conferences, and

30 Ibid.

31 A. Netherwood and A. Flynn, *What Can an Earth Summit Do for Wales* (Report for WWF Cymru 2012).

32 Ibid.

33 P. Williams and A. Thomas, *Sustainable Development in Wales: Understanding Effective Governance* (Joseph Rowntree Foundation 2004).

34 A. Flynn and A. Netherwood, *Communities and Their Quality of Life: How Local Government Is Delivering Sustainable Development*, Working Paper Series No. 16 (Centre For Business Relationships, Accountability, Sustainability and Society 2004).

35 Ibid.

36 Ibid.

37 Ibid.

case studies to support activity. LA21 was given further impetus by a UK Government requirement of local authorities to have a Local Agenda 21 in place by 2000.

This phase of the journey, 'Rio to Devolution', is characterised by a wide range of local authority and NGO engagement in the sustainable development agenda, with a strengthening of the national sustainable development policy through Section 121. From 1997 to 1999 and the Government of Wales Act through to the first National Assembly elections, there was also tremendous upheaval as Wales entered devolution, moving from the Welsh Office through to the National Assembly of Wales and the Welsh Assembly Government (WAG). It could be argued that the absence of a national approach from 1992 to 1998 created a vacuum that was eagerly filled by local government and interest groups. This contributed to both institutional layering, as new ways of working were developed, and policy stretching, as Local Agenda 21 activity continued, even though, with the establishment of the National Assembly for Wales, new governance structures would mean sustainable development policy would become more centralised.

### *Centralisation at Home, Global Focus Away 1998–2003*

Securing the passage of Section 121 in the *Government of Wales Act* 1998 was a considerable achievement for organisations keen to promote sustainable development in Wales. The Assembly, in plenary, formally adopted its first Sustainable Development Scheme Learning to Live Differently in November 2000.[38]

A key theme of the Sustainable Development Scheme and the associated Action Plan was better decision making for sustainable development.[39] The Assembly wished to demonstrate both its commitment to the pursuit of sustainable development and to act as an exemplar to others in Wales. One clear example of how Wales wished to act and to be seen to act was the First Minister's attendance at the WSSD in Johannesburg in August 2002. This was to show to domestic and international audiences the commitment of a senior political figure to sustainable development. One practical outcome of the Summit was the central role played by the Assembly in the Gauteng Declaration that established a global network of regional governments committed to sustainable development, NRG4SD.

According to the Sustainable Development 2003 Annual Report and Action Plan:[40]

> We [the Assembly] now find ourselves in a leadership position internationally in sustainable development, which we never expected when making our Scheme. It doesn't mean that we have all the answers. It does mean that we are firmly at the

[38] National Assembly for Wales, *Learning to Live Differently: Sustainable Development Scheme* (2000).

[39] Ibid.

[40] Welsh Assembly Government Sustainable, *Development 2003 Annual Report and Action Plan* (2003).

forefront in posing the key questions. We have placed ourselves in a wonderful position to access new best practice world-wide, and thus keep ourselves at the cutting edge of new thinking about sustainable development.

In its annual Sustainable Development Report and Action Plan the Assembly Government documents progress in terms of policies and strategies, Action Plan commitments and sustainability indicators.[41] Although 'political' rather than self-critical documents – always keen to indicate achievements rather than challenges – the Annual Reports vividly illustrate the breadth of activity that the Assembly was engaged in. The reports also show an ever-greater confidence in the achievements of the Assembly Government, such that for 2003 it claims that the actions it describes:

show an unprecedented commitment to mainstreaming sustainable development principles as the way Wales does business. This isn't a one-off event, but a cultural change, and as such takes time. Though there is still more to do during the 2 years since the making of the Assembly's Sustainable Development Scheme we have made considerable progress within the Assembly and with its partners and agencies.[42]

There is thus at least considerable rhetoric in support of the impact that organising for sustainability has had on the operations of the Assembly. As the CAC report on the Effectiveness of the Scheme concludes:[43]

The Assembly has established co-ordination mechanisms that sit at the heart of the political and administrative structure of the Assembly. This is a testament to the Assembly's commitment. It has also done well in mainstreaming responsibility for the duty across the organisation.

Nevertheless, the degree of buy-in to sustainability varied both horizontally and vertically within the Assembly (as it did within local government and other public bodies).

The work cited previously for WWF Cymru showed that from a high point of activity on Local Agenda 21 at the turn of the new century a rapid shift in activity occurred.[44] Local Agenda 21 strategies continued to be published by local authorities into 2002, but this seems to be more of a legacy activity than a driver of change. Instead, there was a rebranding of Agenda 21 around this time in Wales. Local Agenda 21 was gradually replaced by a new approach to 'long-term' planning advocated by the WAG, through Community Planning Guidance, encouraging community-level planning over a five-year period and the use of quality of life indicators to engage communities in local 'visions'.[45] Local Agenda 21 seemed to

[41] Ibid.

[42] Ibid.

[43] *How Effectively Has the National Assembly for Wales Promoted Sustainable Development? Report to the Welsh Assembly Government* (CAG 2003).

[44] Netherwood and Flynn, *supra* note 31.

[45] Ibid.

have gone out of 'vogue'. Sustainable development discourse in local government started to focus on 'deliverables', resource efficiency, and institutional change rather than 'visioning' and community involvement. This new 'brand', which replaced Local Agenda 21, was more locally focused, still espousing sustainability but losing the link to the wider international context.

At this time the WAG began to develop a wide-ranging and sophisticated *regional* policy landscape to respond to the issues discussed at Rio and Johannesburg – issuing guidance to local governments and placing them among their delivery partners. Secondly, the WAG began to 'own' the international SD Brand, more than local authorities, through the iterations of the SD Scheme, attendance at Johannesburg, involvement in NRG4SD, and support for partnership work around, for example, Ecological Footprinting, Fairtrade, and Wales for Africa.[46] Thirdly, the WAG took a lead role in framing the national debate around SD and global issues, while local authorities became increasingly focused on delivering local outcomes.[47]

However, also at this time, the third sector began to develop its ideas about supporting sustainable development activity across civil society, while providing critical advice on the Scheme. In 2002, Rod Aspinwall launched Cynnal Cymru – Sustain Wales, the 'Welsh' part of the UK-wide Sustainable Development Commission (appointed by the UK Government), establishing a forum for discussion across Wales sectors to feed into SD policy.[48] In subsequent years, Cynnal Cymru would provide a catalyst for policy input, engagement, and awareness-raising across Wales on this agenda, particularly through its Chair, Morgan Parry.

This phase of the journey is characterised by an increasing centralisation of the WAG's activity, while local authorities and interest groups were required to react to a new institution with emerging policy and ways of working and funding the public sector. This phase also represents a reorganisation of institutional layers and a reframing of policy to delineate between domestic and international SD policy and activity.

## *Rhetoric and Reality 2004–2008*

The research from 2006 shows that the period 2004–2006 was marked by a growing maturity and confidence of Welsh Government in its own legitimacy.[49] The WAG's duty to promote SD was a source of pride across the Assembly. A typical comment at the time was that 'I guess . . . everything that we do is SD proofed . . . the department is all about creating a sustainable environment for the people of Wales [now] and for

46 Ibid.

47 Ibid.

48 Ibid.

49 A. Flynn and T. Marsden, *Aiming Higher: Assessing the Sustainable Development Plans and Actions of the Welsh Assembly Government in Terms of Its Commitments in the UK-wide Strategy* (Sustainable Development Commission 2006).

future generations.'[50] Similarly the interviewee commented: 'The key point to remember is that everything we do is in the context of contributing to sustainable development.'[51] Whilst these *sentiments* would have been shared by other members of staff in the Assembly, the *commitments* of Assembly departments and divisions to the Assembly's SD responsibilities did vary.

An indication of the variability in expectation of how different interests may contribute to SD is contained in the Welsh Government's Action Plan, *Starting to Live Differently*.[52] This document attempted to give meaning to the Government's responsibility to promote SD. It was time-limited to the period of an Assembly Government. The document had sixteen thematic sections which outline policies, commitments, and actions. It featured no discussion of what the challenges might have been in meeting targets or of what meeting (or failing to meet) targets might mean for the corporate delivery of sustainability. It contained a 'top ten' commitments, many of which were quite narrow and specific. Three of them related directly to adapting the National Assembly estate to more sustainable processes (such as renewable energy sources, and uses of building best practice regulations), and four were associated with setting up new projects concerning renewables, new biofuel developments, and energy-efficiency objectives.[53]

Furthermore, there was little indication of how Assembly Sponsored Public Bodies or local authorities might contribute to the Scheme. This was an approach focused firmly on the way the Government was doing its own business, with little thought to how partners might be engaged in shaping the scheme or its delivery. As Flynn and Netherwood concluded in their review of local government experiences of delivering sustainable development,[54] there were significant challenges in making the agenda relevant to community leaders and in ensuring political and senior officer commitment. This was supported by a Wales Audit Office review of local authority SD activity.[55] So, whilst local government had shown itself able to promote innovative sustainable development projects, there was, as with the Assembly Government, little sign of corporate mainstreaming of sustainability.

At this stage, it was becoming increasingly apparent that new ideas and ways of working were competing with older more established ones, as one set of policies began to overlay another. Developmental interests remained powerful, political leaders remained cautious about what they could promise, and key partners in the delivery of sustainable development were not fully engaged in the task. Changing institutional relationships were accompanied by new demands upon the Welsh Government as to what sustainable development meant and how it could be

50 Ibid.
51 Ibid.
52 WAG, *The Sustainable Development Action Plan 2004–2007* (2004).
53 Ibid.
54 Flynn and Netherwood, *supra* note 35.
55 Wales Audit Office, *Sustainable Development in Welsh Local Government* (2005).

TABLE 22.1 *Recommendations from the Effectiveness Review of the Welsh Government Sustainable Development Scheme, 2008*

(a) Articulate what sustainable development looks like – create a route map for sustainable development which sets out what a Sustainable Wales would look like with clear emphasis on how we will get there.
(b) Engage sub-national actors in the articulation of SD and of the role that they can play in delivering sustainable outcomes by:
- developing clear goals, outcomes and targets which the different sectors can understand;
- creating conditions for them to align their activity to the route map;
- enabling them to articulate this locally and drive implementation on the ground.

(c) Concentrate efforts on the 'wicked' and difficult issues and policy conflicts, for example between economic development, transport and ecological limits.
(d) Communicate the sustainable development choices on offer and the pace of change required to partners and the general public.
(e) Articulate the costs and benefits of inaction/action on SD, especially regarding climate change.
(f) Provide meaningful and consistent messages on SD in guidelines, policy development and other networking opportunities with partners, especially local government.
(g) Provide a challenge for Ministerial portfolios and WAG Divisions to identify their high SD impact activity and propose and deliver more sustainable outcomes.
(h) Set clear national targets for sustainable development at a strategic level, and establish and maintain a simple indicator set of well-being (or happiness!).
(i) Ensure that there are clear lines of financial accountability, scrutiny and reporting.
(j) Create the conditions for delivery and bring key actors along with them.

*Source*: A. Flynn, T. Marsden, A. Netherwood, and R. Pitts, *The Sustainable Development Effectiveness Report for Welsh Government* (2008)

delivered. Increasingly, these tensions that were arising from institutional stretching and policy layering were manifesting themselves in day-to-day debates.

In 2007 Netherwood and Flynn, alongside others, were commissioned to undertake an Effectiveness Review of the Sustainable Development Scheme.[56] This review focused on how the Welsh Government could engage nationally to promote sustainable development, encompassing the views of a wide range of institutions discussing strategy, policy, processes, and finance in order to understand what could 'shift' implementation of the Scheme across Wales. A range of recommendations were made which highlighted the opportunities, but the work also highlighted the *absence* of a strategic approach to SD policy and implementation. The recommendations are shown in Table 22.1.

This work suggested that a far more nuanced approach was required to deliver on the Sustainable Development Scheme, one that was outwardly focused and would

[56] A. Flynn, T. Marsden, A. Netherwood, and R. Pitts, *The Sustainable Development Effectiveness Report for Welsh Government* (2008).

engage actors across Wales. The work also illustrated that clarity of approach would be key, a Scheme to make sense of institutional layers and conflicting policy aims. This could be said to be the point at which the rhetoric of the approach of Scheme did not match the reality.

It is interesting more than a decade on to compare these recommendations and hold them up against the architecture of the Well-being of Future Generations Act. There are clear links and similarities, as set out below. It was clear that a 'shift' was needed to make SD policy and delivery a central aim of Government and the public sector. This shift took another eight years, the first of which signified a period of critique, reflection, and shifting paradigms.

### *Critique, Conceptual Wrangling, and Paradigm Shift 2008–2012*

This phase of the journey was informed by a number of external reviews of Wales' approach to SD, which showed variable evidence that policy and strategy was being delivered with SD at its core. The reviews exposed weaknesses in the architecture of SD at the same time as major activity in both domestic and international arenas. Table 22.2 illustrates an incredibly busy picture of strategy and policy making, which was included in successive annual reports on the Scheme. These add to the institutional layering and policy stretching, but also add to the confused picture, picked up in the 2008 review.

There was little sign in the next iteration of the Sustainable Development Scheme that the sorts of shifts suggested in the 2008 review were taking place. The revised Scheme, 'One Wales: One Planet', aspired to place sustainable development at the heart of government as 'the central organising principle'.[57] Three external reviews of the Welsh Government on this issue ultimately showed this not to be the case. One from Wales Audit Office published in 2010 which focused on Welsh Government itself, one commissioned from Netherwood by WWF Cymru in 2011 focusing on policy mechanisms, and the third undertaken by Price Waterhouse Coopers, a formal review on the effectiveness of the Scheme.

The Wales Audit Office Report in January 2010 found that sustainable development was not effectively embedded throughout the civil service.[58] The agenda was seen as one of a number of competing priorities, rather than the means by which the Assembly Government manages its competing priorities. The work also highlighted problems with the culture of the organisation which inhibited integration across the organisation.

[57] Welsh Government, *One Wales: One Planet Sustainable Development Scheme for Wales* (2009).

[58] Wales Audit Office, *Sustainable Decision Making in Welsh Assembly Government* (2010).

TABLE 22.2 *Examples of domestic and international activity, 2008–2011*

| Domestic policy and governance | International activity |
|---|---|
| 2008: WLGA Sustainable Development Framework launched for local government | 2008: Wales signs UNDP climate change action programme for Africa |
| 2009: One Wales: One Planet Revised SD Scheme | 2008: AM Jane Davidson, attends UN climate talks in Poznan |
| 2009: Wales Climate Change Commission established | 2008: Wales becomes first ever Fairtrade Nation 2010 Wales co-chairs global network nrg4SD |
| 2009: Code for Sustainable Homes | 2010: Wales is the UK's only representative at the Quebec climate talks |
| 2010: Zero Waste Strategy launched<br>2010: Wales Climate Change Strategy launched<br>2010: Wales Sustainable Development Charter launched<br>2011: Wales implements carrier bag levy<br>2011: Sustainable Development Commission for Wales closed<br>2011: Wales Sustainable Development Commissioner post established | |

*Source*: A. Flynn and A. Netherwood, *Communities and Their Quality of Life: How Local Government Is Delivering Sustainable Development*, Working Paper Series No. 16 (Centre For Business Relationships, Accountability, Sustainability and Society 2004)

The work undertaken for WWF Cymru highlighted areas of concern,[59] where 'One Wales: One Planet' was *not* featuring in the policy discourse, particularly in economic development, the public sector, transport, and housing. However, there *were* areas where this was featuring strongly: in food and agriculture, energy, waste, and the public sector. The report suggested a need for greater accountability, scrutiny, and monitoring of performance, as well as a route map for long-term, high-level strategy.

The PWC Effectiveness Review of the Scheme, published in December 2011,[60] focused on a lack of leadership within the civil service, marginalisation of the sustainable development agenda, and underdeveloped governance and scrutiny arrangements. Its recommendations focused on the need to develop leadership on SD and more effectively embed this into the workings of the organisation.

59 A. Netherwood, *Progress in Embedding the One Planet Aspiration in Welsh Government* (WWF 2011).

60 PWC, *Effectiveness Review of the Sustainable Development Scheme* (Report for Welsh Government 2011).

The reaction to these pieces of work led to the minister with responsibility for SD challenging directors of government departments on the findings, and a number of policy think pieces emerging from the Director General for Sustainable Development, Clive Bates. These were shared with the Board of Cynnal Cymru for discussion, enabling a thorough exploration of concepts and mechanisms to better frame 'sustainable development' within Welsh Government.[61]

At the same time, the Welsh Local Government Association launched a Sustainable Development Framework in 2008 to support Wales' local authorities on sustainable development policy and practice. This provided consultancy support, policy initiatives, guidance and debate around this agenda for both officers and locally elected politicians.

Unfortunately, in summer 2011, the UK Government department DEFRA announced that the UK Sustainable Development Commission would be closing, withdrawing support and advocacy for the UK administrations.[62] In response, the sustainable development Minister, Jane Davidson, established a new Sustainable Futures Commissioner post in Wales, held by Peter Davies, to act as an advocate for SD and act as a critical friend to Welsh Government.[63]

One of Davies' roles was to produce an independent commentary on Annual Reports of 'One Wales: One Planet', and his commentary in the 2012–2013 Report provided further critique of progress, citing lack of clarity, silo working, the scheme being peripheral to central policy, and the scheme having little traction within the public sector.[64] This phase of the journey was also characterised by a growing realisation that current processes and accountability frameworks would not place SD as a central organising principle of government and the public sector.

It is important to note at this point that there was no great demand from civil society or NGOs for a new Commissioner role. The impetus for change came from a government minister wanting to address the inertia towards sustainable development in governance systems across Wales. It was her intervention which led the Labour Party administration to pursue legislation through the new programme of Government 2011–2016, with the following commitments:[65]

[61] These covered (1) policy context, (2) sustainable development and well-being, (3) ecological limits, (4) hard choices and trade-offs, (5) evidence and science, (6) measurement, (7) behaviour change and mandate, and (8) governance and integration.

[62] M. Kinver, 'UK Government Axes Its Sustainability Watchdog', BBC News (22 July 2010) www.bbc.co.uk/news/science-environment-10725394 accessed 30 November 2017.

[63] 'Written Statement – Commissioner for Sustainable Futures' (Welsh Government 2011) http://gov.wales/about/cabinet/cabinetstatements/previous-administration/2011/sfcommissioner/?lang=en accessed 30 November 2017.

[64] Welsh Government, *One Wales: One Planet The Sustainable Development Annual Report 2012–2013* (Welsh Government 2013).

[65] Welsh Government Programme for Government, 'Chapter 11 Environment and Sustainability' (Welsh Government 2011) http://archive.cynnalcymru.com/sites/default/files/Programme%20for%20Government.pdf accessed 30 November 2017.

- adapting the sustainable development scheme which applied to Welsh Government to a Sustainable Development Bill which would apply across the public sector;
- establishing a statutory sustainable development commissioner; and
- establishing an independent body (from the Government) to provide scrutiny, advice, and support on SD.

This is where the impetus for the FGA came from, a brave move to place sustainable development at the heart of government and public service. This resulted in a White Paper that led to a Sustainable Development Bill,[66] and then an Act.[67] This was a recognition that rather than continue to 'tweak' and 'tinker' with existing approaches, Wales was ready for a fresh approach to both sustainable development policy and institutional change.

### *Evolution: One Wales One Planet to Statute for Future Generations 2011–2015*

From December 2012, onwards this phase signifies an evolution from One Wales: One Planet (which mainly listed government achievements and aspirations) towards a legislative process to embed sustainable development as a central organising principle across the Welsh Public Sector, including the Welsh Government.

During this period, the piece of legislation passed through six ministers, each time evolving in relation to the portfolio. It moved from a predominantly natural resource focused scheme to a Bill and Act focused on future generations, communities, and the public sector. Jane Davidson started the legislative process, which was then passed through John Griffiths to Huw Lewis to Jeff Cuthbert. The change to a broader community-focused Bill reflected the First Minister's priorities.[68] In April 2013, the Welsh Government released a 'White Paper' to consult on a Sustainable Development Bill; by July the consultation had changed its name to a Future Generations Bill at the behest of Huw Lewis.[69]

The White Paper, 'A Sustainable Wales Better Choices for a Better Future – A Consultation on Proposals for a Sustainable Development Bill', ran from December 2012 to March 2013. This covered issues such as governance, accountability, duties on public bodies, the role of a new SD body, and the specific nature of

[66] Welsh Government, *A Sustainable Wales Better Choices for a Better Future – A Consultation on Proposals for a Sustainable Development Bill* (2012).

[67] Welsh Government, Well-being of Future Generations (Wales) Act (2015).

[68] Welsh Government Programme for Government, 'Forward' (Welsh Government 2011) http://archive.cynnalcymru.com/sites/default/files/Programme%20for%20Government.pdf accessed 30 November 2017.

[69] Welsh Government, 'Minutes and Papers of the Meeting of the Cabinet' (Welsh Government 2013) http://gov.wales/about/cabinet/meetings/previous-administration/11jun13/?lang=en accessed 30 November 2017.

a legal duty, and a definition for sustainable development. The responses to this were taken through the legislative process of the National Assembly for Wales, with amendments made towards the end of the process to include aspects of global responsibility.[70]

Other key milestones in the process included consultation on a set of national well-being goals in January 2015,[71] goals which each public body would have to align with. Finally, in May 2015 the Bill was given Royal Assent to be enacted from 1 April 2016. Wales now has a legal definition of sustainable development, and there are legal duties for public bodies to maximise their contribution to SD as corporate entities and as part of new partnership called Public Service Boards – through the application of a *sustainable development principle*.[72] Consultation on Statutory Guidance was undertaken in November 2015 and formally launched in March 2016.[73] Forty-six National indicators were developed and launched in April 2016.[74] The legal definition of sustainable development in the FGA is as follows:

> 'sustainable development' means the process of improving the economic, social, environmental and cultural well-being of Wales by taking action, in accordance with the sustainable development principle, aimed at achieving the well-being goals.[75]

The sustainable development principle is described as five ways of working: (1) *looking to the long term* so that we do not compromise the ability of future generations to meet their own needs; (2) *taking an integrated approach* so that public bodies look at all the well-being goals in deciding on their well-being objectives; (3) *involving a diversity of the population* in the decisions that affect them; (4) *working with others in a collaborative way* to find shared sustainable solutions; and (5) understanding the root causes of issues *to prevent them* from occurring.

Alongside the ongoing legislative process, two major programmes had significant influence on the Bill process and the statutory guidance emerging alongside the Act. The first was the *Wales We Want* conversation, initiated as a pilot exercise by the Welsh Government to mirror the UN 'World We Want' process. Led by Peter Davies, the Commissioner, this involved year-long conversations with individuals, groups, organisations, and communities across Wales.[76] This was facilitated by a third-sector body, Cynnal Cymru, which acted as an 'office' for the Commissioner

[70] Welsh Government, *The Wales We Want* (Welsh Government 2013).

[71] Welsh Government, *How to Measure a Nation's Progress? National Indicators for Wales* (Welsh Government 2016).

[72] Welsh Government, Well-being of Future Generations (Wales) Act 2015, pt. 2, sect. 5.

[73] Welsh Government, *Shared Purpose: Shared Future: Draft Statutory Guidance for the Well-being of Future Generations (Wales) Act 2015* (Welsh Government 2015).

[74] Welsh Government, *supra* note 74.

[75] Welsh Government, *SPSF1: Statutory Guidance for the Well-being of Future Generations Act (Wales) 2015* (Welsh Government 2016).

[76] Welsh Government, *supra* note 73.

on both SD and climate change.[77] Discussions focused on a variety of intergenerational challenges including climate change, poverty, an ageing population, and health inequalities, as well as the opportunities available that require collaborative approaches and integrated solutions.[78] This culminated in a report which identified seven foundations for the well-being of future generations.[79] This informed discussions as the Bill went through the legislative process.

The second was an 'Early Adopter' Programme, involving eleven local authorities and three national parks,[80] led by the Welsh Local Government Association and delivered predominantly by consultancies Price Waterhouse Coopers and Netherwood Sustainable Futures. This ran from June 2014 to December 2015 and engaged these bodies in an assessment for their readiness for the FGA, developed bespoke work on adapting strategy, processes, systems, and governance in readiness for the Act, and developed a range of tools and techniques as a stand-alone resource for public bodies to use. Lessons from this eighteen-month pilot informed the detail of the guidance for both the forty-four bodies covered by the Act, but also the newly charged Public Service Boards. A basic overview of the Act is shown in Tables 22.3 and 22.4 below.

The Act is about changing the Welsh public sector to align it towards SD. The statutory guidance goes into detail about how this should be done. Table 22.4 seeks to summarise changes for both the forty-four bodies, which include Councils, health bodies, and others, as well as the twenty Public Service Boards.

There are other key provisions in the Act: (1) for the establishment of a Commissioner for Future Generations and an Office of the Commissioner; (2) for the Commissioner to publish a report on behalf of Future Generations a year before Welsh Government Elections; (3) for the Auditor General Wales to review the response to the FGA by public bodies; and (4) for the Commissioner to review PSB activity and make recommendations to public bodies.[81]

77 Sustain Wales, 'Wales' Commissioner for Sustainable Futures' (Sustain Wales 2011) http://archive.cynnalcymru.com/commissioner accessed 30 November 2017.

78 Welsh Government, *supra* note 73.

79 Commissioner for Sustainable Futures, *The Wales We Want: A Report on Behalf of Future Generations. The Seven Foundations for the Well-being of Future Generations* (Welsh Government 2015): '1. Children need to be given the best start in life from very early years 2. Future generations need thriving communities built on a strong sense of place 3. Living within global environmental limits, managing our resources efficiently and valuing our environment is critical 4. Investing in growing our local economy is essential for the well-being of future generations 5. Well-being of all depends on reducing inequality and a greater value on diversity 6. Greater engagement in the democratic process, a stronger citizen voice and active participation in decision making is fundamental for the well-being of future generations 7. Celebrating success, valuing our heritage, culture and language will strengthen our identity for future generations.'

80 Councils: Blaenau Gwent, Caerphilly, Cardiff, Merthyr Tydfil, Monmouthshire, Newport; Powys, Swansea, Torfaen, Vale of Glamorgan, Wrexham National Parks: Brecon Beacons; Pembrokeshire Coast; Snowdonia.

81 Well-being of Future Generations (Wales) Act (2015).

TABLE 22.3 *General responsibilities for public sector bodies in Wales under the* Well-Being of Future Generations Act

| | |
|---|---|
| • Adopt the **Sustainable Development Principle** with five ways of working: long term; preventative; collaborative; integrated; involvement.<br>• Work towards seven national **well-being goals,** maximising their contribution to sustainable development<br>  • a prosperous Wales<br>  • a resilient Wales<br>  • a healthier Wales<br>  • a more equal Wales<br>  • a Wales of cohesive communities<br>  • a Wales of vibrant culture and Welsh language<br>  • a globally responsible Wales. | • Focus their work on **Future Generations** (as well as current generations).<br>• Contribute to the work of statutory **Public Service Boards.**<br>• Contribute to the development of a **Well-Being Plan** based on a long-term assessment of the state of communities and 'place' aligned to local authority areas.<br>• Respond to a new **accountability framework** including reporting and review by **Auditor General Wales** for the National Assembly with advice from a **Future Generations Commissioner.**<br>• It also establishes twenty statutory **Public Service Boards** which are tasked to develop and implement a local Well-Being Plan and are also subject to scrutiny by the Commissioner. |

*Source*: Welsh Government, *Shared Purpose: Shared Future SPSF 1: Core Guidance* (2016)

TABLE 22.4 *Specific responsibilities for public sector bodies in Wales under the Well-Being of Future Generations Act*

| | |
|---|---|
| • Maximise contribution to well-being goals in accordance with the sustainable development principle.<br>• Embed the principle in seven core areas<br>  • corporate planning<br>  • risk management<br>  • workforce planning<br>  • performance management<br>  • financial planning<br>  • procurement<br>  • assets.<br>• Define, deliver and report on well-being objectives aligned to the national goals.<br>• Take into account future trends and PSB well-being assessments. | The **Public Service Boards** need to:<br>• work jointly towards all well-being goals<br>• produce a local well-being assessment<br>• produce and implement well-being objectives in a local well-being plan<br>• take reasonable steps to meet objectives in accordance with sustainable development principle<br>• provide annual reports on progress. |

*Sources*: Welsh Government, *Shared Purpose: Shared Future SPSF 1: Core Guidance* (2016); *Shared Purpose: Shared Future SPSF* (2016); *Shared Purpose: Shared Future SPSF* 3 (2016)

This whole approach displays, on paper, a steep change in governance, strategy, corporate activity, planning, and scrutiny in the public sector. It is a very ambitious piece of legislation, which has been embraced by some public bodies and less so by others. At the time of writing, the governance systems are being set up for Public Service Boards and public bodies are beginning to grapple with the ramifications.

The Act clearly represents an attempt to align Welsh government policies, alongside public service, behind a set of statutory goals and principles to apply in public service delivery and institutional reform. The FGA is now the benchmark against which we can apply the concepts of policy stretching and institutional layering, as shown by the role of the Future Generations Commissioner, which draws upon previous commissioner roles and has a wider policy remit.

The Commissioner role is one of advising, supporting, and challenging public sector bodies as they develop their plans, and to provide a report, on behalf of Future Generations, once every five years, prior to an election, to feed into the electoral cycle. This is a change from previous incarnations of the Commissioner role, from a national 'advocate' for sustainable development and the Act, to a role firmly embedded in governance structures. A key question, though, is whether the Act and the Commissioner role will reduce the ideological and institutional tensions described earlier and throughout this chapter. The authors seek to peer into the future to consider this question as part of the next phase on the journey, which discusses how the Government and others might respond to the statute, and what might be expected over the next five years.

### *Adapting Private Sector Machinery 2016–2021*

This leg of the journey is characterised by the FGA starting to influence the way the public sector does its business. The legislation came into force in April 2016. A new Future Generations Commissioner, Sophie Howe, has set up an Office of the Future Generations Commissioner, which has responsibility to scrutinise and monitor the public sector, as well as provide support to forty-four bodies across Wales and twenty local partnerships called Public Service Boards.[82] The Wales Audit Office is charged with auditing responses to the FGA by public bodies are consulting on the most appropriate way to do this.[83] Meanwhile, bodies which are affected by the Act continue to explore its implications including Health Trusts and Local University Health Boards.

[82] Future Generations Commissioner for Wales, 'Our Work' (Future Generations Commissioner for Wales 2017) https://futuregenerations.wales/making-it-happen/# accessed 30 November 2017.

[83] Wales Audit Office, *The Well-being of Future Generations and What It Means for Your Audit.* A consultation by the Auditor General for Wales (2016).

In January 2016, Netherwood and Price Waterhouse Coopers presented the new Commissioner with a list of priorities for the OFGC based on their work with local authorities, which included:[84]

(a) focusing on (and building on) the *seven core areas of change* for the forty-four bodies;
(b) Councils and PSBs establishing a *'whole Council' or 'whole public body' approach* to the FGA;
(c) support for *governance mechanisms* to represent the needs of future generations;
(d) strengthen the link of FGA to *'dominant' public sector agendas* – austerity and service reform;
(e) clarify the relationship between the FGA and other existing and emerging *statute* and integrated approaches to meeting legislative requirements;
(f) build capacity for *policy analysis* in preparing well-being assessments and plans;
(g) clarify the *role of regulators* in stimulating the 'step change' outlined in the FGA;
(h) establish a clear *understanding/baseline of the maturity and capacity of the forty-four bodies' ability* to respond to the Act – to enable a more sophisticated and targeted approach to support;
(i) engage with *groups/professions* and key actors on the detail of adapting current approaches to respond to the FGA;
(j) establish a *public sector network* to develop capacity to respond; and
(k) encourage the *Welsh Government* to communicate what they are doing to help the 'other' forty-three bodies to implement the Act.

These summarise a strategic approach to engage part of the public sector machinery in Wales to progress the Act, but they could be applied equally across the whole sector. The last point is especially important, as the Welsh Government needs to create the conditions for others to implement the Act. To that end, the authors developed a list of key 'asks' of the next Programme of Government, following the Welsh Government election in May 2016. This version focuses not only on key asks, but on what this would enable by 2021 and the 'litmus tests' for whether the Welsh Government and other actors in the public sector were really embedding the sustainable development principle in their activity (Table 22.5).

Some of these litmus tests focus on policy and the extent to which the sustainable development principle has been applied, whereas others apply to the effectiveness of institutional reform and the way in which new partnerships and major projects

[84] Welsh Local Government Association, *Sustainable Development Framework: Well-being of Future Generations Act Early Adopters Final Report* (2016).

TABLE 22.5 *Key 'asks' of Welsh Government, 2016–2021*

| 'Ask' of Welsh Government | By 2021 | Litmus Tests |
|---|---|---|
| Implement a Future Generations Act **change programme** for Welsh Government. | By 2021 WG should be able to clearly show how the Act has been 'a game changer' in the way it has done its business. | Change Programme implemented; Management Training; Performance Reviews; Director General and Cabinet Reports. |
| Apply the principles of the Act to **public sector reform** and other major change programmes. | By 2021 WG should be able show how these programmes have been designed and have started to deliver the goals and the principles. | Local Government Reform; Devolved Powers; Public Service Boards. |
| Adapt approaches to **budgetary planning and finance**. | By 2021 WG should have an understanding of how the sustainable development principle has been applied to the GBP 14 billion spend by Welsh Government per annum. | Local Government Settlements; Health Budget; WG Financial Regulations; Annual Budget Statements, Wales European Funding Office funding. |
| Develop **coherent long-term strategy, targets, milestones**, and outcomes for each well-being goal. | By 2021 WG should be able to show how they and the public sector have shifted the horizons of public sector strategy and developed clear targets, milestones and outcomes for coming decades. | Key WG strategies developed or refreshed 2016–2021, Well-Being Plans, statutory and non-statutory guidance, Future Trends Reports. |
| Work with the **Commissioner for Future Generations** to challenge and catalyse change. | By 2021 There are evidenced examples, of where the Commissioner has challenged and prompted WG to improve their response to the Act. | Key WG strategies; Programme for Government; Welsh Government Annual Reports; Commissioner Reports and published advice. |
| Place **sustainable consumption and production** at the centre of Wales' approach to economic growth. | By 2021 WG should be able to evidence how its own work meets targets for carbon reduction, GHG reduction, footprint reduction, and how it creates the conditions for others to act. | GHGs *and* carbon footprint; Housing Act; City Regions, Well-Being Plans; Infrastructure Strategy; Low Carbon Transition, Climate Change Action Plan. |
| Clear and **integrated policy and reporting** requirements of the public sector. | By 2021 WG will have been communicating consistent requirements to the public sector around the sustainable development principle and well-being goals whatever the area of work. | Documentary evidence; Reporting requirements of the public sector, Ministerial reports, WG Annual Reports; Report on behalf of Future Generations. |

reflect the Act. Key questions will be whether the new 'lens' or 'frame' from the FGA can successfully challenge existing policy approaches sufficiently, to deliver more sustainable outcomes, and whether the institutional reforms suggested by the Act, alter organisational approaches and decision making to the same end.

## CONCLUSION: A NEW 'SUSTAINABLE DEVELOPMENT' AGE OR REVERTING TO TYPE?

The Future Generations Act provides a real opportunity to recalibrate policy and the public sector in Wales. This statute represents a coherent, clear approach which can help to reorder policy layers and be used to help in ongoing public service reform, both at an individual authority level and strategically through proposals for local government reform.[85] It can help to reduce confusion, duplication, policy conflicts, and perverse policy outcomes if it is embraced by the public sector and the Welsh Government. Therein lies a major challenge for leaders in the public sector and government to legitimise long-term and multigenerational thinking, when political and financial cycles and austerity demand shorter-term approaches. Their challenge is not to 'revert to type' and revisit previous unsustainable or ineffective policy layers. The Commissioner role is crucial in this process. It will be a difficult balance for the role to ensure meaningful response to the legislation, while avoiding a 'compliance' response from the public bodies which need to respond to the statute.

Both of the concepts applied in this chronology – policy stretching and institutional layering – have been useful tools to think through Wales' sustainable development journey, as have the distinct phases described. They represent a shift of approach from one that was firmly centred on the policy agenda of a newly established institution to a policy framework of collective responsibility and accountability. Wales has an opportunity through the Future Generations Act to give sustainability greater traction than ever before in the way that it operates as a nation. But at the same time the legislation requires a major culture change across Wales. That is going to be long and difficult. It will perhaps be a future generation in 2050 who can look back on this period and coming decades and think this was the point at which Wales started 'getting it right'.

85 Welsh Government, *White Paper 'Reforming Local Government: Power to Local People'* (Welsh Government 2015).

# 23

# Parliamentary Commissioner for the Environment, New Zealand

*Jonathan Boston*

This chapter explores the role, evolution, and effectiveness of a small but remarkable institution, the New Zealand Parliamentary Commissioner for the Environment (PCE).[1] Established under the Environment Act 1986, the Commissioner's primary functions are, put simply, to serve as an environmental guardian, an independent assessor of environmental policies, systems and processes, and a non-partisan advocate for sound environmental management.[2] The mission is, to quote a recent Commissioner, '[t]o maintain or improve the quality of the New Zealand environment by providing robust independent advice that influences decisions'.[3] While not a 'commission for future generations', to the extent that the PCE is able to promote the wise stewardship of resources, greater policy far-sightedness, and better environmental outcomes, both current and future generations stand to gain.

To date, there have been four Commissioners: Helen Hughes (1987–1996), Dr Morgan Williams (1997–2007), and Dr Jan Wright (2007–2017) were all scientists by training, while the fourth, Hon Simon Upton (who commenced his appointment in mid-October 2017), is a lawyer and politician by background. They have led an

[1] I am most grateful to Helen Hughes, Dr Morgan Williams, Quentin Duthie, and Shaun Killerby for their helpful comments on an earlier draft of this chapter.

[2] There is a modest but growing literature on the history, role, and activities of the Parliamentary Commissioner for the Environment. Amongst the more detailed treatments are K. Bosselmann, 'The Environmental Commissioner – A Guardian for the Environment', in G. Hawke (ed.), *Guardians for the Environment* (Institute of Policy Studies 1997); T. Bührs, *Working within Limits: The Role of the Commission for the Environment in Environmental Policy Development in New Zealand* (PhD Thesis, Auckland University 1991); T. Bührs, 'Barking up Which Trees? The Role of New Zealand's Parliamentary Watchdog' (1996) 48:1 *Political Science* 1–28; G. Hawke (ed.), *Guardians for the Environment* (Institute of Policy Studies 1997); D. Young, *Keeper of the Long View* (Parliamentary Commissioner for the Environment 2007). See also J. Boston, *Governing for the Future: Designing Democratic Institutions for a Better Tomorrow* (Emerald 2017), 338–343.

[3] Parliamentary Commissioner for the Environment, *Annual Report for the Year Ended 30 June 2014* (Parliamentary Commissioner for the Environment 2014) 7.

organization with broad, significant, and demanding roles but only modest resources. For example, in 2017 the Office[4] had close to twenty staff and a budgetary appropriation of about NZD 3.4m (roughly USD 2.5m).[5]

Although small, the PCE is a distinctive and important institution. First, when originally established, it was unique in the democratic world and there were no other public bodies with identical functions and powers. Since the mid-1980s, various OECD countries have created organizations with broadly similar (or overlapping) roles to those of the PCE. These include Canada, Germany, and the Netherlands, and several subnational governments (e.g. the Australia Capital Territory and the Canadian province of Ontario). In some cases, the new bodies were partly inspired by the New Zealand model. Second, the Commissioner is one of only three Officers of Parliament in New Zealand – the others being the Office of the Controller and Auditor-General and the Office of the Ombudsman. As such, the Commissioner is independent of the elected government and accountable only to Parliament. Third, in New Zealand there are no comparable Commissioners for other major policy domains, such as the economy or society. Having said this, there is a Children's Commissioner and a Retirement Commissioner, but they lack the status or independence of being Officers of Parliament. Finally, the PCE can be regarded as a kind of 'commitment device'[6] designed in part to overcome the problem of 'dynamic inconsistency' by providing an authoritative and independent 'voice' in the political arena for environmental integrity and holding policymakers to account for their decisions. While Commissioners cannot enforce compliance with prudent environmental standards, they can certainly exercise a constraining influence and incentivize policy far-sightedness.

This chapter examines the rationale for the PCE, including the logic behind its distinctive roles and governance arrangements. It then outlines the PCE's functions and powers and how these have been applied since its creation in 1987. Following this, the chapter assesses the PCE's performance and explores its contribution to environmental management and outcomes. Finally, consideration is given to whether the PCE provides a useful model for other countries.

4 Strictly speaking, at least in legal terms, there is no 'Office' of the Parliamentary Commissioner for the Environment. The Environment Act 1986 establishes a 'Commissioner', not an 'Office' or a 'Commission'. Nevertheless, the Commissioner is an Officer of Parliament and, as with the other Officers of Parliament, it has become customary in public discourse in New Zealand to refer, more or less interchangeably, to the 'Office' of the PCE and the 'Commissioner'. In common usage, members of the Commissioner's staff are assumed to be part of the 'Office'. Unlike her predecessors, the third Commissioner, Dr Jan Wright, and her staff generally did not use the term 'Office'. However, in keeping with previous practice and much of the relevant literature, I will use the terms 'Office' and 'Commissioner' interchangeably.

5 The size of the Office has varied over the years, from around twelve staff members at the outset to a maximum of about twenty-two.

6 For a brief introduction to the literature on 'commitment devices', see G. Bryan, D. Karlan, and S. Nelson, 'Commitment Devices' (2010) 2 *Annual Review of Economics* 671–698.

## THE POLITICAL AND ENVIRONMENTAL CONTEXT

New Zealand is a highly urbanized, multicultural nation, with around 4.6 million people. The population density is low. Although its land area is modest, the Exclusive Economic Zone (at 4 million square kilometres) is one of the world's largest and about fourteen times the country's landmass. The nation thus has major responsibilities for the marine environment, as well as managing many diverse, vulnerable terrestrial and coastal ecosystems.

Politically, New Zealand is a centralized, unitary state with a unicameral parliament, elected since 1996 via proportional representation.[7] The constitution is not entrenched, so Parliament remains sovereign. Protection of human rights is provided via the Bill of Rights Act and other legal instruments, but there is no explicit legal recognition of environmental rights or the rights of future generations.[8] At the subnational level, there were eleven regional councils and sixty-seven territorial authorities in 2016 (five of which were unitary councils).[9] Subnational government plays a critical role in environment management. Regional councils have responsibility (under the Resource Management Act 1991) for air and water quality and catchment control, while territorial authorities administer local utilities, regulate land use, and give approval for all construction work, including new buildings and significant alterations. Lacking a large manufacturing or industrial base, New Zealand is dependent on its natural resources for most of its export revenues (e.g. from agriculture, horticulture, forestry, fishing, aquaculture, energy supplies, and tourism).[10] While advertising itself internationally as 'clean' and 'green' and '100% pure', the nation's environmental record is unimpressive.[11]

7 For an overview of New Zealand's constitutional and institutional arrangements see J. Hayward (ed.), *New Zealand Government and Politics*, 6th edn. (Oxford University Press 2015) pts. 3 & 6.

8 S. Glazebrook, 'Keeping It Clean and Green: The Case for Constitutional Environmental Protection Rights', in C. Morris, J. Boston, and P. Butler (eds.), *Reconstituting the Constitution* (Springer 2011) 425–458; T. Hayward, *Constitutional Environmental Rights* (Oxford University Press 2005).

9 Unitary councils combine the functions of regional councils and territorial authorities.

10 OECD, *OECD Environmental Performance Reviews: New Zealand 2007* (OECD 2007).

11 See, for instance, Ministry for the Environment, *Environment New Zealand 2007* (Ministry for the Environment 2007); Ministry for the Environment, *Briefing for Incoming Ministers: Environmental Stewardship for a Prosperous New Zealand* (Ministry for the Environment 2014); G. Taylor, 'Environmental Policy-Making in New Zealand, 1978–2013' (2013) 9:3 *Policy Quarterly* 18–27; M. Brown et al., *Vanishing Nature: Facing New Zealand's Biodiversity Crisis* (Environmental Defence Society 2015); M. Joy, *Polluted Inheritance: New Zealand's Freshwater Crisis* (BWB Texts 2105); OECD, *OECD Economic Surveys: New Zealand* (OECD 2015) 24–30; OECD, *OECD Environmental Performance Review: New Zealand 2017* (OECD 2017).

To quote Helen Hughes, the first PCE:

> Our clean green image, up to now, has been due to our low population and low level of industrial development. It has not been due to first class environmental management. There are improvements to be made at all levels of government.[12]

Most of the recent environmental issues in New Zealand mirror those in other jurisdictions: applying the principles of sustainable development and minimizing the environmental impacts of large-scale economic projects; mitigating and adapting to climate change; protecting indigenous habitats and biological diversity; ensuring the sustainable management of conditionally renewable resources, such as fish stocks; and managing waste, contaminated sites and hazardous substances.[13] But some environmental issues have been particularly acute in New Zealand, reflecting its distinctive geography, ecology, land-use patterns, and economic strategies. Amongst these have been the problems associated with introduced pests, such as possums and rabbits, including the complex issues surrounding the safety and effectiveness of pesticides like sodium fluoroacetate or 1080, and biological controls such as myxomatosis and rabbit calic virus. There have also been major challenges for freshwater management arising from the intensification of livestock farming, and the environmental impacts of mining, including oil and gas exploration (both onshore and offshore). Against this, New Zealand has no nuclear power stations and hence is free of the problems of nuclear regulation and the storage of radioactive wastes.

## *The Historical Background*

The origins of the PCE lie in at least five separate, but partly related, developments: the rising tide of concern from the early-to-mid 1960s about humanity's negative environmental impact; the unsatisfactory policy responses to these concerns during the 1970s and early 1980s; the growing tensions between the ambitious economic development agenda of the National government (1975–1984) and the public's increasing environmental consciousness; the findings of an OECD report in 1981 – *Environmental Policies in New Zealand* – which included recommendations to strengthen the provision and quality of environmental advice and create an environmental body with specific audit and oversight functions;[14] and the election of a strongly reformist Labour government in 1984, which included within its senior ranks several people with significant environmental expertise.

[12] Parliamentary Commissioner for the Environment, *Report for the Year Ended 30 June 1992* (Parliamentary Commissioner for the Environment 1992) 4.

[13] OECD, *OECD Environmental Performance Reviews: New Zealand 1996* (OECD 1996); OECD 2007, *supra* note 10; Ministry for the Environment, *supra* note 11; Taylor, *supra* note 11.

[14] OECD, *Environmental Policies in New Zealand* (OECD 1981).

Two main issues during the 1960s sparked a deeper environmental awareness and subsequent policy reform. The first was the gradual loss of the remaining pockets of ancient indigenous forest – including podocarp-hardwood forests and beech forests – due to logging, poor land management, and the introduction of pests by Māori settlers in the thirteenth century (e.g. rats) and European settlers in the nineteenth century (e.g. possums, cats, stoats, deer, and goats). Such forests not only contain a rich diversity of flora and fauna, but also provide vital ecosystem services, not least carbon sequestration. Related to the loss of native forests was another concern, namely the destruction of habitats for many unique species. Since human settlement in New Zealand around 1250, it is estimated that over sixty species have suffered extinction, including at least fifty-one bird species. During the mid-twentieth century many more species were threatened with extinction (currently estimated at over 2,800, with another 3,000 believed to be at risk, out of an estimated 80,000 species of native plants, animals, and fungi).[15] Accordingly, there were calls for greater governmental intervention, for instance, via better pest control, predatory-free sanctuaries, and the protection of the remaining native forests. For many years, this emphasis on 'conservation', rather than 'sustainability', was the critical driver of environmental policy.

Politically, however, it was not forest protection or pest control that proved to be main environmental turning point but rather a massive public campaign to protect Lake Manapouri. The lake is located in the Fiordland National Park and acquired a World Heritage listing in 1990. In the late 1950s it was proposed that the lake level be raised by about 30 metres to increase the output from a proposed underground hydroelectric power station; the electricity was needed for a planned aluminium smelter. A vigorous, decade-long protest movement was born – known as the Save Manapouri Campaign. Considered a landmark in the history of environmentalism in New Zealand, the government eventually backed down on the proposal to raise the lake's level, and subsequently established an independent body – the Guardians of Lake Manapouri and Te Anau – to oversee the management of lake levels. Equally important, however, were the wider political ramifications of the campaign: it heightened citizens' awareness of the threats posed by economic development to many unique flora, fauna, and landscapes, and strengthened New Zealand's environmental movement.[16]

Partly in response, the National government (1960–1972) established a Commission for the Environment in 1972.[17] Its primary role was to prepare audits on the environmental impacts of major development proposals, especially those

[15] Ministry for the Environment, *supra* note 11 at 62.

[16] New Zealand has numerous environmental groups. The most important and influential over the years have been the Environmental Defence Society, the Royal Forest and Bird Society, Fish and Game, and the Environment and Conservation Organizations (which is an umbrella group representing over fifty groups).

[17] Bührs, *supra* note 2; Young, *supra* note 2.

instigated by the government. But the Commission had limited powers, modest resources, constrained independence, and little policy influence. An opportunity to change this state of affairs dawned with the election of the fourth Labour government in July 1984. Taking office in the midst of an economic and constitutional crisis, the new government embarked on sweeping reforms – economic, social, environmental, and constitutional.

### *The Reform of Environmental Administration*

Guiding Labour's reform of environmental administration were four main drivers: (1) a commitment in the party's 1984 election manifesto to replace the Commission for the Environment with a Ministry for the Environment and a separate PCE,[18] influenced no doubt by advocacy for such changes by the country's leading environmental groups;[19] (2) a preference for decentralized (i.e. subnational) decision making for most resource management matters, albeit in the context of a centrally determined regulatory framework and national policy guidelines; (3) a growing interest in using market-based instruments to manage environmental externalities and regulate access to conditionally renewable resources,[20] and (4) various principles of institutional design that informed the overall restructuring of New Zealand's machinery of government during the mid-to-late 1980s.[21]

The precise role of the PCE was not enunciated in Labour's manifesto. But the idea of creating an Officer of Parliament, rather than a Crown entity or some other kind of public institution, was no doubt influenced by the existence of two other statutory bodies that report to Parliament, rather than the government: the Controller and Auditor-General and the Ombudsman. Reporting to Parliament would arguably strengthen the standing, credibility and independence of the proposed body. To quote the former Commissioner, Morgan Williams:

> The status of a Parliamentary officer was considered necessary if the Commissioner was to be an effective guardian of New Zealand's environmental management system in which the Crown plays a key part. The effectiveness of the PCE was envisaged, at that time of restructuring, to be dependent on the Commissioner being sufficiently independent of executive government to review any system or agency the Commissioner considered necessary to enhance environmental management.[22]

At the same time, it was recognized that such governance arrangements would be unusual. There were no comparable bodies elsewhere in parliamentary democracies,

[18] New Zealand Labour Party, 1984 *Policy Document* (New Zealand Labour Party 1984).

[19] C. Wallace, 'An NGO Perspective', in Hawke, *supra* note 2, 85–86.

[20] Bührs, *supra* note 2.

[21] J. Boston et al., *Public Management: The New Zealand Model* (Oxford University Press 1996).

[22] Parliamentary Commissioner for the Environment, *Future Directions: Strategic Focus of the Parliamentary Commissioner for the Environment, 1997–2001* (Parliamentary Commissioner for the Environment 1997) 3.

and no equivalent Officer of Parliament in New Zealand for other major policy domains. Moreover, despite New Zealand being one of the first States to have an Ombudsman, it was never intended that the PCE would primarily undertake such a role (i.e. receiving, investigating, and responding to complaints from citizens about the actions of government agencies). It was not designed, in other words, to replace the Ombudsman in handling complaints about poor environmental administration.

In the event, after widespread consultation with interested groups and the general public, the Labour government announced its decision on the reforms to environmental administration in late 1985, and the new institutional arrangements were established over the course of the following year.[23] The Commission for the Environment was abolished, and a new Environment Act was passed establishing a Ministry for the Environment and a PCE. The Ministry's primary role under the Act is to advise the government on all matters relating to environmental policy and administration. As a government department, it is directly accountable to the Minister for the Environment, and undertakes a work programme as agreed by the Minister. In addition, a new Department of Conservation was established under the Conservation Act 1987. This body brought together staff and resources from a number of government agencies, including the Department of Lands and Survey, the New Zealand Forest Service, and the Department of Internal Affairs. The new Department was given the responsibility of managing the so-called 'conservation estate' – that is, all publicly owned land in New Zealand designated primarily for conservation and protection. Aside from its preservation and protection functions, the Department also provides advice to the Minister of Conservation and is mandated to serve as an 'advocate' for 'the conservation or natural and historic resources' for the benefit of 'present and future generations' (an unusual role for a government department).[24]

The final component of the new environmental management regime was the passage of the Resource Management Act (RMA) in 1991. The RMA combined into one integrated framework the previously fragmented resource-use regimes covering, for instance, land use, forestry, zoning, water, air, and pollution. Significantly, it embraced the principle of 'sustainable management' of natural and physical resources and placed it at the heart of the new framework.[25] All policies, standards, plans, and decision making under the Act were to reflect this fundamental principle. Further, it adopted an 'effects-based' approach to environmental management, thereby replacing the predominantly 'rule-based' or 'activity-based' approach, as previously prescribed under the Town and Country Planning Act (1977) and the

[23] Bührs, *supra* note 2; Hawke, *supra* note 2; H. Hughes, 'Ten Years On', in Hawke, *supra* note 2; Wallace, *supra* note 19; P. Woollaston, 'The Creation of the Position of PCE: The Importance of the Role', in Hawke, *supra* note 2; Young, *supra* note 2.

[24] See Conservation Act 1987, s. 6.

[25] O. Furuseth and C. Cocklin, 'An Institutional Framework for Sustainable Resource Management: The New Zealand Model' (1995) 35:2 *Natural Resources Journal* 243–274.

Water and Soil Conservation Act (1967). In short, the RMA substantially altered the regulatory framework for which the PCE had oversight responsibility.

## THE ROLE AND POWERS OF THE PARLIAMENTARY COMMISSIONER FOR THE ENVIRONMENT

As noted, the PCE was established under the Environment Act 1986. Part 1 of the Act sets out the functions and powers of the Commissioner and the administrative arrangements relating to the Office, while Part 2 enunciates the role of the Ministry for the Environment. As an Officer of Parliament, the Commissioner is appointment by the Governor-General on the recommendation of the House of Representatives.[26] Appointments are for a renewable term of five years. The process of appointments (and reappointments) is overseen by the Officers of Parliament Committee (OPC), which is chaired by Parliament's Speaker.[27] Most, if not all, parliamentary parties are represented on this Committee. While the selection process has differed in the three cases thus far, it is now expected that the Commissioner's position will be advertised, with MPs also invited to suggest suitable appointees. A short list of candidates is then drawn up (e.g. by a recruitment agency in consultation with the Speaker), and these people are interviewed by a sub-Committee of the OPC. Only candidates with sufficient cross-party support are recommended to the House for appointment (or reappointment). Thus far, all Commissioners have enjoyed cross-party support when appointed and all three have been reappointed, again with cross-party backing. This does not imply that each parliamentary party is equally supportive of the preferred candidate, but it does ensure that Commissioners are seen publicly to be 'non-partisan' and 'independent' of the government. This perception is vital if Commissioners are to undertake their statutory roles effectively.

The Commissioner's mandate under the Environment Act is remarkably broad, comprehensive, and open-ended. It covers the operations of both national and subnational agencies, and all matters relating to the natural and built environment. It gives the Commissioner substantial discretion in terms of priority-setting, including how to strike the proper balance between reactive and proactive investigations, what specific environmental issues to monitor and review, and how to allocate resources.

[26] This is very different to the way departmental heads (or 'chief executives' as they are called in New Zealand) are appointed. Departmental heads are appointed under the State Sector Act, with decisions being made by the government on the recommendation of the State Services Commissioner. There is no consultation with opposition parties.

[27] For details of the appointment process, see New Zealand Parliament, 'How Parliament Works: Parliamentary Practice in New Zealand' www.parliament.nz/en-nz/about-parliament/how-parliament-works/ppnz/00HOOOCPPNZ_61/chapter-6-officers-of-parliament-and-other-officers-and#_Toc266888186 accessed 30 November 2017.

As stipulated in Section 16 of the Act, the Commissioner has seven functions, namely to:

(1) Review the system of agencies and processes set up by the Government to manage the allocation, use, and preservation of the country's natural and physical resources, and report the results to Parliament and to such other bodies or persons as deemed appropriate;
(2) Investigate the effectiveness of environmental planning and management by public authorities, and advise them on remedial action;
(3) Investigate any matter where the environment may be or has been adversely affected, whether through natural causes or as a result of the acts or omissions of any person or body, advise on preventative measures or remedial action, and report to Parliament;
(4) Report, on a request from the House or any select committee, on any petition, Bill, or any other matter which may have a significant effect on the environment;
(5) Inquire, on the direction of the House, into any matter that has had or may have a substantial and damaging effect on the environment;
(6) Undertake and encourage the collection and dissemination of information about the environment; and
(7) Encourage preventive measures and remedial actions to protect the environment.

Over the years, two other statutory functions have been added. The first of these, in 2001, gave the PCE the power to audit some of the Electricity Commission's activities. But this provision was somewhat unusual and was repealed in 2010 on the advice of Dr Wright. More significantly, the PCE acquired new responsibilities under the Environment Reporting Act 2015 to review and comment on the synthesis and domain reports produced periodically by the Government Statistician and the Secretary for the Environment.[28]

In fulfilling their various statutory functions, Section 17 of the Environment Act provides guidance to Commissioners on the considerations to which they may wish to 'have regard'. These include:

(1) The maintenance and restoration of ecosystems of importance, especially those supporting habitats or rare, threatened, or endangered species of flora or fauna;
(2) Areas, landscapes, and structures of aesthetic, archaeological, cultural, historical, recreational, scenic, and scientific value;

[28] For the Commissioner's review of the first synthesis report see Parliamentary Commissioner for the Environment, *The State of New Zealand's Environment: Commentary by the Parliamentary Commissioner for the Environment on 'Environment Aotearoa 2015'* (Parliamentary Commissioner for the Environment 2016).

(3) Any land, water, sites, fishing grounds, or physical or cultural resources, or interests associated with such areas, which are part of the heritage of the tangata whenua and which contribute to their well-being; and
(4) Whether any proposals or policies are likely to: increase pollution or the occurrence of natural hazards or hazardous substances; result in the introduction of species or genotypes not previously present within New Zealand (including the territorial sea); have uncertain environmental effects; or result in the allocation or depletion of any natural and physical resources in a way or at a rate that will prevent the renewal by natural processes of the resources.

In undertaking their statutory functions, Commissioners have 'such powers as may be necessary' (Section 16). Amongst these are the powers required to conduct detailed and rigorous investigations, such as obtaining information, summoning people and examining them under oath, and protecting sources of information. Further, in conducting any inquiry requested by Parliament, Commissioners enjoy all the powers conferred on commissions of inquiry under the Commissions of Inquiry Act 1908, together with the immunities and privileges possessed by a Judge in the exercise of the Judge's civil jurisdiction. Similarly, Commissioners have broad powers to report findings and make recommendations. Against this, unlike Courts and Tribunals, they cannot make legally binding rulings or direct that certain policies be implemented. Hence, their influence on decision-makers, whether at the national or subnational levels, must rest on their personal standing, their capacity to persuade through reasoned argument and robust evidence, and their capacity to generate political embarrassment.

### *Political Independence and Relationship with Parliament*

As Officers of Parliament, Commissioners are fully independent of the executive branch and are obliged to execute their functions, duties, and powers without political bias or direction. Consistent with this, the PCE's staff members are not civil servants, but employees of the Commissioner. Likewise, Commissioners do not report to cabinet ministers and, aside from the inevitable constraints imposed by a limited budget, they are free to inquire into such matters as they deem appropriate. They do, of course, brief ministers from time to time.

Commissioners' relationship with Parliament is mediated via the Speaker and the OPC and guided by an explicit, distinctive, but non-binding Code of Practice, originally drafted in 1996 and revised in 2007.[29] The Code is designed to ensure

[29] Report of the Officers of Parliament Committee, *Inquiry into the Review of the Code of Practice for the Provision of Assistance by the Parliamentary Commissioner for the Environment to the House of Representatives, Select Committees, and Members of Parliament* (New Zealand House of Representatives August 2007).

that Parliament's needs can be effectively and appropriately addressed in a manner that 'respects the role and status of select committees, and the Commissioner's independence'.[30]

Four aspects of the relationship with Parliament deserve clarification. First, the nature and extent of formal interactions with the Speaker (and other parliamentarians) have varied over the decades, with much depending on the preferences of the individuals concerned. In some cases, Commissioners and Speakers have met on a regular basis to exchange ideas and in other cases any such meetings have been infrequent. Second, aside from the OPC, Commissioners interact with various other parliamentary select committees from time to time – providing submissions on Bills, supplying expert advice on invitation, and responding to formal requests for investigations to be conducted on particular topics.[31] While requests to undertake investigations have been infrequent, it has been relatively common over the years for Commissioners to be asked to serve as expert advisers. Indeed, on some occasions PCE staff members have offered such assistance informally to select committee clerks, thereby prompting a formal request from the relevant committee. Third, the Commissioner is free to table reports in Parliament when it is sitting and, if Parliament is not in session, such reports can be released at the Commissioner's discretion. Finally, under current arrangements, the OPC is responsible for the PCE's annual budget. The Commissioner prepares an annual bid which is submitted to the Committee for consideration. While the Treasury advises the Committee on such bids, the Committee is not bound to accept its views. For the first decade of the PCE's operations, the Treasury generally opposed any increase in the Commissioner's budget and questioned the need for such an organization. But following the development of a detailed strategic plan in 1997 by the new Commissioner,[32] and detailed consultations between the PCE and Treasury officials, the Treasury has adopted a more favourable disposition and resources have been less constrained.

### *Major Functions*

Over the years, various efforts have been made to summarize succinctly the PCE's main responsibilities. During the tenure of its first Commissioner, the PCE was seen as having three distinct, yet related, functions:[33]

[30] Ibid. at 5–6.

[31] Over the years, Commissioners have provided submissions or advice to a range of select committees – most notably, Local Government and Environment, Primary Production and Transport and Industrial Relations. Currently, the Commissioner reports annually on her performance to the Local Government and Environment Select Committee.

[32] Parliamentary Commissioner for the Environment, *Future Directions: Strategic Focus of the Parliamentary Commissioner for the Environment*, 1997–2001 (Parliamentary Commissioner for the Environment 1997).

[33] Bührs, *supra* note 2.

(1) A system guardian – overseeing and reviewing the national and subnational system of agencies and processes of environmental management and planning;
(2) An environmental auditor – reviewing the performance of public authorities with environmental responsibilities; and
(3) An environmental ombudsman – investigating a wide range of environmental issues or concerns, whether prompted by citizens, community groups, businesses, or parliamentarians.

While this summary has validity, it does not fully reflect how the PCE's role has evolved over time or how priorities have shifted to reflect policy and regulatory changes. Since the late 1980s the balance of activities has altered and other roles – including advising, monitoring, facilitating, brokering, conflict resolution, information sharing, and educating – have often been important. Advocacy, albeit of a particular kind, has also featured. To quote Morgan Williams:

> The Commissioner's role is not one of advocacy for the environment per se but advocacy for good environmental management, in the interests of ensuring our environmental resources can meet the needs of current and future generations. The role is about advancing the development of truly sustainable management by responding to debates and concerns in a balanced and objective manner.[34]

Nevertheless, because the roles of 'system guardian', 'environmental auditor', and 'environmental ombudsman' have frequently been highlighted in the literature on the PCE, some clarification of these roles is desirable.

## *System Guardian*

Under Section 16 of the Environment Act, the first role listed (as noted above) is:

> the objective of maintaining and improving the quality of the environment, to review from time to time the system of agencies and processes established by the Government to manage the allocation, use, and preservation of natural and physical resources, and to report the results of any such review to the House of Representatives and to such other bodies or persons as the Commissioner considers appropriate.

Clearly, this implies that the PCE should review periodically the overall *system* of environmental management in New Zealand, with the aim of identifying systemic weaknesses and gaps and proposing ways to enhance the efficiency, effectiveness, and coherence of the regulatory framework and the related structures and processes. Yet conducting comprehensive and holistic assessments of the performance of the entire environmental management system is demanding. Given the PCE's limited

[34] Parliamentary Commissioner for the Environment, *supra* note 32 at 13.

resources (with only five investigating officers during its early years) and other pressing priorities, Commissioners have undertaken only a few broad, system-wide reviews. The first was the *Report on New Zealand Environmental Management 1987–91*.[35] This was completed in 1991 as part of New Zealand's contribution to the UN Conference on Environment and Development (Earth Summit) in Rio de Janeiro in June 1992. Subsequently, several reviews of the RMA were conducted during the mid 1990s, culminating in a summary report, *Towards Sustainable Management: The Role of the Resource Management Act 1991*.[36] Also, a major PCE report in 2002 – *Creating Our Future: Sustainable Development for New Zealand* – can be regarded as a comprehensive assessment.[37]

Overall, Commissioners have focused on investigating particular aspects of the environmental management system as and when policy deficiencies or regulatory deficits have been evident. Unsurprisingly, matters relating to the implementation, efficiency, and effectiveness of the RMA have figured prominently in their work. For many years, Commissioners repeatedly drew attention to the failure of successive governments to issue National Policy Statements (NPS) on important environmental issues, as intended under the Act. Aside from Coastal Policy Statements, which are mandatory,[38] the first NPS – on electricity transmission – was not issued until March 2008, almost seventeen years after the passage of the Act. Since then four further statements have been promulgated – two dealing with freshwater management (2011 and 2014), one on renewable electricity generation (2011), and one on urban development and capacity (2016).

Additionally, Commissioners have (especially in the 1990s) issued good practice guides to help local councils undertake their responsibilities under the Act (e.g. for coastal management, and historic and cultural heritage management), with particular attention given to developing protocols for consultation with Māori communities and organizations. More recently, guidance on such matters has been handled by the Ministry for the Environment.

In short, rather than focusing primarily on problems of a *systemic* nature or the performance of the environmental management system as a whole, Commissioners have devoted most of their resources to investigating significant environmental policy issues, particularly where critical environmental values have been at risk, and offering practical guidance to improve planning procedures.

[35] Parliamentary Commissioner for the Environment, *Report on New Zealand Environmental Management 1987–91* (Parliamentary Commissioner for the Environment 1991).

[36] Parliamentary Commissioner for the Environment, *Towards Sustainable Management: The Role of the Resource Management Act 1991* (Parliamentary Commissioner for the Environment 1998).

[37] Parliamentary Commissioner for the Environment, *Creating Our Future: Sustainable Development for New Zealand* (Parliamentary Commissioner for the Environment 2002).

[38] Two *New Zealand Coastal Policy Statements* have been promulgated thus far under the Resource Management Act 1991, the first in 1994 and the second in 2010.

### *Environmental Auditor*

Auditing involves the systematic and independent scrutiny of a particular undertaking or organization. The aim is to ensure that specific procedures and processes have been performed in accordance with agreed standards or that various goals have been achieved efficiently and effectively. In terms of auditing, the PCE has a broad statutory role to *assess* 'the effectiveness of environmental planning and management by public authorities, and *advise* them on remedial action'. Plainly, such a function is primarily concerned with effectiveness, rather than compliance. But if undertaken on a comprehensive basis it would be very time-consuming. There are, after all, more than eighty organizations with significant environmental planning and management responsibilities in New Zealand (and many other public bodies whose activities have substantial environmental impacts). Even to review these bodies periodically (e.g. every five or ten years) would be a large undertaking. There is also the potential for overlap with the role of the Auditor-General, whose mandate includes assessing the effectiveness of public agencies, alongside financial audits.

Predictably, therefore, the PCE's audit activities have been modest and targeted. Aside from a broad review of the environmental planning functions of regional government in 1991, the first Commissioner undertook only a few audits of the environmental performance (or planning functions) of public bodies. At the national level, she reviewed aspects of the operations of several organizations (e.g. Transit New Zealand and the Maritime Transport Division of the Ministry of Transport) and collaborated with the Auditor-General on a review of marine fisheries management. At the subnational level she assessed the Gisborne District Council (which is a unitary council) and the Kapiti District Council. In both the latter cases, her assessments were prompted by public concerns over poor environmental performance. In both cases, too, she made it clear that the aim of the investigations was not primarily to apportion blame, but to strengthen the councils' environmental planning systems and processes, thereby enhancing environmental protection.

The two subsequent Commissioners have been even more restrained in auditing the environmental management functions of public bodies. During the term of the second Commissioner, the Office undertook no comprehensive audits of *individual* public bodies, except the Electricity Commission (as required under the 2001 amendments to the Electricity Act noted earlier). Instead, it focused on how local authorities as a whole (or particular subgroups) undertook some of their specific environmental planning functions. Hence, studies were conducted on the management of urban water systems, the handling of suburban amenity values, the approaches taken to sustainable development in peri-urban areas, and the management of urban vegetation. Additionally, the Commissioner collaborated with the Auditor-General in a study comparing the environmental management practices of unitary authorities with those of regional and territorial authorities. The third Commissioner continued the practice (albeit briefly) of reviewing the Electricity Commission's environmental performance. She also undertook reviews in 2008 and 2010 of the environmental management and effects of a landfill (or waste dump) near a North Island town, prompted by concerns over possible failures to comply with relevant planning requirements, and investigated the environmental performance of the country's largest coal company, Solid Energy, which is publicly owned.

One other matter regarding the PCE's audit function deserves comments. Prior to 1987, the Commission for the Environment undertook audits of environmental impact reports which were prepared in relation to major proposed projects. There had been some expectation that the PCE would continue this function. But three factors dictated otherwise. First, the changes to environmental planning brought about by the RMA resulted in environmental impact reports being replaced with assessments of environmental affects and the introduction of new consent processes, which are the responsibility of subnational government. Related to this, the Ministry for the Environment acquired certain regulatory functions, especially for oversight of projects of national significance. These functions have since been transferred to the Environmental Protection Agency following its establishment in 2011. Second, the economic policy reforms instigated by the fourth Labour government ended the major government-funded projects that had absorbed the energies of the former Commission for the Environment. Third, the first Parliamentary Commissioner was keen to avoid devoting her Office's modest resources to project-type audit activities. Hence, the PCE completed several audits that had been commenced by the Commission and then virtually ceased such activities.[39]

### *Environmental Ombudsman*

Whereas the primary role of the Ombudsman in New Zealand is to investigate complaints from citizens, in the case of the PCE there is no reference to such complaints in the Environment Act and Commissioners are not legally obliged to investigate concerns raised with them, except those referred by Parliament. In other words, investigating complaints is discretionary. The first Commissioner emphasized early in her term that while she would seek 'to establish strong links with the public and public interest groups', she had 'no desire to be seen first and foremost as a complaints authority'.[40] Despite such declarations, the number of concerns and complaints raised with her Office steadily increased during the late 1980s and early 1990s – from sixty-eight in the twelve months to 31 March 1988 to a peak of 640 during the 1994–1995 fiscal year.[41] Since then, the number of complaints, or requests for information and advice, has fallen – to several hundred per year during

[39] Hughes, *supra* note 23 at 156.
[40] Quoted by Bührs, *supra* note 2 at 199.
[41] Parliamentary Commissioner for the Environment, *The First 10 Years 1987–96: Summary of an Analysis of Parliamentary Commissioner for the Environment Investigations and Advice on Remedial Action* (Parliamentary Commissioner for the Environment 1997) 1.

the early-to-mid 2000s and less than 100 per year since the late 2000s. About half of these are from individual citizens. Their concerns cover a plethora of matters – from the nuisance caused by unpleasant odours and aircraft noise, to biosecurity issues, water pollution, waste management, traffic congestion, cellphone transmission sites, agricultural spray-drift, the remediation of contaminated sites, and the disposal of hazardous substances.

To manage the workload, the first Commissioner developed criteria for determining which matters to pursue. These criteria evolved over time, but included the environmental significance of the issue in question, whether the matter was related to 'the adequacy of the system or authority management, whether independent scrutiny' was needed, whether the PCE's intervention was likely to improve matters, and whether the issue should be dealt with by another governmental body, such as the Ombudsman.[42] Since the mid 1990s, the role of the PCE in investigating concerns raised by outsiders has diminished, with priority being accorded to other roles.

### *Summary*

In summary, the Environment Act gives Parliamentary Commissioners multiple roles and considerable discretion over how best to balance them. Each Commissioner has struck a different balance, reflecting their particular disciplinary backgrounds and expertise, as well as the evolving legislative, regulatory, and policy contexts. While the PCE was initially viewed as having three primary roles – system guardian, environmental auditor, and environmental ombudsman – these descriptions do not capture the breadth of the Office's statutory responsibilities, nor do they reflect the Commissioners' respective priorities. Accordingly, it is perhaps more accurate to conceive of the Office as an 'environmental guardian' or 'watchdog', rather than as a *system* guardian; as a body that undertakes independent reviews of major environmental policy and regulatory issues, rather than as a auditor of organizational performance; and as a discretionary investigator of serious environmental risks, rather than as an ombudsman responding to citizens' complaints. More simply, to quote the 2006 *Annual Report*, the Office provides 'independent scrutiny, advocacy and advice for a better environment'.[43]

## THE EVOLUTION OF THE PCE

Since 1987 the PCE has produced over 400 reports – an annual average of three to four major reports, and five to ten minor reports or submissions.[44] The highest

[42] Bührs, *supra* note 2 at 200.

[43] Parliamentary Commissioner for the Environment, *Report for the Year Ended 30 June 2006* (Parliamentary Commissioner for the Environment 2006) 7.

[44] Most of these reports are available on the Commission's website www.pce.parliament.nz/ accessed 30 November 2017.

average volume was in the 1990s. The titles of these reports yield a fascinating insight, both in terms of what they reveal about the evolution of domestic and international environmental concerns since the mid 1980s, but also with respect to the perspectives and priorities of the respective Commissioners. Whereas climate change and energy issues, and to a lesser extent mining, have dominated the work of the PCE since around 2000, such issues received much less attention earlier. Likewise, Commissioners have had different views on how best to fulfil their statutory responsibilities. Dr Wright devoted much of her energy to reviewing various governmental policy initiatives and commenting on proposed legislation. By contrast, Dr Williams saw his role as an agent for transformational change. His aim was to reshape the frameworks used for policy analysis – abandoning narrow economic approaches and embracing a paradigm based on biophysical limits and the concept of strong sustainability. His Office was to be a thought leader, influencing policymaking and outcomes not so much by commenting on the specific details of individual policy proposals but rather by changing the mindsets and frameworks within which policy debates are conducted. Such a goal, of course, was ambitious and not quickly achievable.

Under the first Commissioner, Helen Hughes (1987–1997), whose scientific background was in botany, ecology, and conservation, the Office gave priority to five main environmental issues: the sustainable management of land (especially in semi-arid high country areas), including the management of pests (notably possums and rabbits); conservation management (following the establishment and subsequent restructuring of the Department of Conservation); marine and coastal management; the management of waste and hazardous substances; and water-related issues. The following quotation provides a glimpse of the Commissioner's approach to the issue of pest management:

> There was a proposal to introduce myxomatosis to control a rabbit plague in Central Otago. We went down to see for ourselves the damage caused by too much grazing pressure from sheep and rabbits. That was when I realized we were looking at a completely unsustainable system. Central Otago was fast becoming a dust bowl and we were viewing insipient desertification. This was a process I had believed could never happen in New Zealand . . . Two reports later we were recommending a change in land use . . . The rabbits taught us that when land management is unsustainable, the ecosystem is unsustainable, the economy of the area is unsustainable and the human habitation becomes socially unsustainable as people walk off the land.[45]

Aside from audit work and responding to complaints, the first Commissioner's major reports were typically prompted by evidence of poor policy design and/or weak implementation, or even the complete lack of a proper policy framework. As noted,

[45] Quoted from a lecture by H. Hughes at the Yearly Meeting of Quakers in Dunedin, in 'Quakers in Aotearoa' http://quaker.org.nz/helen-hughes accessed 30 November 2017.

her tenure coincided with a remarkable period of regulatory reform in New Zealand with a plethora of new Acts and far-reaching amendments to existing legislation. Many of these legislative changes had significant implications for environmental management. Apart from the landmark RMA, there were reforms affecting biosecurity, building and construction, Crown minerals, electricity, fisheries, forestry, hazardous substances, and maritime transport. Her tenure also occurred during a major reorganization of local government, with around 750 public bodies reconfigured to less than 100. Importantly, too, the period was characterized by a much stronger emphasis on consultation with the Māori community over resource management issues and the commencement of processes to resolve grievances under the Treaty of Waitangi (1840).[46] The latter process was prompted by efforts to compensate iwi (i.e. Māori tribes) for the grave injustices perpetrated during the mid-nineteenth century when European settlers and colonial authorities forcibly acquired large tracts of Māori land. It was thus an era of constant change and adjustment – without doubt a demanding context, especially for a small, fledgling organization seeking to establish its identity and develop new methodologies and robust processes.

Dr Morgan Williams, who succeeded Helen Hughes in 1997, had a scientific background in biology and ecology, having completing a doctorate in population ecology at the University of Bath. Prior to his appointment as Commissioner, he had spent much of his career in in research, management, and policy within the New Zealand Ministry of Agriculture and Fisheries. This included contributing to various projects related to the PCE's early activities, such as the implementation of a new system for managing the control of rabbits in rural areas. During his tenure as Commissioner, Dr Williams initially gave precedence to the urban and marine environments, including energy and transport issues. But he also devoted time to the use of economic instruments for environmental management, conservation management, public participation in resource management, and the growing practice of resource co-management and/or co-governance involving public agencies and bodies representing iwi. Such practices expanded during the 1990s and 2000s as part of the Treaty settlements process.

The pursuit of sustainable economic development dominated the latter part of Williams' tenure. His office produced a series of substantial reports, commissioning several dozen background papers and hosting a major forum.[47] Particularly significant was the publication of *Growing for Good: Intensive Farming, Sustainability and the Environment* in 2004, which highlighted the grave environmental risks associated

[46] See, for instance, H. Matunga, 'A Māori View', in Hawke, *supra* note 2; A. Sharp, *Justice and the Maori* (Oxford University Press 1990).

[47] This approach was developed and encapsulated in his second five-year plan. See Parliamentary Commissioner for the Environment, *Statement of Intent – 2003–2008* (Parliamentary Commissioner for the Environment 2003).

with the intensification of pastoral farming.[48] Not surprisingly, given the critical role of agriculture in the New Zealand economy, this report generated a vigorous public debate about the future of farming and the challenges of protecting environmental values and living within biophysical limits. Over the two years following its publication it generated more than 650 media articles and initiated a community dialogue on issues previously downplayed because of their political sensitivity.

The third Commissioner, Dr Jan Wright, interpreted her role differently to her predecessors, pursuing other priorities and adjusting the mix of expertise within her Office. With a disciplinary background in public policy, physics, energy, and resources, she gave precedence to climate change, both mitigation and adaptation issues.[49] Not merely did she regard climate changes as 'the most important environmental issue of our time',[50] her appointment occurred close to the release of the Fourth Assessment Report of the Intergovernmental Report on Climate Change, a year prior to the passage of legislation establishing the New Zealand Emissions Trading Scheme (ETS), and during a period of unprecedented international diplomacy on climate change, culminating in the Copenhagen summit in late 2009. Moreover, during her tenure the National-led government systematically weakened the ETS and pursued an economic strategy inconsistent with its public pledges to reduce New Zealand's GHG emissions – expanding oil and gas exploration (both onshore and offshore), increasing fossil fuel production, and seeking to double the value of the country's agricultural exports within a decade.[51] The export goal entailed additional land-use change, especially conversion from forestry or sheep/beef farming to dairy farming, and a further intensification of pastoral land use (e.g. more cows per hectare and/or greater fertilizer use). These trends increased

[48] Parliamentary Commissioner for the Environment, *Growing for Good: Intensive Farming, Sustainability and New Zealand's Environment* (Parliamentary Commissioner for the Environment 2004).

[49] The third Commissioner, Dr Jan Wright, developed some new criteria for triaging topics for investigation in 2007. See Parliamentary Commissioner for the Environment, *Annual Report for the Year Ended June 30 2014* (Parliamentary Commissioner for the Environment 2014) 20. To quote: 'The first criterion for adding value is to avoid duplicating the work of others. Instead, I seek out areas where my independence can enable progress on difficult or contested topics, and where I am likely to be able to make practical, effective recommendations. I receive many complaints, information, and suggestions from members of the public. While all the issues raised cannot be investigated, all are considered. Some have led to investigations. However, while it is my job to worry about New Zealand's environment, not everything is of great importance. We strive to get beyond the reactionary and fashionable, and focus attention on what matters most. I pay particular attention to environmental problems that are *irreversible*, *cumulative*, and/or *accelerating*. I also consider their scale and pervasiveness, and whether they threaten to tip a system into another state. Climate change ticks all these boxes and is therefore, in my view, the greatest environmental challenge the world faces.'

[50] Ibid. at 14.

[51] G. Bertram and S. Terry, *The Carbon Challenge: New Zealand's Emissions Trading Scheme* (Bridget Williams Books Ltd 2010); A. Cameron (ed.), *Climate Change Law and Policy in New Zealand* (LexisNexis NZ 2011); A. Macey, 'Climate Change: Towards Policy Coherence' (2014) 10:2 *Policy Quarterly* 49–56.

methane and nitrous oxide emissions and put greater pressure on surface waterways and groundwater. The government also sought, largely unsuccessfully, to weaken the fundamental principles underpinning the RMA. And in 2010 it proposed that certain designated conservation land should be made available for mining. Such actions not only sparked widespread public protests, but also placed the Commissioner regularly in the role of governmental critic. Dr Wright steadfastly promoted 'a much stronger response to climate change',[52] but with little impact.

She described her role as follows:

> The core work of our office is undertaking investigations and providing advice on environmental matters ... The provision of advice is generally done in two ways: either as advice on proposed law changes to select committees or on policy proposals to government agencies ... Investigations arise in a variety of ways. For instance, they may be prompted by letters from the public, or may flow from issues uncovered in earlier investigations. The result of an investigation is in the form of a report tabled in Parliament. Reports usually contain recommendations to Ministers ... My staff and I work hard to ensure reports are accurate and readable, and that recommendations are both practical and effective. While formal reporting is fundamental, we also use a variety of other ways of communicating our work to Parliamentarians and the public, from presentations and speeches, to media comment and videos on our website. Two or three years after a report, a short update on the subject is prepared. These update reports canvass reactions and responses, and sometimes include new developments.[53]

By the end of her tenure in office in early October 2017, Dr Wright had completed over eighty reports, excluding annual reports and statements of intent. Of these, more than half were submissions, briefings, or advice on government bills, proposed regulations, or policy-related documents. A large proportion of such submissions dealt with climate change, energy, or mining issues, including oil and gas exploration. The remaining documents included around two dozen substantive reports covering policy issues and performance audits, and over a dozen update reports. Of the reports, around half focused on climate change, energy, or mining. The remainder covered such topics as freshwater management, pest control, and conservation, together with commentaries on the initial reports prepared under the Environmental Report Act by the Ministry for the Environment and Statistics New Zealand.

## AN ASSESSMENT

Assessing the performance of organizations is problematic. Although there are various commonly used criteria – such as efficiency and effectiveness – these can

52 Parliamentary Commissioner for the Environment, *Annual Report for the Year Ended June 30 2014* (Parliamentary Commissioner for the Environment 2014) 14.

53 Ibid. at 9.

be difficult to apply. Appropriate benchmarks and reliable data are often unavailable. And in terms of assessing impact, there is the fundamental challenge of determining the appropriate counterfactual: what would have happened if the organization in question had not existed? Moreover, organizations vary greatly in their functions, powers, and resources, and even bodies of a broadly comparable nature may face radically different authorizing and operating environments – which may profoundly affect their performance.

As for the PCE, there are no equivalent bodies in New Zealand in other policy sectors, and although there are Environmental Commissioners in some other parliamentary democracies, their functions and powers differ. For instance, the Canadian Commissioner of the Environment and Sustainable Development is appointed by the Canadian Auditor-General, not by the federal Parliament. The primary function of the Commissioner is to conduct performance audits, and the scope of responsibility is limited to federal policies and agencies. Similarly, while the Environmental Commissioner of Ontario, like the PCE, prepares reports on environmental issues of concern,[54] the Office is also mandated to, amongst other things, review the Ontario government's compliance with the Environmental Bill of Rights and its progress in reducing GHG emissions. In Australia there are a number of entities with roles that overlap with the PCE, including the Commissioner for Sustainability and the Environment in the Australian Capital Territory. But in each case, there are marked differences with the PCE either in their functions or operating environments. Hence, the scope for meaningful interagency and interjurisdictional comparisons is limited.

Also, PCEs lack enforcement powers since their influence is limited to making recommendations. Commissioners must therefore rely on the power of persuasion, the force of evidence or the capacity to embarrass. Of course, if they were to have specific enforcement powers, their role would be even more controversial politically and thus their long-term survival and/or effectiveness might be even more at risk. Against this, certain halfway houses might be feasible. For instance, one modest reform option would be to require organizations investigated by the PCE to report within a specified period on how they have responded to the PCE's recommendations. Aside from their limited legal powers, PCEs have operated for three decades with a tiny budget, and thus limited analytical and investigative resources. Such constraints must be properly factored into any evaluation of their performance.[55]

If durability is a relevant measure of success, then the PCE certainly meets this test. And sheer survival is no mean feat, all the more so for an institution with an explicit 'critic and conscience' role. Bear in mind that since the mid 1980s, there

[54] E. Ligeyi, 'The Role of the Environmental Commissioner of Ontario and the Environmental Bill of Rights in Supporting Public Participation in Environmental Decision Making', in Hawke, *supra* note 2.

[55] Bührs, *supra* note 2 at 210–211.

have been no fewer than three changes of government and far-reaching constitutional, policy. and regulatory reforms (as discussed above). Also, major institutional reorganizations and 'terminations' are remarkably common within New Zealand's public sector, and longevity all too rare.[56] Significantly, when the creation of the PCE was under active discussion in the mid 1980s, the Treasury proposed that the relevant legislation contain a sunset clause, on the basis that at least some of the PCE's roles would not be required on a long-term basis. Fortunately, this recommendation was not accepted. Nevertheless, this initially negative disposition by a highly influential department highlights the risks facing a small entity like the PCE. Internationally, moreover, it is not usual for bodies with important environmental responsibilities to be short-lived – the Sustainable Development Commission in the UK provides a prime example. With these considerations in mind, the fact the PCE has survived is no minor achievement. Such durability suggests that the case for an independent environmental 'watchdog' is now widely accepted across New Zealand's political community and that the Office has demonstrated its worth. It also reflects the introduction of proportional representation in 1996. Under the new electoral arrangements, no single party has secured an overall parliamentary majority. Any move to abolish the PCE would thus require the support of at least two or more parties.

Another criterion of institutional performance relates to compliance with, and fulfilment of, the organization's statutory duties. Here, the PCE has an exemplary record. Of course, this is not a particularly demanding test because, as mentioned, Commissioners have a broad mandate and considerable discretion. Hence, matters of compliance are unlikely to arise. Nevertheless, it is important to register that all the Commissioners to date, although interpreting their legislative brief differently, have managed to secure and maintain a reputation for being scrupulously independent in undertaking their statutory duties. Not only have they been appropriately non-partisan, but they have also demonstrated a capacity to work with a wide range of stakeholders, sometimes using their 'neutral' position to assist contending parties to find common ground.

Assessing the PCE's efficiency and effectiveness is harder. There are many possible performance measures, including: the volume and quality of its output; the impact of its investigations, findings and recommendations on policy decisions, environmental planning processes; the quality of environmental management, public understanding of major environmental issues, and the quality of public debate; and – ultimately – its impact on environmental outcomes. Measuring the

[56] Boston et al., *supra* note 21; J. Boston, 'The Eighties: A Retrospective View', paper prepared for a seminar series on *The 100 Years Perspective – History of the Legislation*, 23 October 2012, Wellington, Ministry of Culture and Heritage and the Institute of Public Administration New Zealand.

volume of output is relatively straightforward. But, aside from indicating a certain level of activity, it is not a useful measure of effectiveness.

The quality of the PCE's reports is much more important, but also more difficult to assess. In this regard, Commissioners have pursued various strategies to ensure that their reports meet appropriate standards of accuracy, logic, rigour, clarity, relevance, and timeliness. All reports are peer reviewed; organizations with a direct interest in the subject of the particular inquiry are consulted; and an opportunity is generally provided for any public authorities that are under investigation to conduct a content check (e.g. for accuracy) on relevant parts of draft reports before they are finalized and released.

For such reasons, the PCE's reports have generally been concise, well-documented, clearly presented, and readily accessible, and any policy recommendations or advice on remedial action are explicit. Not surprisingly, therefore, they have been well regarded within the policy community (including parliamentarians, government officials and non-governmental organizations).[57] They have often been widely publicized and quoted in the media, and frequently referred to in Parliament and by public agencies. Generally speaking, policymakers have regarded the PCE's contributions as 'non-partisan, objective, fair and even-handed',[58] and 'well-reasoned and pragmatic'.[59] To quote a long-serving Minister for the Environment, Hon Dr Nick Smith, 'the public has come to trust the office as a brave straight shooter', and the Commissioners have 'carved out a heritage of genuine independence'.[60] To be sure, there have been those who have disagreed vigorously with particular findings or recommendations. But this is to be expected. Many of the PCE's reports have addressed highly controversial issues involving complex policy trade-offs and conflicting values.

As to the impact of the PCE's investigations the record, certainly with respect to acceptance of Commissioners' recommendations, looks impressive, at least at first sight. To date, around 60–70 per cent of the PCE's recommendations have been partially or fully accepted. For instance, during her second term (1992–1997), Helen Hughes made over 800 recommendations. Of these, 46 per cent related to subnational government, 29 per cent to ministers, 19 per cent to parliament or a select committee, and 5 per cent to Crown entities and SOEs. An assessment of the responses to these recommendations revealed there were positive outcomes (that is,

57 Hon G. Brownlee and G. Robertson, comments in the New Zealand Parliament 10 May 2012, 'Appointments – Parliamentary Commissioner for the Environment' 679 Hansard at 2175; Bührs, *supra* note 2; Hawke, *supra* note 2; K. Marshall, 'A Local Government Review of the Commissioner Role', in Hawke, *supra* note 2; G. Robertson, 2012; Hon Dr Nick Smith, 'Measuring Up' – Speech on 25th Anniversary of Parliamentary Commissioner for the Environment, 18 August 2011.

58 Marshall, *supra* note 57 at 13.

59 Hon G. Brownlee, comments in the New Zealand Parliament 10 May 2012, 'Appointments – Parliamentary Commissioner for the Environment' (2012) 679 *Hansard* at 2175.

60 Smith, *supra* note 57.

the recommendations were accepted and/or implemented) in 72 per cent of cases for major reports and 63 per cent for all reports.[61] More recently, as highlighted in Table 23.1, around 60 per cent of the recommendations of the third Commissioner were accepted.[62] Nevertheless, recommendations vary in their significance. The rejection of a few major recommendations may be much more important than the acceptance of many minor ones. Moreover, Commissioners may, having assessed the political context, refrain from making recommendations that they know are bound to be rejected. Assuming, therefore, that the PCE is influential and effective because a relatively high proportion of its recommendations have been accepted may not be valid. Indeed, the point could readily be made that, despite three decades of extensive investigations, reports, submissions, and briefings, there has been, at best, only modest progress on the most serious environmental challenges facing New Zealand and, at worst, repeated policy failure. For instance, many stocks of natural capital, both renewable and non-renewable, continue to be depleted or degraded; efforts to curb GHG emissions remain ineffective; nutrient enrichment of some waterways has worsened; freshwater allocations in some areas with intensifying land use have been poorly managed; urban planning – including of the country's largest city, Auckland – has been deficient, with inadequate investment in public transport and poor traffic management; the identification and remediation of contaminated sites has often been poor; hill country erosion remains a significant problem, not having been helped by inconsistent approaches to forestry management and carbon sequestration; and some fish stocks remain under threat.[63] Clearly, critical sustainability principles, including the need to live within safe biophysical limits, have yet to be adequately embedded in governmental and community decision making. More fundamentally, perhaps, many leading policymakers in New Zealand remain committed to a form of economic development that gives relatively little weight to the economic value of ecosystem services or the ultimate dependence of humanity on a diverse, healthy natural environment. For many, 'progress' continues to be assessed on the basis of narrow measures of flows, such as GDP, rather than trends in capital stocks, not least natural capital. To quote Dr Williams in his final *Annual Report* to Parliament in 2006:

> New Zealand has environmental sustainability challenges. Pressure on our natural capital is growing ... As a nation we have been rapidly increasing our ecological

[61] Parliamentary Commissioner for the Environment, *supra* note 41 at 5.

[62] The decision by the third Commissioner to set a target of having 65 per cent of her recommendations accepted reflected an attempt to balance two competing considerations: on the one hand, a concern that a higher target might result in recommendations that were too unambitious and, on the other hand, a concern that a lower target might result in recommendations that were overly ambitious. There is, of course, no correct target.

[63] Ministry for the Environment, *Environment New Zealand 2007*, *supra* note 11; Taylor, *supra* note 11; E. Eppel, 'Improving New Zealand Water Governance: Challenges and Recommendations' (2014) 10:3 *Policy Quarterly* 66–75; Brown et al., *supra* note 11.

TABLE 23.1 *Parliamentary Commissioner for the Environment performance measures and targets*

| Performance measure | Target for 2014–18 | Actual 2014–15 | Actual 2013–14 | Actual 2012–13 | Actual 2011–12 | Actual 2010–11 | Actual 2009–10 |
|---|---|---|---|---|---|---|---|
| Proportion of recommendations adopted or partially adopted | 65% | 58% | 60% | 61% | 62% | 61% | 53% |
| Number of reports and commentaries | 4–6 | 6 | 3 | 4 | 4 | 2 | 2 |
| Other advice to Parliament | 4–8 | 1 | 4 | 5 | 4 | 1 | 3 |
| Reports and commentaries externally peer reviewed and 'content checked' | 100% | 100% | 100% | 100% | 100% | 100% | 100% |
| Response to public concerns and information requests within required time frames | 100% | 74% | N/A | N/A | N/A | N/A | N/A |

*Source*: Parliamentary Commissioner for the Environment, *Strategic Intentions 2014–2018* (Wellington: Parliamentary Commissioner for the Environment, 2014) 7; Parliamentary Commissioner for the Environment, *Annual Report for the Year Ending 30 June 2015* (Wellington: Parliamentary Commissioner for the Environment, 2015) 26.

> footprint. Over the last 20 years our per capita demand for primary energy, cars, land for housing, and water have all increased. On the cost side of society's ledger, solid wastes, nutrients to waterways, and vehicle emissions have all increased. Most of our economic policies are simply not ones that will ultimately facilitate truly sustainable development.[64]

To blame the PCE for such failures would, of course, be unfair. Changing long-standing mind sets, economic paradigms, and analytical frameworks to reflect ecological principles and biophysical constraints represents a profound challenge – as Dr Williams is well aware. Moreover, a good case can be made that without the PCE environmental outcomes in New Zealand would have been even worse. Yet, it is salutatory that, despite the Office's strenuous efforts, environmental practices have not improved to a greater extent and that on some important measures environmental outcomes have deteriorated. Admittedly, the PCE has helped in 'shifting the system'.[65] But if environmental sustainability is the benchmark, progress has been slow. Likewise, while 'environmental concern' is now 'mainstream' in New Zealand rather the 'preserve of one sector of society' – as Dr Wright noted in her 2007 *Annual Report* – there often remains a large gulf between intentions and practice.[66] New Zealanders may value the environment now more than they did thirty years ago, but the negative impacts of their economic behaviour have, if anything, intensified. Worse, powerful vested interests continue to exercise a disproportionate influence on governmental decision making, often with damaging long-term environmental consequences.[67]

## CONCLUSION

The creation of the PCE in New Zealand represents a remarkable attempt to provide an authoritative voice for better environmental stewardship and an independent check on the capability and performance of the country's rapidly evolving system of environmental management. For three decades, Commissioners with differing backgrounds, expertise, and priorities have sought to fulfil their ambitious mandate. Their task has been constrained by limited resources, an ever-changing policy and regulatory context, and the sheer magnitude, range, and complexity of the environmental issues with which they have been confronted. The pursuit of economic agendas that are incompatible with long-term environmental sustainability has not helped. New Zealand, of course, is not alone in this respect. A fair and

64 Parliamentary Commissioner for the Environment, *Report for the Year Ended 30 June 2006* (Parliamentary Commissioner for the Environment 2006) 12.

65 Parliamentary Commissioner for the Environment, *Report for the Year Ended 30 June 2007* (Parliamentary Commissioner for the Environment 2007) 4.

66 Ibid. at 8.

67 C. James and E. Argyle, 'A Way of Thinking about Vested Interests' (2014) 10:4 *Policy Quarterly* 53–59.

reasonable assessment would suggest that the PCE has performed its statutory duties in a professional, diligent, and dedicated manner and has made a valuable contribution to improving the quality of the country's environmental management. But its many reports and submissions have only occasionally had a decisive impact on policy thinking or major governmental decisions. Similarly, there is little evidence that the PCE has secured enduring or transformative changes – whether to policy-making frameworks, the principles of environmental law, or public attitudes and values. As highlighted in the foregoing discussion, New Zealand governments have repeatedly failed to grapple adequately with a number of critical environmental issues, not least climate change and freshwater management. In such areas, while Commissioners have faithfully defined the nature of the problems and offered evidence-based solutions, they have lacked the statutory authority or political influence to ensure better decisions and outcomes. The quest for a more truly sustainable future thus remains a continuing challenge.

Because of its guardianship role and status as an Officer of Parliament, the PCE is a distinctive public entity internationally. Whether such a model could, or should, be replicated in other parliamentary democracies is a moot question. The appropriateness and utility of the model depends on a country's existing institutional arrangements, constitutional conventions, and regulatory frameworks.[68] Most democracies have already developed their own distinctive institutional, regulatory, and policy mechanisms for addressing environmental matters. It is possible that a body like the PCE could complement their existing arrangements. But other models, including bodies with a broader mandate to speak for future generations, may be preferable, depending on the circumstances.[69] What is clear, however, is that the environmental challenges facing humanity are grave and urgent.[70] Having authoritative, publicly mandated, yet independent voices for environmental sustainability thus remains vital.

[68] See, for instance, Oxford Martin Commission, *Now for the Long Term* (Report of the Oxford Martin Commission for Future Generations 2013); World Future Council, *National Policies & International Instruments to Protect the Rights of Future Generations* (World Future Council 2010); World Future Council, *Guarding Our Future* (World Future Council 2010).

[69] UN, 'High Level Representative for Future Generations', The General Assembly, Draft, 23 July 2013; H. Ward, 'Beyond the Short Term: Legal and Institutional Space for Future Generations in Global Governance' (2011) 22:1 *Yearbook of International Law* 3–36.

[70] IPCC, *Climate Change 2014: Synthesis Report* (IPCC 2014).

# 24

# Canadian Commissioner of the Environment and Sustainable Development

*David Wright and James McKenzie*

Since 1995, Canada's Commissioner of the Environment and Sustainable Development (the Commissioner) has been providing parliamentarians with objective, independent analysis and recommendations on the federal government's efforts to protect the environment and foster sustainable development.[1] This chapter presents an overview of the work of the Commissioner, including the institutional setting within the Office of the Auditor General of Canada. The first section provides the historical background about the office. The second section describes the Commissioner's role and functions, and the third section comments on the audit function as a model for other countries, focusing on attributes of effectiveness. The final section offers concluding comments.

## HISTORICAL BACKGROUND

Momentum toward the creation of a Commissioner of the Environment and Sustainable Development in Canada can be traced back to 1989 when Greenprint Canada – a coalition of twenty-eight organizations, including environmental, conservation, and Aboriginal groups – submitted *A Federal Agenda for the Environment* to the federal government of Canada.[2] This document put forward a comprehensive

[1] For a succinct summary of the Commissioner's mandate see, Office of the Auditor General, 'The Commissioner of the Environment and Sustainable Development' www.oag-bvg.gc.ca/internet/English/au_fs_e_370.html#Commissioner accessed 22 October 2016.

[2] Green Print for Canada Committee, *Greenprint for Canada: A Federal Agenda for the Environment* (Green Print for Canada Committee 1989). It should be noted that several changes in the Office of the Auditor General (OAG) preceded this movement. The OAG began to move beyond its traditional work of looking at the accuracy of financial statements in the 1950s when the Auditor General began to report on "non-productive payments." These were transactions that, while legal, provided no apparent benefit to Canadians. The reports were controversial, however, because government officials believed the Auditor General was commenting on government policy and therefore going beyond his mandate. The 1977 *Auditor*

agenda for the environment, including forty-three recommendations. One of these recommendations was to create an 'independent environmental auditor' to help strengthen accountability within the government with respect to the environment.[3]

Several steps leading to the creation of the Commissioner unfolded in the period between 1989 and 1995.[4] In 1990, the House of Commons Standing Committee on Environment considered the possibility of creating an 'Environmental Auditor General' to monitor the progress of federal departments and agencies in setting and attaining targets for GHG emissions.[5] Shortly thereafter, a private member's bill to establish an Environmental Auditor General was presented to Parliament.[6]

In 1992, the House of Commons Standing Committee on Public Accounts asked the Auditor General for his opinion on the need for an Environmental Auditor General. The Auditor General noted that there were differences of opinion about the nature of the role of an Environmental Auditor General and about who should perform it. In his view, most conceptualizations, including those containing both advocacy and audit, went beyond the mandate and resources of the Office of the Auditor General.[7]

The prospect of creating an Environmental Auditor General was kept alive through the autumn 1993 federal election.[8] In 1994, a new parliamentary committee, the Standing Committee on Environment and Sustainable Development, was tasked with considering the creation of this position and its possible functions.[9] The Standing Committee concluded that the most appropriate way to meet the government's objectives was by creating a Commissioner of the Environment and

*General Act* clarified and expanded the Auditor General's responsibilities. The Auditor General was given a broader mandate to examine how well the government managed its affairs. The new Act maintained the principle that the Auditor General does not comment on policy choices but does examine how policies are implemented. For further historical information, see Office of the Auditor General, 'A Brief History' www.oag-bvg.gc.ca/internet/English/au_fs_e_370.html#history accessed 22 October 2016.

3 Green Print for Canada Committee, *supra* note 2 at 24–25.

4 The historical background presented here has been informed by work completed to produce a report published in 2007. See Office of the Auditor General, *Fulfilling the Potential: A Review of the Environment and Sustainable Development Practice of the Office of the Auditor General* (Report of the Independent Green Ribbon Panel to the Auditor General of Canada, Office of the Auditor General 2007). For further context and commentary, see D. Pond, *The Impact of Parliamentary Officers on Canadian Parliamentary Democracy: A Study of the Commissioner of the Environment and Sustainable Development & The Environmental Commissioner of Ontario* (Canadian Study of Parliament Group 2010) 5–10.

5 House of Commons, *Minutes of Proceedings and Evidence of the Standing Committee on the Environment and Sustainable Development* (October 1990) 42–44.

6 House of Commons, *Commons Debates* (December 1990) 16234–16244.

7 House of Commons, *Minutes of Proceedings and Evidence of the Standing Committee on Public Accounts* (February 1992) 26–27.

8 Creation of this position was promised in the 1993 federal Liberal party "Red Book," a key party platform document. For more commentary about this period, see Pond, *supra* note 5.

9 Letter from the Honourable Sheila Copps to the Chairman of the House Standing Committee on Environment and Sustainable Development (16 March 1994).

Sustainable Development in conjunction with an expanded audit role for the Office of the Auditor General. As proposed, the Commissioner would have been a proactive advocate for sustainable development with two main roles: reviewing how well government policies, programs, and spending support Canada's move to sustainable development; and providing liaison, monitoring, and encouragement to government, Parliament, and the public to support that move.[10]

In its response, the government accepted that all the functions recommended by the Committee were essential but concluded that they could not all be undertaken effectively and efficiently by one body. It proposed a more limited role for the Commissioner, focused on monitoring and audit as part of a broader package of initiatives intended to meet the needs identified by the Committee. The government itself would play the role of advocate for the environment and sustainable development.[11] This was consistent with the view held by some at the time that policy and advocacy work should be left to members of Parliament and government departments.

In December 1995, amendments to the Auditor General Act (the Act) received royal assent,[12] creating the position of the Commissioner of the Environment and Sustainable Development within the Office of the Auditor General,[13] and setting out the Commissioner's mandate and powers. The amendments of 1995 also formally added environmental effects to the considerations that the Auditor General takes into account when determining what to audit and report to the House of Commons.[14] Of note, in the early 1990s, the Office of the Auditor General was already conducting audits related to environmental issues, including audits on issues such as the regulation of Canada's pulp and paper industry, forestry management, and the control and clean-up of freshwater pollution. This experience helped bolster the Commissioner's capacity early in their mandate.

Starting with the first appointment in July 1996, four people have held the position of Commissioner, with three people serving as interim Commissioners:

- Brian Emmett (1996–2000),
- Rick Smith (Interim, 2000),

10 House of Commons, *The Commissioner of the Environment and Sustainable Development, Report of the Standing Committee on Environment and Sustainable Development* (May 1994) xi–xv. For related commentary, see Pond, *supra* note 5.

11 Letter from the Honourable Sheila Copps to the Chairman of the House Standing Committee on Environment and Sustainable Development (16 March 1994).

12 Auditor General Act, RSC, 1985, c. A-17 (Canada).

13 Specifically, the appointment of the Commissioner is a requirement under section 15.1, Auditor General Act: "(1) The Auditor General shall, in accordance with the Public Service Employment Act, appoint a senior officer to be called the Commissioner of the Environment and Sustainable Development who shall report directly to the Auditor General. (2) The Commissioner shall assist the Auditor General in performing the duties of the Auditor General set out in this Act that relate to the environment and sustainable development."

14 Subsection 7(2)(f), Auditor General Act, RSC, 1985, c. A-17 (Canada).

- Johanne Gélinas (2000–2007),
- Ron Thompson (Interim, 2007–2008),
- Scott Vaughan (2008–2013),
- Neil Maxwell (Interim, 2013–2014)
- Julie Gelfand (2014 to 2019), and
- Andrew Hayes (Interim, 2019 to present)

Today, the Commissioner is supported by approximately thirty-five professional staff. The Commissioner and her staff also draw on the broader corporate services capacity of the Office of the Auditor General in areas such as human resources, communications, and audit methodology.[15]

## ROLE AND FUNCTIONS

Appointed by the Auditor General, the Commissioner provides objective independent analysis, and recommendations to Canada's Parliament regarding the federal government's efforts to protect the environment and foster sustainable development. The Commissioner's roles are set out primarily in the Auditor General Act; however, a legislated role also exists under the Federal Sustainable Development Act.[16] Additionally, the Commissioner undertakes other activities from time to time, such as collaboration with provincial auditors general in Canada. These roles and related functions are discussed in the following sections.

Sustainable development is defined in the Auditor General Act.[17] This definition was included in the 1995 amendments and is based on the well-known definition of the Brundtland Commission: "development that meets the needs of the present without compromising the ability of future generations to meet their own needs."[18] Notably, for those interested in looking to Canada as a model for institution creation or reform elsewhere, section 21.1 of the Act builds on the Brundtland definition with a broad description of sustainable development. In the Act, sustainable development is stated to be:[19]

> a continually evolving concept based on the integration of social, economic and environmental concerns, and which may be achieved by, among other things,
>
> (a) the integration of the environment and the economy;
> (b) protecting the health of Canadians;
> (c) protecting ecosystems;

[15] See generally 'Who We Are' www.oag-bvg.gc.ca/internet/English/au_fs_e_370.html#Commissioner accessed 30 November 2017.

[16] Federal Sustainable Development Act SC 2008, c. 33 (Canada).

[17] Section 2, Auditor General Act, RSC, 1985, c. A-17 (Canada).

[18] G.H. Brundtland et al., *Our Common Future: Report of the World Commission on Environment and Development* (Oxford University Press 1987).

[19] Section 21.1, Auditor General Act, RSC, 1985, c. A-17 (Canada).

(d) meeting international obligations;
(e) promoting equity;
(f) an integrated approach to planning and making decisions that takes into account the environmental and natural resource costs of different economic options and the economic costs of different environmental and natural resource options;
(g) preventing pollution; and
(h) respect for nature and the needs of future generations.

Readers involved in working toward creating institutions for future generations at the domestic and international levels may note with interest the explicit reference to "the needs of future generations" in subsection (h).

### *The Commissioner's Role and Functions under the Auditor General Act*

The Commissioner has three primary areas of activity under the Auditor General Act: (1) conducting "performance audits" of federal programs related to the environment and sustainable development; (2) monitoring the implementation of sustainable development strategies of federal departments and their contribution to Canada's Federal Sustainable Development Strategy (FSDS); and (3) overseeing an environmental petitions process. The Commissioner also occasionally publishes studies on environment and sustainable development topics.

**Performance Audits of Environmental and Sustainable Development Issues**

Performance audits, sometimes referred to in other jurisdictions as 'value-for-money audits,'[20] are the main output of the Commissioner. These performance audits are independent and objective assessments of how well the federal public service manages programs and services on behalf of Canadians. The audits typically involve examining departments' management practices, controls, and reporting systems. All performance audit work is conducted in accordance with standards for assurance engagements set by the Chartered Professional Accountants of Canada.[21]

Legislative authority for this work of the Commissioner flows from the broad authority granted by section 23(2) of the Act, which states: "[t]he Commissioner shall, on behalf of the Auditor General, report annually to Parliament concerning *anything* that the Commissioner considers should be brought to the attention of

[20] This terminology is used, for example, by the Sustainable Development Commissioner in the Canadian province of Quebec, who is also part of the Office of the Auditor General of Quebec. See Auditor General of Quebec, 'Mission' www.vgq.gouv.qc.ca/en/en_organisation/en_mission.aspx accessed 22 October 2016.

[21] For more details about how performance audit work is carried out, see Office of the Auditor General *What to Expect – An Auditee's Guide to the Performance Audit Process* (Minister of Public Works and Government Services 2015).

Parliament in relation to environmental and other aspects of sustainable development"[22] (emphasis added).

Performance audits are designed to answer the following questions: (1) are federal programs being run with due regard for economy, efficiency, and environmental effects? and (2) does the government have systems in place to measure the effectiveness of its programs? Final reports of performance audits contain recommendations aimed at improving the way government functions as well as responses to these recommendations from the organization(s) being audited. This work contributes to a public service that is effective and to a government that is accountable to Parliament and Canadians.

An important and fundamental characteristic of the Commissioner's performance audits is that they do not question the merits of federal laws and policies. Rather, the audits examine how well federal laws and policies are being implemented. In doing so, the Commissioner's reports focus on the *federal* government's performance since the activities of Canada's provincial and municipal governments are not within the Commissioner's mandate. Further, it must be noted that the Commissioner does not have prosecutorial or investigative powers. An example of the Commissioner's office refraining from examining merits of laws and policies can be observed in relation to the federal government's recent Responsible Resource Development (RRD) agenda.[23] Part of RRD included substantial changes to several key pieces of federal legislation,[24] including the Fisheries Act,[25] the Navigable Waters Protection Act,[26] and the Canadian Environmental Assessment Act.[27] While these

[22] Section 23(2), Auditor General Act, RSC, 1985, c. A-17 (Canada). It should be noted that s.21.1 articulates the "Purpose" of the Commissioner, which incorporates s.23(3) by reference: "In addition to carrying out the functions referred to in subsection 23(3), the purpose of the Commissioner is to provide sustainable development monitoring and reporting on the progress of category I departments towards sustainable development."

[23] Responsible Resource Development (RRD) was premised on four key outcomes: making resource project review processes more predictable and timely; reducing duplication of project reviews; strengthening environmental protection; and enhancing consultations with Aboriginal peoples. For detailed information, see Natural Resource Canada, 'Responsible Resource Development Backgrounder' www.nrcan.gc.ca/media-room/backgrounders/2012/3269 accessed 22 October 2016; RRD 'Backgrounder' www.nrcan.gc.ca/media-room/backgrounders/2012/3269 accessed 30 November 2017.

[24] A series of bills were tabled to implement RRD, starting with two substantial omnibus bills: Bill C-38, An Act to implement certain provisions of the budget tabled in parliament on March 29, 2012 and other statutes, 1st Sess, 41st Parl, 2012 (Canada); and C-45, A second Act to implement certain provisions of the budget tabled in Parliament on March 29, 2012 and other measures, 1st Sess, 41st Parl, 2012 (Canada).

[25] Fisheries Act, RSC, 1985, c. F-14 (Canada).

[26] Navigable Waters Protection Act RSC, 1985, c. N-22. The above-referenced Bill C-45 amended this Act, making it the Navigation Protection Act, RSC, 1985, c. N-22 (Canada).

[27] Canadian Environmental Assessment Act SC 1992, c. 37 (Canada). The above-referenced Bill C-38 ed this Act, replacing it with the Canadian Environmental Assessment Act, 2012 SC 2012, c. 19, s. 52 (Canada).

changes were the subject of much public attention and controversy,[28] particularly in the environmental community,[29] the Commissioner did not assess or comment on the merits of the new initiative nor the manner in which the legislative changes were brought about through omnibus budget bills. Rather, the office conducted a performance audit of the *implementation* of a key new piece of legislation that was part of RRD: Canadian Environmental Assessment Act, 2012.[30] In short, that audit found that key agencies had put systems and practices in place to implement the new legislation; however, improvements were needed with respect to transparency when determining which projects would undergo assessment and with respect to challenges around meaningful participation of the public and Aboriginal peoples.

A number of factors are considered when identifying the Commissioner's audit topics. An important consideration is the federal government's role and mandate in managing an issue. In Canada, jurisdiction over the environment is shared between the federal and provincial governments. So, while topics such as land-use planning and solid waste management are important environmental issues, they are largely the responsibilities of provincial, territorial, and municipal governments and are therefore outside the scope of the Commissioner's work. In addition to federal jurisdiction, other factors considered when identifying topics to audit include past audit coverage, the significance of the topic to Parliament and Canadians, the likelihood or risk that something could go wrong, and the significance of the impact that this could have on the environment and human health.

Typically, once the Commissioner's report is tabled in Parliament, the House of Commons Standing Committee on Environment and Sustainable Development (ESD Committee) holds a public hearing that the Commissioner attends. During the hearing, the Commissioner provides opening comments on the report and responds to questions that Committee members may have. From time to time, the Commissioner is also called as a witness by the ESD Committee on specific topics. For example, in late 2014 and early 2015, the Commissioner was called as a witness to speak on the subjects of migratory birds as well as pesticide management, both of which have been the subject of audits by the Commissioner. Canada's Senate committees may also call on the Commissioner to present at hearings.

[28] See for example, A. Wherry, 'A Rough Guide to Bill C-38', *Maclean's Magazine*, 6 June 2012 www.macleans.ca/politics/ottawa/a-rough-guide-to-bill-c-38/ accessed 22 October 2016. See also D. Amyot-Bilodeau and M. Gagné, 'Omnibus Bill C-38 – A Major Reform of Federal Environmental Laws' (McCarthy Tetrault 2012) https://mccarthy.ca/article_detail.aspx?id=5957 accessed 22 October 2016; M. Doelle, 'CEAA 2012: The End of Federal EA As We Know It?' (2012) 24 JELP 1, 1–17.

[29] See for example, B. Heelan Powell, 'An Overview of Bill C-38: The Budget Bill that Transformed Canada's Federal Environmental Laws' (Environmental Law Centre 2012). See also A. Gage, 'Bill C-38 and Offloading Fisheries onto the Provinces' (West Coast Environmental Law 2012).

[30] As part of RRD, the government repealed the Canadian Environmental Assessment Act SC 1992, c. 37 (Canada) replacing it with the Canadian Environmental Assessment Act, 2012 SC 2012, c. 19, s. 52 (Canada).

This is particularly the case with the Standing Senate Committee on Energy, the Environment and Natural Resources. In general, information provided by the Commissioner in these venues is based on what has been audited by the office.

Between 1995 and 2014, the Commissioner's staff carried out sixty performance audits. Examples of topics covered by the Commissioner's past performance audits include the following: mitigating and adapting to climate change; environmental monitoring of Canada's oil sands; marine navigation in the Canadian Arctic; conserving biodiversity; responding to oil and chemical spills from ships; cleaning up contaminated sites; and applying and enforcing legislation such as the Canadian Environmental Assessment Act and the Canadian Environmental Protection Act.

**Examples of Performance Audits on Climate Change Tabled by the Commissioner**

Canada's Commissioner of the Environment and Sustainable Development has audited federal government activities related to climate change multiple times. Each audit took a slightly different approach; each was based on government commitments and associated activities at the time. All audit reports employed the same performance audit methodology – looking at what the federal government had committed to and then auditing the performance against that commitment.

For example, in the Commissioner's first report on climate change in 1998, the audit objective was framed around assessing the adequacy of Canada's steps toward implementing its commitment at the time to stabilize GHG emissions at 1990 levels by the year 2000 (Canada had not yet signed and ratified the Kyoto Protocol). That audit found that emissions were headed in the wrong direction and that the National Action Program on Climate Change had been inadequately implemented.

Similarly, a 2012 climate change audit focused on whether Environment Canada had established a plan designed to meet the commitment made by Canada as part of the Copenhagen Accord (17 percent below 2005 levels by 2020). That audit found that the federal government's sector-by-sector approach to regulate GHG emissions lacked an overall implementation plan. It also found that the 2020 target would not be met with measures in place at that time.

The Commissioner's reports on climate change have also focused on specific areas of activity related to climate change mitigation, such as energy efficiency in the 2001 report. As well, in 2006, the Commissioner looked at federal government strategies and action plans in place for adapting to and managing the impacts of climate change.

In 2014, the latest report on climate change by the Commissioner was tabled in Parliament. The audit found some positive developments with respect to estimating and reporting GHG emissions and disbursing climate financing. However, the audit concluded that little had changed with respect to GHG emission reductions since the 2012 audit and that federal measures in place would have little effect on emissions by 2020. It also found that the federal government did not yet have a plan for how it would work toward the greater reductions required beyond 2020.

The 2014 observations were strikingly similar to those of the Commissioner's very first audit on climate change in 1998. In the 1998 report, the Commissioner noted that failure to meet commitments was primarily a result of poor planning and ineffective management. The 2014 report made the overarching observation that, "while the Government of Canada has recognized the need to urgently combat climate change, its planning has been ineffective and the action it has taken has been slow and not well coordinated."

Given Canada's continued efforts and associated commitments in the climate change realm, the Commissioner's latest report on this topic is unlikely to be the last.

In addition to the work of the Commissioner, the Auditor General of Canada has also released audits related to sustainable development and future generations. Such work is underpinned by the Auditor General's broad authority under the Act to report to Parliament on "anything he considers to be of significance and of a nature that should be brought to the attention of the House of Commons."[31] Examples of topics covered by the Auditor General include the following: long-term fiscal sustainability (the Canadian government's capacity to finance its activities and debt obligations in the future without placing an excessive burden on future generations);[32] federal programs and services for First Nations on reserves related to education, drinking water quality, housing, and child and family services; implementation of land claim agreements;[33] official development assistance (foreign

[31] Subsection 7(2), Auditor General Act, 1995. This broad legislative authority may include matters related to the environment and sustainable development and is complemented by the 1995 amendments that added "environment" to the list of dimensions to be considered by the Auditor General when selecting and reporting audits to the House of Commons. Subsection 7(2)(f) contains this reference, indicating that the Auditor General consider whether "money has been expended without due regard to the environmental effects of those expenditures in the context of sustainable development."

[32] OAG, Fall 2012 Report, *Long-Term Fiscal Sustainability* www.oag-bvg.gc.ca/internet/English/parl_oag_201210_07_e_37351.html accessed 30 November 2017.

[33] See OAG May 2006 Report, *Management of Programs for First Nations* www.oag-bvg.gc.ca/internet/English/parl_oag_200605_05_e_14962.html accessed 30 November 2017; see also OAG June 2011 Status Report, *Programs for First Nations on Reserves* www.oag-bvg.gc.ca/internet/English/parl_oag_201106_04_e_35372.html#hd5c accessed 30 November 2017; OAG Fall 2015 Report, *Implementing the Labrador Inuit Land Claims Agreement* www.oag-bvg.gc.ca/internet/English/att__e_41082.html accessed 30 November 2017; OAG *November 2003 Report, INAC – Transferring Responsibilities to the North* www.oag-bvg.gc.ca/internet/docs/20031108ce.pdf accessed 30 November 2017. See generally OAG, *INAC-related Auditor General of Canada Reports* www.aadnc-aandc.gc.ca/eng/1338471861166/1454964057806 accessed 30 November 2017.

aid) supporting poverty reduction;[34] nutrition support programs in northern Canada;[35] sustaining development in the Northwest Territories;[36] and public sector pension plans (including fairness to current and future generations).[37]

The Auditor General of Canada also serves as the Auditor General for Canada's three northern territorial governments. Recent territorial audits with dimensions for future generations include provision of child and family services,[38] safety of schools and childcare facilities,[39] and education.[40]

### *Sustainable Development Strategies*

Since the 1995 amendments to the Auditor General Act, designated federal departments and agencies have been required by law to prepare sustainable development strategies and table them in Parliament. The Commissioner monitors and reports annually on the implementation of these strategies. The 2008 Federal Sustainable Development Act requires the Minister of the Environment to develop an overarching FSDS that includes goals and targets related to topics such as clean air and water.[41] Departmental sustainable development strategies are required to contribute to the FSDS. The Minister is also required to produce a progress report on implementation of the FSDS.

Under section 9(4) of the Federal Sustainable Development Act, the Commissioner is required to review a draft of the FSDS and comment specifically on whether the targets and implementation strategies in the FSDS can be assessed.[42] This work supplements the Commissioner's more targeted performance audits. Under section 23(3) of the Auditor General Act, the Commissioner is also required

[34] See OAG Fall 2009 Report, *Strengthening Aid Effectiveness – Canadian International Development Agency* www.oag-bvg.gc.ca/internet/English/parl_oag_200911_08_e_33209.html accessed 30 November 2017.

[35] OAG Fall 2014 Report, *Nutrition North Canada—Aboriginal Affairs and Northern Development Canada* www.oag-bvg.gc.ca/internet/English/att__e_39985.html accessed 30 November 2017.

[36] OAG Spring 2010 Report, *Sustaining Development in the Northwest Territories* www.oag-bvg.gc.ca/internet/English/parl_oag_201004_04_e_33717.html accessed 30 November 2017.

[37] OAG Spring 2014, *Public Sector Pension Plans* www.oag-bvg.gc.ca/internet/English/att__e_39353.html accessed 30 November 2017.

[38] See e.g. OAG March 2011, *Children, Youth and Family Programs and Services in Nunavut* www.oag-bvg.gc.ca/internet/English/nun_201103_e_35006.html accessed 30 November 2017.

[39] OAG November 2013 Report, *Safety of Schools and Childcare Facilities in Nunavut* www.oag-bvg.gc.ca/internet/English/nun_201311_e_38770.html accessed 30 November 2017.

[40] See e.g., OAG May 2010, *Education in the Northwest Territories—Department of Education, Culture and Employment* www.oag-bvg.gc.ca/internet/English/nwt_201005_e_33873.html#hd3e accessed 30 November 2017.

[41] Federal Sustainable Development Act (S.C. 2008, c. 33).

[42] Section 9(4), Federal Sustainable Development Act (S.C. 2008, c. 33).

to assess and report on the fairness (e.g., balance, completeness) of the information contained in the FSDS progress report.[43]

### *Environmental Petitions*

The 1995 amendments to the Auditor General Act also created an environmental petitions process.[44] Environmental petitions are a way for Canadians to bring their concerns about environmental issues to the attention of the federal government and obtain a formal response. Unlike other public petitions, environmental petitions do not require multiple signatures; rather, they can be submitted by an individual citizen or organization with a concern about environmental issues.

By submitting a petition, residents of Canada can ask certain federal ministers and their departments to explain federal policy, to investigate or take action on an environmental problem, or to examine their enforcement of environmental legislation.[45] The Minister is obligated to provide a response to each petition. While a petition may prompt a Minister and his/her department to act on a certain issue, the Minister is not obligated to take action in response to concerns raised by petitioners. The Commissioner manages the environmental petitions process and monitors the responses of federal ministers. Once a petition is received by the Commissioner's staff, it is forwarded to the appropriate minister(s).

The petitions mechanism is created by section 22 of the Auditor General Act, which requires ministers to provide a response to the petitioner(s) within 120 days.[46] The Commissioner reports annually to Parliament on the petitions process, including the number, nature, and status of petitions received. A guide to the environmental petitions process, called Getting Answers,[47] explains the purpose and mechanics of the petitions process, describes the kinds of requests that can be made, and provides advice on how to prepare a petition. Informing Canadians about the petitions process is a common element in public outreach work by the Commissioner and office staff.

Since 1996, the Commissioner has received more than 400 petitions.[48] These petitions have touched on a wide range of topics such as species at risk, fisheries management, the potential effects of toxic substances on environmental and human health, climate change, environmental assessment, oceans management, and the use of science in decision making. Summaries of petitions and responses from

[43] Section 23(3), Auditor General Act (RSC, 1985, c. A-17).

[44] OAG, *Getting Answers: A Guide to the Environmental Petitions Process* (2014) 1 www.oag-bvg.gc.ca/internet/docs/pet_lp_e_930.pdf accessed 30 November 2017.

[45] Ibid. at 2.

[46] Section 22, Auditor General Act (RSC, 1985, c. A-17).

[47] OAG, *Getting Answers: A Guide to the Environmental Petitions Process* (2014) 1 www.oag-bvg.gc.ca/internet/docs/pet_lp_e_930.pdf accessed 30 November 2017.

[48] See OAG, 'Petitions Catalogue' www.oag-bvg.gc.ca/internet/English/pet_fs_e_929.html accessed 30 November 2017.

the federal government can be found in the Commissioner's online petitions catalogue available on the Office of the Auditor General's website.

### *Studies on Environmental and Sustainable Development Issues*

While less common, the Commissioner has also released studies on various environmental and sustainable development topics.[49] A study differs from an audit in that a study is more descriptive and exploratory and does not include observations or recommendations. Studies also do not comment on the merits or substance of government policy. In some cases, studies are done as an initial step to gather information in anticipation of a planned performance audit.[50]

For example, in 2011, the Commissioner released a study on managing fisheries for sustainability.[51] This study was a step toward identifying a framework and criteria for future audits to determine whether fisheries management practices are supporting sustainable fisheries. The study also identified questions that Canada's Parliament may wish to consider, given its roles to both set the legislative framework for managing fisheries and oversee activities of federal departments and agencies. Examples of other studies conducted by the Commissioner include federal support to the fossil fuel sector,[52] environmental monitoring,[53] a backgrounder on biological diversity,[54] and an overview on climate change.[55]

### *Collaborative Efforts of the Commissioner of the Environment and Sustainable Development*

The Commissioner collaborates from time to time with the province of Ontario's Environment Commissioner and Quebec's Sustainable Development Commissioner. For example, the Quebec Commissioner and the federal

[49] See e.g. CESD Fall 2012 Report, A *Study of Federal Support to the Fossil Fuel Sector* www.oag-bvg.gc.ca/internet/English/parl_cesd_201212_04_e_37713.html accessed 30 November 2017. See also CESD December 2011 Report, A *Study of Managing Fisheries for Sustainability* www.oag-bvg.gc.ca/internet/English/parl_cesd_201112_04_e_36032.html accessed 30 November 2017

[50] See e.g. CESD December 2011 Chapter 4, A *Study of Managing Fisheries for Sustainability*, paragraph 4.7 and Chapter 5, A Study of Environmental Monitoring, paragraph 5.4 www.oag-bvg.gc.ca/internet/English/parl_cesd_201112_e_36027.html accessed 30 November 2017.

[51] CESD December 2011 Report, A *Study of Managing Fisheries for Sustainability* www.oag-bvg.gc.ca/internet/English/parl_cesd_201112_04_e_36032.html accessed 30 November 2017.

[52] CESD Fall 2012 Report, A *Study of Federal Support to the Fossil Fuel Sector* www.oag-bvg.gc.ca/internet/English/parl_cesd_201212_04_e_37713.html accessed 30 November 2017.

[53] CESD Fall 2011 Report, A *Study on Environmental Monitoring* www.oag-bvg.gc.ca/internet/English/parl_cesd_201112_05_e_36033.html accessed 30 November 2017.

[54] CESD Fall 2013 Report, *Backgrounder on Biological Diversity* www.oag-bvg.gc.ca/internet/English/parl_cesd_201311_01_e_38671.html accessed 30 November 2017.

[55] CESD September 2006 Report, *Climate Change – An Overview* www.oag-bvg.gc.ca/internet/English/parl_cesd_200609_00_e_14549.html accessed 30 November 2017.

Commissioner submitted a joint paper to the 2012 Rio+20 Earth Summit under the thematic area "institutional framework for sustainable development."[56] In addition, the Commissioner participates in the Canadian Council of Legislative Auditors (CCOLA) that provides a forum for cooperation and information sharing between the federal and provincial auditors general in Canada.[57]

The Commissioner and staff also actively participate in the International Organization for Supreme Audit Institution's (INTOSAI) Working Group on Environmental Auditing (WGEA).[58] This working group is INTOSAI's largest, with representatives from over seventy countries. Its aim is to encourage audit use in the fields of environmental protection and sustainable development through knowledge sharing, capacity development, and cooperation. Past contributions by the Commissioner's office have included training other Supreme Audit Institutions' officials in environmental auditing.[59] Additionally, Canada chaired the WGEA and hosted its Secretariat from 2001 to 2007 and several of the Commissioner's staff contributed to this work.[60]

The Office of the Auditor General also hosts highly qualified individuals from audit institutions of select developing countries in collaboration with the CCAF-FCVI (formerly named the Canadian Comprehensive Auditing Foundation), a not-for-profit organization dedicated to promoting and strengthening public sector performance auditing, oversight, and accountability in Canada and abroad.[61] This International Fellows Program provides participants with on-the-job and classroom training in performance auditing. Often, at least one Fellow works with the Commissioner's office on a performance audit. Participants in the program are required to develop an audit plan on a topic for implementation in their home country after their fellowship program ends. For example, in 2014–2015, a Fellow from Tanzania completed an audit plan to examine the management of electronic waste in that country.[62]

56 On file with authors.

57 See OAG, *What We Do*, 'Activities within Canada' www.oag-bvg.gc.ca/internet/English/au_fs_e_371.html accessed 30 November 2017; see also Canadian Council of Legislative Auditors, 'About CCOLA' www.ccola.ca/ccola/en/about-ccola accessed 30 November 2017.

58 See OAG, 'International Activities' www.oag-bvg.gc.ca/internet/English/au_fs_e_371.html accessed 30 November 2017

59 Ibid.

60 See INTOSAI WGEA, *2005–2007 Work Plan, October 2004*, 2 www.environmental-auditing.org/Portals/0/wp05-07.pdf accessed 30 November 2017. See also WGEA, 'Message from the Chair of WGEA' (2007) 10 *Greenlines Newsletter* www.environmental-auditing.org/Home/GreenlinesNewsletter/tabid/100/GreenlineId/9/Default.aspx accessed 30 November 2017.

61 Canadian Audit & Accountability Foundation, 'About the Fellowships' www.caaf-fcar.ca/en/international-development-program/fellowships-and-management-internships/about-the-fellowships accessed 30 November 2017.

62 Executive Summary, *Performance Audit Plan on Management Electronic Waste in Tanzania* www.caaf-fcar.ca/images/pdfs/international/fellows/biographies/2014-2015biobooklet.pdf accessed 30 November 2017.

## COMMENTS ON USING THE AUDIT FUNCTION AS A MODEL FOR OTHER COUNTRIES

Reflecting on the experiences of Canada's Commissioner of the Environment and Sustainable Development and of the Auditor General, an audit function can draw attention to and raise awareness of topics important to future generations. For example, past audit work on topics such as mitigating and adapting to climate change, cleaning up contaminated sites, and ensuring the long-term fiscal sustainability of public financing can have impacts on future generations.[63] Further, the audit function can provide advice through recommendations aimed at improving how issues are managed and help improve transparency and accountability of government performance.[64] By its nature, an audit function examines the government's performance in managing important issues.[65] Public reporting on the results of audits can help improve public awareness of how well government programs are being implemented and policies fulfilled.[66]

It is important to reinforce that there are roles that an audit function cannot fulfill. For example, to remain neutral and objective, an audit function does not play the role of an advocate for future generations. Nor do auditors comment on the merits of policy. Other third-party organizations are better suited to fulfilling these functions.

The question of whether the audit-based approach that Canada uses to help safeguard the interests of the environment and future generations could be a model for other jurisdictions is a difficult one to answer. Certainly, there are aspects of the Canadian federal approach that could be relevant and helpful elsewhere; however, context is an important consideration that has to be taken into account. The importance of context has been observed by other commentators in the field.[67] Contextual factors to consider include a jurisdiction's political landscape, existing legislative and institutional arrangements, planned changes to laws and policies, economic and human development realities, and government track records on

63 CESD Fall 2010 Report, 'Adapting to Climate Impacts' www.oag-bvg.gc.ca/internet/English/parl_cesd_201012_03_e_34426.html accessed 30 November 2017; CESD Spring 2012 Reports, 'Federal Contaminated Sites and Their Impacts' www.oag-bvg.gc.ca/internet/English/parl_cesd_201205_03_e_36775.html accessed 30 November 2017; OAG, Fall 2012 Report, *Long-Term Fiscal Sustainability* www.oag-bvg.gc.ca/internet/English/parl_oag_201210_07_e_37351.html accessed 30 November 2017.

64 See OAG *What to Expect*, pt. 3 'Recommendations and Responses' www.oag-bvg.gc.ca/internet/English/meth_lp_e_30860.html#hd2d accessed 30 November 2017.

65 See OAG *What to Expect*, pt. 1, 'Introducing Performance Audits' www.oag-bvg.gc.ca/internet/English/meth_lp_e_30860.html#hd2b accessed 30 November 2017.

66 See OAG *What to Expect* www.oag-bvg.gc.ca/internet/English/meth_lp_e_30860.html accessed 30 November 2017.

67 For a comprehensive account of the context around environmental policy making in Canada, see M. Hessing et al., *Canadian Natural Resource and Environmental Policy*, 2nd edn. (University of British Columbia Press 2005).

adequately taking the interests of future generations into account.[68] Assuming for the moment that such factors align in a way that has a jurisdiction deciding to pursue the creation of an institution for future generations, there are a number of areas in which the institution would need to be strong in order to have a better chance of being effective.

### *Independence*

Independence from the government (and ministries) on which the institution is focused is fundamentally important. This helps ensure that the organization is seen as being an objective third party, which in turn helps build credibility, and credibility is any independent institution's stock-in-trade.

In the case of Canada, the Commissioner benefits from strong independence from government as a result of being embedded in the Office of the Auditor General. This is built into the legislative structure and implemented through rigorous office standards, policies, and procedures, ensuring ongoing integrity of the office. The Auditor General is one of several Officers of Parliament in Canada who are distinguished by their responsibility to Parliament as opposed to serving the government of the day.

### *Access to Relevant Information*

Access to government information is critical for effective fulfillment of the institution's mandate. This is fundamental to generating outputs that are fair, accurate, and useful. Without such access, an institution would lack the relevance and power necessary to analyze and synthesize the activities under scrutiny and would in turn be unable to provide decision makers with insights and information of value.

Canada's Commissioner possesses very strong access to information powers by virtue of the Auditor General Act.[69] In general, this allows the office to understand and examine the issues and entities under audit in a manner not possible by others. Put another way, the Commissioner and the Auditor General are able to add value to Parliament by drawing on and synthesizing information unavailable to other actors in the environment and sustainable development sphere.

[68] See generally ibid. See also, D.V. Wright, 'Options for Oversight in the Provincial Environmental Realm: Examples and Functions of Independent Oversight Offices' (2015) 29 *Journal of Environmental Law and Practice* 216. See also F. Fukuyama, *State-Building: Governance and World Order in the 21st Century* (Cornell University Press 2004) 76.

[69] This is primarily by virtue of s. 13(1) Auditor General Act, RSC, 1985, c. A-17 (Canada). That section states: "Except as provided by any other Act of Parliament that expressly refers to this subsection, the Auditor General is entitled to free access at all convenient times to information that relates to the fulfillment of his or her responsibilities and he or she is also entitled to require and receive from members of the federal public administration any information, reports and explanations that he or she considers necessary for that purpose." Ibid.

### *Communications Tools and Capacity*

Communication of the institution's outputs, as well as making sure such outputs are of sound editorial quality, is of utmost importance, particularly in today's information age and the era of social media. This ensures that the work of the institution is communicated clearly, accurately, and broadly, ultimately in service of the institution's mandate.

In Canada, the Commissioner benefits from the communications and editorial services of the Office of the Auditor General. This organizational support is important to the success of the Commissioner's reporting and outreach activities. Recently, the Commissioner's communications activities have also included increased use of social media, particularly Twitter.

### *Skilled, Multidisciplinary Staff and Advisers*

As with any institution, strong human resources are critical to success. Due to the inherently multidisciplinary nature of environmental and sustainable development issues (including consideration of future generations), it is important for different disciplines to be represented by the people doing the work. This ensures that appropriately diverse knowledge and skills are brought to bear on complex issues at hand.

The Commissioner has a group of staff with a broad range of backgrounds, ranging from environmental sciences to economics to law and public administration and some staff also possess accounting designations.[70] These skills are supplemented by the use of external experts who advise the Commissioner and her staff on specific topics.

### *Sound Management*

Effective management of financial and human resources is key to an organization's longevity and long-term fiscal sustainability. In addition to being a well-managed organization, the adoption of practices that support and enhance transparency is also important. This includes being open and transparent on strategic long-term plans and short-term plans (for example, annual plans), assessing performance against these plans, and publicly reporting on results that an organization is achieving. Being open and transparent about plans and related performance helps ensure accountability for resources being expended. It can also help build and enhance an organization's credibility and trust amongst stakeholders.

[70] See OAG, *Who We Are*, 'Our Employees' www.oag-bvg.gc.ca/internet/English/au_fs_e_370.html#employees accessed 30 November 2017.

## CONCLUSION

More than two decades ago, Canada created the position of the Commissioner of the Environment and Sustainable Development within the Office of the Auditor General. Throughout the years since, under the leadership of Commissioners along the way, the office has generated a significant body of work that has provided parliamentarians and Canadians with independent views of federal government departments' progress or lack of progress toward sustainable development and of how well federal departments and agencies are managing environmental programs. Perhaps of equal importance, the Commissioner has been a respected, credible, and valued voice in the Canadian environmental and sustainable development landscape.[71] These accomplishments are indicative of relative success over the years. However, chronic shortcomings in the implementation of environmental and sustainable development laws, policies, and programs continue to plague the international community. Canada has not been immune to this; the work will never be finished.

Whether the Canadian approach may serve as a model for other jurisdictions depends largely on the many contextual factors in the specific governance and political landscape. However, attributes of the effectiveness of institutions for future generations may be found in how stalwart Canada's Commissioner has been over the years and in the steadiness of the Commissioner's outputs. Strength in the areas of independence plus access to information, communications, staff, and financial management has served the Commissioner well over the course of the position's existence.

Given the intensifying environmental crises at local and global levels and the implications of this for future generations, further institutional development and evolution will undoubtedly unfold, particularly in developing countries as they build capacity. If Canada's experience is helpful in such progress, this would be a welcome contribution by the office.

[71] The above-cited OAG Green Ribbon Panel includes this point on several occasions, noting "strong consensus" that the work of the Commissioner had been useful and had made a difference. See Office of the Auditor General, *Fulfilling the Potential: A Review of the Environment and Sustainable Development Practice of the Office of the Auditor General* (Report of the Independent Green Ribbon Panel to the Auditor General of Canada, Office of the Auditor General 2007) 21, 25, 38.

# 25

# Intergenerational Equity, Peace, and Transitional Justice in Colombia

*Alexandra R. Harrington and Maria del Pilar Vanegas Guzman*

Intergenerational equity is a multifaceted construct, yet at its core sits peace, since without peace there can be little equity at the intragenerational level, let alone to transmit to future generations. In conflict and immediate post-conflict situations, the focus is typically on present-day and short-term concerns, such as ceasing the active hostilities and assisting victims. This is understandable, given the need to construct a durable peace in the present before building on that peace for the future. However, peace agreements can be used to advance intergenerational equity as well as intragenerational equity if they are constructed through mechanisms that understand the importance for working toward equity in the future as a way to build consensus for implementing equitable laws and principles in the current day.

In this context, the example of the peace agreement between the State of Colombia and the Revolutionary Armed Forces of Colombia – People's Army (FARC-EP) stands as a model for drafting an instrument for peace that includes intergenerational equity concepts and needs as part of its bedrock principles. The Peace Agreement was signed in 2016 against the backdrop of a fifty-three-year civil war that saw a legacy of intergenerational upheaval, violence, and hatreds as its legacy. It is an instrument which is being implemented slowly, and with some controversies, yet symbolises an innovative attempt to use concepts of sustainability and concerns over future generations as part of the unifying factors across the parties involved. As this chapter explains, it is an agreement that is at once aspirational and practical for advancing the interests of future generations through intergenerational equity.

## INTERGENERATIONAL EQUITY IN GOALS OF PEACE

At its most fundamental level, the Peace Agreement is just that, an instrument to frame the parameters and mechanisms of peace in the Colombian context. In order to do this, the Agreement establishes that it is built on the foundation of the recognition of individual and collective rights, including rights of and responsibilities for vulnerable populations in general and in particular those groups which have felt the heaviest burden of the conflict.[1] Further, the Agreement emphasises the importance and necessity of sustainability and ecological concerns within the ambit of creating a durable community and legal system for peace.[2] Throughout the terms of the Agreement, the emphasis on non-discrimination and equality in its terms and their application, as well as the ways in which they are construed in current and future situations, is profoundly obvious.[3]

In Chapter 2 of the Agreement, 'Political Participation: A Democratic Opportunity to Build Peace,' the direct links between political participation and access to the political system and equity – present and future – are articulated and given contour.[4] Indeed, as stated in the opening of the chapter, 'peacebuilding is a right and also a mandatory duty, forming the basis for setting Colombia on the road to peace with social justice and to reconciliation, heeding its people's clamour for peace'.[5] There is a dedicated link between including women in society as a whole, especially in terms of the achievement of peace and the entrenchment of equitable principles and practices in society.[6] Additionally, indigenous communities

[1] Final Agreement to End the Armed Conflict and Build a Stable and Lasting Peace (2016) preamble ('Considering that the sum of the accords of which the new Final Agreement is composed, contributes to the fulfilment of fundamental rights, such as political, social, economic and cultural rights; the rights of the victims of conflict to truth, justice and reparations, the rights of boys, girls and adolescents, the right to freedom of faith and its free exercise; the fundamental right of individual and/or collective legal certainty and physical safety; and the fundamental right of each individual and of society to non-recurrence of the tragedy of the internal armed conflict that this Agreement proposes to finally end; Emphasising that the new Final Agreement places special emphasis on the fundamental rights of women, of vulnerable social groups such as indigenous peoples, girls, boys and adolescents, communities of African descent and other ethnically differentiated groups; the fundamental rights of the small-scale farmers, both male and female, and the essential rights of persons with disabilities and of those displaced by the conflict; and the fundamental rights of the elderly and of the LGBTI community').

[2] Ibid. ('Having regard to the fact that the new vision of a Colombia at peace enables us to achieve a sustainable society that is united in diversity and that is based not only on consideration for human rights but on mutual tolerance, protection of the environment, respect for nature and its renewable and non-renewable resources and biodiversity').

[3] Introduction at 6 ('The conditions in order for equality to be real and effective will be guaranteed in its implementation and affirmative measures will be adopted in favour of groups that are discriminated against or marginalised, taking a territorial-based, equity-based and gender-based approach into consideration.')

[4] See generally ibid. at chapter 2.

[5] Ibid.

[6] Ibid. ('Taking account of the fact that women face greater social and institutional barriers in terms of political participation, as a result of deep-rooted discrimination and inequality, as well as structural conditions of exclusion and subordination, there will be significant challenges in guaranteeing their right to participation, and facing up to and transforming these historical conditions will involve developing affirmative measures that will safeguard women's participation in the various areas of political and social representation').

are targeted for recognition and included in the political process and generally in society, and also is the subject of specific attempts for mobilisation and community involvement.[7]

In order to ensure that members of society become engaged in the political system and participate fully as citizens now and in the future, the Agreement provides for the creation of a specialised system at the governmental level to promote the security of the political system and those interacting with it.[8] Specifically, the goal of this specialised system is to

> help to create and to guarantee a culture of peaceful coexistence, tolerance and solidarity that dignifies the exercise of politics and offers guarantees to prevent any form of stigmatisation or persecution of leaders due to their political activities, personal opinion or opposition.[9]

The political security system is designed to be institutionalised and coordinate with many different layers and aspects of the Colombian government. Not only does this require a good deal of present-day activities to generate support for peace and protect the security of the political process, it also creates an 'early warning system', under which prevention of future violence and political issues will be monitored.[10] Further, the Agreement seeks to entrench the democratic political system in within all aspects and avenue of life in Colombia by making it a stable and enduring system for the future.[11] In this way, the peace process is indelibly linked to the stabilisation of democracy and the political process in the State, including the personalisation of the political process through participation and the creation of strong political machinery and party organisations.[12]

In support of these aims, the Agreement creates the National Council for Reconciliation and Coexistence to act as a joint public–private body to advise the national government on issues such as the implementation of the Agreement terms, reconciliation and inclusion of vulnerable communities, human rights issues and protections, creation of a broader media base that incorporates society into the political realm, and implementation of education for peace and reconciliation programmes.[13] Transparency has been identified as essential in this regard, and the Agreement provides that efforts are taken to address issues that can make stable and democratic governance weak, such as electoral fraud and disruption, a lack of general accountability and oversight, and strong institutes of justice and reconciliation.[14]

[7] Ibid. at chapter 2.1.
[8] Ibid. at chapter 2.1.2.
[9] Ibid.
[10] Ibid.
[11] Ibid. at chapter 2.2.
[12] Ibid. at chapters 2.2, 2.3.
[13] Ibid. at chapter 2.2.4.
[14] Ibid. at chapter 2.3.3.1.

Chapter 3 of the Agreement addresses the end of the conflict per se and the immediate measures necessary for the cessation of hostilities, disarmament of hostiles, and verification of these undertakings.[15] An essential part of this chapter, and the Agreement as a whole, is the issue of reintegrating former militants into society and assisting in their economic reintegration as well. To accomplish this, the Agreement addresses the ability of these former fighters to participate in the political life of the nation, the representation of former fighters in political institutions, notably the legislative branch, educational training, societal reintegration, and awareness measures, economic reintegration and especially agrarian economic support, legal recognition and reintegration, protection for children and minors, healthcare protections and assistance, and social security benefits and protections.[16] In return, the demobilising fighters and those associated with rebel activities are required to comply with the terms of the Agreement, cease hostilities and hand in their weapons, and, where appropriate under the terms of the statutes regarding prosecutions, agree to be subject to the jurisdiction of the Special Jurisdiction for Peace.[17] With this in mind, the Agreement creates and operationalises a Special Investigation Unit to investigate activities on all sides which took place during the conflict in contravention of laws and rules.[18]

Further, the Agreement sets out guiding principles for both sides to use as part of ending the conflict, namely 'respect, guarantee, protection and promotion of human rights, safeguard the legitimate monopoly of force and of the use of arms by the state across the country's territories, strengthening the administration of justice, ensuring the monopoly of taxes by the Tax Authorities, territorial-based and equity-based approach, gender-based approach, institutional joint responsibility and coordination, citizen participation, accountability, and guarantees of non-recurrence'.[19] All of these principles require continued monitoring well into the future.[20]

As the Agreement notes, one of the contributors to and contributions of the decades-long conflict in Colombia was the introduction of cultivation of illicit drugs. To address the ongoing threat posed by illicit drugs and the use of agricultural areas to support them, the Agreement contains significant terms at stopping their short- and long-term cultivation and commoditisation.[21] At the same time, the Agreement is aware of and preserves the traditional links between ingestion of certain illicit drugs and indigenous groups for medicinal purposes and, further, recognises that there are potential uses for scientific research into them.[22] Thus,

15 Ibid. at chapter 3.1.
16 Ibid. at chapter 3.2.
17 Ibid. at chapter 3.3.
18 Ibid. at chapter 3.4.4.
19 Ibid. at chapter 3.4.1.
20 Ibid.
21 See generally ibid. at chapter 4.
22 Ibid.

the Agreement preserves the practices of indigenous communities while at the same time seeking to undermine the role that illicit drugs have played in the perpetuation of the conflict. It also highlights the importance of preventing the criminality associated with illicit drug production from infiltrating the governmental system at all levels, in order to create an effective government apparatus for the present day and the future.[23]

Taken together, these terms reflect a wish to create a societal and legal system in which there is a focus on preserving current natural assets and protecting communities which have historically been subject to discrimination and violence so that future generations benefit from the former and can move on from the latter. There is perhaps no better expression of intergenerational equity concerns than this form of provision.

## INTERGENERATIONAL EQUITY IN LAND AND RESOURCES

An essential aspect of the Agreement is the Comprehensive Rural Reform, through which many aspects of lack of social and economic integration are to be remedied. As the Agreement's preamble makes clear, there is a distinct link between land reforms, control over and input into the use of natural resources, and the need for peace, justice, and reconciliation to end the conflict and sustain the momentum in the post-conflict, transitional justice period.[24]

There is also a distinct character to the many areas within Colombia that have been impacted by the conflict in terms of territorial forms, appropriate agricultural and other uses of land, and natural resources access. This is reflected in the terms of the Agreement, which stipulate the need for these unique characteristics to be taken into account to achieve peace and economic and social integration regionally and nationally.[25]

In Chapter 1, the Agreement establishes as a matter of law and practice a system of Comprehensive Rural Reform which forms the backbone of the peace and

[23] Ibid.

[24] Ibid. at preamble ('Extolling and enshrining the justice that is to come inasmuch as it acknowledges essential fundamental rights for new and future generations, such as the right to protected land, the right to the conservation of the human species, the right to be aware of one's origins and identity, the right to know the truth with regard to events occurring before one's birth, the right to exemption from liability for acts committed by earlier generations, the right to the preservation of freedom of choice, and other rights, notwithstanding the rights of victims of any age or generation to truth, justice and reparations').

[25] Ibid. at preamble ('The territorial-based approach of the Agreement requires recognition and consideration of the economic, cultural and social needs, characteristics and peculiarities of Colombia's territories and communities, thereby guaranteeing socio-environmental sustainability; furthermore, it involves implementing the various measures comprehensively and in a coordinated way, with the active participation of all citizens. All of Colombia's regions and territories will contribute to the implementation of the Agreement, with the participation of territorial-based authorities and the various sectors of society').

reconciliation system devised for Colombia.[26] It also comprises a significant step toward protecting the qualities of land and biodiversity in Colombia for the use and enjoyment of current and future generations, as well as seeking to ensure that these assets are protected in order to prevent the social, economic, and legal pressures which can give rise to conflict and violence.[27] The Agreement recognises the specific and special place which land holds for rural communities, and particularly vulnerable members of them, and that this place is different than those in other areas of the country.[28] As part of this, there are provisions for the redistribution of certain conflict associated lands to rural populations, including demobilised fighters and their families, and the acquisition of title to these lands in order to vest the targeted communities with interests in the land now and for their families in the future.[29]

More than simply a matter of distributing legal title and economic incentives, however, the Agreement places a host of reforms at the centre of attempts to achieve rural reform, including increased educational access, infrastructural development, increased and better quality health care access and facilities, access to food and appropriate nutritional components to food access, and the overall promotion of 'well-being and a dignified way of life for the rural population'.[30] These elements are viewed as essential to creating short- and long-term growth in rural areas and among rural communities, allowing them to better integrate into the national economic system and generate sustained and sustainable employment and revenues which will incentivise peace.[31]

26 Ibid. at chapter 1.

27 Ibid.

28 Ibid. ('Within the context of this Agreement to End the Armed Conflict, the Comprehensive Rural Reform [Reforma Rural Integral], hereinafter referred to as CRR, lays the foundation for the structural transformation of the countryside, creates conditions for well-being of the rural population – men and women – thereby contributing to the building of a stable and long-lasting peace. The CRR views Colombia's rural areas as a socio-historic setting of social and cultural diversity in which communities – men and women – play a major role in defining the improvements of their living conditions and in defining the development of the country as part of a vision of urban/rural integration').

29 Ibid. ('A genuine structural transformation of the countryside requires the adoption of measures to promote appropriate use of the land in accordance with its suitable purposes and to stimulate the titling, restitution and equitable distribution thereof, by guaranteeing progressive access to rural property to those who live in the countryside, and, in particular, to rural women and to the most vulnerable communities, and by legalising and democratising property and promoting broader ownership of land, so that it fulfils its social function').

30 Ibid.

31 Ibid. ('Broadly, the CRR acknowledges the fundamental role of the rural, family-run and community-based economies in the development of the countryside, the eradication of hunger, the generation of employment and income, decent and formalised jobs, food production and, in general, in the development of the nation, all in conjunction with and complementary to other forms of agrarian production. The CRR recognises the productive and reproductive role of women and thus their fundamental contribution to rural development and the rural economy, and it will make every endeavour on their behalf and on that of the most vulnerable in society to guarantee conditions of well-being and dignity and to consolidate organisational and production methods').

Overall, the system of Comprehensive Rural Reform reflects several critical, articulated principles: 'structural transformation, comprehensive development of rural areas, equality and a gender-based approach, well-being and quality of life, prioritisation, comprehensive approach', reinstatement of dispossessed victims of conflict, land title system reform and appropriate implementation, nutritional rights, participation by all members of the public, 'benefit, impact and measurement', incorporation of sustainable development in all aspects of policy and planning, effective national involvement in rural matters and rights, and 'democratisation of appropriate use and access to land'.[32] To accomplish these principles and the laws seeking to enforce them, the Agreement crafts the Land Fund, containing at least 3 million hectares of land that will be redistributed from supplies donated by the national government, unclaimed or unused land, lands taken by eminent domain and lands donated by those other than the national government.[33] In addition, the government agrees and is empowered to provide incentives and discounts to those seeking to purchase lands in designated areas.[34] As explained, these lands and methods of assistance in acquiring them will be made available to

> male and female farm workers without land or with insufficient land, with priority being given to the victimised rural population, including associations of victims, rural women, female heads of households and displaced persons. Further beneficiaries may include associations of male and female agricultural workers without land or with insufficient land and also people and communities taking part in settlement and resettlement programmes, with the aim, inter alia, of protecting the environment, substituting crops used for illicit purposes and strengthening food production.[35]

In instances where there are questions of land ownership and associated rights, the Agreement requires that a means of settling these claims peaceably is determined so that conflict is not viewed as a legitimate method of asserting land rights now and in the future.[36] Where, however, land that is granted from the Land Fund or purchased with subsidies or other assistance and is abandoned or used for illegal activities it can be retaken by the state and those who held title and rights to it will forfeit these rights.[37]

To ensure that land use and development in rural areas is done in a manner that protects and preserve the environmental diversity of the nation and its integrity for current and future generations, the Agreement requires that areas of agricultural and environmental importance be designated.[38] These designations include areas which

32 Ibid.
33 Ibid. at chapter 1.1.
34 Ibid. at chapter 1.1.2.
35 Ibid. at chapter 1.1.3.
36 Ibid. at chapter 1.1.5.
37 Ibid. at chapter 1.1.6.
38 Ibid. at chapter 1.1.10.

are not to be developed in order to preserve their integrity and the sustainability of the regions in which they are located.[39] Further, the Agreement creates Peasant Enterprise Zones (Zonas Reservas de Campasina), which seek to use the lessons of free trade zones in other jurisdictions to encourage the growth and development of economics and economic diversification among groups that were historically under included in society.[40] These areas 'are agricultural initiatives that are conducive to peacebuilding, to guaranteeing political, economic, social and cultural rights of rural communities, to development based on socioenvironmental and food sustainability and to reconciliation between Colombian citizens'.[41] As a corollary, the Agreement creates and operationalises Development Programmes with a Territorial-Based Focus to allow for larger communities to move forward with development plans that connect rural and urban communities.[42] In addition to their designated functions, these Programmes are intended to serve as the basic structure for the National Development Plan.[43]

By ensuring that land, and the biodiversity contained on it, is protected and preserved for appropriate use in a way that will not harm society or contribute to conflict, the Agreement's provisions further concerns of intergenerational equity in terms of passing on to future generations land and agricultural use that is sustainable and can be used for the benefit of the larger community. At the same time, the programmes which allow for the inclusion of greater numbers of people in the cultivation of land for legal purposes and in landownership systems ensure that future generations can benefit from economic and ecological ties that otherwise would not exist.

## INTERGENERATIONAL EQUITY IN JUSTICE INSTITUTIONS AND MECHANISMS

The interests of current and future generations in peace are, in the transitional justice setting, intertwined with the implementation and functioning of justice institutions and mechanisms that provide truth as to acts committed during conflict. This is most certainly true in Colombia, where more than five decades of violence and inherited conflicts has generated victims on all sides, and the failure to address this by providing avenues for justice could undermine the value of the Agreement.

From the outset, the Agreement is notable in that it explicitly requires that the application of its terms and the peace generated by them are to be subject to the laws

[39] Ibid.
[40] Ibid. at chapter 1.
[41] Ibid. at chapter 1.1.10.
[42] Ibid. at chapter 1.2.
[43] Ibid. at chapter 1.2.3.

of Colombia as well as international and regional law, including decisions by regional and international courts and legal bodies.[44]

The systems of justice and reconciliation established in the Agreement build on the previously enacted Declaration of Principles for victims' inclusion, namely 'recognition of the victims, acknowledgement of responsibility, realisation of victims' rights, victim participation, historical clarification of the truth, reparations for the victims, guarantees of protection and security, guarantees of non-recurrence, principle of reconciliation, and rights-based approach'.[45] Under the full terms of the comprehensive system for peace, matters of criminal allegations are to be investigated through an institutionalised mechanism.[46] At the end of these investigations, should a finding of prosecution be recommended, another judicial system that is separate from the standard system of justice in Colombia, is to handle the trial.[47] The formalised Comprehensive System is comprised of three organs – the Truth, Coexistence and Non-Recurrence Commission, the Special Unit for the Search or Persons deemed as Missing in the context of and due to the conflict, the Special Jurisdiction for Peace – and two sets of principles – reparations measures for peacebuilding and guarantees of non-recurrence.[48] As the Agreement makes clear, while these entities have their own individual functions and jurisdictions, they are nevertheless intended to work in tandem in order to provide for a comprehensive approach to addressing the issues of the past and ensuring that society is in a position to heal and move into the future together.[49] Indeed, the Agreement makes clear that its purpose is to bring the past conflict and resultant violence to light so that present generations can come to terms with it from a legal and societal point of view.[50]

One of the critical aspects of this system is the attempt to craft a society that is united through an understanding of the past and the use of juridical systems and

[44] Ibid. at preamble ('the new Final Agreement encompasses each and every one of the accords reached in developing the Agenda of the General Agreement signed in Havana in August 2012; and that in order to achieve that, the parties, always and at every stage, have upheld the spirit and scope of the rules of the National Constitution, the principles of international law, international human rights law, international humanitarian law (its conventions and protocols), the stipulations of the Rome Statute (international criminal law), the decisions of the Inter-American Court of Human Rights concerning conflicts and conflict termination, and other resolutions of universally recognised jurisdictions and authoritative pronouncements relating to the subject matters agreed upon').

[45] Ibid. at chapter 5.

[46] Ibid. at chapter 5.1.

[47] Ibid.

[48] Ibid.

[49] Ibid.

[50] Ibid. at chapter 5.1.1.1 ('The end of the conflict is a unique opportunity to satisfy one of the greatest desires of Colombian society and of the victims in particular: to uncover and learn the truth about what happened during the conflict. Colombia needs to know what happened and what must never happen again so as to be able to forge a future in which the well-being and dignified quality of life of everyone is guaranteed, thus helping to break, once and for all, the cycles of violence that have scarred Colombian history').

reparations in order to move forward. Included in this is the understanding that conflict and its legacy had and continues to have unique and enduring impacts on vulnerable members of society, such as women, indigenous groups, and children, and that these legacies must be addressed in order to achieve the goals of peace and reconciliation.[51] However, in order to allow for reconciliation and societal integration in the future, the Agreement is explicit that the mechanisms it creates are not intended to last in perpetuity but rather for as long as necessary to implement their assigned tasks and ensure that their parts in the collective healing and reconstruction of the nation are played.[52] Throughout these mechanisms there is a particular focus on ensuring the use of equity in each aspect of the peace process and the use of law to implement it.[53]

The Truth, Coexistence and Non-Recurrence Commission has a multifaceted mandate that includes working to recognise and highlight the

> human and social impact of the conflict on society, including its impact on economic, social, cultural and environmental rights, and the different ways in which the conflict affected women, children, adolescents, youths and the elderly, persons on the basis of their religion, opinions or beliefs, persons with disabilities, indigenous peoples, rural communities, the Afro-Colombian, black, palenquero and raizal communities, the Roma community, the LGBTI community, displaced and exiled persons, human rights advocates, trade unionists, journalists, farmers, ranchers, traders and businessmen and -women, *inter alia*

as well as bringing to light the past actions and actors involved in the hostilities and the forms of violence and conflict-related impacts experienced by all Colombians.[54]

The Commission is required to serve an investigative and fact-finding function as well as a reconciliation function in the form of bringing communities together to generate dialogue and promote healing at the individual and societal levels, generate a report and implementation system for how to create consensus and reconciliation throughout the State, provide guidance and assistance to victims seeking information and access to justice, and ensure that its work and findings take into account gender equality and inclusion.[55] Additionally, the Agreement provides for an oversight committee for the implementation of recommendations from the Commission.[56]

The Special Unit for the Search or Persons deemed as Missing in the context of and due to the conflict is established to provide an investigative unit leveraging scientific ability and access to information from all sides to the conflict in order to assist family members and others seeking information on the disappeared.[57] In

[51] Ibid.
[52] Ibid. at chapter 5.1.1.1.1.
[53] See generally ibid. at chapter 5.
[54] Ibid. at chapter 5.1.1.1.2.
[55] Ibid. at chapter 5.1.1.1.4.
[56] Ibid. at chapter 5.1.1.1.10.
[57] Ibid. at chapter 5.1.1.2.

addition, the Special Unit is required to establish a national plan for identification of the missing and the provision of information relating to them.[58] Where remains are located, the Special Unit is tasked with ensuring that they are returned to the appropriate family members or others.[59] The Special Unit is also required to maintain a list of burial sites throughout the nation and make this publicly available.[60]

The core justice element of the Agreement is found in the Special Jurisdiction for Peace system. As explained in the Agreement

> a guiding paradigm ... is the idea that the political community is not simply a union of contemporary peers but also a link between generations over time. Justice is forward-looking insofar as it considers that one period in time inevitably influences subsequent ones. This is a forward-looking justice that is respectful of the values of the present and, at the same time, concerned to put an end to conflicts that must not be perpetuated, with the aim of defending the rights of future generations.[61]

Another identified paradigm of the Special Jurisdiction for Peace is

> the application of restorative justice that preferably seeks the restoration of the damage caused and reparations for the victims affected by the conflict, particularly to end the situation of social exclusion generated by their victimisation. Restorative justice is primarily concerned with the needs and the dignity of the victims and is applied using a holistic approach that guarantees justice, truth and guarantees of non-recurrence of what has occurred.[62]

A corollary to this is the recognition that the consequences of the conflict fell particularly hard on vulnerable communities, including gender-based minorities, indigenous communities, and children.[63] Further, the Agreement expressly incorporates international findings that reparations must take these particularised harms into account, especially in the context of those experienced by women.[64]

In instances where certain criteria are met, it is possible for one involved in a the conflict to be subject to an amnesty or pardon, provided the individual benefitting provides information to the Special Jurisdiction or as otherwise required and also agrees to be part of the peace process, to eschew conflict, and to work toward reconciliation.[65] Reflecting this, the Special Jurisdiction for Peace is vested with

58 Ibid.
59 Ibid.
60 Ibid.
61 Ibid.
62 Ibid.
63 Ibid.
64 Ibid.
65 Ibid.

systems to be used in the event that the accused has accepted responsibility and where the accused has not accepted responsibility.[66]

Where individuals admit to or are found to have been involved in crimes established as part of the Agreement, the goal of reparations is not vengeance but rather reintegration into the community and service to the community as a means of preserving balance and achieving growth.[67] For those in rural areas, reparations can take a number of forms, largely aimed at promoting agriculture and forestry, protecting and preserving the environment, building infrastructural capacities, and working toward recovery of communities and their territory.[68] For those in urban areas, the focus of reparations is on the development of infrastructural capacity and growth, particularly in areas where there is a defined need, such as water access and waste systems.[69] Regardless the location of the individual, another form of reparation that is of notable importance is that of landmine and unexploded ordinance clearance.[70] This aspect of reparations involves the individual being physically part of ordinance clearance activities.[71] In instances where an individual has been found guilty of crimes rather than freely acknowledging them, the reparations available become focused on incarceration rather than methods of community reintegration.[72]

At the same time, the reparations section of the Agreement is holistic in that it recognises the need for the national government to create avenues for rehabilitation for all involved in the conflict in terms of mental health and physical health assessments and support, facilitation of the return of those who left Colombia as a result of the conflict, assistance to and repatriation of those displaced by the conflict overall, implementation of land restitution systems, and promoting systems to ensure that similar conflicts will not happen in the future.[73]

66 Ibid. at chapter 5.1.2 (45).
67 Ibid. at chapter 5.1.2 (I)
68 Ibid. at chapter 5.1.2 (I) (A) ('1. Participation in/implementation of effective reparation programmes for displaced rural people; 2. Participation in/implementation of environmental protection programmes for Forest Reserve Areas; 3. Participation in/implementation of infrastructure building and repair programmes in rural areas: schools, roads, health centres, housing, community centres, municipal infrastructure, etc.; 4. Participation in/implementation of rural development programmes; 5. Participation in/implementation of waste disposal programmes where necessary; 6. Participation in/implementation of programmes to improve electrification and connectivity in communications in agricultural areas; 7. Participation in/implementation of programmes to substitute crops used for illicit purposes; 8. Participation in/implementation of environmental recovery programmes for areas affected by crops used for illicit purposes; 9. Participation in/implementation of programmes to build and improve the road infrastructure required to market agricultural products from illicit crop substitution areas').
69 Ibid. at chapter 5.1.2 (I)(B).
70 Ibid. at chapter 5.1.2 (I) (C).
71 Ibid.
72 Ibid. at chapter 5.1.2 (II).
73 Ibid. at chapter 5.1.3.

Finally, as a larger framework, the Agreement seeks to ensure that the terms and principles of international humanitarian law and international human rights law are entrenched in the legal system developed in Colombia in the post-conflict setting.[74] As explicitly stated,

> The Agreement as a whole must contribute to building a shared vision of the need for respect of all human rights. The state will work to guarantee full realisation of these in terms of their universality, comprehensiveness, indivisibility and interdependence, as a basis for justice and materialisation of the recognition of human dignity.[75]

In furtherance of these requirements, the Agreement provides for the operationalisation of systems for monitoring and verification of the implementation of its terms by all parties. This includes the participation of local communities in these processes as well as the oversight of the UN, bringing specifically trained experts to the region.[76] Additionally, the Agreement creates the Commission for Monitoring, Promoting and Verifying the Implementation of the Final Agreement as the national oversight and coordination body.[77]

Taken together, the justice elements of the Agreement demonstrate the will to address the past, even where this is painful, in a context that honours the sacrifices of the victims while at the same time placing these experiences in a larger system of reconciliation and atonement. Rather than being mired in the past, this system allows current and future generations to understand the pain and sacrifices of the victims and to build on this to create a unified society in the future. This is a way to incorporate the wrongs of the past into the shape of the future in a way that is respectful and that creates a stronger fabric of society for the future.

## CONCLUSION

As noted above, peace is a core element of intergenerational equity. In conflict and post-conflict situations, the need to achieve peace and stability is paramount and the impact that peace agreements will have on future generations is not often discussed. However, as this chapter has highlighted, failing to make these connections does a disservice to current and future generations.

Emerging from more than five decades of conflict, Colombia is an excellent example of a peace agreement which works to further intergenerational equity in practice if not in express terminology. As the Colombian peace agreement

[74] Ibid. at chapter 5.2.
[75] Ibid.
[76] Ibid. at chapter 6.1.
[77] Ibid. at chapter 6.1.6.

demonstrates, a holistic understanding of the impacts of conflict on all aspects of law, society, and economy can result in a conclusion to the conflict that seeks to rectify the damage of the past and preserve and protect tangible and intangible assets, experiences, and communities for future generations. If, as the Peace Agreement provides, peace is a right and a duty for all Colombians this means that the inheritance of future generations will be vibrant and based on the shared experiences of conflict and its consequences.

# 26

# Indigenous Peoples and Intergenerational Equity in Mexico

*Odeeth Lara Morales*

Intergenerational equity is directly linked to sustainable development and environmental issues and is committed to equity for future generations.[1] In this regard, land stewardship has many implications for the protection, sustainable use, and degradation or restoration of the environment. Poverty can lead to unbalanced natural ecosystems, loss of diversity, and large-scale deforestation. These factors can have a direct impact on natural resources and are mainly caused by poverty and outmigration.[2] It has also been suggested that in certain situations, damage to the local environment cannot be effectively ceased unless rural livelihood disputes are suitably addressed, and these should be made with an approach that focuses primarily on delivering support for sustainable livelihoods through long-term plans.[3] This is essential to current and future generations, and, as a corollary, to the concept of intergenerational equity.

A second, equally compelling argument complements the understanding of this relationship between poverty and environmental degradation, however. Environmental pressures such as climate change are not caused by poverty, but it is simply the poorest of the poor and the most vulnerable people who suffer their impacts the most, especially indigenous peoples.[4] From this more nuanced

[1] E. Brown Weiss, *Intergenerational Equity: A Legal Framework for Global Environmental Change* (United Nations University 1999).

[2] World Bank, *World Development Report 1997: The State in a Changing World* (Oxford University Press 1997); D. McKenzie, 'Poverty, Inequality, and International Migration: Insights from 10 Years of Migration and Development Conferences' (2017) 25(3) *Revue d'économie du développement* 13–28.

[3] Ibid.

[4] R. McLeman, 'Climate-Related Migration and Its Linkages to Vulnerability, Adaptation, and Socioeconomic Inequality: Evidence from Recent Examples', in *Research Handbook on Climate Change, Migration and the Law* (Edward Elgar 2017); M. Brugnach, M. Craps, and A.R.P.J. Dewulf, 'Including Indigenous Peoples in Climate Change Mitigation: Addressing Issues of Scale, Knowledge and Power' (2017) 140(1) *Climatic Change* 19–32.

viewpoint, the degradation of ecosystems, depletion and overexploitation of land and natural resources, and other more serious damage to the environment is seldom caused by the poor.[5] The poor are, however, the most vulnerable to these effects and impacts. While they may be least responsible, the poor suffer most. And this is a matter of justice.[6] As one compelling example, indigenous communities are very susceptible to climate change impacts since they are commonly based in naturally sensitive regions (e.g. rainforests, deserts, mountains, coastal zones, or the Arctic).[7] Furthermore, they rely on their natural environment for their maintenance and cultural survival.[8]

Alongside the viewpoints of blame and victimisation, it is also essential to recognise that indigenous peoples are often custodians of cultural knowledge that is highly important for securing effective adaptation and mitigation plans to fight against climate change. From this viewpoint, it is possible to go beyond and to respect indigenous peoples' cultures and traditions while supporting the States in which they are located in the creation of plans and actions in order to adapt to a changing environment and to mitigate GHG emissions regarding a low-carbon economy. For instance, in 2008 IWGIA Conference on Indigenous Peoples and Climate Change concentrated on the main constraints that indigenous people face regarding climate change, such as conservation and human rights.[9] Some negotiations went further than climate change affairs and reached discussions of international mitigation policies, actions, and requirements to support indigenous peoples adapting to climate change.[10]

According to the UNFCCC, the majority of issues raised by indigenous peoples regarding climate change are related to decision making and the execution of plans, rights which seem to be fully acknowledged in legal conventions and treaties such as Agenda 21.[11] Working to target specific information and needs of indigenous peoples communities facing climate change, it may be possible to transform passive beneficiaries of sustainable development into active participants and stewards of natural resources and purveyors of their own sustainable livelihoods.[12]

5 Brugnach, Craps, and Dewulf, *supra* note 4.

6 B.J. Richardson, 'Indigenous Peoples, International Law and Sustainability' (2001) 10(1) *Review of European Comparative & International Environmental Law* 1–12; World Bank Group, *World Development Indicators 2014* (World Bank Publications 2014).

7 C. Nilsson, 'Climate Change from an Indigenous Perspective' (2008) (1–2) *Indigenous Affairs* 9–15; Brugnach, Craps, and Dewulf, *supra* note 4.

8 M. Crook, D. Short, and N. South, 'Ecocide, Genocide, Capitalism and Colonialism: Consequences for Indigenous Peoples and Glocal Ecosystems Environments' (2018) 22(3) *Theoretical Criminology* 298–317.

9 Nilsson, *supra* note 7.

10 Ibid.

11 United Nations Permanent Forum on Indigenous Issues, 'Copenhagen Accord,' Advance unedited version (2010).

12 World Bank Group, *World Development Indicators 2014* (World Bank Publications 2014).

The sustainability approach proposed in international conferences, declarations, and treaties continues to focus on respecting indigenous peoples as voices and stewards of vital local and global ecosystems by recognising their role in protecting the biodiversity, including important endangered and threatened species.[13] These principles and subsequent practices also seek to help indigenous peoples towards sustainable livelihoods in today's societies which satisfy the human need for quality of life, while sustaining resources for present and future generations.[14] Indigenous peoples are working to achieve this by preserving the capacity for natural resources or systems to maintain diversity and health, and by increasing their contribution towards sustainable management of natural resources.[15] They deserve, from this point of view, all the possible recognition and support that can be provided. For many indigenous peoples, environmental protection is cultural survival.

## POVERTY AND SOCIAL EXCLUSION OF INDIGENOUS PEOPLES

Indigenous peoples are continuously identified by the UN and international development agencies as among the poorest population groups in remote rural areas which are often located in the least developed communities. Poverty is a problem among indigenous peoples, particularly where they also face tremendous social exclusion challenges such as discrimination, inequality, and lower education.[16] Many indigenous peoples face serious barriers to attaining economic growth, as they are frequently excluded from the conventional economy of their nations. Given this exclusion, such indigenous communities suffer from substantial gaps and weaknesses in infrastructure, for example, water supplies, roads, sewers, schools, or healthcare facilities. Also, discriminatory laws regarding public policies and indigenous rights,

[13] J.J. Armesto, C. Smith-Ramirez, and R. Rozzi, 'Conservation Strategies for Biodiversity and Indigenous People in Chilean Forest Ecosystems' (2001) 31(4) *Journal of the Royal Society of New Zealand* 865–877; United Nations, *Second International Debate on the World's Indigenous Peoples* (UN 2008); United Nations, *A Guidebook to the Green Economy: Issue 1: Green Economy, Green Growth, and Low-Carbon Development – History, Definitions and a Guide to Recent Publications* (New York 2012).

[14] G.H. Brundtland et al., *Our Common Future: Report of the World Commission on Environment and Development* (Oxford University Press 1987).

[15] T. Hák, S. Janoušková, and B. Moldan, 'Sustainable Development Goals: A Need for Relevant Indicators' (2016) 60 *Ecological Indicators* 565–573; L.M. Greathouse-Amador, 'Tourism: A Facilitator of Social Awareness in an Indigenous Mexican Community?' (2005) 22(5) *Review of Policy Research* 709–720; G.J. Martin et al., 'Indigenous and Community Conserved Areas in Oaxaca, Mexico' (2011) 22(2) *Management of Environmental Quality: An International Journal* 250–266; K. Watene and M. Yap, 'Culture and Sustainable Development: Indigenous Contributions' (2015) 11(1) *Journal of Global Ethics* 51–55.

[16] H. Patrinos and G. Psacharopoulos G., *Indigenous People and Poverty in Latin America: An Empirical Analysis* (World Bank 1994); World Bank, *Indigenous Peoples, Poverty and Human Development in Latin America: 1994–2004 Summary* (World Bank 2005); G.H. Hall and H.A. Patrinos, *Indigenous Peoples, Poverty, and Development* (Cambridge University Press 2012).

the loss of their lands and livelihoods are a great contributor to inequality[17]. A number of development agencies have become quite active in working to address the issues directly affecting indigenous peoples, including poverty and social exclusion. However, development interventions for indigenous peoples remain infrequent, inadequate, and often unable to understand or respect their needs or interests. This is normally due to a lack of consultation with indigenous peoples and their lack of participation in decision making. Indigenous peoples have the right and need to be included in the development of strategies and policies that affect their endeavours. Yet, many countries do not take into account Indigenous rights or needs when developing public policies. Furthermore, lack of access to sustainable development threatens the cultural survival of many Indigenous peoples, whose extreme poverty can be exacerbated by ongoing conflicts, deriving from lack of basic recognition that they exist as nations and as the rightful original inhabitants of their territories.[18]

Sustainable development might contribute to the well-being of Indigenous peoples – who have continuously endured injustices and have faced marginalisation, exploitation and exclusion – due to the priorities that it places on ecological concepts of sustainability, and its recognition of the need for economic development and social inclusion.[19] However, it is essential to recognise that although many steps have been taken towards poverty reduction, the report 'Still among the Poorest of the Poor' states that as long as there is poverty for Indigenous peoples, sustainability cannot be achieved.[20] Poverty originates as a result of economic, political, and social exclusion, and for Indigenous peoples this increases alongside environmental and natural resources degradation. Moreover, many indigenous groups are forced to face social exclusion on an everyday basis. For instance, Indigenous women experience multiple forms of discrimination inside and outside their communities. Globally, there are many instances in which the loss of natural resources, access to land, work discrimination, forced migration, lack of opportunities, economic marginalisation, and poverty are wearing down the well-being and, indeed, the right to life, of

[17] ILO, *Brief: Sustainable Development Goals: Indigenous Peoples in Focus* (ILO 2016).

[18] International Fund for Agricultural Development, *Indigenous Peoples and Sustainable Development: Discussion Paper, Roundtable Discussion Paper for the 25th Anniversary Session of IFAD's Governing Council* (IFAD 2003); International Work Group for Indigenous Affairs, *The UN Declaration on the Rights of the Indigenous Peoples* (IWGIA 2012); Hall and Patrinos, *supra* note 16.

[19] R. Scheyvens, 'Promoting Women's Empowerment through Involvement in Ecotourism: Experiences from the Third World' (2000) 8(3) *Journal of Sustainable Tourism* 232–249; J. Hendry, *Reclaiming Culture Indigenous Peoples and Self-Representation* (Palgrave Macmillan 2005); C. Notzke, *The Stranger, the Native and the Land: Perspectives on Indigenous Tourism* (Captus University Press 2006); D.A. Fennell, 'Ecotourism and the Myth of Indigenous Stewardship' (2008) 16(2) *Journal of Sustainable Tourism* 129–149; E. King and D. van de Walle, *Ethno-linguistic Diversity and Disadvantage. Indigenous Peoples, Poverty and Development* (2010) 50.

[20] World Bank, *Still among the Poorest of the Poor.* Indigenous Peoples Country Brief (World Bank 2011).

Indigenous peoples.[21] Social and economic exclusion are costing Indigenous peoples their dignity as human beings, potentially causing the degradation and loss of their valuable and sacred traditional knowledge, culture, languages, and way of life. In many cases, it is existence itself, and cultural survival, that is at stake.[22]

In response to the current crisis, attempts are underway to support the empowerment of poor indigenous communities for recovery or attainment of their rights to political participation, economic development, social inclusion, and cultural survival. For example, in Indonesia, the members of the Suku Anak Dalam indigenous community have been victims of marginalisation and social exclusion.[23] International development agencies provide support to development projects such as the National Program for Community Empowerment (PNPM) Peduli, which supports such communities in finding livelihood opportunities as well as reclaiming their lands.[24] Such efforts are valuable, but small, particularised, and piecemeal. Scaled-up instruments and mechanisms from the national and international community are still needed, in many sectors of the economies of developing countries.[25] For poverty reduction and sustainability, as noted in the 'Still among the Poorest of the Poor', important barriers and key factors remain which prevent the sustainable economic growth and the improvement of national and international policy frameworks for these people.[26] These barriers continue to affect indigenous peoples worldwide.

For example, indigenous peoples in Mexico continue to face notable disadvantages in social and economic development, making them the poorest among the poor. Although official statistics suggest that discrimination against indigenous peoples is decreasing, alongside poverty rates, a great deal remains to be accomplished. In order to improve their socio-economic environment, there is space for great progress through public policy reforms and actions on the ground. Recent research and analysis also suggest that government initiatives and education can be useful and important instruments in this respect.[27]

[21] A. Goodman et al., '"They Treated Me Like Crap and I Know It Was Because I Was Native": The Healthcare Experiences of Aboriginal Peoples Living in Vancouver's Inner City' (2017) 178 *Social Science & Medicine* 87–94.

[22] A. García-Aracil and C. Winter, 'Gender and Ethnicity Differentials in School Attainment and Labor Market Earnings in Ecuador' (2006) 34(2) *World Development* 289–307; FPP, *WPC Recommendation 24: Indigenous Peoples and Protected Areas* (FPP 2003); S. Wiessner, 'The Cultural Rights of Indigenous Peoples: Achievements and Continuing Challenges' (2011) 22(1) *European Journal of International Law* 121–140.

[23] UNESCO, *Social Inclusion: An Indigenous Story* [online video], 4 February 2017 https://en.unesco.org/inclusivepolicylab/learning/social-inclusion-indigenous-story accessed 9 October 2018.

[24] Ibid.

[25] International Institute for Sustainable Development, *What Is Sustainable Development?* (IISD 2012). R. Scheyvens, *Tourism for Development: Empowering Communities* (Prentice Hall 2002).

[26] World Bank, *supra* note 20.

[27] V.A. Garcia-Moreno and H.A. Patrinos, *Indigenous Peoples and Poverty in Mexico. Country Brief* (2011) 7; C. MacIntosh, 'The Role of Law in Ameliorating Global Inequalities in Indigenous Peoples' Health' (2013) 14(1) *Journal of Law, Medicine & Ethics* 74–88.

There is both a promise and an obligation to attempt to achieve these changes as quickly as possible. Indeed, recent sustainable development declarations and agreements specifically build commitments, instruments, and programmes that underline and highlight these issues. The SDGs agenda, and its commitment to the concept of 'no one left behind', may be of great significance to indigenous peoples around the world.[28] These 17 goals encapsulate the importance of a vision that aims to make this a better world. Several key instruments aspire to alleviate economic, environmental, and social vulnerabilities of indigenous peoples. Additionally, achieving poverty reduction (Goal 1), gender equality (Goal 5), decent work and economic growth (Goal 8), reduce inequalities (Goal 10), responsible consumption and production (Goal 12),[29] and other related issues among indigenous peoples represents the potential for meaningful and long-lasting growth that will promote intra- and inter-generational equity.

## MEXICO CASE STUDY

### *Poverty, Migration, and Ecotourism*

The indigenous population of El Alberto, the Hñahñu people, were largely forgotten and ignored by Mexican society and the government, as is the case of many indigenous groups in Mexico. Scattered in small communities across remote regions, their geographical isolation only made it easier to ignore them. The majority of the participants interviewed in 2013 and 2014 recalled always having struggled economically and being unable to earn the necessary income to maintain their households.[30] Lacking economic opportunities in a small community, and been far from big cities, the only jobs available around the area were cultivating and harvesting the lands. Primarily, this involved growing maguey and other types of cactuses, making food or goods with them, collecting fruits, and chopping dead trees for firewood. These products were typically taken to sell in the nearby city of Ixmiquilpan, and sometimes they would go as far as Pachuca.

Poverty and lack of economic opportunities caused some Hñahñu people to start looking for jobs outside the community. Many Hñahñu started to migrate to other cities and states, although the length of their absence depended on the job requirements and the location. Thus, they became construction workers and maids in neighbouring cities (Ixmiquilpan, Pachuca, and Mexico City). Some were able to return to El Alberto on the weekends to see their families. Others, such as the live-in

28 ILO, *supra* note 17.

29 UN, *Transforming Our World: The 2030 Agenda for Sustainable Development. Sustainable Development Knowledge Platform* (United Nations 2015).

30 The following case study was conducted by the author, and the referenced materials and interviews are on file with her.

maids in Guadalajara and Monterrey, were required to stay away for months. Sometimes, years would pass without anyone hearing anything from them. These migrants were very young girls, often as young as 13, who were forced to leave their homes to make their own money and also to save money for their families or an eventual return.

It was not too long after the start of national migration that El Alberto's indigenous members began to inquire and gather information about working wages and living expenses in the US. Older people from El Alberto recalled that national migration started in the early 1960s, and migration to the US started in the late 1980s. They also recall that it was relatively easy to get to the US then, in contrast to the situation today.

Given the data obtained from semi-structured interviews with the local community members, it can be estimated that Hñahñu members who are currently working in the US are located largely in Las Vegas, as well as in Texas and Arizona. Furthermore, while men are mostly employed as construction workers, women are employed in cleaning services (e.g., housemaids, janitors in hotels, restaurants, and convenience stores). Also, results of fieldwork in 2014 suggest that the first group of Hñahñu people from El Alberto who started to migrate illegally were married men with children (two to three children on average), and in an age range of 27–50. These men needed to provide for their families, who were living in deplorable conditions. According to some of the migrants, they were forced to leave because of the lack of economic opportunities in El Alberto, while their wives and children remained on the lands, living on their remittances.

The international migration was initiated because there were not enough opportunities locally and as an effort to improve the quality of life for the migrant's family. Furthermore, the remittances provided by international migration were reflected in El Alberto almost instantly. People no longer starved or spent cold, wet nights, children began to dress better, to wear shoes, and to attend school, and the community, in general, looked healthier. Additionally, houses were rebuilt with more resistant materials such as cement and bricks, and some people even bought televisions and cars.

Findings from the fieldwork demonstrate that the remittances coming from the US caused the community to experience an economic boost, materially and directly increasing their quality of life. These incentives led more community members to leave their lands, and (illegal) international migration rapidly became a trend among El Alberto's members. While migration has been more popular among adults in their early 20s to late 30s in the state of Hidalgo, over the past two decades, young people started to migrate earlier and earlier, some as young as 15. Although, there are no accurate statistics on the number of El Alberto's illegal migrants as confirmed by the Mexican government, it has been estimated by the community authorities that at least 90 per cent of El Alberto's population have migrated illegally to the US at least once, and many of them live their lives between the

US and El Alberto, travelling back and forth. In addition, it is estimated that more than half of those who reside illegally in the US are young men. However, Hñahñu people living in the US seek to remain in contact with each other through different get-togethers. For instance, they have regular reunions to gather money destined for El Alberto, meetings at church, play sports together, and celebrate Mexican holidays.

Notwithstanding the minimal but real economic benefits to the community, illegal immigration has had severe repercussions for the society. During fieldwork at El Alberto, people (mostly the elders) recalled how international migration helped them out of extreme poverty. However, they also explained that in less than a decade they started noticing that it also contributed to significant adverse effects. After remittances assisted families in need, some of those receiving remittances became dependent on them, while some of the women stopped working, children grew up without their fathers, and they had few incentives to achieve in school or contribute to their own people's well-being. The only future for these children was, seemingly, to migrate to the US to earn money, and as a result they became unproductive, dispirited, and troubled. This unproductiveness affected the functionality of the community as a whole.

In many cases, the long periods of absence caused marital problems and sometimes the disintegration of families. Another issue was the behavioural change among the community members themselves, especially the people that returned from the US. According to the interviews, the Hñahñu people who stayed noticed this change in their fellow community members. El Alberto's inhabitants also stated that migrants were not behaving according to the Hñahñu culture anymore. Further, community life was massively reduced because of migration; the community was depopulated, and started to resemble a ghost town. The inhabitants that remained were mostly women, young children, and seniors.

In consequence, the community decided to create a new set of rules before their Hñahñu heritage was lost forever and other issues went further. With the incorporation of those rules, many members were forced to return to claim their lands in order to keep their status as Hñahñu members and to contribute to El Alberto's sustainable development, while others returned under their own volition in order to recover their culture and heritage.

As reported by community members, El Alberto used to look like an abandoned community, and the absence of men between the ages of 20 and 40 was highly noticeable at least for the decade between 1990 and 2000. This absence was reflected in household difficulties and the break-up of relationships between husbands and wives. People tended to notice these issues when it was already too late. Many decided to return to El Alberto for good, and others lived in both places, saving enough money so they could return later and stay with their families for a few months. However, because of controls and security policy changes, the risks of migration and border crossing became pricier and dangerous.

## *Ecotourism*

Given the circumstances of the community, the members of El Alberto themselves originated the idea of creating a tourist attraction that could generate sufficient revenue locally to replace the incomes generated by international migration. Thus, the community assembly of El Alberto created a plan for the development of an ecotourism project that could replace internal and cross-border migration. The project was presented to local and regional authorities that played an important part in the initiation of the ecotourism project. The National Commission for the Development of Indigenous Villages (CDI), a Mexican governmental institution, granted a fund to build toilets and changing rooms for a small swimming pool that the Hñahñu people already owned, one which was fed by natural hot springs. Once this proved successful, in 2004 the CDI granted more funds for the construction of a bigger swimming pool for their water park. However, the water park did not have a good start, since many other hot-spring water parks were already available in the Mezquital Valley. The majority of these water parks were already well established, solid projects that were much bigger than EcoAlberto. Furthermore, the struggling tourism project was not enough motivation for the community members to abandon the town or migration; it was clear that people needed a better incentive to stay. In the face of this, the El Alberto members decided to take advantage of other natural resources. As a result, they created EcoAlberto Ecological Park at el Gran Cañon (the Grand Canyon), a vast landscape with hills and a river. The place started to gain popularity after it integrated an unusual attraction – la caminata nocturna, the 'Night Walk' – a hiking re-enactment of the experiences of El Alberto's people when crossing the border (illegally) between Mexico and the US.

According to the Hñahñu community, the aim of EcoAlberto Ecologic Park was (and still is) to keep fellow community members, particularly young adults, from abandoning the community, and to revive forgotten indigenous traditions and cultural heritage whose loss was accelerated by migration. The initial idea was to offer boat rides and the Night Walk after the construction of a pathway leading to the lowest point of the Grand Canyon. In 2006, the CDI granted funds under the Ecotourism Program for Indigenous Zones (PEZI) and the Program for Alternative Tourism in Indigenous Zones (PTAZI) to build new infrastructure such as traditional cabins for accommodation, a restaurant, toilets and dressing rooms, and a plant to treat the water in order to make it potable for the international palate. Further, after the construction of certain new roads, the community began to implement other adventure and ecotourism attractions such as zipwires and camping areas.

During interviews and informal conversations, participants were asked to share their views on how the development of ecotourism impacted life at El Alberto; few participants cited negative impacts, such as extra work and pollution, and the majority mentioned positive changes such as less migration, more money flowing into the local economy, and better quality of life, especially for the children. Women working at the Ya Mutsi Beñha cooperative explained that even though they did not obtain direct benefits from EcoAlberto, the park attracts tourists who wander around the local community and buy their products.

The majority of the community members agreed that the development of EcoAlberto Ecologic Park has generated tangible and intangible benefits for the community. Even though it may not be possible to evaluate benefits in actual numbers, the gains of the Hñahñu people through ecotourism can be seen in the effects at the community such as the creation of new and better infrastructure. Other positive outcomes include reconciliation among migrants and non-migrants, empowerment of women, and facilitation of community services. A particular benefit has been the clear signs of a revival of the Hñahñu heritage that has also strengthened their connection with the land in terms of its sustainability and has begun to generate a sense of pride among younger generations. Thus, children are learning to feel proud of and identify with their indigenous heritage, no longer seeking to abandon their community with such ease. Furthermore, the development of ecotourism has attracted investment opportunities for locals in different sectors, such as the creation of a cooperative for women for the creation of artisanal souvenirs, and a plant that treats the water from the region.

## CONTRIBUTION OF ECOTOURISM TO ACHIEVING SDGS AT THE HÑAHÑU LOCAL COMMUNITY

TABLE 26.1 *Relevant Sustainable Development Goals*

**Goal 1** End poverty in all its forms
**Goal 5** Gender equality
 **Target 5.1** End all forms of discrimination against all women and girls everywhere
 **Target 5.5** Ensure women's full and effective participation and equal opportunities for leadership at all levels of decision making in political, economic and public life
**Goal 8** Decent work and economic growth: produce sustained, inclusive and sustainable economic growth, full and productive employment and decent work for all.
 **Target 8.1** '... devise and implement policies to promote sustainable tourism that creates jobs and promotes local culture and products'
**Goal 10** Reduce inequalities
 **Target 10.2** '... empower and promote the social, economic and political inclusion of all, irrespective of age, sex, disability, race, ethnicity, origin, religion or economic or other status'
**Goal 12** Responsible consumption and production
 **Target 12.2** '... achieve the sustainable management and efficient use of natural resources'
 **Target 12.b** 'Develop and implement tools to monitor sustainable development impacts for sustainable tourism which creates jobs, promotes local culture and products.'
**Goal 16** Peace and justice, strong institutions
 **Target 16.7** Ensure responsive, inclusive, participatory and representative decision making at all levels

*Source*: UN, *Transforming Our World: The 2030 Agenda for Sustainable Development: Sustainable Development Knowledge Platform* (2015)

### *Community Participation (Goal 16)*

The majority of the indigenous community members at El Alberto are deeply committed to their work. Reportedly, 90 per cent of EcoAlberto's personnel work full time during the year without payment, as a type of social service to the community, which all the Hñahñu members (over the age of 18) do at least once every ten years to keep their status as members of the community. According to the sustainable tourism value chain analysis, this community service is what makes it possible for EcoAlberto to stay in business even if it does not have many visitors for a certain period. In addition, the development of EcoAlberto, as well as the creation of the year of community service, were both strategies to stop Hñahñu members from immigrating to the US and for those who were in the US to able to return to El Alberto and work at home. Nevertheless, not all Hñahñu people welcomed the idea, since having to work for a year without pay is not an easy or practical decision. However, the community as a whole greatly benefits from the scheme, as the inhabitants live in greater transparency, accountability, and harmony, and are fully active and informed about the affairs of the ecotourism company.

### *Resourceful Personnel (Goal 8)*

Even though the indigenous tourism personnel had not been elaborately trained in fields such as customer service and hospitality, their self-perceptions and ability to draw upon cultural and other traditions of hospitality, kindness to guests, and earnest care for visitors assists them in offering culturally appropriate customer service and hospitality to enhance the visitors' ecotourism experience. Other resources such as cooking or the elaboration of artisanal products are also founded upon skills that the indigenous people have practised and passed on through generations among the community members. For instance, the women from the community use their skills to make artisanal crafts and traditional food. Indeed, the Hñahñu women residents have stated that having a market for their artisanal crafts is one of the best parts of the introduction of ecotourism into their community. Correspondingly, the men of the indigenous community have used their traditional and often internationally enhanced skills to work in and manage the construction and farming. While many tasks remain to a certain extent gender-disaggregated, following traditional roles, many of those interviewed also drew certain comfort and traditional security from these differentiations. Furthermore, the development of tourism generates a need for education as well as jobs within the tourism industry.

### *Minor Environmental Impacts (Goal 12)*

The present case study carries very few environmental impacts through well-developed ecotourism projects on their land. The Hñahñu communities located in the region of the Mezquital Valley in the state of Hidalgo in Mexico have continuously asserted that their ancestral roots come from the Otomi people, from whom they have inherited the vocation to conserve the natural resources of their land, especially water and the forest. The development of EcoAlberto's parks on Hñahñu collective land has encouraged them to be aware of climate change and to safeguard natural resources, as this is the prime motivation for the visits to the ecologic parks. Therefore, the region of the Mezquital Valley that hosts the ecotourism projects' infrastructure has suffered few negative impacts, owing to (1) little infrastructure overall, and (2) the infrastructure that exists being built with native material and resources found within the natural surroundings, thus lessening the impact on the environment, with the exception of the plastic toboggans used to slide down in a couple of swimming pools from the water park. It is true that some residents must do community service for a year (i.e. work, but no income) at the ecologic parks, creating some short-term economic loss, and many of the members doing community service also sell firewood, but given that the tinder comes from the dead branches of the trees, it could be argued that this does not bring environmental implications around the forests. Ecotourism is sustainable tourism, and in high seasons such as spring and summer, the number of tourists that arrive at EcoAlberto's parks is controlled by the locals; a committee is charged with patrolling the different areas to prevent the sensitive environment from being damaged by some tourists' reckless behaviour. The committee raises environmental awareness to visitors through guides and other tourism providers, who communicate to the visitors the importance of a healthy environment, and the significance of contributing towards the preservation and conservation of flora and fauna.

### *Empowerment and Economic Improvement of the Hñahñu People (Goals 8 and 10)*

The Hñahñu people of El Alberto, as with many indigenous peoples, were once vulnerable and marginalised. They live in rural areas, where they suffered from inequality, social exclusion, and discrimination in various ways. Nevertheless, the development of EcoAlberto's parks enhanced the well-being of these indigenous peoples and led to their economic, social, psychological, and political empowerment, as well as the enhancement of indigenous pride and female participation.

### *Economic Improvement (Goals 1 and 8)*

The development of ecotourism with the integration of EcoAlberto's parks has produced different options to generate earnings, which also produces sustainable economic development by bringing in long-lasting revenues for the local community. A good portion of ecotourism revenues remain in the local community, and those revenues produce cash flows that have enhanced the well-being of the local community and aid in the reduction of poverty. For instance, part of the revenues is directly used for the construction of schools, clinics, and roads, and part indirectly for housing, the creation of micro-enterprises, and employment. Furthermore, the improvement in the economy of El Alberto has also pushed the local community to towards other types of empowerment.

### *Social Enhancement (Goals 5 and 10)*

In the community of El Alberto, ecotourism has ameliorated and maintained stability among the lives of the Hñahñu inhabitants. In other words, the development of ecotourism has aided the integration of all inhabitants of the community and also those members who live between El Alberto and the US, building a sense of social cohesion. Some examples of social enhancements to which the development of ecotourism has contributed the most include reducing constraints on education, and issues regarding the inclusion of vulnerable groups such as women and youth in social activities. As a result, this has generated psychological empowerment and indigenous pride.

### *Indigenous Dignity (Goals 10 and 12)*

EcoAlberto's ecologic parks took several years to become economically viable. Seeing this project building up day by day, against all the odds, generated a sense of pride and self-esteem among the Hñahñu members, who used ecotourism projects to show their area's natural attractions as well as their distinctive culture and unique traditional knowledge. Yet, 'indigenous dignity' was not born with the inception of EcoAlberto as an ecotourism project per se, but rather as the outside world (e.g., tourists, neighbouring communities, and governmental institutions) started to recognise that it was the Hñahñu people from El Alberto who had come up with the ecotourism idea and that they were able to run not one but two ecologic parks in a sustainable manner. Thus, the Hñahñu inhabitants of El Alberto felt pride and dignity in their culture as well as in the appreciation of 'other' people of their 'native ways'. This, in turn, has motivated them to rescue their long-lost traditions. For instance, the Hñahñu members of El Alberto encountered many types of social discrimination, especially for being part of an indigenous group and speaking a different language, yet as witnessed by the investigator during the fieldwork, the Hñahñu are now very proud (indeed) to wear their native clothes and to talk their traditional tongue, Otomi, as well as to encourage the youth and children to learn it. Thus, El Alberto's ecotourism projects have served as a mechanism to secure the welfare of the Hñahñu community so far.

### *Political Empowerment (Goals 5 and 10)*

The development of the EcoAlberto parks has provided the Hñahñu members of El Alberto a voice with which to claim their indigenous lands and rights of accessing and sustainably using its resources. They have gained many skills, perspectives, and insights into how to deal with the government if there is a need to defend their indigenous rights. Perhaps the clearest example of their political empowerment is the direct and indirect participation of the whole Hñahñu community in the inception and development of EcoAlberto's projects. Additionally, the development of ecotourism has empowered vulnerable groups in the local community, and even aided in empowering vulnerable groups in other neighbouring communities (e.g., women artisans working in cooperatives). Further, it has boosted the creation of various committees to represent the best interests of the Hñahñu people, and this has granted locals the right to participate (through community assemblies) in the decision making regarding EcoAlberto's Parks and to resolve community issues. Furthermore, ecotourism has also moved the Hñahñu community of El Alberto a step closer towards equity between men and women.

### *Women's Empowerment (Goals 5 and 8)*

Men and women have different roles and responsibilities in the Hñahñu community of El Alberto, and Hñahñu women do not have the same rights, access, or control over the common land as men. However, with the international emigration of a very high percentage of Hñahñu men, and the implementation of ecotourism at El Alberto, the division of labour and rights over land started to become more flexible for women. In addition to social and other types of empowerment that ecotourism has boosted for all Hñahñu people, ecotourism development at El Alberto brought particular advantages for women. For instance, while international emigration forced women to fill in for men's duties or the little work that was left at El Alberto (usually done by men), ecotourism stimulates them to propose new initiatives and business ideas. Perhaps the most visible example of female empowerment is the case of the Hñahñu artisans, a group of approximately 300 women from El Alberto and other neighbouring communities in the Mezquital Valley, known as the women's cooperative *Ya munts'i b'ehña*. They formed a sustainable enterprise for the benefit of their families and the region, given the demand for artisanal products by the tourist visiting EcoAlberto's parks. These types of businesses have allowed them to create an income while preserving their culture and traditions.

Additionally, the cooperative and the local government of Ixmiquilpan have worked together to empower women by providing training on gender equality and other types of female issues that they consider important. This involves empowering and training female leaders who can organise and teach educational workshops on different topics such as sexual and reproductive rights, indigenous women's rights, women and sustainability, women and the economy, and women and migration. Thus, since the development of the EcoAlberto parks, women have progressively, although not totally, gained rights to land and to participate in the community's decision-making processes.

## CONCLUSION

Intergenerational equity has become very important in recent decades, especially among countries with high percentages of indigenous peoples and serious problems related to poverty in rural areas. Indigenous communities are valued for their unique features, cultural attractions, and the diversity of their landscapes, yet these communities do not have many options for their subsistence. Ecotourism can be a reliable source for achieving the SDGs in regions with fewer options, as the nature of the ecotourism product can be founded upon the cultural and ecological capital of indigenous peoples, being located in biodiverse natural areas, employing vulnerable local groups, engaging with local businesses, and looking to mitigate climate change.

Ecotourism developments such as EcoAlberto have achieved outstanding results in upholding their socio-cultural heritage. This is handled in a clear hierarchical system with clear roles, highly defined services, active participation of all families, and a community that stands as a great example of how customs and cultural traditions can be saved. The indigenous peoples of this community are active advocates of careful management and governance natural resources, and are promoting a special indigenous-led model of tourism activities based on recognised principles of sustainable tourism.

Before the incorporation of ecotourism there was no social organisation among the community; however, when the members of El Alberto initiated the idea and put their plan into action, they started a community collective system to empower the community as a whole and encourage everyone to become involved in the project. This reinforced their values and assisted in the revival of their culture and traditions, which were rapidly being lost when the Hñahñu people started to migrate to the US Moreover, ecotourism has helped to improve the Hñahñu people's pride and self-esteem as a consequence of tourist interest in their unique traditions and culture. Indeed, by visiting the land that belongs to them, the 'outside world' gives a sign of respect, acknowledging the existence of the Hñahñu people's unique environmental culture and traditions. With the incorporation of ecotourism and the development of the ecologic parks practically on their own, the Hñahñu community have gained a sense of pride in their culture. This has helped them to recover their almost-lost cultural roots and traditions and preserve them for future generations.

Ecotourism opened the door for the development of other local business by creating opportunities to empower women as individuals and as part of the larger community. The rate of Hñahñu people migrating to the US has reduced considerably because of the community service requirements and new local economic opportunities. Subsequently, the development of EcoAlberto and local business, and the return of people form the US, has resulted in the young attending high school, technical courses, and in some cases university in nearby cities. Moreover, the implementation of ecotourism practices is an emerging practice among indigenous communities. It appears likely, from the context of the research, that a less-than-enthusiastic level of interest from policy makers and incomplete commitment on the part of local communities have been the main constraints on the development of these practices in other instances. The example of El Alberto provides an important counterweight to this, demonstrating that indigenous peoples can manage their own business without requiring special qualifications, even if they do need to improve some of their approaches. Consequently, the achievement of substantial benefits is possible if the founding initiatives are carefully conceived and established in a manner that takes into account the needs and interests of the local community as primary considerations.

This case study provides insights into the contribution of ecotourism to achieving the SDGs in an Indigenous community, examining the potential to support the SDGs to achieve poverty reduction (Goal 1), gender equality (Goal 5), decent work and economic growth (Goal 8), and other relevant issues for indigenous peoples (Goal 10). The findings suggest that ecotourism can foster intergenerational equity through the achievement of the global SDGs in regions with few other options, providing a refreshing counter-example to several well-publicised failures and an account of an indigenous community that has succeeded in its ecotourism projects against all odds.

This chapter has sought to contribute to the discussion on whether indigenous empowerment and poverty reduction for sustainable development can realistically be achieved through the implementation of ecotourism projects among indigenous communities. This has immediately evident impacts on indigenous communities and on the larger communities in which they are located. It also offers a perspective on the development and the preservation of cultural heritage and identity that promotes intergenerational equity by ensuring the sustainability of traditional indigenous community land rights and practices for future generations.

# 27

# Legal Innovations for Intergenerational Justice in Sustainable Landscapes Management of Democratic Republic of Congo

*Erick Kassongo*

## INTRODUCTION

The purpose of this chapter is to examine the importance of traditional knowledge (TK) and genetic resources to Indigenous and local communities (ILCs). In the next pages is a broader explanation of the value of TK and genetic resources, as well as examples of industries that depend on access to genetic resources and TK. This chapter will also provide an examination of the threats to access to genetic resources and TK on the part of ILCs, tracing the development of international property rights (IPRs) in this domain. Moreover, there is a survey of the international regimes relating to the protection of TK and access to genetic resources, studying treaties and other international instruments. Incompatibilities can sometimes be observed between IPRs and TK, as well as gaps in the current protections and regimes in place, which will also be examined in this chapter. Finally, the chapter will present case studies in Africa and South America relating to TK and the economic development of ILCs, particularly in the area of agroecology.

## THE IMPORTANCE OF TRADITIONAL KNOWLEDGE AND GENETIC RESOURCES

### *Traditional Knowledge, Access to Genetic Resources, and ILCs*

There is no accepted definition of TK at the international level. However, the CBD suggests that 'traditional knowledge refers to the knowledge, innovations and practices of ILCs around the world, ... developed from experience gained over the centuries and adapted to the local culture and environment'.[1] The collectively

[1] World Intellectual Property Organization, 'Traditional Knowledge' www.wipo.int/tk/en/tk/ accessed 30 November 2017. The definition from the website of the CBD reads as follows: 'Traditional knowledge refers to the knowledge, innovations and practices of indigenous and

owned TK is usually transmitted orally from generation to generation through songs, stories, folklore, proverbs, rituals, and agricultural practices, to name only a few forms. TK often forms part of a community's cultural and spiritual identity and is deeply linked to the connection Indigenous peoples have with the land as they care for and protect Mother Earth and the ecosystems.[2] Indigenous peoples have a profound spiritual connection to Mother Earth, which explains why their culture and territoriality are inextricably linked to biodiversity and TK,[3] as we will discuss in this chapter.

This chapter looks specifically at TK in relation to access to genetic resources, whether from plants, animals, or micro-organisms. Accessing and using genetic resources is 'the process of researching their beneficial properties and using them to increase scientific knowledge and understanding, or to develop commercial products'.[4] Access to genetic resources has not only 'fundamentally altered our understanding of the living world but has also led to the development of new products and practices that contribute to human well-being, ranging from vital medicines to methods that improve the security of our food supplies'.[5] Furthermore, conservation methods that help safeguard global biodiversity have been greatly improved with access to genetic resources.

There is an evident connection between TK, biodiversity, and access to genetic resources. Around the world, most ILCs are located in areas where the vast majority of the world's genetic resources are found. In fact, more than 70 per cent of the world's biological resources are located in ILCs.[6] For millennia, many ILCs have cultivated and used biological diversity sustainably, and still practise the same methods and rely on TK related to this biodiversity today in their daily lives. For

local communities around the world. Developed from experience gained over the centuries and adapted to the local culture and environment, traditional knowledge is transmitted orally from generation to generation. It tends to be collectively owned and takes the form of stories, songs, folklore, proverbs, cultural values, beliefs, rituals, community laws, local language, and agricultural practices, including the development of plant species and animal breeds. Sometimes it is referred to as an oral traditional for it is practiced, sung, danced, painted, carved, chanted and performed down through millennia. Traditional knowledge is mainly of a practical nature, particularly in such fields as agriculture, fisheries, health, horticulture, forestry and environmental management in general'. Convention on Biological Diversity, 'Traditional Knowledge and the Convention on Biological Diversity' www.cbd.int/traditional/intro.shtml accessed 30 November 2017.

2 Z. Whitman, 'Finding Balance: Determining the Relationship between 'Economic Development', Traditional Knowledge and Natural Resource Management in the Context of the Nova Scotia Mi'kmaq' (MA Thesis, Queen's University 2013) at 19–20.

3 S.E. Salako, 'Agrobiotechnology, Indigenous Peoples' Rights and Traditional Knowledge' (2012) 20 *African Journal of International and Comparative Law* 318–332 at 319.

4 Secretariat of the Convention on Biological Diversity, 'Uses of Genetic Resources' www.cbd.int/abs/infokit/factsheet-uses-en.pdf accessed 30 November 2017.

5 Ibid.

6 C. Oguamanam, 'Local Knowledge as Trapped Knowledge: Intellectual Property, Culture, Power and Politics' (2008) 11:1 *Journal of World Intellectual Property* 29–57 at 31.

example, in India 65 per cent of the population has access to traditional systems of medicine, and in Africa 80 per cent of the population uses traditional medicines.[7] It is therefore evident that the defence of biodiversity and the defence of cultural diversity are closely linked. Indeed, in Mexico,

> the preservation of plant species used in traditional medicine or in agricultural polygraphing (for pest control or soil enrichment) cannot be divorced from the cultural knowledge of those techniques [because] if those plants hold the key to a more sustainable future, so do the cultures in which the knowledge of their use and sustainable management is embedded.[8]

Because Mexico is so rich in both biological and cultural diversity, the two are interwoven with special promise.

What is particularly interesting is the reciprocity of the relationship between ILCs and ecosystems. Indeed, ILCs can act as natural resource managers, as some traditional practices 'have been proven to enhance and promote biodiversity at the local level and aid in maintaining healthy ecosystems'.[9] TK has also proven to be an essential factor for the socioeconomic well-being of ILCs. However, there is a need to balance economic development with ecological and cultural sustainability because economic development is essential for the survival of ILCs. This means that a balance should be found between ecological and cultural sustainability and the insurance of a community sustenance strategy, which could mean taking a step closer to Western 'capitalism'.[10] This brings us to the next point: while TK can contribute to the economic well-being of ILCs, the loss of TK often results from socioeconomic pressures. However, some groups embrace the transition as they 'look forward to new opportunities' and have the 'desire to enter the market economy'.[11]

### *Broader Applications of Traditional Knowledge Relating to Genetic Resources*

The value of TK relating to biodiversity and genetic resources is now widely recognized by the global community. The global community not only recognizes that TK is highly valuable for improving the conservation and safeguarding of biodiversity, but also for improving food security, as it encompasses an extensive

[7] K. Bavikatte and D.F. Robinson, 'Towards a Peoples' History of the Law: Biocultural Jurisprudence and the Nagoya Protocol on Access and Benefit Sharing' (2011) 7:1 *Law, Environment and Development Journal* 35–51 at 38.

[8] D.V. Carruthers, 'Agroecology in Mexico: Linking Environmental and Indigenous Struggles' (1997) 10:3 *Society & Natural Resources* 259–272 at 263.

[9] See, e.g., Convention on Biological Diversity, *supra* note 1.

[10] Whitman, *supra* note 2 at 8.

[11] R. Camara-Leret et al., 'Amerindian and Afro-American Perceptions of Their Traditional Knowledge in the Chocó Biodiversity Hotspot' (2016) 70:2 *Economic Botany* 160–175 at 171. See also V. Reyes-García et al., 'Evidence of Traditional Knowledge Loss among a Contemporary Indigenous Society' (2013) 34:4 *Evolution and Human Behavior* 249–257.

knowledge of local environments and ecosystems,[12] and allows us to better adapt to changes in the environment. In fact, for a multitude of generations, farmers have drawn on the diverse plant genetic resources to breed the major crops that feed the world today.[13] The global community also finds TK valuable in numerous commercial applications across a range of industries. Some industries, such as the pharmaceutical industry, industrial biotechnology, and agricultural biotechnology, depend on genetic resources and associated TK.[14]

In fact, TK is essential in the development of drugs and other medical products in the pharmaceutical industry, as three-quarters of the plants that provide active ingredients for prescription drugs came to the attention of researchers because of their use in traditional medicine.[15] In order to give a better perspective, 'only 1 per cent of such species have been documented by science for their medicinal or chemical properties'.[16] The potential for the use of such knowledge is immense. Genetic resources and associated TK also play a crucial role in generating industrial products and processes in the field of industrial biotechnology. In industrial biotechnology, '[e]nzymes are used by textile, detergent, food, feed and other industries to improve the efficiency and quality of their products and production processes'.[17]

Moreover, genetic resources and associated TK are used in the creation of pollution control technologies, as well as the remediation, reclamation, and restoration of former industrial sites.[18] In the case of agricultural biotechnology, the use of genetic resources and associated TK in the seed and crop protection and plant biotechnology industries has led to the improvement of performance and farming efficiency for major crops.[19] Finally, other applications of the use of genetic resources and associated TK can be observed in the cosmetics industry,[20] and even

[12] See, e.g., W. Kelbessa, 'Indigenous Knowledge and Its Contribution to Biodiversity Conservation' (2015) 63 *International Social Science Journal* 143–152.

[13] G. Moore and W. Tymowski, *Explanatory Guide to the International Treaty on Plant Genetic Resources for Food and Agriculture* (2005) at 1.

[14] Secretariat of the Convention on Biological Diversity, *supra* note 4; Bavikatte and Robinson, *supra* note 7 at 38.

[15] G.S. Nijar, 'Traditional Knowledge Systems, International Law and National Challenges: Marginalization or Emancipation?' (2013) 24:4 *European Journal of International Law* 1205–1221 at 1206.

[16] J. Kloppenburg Jr, 'No Hunting! Biodiversity, Indigenous Rights, and Scientific Poaching' (1991) *Cultural Survival Q* 14–18 at 15.

[17] Secretariat of the Convention on Biological Diversity, *supra* note 4 at 2.

[18] See, e.g., J. Sandlosa and A. Keeling, 'Aboriginal Communities, Traditional Knowledge, and the Environmental Legacies of Extractive Development in Canada' (2015) 3 *The Extractive Industries and Society* 278–287.

[19] Secretariat of the Convention on Biological Diversity, *supra* note 4 at 2.

[20] See, e.g., H.O. Elansary et al., 'Diversity of Plants, Traditional Knowledge, and Practices in Local Cosmetics: A Case Study from Alexandria, Egypt' (2015) 69:2 *Economic Botany* 114–126 at 114–115.

in health drinks such as the native brew known as Chullu in India.[21] In essence, the TK systems of ILCs fed, healed, and clothed the world.[22]

### *Threats to Access to Genetic Resources and the Traditional Knowledge of ILCs: The Development of IP Protections for Biodiversity and Genetic Resources TK*

A number of threats face the survival of TK and access to genetic resources.[23] Some of the major concerns that have signalled the need for protection for TK and access to genetic resources are bioprospecting and biopiracy.[24] Biopiracy can be defined as 'the appropriation of the knowledge and genetic resources of farming and indigenous communities by individuals or institutions who seek exclusive monopoly control (patents or intellectual property) over these resources or knowledge'.[25]

Famous instances of biopiracy, related to the basmati, neem, and ayahuasca cases, or the Enola bean controversy,[26] brought to international attention the need for IPR protections for TK.[27] IPRs and access and benefit sharing (ABS) frameworks have therefore been implemented and are intended to limit biopiracy,[28] as we will examine in the next section. However, a weak international framework has been an obstacle to the effective protection of traditional knowledge,[29] and extending IPR protection to TK relating to biodiversity continues to be difficult,[30] owing to a gap in the existing legal mechanisms that has been circumvented through specially designed *sui generis* regimes.[31] Also, the 'lack of concerted international action and the non-inclusion of TK holders in the process' are some of the main obstacles to the protection of TK.[32]

[21] See, e.g., M. Ranjan Saha et al., 'Ethnobotany, Traditional Knowledge and Socioeconomic Importance of Native Drink among the Oraon Rribe of Malda District in India' (2015) 4:1 *Journal of Intercultural Ethnopharmacology* 34–39.

[22] Nijar, *supra* note 15 at 1206.

[23] Ibid. at 1208.

[24] Bavikatte and Robinson, *supra* note 6 at 38; see also: T.K. Mackey and B.A. Liang, 'Integrating Biodiversity Management and Indigenous Biopiracy Protection to Promote Environmental Justice and Global Health' (2012) 102:6 *American Journal of Public Health* 1091–1095.

[25] N. Ross, 'Biopiracy' (2010) 36:6 *Alternatives Journal* 22 at 22 [Ross].

[26] Ross, *supra* note 23 at 22.

[27] U.K. Sarma and I. Barpujari, 'Revisiting the Debate on Intellectual Property Rights and Traditional Knowledge of Biodiversity: Accommodating Local Realities and Perspectives' (2012) 3:4 *The International Indigenous Policy Journal* 1.

[28] Ibid.

[29] Ibid. at 2.

[30] Ibid. at 1.

[31] Ibid.

[32] Ibid.

## INTERNATIONAL REGIMES RELATING TO TRADITIONAL KNOWLEDGE AND GENETIC RESOURCES

Even though it has been previously stated that the framework to protect traditional knowledge presents several obstacles, a number of *sui generis* and national regimes governing biodiversity, genetic resources, and TK do exist. These frameworks include the Indian Biological Diversity Act (2002); Peru's Law No. 27,811 (2002); the Philippines' Indigenous Peoples Rights Act (1997); and Thailand's Act on Protection and Promotion of Traditional Thai Medicinal Intelligence, B.E. 2542 (1999), to name just a few.[33] At the international level, however, the protection of TK related to genetic resources and biodiversity is fragmented across a range of legal regimes – including those governing Indigenous peoples' rights, biodiversity, intellectual property, and trade. Another interesting point is the emergence of the notion of 'biocultural' rights, which makes the link between community and ecosystems.[34] This seems like it may be a new paradigm for protecting natural and cultural resources of Indigenous communities,[35] but it is too early to tell yet.

### *ILO Convention No. 169*

In 1957, the ILO developed and ratified the Indigenous and Tribal Populations Convention, also known as Convention No. 107. Convention No. 107 was an international instrument dedicated to improving the living conditions of Indigenous peoples worldwide. In 1989, Convention No. 107 was revised and renamed the Indigenous and Tribal Peoples Convention (No. 169). It 'recognizes Indigenous peoples' right to self-determination within a nation-state, while setting standards for national governments regarding Indigenous peoples' economic, socio-cultural and political rights, including the right to a land base'.[36] The Convention is law within the nation States that have ratified it. It does not refer specifically to TK with respect to biodiversity or genetic resources. However, it does provide, at Article 15, that '[t]he rights of the peoples concerned to the natural resources pertaining to their lands shall be specially safeguarded. These rights include the right of these peoples to participate in the use, management and conservation of these resources.'

In addition, with respect to benefit sharing, 'successive interpretations of the Convention have repeatedly used a benefit-sharing terminology'.[37] For example,

33 Ibid. at 2.

34 Bavikatte and Robinson, *supra* note 7 at 49–50.

35 C.W. Chen and M. Gilmore, 'Biocultural Rights: A New Paradigm for Protecting Natural and Cultural Resources of Indigenous Communities' (2015) 6:3 *The International Indigenous Policy Journal* https://ojs.lib.uwo.ca/index.php/iipj/article/view/7466/6110.

36 Indigenous Foundations Arts UBC, 'ILO Convention 169' (2009) https://indigenousfoundations.arts.ubc.ca/ilo_convention_169/ accessed 30 November 2017.

37 E. Morgera, 'The Need for an International Legal Concept of Fair and Equitable Benefit Sharing' (2016) 27:2 *European Journal of International Law* 353–383 at 363.

the IACHR and James Anaya, the former UN Special Rapporteur on Indigenous Peoples' Rights,

> have emphasized that 'benefit sharing', as encapsulated in the ILO Convention, refers to an inherent component of indigenous peoples' rights to land and natural resources that is implicit in the American Convention on Human Rights and the UN Declaration on the Rights of Indigenous Peoples.[38]

Moreover, regional human rights case law has built on ILO Convention No. 169

> to clarify that benefit sharing is triggered by the exploitation of traditionally owned lands and natural resources necessary for the survival of indigenous and tribal peoples or by the establishment of environmental protection measures negatively affecting them.[39]

In fact, a few of these cases are *Saramaka People* v. *Suriname* November 2007, *Endorois Welfare Council* v. *Kenya* in 2009, *Community Garífuna Triunfo de la Cruz and Its Members* v. *Honduras* in October 2015, and *Kaliña and Lokono Peoples* v. *Suriname* in November 2015.

### *United Nations Declaration on the Rights of Indigenous Peoples*

The UNDRIP was adopted by the UNGA on 13 September 2007, by a majority of 144 states in favour, with four votes against (Australia, Canada, New Zealand, and the US). Since then, the four countries that voted against have reversed their position and now support the Declaration. The UNDRIP is a key instrument acknowledging and affirming the rights of ILCs in relation to TK.[40] A few Articles focus on the importance of TK for Indigenous peoples and their rights regarding TK. In fact, Article 24 ensures that Indigenous peoples have the right to practise their TK. It provides that 'Indigenous peoples have the right to their traditional medicines and to maintain their health practices, including the conservation of their vital medicinal plants, animals and minerals'. Articles 25 and 29 discuss the

[38] Ibid.

[39] Ibid. at 375, referring to IACtHR, *Case of the Saramaka People* v. *Suriname, Judgment* (Preliminary Objections, Merits, Reparations and Costs) 28 November 2007; *African Commission on Human and Peoples' Rights, Centre for Minority Rights Development (Kenya), and Minority Rights Group International, Endorois Welfare Council* v. *Kenya*, Communication no. 276/2003, 25 November 2009; IACtHR, *Case of the Community Garífuna Triunfo de la Cruz and Its Members* v. *Honduras*, Judgment (Merits, Reparations and Costs), 8 October 2015; IACtHR, *Case of Garífuna Punta Piedra Community and Its Members* v. *Honduras*, Judgment (Preliminary Objections, Merits, Reparations and Costs), 8 October 2015; IACtHR, *Case of the Kaliña and Lokono Peoples* v. *Suriname*, Judgment (Merits, Reparations and Costs) 25 November 2015.

[40] M.-C. Cordonier Segger and F.-K. Phillips, 'Indigenous Traditional Knowledge for Sustainable Development: The Biodiversity Convention and Plant Treaty Regimes' (2015) 20 *Journal of Forest Research* 430–437 at 431.

environment. Article 25 states that 'Indigenous peoples have the right to maintain and strengthen their distinctive spiritual relationship with their traditionally owned or otherwise occupied and used lands, territories, waters and coastal seas and other resources', and Article 29 affirms that 'Indigenous peoples have the right to the conservation and protection of the environment and the productive capacity of their lands or territories and resources.' Finally, Article 31 provides that

> Indigenous peoples have the right to maintain, control, protect and develop their cultural heritage, traditional knowledge and traditional cultural expressions, as well as the manifestations of their sciences, technologies and cultures, including human and genetic resources, seeds, medicines, knowledge of the properties of fauna and flora, oral traditions, literatures, designs, sports and traditional games and visual and performing arts. They also have the right to maintain, control, protect and develop their intellectual property over such cultural heritage, traditional knowledge, and traditional cultural expressions.

### *Convention on Biological Diversity*

The CBD was opened for signature on 5 June 1992 at the UNCED (the Rio 'Earth Summit'). It remained open for signature until 4 June 1993, by which time it had received 168 signatures. The Convention entered into force on 29 December 1993. The CBD has three main objectives. The first is the conservation of the biological diversity, the second is the sustainable use of its components, and the last is the fair and equitable sharing of benefits arising from the use of genetic resources. In the case of TK, Article 8(j) of the CBD is very pertinent, as it is the primary legal basis in international law for the protection of TK. Article 8(j) states that

> each contracting Party shall, as far as possible and as appropriate: (j) Subject to national legislation, respect, preserve and maintain knowledge, innovations and practices of indigenous and local communities embodying traditional lifestyles relevant for the conservation and sustainable use of biological diversity and promote their wider application with the approval and involvement of the holders of such knowledge, innovations and practices and encourage the equitable sharing of the benefits arising from the utilization of such knowledge innovations and practices.

However, this provision was widely criticized for its weak language,[41] as it used terms such as 'promote' and 'encourage'. Parties and stakeholders also 'debated whether the provision contained an obligation for users to require [informed consent] of ILC to access TK as well as an obligation to share the benefits from the utilization of TK'.[42] In response to these debates, the COP 5 established a general principle

[41] K. Koutouki, 'The Nagoya Protocol: Status of Indigenous and Local Communities' (2011) CISDL Legal Working Paper Series at 8–9; Bavikatte and Robinson, *supra* note 7 at 41.

[42] Koutouki, *supra* note 41 at 8–9.

that 'access to TK of ILCs should be subject to the prior informed consent of its holders'.[43]

In regard to access to genetic resources, we have to look at Article 15 of the CBD. However, Article 15 is not focused on ILCs but on States, recognizing 'the sovereign rights of States over their natural resources' and providing that 'the authority to determine access to genetic resources rests with the national governments and is subject to national legislation'. Nevertheless, Article 15 'lays the foundation for ABS by providing some direction for implementing fair and equitable access to genetic resources and the sharing of benefits resulting from their use'.[44]

### *Bonn Guidelines on Access to Genetic Resources and the Fair and Equitable Sharing of Benefits Arising out of Their Utilization*

Formally adopted by the COP to the CBD in 2002, the Bonn Guidelines 'have been used to clarify ethical approaches to prior informed consent and mutually agreed terms on which to gain access and establish benefit-sharing when accessing genetic resources and associated traditional knowledge'.[45] An interesting point to mention about the Bonn Guidelines is that due to their voluntary nature, and without clear national systems of ABS in a number of countries,

> many users of genetic resource and associated traditional knowledge have not necessarily felt obligated to follow principles of prior informed consent and benefit-sharing; and, as a result, many of the bio-diverse developing countries as well as indigenous peoples have sought to develop binding international obligations that built upon the principles enshrined in the Bonn Guidelines.[46]

The Guidelines identify steps in the ABS process, emphasizing the obligation for users to seek the prior informed consent of providers, and identifying the requirements for mutually agreed terms (MAT).[47] Moreover, the Bonn Guidelines 'introduce a proposed list of elements that could be considered as guiding parameters in contractual agreements as well as basic requirements for MAT particularly with regard to ILC and TK (paragraph 43)'.[48] However, they have been criticized for failing to distinguish between the role of ILCs and other stakeholders in managing genetic resources in terms of benefit sharing.[49]

[43] Ibid.

[44] C. Oguamanam, 'Genetic Resources and Access and Benefit Sharing: Politics, Prospects and Opportunities for Canada after Nagoya' (2011) 22 *Journal of Environmental Law and Practice* 87–201 at 96.

[45] Bavikatte and Robinson, *supra* note 7 at 38.

[46] Ibid.

[47] Koutouki, *supra* note 41 at 9.

[48] Ibid.

[49] Ibid. at 10.

### *Aichi Biodiversity Targets*

The Aichi Biodiversity Targets were adopted in decision X/2 during the tenth meeting of the COP held in October 2010 in Nagoya, Aichi Prefecture, Japan. During the Conference, the Parties adopted a revised and updated Strategic Plan for Biodiversity, including the Aichi Biodiversity Targets for the 2011–2020 period.[50] The Aichi Biodiversity Targets are a set of twenty global targets under the Strategic Plan for Biodiversity 2011–2020. Target 14 is that 'by 2020, ecosystems that provide essential services, including services related to water, and contribute to health, livelihoods and well-being, are restored and safeguarded, taking into account the needs of women, indigenous and local communities'. In relation to TK, Target 18 provides that

> by 2020, the traditional knowledge, innovations and practices of indigenous and local communities relevant for the conservation and sustainable use of biodiversity, and their customary use of biological resources, are respected, subject to national legislation and relevant international obligations, and fully integrated and reflected in the implementation of the Convention with the full and effective participation of indigenous and local communities, at all relevant levels.

In regard to access to genetic resources, Target 16 provides that 'by 2015, the Nagoya Protocol on Access to Genetic Resources and the Fair and Equitable Sharing of Benefits Arising from their Utilization is in force and operational, consistent with national legislation'.

### *Nagoya Protocol on Access to Genetic Resources and the Fair and Equitable Sharing of Benefits Arising from their Utilization*

The Nagoya Protocol on Access to Genetic Resources and the Fair and Equitable Sharing of Benefits Arising from their Utilization to the Convention on Biological Diversity was adopted at the tenth meeting of the COP on 29 October 2010, in Nagoya, Japan. Negotiated within the CBD, the Nagoya Protocol 'aims to ensure that TK associated with genetic resources is accessed with prior and informed consent or approval, along with the involvement of local and Indigenous communities'.[51] The Protocol 'was conceived to respond to the many criticisms voiced concerning the Access and Benefits-Sharing (ABS) provisions in the CBD', including criticisms relating to the protection afforded to the TK of ILCs.[52] Ongoing points of contention that were 'put on the table for Nagoya'[53] included

50 www.cbd.int/sp/ accessed 30 November 2017.

51 Sarma and Barpujari, *supra* note 27 at 3.

52 Koutouki, *supra* note 41 at 8.

53 W.P. Nagan, 'Protecting the Economic Patrimony of Indigenous Nations: The Case of the Shuar' (2012) 46 *Policy Sciences* 143–159 at 157.

> An insistence on an inseparable link between genetic resources and traditional knowledge [as well as] clear requirement for informed consent and benefit sharing with regard to traditional knowledge; compliance with traditional law and community expectations when seeking to access community resources and traditional knowledge; the sovereignty of States was circumscribed, so the State has an obligation to facilitate the recognition of indigenous rights and the interpretation of these issues was to be influenced by the recognition of the United Nations Declaration on the Rights of Indigenous People.[54]

The Protocol was, therefore, founded on the premise that ILCs have exclusive right to their TK,[55] and their prior informed consent must be obtained for any access.

The Nagoya Protocol establishes procedural obligations relating to equitable access to TK. Indeed, Articles 7 and 5(5) constitute the NP's core provisions on TK associated with genetic resources, expanding TK and ABS provisions of the CBD.[56] Article 5(5) requires each Party to take legislative, administrative, or policy measures in order that benefits arising from the utilization of TK associated with genetic resources are shared in a fair and equitable way with ILCs holding such knowledge. It further states that such sharing shall be upon mutually agreed terms. Article 7 states that State parties have an obligation to take measures aiming to ensure that TK associated with genetic resources held by ILCs is accessed with their prior informed consent or approval and involvement, based on mutually agreed terms. Furthermore, Article 12 provides that Parties in implementing obligations under the Protocol relating to TK: (1) take into consideration community laws, protocols and procedures relating to access, (2) inform potential users of domestic access requirements, (3) assist ILCs in the development of community protocols, minimum requirements for mutually agreed terms, and model contractual clauses, and (4) refrain from restricting customary use and exchange of GRs and TK in and amongst ILCs.

However, the Nagoya Protocol still presents some problems with respect to the protection of the rights of ILCs. First of all, the language of the NP creates a 'double standard' between the rights of ILCs and the rights of States, using terms such as 'in accordance with domestic law', 'established rights', 'as appropriate', 'as applicable', and 'with the aim of ensuring' (see Articles 6.2, 7, 11, 12, 16.1).[57] Also, the NP fails to address the issue of the IPRs of Indigenous peoples' TK, deferring the issue to the World Intellectual Property Organization (WIPO), while increasing pressure on ILCs through commodification of TK and its subjection to domestic law.[58]

54 Ibid.; Bavikatte and Robinson, *supra* note 7 at 43.

55 The Nagoya Protocol on Access to Genetic Resources and the Fair and Equitable Sharing of Benefits arising from their Utilisation to the Convention on Biological Diversity at art. 7 http://treaties.un.org/doc/source/signature/2010/CN782E.pdf accessed 30 November 2017.

56 T. Greiber et al., *An Explanatory Guide to the Nagoya Protocol on Access and Benefit-Sharing* (IUCN 2012) at 109.

57 Koutouki, *supra* note 41 at 16.

58 Ibid.

*International Treaty on Plant Genetic Resources for Food and Agriculture*

The International Treaty on Plant Genetic Resources for Food and Agriculture (ITPGRFA) was adopted by the Thirty-First Session of the Conference of the UN FAO on 3 November 2001 and entered into force on 29 June 2004. The ITPGRFA's objectives are the conservation and sustainable use of plant genetic resources for food and agriculture, the fair and equitable sharing of benefits derived from their use, the promotion of sustainable agriculture and food security, and the protection of farmers rights.[59] More specifically, the Treaty aims at

> recognizing the enormous contribution of farmers to the diversity of crops that feed the world; establishing a global system to provide farmers, plant breeders and scientists with access to plant genetic materials [and] ensuring that recipients share benefits they derive from the use of these genetic materials with the countries where they have been originated.[60]

Article 9 recognizes the importance of TK by allowing for its preservation and protection through 'farmers rights'. Indeed, Article 9.2 provides that

> The Contracting Parties agree that the responsibility for realizing Farmers' Rights, as they relate to plant genetic resources for food and agriculture, rests with national governments.
>
> In accordance with their needs and priorities, each Contracting Party should, as appropriate, and subject to its national legislation, take measures to protect and promote Farmers' Rights, including: the (a) protection of traditional knowledge relevant to plant genetic resources for food and agriculture.[61]

Article 11.2 also establishes a 'Multilateral System of access and benefit sharing' to facilitate equitable access to designated categories of plant genetic resources for food and agriculture. The Multilateral System is an innovative solution that

> puts 64 of our most important crops – crops that together account for 80 percent of the food we derive from plants – into an easily accessible global pool of genetic resources that is freely available to potential users in the Treaty's ratifying nations for some uses.[62]

The Treaty also prevents the recipients of genetic resources from claiming IPR over them in the form of which they receive them. It ensures that 'access to genetic resources already protected by international property rights is consistent with international and national laws'.[63] Moreover, the members who experience benefits from

[59] Cordonier Segger and Phillips, *supra* note 40 at 432.
[60] www.fao.org/plant-treaty/overview/en/ accessed 30 November 2017.
[61] The International Treaty on Plant Genetic Resources for Food and Agriculture (2001).
[62] FAO www.fao.org/plant-treaty/overview/en/ accessed 30 November 2017.
[63] Ibid.

accessing genetic materials agree to share the benefits through the benefit sharing mechanisms established by the ITPGRFA.

### *Agreement on Trade-Related Aspects of Intellectual Property Rights*

The WTO's Agreement on Trade-Related Aspects of Intellectual Property Rights (TRIPS) was negotiated during the 1986–1994 Uruguay Round and introduced intellectual property rules into the multilateral trading system for the first time. The agreement sets out minimum standards of IPR protection in WTO Member States. The agreement covers five broad issues:

> how basic principles of the trading system and other international intellectual property agreements should be applied; how to give adequate protection to intellectual property rights; how countries should enforce those rights adequately in their own territories; how to settle disputes on intellectual property between members of the WTO and special transitional arrangements during the period when the new system is being introduced.[64]

The agreement does not address the issue of traditional knowledge, but several of its provisions (including those dealing with patents, geographical indications, and protection of undisclosed confidential information) could affect TK.[65] Patent provisions are controversial, as there is no legal obligation on the part of WTO members to protect TK in national legislation, and traditional knowledge often does not meet the patentability criteria of novelty under national regimes.[66] The TRIPS patent criteria actually 'deny recognition to indigenous innovations: the inter-communal and inter-generational context as well as the small-scale production of goods for social exchange and for the common good is not countenanced by the west-inspired IPR regime envisaged by TRIPS'.[67]

### *Intergovernmental Committee (IGC) on Intellectual Property and Genetic Resources, Traditional Knowledge and Folklore established under the World Intellectual Property Organization*

Established in 2000, the WIPO IGC is an international intergovernmental and multi-stakeholder body that serves as the principle forum for negotiations towards a binding instrument relating to TK.[68] WIPO IGC is also 'a forum where WIPO member states discuss the intellectual property issues that arise in the context of

[64] www.ic.gc.ca/eic/site/cipointernet-internetopic.nsf/eng/wr02323.html accessed 30 November 2017.

[65] Sarma and Barpujari, *supra* note 27 at 3.

[66] Ibid.

[67] Nijar, *supra* note 15 at 1206.

[68] F.-K. Phillips, 'Intellectual Property Rights in Traditional Knowledge: Enabler of Sustainable Development' (2016) 32:83 *Utrecht Journal of International and European Law* 1 at 9.

access to genetic resources and benefit-sharing'.[69] Its mandate is to continue facilitating substantive negotiations relating to the Draft Articles for the Protection of Traditional Knowledge renewed through 2017. The Draft Articles on TK were a response to shortcomings of the TRIPS system.[70] The aim of the Committee is to establish a *sui generis* instrument to provide ILCs with a legal framework for protection and enforcement of TK rights.[71] The IGC claims some important achievements such as the increased recognition of TK within the patent system. Moreover, 'in order to provide guidance on the IP aspects of mutually-agreed terms for fair and equitable benefit-sharing related to GRs, WIPO has developed, and regularly updates, an online database of relevant contractual practices' and 'has also prepared draft guidelines on IP clauses in access and benefit-sharing agreements'.[72] Also, as a result of a wide exchange of data and views between member states, the IGC has 'carried out numerous studies and developed other resources (such as glossaries, surveys of national experiences, a laws database and training programmes)'[73] relevant to national experiences and practices to protect TK and traditional cultural expressions. The studies have proved to useful for Member States and others. However, multiple critiques have been made of the limited role of Indigenous groups in the IGC.[74]

## *Sustainable Development Goals*

The 2030 Agenda for Sustainable Development was adopted by all UN Member States in 2015. The SDGs provide targets for the recognition of the role of TK. In fact,

> sustainable development requires establishing a functional balance between socio-economic development and environmental protection. Traditional knowledge plays an integral role in achieving global goals relating to sustainable development, as the practices and knowledge developed by indigenous and local communities implicitly endorses practices of conservation and sustainable use of biodiversity and natural resources.[75]

The inclusion of TK in the SDGs also bolsters the idea that IPRs for traditional knowledge can help enhance the socioeconomic development of ILCs. There are

69 WIPO (2015) www.wipo.int/edocs/pubdocs/en/wipo_pub_tk_2.pdf accessed 30 November 2017.

70 Ibid.

71 Ibid.

72 WIPO, Background Brief No. 2 www.wipo.int/export/sites/www/tk/en/documents/pdf/background_briefs-e-nx2-print.pdf accessed 30 November 2017.

73 Ibid.

74 See, e.g., V. Gordon, 'Appropriation without Representation – the Limited Role of Indigenous Groups in WIPO's Intergovernmental Committee on Intellectual Property and Genetic Resources, Traditional Knowledge, and Folklore' (2014) 16 *Vanderbilt Journal of Entertainment and Technology Law* 629–667.

75 Cordonier Segger and Phillips, *supra* note 40 at 430.

17 goals part of the SDGs. The second SDG, 'Zero Hunger', aims to end hunger, achieve food security and improved nutrition, and promote sustainable agriculture.

In particular, target 2.5 seeks, by 2020, to

> maintain the genetic diversity of seeds, cultivated plants and farmed and domesticated animals and their related wild species, including through soundly managed and diversified seed and plant banks at the national, regional and international levels, and promote access to and fair and equitable sharing of benefits arising from the utilization of genetic resources and associated traditional knowledge, as internationally agreed.

Moreover, the fifteenth goal, 'Life on Land', aims to protect, restore, and promote sustainable use of terrestrial ecosystems, sustainably manage forests, combat desertification, and halt and reverse land degradation and halt biodiversity loss. Indeed, target 15.6 calls on states to '[p]romote fair and equitable sharing of the benefits arising from the utilization of genetic resources and promote appropriate access to such resources, as internationally agreed'.

## CONTINUING TENSIONS BETWEEN TK AND IPRS: CONCEPTUAL AND PRACTICAL DIFFICULTIES

### *Traditional Knowledge and Western Concepts*

There are a number of perceived tensions between TK and IPRs,[76] including 'the dilemmas, the contradictions and some challenges that assail indigenous peoples and other loose categories of non-Western others in their bid to use local knowledge to leverage diverse economic, political and cultural interests'.[77] Besides, there is a history of 'exclusion, derogation and relation of local knowledge within the matrix of colonial culture and power hierarchies',[78] as well as the failure of TRIPS with respect to the protection of ILCs and TK, leaving a 'sour taste in the mouths of indigenous and local communities as well as in developing countries of the South'.[79] There is an 'inherent mismatch' between the notion of IPRs and TK, because the notion of IPRs is extremely Westernized; 'TK at the community level works under customary rules and this context is lost when the knowledge escapes into foreign systems'.[80] TK does not fit easily into Western conceptual categories such as the idea of intellectual property: '[w]hile IPRs aim to commodify or commercialize certain pieces of knowledge, this is generally not the purpose behind customary rights in

76 Phillips, *supra* note 68 at 4–6.
77 Oguamanam, *supra* note 6 at 30.
78 Ibid. at 34.
79 Ibid. at 31–32.
80 Sarma and Barpujari, *supra* note 27 at 2.

TK',[81] and '[t]he idea of "exclusivity" of rights under the IP system may conflict with customary law concepts of how knowledge and resources should be treated'.[82] However, we should also not presume that Indigenous communities do not have the concept of individual ownership of knowledge.[83]

Another issue that highlights the unsuitability of protecting TK in traditional intellectual property categories is the fixation requirement.[84] Patents and copyright tend to be limited in time, 'whereas traditional knowledge or folklore could exist for centuries before it is abandoned or forgotten'.[85] It is inappropriate to reduce the infinitude of TK to finite IPRs. The 'principled objection' here is that 'not all indigenous peoples are willing to commodify their traditional biogenetic resources and related traditional knowledge'.[86] Neoliberalization of the economy, and particularly the marketization and privatization of nature,[87] and even the 'scienticizing'[88] of Indigenous knowledge, are also in complete discordance with traditional Indigenous practices. When reflecting on neoliberalism, even the notion of sustainability differs from a neoliberal perspective versus an Indigenous worldview.[89] In fact, the Mi'kmaq of Nova Scotia explained that:

> Under neoliberalism, sustainability would be framed around self-interest and the market.[90] Differently, mainstream environmentalists would argue environmental preservation is sustainability, concentrating solely on non-human needs.[91] Indigenist theorists would support a community-based idea that includes nature, local economy development and tradition.[92]

One example is the case of the Kani community of southern India and their knowledge of the plant arogyapacha. The Kani shared the knowledge of the arogyapacha's anti-exhaustion potential with researchers from the Tropical Botanic Garden and Research Institute (TBGRI) for the Institute to develop the medicinal

81 Ibid.
82 Ibid.
83 Ibid.
84 Salako, *supra* note 3 at 326.
85 Ibid.
86 Salako, *supra* note 3 at 325–327. See also S. Vermeylen, 'From Life Force to Slimming Aid: Exploring Views on the Commodification of Traditional Medicinal Knowledge' (2008) 28 *Applied Geography* 224–235; Nagan, *supra* note 53 at 155–156.
87 Bavikatte and Robinson, *supra* note 7 at 39–40.
88 Whitman, *supra* note 2 at 25.
89 Ibid. at 95.
90 V. Tauli-Corpus (2006), 'Our Right to Remain Separate and Distinct', in J. Mander and V. Tauli-Corpus (eds.), *Paradigm Wars: Indigenous Peoples' Resistance to Globalization* (Sierra Club Books 2006) 13–21.
91 W. LaDuke, 'Traditional Ecological Knowledge and Environmental Futures' (2005) 5 *Colorado Journal of International Environmental Law and Policy* 127–148. W. LaDuke, *Recovering the Sacred: The Power of Naming and Claiming* (Between the Lines 2005).
92 L. Little Bear, 'Jagged Worldview Colliding', in M. Battiste (ed.), *Reclaiming Indigenous Voice and Vision* (University of British Columbia Press 2000) 77–85.

use of the plant into a drug called Jeevani. In exchange for royalties, the Institute manufactured and distributed Jeenavi, even though 'only a small portion of the Kani community was consulted when the agreement with the company was made' and 'many elders from the community [felt] that their traditional knowledge, including knowledge about arogyapacha, [was] sacred and should never be shared'.[93] While some of the impacts may have been positive, there have been many challenges, such as the conflict within the Kani community. Moreover, the arogyapacha plant is now considered endangered as a result of over-harvesting.

### *The Case of the Karbi and IPRs*

The Karbi are one of the most important indigenous ethnic tribes in Northeast India and especially in the hill areas of Assam. The district of Karbi Anglong is particularly rich in biodiversity and TK based on it. The Karbi used plants to 'treat ailments as varied as leprosy, malaria, ulcers, dysentery, fever, and gynecological problems',[94] and a recent study documents that 'almost 434 species of medicinal and aromatic plants found in Karbi Anglong are used to treat many ailments'.[95] The Karbi people possess two kinds of knowledge: the common knowledge, which is what most men and women know about available herbs and plants, and the specialist knowledge, confined to a few. Unlike common knowledge, specialist knowledge is generally confined to the 'higher' social group in the community and is transmitted from one generation to the next within the same family or clan.[96]

Moreover, specialist knowledge is gendered. The organization around specialist knowledge and who holds such knowledge is extremely complex. The main difference between the two types of knowledge is that while 'the Karbi generally have no reticence regarding the sharing of the common knowledge, the specialist knowledge is, however, closely guarded and remains confined to a very small group in the community'.[97] Even though specialists have been asked about the commercialization of knowledge, they have always been extremely reluctant concerning the idea and explained that commercialization would result in handing over the knowledge to outsiders, 'in whose hands it would fail to have the desired efficacy', and that

93 https://naturaljustice.org/wp-content/uploads/2015/09/Access-and-Benefit-Sharing.pdf accessed 30 November 2017.

94 S.K. Jain and S.K. Borthakur, 'Ethnobotany of the Mikirs of India' (1980) 34(3) *Economic Botany* 264–272.

95 U.K. Sarma and J. Barpujari, 'Revisiting the Debate on Intellectual Property Rights and Traditional Knowledge of Biodiversity: Accommodating Local Realities and Perspectives' (2019) 3(4) *The International Indigenous Policy Journal* https://ir.lib.uwo.ca/iipj/vol3/iss4/1 accessed 30 November 2017.

96 See, e.g., R. Chennells, 'Traditional Knowledge and Benefit Sharing after the Nagoya Protocol: Three Cases from South Africa' (2013) 9:2 *Law, Environment and Development Journal* 163.

97 Sarma and Barpujari, *supra* note 27 at 5.

outsiders would put a price on the knowledge, which would clash with their ethics.[98] This argument is exactly what we have mentioned above: the clash between TK and the neoliberal perspective. The Karbi specialists appear to be apprehensive regarding IPRs.

However, it is extremely interesting to examine the different points of view between the elders of the Karbi society and the youth. In fact, the younger generations,

> particularly those who are educated, are of the view that the tribe should have proprietary rights over its knowledge and if this knowledge is commercialized (which is acceptable to most of them), then the community, in general, and the specialists, in particular, should be entitled to a share of the profits.[99]

Furthermore, young members of the community believe that it is important for the knowledge to be documented and protected through legal means, including IPRs.

### *Romanticizing the Indigenous Ecological Ethos*

Finally, it is important to mention that we must avoid romanticizing the 'Indigenous ecological ethos'.[100] Indeed,

> it is often taken as a given that the worldview and religious beliefs of many Indigenous communities living in close communion with nature are often rooted in nature and speak of affinity with the plant and animal world, which, in turn, leads to sustainable use and conservation of nature.[101]

The term 'ecological ethnicity' is used to describe such cultures and communities. Just like the rest of the world, Indigenous communities' level of ecological consciousness will vary significantly with the material conditions, nature of livelihoods, level of technological development in which they live, and they tend to become 'increasingly drawn into the local, if not world, economy'.[102]

For example, the Karbis have a deep feeling of oneness with the natural world. However, under the impact of modernization and market economy, the Karbis face many changes, including the abandoning of their traditional religion. In fact, in the case of the Karbis of Inglepathar or Chandrasingh Rongigaon, data indicate that youths 'increasingly are being drawn to the lucrative trade of forest produce, such as supplying bamboo to the paper mills, which has resulted in very high levels

98 Ibid.

99 Ibid.

100 Sarma and Barpujari, *supra* note 24 at 5.

101 D. Western, and R.M. Wright, 'The Background to Community-Based Conservation', in D. Western and R. M. Wright (eds.), *Natural Connections: Perspectives in Community-Based Conservation* (Island Press 1995) 1–12.

102 Sarma and Barpujari, *supra* note 27 at 5.

of deforestation in recent times'.[103] The way the bamboo is extracted is unsustainable, as it also leads to the loss of other herbs, roots, etc. which used to play an important role in traditional medicine systems of food for the Karbis. Moreover, it is interesting to observe that because of the deforestation, 'the role of women, who used to collect seasonal herbs, roots, tubers from the nearby forests, is undergoing rapid change' and 'the role of the traditional medicine men, who used to treat common ailments with a combination of divination, medicinal plants and some sacred chanting, is also changing, owing to a preference for modern medicine'.[104] In the case of the Karbis, ecological ethnicity is slowly disappearing as a result of modernization.

### *The Lack of Conceptual Clarity in the Notion of Benefit Sharing*

A growing number of international legal materials refer to benefit sharing 'with regard to natural resource use (extractive activities, forest and water management, tourism, the use of marine resources, land use, and food production), environmental protection (biodiversity conservation and the fight against climate change), and the use of knowledge'.[105] However, there has been an overall lack of conceptual clarity in the notion of benefit sharing as 'benefit sharing is employed in international law to connote a treaty objective, an international obligation, a right, a safeguard, or a mechanism'. The CBD has benefit sharing as one of its objectives (art. 1) but none of the terms 'fair', 'equitable', 'share', or 'benefit' is defined in the Convention. There is no instance in which it has been unequivocally understood, fully developed, or made satisfactorily operational.[106]

Another difficulty regarding benefit sharing lies with power asymmetries in the relations to which benefit sharing applies. On the ground, benefit sharing has been seen as a 'disingenuous win-win rhetoric' that leads to the loss of control and access over resources by the vulnerable through 'narrative framings of the global public good' and 'dominating knowledge approaches'.[107] Therefore, 'a distinction needs to be drawn between benefit sharing among states (inter-state benefit sharing) and benefit sharing within states (intra-state benefit sharing between governments and communities)'[108] for the purposes of conceptual clarity.

Finally, a popular misconception assumes that the benefits of benefit sharing are purely monetary. First of all, 'in those cases where the use of genetic resources is commercial, any royalties arise between ten and twenty years – and sometimes many

[103] Ibid.
[104] Ibid.
[105] Morgera, *supra* note 37 at 356.
[106] Ibid. at 354–355.
[107] A. Martin et al., 'Just Conservation? On the Fairness of Sharing Benefits', in T. Sikor (ed.), *The Justices and Injustices of Ecosystem Services* (Routledge 2014) 69–91 at 84–88.
[108] Morgera, *supra* note 37 at 356.

more – after the original access to genetic resources',[109] and those cases are rather rare. For the development of a new drug, for example, benefit sharing can actually come in non-monetary forms, including sharing of taxonomic and ecosystem information, employment of local people, technology transfer, donation of equipment, and joint authorship on patents.[110] The lack of definitions, explicit benefit sharing requirements, and general clarity around the concept of benefit sharing presents a barrier to its implementation.

One case that embodies the challenges of benefit sharing related to the clarity of the concept is the San and Hoodia case in South Africa. Hoodia is a desert plant traditionally used by the local communities to suppress hunger on long hunting trips. In order to explore the potential for diet products derived from Hoodia, an agreement was signed between a board alliance of San communities and the Council for Scientific and Industrial Research. However, 'the legitimacy of the process and the agreement itself were challenged by the Nama, another community indigenous to Southern African that also traditionally used Hoodia and shared the same knowledge'.[111] Finally, 'the agreement was further undermined by lack of clarity of how the financial benefits would be managed and distributed amongst the communities, with many questioning the accountability of the Hoodia Trust that was established to safeguard the funds', which shows that, again, there is a need for clarification around the concept of benefit sharing.

## CONCLUSION

This chapter has discussed the many facets of the relationship between TK and genetic resources, highlighting the importance of TK for the indigenous communities which possess it and the larger global community which could benefit from it. The chapter also discussed the ways in which this relationship can be beneficial – or detrimental – to current generations of these communities as well as those around the world who could realize important improvements in their health through TK. While this is certainly an issue of the present, it necessarily impacts future generations and the foundations of intergenerational equity and justice because of the effects it can have on the knowledge and resources transferred and available to coming generations.

[109] CBD www.cbd.int/doc/meetings/abs/absep-01/other/absep-01-equitable-en.pdf accessed 30 November 2017.

[110] Ibid.

[111] https://naturaljustice.org/wp-content/uploads/2015/09/Access-and-Benefit-Sharing.pdf accessed 30 November 2017.

# 28

# Local Indigenous Planning Instruments for Intergenerational Equity in Ahousaht Traditional Territories of Canada

*Tara Dawn Atleo*

This chapter explores the planning and policy tools developed by local indigenous communities to approach cultural significance valuation (CSV), and to consider their potential contributions to the promotion of intergenerational equity. As envisioned and applied, these tools offer a unique and essential method of allowing current generations to define the way in which lands and areas of cultural value will be passed on to and experienced by future generations.

Land use planning (LUP), sustainable development, and forest carbon are important today because of the potentially devastating global and local impacts of climate change. Improving and understanding new and culturally appropriate approaches to non-market valuation and issues of resource use in indigenous traditional territories is essential in achieving the SDGs, including SDG 13 on climate change, SDG 1 towards the eradication of poverty, SDG 3 for good health and well-being, and SDGs 14 and 15 for life below water and life on land. This is also crucial for the implementation of the Paris Agreement, as the cultural values of indigenous communities represented in the UNDRIP often align with the values of sustainable development and can be an important part of the solutions.[1]

To achieve the primary purpose, this chapter has four objectives. First, it examines the uses of non-market valuation on issues of cultural heritage, and identifies the challenges and shortcomings pertaining to CSV in the traditional territories of indigenous communities. Next, it summarizes the research findings from three LUP processes that were mandated and guided by the community of Ahousaht for their traditional territories. Third, it uses these findings to discuss a method for calculating cultural significance which utilizes land use designations from the community's own planning tools and adheres to their traditional laws and practices. Finally, it links progress on indigenous valuation with delivering on the global Paris Agreement, and SDG 13 on Climate Action, within the context of the UN DRIP.

[1] Paris Agreement on Climate Change (2015).

## BACKGROUND

### Non-Market Valuation

Non-market valuation is commonly used to assess environmental goods by applying monetary values to goods that do not have a tradeable market. A valuation is done by assessing the use and non-use values of a good through survey or market comparison and then applying a calculated monetary value. Most valuations utilize either use value or non-use value exclusively; however, there is a scenario where both may be used – a valuation of culturally significant areas (CSA) from the perspective of local indigenous peoples. These areas apply both use and non-use values because indigenous people have a connection to the land that cannot be captured solely within the non-use categories of existence, option, or bequest values. As explained by one Ahousaht elder, some areas can be 'so sacred that no one goes there', indicating both a use and non-use value in this case. The concept of applying non-market valuation to CSAs was derived from the techniques used within cultural heritage economics, which aim to value objects and areas with cultural value that cannot be attributed to a market. Using planning tools developed by the local community, such as LUP, and culture variables, such as traditional law, for calculating valuation provides a more accurate account of the good being analysed by specifying the calculation to reflect the interests of the local inhabitants.

### Ahousaht First Nation

The traditional territory of the Ahousaht people, a member nation of the Nuu-chah-nulth, is on the west coast of Vancouver Island in British Columbia (BC), Canada, in an area known widely as Clayoquot Sound. The Ahousaht people have occupied these territories for thousands of years, though have had to work to reclaim rights, governance, and ownership over their traditional territories since the arrival of non-indigenous populations in the 1800s and the implementation of the Indian Act (1985) in Canada in 1876. Despite these violations of rights and traditional land title, Ahousaht adheres to its traditional law and follows the principle of *hišuukiš cawak* (pronounced hish-ook-ish tsa-wok) by applying it throughout their modern dealings with industry and government. The concept of *hišuukiš cawak*, translated to English as 'everything is one and interconnected', is a principle of the Nuu-chah-nulth people and represents the spiritual and historic metaphysical connection that people have to the land.[2] Resource industries, including fisheries, forestry, and finfish and shellfish farming, have been impacting the region since first contact, demonstrating a need for strategic valuation of the CSAs to the people of Ahousaht.

[2] E.R. Atleo, *Tsawalk – A Nuu-Chah-Nulth Worldview* (University of British Columbia Press 2004).

Due to the high impact of industries on the traditional territories, Ahousaht developed conservation work, including watershed planning and recommended forest practices through a scientific panel, to help protect CSAs from development, while sacrificing some areas to pursue opportunities to benefit the community economically.[3] As important as the CSAs are to the Ahousaht people for their cultural practices, spiritual use, and balance within the natural surroundings, the need for economic opportunities in the remote area requires that some areas be allocated for resource development. Non-market valuation can be used as a tool for translating the significance of these areas while ensuring Ahousaht's cultural and economic interests are recognized by those looking to develop or access the traditional territories.[4] This valuation tool could then be used to appropriately appraise specific development opportunities and resource use.

## *Land Use Designations*

A series of community meetings beginning in early 2015 focused on LUP and concluded after the Ahousaht traditional territories were divided into designations for both conservation and development purposes. Out of the several area designations developed, the Forest Management Areas (FMAs) were defined by the community as 'Forested areas suitable for commercial forest restoration, enhancement and development by Ahousaht'.

Allowable activities within these areas include forest harvest, silviculture, and restoration, and the potential for carbon offset projects. Though forest-based carbon credits may appear to be the ideal scenario for LUP because they focus on conservation while simultaneously generating revenue and providing opportunity for other stewardship opportunities such as eco-tourism, a deeper analysis is required to fully understand the costs and benefits associated with the allocation of carbon offsets. Currently, the FMAs are the only areas available for carbon credit projects because of the early conservation work done by the Ahousaht people through watershed planning. This pre-emptive attempt at preservation and protection from industry is a setback in the case of carbon offsets, as these areas cannot qualify under the 'business as usual' policy, discussed later in this chapter, since there is no intent to harvest. The valuation then lies within the accepted loss in potential income, with the community knowing that it would be forgoing economic opportunity that would be brought to traditional territories through harvest, and instead accepting the revenues from a set term of carbon credit sales.

[3] H.S. Mabee and G. Hoberg, 'Protecting Culturally Significant Areas through Watershed Planning in Clayoquot Sound' (2004) 80(2) *The Forestry Chronicle* 229–240.

[4] R. Snyder, D.R. Williams and G. Peterson, 'Culture Loss and Sense of Place in Resource Valuation: Economics, Anthropology, and Indigenous Cultures', in S. Jentoft, H. Minde and R. Nilsen (eds.), *Indigenous Peoples: Resource Management and Global Rights* (Eburon 2003) 107–123.

## VALUATION, INDIGENOUS TRADITIONAL TERRITORIES, AND CULTURAL ECOSYSTEM SERVICES

### *Environmental Valuation*

The application of non-market valuation in economic analysis is a useful tool that is becoming more prevalent in development and natural resource industries. Non-market valuation is defined within welfare economics, and it is used to create a market or market price for a good that does not normally participate in a tradeable market. Though the concept of non-market valuation can seem controversial owing to the application of a monetary value to otherwise non-valuable public goods, attempts have been made to articulate the use of non-market valuation on issues of cultural heritage.[5] Within the study of cultural heritage economics, these valuation techniques are mostly applied to historic buildings and artefacts, as well as landmarks that hold significant value – both use and non-use – to certain people or to the identity of a region.[6]

Although theorists do not specifically address areas with spiritual significance, the application of valuation to objects and places deemed as 'price-less' and 'irreplaceable' is an important concept, as it can include the otherwise excluded social surplus to impact studies.[7] Others have echoed this view, for example by using an analysis of national parks in the US and stressing the importance of value-based analysis in order to incorporate and respect the various interests of a specific place.[8] Such studies, which have provided a definition of 'cultural values' as 'the shared meanings associated with people's lives, environments, and actions that draw upon cultural affiliation' is critical because the definition of 'culture' can be misunderstood or wrongfully defined in some cases, drastically impacting valuation studies.[9] Further, in terms of value, it must be noted here that some studies highlight the ongoing stewardship of indigenous people within their traditional territory, guided by their cultural practices and historical connection, as assisting the resilience of ecosystems within these territories, promoting longevity and diversity.[10]

[5] B. Frey, 'Evaluating Cultural Property: The Economic Approach' (1997) 6(2) *International Journal of Cultural Property* 6 231–246.

[6] S. Navrud and R.C. Ready (eds.), *Valuing Cultural Heritage: Applying Environmental Valuation Techniques to Historic Buildings, Monuments and Artifacts* (Edward Elgar 2002).

[7] See Frey, *supra* note 5.

[8] S. Scheld, D.H. Taplin and S.M. Low, 'The Values-Based Approach for Cultural-Heritage Preservation in US Public Parks' (2014) 45 (2/3) *Association for Preservation Technology International (APT) Bulletin* 49–56.

[9] See ibid.

[10] J. Salick and A. Byg, *Indigenous Peoples and Climate Change* (University of Oxford and Missouri Botanical Garden 2007); A. Johnston, *Is the Sacred for Sale? Tourism and Indigenous Peoples* (Earthscan 2006); P. Hawken, *Blessed Unrest* (Penguin Books 2007).

### *Cultural Significance Valuation*

Culture significance is well defined under cultural ecosystem services (CES), which are defined as 'the non-material benefits people obtain from ecosystems through spiritual enrichment, cognitive development, reflection, recreation and aesthetic experiences'.[11] Generally, the functions of ecosystem services are to 'help capture the economic value of natural assets to local people' by 'making visible the functions of the natural environment in terms of ecological processes that are necessary for human well-being'.[12]

Categories of CES recognized by the Millennium Ecosystem Assessment (MEA) are the following: heritage values, cultural identity, spiritual services, inspiration, aesthetic appreciation of natural and cultivated landscapes, tourism, and recreation.[13] Each of these applies to issues of cultural significance in indigenous traditional territories, indicating a use for CES in such cases. However, what is missing in the CES definition and its categories is a discussion of mutual impact between land and people. For example, Dr E. Richard Atleo, known as *Umeek*, of the Ahousaht people, when discussing the causal link between people and the land, states that although there is no scientific proof of this mutual link, it is a strong belief and practice within the Ahousaht and other indigenous communities that the land and people are interrelated and interconnected.[14] Acknowledging this belief in addition to CES will strengthen valuations of cultural significance pertaining to indigenous traditional territory so that the work and cultural practices of the community can be fully integrated from the initial steps of valuation, and potentially solve challenges that arise in cultural heritage non-market valuation.

Many of the areas of cultural significance being studied for valuation are within the traditional territories of indigenous communities, and in many cases are rich in resources and therefore are at risk of being developed.[15] Though there is a shortage of studies which use the local communities' tools and culture as the baseline in the valuation process, it is important to begin to understand this approach when working

[11] M. Hernández-Morcillo et al., 'An Empirical Review of Cultural Ecosystem Service Indicators' (2013) 29 *Ecological Indicators* 434–444.

[12] R. Kent and A. Dorward, 'Conceptualising Assets and Asset Services in Livelihoods and Ecosystem Analyses: A Framework for Considering Livelihood Responses to Biodiversity Change', Working paper, Centre for Development, Environment and Policy, School of Oriental and African Studies (SOAS), University of London, London (2012).

[13] A. Tengberg, 'Cultural Ecosystem Services Provided by Landscapes: Assessment of Heritage Values and Identity' (2012) 2 *Ecosystem Services* 14–26; Millennium Assessment, 'Ecosystems and Human Well-Being: Current State and Trends: Findings of the Conditions and Trends Working Group', in R. Hassan, R. Scholes and N. Ash (eds.), *Ecosystems and Human Well-Being: Current State and Trends, Volume 1. Findings of the Condition and Trends Working Group of the Millennium Ecosystem Assessment* (Island Press 2005).

[14] E.R. Atleo, *Principles of Tsawalk: An Indigenous Approach to Global Crisis* (University of British Columbia Press 2001).

[15] Mabee and Hoberg, *supra* note 3.

with indigenous communities so that appropriate and locally relevant decisions can be made to help maximize benefits to local inhabitants while also ensuring effective environmental decision making for climate change mitigation and resilience. Local indigenous knowledge will aid nations to comply with the new Paris Agreement on climate change, as they can develop mitigation efforts on a regional basis to better suit the needs and action necessary to reduce emissions.

### *Impact of Industry in British Columbia Indigenous Traditional Territory*

Industry presents many challenges when operating within indigenous traditional territories in BC, notably that

> the potential for destruction and altercation of spiritually significant landscapes typically stems from misunderstanding[.] The problem centres on inadequate definition of what indigenous peoples mean when they assert that the landscape has ancient and profound spiritual significance.[16]

The application of non-market valuation to cultural heritage is highly relevant to living cultures that are active today and are faced with challenges of development and industry encroaching on their lands and way of being, rather than only focusing on historical sites and tourism or recreation attractions. Given its 198 indigenous communities, the most by province in Canada, and expansive natural resource extraction industries working within traditional territories, BC is an ideal location to test this concept.

Though indigenous people have the best understanding and methods of preservation within their traditional territories, these communities also understand that in order to provide economically for their people and ensure that industry does not gain full control over land use, they must be open to exploring development and natural resource extraction opportunities including forestry, mining, fish farms, and now carbon markets.

Carbon markets are a rather new option for forest management in BC, aligning with Article 5.1 of the Paris Agreement's exhortation to 'take action to conserve and enhance, as appropriate, sinks and reservoirs of greenhouse gases as referred to in Article 4, paragraph 1 (d), of the Convention, including forests'.[17] Despite the breadth of forestry activity throughout the province, few studies have focused on the forest management issues of carbon credits versus harvesting.[18]

[16] J. Lewis and S. Sheppard, '"Indigenous" Spiritual Conceptions of Forests and Forest Management', in D.B. Tindall, R.I. Trosper and P. Perreault (eds.), *Aboriginal Peoples and Forest Lands in Canada* (University of British Columbia Press 2013).

[17] UNFCCC, Adoption of the Paris Agreement, 21st Conference of the Parties (2015).

[18] W.S. Schwenk et al., 'Carbon Storage, Timber Production, and Biodiversity: Comparing Ecosystem Services with Multi-Criteria Decision Analysis' (2012) 22(5) *Ecological Applications* 1612–1627. Out of these few studies, Munro is one who mentions the BC First Nations cultural interests, but she specifically states that these interests are not included into

However, omission of the valuation of CSAs weakens the conclusion because of the omission of culture and a significant interest of the affected community.[19] Under BC legislation, carbon credits are applicable only to areas that have plans to be harvested or developed and are therefore allowable in the Ahousaht FMAs. When the sale of carbon credits occurs, the buyer buys the right to pollute up to the amount equal to what would be polluted if the same amount of trees were harvested. Therefore, the seller sells the rights to pollute and gives up the option to harvest. Though harvest cannot happen, areas that have sold carbon credits are still available for economic and cultural activity as long as they do not impact the carbon storage of the forest. Due to Ahousaht's proactive conservation efforts through watershed planning, a minimal area has been set aside for FMAs, meaning that a smaller portion than desired is available for carbon credit allocation due to the 'business as usual' policy, which states that the carbon credit areas must have plans to be developed prior to sale.[20] These FMAs areas also have lower quality trees because they were harvested previously, resulting in lower revenues for carbon credits than would have been available in the pristine areas of Ahousaht territories.

In contrast, other methods of cultural heritage valuations focus on the utility of people who are non-indigenous to the area of study.[21] One method used in these studies is the travel cost method, which focuses mainly on tourism interest by examining transportation and travel costs associated with reaching a particular destination. In other cases, the cultural heritage valuation assesses the cultural good or area as valuable in the past tense, similar to sacred artefacts stored in museums, when in fact the greatest importance and values lie with the local inhabitants who have deep-rooted connections to the lands including but not limited to cultural structures and artefacts within the traditional territories. What these valuations fail to recognize is that, in many cases, the subject areas and artefacts are a part of cultural values which are still practised today, and that, rather than viewing such cultures as that of a luxury good or tourism destination, they should be recognized for their significance to living and thriving communities.[22] The sharing of cultural knowledge has also been a sensitive issue within indigenous communities, as many feel that requests to gain access to this knowledge is another form of resource

her analysis. H. Munro, 'Economic Trade-Offs between Carbon Offset and Timber Opportunities in British Columbia's Central Coast: A Decision Analysis Approach' (Master of Resource Management Thesis, Simon Fraser University 2014).

[19] See Munro, *supra* note 18.

[20] David Suzuki Foundation, *Carbon Offsets* (David Suzuki Foundation 2014).

[21] P. Boxall et al., 'The Contribution of Aboriginal Rock Paintings to Wilderness Recreation Values in North America', in S. Navrud and R.C. Ready (eds.), *Valuing Cultural Heritage: Applying Environmental Valuation Techniques to Historic Buildings, Monuments and Artifacts* (Edward Elgar 2002) chapter 8; M. Boyland, 'The Economics of Using Forests to Increase Carbon Storage' (2006) 36 (September) *Canadian Journal of Forest Research* 2223–2234; Frey, *supra* note 5.

[22] Johnston, *supra* note 10.

exploitation, since many times throughout history this knowledge has been taken out of context and has even been used against indigenous people in order to gain access to the valuable resources within their territories.[23]

As indigenous people become more influential decision makers of development within their traditional territories in BC and Canada, particularly as a result of recent court case decisions, valuations that do not include their cultural interests can be recognized as dismissive and outdated.[24] BC regulation now mandates accommodation of indigenous cultural interests and values, specifically that the communities' interests are worked into forest management plans for all forestry operations in traditional territories.[25]

## *The Importance of Indigenous Perspectives*

The perspective of local inhabitants is a crucial component of accurate valuations, as it represents all of the critical measures evaluated within cultural heritage economic valuations, including but not limited to matters such as tourism. Local input on archaeological inventory is also necessary because it preserves and recognizes sites of ancestral importance to these impacted communities.[26] The indigenous people of Canada are just one example of communities who still practise their culture and face great challenges involving foreign development and industry activity within their traditional territories. An inclusive concept such as this has been missing within the realm of natural resource industry operations in indigenous traditional territories, as there has been a disconnect since first contact between indigenous and non-indigenous in terms of translating the unbreakable bond between indigenous people and the land. As a result of this disconnect, non-indigenous communities have, for the most part, continued extraction to fit their own needs rather than including CSV into management plans. Consultation with indigenous has been made mandatory in BC when operating within traditional territories, and validated through Canada's endorsement of the UN DRIP, although the disconnect still exists because of the significant challenge in finding ways and words to interpret indigenous connection to the land, making it challenging to understand exactly what these territories mean to indigenous people.[27]

[23] M.G. Stevenson, 'Indigenous Knowledge in Environmental Assessment' (1996) 48(3) *Arctic* 278–291.

[24] *Tsilhqot'in Nation* v. *British Columbia* (2014) SCR 257, SCC 44.

[25] A. Mason, 'Cultural Resource Management in the Context of Forestry in British Columbia: Existing Conditions and New Opportunities', in D.B. Tindall, R.L. Trosper and P. Perreault (eds.), *Aboriginal Peoples and Forest Lands in Canada* (University of British Columbia Press 2013) 161–179.

[26] P. Nijkamp and P. Riganti, 'Valuing Urban Cultural Heritage', in L.F. Girard and P. Nijkamp, *Cultural Tourism and Sustainable Local Development* (Ashgate Publishing Limited 2009) 57–72.

[27] Lewis and Sheppard, *supra* note 16.

## APPLICATION OF TOOLS FOR CURRENT AND FUTURE GENERATIONS

For this chapter, data on the use of planning and policy tools for CSV in Ahousaht traditional territories was gathered through observation, interviews, and review of minutes of community meetings. These community meetings were hosted by the hereditary chiefs and held exclusively for Ahousaht members to gather input, opinions, and knowledge around developing a land use plan within the Ahousaht traditional territories. This gathering of qualitative data was done at the community level, and supplemented with individual interviews, to reflect the Assembly of First Nations (AFN) cultural beliefs and practices of engaging the community as a collective whole for decisions that affect well-being for present and future generations.[28]

### *Land Use Planning*

The LUP process was a critical step for the Ahousaht community in their work towards self-governance. The process began in early 2015, and the final community consultation was completed in June of 2016. Results from past studies and consultations were included in the initial planning presented to the community at the first round of meetings, including research and results from the Clayoquot Sound Scientific Panel[29] and the Watershed Plans.[30] New community consultations for primary data collection for this study were carried out through LUP community meetings, which took place in urban areas to involve the off-reserve Ahousaht community members, and also on reserve in the main Ahousaht community of Maaqtusiis. At the first round of community meetings for the LUP process, community members were asked to share their ideal image of the territories, disregarding any systems which were put in place without consulting Ahousaht, such as BC and Canada Parks and private land sales.

The first round of meetings began in Ahousaht, then proceeding to Victoria and Port Alberni. Seventy-seven community members attended this first round of meetings, where the 'ideal future' for the Ahousaht traditional territories was discussed, developing into the land use designations used in this process. The second round of meetings included the same three cities as the first round as well as Nanaimo because of the high population of Ahousaht members residing in the city for post-secondary school and work opportunities.

Additionally, a third round of community meetings took place in Victoria and then Port Alberni, as well as two sessions which took place in Ahousaht: one with high school students and one that was open to all community members. A total of

[28] Atleo 2004, *supra* note 2.

[29] Clayoquot Sound Scientific Panel, *Report of the Scientific Panel for the Sustainable Forest Practices in Clayoquot Sound* (Report Ministry of Forests, Lands and Natural Resources 1994).

[30] Ibid.

162 community members attended the third round of meetings, where they were presented with a finalized copy of the map and designation definitions for their review and approval. All of these meetings prompted discussion regarding past and present LUP, both in the group setting and in informal private sessions.

Indigenous land use designations were developed by the community from these meetings, and once outlined and mapped, were brought back to the community for refinement. These designations included cultural and natural areas, FMAs, shoreline and island management areas, marine harvest bays, watershed management areas, and community development areas. At each round of community meetings, the designations and map boundaries were adjusted according to the community feedback until a final draft could be brought back for community approval. The final draft was approved by the community collectively at meetings held in Victoria, Port Alberni, and Ahousaht in June of 2016. It was concluded that the Ahousaht language being used to describe the designations and the allowable activities within them needed to be worked through further, but the designations and mapping could be finalized.

### *Forest Management Areas*

Once the land use designations were established, the community provided interpretations of these designations in the Ahousaht traditional language to accurately portray the uses and prohibitions within each designation. The definitions and guidelines of each designation along with the interpretation of the traditional names given by the Ahousaht people to each designation indicate a level of cultural significance based on the allowable and prohibited activities within each area.

This was useful not only in the context of the Ahousaht but also for current and future generations wishing to conduct similar activities and ensure significant input into the planning process. Other communities will be able to mimic this model using their own land use visioning relevant to their specific needs without having to adopt Ahousaht's values as their own.

FMAs were designated for 12 per cent of the traditional territories, with the options for development outlined as either harvest or carbon credit allocation, as allowable activities include forest harvesting and associated infrastructure development, forest restoration, and silviculture, as well as road access to these areas. The areas designated as FMAs specifically were chosen for past forestry use, access, and environmental impact. A significant portion of the FMAs has been previously harvested; therefore, harvesting second growth would be the option if harvest were to move forward. These areas are expected to have the lowest cultural significance, as they have been previously accessed for logging; therefore, cultural use, if any, is minimal. The community was open to exploring opportunities for REDD+ carbon offsets, on the condition that the authenticity and intentions of the sales were up to standards, meaning that the sales were to legitimately offset carbon emissions or to be a wholehearted investment in CSR. The community expressed the desire to be knowledgeable about the sale of the credits, and that it is unwilling to participate in sales that are not in accordance with the internationally agreed and legitimate parameters or to organizations whose emissions far exceed offsets available within Ahousaht traditional territories. The reasoning behind this reflects an immediate concern for the impact of carbon offset activities and a concern about the impact of these activities on future generations.

Carbon credit sales work on a contract basis such that the selected forests cannot be harvested for a certain period of time. In the case of the Ahousaht traditional territories, the carbon credit agreement will be based on a 100-year term, meaning that no development can happen within that area during that time. This timeline poses some challenges in the valuation calculation, one example being population growth.[31]

### *Cultural Significance Valuation*

For this analysis the stated preference ordinal scale attribute-based method was identified as being most effective because of the need to consider both use and non-use values in order to adhere to the cultural practices of the Ahousaht people and their rightful ownership over the territories.[32] It is also necessary that the concept of infinity be considered in this unique case to obey the assumptions of the Ahousaht principle of *hišuukiš cawak*.[33] The steps for processing attribute-based methods have been explained as follows:

(1) Characterize the decision problem;
(2) Identify and describe the attributes;
(3) Develop the experimental design;
(4) Develop questionnaire;
(5) Collect data;
(6) Estimate model; and
(7) Interpret results for policy analysis or decision support.[34]

These steps were used to work through this analysis in a manner that can be duplicated in other scenarios.

31 As of June 2016 the population of Ahousaht members, both on and off reserve, was 2,135 and has an average annual growth rate of 2.74 per cent (Statistics Canada 2016).

32 Stated preference ordinal scale attribute-based refers to data collected in a manner by which the respondent ranks their preference against a set number of other options. W. Adamowicz, J. Louviere and J. Swait, *Introduction to Attribute-Based Stated Choice Methods. Report to NOAA Resource Valuation Branch, Damage Assessment Centre* (NOAA 1998).

33 Atleo 2004, *supra* note 2.

34 T. P. Holmes and W.L. Adamowicz, 'Attribute-Based Methods', in P.A. Champ, K.J. Boyle and T.C. Brown, *The Economics of Non-Market Goods and Resources – A Primer on Nonmarket Valuation* (Kluwer Academic Publishers 2003) 176.

Barriers in receiving short-term training for higher level positions mean that Ahousaht people living in the community would, most likely, only be able to access entry-level forestry positions, though in this analysis the highest potential employment income for an Ahousaht person from harvest was used as the benchmark to more accurately represent the maximum economic benefit that the community would be willing to forgo in order to still have access to these areas for cultural use.

Using income in the valuation calculation was not a viable reference, culturally or socially, because of the high poverty rate on Canadian indigenous reserves, which includes the Ahousaht community. Living on reserve, especially remotely, restricts earning capacity and would therefore skew the true valuation in this case. Culture in this case is not a luxury good as implied by other studies showcasing the importance of tourism and preservation for archaeological purposes, but is a real-time necessity for the livelihoods of the people who practise the culture and are rooted to the land. It is also an essential aspect of intergenerational equity preservation, in that it is incumbent upon current generations to provide for the proper valuation of culture so that it can be passed on to the future generations.

The valuation of the cultural significance of the FMAs in this case is the economic opportunity that the community is willing to give up in order to maintain access to these areas for cultural purposes, be it for use or non-use, as a result of the community's decision to zone the FMAs as development areas. As development areas, the FMAs are designed to generate revenue and economic opportunities for the community and it is the choice of the community as to which revenue-generating activity they want to implement, which would be either forestry or carbon offset projects, as they are the two possibilities within the FMAs as stated in their definition. In this way, the community is the repository of decision making and valuation, allowing it to act as a key figure in preserving culture and transmitting it in a way that is mindful of intergenerational equity.

## RESULTS AND IMPACTS FOR CURRENT AND FUTURE GENERATIONS

### *Carbon Offsets vs. Harvest*

Results reflected the community's decision to explore the option of Reducing Emissions from Deforestation and Forest Degradation (REDD), and to investigate the potential of carbon offset projects before agreeing to harvest. This indicates that the FMAs did have a positive value of cultural significance despite being zoned by the community for development. The support for REDD+ as a priority option coincides with the community's concerns for the future that were iterated by one Ahousaht elder in a Port Alberni community meeting: 'climate change is a big concern; we are worried about losing our land, about extinction and loss of resources'. Ahousaht would seek scenarios that avoid this loss.

### *Valuation Estimate*

Using best-case scenario figures, in 2016 the CSV for the FMAs is CAD 125.67 per Ahousaht person. This indicates that Ahousaht people are sacrificing CAD 125.67 potential income for each person, of all ages, in 2016 in order to maintain access to the FMA for cultural use. This valuation will fluctuate from year to year and does not take into consideration the revenues earned by the Ahousaht Forestry Company, which are expected to be put back into the community. This model also assumes that the earnings are spread out over the entire community and does not incorporate incurred expenses for either harvest or carbon credit allocation. Harvest would have various other expenses, while the carbon credit sale would be mainly administrative.

### *Opportunities and Shortcomings of Valuing Indigenous Traditional Territories*

#### Values

From what can be observed through the community consultations and planning processes, the community's willingness to accept economic loss in the case of the FMAs is due to the cultural connection to the land and the community's desires to conserve the FMAs for future generations. Evidence of this was gathered through key statements made by community members at the collective community meetings for the Ahousaht LUP process as cited below:

> I hope that our generation can complete this planning for the next generation. It is good to have a map so that our people and youth know our territories and have an attitude that demonstrates that it is ours. It's up to each of us personally to be out there and taking back these culturally activities.[35]
>
> This process is critically important because it empowers our community to once again fulfil our responsibility of being true stewards of our territories, providing hope and opportunity for future generations, by managing our lands and waters with a respect that is rooted in cultural values, ecological resilience and community well-being.[36]

The monetary loss represents the valuation of cultural significance for the FMAs, as it helps to interpret to the community's choice to implement a revenue-generating project that yields much lower income, though conserves and respects the land according to Ahousaht cultural values. The results reveal that there is cultural significance in the FMAs despite these areas being zoned for development by the community. This is expected, as all areas within the Ahousaht traditional territory

35 Ahousaht member, Port Alberni Land Use Planning Meeting 8 June 2016, transcript on file with the author.

36 Ahousaht hereditary chief in-line, Victoria Land Use Planning Meeting 6 June 6 2016, transcript on file with the author.

have cultural significance to the Ahousaht people in accordance with the traditional Ahousaht law of *hišuukiš cawak* regardless of whether they have already been developed or have no specific physical use.[37]

Physical use, or use value, is unable to fully explain indigenous culture significance for non-market valuation, as the land is such a large piece of everyday way of life; it is more a part of the community than an external entity. Understanding and applying this relationship is where other cultural heritage valuations were lacking, by not understanding that indigenous communities comprise all the things that sustain and surround people as well as people themselves. The valuation of cultural significance reveals the economic opportunity from forestry that the Ahousaht people are willing to sacrifice, and represents the revenue discrepancy between forestry employment income and carbon credit sales revenue.

**Opportunities**

Culture is a key factor in health and well-being in the Ahousaht community, and being able to practise culture affects all aspects of daily life. As an example, those people who are able to practice ceremony or visit a particular place that is sacred to their family and would have otherwise been in a harvest zone experience impacts to their emotional and physical well-being, increasing their capacity to perform at work and school and within their family dynamic.

The CSV calculated within the FMAs is not equal to the monetary loss incurred in reality, as these areas that have allocated carbon credits will have other sustainable business potential so long as the carbon storage within the area is not impacted. Eco-tourism is the most obvious example, as a large portion of Tofino's annual 34 million dollar tourism market is operating within Ahousaht traditional territories, and Ahousaht has begun to enter this market themselves.[38] Therefore, additional potential exists for Ahousaht to make up the cultural significance 'cost' with other streams of revenue so that the sacrifice to maintain cultural access to the FMAs would not be as great.

An important use for this valuation would be to act as a communication tool with industry as a method of explaining and portraying the cultural importance of the traditional territories, and to demonstrate that even areas designated for development have importance to the Ahousaht people. Historically, the connection between indigenous people and the land has been difficult to explain, as the land acts as an extension of one's self and one's community. Industry and government have a difficult time interpreting this, and, as a result, tend to dismiss it as a fabrication or dramatization. Interpreting this valuation in monetary terms may not be the most accurate interpretation of CSAs; however, it is a steppingstone towards cultural

[37] Atleo, *supra* note 2.

[38] Tourism BC, *The Value of Tourism in British Columbia: Trends from 2001 to 2011* (Ministry of Jobs, Tourism and Skills Training 2012).

recognition in a modern economic market. Another use for valuating CSAs would be as a tool for calculating compensation for violations within the territories, such as for unauthorized development or settlements. An example of such a case would be companies interfering with sacred areas while doing maintenance on existing infrastructure or installing new infrastructure, which can result from lack of proper consultation with the local First Nation.[39] Some of these cases can become complicated since the developer and First Nation may not agree on compensation terms due to the fact that there is no documented or calculated justification for the amount that the indigenous may say is required.

This valuation of cultural significance to the local inhabitants of the land is far more impactful than accessing valuations from visitors or newcomers to the area because the pristine nature of Ahousaht traditional territories is the result of the millennia of sustainable use and care by the Ahousaht people, as without their care and protection the lands would not be as attractive to visitors and new comers.[40] Assessing tourism or recreational valuations in this area could have serious impacts on the local inhabitants by either overvaluing or undervaluing areas of significance. For example, if the valuations of visitors or newcomers to the areas were shown to be very high, all development within Ahousaht traditional territories could be halted, as it would be shown as too costly. Employment and business opportunities for the people residing in this area would be interrupted, and their needs would not be taken into consideration by those who do not reside in the area and do not want to jeopardize the pristine nature of the area. This example demonstrates the importance of first considering the valuation from the local perspective rather than the perspective of those who merely visit the area or gain utility knowing such a place exists.

## CONCLUSION

There is value in using locally developed planning and policy tools in CSV studies, with this method being useful for engaging with other stakeholders when faced with development of resource industry in indigenous traditional territories. It is also important to consider other types of indigenous self-governance and engagement within these structures such as modern treaties or land use visioning. In the case of the Ahousaht, the valuation is in the sacrifice of economic opportunity that the community is willing to forgo, not based on income but rather on potential income from a specific project, namely harvesting of the FMAs. In this way, concepts of intergenerational equity can be seen at the core of valuation and decision-making

39 Snyder et al., *supra* note 4.

40 R. Trosper, *Resilience, Reciprocity and Ecological Economics: Northwest Coast Sustainability* (Routledge 2009).

methods that can be enshrined in or protected by legal systems yet still need appropriate methodologies to be implemented in reality.

Indigenous CSAs vary from goods usually valued using these techniques, as they identify with both use value and non-use value characteristics. This is because of the way in which indigenous culture, here using the Ahousaht communities as an example, connects people to their land base and how this connection affects daily life and well-being. This valuation also demonstrates that, despite development, some level of cultural significance can be applied to all of the traditional territories, not just the areas being occupied or used occasionally, as reiterated by one Ahousaht elder in a community meeting: 'it is our job to take care of the land for future generations'. This is also evidenced in community meetings during which there was general agreement among those in attendance to pursue opportunities on carbon offset projects and begin to educate the community on the possibilities. If a carbon offset project was approved, the community would accept the loss of potential economic opportunity in the form of employment that would have been possible through the harvesting of these areas.

Valuation of the CSAs is a controversial method, as it attempts to monetize a factor of health and well-being, though it has the potential to greatly increase communication between indigenous peoples and industries by helping to interpret the connection indigenous people have to the land. This ensures that industry and government are accountable for consultation with local indigenous people and that all interests of the land are included. Also in accordance with the targets towards the SDGs, this will allow for a more mutually beneficial interaction in cases of development and will give local indigenous people more opportunities to conserve and protect what is most important to them, including preserving and protecting the land and areas of cultural value for current and future generations. Each indigenous community is different and has unique laws and values, making the use of LUP or other land use tools made and directed by the community so critical in valuation. For those researchers who are not familiar with cultural practices it is important to integrate the work in the community and become involved with the local people so that the true valuation is not lost in translation.

Around the world, rural indigenous communities are struggling to find culturally appropriate and sustainable livelihoods using local resources, in changing environment and development contexts.[41] Conservation is important to indigenous communities for many reasons, and within these the need for economic opportunities, local employment, and capacity building cannot be ignored. Environmentalists cannot offer sustainable economic opportunity and industry cannot offer long-term

[41] Kent and Dorward, *supra* note 12; P. Hawken, *The Ecology of Commerce* (Harper Business 2010); P. Hawken et al., *Natural Capitalism* (Hachette 1999); M.C. Cordonier Segger and A. Khalfan, *Sustainable Development Law: Principles, Practices, and Prospects* (Oxford University Pres 2004).

conservation that protects the future livelihoods of indigenous peoples. REDD+ offers an option forward, and the SDGs demonstrate the global need for action, but to make it work it is critical that indigenous communities utilize tools such as non-market valuation to protect what is rightfully theirs while also providing opportunities for their people to thrive in their traditional territories. In this way, indigenous communities have the ability to balance and provide for economic and cultural benefits now and in the future, creating a stable path for intergenerational equity to follow.

*Comparative Insights*

# 29

# A Comparative Analysis of Model Institutions: Diversity in Reaching Common Goals

*Judit Pump*

In 2013, the Secretary-General of the UN named eight institutions as models for considering intergenerational solidarity and representing the interests of future generations in policy making.[1] Each institution has its own unique set of characteristics as a result of constitutional backgrounds, functions, and organisational structures, to name only a few characteristics. Additionally each institution has found its own set of theoretical bases and principles upon which to pursue its activities and reach its goals. This comparative study of the model institutions is to identify the set of most important features, including not just references to legal framework, organisational structures, but also missions, aims, and goals, and theories and principles by which they can be characterised. This will be done by placing each institution within this set of criteria, assessed and drawn from existing practice, in which links between the various aspects are highlighted, and it is shown how theories can be operational in practice. The chapter argues for and reflects on the innovative characteristics of model institutions for sustainable development when the theoretical basis – especially legal theory – is lagging behind.

The characteristics are viewed from the perspective of decisions behind the emergence of such institutions, the process of establishment, specificity of characteristics and features compared to already existing institutions, and methods of influencing policy making. For the comparative analysis, Bartee's holistic model of problem solving is applied.[2] His three-dimensional problem-solving space, along with

[1] See the Report Secretary-General on Intergenerational Solidarity and the Needs of Future Generations, 5 August 2013, A/68/x.

[2] E.M. Bartee, 'A Holistic View of Problem Solving' (1973) 20:4 Management Science 439–448. This holistic view consists of a three dimensional problem-solving space (problem taxonomy, problem-solving modes, problem-solving process) and a fourth dimension that is called the chronology of problem solving. Each dimension is broken down further to four layers. Under problem taxonomy four types of problems are recognised: conceptual, empirical, behavioural. and societal. The four basic modes of problem solving are: by individuals, groups, organisations, society. The problem-solving process has four steps: genesis, diagnosis, analysis, synthesis.

the chronology of problem solving, allow one to draw attention to different kinds of aspects that are unique for some reason and could be considered when the question is raised which models to choose for adoption. This comparative analysis has limitations that should be acknowledged: (1) sources of information, and (2) States represented. Regarding the first limitation, the papers found in the previous chapters are the main (though not the only) source of the analysis regarding information on the individual institutions, such as how they were established, what the most important characteristics are, their functions, and the problems faced by them. While it is a limitation, it is also an advantage because it provides a direct source for validation of the findings of the analysis and allows readers to draw their own conclusions. Regarding the second limitation, without exception, all the States named by the Secretary-General belong to the developed economy classification, are members of the OECD (several of them even founding members),[3] and also are members of some other kind of economic cooperation mechanism, be it formal[4] or informal.[5] All of them are governed by some form of Western-style parliamentary regime, and none has a presidential system.[6] The economic power represented by the countries is quite high because they are developed economies and States.[7]

The problems institutions have been established to solve are inherent to industrialised nations. The institutions discussed belong to one particular kind of constitutional family despite their vivid differences in the geographical and the actual institutional settings. These limitations should not be overlooked. Indeed, they can be turned to advantages if the existence of institutions discussed is taken as a warning of problems that can come along with economic development based on industrialisation and that may emerge despite parliamentary democracies. So the adoption of such institutions by both developed and less developed countries with less

The four phases of problem-solving chronology are: personalisation, collaboration, institutionalisation, and socialisation. Ibid. at 441, 444.

3 Canada (10 April 1961); Finland (28 January 1969); Germany (27 September 1961); Hungary (7 May 1996); Israel (7 September 2010); New Zealand (29 May 1973); Norway (4 July 1961); UK (as the home country of the Welsh institution) (2 May 1961).

4 Members of the EU: Finland, Germany, Hungary, UK (at the time of writing), also Norway with a special relationship with the EU.

5 Commonwealth member states: Canada, New Zealand, UK; members of G8: Germany, the UK and Canada; for the review of economic power, see the UN report of 2015 on the World Economic Situation and Prospects 2015 www.un.org/en/development/desa/policy/wesp/wesp_archive/2015wesp_full_en.pdf accessed 30 November 2017.

6 Canada: federal parliamentary democracy (Parliament of Canada) under a constitutional monarchy; Finland: parliamentary republic; Germany federal parliamentary republic; Hungary: parliamentary republic; Israel: parliamentary democracy; New Zealand: parliamentary democracy (New Zealand Parliament) under a constitutional monarchy; Norway: parliamentary constitutional monarchy; the UK: parliamentary constitutional monarchy. See CIA, 'CIA World Factbook' www.cia.gov/library/publications/the-world-factbook/ accessed 30 November 2017.

7 All countries belong to the high-income countries (economies by per capita GNI in 2013) except Hungary, which is in the middle-income group. UN World, *supra* note 1 at 142.

industrialisation and in different constitutional settings may be important from the perspective of prevention.

## THE BIRTH OF THE NEW INSTITUTIONS

The institutions named by the Secretary-General were established at different times and under different conditions. There is one common element that is shared by all of them: the articulation of the need to find an institutional way to change decision making. When reviewing the history of the establishment of these institutions, it is clear that there was dissatisfaction with the way in which political decisions were made concerning economic development. The lack of consideration given to environmental issues in decision making on economic development and its negative impact on the environment and human health was a matter for concern. This was perceived as a situation that should be changed by transformation. The existence of some kind of an institution with a mandate to incorporate the new way of thinking into decision making was perceived as the desired situation.[8]

The first step of the problem-solving process is genesis, that is the recognition of the existence of the problem. The first advocates for setting up such institutions varied from individuals,[9] to non-governmental and other groups,[10] to governments to international bodies.[11] It is noteworthy that among the advocates there were representatives of civil society, academic institutions, and public bodies. The countries can be divided into two main groups depending on whether the initiative for their institutions started within the parliament or outside it. This distinction gains importance when considering the adoptability of the institutions. When reviewing the history of how the institutions were established, two distinctive deliberations can be recognised and should be distinguished: (1) cause group deliberation (CGD), and (2) parliamentary deliberation (PD).

CGD functioned as an informal debate between the members of society – including individuals, groups, and organisations. They as a whole can be considered a *cause*

[8] Bartee distinguishes three different ways in which problems are solved: (1) the perceived present situation transformed into the perceived desired situation; (2) the perceived desired situation transformed into the perceived present situation; and (3) changing perception. Bartee, *supra* note 2 at 439.

[9] Individuals: Norway Anders Bratholm, professor of criminal law; Israel: Joseph Lapid, leader of the Shinui party (in the Parliament); Finland: representatives of the Parliament.

[10] Hungary: a bottom-up initiative coming from Védegylet – Protect the Future! Hungarian Civil Society Organization; Wales: Sustainable Development Charter Group (consisting of twenty-five NGOs, key government agencies, and the Environmental Planning Research Unit at Cardiff University); Greenprint Canada: coalition of environmental conservation and Aboriginal Groups.

[11] New Zealand: working together with the environmental committee of the government, it was the OECD's recommendation to establish some kind of an environmental body, the Labour government took it on, and such changes were advocated by leading environmental groups.

*group*.[12] The problems, as identified by the cause group, were those of economic development not being sustainable and the neglect of the interests of future generations. Various concepts and life experiences were shared, discussed, and analysed within the cause group. The outcome of the CGD was a document containing a proposal to set up some kind of a body or to introduce a special mandate in order to solve the identified problems. During CGD, members could experience all four stages of Bartee's three-dimensional problem-solving space and almost all phases of chronology.[13]

Interestingly, in a cause group the socialisation phase of chronology is not necessarily a follow-up phase of institutionalisation but occurred at the very beginning. Though cause groups are open to everyone, their membership is limited to those accepting and sharing the same social values and ideas that are prerequisites of becoming part of the group. In Bartee's terminology, 'socialisation' means a change in attitude and values of those who previously did not act according to them. The activity of the cause groups reaching out to others having different ideas in order to get them involved is the true socialisation phase if changes are to occur. The diversity, the richness, and the breadth of the membership of the cause group and the number of individuals involved could provide some indication of social embeddedness and success in socialisation.

PD took place within the Parliament among the elected representatives, who were mostly members of political parties. While it was possible to involve experts and other stakeholders in the problem-solving process, the people involved in decision making were limited to politicians, to those having voting power and/or bound not only by their promise to their electors but also to their parties. The whole process was formal, following the rules of the parliament, which was the problem-solving mode of the organisation. The final result of the deliberation was either a piece of legislation providing for the establishment of the institution or the establishment itself.

It is important to point to the difference between parliaments' deliberations depending on whether they were preceded by CGD or not. The end document of CGD was mostly addressed to the parliament, despite the fact that governments are considered to be the main policy makers.[14] The parliament became the target,[15]

12 A cause group is a special pressure group that is formed to promote a particular cause or idea, usually with open membership. P. Norton, 'Introduction: Putting Pressure on Parliaments', in P. Norton (ed.) *Parliaments in Contemporary Western Europe, Volume 2 Parliaments and Pressure Groups in Western Europe* (Routledge 2006) at 3.

13 See Bartee, *supra* note 2.

14 Norton argues that it is the consequence of industrialisation, and the lack of political will of and knowledge at the parliament. Norton, *supra* note 12 at 7.

15 Norton calls on Packenham and reminds that parliament becomes attractive to pressure groups either as a target or as a channel. The distinction between the two is related to the power of bringing about or influencing changes. Seeing parliaments as a target is considered a last resort for pressure groups. Ibid. at 8–9.

because it had the power to bring about the desired changes, that is the establishment of the perceived institution. When PD was preceded by CGD, the outcome of CGD's synthesis step became PD's genesis. The politicians receiving the document were faced with and learned about the questions and answers involved, as well as the conflicts raised and solved during the first deliberation. Note that synthesis reached by CGD was only the synthesis of those having the same ideas and sharing the same values owing to the nature of cause groups.

In that respect, parliaments are different. Ideas of sustainable development or environmental protection, which helped form the cause group, were not inevitably acknowledged by members of Parliaments. The very basic ideas shared by all members of parliaments are related to principles of parliamentary systems, separation of power (legislative, executive and judiciary.)[16] It means that politicians agree on distribution of power and the way in which different ideas are discussed and agreements are reached.[17] When PD was not preceded by CGD, the problem recognition originated from the work of the parliament, and the working experiences and justification of behaviours of its members were discussed during the collaboration phase.

When CGD took place, the parliamentary debate focused more on institutionalisation than on discussing the existence of the substantive problems and its types. Thus, the problem had been transferred, and the focal point shifted to what kind of institution would best fit the purpose. The close follow-up of the debate before the parliament and strong pressure on its members from outside by the cause group ensured that the final solution chosen would be in harmony with the purpose articulated during the CGD, and that the mandate of the new institution would not fall short of previously reached consensus and expectations. It is a good example of how civil society could shape the final result of a PD without being part of the decision-making process and help the social embeddedness of the new institution.

It seems that social embeddedness gains importance not only at the time of foundation. In most of the countries there was a time when the need for such an institution, or even its mere existence, was questioned by politicians. However, experience shows that social support behind such an institution was able to save it.[18]

[16] According to Harlow and Crawlings, '[t]raditional constitutional theory ... vests the law-making function in Parliament; lying behind and legitimating the doctrine of parliamentary sovereignty is the classical English theory of representative democracy, whereby power is delegated from the electors to a representative but independent legislature'. Here executive law-making is legitimated by a parliamentary delegation of power. C. Harlow and R. Rawlings, *Law and Administration* (London 1997) 199.

[17] As shown by authors of Comparative Constitutional Law, there is no single model on the relationship among the three branches (legislature, executive, judiciary), and they may vary significantly. T. Ginsburg and R. Dixon (eds.), *Comparative Constitutional Law* (Edward Elgar 2011).

[18] In the case of Hungary, environmental NGOs and representatives of the Hungarian and international academic community made their voices heard in order to save the position of the ombudsman for future generations.

Conversely, without such backing it could be abolished more easily.[19] The effectiveness of social pressure in keeping the institution alive very much depends on the membership of the cause group. By definition a cause group dissolves after the cause is achieved. However, cause groups are often formed by sectional groups,[20] which are essential parts of the existing establishment, by complementing or taking over governmental duties or becoming part of the policy process. An example is when the government is required to consult with the interest groups prior to passing a piece of legislation.[21] It means that without forming a new cause group the 'old' members and their allies could put pressure on the parliament not to eliminate the institution by targeting the government directly. The pressure on the government reaches the members of parliament as a consequence of the constitutional setup of parliamentary democracy and its party-based election. When an institution reflects the will of the voters, politicians are keener on keeping it. When pressure groups essential to the implementation of governmental policy make clear that there is a strong link between the existence of the institution and their willingness to co-operate, then the question of elimination of such an institution would not be discussed in depth, and it could be taken off the table quite easily.

It should be noted, however, that social support alone is not enough to save these institutions. The performance of such an institution is as important as its social support. In that respect performance should be evaluated from two aspects: (1) usefulness and effectiveness, and (2) disruptiveness. The first can be evaluated against the justification of its establishment, namely the problem to be solved, and the second against the constitutional system they inhabit.[22] From these the following test of adoptability can be developed: (1) social support, (2) expectations met, and (3) constitution-specificity. Experience shows that different sequences of testing should be applied before (ex ante) and after (ex post) the formulation of the institution. Before the introduction of a new institution, the correct sequence of testing correlates with the numbers of test sequences indicated. As demonstrated earlier, the concept of an institution evolves during the first phase of deliberations (CGD or PD). This is the time when the expectations are articulated and elaborated and an institution is chosen that is capable to meet those expectations. Only after the

[19] The example of Israel shows that even though the commissioner had addressed various segments of society there was no social movement that could effectively put pressure on the parliament for keeping the position.

[20] 'Sectional groups exist to promote and defend the interests of a particular section of society, one usually defined by economic activity.' Norton, *supra* note 12 at 3.

[21] Norton refers to who considers such groups as insider groups. By distinguishing between insider and outsider groups Grant reflects on how legitimate they are considered by the government. Ibid. at 3–4. The relationship between the government and the pressure groups is discussed by Norton in detail. Ibid. at 4–6.

[22] Ginsburg uses the term 'constitution-specificity' to mean institutions being organically related to the constitutional schemes they inhabit. T. Ginsburg, 'Constitutional Endurance', in T. Ginsburg and R. Dixon (eds.), *Comparative Constitutional Law* (Edward Elgar 2011) 112–125 at 113.

expectations are known can the institution be named and a review made as to how it can fit into the existing political scheme by either stretching the scope and function of an existing institution or setting up a new one with a new mandate.

However, during the operation of the institution the sequences of testing will be reversed relative to those previously followed. The review process should start with the key question of constitution-specificity, that is, how the institution is perceived to fit into the political system, being organically developed or having the ability to become rooted. The next question is related to meeting expectations within and outside of the parliament – how it can fulfil the role and function it was designed for. The question of social support comes only third in the process. Social support is important when it comes to differences in evaluating whether the work of the institution meets expectations. It may be that the institution is not important for the work of the parliament and/or the government but people are satisfied with its operation and find it fulfils its role as a guarantee. The reason behind the difference in testing lies in the change of the problem. In the first case, the problem was the non-existence of the institution; when it is operating, however, its existence could become the problem. When the institution's performance ends up disrupting or disturbing the proper functioning of the parliament it is likely to be eliminated.[23] A similar result is reached when it does not meet expectations.

The social movements behind the institutions asked for changes in attitude, in establishing guarantees requiring that environmental concerns (one of the pillars of sustainable development) be taken seriously and the interests of future generations be considered in public decision making. It seems that for cause groups the most important aspect of evaluation is whether the institution could serve as a guarantee, a safeguard of public interest, by incorporating those values and aspects into decision making. Reflecting on an environmental problem, such as reducing air pollution, Bartee argues that

> [the] use of formal and legitimate structure and controls is not enough for an eventual solution to this type of problem . . .The ultimate solution to the problem requires that social attitudes, norms, and cultural mores be communicated and changed in the direction of the problem solution.[24]

Thus, in our context, the success of these institutions depends on whether the notion of sustainable development including the protection of the interests of future

[23] The case of Israel shows that even though the high quality of the ombudsman's performance was recognised the institution itself was seen as not having the required constitution-specificity. Based on the minutes of parliamentary deliberation on dissolving the position of commissioner for the future, Teschner states that, beside costs, the primary reason for dissolution was the feeling of MPs that 'the Commission received too much authority to interfere in their work'. N. Teschner, *Official Bodies That Deal with the Needs of Future Generations and Sustainable Development – Comparative Review* (The Knesset Research and Information Centre 2013) 3 www.knesset.gov.il/mmm/data/pdf/me03194.pdf accessed 30 November 2017.

[24] Bartee calls it socialisation, and it is the last phase of the chronology. Bartee, *supra* note 2 at 443.

generations could penetrate decision making at all level and in all problem-solving modes.

There is a significant difference among countries as to how this penetration is conceived. There is no common understanding or working definition of sustainable development even though references are usually made to the Brundtland Report. The work of most institutions is based on this notion; however, their freedom in its interpretation varies greatly. In some of the countries, the notion of sustainable development is broken down into elements and turned into aspects, objectives, or indicators to be considered in the work of the institution.[25] In others its interpretation is left to the institution itself, resulting in freedom to develop the substance and criteria of evaluation when made.[26] The institution is the carrier and transmitter of this substance as a message. The type of institution chosen determines to whom the message on this substance could be transmitted and thus the depth of penetration in the society. The type itself does not necessarily indicate the institution's freedom in determining the substance in the way in which its function, its mandate, and its work do. Two features of the institutions gain importance: (1) who the actors are between whom the institution creates a link, and (2) what the function of the institution is. These analytical questions allow one to see the potential adoptability of the institution in different political systems. The next section will address the answers to those questions.

## INSTITUTIONS

The parliamentary systems of the studied countries vary greatly. However, this comparative analysis will not cover that aspect, and it will not be discussed here. Our focal point is how the various institutions inhabit the constitutional systems in all their uniqueness, and how they improve and complement decision making with long-term thinking. Features of rules or operations that may influence the long-term existence of the institution, including why they could be interpreted as threats to the existing political establishment, are also pointed out.

All institutions are organic developments in the sense that they are a reflection of a country's polity and its institutional structure. The countries' reports show that all of the institutions have some uniqueness compared to those that could be identified as the inspiration for the organisational choice. It seems that the desired perceived function can be named as a determinant factor in organisational choice, and it is also responsible for the uniqueness of each institution. If this desired function is considered as a guarantee, then the choices are not surprising. Those functions include overseeing, monitoring, reviewing, investigating, evaluating, and advising. The question is this: in which context are the functions expected to be practised?

[25] Canada, Germany, and Wales.

[26] New Zealand, Hungary, Israel, Finland, and Norway.

The answer can be given by viewing the institutions as intermediary bodies. Among the institutions there are parliamentary committees, commissions, commissioners, and ombudsmen.

## *Parliamentary Committees*

One could say that there is no parliament without parliamentary committees.[27] However, each parliament has a different committee system that reflects the relationship between the legislature and the executive power, and the rules may significantly differ, regarding how committees may or could participate in parliamentary work. While Yamamoto argues that '[t]he basic function of parliamentary committees is to prepare for deliberation in the full chamber', he also emphasises the special value they add to parliamentary work by making possible informed discussion in the chamber, overseeing government departments and policy enforcement, and being intermediary bodies between interest groups or entry points to citizens.[28] Many of these functions have been developed to promote the idea of separation of powers.[29] Procedural rules help to establish a clear division of labour and power and at the same time can be seen as guarantees for transmitting messages.

Committees are the first place for deliberation of bills. When a committee reviews only bills submitted to the parliament by the government, it means that the committee has an oversight function of government work and acts as an information source. Quality work needs time, so who has the right to set the time limit for such a review is an important question. Setting the time frame within which the committee should formulate its opinion is a very delicate issue. It is not without precedent for such committees to have only a few weeks or even days to give their opinion on bills that have been prepared for months, so that they cannot hamper the legislative work of parliament. Parliaments set their own schedule, so it is up to the specific parliament to determine how much time to set aside for in-depth examination of governmental bills. There are at least two ways in which such a time can be determined: (1) by the number of bills accepted for submission and for deliberation, and (2) by giving an exact time frame within which the opinion has to be formulated by the committees. It is important to note the significant difference between the two cases. In the first case, the lack of time restrictions on the one hand may improve the quality of decision

[27] Issues relevant only to the Finnish and the German parliamentary committees will be discussed under this heading. For a comparative analysis of national parliaments see H. Yamamoto, *Tools for Parliamentary Oversight: A Comparative Study of 88 National Parliaments* (Inter-Parliamentary Union 2007).

[28] Ibid. at 16–17.

[29] The analysis of the legislative-executive relations by Cheibub and Limongi illustrates well the diversity of political systems and the various ways their relations are governed including the processes that are characteristic to them. J.A. Cheibub and F. Limongi, 'Legislative–Executive Relations', in T. Ginsburg and R. Dixon (eds.), *Comparative Constitutional Law* (Edward Elgar 2011) 211–233.

making and sends a message that environmental concerns and the interest of future generations are important. On the other hand, it may give the impression that the committee itself has an indirect right (de facto even if not de jure) to schedule the work of the parliament. In the second case, the time restriction may give the impression that the opinion of the committee is only a formal requirement and that keeping to a schedule is given priority over well-grounded decision.

According to Yamamoto, parliamentary committees are distinguished by their status (permanent or *ad hoc*), their relationship to other committees (general oversight), to legislation (legislative and non-legislative committees), or to governmental structure (departmentally related committees).[30] There are different kinds of general oversight committees, such as those having the ability to review all bills on their constitutional merits. A committee that reviews all bills from the perspective of how legislation promotes long-term thinking, sustainable development, or environmental protection would fit into that list. General oversight committees provide expert opinion to other committees for consideration. Thus, by establishing a special general oversight committee the issues relevant from the perspective of sustainable development and future generations could be highlighted for all committees and committee members.

It is common for bills submitted to a parliament for deliberation to be accompanied by explanatory notes and other background documents giving detailed justification of objectives, reasons, and other information. Thus, the mandate of the committee may extend to review of both the bill and the accompanying documents. When a committee reviews not just the bill but also the accompanying documents it means that oversight is extended to the preparatory phase of the bill. The aim of committee reviews is to enable members of parliament to pursue informed discussions and to take informed decisions. The expert opinion of a committee on the merits of the accompanying materials from the perspective of sustainable development reflects the expectation of the legislature and draws the attention of drafters to the indicators they must consider and respect during the drafting process. This opinion becomes persuasive when it is the result of a consensus between the two sides of the parliament (supporting and in opposition to the government), particularly when a request from the parliament is handed over to the government asking for the provision of additional information or submission of supplementary materials.

Thus, such a committee has a very significant role in helping acknowledgement of the relevance of legislation in moving towards sustainable development by both the parliament and the government.[31] However, it is important to note that problem solving is hampered if scrutiny by the committee is not impartial regarding authorship of the bill (for example, where limited to bills submitted by the government and

[30] Yamamoto, *supra* note 26 at 15.

[31] What Bartee terms the personalisation phase.

not extended to private bills)[32] or its nature (for example, being a new piece of legislation or a modification of an existing one). Such limitations may be interpreted by members of parliament as meaning that sustainability is something that only the government should take seriously and that there might be situations when such aspects could be ignored and that it is the right of MPs to decide when to do so.

The oversight function of parliamentary committees may be extended to secondary legislation.[33] When a parliamentary committee formulates an opinion on secondary legislation, the type of route through which it reaches the government and how its substance has to be considered by the government are important factors. According to an Inter-Parliamentary Union study,

> [t]he outcome of a committee's investigations typically takes the form of a published report, addressed to the government with recommendations, which is laid before parliament as a whole. It is then up to parliament to decide its priority for debate, and how the government response is to be followed up.[34]

There is a significant difference between how committees may reach out to governments directly or through the parliament. Committees usually have a clear right to request information directly from governments and public bodies.[35] However, that does not necessarily mean that they can send their opinions and recommendations directly to them. The setup of the communication routes and rules between the committees and the government is a very delicate issue because it may change or have an effect on the balance of power between the legislative and executive branches. Also, the compelling nature of and the political support behind such opinions can be more powerful if they are allowed to be sent only after a debate or after approval of the parliament.[36]

A non-legislative committee dealing with the future has a very important role in socialisation at the level of the parliament as a whole. Such a committee is an important entry point for involving academics, various public and private bodies, and civil society in parliamentary deliberations. Parliamentary committees plan their own work ahead of time. While the work schedule of a legislative committee is very much influenced and even determined by the legislative programme of the

[32] In this context, private bills refer to bills that are prepared and submitted directly to parliament by members of parliament without the involvement of government.

[33] In this context pieces of legislation passed by the parliament (bills and acts) are referred to as primary legislation, while others that fall under the competence of governments based on delegated power are referred to as secondary legislation, for example, regulations emanating from legislation. Reports on the German and the Israel institutions contain reference to secondary legislation.

[34] D. Beetham, *Parliament and Democracy in the Twenty-First Century – A Guide to Good Practice* (Inter-Parliamentary Union 2006) 130.

[35] The importance of the right to request information by parliamentary committees and other oversight bodies has been widely acknowledged and emphasised not just by the institutions. See ibid. at 130.

[36] From the reports it seems that parliamentary committees have used both methods.

government, a non-legislative committee could fit its work plan to the exact needs of its members. If members of a committee for the future are also members of other committees, then the knowledge gained, the consensus reached, and the importance of aspects on sustainability recognised within this committee could be used as a basis for discussion to those other committees. It should be noted that the nature of the consensus in both sets of committees is the same. It is political, since members of the governing parties or the opposition come to a common understanding of the problems. There is, however, a unique difference between the two. First, people have to see which are the questions falling under the rubric of being political and having long-term effect (thus on future generations) and which are those to which answers have to be left to experts. Also, the different kinds of impact – namely economic, social, and environmental – of technology development, and of research, are discussed and the role of technology in changing culture is recognised.[37] The classical political debate takes place in other committees where political ideas are hashed out in order to solve the problem with or without the support of the opposition.

It may be that the consensus reached within the non-legislative committee would not prevail in other committees; however, there will be at least one representative of this holistic approach that is based on widely held values of sustainable development. Thus, the first committee itself serves as an entry point for views from outside of the parliament by transmitting them to other committees.[38] When considering Bartee's model, such a committee is able to widen the circle of actors involved in the collaboration phase, integrate experience and knowledge of those outside of the parliament, and learn about their motivations that are relevant not just from the perspective of an economic sector or a social or an environmental problem, but from the perspective of future life. It thus changes the formulation of a problem, since the problems of the future can be turned into the questions regarding what life society would like to have and how decisions of today could or would change lives. These are questions that reflect a holistic view that embraces all aspects of life.[39]

The visibility of parliamentary committees is twofold. On the one hand, they act as an entry point for academic and civil society. On the other hand, they could become visible through media coverage, their reports being debated in plenary, or through discussions in the committee.[40] The visibility, and thus the social support,

[37] This kind of debate takes place in the Finnish Committee for Future.

[38] Yamamoto, *supra* note 26 at 11.

[39] This holistic approach is reflected in the book published by the Finnish Committee for the Future, *Black Swans, What Will Change the World Next?* (Finnish Parliament's Committee for the Future 5/2013).

[40] Yamamoto draws attention to how committees and their work may become visible to the public, stating that 'Taking committee reports to debate in the plenary can be valuable both for the committee concerned and for the whole chamber. From the committee's viewpoint, when a committee report is adopted by the full chamber, it then represents the will of parliament as a whole and as such becomes politically more persuasive. Moreover, debate in the plenary gives

of a committee gains importance when it is not a permanent committee or when its existence is to be considered every time by the newly formed parliament after elections. In the latter case, it means that the committee's function has not become an organic part of the parliamentary work and thus the oversight function of the parliament regarding sustainable development may disappear. It is important to point to the special feature of a general oversight parliamentary committee with a mandate to scrutinise sustainable development policy. Such a scrutiny fulfils its function only if it is complex, holistic, and not biased by sectoral interests. The horizontal approach is secured by the existence of a committee that is independent from other departmentally related committees and whose duty is to review bills and background documents from a particular angle.

### *Parliamentary Commissioners: The In-House Commissioner for Future Generations*

When comparing the role of the in-house commissioner with parliamentary committees there are important similarities and striking differences. An in-house commissioner may fulfil the function and position of a permanent oversight committee and a departmentally related committee. He or she may act as a legislative and a non-legislative committee. The most important difference between an in-house commissioner and parliamentary committees is being non-political and being an expert on issues related to future generations. The commissioner is the head of a parliamentary entity that has employees, not members of parliament, and he or she is not a member of parliament chosen by an ad hoc committee. Being politically non-aligned, he or she is not an insider actor of political debate, despite his or her parliamentary position. For the political parties, the in-house commissioner and his or her recommendations will always be considered as expert. The strength of that expert opinion is based on academic and social support, and not on political support for any of the parties.

It is important to see the different nature of the work of experts helping individual representatives or even the committee. Such expertise finds its way into political debate through the members of parliament. Thus, it becomes the opinion of politicians, and the politicians are the ones deciding what kind of expertise is allowed to be considered. This is not the case with the in-house commissioner. The right to choose particular expertise stays with the commissioner, and politicians cannot reject his or her choice. This brings a new dimension into political debates, since all

publicity to the committee's activities. For the plenary, debating committee reports allows issues to be aired in a context of focused deliberation. The content of the reports enables informed discussion, giving both the government and the opposition a chance to present their views.' Yamamoto, *supra* note 26 at 62.

politicians in the parliament and the government have to form an opinion on expert questions and policy solutions that have been formulated by non-politicians.

The actual political debate over the opinion of the in-house commissioner takes place when introduced before the parliamentary committees and the appropriate chamber. In order to gain political support for accepting the commissioner's ideas – including his or her opinion, recommendations, and proposals – he or she has to find a way in which members of parliament and its committees can identify themselves with the problem and its solution. Using Bartee's model, this means that the synthesis to solve a problem reached by the commissioner is presented to the parliament. This synthesis, however, is not the outcome of governmental work or political debate within the parliamentary committees but the deliberation process that took place between academics, members of the civil society, and public bodies, organised, analysed, and evaluated by the commissioner with the help of its employees. From the perspective of the other parliamentary committees, the in-house commissioner's deliberation is very similar to CGDs.

The work of the in-house commissioner is quite similar to the work of background institutions and also to the policy development work of the government. Such a position could help the parliament in gaining more power in policy making and to have more pieces of legislation that are based on self-initiation. There is no doubt among constitutional lawyers that even the legislative work of parliaments is usually based on the bills prepared and submitted by governments.[41] This is said to be the consequence of the lack of expertise and lack of time within parliament. Should a parliament introduce an in-house commissioner with such a mandate and power, it opens the floor for changing the power relationship and the balance between the parliament and the government. Additionally, political parties may see the non-political commissioner as a third actor within parliament (the others being those supporting the government or in opposition) which they cannot control if his or her power may hinder the work of the other committees and the applicable chamber. Designing and establishing such a parliamentary body is thus a very sensitive issue. It should be considered and reviewed from the perspective of how it may influence the balance of power between the legislative and executive branches.

## *The Ombudsman*

Typically, there are two main characteristics of the ombudsman system:[42] (1) having a mandate to oversee government work by *handling complaints from the public* or

[41] See the studies of Ginsburg and Dixon, *supra* note 22.

[42] The term 'ombudsman' is used for the institution. The ombudsman-model is represented by two institutions, those of Hungary and Norway. For comparative studies it is common to use the definition of the International Bar Association from 1974: 'An office provided by the constitution or by action of the legislature or Parliament and headed by an independent high level public official who is responsible to the legislature or Parliament, who receives complaints

*initiating proceedings ex officio*, and (2) independence from the government.[43] Irrespective of which model the ombudsmen belong to,[44] or how independent they are,[45] in this context the common feature is being an intermediary body between the public and the parliament/government (and its public bodies). Thus, they establish a direct link between individuals and the legislature/executive by performing control activities. It should be noted that the kind of intermediary role the ombudsman can play depends on the powers assigned to him or her and the parties between whom he or she intermediates.[46] Also, in this context independence is considered from the aspect of how it affects the playing field of the intermediary role and not of how it affects the oversight function.[47] Only an ombudsman accountable to parliament could become an intermediary body between parliament and the public or parliament and the government.

It is generally understood that the standard of ombudsman's control extends to '1. legal rules 2. principles of "good administration" or "équité" and – as a separate category – 3. human rights.'[48] Beyond the scrutiny of *the legality of administrative conduct*, including the discovery of 'maladministration' and 'negligence', an

from aggrieved persons against government agencies, officials and employers or who acts on his own motion, and has power to investigate, recommend corrective actions and issue reports.' Cited in G. Kucsko-Stadlmayer (ed.), *European Ombudsman-Institutions* (Springer 2008) at 4, referring to Caiden, *International Handbook of the Ombudsman* (Evolution and Present Function 1983) 44.

43 Beetham, *supra* note 35 at 74–79; Yamamoto, *supra* note 26 at 71. For detailed analysis of the ombudsman system in the UK, Ireland, Australia, and New Zealand, see T. Buck, R. Kirkham and B. Thompson, *The Ombudsman Enterprise and Administrative Justice* (Ashgate 2011).

44 There are different approaches to classification of the ombudsman-institutions. Linda Reif makes a distinction between ombudspersons by authority given and comes to two main categories: 'classical ombudsmen' and 'hybrid ombudsmen', while Kucsko-Stadlmayer's model classification refers to types of powers provided for and she differentiates 'basic models', 'rule of law models', and 'human rights models'. The Hungarian ombudsman for future generations was not mentioned in the comparative study because it was established later than the research study performed for the academic foundation of the study. However, the Hungarian ombudsman was evaluated and subsequently based on the powers assigned to it, considered to belong strictly to the human rights model. Changes in the Hungarian ombudsman-system in 2012 show a shift in the ombudsman's practice as it is described by Csink. L. Csink, 'Az ombudsman', in A. Jakab and Gy. Gajduschek (eds.), *A magyar jogrendszer állapota* (MTA Társadalomtudományi Kutatóközpont 2016) 600–616.

45 The Norwegian ombudsman for children did not qualify for Kucsko-Stadlmayer's comparative study because of its independent status. Only those institutions were included in her study that demonstrated independence from government. In that respect an ombudsman as an institution was assumed to be independent if he or she was elected (appointed) by the Parliament. G. Kucsko-Stadlmayer, *European Ombudsman Institutions: A Comparative Legal Analysis Regarding the Multifaceted Realisation of an Idea* (Springer 2008) 5.

46 Compare the tables summarising the powers of the two models: the rule of law model and the human rights model. Ibid. at 63–65.

47 The independence of the ombudsman usually considered with regard to oversight function. It is generally accepted that when an ombudsman is not independent from the government then the effectiveness of oversight function is limited.

48 Kucsko-Stadlmayer, *supra* note 47 at 31–39.

ombudsman may also formulate recommendations on legislation as a corrective measure for the future. The experiences of the institutions show that proposals for legislation are not limited to parliament, but rather any legislative body having the power to correct a troublesome provision may become an addressee. Also, the constitutional control of laws is not necessarily limited to the existing laws but could be extended to new proposals. When the ombudsman is empowered to review proposed legislation, it shifts the ombudsman function from correction to prevention. The generally accepted powers of the ombudsman are corrective in nature. However, when he or she could have a say on the constitutionality of a proposal it places prevention at the forefront.[49] It could be viewed as advice given to the legislature that is based on the experience of the ombudsman's practice or even as a warning when the ombudsman is entitled to appeal against laws before the constitutional court.[50] There is no doubt that such a power is an extension of the standard of control and may change, even significantly, the work of the ombudsman. By becoming part of the legislative process, the ombudsman can shape the legal framework and ensure that values and principles get adequate attention and consideration in the political debate. On the other hand, concerns may be raised about the impact on the efficiency of standard control when the ombudsman is involved in the legislature process.

While the protection of human rights is part of the standard of control of the ombudsmen,[51] their work will differ when one specific human right and the observation of its protection is explicitly assigned. The network established by a specialised ombudsman in protecting children or future generations is unique in that all his or her activity is driven by the principles of that particular field, and complaints are reviewed through that special lens. When ombudsmen are provided with the function of protecting the right to a healthy environment or the right of children, they promote not just the implementation and enforcement of the relevant national laws but also international laws.[52]

The substance and the meaning of the relevant human right is developed and elaborated through the work of the ombudsman. It should be pointed out that those rights are not only interpreted by the ombudsman, but also by national and

[49] In Hungary this special power was first assigned only to the ombudsman for future generations. After reorganisation of the ombudsman's system, this power became general.

[50] The Hungarian ombudsman may turn to the Constitutional Court seeking to nullify any piece of legislation on the ground of being against the Fundamental Law.

[51] Kucsko-Stadlmayer, *supra* note 47 at 39.

[52] See e.g. *The Ombudsman for Children in Norway Supplementary Report to the UN Committee on the Rights of the Child 2009* (Ombudsman for Children, Oslo 2009). Additionally, see the Hungarian ombudsman for future generations work based on the application of the Aarhus Convention referred to in the Report of the Deputy Commissioner responsible for the protection of the interests of future generations in *Report 2013 on the Activities of the Commissioner for Fundamental Rights and His Deputies* (Office of the Commissioner for Fundamental Rights 2014).

international bodies and that may directly or indirectly influence the approach of the ombudsman. Also, interpretations and decisions of a constitutional court[53] may be considered as the baseline for their work.[54] In such a case, not only the constitutional court's interpretation of rule of law or basic human rights are concerned, but also how it interprets the principles of sustainable development, including the protection of natural resources, and of non-derogation.[55] The decisions of a constitutional court are influenced by the constitutionalisation of environmental rights.[56] This kind of strong link established between the two institutions leads to the emergence of a common understanding on the content of the legal requirements of both legislation and application of law.[57]

One could argue that the above-mentioned features are all characteristics of the ombudsman institution in general. The main variations lie not in the powers assigned to specific ombudspersons, but in the degree of restriction to one specific field. While it is possible to say that making the ombudsman responsible for one human right does not extend the standard of control,[58] it does, however, make the ombudsman the 'guardian' of that human right, thus taking away the discretion of the ombudsman to decide what issues to handle based on complaints or *ex officio*.[59] It does require the ombudsman to concentrate his or her effort and activity

53 According to Comella, '[i]t is typical for political institutions (such as the government, a qualified minority of Parliament, the Ombudsman, etc. . . .) to be entitled to challenge statutes in the abstract'. V. Ferreres Comella, 'The Rise of Specialized Constitutional Courts', in Ginsburg, *supra* note 22 at 265–278, 267.

54 This is clearly the case in Hungary. Each report has a part citing Constitutional Court cases relevant to the subject of the report.

55 The non-derogation principle was introduced and elaborated by the Decision 28/1994. (V. 20.) AB of the Hungarian Constitutional Court. It means 'that the state may not let the level of nature protection provided by regulation deteriorate, unless it is unavoidable for exercising another constitutional right or value. Even in such a case, the reduction of the protection level still should not be disproportionate to the goal to be achieved.' It is common that the ombudsmen refer to it. The ombudsman used this principle as baseline in the famous case on the investigation of the of the circumstances of the installation of the Zengő mountain radar station. A. Pánovics, 'National Defence vs. Environmental Protection', in Gy. Bándi (ed.) *Environmental Democracy and Law, Public Participation in Europe, The Avosetta Series (II)* (Europa Law Publishing 2014) 221–233, 225.

56 See J.R. May and E. Daily, *Global Environmental Constitutionalism* (Cambridge University Press 2015).

57 See the decision of the Hungarian Constitutional Court regarding the bill affecting the organisational set up of nature protection (Decision 16/2015. (VI. 5.) AB). The Constitutional Court made reference to accepting some of the arguments in the statement of the ombudsman for future generations asked by the Constitutional Court during the legal process. Since then that decision of the Constitutional Court is regularly cited by both entities in their decisions and reports closing investigations.

58 Kucsko-Stadlmayer argues that '[t]he emphasis placed on human rights protection may have a certain publicity effect; but it does not imply an extended standard of control'. Kucsko-Stadlmayer, *supra* note 47 at 39.

59 On the summary of the right of the European ombudspersons to initiate proceedings see Kucsko-Stadlmayer, *supra* note 47 at 18–22.

to oversee how that human right is respected, and what are the conditions – legal and non-legal – that hinder its protection or lead to its abuse. When the ombudsman is explicitly entrusted with the protection of one specific human right, it means that the institution's work is dedicated solely to it, and annual reports have to be submitted on how the human right was respected and consequent recommendations. The problems arising in regard to that right cannot be ignored. It is the duty of the ombudsman to scrutinise them and to come up with guidance on corrective or preventive measures for their solutions, including considering legislation or application of the law. It is generally recognised that the non-binding nature of the ombudsman's recommendation does not have a negative impact on how persuasive they are viewed as being and how well their work is accepted.[60]

Since ombudsmen are intermediaries, the actor(s) who can be the subject of their investigation is important, whether it is restricted to public bodies of administration or includes other public or private entities.[61] Investigations are important tools for making people aware of the subject examined and the relevant problems and requirements. The longer the list of subjects to be investigated, the wider the group of people the ombudsman can reach. From the perspective of Bartee's model, this means that the list of subjects for investigation indicates whose experience, attitude, and viewpoints the ombudsman can draw upon and when to decide on which of the powers to use and how. From that perspective, the organisational choice for the ombudsman is important.

The independence of an incumbent differs according to the organisational structure of the ombudsman institution. There are three systems of organisation: monocratic, cooperative, and deputy.[62] The experience of the institutions shows that it is possible to set up an organisational structure within which the cooperative model and the deputy model co-exist as a consequence of the difference in powers.[63] Within the deputy system the freedom of the deputy depends on the powers specifically assigned to him or her. Having not just a specific field to be responsible for but also a specific power allows the deputy to act independently and to show authority in his or her field.[64] This independence and authority can be enforced by providing for a special

[60] Buck, Kirkham, and Thompson argue that the non-binding nature is actually a positive feature. Buck et al., *supra* note 45 at 40–42.

[61] On the European experience see Kucsko-Stadlmayer, *supra* note 47 at 23–25.

[62] The systems are differentiated by the number of incumbents appointed and by the relationship between them. Kucsko-Stadlmayer, *supra* note 47 at 11–12.

[63] That is the Hungarian model. However, there are other academic views on the main characteristics. Csink describes the Hungarian ombudsman system as monocratic despite the two deputies appointed by the parliament and the specific mandates assigned to them. Csink, *supra* note 46 at 603.

[64] See powers assigned to the Hungarian ombudsman for future generations in Section 3(1) of the Act CXI of 2011 on the Commissioner for Fundamental Rights www.ajbh.hu/en/web/ajbh-en/act-cxi-of-2011 accessed 30 November 2017. For the functions and powers of the Hungarian Ombudsman for Future Generations, see *infra* ch. 4 in this volume.

title that does not refer to the organisational structure.[65] It is not just a strong message sent out on the significance of that specific field but also an opportunity for the deputy to shape the legal and non-legal requirements against which the conduct and behaviour of natural and legal entities are evaluated. Such a position and power demonstrates the deputy's key role in both the institutionalisation and the socialisation phase of Bartee's model.

### *Supreme Audit Institution*

In general, supreme audit institutions (SAIs) belong to the institutions that oversee the executive.[66] SAIs are respected (1) for their objectivity, secured by strict methodology that was developed over time for elaborating and using objective criteria for evaluations; (2) for being independent from the government and any political movement; (3) for having the right to access to information; and (4) for the expertise of their employees. These characteristics are universally considered as guarantees for enabling SAIs to pursue oversight work.[67] SAIs can reflect on the performance of the executive in regards to sustainable development by conducting a performance audit, also called a value-for-money audit, with regard to economy, efficiency, and effectiveness. While this kind of audit is regularly performed by SAIs, when it comes to sustainable development it is important how the 'three Es'[68] are put into that context and the theoretical background behind the questions raised for review. Comparing reports can reveal striking differences.[69] While national park authorities are guardians of our natural world and national heritage,[70] they are not immune to budgetary

[65] Ibid. at sec. 3(4).

[66] Beetham, *supra* note 35 at 145–146; Yamamoto, *supra* note 26 at 74.

[67] Beetham, *supra* note 35 at 131–132, 145–146; Yamamoto, *supra* note 26 at 74–76.

[68] Under Point 8 of ISSAI 310 the following definition of the three Es is given: 'The principles of economy, efficiency and effectiveness can be defined as follows: a) The principle of economy means minimising the costs of resources. The resources used have to be available in due time, of appropriate quantity and quality, and at the best price. b) The principle of efficiency means getting the most from the available resources. It is concerned with the relationship between resources employed and outputs delivered in terms of quantity, quality and timing. c) The principle of effectiveness concerns meeting the objectives set and achieving the intended results.' INTOSAI: Guidelines on Central Concepts for Performance Auditing, ISSAI 310.

[69] For comparison, see the Canadian 2013 Fall Report of the Commissioner of the Environment and Sustainable Development and the report (November 2012) of the Hungarian State Audit Office on Task Performance and Property Management of National Park Directorates (12106) www.oag-bvg.gc.ca/internet/English/parl_cesd_201311_00_e_38670.html accessed 30 November 2017; The summary of the Hungarian report is available in English https://asz.hu/storage/files/files/Angol_portal/All_reports/2012/12106_nemzeti_parkok_en_vegl.pdf accessed 30 November 2017. The full report only in Hungarian can be accessed at https://asz.hu/storage/files/files/%C3%96sszes%20jelent%C3%A9s/2012/12106j000.pdf accessed 30 November 2017.

[70] According to IUCN, national parks are '[l]arge natural or near natural areas set aside to protect large-scale ecological processes, along with the complement of species and ecosystems characteristic of the area, which also provide a foundation for environmentally and culturally compatible spiritual, scientific, educational, recreational and visitor opportunities. Primary

cutbacks. Whatever decision on adaptation policy to such restrictions the public body managing areas of nature protection and providing information on biodiversity wishes to take, both its negative and positive impacts on tasks and duties should be analysed and evaluated prior to acceptance. For the outcome of the evaluation, it is crucial that the criteria used by the SAI reflect ecological integrity and sustainability. Reducing expenditure on gasoline on the one hand will definitely reduce overhead costs of the public body and help it remain within its budget. On the other hand, it would result in fewer site visits and limitation of the area monitored within the same time frame. For decisions regarding ecological integrity, information on the conditions of ecosystems, the availability of ecosystem services – quantity and quality – and threats to be considered is crucial. That information is not only necessary for making well-grounded decisions on management issues, but is also key for making decisions in other policy areas affecting the natural environment. Making an informed decision requires reliable data drawn from scientific research and systematic monitoring. A decision on reducing the time and area to be covered, for example through reduced use of cars or increasing the hectares visited per person, is by implication a decision on allowing reduced presence in the field and in monitoring activities, jeopardising the credibility of data on ecological integrity. For that reason, evaluation of cost reduction as an answer to austerity measures should be reflected by indicators making such decisions transparent and trade-offs visible. Similar concern should be raised in relation to policy that finds its way out of budgetary constraints by increasing revenues.

Depending on the criteria and indicators used during the performance audit, the outcome and, as a consequence, the message sent will differ significantly. When a decision of a public body struck by an austerity measure is positively acknowledged by SAI for the management choices that allowed it to stay within the budget cut, then the message of the audit office sent to the body responsible for the budgetary cut is that the austerity measure was justified and the cut should be kept in the future. When additional aspects are taken into account – such as how it affects the implementation of conservation plans and whether it would create any information gap, force postponement of research or other monitoring activities, or increase backlog of unfinished work – then the SAI recommendation may take an opposite turn and ask to make previous resources available again in order to secure adequate funding.[71]

objective: To protect natural biodiversity along with its underlying ecological structure and supporting environmental processes, and to promote education and recreation.' See IUCN, *Protected Areas* www.iucn.org/theme/protected-areas/about/protected-areas-categories/category-ii-national-park accessed 30 November 2017.

[71] The Canadian Commissioner for future generations pointed out the need to consider all of them, while there was no reference to any of them when the positive statement on meeting budget constrain was made by the Hungarian Audit Office.

One could ask how it is possible to come to opposite results when the same audit standards are applied all around the world. The answer can be found in the standard itself.[72] The standard provides a sophisticated tool for making the audits; however, the mandate of audit offices and the legal framework of its operation may vary significantly. In general, SAIs have great discretion in determining what and how to audit, choosing from types of audit or audit approach, and setting objectives and criteria. When the act creating the SAI provides for respecting sustainable development and including nature and the needs of future generations, the freedom of the SAI's choice is limited and the aspects having relevance to them become an integral part of all audits.[73] Clearly, this influences priority setting of topics for audit, changes the objectives of individual audits, and influences the criteria to be elaborated and used as a benchmark for evaluation. The result of a performance audit is very much dependent on what criteria are used. Criteria suitable in one country may not be suitable in the other. The context of audit objectives and audit questions within which the principles of economy, efficiency, and/or effectiveness are considered may demonstrate significant difference.

Beyond the legal requirements other causes may explain variations in the substance of audit objectives, audit questions, and criteria leading to different results. In most countries, it is the auditor who identifies the subject matter of a performance audit.[74] Thus, the audit is based on the theoretical approach to the subject accepted by the auditor, and the experiences learned through formal and informal channels by the auditor on problems and their solutions. When a commissioner of the environment and sustainable development whose other mandates include monitoring sustainable development strategies and channelling petitions of civil society and answers from the government and governmental bodies is responsible for a performance audit, monitoring activities and petitions become an important source of information on citizens' concern and governmental approach and solutions. While the use of standards is considered an objective evaluation method, it has subjective elements that are shaped by cultural and social factors beyond the commissioner's academic and personal life experience.[75] Additionally, even though criteria should be objective, their establishment is based on subjective evaluations

[72] 'The International Standard of Supreme Audit Institutions (ISSAI) for Performance Auditing developed by the International Organisation of Supreme Audit Institutions (INTOSAI) aims to promote independent and effective auditing and support the members of INTOSAI in the development of their own professional approach in accordance with their mandates and with national laws and regulations.' INTOSAI: Standard for Performance Auditing ISSAI 3000, Vienna Introduction, point 1.

[73] Auditor General Act of Canada, R.S.C, 1985, c. A-17.

[74] In some countries there are institutions that may request or order SAIs to perform audits. Yamamoto, *supra* note 26 at 20, 76.

[75] The papers on the institutions show changes in priorities following changes in person.

such as 'relevant' or 'complete'.[76] For example, in a society where indigenous people still follow their traditional way of life, the words 'resource management', 'subsistence resource use', 'avoiding adverse effects', and 'primary management objective', to name just a few, carry a different meaning compared to those societies where they are no longer present or cannot have their voice heard or their way of life respected.[77]

According to the INTOSAI's standard, the SAI 'does not question the intentions and decisions of the legislature, depending on the SAI's mandate, but examines whether any shortcomings of the laws and regulations or their implementation have prevented the specified audit objectives from being achieved'.[78] In the context of Bartee's holistic problem-solving system, criteria (indicators) may reflect the acknowledgement by the auditor and his or her team of a problem relevant to sustainable development and future generations' need. By the use of those criteria the auditor could shed light on the nature of the problems and recommend adequate measures to solve them.[79] One could argue that this may contradict the standard. It depends on the legal framework. The auditor's right to establish criteria reflecting sustainable development should not be questioned if his or her mandate includes pursuing such a scrutiny. The same could be said when a constitution consists of provisions on sustainable development, respecting needs of future generations, or protecting the natural environment, and they are made the main organising principles of public and private life. In such a legal environment, the auditor becomes an integral part of those institutions promoting changes in behaviour of all stakeholders based on the norms and values of sustainable development.

### *Independent Advisor to the Government*

All the institutions discussed earlier had a mandate to improve legislation and application of law, but none of them had a mandate to be a catalyst and to advise government on what changes are needed in order to turn the principles of sustainable development into reality. Experience shows that it is possible to establish an institution independent from the government with a mandate to give advice to the government on what to do in order to get the message of sustainable development across the whole society, both private and public sectors. There are three plus one indispensable prerequisites for the existence of such an institution. The first three prerequisites are (1) a strong commitment by the government to sustainable

[76] 'Audit criteria have to be relevant, understandable, complete, reliable, and objective in the context of the subject matter, the audit objective(s) and/or the audit questions', ISSAI 3000, Vienna, point 48.

[77] The populations of Canada, Finland, Norway, and New Zealand include communities of indigenous people.

[78] ISSAI 3000, Vienna, Point 31.

[79] See note 2 on Bartee's holistic problem solving.

development, (2) an acknowledgement that an independent institution is the best advisor, and (3) provision of adequate resources. The plus one prerequisite changes depend on the phase of legal institutionalisation of sustainable development.[80] In this context, this means that the substantive elements of sustainable development are clarified in a piece of legislation along with the duty of (at least) public bodies to meet the indicators developed. In the phase when the meaning of sustainable development and its indicators are to be developed, the fourth prerequisite is the recognition of the need for, and the commitment to, an inclusive deliberative process. Later, however, when the legal institutionalisation is finished and the indicators have been developed, the fourth requirement is the provision of a clear mandate and the assignment of power to the advisor. The variability of the fourth conditions should not be overlooked. Prior to institutionalisation it is in the interest of all public bodies to participate in shedding light on their operation in order to find the best solution. The investigation pursued by the advisor does not have the negative connotation of an official control that always accompanies the work of supervisory bodies, but neither does it mean that the advisor's visits are received positively. However, during the first phase the aim of the investigation is not to match the performance of the public body to requirements and evaluate it accordingly, but rather to involve it in the process of developing the indicators of sustainable development.

The aim of the investigation of the second phase is to see how the public body has adapted to the new requirements in order to meet the goals reflected by the indicators. The attitude towards the advisor may change drastically. The question is whether the positive role of the advisor in the first phase can be kept in the second phase when public accountability is concerned, and when the advisor becomes the guardian of *the ability of future generations to meet their needs*.[81] The trust that the advisor has developed during the first phase is at stake and as a consequence its efficiency in reaching its own aim, that is to remain the catalyst in changing society and promoting a sustainable path. Is it possible to keep that trust? How can the advisor maintain the cooperative nature of the relationship, the openness on both sides, and the positive attitude towards problems related to adaptation that was inherent and self-evident in the first phase?[82] Maintaining trust may be easier if mandates and duties are assigned to other public bodies such as the Auditor General or ombudsman to review the performance of the government and public bodies on

[80] Compare the written statement by the Welsh Assembly Government with the Articles 17-24 of the Well-being of Future Generations (Wales Act 2015) http://gov.wales/about/cabinet/cabinetstatements/previous-administration/2011/sfcommissioner/?lang=en, http://www.legislation.gov.uk/anaw/2015/2/data.pdf accessed 30 November 2017.

[81] Well-being of Future Generations (Wales) Act 2015 art. 18(a)(i).

[82] The problem of and practical difficulties in finding a good balance for sustaining cooperation during investigation is well known in the work of ombudspersons. Buck et al., *supra* note 45 at 149.

how they meet the indicators of sustainable development and to make them accountable by those institutions to the public.

It is important to point to the links between the two phases. The first phase corresponds to the personalisation and the cooperation phase of Bartee's model and the second phase is the institutionalisation phase. The socialisation phase, meaning the acceptance of the norms and values of sustainable development and adapting to them by changing behaviour, may have already started during the first phase prior to the institutionalisation. If indicators are developed on the basis of values and norms agreed by the whole society, it means that the intention and efforts to reach them have been part of moral duties and could be considered as natural obligations.[83] The institutionalisation of such obligations (that is, turning them into legal obligation) would be seen as less intrusive, and acceptance of and compliance with it would be natural. In that respect, the indicators have an essential role, on the one hand in changing behaviours, if important indicators are reflections of natural obligations originating from moral duty generally recognised by the society and/or legal obligations, and on the other hand, in making meeting those obligations possible, if the conditions are in place and secure for the long run. When the advisor's role in the first phase is to promote sustainable development across society and the advisor has the time and resources to meet all stakeholders during a deliberative process, then the chance of finding adequate indicators that are not under- or over-ambitious is higher. Nationwide consultations can help with the acknowledgement of the relationships between obligations and the indicators, and how compliance with legal obligations could promote meeting indicators.

### *Parliamentary Commissioner for the Environment*

The experiences of the institutions show that when environmental degradation is a clear threat to the way of life pursued the demand grows to have an institution with a function of halting such degradation and making decision makers aware of alternative ways of sustaining life and of the need to reconcile conflicting interests. It is axiomatic that economic development of a country is shaped by political decision makers at the highest level, by the legislature, and the executive branch. In societies where the main legislature is the parliament, the governments have wide discretionary power on the choice and means of governance.[84] Policies are usually backed by

[83] Willems argues that natural obligations have become *a bridge between law and morality*. K. Willems, 'The Limits of Law of Obligations', in E. Claes, W. Devroe, and B. Keirsbilck (eds.), *Facing the Limits of the Law* (Springer 2009) 45–56 at 47. Similar conclusions can be drawn from Lauth's arguments differentiating between formal and informal institutions. He draws the attention to the motivation factor in individual decisions when following the pattern of conducts that are socially accepted. H.-J. Lauth, 'Formal and Informal Institutions', in J. Gandhi–Rubén Ruiz-Rufino (eds.), *Routledge Handbook of Comparative Political Institutions* (Routledge 2015) 56–69 at 58.

[84] It comes from the principle of separation of power.

legislation. However, without proper implementation, not just of legal rules but also non-legal measures and strong enforcement of legal obligations, even the best designed environmental policy could fail.[85] Thus, for those who wish to change public decision making on economic development, it may appear self-evident that there is a need for the establishment of an institution that (1) provides systematic information on the state of natural resources, (2) halts economic development that is not in line with sustainable development, and (3) oversees relevant governmental decision making.

As previously shown, parliaments have a wide range of institutional choices for improving their own decision-making process or overseeing the government's performance. However, each institution discussed earlier has some limitation of scope owing to restrictions, such as rights related to subjects to investigate, and methods and powers inherent in the organisational form. One way to overcome this limitation is to establish the position of a parliamentary commissioner with a kind of multifunctional mandate that may integrate functions and mandates similar to other institutions without the bias of organisational restrictions stemming from the particular notion and viewpoints attached to them, such as parliamentary committees, auditors, and ombudsman. This provides for high flexibility in terms of choice of subjects and bodies to review and scrutinise, methods to use, and powers to act.

It is important to emphasise that flexibility does not mean unlimited power. On the one hand, limitation is provided for by legislation and by relevant rules establishing the institution. On the other hand, the institution has to fit its activities into a web of parliamentary institutions with overlapping mandates and to find its niche to avoid duplication and clashes. This second issue is not only a limitation but a prerequisite of its existence from two aspects. In essence, (1) the existence of the multifunctional institution could be justified even if other public bodies exist having similar mandates, and (2) the flexibility ensured by multi-functionality may provide efficiency in adapting to changing social, economic, and legal environments. Multi-functionality with adequate power provides enough room for filling relevant gaps from the perspective of protecting the natural environment.

As in the case of all monocratic bodies, it is the parliamentary commissioner who has the right to prioritise his or her activity. The interpretation of the commissioner's role and of the status quo, including the state of the environment, the economy, and social and cultural status, plays an important part in choosing which set of powers the commissioner wishes to use to fulfil his or her mandate. A wide mandate may be

85 The legal protection of the EU is considered one of the strongest in the world; however, its effectiveness depends on the implementation and enforcement at member state level. The number of infringement procedures regarding lack or inadequate implementation of environmental law initiated by the European Commission against member states shows that problems are present with regard to legislation at member state level let alone application of law; see the statistics of the EU Commission on Environmental Infringements http://ec.europa.eu/environment/legal/law/statistics.htm accessed 30 November 2017.

seen as a tool for creating a special intermediary position reaching and connecting different segments of society. As was shown previously, most of the institutions have a very strong mandate related to oversight of the government and its bodies and to recommend corrective measures. The benchmarks to which the government's performance is compared are important factors in halting degradation of natural resources. The role of the parliamentary commissioner in developing benchmarks is a key factor because it provides the basis of evaluation and recommendations on preventive or corrective measures. The wide mandate that includes system review provides the commissioner enough room to monitor and investigate performance and the impacts of actions and non-actions of the various stakeholders on natural resources. It places conclusions drawn and recommendations on sound basis. The holistic approach is inherently present in such an intermediary role. The commissioner is a key actor in problem solving even if it is not compulsory to follow the recommendations. The commissioner is a constant reminder of the impacts of humans on the natural environment and how they limit alternative choices of human life and life sustenance for future generations.[86]

## COMMON PROBLEMS ADDRESSED

All of the institutions play an important intermediary role and help with penetration of the idea of long-term thinking, sustainable development, and the need to take future generations' interests into account. However, they play this role differently. All of the institutions provide relevant information for decision makers and are dedicated to providing adequate information on problems of today and future and to help long-term thinking. Without exception, they acknowledge the importance of the attitude of people towards environmental protection. The work of the institutions demonstrates that this attitude is very much dependent on what is the source of people's livelihoods and how alienated people are from their natural environment.

In a very simplified way two main groups of people can be recognised. The first group consists of those whose life sustenance from generation to generation is dependent on the state and condition of natural environment. Any human activity negatively affecting the source of their life, such as overexploitation that does not take into account the reproduction capacity of the region under the environmental conditions of the climate, soil, and water availability or disturbing and degrading the state of their natural environment, especially by pollution, demonstrates threats to their very lives. They are sensitive to and acknowledge negative impacts. Thus, they want to learn about all the possible impacts of economic development on natural resources and how this affects its quantity and quality.[87] The second group of people

[86] E.g. the good practice guide of the commissioner on consultations with Māori.

[87] This is reflected in petitions and arguments in all of the countries, not just in those where indigenous people try to pursue their traditional way of life.

are characterised by having income earned mainly by working under some kind of an employment contract. Thus, on the one hand degradation of natural resources may deprive people of the very basic needs of food and water supply. On the other hand, without industrialised work – including the industrialisation of agriculture – people cannot provide an adequate income to cover costs of their life including food and water. Thus, without 'industrialised jobs' they are also deprived of their basic needs.[88] Both sides can argue that their interests should be protected because their interests concern their sustenance,[89] and this can be considered one of the most important paradoxes of political life.[90]

Besides the source of sustenance and survival, there is one more important difference between the two groups that must be considered – the impact of economic activity as an externality on human health. When quantity and quality of natural resources and ecosystem services are crucial for sustenance, the choice of technology is a reflection of that requirement. As a consequence, only technology that is not harmful to human health is used. The knowledge relates to health effects of traditional technologies too, built on the fact that human beings themselves are living creatures, and it has been handed down between generations. It is a knowledge that is part of everyday economic operation, and the user gains first-hand information on the negative impact of technology development. In a technology-based society that outlaws technologies that are harmful to sustenance, and to human health as a result, the culture and cultural pattern including informal institutions would integrate those requirements and expectations.[91]

[88] This narrative is typical with respect to economic development providing industry-related jobs.

[89] This difference becomes crystal clear when the traditional lifestyle and the means of sustenance of indigenous people are threatened and come into conflict with the means of sustaining life based on income generated through employment in an industrialised economy. For a review of this conflict from the perspective of constitutional law see C. Charters, 'Comparative Constitutional Law and Indigenous Peoples: Canada, New Zealand and the USA', in T. Ginsburg and R. Dixon (eds.), *Comparative Constitutional Law* (Edward Elgar 2011) 170–188.

[90] Stones argues that political life is full of paradox and there are several ways in which those can be addressed, e.g. how policies regarding 'the commons' may change depending on the perception of them and the meaning attached to them. D. Stone, *Policy Paradox: The Art of Political Decision Making*, 3rd edn. (W.W. Norton & Company 2012) 59–62.

[91] The term of informal institution used by Lauth refers to 'a norm or set of norms that have a significant impact on the behaviour of individuals' and they are not formally codified. In his interpretation, 'culture indicates a broad concept including rules, values, traditions, and customs. Together, these indicate patterns of a collective identity, which in turn provide a specific interpretation (or construction) of the world and motivate the adoption of common lifestyles (or frame the horizon of possible actions) to a certain degree.' He argues that 'culture and informal institutions are overlapping concepts and informal institutions can be understood as an integral part of cultural patterns'. H.-J. Lauth, 'Formal and Informal Institutions', in J. Gandhi and R. Ruiz-Rufino (eds.), *Routledge Handbook of Comparative Political Institutions* (Routledge 2015) 56–69 at 57, 59.

Contrary to the first group's expectations towards technology, the second group is more permissive regarding the harmful effects on the health and lives of living creatures, within limits set by legislature or authorities based on the opinion of researchers and results of laboratories. Placing technology development, including testing its impact on life, into laboratories has several consequences. It has a strong impact on culture and cultural patterns, on the value system, the attitude towards life, knowledge based on technologies and their harmful impacts, and the relevant informal institutions.[92] Sustainable development policies are decisions on choices. In those decisions, choice of science and technology development plays a key role. The work of the institutions shows that people are concerned and fear loss of control over such decisions, especially in relation to nature and human health. This concern and fear has been turned into the precautionary principle. However, there is no common use of the application of this principle.[93]

Using Bartee's model, it is clear that the societal problems differ in the two groups when it comes to questions such as what the source of sustenance is (what kind of economic activity provides for the support of life) and what should be considered as a health hazard. For the first group there is no difference in how they think about the potential harmful effect of technologies on natural resources and human health, while for the second group their thoughts may become separated, especially for those whose income is directly dependent on the use of such technology. Whose interest is stronger?[94] What is really at stake? Do people have an enforceable individual or collective right to choice of life or healthy environment or is it a question to be decided only by politicians through economic development programmes?[95] How could or should institutions influence decision making? The choice of institution is very much dependent on the answer to those questions.

## CONCLUSION

There are different ways in which the problems related to sustainable development, the protection of the natural environment and future generations can be addressed by establishing special institutions and may be instrumental in solving problems. Despite the differences in organisational structure or constitutional status, the use of a holistic approach to problems, long-term thinking, and the intermediary role are

[92] These differences could be found in materials available on the websites of the institutions.

[93] It is most apparent in relation to GMOs. While in Hungary it is the Fundamental Law that guarantees GMO free agriculture and food production, in Canada the genetic modification of salmons has been permitted and allowed for human consumption. In both countries there is no difference in the knowledge of scientific evidence, the difference is in how and when the precautionary principle is applied.

[94] For examples of conflicts and even violent clashes between the two interests, see e.g. Vandana Shiva's books.

[95] The appearance of environmental constitutionalism (the abundance of environment-related provisions in constitutions) is a sign that the 'rights-based approach' is gaining ground.

key features of such institutions. Their task is to make a link between the present and the future. It is not a choice of those institutions. It should be part of their mandate and they can be held accountable for it.

There is no common understanding of the notion of sustainable development and what the interests of future generations are. However, it is common to use or to refer to the definition of the Brundtland Report, and the functions often correspond to those differentiated by Brown Weiss related to planetary trust.[96] Based on the constitutional system, it is country-specific whether the substance of the notion is elaborated in legally binding documents (in the constitution or legislation) or it is within the discretionary power of the institution to develop it or to decide whose interpretation is accepted as relevant. The questions of whether the interest of future generations can be articulated and who belongs to future generations are decided by the establishment of the institution and by the mandates prescribed.

No general rules can be identified on organisational choice. There is no good or bad choice. However, the choice determines the field of action of the institution, the role it can play in promoting changes in attitude and norms values in order to make the notion of sustainable development a guiding principle for everyone and for all decisions made by both public and private entities, individuals and bodies. When those guiding principles are provided for by the highest level of legislature, the institution has a firm reference point in pursuing its work and promoting penetration of the principles into the whole society. Sustainable development is an attitude to life not at the individual level but at the level of the society.

The institutions may protect the interests of future generations and promote sustainable development by pointing to problems and conflicts of today and the possible long-term effects and impacts relevant for the future. Acknowledging, analysing, and evaluating the impacts of decisions of today on the future and on alternative choices (e.g. if the way life is sustained and life sustenance is secured) is one of the key tools for protecting the interest of future generations. It forces decision makers to weigh and balance different choices. The institution may promote well-informed decision making by channelling adequate information to decision makers and by overseeing public bodies' decision-making process at all phases, from the preparatory phase to the decision-taking phase to surveillance and monitoring.

While one of the most important functions of the institutions is overseeing governmental decision making, their mandate may not be restricted to this. Additional functions may help the institution to play the role of a guardian. As a guardian, the institution may reflect on the decisions of all stakeholders irrespective of their form, regardless of whether they were formulated in the process of legislation or during application of law, or by whom they were taken.

[96] See E. Brown Weiss, 'The Planetary Trust: Conservation and Intergenerational Equity, Ecology Law Quarterly' (1984) 11:4 *Ecology Law Quarterly* 495–582.

The social embeddedness of such institutions is supported, since it is the result of a deliberative process involving society. The long-term existence of the institution may depend on it. The need to have such institutions with a clear scope and mandate might be questioned from time to time. Their existence may be considered a threat to the political establishment, especially to the balance between the legislature and the executive, or they may be viewed as unnecessary in the light of similar or even overlapping mandates. To avoid those conflicts and the jeopardising of the basic functions of the institution, due care has to be taken in the process of its establishment and operation. At the same time, one should never forget that the existence of those kinds of institutions is the outcome of political decisions. Politicians are key actors in what problems are perceived, whether the paradoxes are acknowledged, and what solutions are envisioned and adopted.

# 30

# Comparing Progress in Intergenerational Governance

*Marie-Claire Cordonier Segger, Alexandra R. Harrington, Sébastien Jodoin, Sumudu Atapattu, Salim Nakjavani, and Jaykumar Menon*

For humanity and the Earth, it is crucial that present institutions learn to respect and honour the rights of future generations and to consider the needs of those who are yet to come. The rights of future generations are starting to be recognised as an essential part of policy decisions and even as a legal requirement in an increasing number of countries. Indeed, some countries and communities have begun to design innovative instruments to represent the voices of future generations in their policy-making processes, and to better realise these rights. The need to respect and realise the rights of future generations has also been adopted by the international community through treaty law and through the jurisprudence of eminent courts and tribunals such as the ICJ. Indeed, the UNGA now considers the rights of future generations in its global deliberations, and several proposals have been generated among experts for the creation of new international instruments to represent the voices of future generations in global policy making. Perhaps the most concrete form of policy guidance, and arguably the most visible place, for future generations in the UN context is the 2015 SDGs. At this point in time, it is helpful to summarise and analyse the new domestic and international institutions that work to deliver on the rights of future generations. Indeed, surveying the more progressive national innovations and the principal international trends in this domain make new options possible for policy makers wishing to establish novel instruments to adequately protect the rights of future generations at national and international levels.

This chapter explores instruments that affect the rights of future generations, engage policy making around these rights, and effectively monitor the impacts of such policies on future generations. In particular, it reviews different existing models for enabling the representation of future generations in national governments, including a range of instruments such as Ombudspersons or Parliamentary Commissions for the Rights of Future Generations, providing a brief discussion of their strengths and weaknesses, especially the strength of their mandates for civic engagement and policy intervention. The paper then explores the potential for new international policies, laws, and institutions to monitor the impact of laws on future generations, for instance, through the creation of a renewable mandate for the UN Trusteeship Council, a UN Rapporteur on the Rights of Future Generations or a UN Working Group for the Rights of Future Generations, or an Ombudsperson/Inspection Panel mechanism similar to those used by the World Bank Group of financial institutions. Drawing on the deliberations of the World Future Council's Future Justice Commission, the chapter concludes with recommendations for a new mechanism to represent the rights of future generations nationally and internationally, in light of the predicted impacts and effectiveness in terms of awareness raising and policy change.

## INNOVATIONS AND EXPERIENCES WITH NATIONAL INSTRUMENTS TO REPRESENT THE RIGHTS OF FUTURE GENERATIONS

The rights of future generations are not new, nor is the recognition of the need to respect these rights in laws and policies of countries. Indeed, many constitutions around the world include respect for the rights of future generations and reflect a commitment to sustainable development, with differing degrees of commitment and enforceability depending on the specific culture, political system, and division of powers in each country.

However, to enshrine such rights in constitutional law is not effective unless a State also has institutions and systems in place to ensure that the environment, sustainable development, and the rights of future generations are respected in national policy-making processes, and that initiatives which will impact on the ability of future generations to have their rights protected can be investigated, reviewed, and, if necessary, reconsidered. At present, States are designing and implementing of new instruments to represent and defend the rights of future generations at the national level. Recent experiments have included the design and establishment of National Parliamentary Commissions for Future Generations, for the Environment, for Natural Resources and/or for Sustainable Development, the appointment of National Commissioners for the Environment or for the Environment and Sustainable Development, and even an Ombudsperson for Future Generations. These institutions have different strengths and weaknesses, depending on the mandate, powers, and selection processes for these commissions and commissioners, among other factors.

The recognition of the rights of future generations, and the establishment of national institutions, must also be complemented by a clear indication that national courts will recognise, defend, and uphold these rights. Though progress is still slow and unsteady in this regard, the rights of future generations have been recognised in leading decisions of national courts around the world.

### *Constitutional Protections for the Rights of Future Generations*

Several national constitutions feature explicit references to the rights of future generations. One of the most progressive forms of such recognition involves the implicit or explicit recognition of the needs and rights of future generations, whereby protection of the inherent rights of future generations are seen as part of the *raison d'être* for the governing constitution or charter itself, in a commitment to the Earth and to humanity's future right to survival and prosperity. For instance, the protection of the rights of future generations was cited as one of the reasons for the creation of a Charter of Fundamental Rights and Freedoms in the Czech Republic.[1] Similarly, the French Charter for the Environment is also influenced by the preservation of the rights of future generations.[2] The protection of future generations is an underlying principle behind the Estonian Constitution as well.[3]

In other constitutions, the rights of future generations are seen as part of a commitment to protection of the environment, and a fundamental principle of the constitution itself.[4] Similarly, the rights of future generations are recognised under the Ecuadorean Constitution as guaranteed principles for the State's protection of the environment:

> The constitution recognizes the following environmental principles: The State guarantees a sustainable model of environmentally balanced development, respectful of cultural diversity, to conserve biodiversity and the natural regeneration capacity of ecosystems, and to ensure the satisfaction of the needs of present and future generations.[5]

This recognition is equally clear in the constitution of Argentina, which states that

> All inhabitants are entitled to the right to a healthy and balanced environment fit for human development in order that productive activities shall meet present needs without endangering those of future generations . . .[6]

The South African Constitution also expressly states and affirms the rights of future generations.[7]

Other constitutions operationalise the responsibility for sustainability, and the active pursuit of sustainable development as a policy objective, by delegating it

[1] Charter of Fundamental Rights and Freedoms of the Czech Republic (1991) preamble ('The Federal Assembly, . . . recalling its share of responsibility towards future generations for the fate of life on this earth, . . . has enacted this Charter of fundamental rights and freedom.')

[2] See French Charter for the Environment (2017) preamble ('Considering that, . . . in order to ensure sustainable development, choices designed to meet the needs of present generation should not jeopardise the ability of future generations and other peoples to meet their own needs.')

[3] Constitution of Estonia (2003) preamble.

[4] Constitution of Andorra (1993) preamble.

[5] Constitution of Ecuador (2008) art. 395.

[6] Constitution of Argentina (1994) art. 41 clause 1.

[7] Constitution of the Republic of South Africa (1994) art. 24.

to government institutions. Belgium places a constitutional obligation upon the government to take into account solidarity between generations in enacting State functions:

> In the exercise of their respective powers, the federal state, the communities and the regions pursue the objective of sustainable development, in its social, economic, and environmental dimensions, taking into account solidarity between generations.[8]

Bolivia places the constitutional requirement to protect the rights of future generations onto the State, noting that

> Essential State purposes and functions, in addition to those established by the Constitutional and laws, are: ... To promote and ensure responsible and planned use of natural resources, and promote industrialization through the development and strengthening the productive base in different dimensions and levels as well as environmental conservation, for the welfare of generations present and future.[9]

The same standard is highlighted in the Constitution of Burundi:

> The State guarantees the sound management and the efficient exploitation of the natural resources of the country, while preserving the environment and the conservation of those resources for future generations.[10]

This is also found in the Cuban Constitution, which provides that

> The state protects the environment and natural resources of the country. It recognizes the close links they have with sustainable economic and social development to make human life more rational and to ensure the survival, well-being and security of present and future generations.[11]

Further, the German Constitution requires the State to act in ways that preserve the rights of future generations:

> Mindful also of its responsibility toward future generations, the State shall protect the natural bases of life by legislation and, in accordance with law and justice, by executive and judicial action, all within the framework of constitutional order.[12]

In contrast, the constitution of Bhutan places the responsibility of protecting the rights of future generations onto each and every one of its citizens, providing that

> Every Bhutanese is a trustee of the Kingdom's natural resources and environment for the benefit of the present and future generations ...[13]

[8] Constitution of Belgium (1993) art. 7bis.
[9] Constitution of Bolivia (2007) art. 9(6).
[10] Constitution of Burundi (2018) art. 35.
[11] Constitution of Cuba (1976) art. 27
[12] Basic Law for the Federal Republic of Germany (1949) art. 20a.
[13] Constitution of Bhutan (2008) art. 5 ('Every Bhutanese is a trustee of the Kingdom's natural resources and environment for the benefit of the present and future generations and it is the

### *Innovations of National Instruments for the Environment, Sustainable Development, and Future Generations' Rights*

What exactly are the rights and interests of future generations, and how can they best be defined and protected? One theoretical framework suggests that three elements of sustainable development policy should be prioritised.[14] First, to protect the rights of future generations, it is necessary to conserve options for them. Second, it is necessary to conserve the quality of the environment for future generations. In conjunction with this, third, it is necessary to conserve future generations' access to environmental resources.[15] In the context of conservation options, there is a need for a complete national and international reorientation of legal structures which currently encourage unsustainable resource exploitation that functions against the rights and interests of future generations. For example, instead of encouraging the destruction of biologically valuable tropical forests, this reorientation would entail 'shifting the burden of justification' onto those who seek to deplete the forest resources by requiring them to 'define criteria to justify transformation of forests to other uses, so that areas of rich biological wealth remain and other areas are put to productive, sustainable uses'.[16] In order to undertake the educational and cultural shift towards this view, there is a need for strong and innovative national institutions to defend the rights of future generations, providing a voice for the voiceless. Several States have established commissions on sustainable development and/or environmental issues. Such instruments have, among other points in their mandates, the responsibility to take into account the interests of future generations.

## PARLIAMENTARY COMMISSIONS

### *Commission on Environment and Sustainable Development (Brazil)*

The Brazilian Commission on Environment and Sustainable Development, established in 2004 by Resolution no. 20, is a permanent organ of the Brazilian House of the Representatives.[17] The Commission has the authority to (1) review and vote on bills related to the environment and sustainable development; (2) promote public

fundamental duty of every citizen to contribute to the protection of the natural environment, conservation of the rich biodiversity of Bhutan and prevention of all forms of ecological degradation including noise, visual and physical pollution through the adoption and support of environment friendly practices and policies.')

14 E. Brown Weiss, 'In Fairness to Future Generations and Sustainable Development' (1992–1993) 8 Am. U. J. Int'l L. & Pol'y 19, 22–26.

15 Ibid.

16 Ibid.

17 Comissão de Meio Ambiente e Desenvolvimento Sustentável www2.camara.leg.br/atividade-legislativa/comissoes/comissoes-permanentes/cmads. accessed 30 November 2017.

debates and seminars on the issue; (3) raise environmental concerns before the Parliament; (4) receive citizens' complaints against governmental acts or omissions related to environmental and sustainable development matters; and (5) provide legal opinions on environmental legislation.[18] Examples of activities carried out by the Commission include the proposition of a legislative bill to set out GHG emissions targets for the industrial and energy sectors, and denouncing deforestation to the Ministry of the Environment based on citizens' complaints.[19] Additionally, Brazil recently added two technical advisors to support the Commission's work and is actively considering proposals on biodiversity preservation and reducing the impact of GHG emissions.[20]

### *Commission on Natural Resources, Environment and National Resources (Chile)*

Other commissions have even broader mandates that balance environmental protection with the sustainable use of natural resources and other national heritage. Like its Brazilian counterpart, the Chilean Commission on Natural Resources, Environment and National Resources is a permanent unit of the Parliament with powers to propose and review bills, as well as to promote debates with the community.[21] The Commission has hosted public debates to discuss environmental and related issues such as genetically modified organisms[22] and sustainable use of water resources.[23] Examples of legislative bills proposed by the Commission include (1) the regulation of environmental crimes committed by juridical persons, (2) the establishment of popular action for environmental damages, and (3) the promotion

[18] Articles 24 and 32 of Regimento Interno da Câmara dos Deputados www2.camara.leg.br/atividade-legislativa/legislacao/regimento-interno-da-camara-dos-deputados/RICD%20atualizado%20ate%20RCD%2027-2018.pdf accessed 30 November 2017.

[19] Comissão de Meio Ambiente e Desenvolvimento Sustentável www2.camara.leg.br/atividade-legislativa/comissoes/comissoes-permanentes/cmads. accessed 30 November 2017.

[20] See Ato da Mesa No. 237, Diário da Câmara dos Deputados – Suplemento – 13/7/2018, p. 9 www2.camara.leg.br/legin/int/atomes/2018/atodamesa-237-12-julho-2018-786980-publicacaooriginal-156043-cd-mesa.html accessed 30 November 2017; see also e.g. Câmara Dos Deputados, Comissão De Meio Ambiente E Desenvolvimento Sustentável, Legislative Agenda for 17 October 2018 www.camara.leg.br/internet/ordemdodia/ordemDetalheReuniaoCom.asp?codReuniao=53816 accessed 30 November 2017.

[21] Comisión de Recursos Naturales, Bienes Nacionales y Medio Ambiente www.camara.cl/trabajamos/comision_portada.aspx?prmID=405 accessed 30 November 2017. See also Artículos 213-218 of the Reglamento de La Cámara de Diputados www.camara.cl/camara/media/docs/reglamento_camara_diputados_08.pdf accessed 30 November 2017.

[22] Biblioteca del Congreso Nacional del Chile http://catalogo.bcn.cl/ipac20/ipac.jsp?session=12665DS327587.1326505&profile=bcn&source=~!horizon&view=subscriptionsummary&uri=full=3100001~!115693~!1&ri=1&aspect=subtab146&menu=search&ipp=10&spp=20&staffonly=& &aspect=subtab146&menu=search&ri=1 accessed 30 November 2017.

[23] Ibid.

of respect for animal rights. This Commission attempts to respect the rights of future generations by encouraging environmental protection, though a narrow mandate and lack of resources or institutional support may be limiting factors affecting the success Chilean initiative.

### *Committee for the Future (Finland)*

The Committee for the Future was introduced to Finland during the 1990s and in its initial status functioned on a temporary basis.[24] In 2000, during a national constitutional review period in Finland, the Committee for the Future was elevated to the status of a Parliamentary Standing Committee.[25] One of the key reasons that the Committee for the Future was created in its current form was the realisation that issues related to the future and future generations should be addressed outside the framework of a particular Government and agenda, but rather through a free-standing entity.[26] At present, the Committee for the Future is comprised of Members of Parliament and has the ability to comment on all but budgetary and legislative review issues.[27]

The Committee for the Future has jurisdiction to consider a wide range of issues as they relate to the future and future generations. While it is empowered to consider the impacts of environmental concerns on the future and future generations, the Committee for the Future is not limited to environmental concerns or research.[28] Indeed, the Committee for the Future has produced a series of research reports that address the environment, economy, employment, and science and technology.[29] In the past, the Committee for the Future has engaged in a dialogue with the general Parliament by issuing these reports, in which the focus was on the future and future generations, receiving comments from the Parliament on those reports, and then responding to these comments with future comments on the issues raised by the Parliament.[30] Recent areas of interest for the Committee for the Future include energy and health.[31]

[24] P. Tiihonen, 'Committee for the Future – A New Institution to Discuss the Future in Finland', in B. Jávor and J. Rácz (eds.), *Do We Owe Them a Future?* (Védegylet 2006) 72.

[25] Finnish Parliament, Eduskunnan tyojarjestys, No. 40 section 7 (2000); Tiihonen, *supra* note 24 at 72.

[26] Tiihonen, *supra* note 24 at 72–73.

[27] Finnish Parliament, Eduskunnan tyojarjestys, No. 40 section 7 (2000); Tiihonen, *supra* note 24 at 74.

[28] Tiihonen, *supra* note 24 at 72–88.

[29] Ibid. at 75.

[30] Ibid.

[31] Ibid. at 76–80.

### *Committee for Sustainable Development (Germany)*

The German Parliament has established a Committee for Sustainable Development,[32] the membership of which is derived from Parliament itself.[33] Further, in 2006 the Bundestag created a Parliamentary Advisory Council on Sustainable Development, which is charged with acting as an advocate for issues related to sustainability and future generations within the parliamentary system.[34] Not only is the Advisory Council charged with working within the German governmental apparatus, it is also permitted to liaise with the parliaments of other governments to discuss the issues over which it has jurisdiction.[35]

## SPECIAL COMMISSIONS WITH MANDATES TO SUPPORT A COMMISSIONER

### *National Commission for Future Generations (Israel)*

One of the broader and more flexible instruments to represent and defend the voices of future generations in national policy and law making involves the establishment and operation of a special Parliamentary Commission. For instance, in March 2001, the Israeli Parliament promulgated a chapter in the Knesset law establishing a Commission for Future Generations.[36] The Commission operated as a unit of the Parliament that sought to defend the needs and the rights of future generations, with specific focus on the creation of 'a dimension of the future that would be included in the primary and secondary legislation of the State of Israel'.[37] The Commission's five-year mandate (2001–2006) was broad in scope, including environmental and social-related areas such as natural resources, education, health, technology, law, development, demography, and any other matter of special concern to future generations as determined by the Israeli Constitution, Law and Justice Committee.[38] The Commission had the authority to (1) provide opinions on bills, secondary legislation, and regulations of interest for future generations; (2) provide

[32] Deutscher Bundestag, Drucksache 17/245 (June 12, 2009) section 1.

[33] Ibid.

[34] Parliamentary Advisory Council on Sustainable Development www.bundestag.de/htdocs_e/bundestag/committees/bodies/sustainability/index.html accessed 30 November 2017.

[35] Ibid.

[36] Amendment no. 14– 5761/2001; The Knesset, Commission for Future Generations (Israel: Jerusalem) www. knesset.gov.il/sponsorship/future/eng/future_index.htm accessed 30 November 2017 [Knesset]. For a more detailed analysis of the legislative and 'top-down' process surrounding the enactment of the law which established the Commission see S. Shoham and N. Lamay, 'Commission for Future Generations in the Knesset: Lessons Learnt', in J.C. Tremmel (ed.), *Handbook of Intergenerational Justice* (Edward Elgar 2006) 244–247.

[37] Knesset, *supra* note 36 at 3.

[38] Ibid. at 4 and 18. Nevertheless, national defence and foreign affairs were excluded. See Shoham and Lamay, *supra* note 36 at 246.

the Parliament with recommendations on any issue the Commissioner considered relevant to the rights of future generations; (3) demand any information from institutions 'subject to inspection by the State Comptroller' (i.e. ministries, state corporations, local authorities, etc.); and (4) request a parliamentary committee for 'reasonable time' to collect data and prepare an evaluation regarding certain bills or secondary legislation with particular relevance for future generations.[39] Ultimately, the Commission's mandate was terminated as a matter of law by the Israeli Knesset and has not since been restored.

Given its mandate, the Commission might best be described as an advisory or consultative organ restricted to the legislative work of the Israeli Parliament, with little legal authority to propose bills, carry out inquiries, or adjudicate disputes. Notwithstanding this limited and somewhat reactive role, the Israeli Commission for Future Generations can be regarded as an avant-garde and significant initiative. It challenged 'business as usual' in a troubled region, and provided a representative voice for future generations in policy-making processes, with the ability to participate in activities and processes that cut across environmental, economic, and social topics and fields of policy and law with a commendably holistic perspective.

### *Parliamentary Commissioner for the Environment (New Zealand)*

A second, more focused type of instrument involves the establishment of a Parliamentary Commissioner to protect the environment, with a view to preserving ecosystems in the interest of future generations. For instance, the Parliamentary Commissioner for the Environment (PCE) emerged amidst New Zealand's environmental administrative reform in 1980s.[40] The PCE was empowered by the Environmental Act 1986, which set out the Commissioner's role as an independent environmental ombudsman with a five-year mandate. In this regard, the Commissioner's major authorities include: (1) investigating 'the effectiveness of environmental planning and management carried out by public authorities'; (2) investigating 'any matter in respect of which, in the Commissioner's opinion, the environment may be or has been adversely affected'; (3) reviewing 'the system of agencies and processes established by the Government to manage the allocation, use, and preservation of natural and physical resources'; and (4) if requested by the House of the Representatives, inquiring on matters that have a significant environmental impact.[41] The reviews and investigations carried out by the PCE derive

[39] Knesset, *supra* note 36 at 13–16.

[40] O. Furuseth and C. Cocklin, 'An Institutional Framework for Sustainable Resource Management: The New Zealand Model' (1995) 35 Nat Resources J 253.

[41] The Environment Act 1986 http://legislation.knowledge-basket.co.nz/gpacts/reprint/text/1996/an/015.html accessed 30 November 2017 at S.16.

mainly from the Commissioner's discretion or as a result of citizens or civil association complaints.

Up to the present, the PCE and staff have reviewed and investigated matters related to biodiversity, waste management, lignite, emissions trading schemes, national policy statements and national environmental standards for efficient environmental management, water allocation, and others.[42] It can be said, thus, that the New Zealand Commissioner plays an active role in preventing and remedying environmental harms derived from governmental or private activities which, in turn, have a direct impact on the rights of future generations. Additionally, while their mandate may appear to specifically focus on considering mainly *environmental* impacts in the Commissioner's mandate, in practice the PCE and staff experts have incorporated issues such as social and economic rights within their research. Essentially, the PCE has created a certain latitude to move beyond the purely environmental realm in relation to the protection of future generations. For example, the PCE has issued several studies that examine the relationship between social and economic rights and the protection of future generations.[43]

The PCE has also been commended by world-renowned Māori leaders for their willingness to solicit and respect the views and traditional knowledge of indigenous peoples. One weakness and strength is that under the terms of the creating Act, the emphasis in the PCE mandate is on the Commissioner's discretion, which means that a great deal depends on the actual individual who occupies the position and the advice of the individual's staff. Depending on the individual appointed to the role, the Commissioner may or may not feel the need to take up an active voice as an advocate for the rights of future generations.

### *Environment and Sustainable Development Commissioner (Canada)*

Building on the Parliamentary Environmental Commissioner model, but with a slightly broader original mandate, several countries have established Sustainable Development Commissioners. Canada provides one example. The Canadian proposal for an independent Commissioner originally focused mainly on environmental protection, as advocated in 1989 when a group of twenty-eight environmental NGOs presented a document entitled 'Greenprint for Canada' to the Canadian Ministry of the Environment.[44] The idea gradually won acceptance by the general public and politicians, but the mandate was expanded to include a broader remit for

[42] The Parliamentary Commissioner for the Environment www.pce.parliament.nz/ accessed 30 November 2017.

[43] See 'See Change: Learning and Education for Sustainability', Parliamentary Commissioner for the Environment (2004).

[44] T. Williams, 'Sustainable Development in the Federal Government: The Commissioner of the Environment and Sustainable Development', (2005) Library of Parliament www2.parl.gc.ca/content/lop/researchpublications/prb0512-e.html. accessed 30 November 2017.

sustainable development, and the Commissioner's office was implemented in 1995 through amendments to the Auditor General Act of Canada.[45] The Commissioner's main responsibility is to assist the Auditor during his/her ten-year tenure.[46] According to Subsections 21(1), 22(1), and 23(3) of the Auditor General Act, the Commissioner has a mandate to (1) 'provide sustainable development monitoring and reporting'; (2) 'make any examinations and inquiries that the Commissioner considers necessary'; and (3) receive, record and forward citizens petitions on environmental issues to the appropriate authority.[47] In addition, the Federal Sustainable Development Act (2008) and the Kyoto Protocol Implementation Act (2007) established that the Commissioner has the responsibility to review and report the federal government's progress in implementing the sustainable development action plan and the Kyoto Protocol.[48]

Similar to the New Zealand experience, the Commissioner's actual mandate is not overly broad, though it does include sustainable development, as well as environmental protection, and this implies both social development and economic elements to the work of the Commissioner. A great deal still depends on the individual who is selected for the position, as the Commissioner has discretion to undertake studies and produce reports on issues that they consider necessary. The practice in Canada is to appoint the Commissioner through an independent merit-based civil service recruitment and selection process, which appears laudable. As an agent of the Auditor General, a strong individual has scope to produce high-quality investigations and reports, but not to act independently to secure compliance with Canadian commitments related to the rights of future generations.

### *Deputy Commissioner for Future Generations (Hungary)*

One additional model, which is different from Commissioners who report to Environment Ministers or Auditor Generals, involves the establishment of an ombudsperson to defend the rights of future generations. Under Hungarian law, Parliament is required to select a Deputy Commissioner for Future Generations 'in order to ensure the protection of the interests of future generations'.[49] This position was created as part of an overarching statute creating an Ombudsman for Civil Rights, and the Deputy Commissioner has the same status as a special Ombudsman

[45] Ibid.

[46] Office of the Auditor General of Canada www.oag-bvg.gc.ca/internet/English/esd_fs_e_46.html accessed 30 November 2017. See also Subsection 3(1.1), Auditor General Act, Department of Justice http://laws.justice.gc.ca/en/A-17/FullText.html. accessed 30 November 2017.

[47] Auditor General Act, *supra* note 46.

[48] Office of the Auditor General of Canada, *supra* note 46. For a detailed assessment of Canada's sustainable development policy and strategy see R. Ballhorn, 'The Role of Government and Policy in Sustainable Development' (2005) McGill JSDLP 19.

[49] Fundamental Law of Hungary, art. 30(3). For the functions and powers of the Hungarian Ombudsman for Future Generations, see *infra* ch. 4 in this volume.

as a matter of law.[50] The universe of potential candidates for the Deputy Commissioner position is limited by requirements that candidates be lawyers, have extensive experience with the rights of future generations, and meet a strict set of personal characteristics, as well as by requirements to ensure that there are no conflicts of interest.[51]

Once selected, the Deputy Commissioner has wide jurisdiction. He or she is required to monitor legislative developments and proposals at the State level in order to ensure that they will not pose a threat to the environment and future generations.[52] This requirement includes providing opinions to Members of Parliament, as well as others seeking to take actions that could impact the environment and future generations.[53] The Deputy Commissioner may conduct investigations into potential or alleged violations or threats to the environments and future generations.[54] The Deputy Commissioner's role is not limited to the national government level; he or she is given the ability to review the actions of and assist municipal and other local governments as well.[55] In terms of sanctions, after an investigation, the Deputy Commissioner has the ability to order that an action be stopped or modified in order to protect the interests of the environment and future generations.[56]

The Deputy Commissioner for Future Generations occupies a unique place among the positions discussed above. Although the mandate of the Deputy Commissioner does include environmental concerns, they are expressed in terms of protecting future generations, tying the position directly to future generations rather than the secondary or inferential links found in other positions and their mandates. The Deputy Commissioner is given broad jurisdiction, subject to a set of guidelines for investigations, and has the ability to investigate and sanction public institutions, which gives the position a sense of independence. And the terms of office in this statute are such that they make removal of the Deputy Commissioner difficult without cause, which is important to avoiding the political concerns that have manifested themselves in other systems.

## RECOGNITION OF THE RIGHTS OF FUTURE GENERATIONS IN NATIONAL COURTS

The rights of future generations are also increasingly being upheld in national courts, although they constitute only the beginning of sustained national jurisprudence on the topic.

[50] Act CXI of 2011 on the Commissioner for Fundamental Rights, art. 5.
[51] Ibid.
[52] Ibid. at art. 3(1).
[53] Ibid.
[54] Ibid.
[55] Ibid.
[56] Ibid.

### *Massachusetts v. EPA (United States)*

In April 2007, the Supreme Court of the US decided a case filed by twelve states and several cities against the US Environmental Protection Agency (EPA), the national environmental regulatory entity. The plaintiffs challenged the EPA's alleged omissions in regulating carbon dioxide and other GHGs. Justice Stevens' majority opinion supported the standing of the State of Massachusetts to bring the suit,[57] finding that

> While it may be true that regulating motor-vehicle emissions will not by itself reverse global warming, it by no means follows that we lack jurisdiction to decide whether EPA has a duty to take steps to slow or reduce it. See also Larson v. Valente, 456 U.S. 228, 244, n. 15, 102 S. Ct. 1673, 72 L. Ed. 2d 33 (1982) . . . Because of the enormity of the potential consequences associated with man-made climate change, the fact that the effectiveness of a remedy might be delayed during the (relatively short) time it takes for a new motor-vehicle fleet to replace an older one is essentially irrelevant. Nor is it dispositive that developing countries such as China and India are poised to increase greenhouse gas emissions substantially over the next century: A reduction in domestic emissions would slow the pace of global emissions increases, no matter what happens elsewhere . . . In sum – at least according to petitioners' uncontested affidavits – the rise in sea levels associated with global warming has already harmed and will continue to harm Massachusetts. The risk of catastrophic harm, though remote, is nevertheless real. That risk would be reduced to some extent if petitioners received the relief they seek. We therefore hold that petitioners have standing to challenge EPA's denial of their rulemaking petition.[58]

On this basis, the Supreme Court considered the actual harm as well as the risk of harm from global warming to Massachusetts' shoreline which suggests, although not explicitly, that states might 'serve as representatives for future generations' before US Courts.[59]

### *Minors Oposa v. Secretary of the Department of Environment and Natural Resources (Philippines)*

One domestic court decision on intergenerational equity, as well as intragenerational equity, is the landmark 1993 Philippine Supreme Court Case, *Minors Oposa* v. *Secretary of the Department of Environment and Natural Resources* ('DENR'). The case addressed intergenerational equity in the context of state

[57] Ibid. at 1455–1459.

[58] *Massachusetts* v. *EPA*, 549 US 497 (2007) (QL).

[59] B.C. Mank, 'Standing and Future Generations: Does *Massachusetts* v. *EPA* open standing for generations to come?' (2009) 34 *Colum J Envtl* L 71–72.

management of public forest land. In a novel situation under Philippine law, the Philippine Supreme Court permitted a class action brought by Filipino children acting as representatives for themselves and for future generations. The petitioners wanted to halt governmentally licensed timber cutting within the remaining national forests, which had been significantly reduced. The plaintiffs alleged that present and continued logging violated their right to a healthy environment under the Philippine Constitution and would entail irreparable harm to them and future generations of the nation. The Court considered the issue of intergenerational responsibility and decided that the petitioners had *locus standi*, i.e., were qualified to sue, on behalf of present and future generations in the Philippines. In rendering its decision, the Court accepted the petitioners' statistical evidence regarding the amount of forest cover required to maintain a healthy environment for present and future generations.

These cases and other more recent cases are worth noting because they are in countries that do not include the rights of future generations in their constitutions and have not established institutional mechanisms for protecting the rights of future generations. Despite a lack of precedent, however, both cases indicate willingness on the part of countries that are vastly different in terms of development and wealth to examine the issue of the rights of future generations at the judicial – if not political – level.

## SURVEY OF INTERNATIONAL PROPOSALS FOR WAYS TO REPRESENT THE GLOBAL RIGHTS OF FUTURE GENERATIONS

### *Evolution of International Jurisprudence Respecting and Taking into Account the Rights of Future Generations*

Reference to the need to respect and take into account the rights of future generations can be seen in seminal documents of international law as the Charter of the UN and the ICESCR.[60] Indeed, the UN Committee on Economic, Social and Cultural Rights has interpreted provisions of the ICESCR to include rights which affect future generations, such as the right to water, in a way that seeks to implicitly protect, as well as recognise, the rights of future generations.[61] The need to respect the rights of future generations was also recognised in the UNFCCC, and its Kyoto Protocol, among other international treaties on sustainable development.[62]

60 See Charter of the United Nations (1945); International Covenant on Economic, Social and Cultural Rights (1966).

61 See 'Substantive Issues Arising in the Implementation of the International Covenant on Economic, Social and Cultural Rights, General Comment No. 15, The Right to Water', United Nations Committee on Economic, Social and Cultural Rights (2002).

62 United Nations Framework Convention for Climate Change (1992) preamble, art. 3; Kyoto Protocol to the United Nations Framework Convention on Climate Change (1998).

More recently, the 2016 Paris Agreement to the UNFCCC overtly included, and indeed embraced, sustainable development and the rights of future generations as key and essential elements for the international community to attend to now and in the years to come. Additionally, the rights of future generations are protected in a variety of regional agreements, and the 2015 SDGs, the successors to the MDGs have the rights of future generations and intergenerational equity at their core.[63]

The intergenerational aspects of State activities have been addressed at the international level in judgments of the ICJ. There, the implications of intergenerational equity were discussed in Judge Weeramantry's lengthy separate opinion on 'equity' in the *Maritime Delimitation in the Area between Greenland and Jan Mayen* case (*Denmark* v. *Norway*) case, and in his dissent in the *Nuclear Tests* case (*New Zealand* v. *France*). In *Denmark* v. *Norway*, Judge Weeramantry's comments referred to intergenerational equity, and specifically to 'the concept of wise stewardship [of natural resources]... and their conservation for the benefit of future generations'. In his dissenting opinion in the *Nuclear Tests* case, Judge Weeramantry stated that

> The case before the court raises, as no case before the court has done, the principle of intergenerational equity – an important and rapidly developing principle of contemporary environmental law... The court has not thus far had occasion to make any pronouncement on this rapidly developing field ... [The case]... raises in pointed form the possibility of damage to generations yet unborn.

Furthermore, in the 1997 *Gabcikovo-Nagymaros* case, the ICJ found that there is a need to balance between the needs of protecting the environment and development.[64] Separate and dissenting opinions such as those provided by Judge Weeramantry in this and the above cases are useful in offering alternative interpretations on the relevant subject matter and often contribute to the ICJ's role in developing and clarifying international law.

The precautionary principle is directed at addressing the issue of potential harm in the face of scientific uncertainty. It has been employed across the spectrum of international environmental issues in many instruments, from regulation of the transport and disposal of hazardous wastes in the Bamako Convention[65] to conservation of living natural resources, as demonstrated in the UN CBD and the UN

[63] See, e.g., Tokyo Declaration for the Dynamic and Enduring ASEAN-Japan Partnership in the New Millennium, Association of South East Asian Nations (2003); North American Agreement on Environmental Cooperation (1994).

[64] *Case Concerning the Gabcikovo-Nagymaros Project (Hungary v Slovakia) Judgment* [1997] ICJ Reports p. 7 (25 September 1997).

[65] Bamako Convention on the Ban of the Import into Africa and the Control of Transboundary Movement and Management of Hazardous Wastes Within Africa (1991).

Convention on the Law of the Seas Straddling Stocks Agreement.[66] The precautionary principle is most commonly expressed in the words found at Principle 15 of the Rio Declaration:

> In order to protect the environment, the precautionary approach shall be widely applied by States according to their capabilities. Where there are threats of serious or irreversible damage, lack of full scientific certainty shall not be used as a reason for postponing cost-effective measures to prevent environmental degradation.[67]

Thus, through these and a number of national and regional courts, the rights of future generations have slowly worked their way into international jurisprudential thought. This progression in recognition and discussion is important to the framing of the rights of future generations.

### *International Proposals for Institutions to Respect and Take into Account the Rights of Future Generations*

Several proposals have been raised to recommend that the international community better take into account and protect the rights of future generations. These proposals include establishing a new mandate of Trustee for Future Generations for the UN Trusteeship Council; advocating the creation of an international body built on the model of the World Bank Inspection Panel, to safeguard the rights of future generations in all international projects and initiatives; and activating the special procedures of the UN Human Rights Council to appoint a Special Rapporteur on the Rights of Future Generations, or establish a Working Group on the Rights of Future Generations. This third option, together with the recommendation that regional 'future generations ombudsperson' instruments should be further investigated and recommended for supra national organisations such as the EU, was considered the most reasonable and viable by the World Future Council's Future Justice Experts Commissions.

### *UN Trusteeship Council*

One proposal that has been put forward by experts would involve replacing the mandate of the UN Trusteeship Council with a new mandate to protect the environment, or to represent the interests of future generations.[68]

[66] United Nations Convention on Biological Diversity (1992). United Nations Agreement for the implementation of the Provisions of the United Nations Convention on the Law of the Sea of 10 December 1982 relating to the Conservation and Management of Straddling Fish Stocks and Highly Migratory Fish Stocks (2001).

[67] Rio Declaration on Environment and Development (1992) Principle 15.

[68] P.H. Sand, 'Sovereignty Bounded: Public Trusteeship for Common Pool Resources?' (2004) 4: 1 *Global Environ Politics* 47–71. See also I. Kaul, I. Grunberg, and M.A. Stern (eds.), *Global Public Goods: International Cooperation in the 21st Century* (Oxford University Press 1999).

The Trusteeship Council was made up of the five permanent members of the UNSC: China, France, Russian Federation, the UK and the US. In setting up the International Trusteeship System, the States that drafted the UN Charter established the Trusteeship Council as an organ of the UN and assigned to it the task of supervising the administration of Trust Territories placed under the Trusteeship System. The aims of the Trusteeship System were deemed to have been fulfilled when all Trust Territories had attained self-government or independence, either as separate States or by joining neighbouring independent States. As such, the UN Trusteeship Council suspended its operations on 1 November 1994, with the independence of Palau, the last remaining Trust Territory, on 1 October 1994. By a resolution adopted on 25 May 1994, the Council amended its rules of procedure to drop the obligation to meet annually and agreed to meet as occasion required.

The original mandate and operational modes of the UN Trusteeship Council are both more conscribed than and extremely different from the mandates of the national parliamentary commissions and councils for future generations and the environment that are analysed above. As such, completely new mandates, operational methods, and institutional models would likely be needed to transform the UN Trusteeship Council into an environmental institution. Furthermore, the UN Trusteeship Council, while likely a valuable institution during a certain period of history, was questioned by many developing countries, particularly as these countries continue their struggle to survive and overcome combined legacies of colonialism, mercantilism, and military dominance from overseas empires.[69]

### *Building on World Bank Ombudsperson and Inspection Panel Experiences*

A second option might be to seek to establish a quasi-judicial ombudsperson or inspection panel for international initiatives and projects that might impact on the rights of future generations. A related aspect of this choice could be to seek more explicit recognition of a responsibility to protect the rights of future generations within the mandate of the World Bank Inspection Panel itself, and expand the scope of the existing Panel's responsibilities to extend beyond projects funded by the World Bank Group.

The World Bank Group includes an International Finance Corporation (IFC), which is one of the key financiers that aim to involve civil society as an important

[69] See e.g., Second International Decade for the Eradication of Colonialism (2001–2010) A/56/61 March 4 2001; G.W. Morrell, 'A Higher Stage of Imperialism? The Big Three, the UN Trusteeship Council and the Early Cold War', in R.M. Douglas, M.D. Callahan, and E. Bishop (eds.), *Imperialism on Trial: International Oversight of Colonial Rule in Historical Perspective* (Lexington Books, 2006); T. Collier, *The Bottom Billion* (Oxford University Press 2004).

stakeholder in projects.[70] The IFC's mission is to reduce poverty and improve lives. It entertains this sector's contribution from policy development to project-specific input. IFC materials highlight promoting community consultation, participation, and environmental protection; extending project reach and benefits to the poorest and most vulnerable; and introducing flexible and innovative approaches to difficult environmental and social concerns. As a sustainable policy rule, IFC measures development results of investment projects using criteria that include a project's business success (or financial performance); its return to society (or economic performance); its social and environmental performance; and private sector development impacts (such as demonstration effects, linkages, impacts on the investment climate, or corporate governance aspects). The IFC reports on its development effectiveness at least once a year, and approaches sustainability with programming on climate change, poverty, corruption, HIV/AIDS, participation of women in private sector development, and the preservation of natural resources.[71] In the IFC, one mechanism of interest to the present study is the independent Compliance Advisor/Ombudsman (CAO), which offers recourse to communities that are directly affected by IFC projects. This legal body was formed in 1999. They have engaged in public consultation in maintaining environmental and social safeguards.[72] The three functions[73] of the CAO office involve (1) compliance (audits) to independently assess whether IFC and MIGA have complied with their environmental and social Safeguard Policies, guidelines and procedures, in investing in (IFC) or providing political risk insurance to (MIGA) projects; (2) advisory services (advisory projects) to provide independent, timely, and objective advice to the president of the World Bank Group and management of the IFC and MIGA; this advice relates only to broader environmental and social policies, guidelines, procedures, resources, and systems; and (3) ombudsman (complaint resolution) to provide an accessible and effective mechanism for handling complaints from persons who are affected (or are likely to be affected) by the social and environmental impacts of IFC- or MIGA-sponsored projects.

A related mechanism also worth certain consideration is the World Bank Inspection Panel. The Inspection Panel was established by the Executive Directors of the International Bank for Reconstruction and Development (IBRD) and the International Development Association (IDA) on 22 September 1993.[74] The primary purpose of the Inspection Panel is to address the concerns of the people who may be

[70] IDLO-CISDL, *Compendium of Legal Best Practices on Climate Change* Policy (IDLO-CISDL 2011).

[71] For further information see www.ifc.org/ngo accessed 30 November 2017.

[72] For further information see www.ifc.org/ifcext/enviro.nsf/AttachmentsByTitle/p_2005SustReport_4/$FILE/Listening.pdf accessed 30 November 2017.

[73] For further information see www.cao-ombudsman.org/ accessed 30 November 2017.

[74] See Inspection Panel – About Us, The World Bank http://web.worldbank.org/WBSITE/EXTERNAL/EXTINSPECTIONPANEL/0,,menuPK:64129249~pagePK:64132081~piPK:64132052~theSitePK:380794,00.html accessed March 30, 2010.

affected by Bank projects and to ensure that the Bank adheres to its operational policies and procedures during design, preparation, and implementation phases of projects. The Inspection Panel consists of three members who are appointed by the Board for non-renewable periods of five years.[75] Members are selected on the basis of their ability to deal thoroughly and fairly with the requests brought to them, their integrity and independence from the Bank Management, and their exposure to developmental issues and living conditions in developing countries.[76] Because this is the first body of its kind to give voice to private citizens in an international context, the Panel's operational procedures and its operations appear to have stayed fairly innovative and fluid.[77] During a normal process, the Panel receives a request and decides whether the request is within its mandate.[78] If the Board approves a recommendation to investigate, the Panel proceeds with the investigation. When the Panel finishes an investigation, it sends the findings to the Board and to Bank Management. Bank Management then has six weeks to submit its recommendations to the Board on what actions the Bank should take in response to the Panel's findings. Based on the Panel's findings and Bank Management's recommendations, the Board takes the final decision on what should be done.[79]

Such inspection panel or ombudsperson roles partly resemble the final national model of the more juridical Future Generations Ombudsperson or Parliamentary Commissioner discussed above. In that model, the authority of the Commissioner is not constrained to an auditing role, but rather is focused on reviewing projects and initiatives for compliance with operating procedures and policy objectives, and where necessary even recommending alternatives. If independent, the panel would have both the advantages and disadvantages of a completely new institution or project, with no legacy to overcome, but also no support from existing systems and institutions, and an acute vulnerability to 'regulatory capture'.

### *Special Procedures of the UN Human Rights Council*

A second proposal might involve establishing a new Special Rapporteur on the Rights of Future Generations, or a Working Group on the Rights of Future Generations under the Special Procedures of the UN Human Rights Council. Special procedures is the general name given to the mechanisms established by the UNHCR and assumed by the Human Rights Council to address either specific country situations or thematic challenges that are global in nature.

Special procedure mandates usually call on mandate holders to examine, monitor, advise, and publicly report on human rights situations in specific countries or

75 Ibid.
76 Ibid.
77 Ibid.
78 Ibid.
79 Ibid.

territories, known as country mandates, or on major phenomena of human rights violations worldwide, known as thematic mandates. Various activities are undertaken by special procedures, including responding to individual complaints, conducting studies, providing advice on technical cooperation at the country level, and engaging in general promotional activities.

Special procedures are either an individual (called 'Special Rapporteur', 'Special Representative of the Secretary-General', or 'Independent Expert') or a Working Group usually composed of five members, one from each region. The mandates of the special procedures are established and defined by the resolution creating them. These resolutions must be proposed, negotiated, and agreed by the States in the UN Human Rights Councils.

Depending on the mandate and terms of reference, the initiation of a Special Rapporteur for the Rights of Future Generations would resemble the domestic Commissioners for the environment, sustainable development, or future generations, as analysed above. The advantages and disadvantages of such an approach are clear – a great deal would depend on the individual chosen and the scope of their mandate, and such a person would likely at best play the role of an auditor rather than an intervenor. However, UN Human Rights Special Rapporteurs have an excellent reputation, and are famed for their ability to bring issues forward and give them legitimacy in the eyes of the world.

## CONCLUSION

There is considerable potential for policy innovation for the voices and rights of future generations, while at the same time this is an area which has already seen a great deal of innovation and significant reconceptualisation of law and rights holders. As noted above, there are a number of key lessons that can be drawn for the future of implementing intergenerational equity.

First, at the national level, it is clear that a number of States have begun to include the rights of future generations in national constitutions, and have started to adopt new instruments to give voices for future generations in national policy-making structures. These instruments are specific to the ecological conditions, political and social realities, and level of economic resources available in each country; however, they are a valiant first step and offer valuable lessons for international and other national decision makers. Further, in some jurisdictions that have not made future generations a priority, courts are still willing to enforce a certain minimum standard of respect, and even standing.

Second, at the international level, it is clear that many treaties have been negotiated and ratified, some with nearly universal membership, which recognise and respect the principle of intergenerational equity. International courts and tribunals have also begun to pronounce on this issue, and will likely soon be offered an opportunity to make decisive statement with regards to the rights of future generations, perhaps guided by ancient wisdom and the courageous advice of jurists who traced the initial juridical pathways in this area.

Third, there is an opportunity to advance the proposal that new instruments are needed to represent these interests globally. A UN Human Rights Council Special Rapporteur or Working Group instrument could be further investigated as a method of protecting and promoting the rights of future generations. Both these options have their challenges, given the limitations and history of existing international institutions, voting, and geopolitical considerations, but they also have considerable potential to investigate and raise questions specific to the rights of future generations in international society, and to stimulate independent international deliberations, research, analysis, debate, and policy dialogue that is much needed today. There is a delicate balance between the rights of future generations of all regions, and it is important not to recommend the creation of an instrument that would guard the rights of present and future generations in one region to the detriment of the rights of the poor and future generations in another region.

# 31

# International Institutions for Future Generations and Democratic Legitimacy

*Peter Lawrence*

Arrival of the Anthropocene has focused attention on human beings' impacts on functioning global ecosystems and made increasingly urgent the need to focus on global institutional reform. The Anthropocene involves the notion that we have entered into a new era in which human beings have permanently modified global ecosystems, including the climatic system. Evidence mounts that the Earth's climatic system is approaching tipping points with potentially catastrophic consequences. This has led John Dryzek to call for a rethink of political institutions appropriate for this new era based on 'ecosystemic reflexivity' as a first overriding virtue.[1] 'Ecosystemic reflexivity' involves incorporating better ways of listening to ecological systems with broader participation – taking in both nature and future generations – into human institutions.[2]

One such global institutional reform proposal which would seem to meet well the requirements of ecosystemic reflexivity is the proposal for a UN High Commissioner for Future Generations (UNHCFG). This chapter takes as its starting point the position that we as a society do not have time to develop radically new institutions,[3] but that the proposed UNHCFG could be a valuable element in reforming existing global institutions to make them more responsive to the demands of the Anthropocene and increasing pressure on governments to take stronger action on climate change and related threats to global ecosystems.

The focus in this chapter is on the democratic legitimacy of such proposals, which has tended to be neglected. This neglect has stemmed from international relations literature only relatively recently focusing on democratic legitimacy at the

1 J. Dryzek, 'Institutions for the Anthropocene: Governance in a Changing Earth System' (2015) *British Journal of Political Science* 1.

2 Ibid. at 12.

3 T. Hale, 'Transparency, Accountability, and Global Governance' (2008) *Global Governance* 73, 90.

global level.[4] It has also stemmed from the view that democratic legitimacy cannot apply at the international level.

This chapter takes as its starting point the position that maximising democratic legitimacy at the international level is important for the same reason it is at the national level. Democracy involves at its heart the notion of governments being responsive to the will of the people. A powerful rationale for democracy is that – when compared to alternative models – it is more likely to result in just decisions.[5] The international community has endorsed this position in its consensus support for various resolutions by UN bodies. It remains important to strive to make international institutions, including institutions purporting to represent the interests of future generations, as responsive as possible to people affected by their decisions and activities, and maximise accountability to avoid such institutions being instruments of tyranny.

While there is no single theory of democracy, this chapter applies Dingwerth's criteria for democratic legitimacy,[6] which incorporate elements found across a wide spectrum of theories: the notion of inclusiveness or fair representation, the notion of democratic control (accountability and transparency), and deliberation.[7] First, this chapter aims to examine whether it is coherent to apply these criteria of democratic legitimacy to a proposed UNHCFG. Second, it examines what these criteria require in terms of a mandate for such an institution. The elements of a mandate for a proposed UNHCFG are discussed in a general way, and whether this is best achieved by a requirement to report for example to the UN General Assembly or the UN Secretary-General is not considered.

This chapter is structured as follows. The next section introduces recent proposals for a UNHCFG. The third section explains why democratic legitimacy is important in considering global governance reform proposals for a UNHCFG. The fourth section applies the criteria of democratic legitimacy to a proposed UNHCFG, considering in turn inclusiveness, democratic control, and deliberation. Each criterion is shown to dictate particular key elements in the mandate of a proposed UNHCFG. The fifth section turns to examine what mandate a UNHCFG should

4 But see K. Dingwerth, 'The Democratic Legitimacy of Public–Private Rulemaking: What Can We Learn from the World Commission on Dams?' (2005) *Global Governance* 65.

5 Amartya Sen uses evidence of the role of democracy in reducing famines and interstate conflict, so not direct measures of justice but perhaps useful proxies. He writes: 'Attention must be paid to the extensive evidence that democracy and political and civil rights tend to enhance freedoms of other kinds (such as human security) through giving a voice, at least in many circumstances, to the deprived and the vulnerable'. A. Sen, *The Idea of Justice* (Allen Lane 2009) 348.

6 K. Dingwerth, *The New Transnationalism: Transnational Governance and Its Democratic Legitimacy* (Palgrave Macmillan 2007).

7 K. Dingwerth, 'Global Democracy and the Democratic Minimum: Why a Procedural Account Alone Is Insufficient' (2014) 20(4) *European Journal of International Relations* 1124.

have, particularly from the point of view of ensuring democratic control through accountability. The final section draws conclusions.

## PROPOSALS FOR INTERNATIONAL INSTITUTIONAL REFORM: A UN HIGH COMMISSIONER FOR FUTURE GENERATIONS

There has been increasing attention in recent years to *national* institutional mechanisms designed to give greater weight to future generations, such as Commissioners or Parliamentary Committees for the Future.[8] Less attention has been paid to *international* institutional reform proposals aimed at increasing long-term thinking through a specific mandate to consider the interests of future generations. One such international reform proposal is the proposal to establish a UNHCFG. During the lead up to the 2012 Rio +20 UN Conference on Sustainable Development, civil society and a number of governments proposed the establishment of a UNHCFG to have the following functions:

(a) acting 'as an advocate for intergenerational solidarity through interactions with Member States and other stakeholders, as well is across United Nations entities';
(b) 'undertaking research and fostering expertise on policy practices to enhance intergenerational solidarity in the context of sustainable development';
(c) at the request of the United Nations or any of its entities or specialised agencies, offering advice on the 'implementation of existing intergovernmental commitments to enhance the rights and address the needs of future generations';
(d) upon request, offering 'support and advice, including to individual member states, on best practices and on policy measures to enhance intergenerational solidarity'.[9]

Under some civil society proposals, a UNHCFG would have a mandate to bring intergenerational justice issues to the attention of UN organs, participate in treaty negotiations, and request advisory opinions from the ICJ.[10] The latter proposal reflected the call by many civil society groups for the establishment of ombudsmen for future generations at both the national and international level. Under these

[8] Report of the Oxford Martin Commission for Future Generations, *Now for the Long Term* (Oxford University Press 2013).

[9] *Intergenerational Solidarity and the Needs of Future Generations*, UN Secretary-General (2013), UNGA, 68th session item 19(a), UN Doc A/68/322 (15 August 2013) at para. 63.

[10] H. Ward, *Committing to the Future We Want: A High Commissioner for Future Generations at Rio+20*, (2012) Foundation for Democracy and Sustainable Development, World Future Council www.fdsd.org/wordpress/wp-content/uploads/ Committing-to-the-future-we-want-main-report.pdf 30 November 2017.

proposals, the function of such a national institution would include not only advocacy for sustainable development and its implementation in policy practices, but also responding to citizen petitions, with the power to 'investigate claims of environmental crimes and engage in either conciliation or litigation'.[11] A new international ombudsman was envisaged as providing an overarching support for such national mechanisms.

It is important to emphasise that the recent proposals to create a UNHCFG did not involve the transfer of sovereignty from nation states to an international organisation. The UNHCFG would not be authorised to take decisions but rather seek to exert pressure on states by reminding them of their obligations towards future generations, similar to the role played by the existing UN Commissioners for human rights and refugees.[12] In spite of this, the proposal was seen as too intrusive by a number of developing countries, and as favouring developed country interests against developing countries, and was rejected.[13]

## THE IMPORTANCE OF DEMOCRATIC LEGITIMACY

Support for the core notion of democracy as 'governance based on the will of the people' is not limited to democratic Western governments or theorists, and the international community has expressed support for the democratic ideal. While the term 'democracy' does not appear in the UN Charter, it indirectly bases its legitimacy on democracy through use of the opening words 'We the Peoples of the United Nations'. The Universal Declaration of Human Rights, adopted by the General Assembly in 1948, went further, proclaiming that 'the will of the people shall be the basis of the authority of government' and guaranteeing to everyone rights essential for effective political participation. The ICCPR, adopted by the General Assembly in 1966, imposed obligations on states to respect the right of individuals to participate in public affairs. More recently, the UN Millennium Declaration, adopted by the General Assembly in 2000, states that '[d]emocratic and participatory governance based on the will of the people' best ensures 'dignity' and a range of human rights including rights to be free from hunger, free of violence, oppression, and injustice.[14] The UN Human Rights Council has gone one step further in making an explicit link between legitimacy and democracy, stating that '[a] functioning democracy, strong and accountable institutions, transparent and inclusive decision-

[11] *Intergenerational Solidarity and the Needs of Future Generations*, *supra* note 9 at para. 54.

[12] S. Caney, 'Applying the Principle of Intergenerational Equity to the 2015 Multilateral Processes' (2014) Background Paper (Mary Robinson Foundation Climate Justice 18).

[13] Ibid.

[14] United Nations Millennium Declaration, Resolution adopted by the General Assembly (UN doc.A/RES/55/2 (18 September 2000)) www.un.org/millennium/declaration/ares552e.pdf accessed 30 November 2017 para. 6.

making and effective rule of law is essential for a legitimate and effective Government that is respectful of human rights'.[15]

While the language of the UN Millennium Declaration and UN Human Rights Council seems to reflect an instrumental (or epistemic) view of democracy, this chapter does not take a particular position on this issue. Rather, democratic legitimacy criteria common to a number of theories of democracy synthesised by Dingwerth are used as the basis of analysis to evaluate proposals for a UNHCFG.[16] Under this approach, a rulemaking process is considered 'democratically legitimate' to the extent that it involves procedures that are considered 'rightful' or 'justifiable'.[17] The focus here is on normative legitimacy, in other words, the justification of institutional authority from a normative point of view, rather than 'sociological' legitimacy, which refers to whether an institution is actually considered authoritative.[18]

The idea of democratic legitimacy rests on the *ideal* of democracy. In the view of some authors, the ideal of democracy rests on the all affected principle (AAP), according to which any person potentially affected by a decision should have a say in relation to that decision.[19] Some argue that international institutions can never meet any minimal criteria of democratic legitimacy because they are the creatures of states, many of which are not democratic.[20] But David Held has pointed out that the idea of democracy being necessarily linked and limited to sovereign states ignores the dramatic change over the last decades with states (especially in Europe) now interlocked through complex international structures, including in relation to defence, responses to environmental problems, and human rights mechanisms. Held argues in favour of creating much-needed innovative and deliberative decision-making centres beyond national territories, to supplement existing national political units on the basis of the AAP and a notion of cosmopolitan democracy.[21]

15 Human Rights, Democracy and the Rule of Law, United Nations Human Rights Council (2012), resolution 19/36 UN GA doc. A/HRC/RES/19/36 (19 April 2012) para. 5.

16 Dingwerth, *supra* note 6; Dingwerth, *supra* note 7.

17 Dingwerth, *supra* note 6 at 15.

18 D. Bodansky, 'The Legitimacy of International Governance: A Coming Challenge for International Environmental Law?' (1999) 93 *American Journal of International Law* 596.

19 R. Goodin, 'Enfranchising All Affected Interests, and Its Alternatives' (2007) 35(1) *Philosophy and Public Affairs* 40 at 49. See B. Saunders, 'Democracy and Future Generations' (2014) 4(2) *Philosophy and Public Issues* 11. Arrhenius points out that this criticism is misdirected, as weak implementation does not per se demonstrate that the principle itself is unjustified as a democratic ideal. G. Arrhenius, 'The Boundary Problem in Democratic Theory', in F. Termsan (ed.), *Democracy Unbound: Basic Explorations I* (Filosofiska Institutionen, Stockholms Universitet 2005) 14.

20 R. Dahl, 'Can International Organisations Be Democratic? A Sceptic's View', in I. Shapiro and C. Hacker-Cordon (eds.), *Democracy's Edges* (Cambridge University Press 1999). See also T. Christiano, 'Is Democratic Legitimacy Possible for International Institutions?', in D. Archibugi, M. Koenig-Archibugi, and R. Marchetti (eds.), *Global Democracy: Normative and Empirical Perspectives* (Cambridge University Press 2011) 69 at 81.

21 D. Held, *Democracy and the Global Order* (Polity Press 1995).

Dingwerth sets out a valuable framework for measuring democratic legitimacy at the international level based on 'inclusiveness', 'democratic control', and 'discursive quality' (deliberation).[22] This model contains elements common to many theories of democracy.[23] 'Inclusiveness' refers to the extent to which those 'subject to a decision have been included in the decision-making process' with an equal opportunity to participate.[24] 'Democratic control' is the notion that those who govern should be subject to the control of those who are governed.[25] Democratic control is aimed at ensuring that those who govern are responsive to those who are governed and act in accordance with the interests of constituencies achieved through accountability and transparency.[26] 'Discursive practice' incorporates deliberative democracy approaches that focus on the quality of discourses involved in the decision-making process. The qualities of inclusiveness, equality, and freedom from coercion and rationality are seen as essential prerequisites for democratic discourse.[27]

These broad criteria for democratic legitimacy provide a set of democratic values rather than a rigid model to be applied to international institutions.[28] And as we have seen above, the international community has affirmed these values as being essential for maximising implementation of human rights. The precise form which these criteria take needs to be adapted to the specific institution in question. Macdonald and Macdonald have demonstrated, in their study applying democratic legitimacy criteria to the transnational garments industry,[29] that it is vital to consider the *underlying purpose* that electoral accountability principles play at the *national* level – making the exercise of public power responsive to those affected by decision making – when considering the particular power relationships and accountability chains in any particular *international* context. Applying this insight here, accountability chains in relation to institutions purporting to represent future generations cannot take the same form as in other contexts given the necessarily indirect manner in which future generations can hold proxies to account. In spite of this limitation,

22 Dingwerth, *supra* note 6 at 27.

23 Dingwerth, *supra* note 7 at 1126. See also S. Karlsson-Vinkhuyzen and A. Vihma, 'Comparing the Legitimacy and Effectiveness of Global Hard and Soft Law: An Analytical Framework' (2009) 3 *Regulation & Governance* 400; P. Van Ham 'Transnational Governance and Democratic Legitimacy, A Conceptual Overview', in The Hague Institute for Global Justice and Netherlands Institute of International Relations Clingendael, Special Report on Transnational Governance and Democratic Legitimacy (July 2014) 5–22 www.clingendael.nl/sites/default/files/Transnational%20Governance%20and%20Democratiy%20Legitimacy%20-%20Special%20Report.pdf accessed 30 November 2017.

24 Dingwerth, *supra* note 6 at 28.

25 Ibid. at 29.

26 Ibid.

27 Ibid. at 23.

28 Dingwerth, *supra* note 6 at 18.

29 T. Macdonald and K. Macdonald, 'Non-Electoral Accountability in Global Politics: Strengthening Democratic Control within the Global Garment Industry' (2006) 17(1) EJIL 89.

the underlying purpose of seeking to ensure that institutions are in place to provide individuals equal protection against oppressive forms of power remains crucial.

A further problem in applying the criteria sketched above in relation to international institutions purporting to represent the interests of future generations is whether it is meaningful to apply the concept of inclusion or responsiveness in relation to unborn persons who cannot express preferences in terms of political decisions taken now. Application of the notion of inclusion or responsiveness and the AAP in relation to future generations implies that the *demos* can be legitimately extended into the future. Arguably, if the basis of the AAP is linked to being potentially affected by a decision, it is logical to extend the notion of 'being affected' to include future people likely to be affected by decisions taken by contemporaries to the extent that the impacts on the interests of future generations are reasonably predictable.[30] One objection to this approach (the so-called epistemic objection) is that it may place an impossibly high threshold on decision makers. How can decision makers know what impacts current decisions will have on the interests of future generations and what assumptions can they make about the values of future generations?

The proviso that decision makers reasonably be held to take into account the interests of future generations *to the extent that these are reasonably predictable* helps deal with the first objection. Thus, for example, while we may be uncertain as to future generations' values, we can make reasonable assumptions that they will share our basic interests in functioning climate system, a global ecosystem that has not been irreversibly harmed, and minimum needs for water, food, and shelter.[31] Indeed, all that is necessary as a prerequisite for political representation of future generations is that one knows enough about the interests of future people, or at least a significantly large number of generations, to be able to make 'probabilistic, nonrandom judgments about the effects of policies' on their interests.[32]

In summary, the value of democracy in increasing the likelihood of just decisions has been endorsed by the international community. In addition, Dingwerth sets out some broad criteria for democratic legitimacy in relation to international institutions common to many theories, including inclusiveness, government control, and deliberation. Objections to application of democratic legitimacy criteria to international institutions purporting to represent future generations' interests were not convincing, since taking into account the interests of unborn persons does not impose an overly burdensome obligation because we can make reasonable predictions

[30] R. Goodin, 'Enfranchising All Affected Interests, and Its Alternatives' (2007) 35(1) *Philosophy and Public Affairs* 40.

[31] R.P. Hiskes, *The Human Right to a Green Future: Environmental Rights and Intergenerational Justice* (Cambridge University Press 2009).

[32] G. Kavka and M. Warren, 'Political Representation for Future Generations', in R. Elliot and A. Gare (eds.), *Environmental Philosophy* (University of Queensland Press 1983) 25.

about future persons' basic needs. While there are challenges to the application of democratic standards to international institutions owing to the undemocratic nature of many states, seeking to maximise the democratic legitimacy of such institutions remains important. If the ideal of democracy is abandoned at the international level, it takes with it the ability to ensure that institutions reflect the interests of people who they purport to represent.

## THE ELEMENTS OF DEMOCRATIC LEGITIMACY

### *Inclusion/Fair Representation*

Application of notions of representation raises challenging issues about *who* is to be represented and *how* they are to be represented. Turning to the latter issue first, we need a concept of representation. Hannah Pitkin's influential definition of representation includes two arms – firstly, the notion of 'substantive acting for others interests' and secondly, the notion of a representative acting as an agent for another.[33] The first arm of the definition is broad enough to allow for representation of future generations by proxies on the basis that future generations possess interests.[34] Just as we accept that it is legitimate for a guardian to represent the interests of a disabled child, there is no reason in principle that a proxy cannot represent the interests of future generations.[35] But the notion of a 'proxy' in the sense of someone standing in the shoes of a particular person is perhaps misleading, as it conceals the context within which this 'substitution' occurs. For example, the legitimacy of a guardian's claim to represent disabled children does not happen in a vacuum and entails a range of accountability mechanisms, for example a closely defined mandate contained in legislation and oversight mechanisms. Moreover, the guardianship analogy is imperfect in that its scope is usually linked to decisions limited to basic needs such as accommodation and healthcare. In contrast, a proxy for future generations can purport to represent this category of persons' interests in relation to broader public policy making.

Michael Saward's concept of representation is helpful in clarifying how we can conceive of a 'proxy for future generations', in terms of democratic legitimacy. Saward has proposed the idea of representation as a claim, rather than a fact resulting from (free and fair) elections.[36] This approach opens up the possibility of valid representation outside the electoral context. The essence of such claims is that

[33] H. Pitkin, *The Concept of Representation* (University of California Press 1967) 209.

[34] R. Goodin, 'Enfranchising the Earth, and Its Alternatives' (1996) *Political Studies* 835, 843; T. Ball, 'Democracy', in A. Dobson and R. Eckersley (eds.), *Political Theory and the Ecological Challenge* (Cambridge University Press 2006) 137.

[35] Ibid.

[36] M. Saward, 'Representation and Democracy: Revisions and Possibilities' (2008) 2(3) *Sociology Compass* 1000, 1003.

'someone represents the interests of a specified group viz: I/he/she represents these people's interest because of X'.[37]

Saward shows that 'X' can constitute a number of factors including ties to a tradition, in the case of a religious leader. Importantly this notion of representation involves a particular group accepting the purported claim of representation, which is clearly not possible in relation to future generations. But Saward's concept of representation also includes the notion of 'surrogacy for wider interests' and stakeholders,[38] which are more relevant to the intergenerational context. Representation by 'surrogacy' arises owing to structural limitations and 'important perspectives not being heard'.[39] The category of 'stakeholders' involves those with a stake in the decision having a right to have their interests included in the process.[40] Both these latter two categories of surrogacy and stakeholder-based representation apply in relation to future generations, albeit the stakeholder notion can only apply indirectly owing to the stakeholders (future generations) not yet being in existence.

Criteria are also required for evaluating non-electoral representative claims. To this end, Saward proposes a number of criteria. One of these (the 'confirming' criterion) involves a constituency accepting a claim that clearly could not apply to institutions purporting to represent future generations except in a retrospective sense. However, Saward's authenticity criterion emphasises whether a particular representative appears to speak 'genuinely' on behalf of relatively marginalised persons would apply to claimed representatives of future generations.[41] The idea here is that, absent evidence to the contrary, we can make an assumption that an organisation or individual purporting to represent a marginalised group is genuine.

This test of 'authentic representation' would seem, however, to be too easy. Two comments can be made at this point. Firstly, representation by 'proxy', while not perfect, is better than no representation at all.[42] Secondly, recalling the checks and balances involved in the representation by a guardian of a disabled person, additional checks and balances were essential to the legitimacy of this form of representation. Thus, in the context of a proxy for future generations it is necessary to ensure that future generations' interests are appropriately reflected in the mandate of a UNHCFG. This, together with a mandate giving NGOs a strong role, provides a further guarantee that such representation is 'authentic' and accountable. Thus, authentic representation needs to be linked to accountability and transparency mechanisms.

[37] M. Saward 'Authorisation and Authenticity: Representation and the Unelected' (2009) 17(1) *Journal of Political Philosophy* 1, 9.

[38] Ibid. at 12.

[39] Ibid.

[40] Ibid. at 13.

[41] Ibid. at 20.

[42] R. Eckersley, 'Deliberative Democracy, Ecological Representation and Risk: Towards a Democracy of the Affected', in M. Saward (ed.) *Democratic Innovation, Deliberation, Representation and Association* (Routledge 2000) 117.

### *Accountability and Transparency*

Democratic control requires wielders of public power being held accountable. Accountability is closely linked to the concept of democratic representation. Thus Marc Warren and Dario Castiglione argue that 'democratic representation involves a representative X being held accountable to constituency Y with regard to interests Z'.[43] Accountability traditionally involves the notion that if an elected representative does not represent the interests of his or her constituency, he or she can be sanctioned by removal.

Ruth Grant and Robert Keohane have demonstrated that this traditional notion of accountability needs to be reconfigured when we examine global politics. They emphasise the need to distinguish between a *participation* model of accountability where performance of a wielder of power is evaluated by those affected by their decisions, from a *delegation* model of accountability whereby performance is evaluated by those entrusting them with powers.[44] They point out that in the global system it is essential to distinguish between these two types of accountability given the fragmented global *demos*. There is no global democratic organisation. The UN organisation and treaty-related institutions and bodies do not involve any direct representation by citizens. Decisions are made by states, often with some role for NGOs. While one could seek to argue that the UN derives its democratic legitimacy from the authority delegated by democratic states (in turn representing citizens) to this organisation, this argument is flawed for three reasons. First, a substantial minority of countries around the world are not democratic.[45] Second, even within representative-style democratic governments, foreign policy decisions relating to the negotiation and entry into treaties tend to be conducted with little parliamentary scrutiny.[46] Third, treaty negotiations often take place within negotiating blocks such as the G77 or EU, with individual countries having limited capacities to influence positions of the negotiating group.[47]

Grant and Keohane point out that some international organisations, while having weak accountability in terms of participation, nevertheless have strong accountability in terms of the delegation model as member states hold to account the performance of the particular organisation.[48] Their analysis is particularly useful

[43] M. Warren and D. Castiglione, 'The Transformation of Democratic Representation' (2004) 2 (1) *Democracy and Society* 20.

[44] R. Grant and R. Keohane, 'Accountability and Abuses of Power in World Politics' (2005) 99(1) *American Political Science Review* 29 at 31.

[45] *Freedom in the World – Electoral Democracies* (Freedom House 2014) https://freedomhouse.org/sites/default/files/Electoral%20Democracy%20Numbers%2C%20FIW%201989-2014.pdf accessed 30 November 2017.

[46] J. Crawford, 'Democracy and International Law' (1994) 64 *British Yearbook of International Law* 113.

[47] Karlsson-Vinkhuyzen, *supra* note 23.

[48] Grant and Keohane, *supra* note 44.

in terms of accountability requirements for institutions to protect future generations. Accountability through participation is not possible in a direct manner. Nor is accountability through delegation. Nevertheless, accountability can occur *indirectly* via both means. Thus a UNHCFG established by member states could be held accountable in terms of the delegation of powers by those states establishing such a body. Direct representation in a delegation sense is not possible for future unborn persons. Nevertheless, accountability is possible by ensuring that a UNHCFG acts in accordance with standards laid down in the instrument establishing its mandate. A significant weakness in this approach, however, is that states are reluctant to accept strong obligations of intergenerational justice, both on the ethical plane and in international law.[49] This, therefore, lessens the likelihood of a strong mandate on which accountability could be based.

In spite of these limitations, transnational civil society provides a further 'channel of accountability' by providing a linkage to external actors outside the particular institutions.[50] International civil society may play an essential role in checking that information is reliable and ensuring its broader dissemination. This in turn can help ensure accountability in that the terms of accountability (i.e. the relevant standards) can be appropriately revised in a dynamic fashion.[51]

Transparency is linked to accountability as information must be made public in order to hold decision makers to account.[52] Again, this flows from the AAP in that the provision of information can ensure that those potentially affected by a decision have meaningful input even if the input is provided by a proxy representing future generations. A key objective of proposals for a UNHCFG includes making the impacts of decisions on future generations more transparent, and an important role for international civil society is integral to many proposals for this to occur.[53] Indeed, one such proposal would provide the mandate for a UNHCFG for complaints to be received from NGOs and affected persons' violations of the right to a healthy environment.[54]

To sum up, the accountability element of democratic legitimacy dictates that a UNHCFG be held to account by being required to undertake its functions in accordance with an agreed mandate. Indeed, this and other elements of accountability have been reflected in the proposals for a UNHCFG in the lead up to the Rio +20 Conference. Accountability was reflected in proposals to require a UNHCFG

49 P. Lawrence, *Justice for Future Generations: Climate Change and International Law* (Edward Elgar 2014). This is so despite powerful arguments supporting an ethical obligation on contemporaries towards future generations; see A. Gosseries and L. Meyer (eds.), *Intergenerational Justice* (Oxford University Press 2009).

50 A. Buchanan and R. Keohane, 'The Legitimacy of Global Governance Institutions' (2006) 20(4) *Ethics and International Affairs* 405, 432.

51 Ibid.

52 Van Ham, *supra* note 23.

53 Ward, *supra* note 10.

54 Ibid. at 5.

to report to UN organs in which all UN member states are represented. This was to be facilitated by the UNHCFG's activities being fully transparent, with broad participation of stakeholders and encouraging both governments and the public to make recommendations on matters falling within the mandate of the UNHCFG.[55] In addition, transparency would be ensured by all reports being made publicly available.[56]

A key potential weakness in all these proposals is that accountability would be only as strong as the mandate of a UNHCFG. Empirical evidence suggests that transparency can help ensure accountability in holding international institutions to account in terms of their own standards but this is most effective when combined with a well-targeted NGO campaign.[57] A weakness in this approach is that it may be difficult to agree on sufficiently specific standards in a mandate for a UNHCFG. As discussed below, a general mandate including core human rights or sustainable development may be sufficient in providing a basis for a UNHCFG playing an advocacy role with a corresponding accountability function. However, this would be arguably too vague to serve as a basis for accountability for a UNHCFG taking on a complaints function which would necessarily involve more precise standards.[58] Based on experience to date, it may be difficult to obtain agreement on a sufficiently strong mandate in terms of protection of the interests of future generations.

### *Deliberation*

According to theories of 'deliberative democracy', the process of deliberation is an essential ingredient of democratic legitimacy.[59] Deliberation entails equal consideration of all arguments and positions.[60] If one accepts that the interests of future generations can be represented through proxies, then the question arises as to whether the participation of such proxies in the deliberative process is sufficient to meet the requirement of deliberation entailed in such theories. If one accepts the notion of representation as entailing necessarily partial representation of interests rather than agency, there seems no reason in principle why proxies cannot be part of the process of deliberation.

A further possibility arises out of John Dryzek and Simon Niemeyer's theory of deliberative democracy comprising the representation of 'discourses' rather than individuals. These authors define discourses as 'a set of categories and concepts

55 Ibid. at 6.
56 Ibid. at 3.
57 T. Hale, 'Transparency, Accountability, and Global Governance' (2008) 14 *Global Governance* 73.
58 J. Anstee-Wedderburn, 'Giving a Voice to Future Generations: Intergenerational Equity, Representatives of Generations to Come, and the Challenge of Planetary Rights' (2014) 1(1) *Australian Journal of Environmental Law* 37.
59 Dingwerth, *supra* note 6 at 2.
60 Van Ham, *supra* note 23 at 18.

embodying specific assumptions, judgments, contentions, dispositions, and capabilities'.[61] Dryzek and Niemeyer emphasise the rational basis of democracy in producing better collective outcomes than its alternatives by providing the possibility for policy proposals to be criticised from a variety of points of view. They argue that, accordingly, it is more crucial that the varying perspectives be represented than 'proportional representation of those who subscribe to the various positions'.[62] They further argue that it is not representation of persons as such but elements of their 'interests, identities, and values' that is important.[63] They go on to argue that what counts is that all the various discourses be represented rather than individuals, with democratic legitimacy 'generated to the extent to which collective decisions are consistent with the constellation of discourses existing in the public sphere'.[64]

On the face of it, this theory is attractive in allowing the representation of the interests of future generations through discourses which reflect their interests, thus ensuring their democratic legitimacy. A proxy for future generations could help to ensure such discourses are factored into policy making. This approach would avoid the need for demonstrating some type of agency of future persons. However, a weakness of this approach is that it relies on social science methodologies to identify the relevant discourses, thus opening up the possibility of an unaccountable scientific elite.[65]

In spite of these concerns, deliberation is a vital ingredient in many theories of democracy, as it is more broadly seen as part of the process by which citizens' views are conveyed to representative institutions.[66] Thus, deliberative democracy provides a strong justification for a proxy to represent the interests of future generations in the deliberative process. Thus deliberative democracy could underpin the advocacy element containing proposals for a UNHCFG.

## OBJECTIVE AND EFFECTIVENESS

As foreshadowed above, a UNHCFG would need to operate on the basis of a clearly defined and appropriate mandate to ensure accountability. Moreover, the precise mandate of the UNHCFG would be vital in terms of the potential for such an institution to be effective in furthering intergenerational justice. As pointed out by

[61] J. Dryzek and S. Niemeyer, 'Discursive Representation' (2008) 102(4) *American Political Science Review* 481.

[62] Ibid. at 482.

[63] Ibid. at 483.

[64] Ibid. at 484.

[65] Dryzek and Niemeyer recognise this issue and seek to address it. Dryzek and Niemeyer, supra note 61 at 487.

[66] M. Saward, 'Less Than Meets the Eye: Democratic Legitimacy and Deliberative Theory', in M. Saward (ed.), *Democratic Innovation, Deliberation, Representation and Association* (Routledge 2000) 66–77.

Dingwerth,[67] the need to address the structural preconditions necessary for individuals to participate in democracy (basic human rights to subsistence, health, and education) shows how democratic legitimacy and justice are inexorably linked. Thus, representation of future generations through a proxy in the form of a UNHCFG which includes in its mandate basic human rights has an attraction in terms of furthering intergenerational justice.

However, options for the mandate of a UNHCFG involve a range of options, including possible references to intergenerational solidarity or justice, human rights, sustainable development, and protection of the global ecological system. Space precludes fully discussing these options here, but some comments are made in terms of how these options relate to democratic legitimacy criteria.

An interesting threshold question is how precise the objective or mandate should be, given that, as mentioned above, a more precise standard would facilitate greater accountability but could be very difficult to negotiate. One could conceivably have UNHCFGs in relation to sectors of policy making (e.g. the oceans, atmosphere, and biodiversity),[68] which could ensure more precise benchmarks; however, this would require the necessary political will to invest the negotiation capital in such an exercise.

Arguably it would be preferable to incorporate a goal highlighting core human rights and a strong version of sustainable development in the mandate of a UNHCFG. One option would be to base the mandate of a UNHCFG on intergenerational justice, defined as future generations' interests and core human rights to life, health, and subsistence being considered to be of equal weight to current persons.[69] To this end, the purpose should be to highlight the particular interests of future generations in relation to international action to address global environment, development, and social and economic issues. One may object that the equal weight requirement ignores the reality that for many developing countries the need to address poverty should prevail over the interests of future generations. However, given the systematic failure of current policy makers to consider the interests of future unborn generations across a wide range of issues,[70] the idea of the 'future mechanism' is that it functions to ensure consideration of the distinctive interests of future generations. Such a mechanism would not pre-empt the process involved in deciding the balance between current and future generations' needs. The extent to which a new international mechanism focused on the interests of future generations seeks to enshrine human rights beyond the core rights is a difficult issue. Some may argue for a more comprehensive list of human rights. However, this needs to be

[67] Dingwerth, *supra* note 7.

[68] C. Stone, *Should Trees Have Standing? Law, Morality, and the Environment*, 3rd edn. (Oxford University Press 2010) 104.

[69] S. Caney, 'Climate Change, Human Rights and Moral Thresholds', in S. Humphreys (ed.), *Human Rights and Climate Change* (Cambridge University Press 2009) 69.

[70] Ward, *supra* note 10.

balanced against political feasibility, as some states' hackles may be raised about inclusion of an extensive list of human rights.[71]

A further option would be to include in the mandate the objective of sustainable development as defined in the Brundtland sense of 'meeting the needs of the present without compromising the ability of future generations to meet their own needs'.[72] This flows from the dependence of human beings on the global ecological system and the intergenerational justice principle. This would link well with the criteria of inclusion/fair representation: without sustainable development being part of the mandate, there is a risk that future generations' interests would be unfairly underrepresented.

Putting 'sustainable development' centre stage in the mandate of the proposed body is attractive in that this concept, despite its ambiguity, has been widely endorsed by the international community (e.g. the Rio Declaration on Environment and Development 1992, Principle 3).[73] There is nevertheless a danger that the economic development aspect of sustainable development is emphasised at the expense of the environment.[74] Moreover, one could argue that the Anthropocene requires the mandate of a UNHCFG to explicitly include the objective of preserving the global ecological system in its mandate, on the grounds that sustainable development and human rights are inadequate to the task at hand.

In relation to institutions aimed at protecting the welfare of future generations this issue is challenging in that one can only assess in the future how effective such an institution is in terms of impacts on future generation's welfare. But this challenge can be overstated. One can assess in the short term, for example, how effective a new UNHCFG would be in factoring in the interests of future generations into current policy making.

A further potential challenge is an argument that a UNHCFG would end up pre-empting difficult policy decisions on how to balance current and future generations' interests. Indeed, Karsten Klint Jensen has argued that a proxy for future generations is inherently undemocratic in the sense that it entails the notion of giving a particular category of persons greater representation than other groups.[75] This, however, ignores the context which involves the current underrepresentation of future generations. Moreover, a UNHCFG would not be directly making decisions but rather would conceivably have a mandate to highlight long-term interests of

[71] Buchanan and Keohane, *supra* note 50.

[72] G.H. Brundtland et al., *Our Common Future: Report of the World Commission on Environment and Development* (Oxford University Press 1987) 43; Ward, *supra* note 10.

[73] The Rio Declaration on Environment and Development in Principle 3 states that 'the right to development must be fulfilled so as to equitably meet development and environmental needs of present and future generations'.

[74] K. Bosselmann, *The Principle of Sustainability: Transforming Law and Governance* (Ashgate 2008).

[75] K.K. Jensen, 'Future Generations in Democracy: Representation or Consideration?' (2015) 6(3) *Jurisprudence* 535.

future generations and advocate the incorporation of these interests into policy making. This would not pre-empt government and global decision making, but arguably would ensure that it is better informed and conditioned by a wider range of relevant interests.

## CONCLUSION

Democratic legitimacy criteria can and should be applied to international institutional proposals purporting to represent future generations. This is because maximising the democratic legitimacy of institutions purporting to represent future generations will increase the likelihood that they deliver just outcomes and redress to at least to some extent the short-term focus of current governance structures.

However, democratic governance is necessary but not sufficient to guarantee just or sustainable outcomes. For this to occur, one needs to address political-economic structures that constitute barriers to participation of the less powerful in the political process.[76] Both national and international governance operates within an economic system geared towards rapid economic growth rather than sustainability.[77] Thus, while it is worthwhile pressing for more democratic international institutional structures, this alone will be insufficient to deliver the policy outcomes necessary to protect the interests of future generations and the global ecological system. Crucially, however, this does not detract from the importance of the democratic ideal as a benchmark for pressing to make governance structures more democratic.[78]

The democratic legitimacy criteria applied in this chapter reflects the ideal of democracy which has been endorsed by the international community as a precondition for the fulfilment of human rights. Democratic legitimacy criteria can coherently be applied to institutions purporting to represent future generations if, firstly, it is adopted on an interests-based (rather than delegation) notion of representation by proxies, and secondly, if its criteria are tailored to the particular features of both the international system and future generations.

In terms of the first issue, we have seen that Saward's notion of representation of non-electoral claims provides a workable framework for assessing the validity of representative claims including in relation to proxies purporting to represent the interests of future generations. Acceptance of an assumption of authentic representation, until proven otherwise, is rather weak, and strong accountability through appropriate transparency mechanisms is also required. Moreover, proxy representation is better than no representation at all. This was combined with the argument that the *demos* can reasonably extended into the future to include future people

[76] D. Schlossberg, *Defining Environmental Justice, Theories, Movements, and Nature* (Oxford University Pres 2007) 28.

[77] Bosselmann, *supra* note 74.

[78] D. Coady and R. Cory, *The Climate Change Debate: An Epistemic and Ethical Enquiry* (Palgrave McMillan 2013) 82.

likely to be affected by decisions taken by contemporaries to the extent that the impacts on the interests of future generations are reasonably predictable. Proxies for future generations can reasonably make assumptions that future generations share our basic interests in terms of core human rights, and a functioning climate and global ecological system upon which human beings all depend.

In terms of accountability, we saw that Grant and Keohane's theory provides a basis for criteria applicable to institutions aimed at protecting future generations: such institutions can be 'held to account' by ensuring that they comply with a mandate carefully crafted to ensure that intergenerational justice is promoted. The weak point, however, in establishing such accountability remains the reluctance of states to accept obligations towards future generations. However, transnational NGO networks can, at least to some extent, rectify this weakness.

The argument made here is that 'democratic legitimacy' is not an all-or-nothing concept, but rather an important ideal. Even if the non-democratic nature of many governments operates as a significant barrier to making international institutions democratic in a sense comparable to national governments, democratic legitimacy remains an important ideal at the international level. This is because it involves such institutions taking into account as much as possible the impact of their decisions and activities on persons affected by these decisions. These arguments apply with equal force in relation to institutional mechanisms purporting to represent future generations. International institutions operate in the context of economic structures and discourses dominated by short-term unsustainable thinking which is difficult to shift. However, given the systematic neglect of the interests of future generations by existing institutions, one can be cautiously optimistic that institutions with an explicit mandate to represent future generations can potentially make matters marginally better. Given the current failure to incorporate the interests of future generations into policy making and the threat to the global ecological system, there are powerful arguments for supporting the establishment of a UNHCFG to give a voice to these interests. The democratic legitimacy of such an institution will be furthered by a mandate which places core human rights and strong sustainability centre stage. Accountability would be best achieved by such an institution having an advocacy rather than complaints role, with transparency in relation to long-term policy impacts being linked to a strong role for NGOs to facilitate accountability.

# PART V

# Regional Trends in Intergenerational Justice

# 32

# A European Human Rights Perspective on National Sustainable Development Institutions

*Christina Binder*

The protection of the environment is a cornerstone of intergenerational justice and a main objective of national sustainable development institutions. Different approaches to the protection of the environment are possible. One approach is to consider the protection of the environment in its own right. Examples of international treaties adhering to this approach include instruments for the protection of the ozone layer, forests, biodiversity, and seas.[1] Also, in some national constitutions the protection of the environment is considered as a good in its own right. Another approach to the protection of the environment is a human-centred perspective which defines the environment from the perspective of its value for human beings.[2] Relevant rights under this approach include third-generation/

[1] E.g. Vienna Convention for the Protection of the Ozone Layer (entered into force 22 September 1988) 1513 UNTS 293; International Convention for the Prevention of Pollution from Ships (entered into force 2 October 1983) 1340 UNTS 184; International Tropical Timber Agreement (entered into force 7 December 2011) 2797 UNTS Doc. TD/TIMBER.3/12; Convention on Biological Diversity (entered into force 29 December 1993) 1760 UNTS 79; Convention on Wetlands of International Importance Especially as Waterfowl Habitat (entered into force 21 December 1975) 996 UNTS 243; UN Convention on the Law of the Sea (entered into force 16 November 1994) 1988 UNTS 3. For further examples see also U. Beyerlin and J. Grote Stoutenburg, 'Environment, International Protection', *The Max Planck Encyclopedia of International Law* Vol. 3 (Oxford University Press 2012) 461. Note, however, that often the protection of the environment serves to fulfil economic objectives, again part of a human-centred perspective. For example, while the preamble to the Whaling Convention (International Convention for the Regulation of Whaling [entered into force 10 November 1948] 181 UNTS 364) recalls as an objective to safeguard 'for future generations the great natural resources represented by the whale stocks', it later elaborates that 'increases in the size of whale stocks will permit increases in the number of whales which may be captured without endangering these natural resources'.

[2] This is also the approach opted for in the 1972 Stockholm Declaration: 'Man has the fundamental right to freedom, equality and adequate conditions of life, in an environment of a quality that permits a life of dignity and well-being, and he bears a solemn responsibility to protect and improve the environment for present and future generations. In this respect,

collective rights such as the right to a healthy environment or the right to development, as *inter alia* enshrined in a number of General Assembly Resolutions.[3]

While these are *a priori* non-binding instruments at the universal level, the African Charter on Human and Peoples' Rights in particular has incorporated the content of these resolutions at the regional level in binding form.[4] Also, individual (human) rights may be at stake in case of environmental degradation. Most obviously, this might concern economic and social rights such as the right to health or the right to an adequate standard of living. However, as can be seen in the case law of regional human rights bodies, civil and political rights may also be of relevance. Damages to the environment are thus considered as possible encroachments of human beings' right to private and family life, the overarching right to life, or the protection of property.[5] The European context is a particularly good example since, owing to the volume of the ECtHR's jurisprudence in comparison to other human rights bodies,[6] valuable findings may be made with regard to how civil and political rights can serve the protection of the environment.

policies promoting or perpetuating apartheid, racial segregation, discrimination, colonial and other forms of oppression and foreign domination stand condemned and must be eliminated.' Stockholm Declaration of the United Nations Conference on the Human Environment (16 June 1972) UN Doc. A/CONF.48/14. The 1992 Rio Declaration proclaims in Principle 1 that 'Human beings are at the centre of concerns for sustainable development. They are entitled to a healthy and productive life in harmony with nature.' 'Rio Declaration on Environment and Development', Report of the United Nations Conference on Environment and Development (10 August 1992) UN Doc. A/CONF.151/26 (Vol. I).

3 UNGA Res 41/128 'Declaration on the Right to Development' (4 December 1986) UN Doc A/RES/41/128; Principle 3, 'Rio Declaration on Environment and Development' Report of the United Nations Conference on Environment and Development (10 August 1992) UN Doc. A/CONF.151/26 (Vol. I); 'Point I.5, Plan of Implementation of the World Summit on Sustainable Development' (4 September 2002) UN Doc. A/CONF.199/L.1; UNGA Res 45/94 'Right to a Healthy Environment for the Well-Being of Individuals' (14 December 1990) UN Doc. A/RES/45/94.

4 African Charter on Human and Peoples' Rights (entered into force 21 October 1986) 1520 UNTS 217 (Banjul Charter) arts. 22 (right to economic, social and cultural development) and 24 (right to a general satisfactory environment).

5 The right to property is at stake in the Americas and in relation to indigenous peoples. Given these communities' intertwined relationship to their territory, which is also protected by art. 21 of the American Convention on Human Rights (ACHR) (right to property) in the interpretation of the IACHR, degradations of the environment may be considered as violations of art. 21 ACHR, e.g. *Saramaka People* v. *Suriname* (Judgment on Preliminary Objections, Merits, Reparations and Costs) Inter-American Court of Human Rights Series C No.172 (28 November 2007).

6 This is especially the case in comparison to human rights bodies dealing with economic, social, and cultural rights. For example, only in 2013 was an Optional Protocol to the ICESCR adopted to permit the Committee on Economic, Social and Cultural Rights (CESCR) to receive individual complaints. So far, only approximately thirteen complaints have been received. (As of May 2016, See UN Committee on Economic, Social and Cultural Rights, 'Statistical Survey on Individual Complaints' www.ohchr.org/EN/HRBodies/CESCR/Pages/CESCRIndex.aspx accessed 2 October 2016.

Accordingly, this chapter examines environmental protection through the lens of the case law of the ECtHR.[7] It will start with a brief overview of the protection of the environment in the framework of the CoE in the next section. Then, the third section argues that the right to a healthy environment is increasingly well protected in the dynamic case law of the ECtHR. Still, there are important challenges to the protection of the environment through the ECtHR's jurisprudence. These include the victim requirement under the European Convention of Human Rights (ECHR), a generally wide margin of appreciation granted to states and the ECtHR's understandable self-restraint regarding reparations once a violation is established. This will be discussed in the fourth section. While there are certain indicia of improvement – as shown in the fifth section – there is still a long way to go. Against that background, the final section discusses the considerable need for national sustainable development institutions to achieve a truly effective protection of the environment, therewith complementing the protection of the ECtHR.

## BACKGROUND: THE PROTECTION OF THE ENVIRONMENT IN THE FRAMEWORK OF THE COE

Since the early 1990s, the necessary protection of the environment has gained prominence in the framework of the CoE. In particular, the Parliamentary Assembly of the CoE has repeatedly pushed for an enforceable right to a healthy environment. As early as 1990, the Parliamentary Assembly recommended that the Committee of Ministers adopt a 'European Charter and a European Convention on environmental protection and sustainable development', which included *inter alia* a fundamental right to an environment and living conditions conducive to the health of every person.[8] In 1999, the Parliamentary Assembly recommended that the Committee of Ministers draft 'an amendment or an additional protocol to the ECHR concerning the right of individuals to a healthy and viable environment'.[9] Similarly, in 2003 the Parliamentary Assembly recommended the drawing up of an additional Protocol to the ECHR 'concerning the recognition of individual procedural rights intended to enhance environmental protection, as set out in the Aarhus

[7] This contribution, accordingly, does not deal with the protection achieved through the (revised) European Social Charter. For relevant case law by the European Social Committee, see e.g. M. Trilsch, 'European Committee of Social Rights: The Right to a Healthy Environment' (2009) 7 International Journal of Constitutional Law 529. For the case of the European Social Committee, see http://hudoc.esc.coe.int/eng# accessed 30 November 2017.

[8] CoE (European Parliamentary Assembly), 'Formulation of a European Charter and a European Convention on Environmental Protection and Sustainable Development, Recommendation 1130 (1990)' (28 September 1990), Doc 6286.

[9] CoE (European Parliamentary Assembly), 'Future Action to Be Taken by the Council of European in the Field of Environment Protection, Recommendation 1431 (1999)' (4 November 1999) Doc 8560.

Convention'.[10] Other attempts, for instance on the preparation of a recommendation for the implementation of urgent practical measures for better prevention of environment related hazards, followed in 2009.[11] The Parliamentary Assembly likewise again recommended an Additional Protocol to the ECHR concerning the right to a healthy environment.[12]

Still, the Committee of Ministers has not given due practical effect to the respective recommendations. Among the reasons put forward are that other international instruments, including the ECHR in the dynamic interpretation by the ECtHR, would already sufficiently contribute to the protection of the environment.[13] Can this be considered correct?

## PROTECTION AGAINST ENVIRONMENTAL DEGRADATION IN THE CASE LAW OF THE ECTHR

Inherent limitations of the protection of the environment arise from the fact that the ECHR is not a specific instrument for environmental protection. The protection of the environment by the ECtHR occurs from a human rights-centred perspective, thus the protection always takes the value of the environment for human beings into consideration. In contrast, the ECtHR does not protect the environment for its own sake. In this vein, the ECtHR found in *Kyrtatos* v. *Greece*, concerning the application of house owners who complained under Article 8 ECHR that a construction project had led to the destruction of a swamp near their property and that the area around their home had lost its 'scenic beauty', that:

> the crucial element which must be present in determining whether, in the circumstances of a case, environmental pollution has adversely affected one of the rights safeguarded by paragraph 1 of Article 8 is the existence of a harmful effect on a person's private or family sphere and not simply the general deterioration of the environment. Neither Article 8 nor any of the other Articles of the Convention are specifically designed to provide general protection of the environment as such; to that effect, other international instruments and domestic legislation are more pertinent in dealing with this particular aspect.[14]

[10] CoE (European Parliamentary Assembly), 'Environment and Human Rights, Recommendation 114 (2003)' (27 June 2003) Doc 9791.

[11] CoE (European Parliamentary Assembly), 'Environment and Health: Better Prevention of Environment Related Health Hazards, Recommendation 1863 (2009)' (13 March 2009) Doc 11788. See also CoE (European Parliamentary Assembly), 'The Challenges Posed by Climate Change, Recommendation 1883 (2009)' (29 September 2009) Doc 12002.

[12] CoE (European Parliamentary Assembly), 'Drafting an Additional Protocol to the European Convention on Human Rights Concerning the Right to a Healthy Environment, Recommendation 1885 (2009)' (30 September 2009) Doc 12003.

[13] CoE (Committee of Ministers), 'Reply to Parliamentary Assembly Recommendation 1863 (2009)' (21 October 2009) Doc 12075.

[14] *Kyrtatos* v. *Greece*, ECHR 2003-VI, para. 52. *Aydin and Others* v. *Turkey*, ECHR 1997-VI, where the ECtHR rejected a complaint under Article 8 of the ECHR as manifestly ill-founded.

On this basis, the ECtHR dismissed the complaint regarding Article 8 ECHR.

There is thus no direct protection of the environment. However, as a slight caveat, it might be added that the increased concern for the state of the environment has been recognised as constituting a legitimate ground for interference with a particular right.[15] Moreover, since the 1980s and 1990s, both the European Commission on Human Rights and the ECtHR have interpreted the ECHR in such a way as to apply to environmental degradation analysis where it concerns the rights of individuals. Although there is no explicit right to a healthy environment incorporated in the ECHR, other provisions of the ECHR have been understood in a way as to grant according relief. Of comparatively greatest importance are the rights to private and family life (Article 8) and to life (Article 2).[16]

### *Right to Private and Family Life (Article 8 ECHR)*

Most of the jurisprudence on environmental matters has concerned Article 8 of the ECHR, which reads: 'Everyone has the right to respect for his private and family life, his home and his correspondence.' Although the wording of the provision does not readily lend itself to the protection of the environment, the ECtHR has recognised, in its dynamic interpretation of Article 8, a substantive right to be protected against pollution/environmental degradation. More particularly, the ECtHR has emphasised positive state obligations concerning either existing environmental nuisances

The applicants had complained about the impact of an intended construction of dams and hydroelectric power plants on the ecosystem of a valley where a national park was located. Still, they had not given an indication of how the construction of the dam would directly affect their way of life.

15 For the recognition that environment increasingly constitutes a legitimate concern, see e.g. *Mangouras* v. *Spain* ECHR 2010, para. 86; *Pine Valley Developments Ltd* v. *Ireland* ECHR (1991) Series A no. 222, para. 57; *Buckley* v. *United Kingdom* ECHR 1996-IV.

16 Of more limited relevance are the right to fair trial (Article 6 ECHR) as well as to an effective remedy (Article 13 ECHR), where insufficient procedures are established or no effective remedy is granted, the right to property (Article 1 of Protocol No 1 to the ECHR), and the right to freedom of expression (Article 10 ECHR) as regards the right to receive information on environmental degradation. Regarding Articles 6 and 13 ECHR (access to justice and other remedies in environmental matters) see e.g. *Zander* v. *Sweden*, ECHR (1993) Series A 279-B (where the ECtHR found that a claim by the application with regard to the use of water in their well for drinking purposes constituted a 'civil right' in the sense of Article 6 ECHR and that it was thus necessary to have the ability to have a government's decision reviewed by a court); *Hatton and Others* v. *United Kingdom*, ECHR 2003-VIII (finding a violation of Article 13 ECHR with regard to the domestic remedies available to the applicants concerning their rights under Article 8 ECHR). Regarding Article 10 ECHR see *Steel and Morris* v. *United Kingdom*, ECHR 2005-II (where the ECtHR discussed the right of environmental activities to distribute information and ideas on matters of general interest such as the environment). Regarding Article 1 of Protocol No 1 to the ECHR, see e.g. *Taşkin and Others* v. *Turkey*, ECHR 2004-X (finding that even though the protection of one's possessions needs to be 'practical and effective' this does not mean that one has the right to continue to enjoy one's property in a pleasant environment).

such as in *López Ostra*,[17] or impending environmental risks as in *Guerra*[18] and *Tătar*.[19] The ECtHR has accordingly read a positive obligation of states into Article 8, such as providing citizens with essential information on the potential risks and consequences of hazardous activities to ensure the effective protection of the rights guaranteed under Article 8.

Three cases are particularly illustrative examples of this. Perhaps best known is *López Ostra* v. *Spain* (1994).[20] This was the first case where the ECtHR found a breach of the ECHR as a consequence of environmental harm and established that the effective enjoyment of private and family life was violated by the health problems and nuisance caused by a wastewater plant operating in the vicinity of the applicant's home. More particularly, the ECtHR considered that severe environmental pollution might affect individuals' well-being and prevent them from enjoying their homes in such a way as to affect their private and family lives adversely, without, however, seriously endangering their health. In all instances, regard had to be had for the fair balance that must be struck between the competing interests of the individual and the community's well-being as a whole. In light of the State's failure to strike such a fair balance, the ECtHR concluded that a violation of Article 8 had occurred.

An even clearer example can be found in *Guerra* v. *Italy* (1998),[21] decided four years later. In this case, the ECtHR established a breach of Article 8 because of the Italian government's inaction and its failure to provide the local population with information about the pollution risk factor and how to proceed in the event of an accident at a nearby chemical factory. In so doing, the ECtHR thus read a positive obligation of the Italian government into Article 8, namely to inform the population about possible environmental risks.

A similar judgment was handed down in 2009 in *Tătar* v. *Romania* (2009),[22] where the ECtHR established a breach of Article 8 on the basis of the State's inaction. More specifically, the ECtHR found that Romania had not lived up to its obligations to assess the risks and consequences of a hazardous industrial process (gold mining operations) and to keep the public informed. In its reasoning, the ECtHR referred to the precautionary principle, which requires that States do not delay preventive action simply because of scientific uncertainty.[23]

[17] *López Ostra* v. *Spain* (1994) Series A no 303-C.

[18] *Guerra and Others* v. *Italy* ECHR 1998-I.

[19] *Tătar* v. *Romania* App no 67021/01 (ECtHR, 27 January 2009).

[20] *López Ostra*, *supra* note 17.

[21] *Guerra*, *supra* note 18.

[22] *Tătar*, *supra* note 19.

[23] In other contexts, however, the ECtHR has not followed the precautionary principle, instead giving priority to the margin of appreciation doctrine. For example, *Luginbühl* v. *Switzerland*, App No 42756/02 (Decision on Admissibility) (ECtHR, 17 January 2006), with regard to emissions causes by electromagnetic radiation of mobile phone antennas.

### Right to Life (Article 2 ECHR)

In the most severe cases, which involved the loss of life through dangerous activities or natural disasters, the ECtHR has gone so far as to establish a violation of Article 2 ECHR (right to life). Perhaps the best-known case is the Grand Chamber decision, *Öneryildiz* v. *Turkey*,[24] from 2004. In this case, the ECtHR held that a lack of adequate protection to safeguard the right to life and the lack of preventive measures which should have been taken by the State to prevent a methane gas explosion on a rubbish dip implied a violation of Article 2 (as well as of Article 1 of Protocol No 1, Article 6 ECHR, and Article 13 ECHR). The explosion had destroyed dwellings built on land surrounding the rubbish tip and caused the deaths of several dwellers. The ECtHR also read a procedural dimension into Article 2, holding that the applicant's right to information had been ignored. Based on the ECtHR's approach in this case, some authors have even found that it implied a new 'basic human right' of clear and full information.[25]

These findings were reiterated in *Budayeva and Others* v. *Russia* (2008).[26] Here, the ECtHR found that the failure by authorities to implement land-planning and emergency relief policies in light of a foreseeable risk of a mudslide, which caused the death of several persons, violated Article 2. While the case did not directly involve environmental dangers, it showed that the ECtHR is 'serious about insisting that governments have a duty not to leave citizens exposed to serious harm'.[27]

At the same time, the ECtHR has emphasised that the State's obligation to prevent an applicant's life being put at risk only arose in cases where the risks were foreseeable to the State. Thus, in *LCB* v. *United Kingdom* (1998), the ECtHR assessed whether, in the late 1950s, UK authorities could or should have foreseen the risks arising from nuclear testing conducted near the Christmas Islands and could have therefore reasonably been expected to provide advice to the parents of the applicant, who later contracted leukaemia, to monitor her health. '[G]iven the information available to the State at the relevant time ... concerning the likelihood of the applicant's father having been exposed to dangerous levels of radiation and of this having created a risk to her health',[28] the ECtHR found that these risks had not been foreseeable and that, therefore, the State could not have been expected to take such action.

[24] *Öneryildiz* v. *Turkey*, ECHR 2004-XII.

[25] S. Kravchenko and J.E. Bonine, 'Interpretation of Human Rights for the Protection of the Environment in the European Court of Human Rights' (2012) 25 *Global Business & Development Law Journal* 245 at 279.

[26] *Budayeva and Others* v. *Russia*, ECHR 2008 (extracts).

[27] Kravchenko and Bonine, *supra* note 25 at 279.

[28] *LCB* v. *United Kingdom*, ECHR 1998-III, para. 41.

### Appreciation

Overall, increasingly clear standards can be gained from the ECtHR's jurisprudence for the protection of the environment. This is especially the case with regard to the procedural dimension induced by the ECtHR into certain rights, for example that the population has the right to be informed about serious environmental risks. In *Guerra* v. *Italy*, the ECtHR established the government's duty to provide information.[29] In *Tătar* v. *Romania*, the ECtHR went so far as to draw on the precautionary principle regarding the government's positive duty to keep the public informed.[30] At times, the ECtHR has also utilised other instruments, such as the Aarhus Convention, and referred to the case law of other judicial bodies to further the right to environmental protection.[31] What is more, in most severe cases (for example when lives are lost), protection can be gained likewise from Article 2. Still, the possible reliance on Article 2 is very restricted. The ECtHR seems to be willing to rely on Article 2 ECHR only in the context of environmental degradation when there was an actual loss of life and where real risks were at minimum foreseeable, for example when states were not acting in the face of an imminent danger, as in *Öneryildiz*. Hence, Article 8 appears as the most important provision to bring environmental protection within the scope of the ECHR.[32] However, there are important challenges to the protection of the right to a healthy environment by the ECtHR.

## CHALLENGES TO THE ECTHR'S PROTECTION OF THE ENVIRONMENT

Among the numerous challenges to the ECtHR's protection of the environment,[33] three are of particular importance. They include – in addition to the above-

[29] *Guerra, supra* note 18 at para. 60.

[30] *Tătar, supra* note 19 at para. 109: 'La Cour rappelle qu'en droit roumain le droit à un environnement sain est un principe ayant valeur constitutionnelle. Ce principe a été repris par la loi no 137/1995 sur la protection de l'environnement, qui était en vigueur à l'époque des faits (voir pp. 16–17, a et b). Par ailleurs, le principe de précaution recommande aux États de ne pas retarder l'adoption de mesures effectives et proportionnées visant à prévenir un risque de dommages graves et irréversibles à l'environnement en l'absence de certitude scientifique ou technique (voir p. 27, h).' Kravchenko and Bonine, *supra* note 25 at 275.

[31] The potential for further evolution of this standard is also given, in view of the fact in more recent cases the Court has based its reasoning *inter alia* on the precautionary principle, increasingly recognized as CIL. See P. Sands and J. Peel, *Principles of International Environmental Law*, 3rd edn. (Cambridge University Press 2012) 228.

[32] Put differently, States are under an obligation to ensure that adequate protection of the rights of individuals is given and must for this purpose take preventive measures where risks are foreseeable. This includes an obligation to 'regulate and control environmental problems where they impair the exercise of convention rights'. A. Boyle, 'Human Rights or Environmental Rights? A Reassessment' (2007) 18 *Fordham Environmental Law Review* 481 at 486.

[33] Other challenges include the scope of application of the ECHR, which is limited to factual situations occurring within the jurisdiction of State Parties (Article 1 ECHR). This largely

mentioned limitations arising from the ECHR's scope (protection of the environment *only* where it interferes with the protected rights of individuals)[34] – the victim requirement, the traditionally broad margin of appreciation of States when it comes to measures of environmental protection, and the general self-restraint of the ECtHR in the area of reparations.

### Victim Requirement

A first obstacle to an effective protection of the environment in the ECtHR's case law is the 'victim requirement' as regards individual applications. It relates to the fact that, to file an individual application, Article 34 ECHR requires the applicant to be individually affected. Put differently, there has to be a sufficient link between the damage and the repercussions on the victim. While the ECtHR's case law is somewhat inconsistent,[35] the ECtHR has repeatedly rejected cases because the applicant(s) was/were not individually affected. This limits the possibility of public interest claims for the sake of environmental protection, such as *actio popularis* claims.

For example, the ECtHR denied the existence of the victim requirement in *Asselbourg and Others* v. *Luxembourg*. In the case at issue, the ECtHR rejected an application by individuals who lived in an area where a company had received a

relates to a territorial understanding of jurisdiction (*Banković and Others* v. *Belgium and others*, ECHR 2001-XII, para. 59). While there have been a number of cases recognizing the extraterritorial applicability of the ECHR in certain circumstances, these usually involved cases where a State exercised 'effective control' over another State's territory (*Loizidou* v. *Turkey*, ECHR 1996-VI) or authority and control over individuals located abroad (*Al-Skeini and Others* v. *United Kingdom*, ECHR 2011). It would therefore be difficult for transboundary pollution to reach this threshold. So far, the ECtHR has not decided on cases relating to transboundary environmental protection. In two cases which perhaps would have raised extraterritorial issues in the context of environmental pollution (nuclear testing), the ECtHR dismissed the facts for other reasons (*LCB* v. *United Kingdom*, *supra* note 28); *McGinley and Egan* v. *United Kingdom*, ECHR 1998-III). However, see H.E. Heiskanen and J. Viljanen, 'Reforming the Strasbourg Doctrine on Extraterritorial Jurisdiction in the Context of Environmental Protection' (2014) *European Law Reporter* 285, arguing for the extension of the current jurisprudence to situations where significant environmental damage is caused abroad, e.g. by corporations. This is different in the Banjul Charter, which does not contain a jurisdictional clause. Human Rights Council, 'Analytical Study on the Relationship between Human Rights and the Environment' Report of the UN High Commissioner for Human Rights (16 December 2011) UN Doc. A/HRC/19/34, para. 69 (which indicates the Banjul Charter's potential in the field of extraterritorial environmental damage). Another challenge is the partial lack of proof of the causality link between an act of environmental pollution and the impact on the individual.

34 Particularly exemplary is the statement by the ECtHR in *Kyrtatos* v. *Greece*, *supra* note 14 at para. 53, where the ECtHR explained that it could not 'accept that the interference with the conditions of animal life in the swamp constitutes an attack on the private or family life of the applicants'.

35 See also below for less restrictive cases. For an overview see R. Pavoni, 'Public Interest Environmental Litigation and the European Court of Human Rights: No Love at First Sight', in F. Lenzerini and A.F. Vrdoljak (eds.), *International Law for Common Goods: Normative Perspectives on Human Rights, Culture and Nature* (Hart 2014) 331.

licence to change its production methods and to produce steel from scrap instead of iron. The applicants had complained that they were denied effective access to a court in the licence procedure and criticised the company for not being required to use the best possible technology to avoid pollution, claiming a violation of Article 6 ECHR. The ECtHR held that the link/individual effect was too remote and thus not sufficiently direct:

> The mere mention of the pollution risks inherent in the production of steel from scrap iron is not enough to justify the applicants' assertion that they are the victims of a violation of the Convention. They must be able to assert, arguably and in a detailed manner, that for lack of adequate precautions taken by the authorities the degree of probability of the occurrence of damage is such that it can be considered to constitute a violation on condition that the consequences of the act complained are not too remote.[36]

Consequently, the ECtHR found the claim manifestly ill-founded and dismissed the application as inadmissible.

Likewise, in *Ivan Atanasov* v. *Bulgaria*,[37] the ECtHR rejected an application concerning a reclamation scheme to clean up the pollution of a tailings pond previously used by a copper mine site approximately one km from the applicant's home in a village for lack of proof of direct impact on the applicant or his family's life.[38] More precisely, the ECtHR found Article 8 of the ECHR not to be triggered since the applicant lived 'at a considerable distance from the pollution source' and there were no materials showing that the pollution in and around the pond had caused an increase in the morbidity rate of the residents of the applicant's village or sufficient adverse impact on the applicant's enjoyment of the amenities of his home and the quality of his private and family life.[39]

In fact, the European Commission of Human Rights had already held in *Tauira* v. *France* that applicants have to be individually affected for the complaint to be admissible and that the ECHR does not provide for an *actio popularis*.[40] The applicants, residents of French Polynesia who lived separately from each other and a few 100 km away from the Mururoa atoll where a series of nuclear underground tests had been conducted between 1966 and 1992, had claimed that the French President's decision to resume underground testing of nuclear weapons in that area between 1995 and 1996 constituted a violation of several rights, *inter alia* of Articles 2

36 *Asselbourg and 78 Others and Greenpeace Association-Luxembourg* v. *Luxembourg*, ECHR1999-VI.

37 *Ivan Atanasov* v. *Bulgaria*, App no 12853/03 (ECtHR, 2 December 2010).

38 This scheme, which consisted of laying sludge containing heavy metals coming from a waste-water treatment plant on the pond, had been approved by relevant authorities even though a government report had found that 'there was a risk of heavy-metal contamination impacting on the population's health within a ten-kilometre perimeter around the pond'. Ibid. at para. 32.

39 Ibid. at paras. 76–79.

40 *Noel Narvii Tauira and Eighteen Others* v. *France*, (1995) 83-B DR 112.

and 8 of the ECHR. The applicants called into question the environmental monitoring process and argued that the radiation from the nuclear tests might have serious consequences on the health of the local population. The European Commission declared the complaint inadmissible, stating that '[i]n order for an applicant to claim to be a victim of a violation of the Convention, there must be a sufficiently direct link between the applicant and the loss which he considers he has suffered as a result of the alleged violation' and further highlighted that '[m]erely invoking risks inherent in the use of nuclear power, whether for civil or military purposes, is insufficient to enable the applicants to be victims of a violation of the Convention'.[41]

Thus, in view of the necessary requirement to be individually affected and to be the 'victim' of a violation, 'public interest litigation' for the general protection of the environment is generally not possible. A so-called *actio popularis* by NGOs complaining, for instance, about environmental degradation as a common good, is generally impeded.[42] While this must be distinguished from cases where an NGO is appearing as a representative of its members' interests, which all are actual or potential victims of the alleged human rights violation ('common interest litigation'),[43] it still limits the operationalisation of the ECHR for the general protection of the environment.

### *Wide Margin of Appreciation of States*

A further obstacle to the effective protection of the environment in the case law of the ECtHR is the generally wide margin of appreciation left to States in case of alleged violations of the ECHR in the context of environmental degradation.[44]

As explained by the ECtHR in *Buckley* v. *United Kingdom*,

> [t]he scope of [the] margin of appreciation is not identical in each case but will vary according to the context . . . Relevant factors include the nature of the Convention right in issue, its importance for the individual and the nature of the activities concerned.[45]

41 Ibid. at paras. 131 and 133.

42 Note that this is different in the Americas, before Inter-American human rights institutions, as well as in Africa since neither the American Convention on Human Rights (art. 44) nor the Banjul Charter (art. 55) establish a victim requirement.

43 J. Verschuuren, 'Contribution of the Case Law of the European Court of Human Rights to Sustainable Development in Europe', in W. Scholtz and J. Verschuuren (eds.), *Regional Environmental Law – Transregional Comparative Lessons in Pursuit of Sustainable Development* (Edward Elgar 2015) 363 at 372 (referring to the example of *Gorraiz Lizarraga and Others* v. *Spain*, ECHR 2004-III).

44 H. Müllerová, 'Environment Playing Short-Handed: Margin of Appreciation in Environmental Jurisprudence of the European Court of Human Rights' (2015) 24(1) *Review of European Community & International Environmental Law* 83.

45 *Buckley* v. *United Kingdom*, *supra* note 15 at para. 74.

In the context of environmental concerns, the ECtHR assesses whether a fair balance has been struck between the competing interests of the individual affected and of the community as a whole to, for example, have a certain industrial or economic activity conducted. However, due to the 'direct and continuous contact with the vital forces of their countries, the national authorities are in principle better placed than an international court to evaluate local needs and conditions',[46] which is particularly so in the case of town or country planning measures or other cases involving environmental issues.[47]

*Hatton* v. *United Kingdom* (2003) demonstrated that the ECHR does not lend itself to broad environmental reform. In this case, several persons had lodged a complaint against excessive noise from take-offs and landings at Heathrow Airport. The ECtHR's Grand Chamber – contrary to the Chamber – did not establish a violation of Article 8 of the ECHR but rather assessed that 'a fair balance was struck between the competing interests of the individuals affected by the night noise and the community as a whole'.[48] More particularly, the ECtHR held:

> Environmental protection should be taken into consideration by States in acting within their margin of appreciation and by the Court in its review of that margin, but it would not be appropriate for the Court to adopt a special approach in this respect by reference to a special status of environmental human rights.[49]

In determining whether a fair balance has been struck – and in consideration of the wide margin of appreciation granted to states – the ECtHR takes the severity of interference (such as, quite possibly, the extent of environmental damage caused) into consideration and contrasts it with the measures taken by the state to prevent, mitigate or compensate such.[50]

As can be seen in *Fadeyeva* v. *Russia*, the scale will only tip in favour of the applicant where

> there has been a manifest error of appreciation by the national authorities in striking a fair balance between the competing interests of different private actors in this

[46] Ibid. at para. 75.

[47] On the explicit confirmation that 'in cases raising environmental issues the State must be allowed a wide margin of appreciation' see e.g. *Hatton*, *supra* note 16 at para. 101; *Hardy and Maile* v. *United Kingdom*, App no 31965/07 (ECtHR, 9 July 2012) para. 218; *Koceniak* v. *Poland*, App no 1733/06 (ECtHR, 17 June 2014) para. 59; *Dubetska and Others* v. *Ukraine*, App no 30499/03 (ECtHR, 10 February 2011) para. 141.

[48] *Hatton*, *supra* note 16 at para. 224.

[49] Ibid. at para. 122.

[50] *Koceniak* v. *Poland*, App no 1733/06 (ECtHR, 17 June 2014) para. 58: 'However, under Article 8 the alleged nuisance must have attained the minimum level of severity required for it to amount to an interference with applicants' rights to respect for their private lives and their homes. The assessment of that minimum is relative and depends on all the circumstances: the intensity and duration of the nuisance, its physical or mental effects, the general context, and whether the detriment complained of was negligible in comparison to the environmental hazards symptomatic of life in every modern city . . .'

> sphere ... [T]he complexity of the issues involved with regard to environmental protection renders the Court's role primarily a subsidiary one.[51]

In the given instance, the State had authorised the operation of the steel plant and established by legislation a buffer zone around its premises where affected individuals were to be resettled. However, those legislative measures were never implemented. The ECtHR concluded therefore:

> [T]he state did not offer the applicant any effective solution to help her move away from the dangerous area. Furthermore, although the polluting plant in issue operated in breach of domestic environmental standards, there is no indication that the State designed or applied effective measures which would take into account the interests of the local population, affected by the pollution, and which would be capable of reducing the industrial pollution to acceptable levels.[52]

Therefore, and despite the wide margin of appreciation granted to states in an environmental context, in the *Fadeyeva* case, the State had failed to strike a fair balance between the interests of the community and the applicant's effective enjoyment of the right to respect for home and private life. The ECtHR accordingly found a violation.

The wide margin of appreciation in environmental matters and the self-restraint on the part of the ECtHR is understandable given the necessary room for manoeuvre of national authorities as regards the implementation of domestic policies.[53] Still, it restricts the effectiveness of the ECtHR to function as a promoter of environmental protection and reform.

### *The ECtHR's Self-Restraint as Regards Reparations*

Even if the ECtHR establishes a violation of the ECHR, it seems reluctant to award (specific) reparations. This self-restraint on the part of the ECtHR in awarding far-reaching reparations in cases of a breach further limits its ability to effectively address issues of environmental degradation.[54] In fact, the ECtHR's role regarding reparations is restricted by the wording of Article 41 ECHR, which establishes that

> [i]f the Court finds that there has been a violation of the Convention or the protocols thereto, and if the internal law of the High Contracting Party concerned allows only partial reparation to be made, the Court shall, if necessary, afford just satisfaction to the injured party.

51 *Fadeyeva* v. *Russia*, ECHR 2005-IV, para. 105.

52 Ibid. at para. 133.

53 Müllerová, *supra* note 45 at 84.

54 For the conceptual background thereto cf. M. Fyrnys, 'Expanding Competences by Judicial Lawmaking: The Pilot Judgment Procedure of the European Court of Human Rights'. in A. Von Bogdandy and I. Venzke (eds.), *International Judicial Lawmaking* (Springer 2012) 329 at 336–339.

Article 41 delineates the role of the ECtHR and was generally understood to prevent further going reparations, as for example, *restitutio in integrum*.[55]

This also is reflected in cases concerning the environment. The ECtHR seems unwilling to order specific actions that would mitigate damage to the environment. Instead, it satisfies itself with small awards of compensation or does not award any compensation at all. For example, in *Guerra* v. *Italy* the ECtHR awarded some monetary compensation for the violation of the rights of Ms Guerra and the other applicants. It did not, however, order a clean-up of the industrial estate where the explosion had occurred:

> The Court notes that the Convention does not empower it to accede to such request. It reiterates that it is for the State to choose the means to be used in its domestic legal system in order to comply with the provisions of the Convention or to redress the situation that has given rise to the violation of the Convention . . .[56]

In *Tătar* v. *Romania*, the ECtHR did not award any compensation at all given the lack of a causal link between the exposure to poisonous gases caused by the widespread pollution of the gold mine and the aggravation of the applicant's asthma. Rather, it contented itself with establishing a breach of the ECHR.[57] This trust in the good faith of local authorities on the part of the ECtHR was criticised as 'naive' and for limiting the ECtHR's role in terms of environmental protection.[58]

### *Appreciation*

Overall, important limitations reduce the ECtHR's role as a promoter of the protection of the environment. A narrow understanding of the victim requirement, the States' general broad margin of appreciation and the ECtHR's self-restraint as regards reparations combine to reduce the impact of its case law. Still, there are also certain indications of positive trends in the jurisprudence of the ECtHR.

## TRENDS FOR IMPROVEMENT AS REGARDS THE ECTHR'S PROTECTION OF THE ENVIRONMENT

Various possibilities exist to enhance the ECtHR's protection of the environment. And, indeed, some tentative indications in the ECtHR's case law seem to point towards a stronger protection. These include methods to circumvent the strict application of the victim requirement (Article 34 ECHR), as well as a strengthening

[55] J. Frowein and W. Peukert, *Europäische Menschenrechtskonvention. EMRK Kommentar*, 3rd edn. (Engel 2009) 536; P. van Dijk, F. van Hoof, A. van Rijn, and L. Zwaak (eds.), *Theory and Practice of the European Convention on Human Rights*, 4th edn. (Intersentia 2006) 245ff.

[56] *Guerra*, *supra* note 18 at para. 230.

[57] *Tătar*, *supra* note 19 at para. 132.

[58] Kravchenko and Bonine, *supra* note 25 at 281.

of material standards to limit the margin of appreciation of states by means of judicial dialogue. Also, the ECtHR has adopted an increasingly strong stand regarding reparations.

### *Victim Requirement Less Marked*

A first possibility to facilitate the application of the ECHR to cases of environmental pollution is to focus on those cases which evidence a less strict understanding of the victim requirement. In fact, in some cases, positively, the ECtHR adopts a rather generous approach to the need to be personally affected.

This was the case in *Okyay and Others* v. *Turkey*.[59] The applicants had introduced domestic proceedings against three thermal plants – apparently constituting a general threat to public health and the environment – located approximately 250 km from their home. They complained under Article 6 of the ECHR about the administrative authorities' failure to comply with an injunction suspending the plants' activities. The government argued, *inter alia*, that the applicants had admitted that they had not been personally affected by the power plants but that they were solely concerned about their country's environmental problems. The ECtHR, however, found Article 6 to be applicable and noted thereby that the hazardous gas emitted by the power plants extended over an

> area in which the applicants live and brings into play their right to protection of their physical integrity, despite the fact that the risk which they run is not as serious, specific and imminent as that run by those living in the immediate vicinity of the plants.[60]

In light of the failure of national authorities to comply with judgments suspending the project, the ECtHR found that Article 6 ECHR was deprived of any useful effect and had consequently been violated.

Likewise, in *Taşkin* v. *Turkey*, the ECtHR found a violation of Articles 6 and 8 of the ECHR in the case of a complaint lodged by ten inhabitants of a municipality, living between 300 m and 10 km from a gold mine.[61] In particular, it found that Article 8 also applied to cases where

> the *dangerous effects of an activity* to which the individuals concerned are likely to be exposed have been determined as part of an environmental impact assessment procedure in such a way as to establish a *sufficiently close link* with private and family life for the purposes of Article 8 of the Convention.[62]

[59] *Okyay and Others* v. *Turkey*, ECHR 2005-VII.
[60] Ibid. at para. 66.
[61] *Taşkin*, *supra* note 16.
[62] Ibid. at para. 113 (emphasis added).

The ECtHR also found a violation of Articles 6 and 8 ECHR with respect to the application of 315 Turkish nationals living in a district where the gold mine was sited (*Öçkan and Others* v. *Turkey*)[63] as well as in case of an applicant living about 50 km away from the gold mine (*Lemke* v. *Turkey*).[64] In the *Lemke* case, the ECtHR responded to Turkey's objection on the applicant not fulfilling the victim requirement in reference to *Taşkin* v. *Turkey* that the applicant – who lived 50 km from the gold mine in question – was entitled under Turkish national law to seek remedies against the activity and therefore his complaints related to the defence of a specific duty which was recognised by national law.

Further, in *Di Sarno and Others* v. *Italy*,[65] the ECtHR found a violation with regard to Italy's continued liability to deal with the 'waste crisis' in the Campania region. The eighteen applicants living or working in the affected municipality had complained, *inter alia*, in reliance on Article 8 of the ECHR that Italy had failed to take the necessary measures to ensure the appropriate functioning of the public waste collection service, which had caused serious environmental impairment in their region and had placed their life and health at risk. The Italian government had argued, *inter alia*, that the applicants simply alleged the general deterioration of the environment and thus could not claim victim status. The ECtHR noted respectively that the applicants were indeed denouncing a situation affecting the whole population in the region, namely the detriment to the environment caused by the improper functioning of the waste collection treatment and disposal service. The ECtHR thus found that the environmental damage complained of by the applicants had been such as to directly affect their own well-being and established a violation of Article 8.[66]

*Di Sarno and Others* v. *Italy* thus comes close to a class action where several applicants allege environmental protection as a common good. As was rightly observed by Pavoni:

> The victim and similar requirements in the ECHR only imply that the applicants be personally affected by the violation, not that they be *specially affected* so as to distinguish their own situation from that of other potential complainants. And this type of litigation cannot be assimilated to an *actio popularis strico sensu*, where in principle no specific personal injury can be identified. It is more akin and amenable to the notion of class action. At the same time, given the magnitude of the environmental problems at stake with the resulting large number of potential victims and extensive coverage of the concerned areas and ecosystems, the adjudication of these disputes inevitably contributes to the defence of the environment as a common good.[67]

63 *Öçkan and Others* v. *Turkey*, App no 46771/99 (ECtHR, 28 March 2006).
64 *Lemke* v. *Turkey*, App no 17381/02 (ECtHR, 5 June 2007).
65 *Di Sarno and Others* v. *Italy*, App no 30765/08 (ECtHR, 10 January 2012).
66 Ibid. at para. 81.
67 Pavoni, *supra* note 36 at 343.

To explore avenues of possible class action as common interest litigation – therewith cautiously widening a strict application of the need to be individually affected – thus seems as a move towards an easier protection of the environment.[68] In fact, the ECtHR appears especially inclined to a more lenient understanding of the victim requirement where the concerned persons are granted a legal position under domestic law.[69]

Another possibility would be, of course, not to rely on individual applications but rather to consider interstate complaints. Interstate complaints do not have to assert the rights of a specific person to be violated and might thus be a means to circumvent the victim requirement. Such complaints can refer to the incompatibility of a State's legislation or administrative practice with the ECHR in general terms and therefore may adopt the character of an *actio popularis*.[70] They thus could have a wide field of application with regard to actions and omissions of states and according environmental impairment. There could also be a possibility to complain about environmental risks concerning future human rights violations. However, in this context it must be noted that interstate complaints have been rare, with only twenty having been brought so far,[71] and these mostly in the context of interstate conflicts. Whether this offers real potential for environmental protection is thus questionable, particularly in light of the comparatively limited, albeit growing, number of international disputes dealing with environmental obligations.

## *Judicial Dialogue: Stricter Standards*

Other means to strengthen the ECtHR's protection of the environment include reducing the margin of appreciation of states via the recognition and incorporation of stricter environmental law standards. This includes the ECtHR's approach of resorting to a dynamic interpretation of the ECHR by reference to other treaties (for example the Aarhus Convention,[72] the International Convention on Civil Liability for Oil Pollution Damage,[73] the UN Convention on the Law of the

68 Note, however, that an *actio popularis strictu sensu* – without victim requirement – remains impermissible in the European system of human rights protection. See Article 34 ECHR.

69 E.g. the ECtHR's explanation in *Lemke* v. *Turkey* that the applicant was entitled to seek remedies under national law, *Lemke* (note 65 above) para. 36. Also see the Dissenting Opinion in *Balmer-Schafroth*: 'It can be said that the national law of European States has raised the "standard" of court protection to a very high level and that the "standard" of the protection afforded by the European Convention on Human Rights cannot be lower.' *Balmer-Schafroth and Others* v. *Switzerland*, ECHR 1997-IV.

70 Van Dijk et al., *supra* note 56 at 49.

71 For an overview see ECtHR, 'Inter-State Applications' www.echr.coe.int/Documents/InterStates_applications_ENG.pdf accessed 2 October 2016.

72 *Taşkin*, *supra* note 16 at para. 99; *Ivan Atanasov*, *supra* note 38 at para. 55; *Di Sarno*, *supra* note 67 at para. 107; *Grimkovskaya* v. *Ukraine*, App no 38182/03 (ECtHR, 21 July 2011), paras. 39, 69; *Demir and Baykara* v. *Turkey*, ECHR 2008.

73 *Mangouras*, *supra* note 15 at para. 22.

Sea,[74] the Convention on Civil Liability for Damage resulting from Activities Dangerous to the Environment,[75] and the Convention on the Protection of the Environment through Criminal Law)[76] or IEL standards,[77] more particularly the right to a healthy environment,[78] and the precautionary principle,[79] as well as a judicial dialogue between the ECtHR and other judicial bodies (for example the Aarhus Compliance Committee,[80] the International Court of Justice,[81] and the International Tribunal for the Law of the Sea).[82] Notably, the ECtHR does so even if the respondent State in question has not signed or ratified these instruments.

To refer to international standards on environmental protection seems warranted since the ECHR remains silent on the state of the law in this regard.[83] Advantages of stricter standards have already been demonstrated in cases such as *Tătar* v. *Romania*, where the ECtHR relied on the precautionary principle in finding that Romania had breached its obligations under Article 8 ECHR.[84] In order to establish this as the applicable international norm, the ECtHR drew reference *inter alia* from soft law instruments (the Stockholm Declaration and the Rio Declaration), international treaties (the Aarhus Convention), decisions by other judicial bodies (the *Gabčikovo-Nagymaros* judgment by the International Court of Justice, and *National Farmer's Union* (C-157/96) by the European Court of Justice) and EU legislation.

Such cross-references might also situate the ECHR in the broader context of applicable environmental standards and enhance the legitimacy of the ECtHR's dynamic interpretation of the ECHR accordingly. Reducing States' margin of appreciation on the basis of such case law may thus have positive effects for the ECtHR's protection of the environment.

74 Ibid. at para. 44.

75 *Öneryildiz, supra* note 24 at para. 59; *Mangouras, supra* note 15 at para. 34.

76 *Öneryildiz, supra* note 24 at para. 59.

77 *Borysiewicz* v. *Poland*, App no 71146/01 (ECtHR, 1 July 2008), para. 53; *Mangouras, supra* note 15.

78 As included, *inter alia,* in Principle 10 of the 'Rio Declaration on Environment and Development' Report of the United Nations Conference on Environment and Development (10 August 1992) UN Doc. A/CONF.151/26 (Vol. I). e.g. *Okyay, supra* note 60 at para. 51; *Taşkin, supra* note 16 at para. 98.

79 *Tătar, supra* note 19 at para. 69

80 *Lesoochranárske Zoskupenie Vlk* v. *Slovakia*, App no 53246/08 (ECtHR, 2 October 2012) paras. 60ff.

81 *Tătar, supra* note 19 at para. 69.

82 *Mangouras, supra* note 15 at para. 46.

83 This was notably recognized in *Kyrtatos, supra* note 14 at para. 52, where the ECtHR stated: 'Neither Article 8 nor any of the other Articles of the Convention are specifically designed to provide general protection of the environment as such; to that effect, *other international instruments* and domestic legislation are more pertinent in dealing with this particular aspect' (emphasis added).

84 See also above in more detail.

### Firmer Action of the ECtHR in Case of Reparations

Finally, a more affirmative stand by the ECtHR in reparations and its more precise indications as to which measures States have to adopt to remedy a situation might be of use in situations of environmental pollution.

The ECtHR could therewith take the IACHR as an example. In fact, the IACHR lists in great detail which measures a State must adopt to remedy a situation, including the demarcation of indigenous territories in case of timber logging activities,[85] and the adoption of relevant legislative measures[86]. True, Article 41 of the ECHR is more restrictive than Article 63(1) ACHR,[87] and the ECtHR is thus more limited in terms of competences to order reparations than the IACtHR. Still, there is room for a more affirmative stand – especially when Article 41 is read in conjunction with Article 46 ECHR on the binding force and execution of judgments.[88]

Positively, in some cases, the ECtHR has moved away from its general deference towards States as regards reparations. Recent case law seems to indicate that the ECtHR is slowly relying on other forms of reparation and started to address as far as possible the effects, moving towards a *restitutio in integrum*.[89] This might be

[85] E.g. *Mayagna (Sumo) Awas Tingni Community* v. *Nicaragua*, (Judgment on Merits, Reparations and Costs) Inter-American Court of Human Rights Series C No 79 (31 August 2001); *Yakye Axa Indigenous Community* v. *Paraguay* (Judgment on Merits, Reparations and Costs) Inter-American Court of Human Rights Series C No 125 (17 June 2005).

[86] E.g. *The Girls Yean and Bosico* v. *Dominican Republic* (Judgment on Preliminary Objections, Merits, Reparations and Costs) Inter-American Court of Human Rights Series C No 130 (8 September 2005); *Xákmok Kásek Indigenous Community* v. *Paraguay*, (Judgment on Merits, Reparations and Costs) Inter-American Court of Human Rights Series C No 214 (24 August 2010).

[87] Article 63(1) ACHR: 'If the Court finds that there has been a violation of a right or freedom protected by this Convention, the Court shall rule that the injured party be ensured the enjoyment of his right or freedom that was violated. It shall also rule, if appropriate, that the consequences of the measure or situation that constituted the breach of such right or freedom be remedied and that fair compensation be paid to the injured party.'

[88] Cf. F. Vanneste, *General International Law before Human Rights Courts. Assessing the Specialty Claims of International Human Rights Law* (Intersentia 2010), 515ff.

[89] As stated in *Verein gegen Tierfabriken Schweiz (VgT)* v. *Switzerland (No. 2)*, ECHR 2009, para. 88: '[I]n certain special circumstances the Court has found it useful to indicate to a respondent State the type of measures that might be taken to put an end to the situation – often a systemic one – which has given rise to the finding of a violation (for example, *Öcalan* v. *Turkey*, para. 210 in fine, ECHR 2005-IV, and *Popov* v. *Russia*, App no 26853/04 (ECtHR, 11 December 2006), para. 263. Sometimes, the nature of the violation does not even leave any choice as to the measures to be taken (*Assinadze* v. *Georgia*, ECHR 2004-II, para. 202).' In this regard, cf. e.g. *Scozzari and Giunta* v. *Italy*, ECHR 2000-VIII, para. 249; *Assinadze* v. *Georgia*, ECHR 2004-II, para. 202. See especially the detailed indications given to states in pilot judgments (*Broniowski* v. *Poland*, ECHR Reports 2004-V; *Broniowski* v. *Poland*, ECHR 2005-IX; *Ananyev and Others* v. *Russia*, ECtHR) For further reference on pilot judgments D. Haider, *The Pilot-Judgment Procedure of the European Court of Human Rights* (Martinus Nijhoff 2013).

beneficial likewise for instances of environmental pollution where States frequently are in need of enhanced guidance.

### *Appreciation*

As explored above, there are numerous possibilities to improve the protection of the environment through the ECtHR. These include a more generous approach to the victim requirement, tighter substantial standards, *inter alia*, through judicial dialogue and a more affirmative stand by the ECtHR in case of reparations. Certain tendencies in the ECtHR's case law seem to indicate that it has indeed moved in this direction. Still, these are only slow beginnings. The above-mentioned trends notwithstanding, important shortcomings remain.

## CONCLUSION

Against this background, one may wonder about the possible role for national sustainable development institutions. And, more specifically, what can be gained for them from the case law of the ECtHR? Three possible considerations come to mind: legitimacy, substantive standards, and institutional complementarity concerning implementation.

First, the increasing recognition of the right to a healthy environment and the growing protection against environmental degradation in the case law of the ECtHR confers considerable legitimacy on national sustainable development institutions. They are institutions to 'operationalise and implement' the 'protection of the environment' at domestic level. The authoritative findings of the ECtHR and its increasing protection of the environment may strengthen their position accordingly. Conversely, the relevance of the domestic is also recognised by the ECtHR which draws on domestic law when developing standards and analysing a particular case.[90]

A second benefit can be gained from the increasing clarification of substantive standards. The ECtHR's case law with regard to environmental issues is more and more extensive. Accordingly, the ECtHR provides valuable yardsticks to guide the work of national sustainable development institutions. The development and affirmation of procedural rights and the public participation dimension in the case law of the ECtHR seem especially promising.[91] At the same time, and notwithstanding these improvements, the ECtHR continues to leave States a broad margin of appreciation when dealing with environmental issues through the lens of individual rights. There is thus a certain protection gap. National sustainable development

[90] *Kyrtatos*, *supra* note 14 at para. 52.

[91] Also, the increasingly broad recognition of environmental standards in the case law of the ECtHR, by means of judicial dialogue and with reference to a variety of environmental norms – including soft law instruments – is beneficial.

institutions could fill this gap, alongside with national courts, and concretise the rather broad environmental standards in the specific domestic context.

Finally, in view of the ECtHR's reluctance to award far-reaching reparations, national sustainable development institutions may valuably complement the Court institutionally by finding the best manner to implement its judgments. In doing so, national sustainable development institutions can contribute to the protection of the environment on the basis of the findings of the ECtHR.

In a nutshell, the increased protection of the environment in the case law of the ECtHR valuably informs the work of national sustainable development institutions. At the same time, these institutions are crucial domestic complements which give effect to the findings of the ECtHR (in the broad sense). In the ideal, the benefits for the ECtHR and national sustainable development institutions are thus mutual.

# 33

# Embedding Intergenerational Justice across Government: Regional Trends in Africa

*Damilola Olawuyi*

In the context of global commitments to intergenerational equity, this chapter surveys and evaluates governance arrangements across Africa aimed at achieving sustainable development and securing the environment for future generations. It has been over twenty years since sustainable development was internationally recognized as the overarching legal and policy context for efforts to promote development 'that meets the needs of the present without compromising the ability of future generations to meet their own needs'.[1] Over that period, varying levels of attention have been given to the challenge of safeguarding and implementing sustainable development in resource utilization across Africa.[2]

Although Africa is not one homogeneous geographical unit, approaches adopted to institutionalize and implement intergenerational commitments have been largely

[1] G.H. Brundtland et al., *Our Common Future: Report of the World Commission on Environment and Development* (Oxford University Press 1987).

[2] For example, in 2006 the Southern African Development Community (SADC) adopted a 'Framework for the Harmonization of Mining Policies Standards and Regulatory Frameworks' to create policy guidelines in key areas such as sustainable development, environmental management, and public participation. Similarly, in 2007, the UN Economic Commission for Africa (ECA) convened the Big Table meeting on 'Managing Africa's Natural Resources for Growth'. The Big Table meeting triggered initiatives, such as the Extractive Industries Transparency Initiative (EITI++) and the International Study Group to Review Africa's Mining Regimes (ISG), aimed at establishing sustainability safeguards in resource extraction projects. See UN Economic Commission for Africa, *Africa Review: Report on Mining (Executive Summary)* (UN 2008) 7–12 uneca.org/sites/default/files/PublicationFiles/aficanreviewreport-on-miningsummary2008.pdf accessed 30 November 2017. One of the most recent of these is the adoption of an *African Resolution on a Human Rights-Based Approach to Natural Resources Governance* by the African Commission on Human and Peoples' Rights (African Commission) at its 51st Ordinary Session held from April 18th to May 2nd, 2012 in Banjul, Gambia achpr.org/sessions/51st/resolutions/224 accessed 30 November 2017. It calls on all African countries to respect, protect, and fulfil human rights and sustainable development commitments in the utilization of natural resources.

similar and consistent across the continent.[3] This is mainly the approach of utilizing extant political systems and institutions to protect, preserve, and defend the interests/needs of present and future generations (the 'Linkage Approach'). While there is no direct equivalent of a 'Parliamentary Commissioner for Future Generations' or a distinct 'Ombudsman for the Environment or Future Generations' in Africa, there are over 100 distinct committees, departments, and agencies established across different levels of government with mandates to protect the environment, preserve cultural heritage, and ensure sustainable utilization of natural resources for present and future generations.[4]

However, despite the proliferation of institutions, agencies, and committees on sustainable development across Africa, the continent remains mired in complex sustainability challenges that threaten the abilities of future generations to find the African continent in a liveable or usable state. Entrenched problems of environmental pollution and economic mismanagement have seen the resource-rich African continent struggle in terms of social, environmental, and economic development.[5] Even though the continent has perennially accounted for a significant

[3] With fifty-four countries, Africa is the world's second-largest and second most populous continent covering about over 30 million square kilometres. With 1.1 billion people as of 2013, it accounts for about 15 per cent of the world's human population. See 'Getting to Know Africa: 50 Interesting Facts (National Geographic 2013) http://voices.nationalgeographic.com/2013/10/31/getting-to-know-africa-50-facts/ accessed 30 November 2017.

[4] There is a plenitude of examples across Africa. See for example Kenya's National Environment Council (NEC) established under the Section 4 (1) of Kenya's Environmental Management and Coordination Act No. 8 of 1999; Kenya's National Environment Management Authority (NEMA) Environmental Management and Coordination Act (EMCA) No. 8 of 1999: South Africa's Department of Environmental Affairs; the Nigerian National Environmental Standards and Regulations Enforcement Agency (NESREA) established under the NESREA Act (NESREA) Act; the Niger Delta Development Commission (NDDC) of Nigeria established under the NDDC Act: the Energy Commission of Nigeria, the National Oil Spill Detection and Response Agency (NOSDRA), National Water Resources Institute (NWRI) and the Nigerian Tourism Development Corporation (NTDC). Recently, the Government of Nigeria established the Hydrocarbon Pollution Restoration Project (HYPREP) to investigate, evaluate, and make recommendations on the clean-up of hydrocarbon impacted sites in the Niger Delta region of Nigeria.

[5] For example, decades of oil spillage, gas flaring, and effluent discharge in Nigeria's Niger Delta have severely damaged the ecosystem and environment of that region. According to a 2011 report of the UN, reversing many of the environmental and social consequences of oil spillage in the Niger Delta is possible but may take twenty-five to thirty years. UNEP, 'Environmental Assessment of Ogoniland' (UNEP 2011) 12 postconflict.unep.ch/publications/OEA/UNEP_OEA.pdf accessed 30 November 2017. See generally O. Oluduro, 'Oil Exploitation and Human Rights Violations in Nigeria's Oil Producing Communities' (2014) 25:2 *Afrika Focus* 160 at 165 (providing an account of the nature and scope of the problems discussed); see also Human Rights Watch, *The Price of Oil: Corporate Responsibility and Human Rights Violations in Nigeria's Oil Producing Communities* (Human Rights Watch 1999) 47 hrw.org/reports/1999/nigeria/nigeria0199.pdf accessed 30 November 2017 (discussing the impacts of governmental corruption, in the form of systematic kickbacks for the award of contracts, special bank accounts in the control of the presidency, and fraudulent allocation of oil or refined products to political favourites, on sustainable resource governance in Nigeria).

portion of global resource production and supply,[6] Africa remains home to the poorest nations on earth.[7] In 2014, thirty-four of forty-two nations identified as having 'low human development' on the UN HDI are African States.[8] Furthermore, thirty-four of the forty-eight nations on the UN list of least developed States are African States.[9] African States also have the lowest life expectancy rates, with a continental average of 48, an abysmally low figure when compared to other resource-rich countries such as Canada (82), the US (79), the UK (82), and Qatar (83).[10] Therefore, for several decades, resource-rich African States have been identified as fitting global examples of resource-cursed nations – the paradox of countries having more resources, yet less economic, social, and environmental development and growth.[11]

Apart from entrenched problems resulting from unsustainable resource utilization, the destruction of cultural sites and theft of cultural artefacts by militant and

[6] In 2008, Africa produced about 483 tons of gold, or 22 per cent of the world's total production. See British Petroleum, 'BP Statistical Review of World Energy June 2014' (2014) 9 www.bp.com/content/dam/bp/pdf/Energy-economics/statistical-review-2014/BP-statistical-review-of-world-energy-2014-full-report.pdf accessed 30 November 2017; see also African Development Bank and the African Union, *Oil and Gas in Africa* (July 2009) xxvii www.afdb.org/fileadmin/uploads/afdb/Documents/Publications/Oil%20and%20Gas%20in%20Africa.pdf accessed 30 November 2017.

[7] Seventy-five per cent of the world's poorest countries are located in Africa. See The World Bank, 'Poverty Headcount Ratio at $2 a day (PPP) (% of Population)' (2015) (displaying geographic areas with the percentage of the population living on less than two dollars per day); see also The Borgen Project, 'Top 10 Poverty in Africa Facts' (2014). Food insecurity threatens millions of Africans each year, especially in the Horn and Southern African sub-regions, and Africa is home to more malnourished people than any other continent. Chronic food insecurity affects more than a quarter of the population and interacts with pandemic diseases such as the Ebola virus disease and HIV/AIDS to form a web of multidimensional emergency in many areas. See United Nations Conference on Trade and Development, 'UN List of Least Developed Countries' (UN 2013) http://unctad.org/en/pages/aldc/Least%20Developed%20Countries/UN-list-of-Least-Developed-Countries.aspx accessed 30 November 2017; World Bank, 'World Development Indicators' (2015) http://data.worldbank.org/data-catalog/world-development-indicators accessed 30 November 2017; J.A. Salomon et. al., 'Healthy Life Expectancy for 187 Countries, 1990–2010: A Systematic Analysis for the Global Burden Disease Study 2010' (2013) 380 *The Lancet* 2144, 2155.

[8] Human Development Report, *Sustaining Human Progress: Reducing Vulnerabilities and Building Resilience* (United Nations Development Programme 2014) 8–13; see also S. Alkire et. al., *Multidimensional Poverty Index 2014: Brief Methodological Note and Results* (Oxford University Press 2014) 178.

[9] United Nations Conference on Trade and Development, *supra* note 7.

[10] World Bank, 'World Development Indicators', *supra* note 7; Salomon et. al., *supra* note 7 at 2144, 2155.

[11] J.D. Sachs and A.M. Warner, 'The Curse of Natural Resources' (2001) 45 *Eur Econ Rev* 827 at 827; L. Wenar, 'Property Rights and the Resource Curse' (2008) 36 *Philos Pub Affairs* 3, at 5–7; B. Okeke and E.T. Aniche, 'A Critique of the Enforcement of Nigeria Extractive Industries Transparency Initiative (Neiti) Act 2007 in Nigerian Oil and Gas Sector' (2013) 14 *Brit J Arts Soc Sci* 98 at 99; X. Sala-i-Martin and A. Subramanian, *Addressing the Natural Resource Curse: An Illustration from Nigeria* (Oxford University Press 2003) 13–15.

terrorist groups such as the Boko Haram group in West Africa, the Al Shabaab in East Africa, and the Ansar Dine in the historic Malian city of Timbuktu, present arguably more complex and urgent social concerns to current and future generations.[12] The destruction of cultural heritage might mean that future generations may never be able to enjoy the benefit of shared cultural identity showcased through ancient African museums, mausoleums, and cultural sites. These concerns emphasize the need for a workable and overarching model of governance across Africa that give greater priority and profile to the protection of the environment and cultural heritage for the use of future generations. Embedding intergenerational equity across government means providing decision makers with the skills and resources to fully consider the consequences of government programmes and policies on the environment, cultural heritage, and wider society such that future generations have at least the same opportunities to meet their own needs as the generation governing today.[13]

Despite the evident need for a more robust institutionalization of intergenerational equity in governments across Africa, approaches adopted by many African States have remained uncoordinated, non-committal, fragile, mostly *ad hoc*, and generally fall short of what is necessary to protect, preserve, and defend the interests and needs of future generations. While some States in Europe and Australasia have established or appointed distinct future generations institutes and Commissioners, the tasks of protecting cultural sites and the environment for future generations have not been accorded such distinct recognition in Africa.[14] Regulatory and institutional intervention have been mainly in the form of the Linkage Approach, which has so far failed to address the complex sustainability challenges facing African States. Due to the absence of a focal lead agency or committee on future generations, interventions have been framed mostly in general environmental protection terms. This leaves out other unique concerns facing intergenerational equity in Africa.

This chapter evaluates the rationale and functionality of the Linkage Approach to intergenerational equity, as adopted across Africa, for achieving sustainable development and securing the environment for future generations. Drawing specific examples from four countries across the African subregions – Nigeria (West Africa),

[12] 'Timbuktu's Destruction: Why Islamists Are Wrecking Mali's Cultural Heritage' The Time (2012) http://world.time.com/2012/07/02/timbuktus-destruction-why-islamists-are-wrecking-malis-cultural-heritage/ accessed 30 November 2017. See also *Islamic State Destroying Ancient Cultural Treasures* (The Clarion Project 2015) http://www.clarionproject.org/analysis/islamisms-totalitarian-vision-control-or-destroy-all-culture accessed 30 November 2017.

[13] This definition draws extensively from the definition in Great Britain Parliament, Environmental Audit Committee, *Embedding Sustainable Development across Government, After the Secretary of State's Announcement on the Future of the Sustainable Development Commission* (Volume 504 of HC (Series) (House of Commons 2011) 7.

[14] See for example Hungary, which appointed Professor Marcel Szabó as the Ombudsman for Future Generations in 2012. See also New Zealand's Parliamentary Commissioner for the Environment (PCE).

Kenya (East Africa), South Africa (Southern Africa), and Egypt (North Africa) – this chapter analyses why the Linkage Approach, as opposed to distinct institutionalization model, may not be a functional and expedient model for the representation of future generations in Africa.[15]

The thesis of this chapter is straightforward: for Africa to make real progress in protecting, preserving, and defending the interests and needs of future generations, there is an urgent need to reassess and revitalize the architecture for delivering sustainable development and intergenerational justice. The chapter discusses the need for African States to transcend the prevailing Linkage Approach to a more strategic, focused, and independent framework for sustainable development. This will be in the form of appointing distinct 'Parliamentary Commissioners for Future Generations' or 'Ombudsmen for the Environment or Future Generations' with the mandate of institutionalizing sustainable development in policy making. As a model of governance, the appointment of a focal future generations institution or officer would not only assist governments to better reflect and develop robust future generations' interests in policy making, the focal officer will also be well placed to authoritatively develop, evaluate, monitor, and access the performance of government departments and agencies against sustainable management targets and threshold. Such a focal body will also provide leadership by assisting government departments to develop the skills and resources they need to make more sustainable decisions.

This chapter is divided into five sections. After this introduction, the second section evaluates the efficacy of public bodies involved in implementing sustainable development programmes in Nigeria, Kenya, South Africa, and Egypt. A third section develops a case for a more committed, independent, and distinct institutionalization of future generations concerns. The fourth section proposes legal pathways for effectively mobilizing future generations institutions in Africa, discussing guiding principles and approaches through which future generations institutions can be established to be independent, focused, and non-partisan across Africa. The chapter concludes in a fifth section.

## IMPLEMENTING INTERGENERATIONAL JUSTICE: REGIONAL TRENDS IN AFRICA

This section examines and evaluates the efficacy of regional trends and approaches for the implementation of future generations programmes. As noted earlier,

[15] Apart from allowing for a balanced geographical spread, these countries are also selected for their dominant roles as key economic powers in Africa. Nigeria, Kenya, Egypt, and South Africa are historical giants in Africa's extractive industry, ranging from mining, oil and gas, drilling, and agriculture. These countries have also been the epicentre of major environmental and future generations concerns associated with oil production and mining in Africa. See US Energy Information Administration, 'Oil and Natural Gas in Sub-Saharan Africa' (USEIA 2013) eia.gov/pressroom/presentations/howard_08012013.pdf accessed 30 November 2017.

although there are a number of public bodies involved in environmental protection and sustainable development, few have the specific mandate of protecting the interests and needs of future generations. Generally, the African States surveyed do not appear to have already established effective and distinctive governance bodies or offices for future generations. Consequently, future generations' interests arise as part of wider general mandates on environmental protection and sustainable development. Discussed below are an illustrative selection of key governance arrangements and tools utilized to embed intergenerational justice into governments.

### *Department or Ministry of the Environment (MoE)*

All African States have established ministries or departments responsible for implementing governmental policies on environmental protection and sustainable development.[16] These entities range from the Federal Ministry of Environment in Nigeria, established in 1999, the Ministry of Environment and Natural Resources in Kenya, the Department of Environmental Affairs in South Africa, first established in 1994 as the Department of Environmental Affairs and Tourism, and the Ministry for Environmental Affairs in Egypt established in 1997.[17] The broad mandates of MoEs include (1) formulating and implementing environmental policies; (2) preparing the necessary action plans for environmental protection; (3) stipulating procedures for EIA for projects; (4) managing and protecting oceans and coastal resources, promoting conservation and the sustainable use of natural resources; (5) promoting cooperation in environmental science and conservation technology; and (6) cooperating with federal and state Ministries, local government, statutory bodies, and research agencies on matters relating to the protection of the environment and the conservation of natural resources.[18] Typically headed by a cabinet minister or Secretary for Environment, MoEs supervise and enforce environmental protection measures on water quality, effluent limitations, air quality, atmospheric protection, ozone protection, and noise control, as well as the removal and control of hazardous substances. At provincial or state levels, ministries of environment also play similar roles and are supervised by commissioners for environment.

The broad mandates of African MoEs arguably cover conserving natural resources and protecting the environment for present and future generations. While they are

[16] For a comprehensive list of all environment ministries in Africa, see World Bank, 'Africa Environmental Agencies' (World Bank 2015) http://web.worldbank.org/archive/website01004/WEB/0__CO-75.HTM accessed 21 September 2015.

[17] See Kenya Ministry of Environment and Natural Resources, 'About Us' (Ministry of Environment and Natural Resources 2015) www.environment.go.ke/?page_id=2 accessed 21 September 2015); see also South Africa Department for Environmental Affairs, 'Introduction and Background' (Department for Environmental Affairs 2015) www.environment.gov.za/aboutus/department accessed 21 September 2015).

[18] Ibid.

not 'ministries for future generations', to the extent that the MoEs promote environmental protection and the wise stewardship of natural resources, both current and future generations stand to gain. However, since their respective establishment in the 1990s, African MoEs have been inconsistent in the design and implementation of future generations programmes. Owing to differing priorities placed on environmental matters by successive governments, future generations policies and projects are inconsistently implemented in accordance with the visions and priorities of the government in power. This lack of continuity and political commitment often results in gaps or the disappearance of programmes and structures designed for embedding sustainable development across the government.

Similarly, since MoEs are supervised by cabinet ministers, they are accountable to the government and therefore arguably lack the required level of institutional independence required to hold policy makers to account for their actions. MoEs lack the status and independence needed to serve as 'watchdogs' to monitor and report on the sustainability of government operations and policies. Equally intertwined with this is the lack of independent funding opportunities for MoEs to drive and implement future generations programmes. The abilities of MoEs to launch and implement long-term future generations programmes have been hampered by a lack of consistent funding for sustainable development by successive governments. In Nigeria, for example, activities of the Nigerian MoE have often been hampered due to diversion of funds meant for the it and also because the political will to fund it has not been maintained by successive governments.[19]

The above problems do not imply that MoEs are irrelevant or inimical to sustainable development. They do, however, underscore the need for African governments to reassess and revitalize the architecture for delivering sustainable development to make them more focused, holistic, and consistent. Future generation policies and programmes can be strengthened if independently implemented and consistently pursued irrespective of the government in power.

### *Presidential Advisors on Sustainable Development, Environment, and Energy*

Another tool utilized by African States to embed sustainable development in government is the appointment of special advisors, consultants, and quasi-state officials on energy, environment, and sustainable development issues.[20] In African States

[19] 'Nigeria ICPC Returns N1 Billion Looted Funds to Environment Ministry' (AllAfrica 2015) http://allafrica.com/stories/201509160545.html accessed 21 September 2015.

[20] See for example Office of the Special Advisor to the Presidency on Food and Climate Change, Government of Kenya, currently occupied by James Karanja Nyoro. His responsibilities includes providing strategic direction to the Government to systematically and sustainably formulate, facilitate, and implement policies and programmes that will ensure that Kenya attains its food security and climate change programmes and plans, Government of Kenya www.deputypresident.go.ke/index.php/advisor-food-climate-change accessed 23 September 2015).

such as Nigeria, Kenya, Egypt, and South Africa, the respective presidents have constitutional powers to appoint and designate a number of special advisors to provide expert advice on thematic policy issues. In Nigeria, for example, this power has been leveraged by successive presidents to appoint special advisors on energy, environment, and, more recently, on Niger Delta affairs.[21] Special advisors are direct appointees and staffs of the Office of the President, and are therefore not constitutionally empowered to play direct governance or enforcement roles. Similarly, it is discretionary for a sitting president to determine whether he/she requires any 'special advice' and the priority policy areas for which such 'special advice' is required. While some governments have appointed Special Advisors on Environment and Sustainable Development, others have overlooked such appointments. This lack of continuity often results in gaps or the disappearance of policy initiatives or programmes put in place by a president and his/her team of special advisors. Similarly, in all African countries surveyed none has designated or appointed a special advisor on future generations.

Furthermore, the Office of Special Advisors has been largely duplicative and redundant in many African countries. Offices of Special Advisors are also perceived as corrupt political creations designed to reward political associates.[22] In Kenya, for example, the President has been accused of appointing a large number of advisors, consultants, and quasi-State officials on special terms, and accruing an unsustainable annual wage bill of almost $2 million.[23] In a State where many citizens live on less than $1 a day, the appointment of special advisors without designated real enforcement and governance roles is by itself an affront to sustainable development.[24] Some of the special advisor roles are also duplicative. For example, in Nigeria, former president Goodluck Jonathan appointed eighteen special advisors, including a special advisor on social development, another on energy, and another on Niger Delta affairs.[25] All of these roles touch on sustainable development and could arguably have been assigned to a single special advisor on sustainable development. Furthermore, due to the absence of legislative backing for the special advisors, incumbents of such offices often end up duplicating the functions of career civil servants, ministry officials, and agencies. [26]

Offices of presidential special advisors, as currently utilized and composed in Africa, arguably fall short of what is necessary to protect, preserve, and defend the

21 'President Jonathan Swears in 13 Special Advisers', *The Vanguard* (2011) www.vanguardngr.com/2011/07/jonathan-swears-in-13-special-advisers/ accessed 30 November 2017.

22 See 'Kenya: The Clique of Public Servants on Special Terms', *Daily Nation* (15 March 2014) http://mobile.nation.co.ke/news/The-clique-of-public-servants-on-special-terms-/-/1950946/2245914/-/format/xhtml/-/dpn389z/-/index.html accessed 23 September 2015.

23 Ibid.

24 Kenya is one of the countries identified by the World Bank as having one of the highest incidents of poverty. See World Bank, 'Poverty Headcount Ratio', *supra* note 7.

25 'President Jonathan Swears in 13 Special Advisers', *supra* note 21.

26 See 'Kenya: The Clique of Public Servants on Special Terms', *supra* note 22.

interests/needs of future generations. However, being close to the corridors of power, special advisors can meaningfully contribute to sustainable development and future generations programmes by providing robust independent advice that influences decisions. While special advisors cannot enforce compliance with prudent sustainability standards, they can certainly exercise a constraining influence and help to encourage government commitment to future generations programmes. However, for special advisors to deliver real value their offices must be legislatively recognized and their mandates clearly delineated.

### *Environment and Sustainable Development Agencies and Commissions*

Another trend, adopted in the African region to embed sustainable development in government, is the creation of special commissions and agencies mandated to monitor, enforce, and report on environmental protection and the sustainability of government operations and policies. Examples include Nigeria's National Oil Spill Detection and Response Agency (NOSDRA), the National Environmental Standards Regulatory and Enforcement Agency (NESREA), National Parks Service (NPS), the Niger Delta Development Commission (NDDC), and, at the substate level, the Rivers State Sustainable Development Agency (RSSDA).[27] All these agencies have the protection of the environment and cultural heritage for present and future generations as part of their broad mandates. In Kenya, there are similar agencies such as the National Environment Management Authority (NEMA), Kenya Water Towers Agency (KWTA), Kenya Wildlife Service (KWS), Kenya Forest Service (KFS), and Kenya Forest Research Institute (KEFRI). These agencies are established to ensure that development activities 'do not compromise the capacity of the resource base to meet the needs of the present generation as well as those of future generations'.[28] Similarly, the Egyptian Environmental Affairs Agency is mandated, amongst other things, to prepare studies on the state of the environment, formulate the national plan for the protection of the environment, and monitor the implementation of international and regional conventions related to the environment.

All of the African sustainable development agencies and commissions surveyed describe their work under four headings: (1) advocacy – raising awareness of the concept of sustainable development and responding to government policy initiatives; (2) capacity-building – establishing good working relationships with and between key parts of the government, and developing skills in departments; (3) policy and advice – drawing on expert opinion to provide evidence-based advice to the government on sustainable development; and (4) watchdog – monitoring performance against targets

[27] See 'Federal Ministry of Environment of Nigeria' (Federal Republic of Nigeria 2015) www.nigeria.gov.ng/index.php/2016-04-06-08-40-29/executive/147-federal-ministry-of-environment accessed 25 September 2015.

[28] Environmental Management and Coordination Act (EMCA) (1999) sec. 3.

and reporting on them. Generally, sustainable development agencies and commissions spearhead national implementation of norms of sustainable development and intergenerational justice envisioned by international treaty law. They also serve as watchdogs in scrutinising and monitoring the government's progress on implementing the treaty obligations and national environmental plan and strategies. They further stipulate penalties for activities of the public that are detrimental to the environment.

While the contributions and roles of sustainable development agencies in implementing programmes that promote fairness between generations and the maintenance of the environment cannot be denied, a major drawback is that these agencies do not have specialized mandates for future generations. African States are yet to appoint agencies or commissions exclusively committed to future generations' interests and needs, the implication being that future generations programmes are implemented haphazardly as part of general environmental protection mandates and mostly scattered across diverse agencies. The danger in this governance model is that the unique needs of future generations often get lost in bureaucratic processes. With several agencies mandated to tackle various aspects of environmental protection and intergenerational justice, the result is a one-pipe-at-a-time approach to intergenerational equity, as opposed to a proactive and holistic political leadership that ensures that actions and programmes necessary to protect future generations' interests are implemented. For example, despite the proliferation of environmental agencies in Nigeria, a lack of coherent and holistic approach often means that different agencies pursue parallel and at times conflicting programmes without fully delineating the entire scope of future generation needs.

This lack of coordinated response to intergenerational equity issues underscores the need for a focal body or office for future generations that provides holistic evaluation, review, and monitoring of a wide range of intergenerational issues ranging from environmental concerns to the protection of cultural heritage and the investigation of bioethical concerns. This integrated approach may be particularly fitting for several African States such as Nigeria, South Africa, and Kenya, where lack of interagency coordination is arguably one of the key barriers to sustainable development and growth.

### *Parliamentary Committees on Sustainable Development*

Another trend in African States is the establishment of parliamentary committees on environment and sustainable development. Such parliamentary committees work within the parliamentary system to consider the extent to which policies and programmes of government departments contribute to environmental protection and sustainable development. They also review and evaluate government performance against national sustainable development and environmental protection goals. In Nigeria, for example, both parliamentary houses under its bicameral structure have committees established to review and evaluate the government's sustainable development policies and programmes.[29] These include the Senate Committee on Environment, the Senate Committee on Niger Delta Development, the House Committee on the Environment, and the House Committee on Niger Delta Development. Kenya's Senate and National Assembly also have respective Environment and Natural Resources Committees that evaluate and support government sustainable development programmes. Generally, parliamentary committees perform oversight functions aimed at evaluating matters relating to environment management and conservation. These committees play diverse roles, including supporting the government with recommendations on medium- and long-term planning, and developing goals, measures, and instruments for the long run. They consider the extent to which the policies and programmes of government departments and non-departmental public bodies contribute to environmental protection and sustainable development, and also audit the government's performance against national sustainable development and environmental protection policies and goals. While none of the African States has established a 'Parliamentary Committee on Future Generations', to the extent that extant committees evaluate and promote the conservation of natural resources and the protection of the environment, both current and future generations stand to gain.

Although parliamentary committees play oversight roles in keeping government on track for delivering intergenerational justice and sustainable development, they have limited powers and mandates to monitor and enforce policy implementation. In presidential systems of government, operational in Nigeria, Kenya, Egypt, Benin, Algeria, Liberia, and many other parts of Africa, the executive arm of government leads policy execution, while parliament's principal role is to make laws.[30] Consequently, unlike the Parliamentary Commissioner in New Zealand or the Ombudsman in Hungary, who are experts directly appointed and independent of the elected government, parliamentary committees comprise mainly elected lawmakers. This limits the abilities of such committees to function independently or to act as non-partisan advocates for sound environmental management.

[29] There are currently fifty-seven standing committees in the Nigerian Senate, while the House of Representatives currently eighty-nine standing committees. See Nigerian National Assembly, 'Committees' (Nigerian National Assembly 2015) www.nass.gov.ng/committee accessed 30 November 2017.

[30] See Federal Republic of Nigeria, 'Government' (Federal Republic of Nigeria 2017) www.nigeria.gov.ng/# accessed 30 November 2017; Government of Kenya, 'Home' (Government of Kenya 2017) www.mygov.go.ke/ accessed 30 November 2017; Government of Egypt, 'GovGuide' (Government of Egypt 2017) www.egypt.gov.eg/english/home.aspx accessed 30 November 2017; Government of Benin, 'Benin: Government' (Government of Egypt 2017) https://globaledge.msu.edu/countries/benin/government accessed 30 November 2017; Government of Algeria, 'Government' (Government of Algeria 2017) https://globaledge.msu.edu/countries/algeria/government accessed 30 November 2017; *Government of Liberia*, 'Ministry of Information' (Government of Liberia 2017) www.micat.gov.lr/ accessed 30 November 2017.

Parliamentary committees also face the problem of continuity in governance as they are often reconstituted or dissolved at the end of the constitutional term of the parliament. Considering the importance of continuity and consistency in achieving intergenerational justice, there is a need to reassess how future generations programmes can be better embedded in governance through focused, holistic, and stable governance models. In general, while parliamentary committees play vital roles in ingraining the principles of sustainable development and long-term thinking in politics, they are mostly *ad hoc*, and generally fall short of what is necessary to consistently protect, preserve, and defend the interests/needs of future generations in Africa.

Equally important is the concern that parliamentary committees, like many of the other surveyed governance institutions, are not properly constituted to reflect the voice of children and youths. In many African States, youths are marginalized and are not given prominent roles in government. The end result is that youths, who could provide better perspectives on the concerns and injustices facing future generations, are unable to play active roles under prevailing political arrangements. In Nigeria, for example, no youth or individual under the age of thirty years has ever been elected to the federal parliament. Similarly, youths are often overlooked for appointments as ministers, agency heads, or representatives on government committees and agencies for sustainable development. Current governance institutions are therefore incapable, owing to their constitution and approach, of engaging meaningfully in dialogue with youths, children, and society as a whole to promote fairness between generations and the maintenance of the Earth's ecosystem.

It is evident from the foregoing that the prevailing paradigm of embedding intergenerational equity as part of wider general mandates on environmental protection and sustainable development has not delivered real progress in Africa. Faced with problems of lack of continuity, low levels of transparency, inadequate funding, limited engagement with youth, lack of functional independence, lack of coordination, and lack of commitment, the Linkage Approach to intergenerational justice generally falls short of what is required to consistently protect, preserve, and defend the interests and needs of future generations in Africa. Therefore, new viable paths must be developed. New governance arrangements, processes, tools, and mechanisms must be adapted to give a higher profile to sustainable development and intergenerational justice issues. The next section discusses the importance of appointing future generation institutions to play this important role.

## IMPROVING THE SUSTAINABILITY ARCHITECTURE: THE NEED FOR AN INDEPENDENT FUTURE GENERATIONS BODY OR OFFICE

Future generations policies and programmes can be strengthened if independently implemented and consistently pursued irrespective of the government in power. For

African governments to deal with the long-term effects of anthropogenic activities in a focused, committed, and effective manner, there is a need to transcend the prevailing Linkage Approach to a more strategic and independent framework for sustainable development. This will be in the form of appointing distinct 'Parliamentary Commissioners for Future Generations' or 'Ombudsmen for the Environment or Sustainable Development' with the mandate to institutionalize intergenerational equity in policy making across government and to collate data from departments on performance against targets for sustainable operations and intergenerational justice.

As a model of governance, the appointment of a focal future generations institute or officer will give a higher profile to sustainable development and intergenerational justice issues in Africa. By taking such a bold step of appointing a distinct future generations officer or institution, African governments will be sending a strong message to business enterprises and stakeholders that resource utilization, investments, planning, and development must not jeopardize the well-being of future generations. Such commitment on the part of government would also encourage government agencies and even private sector corporations to develop future generation programmes.

Secondly, appointing a future generations body or officer would assist governments to better focus on and develop robust future generations interests in policy making. The prevailing circumstances, in which sustainability initiatives are scattered across several agencies, commissions, arms of government, and bodies such that one might require a compass to steer through who is doing what, have proven to be a wrong model for Africa. A focal institution or officer could help bring together and coordinate the several competing and at times overlapping programmes, and supervise their coherent implementation. A coherent approach to implementation not only saves time and costs, it also ensures systemic coordination and better delivery of programmes to policy areas where they are needed the most.

Thirdly, a focal institution or officer will also be well placed to authoritatively develop, evaluate, monitor, and access the performance of government departments and agencies against sustainable management targets and thresholds. Future generations programmes will be better enhanced when spearheaded by experts with qualifications, experience, and recognitions in sustainable development to spearhead future generation programmes. For example, Hungary established the position of Ombudsman for Future Generations in 2008, although the tasks and responsibilities have varied over time since then.[31] The former ombudsman, Professor Marcel Szabó, a renowned international sustainable development expert, was appointed in 2012 and remained in office until 2016, when he joined the Hungarian Constitutional Court. By appointing experienced professionals to spearhead future generation programmes, the focal institute or office can authoritatively

[31] See Sándor Fülöp's chapter in this volume. For the functions and powers of the Hungarian Ombudsman for Future Generations, see *infra* ch. 4 in this volume.

develop best practices, strategies, programmes, and tools that would enhance governments to better reflect intergenerational equity in governance.

Similarly, a focal future generations body or officer could foster capacity development programmes that would assist government departments to develop the skills and resources they need to make more sustainable decisions, through capacity-building programmes, training, and events. One of the problems facing sustainable development and intergenerational equity in Africa is the widening gap in available capacity to implement international treaties and best practice. Appointing a focal officer or institute to spearhead sustainability education will develop and deepen the capacity of government officials to implement future generation programmes.

Lastly, institutionalizing a distinct focal institution or officer to implement future generations programmes would prevent the problems of political inconsistency and lack of continuing political will to implement future generations programmes. The prevailing lack of continuity or ongoing commitments by successive governments to pursue or retain existing sustainable development programmes can be addressed by institutionalizing a focal institute or officer that can carry on future generation programmes irrespective of any change in government.

Although some scholars might decry the proliferation of institutions as a reason for lumping intergenerational justice under existing bodies, the overwhelming evidence of unsustainability in resource utilization, energy insecurity, environmental degradation, and stunted economic growth in Africa suggests that the Linkage Approach has simply not delivered results for Africa. In light of many governmental and political challenges facing the effective delivery of sustainable development and intergenerational justice under the linkage model, intergenerational justice must be prioritized and institutionalized in Africa, more so than any other region in the world. The delivery of sustainable development and intergenerational justice programmes can be enhanced and revitalized by African governments by adopting a committed, focused, and institutionalized approach.

In the next section, it is suggested that there are practical approaches for ensuring the effective implementation of the institutionalisation approach to intergenerational justice.

## SUGGESTED APPROACHES

The institutions needed to represent future generations will vary for different African countries depending on the differences among existing political systems and the interplay of extant institutions. Institutionalising future generations programmes can occur through the appointment of a future generations officer or chief sustainability officer, as an officer of government, with the same rank and recognition as officers such as the Auditor General or Accountant General. It can also occur through the appointment of Parliamentary Commissioners for Future Generations or an Ombudsman for the Future Generations, or by expanding the roles of any of the extant agencies or institutions to include a future generations officer. Whatever the designation or approach adopted, the most important requirement is to ensure that the structural conditions, processes, and outcomes of such mechanisms and institutions enables them to act as independent watchdogs, advisors, and a non-partisan advocate for sound environmental management.

### *Structural Conditions*

Before one can speak of embedding intergenerational equity into governance, extant laws must be updated to recognize and establish a distinctive role for a future generations commission or officer. States such as New Zealand and Hungary have been able to appoint sustainable development commissioners or officers because of express statutory allowances for such offices. In Hungary, for example, in 2011 the Parliament recognized the need to protect natural resources at constitutional level by stating in the Fundamental Law that:

> agricultural land, forests and drinking water supplies, biodiversity – in particular native plant and animal species – and cultural assets are part of the nation's common heritage, and named the State and every person to be obliged to protect, sustain and preserve them for future generations.[32]

This recognition paved the way for the institutionalisation of the Office of the Ombudsman for Future Generations.[33] Similarly, in New Zealand, the office of a Parliamentary Commissioner for Environment was established under the Environment Act 1986.[34]

A starting point, therefore, is to put in place adequate structural conditions in terms of legal and institutional frameworks that recognize the need to protect, sustain, and preserve natural resources, native plant and animal species, and cultural assets for future generations. While environmental laws in many parts of Africa already recognize environmental protection for present and future generations, it is imperative to take a step further by updating the laws to establish sustainability institutions to monitor, review, and enforce the preservation and protection of resources and the protection of national heritage for the interests of future generations.

Such a focal institution or officer must be legally empowered to investigate any matter where resource conservation or the environment may be, or has been, adversely affected, collate data from departments on performance against targets for sustainable operations and sustainable management, measure and monitor compliance with sustainable development plans, and provide evidence-based advice to the government on preventive measures and remedial actions to protect the

32 The Fundamental Law of Hungary (2013) art. P.

33 See Sándor Fülöp's chapter in this volume.

34 New Zealand Environment Act (1986) pt. I. Section 4 specifically provides that 'There shall be appointed, as an officer of Parliament, a Parliamentary Commissioner for the Environment.'

environment. They should also be empowered to monitor policy developments and legislative proposals to ensure that they do not pose severe or irreversible threats to the interests of future generations.

The future generations institution can perform these roles in a non-confrontational, non-judicial, and consultative manner in order to ensure that government policies, actions, and programmes do not stifle sustainable development. They can be involved in the elaboration of non-binding statements and proposals to any public authority, including the government, in order to ensure that the direct link between the State's common heritage and the fundamental rights of all generations – including future generations – are respected and not forgotten.

### *Process*

A second prerequisite is to establish procedures to ensure that such officers are practically able to deliver sustainability outcomes. A future generations officer should not exist only on paper. In this context, 'process' refers to how effective the body or officer is in delivering practical outcomes. A future generations officer should be set up to serve as an independent assessor of government policies, systems, and processes, and a non-partisan advocate for the protection of future generations interests. Independence and autonomy are very important in frail democracies, as is the case in many parts of Africa, to ensure that future generations officers are not influenced or impacted by political considerations or governmental pressure. Furthermore, a future generations officer should be procedurally empowered to perform spot assessments, fact-findings, and investigations, such that they are able to gather first-hand information on the true impacts of a project on sustainable development. Similarly, adequate institutional resources must be provided to ensure that such officers can consult widely and interact with the public to properly determine pressing needs. One important way of ensuring financial independence in the African socio-political context is to ensure that such an institution is given a direct budgetary allocation from the national account such that its future will not be tied to the priorities of the government in power.

### *Monitoring Outcomes*

It is not enough to establish future generations offices or institutions; governments must be committed to implementing the recommendations and advice emanating from such offices. There is a need to put in place accountability mechanisms and public reporting through which the public can monitor how much of the recommendations or programmes of the future generations officers are translated into action. Periodic mandate review and monitoring will enable the public to determine whether the structural conditions and processes are actually bringing about results in preserving the needs of future generations in policy implementation and project planning and execution. Similarly, while the outcome may tell us whether sustainable development is delivered, structural conditions and processes tell us how they are delivered. Outcome indicators assess, for example, the extent to which government departments are complying with project threshold and methodologies approved by the future generations officer. Through public disclosure, periodic compliance reviews, and mandatory reporting obligations for government agencies, governments will be able to demonstrate to the public that future generations programmes are executed in line with guidelines approved and mandated by the future generations office.

The importance of measuring outcomes cannot be overemphasized in developing democracies where governments often pay lip service to sustainable development. It is easy for government agencies to lay claim to intergenerational justice and sustainable development during the design and execution of a project. However, there is a need for the future generations office to perform oversight functions of gathering on-the-ground facts and to investigate whether projects are proceeding as approved. Accountability moves beyond examining whether a government agency has complied with national sustainable development plans and policies to include reviewing and monitoring the methodology and approaches adopted in doing so.

The three elements must be given robust consideration by African governments in setting up a future generations office. In the light of prevailing circumstances where investments, development programmes, and projects affect sustainable development, governments must show more commitment in revitalizing the delivery of intergenerational justice programmes in order to ensure that the ability of future generations to live and thrive in Africa are not jeopardized.

## CONCLUSION

While the creation of a future generations institution will not solve all of the entrenched problems of sustainable development and intergenerational equity in Africa, it can certainly revitalize and influence the delivery of sustainable development programmes and policies across the continent. As a model of governance, the appointment of a focal future generations body or officer could help overcome problems of lack of continuity, low levels of transparency, inadequate funding, limited engagement with youth, lack of functional independence, lack of coordination, and lack of commitment that have stifled previous approaches to institutionalization of intergenerational justice in Africa.

As African States grapple with several complex environmental, social, economic, and security challenges that threaten the interests of future generations, it is important to reassess how extant legal and institutional frameworks can be reformed to prioritize the institutionalization of intergenerational equity. Depending on the socio-political structures and realities in respective African States it is possible that a future generations institution could complement existing institutional arrangements, for example, by granting special advisors more independent mandates and powers to serve as future generations officers. The alternative, a distinct institutionalization model which involves a body or officer with a focused, independent, and broader mandate to speak for future generations, may be preferable, to provide authoritative and non-partisan monitoring and assessment of sustainability programmes. Whatever approach or model is adopted, what is clear is that the problems of sustainable development and intergenerational justice in Africa are complex and therefore require urgent, sustained, and committed action.

# 34

# Intergenerational Equity, Justice, and Modern Treaties between First Nations Communities and Canada

*Tara Dawn Atleo, Marie-Claire Cordonier Segger and Alexandra R. Harrington*

As the debates in this volume demonstrate, although intergenerational equity may appear simple at its core, whereby current generations respect the interests of generations to come, there are complexities and nuances in the implementation of the principle across economic, social and cultural, and environmental law and policy. Considerations of intergenerational justice apply to all actors and jurisdictions, and while it is essential that the present and future needs of the most underrepresented, marginalised, and vulnerable communities be taken into account, the most effective ways and means are often difficult to discern. In this context, legal experiences of States and indigenous nations may offer important lessons in ways that key actors assert agency and influence relevant policies and practices affecting current and future generations.

This chapter explores how intergenerational equity and justice, along with other international principles related to sustainable development, may be furthered and supported through the 'modern treaties' in existence between the Government of Canada and a number of First Nations communities. These legal instruments, negotiated between the parties in order to address land claims, indigenous self-governance and other priorities, touch on the global SDGs for entire peoples, their nations, and their territories. The modern treaty experiences offer warnings, but also an opportunity and a series of binding commitments which are worthy of awareness, analysis, and dialogue, as well as implementation on all levels. In this chapter, the analysis of the modern treaties in Canada in terms of their potential for respecting the needs and interests of future generations can be advanced through the discussion of how the accords reflect Canada's targets under the SDGs, which themselves seek to advance intergenerational equity and justice considerations. By analysing how modern treaties could contribute to the SDGs, it is possible to tease out binding obligations upon both Canada and First Nations, which seek to improve economic, environmental, and socio-cultural conditions for both present and future generations.

Building on the findings of an exploratory project engaging indigenous and non-indigenous collaborators supported by the Canadian Social Sciences and Humanities Research Council (SSHRC) at the School of Environment, Enterprise and Development (SEED) of the University of Waterloo,[1] this chapter briefly discusses Canada's commitments to the SDGs in relation to the principle of intergenerational equity and justice, examining how this principle is furthered and promoted by the seventeen SDGs and their 169 targets in the context of indigenous sustainable development and providing a context within which to view and evaluate the terms of Canada's modern treaties with First Nations, as instruments for advancing the needs and interests of future generations. Following this, specific provisions from case studies of modern treaties between Canada and certain First Nations are examined in light of their contributions to intergenerational equity and selected SDG targets, before lessons learned from analysis of experiences implementing Canada–First Nations modern treaties are offered, as a contribution to efforts to strengthen and improve implementation of the SDGs for present and future generations.

## SCOPE OF ANALYSIS: A SELECTION OF CANADA'S TREATIES WITH FIRST NATIONS

The term 'modern treaties' refers to those treaties that have been negotiated and signed between various First Nations communities in Canada and the Canadian government in the most recent decades. This is a significant period to examine as it is the result of attempts to reconfigure the relationship between indigenous communities and the national and provincial governments in Canada.[2] In this period, the principle of intergenerational equity was also further defined and applied in international and national law.[3] Previously concluded treaties, often referred to as 'historical treaties', are important but outside the scope of the current discussion.[4]

To date, there have been over thirty modern treaties signed between First Nations communities and the Canadian Government, spanning a wide swathe of geography and community identity. For analysis, this chapter focuses on an initial selection of fifteen modern treaties from different areas of Canada.

1 For more information about this research project, see https://uwaterloo.ca/scholar/mcordoni/home accessed 18 May 2020.

2 Crown–Indigenous Relations and Northern Affairs Canada, 'Treaties and Agreements' www.rcaanc-cirnac.gc.ca/eng/1100100028574/1529354437231 accessed 20 June 2019.

3 Ibid.

4 Ibid.

## CANADA'S COMMITMENT TO THE SDGS AND INTERGENERATIONAL EQUITY

Canada has adopted the world's seventeen SDGs, and is committed to the advancement of 169 important targets for all peoples across Canada. The government is also committed to cooperation for the achievement of the SDG targets globally, including through implementation of myriad related binding international treaties that are discussed elsewhere in this volume. While the SDGs are not a binding international legal instrument, they set a framework and targets to guide the policies and practices of the Canadian and other governments on all levels, and, in many instances, also reflect other treaty law commitments, both internationally and within Canada in terms of binding accords with First Nations. Indeed, achievement of the commitments enshrined in the seventeen global SDGs could make a significant contribution to intergenerational equity globally, advancing efforts on all levels towards a more sustainable future for all by 2030.[5]

As an initial example, Canada's federal, provincial and municipal governments are committed to achieving SDG 1 to end extreme poverty by 2030 and reduce all poverty.[6] With this in mind, in target 1.1, states seek to 'eradicate extreme poverty for all people everywhere', setting the amount of $1.25 per day as the poverty rate at a global level.[7] This ambitious aim is somewhat tempered by SDG target 1.2, which establishes a threshold of at least halving the 'the proportion of men, women and children of all ages living in poverty in all its dimensions according to national definitions'.[8] Recognising the many forms of connection between vulnerable populations and communities and the reduction of poverty,[9] in several other SDG 1 targets, states provide for further general national protections for these populations and communities, as well as for economic, financial, and property rights and protections.[10] Further, at the international and national levels, SDG 1 encourages the creation of 'sound policy frameworks at the national, regional and international levels, based on pro-poor and gender-sensitive development strategies, to support accelerated investment in poverty eradication actions'.[11] Canada's commitments to the targets in SDG 10 are also very important for intergenerational equity, as commitments focus on promoting the reduction of inequalities and poverty rates within current generations, including through the enhancement of economic opportunities and the development of better social and economic conditions.[12] These

5 See UNGA, *Transforming Our World: The 2030 Agenda for Sustainable Development*, A/RES/70/1 (25 September 2015).

6 Ibid. at Goal 1 ('End poverty in all its forms everywhere').

7 Ibid. at para. 1.1.

8 Ibid. at para. 1.2.

9 Ibid. at para. 1.3.

10 Ibid. at para. 1.4.

11 Ibid. at para. 1.B.

12 Ibid. at Goal 10.

targets promote intergenerational equity by ensuring that future generations can benefit from societies in which poverty is reduced – if not eradicated – and vulnerable populations and communities are given recognition of rights that allow them to move out of poverty in the present and future. However, concern for the needs and interests of future generations permeates the other SDGs, as well, in further profound ways.

For instance, in SDG 2, by focusing on hunger and nutrition issues, Canada and other countries recognise the importance of food security for current and future generations, while also emphasising that efforts to promote food security should not harm future generations and instead expand local and indigenous community capacities and protections for the future.[13] In target 2.5, Canada and other countries identify a need for the protection of agricultural products, including those used or maximised through traditional knowledge, and the growth of 'access to and fair and equitable sharing of benefits arising from the utilisation of genetic resources'.[14] In this way, the SDGs promote intergenerational equity through the preservation of agricultural products and food sources as well as in terms of protections for and the preservation of traditional knowledge and practices, many of which are integral to indigenous community heritage. In conjunction, and as a further illustrative example, Canada's commitments to achieve SDG 6 on clean water and sanitation can be generally linked to intergenerational equity by ensuring that improvements in access to water and investment in better sanitation will be enjoyed by both current and future generations,[15] by protecting water supplies and the watersheds that affect them against chemical and other pollution, and through preserving fresh water resources.[16] As an additional example, the protection of cultural heritage and traditional knowledge is carried out directly in the interest of preserving knowledge and culture for the present but also for the generations to come. Importantly, the targets adopted by Canada and other countries under SDG 11 provide for the enhancement of protections and safeguards for cultural heritage sites at the international and national levels.[17]

Further, SDG 3 on health and access to health care has tangible links to intergenerational equity, as through efforts to achieve this SDG, Canada and other countries seek to ensure lower mortality rates for children, to create healthier

[13] Ibid. at Goal 2; Ibid. at para. 2.4 ('By 2030, ensure sustainable food production systems and implement resilient agricultural practices that increase productivity and production, that help maintain ecosystems, that strengthen capacity for adaptation to climate change, extreme weather, drought, flooding and other disasters and that progressively improve land and soil quality.') These provisions are furthered by indicator 2.4.1, which uses the 'proportion of agricultural area under productive and sustainable agriculture' as a measurable entity for national assessment of progress toward achieving SDG 2.

[14] Ibid. at para. 2.5.

[15] Ibid. at para. 6.

[16] Ibid. at paras. 6.3, 6.4.

[17] Ibid. at Goal 11, para. 11.4.

populations that are empowered with better knowledge regarding health care for themselves and their children, and to create a healthier basis on which future generations can build.[18] Links between health protection and intergenerational equity are also implied, as access to health services is a key determinant of greater equity in well-functioning social systems, laying foundations for healthier populations into the future. Similarly, in SDG 4 on education, the targets adopted by Canada and other countries are critical for the achievement of greater intergenerational equity, since efforts to improve access to education systems for students and learners across all levels of educational need can help different generations of learners to improve their lives, and to express their voices in decision-making.[19] Of particular note is the way in which Canada's commitments under SDG 4 encourage the inclusion of women and girl children in national education systems, and the inclusion of vulnerable and underrepresented students.[20] By generating stronger education systems which provide for the full education of the entire population throughout an individual's life and in the face of changing needs and educational advances, SDG 4 establishes a significant platform for growth and development by current and future generations.[21] There is a dual focus in this SDG on both individual students and learners and society as a whole.

Achieving gender equality is an essential aspect of intergenerational equity, ensuring that the biases and limitations of the past do not transmit themselves to the future. Beyond equality concepts per se, Canada's commitments to SDG 5 provide for protection of women and girls from violence at all levels – public and private[22] – and also provides for the valuation of household work and child-rearing activities 'through the provision of public services, infrastructure and social protection policies and the promotion of shared responsibility within the household and the family as nationally appropriate'.[23] Creating a system in which gender biases are reduced and in which there is full legal and societal recognition and valuing of the infrastructural values of work by all is necessary for advancing the interests of current generations and allows for more robust systems of equity for future generations.

On a larger scale, the commitments of Canada and other countries in SDG 8 relate to economic growth and development in a sustainable and holistically meaningful manner, one that also promotes growth of decent employment opportunities and training.[24] In conjunction, in SDG 9 on the development of inclusive and sustainable infrastructure at the national and subnational levels, intergenerational

[18] Ibid. at Goal 3.
[19] Ibid. at Goal 4 ('Ensure inclusive and equitable quality education and promote lifelong learning opportunities for all.')
[20] Ibid. at paras. 4.1, 4.2, 4.3.
[21] See generally ibid.
[22] Ibid. at Goal 5, paras. 5.2, 5.3.
[23] Ibid. at 5.4.
[24] Ibid. at Goal 8.

equity can be advanced by aiming to craft infrastructure for current needs that is also likely to bring improvements for future generations.[25] Through development of small-scale infrastructure and small or micro sustainable business opportunities, systems can be put in place for future growth.[26] Additionally, in SDG 9, Canada and other states commit to encourage scientific and technical research and skills across all segments of society, improving education of workers so as to allow them to participate more fully in the workforce.[27] Through inclusion and continuing involvement of increasingly capable people, it is possible to improve equity for the present and future needs of both the economy and the society, while advancing opportunities to pass on knowledge and advanced insights and training to future generations.

Closely related to this are the terms and targets of SDG 12 relating to sustainable consumption and production patterns and the ways in which consumers and producers interact in order to create a lasting pattern of sustainability.[28] This is clearly articulated in target 12.8, which provides that '[b]y 2030, ensure that people everywhere have the relevant information and awareness for sustainable development and lifestyles in harmony with nature'.[29] In their work to address these targets, states and others seek to improve natural resources management and the use – and restriction of use – of chemicals and chemical waste so as to provide for responsible use and management.[30] Also under the aegis of SDG 12, Canada and other states prioritize the need for public procurement to 'promote ... practices that are sustainable, in accordance with national policies and priorities'.[31] The creation of sustainable consumption and production patterns will have impacts well beyond 2030, as it will allow for the generation of innovation that assists future generations and seeks to ensure that the systems of consumption and production inherited by future generations are stronger and better able to adapt to changing realities than those inherited by the current generation.

Perhaps one of the most pressing challenges for efforts to promote greater intergenerational equity involves maintaining and supporting marine and terrestrial ecosystems, and preventing and mitigation climate change impacts and effects. Destruction of habitat, the living systems on which all beings on Earth depend, and degradation of the world's climate threaten the interests of all future generations. In this regard, Canada's commitments to advance SDGs 13, 14, and 15 are of particular importance, encompassing targets related to climate change, life below water, and life on land, respectively. Fundamentally, the impacts of climate

[25] Ibid. at Goal 9.
[26] Ibid. at para. 9.3.
[27] Ibid. at para. 9.5.
[28] See generally Goal 12.
[29] Ibid. at para. 12.8.
[30] Ibid. at paras. 12.2, 12.4, 12.5.
[31] Ibid. at para. 12.7.

change on both present and future generations are likely to prevent any hope of improving intergenerational equity. In SDG target 13.1, Canada and other countries prioritize actions that can strengthen adaptation and resilience to climate-change-related effects, notably disasters.[32] To further this, in other SDG 13 targets, Canada and other stages prioritize the need to develop national policies which prevent and mitigate climate changes, as well as advancing educational programmes and awareness campaigns for all levels of society, including children and teachers.[33] Climate change impacts could foreclose on all options for future generations, and by recognising the need to implement the decisions of the UNFCC, in this SDG, Canada and other states integrate the intergenerational protections established in later binding treaties under the UNFCCC such as the Paris Agreement that was adopted a few months after the SDGs. In the many targets agreed by Canada and other countries under SDG 14 relating to life below water – including oceans, rivers, lakes, and wetlands – governments prioritize the protection of these areas and their ecosystems for current and future generations, promoting the equitable transfer of water and water resources.[34] Further priorities are set by the targets agreed in SDG 15 relating to protecting life on land – including mountain, forest and other ecosystems, also biodiversity and species conservation.[35] Without such protections, and related restoration, these biological and ecological resources would not be available for the enjoyment of future generations of humans or the millions of other species.

Another key aspect of the intergenerational equity principle which is reflected in the SDGs is the need for greater stability in societies, to which the promotion of peace and justice within society at a multitude of levels, from the international to the regional to the national to the most local, contributes. Recognising this, in SDG 16 Canada and other governments prioritize the need to 'promote peaceful and inclusive societies for sustainable development, provide access to justice for all and build effective, accountable and inclusive institutions at all levels'.[36] Overall, SDG 16 aims to create societies in which all aspects of these needs are holistically embraced and addressed, ranging from violence to human trafficking to illicit activities and beyond.[37] Significantly, this includes the development and implementation of governance mechanisms that promote inclusion of vulnerable and underrepresented groups,[38] ensure that all voices are included in policy and other evaluation,[39] and address the scourges caused by bribery and corruption across all

[32] Ibid. at para. 13.1.
[33] Ibid. at para. 13.2.
[34] Ibid. at Goal 14.
[35] Ibid. at Goal 15.
[36] Ibid. at Goal 16.
[37] Ibid.
[38] Ibid. at para. 16.6.
[39] Ibid. at para. 16.7.

sectors.[40] As envisioned in the SDG system, these mechanisms are flexible in their structure provided that they are focused on the function of achieving inclusion and justice within society.

Finally, in SDG 17, there are provisions for the strengthening and forging of relationships between institutions and entities involved in the funding and implementation of policies and plans which seek to implement the SDGs as a whole. The role of these strengthened institutions is intended to be a sustainable set of international and national entities that have the ability to provide these forms of assistance now and into the future generations.[41] An essential aspect of this challenge, with regard to setting in place cooperative, long-term engagements that could contribute to greater intergenerational equity, can be found in target 17.17, which provides for '[e]ncourage[ment] and promot[ion of] effective public, public-private and civil society partnerships, building on the experience and resourcing strategies of partnerships'.[42] This is accompanied by aims to increase capacity-building and technology transfer across constituencies at all levels.[43]

## INTERGENERATIONAL EQUITY THROUGH FIRST NATIONS TREATIES WITH CANADA FOR THE SDGS

With potential to contribute to a lasting society that fosters inclusion of all members of society, especially vulnerable members and communities, the provisions of modern treaties seek improvements through a variety of means across the legal and cultural spectrum. For example, as part of these treaties, the Canadian Government has agreed to provide financial settlements and payments for forest resources that are specifically to be used for economic development of the applicable communities.[44] Some of these treaties make specific provision for forms of corporations or other entities to be used in the disbursement of these funds, while others simply provide for the funding and allow the communities to determine how best to address the needs of their constituencies.[45] Additionally, a number of these treaties allow for the ability

40 Ibid. at para. 16.5.

41 Ibid. at Goal 17.

42 Ibid. at para. 17.17.

43 Ibid. at Goal 17.

44 Tsawwassen First Nation Final Agreement (2007) ch. 10(5).

45 Ibid.; Land Claims Agreement between the Inuit of Labrador and Her Majesty the Queen in Right of Newfoundland and Labrador and Her Majesty the Queen in Right of Canada (2005) pts. 4,7 [Inuit of Labrador]; Carcross/Tagish Agreement among the Government of Canada, the Carcross/Tagish First Nation and the Government of the Yukon (2005) chs. 5, 12; Champagne and Aishihik First Nations Final Agreement between the Government of Canada, the Champagne and Aishihik First Nations and the Government of the Yukon (1992) chs. 13, 20, 22; Kwanlin Dun First Nation Final Agreement among the Government of Canada, the Kwanlin Dun First Nation and the Government of the Yukon (2005) chs. 13, 20, 22; Kluane First Nation Final Agreement among the Government of Canada, the Kluane First Nation and the Government of the Yukon (2003) chs. 13, 20, 22; Little Salmon/Carmacks

of indigenous communities to act directly on issues and practice relating to the exploitation of natural resources located on community territory.[46] In this way, the modern treaties reflect essential elements of intergenerational equity and assist in the creation of a society at the local, regional, and national levels that is more inclusive and that is able to equitably preserve the natural resources found in Canada as well as the traditional knowledge and practices associated with them. Indeed, the terms of the modern treaties reflect a number of SDGs in this context, particularly SDG 1 and SDG 10.

There are several mechanisms through which the treaties contain provisions that seek to improve the agricultural productivity and sustainability of indigenous communities and their conduct on indigenous territorial lands. The encouragement and development of sustainable, traditional agriculture is advanced through legal and societal recognition and protection of traditional practices, knowledge, and land rights. Such recognition and protection is provided in some of the modern treaties through the legal enshrinement of community land holding rights, including territories used for agricultural practices,[47] and the ability of indigenous communities to craft and enact their own laws under the terms of many self-governance treaty terms.[48] This is directly connected with the need to implement sustainable and resilient agricultural practices and patterns, as seen in the terms of many modern treaties which relate to the involvement of the indigenous community and the provincial and governmental communities in determining allowable catches per year, as this has an impact on agricultural ecosystems and conditions as well.[49] The links between these aspects of the modern treaties and intergenerational equity are perhaps obvious, in that incorporating the elements of traditional

First Nation Final Agreement among the Government of Canada, the Little Salmon/Carmacks First Nation and the Government of the Yukon (1997) chs. 13, 20, 22; Ta'an Kwac'han Final Agreement among the Government of Canada, the Ta'an Kwac'han First Nation and the Government of the Yukon (2002) chs. 13, 20, 22; Land Claims and Self-Government Agreement among the Tlicho and the Government of the Northwest Territories and the Government of Canada (2005) chs. 24, 25, 26; Maa'Nulth First Nations Final Agreement (2009) chs. 10, 16, 17; Tla'Amin Final Agreement (2016) chs. 8, 18, 19; Governance Agreement between Sioux Valley Dakota Nation and Her Majesty the Queen in Right of Canada (2013) art. 23; Comprehensive Land Claim Agreement between Her Majesty in Right of Canada and the Gwich'in (1992) chs. 7–10.

[46] Inuvialuit Final Agreement (1987) arts. 10, 13, 14; Inuit of Labrador Agreement, *supra* note 45 at pts. 5, 12, 13; Sioux Valley Dakota Agreement, *supra* note 45 at art. 15; Carcross/Tagish Agreement, *supra* note 45 at chs. 2, 12; Gwich'in Agreement at ch. 12.

[47] See e.g. Tsawwassen Agreement, *supra* note 44 at ch. 6(4).

[48] Ibid. at ch. 9.

[49] See ibid. at chs. 9, 10; Champagne and Aishihik Agreement, *supra* note 45 at ch. 16; Little Salmon/Carmacks Agreement, *supra* note 45 at ch. 16; Tlicho Agreement, *supra* note 45 at chs. 7, 12; Maa'Nulth Agreement, *supra* note 45 at chs. 10, 11; Inuvialuit Agreement, *supra* note 46 at ch. 12; Inuit of Labrador Agreement, *supra* note 45 at pts. 5, 12, 13; Sioux Valley Dakota Agreement, *supra* note 45 at art. 15; Carcross/Tagish Agreement, *supra* note 45 at chs. 2, 12; Gwich'in Agreement, *supra* note 45 at ch. 12.

agricultural practices that have sustained food sources and security for centuries into current and future practices hold the potential to benefit both current and future generations by providing for reliable food supplies over time. In this way, the terms of modern treaties in this context further implementation of commitments to achieve the SDG 2 targets.

The majority of modern treaties, especially those with self-governance mechanisms for the applicable indigenous communities, provide for some form of devolution of many health-related laws and rules to the local communities.[50] In terms of addressing and preventing potential health-related aspects of pollution and contamination, many of the modern treaties also provide for the use of EIAs as tools to engage communities and improve protection of health and the environment.[51] Control over education and the inclusion of cultural and traditional heritage and knowledge in the curricula at all levels play a significant part of the modern treaties.[52] In terms of gender equality measures, while the majority of the modern treaties reviewed are silent on gender equality and/or mainstreaming, they are notable for their use of gender-neutral language and terminology.[53] Taken together, gender equality and education that is available to vulnerable groups in society while taking into account the needs and knowledge of minority communities promotes the accomplishment of intergenerational equity by striving to eliminate bases of bias for the future. Additionally, these measures will allow for the participation of a greater section of society in public life in the future, empowering First Nations to promote equity as well as equality. Improved capacities and opportunities on these points could advance the achievement of the SDGs, particularly SDG 3, 4, and 5.

To secure improved access to water and clean sanitation, the modern treaties are largely protective of the rights of indigenous community members over water

[50] Inuit of Labrador Agreement, *supra* note 45 at ch. 17; Sioux Valley Agreement, *supra* note 45 at pt. 19; Tsawwassen, *supra* note 44 at ch. 16; Kluane Agreement, *supra* note 45 at ch. 24; Little Salmon/Carmacks Agreement, *supra* note 45 at ch. 24; Ta'an Agreement, *supra* note 45 at ch. 24; Tlicho Agreement, *supra* note 45 at ch. 7; Maa'Nulth Agreement, *supra* note 45 at ch. 13.22.

[51] Inuit of Labrador, *supra* note 45 at ch. 11; Tsawwassen, *supra* note 44 at ch. 15; Champagne and Aishihik Agreement, *supra* note 45 at ch. 14; Kwanlin Dun Agreement, *supra* note 45 at ch. 14; Kluane Agreement, *supra* note 45 at ch. 14; Little Salmon/Carmacks Agreement, *supra* note 45 at ch. 14; Ta'an Agreement, *supra* note 45 at ch. 14.

[52] Inuit of Labrador Agreement, *supra* note 45 at pt. 17; Sioux Valley Dakota Agreement, *supra* note 45 at pt. 18; Carcross/Tagish Agreement, *supra* note 45 at chs. 23, 24; Gwich'in Agreement, *supra* note 45 at chs. 11, 16; Tsawwassen Agreement, *supra* note 44 at chs. 14, 16; Champagne and Aishihik Agreement, *supra* note 45 at chs. 13, 24; Kwanlin Dun Agreement, *supra* note 45 at chs. 13, 24; Kluane Agreement, *supra* note 45 at chs. 13, 24; Little Salmon/Carmacks Agreement, *supra* note 45 at chs. 13, 24; Ta'an Agreement, *supra* note 45 at chs. 13, 14; Tlicho Agreement, *supra* note 45 at ch. 7; James Bay and Northern Quebec Agreement (1978) secs. 8, 16; Maa'Nulth Agreement, *supra* note 45 at chs. 13.20, 13.21; Tla'min Agreement, *supra* note 45 at chs. 13.20, 13.21.

[53] See generally ibid.

resources located within their territories.[54] In particular, the treaties make clear protections for water management and water rights, including provisions that impact on the availability of water for drinking and other purposes within the community and outside the community.[55] This includes powers directly devolved to the community governments through the terms of applicable treaties.[56] The overall protection of natural resources related to water, especially lakes, rivers, and waters in the territories of national parks and preserve areas, is also expressly provided for and understood as a key aspect of community rights.[57] In this way, the modern treaties provisions can be seen as ensuring intergenerational equity in terms of continued access to vital natural resources that are needed for survival as well as development. Further, the modern treaty terms relating to water, sanitation, and associated practices can contribute to Canada fulfilling its commitments under SDG 6.

In the context of sustainable economic growth and employment opportunities, over half of the modern treaties contain overlapping requirements regarding the use and exploitation of natural resources for economic development and job creation.[58] This includes the use of concession fees and similar arrangements under which natural resources can be extracted from indigenous community territories subject to restrictions on the economic, environmental, and societal impacts in the long and short term.[59] Some of these treaties pay particular attention to balancing the ability to use cultural heritage resources for economic and employment-based development with the protection of the cultural resources for current and future generations.[60] Most of the treaties contain provisions that assist indigenous communities through funding and knowledge transfer that results in sustainable and environmentally protective actions and development.[61] Further, in the modern treaties

[54] See generally ibid.

[55] Inuit of Labrador Agreement, *supra* note 45 at ch. 5; Carcross/Tagish Agreement, *supra* note 45 at chs. 14, 16; Gwich'in Agreement, *supra* note 45 at chs. 12, 19, 24; Kwanlin Dun Agreement, *supra* note 45 at ch. 14; Kluane Agreement, *supra* note 45 at 14; Little Salmon/Carmacks Agreement, *supra* note 45 at ch. 14; Tlicho Agreement, *supra* note 45 at ch. 18; Tla'Amin Agreement, *supra* note 45 at ch. 7.2.

[56] Sioux Valley Dakota Agreement, *supra* note 45 at ch. 16.01; Champagne and Aishihik Agreement, *supra* note 45 at ch. 14; Kwanlin Dun Agreement, *supra* note 45 at ch. 14; Kluane Agreement, *supra* note 45 at 14; Little Salmon/Carmacks Agreement, *supra* note 45 at ch. 14; Ta'an Agreement, *supra* note 45 at ch. 14; Tlicho Agreement, *supra* note 45 at ch. 18.

[57] Inuit of Labrador Agreement, *supra* note 45 at chs. 6, 9; Tsawwassen, *supra* note 44 at ch. 15; Kluane Agreement, *supra* note 45 at 10; Ta'an Agreement, *supra* note 45 at ch. 14; Tlicho Agreement, *supra* note 45 at ch. 22.

[58] Inuvialuit Agreement, *supra* note 46; James Bay Agreement, *supra* note 52 at sec. 8.

[59] Inuvialuit Agreement, *supra* note 46; Inuit of Labrador Agreement, *supra* note 45; Sioux Valley Dakota Agreement, *supra* note 45; Carcross/Tagish Agreement, *supra* note 45; Gwich'in Agreement, *supra* note 45; Tsawwassen Agreement, *supra* note 44 at chs. 9, 16.

[60] Champagne and Aishihik, *supra* note 45 at ch. 13; Kwanlin Dun Agreement, *supra* note 45 at ch. 13; Kluane Agreement, *supra* note 45 at ch. 13; Little Salmon/Carmacks Agreement, *supra* note 45 at ch. 13; Ta'an Agreement, *supra* note 45 at ch. 13.

[61] Tlicho Agreement, *supra* note 45 at ch. 23;

reviewed, First Nations and Canada provide an articulated connection between small-scale business and infrastructural concerns as well as for the larger development of infrastructure within the provincial and national communities.[62] For many of the self-governance mechanisms, the sustainable development of infrastructure is a key priority.[63] Providing for sustainable and technologically advanced industries – and associated employment opportunities – places the modern treaties in a position to fulfil essential aspects of intergenerational equity, and by implementing the treaty fully, Canada has an opportunity to support efforts to achieve SDGs 8 and 9.

In relation to cultural heritage and preservation for future generations, it is notable that in the vast majority of the modern treaties, Canada and First Nations make significant provisions for the protection of a number of forms of cultural heritage, including tangible and intangible heritage and knowledge.[64] Again, devolved powers under the terms of the self-governance agreements play a vital role in establishing the ability of the indigenous communities to preserve, protect, and honour their heritage and traditional forms of knowledge.[65] Taken together with cultural heritage resource preservation and protection, the sustainable management and use of natural resources in the territories of impacted indigenous communities is critical to advancing intergenerational equity.[66] For example, these measures have been implemented in regards to fish, wildlife, and bird species and resources,[67] as well as forests and other ecosystem resources.[68] Additionally, some modern treaties contain requirements regarding derogation and jurisdiction sharing in regards to

62 Inuvialuit Agreement, *supra* note 46; Inuit of Labrador Agreement, *supra* note 45.

63 Inuit of Labrador Agreement, *supra* note 45; Sioux Valley Dakota Agreement, *supra* note 45.

64 Inuit of Labrador Agreement, *supra* note 45 at ch. 15; Carcross/Tagish Agreement, *supra* note 45 at chs. 2, 13; Gwich'in Agreement, *supra* note 45 at ch. 1; Champagne and Aishihik Agreement, *supra* note 45 at chs. 10, 13; Kwanlin Dun Agreement, *supra* note 45 at chs. 10, 13; Kluane Agreement, *supra* note 45 at chs. 10, 13; Little Salmon/Carmacks Agreement, *supra* note 45 at chs. 10, 13; Ta'an Agreement, *supra* note 45 at ch. 13; Tlicho Agreement, *supra* note 45 at ch. 17; Maa'Nulth Agreement, *supra* note 45 at chs. 13, 21; Tla'Amin Agreement, *supra* note 45 at ch. 14.

65 Champagne and Aishihik Agreement, *supra* note 45 at ch. 24; Kwanlin Dun Agreement, *supra* note 45 at ch. 24; Kluane Agreement, *supra* note 45 at ch. 24; Little Salmon/Carmacks Agreement, *supra* note 45 at ch. 24; Ta'an Agreement, *supra* note 45 at ch. 24; Tlicho Agreement, *supra* note 45 at ch. 7; Tla'Amin Agreement, *supra* note 45 at ch. 15.

66 See ibid.

67 Tsawwassen Agreement, *supra* note 44 at chs. 9–12; Champagne and Aishihik Agreement, *supra* note 45 at chs. 10, 16, 17; Kwanlin Dun Agreement, *supra* note 45 at chs. 10, 16, 17, 27; Kluane Agreement, *supra* note 45 at chs. 10, 16, 17, 27; Little Salmon/Carmacks Agreement, *supra* note 45 at chs. 10, 16, 17, 27; Ta'an Agreement, *supra* note 45 at chs. 10, 16, 17, 27; Maa'Nulth Agreement, *supra* note 45 at ch. 7; Tla'Amin Agreement, *supra* note 45 at ch. 8; Inuit of Labrador Agreement, *supra* note 45 at chs. 12, 13; Carcross/Tagish Agreement, *supra* note 45 at chs. 13, 16, 27; Gwich'in Agreement, *supra* note 45 at ch. 14.

68 See Tlicho Agreement, *supra* note 45 at chs. 6, 9, 12, 22; James Bay Agreement, *supra* note 52 at chs. 5, 6, 7; Maa'Nulth Agreement, *supra* note 45 at ch. 9; Tla'Amin Agreement, *supra* note 45 at ch. 12; Inuvialuit Agreement, *supra* note 46 at chs. 13, 14; Inuit of Labrador Agreement, *supra* note 45 at chs. 4–6, 9; Carcross/Tagish Agreement, *supra* note 45 at chs. 10, 11, 17, 18; Gwich'in Agreement, *supra* note 45 at chs. 12, 13, 15, 19, 21, 24, 26;

waste and other forms of pollution remediation and prevention.[69] The terms of the modern treaties which address cultural heritage and natural resources protection directly impact intergenerational equity by ensuring that the resources and heritage passed to the current generation will be available for future generations. These protections, if implemented effectively, would support Canada's commitments under the SDGs, notably SDGs 11 and 12.

Commitments to respond to the threat of climate change play an important, if potentially unintended, role in modern treaty interpretation. This is perhaps best illustrated by the requirement for the use of EIAs for indigenous community, provincial, and national development activities as well as the need to involve indigenous communities in these EIAs and associated decision making regarding development.[70] Additionally, there are laws regarding indigenous community development and preservation that can also relate to strengthening capacity and resilience.[71] General EIA requirements are further supplemented by provisions relating to EIAs in maritime contexts in many of the modern treaties.[72] This includes provisions requiring the joint administration of maritime resources and implementation of laws and rules by the national, provincial, and indigenous authorities.[73] Similar requirements are included in the treaties for EIAs and other forms of administrative monitoring, consultation and oversight of development that impacts indigenous communities in the context of forests, wetlands, and other forms of terrestrial ecosystems.[74] Included in these are specialised Wildlife Impact Assessments, which can be required in key contexts.[75] Related provisions hold that,

69 See Sioux Valley Dakota Agreement, *supra* note 45 at pt. 16.

70 Ibid. at pt. 16.03; Inuvialuit Agreement, *supra* note 46 at chs. 11, 12; Inuit of Labrador Agreement, *supra* note 45 at chs. 10, 11, 17.

71 Inuvialuit Agreement, *supra* note 46 at chs. 11, 12; Inuit of Labrador Agreement, *supra* note 45 at chs. 10, 11, 17; Sioux Valley Dakota Agreement, *supra* note 45 at pt. 16.02; Carcross/Tagish Agreement, *supra* note 45 at pts. 16.9–16.11; Tsawwassen Agreement, *supra* note 44 at ch. 15.

72 Tsawwassen Agreement, *supra* note 44 at chs. 12, 15; Inuvialuit Agreement, *supra* note 46 at secs. 7, 8, 13; Sioux Valley Dakota Agreement, *supra* note 45 at ch. 15.

73 Champagne and Aishihik Agreement, *supra* note 45 at ch. 14(6); Kwanlin Dun Agreement, *supra* note 45 at ch. 14; Kluane Agreement, *supra* note 45 at ch. 14; Little Salmon/Carmacks Agreement, *supra* note 45 at ch. 14; Ta'an Agreement, *supra* note 45 at ch. 14; Inuvialuit Agreement, *supra* note 46 at secs. 7, 8, 13; Inuit of Labrador Agreement, *supra* note 45 at 5, 6, 11, 17; Carcross/Tagish Agreement, *supra* note 45 at chs. 14, 16, 22, 27; Gwich'in Agreement, *supra* note 45 at chs. 12, 19, 24.

74 Inuvialuit Agreement, *supra* note 46 at ch. 10; Inuit of Labrador Agreement, *supra* note 45 at chs. 4, 7, 10, 11; Sioux Valley Dakota Agreement, *supra* note 45 at chs. 15, 16; Carcross/Tagish Agreement, *supra* note 45 at chs. 11, 16, 17; Gwich'in Agreement, *supra* note 45 at 12, 13, 15, 24; Tsawwassen Agreement, *supra* note 44 at ch. 15; Champagne and Aishihik Agreement, *supra* note 45 at chs. 10, 11; Kwanlin Dun Agreement, *supra* note 45 at chs. 10, 11; Kluane Agreement, *supra* note 45 at chs. 10, 11; Little Salmon/Carmacks Agreement, *supra* note 45 at chs. 10, 11; Ta'an Agreement, *supra* note 45 at chs. 10, 11; Tlicho Agreement, *supra* note 45 at ch. 22.2; James Bay Agreement, *supra* note 52 at ch. 5.1.7; Maa'Nulth Agreement, *supra* note 45 at ch. 23; Tla'Amin Agreement, *supra* note 45 at ch. 13.

75 Inuvialuit Agreement, *supra* note 46 at ch. 13.

in most instances applicable, it is important to protect and legally recognise the role of bivalves and other forms of marine wildlife for current and future generations within a particular indigenous community and across Canada as a whole.[76] Of special note for terrestrial resources, the modern treaties contain significant protections for the harvesting of many different forms of wildlife, including those such as caribou, which are of particular import to specific communities and ecosystems.[77] Taken together, these aspects of the modern treaties are geared toward ensuring that intergenerational equity is advanced through protections of natural resources and territories as well as thorough evaluation and understanding of the impacts of potential development practices. In this manner, these modern treaty provisions could directly contribute to the advancement of efforts to achieve SDGs 13, 14, and 15 across Canada.

One of the enduring elements of the modern First Nations treaties with the Canadian government involves the establishment of a variety of governance mechanisms, including committees and boards at the local, provincial, and national levels.[78] While many of these mechanisms are unique to the needs of the communities and territories over which they have jurisdiction, there are some forms that are fairly uniform among the modern treaties.[79] These include joint and cooperative entities for the regulation of hunting and fishing activities, land development, resources management, research activities, and permitting activities.[80] Not only do these mechanisms ensure equality of participation opportunity, they also promote transparency in the governance processes and the inclusion of accountability at all levels of law, policy, regulation, and society.[81] This is essential for passing on equitable and just governance mechanisms to future generations as well as ensuring that future generations exist in a legal system that has entrenched these mechanisms within a sustainable and flexible structure. These provisions and the full implementation of relevant mechanisms for governance, transparency, and accountability at

[76] Tsawwassen Agreement, *supra* note 44 at ch. 9; Champagne Agreement, *supra* note 45 at ch. 16; Kwanlin Dun Agreement, *supra* note 45 at ch. 16; Kluane Agreement, *supra* note 45 at ch. 16; Little Salmon/Carmacks Agreement, ch. 16; Ta'an Agreement, *supra* note 45 at ch. 16; Maa'Nulth Agreement, *supra* note 45 at ch. 10; Tla'Amin Agreement, *supra* note 45 at ch. 9; Inuit of Labrador Agreement, *supra* note 45 at chs. 5, 8, 9; Carcross/Tagish Agreement, *supra* note 45 at ch. 16; Gwich'in Agreement, *supra* note 45 at ch. 12.

[77] Inuvialuit Agreement, *supra* note 46 at chs. 14, 24; Inuit of Labrador Agreement, *supra* note 45 at ch. 12; Carcross/Tagish Agreement, *supra* note 45 at ch. 16; Tsawwassen Agreement, *supra* note 44 at chs. 9–12; Kluane Agreement, *supra* note 45 at ch. 16; Champagne and Aishihik Agreement, *supra* note 45 at ch. 16; Kwanlin Dun Agreement, *supra* note 45 at ch. 16; Little Salmon/Carmacks Agreement, *supra* note 45 at ch. 16; Ta'an Agreement, *supra* note 45 at ch. 16.

[78] See generally ibid.

[79] See ibid.

[80] See ibid.

[81] See ibid.

all governmental levels is also an important way to advance efforts to achieve SDGs 16 and 17 across Canada.

## INITIAL CONCLUSIONS AND FURTHER RESEARCH NEEDS

First Nations negotiated hard, often for many years, to come to terms with the Canadian government in the modern treaties. The accords, in preliminary review, appear to offer an important opportunity to advance greater equity across Canada, particularly for First Nations communities, laying the foundations for implementation that strengthens intergenerational equity. In addition, the terms of the modern treaties demonstrate numerous linkages with and between specific areas of law and policy which could further advance intergenerational equity for indigenous peoples and all Canadians.

As has been demonstrated above, modern treaties include commitments which, if implemented effectively, could greatly enhance efforts to achieve the SDGs across Canada, especially for indigenous peoples. Indeed, nearly every modern treaty reviewed in this chapter has multiple areas of confluence with the SDGs and their targets. At a minimum, there can be identified an opportunity to learn new lessons for ways in which indigenous communities can be brought into discussions on ways to achieve the SDGs on local, regional, provincial and national levels. Further, the interconnections suggest that the implementation of modern treaties and efforts to strengthen and advance the SDGs can be assessed, monitored and analysed together, through the lens of promoting intergenerational equity in new and flexible methods and mechanisms. Further research is need to identify specific instances in which progress in implementing the modern treaties has actually led to improvements in meeting the SDGs by and with First Nations, and to generate key insights into the means by which compliance with treaty obligations for achievement of the SDG targets can improve the lives and livelihoods of current and future generations across Canada.

# 35

# Institutions for Future Generations in Asia

*Antonio G.M. La Viña and Gregorio Rafael P. Bueta*

An unprecedented wave of change has been taking place in the past few decades in the field of environment. The concept of sustainable development is now commonly understood by many people around the world – from its origins during the 1972 UN Conference on the Human Environment (more commonly known as the 1972 Stockholm Conference), up to the recently agreed upon Post-2015 Agenda and the SDGs.[1] The roots of sustainable development go back to the early 1970s, when the UN Declaration in Stockholm proclaimed the second UN Development Decade and the Stockholm Convention first clearly emphasized that environmental protection and economic development must be understood as compatible and mutually reinforcing goals.[2] It has been defined as 'development that meets the needs of the present without compromising the ability of future generations to meet their own needs'.[3]

References to sustainable development conjure ideas of eco- and green living, recycling and reusing, organic products, renewable energy, green buildings, and

[1] See generally UN, *Sustainable Development Goals* www.un.org/sustainabledevelopment/sustainable-development-goals/ accessed 30 November 2017.

[2] U. Beyerlin, 'Different Types of Norms in International Environmental Law: Policies, Principles and Rules', in D. Bodansky et al. (eds.) *The Oxford Handbook of International Environmental Law* 425 at 443 (Oxford University Press 2007); see also A.B.M. Marong, 'From Rio to Johannesburg: Reflections on the Role of International Legal Norms in Sustainable Development' (2000) 16 *Georgetown International Environmental Law Review* 21 (II. Brief History of Sustainable Development, where he says that state practice, cultural norms of indigenous societies, and contemporary non-state actors have contributed to the development of the concept). Marong also adds, '1972 Stockholm Conference is particularly important because even without using the term "sustainable development," the Conference laid a foundation for the integrated consideration of environment and development issues, and established a substratum of understanding especially between developed and developing countries upon which future progress was built' (referring to the preambular paras. 8, 9, 10, 11, and 13 of the Declaration as basis).

[3] G.H. Brundtland et al., *Our Common Future: Report of the World Commission on Environment and Development* (Oxford University Press 1987) 43.

electric cars, to name only a few. However, often left out of the discussion, and not quite regarded as a reason for sustainable development, is the part which refers to the ability of future generations to meet their own needs. People change their lifestyle and habits and change their views and outlook on the environment to ensure a better future for themselves – not necessarily for the generations that will come after.

This is where the concept of intergenerational justice, or intergenerational equity, comes in. One author notes that the concept has been much cited in both official and scholarly circles, and that it rests comfortably in all disciplines.[4] Often regarded as the pioneering definition is Edith Brown Weiss's 1989 doctrine of intergenerational equity, which provides that each generation holds the planet on trust, obliged to pass it to all future generations in no worse condition than that in which they enjoyed it and to provide equal access to its cultural and natural resources.[5] Professor Brown Weiss also cited three basic principles of intergenerational ecological equity: conservation of options, conservation of quality, and conservation of access.[6] The concept of intergenerational equity presents a potential solution to environmental problems whose effects are likely to be spread unevenly over time, or across generations, because of its explicit reference to future generations.[7] Another interesting definition of intergenerational equity was offered by the Foundation for the Rights of Future Generations, which draws upon different disciplines, to wit:

> Intergenerational Justice means that today's children and future generations must be capable to [sic] meet their own needs and fulfil their rights and aspirations to at least the same extent as the generation governing today.[8]

One important method through which intergenerational justice is given life and meaning is inclusion in institutions. These bodies, be they public and governmental instrumentalities or from the private sector, play a key role in promoting and achieving intergenerational justice, and also sustainable development. These institutions work within their respective legal and political frameworks. At the national level, numerous legislative instruments seek to protect the environment for the benefit of present and future generations.[9] As one author puts it, the idea of taking into account the needs of future generations appears in national laws, constitutions,

4 See B.H. Weston, 'Climate Change and Intergenerational Justice: Foundational Reflections' (2008) 9 *Vermont Journal of Environmental Law* 3.

5 E. Brown Weiss, *In Fairness to Future Generations: International Law, Common Patrimony, and Intergenerational Equity* (United Nations University 1989).

6 Ibid.

7 C. Woods, *Intergenerational Equity in Law and Practice* (Oxford University Press 2011).

8 See generally www.intergenerationaljustice.org/ accessed 30 November 2019.

9 J. Anstee-Wedderburn, 'Giving a Voice to Future Generations: Intergenerational Equity, Representatives of Generations to Come, and the Challenge of Planetary Rights' (2014) 1(1) *Australian Journal of Environmental Law* 42.

and international instruments including non-binding declarations, preambles of MEAs, and, most notably, the operative provisions of the UNFCCC.[10]

This chapter will look at how institutions in Asia contribute to the development and fulfilment of intergenerational justice around the world. First will be a brief look at the climate change challenges facing Asia – an area marked by crisis situations which make intergenerational justice seem elusive. This will be followed by an overview of the Asian legal framework for sustainable development and intergenerational justice, looking at constitutional provisions, laws, declarations, resolutions, and some responses to the climate change problem by governments and institutions. A discussion on some significant and noteworthy sustainable development institutions will be made, along with a discussion of best practices. Evolving jurisprudence on sustainable development and intergenerational equity from Asia will be presented, discussing significant cases and recent judicial initiatives and innovations. Finally, challenges faced by institutions for future generations will be identified, followed by lessons learned and recommendations. For the purposes of this chapter, the discussions on Asia will be limited to Southeast and South Asia because of the availability of examples of institutions and case law. East Asia, particularly China, is excluded from this article, as other chapters in the volume tackle these experiences.

## CLIMATE CHANGE IN ASIA: A CRISIS SITUATION

The UNFCCC defined the term as 'a change of climate which is attributed directly or indirectly to human activity that alters the composition of the global atmosphere and which is in addition to natural climate variability observed over comparable time periods'.[11] Climate change as a global concern has risen in prominence and dialogue over the past few decades, owing to its increased impacts on people's lives and property. Climate change is fundamentally a problem of distributive justice for present and future generations and, as such, it is of great urgency to protecting human welfare over the long run.[12]

As the Paris Agreement puts it, climate change represents an urgent and potentially irreversible threat to human societies and the planet.[13] The Agreement further states:[14]

> Climate change is a common concern of humankind, Parties should, when taking action to address climate change, respect, promote and consider their respective obligations on human rights, the right to health, the rights of indigenous peoples,

[10] Ibid. at 38–39.

[11] United Nations Framework Convention on Climate Change (1992) art. 1(2).

[12] M. Zehairi, 'Justice in a Warming World: Global and Intergenerational Justice and Climate Change' https://macsphere.mcmaster.ca/bitstream/11375/11604/1/fulltext.pdf accessed 30 November 2017.

[13] Paris Agreement on Climate Change (2015).

[14] Ibid.

local communities, migrants, children, persons with disabilities and people in vulnerable situations and the right to development, as well as gender equality, empowerment of women and intergenerational equity.

The impacts of climate change are nowhere more evident and devastating than in Asia. The Asia Pacific region is projected to be one of the regions most impacted by climate change, partly because of its high exposure to climate impacts and partly because of the great vulnerability of some areas.[15] These statistics point to the grim reality of climate change in Asia:[16] six of the ten most vulnerable nations to climate change are in Asia and the Pacific;[17] by 2025, 410 million urban dwellers and 341 million people in inland areas will be at increased risk; $63.1 billion in annual damage is caused by disasters in Asia and the Pacific; and 64 million Asians will be pushed into poverty for every 10 per cent rise in food prices due to fewer crop yields. Southeast Asia is highly vulnerable to climate change, as a large proportion of the population and economic activity is concentrated along coastlines, the region is heavily reliant on agriculture for livelihoods, there is a high dependence on natural resources and forestry, and the level of extreme poverty remains high.[18]

More recently, in the IPCC's Fifth Assessment Report, the following significant observations were made on the impact of climate change in Asia.[19] First, warming trends and increasing temperature extremes have been observed across most of the Asian region over the past century. Second, coastal and marine systems in Asia are under increasing stress from both climatic and non-climatic drivers. Third, multiple stresses caused by rapid urbanization, industrialization, and economic development will be compounded by climate change. Fourth, extreme climate events will have an increasing impact on human health, security, livelihoods, and poverty, with the type and magnitude of impact varying across Asia.

The brief discussion above points to a climate crisis situation facing Asia. As the world tries to grapple with the phenomenon and as world leaders and nations prepare to implement new commitments to reduce warming through the Paris Agreement, people across the globe need to continue dealing with the impacts of climate change. In addition, as the crisis situation worsens, the prospects of

[15] Asian Development Bank, *Addressing Climate Change and Migration in Asia and the Pacific* (Asian Development Bank 2012) 19.

[16] See Asian Development Bank, 'Climate Change in Asia and the Pacific' www.adb.org/news/infographics/climate-change-asia-and-pacific accessed 30 November 2017.

[17] These countries are the Philippines, Cambodia, India, Pakistan, and Lao PDR.

[18] ASEAN, *ASEAN Cooperation on Environment* http://environment.asean.org/asean-working-group-on-climate-change/ accessed 30 November 2017.

[19] See generally Y. Hijioka et al., 'Asia', in V.R. Barros et al. (eds.), *Climate Change 2014: Impacts, Adaptation, and Vulnerability. Part B: Regional Aspects. Contribution of Working Group II to the Fifth Assessment Report of the Intergovernmental Panel on Climate Change* (Cambridge University Press 2014) 1327–1370.

achieving true and meaningful intergenerational equity seem bleak. However, all is not lost, and positive developments through various institutions in Asia have given hope to the fulfilment of this generation's responsibility to the next.

## ASIAN LEGAL FRAMEWORK FOR SUSTAINABLE DEVELOPMENT AND INTERGENERATIONAL JUSTICE

Asia is not only at the forefront of the impacts of climate change, it is also developing a pool of significant legal frameworks for sustainable development and intergenerational justice. Many laws in response to the challenge of climate change have been drawn up despite the varying politics of climate change in the region.[20] Regional organizations and bodies have also taken steps to address one of the biggest challenges facing the people of the region, although they have yet to develop much of a profile in creating common policies and response initiatives.[21]

### *Southeast Asia*

The legal framework for sustainable development and intergenerational justice can be found regionally and in several national constitutions in Southeast Asia. The Association of Southeast Asian Nations (ASEAN) was established in 1967 as the regional body for cooperation of the Southeast Asian nations. Its aims and purposes involve cooperation in economic, social, cultural, technical, educational, and other fields, and in the promotion of regional peace and stability through abiding respect for justice and the rule of law and adherence to the principles of the UN Charter.[22] Recognizing the importance of environmental cooperation for sustainable development and regional integration, ASEAN members have, since 1977, cooperated closely in promoting environmental cooperation.[23] ASEAN environmental cooperation focuses on the following priority areas of regional importance

20 See generally C.W. Freeman, III and A. Searight, 'The Politics of Climate Change in Asia (3)', in Center for Strategic and International Studies, *Asia's Response to Climate Change and Natural Disasters: Implications for an Evolving Regional Architecture* (CSIS 2010).

21 T. Schaffer, 'Asian Regional Institutions and Climate Change (45)', in Center for Strategic and International Studies, *Asia's Response to Climate Change and Natural Disasters: Implications for an Evolving Regional Architecture* (CSIS 2010). The author adds, 'Because Asia does not have a single dominant institutional architecture, the consensus-building role is diffused over a variety of organizations and discussion channels with different degrees of authority and varied membership.' Ibid. at 45.

22 ASEAN, ASEAN History http://asean.org/asean/about-asean/history/ accessed 30 November 2017.

23 ASEAN, Environment: About Us http://environment.asean.org/about-us-2/ accessed 30 November 2017.

as reflected in the Blueprint for the ASEAN Socio-Cultural Community (ASCC Blueprint)[24] 2009–2015:[25]

(a) Addressing global environmental issues;
(b) Managing and preventing transboundary environmental pollution;
(c) Promoting sustainable development through environmental education and public participation;
(d) Promoting environmentally sound technology;
(e) Harmonizing environmental policies and databases;
(f) Promoting sustainable use of coastal and marine environment;
(g) Promoting sustainable management of natural resources and biodiversity;
(h) Promoting the sustainability of freshwater resources;
(i) Responding to climate change and addressing its impacts; and
(j) Promoting sustainable forest management.

ASEAN has also provided for an institutional framework for environment,[26] establishing working groups hosted by each Member State on some of the priority areas above.

Climate change has also been a priority for ASEAN. ASEAN has played an active leadership role in addressing climate change in the global community, and stewardship of these initiatives comes from the ASEAN Heads of State and Government themselves.[27] In a joint statement on climate change during the 28th and 29th ASEAN Summits in Vientiane, Laos PDR,[28] the ASEAN leaders expressed grave concern about the impacts of climate change throughout the ASEAN region in areas such as extreme climate event, food, water and energy security, livelihoods, health, land use, and biodiversity, including disproportionate impacts on women and children. However, they reaffirmed their commitment to the UNFCCC, to the Paris Agreement, and to efforts to address climate change that should be consistent with broader SDGs.[29]

In addition, during the 19th ASEAN +3 (China, Japan, and Korea) Summit held in Vientiane, Laos, the States issued a statement on Promoting Sustainable

[24] See ASEAN, ASCC Blueprint www.asean.org/wp-content/uploads/2012/05/8.-March-2016-ASCC-Blueprint-2025.pdf accessed 30 November 2017.

[25] ASEAN, Environment: About Us, *supra* note 23.

[26] See ASEAN, Institutional Framework – ASEAN Cooperation on Environment http://i1.wp.com/environment.asean.org/wp-content/uploads/2015/07/INSTITUTIONAL-FRAMEWORK-ASEAN-COOPERATION-on-ENVIRONMENT.jpg accessed 30 November 2017.

[27] ASEAN, Climate Change http://environment.asean.org/climate-change-page/ accessed 30 November 2017.

[28] ASEAN Joint Statement on Climate Change to the 22nd Conference of the Parties (COP-22) to the United Nations Framework Convention on Climate Change (UNFCCC) http://asean.org/storage/2016/09/ASEAN-Joint-Statement-on-Climate-Change-28th-and-29th-AS-Final.pdf accessed 30 November 2017.

[29] See UN, Sustainable Development https://sustainabledevelopment.un.org/?menu=1300 accessed 30 November 2017; ASEAN Joint Statement, *supra* note 28.

Development Cooperation.[30] The heads of state reaffirmed their commitment to the SDGs and the Paris Agreement and agreed on the promotion of sustainable micro, small, and medium enterprises, as well as sustainable tourism.

The commitment to environmental protection, sustainable development, and intergenerational justice can also be found in several constitutional provisions of select ASEAN States. In Cambodia, article 59 of the Constitution,[31] under Chapter V on the economy, requires the State to preserve and protect the environment and the balance of natural resources.[32] The Constitution of Indonesia, under article 28H (1),[33] states that every person shall have the right to obtain a proper and healthy living environment.[34] In addition, article 33(4) also provides that the organization of the national economy shall be conducted on the basis of environmental perspective, among others.[35] The Lao People's Democratic Republic's article 19 of the Constitution,[36] under Chapter 2 of the Socio-Economic Regime, calls on all organizations and people to protect the environment and natural resources.[37]

The Philippine Constitution contains several provisions relating to the environment.[38] Section 16, in article II on Principles and State Policies, mandates the State to protect and advance the right of the people to a healthful and balanced ecology.[39]

30 ASEAN Plus Three Leader's Statement on Promoting Sustainable Development Cooperation (07 September 2016) http://asean.org/storage/2016/09/Final-ASEAN-Plus-Three-Leaders%E2%80%99-Statement-on-Promoting-Sustainable-Development-Final.pdf accessed 30 November 2017.

31 Constitution of Cambodia www.ccc.gov.kh/english/basic_text/Constitution%20of%20the%20Kingdom%20of%20Cambodia.pdf accessed 30 November 2017.

32 Article 59, Constitution of the Kingdom of Cambodia states, 'The State shall preserve and protect the environment and the balance of natural resources, by organizing a precise planning for the management, especially of the land, water atmosphere, air, geology, ecological systems, mines, energy, petroleum and gas, rocks, sand, gems, forest and forest by-products, wildlife, fish and aquatic resources.' Ibid. at art. 59.

33 Constitution of Indonesia www.setneg.go.id/images/stories/kepmen/legal_product/uud_1945.pdf accessed 30 November 2017.

34 Article 28H(1) of the Constitution of the Republic of Indonesia states, 'Every person shall have the right to lead a physically and mentally prosperous life, to have residence, and to obtain a proper and healthy living environment as well as to obtain health services.' Ibid. at art. 28H(1).

35 Article 33(4), Chapter XIV provides: 'The organisation of the national economy shall be conducted on the basis of economic democracy upholding the principles of togetherness, efficiency with justice, continuity, environmental perspective, self-sufficiency, and keeping a balance in the progress and unity of the national economy.' Ibid. at Article 33(4), Chapter XIV.

36 Constitution of the Lao People's Democratic Republic www.ilo.org/wcmsp5/groups/public/@ed_protect/@protrav/@ilo_aids/documents/legaldocument/wcms_117348.pdf accessed 30 November 2017.

37 Article 19, Chapter 2, Laos PDR Constitution states, 'All organisations and citizens must protect the environment and natural resources: land surfaces, underground [resources,] forests, animals, water sources and the atmosphere.' Ibid. at art. 19.

38 Copy available at www.gov.ph/constitutions/1987-constitution/ accessed 30 November 2017.

39 Section 16, Article II, Constitution of the Republic of the Philippines: 'The State shall protect and advance the right of the people to a healthful and balanced ecology in accord with the rhythm and harmony of nature.'

Another provision enjoins the State to ensure the people's right to health.[40] Article 29 of Vietnam's Constitution, in Chapter 2 on the Economic System,[41] mandates State organs, social bodies, and all individuals to abide by State regulations on the environment.[42] Article 112(5) also provides as one of the powers and duties of the State to take measures to protect the environment.[43] Malaysia and Singapore do not have specific provisions in their constitutions on environmental protection. Brunei Darussalam's constitution also does not have a specific provision on environmental protection, but in a speech during the signing of the new constitution, there was mention of the need to make sacrifices for future generations.[44]

### *South Asia*

South Asia is another region with a long tradition of legal frameworks for environmental protection, sustainable development, and intergenerational equity.[45] At the regional level, the South Asian Association for Regional Cooperation (SAARC) is the regional IGO of States in South Asia. Established in 1985, SAARC has as one of its objectives to promote the welfare of the peoples of South Asia and to improve their quality of life.[46] One of the areas of cooperation identified by SAARC is the environment.[47] With the increasing urgency of responding to its effects,

[40] Section 15, Article II, Constitution of the Republic of the Philippines: 'The State shall protect and promote the right to health of the people and instill health consciousness among them.'

[41] Constitution of Vietnam www.moj.gov.vn/vbpq/en/lists/vn%20bn%20php%20lut/view_detail.aspx?itemid=10450 accessed 30 November 2017.

[42] Article 29, Chapter 2, Constitution of the Socialist Republic of Vietnam: 'State organs, units of the armed forces, economic and social bodies, and all individuals must abide by State regulations on the rational use of natural wealth and on environmental protection. All acts likely to bring about exhaustion of natural wealth and to cause damage to the environment are strictly forbidden.' Ibid. at art. 29(2).

[43] Article 112(5), Constitution of the Socialist Republic of Vietnam: 'To take measures to protect the rights and legitimate interests of the citizen, to create conditions for him to exercise his rights and fulfil his duties, to protect the property and interests of the State and society; to protect the environment.' Ibid. at art. 112(5).

[44] Constitution of the Sultanate of Brunei (2004). 'We have to be prepared to make sacrifices and work harder for a resplendent future, especially for the future generation'; speech by His Majesty Sultan Haji Hassanal Bolkiah Mu'izzaddin Waddaulah ibni Al-Marhum Sultan Haji Omar 'Ali Saifuddien Sa'adul Khairi Waddien, Sultan and Yang di-Pertuan of Brunei Darussalam at the official signing ceremony of the Constitution of Brunei Darussalam (Amendment) Proclamation at the Lapau, Bandar Seri Begawan, Brunei Darussalam, 29 September 2004.

[45] For purposes of this article, South Asia shall be composed of the following countries: Afghanistan, Bangladesh, Bhutan, India, Maldives, Nepal, Pakistan, and Sri Lanka.

[46] See generally the SAARC Charter http://saarc-sec.org/SAARC-Charter/5/ accessed 30 November 2017.

[47] See SAARC, Areas of Cooperation http://saarc-sec.org/areaofcooperation/cat-detail.php?cat_id=54 accessed 30 November 2017.

climate change has become a core issue for SAARC.[48] The Heads of State or Government of the Member States of SAARC have, at successive Summits since 1987, reiterated the need to strengthen and intensify regional cooperation to preserve, protect, and manage the diverse and fragile ecosystems of the region, including the need to address the challenges posed by climate change and natural disasters. The preservation and protection of the environment, including disaster risk reduction and management, remains a high priority on the agenda of cooperation being pursued by the Member States of SAARC.[49]

Regional centres have been established by SAARC to address diverse aspects of environmental issues, climate change, and natural disasters. These centres include the SAARC Coastal Zone Management Centre;[50] the SAARC Forestry Centre;[51] the SAARC Disaster Management Centre;[52] and the SAARC Meteorological Research Centre.[53] A Technical Committee on Environment was also established in 1992 to monitor recommendations of regional studies and to focus on environment, climate change, forestry, and natural disasters.

Several documents issued by SAARC embody its concern for the environment and climate change.[54] The 1997 SAARC Environment Action Plan identified some of the key concerns of Member States and set out the parameters of and modalities for regional cooperation. Another important document is the 2008 Dhaka Declaration and SAARC Action Plan on Climate Change. The Dhaka Declaration requires Member States to undertake activities (1) to promote advocacy programmes and mass awareness on climate change; cooperation in capacity building including the development of clean development mechanism (CDM) projects and designated national authorities, and on incentives for removal of GHG by sinks; (2) to exchange information on best practices, sharing of the results of research and development for mitigating the effects of climate change and undertaking adaptation measures, and for enhancing South–South cooperation on technology development and transfer, as per established SAARC norms; and (3) to initiate and implement programmes

[48] B. Majaw, 'Climate Change and South Asian Association for Regional Cooperation: A Regional Response' (2012) 4:2 *International Journal of Social Sciences* 73 www.sobiad.org/ejournals/journal_ijss/arhieves/2012_2/baniateilang_majaw.pdf accessed 30 November 2017.

[49] Ibid.

[50] See generally SAARC, SAARC Coastal Zone Management Center www.sczmc.org accessed 30 November 2017.

[51] See generally SAARC, SAARC Forestry Centre www.saarcforestrycentre.org accessed 30 November 2017.

[52] See generally SAARC, SAARC Disaster Management Centre www.saarc-sdmc.nic.in accessed 30 November 2017.

[53] See generally SAARC, SAARC Meteorological Research Centre www.saarc-smrc.org accessed 30 November 2017.

[54] See SAARC, Areas of Cooperation http://saarc-sec.org/areaofcooperation/cat-detail.php?cat_id=54 accessed 30 November 2017.

and measures as per SAARC practice for adaptation for dealing with the onslaught of climate change to protect the lives and livelihood of the people.[55]

Complementing the Dhaka Declaration, the objectives of the Action Plan are to identify and create opportunities for activities achievable through regional cooperation and South–South support in terms of technology and knowledge transfer.[56] It also identifies seven thematic areas of cooperation: (1) adaptation, (2) mitigation, (3) technology transfer, (4) finance and investment, (5) education and awareness, (6) management of impacts and risks, and (7) capacity building for international negotiations.

The events in Dhaka in 2008 were followed in Thimphu, Bhutan by the 2010 Thimphu Statement on Climate Change.[57] The Statement outlines a number of important initiatives at the national and regional level to strengthen and intensify regional cooperation to address the adverse effects of climate change in a focused manner, particularly the convening of the Inter-governmental Expert Group on Climate Change.[58]

At the national level, SAARC Member States have also provided their own legal and policy framework for environmental protection and sustainable development. Most SAARC members have climate change action plans and policies in place.[59] National environmental and planning agencies have also been given the task of implementing and monitoring SDGs and initiatives.[60]

Almost all SAARC countries have provisions in their constitutions dealing with the environment. In the 2004 Constitution of Afghanistan,[61] one of the goals cited was the attainment of a sound environment for all inhabitants.[62] Two articles

55 Ibid.

56 Majaw, *supra* note 48 at 75–76.

57 SAARC, Thimpu Statement in Climate Change www.saarc-sec.org/userfiles/ThimphuStatementonClimateChange-29April2010.pdf accessed 30 November 2017.

58 See SAARC, Areas of Cooperation http://saarc-sec.org/areaofcooperation/cat-detail.php?cat_id=54 accessed 30 November 2017

59 See National Climate Change Adaptation for Sri Lanka 2011–2016; National Action Plan on Climate Change of India; National Climate Change Policy in Pakistan; 'Bhutan 2020: A Vision for Peace, Prosperity and Happiness'; Bangladesh Climate Change Strategy and Action Plan (BCCSAP). The Maldives has drafted the National Greenhouse Gas Inventory, National Mitigation Plan, Vulnerability Assessment and Adaptation Options. Nepal has a National Strategy for Sustainable Development (NSSD) under the name of the Sustainable Development Agenda for Nepal (SDAN).

60 See generally United Nations Economic and Social Commission for Asia and the Pacific, *Achieving the Sustainable Development Goals in South Asia: Key Policy Priorities and Implementation Challenges* (UN 2016) 16.

61 Constitution of Afghanistan www.afghanembassy.com.pl/afg/images/pliki/TheConstitution.pdf accessed 30 November 2017.

62 Preamble, Constitution of the Islamic Republic of Afghanistan: 'Attain a prosperous life and sound living environment for all inhabitants of this land . . .' Ibid.

subsequently deal with the environment: article 9 provides that the protection and utilization of natural resources shall be regulated by law;[63] and article 15 obligates the State to protect and preserve forests and the living environment.[64] The Constitution of Bangladesh, in article 18A,[65] provides for the protection and improvement of the environment for present and future citizens.[66]

The Constitution of Bhutan is replete with provisions on the environment.[67] Article 5 on the environment provides for several provisions on environmental protection – the duty of citizens as trustees for the present and future generations; the duties of the government and power holders to enact needed legislation; and the maintenance of 60 per cent forest cover for all time.[68] Article 8(2) states that protection and respect for the environment is a fundamental duty of all Bhutanese.[69] In addition, Article 9(2)

63 'Mines and other subterranean resources as well as historical relics shall be the property of the state. Protection, management and proper utilization of public properties as well as natural resources shall be regulated by law.' Ibid. at art. 6, ch. 1.

64 'The state shall be obligated to adopt necessary measures to protect and improve forests as well as the living environment.' Ibid. at art. 15, ch. 1.

65 Constitution of Bangladesh http://bdlaws.minlaw.gov.bd/pdf_part.php?id=367 accessed 30 November 2017.

66 'Protection and improvement of environment and biodiversity – The State shall endeavour to protect and improve the environment and to preserve and safeguard the natural resources, bio-diversity, wetlands, forests and wild life for the present and future citizens.' Ibid. at art. 18A, pt. II.

67 Constitution of the Kingdom of Bhutan www.nationalcouncil.bt/assets/uploads/files/Constitution%20%20of%20Bhutan%20English.pdf accessed 30 November 2017.

68 Article 5 Environment, Constitution of the Kingdom of Bhutan: '(1) Every Bhutanese is a trustee of the Kingdom's natural resources and environment for the benefit of the present and future generations and it is the fundamental duty of every citizen to contribute to the protection of the natural environment, conservation of the rich biodiversity of Bhutan and prevention of all forms of ecological degradation including noise, visual and physical pollution through the adoption and support of environment friendly practices and policies. (2) The Royal Government shall: (a) Protect, conserve and improve the pristine environment and safeguard the biodiversity of the country; (b) Prevent pollution and ecological degradation; (c) Secure ecologically balanced sustainable development while promoting justifiable economic and social development; and (d) Ensure a safe and healthy environment. (3) The Government shall ensure that, in order to conserve the country's natural resources and to prevent degradation of the ecosystem, a minimum of sixty percent of Bhutan's total land shall be maintained under forest cover for all time. (4) Parliament may enact environmental legislation to ensure sustainable use of natural resources and maintain intergenerational equity and reaffirm the sovereign rights of the State over its own biological resources. (5) Parliament may, by law, declare any part of the country to be a National Park, Wildlife Reserve, Nature Reserve, Protected Forest, Biosphere Reserve, Critical Watershed and such other categories meriting protection.' For an additional discussion of these articles, see L. Sonam Tobgye, *The Constitution of Bhutan: Principles and Philosophies* (Royal Court of Justice of Bhutan 2015) 125–129.

69 Article 8(2), Constitution of the Kingdom of Bhutan: 'A Bhutanese citizen shall have the duty to preserve, protect and respect the environment, culture and heritage of the nation.'

requires the government to ensure conditions for the achievement of Gross National Happiness,[70] one of the tenets of which is a sustainable lifestyle.[71]

In India, articles 48A[72] and 51A(g)[73] of the Constitution contain environment-related provisions,[74] both for the government and the citizens. Article 48A requires the State to protect and preserve the environment, while article 51A(g) lists as one of the duties of Indian citizens the protection and improvement of the natural environment.[75] In the Maldives Constitution,[76] article 22 provides that the State has the fundamental duty to protect and preserve the environment for the present and future generations, and to pursue economic and social goals through ecologically balanced sustainable development.[77] To complement the previous requirement, article 23(2) provides that one of the rights guaranteed by the State is the right to a healthy and ecologically balanced environment.[78]

The youngest constitution among SAARC members belongs to Nepal and was adopted and promulgated in September 2015.[79] Despite its youth, the Nepalese Constitution has the greatest number of provisions relating to environment and sustainable development. Article 30 provides for the right to a clean and healthy environment, which includes the right of a victim of environmental degradation to be compensated, and for the balancing of environment and development.[80]

70 Gross National Happiness has been defined as a concept implying that sustainable development should take a holistic approach towards notions of progress and give equal importance to non-economic aspects of well-being

71 Article 9(2), Constitution of the Kingdom of Bhutan: 'The State shall strive to promote those conditions that will enable the pursuit of Gross National Happiness.'

72 Article 48A, the Constitution of India: 'The State shall endeavour to protect and improve the environment and to safeguard the forests and wild life of the country.'

73 Article 51A(g), the Constitution of India: 'It shall be the duty of every citizen of India: . . . (g) to protect and improve the natural environment including forests, lakes, rivers and wild life, and to have compassion for living creatures.'

74 Ibid.

75 Ibid. at art. 48A.

76 Constitution of the Republic of the Maldives www.presidencymaldives.gov.mv/Documents/ConstitutionOfMaldives.pdf accessed 30 November 2017.

77 Article 22, Constitution of the Republic of the Maldives: 'The State has a fundamental duty to protect and preserve the natural environment, biodiversity, resources and beauty of the country for the benefit of present and future generations. The State shall undertake and promote desirable economic and social goals through ecologically balanced sustainable development and shall take measures necessary to foster conservation, prevent pollution, the extinction of any species and ecological degradation from any such goals.' Ibid.

78 Article 23, Constitution of the Republic of the Maldives: 'Every citizen has the following rights pursuant to this Constitution, and the State undertakes to achieve the progressive realisation of these rights by reasonable measures within its ability and resources: . . . (d) a healthy and ecologically balanced environment.'

79 Constitution of Nepal www.ilo.org/dyn/natlex/docs/MONOGRAPH/100061/119815/F-1676948026/NPL100061%20Eng.pdf accessed 30 November 2017.

80 Article 30, Part II, Constitution of Nepal: Right regarding clean environment: '(1) Each person shall have the right to live in a healthy and clean environment. (2) The victim of environmental pollution and degradation shall have the right to be compensated by the pollutant as provided

Article 35 provides for the right to health care, particularly access to clean water and hygiene.[81] Several policies under article 51 are relevant to sustainable development: proper land utilization by maintaining environmental balance;[82] strategies and programmes for sustainable socio-economic development;[83] and on the conservation, management, and use of natural resources.[84] Sri Lanka's Constitution also has several provisions on the environment.[85] Notably, article 27(14) provides that the protection, preservation, and improvement of the environment are to be part of the directive policies of the State.[86] Additionally, article 28(f) further provides for every citizen's duty to protect nature.[87]

for by law. (3) Provided that this Article shall not be deemed to obstruct the making of required legal provisions to strike a balance between environment and development for the use of national development works.'

81 Article 35, Part II, Constitution of Nepal: 'Right to health care: ... (4) Each citizen shall have the right to access to clean water and hygiene.'

82 Article 51(e)(4), Part III, Constitution of Nepal: '(e) Policies regarding agriculture and land reform: ... (4) Making proper utilization of land through proper regulation and management on the basis of productivity of land, its nature, and also by maintaining environmental balance ...'

83 Article 51(f)(1), Part III, Constitution of Nepal: '(f) Development policy: (1) Formulating strategies and programs for sustainable socio-economic development under regional development plans for balanced and inclusive regional development and to implement them in a coordinated manner ...'

84 Article 51(g), Part III, Constitution of Nepal: 'Policy regarding the conservation, management and use of natural resources: (1) The State shall pursue a policy of conserving the natural resources available in the country by imbibing the norms of inter-generation judicious use of it and for the national interest. It shall also be about its sustainable use in an environmentally friendly way. The policy shall ensure the fair distribution of the benefits generated by it by giving local people the priority and preferential rights. (2) The State shall pursue a policy of prioritizing national investment in water resources based on people's participation and making a multiutility development of water resources. (3) The State shall pursue a policy of developing and producing renewable energy, ensuring cheap, easily available and dependable supply of energy, and making an appropriate use of it to meet the basic needs of the citizens. (4) Developing a sustainable and dependable irrigation system by controlling water-related natural disasters with the management of the river systems. (5) The State shall pursue a policy of making a sustainable use of biodiversity through the conservation and management of forests, fauna and flora, and by minimizing the negative impacts of industrialization and physical development by promoting public awareness on environmental cleanliness and protection. (6) The State shall pursue a policy of keeping necessary landmass as forest area in order to strike an environmental balance. (7) The State shall pursue a policy of adopting appropriate ways of minimizing or stopping negative effects on environment if it is there, or if there is a possibility of such an impact on nature, environment, or biodiversity. (8) The State shall formulate policies and enact laws on the basis of the principle of sustainable environment development based on prewarning and pre-informed agreements regarding environmental protection. (9) The State shall formulate and pursue a policy of designing a prewarning system, disaster preparedness, rescue, relief works and rehabilitation in order to minimize the risks of natural disasters.'

85 Constitution of the Democratic Socialist Republic of Sri Lanka www.parliament.lk/files/pdf/constitution.pdf accessed 30 November 2017.

86 Article 27(14), Constitution of the Democratic Socialist Republic of Sri Lanka: 'The State shall protect, preserve and improve the environment for the benefit of the community.'

87 Article 28(f), Constitution of the Democratic Socialist Republic of Sri Lanka: 'The exercise and enjoyment of rights and freedoms are inseparable from the performance of duties and

The above discussion points to clear mandates for environmental protection in the fundamental laws of almost all Southeast and South Asian States. Indirectly, these provisions can be linked to a desire by these States to achieve sustainable development, and even intergenerational equity. Some constitutions – such as those of Bhutan, the Maldives, and Nepal – explicitly mention the goal of sustainable development in its provisions. More interestingly, some constitutions – such as in Bangladesh, Bhutan, the Maldives, and Nepal – make specific mention of preserving the environment and natural resources for the present and future generations.[88] Asia is not alone, and similar provisions on intergenerational justice in constitutions can be seen in other parts of the world.[89]

There is a strong legal framework in Asia not just for environmental protection but also for achieving the goals of sustainable development and the fulfilment of intergenerational justice. The provisions in these constitutions are translated into laws, policies, and even jurisprudence. This then gives institutions that work for sustainable development the legal mandate needed to pursue their goals and objectives.

## SUSTAINABLE DEVELOPMENT INSTITUTIONS IN ASIA

Institutions play a crucial role in the fulfilment and achievement of sustainable development. It is through these institutions that the goals of sustainable development are given life and meaning and are made a reality for the people. As one study puts it, the successful adoption of policies that ensure sustainability will depend

obligations and accordingly it is the duty of every person in Sri Lanka – . . . (f) to protect nature and conserve its riches.'

88 As noted previously, the preamble of Brunei's Constitution makes mention of future generations.

89 See Anstee-Wedderburn, *supra* note 9 at 43: Bolivia's constitution includes a right to a healthy environment safeguarding the rights of future generation. Political Constitution of the State 2009 (Bolivia) art. 9. Ecuador's constitution provides that 'the State shall exercise sovereignty over biodiversity, whose administration and management shall be conducted on the basis of responsibility between generations'. Constitution of 2008 (Republic of Ecuador) art. 400. Norway's constitution provides for a right to an environment that is conducive to health safeguarded for future generations. Constitution of Norway 1814 (Norway) art. 110(b). South Africa's constitution provides that 'everyone has the right to have the environment protected for the benefit of present and future generations'. Constitution of the Republic of South Africa 1996 (South Africa) art. 24. Kenya's constitution provides for the right to a 'clean and healthy environment . . . protected for the benefit of present and future generations'. The Constitution of Kenya 2010 (Kenya) art. 42. The constitutions of Guyana, Papua New Guinea, Germany, and Vanuatu impose duties to conserve the environment including for future generations. Constitution of the Co-operative Republic of Guyana Act 1980 (Guyana) art. 36; Constitution of the Independent State of Papua New Guinea 1975 (Papua New Guinea) art. 4; Basic Law for the Federal Republic of Germany 1949 (Germany) art. 20a; Constitution of the Republic of Vanuatu 1980 (Vanuatu) art. 7.

crucially on the institutions of a given State.[90] Another study points out that, given the wide range of objectives under the SDGs, a national coordinating and steering agency is critical for effective implementation of the SDGs.[91] Although specifics may vary, all major internationally agreed documents on sustainable development since the Earth Summit emphasized general features that institutions for sustainable development should have:[92] (1) the ability to address the economic, social, and environmental dimensions in a balanced manner; (2) the ability to adopt integrated planning across sectors as much as possible (integrated planning, horizontal coordination, coherence, and consistency); (3) the ability to consider the interests of future generations; (4) the ability to strive to meaningfully to engage all relevant stakeholders in decision-making processes, maintaining an effective balance between top-down and bottom-up processes (participation); and (5) the ability to strive to improve access to information and access to justice.

In Asia, institutions at the regional and national level are also at the forefront of promoting sustainable development and intergenerational justice.

### *Regional Institutions*

Asia's regional organizations differ in membership, scope, and ambition. Within this setting, they have not developed the supranational authority of, for example, the EU, and there seems little appetite in the region for this level of political, economic, and regulatory integration.[93] This becomes relevant given the nature of and challenges brought about by climate change and sustainable development, since an integrated and regional approach is needed to tackle transboundary issues. Each State can also learn from best practices from around the region. It is in this context that the initiatives on sustainable development of these institutions will be discussed.

One study noted the following advantages of regional institutions:[94] (1) regional organizations have a special role, perhaps a unique one, in addressing climate change related issues; (2) regional organizations can also be useful in developing mechanisms for sharing or coordinating physical infrastructure, and in harmonizing

[90] See B. Mueller and C. Mueller, 'The Role of Institutions in Sustainable Development', in Y.- K. Ng and I. Wills (eds.), *Welfare Economics and Sustainable Development, Vol II* (EOLSS 2009).

[91] United Nations Economic and Social Commission for Asia and the Pacific, *Achieving the Sustainable Development Goals in South Asia: Key Policy Priorities and Implementation Challenges* (UN 2016) 16.

[92] United Nations Department of Economic and Social Affairs, *National Institutions for Sustainable Development: A Preliminary Review of the Institutional Literature* (UN 2012) 5 https://sustainabledevelopment.un.org/content/documents/1372Study2_final.pdf accessed 30 November 2017.

[93] T. Schaffer, *supra* note 21. The author adds: 'Because Asia does not have a single dominant institutional architecture, the consensus-building role is diffused over a variety of organizations and discussion channels with different degrees of authority and varied membership.' Ibid. at 46.

[94] Ibid. at 57–58.

standards and policies; (3) regional organizations have an advantage in developing networks of cooperation; and (4) regional organizations play an important role in establishing norms and expectations for regional policies.

Earlier in this chapter, the ASEAN and SAARC initiatives on environment and sustainable development were discussed. To recall, these intergovernmental bodies have committed to the protection and preservation of the environment, and to sustainable development in various ways, be it through documents and declarations, or through the creation of multi-stakeholder institutions to tackle specific issues. Both have also been key players in the international arena, ably representing and attempting to push for the needs and aspirations of the people of the regions.

Another key institution in Asia and the Pacific is the Asia Pacific Economic Cooperation (APEC). It is a regional economic forum established in 1989 to leverage the growing interdependence of the Asia Pacific region. The twenty-one Member States[95] aim to create greater prosperity for the people of the region by promoting balanced, inclusive, sustainable, innovative, and secure growth and by accelerating regional economic integration.[96] Although primarily an economic and trade partnership, APEC as an institution has also worked on the issues of climate change and sustainable development, perhaps in recognition that inclusive economic growth cannot be achieved without addressing these issues.

As early as 1993, APEC's leaders elaborated their mandate for sustainable development: 'our environment is improved as we protect the quality of our air, water and green spaces and manage our energy resources and renewable resources to ensure sustainable growth and provide a more secure future for our people'.[97] This has been followed by further commitments to sustainable development and to its integration into the work of APEC. Sustainable cities, cleaner production, and sustainability of the marine environment were also identified as key areas of concern. In 2007, APEC leaders adopted the Sydney Declaration on Climate Change, Energy Security, and Clean Development.[98] This historic measure, under the leadership of Australia, formally placed climate change on APEC's agenda.[99]

[95] APEC's members include: Australia, Brunei Darussalam, Canada, Chile, the People's Republic of China, Hong Kong, China, Indonesia, Japan, Republic of Korea, Malaysia, Mexico, New Zealand, Papua New Guinea, Peru, the Philippines, the Russian Federation, Singapore, Chinese Taipei, Thailand, the US, and Vietnam.

[96] APEC, About Us www.apec.org/About-Us/About-APEC.aspx accessed 30 November 2017.

[97] APEC, Sustainable Development www.apec.org/Groups/Other-Groups/Sustainable-Development.aspx accessed 30 November 2017.

[98] APEC, Leaders Declarations www.apec.org/Meeting-Papers/Leaders-Declarations/2007/2007_aelm/aelm_climatechange.aspx accessed 30 November 2017.

[99] T. Schaffer, *supra* note 21 at 47.

In the Leader's Declaration during the 2015 APEC Summit held in Manila, Philippines,[100] the heads of government and of State reiterated its commitment to achieving the SDGs,[101] to building sustainable and disaster-resilient communities,[102] and to tackling climate change by supporting the Paris Agreement.[103]

## *National Institutions*

National institutions also play an important role in making sustainable development and intergenerational justice a reality for the people of Asia. In fact, without these bodies and organizations, the goals and aspirations agreed upon by the international community cannot be implemented or become a reality. National institutions translate internationally agreed upon commitments to local laws, policies, plans, and programmes. Some institutions, such as enforcement agencies and the courts, protect and uphold these goals through their actions and decisions. For the purpose of this chapter, the national institutions to be discussed and to be given as examples shall be limited to executive branch agencies, and judicial and quasi-judicial bodies.

[100] APEC, Leaders Declarations www.apec.org/Meeting-Papers/Leaders-Declarations/2015/2015_aelm.aspx accessed November 2017.

[101] 'We reaffirm our commitment to implementing the 2030 Agenda for Sustainable Development ("2030 Agenda"), which sets a comprehensive, universal, and ambitious framework for global development efforts for the next 15 years, and to ensuring that no one is left behind in our efforts to eradicate poverty and build an inclusive and sustainable future for all. We also reaffirm our commitment to implementing the Addis Ababa Action Agenda, which provides a comprehensive roadmap to help economies implement policies to attract and mobilize diverse sources of financing critical for the realization of the Sustainable Development Goals.' Ibid.

[102] 'We welcome and adopt the APEC Disaster Risk Reduction (DRR) Framework to facilitate collective work in building adaptive and disaster-resilient economies supporting inclusive and sustainable development in the face of the "new normal". Through the APEC DRR Framework, we will minimize the losses we endure and ensure that our communities have the support to overcome adversity and to build back better. We instruct Ministers to craft an action plan in 2016 to operationalize the APEC DRR Framework and renew existing efforts such as business continuity planning, strengthening early warning systems, search and rescue, post-disaster recovery, promoting appropriate donations, and enhancing capacity building. We welcome the APEC Principles for the Movement of Humanitarian Goods and Equipment during Emergencies to better protect lives and livelihoods. We also note the Sendai Framework for Disaster Risk Reduction 2015–2030.' Ibid.

[103] 'In line with our goal to promote sustainable communities, we are firmly committed to achieving a fair, balanced, ambitious, durable, and dynamic agreement on climate change at the Paris Climate Conference (COP21) in December. We therefore reaffirm our aspirational goals to reduce aggregate energy intensity by 45 percent by 2035 and double renewable energy in the regional energy mix by 2030 to achieve sustainable and resilient energy development within the Asia-Pacific.' Ibid.

### *Executive Branch Agencies*

The executive branch is broadly the administrative arm of the government, tasked with the implementation and enforcement of laws and policies. In other words, agencies in this part of the government are in charge of the day-to-day working and operations of the State. These are ministries and departments, planning commissions, police and other law enforcers, prosecutors, and other specialized agencies, among others. The same government instrumentalities are given the task of implementing and putting into effect international treaty commitments of their respective countries, which include environmental treaties and SDGs. Examples of these executive branch agencies from the Philippines will be discussed.

### *Climate Change Commission of the Philippines*

The Climate Change Commission of the Philippines (CCC) is the lead policy-making body mandated by the government to coordinate, monitor, and evaluate programmes and action plans relating to climate change pursuant to the Climate Change Act of 2009.[104] The Philippines is the only State in Asia with a climate-change-specific law, which makes the CCC a unique institution, given that its legal mandate comes from a law specifically aimed at tackling climate change.[105] Of note is the state policy declared by the Climate Change Act:

> It is the policy of the State to afford full protection and the advancement of the right of the people to a healthful ecology in accord with the rhythm and harmony of nature. In this light, the State has adopted the Philippine Agenda 21 framework which espouses sustainable development, to fulfill human needs while maintaining the quality of the natural environment for current and future generations.
>
> Towards this end, the State adopts the principle of protecting the climate system for the benefit of humankind, on the basis of climate justice or common but differentiated responsibilities and the Precautionary Principle to guide decision-making in climate risk management.[106]

The law mandates that the CCC and the government's work on climate change be guided by two main documents, the National Framework Strategy on Climate

[104] See generally Government of the Philippines, Climate Change Commission of the Philippines http://climate.gov.ph/ accessed 30 November 2017.

[105] Other climate change government agencies in Asia include, among others, the Ministry of Climate Change in Pakistan, the National Council on Climate Change in Indonesia (created through Presidential Regulation), and the Climate Change Secretariat in Sri Lanka.

[106] Section 2: Declaration of Policy, Republic Act No. 9729 Climate Change Act of 2009 (Philippines).

Change[107] and the National Climate Change Action Plan.[108] These will then be translated into Local Climate Change Action Plans by all the local government units of the country. Some interesting programmes of the CCC include the Communities for Resilience (CORE)[109] and the implementation of the People's Survival Fund.[110]

### *Philippine Environmental Ombudsman*

An ombudsman has been defined as a government official appointed to receive and investigate complaints made by individuals against abuses or capricious acts of public officials.[111] The institution of the ombudsman, first created in Sweden more than 200 years ago, is designed to provide protection for the individual where there is a substantial imbalance of power.[112] Generally understood in most jurisdictions to deal with graft and corruption cases, or to hold public officials accountable, there is increasing recognition of an ombudsman's (or ombudsperson's) role in environmental matters. In an early study, it was stated that, 'The creation of an Office of Environmental Ombudsman ... would provide the citizen with an effective means of challenging the complex bureaucracy of environmental decision-making'.[113] Currently, most ombudsmen have the jurisdiction to deal with environmental issues

107 Government of the Philippines, National Framework Strategy on Climate Change www.neda.gov.ph/wp-content/uploads/2013/10/nfscc_sgd.pdf accessed 30 November 2017.

108 Government of the Philippines, National Climate Change Action Plan www.dilg.gov.ph/PDF_File/reports_resources/DILG-Resources-2012116-d7b64f9faf.pdf accessed 30 November 2017.

109 Through CORE (Communities for Resilience), an improved Ecotown programme, the CCC intends to promote the understanding of climate and disaster risk, especially by communities identified by experts to be more vulnerable to disasters caused by climate change, and strengthen the technical knowledge and capacity of LGUs in developing the Local Climate Change Action Plan (LCCAP) through a series of convergence consultations and trainings; see http://climate.gov.ph/index.php/content/?id=67&Itemid=10 accessed 30 November 2017.

110 The People's Survival Fund (PSF) was created by Republic Act 10174 as an annual fund intended for local government units and accredited local/community organizations to implement climate change adaptation projects that will better equip vulnerable communities to deal with the impacts of climate change. It supplements the annual appropriations allocated by relevant government agencies and local government units for climate-change-related programmes and projects. The Philippine government programmed at least P1 billion into the PSF which will be sourced from the national budget; see http://psf.climate.gov.ph/ accessed 30 November 2017. Other countries with a similar climate change fund include, among others, Bangladesh (Climate Change Trust Fund Act 2010) and the Maldives (Climate Change Trust Fund, supported by the World Bank).

111 Merriam-Webster, Ombudsman www.merriam-webster.com/dictionary/ombudsman accessed 30 November 2017.

112 Ombudsman Association, *About the Role of an Ombudsman* www.ombudsmanassociation.org/about-the-role-of-an-ombudsman.php accessed 30 November 2017.

113 See generally K.J. Ege, 'Enforcing Environmental Policy the Environmental Ombudsman' (1971) 56 *Cornell Law Review* 847 http://scholarship.law.cornell.edu/clr/vol56/iss5/5 accessed 30 November 2017.

indirectly when administrative conduct is involved.[114] Some human rights ombudsmen can also investigate matters involving human rights to the environment if environmental rights are contained in the constitution or other domestic law in the state where they operate.[115] With these developments as background, another unique and interesting development from the Philippines is the designation of an Environmental Ombudsman.[116] Established in 2012, the Environmental Ombudsman has jurisdiction over violations of environmental laws involving public officials and employees. A thirty-person environmental team was designated, with a specific caseload on environmental matters.

One of the first initiatives to be implemented was the Solid Waste Management Compliance Program. It aims to monitor the local government units' compliance with the Philippines' Republic Act No. 9003, or the Ecological Solid Waste Management Act of 2000. The programme is in consonance with the constitutional mandate of the Ombudsman to mobilize State resources, improve governance, and promote the rule of law.[117] Another initiative is the creation of a manual for environmental crime scene investigation for the successful prosecution of cases involving public officials.

### *Judicial and Quasi-Judicial Bodies*

The role of judicial and quasi-judicial bodies is traditionally seen as regards the resolution of commercial and civil disputes, and those related to criminal law. There is, however, growing international recognition that the courts have a crucial role to play in the environmental movement, as recognized in the concept of environmental justice and access to justice – developments in the international sphere have made the courts and the justice system key players in addressing the problems of environmental degradation, global warming, and climate change.[118] This has coincided with the development over the past few decades of environmental law, emerging as one of the youngest fields of law. It is undergoing a process of rapid development caused partly by a quantum leap in our understanding of the environmental challenge[119] and partly by the urgent need for the law to respond in an effective manner.[120]

[114] L.C. Reif, *The Ombudsman, Good Governance, and the International Human Rights System* (Springer 2004) 11.

[115] Ibid.

[116] See generally Environmental Ombudsman, A *Briefing Paper* www.ombudsman.gov.ph/docs/investmentOmbudsman/EnviTeam.pdf accessed 30 November 2017.

[117] Ibid.

[118] See generally C. Redgwell, 'National Implementation', in D. Bodansky, et al. (eds.), *The Oxford Handbook of International Environmental Law* (Oxford University Press 2007).

[119] Judge C.G. Weeramantry, 'Introduction: Judges and Environmental Law', in D. Sheldon and A. Kiss, *Judicial Handbook on Environmental Law* (UNEP 2005) xvii.

[120] B.J. Preston, 'The Role of the Judiciary in Promoting Sustainable Development: The Experience from Asia and the Pacific', paper presented at the Second Kenya National Judicial Colloquium on Environmental Law, Mombasa, Kenya, 17–22 April 2006 http://ssrn.com/abstract=1124804 accessed 30 November 2017.

One area of increasing importance, which has been comparatively little explored in judicial decisions, is the law concerning sustainable development. International, national, provincial, and local law and policymaking bodies may have embraced the principles of sustainable development, but they have been reticent in explicating the meaning, circumstances of application, and precise details of the means of implementation.[121] Since the adoption of sustainable development as the development paradigm, the concept of sustainable development has influenced not only the legal structures governing policymaking but also those concerning dispute settlement.[122]

The recognition of the court's role in environmental matters and in sustainable development has resulted in an increase in environmental courts and tribunals (ECTs).[123] It was recently reported that there are more than 800 authorized ECTs worldwide.[124] These institutions can be the more formal and common judicial bodies such as the regular courts, or quasi-judicial bodies such as environmental tribunals or adjudication boards.

As will be seen in the sample of jurisprudence presented below, judicial and quasi-judicial institutions play an important role in the attainment of sustainable development and the fulfilment of intergenerational equity. It is important to stress the significance of the strong role judges have in determining the content of the principle of intergenerational equity.[125] The leadership role which judges play will be important in bringing the entire legal profession together to meet these objectives since judges influence the development of the practice of law through their decisions and their interaction with lawyers. Their decisions will also help shape government policies towards sustainable development and intergenerational equity. In addition, disputes brought before the courts presenting competing interests can be decided through the lens of sustainable development and the impacts on generations yet to come.

## EVOLVING ASIAN JURISPRUDENCE ON SUSTAINABLE DEVELOPMENT AND INTERGENERATIONAL JUSTICE

Courts have been constantly called upon to protect people's environmental rights and to resolve disputes which may impact the environment. Since the emergence of

[121] Ibid.

[122] M. Orellana, 'Introduction' (2009) X:1 *Sustainable Development Law and Policy* 2.

[123] An environmental court and tribunal has been defined as a public judicial or administrative body, chamber, or official specializing in deciding disputes about environmental, natural resources, land use, development, or related issues. G. Pring and C. Pring, 'Twenty-First Century Environmental Dispute Resolution – Is There an "ECT" in Your Future?' (2015) 33:1 *Journal of Energy & Natural Resources Law* 10.

[124] See generally ibid. The authors noted that 'authorized' does not always mean actually operating. A number of countries have authorized ECTs, but have not followed through and actually set them up or have discontinued them, for budgetary, political, or other reasons.

[125] C. Woods, *Intergenerational Equity in Law and Practice* (Oxford University Press 2011) 20 and www.geog.ox.ac.uk/research/transformations/cewf/wpapers/wpg11-06.pdf accessed 30 November 2017.

the environmental law movement in the 1970s, there has been a steady increase of environment-related jurisprudence around the world. These cases range from the enforcement of environmental laws and regulations and public interest litigation (PIL), to action claimed on the basis of environmental rights enshrined in constitutions or fundamental laws. PIL cases in countries such as the Philippines and India have focused on the following: infringement of the constitutional right to life, enforcement of statutory rights and duties, and giving voice to marginalized or vulnerable sectors of society.[126]

In recent years, due to the increasing impacts of climate change and the heightened awareness that it has brought, environmental litigation has focused on climate change issues and adaptation and mitigation. According to a study by the Sabin Center for Climate Change at Columbia Law School, as cited by the ADB, there have already been more than 500 climate change litigation cases in the US and about 200 cases in the rest of the world.[127] The aim of climate change litigation is to plug the regulatory gaps where possible and call upon the judiciary, which tends to be the least politicized branch of government in most countries, to hold government to its legal responsibilities of protecting people from the immediate and the long-term impacts of climate change.[128] Climate change litigation has been described as a phenomenon that has unfolded with 'breathtaking speed'.[129] Litigation is being utilized both to encourage and challenge consideration of climate change.[130]

The continued development of jurisprudence on environment, climate change, and other related principles will ensure the continued development of case law doctrines for the protection of the environment, more so for sustainable development and intergenerational justice. Given the complex issues surrounding climate change and other competing interests and issues, one can expect an increase in litigation and disputes brought before the courts. Judiciaries will thus be called to task to ensure that sustainable development, a globally agreed upon development paradigm, and intergenerational justice are given life, fulfilment, and meaning through jurisprudence.

In some of the sample cases below, sustainable development and intergenerational justice were not directly discussed nor used as basis by the courts. However, these cases demonstrate the openness and willingness of Asian judiciaries to make decisions in favour of nature, the people's right to a clean and healthy environment,

126 J. Lin, 'Litigating Climate Change in Asia' (2014) 4(4) *Climate Law* 140–149 at 143.

127 Welcome Remarks by ADB President Takehiko Nakao at the Third Asian Judges Symposium on Law, Policy and Climate Change, 26 September 2016, Manila, Philippines www.adb.org/news/speeches/welcome-remarks-third-asian-judges-symposium-law-policy-and-climate-change-takehiko accessed 30 November 2017.

128 Lin, *supra* note 126 at 142.

129 R.F. Blomquist, 'Comparative Climate Change Torts' (2012) 46 *Valparaiso University Law Review* 1053.

130 M. Wilensky, *Climate Change in the Courts: As Assessment of Non-US Climate Change Litigation* (Sabin Center for Climate Change Law 2015) at 35.

and conserving and developing our resources in a sustainable manner to protect the interests of generations to come.

## Bangladesh

### *Farooque* v. *Government of Bangladesh*

The petitioner sought government action against vehicle generated pollution, owing to the worsening air quality in Dhaka, the capital of Bangladesh.[131] The Supreme Court of Bangladesh ruled that the government failed to safeguard the citizen's fundamental constitutional rights by allowing vehicular pollution to pose a deadly threat despite the enactment of legislation and regulations. The Court ordered the government to take urgent preventive measures, including compliance with and enforcement of international petroleum standards and the phasing out of two- and three-wheelers.

### *Bangladesh Environmental Lawyers Association* v. *Bangladesh*

The case concerned ship breaking yards that pose environmental, safety, and health hazards to the public, particularly child labourers.[132] The Supreme Court of Bangladesh directed the closing of ship breaking yards that were operating without the necessary environmental clearance. The Court also directed various actions to be undertaken by the government to prevent future environmental harm, and a committee was established to monitor compliance with court orders.

## India

### *MC Mehta* v. *Union of India*

This case has been credited with starting the public interest litigation movement in India.[133] MC Mehta, an environmentalist and advocate, filed the petition highlighting the chaotic traffic conditions and air pollution in the Indian capital, Delhi. In granting the petition and the adoption of the continuing mandamus procedure, several orders have been issued spanning a period of more than thirty years, with some orders being issued as recently as 2015.

Some of the more significant orders issued by the Supreme Court of India are the following: all government-owned vehicles to run on compressed natural gas (1995); plying of commercial vehicles fifteen years and older prohibited beginning 1998 (1998); creation of an Environmental Pollution (Prevention and Control)

[131] 22 BLD 345 (2002)

[132] Writ Petition 7260 of 2008.

[133] Writ Petition No. 13029 in 1985.

Authority (1998), which has subsequently issued numerous orders; and imposition of an environmental protection charge on the purchase of luxury diesel vehicles (2016).

### *MC Mehta* v. *Kamalnath and Others*

The Supreme Court of India had occasion to use the polluter pays principle and the public trust doctrine in this case.[134] A private company had built a motel on the banks of the River Beas. It eventually encroached on adjacent land and conducted works to change the flow of the river, resulting in flooding and blockage of the river's natural flow. The Court had this to say on the public trust doctrine: 'The State as a trustee is under a legal duty to protect the natural resources. These resources meant for public use cannot be converted into private ownership. Thus the public trust doctrine is part of the law of the land.'

### *Animal Welfare Board* v. *A. Nagaraja*

In this case,[135] which involved the ban on the use of bulls in *jallikattu*,[136] bull races, bullfights, or any other type of performance, the Supreme Court of India had occasion to enunciate a species best interest standard:

> Every species has an inherent right to live and shall be protected by law, subject to the exceptions provided out of necessity. Animal has also honour and dignity which cannot be arbitrarily deprived of and its rights and privacy have to be respected and protected from unlawful attack.[137]

### *MC Mehta* v. *Union of India*

In this case, known as the *Taj Trapezium* case, the Supreme Court of India applied the principle of sustainable development while taking note of the disastrous effects that the emissions from the Mathura Oil Refinery had on the Taj Mahal.[138] The Court also passed various orders and monitored compliance with the same.

### *State of Himachal Pradesh* v. *Ganesh Wood Products*

In this case, Ganesh Wood Products challenged an order of the State refusing the establishment of katha factories on the ground that this will lead to indiscriminate felling of the so-called khair trees, which would have a deep and adverse effect

[134] 1 SCC 388 (1997).

[135] 7 SCC 547 (2014).

[136] *Jallikattu* is a traditional bull-baiting sport played in Tamil Nadu, India as a part of Pongal celebrations on Mattu Pongal day.

[137] See *supra* note 134.

[138] AIR 1997 SC 734.

upon the environment and ecology of the State.[139] Using the principles of intergenerational equity and sustainable development, the Supreme Court of India upheld the decision of the State government, remanded the case to the lower courts for additional hearings, and prohibited industries from setting up factories until matters have been settled in the lower courts.

### *Nepal*

***Prakash Mani Sharma* v. *His Majesty's Government Cabinet Secretary et al.***

The petition sought to quash a government decision allowing unfettered import of diesel taxies and leaded petrol from India.[140] The Supreme Court of Nepal held that a healthy environment is a prerequisite to the protection of the right to personal freedom under the Indian Constitution and that the State has a primary obligation to protect the right to personal liberty by reducing environmental pollution as much as possible. Based on the concept of sustainable development, the Court stated that the environment cannot be ignored for development. The Court issued a directive to enforce essential measures within a maximum of two years in order to reduce vehicular pollution in the Kathmandu Valley.

### *Pakistan*

***Ashgar Leghari* v. *Federation of Pakistan***

The petitioner, Leghari, a law student, claimed that government's failure to implement its climate change policies offended his fundamental rights, in particular the constitutional principles of social and economic justice.[141]

He also submitted that international environmental principles such as the doctrine of public trust, sustainable development, the precautionary principle, and intergenerational equity form part of the fundamental rights. As a response and in an unprecedented move, the Lahore High Court ordered the establishment of a Climate Change Commission to effectively implement the climate change policies of the region. The Commission is multi-sectoral and multi-stakeholder, composed of twenty-one representatives from relevant government agencies as well as from non-government organizations. Regular reports on implementation are to be submitted to the court for monitoring.

[139] AIR 1996 SC 149.
[140] Writ Petition No. 3440 1996, 2003 decision of the Supreme Court of Nepal.
[141] Writ Petition No. 25501 2015, Lahore High Court.

## Philippines

### *Minors Oposa* v. *Factoran*

The most celebrated decision on intergenerational justice from the Philippines Supreme Court was in *Minors Oposa* v. *Factoran*,[142] in which the petitioners asserted, and the Court accepted, that they represented both their own interests and those of future generations.[143] The petitioners prayed for the cancellation of all existing timber licence agreements (TLAs) and the cessation of the issuance of new TLAs. The petitioners claim that 'they represent their generation as well as generations yet unborn'.[144] The respondent Secretary of Environment and Natural Resources argued that the issue is a political question beyond the ambit of the courts. In allowing the petitioners to sue on behalf of unborn generations on the grounds of intergenerational justice, the Court granted the petition on the basis of the Philippine Constitution's declared state policy on the right to a balanced and healthful ecology. The Court also said that this right has a correlative duty to refrain from impairing the environment. The Philippine Supreme Court has repeatedly used the *Oposa* case as basis for allowing citizen's suits for and on behalf of future generations.[145]

### *Metropolitan Manila Development Authority* v. *Concerned Residents of Manila Bay*

In this case, the Philippine Supreme Court had occasion to issue a Writ of Continuing Mandamus in the implementation of its decision.[146] The government agencies went on to appeal a decision of the Regional Trial Court, finding them liable for the pollution and unsafe water quality in Manila Bay. The concerned residents argued that the water quality in the Bay had fallen below acceptable standards and the government did not take heed of the dangers that this posed to public health and to marine life. The Court ordered the relevant government agencies to clean up Manila Bay and to submit regular reports on its status, pursuant to the writ of continuing mandamus issued. A multi-sectoral committee was also created to comply with the Court's order.

[142] G.R. No. 101083, July 30, 1993, 224 SCRA 792.

[143] Anstee-Wedderburn, *supra* note 9 at 43.

[144] See *supra* note 142.

[145] See *Arigo* v. *Swift*, G.R. No. 206510, September 16, 2014, concerning damage by an American warship to the Tubbataha Reef protected area; *Collado* v. *Court of Appeals*, G.R. No. 107764, 04 October 2002, 390 SCRA 343, holding that protection of watersheds is an intergenerational responsibility.

[146] G.R. Nos. 171947–48, December 18, 2008, 574 SCRA 661.

***Resident Marine Mammals* v. *Reyes***

The Philippine Supreme Court gave standing to the resident marine mammals of Tañon Strait,[147] as represented by individuals known as Stewards.[148] The petitioners challenged a petroleum service contract entered into by the government on the grounds that said exploration activities will cause adverse ecological impact. The Court stated that owing to the enactment of the Rules of Procedure for Environmental Cases,[149] wherein citizens suits are allowed and citizens can file petitions as stewards of nature, the petitioners and the Stewards have standing to sue. As regards the petroleum exploration contract, the Court also ruled that it violated environmental laws for being within a protected area (a marine reserve) and for non-compliance with Philippine EIA laws.

***ISAAA* v. *Greenpeace Southeast Asia (Philippines)***

Petitioners Greenpeace Southeast Asia (Philippines) challenged the *Bt talong* (genetically modified eggplants), which they argued were not fit for human consumption and harmful to the environment.[150] Petitioners asked the Court to apply the precautionary principle since the real effects of genetically modified eggplants have not been fully studied and tested. The Philippine Supreme Court, affirming the Court of Appeals, ruled that, on the basis of the precautionary principle, the Philippine National Biosafety Framework needed to be operationalized first before any further testing could be conducted. The Court also took cognizance of the experience of India with genetically modified eggplants and that the Supreme Court of India had issued an indefinite moratorium on all testing and commercialization of such products until government amended the regulations. Recently, however, the Supreme Court reversed itself and dismissed the petition as being moot and academic since the field trials had already been completed by the time the Court of Appeals made the decision to stop them.

## *Sri Lanka*

***Bulankulama* v. *Secretary, Ministry of Industrial Development* (the Eppawela Case)**

This case involved a proposed agreement between the government and a private company on the potential mining of phosphate and other minerals in the Eppawela area.[151] Many residents of Eppawela objected, claiming that the mining activities

[147] The 'Resident Marine Mammals' in the petition are the toothed whales, dolphins, porpoises, and other cetacean species that inhabit the waters in and around the Tañon Strait.

[148] See https://www.elaw.org/ph.tanon.15 accessed 18 May 2020.

[149] See discussion below.

[150] G.R. No. 209271, 8 December 2015; see Resolution, 26 July 2016.

[151] Application No. 884/99, Supreme Court of Sri Lanka 243 (7 April 2000).

will result in environmental and economic disaster. The Supreme Court of Sri Lanka observed that the government was the 'trustee' of natural resources in Sri Lanka and, as such, the individual residents had standing to sue. The Court recognized that the public trust doctrine includes the notion of public guardianship as 'the organs of state are guardians to whom the people have committed the care and preservation of the resources of the people'.[152]

***Watte Gedara Wijebanda* v. *Conservator General of Forest***

This case concerned the denial of petitioner's application for a mining/quarrying permit by the concerned government authority.[153] The government argued that the mining site was near a national reserve and some archaeological sites. The Supreme Court of Sri Lanka held that, while environmental rights are not specifically alluded to under the fundamental rights chapter of the Sri Lankan Constitution, the right to a clean environment and the principle of intergenerational equity with respect to the protection and preservation of the environment are inherent in a meaningful reading of equal protection provisions of the Constitution.

## JUDICIAL INITIATIVES

### *Philippine Environmental Rule of Procedure*

The Supreme Court promulgated, in 2010, the *Rules of Procedure for Environmental Cases* (Rules).[154] They were crafted 'to primarily protect and advance the constitutional right of the people to a balanced and healthful ecology'[155] and

> to provide a simplified, speedy, and inexpensive recourse for the enforcement of environmental rights and duties by introducing and adopting innovations and best practices to ensure the effective enforcement of remedies and redress for violation of environmental laws.[156]

More importantly, the Rules expressly enable 'the courts to monitor and exact compliance with orders and judgments in environmental cases'.[157]

As discussed earlier, in *Oposa* v. *Factoran*,[158] the Supreme Court liberalized the rules on standing by recognizing the principle of intergenerational equity. The Rules carry on this tradition by further liberalizing the requirements on *locus standi*. Environmental cases for the enforcement of rights and obligations under

[152] Ibid.
[153] SC Application No. 118/2004, Supreme Court of Sri Lanka.
[154] A.M. No. 09-6-8-SC, April 2010.
[155] A. La Viña, *Philippine Law and Ecology, Vol. II* (2012), 197–198.
[156] Ibid.
[157] Ibid.
[158] G.R. No. 101083, 30 July 1993.

environmental laws may be initiated through a citizen suit filed by a Filipino citizen in representation of others, including minors or generations yet unborn.[159]

The provision on citizen suits must be read in relation to Rule 2, Section 4, which requires civil actions to be brought by any real party in interest, including the government and juridical entities authorized by law. The term 'real party in interest' must be understood in its ordinary meaning in which the environmental action must be brought by the party who stands to benefit from or be injured by the judgment in the suit, or the party entitled by the avails of the suit. Hence, Section 4 requires that the civil action is initiated by the real party in interest, while Section 5 requires only that one is a Filipino citizen and that the suit is filed in the public interest, with no proof of personal injury needed.[160]

In citizen suits, courts may grant relief which may include the protection, preservation, or rehabilitation of the environment and the payment of attorney's fees, costs, and other litigation expenses. A court may also require the violator to submit a programme for rehabilitation or restoration of the environment and contribute to a special trust fund to finance implementation of that programme.[161]

A particularly interesting provision included in the Rules is the Strategic Lawsuit against Public Participation (SLAPP). This refers to any legal action filed against any person who is involved in the enforcement of environmental laws, the protection of the environment, or the assertion of environmental rights, as a means to harass, vex, exert undue pressure on, or stifle any legal recourse by the defendant. In other words, true to its abbreviation, a SLAPP is a retaliatory suit to stifle a person or office that seeks to enforce environmental laws or assert environmental rights.[162]

This defendant, in such an action, can assert that the case filed against them is a SLAPP and hope for damages, attorney's fees, and costs of suit. A responsibility is then placed upon the petitioner to prove that their complaints are not simply meant to discourage or dissuade the defendant from a separate legitimate action against them.

The inclusion of this provision in the Rules is an excellent example of an exercise in foresight on the part of the Court. It anticipates both delaying and retaliatory action from violators of environmental rights, and protects individuals and institutions that uphold these rights. It likewise safeguards the sanctity of the judicial process and the right of recourse to the courts.

Another useful remedy provided in the Rules is the Writ of Continuing Mandamus earlier established by jurisprudence in *MMDA* v. *Concerned Residents of Manila Bay*. Under the Rules, a continuing mandamus is available as a remedy when a government agency or officer unlawfully neglects a duty imposed upon it by

[159] Rule 2, § 5, Rules of Procedure for Environmental Cases.
[160] La Viña, *supra* note 156 at 197–198.
[161] Rule 5, § 1, Rules of Procedure for Environmental Cases.
[162] La Viña, *supra* note 156 at 197–198.

law in connection with the enforcement or violation of environmental laws, rules, and regulations, or rights, or unlawfully excludes another from the use or enjoyment of such right.[163]

This writ allows the court to require the government agency or officer to perform an act or series of acts until the judgment is fully satisfied and to submit periodic reports on its progress. The court may evaluate and monitor compliance with its judgment, by itself or through a commissioner or appropriate government agency.[164] The remedy of continuing mandamus is further unique in that it allows the award of damages where government agencies or officers maliciously neglect to perform their duties.[165]

Finally, the Rules of Procedure created the Writ of *Kalikasan* (nature), a judicial remedy in case of 'environmental damage of such magnitude as to prejudice the life, health or property of inhabitants in two or more cities or provinces'.[166] A petition for the issuance of the Writ of *Kalikasan* is a form of special civil action in environmental cases. Currently, the trend is for the Supreme Court to remand the petition to the Court of Appeals for reception of evidence and rendition of judgment. So far, none of the Court of Appeals' decisions have been brought up to and decided upon by the Supreme Court.

## ASIAN JUDGES NETWORK ON ENVIRONMENT

The Asian Judges Network on Environment (AJNE) was formally launched during the Second Asian Judges Symposium on Environment, held in Manila in December 2013.[167] Supported by a project with the ADB, AJNE is an information- and experience-sharing arrangement among senior judges of ASEAN and SAARC Member States, committed to providing a dynamic forum for judicial capacity building and multilateral exchanges on environmental adjudication. AJNE's website also contains environment-related laws, rules, regulations, and case law of various Asian countries. Under the AJNE, a combination of roundtables, which serve as capacity development events, and various knowledge products have resulted in significant achievements in various judiciaries in Asia.[168] Green benches have been established in Bhutan, Malaysia, Pakistan, and the Philippines.[169] In Pakistan, the Supreme Court constituted a Committee on Enhancing Environmental Justice to

[163] Rule 8, Sec. 1. Rules of Procedure for Environmental Cases
[164] Ibid. at § 7.
[165] Rule 8, § 1, Rules of Procedure for Environmental Cases.
[166] FN To come
[167] See generally www.ajne.org accessed 30 November 2017.
[168] See ibid.
[169] See G.R.P. Bueta, Opening Remarks, Strengthening Capacity for Environmental Law in Malaysia's Judiciary: Train-the-Judges Program, 10–13 July 2017, Bangi, Malaysia www.ajne.org/sites/default/files/event/7112/session-materials/opening-remarks-ttj.pdf accessed 30 November 2017.

oversee judicial efforts on environmental justice, such as development of an environmental law curriculum for judicial academies.[170] In Sri Lanka, a South Asian Judges Training Centre on Environmental Rule of Law and Sustainable Green Development was created with support from its President.[171] Indonesia has also instituted a Judicial Certification Program on the Environment.[172] At a regional level, the ASEAN judiciaries have convened a Judicial Working Group on the Environment.[173]

## CONCLUSION

The discussions in this chapter show that Asia as a region has the potential to continue working for sustainable development and future generations. In most States, the necessary legal framework, through constitutions and fundamental laws, is in place, and there is thus sufficient awareness and understanding of the magnitude of the environmental problems the region faces, particularly climate change. This is then supported by the various institutions such as executive branch agencies and the judiciary.

Of particular note are developments in the various judiciaries of Asia. As one eminent judge puts it, the role of the judiciary in relation to the law of sustainable development is thus of the greatest importance.[174] The jurisprudence and cases discussed – and there are many more available – show the judges' commitment to environmental protection and sustainable development. Judiciaries in Asia are willing to do their part to protect nature and promote intergenerational justice. One recent study made the following observation on Asian judiciaries:[175]

> First, most if not all constitutions confer protection on the fundamental right to life. It is open to judiciaries to interpret the right to life to include ecological balance and the right to a healthy environment. Secondly, while the public-trust doctrine that underlies the 'atmospheric trust' cause of action that was pursued in the road-sharing case has developed extensively through common law, it is not inapplicable in civil-law systems . . . Even in civil-law systems that do not use the nomenclature

[170] Asian Development Bank, *South Asia Conference on Environmental Justice: Bhurban, 24–25 March 2012* (ADB 2013).

[171] I. Ahsan, *ADB's Role in Strengthening Environmental Governance and the Asian Judges Network on Environment*, presentation during the Fourth South Asia Judicial Roundtable on Environment, 28–29 November 2015, Kathmandu, Nepal www.ajne.org/sites/default/files/event/9/session-materials/01-ms.-irum-ahsan.pdf accessed 30 November 2017.

[172] Ibid.

[173] Ibid.

[174] B.J. Preston, 'The Role of the Judiciary in Promoting Sustainable Development: The Experience from Asia and the Pacific', paper presented at the Second Kenya National Judicial Colloquium on Environmental Law, Mombasa, Kenya, 17–22 April 2006 http://ssrn.com/abstract=1124804 accessed 30 November 2017.

[175] Lin, *supra* note 126 at 148–149.

> of the public trust, functional equivalents of the doctrine can be found. The public-trust doctrine offers a promising avenue for climate change litigation that should be explored in both common-law and civil-law jurisdictions. Finally, there are good reasons to be cautious about judicial overreach into the policy arena or having unrealistic expectations about the role of the judiciary in climate governance. However, at this stage of nascent development of climate change litigation in Asia, it can be argued that such concerns are premature. At this point in time, more, not less, involvement by the three branches of government is warranted.

Efforts to work with judiciaries to build their capacity to handle more environmental cases, particularly with the impending increase in climate change litigation, should be scaled up. Judicial networks and initiatives such as the AJNE can be supported, allowing Asian judges to learn from the experiences of judges from other regions around the world. Information and experience sharing between judiciaries can also be improved, with best practices being replicated in handling specific cases. Specialist judges, green benches, and even ECTs can be designated and established. Judges and other institutions for future generations need the support of the general public to enable them to do their work. Executive branch agencies, most with limited capacity and resources, need assistance from NGOs and other civil society organizations in areas such as enforcement of environmental laws and capacity building. Implementation of laws, a perennial challenge for many governments, can also be strengthened through cooperation. Most countries have good environmental laws, and the problem is with enforcement and putting things on paper into practice. Judiciaries also need the public's help, since good decisions cannot be made if cases are not brought before the courts. Courts should be seen as partners in the protection of the environment and the promotion of sustainable development. Expert witnesses, assistance in understanding scientific evidence, and cooperation with court orders are also possible areas of collaboration and assistance.

As new development goals have been set through the SDGs, future generations can see a glimmer of hope from institutions in Asia. However, the road ahead will be challenging, as climate change's impacts are set to increase, and these institutions' commitment to sustainable development and intergenerational justice will be put to the test. For executive agencies, implementation of environmental laws and the provision of basic services will be harder. As for judiciaries, their already clogged dockets will see more environment and climate change litigation and disputes over competing interests. These institutions cannot do it alone – it is up to all citizens to support these institutions to ensure a healthy and liveable future for generations to come.

# PART VI

# Future Trends

# 36

# Equity across Generations in Implementing International Law on Water

*Otto Spijkers*

Water law regulates the use of freshwater resources, such as rivers, lakes, wetlands, aquifers, and glaciers. A considerable challenge is to ensure that these resources remain in good health, so that future generations can make use of them as well. The most urgent problems facing efforts to ensure the sustainable utilization of these freshwater resources include water pollution, depletion of non-rechargeable underground water and fossil water, and diversion of freshwater resources in a way that negatively affects the ecosystem of which such resources often constitute the beating heart.[1]

If one cares about the needs and interests of future generations, it is thus necessary for the present generation to use these freshwater resources sustainably, in a way that does not compromise the ability of future generations to benefit from the same resources. There are different ways to give substance to this obligation of sustainable use.[2] It could be argued that the present generation must leave freshwater resources

[1] On freshwater ecosystems, see e.g. O. McIntyre, 'The Protection of Freshwater Ecosystems Revisited: Towards a Common Understanding of the "Ecosystems Approach" to the Protection of Transboundary Water Resources' (2014) 23:1 *Review of European Community and International Environmental Law* 88–95.

[2] See e.g. E. Brown Weiss, *In Fairness to Future Generations: International Law, Common Patrimony, and Intergenerational Equity* (United Nations University 1989); S. Roy Chowdhury, 'Intergenerational Equity: Substratum of the Right to Sustainable Development', in S. Roy Chowdhury and E. Denters (eds.), *The Right to Development in International Law* (Nijhoff 1992) 233–257; E. Brown Weiss, 'Intergenerational Equity: A Legal Framework for Global Environmental Change', in E. Brown Weiss (ed.), *Environmental Change and International Law: New Challenges and Dimensions* (United Nations University Press 1992); E. Brown Weiss, 'Intergenerational Equity and Rights of Future Generations', in T. Buergenthal and P. Nikken (eds.), *The Modern World of Human Rights: Essays in Honour of Thomas Buergenthal* (IIDH 1996) 601–619; K.I. Vibhute, 'Environment, Present and Future Generations: Intergenerational Equity, Justice and Responsibility' (1998) 38:1 *Indian Journal of International Law* 65–73; L.M. Collins, 'Revisiting the Doctrine of Intergenerational Equity in Global Environmental Governance' (2007) 30:1 *Dalhousie Law Journal* 79–140; M. Fitzmaurice, 'Intergenerational Equity Revisited', in G. Hafner and I. Buffard (eds.), *International Law*

in the exact same condition in which it found them. According to a report of the UN Secretary-General, 'nearly all human traditions recognize that the living are sojourners on Earth and temporary stewards of its resources'.[3] It could also be argued that the present generation can fully exploit these resources, as long as it provides future generations with a viable alternative, or that the present generation can fully exploit the resources as long as the present generation provides future generations with the means (technologies) to repair what the present generation has destroyed. Of course, a middle position is also available: one could argue that the present generation must find an equitable balance between satisfying its own needs and leaving enough for future generations to satisfy their needs. Leaving an *equitable* share of the benefits and burdens of freshwater utilization to future generations is not the same as leaving them an *equal* share, but it means more than leaving to future generations only the minimal resources they need to stay alive. After all, from the previous generations, the present generation inherited much more than that. It could be argued that what the past generations offered to the present generation, the present generation now owes to future generations. In short, the general question of equity across generations also resurfaces in the context of water resources management and exploitation.

The aim of this chapter is not to go into the philosophical debate on what exactly is owned to the future generations, and why, and how much. The aim is more modest. It is to give an overview of some actual examples of how international water law agreements have attempted to achieve an equitable intergenerational balance. This intergenerational balance needs to be found within the legal framework of (international) water law. The foundational principles of this framework are (1) the principle of equitable and reasonable utilization, and (2) the no harm rule, which calls upon States to do all they can – the due diligence obligation – to prevent significant harm, done from the territories under their control, to other States. The

*between Universalism and Fragmentation: Festschrift in Honour of Gerhard Hafner* (Nijhoff 2008) 195–229; D. Shelton, 'Intergenerational Equity', in R. Wolfrum and C. Kojima (eds.), *Solidarity: A Structural Principle of International Law* (Springer 2010); E. Brown Weiss, 'Implementing Intergenerational Equity', in M. Fitzmaurice, D.M. Ong, and P. Merkouris (eds.), *Research Handbook on International Environmental Law* (Elgar 2010); G.E. Henderson, 'Rawls and Sustainable Development' (2011) 7:1 *McGill International Journal of Sustainable Development Law and Policy* 1–32; C. Wolf, 'Environmental Ethics, Future Generations and Environmental Law', in A. Marmor (ed.), *The Routledge Companion to Philosophy of Law* (Routledge 2012) 397–413; B.H. Weston, 'The Theoretical Foundations of Intergenerational Ecological Justice: An Overview' (2012) 34:1 *Human Rights Quarterly* 251–266; P. Lawrence, 'Justice for Future Generations: Environment Discourses, International Law and Climate Change', in B. Jessup and K. Rubenstein (eds.), *Environmental Discourses in Public and International Law* (Cambridge University Press 2012) 23–46; *Intergenerational Solidarity and the Needs of Future Generations*, Report of the Secretary-General of the United Nations, UN Doc. A/68/322 (15 August 2013).

3 *Intergenerational Solidarity and the Needs of Future Generations*, *supra* note 2 at 4.

focus in this contribution is on the first principle, because this is the principle which can most naturally connect with the principle of intergenerational equity.

First, it is necessary to briefly explain why the no harm rule has much less potential to become an intergenerational equity protection principle. The no harm rule reflected in Article 7 of the Convention on the Non-Navigational Uses of International Watercourses ('Watercourses Convention'),[4] is as follows:

> Watercourse States shall, in utilising an international watercourse in their territories, take all appropriate measures to prevent the causing of significant harm to other watercourse States.

The general no harm rule applies *intra*generationally: it applies in the relations between neighbouring States. It does not apply *inter*generationally: it does not protect future generations from harm caused by the present generation. It is important to note here that the provision on preventing pollution, Article 21 of the Watercourses Convention, allows for a more intergenerational interpretation. It calls upon States to prevent the pollution of an international watercourse 'that may cause significant harm to other watercourse States *or to their environment*, including harm to human health or safety, to the use of the waters for any beneficial purpose *or to the living resources of the watercourse*'.[5]

In any case, in scholarship, there is little support for an intergenerational interpretation of the general no harm rule, and there appear to be no hints supporting such an intergenerational approach. And, thus, the more promising route to take is to focus on an intergenerational interpretation of the equitable use principle, as reflected *inter alia* in Article 5 Watercourses Convention, on which more below. The central question of this contribution is thus: *What is the link between the principle of intergenerational equity and the principle of equitable and reasonable utilization in (transboundary) water law?*

The research question refers to the principle of intergenerational equity, and not to sustainable development. Many of the agreements that will be analysed in this contribution refer to the latter. For example, Article 5 of the Watercourses Convention links equitable and reasonable utilization to sustainable utilization, and not explicitly to intergenerational equity. It is thus apt to say a few words about the relationship between sustainable utilization (or sustainable development) and the principle of intergenerational equity.

According to the highly influential UN report 'Our Common Future', the essence of sustainable development is that the development policy of States must meet the needs of the present generation without compromising the ability of future

4 Convention on the Law of the Non-Navigational Uses of International Watercourses (entry into force 17 August 2014), UNDoc. A/51/869, or as annex to UNGA Resolution A/RES/51/229 of 21 May 1997.

5 See O. McIntyre, *Environmental Protection of International Watercourses under International Law* (Ashgate 2007).

generations to meet their own needs.[6] And the essence of the legal principle of intergenerational equity is that States ought to conserve and use the environment and natural resources for the benefit of both present and future generations.[7] In short, to understand how sustainable development and intergenerational equity relate to each other in the language of international law, it is best to see the former as an *objective* of the international community and the latter as one of the *legal principles* that must be applied in order to achieve this objective. Intergenerational equity is not the only legal principle relevant for realizing the objective of sustainable development. Other relevant principles include *intra*generational equity, public participation, and the principle of integration of the social, economic, environmental, and human rights aspects of development.[8] The latter has been linked in interesting ways to the intergenerational equity principle, raising the (philosophical) question about the possibility of human rights of future generations.[9]

Before directly addressing the central question, it is perhaps useful to further delineate the research by clarifying what this contribution is *not* about. First of all, this contribution does not purport to analyse the principle of intergenerational equity in a general sense, but only in its application to water resources. The principle might have a different meaning depending on the natural resource and context to which it is applied – be it air, sunlight, oil, gas, forests, plants, animals, or water. Or it might permit a cross-cutting application, regardless of the resource, as is proposed for example in the so-called 'sustainable landscape approach to development'.[10] In this

[6] *'Our Common Future': Report of the World Commission on Environment and Development*, transmitted to the General Assembly by the Secretary-General on 4 August 1987, UN Doc. A/42/427, para. 27.

[7] Summary of Proposed Legal Principles for Environmental Protection and Sustainable Development, adopted by the WCED Experts Group on Environmental Law, published in *Our Common Future*, principle 2.

[8] See especially the Rio Declaration on Environment and Development, published in the Report of the UNCED, held in Rio de Janeiro, between 3 and 14 June 1992, UNDoc. A/CONF.151/26/Rev.I (Vol I) ('Rio Declaration on Environment and Development'). The UN General Assembly unanimously endorsed this declaration in resolution 47/190, adopted 22 December 1992. And see the New Delhi Declaration of Principles of International Law relating to Sustainable Development, adopted by the International Law Association (April 2002) UN Doc. A/CONF.199/8, and published, with an introduction by N. Schrijver (2002) *Netherlands International Law Review* 299–305.

[9] On the human right to water, see General Comment No. 15 adopted by the UN Committee on Economic, Social and Cultural Rights in 2002. Besides reference in human rights documents, the human right to water is also referred to in typical water law agreements such as the London Protocol on Water and Health to the 1992 Helsinki Convention, the Charter of the Senegal Waters of 2002, the Charter of the Niger Waters of 2008, and the 2012 Water Charter of the Lake Chad Basin. This is seldom if at all linked to any rights future generations may have. See also O. McIntyre, 'Environmental Protection and the Human Right to Water: Complementarity and Tension', in L. Westra, C.L. Soskolne, and D.W. Spady (eds.), *Human Health and Ecological Integrity: Ethics, Law and Human Rights* (Routledge 2012).

[10] See e.g. D. Treguer and E. Pehu, *Moving toward a Sustainable Landscape Approach to Development* (World Bank Group 2014).

contribution, a position in this debate will not be taken, and limit ourselves to an analysis of the water law context. This is not to suggest that the principle of equity has evolved in that context in splendid isolation. Indeed, developments elsewhere – take the law of the sea as an example – do feed into the process of evolution of the principle as applied to water resources.[11] But an examination of this cross-fertilization falls beyond the scope of this paper.

Second, this is a chapter about water *law*; it is only indirectly about moral or philosophical obligations or theories of intergenerational equity. Third, the focus is on an analysis of *existing* international and domestic water law, not on how the law *ought* to read. This chapter is thus largely descriptive in nature, not normative. At the same time, the international and domestic regulations and policies referred to in this paper might serve as examples for States that have not yet adopted similar regulations and policies. They have been selected because they contain interesting ideas on how to give meaning to intergenerational equity in the framework of water law. They are to be considered *best practices*, and, as mentioned above, thus do not necessarily paint a representative picture of the current state of water law. Most water law pays much less attention to intergenerational equity than the examples referred to in this paper.

Fourth, this chapter does not look at *regional* water law, such as the water law of the EU. To do so would require an exploration of the particularities of this specific regional legal order, without which it is difficult to understand the EU legislation in this field. At the same time, it must be kept in mind, when we analyse some of the agreements between States that are members of the EU, and when we analyse the domestic water law of some EU Member States, that these are heavily influenced by EU water law, especially the Water Framework Directive of 2000.[12]

This chapter is structured as follows. The next section examines the principle of intergenerational equity as reflected in the Watercourses Convention. This Convention is selected as starting point because it is the only convention on general international water law that was prepared and drafted at the global level – the level of the UN – in part with the aim of codifying already existing CIL. This was certainly the case for Article 5 of the Watercourses Convention, the provision which contains the principle of equitable and reasonable use. The idea is that this

[11] See T. Cottier, *Equitable Principles of Maritime Boundary Delimitation: The Quest for Distributive Justice in International Law* (Cambridge University Press 2015).

[12] Water Framework Directive, directive 2000/60/EC, adopted by the European Parliament and the Council of Ministers of the EU on 23 October 2000. The aim of the Directive was to promote a more coherent water policy with the adoption of a European framework for water management and water protection for each river basin district. There are plenty of references to sustainable development therein. Most importantly, Article 1 identified the establishment of a framework for the protection of water resources which 'prevents further deterioration and protects and enhances the status of aquatic ecosystems' and 'promotes sustainable water use based on a long-term protection of available water resources' as one of the purposes of this Directive.

will help get an accurate picture of the content of this fundamental principle of international water law. The third section of the chapter looks at more specific international regulations in the field of freshwater management. The agreements referred to have all been selected because they contain interesting ideas on how to give meaning to intergenerational equity in the framework of international water law. Together they constitute a collection of innovative and progressive suggestions of how to build on the fundamental principles of international water law, adding a more pronounced intergenerational, or 'green', layer to them. Taken together, the selected international regulations certainly do not provide a representative picture of the current state of international water law. Not all water-related agreements pay as much attention to intergenerational equity as the examples referred to in this paper. What they do is provide an interesting collection of best practices. The fourth and fifth sections of the chapter look at examples of domestic law and policies in which the principle of intergenerational equity has been applied in the context of water management in an interesting way. Finally, the chapter ends with a general conclusion.

## THE PRINCIPLE OF INTERGENERATIONAL EQUITY IN THE WATERCOURSES CONVENTION

How does the principle of intergenerational equity take shape in international water law? To find the answer, the Watercourses Convention is the starting point. This multilateral treaty is generally considered to provide the global legal framework. It does not have that many State Parties; however, it is generally considered to reflect CIL, binding on all States.[13]

International water law deals mostly with the shared utilization of transboundary rivers, lakes, aquifers, and their ecosystems. Traditionally, international water law was primarily about obligations one State owed to another State with which it happened to share a particular freshwater resource. This explains the predominance in international water law of the so-called 'no harm principle', which says that any State must take all appropriate measures to prevent any use of an international watercourse, located within its territory, causing significant harm *to another State*. A similar provision is Article 2 of the Convention on the Protection and Use of Transboundary Watercourses and International Lakes of the UNECE, according to which States must 'prevent, control and reduce any transboundary impact'.[14] Transboundary impact is defined, in Article 1(2) of the same convention, as 'any significant

[13] As of September 2017, the Convention has thirty-six State parties.

[14] Convention on the Protection and Use of Transboundary Watercourses and International Lakes (entry into force 6 October 1996). The Convention had forty-one State parties by September 2015.

adverse effect on the environment . . . within an area under the jurisdiction of another Party'.[15] The UNECE Convention is the other global convention on international water law, coexisting together with the Watercourses Convention.

The no harm rule thus protects one State from harmful effects caused by activities of another State – or activities taking place within the territory of another State. But, as explained already briefly above, it does not protect the future generations from harmful effects caused by the present generation. In recent years, attention is increasingly paid to obligations the present generation owes to future generations with whom it also 'shares' a freshwater resource. How can and does international water law deal with these concerns? This is a question about *inter*generational equity, i.e. the relationship between the present generation and future generations, and not about *intra*generational equity, i.e. the relationship between different communities (States) existing within the present generation.[16] One could imagine a version of the no harm rule which prohibits both intra- and inter-generational harm:

> *Watercourse States shall, in utilising an international watercourse situated within their territories, take all appropriate measures to prevent the causing of significant harm to both the present and future generations of other watercourse States as well as their own.*

Such an approach to the no harm rule is so far not reflected in existing international water law.[17] But existing international water law is not formulated in such a way as to explicitly exclude such an intra- and inter-generational version of the no harm rule interpretation, or hinder its emergence through practice.

Existing international water law is not entirely silent when it comes to intergenerational relations and concerns. The Watercourses Convention's Preamble already makes it explicit that ensuring the promotion of the sustainable utilization of international watercourses is done 'for present and future generations'. It thus links sustainable utilization to the principle of intergenerational equity in a way that

[15] Article 2 of the UNECE Convention.

[16] For some recent scholarship on the principle of intergenerational equity, see e.g. J. Spier, 'Intergenerational Equity: An Aspiration or an Effective Weapon?', in A. Papaux and S. Zurbuchen (eds.), *Philosophy, Law and Environmental Crisis* (Swiss Institute of Comparative Law 2016); Z. Hadjiargyrou, 'A Conceptual and Practical Evaluation of Intergenerational Equity in International Environmental Law' (2016) 18: 3–4 *International Community Law Review* 248–277; C. Redgwell, 'Principles and Emerging Norms in International Law: Intra- and Inter-generational Equity', in C.P. Carlarne, K.R. Gray, and R.G. Tarasofsky (eds.), *The Oxford Handbook of International Climate Change Law* (Oxford University Press 2016); C. Molinari, 'Principle 3: From a Right to Development to Intergenerational Equity', in J.E. Viñuales, *The Rio Declaration on Environment and Development: A Commentary* (Oxford University Press 2015).

[17] See also the Berlin Rules, Commentary to Article 8. The Berlin Rules on Water Resources, approved by the ILA's Water Resources Law Committee in 2004 (2004) 71:II *International Law Association Reports of Conferences* 334–421.

was explained above. But the most relevant provision is Article 5 Watercourses Convention, which reads as follows (where relevant):[18]

> Watercourse States shall in their respective territories utilise an international watercourse in an equitable and reasonable manner. In particular, an international watercourse shall be used and developed by watercourse States with a view to attaining optimal and sustainable utilisation thereof and benefits therefrom, taking into account the interests of the watercourse States concerned, consistent with adequate protection of the watercourse.

Article 5 does not make explicit whether the obligation of equitable utilization is restricted to balancing the uses of different States sharing a watercourse at present times (*intra*generational equity) or whether it includes an obligation to balance the rights and uses of the present and the future generation (*inter*generational equity).

One might expect the reference to 'sustainable utilization' in Article 5 to be of some relevance here. But the International Law Commission (ILC), which is responsible for the drafting of the provision, said very little about the intended meaning of 'sustainable utilization'.[19] And thus others jumped in to provide a definition. An interesting proposal came from the International Law Association. In 2004, it defined 'sustainable use' as follows:

> The integrated management of resources to assure efficient use of and equitable access to waters for the benefit of current and future generations while preserving renewable resources and maintaining non-renewable resources to the maximum extent reasonably possible.[20]

The suggestion was to link sustainable use to equitable use in such a way that equitable use implies an obligation to ensure equitable access to waters for both present and future generations. If Article 5 of the Watercourses Convention makes one thing clear, it is that the obligation of equitable and reasonable utilization of an international watercourse includes sustainable utilization thereof. But what does

[18] According to the Convention's Preamble, the Watercourses Convention was inspired by a shared conviction among States that 'a framework convention will ensure the utilization, development, conservation, management and protection of international watercourses and the promotion of the optimal and sustainable utilization thereof for present and future generations'.

[19] International Law Commission, 'Draft Articles on the Law of the Non-Navigational Uses of International Watercourses and Commentaries Thereto' (1994) II *Yearbook of the International Law Commission* Pt. Two. This has a good reason: the reference to 'sustainable use' was added at the request of the Netherlands and Finland, when the ILC's Draft Articles on the Law of the Non-Navigational Uses of International Watercourses, which were finished in 1994 and constituted the basis of the text of the Watercourses Convention (which was itself adopted in 1997), were discussed by the States. See the Summary records of the 15th meeting of the Sixth Committee of the UN General Assembly, held on Tuesday, 8 October 1996, UN Doc. A/C.6/51/SR.15, p. 2.

[20] Berlin Rules, Article 3(19). The Commentary explains that this definition was derived from declarations on sustainable development, such as the Rio Declaration of 1992.

this mean concretely? Article 6 of the Watercourses Convention might be of some help here. This provision reads as follows (where relevant):

> Utilization of an international watercourse in an equitable and reasonable manner within the meaning of article 5 requires taking into account all relevant factors and circumstances, including ... existing *and potential* uses of the watercourse.

In the ILC commentary accompanying this provision, it is explained that inclusion of this factor in the list was done 'in order to emphasize that neither [existing nor potential use] is given priority, while recognizing that one or both factors may be relevant in a given case'.[21] In other words, the existing and potential uses of the watercourse must be balanced against each other.

The UNECE Convention has a clear reference to future generations. According to this Convention, State Parties to the Convention shall be guided, *inter alia*, by the principle that 'water resources shall be managed so that the needs of the present generation are met without compromising the ability of future generations to meet their own needs'.[22] This is a clear reference to the concept of sustainable development as defined in the Brundtland Report.

## FUTURE GENERATIONS IN SPECIFIC INTERNATIONAL AGREEMENTS

How is the principle of intergenerational equity reflected in specific international agreements regulating the use of a particular transboundary watercourse? That is the question to be addressed in this section.

This chapter looks at the agreements regulating the joint management of the River Danube,[23] the River Meuse,[24] the Orange-Senqu River,[25] the river between

[21] ILC, *Draft Articles and Commentaries Thereto Adopted by the Drafting Committee on Second Reading* (ILC 1994) 101.

[22] UNECE Convention art. 2(5)(c). See O. Spijkers, 'The Sustainable Development Goals as Catalyst for the Sustainable Management of Water Resources' (2015) 24 *Journal of Water Law* 115–125; O. McIntyre, 'The Principle of Equitable and Reasonable Utilisation', in A. Tanzi, O. McIntyre, A. Kolliopoulos, A. Rieu-Clarke, and R. Kinna (eds.), *The UNECE Convention on the Protection and Use of Transboundary Watercourses and International Lakes* (Brill Nijhoff 2015).

[23] Convention on Co-operation for the Protection and Sustainable Use of the River Danube (entry into force in 1998). The text is available at the official website of the International Commission for the Protection of the Danube River www.icpdr.org/ accessed 30 November 2017.

[24] Accord concernant la protection de la Meuse (Agreement on the protection of the Meuse) (signed on 26 April 1994, no longer in force); Accord international sur la Meuse (International Agreement on the Meuse) (entry into force in 2006) www.meuse-maas.be/ accessed 30 November 2017.

[25] Agreement for the Establishment of the Orange-Senqu Commission (signed 3 November 2000). The text is available on the website of the Orange-Senqu River Commission (ORASECOM) at www.orasecom.org/about/agreements.aspx accessed 30 November 2017.

Senegal and Mauritania,[26] Lake Tanganyika,[27] and the Niger River basin,[28] the Guarani Aquifer,[29] and the transboundary rivers shared by Kazakhstan and China.[30] The agreements are examined in chronological order below.[31]

### *Danube*

The Danube Convention is full of references to the imperative need for a balance between present and future generations' interests, short and long term, economy and the environment.[32] Already in the Preamble, the States expressed concern 'over the occurrence and threats of adverse effects, in the short or long term, of changes in conditions of watercourses within the Danube River Basin on the environment, economies and well-being of the Danubian States'. This has motivated the States to strive for a 'lasting improvement and protection' of the Danube River and 'sustainable water management'.[33]

[26] Charte des Eaux du Fleuve Sénégal (Charter of Senegal River Waters) (signed on 28 May 2002). The text is available at the website of the Organisation pour la Mise en Valeur du fleuve Sénégal (OMVS) www.portail-omvs.org/ accessed 30 November 2017.

[27] Convention on the Sustainable Management of Lake Tanganyika (entry into force in 2005) http://lta.iwlearn.org/documents/the-convention-on-the-sustainable-management-of-lake-tanganyika-eng.pdf accessed 30 November 2017.

[28] La Charte de l'eau du bassin du Niger (Niger Basin Water Charter) (signed on 30 April 2008). The text is available at the website of the Autorité du Bassin du Niger www.abn.ne/ accessed 30 November 2017.

[29] Guarani Aquifer Agreement (signed on 2 August 2010, entry into force 26 November 2020) http://faolex.fao.org/docs/pdf/mul-143888English.pdf accessed 30 November 2017.

[30] Agreement between the Government of the Republic of Kazakhstan and the People's Republic of China on water quality protection of transboundary waters (into force on 22 February 2011) http://faolex.fao.org/docs/texts/bi-110874.doc (only in Chinese and Russian) accessed 30 November 2017. On this treaty, see O. Spijkers, X. Li, and L. Dai, 'Sustainable Development in China's International and Domestic Water Law' (2015) 24(5/6) *Journal of Water Law* 207 at sec. 2.1.

[31] The aim is not completeness, but to identify certain interesting examples. This discussion could also have referred to, *inter alia*, Agreement on the Cooperation for the Sustainable Development of the Mekong River Basin (adopted 5 April 1995); Agreement on the Nile River Basin Cooperative Framework of 2009. For a useful collection of water law materials, see http://internationalwaterlaw.org/documents/ accessed 30 November 2017.

[32] For some recent scholarship, see R. Moynihan, 'The Contribution of the UNECE Water Regime to Transboundary Cooperation in the Danube River Basin', in A. Tanzi, O. McIntyre, A. Kolliopoulos, A. Rieu-Clarke, and R. Kinna, *supra* note 22; M. Ambrus, 'Legitimacy Narratives in Polycentric Water Law and Governance: The Strategies of the Danube Commission' (2014) 11 *International Organizations Law Review* 83–113; I. Grexa, 'La gestion commune des fleuves internationaux: l'exemple de la Convention sur le Danube de 1948', in B. Aurescu and A. Pellet (eds.), *Actualité du droit des fleuves internationaux: acte des journées d'etude des 24 et 25 octobre 2008* (Pedone 2010); M. Koyano, 'Effective Implementation of International Environmental Agreements: Learning Lessons from the Danube Delta Conflict', in T. Komori and K. Wellens (eds.), *Public Interest Rules of International Law: Towards Effective Implementation* (Ashgate 2009).

[33] Danube Convention, *supra* note 23 at preamble.

Looking at the operative paragraphs, one sees that Article 2 of the Danube Convention defines as the objective to 'strive at achieving the goals of a sustainable and equitable water management'. The Danubian States pledge to take measures aimed at the 'sustainable development and environmental protection of the Danube River', in particular the 'sustainable use of water resources for municipal, industrial and agricultural purposes as well as the conservation and restauration of ecosystems'. Here, we thus find a clear reference to a 'green' version of the principle of equitable utilization, taking intergenerational and sustainable interests into account.

Article 5, on prevention, control, and reduction of transboundary impact, imposes an obligation on States to take all sorts of measures 'to ensure efficient water quality protection and sustainable water use and thereby also to prevent, control and reduce transboundary impact'.[34] It is clear from this formulation that the obligation to prevent transboundary impact or harm is secondary to the obligation of equitable and sustainable use.[35] Clearly, then, the intergenerational references in the treaty are linked to equitable utilization, and not to the no harm rule.

### *Meuse*

The purpose of the old Accord concernant la protection de la Meuse was to 'preserve and improve the quality of the Meuse'.[36] The Agreement urged States to abide by certain principles that are all central to sustainable development, including the precautionary principle, the principle of prevention, and the polluter pays principle.[37] The States also pledged to consult each other in order to ensure the sustainable development of the river.[38] The Agreement did not refer to equitable

[34] For the linkage between the Danube and the UNECE Convention, see e.g. Moynihan, 'The Contribution of the UNECE Water Regime to Transboundary Cooperation in the Danube River Basin', *supra* note 32.

[35] Transboundary impact is defined as follows: 'Any significant adverse effect on the riverine environment resulting from a change in the conditions of waters caused by human activity and stretching out beyond an area under the jurisdiction of a Contracting Party. Such changes may affect life and property, safety of facilities and the aquatic ecosystems concerned.' Ibid. at art. 1(c). Article 6 elaborates on the measures States must take to avoid transboundary impact and strive towards sustainable and equitable use of the water resources.

[36] Accord concernant la protection de la Meuse at art. 2(1). On this old agreement, see e.g. J. Verhoeven, 'De La Haye à Gand en passant par Charleville-Mézières: histoires d'Escaut et de la Meuse', in R. Andersen et al. (eds.), *En hommage à Francis Delpérée: itinéraires d'un constitutionnaliste* (Bruylant 2007); J. van Dunné, 'Transboundary Pollution and Liability Issues: Private Law vs Public International Law Approaches: The Cases of the Rivers Rhine and Meuse' (1999) *Acta juridica* 303–338; J. Verhoeven, 'Les accords de Charleville-Mézières du 26 avril 1994 sur l'Escaut et sur la Meuse' (1997) 43 *Annuaire français de droit international* 799–809; Pierre d'Argent, 'L'évolution du Statut juridique de la Meuse et de l'Escaut: une mise en perspective des Accords de Charleville-Mézières du 26 avril 1994' (1997) 30 *Revue belge de droit international* 133–171.

[37] Accord concernant la protection de la Meuse at art. 3(2).

[38] Ibid. at art. 3(5).

utilization. The no harm principle was only referred to in the paragraph on the precautionary principle, in the sense that States may not use lack of scientific certainty as excuses not to take measures to prevent transboundary impact.[39]

The new Accord international sur la Meuse, adopted a few years later, was made to replace the older agreement.[40] Again, there is no explicit reference to the two foundational principles of international water law, but there is again a reference to the same principles of sustainable development referred to in the previous agreement.[41]

### *Orange-Senqu River*

Another interesting example is the Agreement for the Establishment of the Orange-Senqu Commission.[42] In the Preamble, the States express a commitment 'towards the realization of the principle of equitable and reasonable utilization, as well as the principle of sustainable development with regard to the River System'.[43] The two principles thus need to be taken into account, but that says little about how the two relate to each other.

If one looks at the provision on the tasks of the Council – the highest body of the Orange-Senqu Commission – one sees that one of its tasks is to advise the Parties on 'the equitable and reasonable utilization of the water sources in the River System to support sustainable development in the territory of each Party'.[44] This suggests that equitable use must be regarded as a means to ensure sustainable development. That is a clear indication that we must interpret the principle of equitable use in a sustainable context, i.e. as referring to both intra- and inter-generational equity.

The Agreement also contains an article outlining the obligations of the States themselves. These provisions are very much modelled after the Watercourses Convention. The equitable utilization principle reads as follows:

> The Parties shall, in their respective territories, utilise the resources of the River System in an equitable and reasonable manner with a view to attaining optimal and sustainable utilisation thereof, and benefits therefrom, consistent with adequate protection of the River System.[45]

39 Ibid. at art. 3(2).

40 For some background on implementation, see A. van Heezik, 'In Troubled Waters: Transboundary Meuse River Basin Politics', in N. Disco and A. van Heezik (eds.), *Different Strokes for Different Folks: 50 Years of Agreements and Disagreements in the Rhine, Meuse, Scheldt and Ems River Basins* (Eburon Academic Publishers 2014).

41 Accord international sur la Meuse at art. 3(1).

42 For some background and context, see e.g. I. Jacobs, *The Politics of Water in Africa: Norms, Environmental Regions and Transboundary Cooperation in the Orange-Senqu and Nile Rivers* (Continuum 2012).

43 Agreement for the Establishment of the Orange-Senqu Commission, Preamble.

44 Ibid. at art. 5.2.2.

45 Ibid. at art. 7.2.

Similarly, the no harm rule is worded as follows:

> The Parties shall, in utilising the resources of the River System in their territories, take all appropriate measures to prevent the causing of significant harm to any other Party.[46]

This general no harm rule is worded in a purely inter-State way. But further down, one finds an interesting application of the no harm principle, which is formulated as follows:

> The Parties shall individually and jointly prevent, reduce and control pollution of the River System that may cause significant harm to one or more of the Parties, including harm to the environment, or to human health or safety, or to the ecosystem of the River System.[47]

Especially the latter phrase suggests a more expansive interpretation of the no harm rule, one that also protects the environment itself from harm, regardless of whether neighbouring States may suffer the consequences.

Since frequent reference is made in the Agreement to the Revised Protocol on Shared Watercourses in the Southern African Development Community (SADC),[48] it might be interesting to take a look at this regional treaty as well.[49] The Protocol was inspired by a conviction of the 'need for coordinated and environmentally

[46] Ibid. at art. 7.3.

[47] Ibid. at art. 7.13.

[48] According to Articles 7.3 and 7.13 of the Agreement for the Establishment of the Orange-Senqu Commission, both the terms 'equitable and reasonable' and 'significant harm' must be interpreted in line with the Revised Protocol on Shared Watercourses in the Southern African Development Community.

[49] See e.g. F. Sindico and S. Hawkins, 'The Guarani Aquifer Agreement and Transboundary Aquifer Law in the SADC' (2015) 24(3) *Review of European, Comparative & International Environmental Law* 318–329; R. Kinna, 'The UNECE Water Convention Viewed from the Perspective of the SADC Revised Protocol on Shared Watercourses', in A. Tanzi (ed.), *The UNECE Convention on the Protection and Use of Transboundary Watercourses and International Lakes* (Brill 2015); D. Malzbender and A. Earle, 'Southern Africa', in F.R. Loures and A. Rieu-Clarke (eds.), *The UN Watercourses Convention in Force: Strengthening International Law for Transboundary Water Management* (Earthscan 2013); P. Canelas de Castro, 'Regional Responses to the Glocal Water Crisis: the EU and SADC Experiences compared', in F. Laursen (ed.), *The EU and Federalism: Polities and Policies Compared* (Ashgate 2011); S. Lindemann, 'Success and Failure in International River Basin Management: The Case of Southern Africa', in H.G. Brauch (ed.), *Facing Global Environmental Change: Environmental, Human, Energy, Food, Health and Water Security Concepts* (Springer 2009); P. van der Zaag, 'Southern Africa: Evolving Regional Water Law and Politics', in J. Dellapenna and J. Gupta (eds.), *The Evolution of the Law and Politics of Water* (Springer 2009); L.J. Kotzé, 'The Southern African Development Community Experience in Shared Watercourse Governance', in S. Hart (ed.), *Shared Resources: Issues of Governance* (IUCN 2008).

sound development of the resources of shared watercourses in the SADC Region in order to support sustainable socioeconomic development'.[50]

Pursuant to this conviction, one of the protocol's principal objectives is to 'promote a coordinated and integrated environmentally sound development and management of shared watercourses'.[51] The term 'management' is defined in the framework of sustainable development, as follows:

> 'Management of a shared watercourse' means ... planning the sustainable development of a shared watercourse [and] promoting the rational, equitable and optimal utilisation, protection, and control of the watercourse.[52]

Another principal objective is to 'advance the sustainable, equitable and reasonable utilisation of the shared watercourses'.[53] The States are free to use the watercourses within their territory, as long as this is done in accordance with the protocol's principles. Different ways of using the watercourse are identified, including environmental use.[54] The latter is defined as 'the use of water for the preservation and maintenance of ecosystems'.[55] This is obviously a permitted type of use, but it is just one of many.

As noted, the Protocol obliges States to comply with certain principles when using their watercourses. In this list of general principles, the need for a balance between interests of present and future generations clearly is reflected, as the protocol requires that

> State Parties shall maintain a proper balance between resource development for a higher standard of living for their people and conservation and enhancement of the environment to promote sustainable development.[56]

There is also a variation of the equitable use principle, worded as follows:

> Watercourse States shall in their respective territories utilise a shared watercourse in an equitable and reasonable manner. In particular, a shared watercourse shall be used and developed by Watercourse States with a view to attain optimal and sustainable utilisation thereof and benefits therefrom, taking into account the interests of the Watercourse States concerned, consistent with adequate protection of the watercourse for the benefit of current and future generations.[57]

[50] Revised Protocol on Shared Watercourses in the Southern African Development Community (1995) preamble.
[51] Ibid. at art. 2(c).
[52] Ibid. at art. 1.
[53] Ibid. at art. 2(b).
[54] Ibid. at art. 3(2).
[55] Ibid. at art. 1(1); ibid. at art. 4(2).
[56] Ibid. at art. 3(4).
[57] Ibid. at art. 3(7)(a).

This is almost entirely the same as the provision in the Watercourses Convention, but the addition at the end is interesting. It is an explicit reference to the need to find an intergenerational balance, a reference not found in the Watercourses Convention.

There is also a reference, in the list of principles, to the no harm rule:

> State Parties shall, in utilising a shared watercourse in their territories, take all appropriate measures to prevent the causing of significant harm to other Watercourse States.[58]

There is no reference to the interests of future generations. But a bit further down, a variation of the no harm rule focusing on pollution can be found:

> State Parties shall, individually and, where appropriate, jointly, prevent, reduce and control the pollution *and environmental degradation* of a shared watercourse that may cause significant harm to other Watercourse States or to their environment, including harm to human health or safety, to the use of the waters for any beneficial purpose or to the living resources of the watercourse.[59]

Again, the addition – in italics – to the otherwise copy-pasted text of the provision in the Watercourses Convention is telling here.

### *Senegal River*

Another interesting example is the Charter of Senegal River Waters.[60] Like the Orange-Senqu Agreement, the Senegal River Charter also refers to various kinds of uses of the waters and the need to divide the scarce resources between all these different uses. In the Preamble, States are reminded that, when allocating the

[58] Ibid. at art. 3(10)(a).

[59] Ibid. at art. 4(2)(b)(i).

[60] See e.g. M.M. Mbengue, 'A Model for African Shared Water Resources: The Senegal River Legal System' (2014) 23 *Review of European, Comparative and International Environmental Law* 59–66; F. Padt and J.C. Sanches, 'Creating New Spaces for Sustainable Water Management in the Senegal River Basin' (2013) 53 *Natural Resources Journal* 265–284; M.M. Mbengue, 'The Senegal River Legal Regime and Its Contribution to the Development of the Law of International Watercourses in Africa', in L. Boisson de Chazournes, *International Law and Freshwater* (Oxford University Press 2013); U. Alam, 'Cooperating Internationally over Water: Explaining L'espace OMVS' (2012) 50 *Journal of Modern African Studies* 175–199; M. Kipping, 'Water Security in the Senegal River Basin: Water Cooperation and Water Conflicts', in H.G. Brauch (ed.), *Facing Global Environmental Change* (Springer 2009); M. Vick, 'The Senegal River Basin: A Retrospective and Prospective Look at the Legal Régime' (2006) 46 *Natural Resources Journal* 211–243; A.S. Ba and M.M. Mbengue, 'Le Régime juridique du fleuve Sénégal: aspects du droit des cours d'eau dans un contexte régional' (2006) 12 *African Yearbook of International Law* 309–347; M. Kipping, *Konflikte und Kooperation um Wasser: Wasserpolitik am Senegalfluss und internationales Flussmanagement im Südlichen Afrika* (Auflage 2005).

freshwater resources for the different uses, they should always 'take into account the objective of sustainable development'.[61]

Article 4 further elaborates on this obligation by requiring States to take into account certain principles when distributing freshwater resources among the different uses. Explicitly mentioned is the principle of equitable and reasonable use of the waters of the River, and the obligation to preserve the environment.[62] So both principles – equitable and sustainable use – are included.

In subsequent articles, we find more concrete commitments. Article 5 requires States to take into account the availability and continuity of the freshwater resources, and to ensure the sustainable maintenance of favourable ecological conditions in the river basin. Article 7 requires States to consider the preservation and protection of the environment when distributing water resources. Importantly, Article 6 emphasizes that the principles set out in Article 7 are secondary to the need to satisfy basic needs, and to ensure that reasonable satisfaction of all present-day water needs is possible. The treaty thus tries to find a balance between environmental considerations and immediate water needs of the present generation.

Article 4 refers explicitly to the principle of equitable use, further detailing it in the context of sustainable development. But one does not find all that many references to the no harm rule. Only in the Part on Protection and Environmental Preservation (Part 4) is there an interesting variation. Article 16 requires States to take measures to 'prevent, reduce or control activities or conditions, resulting from natural causes or human activity, that may cause injury to other States, to the environment of the River, or to the health or safety of human beings'.[63] Clearly, this is yet another example of a more expansive version of the no harm rule, not limited strictly to harm caused by one State to the other.

### *Lake Tanganyika*

Another interesting example is the Convention on the Sustainable Management of Lake Tanganyika. According to its preamble, the Convention is motivated by a realization that 'the riparian States share a common interest in the conservation and equitable utilization of the resources of Lake Tanganyika'. The principal objective is to 'ensure the protection and conservation of the biological diversity and the sustainable use of the natural resources of Lake Tanganyika'.[64] To achieve this, the States must 'accord particular attention to ensuring that present and future

[61] Charter of Senegal River Waters (2009) preamble.
[62] Ibid. at art. 4.
[63] Ibid. at art. 16. See also the definition of 'pollution', in Article 1(15). This is also defined beyond the transboundary context.
[64] Lake Tanganyika Convention (2008) art. 2(1).

communities living near the Lake benefit from the sustainable use of the Lake's natural resources'.[65] One of the Convention's general principles states that

> the natural resources of Lake Tanganyika shall be protected, conserved, managed, and used for sustainable development to meet the needs of present and future generations in an equitable manner.[66]

Taken together, all these proclamations can lead to the conclusion that a better marriage between the principles of equitable use and sustainable use is hardly imaginable. The Convention also refers to the no harm rule. Article 6 asks all States to 'ensure that activities within their jurisdiction or control do not cause transboundary adverse impacts'. The latter term is defined as 'any adverse impact that extends beyond the territory of the Contracting State in which the physical origin of the adverse impact is situated'.[67] The term 'adverse impact' is defined in the Convention as follows:

> Any actual or potential detrimental effect on the Lake's environment and any actual or potential consequential detrimental effect on legitimate uses of the Lake, on the health of the people of a Contracting State or on their ability to provide for their health, safety and cultural and economic well-being.[68]

Even in the definition of *transboundary* adverse impact, no reference to the interests of the other State is made. It only refers to impact felt beyond the State's own territory. At the same time, it requires some imagination to interpret this as a prohibition to cause harm to the State's own future generations as well.

### *Niger Basin*

From the Preamble of the Niger Basin Water Charter, it is clear that the agreement seeks to find an intergenerational balance between, on the one hand, promoting the economic and social progress of the States and contributing to the fight against poverty, and, on the other hand, ensuring sustainable development.[69]

65 Ibid. at art. 2(2).
66 Ibid. at art. 5(2).
67 Ibid. at art. 1.
68 Ibid.
69 On the management of the Niger Basin, see e.g. M. Ngaide, 'La contribution de l'Afrique à la gestion des ressources en eau transfrontalières: l'exemple la Charte de l'eau du Bassin du Niger' (2012) 66 *Revue juridique et politique des États francophones* 263–316; K. Sangbana, 'Les gestion intégrée des ressorces en eaux partagées et les organismes de bassin en Afrique: les cas de l'Autorité du Bassin du Niger et de l'Autorité du Bassin de la Volta', in *Société française pour le droit international, L'eau en droit international: Colloque d'Orléans* (Pedone 2011); U. Umoh, I. Ekpoh, and S. Kumar, 'Water Conflict in West Africa: The Niger River Basin Experience', in V. Grover (ed.), *Water: A Source of Conflict or Cooperation?* (Science Publishers 2007). For some background on earlier treaties, see e.g. T. Maluwa, 'Legal Aspects of the Niger River under the Niamey Treaties' (1988) 28 *Natural Resources Journal* 671–697; B.A. Godana, *Africa's*

The main objective of the Charter is to 'encourage cooperation based on solidarity and reciprocity for a sustainable, equitable and coordinated use' of the Niger Basin.[70] Article 4 further elaborates on the principle of equitable and reasonable use. Here a desire to come to an agreement on what is equitable towards future generations is also reflected. Factors to be taken into account include 'past, present and future uses of the Basin's water resources', the 'economic and social needs of the States and their populations', and the 'need to avoid wasteful use of the Basin's waters'.[71] This is complemented *inter alia* by Article 12, which is entirely devoted to the preservation and protection of the environment.[72] On the other hand, Article 14, proclaims that the Basin's water must be used in a 'fair and equitable manner' to meet the present-day needs for human consumption, agriculture, fisheries, industry, tourism, etc. This raises the question what comes first in case of water scarcity. On this, Article 15 says that, when not all uses can be satisfied at the same time, 'particular attention must be paid to essential human needs'.

There is also a reference to the no harm rule, in Article 5, which reads as follows:

> States Parties shall ensure that activities carried out within their territory cannot cause damage to other States Parties, in accordance with Article 4 of the Revised Convention establishing the Niger Basin Authority.[73]

The provision referred to in the last part of the sentence requires States to refrain from carrying out 'any works likely to pollute waters or adversely modify the biological features of the fauna and flora'.[74] This could be interpreted as a more expansive interpretation of the no harm rule, not unlike the Revised Protocol on Shared Watercourses in the Southern African Development Community referred to above. The search for an intergenerational balance is also reflected in the definition of 'integrated water resources management', which is defined as

> the process which encourages the coordinated development and management of water, land and related resources with a view to maximizing, in an equitable manner, the resulting economic and social welfare without compromising the sustainability of essential ecosystems.[75]

*Shared Water Resources: Legal and Institutional Aspects of the Nile, Niger and Senegal River Systems* (Pinter 1985).

70 Niger Basin Water Charter, *supra* note 28 at art. 2.

71 Ibid. at art. 4.

72 See also Annex No. 1 on the Protection of the Environment of the Niger Basin, Annexed to the Niger Basin Water Charter (2008).

73 Transboundary impact is defined as 'any significant impact, such as the modification of the characteristics of transboundary waters caused by human activity'. Ibid. at art. 1(17).

74 Convention révisée portant création de l'autorité du Bassin du Niger (Revised Convention Establishing the Niger Basin Authority) (29 October 1987) art. 4.

75 Niger Basin Water Charter, *supra* note 28 at art. 1(15).

Interesting is also the definition of 'pollution':

> Any change harmful to the composition or the quality of the water of an international watercourse resulting directly or indirectly from human behaviour, which is likely to cause harm to one or more watercourse States or their environment, including harm to the health or the safety of humans, or to any use of water, or to the biological resources of the watercourse.[76]

This definition is immediately followed by a definition of 'transboundary pollution', which reads that 'any pollution which is caused by activities carried out on the territory or under the control of one State, and producing harmful effects to the environment of one or several other States'.[77] This brings pollution back within a transboundary context.

### *Guarani Aquifer*

The Guarani is an underground aquifer and, as such, the Watercourses Convention does not govern its utilization. A watercourse is defined in the Convention as 'a system of surface waters and groundwaters constituting by virtue of their physical relationship a unitary whole'.[78] A system without surface waters is thus not covered by the Watercourses Convention. Reference must then be made here to the Draft Articles on the Law of Transboundary Aquifers prepared by the ILC in 2008.[79]

Article 4 of these articles contains a variation of the equitable utilization principle, applicable to transboundary aquifers. This is not a copy-paste from the Watercourses Convention because there is a big difference between surface water and groundwater. As the ILC explains, the Watercourses Convention deals with 'renewable

[76] Ibid. at art. 1(25).

[77] Ibid. at art. 1(26).

[78] Watercourses Convention, *supra* note 4 at art. 2(a).

[79] ILC, Draft Articles on the Law of Transboundary Aquifers, with Commentaries, adopted by the International Law Commission at its sixtieth session (2008), UN Doc. A/63/10. See e.g. O. McIntyre, 'International Water Resources Law and the International Law Commission Draft Articles on Transboundary Aquifers: A Missed Opportunity for Cross-Fertilisation?' (2011) 13:3 *International Community Law Review* 237–254; N. Sánchez Castillo, 'Differentiating between Sovereignty over Exclusive and Shared Resources in the Light of Future Discussions on the Law of Transboundary Aquifers' (2015) 24 *Review of European, Comparative and International Environmental Law* 4–15; A. Tanzi and A. Kolliopoulos, 'The International Water Law Process and Transboundary Groundwater: Supplementing the Water Convention with the 2012 UNECE Model Provisions', in A. Tanzi, *The UNECE Convention on the Protection and Use of Transboundary Watercourses and International Lakes* (Brill 2015); G. Eckstein and F. Sindico, 'The Law of Transboundary Aquifers: Many Ways of Going Forward, but Only One Way of Standing Still' (2014) 23 *Review of European, Comparative and International Environmental Law* 32–42; J.W. Dellapenna, 'The Law of Transboundary Groundwater', in L. Westra and M. Vilela, *The Earth Charter, Ecological Integrity and Social Movements* (Routledge 2014); R. Frink, 'Preserving Trans-Boundary Aquifers: A Precious Resource for Our Future Generations' (2013) 26 *Pacific McGeorge Global Business and Development Law Journal* 503–530.

waters which receive substantial recharge and in that context the principle of sustainable utilization fully applie[s]'; whilst 'the waters in aquifers, whether recharging or non-recharging, are more or less non-renewable', and thus one cannot expect of the present generation to leave these waters in the same shape – in terms of quality and quantity – as it found them. The objective is more modest: *inter alia*, to 'aim at maximizing the long-term benefits derived from the use of water contained [in the aquifer]', to 'tak[e] into account present and future needs of, and alternative water sources for, the aquifer States', and 'not [to] utilize a recharging transboundary aquifer or aquifer system at a level that would prevent continuance of its effective functioning'.[80]

Article 6 sets out the obligation not to cause significant harm. It basically obliges one Aquifer State to take all appropriate measures to prevent the causing of significant harm to other Aquifer States.[81] Article 12, on pollution, follows the same model: it obliges Aquifer States to prevent, reduce, and control pollution of the transboundary aquifers or aquifer systems situated on their territory that may cause significant harm to other Aquifer States.[82]

From the above, it can be concluded that the principle of equitable utilization and the no harm rule also govern the exploitation and management of transboundary aquifers. Let us now turn to the Guarani Aquifer Agreement, and see how these two foundational principles of international water law are linked to intergenerational equity. In the Preamble, the States acknowledge they are 'conscious of the responsibility to promote the sustainable development [of the Guarani Aquifer System] *for the benefit of* present and future generations'.[83] This is a very explicit reference to the interests of future generations. So how does this approach affect the interpretation of the principles?

In Article 3, there is a pledge by each State to use the Guarani Aquifer's resources 'on the basis of reasonable and sustainable uses criteria, respecting the obligation of

80 Draft Articles on the Law of Transboundary Aquifers, *supra* note 79 at commentary to art. 4, para. (4).

81 Ibid. at art. 6.

82 Ibid. at art. 12.

83 Guarani Aquifer Agreement, *supra* note 29 at preamble. On the Agreement, see e.g. C. Tinker, 'The Guarani Aquifer Accord: Cooperation in South America towards Prevention of Harm and Sustainable, Equitable Use of Underground Transboundary Water' (2016) 15:2 *Law and Practice of International Courts and Tribunals* 249–263; F. Sindico and S. Hawkins, 'The Guarani Aquifer Agreement and Transboundary Aquifer Law in the SADC: Comparing Apples and Oranges?' (2015) 24 *Review of European, Comparative and International Environmental Law* 318–329; L. del Castillo-Laborde, 'The Guaraní Aquifer Framework Agreement (2010)', in L. Boisson de Chazournes, C. Leb, and M. Tignino (eds.), *International Law and Freshwater: The Multiple Challenges* (Elgar 2013); D. Cassuto and R. Sampaio, 'Hard, Soft and Uncertain: The Guarani Aquifer and the Challenges of Transboundary Groundwater' (2013) 24 *Colorado Journal of International Environmental Law and Policy* 1–41; B. Green, 'Contemporary Governance of Transboundary Groundwater Resources: The Guarani Aquifer Project' (2010) 21 *Journal of Water Law* 232–240.

not causing significant harm to the other Parties or the environment'. The latter three words are interesting, as they provide room for an intergenerational interpretation of the no harm rule. Article 6 complements this provision by requiring that the States 'adopt all the necessary measures to avoid causing significant harm to the other Parties or the environment' when utilizing the water resources of the Guarani Aquifer System.[84]

Article 4 contains a reference to equitable utilization, worded as follows: 'The Parties shall promote the conservation and environmental protection of the Guarani Aquifer System so as to ensure multiple, reasonable, sustainable, and equitable use of its water resources.' Clearly, equitable use is closely linked to sustainable use here, and thus there is plenty of support for an intergenerational interpretation of the equitable use principle.

### *Rivers of Kazakhstan and China*

In February 2011, Kazakhstan and China signed an Agreement on water quality protection of transboundary waters.[85] In the preamble, the two States acknowledge 'their responsibility to present and future generations for the preservation of the aquatic environment, the protection of transboundary rivers from pollution and the protection of the water quality of transboundary rivers'.[86] The fact that this obligation is owed to both present and future generations should be emphasized here.

But how to balance the interests between the different generations? Must this be done on the basis of equity? The Agreement contains no explicit reference to the principle of equitable utilization, but it does have multiple references to the no harm rule, or the rule obliging States to prevent transboundary impact. The latter term is defined in the agreement in a traditional sense, i.e. as an obligation to try and avoid harmful effects felt on the territory of one Party caused by activities that take place in the territory of the other Party.[87]

## FUTURE GENERATIONS IN DOMESTIC WATER LAW

References to the interests of future generations in the utilization of freshwater resources can also be found in the domestic law of various States. In this section,

[84] See also Guarani Aquifer Agreement, *supra* note 29 at art. 7.

[85] More in general about water agreements between Kazakhstan and its neighbours, see e.g. N. Kipshakbaev, 'Cooperation of the Republic of Kazakhstan with Adjoining States on Transboundary Water Issues', in UNECE, *Transboundary Water Cooperation: Trends in the Newly Independent States* (UN 2006).

[86] Agreement between Kazakhstan and China, *supra* note 30 at preamble.

[87] Ibid. at art. 2.

a selection of more recent examples of such domestic legislation is offered.[88] The examples have been selected in such a way as to show the great variety of States involved.[89] For example, the first provision of the recently adopted Austrian Federal Constitutional Act on Sustainability states that

> the Republic of Austria is committed to the principle of sustainability in using natural resources to ensure that future generations will also benefit from optimal quality of life.[90]

The word 'also' indicates the commitment to search for a balance in order to ensure an optimal quality of life for both present and future generations.

One of the principal objectives of the recently adopted Water Law of the Central African Republic is to:

> Mobilize and manage water resources, to ensure the conditions for sustainable development, through rational use, while preserving the interest of current and future generations.[91]

Article 36 of the Congolese law on the planning and development of the territory and its natural resources proclaims that

> the exploitation of natural resources must take into account the indispensable preservation of the environment, so as to meet the needs of present and future generations.[92]

The new Land Law of the Macao Special Administrative Region of the People's Republic of China, adopted in 2013, refers to the principle of sustainability as requiring a 'coordinated and balanced' development policy:

> ... so as to ensure meeting the needs of the present generation whilst transmitting to the future generations a properly planned and ordered region.[93]

The Code of the Environment in Burkina Faso calls for sustainable production and consumption, defined as

[88] Not all examples apply to the utilization of freshwater resources alone. Examples of domestic environmental law applicable *inter alia* to freshwater resources – but also to other natural resources – are also included.

[89] For more examples, see e.g. Brown Weiss, *supra* note 2 at 10–11.

[90] Federal Constitutional Act on Sustainability, Animal Protection, Comprehensive Environmental Protection, on Water and Food Security as well as Research, adopted 11 July 2013, para. 1 www.ris.bka.gv.at/Dokumente/Erv/ERV_2013_1_111/ERV_2013_1_111.html accessed 30 November 2017.

[91] Water Law of the Central African Republic (2006) art. 2 http://faolex.fao.org/docs/pdf/caf107433.pdf accessed 30 November 2017.

[92] Law No. 43-2014 of 10 October 2014, on the Planning and Development of the Territory (2014) art. 36 http://faolex.fao.org/docs/pdf/con143310.pdf accessed 30 November 2017.

[93] Land Law of the Special Administrative Region of Macau, Law No. 10/2013, art. 2(1) (2013) http://images.io.gov.mo/bo/i/2013/36/lei-10-2013.pdf accessed 30 November 2017.

> mechanisms of production and use of goods and services that meet basic needs, and contribute to improving the quality of life, while minimizing the use of natural resources, so as not to endanger needs of future generations.[94]

The same Code also makes explicit reference to the principle of sustainable development, according to which 'the present generation should meet its needs without compromising the ability of future generations to meet their own needs'.[95] And 'natural resources which contribute to the satisfaction of human needs must be exploited to meet the needs of the present generation without compromising the ability of future generations to meet their own needs'.[96]

Article 112 of the Norwegian Constitution reads as follows:

> Every person has the right to an environment that is conducive to health and to a natural environment whose productivity and diversity are maintained. Natural resources shall be managed on the basis of comprehensive long-term considerations which will safeguard this right for future generations as well.[97]

Finally, a very interesting example is the Maltese Sustainable Development Act, which includes the following provision:

> There shall be a Guardian of Future Generations with the aim of safeguarding intergenerational and intragenerational sustainable development in Malta.[98]

This Guardian has the mandate to, *inter alia*, 'direct the focus of the competent authority to safeguard future generations'.[99] This reminds one a bit of the Hungarian Parliamentary Commissioner for Future Generations, a position established in 2008 and replaced by a Deputy Commissioner for Fundamental Rights responsible for the protection of the interests of future generations in 2012.[100] A handful of States have established similar institutions.[101]

With the exception of the above-mentioned examples, future generations do not play a role in the process of utilizing a State's freshwater or other natural resources.

[94] Environmental Code of Burkina Faso, Law No 006-2013 (2013) art. 4 www.assembleenationale.bf/IMG/pdf/loi_n0006_portant_code_de_l_environnement.pdf accessed 30 November 2017.

[95] Ibid. at art. 9.

[96] Ibid. at art. 18.

[97] Translation available at www.stortinget.no/globalassets/pdf/english/constitutionenglish.pdf accessed 30 November 2017.

[98] Maltese Sustainable Development Act (Chapter 521), Act X of 10 July 2012, pt. IV, art. 8 http://justiceservices.gov.mt/DownloadDocument.aspx?app=lom&itemid=11917&l=1 accessed 30 November 2017.

[99] Ibid. at arts. 8, 4, j.

[100] See Hungarian Act LIX of 1993 on the Parliamentary Commissioner for Civil Rights (Ombudsman), provision 27; Hungarian Act CXI of 2011 on the Commissioner for Fundamental Rights, as amended by Act CCXXIII of 2013, ch. I, sec. 3 www.ajbh.hu/en/web/ajbh-en/act-cxi-of-2011 accessed 30 November 2017. See also ch. 4 in this volume.

[101] See Brown Weiss, *supra* note 2 at 11–13.

Instead, those participating in this process in the present are obligated not to endanger or compromise the interests of future generations in the same freshwater resources.

## FUTURE GENERATIONS IN DOMESTIC WATER PLANS AND POLICIES

Many national water resource plans and policies also increasingly refer to the interests of future generations. It is interesting to examine how this balance is sought in various cases.

An early example is the national water policy of Bangladesh, adopted in 1999. This policy begins with the following proclamation:

> Every public agency, every community, village and each individual has an important role to play in ensuring that the water and associated natural resources of Bangladesh are used judiciously so that the future generations can be assured of at least the same, if not better, availability and quality of those resources.[102]

Here, the balance between the benefits and burdens of freshwater resources utilization tilts in favour of the future generations, which is somewhat unusual. There are very few examples of such an approach.

It is also difficult to surpass the Bangladeshi formulation in terms of clarity and specificity. But the National Water Sector Strategy and Investment Program of Yemen, adopted in 2004, clearly surpassed the Bangladeshi report in the urgency with which the protection of the interests of future generations was described. The various working groups that prepared this strategy began from a series of considerations, one of which was that

> exhausting and wasting or polluting water is considered a criminal act, contravening all religions and can almost be considered an act of terror against the rights of present and future generations.[103]

Here, the act of unsustainable exploitation of freshwater resources is condemned in extremely strong terms, but this in itself does not mean the interests of future generations are preferred over those of the present.

The Ghanaian National Water Policy of 2007 is a more cautiously formulated example. Its overall goal is to

[102] National Water Policy, published in 1999 by the Ministry of Water Resources of the Government of the People's Republic of Bangladesh, 4 http://faolex.fao.org/docs/pdf/bgd146075.pdf accessed 30 November 2017.

[103] National Water Sector Strategy and Investment Program (NWSSIP) of Yemen, published in December 2004 by the Ministry of Water and Environment, 3 www.yemenwater.org/wp-content/uploads/2013/05/NWSSIP_2004_English1.pdf accessed 30 November 2017.

> achieve the sustainable development, management and use of Ghana's water resources, to improve health and livelihoods, reduce vulnerability, while assuring good governance for present and future generations.[104]

If the reference to future generations refers back only to good governance, then this quote says little about the exact intergenerational balance of burdens and benefits.

A Croatian regulation referred, in 2008, to the principle of sustainable development, according to which water should be managed in such a way as to

> meet the needs of the present generation without compromising the right and ability of future generations to realize their needs for themselves.[105]

One clearly sees the Croatian authorities took their inspiration from the Brundtland report.

The National Action Plan for Integrated Management of Water Resources of Cape Verde, adopted in November 2010, also advocated for sustainable development, interpreted as an

> economic and social policy that respects the environment, is specifically focused on the prudent and rational utilization of natural resources and respect for safeguarding the interests of future generations.[106]

In the same year, the Water Conservation Strategy of the United Arab Emirates was adopted. This strategy identified eight initiatives that needed to be implemented, of which the first was to

> develop legislation, standards and Federal mechanisms for integrated water resources management [in order to] preserve, protect and enhance water resources management in UAE, and to appropriately allocate and effectively use water resources for the benefit of current and future generations.[107]

And finally, the Guatemalan National Plan of 2014 identified five axes of importance, of which the fourth was this:

> The development of a natural resources plan for today and for the future [requiring, *inter alia*, the] sustainable management of lake and river systems.[108]

[104] National Water Policy, adopted in 2007 by the Ghanaian Ministry of Water Resources, Works and Housing, 19 www.purc.com.gh/purc/sites/default/files/WATERPOLICY.pdf accessed 30 November 2017.

[105] Croatian Regulation on the water management strategy, published 15 July 2008 http://faolex.fao.org/docs/texts/cro129713.doc accessed 30 November 2017.

[106] National Action Plan for Integrated Water Resources Management of Cape Verde, annexed to resolution No. 66/2010 of 24 November 2010, 33 http://faolex.fao.org/docs/pdf/cvi119727.pdf accessed 30 November 2017.

[107] United Arab Emirates, Water Conservation Strategy (2010) 68 http://faolex.fao.org/docs/pdf/uae147095.pdf accessed 30 November 2017.

[108] See Plan Nacional de Desarrollo K'atun: nuestra Guatemala 2032 (2004) 12–13, 59, 239–295 http://faolex.fao.org/docs/pdf/gua143736.pdf accessed 30 November 2017.

There are many other examples of water plans and policies which make reference to future generations, such as the Panamanian National Water Resources Policy, adopted 23 April 2013,[109] and the Sustainable and Integrated Water and Sanitation Policy 2012–2021 of Tuvalu.[110] All of these plans seek to give meaning to the intergenerational equity principle in their own way by searching for an acceptable distribution of burdens and benefits between present and future generations.

## CONCLUSION

This chapter first examined the relationship between the principle of intergenerational equity and the two most fundamental principles of international water law – the no harm rule and the principle of equitable utilization – as reflected in the UN Watercourses Convention. It then looked at how this relationship between intergenerational equity and water law's foundational principles played out in specific agreements regulating a particular transboundary watercourse. Many of these agreements use the Watercourses Convention's proclamation of the principles as starting point, but then add more intergenerational elements to them. It appears that States are more and more confident in doing so, and thus the principles slowly evolve into more sustainable, intergenerational versions of themselves.

We also see this evolution in domestic law and policies. All examples referred to above have attempted to find a way to share the burdens and benefits of freshwater resource management and utilization among the present and future generations. The exact formulation of this balance differs. Sometimes the present generation has an obligation to ensure that future generations have at least as many resources and opportunities as the present generation currently has. Sometimes the present generation is asked only to keep the interests of future generations in mind when utilizing the freshwater resources. Very few legal frameworks give a role to representatives of future generations as participants. It is more common for the present generation to simply accept an obligation for itself to take into account the interests of future generations, without giving the latter any means to ensure compliance with this commitment. If we take all these examples together, we find an interesting laboratory of intellectual experiments, most of them of very recent date, which may provide a source of inspiration. The question of how to ensure compliance with these water laws remains beyond the scope of this chapter, but the next step is to faithfully carry out those plans and to respect the commitments that have been made to present and future generations.

109 Panamanian National Water Resources Policy (2013) http://faolex.fao.org/docs/pdf/pan123087.pdf accessed 30 November 2017.

110 Adopted by the Office of the Deputy Prime Minister and Ministry of Public Utilities in 2012 http://faolex.fao.org/docs/pdf/tuv143758.pdf accessed 30 November 2017. Faolex is a legislative database with domestic laws and regulation relating to renewable natural resources. It has an excellent collection, which is easily searchable.

# 37

# Intergenerational Justice in the Paris Agreement on Climate Change

*Marie-Claire Cordonier Segger*

Climate change is the justice challenge of our century.

*Hon. Mary Robinson, former President of the Republic of Ireland and winner of the Right Livelihood Award*

Climate change is a crucial challenge for both intragenerational and intergenerational equity, offering the world an unprecedented opportunity to demonstrate its commitment to the principles and practice of sustainable development. In 2016, through *Transforming Our World: The 2030 Agenda for Sustainable Development*, the UN and its member States agreed on seventeen SDGs for the world, identifying time-bound targets and implementation methods.[1] As legal reviews have revealed, the targets adopted in the SDGs are not just aspirational goals and objectives, as many can also be found in the object and purpose of many important international treaties among states.[2] Achieving SDG 13 to take urgent action to combat climate change and its impacts will be implemented in part through the 2015 Paris Agreement.[3] Indeed, in SDG 13, States acknowledge that the 1992 UNFCCC and its instruments are the primary international, intergovernmental forum for negotiating the global response to climate change.[4] Other SDGs, for instance on energy, water, hunger, poverty, biodiversity, oceans, cities, and infrastructure, are also highly relevant to climate change, including SDG 10 to reduce inequality within and among countries and, as such, offer crucial opportunities to either frustrate or foster intergenerational equity and justice.[5]

1 UNGA Res 70/1.
2 See M.-C. Cordonier Segger and E. Mrema (eds.), 'The Contribution of International Law, Policy and Governance to the Sustainable Development Goals' (Issue Briefs, CISDL/UNEP 2016).
3 Paris Agreement on climate change (2015).
4 United Nations Framework Convention on Climate Change (1992).
5 UNFCCC https://unfccc.int/action-on-climate-and-sdgs.

The international regime to address climate challenge developed in an interactional manner over decades,[6] as countries struggled to find an appropriate international cooperative framework for sustainable development more broadly. As part of these debates, collaboration efforts on climate change have not been simple, nor straightforward for diverse countries to agree.[7] Prior to the 1977 World Conference on Climate Change at Geneva through to the 1992 signing of the UNFCCC in Rio de Janeiro and its 1997 Kyoto Protocol, countries sought consensus on cooperative approaches that had a chance of success. In 2015, the 197 Parties to the UNFCCC finally concluded an international agreement on climate change at the 21st COP (COP21) in Paris. At the 2016 UNFCCC COP22 in Marrakesh, Morocco, the following year, the Paris Agreement entered rapidly into force, after more than fifty-five Parties to the Convention accounting for over 55 per cent of the total global GHG emissions had ratified.[8] At the 2018 COP24 in Katowice, Poland, negotiations on modalities and implementation guidelines further led to the adoption of the 'Katowice Outcomes', a package of decisions guiding how the Paris Agreement is implemented, and in the 2019 COP25 at Madrid, Spain, hosted by the Government of Chile, even as consensus proved elusive on several remaining points, the Paris Agreement's Committee on Compliance and Implementation was established.[9]

The Paris Agreement and the Katowice Outcomes aim to strengthen the global response to the threat of climate change in the context of sustainable development and efforts to eradicate poverty. Parties seek to hold increases in global temperatures well below 2 °C, pursuing efforts toward a 1.5 °C limit; to increase adaptation to climate impacts and foster resilience; and to harness finance flows for low GHG emissions and climate-resilient development.[10] The Paris Agreement sets a 'high-ambition' framework for new climate mitigation, adaptation, and finance commitments by countries, backed by measures for intergovernmental cooperation on loss and damage, forests and land management, technology development and transfer, education and capacity-building, with a fit-to-purpose framework of transparency, peer review, stocktaking, and compliance support. Adopting a 'bottom-up' approach, it facilitates submissions of climate action plans to the UNFCCC by over 188 countries, as Nationally Determined Contributions (NDCs) to the global response to climate change.

A focus on the legal dimensions of intergenerational equity in the Paris Agreement, in the context of global commitments to sustainable development, is

[6] For more, see J. Brunnée and S.J. Toope, *Legitimacy and Legality in International Law: An Interactional Account* (Cambridge University Press 2010).

[7] See M. Doelle, 'The Paris Agreement: Historic Breakthrough or High Stakes Experiment?' (2016) 6:1–2 *Climate Law* 1–20.

[8] UNFCCC COP22 Press Statement 2016.

[9] UNFCCC COP24 Press Statement 2018; UNFCCC COP24 Decision on Katowice Outlines (Paris Agreement Work Programme PAWP).

[10] Paris Agreement, *supra* note 3 at art. 2.1.

especially relevant for the global youth leading 'climate strikes' which have engaged over 1.6 million students from over 2,200 cities and towns in 120 countries worldwide.[11] Intergenerational equity is also key for leading high-ambition countries and emerging economies, as well as for the most vulnerable countries that are otherwise often excluded from international law-making. Indeed, legal research by the CISDL notes that out of 187 countries with intended nationally determined contributions (iNDCs) published online by the UNFCCC registry, 156 countries explicitly prioritise an intention to undertake legal and institutional reforms in order to meet their commitments.[12] Further, 120 countries are calling for capacity-building and support from the international community, with fifty-one stressing specifically the need for legal and institutional capacity-building.

Building on the work of the Climate Law and Governance Initiative in partnership with the UNFCCC Secretariat,[13] this chapter provides an overview of the potential contributions of the new Paris Agreement towards intergenerational justice. From a broad-brush perspective, as this chapter explains, the UNFCCC Paris Agreement reflects intergenerational equity in several ways – through its principles, its purpose, its operational provisions, and its institutional arrangements for implementation.

## THE INTERGENERATIONAL EQUITY PRINCIPLE FOR CLIMATE CHANGE RISKS AND IMPACTS

Climate change poses crucial challenges for sustainable development, and particularly for the needs and interests of future generations. The impacts of climate change threaten to undermine decades of social and economic development, to severely constrain efforts to protect the environment, and to affect a wide range of human rights, such as the rights to life, health, water, food, shelter, and an adequate standard of living.[14] As the IPCC has noted, from 1880 to 2012, average global

[11] BBC, 'Schools' Climate Change Protests' www.bbc.com/news/topics/czmw21ewkzqt/schools-climate-change-protests (last visited 12 September 2019); TIME, 'It's Literally Our Future' 20 March 2019 (online: http://time.com/5554775/youth-school-climate-change-strike-action/); TIME, 'Swedish Teen Climate Activist Greta Thunberg Has Been Nominated for the Nobel Peace Prize Nobel Prize Nomination' 14 March 2019 http://time.com/5551172/climate-greta-thunberg-nobel-nominated/.

[12] M.-C. Cordonier Segger, M. Reiner, and A. Scott, 'Countries Stress Importance of Legal and Institutional Reforms in Their iNDCs' (Climate Law and Governance Initiative September 2016) 4 www.climatelawgovernance.org/knowledge-centre.html accessed 07 April 2019.

[13] Climate Law and Governance Initiative partners include the CISDL, the ILA, and expert colleagues from McGill University, University of Cambridge, Yale University, University of Waterloo, University of Chile, University of Madrid, Ateneo School of Governance, University of Zambia Faculty of Law, and the University of Nairobi Faculty of Law, among others, in collaboration with IDLO, UNDP, UNEP, CIFOR, EBRD, and the IUCN World Commission for Environmental Law. See www.climatelawgovernance.org for details.

[14] UNCHR Res 7/23 (2008) UN Doc A/HRC/RES/7/23; UNGA Res 63/32 (26 November 2008) UN Doc A/RES/63/32; UNCHR Res 10/4 (2009) UN Doc A/HRC/RES/10/4; UNGA Res 63/281

temperature increased by 0.85 °C.[15] Global emissions of carbon dioxide ($CO_2$) have increased by almost 50 per cent since 1990, and emissions grew more quickly between 2000 and 2010 than in each of the three previous decades.[16] Given current concentrations and ongoing GHG emissions, it is likely that by the end of this century, the increase in global temperature will exceed 1.5 °C compared to the 1850–1900 period.[17]

Such changes have already led to serious repercussions and give rise to significant further risks worldwide. Food security is threatened. For each degree of temperature increase, grain yields decline by about 5 per cent. Maize, wheat, and other major crops experienced significant yield reductions at the global level of 40 megatonnes per year between 1981 and 2002 owing to a warmer climate.[18] Oceans have warmed, with snow and ice diminishing and sea levels rising. The extent of Arctic sea ice has decreased since 1979, with 1.07 million km$^2$ of ice loss every decade.[19] From 1901 to 2010, the global average sea level rose by 19 cm as ice melted and oceans expanded, with a further rise predicted of 24–30 cm by 2065 and 40–63 cm by 2100.[20] At the same time, studies comparing eight-eight recent forest 'die-offs' show that increases in drought and heat stress are fundamentally altering forests in many regions, with a rise in tree mortality associated with climate-induced stress, insect outbreaks, and wildfire.[21] Reports suggest that the costs of climate change adaptation will reach between USD 70 and USD 100 billion a year by 2050.[22]

This is a challenge to intergenerational equity. Most effects of climate change will persist for many centuries even if emissions were halted immediately. The

(3 June 2009) UN Doc A/RES/63/281; Report of the Secretary-General 'Climate Change and Its Possible Security Implications' (2009) UN Doc A/64/350; UNSC Presidential Statement (2011) UN Doc S/PRST/2011/15; UNCHR Res 18/22 (2011) UN Doc A/HRC/RES/18/22.

15 IPCC, 'Climate Change 2014 Synthesis Report' (Summary for Policy Makers [SPM] Geneva 2015) www.ipcc.ch/pdf/assessment-report/ar5/syr/SYR_AR5_FINAL_full_wcover.pdf accessed 3 June 2016, Section SPM 1.1, 2 (IPCC 2014 Report).

16 Ibid.; UNGA Res 70/1 (25 September 2015) UN Doc A/RES/70/1.

17 It should be noted that a 1.5 °C increase only constitutes the most certain scenario, with other outcomes carrying considerable percentages of likelihood as well. See IPCC 2014 Report (n 2), Section E1, 20, which shows that global surface temperature change for the end of the twenty-first century is likely to exceed 1.5 °C relative to 1850 to 1900 for all RCP scenarios except RCP2.6. It is likely to exceed 2 °C for RCP6.0 and RCP8.5, and more likely than not to exceed 2 °C for RCP4.5.

18 Maize, wheat, and other major crops have experienced significant yield reductions at the global level of 40 megatonnes per year between 1981 and 2002 owing to a warmer climate. IPCC 2014 Report (n 2).

19 IPCC 2014 Report (n 2).

20 Ibid.

21 C.D. Allen et al., 'A Global Overview of Drought and Heat-Induced Tree Mortality Reveals Emerging Climate Change Risks for Forests' (2010) 259 *Forest Ecology and Management* 660.

22 M. Chambwera and others, 'Economics of Adaptation', in C.B. Field et al., *Climate Change 2014: Impacts, Adaptation, and Vulnerability. Part A: Global and Sectoral Aspects. Contribution of Working Group II to the Fifth Assessment Report of the Intergovernmental Panel on Climate Change* (Cambridge University Press 2014) 945 at 959.

impacts of climate change reach far into the future, threatening the potential lives and livelihoods, indeed the very existence, of generations to come. Already, some countries are seriously at risk of losing the entirety of their national territories. According to studies, the current trajectory of global warming will – if left unchecked – surpass 1.5 °C by 2030, costing millions of lives and terrible loss and damage for human civilisation.[23] Further, millions of other entire species are also threatened with extinction due to human-induced climate change and related changes.[24] Perhaps most troubling, current regulatory and financial regimes guiding development continue to privilege carbon-intensive, unsustainable options, rather than promoting sustainable development, and making finance flows consistent with a pathway towards low-GHG and climate-resilient alternatives, as sought by the 2015 Paris Agreement and its 2018 Katowice Rulebook.

However, as this chapter argues, it may still be possible, using a wide array of legal and institutional measures, to limit the increase in global mean temperature to well below 2 °C above pre-industrial levels. Major regulatory, institutional, economic, and technological transformations, if carried out immediately, offer the world a chance to limit dangerous consequences to below this threshold, although they would still carry serious possible consequences for future generations. Such transformations, guided by legal and institutional reforms, can be carried out in accordance with the principles of international law on sustainable development, in particular, the principle of intergenerational equity.[25]

The contours of international attempts to secure greater equity and the eradication of poverty, particularly in relation to the emerging principles of international law on sustainable development, are discussed elsewhere in this volume and bear only a brief mention here. As noted in the introductory chapters of this volume, in 2002, the ILA's Committee on the Legal Aspects of Sustainable Development, after ten years of study, released the New Delhi ILA Declaration on Principles of International Law relating to Sustainable Development as a Resolution of its 70th Conference.[26] The New Delhi Declaration notes that 'sustainable development is

[23] UNEP 2018 Adaptation Gap Report; IPCC 2018 1.5 Degrees Report.

[24] IPBES 2019 Biodiversity Assessment Report.

[25] M.-C. Cordonier Segger, 'Significant Developments in Sustainable Development Law and Governance: A Proposal' (2004) 28 *Natural Resources Forum* 61; M.-C. Cordonier Segger et al., 'Prospects for Principles of International Sustainable Development Law after the WSSD: Common but Differentiated Responsibilities, Precaution and Participation' (2003) 12 RECIEL 54.

[26] It is argued that States have a duty to respect the following principles: (1) sustainable use of natural resources whereby States have sovereign rights over their natural resources, and a corresponding duty not to cause, or allow, undue damage to the environment of other States in the use of these resources; (2) inter- and intra-generational equity and the eradication of poverty; (3) common but differentiated responsibilities and respective capabilities; (4) the precautionary approach to human health, natural resources, and ecosystems, transferring the burden of proving lack of significant harm from an undertaking to the proponent, in cases of scientific uncertainty; (5) public participation, backed by access to information and justice;

now widely accepted as a global objective and that the concept has been amply recognised in various international and national legal instruments, including treaty law and jurisprudence at international and national levels'. In the 2002 New Delhi Declaration, seven principles of international law are highlighted which characterise treaties related to sustainable development[27] and are reflected in decisions of international courts and tribunals.[28] The ILA underlined that States have a duty to respect key principles, including a principle of inter- and intra-generational equity and the eradication of poverty.[29] As one of the 'sustainable development principles', this commitment to equity is gaining certain recognition by States and other actors in international law. It may not yet be recognised by all countries as a rule of CIL. However, the principle is increasingly reflected and made operational in binding international treaties, forming part of international law and policy in the field of sustainable development, including in the UNFCCC and its Paris Agreement.[30]

In the ILA New Delhi Declaration, the importance of equity and the eradication of poverty are underlined, with experts findings that the 'principle of equity is central to the attainment of sustainable development'. In the Declaration, ILA experts refer to both intergenerational equity (the right of future generations to enjoy a fair level of the common patrimony) and intragenerational equity (the right of all peoples within the current generation of fair access to the current generation's entitlement to the Earth's natural resources) (2.1); noting that the 'present generation has a right to use and enjoy the resources of the Earth but is under an obligation to take into account the long-term impact of its activities and to sustain the resource base and the global environment for the benefit of future generations of humankind' (2.2); and that the 'right to development must be implemented so as to meet developmental and environmental needs of present and future generations in a sustainable and equitable manner. They highlight 'the duty to cooperate for the eradication of poverty in accordance with Chapter IX on International Economic

(6) good governance, with measures to support rule of law, coherence, and anti-corruption; and (7) integration and interrelationship of human rights and social, economic, and environmental objectives. See ILA, 'New Delhi Declaration on the Principles of International Law Related to Sustainable Development', Resolution 3/2002, available online: https://cisdl.org/public/docs/new_delhi_declaration.pdf; N. Schrijver and F. Weiss (eds.), *International Law and Sustainable Development: Principles and Practice* (Martinus Nijhoff 2004) 1–152, 699–706; D. French, *International Law and Policy of Sustainable Development* (Manchester University Press 2005); See also 7 CISDL Legal Working Papers detailing the meaning, scope and existing status in international law of each proposed ILA New Delhi Declaration Principle http://cisdl.org/public/docs/new_delhi_declaration.pdf accessed 12 June 2016.

27 M.-C. Cordonier Segger and C.J. Weeramantry (eds.), *Sustainable Justice* (Martinus Nijhoff 2004) 561–592.

28 M.-C. Cordonier Segger with C.J. Weeramantry (eds.), *Sustainable Development in International Courts and Tribunals* (Routledge 2017).

29 M.-C. Cordonier Segger, 'Sustainable Development in International Law', in D. Armstrong (ed.), *Routledge Handbook on International Law* (Routledge 2009) 355.

30 Ibid.

and Social Co-operation of the Charter of the UN and the Rio Declaration on Environment and Development as well as the duty to cooperate for global sustainable development and the attainment of equity in the development opportunities of developed and developing countries' (2.3); and state that while 'it is the primary responsibility of the State to aim for conditions of equity within its own population and to ensure, as a minimum, the eradication of poverty, all States which are in a position to do so have a further responsibility, as recognised by the Charter of the United Nations and the Millennium Declaration of the United Nations, to assist States in achieving this objective' (2.4).[31]

The Millennium Declaration was the forerunner for the 2015 SDGs, which identify several crucial targets for achieving greater equity – or at least reducing inequality – by 2030. Indeed, in SDG 10 to reduce inequality within and among countries, governments and a wide array of stakeholders prioritised several crucial targets, committing to adjust economic endeavours in order to increase equity among current generations; to reduce discrimination and promote greater inclusion; and to address the needs and voices of vulnerable developing countries and peoples, especially migrants. Addressing economic activities, for instance, in SDG 10 countries set targets to 'progressively achieve and sustain income growth of the bottom 40 per cent of the population at a rate higher than the national average' by 2030 (10.1); to 'adopt policies, especially fiscal, wage and social protection policies, and progressively achieve greater equality' (10.4); and to 'improve the regulation and monitoring of global financial markets and institutions and strengthen the implementation of such regulations'(10.5).[32] To reduce discrimination through inclusion, for instance, in SDG 10 countries also set targets to, by 2030, 'empower and promote the social, economic and political inclusion of all, irrespective of age, sex, disability, race, ethnicity, origin, religion or economic or other status' (10.2) and to 'ensure equal opportunity and reduce inequalities of outcome, including by eliminating discriminatory laws, policies and practices and promoting appropriate legislation, policies and action in this regard' (10.3).[33] They also prioritised, with regards the most vulnerable countries, to 'ensure enhanced representation and voice for developing countries in decision-making in global international economic and financial institutions in order to deliver more effective, credible, accountable and legitimate institutions' (10.6) and to 'facilitate orderly, safe, regular and responsible migration and mobility of people, including through the implementation of planned and well-managed migration policies' (10.7).[34] Among other means, these targets are to be implemented by encouraging 'official development assistance and financial flows, including foreign direct investment, to States where the need is

[31] ILA New Delhi Declaration of Principles of Sustainable Development (2009).

[32] Sustainable Development Goals Knowledge Platform, Sustainable Development Goals 10 https://sustainabledevelopment.un.org/sdg10 accessed 12 September 2019.

[33] Ibid.

[34] Ibid.

greatest, in particular least developed countries, African countries, small island developing States and landlocked developing countries, in accordance with their national plans and programmes' (10.b).[35]

This mandate is directly relevant to climate change. Climate change requires significant adjustments to economic endeavours, and this transformation may either increase equity among current generations or greatly worsen conditions for many – ensuring a 'just transition' is essential for success. Further, both climate change impacts themselves, and also measures to address climate mitigation and adaptation, can either reduce discrimination and promote greater inclusion or disproportionately affect people who already face discrimination and exclusion. Of great relevance to the Paris Agreement, finally, it will be essential to address the needs and voices of the most vulnerable peoples, especially migrants whose lives and livelihoods are impacted by climate change, and future generations whose opportunities and options will be restricted, perhaps irreparably, by climate change. Climate change, including extreme weather events such as hurricanes and storms, heatwaves, wildfires, desertification and drought, and dangerous floods, already disproportionately affect least developed countries, African countries, SIDS and landlocked developing countries. The needs of these 'highly climate vulnerable countries' can and must be addressed in efforts to implement the Paris Agreement.

As the rest of this chapter argues, the principle of intergenerational equity and poverty eradication, especially, permeates the 2015 Paris Agreement and the 2018 Katowice Outcomes and further decisions. Further, these international instruments on climate change and the domestic measures taken for their implementation hold the potential to either assist countries in making progress towards achievement of related SDGs, including SDG 10 to reduce inequality within and among countries, or to exacerbate current conditions, leading to greater inequality and significant injustices both within current generations and for the future.

## CONTRIBUTIONS OF THE GLOBAL CLIMATE REGIME, PARTICULARLY THE PARIS AGREEMENT, TO INTERGENERATIONAL EQUITY

The UNFCCC was concluded in 1992 and is the central framework for global efforts to avoid the dangers of climate change.[36] While the Treaty itself does not contain binding GHG emission limits or enforcement mechanisms, it does provide a framework for the negotiation of further protocols and instruments. The Kyoto Protocol includes binding emissions reduction targets for Parties,[37] and is based

[35] Ibid.

[36] Framework Convention on Climate Change (adopted 9 May 1992, entered into force 21 March 1994) 1771 UNTS 107 (UNFCCC).

[37] Kyoto Protocol to the United Nations Framework Convention on Climate Change (adopted 11 December 1997, entered into force 16 February 2005) 2303 UNTS 148 (Kyoto Protocol).

on the principle of common but differentiated responsibilities and respective capabilities (CBDRRC).[38] The first commitment period under the Protocol ended in 2012; however, efforts have fallen short of what is needed to mitigate and adapt to dangerous climate change. Indeed, only thirty-seven countries accepted binding targets under the second commitment period of the Kyoto Protocol, and current projections for average global temperature rise by the end of the century place warming well above the 1.5–2 °C limit necessary to avoid dangerous climate change.

The Paris Agreement adopted by the UNFCCC COP21 on 12 December 2015 entered into force in 2016,[39] and was supplemented by the Katowice Outcomes agreed by the Ad Hoc Working Group on the Paris Agreement (APA) that was established at the 44th UNFCCC Subsidiary Bodies meeting in Bonn, Germany in May 2016. The Treaty[40] and its Adoption Decision[41] seek to establish a universally acceptable framework to limit climate change well below 2 °C, pursuing efforts toward a 1.5 °C limit, to support adaptation and resilience, and to mobilise climate finance, equitably promoting sustainable development and poverty eradication. In essence, the Paris Agreement presents a core triangle of obligations. First, countries must take nationally determined, quantifiable, and progressive action for climate mitigation and adaptation; second, these actions are incentivised by changes in financial flows and related technology transfer, capacity-building, education, and other cooperative measures; and third, enforcement is achieved through transparency and reporting, peer review, periodic stocktaking, public participation, and compliance mechanisms.

While all Parties, including those with the least historical contributions to global emissions, begin to play a role in emissions reduction, they also benefit from new investment and collaboration for low-GHG pathways for sustainable development and poverty eradication. As an important instrument in the climate regime, the Paris Agreement holds all the hallmarks of a sustainable development accord.[42]

The Paris Agreement is predicated upon an expectation that, if NDCs can be shaped and supported by peer review and public awareness, new scientific data on risks, actual impacts, and greater political attention will lead to ever-higher ambition from all levels of governments, along with non-State actors in the private sector and

38 S. Maljean-Dubois and P. Moraga Sariego, 'Le principe des responsabilités communes mais differenciées dans le régime international du climat' (2014) 55 *Cahiers de Droit* 83.

39 Paris Agreement (adopted 12 December 2015) UN Doc FCCC/CP/2015/L.9/Rev.1.

40 While a certain ambiguity may exist on this point, the Paris Agreement can be seen as a Treaty in the sense of art. 2(a) of the Vienna Convention on the Law of Treaties (adopted May 1969, entered into force January 1980) 1155 UNTS 331. One indication is the need for ratification for its entry into force.

41 Conference on the Adoption of the Paris Agreement (12 December 2015, opened for signature 21 April 2016) UN Doc FCCC/CP/2015/L.9/Rev.1.

42 M.-C. Cordonier Segger and A. Khalfan, *Sustainable Development Law: Principles, Practices, and Prospects* (Oxford University Press 2004). See also C. Voigt, *Sustainable Development as a Principle of International Law: Resolving Conflicts between Climate Measures and WTO Law* (Brill 2009).

civil society. Some hope that countries, perhaps in clubs with higher ambition, can move towards setting and achieving absolute emissions reduction targets, diversified enhanced mitigation actions, or arrangements among donors and beneficiaries to address key sectors. The former would seek to bind Parties to attain net zero emissions levels over the long term through a quantifiable standard. The latter would set higher ambitions, whether or not remaining recalcitrant countries also accepted such actions as obligatory.

The UNFCCC Paris Agreement reflects intergenerational equity in four key ways. First, like the UNFCCC under which the Paris Agreement operates, the accord implicitly recognises the principle of intra- and inter-generational equity. In both the treaty and its agreement, the potential dangers of anthropogenic climate change for present and future generations are recognised as crucial motivating factors for action. Second, in its object and purpose, the Paris Agreement attempts to slow rising emissions levels, provide for adaptation, and redirect financial flows in order to prevent the harm to future generations that would result from current policies and trends. Third, and perhaps of greatest interest for scholars, in its operational provisions, the agreement seeks to shape future economic, social, and environmental factors for decisions, changing the parameters that are causing climate change towards a more sustainable development. Finally, in its institutional arrangements, including for transparency, stocktaking, capacity, awareness and education, and compliance, the accord sets in place regimes that should, if implemented, offer continuing guidance to future generations in regulating anthropogenic climate change.

### *Commitments to Intergenerational Equity in the Principles of the UNFCCC and the Paris Agreement*

In the Preamble of the Treaty, as mentioned above there are two references to equity and intergenerational equity, which also appear in the Preamble of the Adoption Decision. The new Treaty seeks to enhance implementation of the UNFCCC, which sets out its ultimate objective as the

> stabilization of greenhouse gas concentrations in the atmosphere at a level that would prevent dangerous anthropogenic interference with the climate system ... within a time frame sufficient to allow ecosystems to adapt naturally to climate change, to ensure that food production is not threatened and to *enable economic development to proceed in a sustainable manner.*[43]

[43] Emphasis added. While this Article establishes an unequivocal link between the Paris Agreement and the UNFCCC, as do the common implementation mechanisms discussed below, the Agreement remains silent on the actual nature of the relationship between the two documents. The Paris Agreement could be said to constitute a de facto Protocol to the UNFCCC but may also be characterised as a subsequent agreement. The latter option would give more room for an interpretation of the terms of the Paris Agreement independent of the meaning contained in the UNFCCC. See in that regard A. Savaresi, 'The Paris

Specifically, the Paris Agreement aims to implement the commitments in article 4 UNFCCC in accordance with the principles reflected in article 3 UNFCCC.[44]

Further, the commitment to intergenerational equity in the context of sustainable development permeates the Adoption Decision of the Paris Agreement. Indeed, the Decision begins by welcoming UNGA Res 70/1 on the global SDG, particularly Goal 13,[45] and acknowledging that climate change is a common concern of humankind. The Adoption Decision also recognises that when taking action on climate change, States must respect, promote, and consider their human rights obligations; the right to development; the rights of indigenous peoples, children, and others in vulnerable situations; gender equality and empowerment; and intergenerational equity. In essence, important sustainable development principles such as transparency and public participation, integration of environmental concerns and human rights into economic decision-making, good governance, precaution, intergenerational equity, CBDRRC, and sustainable use of natural resources such as energy, are reflected in the Preamble to the Adoption Decision.[46] This commitment is also reflected in principle in the Katowice Rulebook, which provides modalities and guidelines for implementation of Paris Agreement.

### *Commitments to Intergenerational Equity in the Purpose of the Paris Agreement*

Under article 2, the Paris Agreement aims to strengthen the global response to the threat of climate change, in the context of sustainable development and efforts to eradicate poverty, by holding the increase in the global average temperature to 'well below 2 °C above pre industrial levels' and pursuing efforts to limit the temperature increase to 1.5 °C; by increasing the ability to adapt to the adverse impacts of climate change as well as foster climate resilience and low GHG emissions development; and by making finance flows consistent with a pathway towards low GHG emissions and climate-resilient development.[47]

Agreement: A Rejoinder' (EJIL: *Talk!* 16 February 2016) www.ejiltalk.org/the-paris-agreement-a-rejoinder/ accessed 12 June 2016.

44 The principles in article 3 UNFCCC (n 10) include intergenerational and intragenerational equity, common but differentiated responsibility, precaution, right to sustainable development, and nondiscrimination.

45 SDG 13 requires 'urgent action to combat climate change and its impacts, acknowledging that the UNFCCC is the primary international, intergovernmental forum for negotiating the global response to climate change'. See UNGA Res 70/1 (n 3) 14.

46 See J.H. Knox, 'Linking Human Rights and Climate Change at the United Nations' (2009) 33 *Harvard Environmental Law Review* 477; J.H. Knox, 'Climate Change and Human Rights Law' (2009) 50 *Virginia Journal of International Law* 163.

47 Paris Agreement, *supra* note 3.

Article 2 further specifies that the agreement will be implemented to 'reflect equity and the principle of CBDRRC, in the light of different national circumstances'.[48] The legal obligations of developing countries under the Paris Agreement are thus variable in order to equitably reflect their historical, economic, and social circumstances in comparison with those of other states. Article 3 of the Paris Agreement underscores that all Parties will undertake and communicate ambitious efforts (as defined in articles 4, 7, 9, 10, 11, and 13) to achieve the aim of the agreement through NDCs to the global response to climate change. In doing so, it recognises, the efforts of all Parties will progress over time, and that there is a need to support developing country Parties for effective implementation.

The Paris Agreement aims to achieve climate mitigation, adaptation and finance through a series of cooperative frameworks and mechanisms, each of which establishes different legal rights and obligations for Parties, and explicitly makes provision for the needs of developing country Parties, especially the most vulnerable. These are intended to achieve NDCs to mitigation and adaptation, through mobilisation of resources, transparency, global stocktaking and review, a sustainable development mechanism and non-market approaches, technology transfer, and further implementation measures, such as capacity-building, education, and a compliance mechanism. In the Katowice Rulebook, the objectives for the modalities and guidelines for implementation recognise the commitment of Parties to greater intergenerational and intragenerational equity.

### *Commitments to Intergenerational Equity in the Operations of the Paris Agreement*

Commitments to equity arises frequently in the operational provisions Paris Agreement, as was posited prior to the conclusion of the Paris Agreement by leading legal scholars.[49] In the operational provisions of the Paris Agreement, it is noted that Parties should protect the climate on the basis of equity and the principle of CBDRRC. The importance of efforts to eradicate poverty are also highlighted (Preamble, paragraphs 8 and 9), in the statement of the general objective of the Agreement (Article 2), and in relation to cooperation to implement NDCs (Article 6). In the Katowice Rulebook, equity is also highlighted.

Several other operational provisions further seek to secure, in a practical way, intergenerational equity. While a comprehensive analysis is beyond the scope of this chapter, six key mechanisms in the Paris Agreement which specifically address

48 Note the shift from differentiation as adopted by the UNFCCC.

49 C. Voigt, 'Equity in the 2015 Climate Agreement' (2014) 4 *Climate Law* 50.

efforts to reduce inequality, and reflect the principle of inter- and intra-generational equity, can be highlighted.

### *Nationally Determined Contributions to Global Climate Mitigation and Adaptation*

One of the central aspects of the Paris Agreement is its 'bottom-up' approach. Paragraph 2(b) of UNGA Decision 1/CP.19 invited all parties to communicate to the UNFCCC Secretariat their 'intended Nationally Determined Contributions (iNDCs) for GHG emissions reductions'. By COP21, 185 countries had submitted their iNDCs. Under article 3 of the Paris Agreement, Parties commit that they 'shall prepare, communicate and maintain' successive NDCs and pursue domestic mitigation measures to achieve their commitments. Rather than setting out specific mitigation or adaptation targets for each country, the Paris Agreement commits Parties to nationally determine and transparently communicate their own objectives, to inform the international community of the progress in implementing and achieving them, and to participate in periodic global stocktaking to inform progressively higher ambition. Paragraph 13 of the Paris Agreement Adoption Decision recalls this invitation for Parties who have not done so already, for the pre-2020 period. The NDCs will be communicated every five years (i.e. 2020, 2025, 2030, etc.). A Party may at any time adjust its existing NDC to enhance its level of ambition (article 4.3, article 4.11). These NDCs, once submitted by the government of a country, shall be recorded in a public registry maintained by the UNFCCC Secretariat. The information that must be included in the communication of NDCs, so as to facilitate clarity, transparency, and understanding, is explained in paragraph 27 of the Adoption Decision (see also Decision 1/CP.20, paragraph 14). Furthermore, Parties shall account for their NDCs and, in accounting for GHG emissions and removals corresponding to the NDCs, Parties shall promote environmental integrity, transparency, accuracy, completeness, comparability, and consistency, and avoid double-counting in accordance with guidance from Parties in the CMA (article 4.13).

### *GHG-Emission Mitigation, Low-Carbon GHG-Emission Development Strategies, and GHG Sinks and Reservoirs*

In article 4 of the Paris Agreement, the Parties aim to reach global peaking of GHG emissions as soon as possible, recognising that this will take longer for developing country Parties, and to undertake rapid reductions thereafter in accordance with the best available science, so as to balance emissions by sources and removals by sinks in the second half of this century (article 4.1). The notion of balancing emissions and removals can be understood as an objective of 'net zero' emissions, whereby any residual anthropogenic GHG emissions would be annulled by activities removing

GHG from the atmosphere. Such a sequestration of GHG could occur through expansion of the activities of natural carbon sinks and reservoirs, such as forests or oceans, or through the deployment of carbon capture technologies.[50]

In this respect and in line with the principle of equity, article 4 of the Paris Agreement recognises that developed countries should take the lead by undertaking economy-wide absolute emission reduction targets, while developing countries should continue enhancing mitigation efforts, moving over time towards economy-wide targets (article 4.4, see also Preamble paragraph 16). Support shall also be provided to developing country Parties for the implementation of mitigation efforts, recognising that enhanced support for developing country Parties will allow for higher ambition in their actions (article 4.5, see also articles 9, 10 and 11). The least developed countries (LDCs) and SIDS may prepare strategies that reflect their special circumstances (article 4.6). Parties shall take into consideration in the implementation of this Agreement the concerns of Parties with economies most affected by the impacts of response measures, particularly developing country Parties (article 4.15). Further, over and above their NDCs, all Parties should strive to formulate and communicate long-term Low GHG Emission Development Strategies (LEDS), taking into account CBDRRC, in light of different national circumstances (article 4.19).

### *Adaptation Goal and Communications, and Efforts to Address Loss and Damage*

By virtue of article 7, a global goal on adaptation is established to enhance adaptive capacity, strengthen resilience, and reduce vulnerability to climate change, with a view to contributing to sustainable development and ensuring an adequate adaptation response (article 7.1). Each Party should submit and periodically update an Adaptation Communication, which may include a national adaptation plan, priorities, implementation and support needs, plans, and actions, without creating additional burdens for developing country Parties (article 7.10, article 7.11). The Adaptation Communications shall be recorded in a public registry maintained by the UNFCCC Secretariat (article 7.12). Of great relevance to intergenerational equity, in article 7 the Paris Agreement provides that adaptation is recognised as a global challenge faced by all with multiple dimensions, taking into account the

[50] The utilisation of both carbon sinks (including afforestation) and carbon dioxide capture and storage (CCS) as well as bioenergy with carbon dioxide capture and storage (BECCS) feature prominently in several of the mitigation scenarios developed by the UNFCCC. This applies not only to overshoot scenarios (where the declared targets are exceeded for certain periods) but also to compensate for industries in which mitigation is more costly. However, there are also concerns associated with the deployment of CCS and BECCS. See IPCC 2014 Report (n 2) SPM 3.4, as well as Full IPCC Report, Box 3.3 'Carbon Dioxide Removal and Solar Radiation Management Geoengineering Technologies – Possible Roles, Options, Risks and Status' at 89.

urgent and immediate needs of those developing country Parties that are particularly vulnerable to the adverse effects of climate change (article 7.1). The adaptation efforts of developing country Parties shall be recognised, in accordance with the modalities to be adopted by the first COP meeting of the Paris Agreement Parties (article 7.3), and the Adaptation Committee and the Least Developed Countries Expert Group (LEG) should be involved in this process (Adoption Decision, paragraph 42). The Green Climate Fund is to expedite support for the LDCs and other developing country Parties for the formulation of National Adaptation Plans (Adoption Decision, paragraph 47). Parties should strengthen their cooperation on enhancing action on adaptation, taking into account the Cancun Adaptation Framework (article 7.7), and the global stocktake shall recognise and enhance these efforts, reviewing the adequacy and effectiveness of adaptation and support for it, and overall progress (article 7.14, also article 14). Continuous and enhanced international support shall be provided to developing country Parties for the implementation of commitments to enhance action on adaptation, to engage in adaptation planning, and to prepare, submit, and periodically update their Adaptation Communications (article 7.13, also articles 7.7, 7.9, 7.10, and 7.11). The Paris Agreement recognises the importance of averting, minimising, and addressing loss and damage associated with the adverse effects of climate change, including extreme weather events as well as slow onset events, and it specifically highlights the importance of sustainable development in reducing the risk of loss and damage (article 8.1). The Paris Agreement also addresses the Warsaw International Mechanism for Loss and Damage associated with Climate Change Impacts, noting that this shall be subject to the authority and the guidance of the COP serving as the MOP to the Paris Agreement (the new CMA), and notes that Parties should enhance understanding, action, and support on a cooperative and facilitative basis with respect to loss and damage associated with the adverse effects of climate change (article 8.3, also article 8.2). Certain key priorities for cooperation and facilitation are identified in the Paris Agreement, such as early warning systems, emergency preparedness, slow onset events, events that may involve irreversible and permanent loss and damage, comprehensive risk assessment and management, risk insurance facilities, climate risk pooling and other insurance solutions, and non-economic losses, as well as resilience of communities, livelihoods and ecosystems (article 8.4). The Treaty commits to ensuring that the Warsaw International Mechanism (WIM) collaborates with existing bodies and expert groups, as well as relevant actors outside the Agreement (article 8.5). It does not go further to define, deny, or designate liability or compensation. In the Adoption Decision, while a new clearing house for risk transfer is established to serve as a repository for information on insurance and risk transfer to facilitate Parties' efforts to develop and implement comprehensive risk management strategies (Adoption Decision, paragraph 49), it is simply stated that article 8 of the Treaty does not involve or provide a basis for any liability or compensation (Adoption Decision, paragraph 52). In essence, the Treaty neither confirms nor denies whether liability exists or compensation should be provided, a stalemate in legal terms. In the Katowice Outcomes, guidelines are provided for operationalising this key aspect of the Paris Agreement.

### *Mobilisation and Directing of Climate Finance*

The provision of climate finance is also crucial for intergenerational and intragenerational equity, and to meet the targets of SDG 10 discussed above. Under article 9 of the Paris Agreement, developed country Parties shall provide financial resources to assist developing country Parties with respect to both mitigation and adaptation, in continuation of their existing UNFCCC obligations (article 9.1), while other Parties are encouraged to provide financial support voluntarily (article 9.2). At the same time, it holds, all Parties should increase their efforts in mobilising climate finance from a wide variety of sources, instruments, and channels, noting the significant role of public funds and taking into account the priorities and needs of developing country Parties, with the greater onus being on developed country Parties which shall take the lead (article 9.3). Prior to 2025, the COP shall set a new collective quantified goal from a floor of USD 100 billion per year, taking into account the needs and priorities of developing countries (Adoption Decision, paragraph 54). Developed country Parties are strongly urged to scale up their level of financial support, with a concrete roadmap to achieve this goal by 2020 for mitigation and adaptation, while significantly increasing adaptation finance from current levels, and to provide appropriate technology and capacity-building support (Adoption Decision, paragraph 115). Developed country Parties shall biennially communicate indicative quantitative and qualitative information related to scaling up the provision and as regards mobilising financial resources, including as to the balance between adaptation and mitigation (as per articles 9.1 and 9.3), as applicable, with the financial mechanism of the UNFCCC serving as the mechanism for the Paris Agreement. The provision of scaled-up financial resources should attempt to balance the provision of mitigation and adaptation resources and take into account country-driven strategies and the priorities and needs of developing country Parties, especially those that are particularly vulnerable to the adverse effects of climate change and have significant capacity constraints, such as LDCs and SIDS, considering the need for public and grant-based resources for adaptation (article 9.4). In the Katowice Rulebook, guidelines are provided for operationalising this key aspect of the Paris Agreement.

### *Transparency, Global Stocktaking, and Peer Review*

By virtue of article 13, in addition to reporting on mitigation and adaptation, Parties should also regularly provide Communications on a national inventory report of GHG emissions by sources and removals by sinks, prepared using good practice methodologies accepted by the IPCC (article 13.7(a)), and the information necessary to track progress made in implementing and achieving NDCs (article 13.7(b)). They should also provide information regarding climate change impacts and adaptation (article 13.8).

Of particular interest to developing countries, article 13 contains further transparency provisions. For developing country Parties, information may be presented on financial, technological, and capacity-building support needed and received under article 9 on climate finance, article 10 on technology transfer, and article 11 on capacity-building (article 13.10). For developing country Parties, information may be presented on progress made on implementing capacity-building plans, policies, actions, or measures to implement the Paris Agreement (article 11.4). The LDCs and SIDS may submit the information required at their discretion (Adoption Decision, paragraph 91). The national inventory reports on GHG emissions by sources and removals by sinks, and the information for tracking progress, as well as the level of support by developed countries to developing countries, will be the object of a technical expert review and also of a multilateral consideration of progress (article 13.11, article 13.12, article 13.13). The review process shall pay particular attention to the respective national capabilities and circumstances of developing country Parties. Support shall be provided to developing countries for the implementation of transparency framework (article 13.14), and for building the capacity of developing country Parties to participate in the process, on a continuous basis (article 13.15). The 'enhanced transparency framework' shall build on the transparency arrangements under the UNFCCC (including reporting, verification, and monitoring measures) and be implemented with common modalities, guidelines, and procedures in a manner that is facilitative, non-intrusive, non-punitive, respectful of national sovereignty, and avoids placing undue burdens on Parties (article 13.3). It shall supersede existing guidance (Adoption Decision, paragraph 88). As a further ambition/transparency measure, the Paris Agreement stipulates that its Meetings of the Parties shall periodically take stock of the Treaty's implementation, to assess collective progress towards achieving the Treaty's purpose and long-term goals, referred to as the 'global stocktake', which shall be conducted in the light of equity and the best available science (article 14.1).

### *Sustainable Development Market Mechanism and Non-Market Approaches*

Under article 6, Parties may engage in 'international transfers of mitigation outcomes' towards their NDCs, through voluntary cooperation, to allow for 'higher ambition in their mitigation and adaptation actions and to promote sustainable development and environmental integrity' (article 6.1). When using internationally transferred mitigation outcomes, Parties shall promote sustainable development and ensure environmental integrity and transparency, applying robust accounting and governance to avoid double-counting, consistent with guidance to be adopted by the

COP MOP to the Paris Agreement (article 6.2).[51] Further, a 'sustainable development mechanism' is established to promote mitigation of GHG emissions while fostering sustainable development; to incentivise and facilitate GHG mitigation by public and private entities authorised by a Party; to contribute to the reduction of emission levels in the host Party, which will benefit from mitigation activities resulting in emission reductions that can also be used by another Party to fulfil its NDC; and to deliver an overall mitigation in global emissions (Article 6.4). It is established under the authority of the COP meeting of the Paris Agreement Parties, for use by the Parties on a voluntary basis, and is to be supervised by a body designated by the COP MOP (article 6.4). Rules, modalities, and procedures for its operation should be forthcoming (article 6.7). The new mechanism might draw upon certain experience accumulated through the Clean Development Mechanism (CDM) under the Kyoto Protocol. However, the key question is how this mechanism will work in a world of NDCs, where developing countries (as potential hosts) also have agreed baselines and/or reference levels. Provisions of interest to vulnerable developing countries include a commitment that a share of proceeds from the mechanism shall be dedicated to cover administrative expenses and to assist developing country Parties particularly vulnerable to climate change to meet adaptation costs (article 6.7). There is also recognition of the importance of non-market approaches, and the definition of a framework to promote them, including public and private sector participation and coordination across instruments and relevant institutional arrangements (article 6.8 and 6.9). It is not enough, perhaps many would argue, but provides a platform to build on.

### *Technology Mechanism*

The Technology Mechanism established under the UNFCCC shall also serve the Paris Agreement (article 10.3). Parties recognise the importance of technology for the implementation of mitigation and adaptation actions under the Paris Agreement, and commit to strengthening cooperative action on technology development and transfer (article 10.2). They also establish a framework to guide the operation of the Technology Mechanism (Article 10.4). Of interest to vulnerable developing countries, Parties agree to focus on collaborative approaches to research and development, and on facilitating access to technology, in particular for early stages of the technology cycle, for developing country Parties (article 10.5). Support, including financial support, shall be provided to developing country Parties,

[51] See K. Khoday, 'Mobilizing Market Forces to Combat Global Environmental Change: Lessons from UN-Private Sector Partnerships in China' (2007) 16 *Rev Euro Comm & Int'l Envt* 173; S. Bernstein et al., 'A Tale of Two Copenhagens: Carbon Markets and Climate Governance' (2010) 39 *Millenn J Int Stud* 161; C. Voigt 'WTO Law and International Emissions Trading: Is There Potential for Conflict?' (2008) 2 CCLR 54.

including for strengthening cooperative action on technology development and transfer at different stages of the technology cycle. Further, as the Adoption Decision also clarifies, the Subsidiary Body for Scientific and Technological Advice will undertake a work programme under the framework for non-market approaches to sustainable development referred to in article 6 of the Paris Agreement (paragraph 40). All UN agencies and financial institutions are invited to provide information on how their development assistance and climate finance programmes incorporate climate-proofing and climate resilience measures (paragraph 44). The link between adequate and predictable financial resources and sustainable management of forests is recognised (article 55), as are the co-benefits of voluntary mitigation actions for adaptation, health, and sustainable development (article 109). In addition, the Decision underlines the importance of taking national sustainable development priorities into account in the existing technical examination process on mitigation (paragraph 110(a)), and encourages Parties to make effective use of the Climate Technology Centre and Network to obtain assistance to develop economically, environmentally and socially viable project proposals in the high mitigation potential areas identified in the process (paragraph 110(d)). In the Katowice Outcomes, guidelines are provided for operationalising this key aspect of the Paris Agreement.

## COMMITMENTS TO INTERGENERATIONAL EQUITY IN THE INSTITUTIONAL FRAMEWORKS OF THE PARIS AGREEMENT

### *Cooperation for Capacity-Building*

Capacity-building under the Paris Agreement, according to article 11, should enhance the capacity and ability of developing country Parties to take effective climate action, particularly 'countries with the least capacity, such as the LDCs, and those that are particularly vulnerable to the adverse effects of climate change' (article 11.1). All countries should cooperate to achieve this, and there is a specific provision that developed country Parties should enhance support for capacity-building actions in developing country Parties (article 11.3). Capacity-building should be country-driven and responsive to national needs, and it should foster country ownership of Parties, including at the national, subnational, and local levels, in particular for developing country Parties (article 11.2). In essence, an effective, iterative process is called for: one that is participatory, cross-cutting, and gender-responsive (article 11.2). Capacity-building should be guided by lessons learned, including those from previous activities under the UNFCCC. There will be regular communication by all Parties that support capacity-building about their actions and measures (including the capacity-building done under regional, bilateral, and multilateral approaches). Capacity-building will not just assist with technical capacity for implementing adaptation and mitigation actions, the facilitation of technology development, dissemination and deployment, and access to climate finance, but it will also support education, training, and public awareness, and the transparent, timely, and accurate communication of information (article 11.1, article 11.4, see also article 13.15).

The Paris Agreement calls for capacity-building activities to be enhanced through appropriate institutional arrangements, to be created in the APA and followed up in the COP serving as the MOP to the Paris Agreement, known as the CMA (article 11.5). The Paris Committee on Capacity-building is also created, with the aim of addressing gaps and needs in implementing capacity-building in developing country Parties and further enhancing capacity-building efforts, including with regard to coherence and coordination in capacity-building activities under the Convention (Adoption Decision, paragraph 72). Further, a Capacity-building Initiative for Transparency is created by the Adoption Decision, in order to build institutional and technical capacity, both pre- and post-2020. Of importance for the principle of intergenerational equity and SDG 10, this initiative will support developing country Parties, upon request, in meeting enhanced transparency requirements as defined in article 13 of the Agreement in a timely manner (Adoption Decision, paragraph 85). In the Katowice Outcomes, guidelines are provided for operationalising this key aspect of the Paris Agreement.

### *Education and Public Awareness*

The Paris Agreement affirms that Parties shall cooperate in taking measures, as appropriate, to enhance climate change education, training, public awareness, public participation, and public access to information, recognising the importance of these steps with respect to enhancing actions under the Agreement (article 12).

### *Implementation and Compliance Mechanism*

A mechanism to facilitate implementation of the agreement and promote compliance is established (article 15.1). This mechanism is structured as an expert-based and facilitative committee and operates in a transparent, non-adversarial, and non-punitive way, according to procedures to be defined by the first MOP. The Compliance Committee shall pay particular attention to the respective national capabilities and circumstances of Parties. The committee consists of twelve members with recognised competence in relevant scientific, technical, socio-economic, or legal fields, to be elected by the COP on the basis of equitable geographical representation, with two members each from the five regional groups of the UN and one member each from the SIDS and the LDCs, taking gender balance into account (Adoption Decision, paragraph 103). In the Katowice Outcomes, guidelines are provided for operationalising this 'crown jewel' of the Paris Agreement.

### Governance and Dispute Settlement

The Paris Agreement adopts the UNFCCC rules of procedure and secretariat (article 16 and article 17); its governance structure, including the subsidiary body for scientific and technological advice (UNFCCC article 9) and the subsidiary body for implementation (UNFCCC article 10); the arrangements for voting and observer participation (article 18, article 19); and its dispute settlement mechanism (article 24, see also UNFCCC article 14). The Treaty opens for signature from 22 April 2016 to 21 April 2017, and thereafter for accession (article 20.1), and shall enter into force thirty days after fifty-five Parties to the UNFCCC accounting for at least 55 per cent of global GHG emissions have joined (article 21.1).

### Institutionalisation of Respect for Human Rights and Equity in the Paris Agreement

Following the Cancun Agreements, which recognised the importance of respecting human rights in all climate-related actions, the Paris Agreement also contains several references to respect for human rights. Human rights considerations – arising from the effects of climate change itself, as well as from Parties' climate change response measures – shall be taken into account at the national level. At its latest session, the Human Rights Council reaffirmed the importance of respect for human rights in the efforts to address climate change, building on previous statements to the same effect.[52] In addition, as observed by the Office of the UN High Commissioner for Human Rights, respect for the right to public participation and access to information are guaranteed under international human rights law and, along with other fundamental rights, are critical to the success of efforts to address climate change.[53] Further, to respect the principle of equity, climate response measures should recognise the specific rights of Indigenous peoples, as affirmed in the UN Declaration on the Rights of Indigenous Peoples and other binding international human rights treaties.[54] Indigenous peoples can be included in participatory processes relating to climate change. The principle of free, prior and informed consent may also be applicable in climate-related projects that affect the lands of indigenous peoples, and the traditional knowledge of indigenous peoples and local communities must be considered in climate actions at the domestic level. Finally, as the

[52] UNCHR Draft Res (2015) UN Doc A/HRC/29/L.21; UNCHR Res 7/23 (2008) UN Doc A/HRC/7/78; UNCHR Res 10/4 (2009) UN Doc A/HRC/10/L.11.

[53] OHCHR (2009) UN Doc A/HRC/10/61 paras. 78–79. See also OHCHR (2011) UN Doc A/HRC/19/34. See also S. Atapattu, 'Climate Change, Human Rights and Forced Migration: Implications for International Law' (2009) 27 *Wis Int'l LJ* 607; S. Atapattu, 'Global Climate Change: Can Human Rights (and Human Beings) Survive This Onslaught?' (2008) 20 *Colo J Int Environ Law Policy* 35.

[54] UNGA Res 61/295 (13 September 2007) UN Doc. A/61/PV.107.

Office of the UN High Commissioner for Human Rights has noted, the 'effects of climate change will be felt most acutely by those segments of the population who are already in vulnerable situations due to factors such as poverty, gender, age, minority status, and disability'.[55] Parties can adopt new measures to mainstream consideration for the right to non-discrimination of historically vulnerable groups across their climate policies and climate-related legislation, and take the necessary affirmative actions to ensure that climate change harms and climate response measures do not impact on substantive equality.

## CONCLUSION

Given available scientific findings, solving climate change is a matter of urgent attention for intergenerational justice. There can be no sustainable development for future generations if the worst-case scenarios for climate change are not averted. Compliance with the Paris Agreement, with due consideration of the applicable principles of international law, is crucial to achieve all global SDGs.[56] In this article, key international and domestic law and governance issues raised in the Paris Agreement have been identified and discussed.

The new global commitment to climate justice has transformed and informed the roles and engagement of all the actors involved in the UNFCCC COP21, including State delegations, non-State observers from civil society, academia, and the private sector, among others, and IGOs. Jurists, legal institutes and associations, law schools, judges networks, decision-makers, advocates, and other members of the law and governance community worldwide have long sought legal and institutional reforms on multiple levels, including international, regional, national, and subnational level, to facilitate, incentivise, and mandate effective action on climate change.[57] Indeed, the International Bar Association has highlighted that '[t]he need for climate change justice is ... apparent in the unequal geographic distribution of its environmental effects'.[58] As ILA Climate Change Principles affirm, States have an obligation 'to employ due diligence efforts to mitigate climate change impacts' in the design of any social and economic development plan which may result in significant emissions of GHGs (paragraph 5).[59] The ILA's Committee on

[55] OHCHR (2009) UN Doc A/HRC/10/61 para. 42.

[56] M.-C. Cordonier Segger and E. Mrema (eds.), 'Contributions of International Law to Implementing the Sustainable Development Goals' (CISDL/UNEP 2016). See also U. Natarajan and K. Khoday, 'Locating Nature: Making and Unmaking International Law' (2014) 27 *LJIL* 573.

[57] K. Levin et al., 'Overcoming the Tragedy of Super Wicked Problems: Constraining Our Future Selves to Ameliorate Global Climate Change' (2012) 45 *Policy Sciences* 123.

[58] IBA Climate Change Justice and Human Rights Task Force (2014) 45.

[59] ILA 'Legal Principles Relating to Climate Change' (2014). See also Expert Group on Global Climate Obligations, 'Oslo Principles on Global Obligations to Reduce Climate Change' (2015).

International Law on Sustainable Development, and its follow-up Committee on the role of International Law in Sustainable Natural Resources Management, are further working to illuminate the principles and good practices of international law which guide efforts in this field.[60]

Building on more than a decade of international symposia and conferences, backed by independent research and analysis, a consortium of law faculties from leading universities, together with key research institutes, intergovernmental agencies, law associations, judges' networks, expert commissions, and others, leads Climate Law and Governance Initiative, as a special forum for informed dialogue between experts, practising jurists, and decision-makers.[61] For effective responses to climate change under international law, interactional forms of international law-making under framework treaties are proving essential.[62] Many countries plan to reform their laws and institutions across diverse economic, environmental, and social sectors in order to respond to the challenges of climate mitigation, resilience, technology, finance, and accountability.[63] There is a pressing need for innovative legal knowledge, expertise, and capacity-building to ensure a strengthened agenda for the implementation of the Paris Agreement and the broader global SDGs, in accordance with the principle of intergenerational equity, in the interest of present and especially future generations.

60 ILA, 'New Delhi Declaration of Principles of International Law Relating to Sustainable Development' (2009). See also Committee on the Legal Principles Relating to Climate Change, 'International Law on Sustainable Development' (ILA 2012).

61 Report from Climate Law and Governance Day, Sorbonne Faculty of Law, Panthéon-Sorbonne University, Paris, 04 December 2015 (CISDL/LCIL/IREDIES/IDLO/CIFOR/UNEP/UNDP Paris 2015); Report from Climate Law and Governance Official Side Event to the UNFCCC COP21 in Paris, 11 December 2014 (CISDL/NCCSD/ASOG, Paris 2015) www.climatelawgovernance.org.

62 Brunnée and Toope, *supra* note 6.

63 See for instance R. Kibugi, 'Mainstreaming Climate Change into Public Policy Functions: Legal Options to Reinforce Sustainable Development of Kenya' (2012) 8 *Fla A & M UL Rev* 205; R. Kibugi, 'Legal Options for Mainstreaming Climate Change Disaster Risk Reduction in Governance for Kenya', in K.O.H. Kheng-Lian (ed.), *Adaptation to Climate Change, ASEAN and Comparative Experiences* (WSPC 2015) 409; J. Ramon, T. Villarin, M. Antonia, Y. Loyzaga, and A.G.M. La Viña, 'In the Eye of the Perfect Storm: What the Philippines Should Do about Climate Change' (SCJ Professorial Lecture Working Paper July 2008) http://ohm.ecce.admu.edu.ph/wiki/pub/Main/EandEMaterials/SCJ_doc.pdf accessed 14 June 2016.

# 38

# The Four-Branches Model of Government: Representing Future Generations

*Joerg Chet Tremmel*

[O]nly present interests make themselves heard and felt and enforce their consideration. It is to them that public agencies are accountable, and this is the way in which concretely the respecting of rights comes about (as distinct from their abstract acknowledgment). But the future is not represented, it is not a force that can throw its weight into the scales. The nonexistent has no lobby, and the unborn are powerless. Thus accountability to them has no political reality behind it in present decision-making, and when they can make their complaint, then we, the culprits, will no longer be there.

H. Jonas, *The Imperative of Responsibility* (1984), 22

Only recently, in the past two decades, have scholars of philosophy, law, and political science engaged in a burgeoning debate about the 'presentism' of the democratic form of government.[1] Since these studies are quite new, concept formation still

[1] R. Schlickeisen, 'Protecting Biodiversity for Future Generations: An Argument for a Constitutional amendment' (1994) 8(1) *Tulane Environmental Law Review* 181–221; A. Dobson, 'Representative Democracy and the Environment', in W.M. Lafferty and J. Meadowcroft (eds.), *Democracy and the Environment* (Edward Elgar 1996) 124–139; R.E. Goodin, 'Enfranchising the Earth, and Its Alternatives' (1996) 44(5) *Political Studies* 835–849; T. Stein, 'Does the Constitutional and Democratic System Work? The Ecological Crisis as a Challenge to the Political Order of Constitutional Democracy' (1998) 4(3) *Constellations* 420–449; T. Stein, 'Zum Problem der Zukunftsfähigkeit der Demokratie', in B. Gesang (ed.) *Kann Demokratie Nachhaltigkeit?* (Springer 2014) 47–63; J. Barry, *Greening Political Theory* (Sage 1999); J. Doeleman and T. Sandler, 'The Intergenerational Case of Missing Markets and Missing Voters' (1998) 74(1) *Land Economics* 1–15; R. Eckersley, *The Green State: Rethinking Democracy and Sovereignty* (MIT 2004); P. Wood, 'Intergenerational Justice and Curtailment on the Discretionary Powers of Governments' (2004) 26(4) *Environmental Ethics* 411–428; K.S. Ekeli, 'Giving a Voice to Posterity – Deliberative Democracy and Representation of Future People' (2005) 18(5) *Journal of Agricultural and Environmental Ethics* 429–450; J.C. Tremmel, 'Establishment of Intergenerational Justice in National Constitutions', in J.C. Tremmel (ed.), *Handbook of Intergenerational Justice* (Edward Elgar 2006) 187–214; D.F. Thompson, 'Representing Future Generations: Political 'Presentism' and Democratic Trusteeship' (2010) 13(1) *Critical Review of International Social and Political Philosophy* 17–37; R. Read, *Guardians of the Future: A Constitutional Case for Representing and Protecting Future*

remains unfinished. To be sure, having an adequate terminology is essential – after all, just as concepts without corresponding phenomena are empty, so too are existing phenomena inaccessible to human reason without appropriate concepts.[2] For instance, the concepts of 'presentism' and 'short-termism' do not mean the same. 'Presentism' stands in sharp contrast to the noble idea of 'intergenerational justice',[3] but the same is not necessarily true for the phrase 'short term'. Take, for example, the political right of generations to self-determination. Constitution-making is a case in point that has been discussed regularly in political philosophy, and at great length in particular by Jefferson, Madison, and Paine during the founding of the US. Constitutions enshrine the fundamental values of a people and they build a framework for a state's public policy. With regard to intergenerational justice, their long-term endurance gives rise to two concerns: the (forgone) welfare concern and the sovereignty concern. A procedure for constitution-amending that is intergenerationally just must not be too rigid and long-term-oriented.[4] One must thus be careful with criticizing short-termism and praising long-termism in general. Not every short-term action is a form of myopia that overdiscounts the interests of future generations. Another remark regarding terminology: speaking of 'institutions for the future' is not wrong but a little imprecise. The future itself is no moral patient. It can neither be harmed nor benefited. If one seeks to address the members of future generations of the human species, one should say so. Terminologically, the use of specific concepts such as 'institutions for future generations' is preferable to concepts such

*People* (Green House 2011); Oxford Martin Commission for Future Generations, *Now for the Long Term* (2013) www.oxfordmartin.ox.ac.uk/policy/commission/ accessed 12 September 2017; B. Gesang (ed.), *Kann Demokratie Nachhaltigkeit?* (Springer 2014); M. Kates, 'Justice, Democracy, and Future Generations' (2015) 18(5) *Critical Review of International Social and Political Philosophy* 508–528; J.C. Tremmel, 'Parliaments and Future Generations – The Four-Powers Model', in D. Birnbacher and M. Thorseth (eds.), *The Politics of Sustainability: Philosophical Perspectives* (Routledge 2015) 212–233. Research on institutions for future generations has even gained momentum in the last years. In 2016/2017 alone, several remarkable volumes addressed institutional responses to the widespread problem of 'presentism' in democracies. See I. González-Ricoy, 'Constitutionalizing Intergenerational Provisions', in I. González-Ricoy and A. Gosseries (eds.), *Institutions for Future Generations* (Oxford University Press 2016) 170–184; J. Boston, *Governing for the Future: Designing Democratic Institutions for a Better Tomorrow* (Emerald 2017); L. Köhler, *Die Repräsentation von Non-Voice-Partys in Demokratien* (Springer 2017); M. Rose, *Zukünftige Generationen in der heutigen Demokratie. Theorie und Praxis der Proxy-Repräsentation* (Springer 2017).

2 Paraphrasing a famous remark by Kant: 'Thoughts without content are empty, intuitions without concepts are blind.' I. Kant, *Kritik der reinen Vernunft, Werkausgabe Bd. III, Herausgegeben von Wilhelm Weischedel* (Suhrkamp 1968 (first published 1781)) 98 (B 75).

3 For an overview of definitions and theories of 'intergenerational justice', see J.C. Tremmel, *Eine Theorie der Generationengerechtigkeit* (mentis 2012); J.C. Tremmel, *A Theory of Intergenerational Justice* (Earthscan 2009); A. Gosseries and L.H. Meyer (eds.), *Intergenerational Justice* (Oxford University Press 2009).

4 In search of middle ground between perpetual constitutions (responsibility in difficult-to-change constitutions) and sunset constitutions, Tremmel proposes recurrent constitutional reform commissions. See J.C. Tremmel, 'Constitutions as Intergenerational Contracts: Flexible or Fixed?' (2017) 9(1) *Intergenerational Justice Review* 4–17.

as 'future-beneficial institutions' or 'institutions for the future'. This chapter will critique the concept of 'presentism' (harmful short-termism) and discuss 'institutions for future generations' in general and 'offices for future citizens of specific states' in particular.

## THE REASONS FOR ENDEMIC PRESENTISM IN DEMOCRACIES

### *The Electorate*

Democracies are skewed in favour of presentism. From this assessment, some studies arrive at conclusions which can be taken as a critique of elected politicians or, to use a pejorative term, 'the political class'. These theorists argue that politicians are inclined to adopt policies that let them reap short-term benefits while avoiding policies that have near-term costs and delayed benefits.[5] But this underestimates the influence of voters as the root cause. The constituency usually tends to seek advantages that can be realized in the present or near future, or at the very least within its lifetime. Faced with the choice between receiving a certain state benefit (or tax concession) either now or at a slightly later point in time, for example in a year, most voters opt for the present day for what appear to be rational reasons. Pure time preference might be myopic and irrational but the reduction of uncertainty is not – and the future, especially the distant one, is less certain than the present. And as no one knows the day of his own death, it is arguably not irrational to strive for a good life *before* one dies. Measuring 'time preference'[6] is an interdisciplinary topic with an abundance of literature on it in each of the related disciplines (inter alia, philosophy, political science, sociology, economics, and biology). For economics as a discipline, it is simply axiomatic to assume that any sum of money due in the future has a different value from the same sum due in the present. Interest rates balance the present value and the future value of given sums of money. Biologists have pointed to the fact that the growth of the frontal lobe in the human brain of homo sapiens was a precondition for the very possibility of certain forms of the deferment of preference satisfaction.

This chapter restricts itself to *political* presentism. In some theories of voters' presentism it is assumed that older voters tend to have stronger short-term interests than younger ones because the former are not as likely to experience the delayed costs of today's presentist actions.[7] It has been empirically shown that there is an age effect in the acceptance of public policy measures directed at different age groups.

5 G.S. Kavka and V. Warren, 'Political Representation for Future Generations', in R. Elliot and A. Gare (eds.), *Environmental Philosophy: A Collection of Readings* (Pennsylvania State University Press 1983) 20–39.

6 To use a term introduced by Frederick. See S. Frederick, 'Measuring Intergenerational Time Preference: Are Future Lives Valued Less?' (2003) 26(1) *Journal of Risk and Uncertainty* 39–53.

7 For example, P. Van Parijs, 'The Disfranchisement of the Elderly, and Other Attempts to Secure Intergenerational Justice' (1998) 27(4) *Philosophy & Public Affairs* 292–333.

With every year gained in life, the odds of supporting a significant increase in child benefits decrease by around 4 per cent. Childlessness has an important effect: the odds of childless elderly people being in favour of the proposed policy measure are 53 per cent lower than for parents.[8]

It comes as no surprise that in direct democracies such as Switzerland, a 'presentism' of the electorate can be ascertained by looking at the relevant referendums.[9] It is thus inappropriate to equate more direct democracy, especially in ageing societies, with less 'presentism'.

## *Politicians and Their Need to Campaign*

In democracy, opposition politicians take an interest in being elected, as do governing politicians in being re-elected. This is not to say that, as a group, politicians are exclusively motivated by power, position, and privileges. Even those who seek to shape sensible policy have to exert power to do so, and the only way to obtain that kind of power is by holding an office (or mandate). Therefore, during campaigns, political parties have to focus on the current preferences of the current electorate. Future people cannot vote today and they cannot be included in the calculus to maximize votes. Political competitions between two politicians, one of whom promises some benefits to occur in the near future, while the other one pledges the same but in the further future, will not end in favour of the latter.[10] Future-awareness amongst politicians cannot translate into sustainable decision-making under the dictates of frequent electoral campaigns. Necessarily, the rhythm of democracy conforms to the timing of election periods (i.e. periods of four to five years), thereby exhibiting structural incentives for a politics of 'glorifying the present and disregarding the future'.[11] For this reason, appeals to the conscience of politicians, asking them to consider the interests of future people more deeply, are likely to go unheard. *Mutatis mutandis*, John Stuart Mill's insight from 1861 still holds true today:

[8] H. Wilkoszewski, 'Demographic Pressure and Attitudes towards Public Intergenerational Transfers in Germany – How Much Room Left for Reforms?', in J.C. Tremmel (ed.), *Demographic Change and Intergenerational Justice* (Springer 2008) 202.

[9] G. Bonoli and S. Häusermann, 'Who Wants What from the Welfare State? Socio-Structural Cleavages in Distributional Politics: Evidence from Swiss Referendum Votes', in J.C. Tremmel (ed.), *A Young Generation under Pressure? The Financial Situation and the 'Rush Hour' of the Cohorts 1970–1985 in a Generational Comparison* (Springer 2009) 187–205.

[10] Alleged tools of political education can play their part in this. For their seeming objectification of the vote decision may lead to a concentration on one's own interests ('What would your purse choose?') and not focusing on the common good.

[11] As stated by the former German president Richard von Weizsäcker in an interview. See H. von Friedrich, M. Mändler, and E. von Kimakowitz, *Die Herausforderung Zukunft: Deutschland im Dialog: Ein Appell der jungen Generation* (Ullstein 1998) 53. Also see the statement of former Japanese Prime Minister Yoshihiko Noda: 'The structure invites politics that burden silent generations and puts problems off' (*The Washington Post*, 1 October 2013, A19).

> Rulers and ruling classes are under a necessity of considering the interests and wishes and wishes of those who have the suffrage; but of those who are excluded, it is in their option whether they will do so or not; and, however honestly disposed, they are, in general, too fully occupied with things which they *must* attend to to have much room in their thoughts for any thing which they can with impunity disregard.[12]

### *Breach of the All-Affected Principle*

The result of voters' presentist attitudes on the one hand and politicians' need to campaign frequently on the other hand is a breach of the all-affected principle.[13] Present citizens' decisions will affect people of tomorrow, too. According to the *all-affected principle*, all citizens who are affected by decisions – both current and future citizens – should have their say on the laws that rule their lives.[14] This right to participate in the decision-making process is an important normative justification for democracy (just recall the famous maxim 'no taxation without representation'). But future generations of the citizenry cannot vote (or participate otherwise) today. Conflicts of interest are decided according to the opinion of the majority of eligible voters, not the majority of those affected by the decision. This presents an internal deficiency of present democratic systems that brings into being a special form of 'representation gap'. This gap is different from the lack of electoral representation for societal minorities or other groups whose lack of representation is often lamented, such as women, the elderly, foreigners, and minors.[15] These groups are present in

[12] J.S. Mill, *Considerations on Representative Government, Edited with an Introduction by Currin V. Shilds* (Liberal Arts Press 1958. First published 1861) 131.

[13] This is not to say that there are not additional drivers for presentism in democracies. Businesses with short time frames play a role as well. Politicians who want to be (re)elected are often dependent on the support of firms. Another driver of presentism in democracies is the twenty-four-hour news cycle that puts pressure on politicians to be able to respond quickly to show that they are taking action. S. Caney, 'Political Institutions for the Future: A Fivefold Package', in González-Ricoy and Gosseries (eds.), *Institutions for Future Generations, supra* note 1 at 135–155; Boston, *Governing for the Future, supra* note 1.

[14] For different versions of the so-called 'all-affected principle', see L. Beckman, 'Democracy and Future Generations. Should the Unborn Have a Voice?', in J.-C. Merle (ed.), *Spheres of Global Justice, Vol. 2: Fair Distribution – Global Economic, Social and Intergenerational Justice* (Springer 2013) 778; J. Dryzeck, 'Transnational Democracy' (1999) 7(1) *Journal of Political Philosophy* 44; Dobson, 'Representative Democracy and the Environment', *supra* note 1 at 124; I. Shapiro, *Democracy's Place* (Cornell University Press 2006); R. Goodin, 'Enfranchising All Affected Interests, and Its Alternatives' (2007) 35(1) *Philosophy & Public Affairs* 40–68.

[15] With regard to the case of minors, Tremmel and Wilhelm advocate a 'flexible voting age' building on the willingness of minors to participate in elections. This proposal takes into account that babies, young children, and many younger adolescents have no interest in political participation anyway. The 'flexible voting age' proposal contains a need for adolescents to register in voting lists and must thus strictly distinguished from proposals that come under the name of 'voting from birth on' or 'voting age zero'. See J.C. Tremmel and

the here and now; they can take part in political discourse, write letters, appear on talk shows, and in many cases vote in elections. None of this applies to future generations. If future generations were able to claim their interests in the political decision-making process, the majority stakes in important political decisions would be different. Consider the example of energy policy. The current form of energy production, with its emphasis on fossil energy sources, enables a high standard of living in the present. However, with such a policy come grave disadvantages in the medium term (fifty to a hundred years from now).[16]

Assuming that only those born within the next 200 years were to have a say on energy policy in the next general election, all political parties would hasten to rewrite their programmes in order to facilitate a much faster reduction in GHG emissions. This further substantiates the asymmetry between the two alleged two drivers of political presentism: voters and politicians.

The problem of political presentism cannot be solved, only alleviated. But limiting the size of this problem would be no small achievement – in fact, it is of paramount importance for the future of mankind. Offices for future generations (OFG) were proposed in the literature,[17] and already realized in practice in pioneering jurisdictions, to precisely do this job: to represent the interests of *future* citizens in *today's* decision-making. In order to 'outwit' the presentist part of the electorate, as it were, the future-oriented part of the political class should take a genuine interest in amending the rules of the game so as to include a self-commitment of the entire political class. This nourishes the hope that OFGs will eventually come into existence.

Independent bodies, such as overseers, auditors, supervisors, and later constitutional courts and public ombudsmen, have been a fundamental part of democratic architecture since classical Athens. The role of such bodies is supportive for democracy, as it equips democracy against the anxieties of the majoritarian principle.

J. Wilhelm, 'Democracy or Epistocracy? Age as a Criterion of Voter Eligibility', in J.C. Tremmel, A. Mason, I. Dimitrijoski, and P.G. Petter (eds.), *Youth Quotas in Ageing Societies* (Springer 2015) 125–147.

16 Scientific analyses indicate that current energy policy intensifies the natural greenhouse effect and causes the global average temperature to rise. IPCC (ed.), *Climate Change: The IPCC Scientific Assessment* (Cambridge University Press 1990). Post-1990 – the year in which the IPCC's First Assessment Report assessed a connection between anthropogenic carbon dioxide emissions and climate change with a 90 per cent probability – presently living generations can no longer legitimately claim ignorance of the consequences of their actions. Anthropogenic climate change has already cost hundreds of thousands of human lives. And the prospects for the future look even direr. For estimations of current and future casualties, see WHO, *Global Health Risks: Mortality and Burden of Disease Attributable to Selected Major Risks* (WHO 2009) 50; Global Humanitarian Forum, *Human Impact Report. Climate Change – The Anatomy of a Silent Crisis* (Global Humanitarian Forum 2009) 11; World Bank, *Turn Down the Heat: Climate Extremes, Regional Impacts, and the Case for Resilience* (World Bank 2013) XXV.

17 See *supra* note 1.

OFGs are democratically legitimized as long as they are granted their status by law and as long as this status can be revoked by law as well.[18]

From the analysis of the root causes of political presentism it follows that having the members of OFGs elected in general elections is not adequate. Is the alternative, the *appointment* of the members of the OFG, justified? While an election by the entire population would indeed maximize the formal independence of the organization's members – in particular vis-à-vis the legislative, executive, and judicial branches – there would be downsides as well. For instance, there would be election campaigns which in principle would follow the same logic as the well-known campaigns for parliamentary mandates. In view of an electorate that is itself biased in favour of the present, those candidates who promise to cater for the short-term wishes of their constituencies would have an advantage. If the candidates for the OFG would have to run campaigns and court for votes, they would turn into de facto politicians. No longer would knowledge and expertise be the decisive qualities, but rather eloquence and smoothness in the political arena. Unelected representatives for future citizens, appointed *by* elected politicians but not *for* their pleasure,[19] are a necessary and legitimate instrument against political presentism.

### *The Anthropocene Concept as a Wake-Up Call for Reforming Democracy*

It is only since the twentieth century that the pace of humankind and the environment have started to fall apart so dramatically.[20] In environmental issues, more than elsewhere, the effects of current actions reach far into the future and can have a deeply negative impact on the quality of life for numerous future generations. Prompted by humanity's unprecedented ability to influence its geophysical surroundings, scientists have recently begun to speak of the beginning of a new geological period, the Anthropocene.[21]

As a result of urbanization, large areas are by now covered by a mixture of concrete, glass, and metal. Even if humankind were to go extinct tomorrow, those structures would remain where they are for millennia to come. If, in a few thousand years from now, geologists were to visit the place where a large city is standing today,

[18] P. Rosenvallon, *Democratic Legitimacy: Impartiality, Reflexivity, Proximity* (Princeton University Press 2011) chs. 4, 5.

[19] See P. Pettit, *On the People's Terms: A Republican Theory and Model of Democracy* (Cambridge University Press 2012) 306.

[20] The problem of 'presentism' in democracies is not limited to environmental issues. Long before the advent of the modern environmental movement, excessive public debt was a prime example of the careless use of the future. See T. Jefferson, 'Letter to John Taylor' (28 May 1816) http://teachingamericanhistory.org/library/index.asp?document=308 accessed 24 October 2017. Underinvestment in education or lack of adjustments to social security systems are other examples of a lack of future orientation in political systems.

[21] At the 35th International Geological Congress in Cape Town (September 2016), the members of the sub-commission voted almost unanimously in favour of changing the classification of geological epochs and of declaring a new world age – the Anthropocene.

they would discover fragments of concrete, rusted iron, bitumen from pavements, glass from fibre-optic cables, and an amount of aluminium which as such is not found in nature. The shifting from wilderness to grasslands is another unforeseen sign of the enormous changes humanity has brought upon the Earth's surface. While the proportion of non-wilderness was minimal 12,000 years ago, more than a third of the Earth's surface is being used as grassland for livestock today. If one were to place all mammals on a huge scale, one would find that humans and their livestock have amounted for 0.1 per cent of all biomass at the beginning of the Holocene, while today this share has increased to 90 per cent of all biomass.

Further examples of the unprecedented depth of human interventions cut across many topic areas, with the following representing essential examples. (1) The harvesting of subterranean forests, that is, the extraction of coal, oil and gas from the lithosphere. If at all possible, it would take hundreds of millions of years for these resources to regenerate. (2) The anthropogenic contamination by radioactivity, the timescale of which is likewise only measurable in millions of years. (3) The species extinction caused by the human race. Nature is always in the process of creating new species, so it is indeed only a matter of time until the ramifications of the sixth mass extinction will have been 'processed' by nature. However, this too will run into the low millions of years. (4) Climate change, by comparison, is reversible within a much shorter time frame, but here too we are dealing with tens of thousands of years. And finally, (5) space debris has accumulated in the orbit since the beginning of space travel, without the forces of nature being able to dispose of it on their own within the next thousands of years.

It is not very controversial in philosophy that the 'neighbour ethics' that was very useful in the Holocene is of limited use for the future in this new era.[22] But it is less understood that the ecological crisis is also a crisis of democracy as a form of government. Democracy, as we know it, has been designed in and for the Holocene. The transition into a new phase of geology necessitates a reform of democracy as a form of government. One can think of 'the Anthropocene concept' as just another frame, but one could also understand it as a wake-up call to reform democracy.

Before outlining how such a reform could look, two caveats seem to be necessary, one with regard to the superiority of democracy to all other forms of political rule and the other with regard to the limited use of posterity protection clauses in constitutions.

## DEMOCRACY AS A VALUABLE INHERITANCE FOR FUTURE GENERATIONS

Reforming democracy, to be sure, does not mean putting it into question. It cannot be overstated that democracy as a form of government is one of the most valuable

[22] Tremmel, *supra* note 3 at 3.

legacies which future generations can inherit from present generations. After a series of failed UN climate conferences between 2009 and 2014 before the success in Paris 2015 (and then again when US president Donald Trump opted out of this accord in 2017), there was an increase in contributions asking the question of whether democracy is the best form of government to cope with ecological challenges.[23] This provocative question is misleading regardless of whether it is answered in the affirmative.

At any rate, the international climate conferences are a bad case in point, given that not only democratic but also non-democratic States contributed to the failure of the negotiations. Comparative studies have shown that the environmental performance of authoritative regimes is worse than that of democracies.[24] Dictatorial regimes display, on average, less concern for the long-term interests of their citizens than democratic ones.[25] So-called epistocrats could reply in return that they do not advocate for dictatorship *per se*, but rather an enlightened authoritarian rule.[26] But one lesson from history is that there is no way to ensure that an enlightened dictator does not abandon his benevolence eventually. One hundred and fifty years ago, at a time when intellectuals open-mindedly discussed whether or not democracy is better than monarchy or aristocracy, Mill wrote sensible words that are still (or again) worth reading today: 'In no government will the interests of the people be the object, except where the people are able to dismiss their rulers as soon as the devotion of those rulers to the interests of the people becomes questionable'.[27]

In the long run, no form of government other than democracy is better suited to solve the global environmental problems, as it is, in Churchill's words, 'the worst form of Government except all those other forms that have been tried from time to time'.[28]

[23] See, e.g., D. Shearman and J.W. Smith, *The Climate Change Challenge and the Failure of Democracy* (Praeger Publishers 2007); J. Randers, *2052: A Global Forecast for the Next Forty Years* (Chelsea Green Publishing 2012).

[24] H. Weidner and M. Jänicke (eds.), *Capacity Building in National Environmental Policy: A Comparative Study of 17 Countries* (Springer 2002); M. Jänicke, 'Democracy as a Condition for Environmental Policy Success', in W.M. Lafferty and J. Meadowcroft (eds.), *Democracy and the Environment* (Edward Elgar 1996) 71–85; M. Jänicke, 'Conditions for Environmental Policy Success: An International Comparison' (1992) 12(1) *Environmentalist* 47–58.

[25] J. Boston, 'Safeguarding the Interests of Future Generations: Countering the Presentist Bias in Democratic Policy-Making', in F. Ciaramelli and F. Menga (eds.), *Responsabilità verso le future generazioni future* (Editoriale Scientifica 2017b) 252. See also Boston, *supra* note 1.

[26] See J. Brennan, *Against Democracy* (Princeton University Press 2016).

[27] J.S. Mill, *The Collected Works of John Stuart Mill, Vol. 18. Essays on Politics and Society*, ed. by J. Robson (Routledge & Kegan Paul 1977) 73.

[28] In full: 'No one pretends that democracy is perfect or all-wise. Indeed, it has been said that democracy is the worst form of Government except all those other forms that have been tried from time to time; but there is the broad feeling in our country that the people should rule, continuously rule, and that public opinion, expressed by all constitutional means, should shape, guide, and control the actions of Ministers who are their servants and not their masters.'

## POSTERITY PROTECTION PROVISIONS IN CONSTITUTIONS DO NOT SUFFICE

The growing acceptance of responsibility for future generations has led to the trend of including posterity protection clauses in constitutions. Insofar as many constitutions have been newly adopted, there are significant examples of the inscription of future generations as part of the constitutional structure, for example in Eastern Europe and Central Asia after 1989, or in South Africa after the end of apartheid. Even well-established constitutions have been changed in order to reflect the increasing future-mindedness of citizenries around the world.[29] Five constitutions speak explicitly of 'rights of future generations': Norway,[30] Japan,[31] Iran,[32] Bolivia,[33] and Malawi.[34] In other constitutional texts, for instance the constitution of the Republic of Georgia,[35] the 'interests' of future generations are addressed; alternatively, their 'needs' are recognized in the constitution of Uganda.[36]

The number of constitutions with posterity protection clauses is already considerable, and it continues to grow. But does this make any difference? A sobering conclusion seems in order. The establishment of such clauses has resulted neither in the phasing out of nuclear power nor in serious climate action in the respective countries. Constitutional courts are obviously not optimal to serve as the guardians of future generations' interests since they cannot represent such interests with full commitment for the simple reason that they typically have no mandate to do so.

It makes a substantial difference whether a new institution is created with its own budget, whether people come to hold new positions, and whether new office spaces are furnished for a devoted new cause or whether, by contrast, existing

Hansard Parliament Bill. November 1947, Band 444. S. 203-321 http://hansard.millbanksystems.com/commons/1947/nov/11/parliament-bill accessed 31 December 2017.

29 For details, see E. Brown Weiss, *In Fairness to Future Generations* (United Nations University/Transnational Publishers 1989); T. Hayward, *Constitutional Environmental Rights* (Oxford University Press 2005); Tremmel, *supra* note 3 at 192–197; E. Brandl and H. Bungert, 'Constitutional Entrenchment of Environmental Protection' (1992) 16(1) *Harvard Environmental Law Review* 1–100; H.S. Cho and O. Pedersen, 'Environmental Rights and Future Generations', in M. Tushnet, T. Fleiner, and C. Saunders (eds.), *Routledge Handbook on Constitutional Law* (Routledge 2013) 435–447; K.S. Ekeli, *Green Constitutionalism: The Constitutional Protection of Future Generations* (Ratio Juris 2007) 20 (3), 378–401; González-Ricoy, *supra* note 1; M.K. MacKenzie, 'Institutional Design and Sources of Short-Termism', in Gosseries and González Ricoy, *supra* note 1 at 24–48.

30 Constitution of Norway, art. 110b (2014).

31 Constitution of Japan, art. 11 (1946).

32 Constitution of the Islamic Republic of Iran, art. 50 (1979).

33 Constitution of Bolivia, art. 7 (2009).

34 Constitution of Malawi, arts. 11, 13 (1994).

35 Constitution of the Republic of Georgia, arts. 4, 37 (1995).

36 Constitution of the Republic of Uganda, art. XXVII ii (1995).

courts are entrusted with new tasks by legal extensions. The approach advocated below is based on the need to create a new OFG for the representation of future generations.[37]

## PARADIGM SHIFT FROM A THREE- TO A FOUR-POWER-MODEL

What is required is no less than a paradigm shift.[38] The new paradigm would entail a 'future branch' and regard it as a legitimate and necessary part of a democratically constituted community.[39] The linchpin of this paradigm would be that the age-old separation of powers into legislative, executive, and judicial branches is no longer appropriate today. The present-day demos of the twenty-first century can affect the living conditions of a future demos far more than it used to do in former times. Just like in the eighteenth century, when in the course of first establishing a democracy in a large territorial state, the *Federalist Papers* considered a system of 'checks and balances' to protect minorities against the 'tyranny of majority',[40] so today we are in need of 'checks and balances' against the tyranny of the present over the future.

The historical roots of the separation of powers are usually associated with the political theorists John Locke and Charles de Montesquieu. However, even as early a philosopher as Aristotle recommended a mixed constitution or, more specifically, a mixture of democracy and oligarchy designed to prevent an excessive concentration of power, which he called 'polity'. In his *Two Treatises of Government*, published in 1690, John Locke distinguishes between legislative and executive, but leaves no room for an independent third judicial power. Locke introduces a clear hierarchy of powers when he writes that 'this *legislative* is not

[37] In much of the literature, such bodies (e.g. the Commission for Future Generations in Israel or the Parliamentary Commissioner for Future Generations in Hungary) are referred to as 'institutions'. In the social sciences, there are a variety of conflicting definitions of the term 'institution'. Some theories define the term so as to not cover organizations. In the following, however, a concept of institutions is employed which also includes organizations or permanently organized associations of individuals.

[38] The proposal of a four-power model is outlined in greater detail in Tremmel, 'Parliaments and Future Generations – The Four-Powers-Model', *supra* note 1; J.C. Tremmel, *Responsibility for Future Citizens in the Realm of Politics* (forthcoming).

[39] The idea of an extension of the three-branch-model of government by a future branch is quite new and thus it has not yet been perused in political science, law, or philosophy. While a number of scholars and institutions demand that a transformation of our political system must go beyond marginalia, they have not called for a four-power model. At least Pierre Rosenvallon noted, however, that for a justification of independent agencies that reduce the scope of administrative-executive power significantly, 'the traditional concept of separation of powers has had to be stretched'. Rosenvallon, *supra* note 18 at 75.

[40] The term was coined by Tocqueville. See A. de Tocqueville, *Democracy in America* (1835/1840) www.gutenberg.org/files/815/815-h/815-h.htm accessed 18 December 2017.

only the *supreme power* of the common-wealth, but sacred and unalterable in the hands where the community has once placed it'.[41]

Charles de Montesquieu, the actual 'father' of the tripartite separation of powers doctrine, applies the classical division of legislative, executive and judiciary power in his *De l'esprit des lois* of 1748. In the sixth chapter of the eleventh book,[42] which mainly deals with the English constitution, he is concerned with the sharing and balancing of powers. He writes, 'In every government there are three sorts of power: *the legislative; the executive, in respect to things dependent on the law of nations; and the executive, in regard to things that depend on the civil law.*'[43] Following this statement, Montesquieu explains that this latter power is to be referred to as the judiciary power of the state. This brings us to the classic tripartite division of legislative, executive, and judicial power.

The *trias politica* was conceived by thinkers in the seventeenth and eighteenth century and is now universally established in Western democracies. The view of our present three-power model changes when we learn about the evolution from a two- to a three-power model in the approaches of Locke and Montesquieu. The most important lesson from the history of ideas seems to be that even the supposedly definitive present is only a stage between past and future. The tripartite division was sufficient for the past, but in the twenty-first century it does not suffice anymore.

A few remarks with regard to the 'vertically' directed separation of powers seem appropriate. In federal states like Germany, for example, the federalization of political systems means the division of labour between a local level, a *Länder* level, and a national level, complemented by the EU. All levels from the Länder level upwards have governments, parliaments, and constitutional courts.[44] They should thus also have future branches to complement their 'horizontal' separation of powers. This could (and should) be complemented by a future branch.

Apart from the horizontal and vertical 'separation of powers', further overloading the term is of little use. The media is also often referred to colloquially as 'the fourth power'. The same applies for interest groups such as trade unions or employers' associations. It is true that the power of the political system does not autonomously penetrate other areas such as business, science, media, religion, and private relationships. However, to prevent confusion, the term 'separation of powers' should continue to refer to the organization of state power. The terminology used here

[41] J. Locke, *Two Treatises of Government* (McMaster University Archive 1823) http://socserv.mcmaster.ca/econ/ugcm/3ll3/locke/government.pdf accessed 11 Nov 2017 (first published 1690) ch. XI, § 134.

[42] C. de Montesquieu, *The Spirit of Laws, Translated by T. Nugent* (Batoche Books 2011, original edn. *De l'esprit des lois*, 1748) 173–184; 92–93.

[43] Ibid. at 173.

[44] The European level also displays a parliament (the European Parliament), a court (European Court of Justice), and a (sort of) government (the European Commission).

counts only the 'branches of government' (not society) and adds a fourth such branch to the existing three.

The legislative branch passes the law, the executive branch implements it, and the judiciary controls its abidance. Where does the future branch fit in here? Constitutional courts check the *constitutionality* of laws after the legislative branch has passed them. OFGs *could* be designed as a body which checks the *sustainability* of laws and quashes them if they harm future citizens. Alternatively, it is possible to see an OFG as somewhat closer to the legislative than to the judicative branch, namely as a body with the right to initiate legislation instead of preventing it.

It should not be forgotten that the idea of the *trias politica* currently varies from country to country as a result of different traditions of political thought.[45] With regard to institutions for future generations, there cannot be a one-size-fits-all solution; rather, it seems apt to conceive of such a representative body differently for each country.

The 'fourth branch of government' is an umbrella term that does not designate a particular model. Instead, it refers to all OFGs that are powerful enough to credibly represent the needs and interests of future citizens. However, if an OFG has no bargaining power at all, it does not qualify as an embodiment of the future branch.

## COUNTERARGUMENTS AGAINST A POWERFUL INSTITUTION FOR FUTURE CITIZENS

### *'Only the Contemporary Citizens Constitute the Demos!'*

There are, of course, counterarguments against the establishment of a powerful institution for the representation of future generations of the citizenry. First, the claim that only present citizens constitute the demos will be scrutinized. 'Who constitutes the demos?' is one of the great questions in political theory. To pose the question this way is not self-evident or undisputed, but arguably this framing of the question is preferable to a formulation such as 'Who should be included in the demos?' The latter might lead us to think of an existing authorized decision group and thereby to block out the more decisive question of how the original composition of an authorized group can be justified.[46] The idea of who is part of the demos is

[45] Take the example of France. To this day, popular sovereignty is equated much more strongly with parliamentary sovereignty in France than it is in Germany. The powers exercised by Germany's constitutional court continue to astonish many in France. In the midst of the Euro crisis, many French rubbed their eyes in disbelief when the European Stability Mechanism (ESM) threatened to fail at the hands of the Federal Constitutional Court.

[46] R. Goodin, *supra* note 14. The question of the constitution of the demos was already central to political thinkers in ancient and medieval times. In modern times, it has still occupied generations of political scientists. It is reminiscent of Robert Dahl's still relevant quote: '[The problem of inclusion] is an embarrassment to all normative theories of democracy, or would be

subject to historical change.[47] Two hundred and fifty years ago, in most democracies the demos was formed of those men who paid the 'right' tax revenue, had the 'right' skin colour, and were of the 'right' religion and the 'right' age.

It is crucial that, for reasons of logic, the issue of the original composition of the demos cannot decided democratically. Goodin writes: 'It is logically incoherent to let the composition of the initial demos be decided by a vote of the demos, because that demos cannot be constituted until after the demos votes.'[48] To illustrate this point, one might imagine the 1959 vote on women's suffrage in Switzerland. Two-thirds of the men refused the extension of suffrage and thus defined themselves, alone, as the voting demos, at that time and also in the future. Today, hardly anyone would consider this decision to be legitimate.[49]

Rather, the consideration of upstream normative principles must form the basis of deciding how the demos should be constituted. The *all-affected principle* leads to the conclusion that both current and future citizens can be considered as bearers of popular sovereignty.

But, it might be asked, is it not the case that the principle of representation is generally incompatible with the idea of democracy? In a world in which most democracies happen to be *representative* democracies, the struggle for the principle of representation itself (as it prominently features in Kant's distinction between the republic and democracy) has long been settled. According to a dictum by Abraham Lincoln in his Gettysburg Address, democracy is characterized by 'government of the people, by the people, for the people'.[50]

However, most democracies today are based on the principle of representation: government of *all* members of the people (with few exceptions), by *some* elected representatives from the people, for *all* members of the people. Thus, in accordance with common knowledge, representation and democracy do not seem to conflict. Extending the principle of representation to future citizens merely amounts to a consistent extension of this principle. Representation, in the broadest sense, should be understood as a visualization of the absent, since it means making the invisible

were it not ignored.' R.A. Dahl, *Dilemmas of Pluralist Democracy* (Yale University Press 1982) 98.

47 The Greek term *dēmos* designates the citizenry within a people, while the term *ethnos* refers to a nation as an ethnic group. Historically, the establishment of demes as fundamental units of the state by Cleisthenes in 508 BC was an important step in the evolvement of political order out of kin structures.

48 Goodin, *supra* note 14 at 47.

49 In Germany, a contradictory provision is still in force: section 2 (2) of the Scrutiny Act (*Wahlprüfungsgesetz*) specifies that only eligible voters are able to challenge the validity of an election. Thus, the part of the German people to whom the right to vote is denied on grounds of age is unable to challenge its situation by taking legal action.

50 A. Brooks Lapsley, *The Papers and Writings of Abraham Lincoln, Vol. 7* (2012) www.gutenberg .org/files/2659/2659-h/2659-h.htm#link2H_4_0028 accessed 25 October 2017.

visible and the absent present.[51] Representation as such is thus not an obstacle but a requirement when it comes to the case of yet-unrepresented groups of future citizens of a state or political entity.

### *'We Do Not Have Any Obligations towards Future People Because of the Non-Identity Principle'*

The non-identity problem has often been viewed as a serious challenge to theories of intergenerational justice and models of representation of future generations. Advocacy for OFGs implies that we *have* obligations towards future people in the first place. Viewed strictly, if the non-identity principle (NIP) were a single irrefutable 'no-obligation' argument, it would necessarily and with one blow spell the end to any accounts of the representation of future generations. But the non-identity problem does not present an irrefutable argument against representation of future citizens.[52]

A look into the history of future ethics is instructive here. The NIP has been viewed as such a serious challenge to the justification of *any* obligation towards future generations that the debate over the extent of such obligations, which began during the 1970s with a number of remarkable collections of essays,[53] has ebbed. Tim Mulgan has noted that the non-identity challenge is to this day 'plaguing present Western theories of generational justice'.[54]

By the same token, Clark Wolf states that 'the non-identity problem calls into question whether distant future persons might claim rights against members of the present generation ... For this reason, some theorists have more or less abandoned the idea of intergenerational justice altogether.'[55] Derek Parfit, too, emphasizes the significance of the non-identity problem, claiming:

> We may be able to remember a time when we were concerned about effects on future generations, but had overlooked the Non-Identity Problem. We may have thought that a policy like depletion would be against the interest of future people.

[51] G. Göhler, 'Politische Repräsentation in der Demokratie', in T. Leif (ed.), *Die politische Klasse in Deutschland. Eliten auf dem Prüfstand* (Bouvier 1992) 109; W. Thaa, *Politisches Handeln. Demokratietheoretische Überlegungen im Anschluss an Hannah Arendt* (Nomos 2011) 151.

[52] For its refutation in the context of offices for future generations, see Tremmel, *Eine Theorie der Generationengerechtigkeit*, *supra* note 3 at 72–92; J.C. Tremmel, 'The Non-Identity Problem: An Irrefutable Argument against Representation of Future Generations?', in J. Enders and M. Remig (eds.), *Theories of Sustainable Development* (Routledge 2015) 126–144.

[53] R. Sikora and B. Barry (eds.), *Obligations to Future Generations* (Temple University Press 1978); E. Partridge (ed.), *Responsibilities to Future Generations* (Prometheus Books 1980a).

[54] T. Mulgan, 'Neutrality, Rebirth and Intergenerational Justice' (2002) 19(1) *Journal of Applied Philosophy* 8.

[55] C. Wolf, 'Do Future Persons Presently Have Alternate Possible Identities?', in M.A. Roberts and D.T. Wassermann (eds.), *Harming Future Persons: Ethics, Genethics and the Nonidentity Problem* (Springer 2009) 96.

> When we saw that this was false, did we become less concerned about effects on future generations?[56]

Parfit's statement can be interpreted to the effect that NIP is difficult to refute. And, indeed, for a time, it did achieve the status of a kind of paradigm in the Kuhnian sense among philosophers,[57] who ceased discussing the rights or wrongs of it and were concerned with researching issues within the paradigm itself.

The NIP can be formulated as follows: the present actions of members of the currently living generation determine not only what the conditions of life of future people will be, but also which people will exist.[58] The refutation focuses on the medical-reproductive underpinning of the NIP, and its short form could proceed as follows. A proponent of the NIP claims this: 'If we deplete natural resources rapidly in the next 10 years, this might be bad for future generations, but it will also impact who will be meeting, mating, and making children with whom. As a result, a different set of people will come into existence compared with any alternative policy.' His listener might answer, 'Okay, your claim sounds 100 per cent correct.'

But then a bystander steps in and argues as follows: 'Well, but this is not the only factor that will have an impact on who will be meeting, mating, and making children with whom. I have heard that the government will prolong the opening times in bars from 11 pm to 3 am. This will also have an impact on who will be meeting, mating, and making children with whom, won't it?' Her counterpart nods and replies: 'Well, this is also correct. But then the first factor (depletion policy) might account for 50 per cent of the stated effect, and the curfew change will account for the other 50 per cent.' But then another bystander intervenes: 'According to serious forecasts the number of female students at universities will double in the next ten years. This will definitely have an impact on who will be meeting, mating, and making children with whom.' The other two contend: 'Then all three factors that were mentioned may account for 33 per cent each.' Another bystander steps in and adds: 'Don't forget the new dating app for smartphones! It will also have an impact on who will be meeting, mating and making children with whom.' And then the group catches sight of a huge crowd of people who are queuing in order to add yet more factors that have a bearing on who will be meeting, mating, and making children with whom. The takeaway from this story is that myriad factors affect who comes into existence and who does not. The impact of the depletion policy, as one single factor, is miniscule. Thus, it is misleading to say that the depletion policy will be causal in determining who comes into

56 Parfit supports the 'no-difference view'. However, his statement also makes clear that he has absolutely no doubts regarding the validity of the non-identity problem. D. Parfit, *Reasons and Persons*, 3rd rev. edn. (Oxford University Press 1987) 367.

57 T.S. Kuhn, *The Structure of Scientific Revolutions* (University of Chicago Press 1963).

58 G.S. Kavka, 'The Futurity Problem', in Sikora and Barry, *supra* note 53 at 192.

existence. Words like 'caused', 'because of', or 'due to' imply a concept of causality that is inadequate here.

But is it still not the case that several choices have a 100 per cent impact on who will live at a certain point in the future? This depends on one's notion of causality. It is misleading to construct a monocausal relationship from a weak multicausal context. When we think about what 'caused' something, we might hold variable A responsible for 50 per cent of the effect, variable B for 30 per cent, and variable C for 19 per cent. We know in the back of our mind that there is an undefinable number of additional variables that sum up to the last 1 per cent, but we normally don't understand causality in that way. When a judge lists the causes of a car accident in his writ, he will say that a slight drunkenness was 50 per cent responsible and a dispute in the car with the passenger was to blame for the rest. He will not say: 'Another cause is that no comet recently hit the area where the accident occurred and as a result the road was intact.' But this statement would be not completely false, for if there had been such a comet impact, the accident would not have happened in this specific road. To sum up, the NIP might be an interesting thought from the philosophical ivory tower, but it is overrated in the context of institutions for future generations.

### *'We Cannot Act in the Best Interest of Future People Because We Do Not Know Their Interests'*

It is in principle impossible to ascertain the interests, preferences, and values of people who live in a distant future. If circumstances change, the interests of future generations might change as well. That circumstances will change in the future is very likely, given the rapid change in the past 300 years. Advocates of need-based conceptions of intergenerational justice, such as Ernest Partridge, Lukas Meyer, Ian Gough, and Jörg Tremmel, do not deny this but they counter that it is 'needs' that matter, not 'preferences'. The basic needs of every member of every generation are identical, no matter which age, culture, or context he or she lived (lives, will live) in. Future individuals will also need air to breathe and water to drink, and thus they will need croplands and watersheds to supply their food and water.[59] Therefore, the argument that there are no obligations towards future generations because it is impossible to know their higher preferences loses ground.[60]

59 See Kavka, *supra* note 58 at 189; Tremmel, *A Theory of Intergenerational Justice*, *supra* note 3 at 113.

60 Partridge contends: 'The very enormity of the changes that are projected, or imminent, may render a finely tuned science of forecasting somewhat irrelevant. For whatever their tastes in music or poetry, or whatever their preferences in sports and other amusements, our descendants will need croplands and watersheds to supply their food and water.' E. Partridge, 'Introduction', in E. Partridge (ed.), *Responsibilities to Future Generations* (Prometheus Books 1980) 2.

Although the distinction between basic needs and higher preferences is helpful in theory, it does not really help for the practice of OFGs, as examples show. Drawing on the documented decisions of the Israeli and the Hungarian Commissioners for Future Generations,[61] it is difficult to say which of the issues they were confronted with in their daily work were needs versus interests issues. In an interview, the Hungarian Ombudsman for Future Generations (FGO) stated:

> Thousands of hectares of last green spots around the larger cities of Hungary were saved by the FGO (decreasing our popularity amongst real estate speculators, strong allies of several political parties), large polluting enterprises (such as the 50 MW Szerencs Power Plant in the buffer zone of the Tokaj World Heritage Site) were prevented and we could even cross out the plans of the Ministry of Defense to put a radio locator with strong and long lasting non-ionizing radiation on the top of a hill in Pécs (South Hungarian city with 160,000 dwellers).[62]

In this instance, the task of the FGO was mainly environmental and included obligations to protect the health and living conditions of present and future generations and to preserve the common heritage of humanity as well as the quality of life and the unhindered access to natural resources.[63] The bulk of the FGO's activities consisted of mediation and handling citizens' petitions against public administration.

In addition, the FGO was endowed with a number of powerful and very specific authorities reminiscent of those of an Attorney General, comparable to the position of the Federal Prosecutor in the Brazilian *Ministério Publico*.[64] The regulations added to the Ombudsman Act in 2007 authorized the FGO 'to repeal the enforcement of governmental decisions, if otherwise the environment were to suffer from severe damages'.[65] Apart from this powerful weapon, he also had the right to participate in certain civil and administrative trials. This could happen either by

[61] For detailed accounts of these two OFGs, see for Hungary Act No. CXI of 2011 on the Commissioner for Fundamental Rights; Éva Ambrusné Tóth, 'The Parliamentary Commissioner for Future Generations in Hungary and Its Impact' (2010) 10(1) *Intergenerational Justice Review* 18–24; S. Fülöp, 'Die Rechte, Pflichten und Tätigkeiten des ungarischen Parlamentsbeauftragten für zukünftige Generationen', in B. Gesang (ed.), *Kann Demokratie Nachhaltigkeit?* (Springer 2014) 67–84. For Israel, see S. Shoham and N. Lamay, 'Commission for Future Generations in the Knesset: Lessons Learnt', in J.C. Tremmel (ed.), *Handbook of Intergenerational Justice* (Edward Elgar 2006) 244–262 (including the Knesset Law that established the commission 2001); S. Shoham, *Future Intelligence* (Verlag Bertelsmann Stiftung 2010).

[62] Manuscript of S. Fülöp at the Workshop European Science Foundation ENRI Representing Future Generations (4 May 2013, Munich).

[63] Act No. CXI of 2011 (Hungary), § 3.

[64] In an interview with the German magazine *Der Spiegel* (Utler 2010, 2), Fülöp himself characterized his task as follows: 'I am, so to speak, a state prosecutor for the citizens, called into action whenever the government fails.'

[65] Fülöp, *supra* note 62 at 73.

his initiating a lawsuit or by joining a lawsuit initiated by a third party as an amicus curiae. The FGO was to be consulted on every draft bill and government initiative that could have an impact on the environment and sustainable development. Further, he could argue his case in parliamentary committees and had the right to speak in plenary sessions – and used both of these abilities.

How did the Hungarian FGO deal with the problem of competing interests of future generations? How could he know which alternative political action would prove (most) advantageous to future citizens of Hungary? In what was seen as particularly controversial at the time, the FGO deployed all legal instruments at his command in order to prevent a huge biomass facility made up for 50 MW in the buffer zone of Tokaj, a wine region and World Cultural Heritage site. It should not go unnoticed that biomass is a renewable energy that plays a decisive role if a country wants to phase out both fossil and nuclear energies. In this instance, the question was what serves posterity more – an increase in the country's share in renewable energy or the aesthetic value of a preserved cultural rural site? In cases like these, it is almost impossible to scientifically determine how the needs and interests of future generations would be served best. Likewise, the Israeli commissioner once exhausted his far-reaching competencies in a case in which the perspective of intergenerational justice could be claimed by both sides. Simply put, he advocated a law for the inclusion of disabled young people which the Finance Minister had rejected for cost reasons.[66]

Evidence suggests that the 'uncertainty argument' deserves to be taken seriously. Failing to adequately cope with this counterargument might have contributed to the disempowerment of the FGO in Hungary,[67] and the demise of the Knesset Commission for Future Generations in Israel. This, however, does not belittle the credit due to those states that first installed representatives of future generations, and, in so doing, altered the institutional setting of their respective political landscapes in spirited and innovative ways.

[66] Shoham and Lamay, *supra* note 61 at 248f.

[67] The Hungarian system of ombudspersons before 2008 consisted of the 'general ombudsperson' primarily in charge of civil rights, and two 'special ombudspersons' in charge of ethnical minorities' rights, data privacy, and freedom of information. Hence, the FGO that was installed 2008 was third in the line of 'special ombudspersons'. In 2011, with a change in the Hungarian constitution, the FGO was converted into a Deputy Ombudsman for Future Generations under the General Ombudsman. In comparison to the original FGO, the new institution has much lesser resources and no right of investigation without the agreement of the General Ombudsman. From 2012 to 2016, Marcel Szabó, a professor of law, was the incumbent of the new Deputy FGO post. Following Szabó's appointment to the Constitutional Court, Gyula Bándi, also a professor of law, was appointed to the post. The disarming of the FGO in 2011 is usually seen as a major setback by the scientific community. But Rose still lists the Deputy FGO in Hungary (as it is since 2011) among the most powerful institutions for future generations worldwide. Rose, *supra* note 1 at 258–264. For the functions and powers of the Hungarian Ombudsman for Future Generations, see *infra* ch. 4 in this volume.

## TYPOLOGIES OF OFGS

Across the globe, there is by now a considerable number of institutions with a mandate for sustainability and intergenerational justice.[68] To bring some order to this 'messy landscape'[69] is a vital feat to achieve. But classifying these institutions is complicated, because they differ on multiple dimensions: their regional ambit (e.g. national or supranational), the scope of their competencies, their statutory basis, their governance and accountability arrangements, their composition, and their size and resourcing.[70]

In addition to verbal attempts,[71] a three-axis graphic model visualizes some of the most important dimensions of OFGs. The 'cuboid of offices for future generations' is heuristically well suited to exploring the uncharted territory in the 'universe of cases' of OFGs. Some sub-cuboids are (or were) filled already, others might be filled in the future. Each sub-cuboid represents a potential separate case study. The model applies to powerful OFGs only and, more specifically, it applies to OFGs which have the right to intervene in legislative procedures. This is decisive in whether such offices have 'hard power' and are distinguishable from those institutions that enjoy merely consultative status and thus exercise little actual power in a Weberian sense.[72] Moreover, this tool relates to OFGs that are designed for the national level. These OFGs are aimed at ensuring the representation of the future *demos* of a

[68] A UN report mentions the following eight institutions on a national level as the allegedly most influential ones: Finland (Committee of the Future); Germany (Parliamentary Advisory Council on Sustainable Development); Israel (Commissioner for Future Generations [2001–2006]); Hungary (Ombudsman for Future Generations [2008–2011]); Canada (Principal for Sustainable Development Strategies); Wales (Commissioner for Sustainable Futures); Norway (Ombudsman for Children); New Zealand (Parliamentary Commissioner for the Environment). On the UN level, the report brings the creation of a 'High Commissioner for Future Generations' into discussion. Applying a very wide definition of 'institutions' that includes not just OFG but also constitutional posterity protection provisions and cross-cutting policies, Boston (2017b) lists eighty institutions. Rose comes up with twenty-nine institutions but states that he has deliberately left out those that seem too powerless. See Rose, *supra* note 1 at Appendix I.

[69] Boston, *supra* note 1 at 321.

[70] Cf. ibid. at 322.

[71] Rose's elaborated typology employs a sophisticated thirteen-criteria scheme in which each criterion can have two or more values. See Rose, *supra* note 1. For previous examples, see B. Jávor and J. Rácz (eds.), *Do We Owe Them a Future? The Opportunities of a Representation for Future Generations in Europe* (Védegylet 2006); M. Göpel and M. Arhelger, 'How to Protect Future Generations' Rights in European Governance' (2010) 10(1) *Intergenerational Justice Review* 3–10; N. Teschner, *Official Bodies That Deal with the Needs of Future Generations and Sustainable Development: Comparative Review* (The Knesset Research and Information Centre 2013).

[72] '*Power* means every chance in a social relation to have one's own will even again the resistance of others.' M. Weber, *Wirtschaft und Gesellschaft: Grundriss der verstehenden Soziologie, published by Johannes Winckelmann* (Mohr-Verlag 1972, first published 1921/1922), § 16.

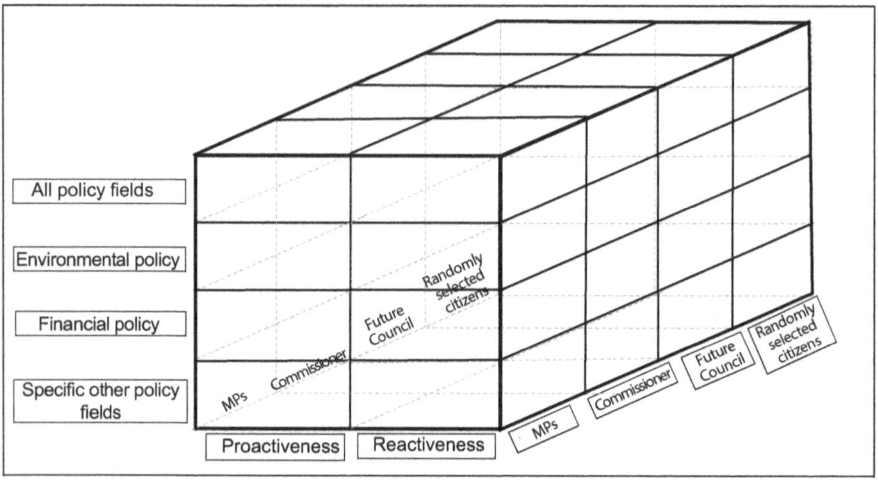


FIGURE 38.1 The cuboid of offices for future generations

specific people but not of future generations of mankind.[73] The three dimensions of the cuboid below are 'agency', 'policy fields', and 'composition/membership'.

Proactiveness and reactiveness are the two values of the dimension 'agency' that make up the cuboid's horizontal axis. Proactiveness means that the OFG has the right to take the political initiative, that is, to start the legislative process. This can happen directly or indirectly, depending on the concrete channels offered in the institutional architecture. Reactive power means that the OFG has the right to stop the lawmaking process or, put differently, OFGs can get competencies either on the output side or input side of the political process.

The vertical axis of the cuboid categorizes OFGs according to the policy fields they treat. The values are: (a) 'monothematically the environment'; (b) 'monothematically the finances'; (c) 'monothematically a specific other policy field'; and (d) 'multithematically all policy fields'.

Those OFGs dealing with all areas of policy making must be distinguished from those which deal with only a few selected policy fields. In the case of the latter, the policy areas in question are usually environmental or financial policy. However, other policy fields are also conceivable (e.g. education or labour market policy). While the Israeli OFG (2001–2006) was empowered to engage on any subject on the parliament's agenda, excluding defence and foreign affairs, the Hungarian OFG (2008–2011) was 'solely' tasked to sustain and preserve the environment for future generations.

[73] Of course, the members of each specific people are part of mankind, but we should avoid ambiguous terminology.

The diagonal plane of the cuboid represents the composition of the OFG. The values are: (a) members of parliament; (b) commissioner; (c) future council; and (d) randomly selected citizens. Members of parliament can, in theory and practice, form parliamentary committees for future generations. Examples are the Committee for the Future in Finland and the Parliamentary Advisory Council for Sustainable Development in Germany. The term of office of the members of these OFGs overlaps with that of the other members of parliament. Commissioners, and also ombudsmen or guardians, are independent in the sense that they are not members of the legislative or executive branch, notwithstanding that they are appointed by the legislature or the government. The Hungarian, Israeli, and Welsh OFGs fall into this category.

Future councils are expert groups that are appointed by the legislature and the government, just like commissioners. One important difference is that these OFGs are less person-centred and less vulnerable. These independent bodies exist in most countries, albeit without assertive competencies. Future councils with 'hard power' – the right to initiate, to delay, or to stop legislation – have been proposed in the literature.[74] Finally, participatory/deliberative theory has made the case for randomly selected citizens' committees. In practice, such assemblies were established on a temporary basis to deal with a variety of issues. Arguably, the most prominent examples for that approach were the citizens' committee for the constitution of Iceland[75] and the British Columbia Citizens' Assembly in Canada.[76] In the literature, a permanent citizens' chamber to represent future generations has been proposed, either with or without veto rights.[77]

The core questions for each citizenry that embarks on the endeavour of implementing an OFG are the following:

[74] Tremmel, 'Parliaments and Future Generations – The Four-Powers Model', *supra* note 1; Tremmel, *Responsibility for Future Citizens in the Realm of Politics*, *supra* note 38; J.C. Tremmel, 'Zukunftsräte zur Vertretung der Interessen kommender Generationen. Ein praxisorientierter Vorschlag für Deutschland', in T. Mannewitz (ed.), *Die Demokratie und ihre Defekte* (Springer forthcoming); J. Rux, 'Der ökologische Rat – Ein Vorschlag zur Änderung des Grundgesetzes', in Stiftung für die Rechte zukünftiger Generationen (ed.), *Handbuch Generationengerechtigkeit* (oekom 2003) 471–490; Stein, 'Zum Problem der Zukunftsfähigkeit der Demokratie', *supra* note 1.

[75] H. Landemore, 'Inclusive Constitution-Making: The Icelandic Experiment' (2015) 23(2) *Journal of Political Philosophy* 166–191.

[76] M.E. Warren and H. Pearse (eds.), *Designing Democracy: The British Columbia Citizens' Assembly* (Cambridge University Press 2008).

[77] See e.g. M.K. MacKenzie, 'A General-Purpose, Randomly Selected Chamber', in Gosseries and González Ricoy, *supra* note 1 at 282–298; Read, *supra* note 1. More cautiously, Smith argues that OFGs can enhance their legitimacy through embedding systematic public participation in their activities. G. Smith, 'Enhancing the Democratic Legitimacy of Independent Offices for Future Generations: The Case for Embedded Public Participation', Conference paper presented at the Institute for Futures Studies Symposium, Stockholm, 7–8 December 2017.

(a) Should the representative body for future generations be entitled to initiate legislation, to put a substantive veto on it, or even to prevent it completely?
(b) Should the domain of the new institution be limited to certain areas of policy and, if so, which ones?
(c) How should the new institution be constituted? Should their members be appointed? By which procedure and by whom?
(d) How many members should the institution for future citizens have? How long should the new institution's members be in office, and to what kind of resources should they be entitled?
(e) Would the constitution of a particular country have to be amended in order to establish such a new institution and, if yes, how exactly?

Tentative answers to these questions have been offered by devising an institution for Germany,[78] the UK,[79] and New Zealand.[80] These models are not transferable from one country to another, as they factor in the existing political institutions and traditions of each country. However, are there not characteristics that all (or almost all) institutions for future citizens should have an involvement in? Even if it seems apt to design OFGs differently for each country's political system, two design features seem generalizable to a large extent.

## THE RIGHT TO INITIATE LEGISLATION AS A KEY DESIGN CRITERION OF OFGS

The key criterion suggested here is 'constructive input' in the sense of a right to initiate legislation, as opposed to the possibility of destructive input, that is, all rights intended to suspend laws and programmes temporarily or permanently. The logic of proactiveness seeks first to prevent another 'veto player' and second to render the charge of an 'eco-dictatorship' moot.

### *The Prevention of an Additional Veto Player*

This first argument runs as follows. Separation of powers is meant to create an internal control mechanism among the government bodies so as to prevent the abuse of power. At the same time, separation of powers should not diffuse the state authority to the effect that the state itself becomes powerless, for a powerless state will find itself unable to guarantee the liberty, security, and equality of its

[78] Tremmel, *Responsibility for Future Citizens in the Realm of Politics*, *supra* note 38; Tremmel, 'Zukunftsräte zur Vertretung der Interessen kommender Generationen', *supra* note 74.

[79] Read, *supra* note 1.

[80] J. Boston, *Safeguarding the Future: Governing in an Uncertain World* (Bridget Williams Books 2017).

citizens. In the best case, separation of powers amounts to a sort of division of labour. In the worst case, the different branches neutralize each other as 'veto players', thereby making it impossible for any governing to take place at all. Traditionally, institutionalists examined dichotomous classifications (i.e. unitary vs. federalist, parliamentarian vs. presidential). By contrast, George Tsebelis's theory of veto players asks how many actors must consent to a decision or are able to veto it.[81] Multilevel parliamentarianism already features a high number of veto players, such as the second legislative chamber, the constitutional court, the president (if he or she has to formally sign laws in parliamentarian systems), and the people itself, insofar as it makes itself heard through referendums.

There is certainly a risk that creating a fully operational OFG will bring about the addition of a new veto player, thereby increasing the chances of gridlock of the political system. Therefore OFGs should have the right to initiate legislation but not to prevent it.

The right to delay lawmaking (for a limited period of time, not indefinitely) seems to be somewhat in between the input and the output side of the political process. But it is in fact also a reaction, not an initial action, and thus part of a reactive capacity. It can be a sharp sword, as Shlomo Shoham, the one and only Knesset Commissioner for Future Generations, explains:

> The right to be given enough time to prepare an opinion is an implied authority to create a delay in the legislative process. Such a delay may be crucial for the parliamentary work when it comes to bills discussed the framework of the state's budget. In that case, the time factor is vital since the implication of not voting on the state's budget for the next year is . . . that parliament must dissolve itself and go to elections.[82]

While this might be a peculiarity of the political system in Israel, the American experience with filibustering at the national level highlights that delaying resistance is often difficult to overcome at all.

## *Silencing the Charge of 'Dictatorship'*

Expertocracy, the rule of experts, has been discussed in political theory for a long time,[83] arguably since Plato promoted it for Kallipolis, the utopian city in his dialogue *The Republic*. It has been both hailed and condemned. The devil lies in the details. For example, a future council, endowed with a right of initiative, is allowed to introduce proposals for new legislation into the parliament. Lest it be

[81] See G. Tsebelis, *Veto Players: How Political Institutions Work* (Princeton University Press 2002).

[82] Shoham and Lamay, *supra* note 61 at 248.

[83] One comprehensive account is provided by Frank Fischer. See F. Fischer, *Technocracy and the Politics of Expertise* (SAGE Publications 1990).

misunderstood, such an expert council would not have the right to decide these parliamentary processes. The future council would not be allowed to pass laws; it would only have the power to place bills on the formal voting agenda of the legislature. In order to allow this, most parliaments would have to change their rules of procedure, not their constitutions. Currently, parliamentary rules of procedure usually state that bills have to be signed either by a party fraction or, interfractionally, by five per cent of all members of the parliament. The motions of the future council would be similar to those interfractional motions the proceedings of which are often referred to as 'the shining hours of parliamentarianism' in the literature.[84]

Strengthening the scientific and academic input on politics by an OFG, as suggested here, therefore does not imply that politicians must necessarily follow scholarly advice. Indeed, it would be naïve to believe that the legislature would take up and implement each and every proposal made by the future council in the form in which it has been sketched here. Rather, it stands to reason that parliament would pass on most of its legislative initiatives to committees, where they would face a silent death by non-action.[85] However, there is legitimate hope that, at least in some cases, the legislative initiatives brought forth by the new institutions might be able to garner the support of future-oriented lawmakers, as well as that of the press and public opinion.

By limiting itself to a purely constructive role, the legitimacy of the new future council is ensured. The charge of an 'eco-dictatorship' cannot be directed against such a future council, as this charge only makes sense when talking about organizations with veto rights, for only these can override decisions made democratically by parliament.

To be sure, the model of a future council as presented here transcends the dualist interpretation of science and politics spelled out in their respective binary codes of 'wisdom' and 'power'. Unlike paid political consultants, the independent members of a future council would not approach politicians as mere supplicants, hoping for a willing ear that may be lent but that does not have to be. While, on the one hand, the power of decision-making remains fully with the politicians, the element of long-term rationality, on the other hand, is strengthened by parliament's obligation to at

[84] U. Kranenpohl, 'Konsens im Konflikt? Inter- und überfraktionelle Initiativen im Deutschen Bundestag' (2001) 32(4) *Zeitschrift für Parlamentsfragen* 733–758.

[85] It was in this manner that an attempt to adopt a stronger reference to future generations in the Basic Law also failed – an attempt that had been undertaken in the years 2003–2009 by young members of parliament and which had been initiated by the Foundation for the Rights of Future Generations. For further readings on the initiative for an Intergenerational Justice Act, which had considered several formulations, but never a direct intrusion into the separation of powers model, see Tremmel, *Eine Theorie der Generationengerechtigkeit*, *supra* note 3 at 109–111; J.C. Tremmel, 'Verankerung von Generationengerechtigkeit in der Verfassung' (2005) 8/2005 *Aus Politik und Zeitgeschichte* 18–28; M. Wanderwitz, P. Friedrich, A. Lührmann, and M. Kauch, 'Changing the German Constitution in Favor of Future Generations – Four Perspectives from the Young Generation', in J.C. Tremmel (ed.), *Demographic Change and Intergenerational Justice* (Springer 2008) 163–173.

least consider the future council's proposals. The endemic problem of politics' resistance to advice is not entirely solved but rather mitigated.

In the current global political climate, where politicians and other decision influencers have taken to disregarding scientific insights, there is the need for a stronger coupling of politics and science. This highlights the argument that knowledge ought to play a role in political decision-making.

## CONCLUSION

Another important design feature of OFGs is their leadership structure. It is an interesting question whether institutions that are led by a group are better suited, in theory and practice, to represent future citizens than those that are led by a single person. In this context, 'led by a single person' is defined as having one single individual in the driving seat of the institution for future generations, independently of his or her leadership style. Even if a chairperson of an institution for future generations consulted regularly with his or her subordinates, and listened to their advice, this would count as a case of single leadership, as one individual alone is legally responsible and more visible for the media and the public than the rest of the staff.

Compared with other branches of government, individual-led OFGs are a peculiarity. In constitutional courts, the chairperson is usually not more than a *primus inter pares*. Likewise, in the legislature, the role of the parliament's chairperson enjoys comparably little additional power compared to other members of parliament.[86] The effects of the variable 'collective leadership', as opposed to 'individual leadership', for the success of OFGs cannot be ascertained in a scientific sense for epistemological reasons. There is no alternative history that tells us if, for instance, the Commissioner for Future Generations in Israel would not have been disbanded if this institution would have been devised as a group-led institution from the beginning. But what can be done is a test of the plausibility of the thesis that institutions that are led by a group are better suited to represent future citizens than those that are led by a single person.

Critics of any institution for future citizens anywhere in the world have the chance to zero in on its personal embodiment. Even if the integrity of the office-holders is beyond doubt, his or her unique position does provide an additional target. The only possibility of avoiding this is to have no single individual in such an exposed position. A collective body is better shielded from criticisms that are ostensibly directed against a person but in fact aimed at delegitimatizing the institution. It should not be forgotten that OFGs have many foes just because of the nature of their mandates:

[86] This is of course different with regard to the leaders of the executive branch (the government), such as presidents, prime ministers, or chancellors.

> [A]ny commission (or other public entity) for future generations runs the risk of having few friends and defenders. At the same time, it is bound to generate enemies. Among these will be all those with a vested interest in existing policy arrangements and who expect to be net losers from the kinds of policy investments advocated by a future-oriented institution. Ironically, therefore, such institutions are destined to encounter the same political challenges and temporal asymmetries that they are designed to alleviate. If they fail to meet these challenges, they will become yet further victims of the presentist bias.[87]

The optimal group size of collectively led OFGs is up for discussion and further research.[88] Every composition of the steering board of an OFG that has more than a single leader can bring about the positive effects known from bipartisan bodies in highly polarized political systems. For the productive exchange of arguments, two members would be the minimum to develop a 'deliberative stance'[89] and fruitfully exchange arguments.

87 Boston, *supra* note 1 at 331.

88 John Rawls, for instance, was particularly optimistic about the chances of success of deliberation within the US Supreme Court. J. Rawls, *Political Liberalism* (Columbia University Press 1993) §6 (The Supreme Court as Exemplar of Public Reason).

89 S. Niemeyer and J. Jennstål, 'The Deliberative Democratic Inclusion of Future Generations', in González-Ricoy and Gosseries (eds.), *Institutions for Future Generations*, *supra* note 1 at 247.

# 39

# Intergenerational Equity in Sustainable Development Treaty Implementation

*Marcel Szabó, Marie-Claire Cordonier Segger, and Alexandra R. Harrington*

International law reflects the values shared by States and has helped them face the most consequential challenges of the day. After the Second World War, the most significant challenge was to preserve international peace and security, as well as to guarantee basic human rights. In the twenty-first century, States face a new challenge: climate change and its consequences, and, ultimately, the survival of all mankind. Unfortunately, the consequences of climate change are highly visible – for example, extreme weather conditions (droughts, heatwaves and devastating storms, floods in areas where people have never experienced similar events before), melting ice in the Arctic, the extinction of some native plant and animal species and the appearance of unknown invasive species in the same area.[1]

While climate change impacts can be localised, the main means of intervention against such impacts is through international law since, once these laws have been properly ratified, States are responsible for applying the provisions fully and unconditionally within their own legal systems. This, however, requires intensive cooperation among the various fields of study. So, for example, in politics and economics (including both the level of individual companies and that of the national economy), scholars and decision-makers must also accept that preservation of the environment and the responsible management of resources are as important as short-term political and economic advantages.

In determining the scope of interventions for preserving the environment, the latest results of research in natural sciences must also be taken into account. In this context, jurisprudence shall elaborate upon and apply new regulatory methods that encourage economic operators, consumers and public authorities to

[1] Living Planet Report 2018, pp. 11, 90 and 119 https://wwf.panda.org/knowledge_hub/all_publications/living_planet_report_2018/; Camilo Mora and Peter Sale, *Ongoing Global Biodiversity Loss and the Need to Move Beyond Protected Areas: A Review of the Technical and Practical Shortcomings of Protected Areas on Land and Sea* (Marine Ecology Progress Series, 2011) 251–255.

manage resources responsibly and that reward them for responsible management. Such new methods can include supporting the introduction of new technologies, encouraging consumer awareness and conscious economic behaviour through tax incentives or otherwise and applying consistently the 'polluter pays' principle, one of the oldest principles of international environmental law.

A further significant consideration is that the Earth's population continues to increase. Currently, it is approximately 7.5 billion persons, but according to UN estimates it may exceed 11 billion persons by 2100.[2] Population growth will require increases in food production and agricultural land, which may be to the detriment of forests. According to an FAO report, the size of forests in tropical States decreased by 7 million hectares annually between 2000 and 2010, while the size of agricultural land increased by 6 million hectares annually.[3] At the same time, the reduction of forests automatically entails an increase in carbon dioxide in the atmosphere, as forests play a particularly important role in carbon sequestration.

In its special report, the IPCC confirmed that the rate of global warming will reach the threshold of 1.5 °C between 2030 and 2052,[4] and an increase in temperature of 2 °C is the maximum that humankind can tolerate. In case of an increase of 2.2 °C, large African mammals are expected to become extinct, while an increase of 2.8 °C would result in the destruction of the Amazon rainforests and the coral reefs around Australia. An increase of approximately 4 °C would result in the destruction of all mankind, as in natural circumstances humans can tolerate a maximum temperature of approximately 35 °C (the so-called wet-bulb temperature).

At the same time, global warming triggered by the reduction of forests decreases the average production of agricultural land. Therefore, in order to maintain production rates in the regions that are most affected by global warming and are overpopulated, additional land must be given over to agricultural production or production must be intensified by monoculture production and fertiliser use, leading to the fast depletion of soils.

It is, therefore, particularly important for today's generations to take into account the interests of future generations in all areas of life. Furthermore, it is essential to raise awareness about the fact that climate change is not a future issue affecting generations that are still to be born. On the contrary, the global consequences of current environmental changes will be felt within several years or decades, so they will also affect today's generations. This means that if circumstances remain unchanged, within thirty years today's generations will not be able to fully enjoy the results of economic development. In relation to the fight against climate change, the most important political guideline may be that 'after a flood, it only matters who made the ship on time'. Thus, while the history of past centuries is

[2] World Population Prospect 2019 https://population.un.org/wpp/.

[3] FAO, State of the World's Forests (2016).

[4] IPCC, Special Report: Global Warming of 1.5 °C, Summary for Policymakers (2018) 6.

primarily about wars and conquests, today's statesmen and stateswomen may gain recognition and respect from the next generation by thinking and acting responsibly in the interest of future generations instead of using arms.

In this context, policy and lawmakers need to take into account the interests of future generations mainly in the fields of ethics, law and economics.

## ETHICAL ASPECTS OF INTERGENERATIONAL EQUITY

For centuries, the main driving force of human history has been that the world is gradually getting better and better, under the guidance of wise people. Technical means are always being perfected, the environment is improving, and quality of life is increasing, so everyone will live an increasingly better life and be able to consume more and more. This approach, however, may only be valid if it is assumed that resources are endless and can be used without limits.

The phenomenon of climate change, however, has clearly shown that this assumption does not hold true. Future generations will hardly be able to increase their use of resources and consume more than today's generations. On the contrary, a significant decrease in resources available for consumption is expected in terms of both their absolute value and their value *per capita*. However, the responsibility of today's generations for future generations requires the posing of a fundamental question: if it is already certain that we cannot improve our lives and living conditions, what sacrifice should we make in order not to impair the living conditions of our children and grandchildren and to provide them with the opportunity of free choice? Even though the responsibility of today's generations for future generations is set out in an increasing number of legal documents, this issue can be considered primarily as an ethical one.

Furthermore, the responsibility for future generations sheds light on an additional issue. The concept of future generations is linked to specific societies instead of specific individuals, and therefore responsibility for future generations can be understood at the level of the society as a whole rather than for specific individuals. However, the question of whether preserving living conditions for future generations requires the same level or at least the same proportion of sacrifice from all members of today's generations, regardless of whether they are citizens of a developed or a developing country, is unaddressed. In this situation, differences among living and other conditions in developed and developing countries should be taken into account in determining the scope of their responsibility for next generations. Intragenerational equity requires each nation to ensure the survival of its own descendants, knowing and hoping that the other nations are subject to similar responsibility and sacrifice in connection with their own future generations. While ethically it may be expected that everyone will take the necessary measures in the interests of their own descendants, the approach requiring action from today's generations in the interest of future generations of nations living in other parts of the world is undermined by significant economic, geographical, political and other objective differences.

The cornerstone of thinking about future generations is that the members of a nation can answer together the questions of identity, shared cultural and ethical values that will be bequeathed to children and grandchildren, and how to change consumption patterns and lifestyles to allow these values to be passed on. In his encyclical letter *Laudato Si'*, Pope Francis underlines that the meaning of the life of today's generations may be questioned if they leave an unliveable world to subsequent generations.[5]

It is generally true that the community is willing to make a larger sacrifice where there is already a direct and institutionalised link between today's generations and future generations. While international law introduced *inter alia* the category of intergenerational equity, it still lacks real means to support the implementation of such equity. On the contrary, the national law of certain States already contains institutions (mostly falling within the scope of the social care system) which are aimed at implementing intergenerational cooperation. Such institutions include, for example, old-age pensions or childbirth allowances. Therefore, where the institutions of international law are suitable for designating the scope of intergenerational equity, nations and States are to be responsible for determining its content.

## LEGAL ASPECTS OF INTERGENERATIONAL EQUITY

Although the responsibility for future generations may primarily be assessed at national level, an approach beyond the State level must be applied in relation to the protection of human rights, including for so-called second- and third-generation human rights. Article 1 of the ICESCR provides that '[a]ll peoples may … freely dispose of their natural wealth and resources … In no case may a people be deprived of its own means of subsistence.' While each State is required to enforce basic human rights within its own territories (having regard to their own legal systems and cultures), the same States may fail to take into account whether, within their jurisdiction, economic operators (including in particular multinational companies) respect basic human rights in their foreign operations.

Similarly, where a State adopts a specific regulation in respect of its resident citizens or resident legal entities, the regulation may not take into account the global impacts that would result therefrom. For example, a direct link exists where rules on water resources have an impact on neighbouring States using the water base or where emissions of pollutants affect the territory of neighbouring States. An indirect link exists, however, if the effect on other States and citizens can only be demonstrated as a secondary impact. In this context, an international legal environment

[5] *Encyclical Letter Laudato Si' of the Holy Father Francis on Care for Our Common Home*, 2015, para. 206.

that allows responsibility to be established not only for direct links but also in case of scientifically supported indirect links would also be suitable for enforcing responsibility for future generations, thereby promoting responsible management of resources. In this case, taking into account the 2011 UN Draft Articles on the International Legal Responsibility of States, State responsibility may be based on non-compliance with the due diligence obligations in addition to responsibility for specific human rights violations.[6]

Certain international agreements, primarily those on the environment or human rights, already apply monitoring requirements and from time to time analyse Contracting Parties' practices in relationship to a treaty regime's terms.[7] Extending the monitoring system beyond the purely human rights context may relate to the specific issues of climate change and therefore to the issue of responsibility for future generations, and can provide a suitable basis for a certain kind of global solidarity, thereby reducing intragenerational inequality.

Furthermore, determining the applicable consequences is a significant element of the regulation of responsibility for future generations. The current rules of international law, in particular those relating to climate change, are much more focused on remedying damage that has arisen rather than preventing damage or restoring the original condition (if applicable). So, for example, the inclusion of persons fleeing from impossible living conditions requires significant economic and social resources from the States concerned. With careful planning, such resources could also be used to prevent the reasons underlying the flight of populations and/or solving problems at their source. This is important because, while the living conditions of billions of people may become impossible due to climate change, the number of refugees the EU may be able to receive is not proportional to the climate activity of this organisation.

Intragenerational solidarity, however, requires a change in today's perspective that is primarily, and in many cases exclusively, based on economic interests. The classic liberal economic policy of Adam Smith and David Ricardo is based on the self-regulating power of the market and assumes that free market processes that are free from government interventions create an economic order that is ideal for everyone. While it is unquestionable that the extension of economic cooperation was successful in several instances (for example, the EU or the WTO), intragenerational solidarity requires State and international law intervention and the subjection of classic free market processes to legal and ethical limits.

6 Timo Koivurova, 'Due Diligence' (2010) Max Planck Encyclopedia of Public International Law https://opil.ouplaw.com/view/10.1093/law:epil/9780199231690/law-9780199231690-e1034 accessed 30 June 2019.

7 Examples of monitoring: regular country visits by elected or appointed experts; ad hoc onsite inspections by experts; evaluations based on questionnaires; written reporting, carried out by Member States (self-assessment).

Two issues arise in this respect. On the one hand, legal and ethical limits are not established within these systems. For example, it is hardly justifiable from a legal or ethical point of view that in the framework of the WTO, mineral water is a commodity just like any other product,[8] and therefore, based on market processes and interests only, the water resources of a developing country may also be used to supply a developed country so that it may 'keep in reserve' its own water resources. Furthermore, the regulatory State (or, as the case may be, the community of States) should be strong enough even when, owing to rationalisation of economic processes and increased efficiency of production, the business interests of market players become contrary to the legal and ethical rules in place and their lobbies try to soften those rules.

Similar trends apply where agricultural land is acquired or leased by foreign market players. International law and EU law, as well as the national law of several States, allow for the lease and acquisition of arable land by foreigners, and certain developed countries may satisfy the needs of their citizens by using the resources of other States, thereby saving their own arable land. The importance of such an approach is well demonstrated by the fact that, for example, within the European Union arable land is regulated as an investment vehicle in connection with the free movement of capital, and Member States may only exceptionally subject this to restrictions. Furthermore, Member States shall allow for the acquisition of their arable land by the citizens of other Member States, according to the provisions of EU law.

Another example of the conflict between legal and ethical aspects of intergenerational equity is the regulations and practices concerning the prohibition of child labour.[9] In principle, all States support the prohibition of child labour; however, certain States and international organisations have failed to take truly effective action against multinational companies that obtain advantages on the market through the indirect use of child labour. Currently, action against such market players is primarily based only on the ethical values of the society.

This also holds true for the obligation to preserve natural resources for future generations. Several natural resources may be fully exhausted within several decades if their current use is maintained. Although several decades is a short period in the context of human history, in the world of short political objectives it is long enough to be the focus of political thinking. For example, in its decision No. 28/2017. (X. 25.), the Hungarian Constitutional Court found that the obligation to preserve biological diversity is 'a peremptory norm of the international law and it reflects also the intention of the international community as a whole'.[10] Legal solutions engaging similar existing legal means in order to preserve natural resources may

[8] Mike Muller and Christophe Bellmann, *Trade and Water – How Might Trade Policy Contribute to Sustainable Water Management?* (International Centre for Trade and Sustainable Development, 2016) 14–17.

[9] The ILO Conventions and Recommendations concerning child labour are available at www.ilo.org/ipec/facts/ILOconventionsonchildlabour/lang--en/index.htm accessed 30 June 2019.

[10] Decision No. 28/2017. (X. 25.) AB, Reasoning [38].

constitute an example for legislators, those applying the law and courts (constitutional courts) globally.

Further to strategic documents, several national parliaments have a body that is mainly responsible for taking into account sustainable development (or, in a broader sense, the interests of future generations), including for example the National Council for Sustainable Development in Hungary, which was set up in 2008, is headed by the vice president of Parliament and is a consultative and advisory body of Parliament on matters relating to sustainable development.[11] What is common to those bodies is that their members come from professional and scientific research institutes, universities and civil society organisations in addition to politics, and they are responsible for *inter alia* taking positions on whether legislative bills comply with the concept of sustainable development and may, where applicable, initiate activities through the legislative process. Unfortunately, even though such institutions exist in several States, their findings are in many cases fully ignored by legislators.

Whereas certain strategic documents are to be adopted only at the national level, protection of the interests of future generations may also be realised universally. Several international civil society organisations requested the creation of a position similar to that of an ombudsman or high commissioner as an element of UN reform at the Rio+20 summit. Even though this institution has not yet been established, the UN Secretary-General was invited to prepare a report on the situation of future generations under the auspices of the UN.[12]

## ECONOMIC ASPECTS OF INTERGENERATIONAL EQUITY

Today's economic model is based on increasing consumption and production and on the assumption that the continuous development thereof can satisfy the needs of an ever-increasing world population. The major weakness of this model is that the Earth's resources are limited. While citizens of developed states already use natural resources very intensively in order to ensure their own well-being and quality of life, citizens of developing countries are seeking to reach such levels of well-being. This effort, however, will result in an unsustainable situation, even in the short term, and by 2050 according to certain pessimistic forecasts.

According to Principle 8 of the 1992 Rio Declaration, '[t]o achieve sustainable development and a higher quality of life for all people, States should reduce and eliminate unsustainable patterns of production and consumption and promote appropriate demographic policies'. Therefore, it can be said that due consideration of the interests of future generations and responsible management of the Earth's resources require changing the ethical and legal approach, as well as revisiting the

[11] See in detail www.parlament.hu/web/ncsd/national-council-for-sustainable-development accessed 30 June 2019.

[12] Intergenerational Solidarity and the Needs of Future Generations. Report of the Secretary General, A/68/100, 2013.

basic economic approach. A key element may be decoupling,[13] that is, separating the economic concept of growth from natural growth in terms of consumption. Although statistical growth is virtually unlimited, at least in theory, the Earth's limited resources constitute an absolute limit for physical growth.

Implementation of decoupling is by no means impossible. Decoupling would be supported, for example, by making public administration eco-friendly, by the obligatory recycling of raw materials in the construction of infrastructure or obligatory consideration of calculations regarding the efficiency of certain investments and proper accounting of their efficiency. However, the issue in this respect is how to obtain the support of stakeholders. Market players will refrain from adopting a different market practice as long as they consider its introduction to be a competitive disadvantage that would threaten their own position.

According to this approach, when establishing product value we should not consider ecological services as externalities.[14] Nevertheless, discounting is another essential element in today's economic approach. By recognising future damage at a lower current value, discounting creates a link between ecological damage that is certain to arise in the distant future and financial advantage that may be realised in the immediate future.[15] This approach itself prefers current economic advantage even at the cost of mid-term and long-term damage.

However, a great deal of work is being done today to advance greener, more sustainable economics.[16] Green economics assigns a value to ecological services, thereby taking them into account in the analysis of economic processes. Today this approach may continue to be pushed into the background by mainstream economic studies, but it is also clear that ideas for reform that would achieve more sustainable development and responsible management of environmental resources, as against the unconditional achievement of short-term economic advantages, also exist in the field of economics.

## LESSONS FOR INTERGENERATIONAL EQUITY

This volume is structured in six parts, each of which has highlighted the place of and lessons for and from intergenerational equity. After a brief introduction from the

[13] See OECD Environment Programme, Indicators to Measure Decoupling of Environmental Pressure from Economic Growth. Executive Summary, 1–3 www.oecd.org/environment/indicators-modelling-outlooks/1933638.pdf accessed 30 June 2019.

[14] See in general TEEB Report for Business: The Economics of Ecosystems and Biodiversity www.teebweb.org/wp-content/uploads/Study%20and%20Reports/Reports/Business%20and%20Enterprise/TEEB%20for%20Business%20Report/TEEB%20for%20Business.pdf accessed 30 June 2019.

[15] Cedric Philibert, 'Discounting the Future' (2003) Internet Encyclopaedia of Ecological Economics.

[16] Cameron Allen and Stuart Clouth (eds.), *A Guidebook to the Green Economy* (UN Division for Sustainable Development, 2012).

editors, the opening of the volume featured the voice of Edith Brown Weiss, who argued that the concept of intergenerational equity provides a valuable framework to address the most challenging issues featuring the new Anthropocene epoch, i.e. human activities that are shaping the planet's environment on an unprecedented scale. She highlighted that, since the temporal aspect of human activities has been understood, humankind's responsibility for its descendants has become a major concern for many. In this context, the notion of intergenerational equity is a tool for the reconciliation of solidarity between past, present and future generations. Basic principles of intergenerational equity are threefold: humanity must conserve comparable quality, options, and access to all basic resources of the Earth's environment for future generations to enjoy and to decide for themselves. The chapter explored the substantial and institutional criteria for individual national institutions to take a role in realising these universal principles guaranteed by international law on a national level.

Part I of the volume then provided the foundations for the book by highlighting the relevant international conventions enshrining the basic exigencies of intergenerational justice and sustainable development, focusing in particular on treaties such as the 1992 Convention on Biological Diversity, the 1992 UN Framework Convention on Climate Change, the 1972 Convention Concerning the Protection of the World Cultural and Natural Heritage and the 1998 UNECE Aarhus Convention on Access to Information, Public Participation in Decision-making and Access to Justice in Environmental Matters. The chapters in this part defined the theoretical background underpinning the principle of intergenerational equity and obligations related to intergenerational justice in international law on sustainable development, their implementation and implications.

Part II moved on to focus on the contours of intergenerational justice, equity and the rights of future generations, providing perspectives on the concept and its implications for law and policy. The chapters in this part scoped the international acceptance and dissemination of these norms, focusing on the key issues related to intergenerational justice for national implementation, with contributions concentrating on the main problems, relevant models, similarities and discrepancies. Following this, Part III highlighted several key challenges for national implementation of intergenerational equity and justice in principle, exploring recent trends and innovations in the development of constitutional legal norms and arrangements, economic instruments, mechanisms for transparent public participation and access to justice, and measures to address science, precaution and uncertainty.

Part IV of the volume provided original case studies on prominent national sustainable development institutions of model character, analysing different solutions to the complex problem of policy integration and the representation of the interests of future generations. The chapters in this part examined comparative insights from different experiences and traditions, generating areas of commonality and difference in the development of intergenerational equity concepts. The cases revealed and analysed the ability and means of national sustainable development institutions to measure progress in their work for a more intergenerationally just society, demonstrating numerous challenges encountered by these institutions in their efforts. Finding the right places to intervene in the current socio-economic system as well as choosing the appropriate methodologies for impact assessment presented particular challenges, given the complexity and interconnectedness of factors influencing an outcome as well as the timescale of the problems to be considered. The more deeply a potential solution affects present societal values, the more impact it can have on future well-being.

The chapters in Part V shed light on current regional trends and innovations in this field, focusing on recent developments at regional levels and proposals for institutionalising the representation of future generations in Europe, Africa, Asia, Latin America and the Caribbean. Finally, in Part VI, several chapters scoped future directions and options for particular sectors of law and policy, distilling lessons learned from current practices, and options for reform of political and legal institutions at the national, regional and global levels. They summarised the findings of the volume, noting that education and the development of values-based legal institutions with effective authority on behalf of future generations could play key roles in delivering and disseminating intergenerational justice.

## CONCLUSIONS

From the analysis in this volume, it follows that ethical, legal and economic fundamentals that could be suitable for duly considering mid-term and long-term aspects relating to the limited nature of the Earth's resources, instead of short-term economic aspects, already exist. Unfortunately, in human history, in almost every case a serious catastrophe has been necessary to change the prevailing political, economic and legal approach. Today, many people still think that climate change and other potential sources of danger may threaten the generations of the distant future only, and that they pose existential risks to humans only. Recognising that this does not hold true will hopefully lead to creating the foundations for the necessary change of the ethical, legal and economic paradigm. While it is true that the primary effects of climate change will affect the most vulnerable developing countries to a larger extent, developed countries should also take into account the secondary effects including, for example, the challenges of international migration related to climate change, internal and international conflicts, and loss of entire ecosystems on which livelihoods depend.

To respect the needs and interests of future generations, an important task is raising the awareness of all mankind about the dramatic changes and threats which are faced because of current (less than sustainable) development pathways. Today, numerous scientists have already abolished their earlier practice of publishing their latest research outcomes only in highly ranked scientific forums that meet academic standards, owing to concerns that their discoveries will remain almost unknown to the wider public. They expressly seek to help students and the broader public to become aware of scientific results, thereby calling the attention of society, politics and economics to the threats that are faced. This change in approach, and the resulting popularisation of scientific findings, is becoming so widespread that it might even be called a 'revolution of scientists'. The future of our planet depends in large part on whether this revolution of scientists will be followed by a revolution of politicians, economists and jurists, that is, whether it will be followed by a process in which politics, economics and jurisprudence will reach beyond their traditional frameworks in order to prevent these extremely serious threats in a timely manner and to support the efforts of all humanity to move towards a more sustainable and enlightened world for future generations.

# Afterword

*H.E. Justice C.G. Weeramantry*

The sustainability problems now facing humanity pose the most serious danger to mankind since the human race began. Not only is our current situation fraught with unprecedented threats to the human future. These are also problems of the utmost urgency, and they demand concerted global action at all levels within the next ten to fifteen years. The time available to implement solutions is running out at an alarming rate. Humanity is racing towards the abyss of environmental devastation with such a blinkered vision that the impending peril is scarcely perceived by the vast bulk of the global population.

It is indeed sad to note that, in this age in which information is more easily available to all levels of the population than ever before, so many are still unaware of the extent of this danger, its immediacy, its irreversibility, its impact on thousands of generations now and to come, the fact that it could be prevented through concerted action, its violation of every principle known to law and religion, and its potential for the destruction of all civilisation. All these are scarcely known or perceived by the generation perpetrating this damage. Indeed, those perpetrating the damage rarely bring the problems to the attention of the general public and, indeed, often try to conceal it. Consequently, this danger is permitted to grow at an exponentially increasing rate, without a voice of protest reaching the corridors of power – economic power, political power, military power and technological power – where decisions are taken on a daily basis that will impair the environment even further.

I recall, during the period in which the ICJ was hearing submissions regarding the Legality of Nuclear Weapons, one of the lawyers for the anti-nuclear powers observed that if Stone Age men had been able to damage our environment 25,000 years ago we would have condemned them as savages, brutes and barbarians. Even if people of the Stone Age could have caused such damage, they would not have known what they were doing. On the other hand, we know full well that we have been damaging the environment for multiples of 25,000 years. Yet we continue to do so with full knowledge of the damage we are causing to future generations.

If prehistoric men could be condemned as savages, brutes and barbarians for such conduct, I wonder what language future generations would adopt to describe our generation, who are polluting our environment with full knowledge that we are doing so. The conclusion at which we arrive is that our generation is clearly the most rapacious generation that has ever existed since the human race began. A society claiming to be civilised, advanced and law-abiding cannot permit such a reversal of all the human duties towards our children and our children's children which has been built up through untold centuries of effort and sacrifice.

President Eisenhower, in his celebrated farewell address, warned the American people of the dangers of the military/industrial complex which was entering into every detail of their daily lives and of the danger to privacy and human rights resulting from the activities of this conglomerate of power. The dangers he so wisely perceived were only a smattering of the dangers that prevail today. If this great military commander were alive in our time, he would have been aghast at the dangers that are proliferating while those in authority, as well as the general public, turn a blind eye to them.

## THE URGENCY OF THE PROBLEM

Carbon emissions to the atmosphere, pollution of the water resources, testing of nuclear weapons, surreptitious disposal of nuclear waste, deforestation, endangering of fauna and flora, uncontrolled disposal of industrial waste and depletion of the Earth's resources are proceeding at an ever-increasing rate. This is regardless of the fact that the damage already done has been so great that it has even caused significant climate change in our time, which will increase exponentially if preventive action is not taken immediately. If such operations are continued even at the present rate, the environment will, in the next decade or two, have deteriorated to levels which will not be able to support the global population as we now know it.

There is no safe method of disposing of waste from nuclear reactors, and all of this is accumulating. Even the IAEA has no record of the waste produced by each nuclear energy installation. The surreptitious disposal of these emissions pollutes the environment for multiples of 25,000 years, which is only the half-life of some of these chemicals. This is an untold danger to future generations, and children for thousands of years will be playing and living on ground which discharges radioactive emissions. The fish in polluted waters are even damaged genetically, and such pollution to ocean space anywhere is a pollution to ocean space everywhere. In addition, accidents are inevitable in all industrial establishments. The Bhopal incident in India has caused damage to thousands of people, and its effects will continue for many years to come. Chernobyl and Fukushima have displayed to the world the tremendous danger of nuclear accidents resulting from the fact that nuclear plants cannot be supervised every millisecond, as required. Hundreds of nuclear reactors are functioning all over the world, each of which is a source of hidden and uncontrollable danger.

All these factors in combination make this a problem of the greatest urgency. Of even greater importance, nuclear weapons testing still takes place today, despite the harrowing sufferings and terrible genetic defects these weapons induce. Such problems were well described to the International Court in the case of *New Zealand* v. *France*. Witnesses from territories in which nuclear testing took place appeared in Court and gave us glimpses of the horrific genetic deformities of children born after the bombings. The deformities were so great that some children born after the testing could scarcely be recognised as human and were swiftly buried. Among them were children born with two heads, with knees joined, and some who looked like objects with a palpitating heart under a translucent skin.

The possibility of the use of a nuclear weapon grows by the day as more and more states and organisations seek to lay their hands on nuclear weapons, and the knowledge necessary for their construction proliferates through the Internet to the point where the knowledge necessary to make a crude nuclear weapon is widely available. The materials necessary to make such a weapon are also available, owing to the proliferation of nuclear reactors whose waste is secretly disposed of.

If an irresponsible organisation lays its hands on a nuclear weapon, the danger of its use is ever-present, and the next use of a nuclear weapon will not be on a sitting target like Hiroshima or Nagasaki, which were unable to retaliate. The next use of a nuclear weapon will provoke the use of a nuclear weapon in return, resulting in a nuclear winter which will destroy global vegetation and spell the end of civilisation as we know it.

This situation was well described by the Soviet scientist Pyotr Kapitsa, giving evidence before the US Senate in 1983 and before the UN in 1985, where he described the total darkness that will fall upon the Earth in such an event: 'It will cause such profound and severe effects on the climate causing cold weather and blocking sunlight for a period of months or even years by emission of large amounts of firestorm, smoke and soot into the Earth's stratosphere.'

This multiplicity of dangers strangely passes unheeded by the legal profession, by the general public and by the powers that be, leaving us with the clear impression that mankind is heading towards its doom unless these dangers are brought under control.

## OBSTACLES TO BE OVERCOME

All of this prompts an enquiry regarding the factors that stand in the way of attention to this problem.

The first is the cloak of secrecy surrounding most of these environment endangering operations, such as nuclear testing, disposal of nuclear waste, discharge of waste by factories and carbon emissions. All of these are done with careful attention to keeping this information away from the general public. It is important that the principle of transparency at every level be insisted upon and that organisations like Transparency International continue to do the steering work in this connection, which needs to be better known and amplified.

Another major obstacle is the strength of the military/industrial/technological complex, which is responsible for well over 90 per cent of the pollution that now takes place. All of these entities are focused on short-term results, whether they be next year's balance sheet or the next election, which will take place in two or three years' time. The long-term perspectives spanning generations yet to come are totally outside their purview.

By way of contrast, native American tribes thought of the impact of their actions for seven generations to come, and all religions have emphasised the concept of trusteeship of the Earth's resources, which are meant to be enjoyed by us and not damaged or depleted. Scripture from every religion can be cited in support of this, but, strangely, modern legal systems, both domestic and international, seem to have lost sight of this important perspective.

When we consider that each of the entities involved in this conflict has powers which far exceed even the power of most nation states, we will realise how difficult it is to impose controls on them. This is where national legal systems and international law have to rise to the challenge, and this will be dealt with in a later section. The strength of the military complex is immense in terms of its enormous budgets, its closeness to the centre of political power and its linkage with problems of national security. What the military demands is hard to resist, and the argument of national security tends to override all other considerations.

Likewise, the strength of the corporate establishment, often functioning through multinational corporations, is difficult to resist. Several major corporations have greater budgets than over 150 of the nations of the world. They often deal with the governments of nation states on a theoretical footing of equality, when in fact they are in a position to lay down and dictate terms to the poor country in which they propose to operate. The legal principle that the letter of the contract must be obeyed prevails over the need to consider the manifest unfairness of a contract heavily weighted in favour of the more powerful contracting party.

Likewise, the strength of the technological establishment, combined with the expert scientific knowledge at its command, makes it difficult for its power to be resisted. The need for ethical codes for scientists engaged in activities that pose a danger to human rights has been grossly overlooked. I myself have had the privilege of drafting an ethical code for nuclear scientists that stresses their responsibility for the eventual outcome of their scientific work.[1] Such codes need to be drawn up and adopted by all bodies of scientists, because the effect of their work goes far beyond

[1] Reproduced in the *Encyclopedia of Social Inventions* (London 1991).

their laboratories and can cause untold damage to the human body, human society and the environment.[2]

When these forces are combined, as they often are, their power is nearly irresistible, even by nation states. Every component element of the military/industrial/technological complex focuses on short-term objectives for reasons already stated, and the long-term objective of future generations is furthest from their contemplation.

## PUBLIC APATHY

A major problem to be overcome in countering environmental damage done by major actors on the international scene is the almost total apathy of the general public, who do not raise their voices in protest. They adapt this quiescent attitude for several reasons. One reason is lack of information; another is a feeling of helplessness in the face of such conglomerations of power; yet another reason is the feeling that, however much they may protest, their protest will be unheeded for lack of enforcement power. A further reason is their belief that the legal system is weighted against them and that, even if they go to court to assert their rights, they will have little chance of success.

All these reasons in combination leave the perpetrators of environmental damage free to pursue their activities in the confidence that the voice of protest, if any, will be ineffective. An important task awaiting attention is the task of spreading information to the general public about the numerous organisations working in this field. The steps already taken by UN organisations, churches, environmental organisations and others are meaningful and can be strengthened by popular participation. An outstanding example is the Assisi Declaration (1986), a combined declaration of all religions on our duties to protect and preserve the environment. This Declaration was named after Saint Francis of Assisi (1181–1216), who was very sensitive to the concept of human duties towards the environment.

## SHORTCOMINGS OF LEGAL SYSTEMS

All this damaging activity and the ineffectiveness of protest occur against the background of the failure of national legal systems and of international law to take meaningful steps to ensure and protect the rights of future generations to an environment undefiled by us.

Current legal systems are structured on the basis that, if one's rights are being infringed, one must appear in court to protect them. There are organisations that may espouse one's calls, but the citizen's ultimate recourse is the judicial system. Legal systems around the world are structured on this basis. If the party affected does

[2] See *The Slumbering Sentinels: Law and Technology in the Wake of Technology* (Penguin 1983).

not complain, the violation of rights that have been committed goes ahead without any restraint from the law. In this day and age, it is perplexing that legal systems should still function on this basis, especially when one considers that the people whose rights are trampled upon are not yet born and cannot possibly appear in court to defend their rights. This is a curious anomaly and a strange gap in our legal systems, especially in this twenty-first century, which is supposedly so advanced in the protection of basic rights.

Institutions such as an Ombudsman for Future Generations are a sterling way of remedying this shortcoming, and it is wonderful to see this institution already adopted in Hungary and some other countries. Yet much work remains to be done in giving such Ombudsmen the power to appear in court, to present the case for future generations and to obtain a decree that will be binding on the highest authorities.

No legal system can claim to be adequate if it fails to provide such a basic mechanism for the protection of the rights of future citizens merely because they are not yet in existence. In fact, this would even appear ludicrous in the eyes of an impartial observer assessing the value of any legal system, given that even the most ancient human societies attached great importance to the protection of their posterity. It would be absurd to contend that this protection is restricted only to the rights of children already born. Children not yet born have an even greater right to the protection of their basic entitlements as human beings.

All customary systems of law and all religions stress this duty towards those who are unable to assert their rights. Just one illustration is a statement by Jesus Christ himself that it would be better for those who place obstacles in the way of children to have a millstone tied around their necks and to be drowned in the sea than to continue placing obstacles in the way of children.[3] Similar quotations can be made from the scriptures of all religions; for example, in ancient Hinduism, in such treatises as Kautilya's *Arthasastra*, the duties of kings to protect the environment in all its aspects were minutely specified as early as the third century BC. Buddhism teaches very clearly that the environment is to be enjoyed by us, but only on the basis of trusteeship, with a duty to preserve it for those who would enjoy it after us. In Islam, the Qur'an clearly states that it is our duty to 'tread lightly on the Earth' and that 'it is He who made you trustees of the Earth',[4] using it but not in such a manner as to lessen its value for future generations. Yet civilised society and the legal systems of today seem to permit environmentally damaging conduct that has been universally condemned since the beginnings of civilised society. How much worse would it be if those affected are our children's children and their children, ad infinitum?

[3] Matthew 18:6.

[4] Qur'an 25:53 and 6:165.

## A CALL TO ACTION

We arrive at the conclusion that this crucial gap in all legal systems urgently needs to be filled, and it is the business of all who value the human future to rise to their responsibilities and remedy this defect which runs through all legal systems.

Even more importantly, international law must look upon itself as the custodian of the human future. It needs to strengthen its resources in safeguarding these future members of the global family who do not as yet have a voice to speak for themselves. Trampling on their rights because they do not protest seems barbaric and absurd. If international law is to be true to its mission of achieving and strengthening a world of peace and justice, this major defect needs to be remedied urgently.

This is a call to international lawyers to take a wider view of the reach of their discipline and extend its frontiers to the point where it protects unborn generations from the rapaciousness of the present. International law would be failing in its mission if it did not discharge this trust. This message is a call to all levels of society to do whatever they can as individuals and as groups to prevent the pillage of future generations that is now occurring without let or hindrance from the law. Every individual has a duty to interest himself or herself in this damage now being done to his or her children and their children. The feeling of apathy, now so widely prevalent, needs to be shaken off. The contribution of every individual matters. Social and community groups, churches, religious associations, political parties, universities, learned societies and all other citizen groups need to realise the urgency of this call and to interest themselves in this fundamental problem endangering the human future.

Organisations such as the Hungarian Ombudsman's Office, the World Future Council, the Oxford Martin Commission for Future Generations, the Centre for International Sustainable Development Law and others too numerous to mention have done considerable work in relevant fields, which needs to be known by the global public. All these must be brought together and a collective action formulated on such matters as peace education, transparency, coalitions for collective action, cross-cultural and interreligious understanding, sensitising multinational cooperations to their environmental obligations, researching areas of immediate danger, reducing poverty levels and organising a public information service on the environmental danger.

The voice of protest must be raised to the extent that those in political power will realise that the votes they obtain are dependent on their concern as human beings for our children and our children's children. I draw attention in this connection to the UNGA Resolution on the Historical Responsibility of States for the Preservation of Nature for the Present and Future Generations (General Assembly Resolution 35/8 of 30 October 1980). A concerted campaign needs to be mounted to draw the attention of every state to its responsibilities under this resolution, and in particular to Article 3, which calls upon states to take measures including legislative measures necessary for this purpose.

A necessary step in this direction is the education of the general public at all levels. There needs to be dissemination of information from schoolrooms to the boardrooms of major companies and from the village level to the level of national parliaments. Let there be a universal call to action through universal education from the schoolroom upwards regarding the magnitude of this danger.

If a country is under attack, all citizens join together to defend it. Human civilisation is now under attack, and the citizens of all countries cannot continue to remain silent and inactive. This is an urgent message to all who are concerned with the human future to discard their apathy and rise to the defence of humanity and civilisation.

# Table of Authorities

## INTERNATIONAL TREATIES AND INSTRUMENTS

Convention Concerning the Protection of the World Cultural and Natural Heritage (1972)
Convention for the Protection of Cultural Property in the Event of Armed Conflict (1945)
Convention on Co-operation for the Protection and Sustainable Use of the River Danube (1998)
Convention on International Trade in Endangered Species of Wild Fauna and Flora (1973)
Convention on the Elimination of All Forms of Racial Discrimination (1969)
Convention on the Elimination of All Forms of Discrimination against Women (1981)
Convention on the Law of the Non-Navigational Uses of International Watercourses (2014)
Convention on the Prevention and Punishment of the Crime of Genocide (1948)
Convention on the Protection and Use of Transboundary Watercourses and International Lakes, Adopted in Helsinki (1996)
Convention on the Rights of Persons with Disabilities (2006)
Convention on the Rights of Persons with Disabilities (2008)
Convention on the Rights of the Child (1990)
Convention on the Sustainable Management of Lake Tanganyika (2005)
Convention on Wetlands of International Importance Especially as Waterfowl Habitat (1975)
Convention révisée portant création de l'autorité du Bassin du Niger (1987)
Declaration of Principles Governing the Sea-Bed and the Ocean Floor, and the Subsoil Thereof, beyond the Limits of National Jurisdiction (1970)
Declaration of the United Nations Conference on the Human Environment (1972)
Draft International Covenant on Environment and Development, 4th Edition (2010)
European Convention for the Protection of Human Rights and Fundamental Freedoms (1950)
Goa Guidelines on Intergenerational Equity (1988)
Guarani Aquifer Agreement (2010)
Inter-American Commission on Human Rights (1959)
International Covenant on Civil and Political Rights (1976)
International Covenant on Economic, Social and Cultural Rights (1976)
International Convention for the Prevention of Pollution from Ships (1983)
International Convention for the Regulation of Whaling (1948)
International Law Association New Delhi Conference, Fifth and Final Report of the Committee on Legal Aspects of Sustainable Development (2002)

International Law Commission Draft Articles on the Law of the Non-navigational Uses of International Watercourses and Commentaries Thereto (1994)
International Tropical Timber Agreement (2011)
Kyoto Protocol to the United Nations Framework Convention on Climate Change (1997)
London Protocol on Water and Health to the 1992 Helsinki Convention (1996)
North American Agreement on Environmental Cooperation (1994)
Optional Protocol to the Convention on the Rights of the Child on a Communications Procedure (2012)
Outer Space Treaty (1967)
Protocol to the African Charter on Human and Peoples' Rights on the Establishment of an African Court on Human and Peoples' Rights (1988)
Protocol to the American Convention on Human Rights in the Area of Economic, Social and Cultural Rights (Protocol of San Salvador) (1988)
Revised Protocol on Shared Watercourses in the Southern African Development Community (2000)
Rio Declaration on Environment and Development (1992)
San Francisco de Quito Declaration (1989)
Sofia Guiding Statements on the Judicial Elaboration of the 2002 New Delhi Declaration of Principles of International Law Relating to Sustainable Development (2012)
Stockholm Declaration of the United Nations Conference on the Human Environment (1972)
Tokyo Declaration for the Dynamic and Enduring ASEAN–Japan Partnership (2003)
Transforming our World: The 2030 Agenda for Sustainable Development. Sustainable Development Knowledge Platform (2015)
United Nations Agreement for the Implementation of the Provisions of the United Nations Convention on the Law of the Sea of 10 December 1982 Relating to the Conservation and Management of Straddling Fish Stocks and Highly Migratory Fish Stocks (2001)
United Nations Charter of Economic Rights and Duties of States (1975)
United Nations Convention on Biological Diversity (1993)
United Nations Convention on the Law of the Sea (1994)
United Nations Convention on the Protection and Use of Transboundary Watercourses and International Lakes (1996)
United Nations Declaration on Human Environment (1972)
UNECE (Pan-European) Convention on Access to Information, Participation and Justice in Environmental Decision-Making Procedures (1998)

United Nations Framework Convention on Climate Change (1992)
United Nations Framework Convention on Climate Change, Adoption of the Paris Agreement (2015)
Vienna Convention on the Law of Treaties (1969)
Vienna Convention for the Protection of the Ozone Layer (1988)
Water Charter of the Lake Chad Basin (2012)
World Heritage Convention (1975)

## NATIONAL LAWS AND INSTRUMENTS

### *Islamic Republic of Afghanistan*

Constitution of the Islamic Republic of Afghanistan (2015)

### *Principality of Andorra*

Constitution of the Principality of Andorra (1993)

### *Angola*

Constitution of Angola (1992)

### *Argentine Republic*

Constitution of the Argentine Republic (1994)

### *Republic of Armenia*

Constitution of the Republic of Armenia (2015)

### *Austria*

Federal Constitutional Act on Sustainability, Animal Protection, Comprehensive Environmental Protection, on Water and Food Security as well as Research (2013)

### *Republic of Azerbaijan*

Constitution of the Republic of Azerbaijan (1995)

*People's Republic of Bangladesh*

Bangladesh Climate Change Strategy and Action Plan (2016)
National Water Policy (1999)

*Belgium*

Constitution of Belgium (1831)

*Plurinational State of Bolivia*

Political Constitution of the State (2009)

*Kingdom of Bhutan*

Bhutan 2020: A Vision for Peace, Prosperity and Happiness (2016)
Constitution of the Kingdom of Bhutan (2008)

*Burkina Faso*

Environmental Code of Burkina Faso, Law No 006-2013 (2013)

*Burundi*

Constitution of Burundi (2018)

*Federative Republic of Brazil*

Constituição da República Federative do Brasil (1988)
STJ Resp 889766-SP 2ªT DJ 18/10/2007 (2007)
STJ Resp 1098028/SP 1ª T 09/02/2010 (2010)

*Cape Verde*

National Action Plan for Integrated Water Resources Management of Cape Verde, Resolution No. 66/2010 of 24 November 2010 (2010)

*Kingdom of Cambodia*

Constitution of the Kingdom of Cambodia (1993)

## *Canada*

Auditor General Act, RSC, 1985, c A-17 (1985)
Canadian Environmental Assessment Act, 2012 SC 2012, c 19, s. 52 (2012)
Carcross/Tagish Agreement among the Government of Canada, the Carcross/Tagish First Nation and the Government of the Yukon (2005)
Champagne and Aishihik First Nations Final Agreement between the Government of Canada, the Champagne and Aishinik First Nations and the Government of the Yukon (1992)
Comprehensive Land Claim Agreement chs between Her Majesty in Right of Canada and the Gwich'in (1992)
Federal Sustainable Development Act SC 2008, c 33 (2008)
Fisheries Act, RSC, 1985, c F-14 (1985)
Governance Agreement between Sioux Valley Dakota Nation and Her Majesty the Queen in Right of Canada (2013)
Inuvialuit Final Agreement (1987)
Kluane First Nation Final Agreement among the Government of Canada, the Kluane First Nation and the Government of the Yukon (2003)
Kwanlin Dun First Nation Final Agreement among the Government of Canada, the Kwanlin Dun First Nation and the Government of the Yukon (2005)
Land Claims Agreement between the Inuit of Labrador and Her Majesty the Queen in Right of Newfoundland and Labrador and Her Majesty the Queen in Right of Canada (2005)
Land Claims and Self-Government Agreement among the Tlicho and the Government of the Northwest Territories and the Government of Canada (2005)
Little Salmon/Carmacks First Nation Final Agreement among the Government of Canada, the Little Salmon/Carmacks First Nation and the Government of the Yukon (1997)
Maa'Nulth First Nations Final Agreement (2009)
Navigation Protection Act, RSC, 1985, c N-22 (1985)
Ta'an Kwac'han Final Agreement among the Government of Canada, the Ta'an Kwac'han First Nation and the Government of the Yukon (2002)
Tla'Amin Final Agreement (2016)
Tsawwassen First Nation Final Agreement (2007)

## *Central African Republic*

Water Law of the Central African Republic (2006)

### *Republic of Chile*

Reglamento de La Cámara de Diputados (1996)

### *Republic of Colombia*

Final Agreement to End the Armed Conflict and Build a Stable and Lasting Peace (2016)

### *Republic of Croatia*

Croatian Regulation on the water management strategy (15 July 2008)

### *Republic of Cuba*

Constitution of the Republic of Cuba (1976)

### *Czech Republic*

Charter of Fundamental Rights and Freedoms of the Czech Republic (1991)

### *Democratic Republic of Congo*

Law No. 43-2014 of 10 October 2014, on the Planning and Development of the Territory

### *Republic of Ecuador*

Constitution of 2008 (2008)

### *European Union*

Charter of Fundamental Rights and Freedoms, OJ 2010/C 83/02 (2010)
Council Decision of 3 December 2013 Establishing the Specific Programme Implementing Horizon 2020 – the Framework Programme for Research and Innovation (2014–2020) (2013/743/EU), OJ L 347, 20.12.2013, 965
Council Directive 85/337/EEC of 27 June 1985 on the Assessment of the Effects of Certain Public and Private Projects on the Environment [1985] OJ L 175/40 (1985)

EU Birds Directive, Directive 2009/147/EC (2009)
EC Council Directive No. 80/779 on Air Quality Limit Values, 15 July 1980, L 229, O.J.E.C. 30 (1980)
EC Council Directive No. 85/201 on Air Quality Standards for Nitrogen Dioxide, 7 Mar. 1985, L 87 O.J.E.C. (1985)
EU Council, Doc. 9668 (2003)
EU Directive 2011/92/EU [2011] L 26/1 (2011)
EU Habitats Directive, Directive 92/43/EEC (1992)
Regulation (EU) No 1291/2013 of the European Parliament and of the Council of 11 December 2013 Establishing Horizon 2020 – the Framework Programme for Research and Innovation (2014–2020) and Repealing Decision No 1982/2006/EC, OL J 304, 20.12.2013, 104.
Treaty on the Functioning of the European Union (2007)
Water Framework Directive, Directive 2000/60/EC (2000)

### *Estonia*

Constitution of Estonia (2013)

### *Finland*

Finnish Parliament, Eduskunnan tyojarjestys (2000)

### *France*

French Charter for the Environment (2004)

### *Federal Republic of Germany*

Act on Nature Conservation and Landscape Management (Federal Nature Conservation Act) (2009)
Basic Law for the Federal Republic of Germany 1949 (Germany)
Deutscher Bundestag, Drucksache 17/245 (June 12, 2009)Promulgation of the Amendment to the Waste Water Charges Act of 18 January 2005 (2005)
Deutscher Bundestag, Parlamentarischer Beirat für nachhaltige Entwicklung/Unterrichtung – 20.06.2017 (hib 381/2017)
Federal Constitutional Court, ruling of 13 March 2007 (2007)
Federal Emission Control Act (2013)
Federal Water Act (1957)

### *Republic of Ghana*

National Water Policy, adopted in 2007 by the Ghanaian Ministry of Water Resources, Works and Housing (2007)

### *Republic of Guatemala*

Plan Nacional de Desarrollo K'atun: nuestra Guatemala (2014)

### *Co-operative Republic of Guyana*

Constitution of the Co-operative Republic of Guyana Act 1980 (1980)

### *Hungary*

2013 Annual Report of the Commissioner for Fundamental Rights (AJBH 2014)
2016 Annual Report of the Commissioner for Fundamental Rights (AJBH 2017)
Act. LIII of 1995 on the General Rules of Environmental Protection
Fundamental Law of Hungary (2012)
Hungarian Act LIX of 1993 on the Parliamentary Commissioner for Civil Rights (Ombudsman) (1993)
Hungarian Act CXI of 2011 on the Commissioner for Fundamental Rights, as amended by Act CCXXIII of 2013 (2013)
Hungary Constitutional Court Decision No. 3104/2017 (V. 8.) AB (2017)
Hungary Constitutional Court Decision No. 28/2017 (X. 25.) AB (2017)
Hungary Constitutional Court Decision No. 14/2020 (VII. 6.) AB (2020)
Hungary Parliament decree No. 84/1995 (VII. 6.) (1995)

### *Republic of India*

National Action Plan on Climate Change of India (2008)

### *Republic of Indonesia*

Constitution of the Republic of Indonesia (1945)

### *State of Israel*

Knesset Law 1994 (Amendment No. 14), 5761-2001 (2001)
Knesset Law (Amendment) – Dissolution of the Knesset Commission for Future Generations, 5770-201 (2003)

Knesset Legislation No. P/17/1629 (4 Dec. 2007)
State Comptroller Act 5718-1958 (2000)

*State of Japan*

Constitution of the State of Japan (1946)

*Republic of Kenya*

Kenya's Environmental Management and Coordination Act no. 8 of 1999 (1999)

*Lao People's Democratic Republic*

Constitution of the Lao People's Democratic Republic (1991)

*Macao Special Administrative Region of the People's Republic of China*

Land Law of the Special Administrative Region of Macao, Law No. 10/2013 (2013)

*Republic of Maldives*

Maldives National Greenhouse Gas Inventory, National Mitigation Plan, Vulnerability Assessment and Adaptation Options (2010)
Constitution of the Republic of the Maldives (2008)

*Malta*

Maltese Sustainable Development Act, Act X of 10 July 2012 (2012)

*Nepal*

Nepal National Strategy for Sustainable Development (2015)

*New Zealand*

Environment Act (1986)

*Federal Republic of Nigeria*

Niger Delta Development Commission Act (1998)

Nigerian National Environmental Standards and Regulations Enforcement Agency Act (2007)

*Kingdom of Norway*

Act relating to Adoption (1986)
Act relating to Child Welfare Services (1992)
Act relating to Children and Parents (1981)
Act relating to Land (1995)
Act relating to Mediation and Procedure in Civil Disputes (1915)
Act relating to Procedure in Cases concerning the Public Administration (1967)
Act Relating to the Protection of the Environment in Svalbard (2001)
Act Relating to the Strengthening of the Status of Human Rights in Norwegian Law (1999)
Aquaculture Act (2005)
Constitution of the Kingdom of Norway (as amended in 1992)
Forestry Act (2005)
Gene Technology Act (1993)
General Civil Penal Code (1902)
Local Government Act (1992)
Marine Resources Act (2008)
Minerals Act (2009)
Nature Diversity Act (2009)
Ombudsman for Children Act (1981)
Planning and Building Act (2008)

*Republic of Panama*

Panamanian National Water Resources Policy (2013)

*Papua New Guinea*

Constitution of the Independent State of Papua New Guinea (1975)

*Republic of the Philippines*

Constitution of the Republic of the Philippines (1987)
Declaration of Policy, Republic Act No. 9729 Climate Change Act of 2009 (2009)
National Climate Change Action Plan (2017)

National Framework Strategy on Climate Change (2017)
Republic Act 10174 (2017)

*Republic of Poland*

Constitution of the Republic of Poland (1971)

*Portugal*

Constitution of Portugal (1976)

*Russian Federation*

Constitution of the Russian Federation (1993)

*Republic of South Africa*

Constitution of the Republic of South Africa (1996)

*Democratic Socialist Republic of Sri Lanka*

National Climate Change Adaptation for Sri Lanka 2011–2016 (2011)

*Sweden*

Constitution of Sweden (1974)

*Swiss Confederation*

Constitution of the Swiss Confederation (2000)

*Ukraine*

Constitution of Ukraine (1996)

*United Arab Emirates*

Water Conservation Strategy (2010)

*Republic of Vanuatu*

Constitution of the Republic of Vanuatu (1980)

*Socialist Republic of Vietnam*

Constitution of the Socialist Republic of Vietnam (2013)

*Wales*

UK Government of Wales Act (1998)
Well-being of Future Generations (Wales) Act 2015 (2015)

*Republic of Yemen*

National Water Sector Strategy and Investment Program (2004)

## SELECTED BOOKS AND GOVERNMENTAL PUBLICATIONS

Adamowicz, W., J. Louviere, and J. Swait, *Introduction to Attribute-Based Stated Choice Methods. Report to NOAA Resource Valuation Branch, Damage Assessment Center* (National Oceanic and Atmospheric Administration/US Department of Commerce 1998).

Agius, E., and S. Busuttil (eds.) *Future Generations and International Law* (Earthscan 1998).

Alam, S., S. Atapattu, C.G. Gonzalez, and J. Razzaque, *International Environmental Law and the Global South* (Cambridge University Press 2015).

Alkire, S., A. Conconi, and S. Seth, *Multidimensional Poverty Index 2014: Brief Methodological Note and Results* (Oxford Poverty and Human Development Initiative 2014).

Aristotle, *Nicomachean Ethics, Book V*, ed. and trans. R. Crisp (Cambridge University Press 2000).

Asian Development Bank, *Addressing Climate Change and Migration in Asia and the Pacific* (Asian Development Bank 2012).

Atleo, E.R., *Principles of Tsawalk: An Indigenous Approach to Global Crisis* (University of British Columbia Press 2001).

*Tsawalk: A Nuu-Chah-Nulth Worldview* (University of British Columbia Press 2004).

Baslar, K., *The Concept of Common Heritage of Mankind in International Law* (Brill 1998).

Beetham, D., *Parliament and Democracy in the Twenty-First Century: A Guide to Good Practice* (Inter-Parliamentary Union 2006).

Berleant, A., *The Aesthetics of Environment* (Temple University Press 1992).

Bifulco, R., *Diritto e generazioni future* (Franco Angeli 2008).

Bonvillian, W., and C. Weiss, *Technological Innovation in Legacy Sectors* (Oxford University Press 2015).

Boston, J., *Governing for the Future: Designing Democratic Institutions for a Better Tomorrow* (Emerald 2017).

Bowman, M., and C. Redgwell, *International Law and the Conservation of Biological Diversity* (Kluwer Law International 1996).

Brand, S., *The Clock of the Long Now* (Basic Books 1999).

Bratholm, A., *Umyndige personer* (Universitetsforlaget 1969).

Brown Weiss, E., *In Fairness to Future Generations: International Law, Common Patrimony, and Intergenerational Equity* (United Nations University 1989).

*Intergenerational Equity: A Legal Framework for Global Environmental Change* (United Nations University 1999).

Buck, T., R. Kirkham, and B. Thompson, *The Ombudsman Enterprise and Administrative Justice* (Ashgate 2011).

Brown, M., R.T.T. Stephens, R. Peart, and B. Fedder, *Vanishing Nature: Facing New Zealand's Biodiversity Crisis* (Environmental Defence Society 2015).

Bührs, T., 'Working Within Limits: The Role of the Commission for the Environment in Environmental Policy Development in New Zealand' (PhD Thesis, Auckland University, 1991).

Burke, E., *Reflections on the Revolution in France* (Hackett 1987).

Clayoquot Sound Scientific Panel, *Report of the Scientific Panel for the Sustainable Forest Practices in Clayoquot Sound* (Report Ministry of Forests, Lands and Natural Resources 1994).

Common Cause Foundation, *Perceptions Matter: The Common Cause UK Values Survey* (Common Cause Foundation 2016).

Cordonier Segger, M.-C., and A. Khalfan, *Sustainable Development Law: Principles, Practices, & Prospects* (Oxford University Press 2004).

Cottier, T., *Equitable Principles of Maritime Boundary Delimitation: the Quest for Distributive Justice in International Law* (Cambridge University Press 2015).

David Suzuki Foundation, *Carbon Offsets* (David Suzuki Foundation 2014).

Davies, P., *Representation of Future Generations* (Oxford University Press 2013).

Detrick, S., *A Commentary on the United Nations Convention on the Rights of the Child* (Martinus Nijhoff 1999).

Dworkin, R., *Taking Rights Seriously* (Harvard University Press 1977).

Edenhofer, O., et al. (eds), *Mitigation of Climate Change: Summary for Policymakers, Contribution of Working Group III to the Fifth Assessment Report of the Intergovernmental Panel on Climate Change* (Cambridge University Press 2014).

Environmental Audit Committee, *Embedding Sustainable Development Across Government, After the Secretary of State's Announcement on the Future of the Sustainable Development Commission* (HC 504) (House of Commons 2011).

European Environment Agency (EEA), *Global Megatrends Assessment 2015* (EEA 2015).

Evernden, N., *The Social Creation of Nature* (Johns Hopkins University Press 1992).

Ferrer Ortega, L.G., *Los derechos de las futuras generaciones desde la perspectiva del derecho internacional: el pinrcipio de equidad intergeneracional* (Universidad Nacional Autónoma de México 2014).

Finnish Committee for the Future, *Black Swans, What Will Change the World Next?* (Finnish Parliament's Committee for the Future 2013).

Francis, Pope, *Laudato Si': On Care for Our Common Home* [Encyclical] (Vatican Press 2015).

Frowein, J., and W. Peukert, *Europäische Menschenrechtskonvention. EMRK Kommentar*, 3rd edn. (Engel 2009).

Fukuyama, F., *State-Building: Governance and World Order in the 21st Century* (Cornell University Press 2004).

Fülöp, S., *A jövő nemzedékek országgyűlési biztosának beszámolója 2008–2009. [The report of the Parliamentary Commissioner for Future Generations 2008–2009]* (Országgyűlési Biztos Hivatala 2010).

Göpel, M., *Ombudspersons for Future Generations as Sustainability Implementation Units* (World Future Council 2012).

Göpel, M. and C. Pearce, *Guarding Our Future: How to Include Generations in Policy Making* (World Future Council 2013).

Gore, A., *Earth in the Balance: Ecology and the Human Spirit* (Houghton Mifflin 1992).

Hunter, D., J. Salzman, and D. Zaelke, *International Environmental Law and Policy*, 2015 edn. (Foundation Press, 2015).

Forest Peoples Programme (FPP), *WPC Recommendation 24: Indigenous Peoples and Protected Areas* (FPP 2003).

Garcia, B., *The Amazon from an International Law Perspective* (Cambridge University Press 2011).

Ginsburg, T., and R. Dixon (eds.), *Comparative Constitutional Law* (Edward Elgar 2011).

Haider, D., *The Pilot-Judgment Procedure of the European Court of Human Rights* (Martinus Nijhoff 2013).

Hanna, S., C. Folke, and K.-G. Mäler (eds.), *Rights to Nature: Ecological, Economic, Cultural, and Political Principles of Institutions for the Environment* (Island Press 1996).

Harlow, C., and R. Rawlings, *Law and Administration* (Cambridge University Press 1997).

Hart, H.L.A., and T. Honoré, *Causation in the Law*, 2nd edn. (Oxford University Press 1985).

Hawken, P., *The Ecology of Commerce* (Harper Business, 2010).

Hawken, P., A. Lovins, and L. Hunter Lovins, *Natural Capitalism* (Hatchette, 1999).

Hayward, J. (ed.), *New Zealand Government and Politics*, 6th edn. (Oxford University Press 2015).

Hayward, T., *Constitutional Environmental Rights* (Oxford University Press 2005).

Heinzerling, L., and F. Ackerman, *Pricing the Priceless: Cost–Benefit Analysis of Environmental Protection* (Georgetown Environmental Law and Policy Institute 2002).

Hendry, J., *Reclaiming Culture Indigenous Peoples and Self-Representation* (Palgrave Macmillan, 2005).

Hessing, M., M. Howlett, and T. Somerville, *Canadian Natural Resource and Environmental Policy*, 2nd edn. (University of British Columbia Press 2005).

Hofstede, G., G.J. Hofstede, and M. Minkov, *Cultures and Organizations: Software of the Mind*, 3rd edn. (McGraw-Hill 2010).

House of Commons, *Minutes of Proceedings and Evidence of the Standing Committee on the Environment and Sustainable Development* (October 1990).

*Commons Debates* (December 1990).

*Minutes of Proceedings and Evidence of the Standing Committee on Public Accounts* (February 1992).

*The Commissioner of the Environment and Sustainable Development, Report of the Standing Committee on Environment and Sustainable Development* (May 1994).

International Fund for Agricultural Development (IFAD), *Indigenous Peoples and Sustainable Development: Discussion Paper, Roundtable Discussion Paper for the 25th Anniversary Session of IFAD's Governing Council* (IFAD 2003).

International Institute for Sustainable Development (IISD), *What is Sustainable Development?* (IISD 2012).

International Labour Organization (ILO), *Brief, Sustainable Development Goals: Indigenous Peoples in Focus* (ILO 2016).

International Work Group for Indigenous Affairs (IWGIA), *The UN Declaration on the Rights of the Indigenous Peoples* (IWGIA 2012).

Jacobs, I., *The Politics of Water in Africa: Norms, Environmental Regions and Transboundary Cooperation in the Orange-Senqu and Nile Rivers* (Continuum 2012).

Jasanoff, S., *The Fifth Branch: Science Advisers as Policymakers* (Harvard University Press, 1990).

Johnston, A., *Is the Sacred for Sale? Tourism and Indigenous Peoples* (Earthscan, 2006).
Joy, M., *Polluted Inheritance: New Zealand's Freshwater Crisis* (BWB Texts 2105).
Justinian, *Institutes: Book II On the Law of Things, Title I, Of the Different Kinds of Things*, trans. J.B. Moyle, 5th edn. (Oxford University Press 1913).
Hawken, P., *Blessed Unrest* (Penguin Books 2007).
Kelsen, H., *Pure Theory of Law*, trans. M. Knight (University of California Press 1969).
Kipping, M., *Konflikte und Kooperation um Wasser: Wasserpolitik am Senegalfluss und internationales Flussmanagement im Südlichen Afrika* (LIT 2005).
Kloepfer, M., *Zur Geschichte des deutschen Umweltrechts* (Duncker & Humblot 1994).
Kucsko-Stadlmayer, G. (ed.), *European Ombudsman-Institutions* (Springer 2008).
La Viña, A., *Philippine Law and Ecology, Vol. II* (University of the Philippines College of Law 2012).
Lazarus, R.J., *The Making of Environmental Law* (University of Chicago Press 2004).
Lyle, J.T., *Regenerative Design for Sustainable Development* (Wiley 1996).
Mannermaa, M., *Democracy in the Turmoil of the Future Societal Influence within a New Frame of Reference* (Committee for the Future Eduskunta, Parliament of Finland 2007).
Meadows, D.H., *Leverage Points: Places to Intervene in a System* (The Sustainability Institute 1999).
May, J.R., and E. Daly, *Global Environmental Constitutionalism* (Cambridge University Press 2015).
McLellan, R. (ed), *Living Planet Report 2014: Species and Spaces, People and Places* (World Wildlife Fund 2014).
Meyers, N., *The Sinking Ark* (Pergamon Press 1979).
Millennium Ecosystem Assessment, *Ecosystems and Human Wellbeing: Synthesis* (Island Press 2005).
Ministry for the Environment, *Environment New Zealand 2007* (Ministry for the Environment 2007).
*Briefing for Incoming Ministers: Environmental Stewardship for a Prosperous New Zealand* (Ministry for the Environment 2014).
Mulgan, T., *Ethics for a Broken World: Imagining Philosophy after Catastrophe* (Routledge 2014).
Navrud, S., and R.C. Ready (eds.), *Valuing Cultural Heritage: Applying Environmental Valuation Techniques to Historic Buildings, Monuments and Artifacts* (Edward Elgar, 2002).
New Zealand Labour Party, 1984 *Policy Document* (New Zealand Labour Party 1984).
Notzke, C., *The Stranger, the Native and the Land: Perspectives on Indigenous Tourism* (Captus University Press 2006).
Office of the Auditor General (OAG), *INAC – Transferring Responsibilities to the North*, November 2003 Report (Office of the Auditor General 2003).
*Management of Programs for First Nations*, May 2006 Report (Office of the Auditor General 2006).
*Fulfilling the Potential: A Review of the Environment and Sustainable Development Practice of the Office of the Auditor General*, Report of the Independent Green Ribbon Panel to the Auditor General of Canada (Office of the Auditor General 2007).
*Strengthening Aid Effectiveness—Canadian International Development* Agency, Fall 2009 Report (Office of the Auditor General 2009).
*Sustaining Development in the Northwest* Territories, Spring 2010 Report (Office of the Auditor General 2010).

*Education in the Northwest Territories—Department of Education, Culture and Employment*, May 2010 Report (Office of the Auditor General 2010).
*Children, Youth and Family Programs and Services in* Nunavut, March 2011 Report (Office of the Auditor General 2011).
*Programs for First Nations on* Reserves, June 2011 Status Report (Office of the Auditor General 2011).
*Long-Term Fiscal Sustainability*, Fall 2012 Report (Office of the Auditor General 2012).
*Safety of Schools and Childcare Facilities in Nunavut*, November 2013 Report (Office of the Auditor General 2013).
*Getting Answers: A Guide to the Environmental Petitions Process* (Office of the Auditor General 2014).
*Public Sector Pension Plans*, Spring 2014 Report (Office of the Auditor General 2014).
*Nutrition North Canada—Aboriginal Affairs and Northern Development* Canada, Fall 2014 Report (Office of the Auditor General 2014).
*What to Expect – An Auditee's Guide to the Performance Audit Process* (Minister of Public Works and Government Services 2015).
*Implementing the Labrador Inuit Land Claims Agreement*, Fall 2015 Report (Office of the Auditor General 2015).
Organisation for Economic Co-operation and Development (OECD), *OECD Environmental Performance Reviews: New Zealand 1996* (OECD 1996).
*OECD Environmental Performance Reviews: New Zealand 2007* (OECD 2007).
*OECD Environmental Outlook to 2050* (OECD 2012).
*OECD Economic Surveys: New Zealand* (OECD 2015).
*OECD Environmental Performance Review: New Zealand 2017* (OECD 2017).
Osiatyński, W., *Human Rights and Their Limits* (Cambridge University Press 2009).
Parfit, D., *Reasons and Persons* (Oxford University Press 1984).
Patrinos, H., and G. Psacharopoulos, *Indigenous People and Poverty in Latin America: An Empirical Analysis* (World Bank 1994).
Peel, J., *Science and Risk Regulation in International Law* (Cambridge University Press 2010).
Peel, J. and H.M. Osofsky, *Climate Change Litigation* (Cambridge University Press 2015).
Pond, D., *The Impact of Parliamentary Officers on Canadian Parliamentary Democracy: A Study of the Commissioner of the Environment and Sustainable Development and the Environmental Commissioner of Ontario* (Canadian Study of Parliament Group 2010).
Ramos, Jr., D., *Meio ambiente e conceito jurídico de futuras gerações* (Juruá Editora Juvevê 2012).
Rawls, J., *A Theory of Justice* (Harvard University Press 1971).
Read, R., *Guardians of the Future: A Constitutional Case for Representing and Protecting Future People* (Green House 2012).
Redgwell, C., *Intergenerational Trusts and Environmental Protection* (Manchester University Press 1999).
Reif, L.C., *The Ombudsman, Good Governance, and the International Human Rights System* (Springer 2004).
Reiss, H. (ed.), *Kant's Political Writings* (Cambridge University Press 1970).
Salick, J. and A. Byg, *Indigenous Peoples and Climate Change* (University of Oxford and Missouri Botanical Garden, 2007).
Samararatne, D., *Public Trust Doctrine the Sri Lankan Version* (International Centre for Ethnic Studies 2010).

Sands, P., and J. Peel, *Principles of International Environmental Law*, 3rd edn. (Cambridge University Press 2012).

Scheyvens, R., *Tourism for Development: Empowering Communities* (Prentice Hall 2002).

Science and Environmental Health Network and The International Human Rights Clinic at Harvard Law School, *Models for Protecting the Environment for Future Generations* (Harvard University Press 2008).

Shoham, S., *Future Intelligence* (Bertelsmann Stiftung 2010).

Singer, P., *The Expanding Circle* (Princeton University Press 2011).

Smith, G., *The Democratic Case for an Office for Future Generations*, Foundation for Democracy and Sustainable Development Report (FDSD 2015).

Stone, C.D., *Should Trees Have Standing? and Other Essays on Law, Morals and the Environment* (Oceana Publications 1996).

Stone, D., *Policy Paradox: The Art of Political Decision Making*, 3rd edn. (W.W. Norton & Company 2012).

Sustainable Development Commission – United Kingdom (SDC-UK), *Working Together for a Sustainable Future: New Arrangements in Wales* (SDC-UK 2011).

Szarka, J., *The Shaping of Environmental Policy in France* (Berghahn Books 2002).

Tarasofsky, R.G. (ed), *The Oxford Handbook of International Climate Change Law* (Oxford University Press 2016).

TEEB (The Economics of Ecosystems and Biodiversity), *An Interim Report, European Communities* (TEEB 2008).

Teschner, N., *Official Bodies That Deal with the Needs of Future Generations and Sustainable Development: Comparative Review* (The Knesset Research and Information Center 2013).

Tobgye, L.S., *The Constitution of Bhutan: Principles and Philosophies* (Royal Court of Justice of Bhutan 2015).

Tourism British Columbia (Tourism BC), *The Value of Tourism in British Columbia: Trends from 2001 to 2011* (Ministry of Jobs, Tourism and Skills Training 2012).

Treguer, D., and E. Pehu, *Moving toward a Sustainable Landscape Approach to Development* (World Bank Group 2014).

Tremmel, J.C. (ed.) *Handbook of Intergenerational Justice* (Edward Elgar 2006).

Trosper, R., *Resilience, Reciprocity and Ecological Economics: Northwest Coast Sustainability* (Routledge 2009).

Tyler, T., *Why People Obey the Law* (Princeton University Press 2006).

Twining, W., and D. Miers, *How to Do Things with Rules*, 4th edn. (Butterworths 1999).

Union of International Associations, *Yearbook of International Organizations (2016–2017)* (Brill 2016).

United Nations Department of Economic and Social Affairs (UNDESA), *A Guidebook to the Green Economy: Issue 1: Green Economy, Green Growth, and Low-Carbon Development – History, Definitions and a Guide to Recent Publications* (UNDESA 2012).

*National Institutions for Sustainable Development: A Preliminary Review of the Institutional Literature* (UNDESA 2012).

United Nations Environment Programme World Future Council (UNEP-WFC), *Global Conference on Implementing Intergenerational Equity: Bringing Future Perspectives to the Status Quo – Conference Synopsis* (UNEP-WFC 2013).

Van Dijk, P., F. van Hoof, A. van Rijn, and L. Zwaak (eds.), *Theory and Practice of the European Convention on Human Rights*, 4th edn. (Intersentia 2006).

Vanneste, F., *General International Law before Human Rights Courts: Assessing the Specialty Claims of International Human Rights Law* (Intersentia 2010).

Vinuales, J., *The Rio Declaration on Environment and Development: A Commentary* (Oxford University Press 2015).
Ward, H., *Democracy in the Face of Climate Change: Exploring the Present, 2050, and Beyond*, Foundation for Democracy and Sustainable Development Report (FDSD January 2016).
Westall, A., *The Relationship between Democracy and Sustainable Development*, Foundation for Democracy and Sustainable Development Briefing (FDSD 2015).
Wilson, A., *The Culture of Nature: North American Landscape from Disney to the Exxon Valdez* (Blackwell Publishing 1992).
Wilson, E.O., *The Diversity of Life* (Harvard University Press 1992).
*Half-Earth: Our Planet's Fight for Life* (Liveright 2016).
Wilson, E.O. (ed.) *Biodiversity* (National Academy of Sciences 1988).
Woods, C., *Intergenerational Equity in Law and Practice* (Oxford University Press 2011).
World Bank, *World Development Report 1997: The State in a Changing World* (Oxford University Press 1997).
*Indigenous Peoples, Poverty and Human Development in Latin America: 1994–2004 Summary* (World Bank 2005).
*Still among the Poorest of the Poor. Indigenous Peoples Country Brief* (World Bank 2011).
World Bank Group, *World Development Indicators 2014* (World Bank 2014).
Yamamoto, H., *Tools for Parliamentary Oversight: A Comparative Study of 88 National Parliaments* (Inter-Parliamentary Union 2007).
Young, D., *Keeper of the Long View* (Parliamentary Commissioner for the Environment 2007).

## ACADEMIC LITERATURE AND SECONDARY SOURCES

Alam, U., 'Cooperating Internationally over Water: Explaining L'espace OMVS' (2012) 50(2) *Journal of Modern African Studies* 175–199.
Allen, T., 'The Philippine Children's Case Recognizing Legal Standing for Future Generations' (1994) 6 *Georgetown International Environmental Law Review* 713–741.
Ambrus, M., 'Legitimacy Narratives in Polycentric Water Law and Governance: the Strategies of the Danube Commission' (2014) 11(1) *International Organizations Law Review* 83–113.
Ambrusné, É.T., 'The Parliamentary Commissioner for Future Generations of Hungary and His Impact' (2010) 10 *Intergenerational Justice Review* 18–23.
Anstee-Wedderburn, J., 'Giving a Voice to Future Generations: Intergenetarional Equity, Representatives of Generations to Come, and the Challenge of Planetary Rights' (2014) 1(1) *Australian Journal of Environmental Law* 37–70.
Armesto, J.J., C. Smith-Ramirez, and R. Rozzii, 'Conservation Strategies for Biodiversity and Indigenous People in Chilean Forest Ecosystems' (2001) 31(4) *Journal of the Royal Society of New Zealand* 865–877.
Ba, A.S., and M.M. Mbengue, 'Le Régime juridique du fleuve Sénégal: aspects du droit des cours d'eau dans un contexte régional' (2006) 12(1) *African Yearbook of International Law* 309–347.
Ballhorn, R., 'The Role of Government and Policy in Sustainable Development' (2005) 1(1) *McGill International Journal of Sustainable Development Law and Policy* 19–27.
Barral, V., 'Sustainable Development in International Law: Nature and Operation of an Evolutive Legal Norm' (2012) 23(2) *European Journal of International Law* 377–400.

Barresi, P.A., 'Beyond Fairness to Future Generations: An Intragenerational Alternative to Intergenerational Equity in the International Environmental Arena' 11 (1997) *Tulane Environmental Law Journal* 59–88.

Bartee, E.M., 'A Holistic View of Problem Solving' (1973) 20(4) *Management Science* 439–448.

Besthorn, F.H., 'Deep Ecology's Contributions to Social Work: A Ten-Year Retrospective' (2012) 21(3) *International Journal of Social Welfare* 248–259.

Beven, K., 'Facets of Uncertainty: Epistemic Uncertainty, Non-Stationarity, Likelihood, Hypothesis Testing, and Communication' (2016) 61(9) *Hydrological Sciences Journal* 1652–1665.

Blomquist, R.F.'Comparative Climate Change Torts' (2012) 46 *Valparaiso University Law Review* 1053–1075.

Blumm, M.C., 'Public Property and the Democratization of Western Water Law: A Modern View of the Public Trust Doctrine' (1989) 19 *Environmental Law* 573–604.

Blumm, M.C., and R.D. Guthrie, 'Internationalizing the Public Trust Doctrine: Natural Law and Constitutional and Statutory Approaches to Fulfilling the Saxion Vision' (2011) 45 *University of California Davis Law Review* 741–808.

Bowling, C., E. Pierson, and S. Ratté, *The Common Concern of Humankind: A Potential Framework for a New International Legally Binding Instrument on the Conservation and Sustainable Use of Marine Biological Diversity in the High Seas* <www.un.org/depts/los/biodiversity/prepcom_files/BowlingPiersonandRatte_Common_Concern.pdf> accessed 30 November 2017.

Boyland, M., 'The Economics of Using Forests to Increase Carbon Storage' (2006) 36(9) *Canadian Journal of Forest Research* 2223–2234.

Boyle, A., 'Human Rights or Environmental Rights? A Reassessment' (2007) 18 *Fordham Environmental Law Review* 471–511.

Brennan, T.A., 'Causal Chains and Statistical Links: The Role of Scientific Uncertainty in Hazardous-Substance Litigation' (1987) 73 *Cornell Law Review* 469–533.

Brennan, T.J., 'Discounting the Future: Economics and Ethics' (1995) 120 *Resources* 3–6.

Brown, J.D., 'Prospects for the Open Treatment of Uncertainty in Environmental Research' (2010) 34(1) *Progress in Physical Geography* 75–100.

Brown Weiss, E., 'A Planetary Trust: Conservation and Intergenerational Equity' (1984) 11 *Ecology Law Quarterly* 495–582.

'Our Rights and Obligations to Future Generations for the Environment' (1990) 84(1) *American Journal of International Law* 198–207.

'In Fairness to Future Generations and Sustainable Development' (1992) 8(1) *American University International Law Review* 19–26.

'Climate Change, Intergenerational Equity, and International Law' (2008) 9 *Vermont Journal of Environmental Law* 615–627.

'International Law in a Kaleidoscopic World' (2011) 1(1) *Asian Journal International Law* 21–32.

Brugnach, M., M. Craps, and A.R.P.J. Dewulf, 'Including Indigenous Peoples in Climate Change Mitigation: Addressing Issues of Scale, Knowledge and Power' (2017) 140(1) *Climatic Change* 19–32.

Bryan, G., D. Karlan, and S. Nelson, 'Commitment Devices' (2010) 2(1) *Annual Review of Economics* 671–698.

Bryner, N.S., 'Brazil's Green Court' (2012) 29 *Pace Environmental Law Review* 470–537.

Bührs, T., 'Barking Up Which Trees? The Role of New Zealand's Parliamentary Watchdog' (1996) 48(1) *Political Science* 1–28.

Cassuto, D., and R. Sampaio, 'Hard, Soft & Uncertain: The Guarani Aquifer and the Challenges of Transboundary Groundwater' (2013) 24 *Colorado Journal of International Environmental Law and Policy* 1–41.

Collins, L.M., 'Revisiting the Doctrine of Intergenerational Equity in Global Environmental Governance' (2007) 30 *Dalhousie Law Journal* 73–134.

Cook, C.N., M.B. Mascia, M.W. Schwartz, H.P. Possingham, and R.A. Fuller, 'Achieving Conservation Science That Bridges the Knowledge–Action Boundary: Achieving Effective Conservation Science' (2013) 27(4) *Conservation Biology* 669–678.

Cordonier Segger, M.-C., 'Sustainability, Global Justice, and the Law: Contributions of the Hon. Justice Charles Doherty Gonthier' (2010) 55(2) *McGill Law Journal* 337–355.

Costanza, R., and B.C. Patten, 'Defining and Predicting Sustainability' (1995) 15(3) *Ecological Economics* 193–196.

Crook, M., D. Short, and N. South, 'Ecocide, Genocide, Capitalism and Colonialism: Consequences for Indigenous Peoples and Glocal Ecosystems Environments' (2018) 22(3) *Theoretical Criminology* 298–317.

Crutzen, P.J., and E.F. Stoermer, 'The "Anthropocene"' (2000) 41 *Global Change Newsletter: International Geosphere: Biosphere Programme* 17–18.

D'Argent, P., 'L'évolution du Statut juridique de la Meuse et de l'Escaut: une mise en perspective des Accords de Charleville-Mézières du 26 avril 1994' (1997) 30 *Revue belge de droit international* 133–171.

Deter, G., '"Nationale Nachhaltigkeitsstrategie" und Grundgesetz' (2012) 3 *Zeitschrift für Umweltrecht* 157–163.

DeMarco, J.V., 'Law of Future Generations: The Theory of Intergenerational Equity in Canadian Environmental Law' (2004) 15(1) *Journal of Environmental Law and Practice* 1–46.

Dirzo, R., and P.H. Raven, 'Global State of Biodiversity and Loss' (2003) 28 *Annual Review of Environment and Resources* 137–167.

Dismukes, G.C., V.V. Klimov, S.V. Baranov, Y.N. Kozlov, J. DasGupta, and A. Tyryshkin, 'The Origin of Atmospheric Oxygen on Earth: The Innovation of Oxygenic Photosynthesis' (2001) 98(5) *Proceedings of the National Academy of Sciences* 2170–2175.

Dror, G., 'Cancellation of Commission for Future Generations: Between Politics and Ethics' (2012) 3(2) *Ecology and Environment – Journal of Environmental Sciences and Policy* 161–165.

Durack, P.J., S.E. Wijffels, and R.J. Matear, 'Ocean Salinities Reveal Strong Global Water Cycle Intensification during 1950–2000' (2012) 336(6080) *Science* 455–458.

Ege, K.J., 'Enforcing Environmental Policy the Environmental Ombudsman' (1971) 56 *Cornell Law Review* 847–863.

Farber, D.A., 'Uncertainty' (2011) 99 *Georgetown Law Journal* 901–959.

Feeny, D., F. Berkes, B.J. McCay, and J.M. Acheson, 'The Tragedy of the Commons: Twenty-Two Years Later' (1990) 18(1) *Human Ecology* 1–19.

Fennell, D.A., 'Ecotourism and the Myth of Indigenous Stewardship' (2008) 16(2) *Journal of Sustainable Tourism* 129–149.

Frey, B., 'Evaluating Cultural Property: The Economic Approach' (1997) 6(2) *International Journal of Cultural Property* 231–246.

Frink, R., 'Preserving Trans-Boundary Aquifers: A Precious Resource for Our Future Generations' (2013) 26 *Pacific McGeorge Global Business and Development Law Journal* 503–530.

Furuseth, O., and C. Cocklin, 'An Institutional Framework for Sustainable Resource Management: The New Zealand Model' (1995) 35 *Natural Resources Journal* 243–273.

García-Aracil, A., and C. Winter, 'Gender and Ethnicity Differentials in School Attainment and Labor Market Earnings in Ecuador' (2006) 34(2) *World Development* 289–307.

Gatmaytan, D.B., 'The Illusion of Intergenerational Equity: Oposa v. Factoran as Pyrrhic Victory' (2003) 15 *Georgetown International Environmental Law Review* 457–485.

Goodman, A., K. Fleming, N. Markwick, T. Morrison, L. Lagimodiere, and T. Kerr, '"They Treated Me Like Crap and I Know It Was Because I Was Native": The Healthcare Experiences of Aboriginal Peoples Living in Vancouver's Inner City' (2017) 178 *Social Science & Medicine* 87–94.

Greathouse-Amador, L.M., 'Tourism: A Facilitator of Social Awareness in an Indigenous Mexican Community?' (2005) 22(5) *Review of Policy Research* 709–720.

Green, B., 'Contemporary Governance of Transboundary Groundwater Resources: the Guarani Aquifer Project' (2010) 21(6) *Journal of Water Law* 232–240.

Green, R.M., 'Intergenerational Distributive Justice and Environmental Responsibility' (1977) 27(4) *BioScience* 260–265.

Grubler, A., Y. Ermoliev, and A. Kryazhimskiy, 'Coping with Uncertainties: Examples of Modeling Approaches at IIASA' (2015) 98 *Technological Forecasting and Social Change* 213–222.

Gundling, L., 'What Obligation Does Our Generation Owe to the Next? An Approach to Global Environmental Responsibility: Our Responsibility to Future Generations' (1990) 84(1) *American Journal of International Law* 190–198.

Fauchald, O.K., 'Forfatning og miljøvern – en analyse av Grunnloven § 110 b' (2007) 120(1–2) *Tidsskrift for rettsvitenskap* 1–84.

'Hva er konsekvensene av Grunnlovens miljøparagraf?' (2015) 200 *PrivIus Journal of Private Law* 30–31.

French, D.A., 'International Environmental Law and the Achievement of Intragenerational Equity' (2001) 31 *Environmental Law Reporter* 10469–10485.

Furuseth, O., and C. Cocklin, 'An Institutional Framework For Sustainable Resource Management: The New Zealand Model' (1995) 35 *Natural Resources Journal* 243–273.

Göpel, M., and M. Arhelger, 'How to Protect Future Generations' Rights in European Governance' (2010) 10 *Intergenerational Justice Review* 3–9.

Hadjiargyrou, Z., 'A Conceptual and Practical Evaluation of Intergenerational Equity in International Environmental Law' (2016) 18 (3–4) *International Community Law Review* 248–277.

Hák, S., S. Janoušková, and B. Moldan, 'Sustainable Development Goals: A Need for Relevant Indicators' (2016) 60 *Ecological Indicators* 565–573.

Harmon, S.H.E., 'From Engagement to Re-engagement: The Expression of Moral Values in European Patent Proceedings, Past and Future' (2006) *European Law Review* 31(5).

Harwood, J., and K. Stokes, 'Coping with Uncertainty in Ecological Advice: Lessons from Fisheries' (2003) 18(12) *Trends in Ecology & Evolution* 617–622.

Heiskanen, H.E., and J. Viljanen, 'Reforming the Strasbourg Doctrine on Extraterritorial Jurisdiction in the Context of Environmental Protection' (2014) 11 *European Law Reporter* 285–295.

Henderson, G.E., 'Rawls and Sustainable Development' (2011) 7(1) *McGill International Journal of Sustainable Development Law and Policy* 1–32.

Hernández-Morcillo, M., T. Plieninger, and C. Bieling, 'An Empirical Review of Cultural Ecosystem Service Indicators' (2013) 29 *Ecological Indicators* 434–444.

Kahl, W., 'Staatsziel Nachhaltigkeit und Generationengerechtigkeit' (2009) 62(2) *Die Öffentliche Verwaltung* 2–13.

Kim, R.E., and K. Bosselmann, 'Operationalizing Sustainable Development: Ecological Integrity as a *Grundnorm* of International Law' (2015) 24(2) *Review of European Community and International Environmental Law* 194–208.

Klass, A.B., 'Modern Public Trust Principles: Recognizing Rights and Integrating Standards' (2006) 82 *Notre Dame Law Review* 699–754.

Knox, J.H., 'Linking Human Rights and Climate Change at the United Nations' (2009) 23 *Harvard Environmental Law Review* 477–498.

Kravchenko, S., and J.E. Bonine, 'Interpretation of Human Rights for the Protection of the Environment in the European Court of Human Rights' (2012) 25(1) *Global Business & Development Law Journal* 245–287.

Kriebel, D., 'How Much Evidence Is Enough? Conventions of Causal Inference' (2009) 72(1) *Law and Contemporary Problems* 121–136.

Lányi, A., 'Az ökológia mint politikai filozófia (Ecology as a political philosophy)' (2012) *Politikatudományi Szemle* XXI 105–130.

Lenton, T.M., H. Held, E. Kriegler, J.W. Hall, W. Lucht, S. Rahmstorf, and H.J. Schnellnhuber, 'Tipping Elements in the Earth's Climate System' (2008) 105 *Proceedings of the National Academy of Sciences of the Unites States of America* 1786–1793.

Lowe, V., 'The Role of Equity in International Law' (1989) 12(1) *Australian Yearbook of International Law* 54–81.

Ludwig, D., M. Mangel, and B. Haddad, 'Ecology, Conservation, and Public Policy' (2001) 32(1) *Annual Review of Ecology and Systematics* 481–517.

Mabee, H.S., and G. Hoberg, 'Protecting Culturally Significant Areas through Watershed Planning in Clayoquot Sound' (2004) 80(2) *Forestry Chronicle* 229–240.

MacIntosh, C., 'The Role of Law in Ameliorating Global Inequalities in Indigenous Peoples' Health' (2013) 41(1) *Journal of Law, Medicine & Ethics* 74–88.

Maggio, G.F., 'Inter/Intragenerational Equity: Current Applications under International Law for Promoting the Sustainable Development of Natural Resources' (1997) 4(2) *Buffalo Environmental Law Journal* 161–223.

Maluwa, T., 'Legal Aspects of the Niger River under the Niamey Treaties' (1988) 28 *Natural Resources Journal* 671–697.

Manguiat, M.S.Z., and V.P.B. Yu III, 'Maximizing the Value of Oposa v. Factoran' (2003) 15 *Georgetown International Environmental Law Review* 487–496.

Mank, B.C., 'Standing and Future Generations: Does *Massachusetts* v *EPA* Open Standing for Generations to Come?' (2009) 34(1) *Columbia Journal of Environmental Law* 1–97.

Martin, G.J., C.I. Camacho Benavides, C.A. Del Campo García, S.A. Fonseca, F.C. Mendoza, and M.A. González Ortíz, 'Indigenous and Community Conserved Areas in Oaxaca, Mexico' (2011) 22(2) *Management of Environmental Quality: An International Journal* 250–266.

Martin-Nagle, R., 'Fossil Aquifers: A Common Heritage of Mankind' (Winter 2011) *Journal of Energy & Environmental Law* 39–60.

Marong, A.B.M., 'From Rio to Johannesburg: Reflections on the Role of International Legal Norms in Sustainable Development' (2000) 16 *Georgetown International Environmental Law Review* 22–26.

Mbengue, M.M., 'A Model for African Shared Water Resources: The Senegal River Legal System' (2014) 23(1) *Review of European, Comparative and International Environmental Law* 59–66.

McIntyre, O., 'The Protection of Freshwater Ecosystems Revisited: Towards a Common Understanding of the 'Ecosystems Approach' to the Protection of Transboundary

Water Resources' (2014) 23(1) *Review of European Community and International Environmental Law* 88–95.

'International Water Resources Law and the International Law Commission Draft Articles on Transboundary Aquifers: A Missed Opportunity for Cross-Fertilisation?' (2011) 13(3) *International Community Law Review* 237–254.

McKenzie, D., 'Poverty, Inequality, and International Migration: Insights from 10 Years of Migration and Development Conferences' (2017) 25(3) *Revue d'économie du développement* 13–28.

Meadows, D.H., 'Dancing with Systems' (2002) 13 *Systems Thinking* 58–63.

Mora, C., and P. Sale, 'Ongoing Global Biodiversity Loss and the Need to Move beyond Protected Areas: A Review of the Technical and Practical Shortcomings of Protected Areas on Land and Sea' (2011) 434 *Marine Ecology (Progress Series)* 251–266.

Morse, W.L., 'International Law: The Bridge to International Justice' (1972) 4(1) *Akron Law Review* 1–26.

Muers, R., 'Pushing the Limit: Theology and Responsibility to Future Generations' (2003) 16(2) *Studies in Christian Ethics* 36–51.

Mullally, S., 'Defining the Limits of Citizenship: Family Life, Immigration and 'Non-Nationals' in Irish Law' (2004) 39 *Irish Jurist* 334–351.

Müllerová, H., 'Environment Playing Short-Handed: Margin of Appreciation in Environmental Jurisprudence of the European Court of Human Rights' (2015) 24(1) *Review of European Community & International Environmental Law* 83–92.

Ngaide, M., 'La contribution de l'Afrique à la gestion des ressources en eau transfrontalières: l'exemple la Charte de l'eau du Bassin du Niger' (2012) 66(3) *Revue juridique et politique des États francophones* 263–316.

Nilsson, C., 'Climate Change from an Indigenous Perspective' (2008) 1–2 *Indigenous Affairs* 9-15.

O'Connor, P., 'Careful What You Wish For: Positive Freehold Covenants' (2011) 3 *Conveyancer and Property Lawyer* 191–207.

O'Neill, O., 'Environmental Values, Anthropocentrism and Speciesism' (1997) 6 *Environmental Values* 127–142.

O'Reilly, J., K. Brysse, M. Oppenheimer, and N. Oreskes, 'Characterizing Uncertainty in Expert Assessments: Ozone Depletion and the West Antarctic Ice Sheet' (2011) 2(5) *Wiley Interdisciplinary Reviews: Climate Change* 728–743.

Okeke, B., and E. Taniche, 'A Critique of the Enforcement of Nigeria Extractive Industries Transparency Initiative (Neiti) Act 2007 in Nigerian Oil and Gas Sector' (2013) 14(2) *British Journal of Arts and Social Sciences* 98–108.

Oluduro, O., 'Oil Exploitation and Human Rights Violations in Nigeria's Oil Producing Communities' (2014) 25(2) *Afrika Focus* 160–166.

Orellana, M., 'Introduction' (2009) X(1) *Sustainable Development Law and Policy* 2.

Padt, F., and J.C. Sanches, 'Creating New Spaces for Sustainable Water Management in the Senegal River Basin' (2013) 53 *Natural Resources Journal* 265–284.

Pan, Y., R.A. Birdsey, J. Fang, R. Houghton, P.E. Kauppi, W.A. Kurz, et al., 'A Large and Persistent Carbon Sink in the World's Forests' (2011) 333(6045) *Science* 988–993.

Payne, M.R., M. Barange, W.W.L. Cheung, B.R. MacKenzie, H.P. Batchelder, X. Cormon, et al., 'Uncertainties in Projecting Climate-Change Impacts in Marine Ecosystems' (May 2016) 73(5) *ICES Journal of Marine Science: Journal Du Conseil* 1272–1282.

Pring, G., and C. Pring, 'Twenty-First Century Environmental Dispute Resolution: Is There an 'ECT' in Your Future?' (2015) 33(1) *Journal of Energy & Natural Resources Law* 10–33.

Regan, H.M., M. Colyvan, and M.A. Burgman, 'A Taxonomy and Treatment of Uncertainty for Ecology and Conservation Biology' (2002) 12(2) *Ecological Applications* 618–628.

Reimer, F., 'Nachhaltigkeit durch Wahlrecht? Verfassungsrechtliche Möglichkeiten und Grenzen eines "Wahlrechts von Geburt an"' (2004) 35(2) *Zeitschrift für Parlamentsfragen* 322–339.

Richardson, B.J., 'Indigenous Peoples, International Law and Sustainability' (2001) 10(1) *Review of European Comparative & International Environmental Law* 1–12.

Rockström, J., W. Steffen, K. Noone, et al., 'A Safe Operating Space for Humanity' (2009) 461(7263) *Nature* 472–475.

Rowell, A., 'Time in Cost–Benefit Analysis' (2014) 4(4) *University of California Irvine Law Review* 1215–1239.

Sachs, J.D., and A.M. Warner, 'The Curse of Natural Resources' (2001) 45(4–6) *European Economic Review* 827–838.

Salomon, J.A., H. Wang, M.K. Freeman, T. Vos, A.D. Flaxman, A.D. Lopez, and C.J.L. Murray, 'Healthy Life Expectancy for 187 Countries, 1990–2010: A Systematic Analysis for the Global Burden Disease Study 2010' (2013) 380(9859) *The Lancet* 2144–2162.

Sánchez Castillo, N., 'Differentiating between Sovereignty over Exclusive and Shared Resources in the Light of Future Discussions on the Law of Transboundary Aquifers' (2015) 24(1) *Review of European, Comparative and International Environmental Law* 4–15.

Sand, P.H., 'Sovereignty Bounded: Public Trusteeship for Common Pool Resources?' (2004) 4(1) *Global Environmental Politics* 47–71.

Scheld, S., D.H. Taplin, and S.M. Low, 'The Values-Based Approach for Cultural-Heritage Preservation in US Public Parks' (2014) 45(2/3) *Association for Preservation Technology International (APT) Bulletin* 49–56.

Scheyvens, R., 'Promoting Women's Empowerment through Involvement in Ecotourism: Experiences from the Third World' (2000) 8(3) *Journal of Sustainable Tourism* 232–249.

Schickhardt, C., 'Kinder im Wahlrecht und in Demokratien. Für eine elterliche Stellvertreterwahlpflicht' (2015) 2(1) *Zeitschrift für Praktische Philosophie* 191–248.

Schwenk, W.S., T.M. Donovan, W.S. Keeton, and J.S. Nunery, 'Carbon Storage, Timber Production, and Biodiversity: Comparing Ecosystem Services with Multi-Criteria Decision Analysis' (2012) 22(5) *Ecological Applications* 1612–1627.

Smith, C., 'Policy Implications of Uncertainty' (2011) 369(1956) *Philosophical Transactions of the Royal Society A: Mathematical, Physical and Engineering Sciences* 4932–4937.

Sohn, L.B., and E. Brown Weiss, 'Intergenerational Equity in International Law' (1987) 81 *Proceedings of the Annual Meeting, American Society of International Law* 126–133.

Spijkers, O., 'The Sustainable Development Goals as Catalyst for the Sustainable Management of Water Resources' (2015) 24 *Journal of Water Law* 115–125.

Stevenson, M.G., 'Indigenous Knowledge in Environmental Assessment' (1996) 48(3) *Arctic* 278–291.

Sunstein, C.R., and A. Rowell, 'On Discounting Regulatory Benefits: Risk, Money, and Intergenerational Equity' (2007) *University of Chicago Law Review* 171–208.

Tengberg, A., 'Cultural Ecosystem Services Provided by Landscapes: Assessment of Heritage Values and Identity' (2012) 2 *Ecosystem Services* 14–26.

Thompson, D., 'Representing Future Generations: Political Presentism and Democratic Trusteeship' (2010) 13(1) *Critical Review of International and Political Philosophy* 17–37.

Tinker, C., 'The Guarani Aquifer Accord: Cooperation in South America towards Prevention of Harm and Sustainable, Equitable Use of Underground Transboundary Water' (2016) 15(2) *The Law and Practice of International Courts and Tribunals* 249–263.

Trilsch, M., 'European Committee of Social Rights: The Right to a Healthy Environment' (2009) 7(3) *International Journal of Constitutional Law* 529–538.

Van der Schyff, E., 'Unpacking the Public Trust Doctrine: A Journey into Foreign Territory' (2010) 13(5) *PER: Potchefstroomse Elektroniese Regsblad* 122–189.

Van Dunné, J., 'Transboundary Pollution and Liability Issues: Private Law vs Public International Law Approaches: The Cases of the Rivers Rhine and Meuse' (1999) *Acta Juridica* 303–338.

VanderVen, K., and A.J. Schneider-Munoz, 'As the World Ages: Attaining a Harmonious Future World through Intergenerational Connections' (2012) 10(2) *Journal of Intergenerational Relationships* 115–130.

Veinla, H., 'Sustainable Development as the Fundamental Principle of Europe's Environmental Ius Commune' (2005) X *Juridica International* 115–125.

Verhoeven, J., 'Les accords de Charleville-Mézières du 26 avril 1994 sur l'Escaut et sur la Meuse' (1997) 43(1) *Annuaire français de droit international* 799–809.

Vibhute, K.I., 'Environment, Present and Future Generations: Inter-generational Equity, Justice and Responsibility' (1998) 38(1) *Indian Journal of International Law* 65–73.

Vick, M., 'The Senegal River Basin: A Retrospective and Prospective Look at the Legal Régime' (2006) 46 *Natural Resources Journal* 211–243.

Ware, D., 'The Amazon Treaty: A Turning Point in Latin America Co-operation?' (1980) 15 *Texas International Law Journal* 118–137.

Watene, K., and M. Yap, 'Culture and Sustainable Development: Indigenous Contributions' (2015) 11(1) *Journal of Global Ethics* 51–55.

Wenar, L., 'Property Rights and the Resource Curse' (2008) 36(3) *Philosophy and Public Affairs* 5–7.

Weston, B.H., 'The Theoretical Foundations of Intergenerational Ecological Justice: An Overview' (2012) 34(1) *Human Rights Quarterly* 251–266.

Wiessner, S., 'The Cultural Rights of Indigenous Peoples: Achievements and Continuing Challenges' (2011) 22(1) *European Journal of International Law* 121–140.

Wood, M.C., 'Advancing the Sovereign Trust of Government to Safeguard the Environment for Present and Future Generations (Part II): Instilling a Fiduciary Obligation in Governance' (2009) 39(1) *Environmental Law* 91–139.

Wood, M.C., and D. Galpern, 'Atmospheric Recovery Litigation: Making the Fossil Fuel Industry Pay to Restore a Viable Climate System' (2015) 45(2) *Environmental Law* 259–337.

Wright, D.V., 'Options for Oversight in the Provincial Environmental Realm: Examples and Functions of Independent Oversight Offices' (2015) 29 *Journal of Environmental Law and Practice* 199–220.

Yodzis, P., 'Must Top Predators Be Culled for the Sake of Fisheries?' (2001) 16(2) *Trends in Ecology & Evolution* 78–84.

Printed by Integrated Books International,
United States of America